P9-DWG-544

THE PAPERS OF

Andrew Johnson

Sponsored by

The University of Tennessee

The National Historical Publications and Records Commission

The Tennessee Historical Commission

Andrew Johnson in Nashville: a photograph by C. G. Giers.
Courtesy Margaret Johnson Patterson Bartlett.

THE PAPERS OF

Andrew Johnson

Volume 6, 1862 - 1864

LEROY P. GRAF AND RALPH W. HASKINS
EDITORS

PATRICIA P. CLARK, ASSOCIATE EDITOR

MARION O. SMITH, RESEARCH ASSOCIATE

1983
THE UNIVERSITY OF TENNESSEE PRESS
KNOXVILLE

Clothbound editions of University of Tennessee Press books are printed on paper designed for an effective life of at least 300 years, and binding materials are chosen for strength and durability.

Library of Congress Cataloging in Publication Data (Revised)

Johnson, Andrew, Pres. United States, 1808-1875.
The papers of Andrew Johnson.
Includes bibliographical references and index.
CONTENTS: v. 1. 1822-1851.—v.2. 1852-1857.—v. 3. 1858-1860. [etc.]
1. United States—Politics and government—1849-1877—Sources. 2. Johnson, Andrew, Pres. U.S., 1808-1875. 3. Presidents—United States—Correspondence.
I. Graf, LeRoy P. and Haskins, Ralph W., eds.
E415.6.J65 1967 973.8'1'0924 [B] 67-25733
ISBN 0-87049-346-9

TO

Alvin Herborg Nielsen

SCIENTIST, ADMINISTRATOR, SUPPORTER
OF THE ARTS, AND NOT LEAST OF ALL,
FRIEND

Contents

1862

1864

Illustrations

Introduction

ANDREW JOHNSON: MILITARY GOVERNOR, 1862-1864

Early in June, 1864, shortly after Andrew Johnson was named Lincoln's running mate on the Union Party ticket, Nashville became the scene of a political jubilee whipped up by Sam Carter, the governor's hosteler and "whiskey-man." Not only had the Baltimore convention reached into rebel territory and chosen a Tennessean for the second highest office in the land, but fortunes of war east and west smiled upon the northern cause, and the state itself was anticipating an early resumption of civil government. Plainly a jollification was in order for the unionists, who notwithstanding the long Federal occupation, remained something of an archipelago in a sea of secessionists. For a throng of several thousand, lured by a band of music and a salvo of cannon, the climax of an oppressively hot evening was an address by the governor, holding forth from the steps of the St. Cloud Hotel.[1] His appearance before a Nashville audience presented no great novelty, for he had from time to time harangued the locals during both the civil and military governorships. Yet for Johnson this was an auspicious occasion, signalizing as it did another stride forward in a public career encompassing more than three decades. These remarks, extending over little more than an hour, afford an insight into his views, some of them immutable and others changing, during nearly two years of the military governorship.

In what may charitably be called an acceptance speech, Johnson permitted himself a modest disclaimer: far from seeking the candidacy, he had avoided it; but now, "Come weal or woe, success or defeat, sink or swim, survive or perish, I accept the nomination on principle, be the consequences what they may." Dwelling momentarily on the proceedings at Baltimore, the speaker interpreted Lincoln's nomination as confirmation of the Union's resolve "to maintain and carry out the principles of free government" and his own as a declaration that "a State cannot put itself from under the national authority," that "the rebellious States are still in the Union," and that "their loyal citizens are still citizens of the United States." The Plebeian reaffirmed his steadfast faith in man's capability for self-government, be he laborer or shoemaker, tailor or grocer. Anathematizing a favorite foe, he recalled the chivalry's aversion to one "of humble origin—a railsplitter"—and waggishly inquired, "if this aristocracy is so violently opposed to being governed by Mr. Lincoln, what in the name of

1. Speech on Vice-Presidential Nomination, June 9, 1864.

conscience will it do with Lincoln and Johnson?" This erstwhile defender of the peculiar institution, become a latter-day convert to abolition, had already decreed that slavery was dead. Now he urged emancipation both because "it is right in itself" and because it destroys the slavocracy, thereby "freeing more whites than blacks in Tennessee." For the beneficiaries of right in itself, Johnson had a stern admonition: "liberty means liberty to work, and enjoy the fruits of your labor. Idleness is not freedom." The incubus of slavery exorcised and the doors thrown open, he envisioned a flood tide of newcomers from all over the nation. "Come on!" beckoned the self-appointed commissioner of immigration: "We need your labor, your skill, your capital. We want your enterprise and invention." At some future time, when the state vied with New England in the mechanic arts, patent office visitors "need not blush that Tennessee can show nothing but a mousetrap." Strange sentiments, coming from a hardy provincial who had once marshalled an impressive array of statistics designed to demonstrate Tennessee's superiority over New Hampshire.[2] Truly the Americanization of this southerner was proceeding apace.

But what of the restoration of civil government in Tennessee and, by implication, in the South? One thing certain—parricides should have no part in the great task. Sounding again the Catonian cliché which would render him so palatable to ultras who demanded a fundamental change in the southern system, he intoned that "Treason must be made odious, and traitors must be punished and impoverished," elaborating that "Their great plantations must be seized and divided into small farms, and sold to honest, industrious men." Thundering that "the traitor has ceased to be a citizen" and become "a public enemy," the governor prescribed "a severe ordeal before he is restored to citizenship." Instead let those "true and faithful men," be they but five thousand in number—an estimate at variance with his asseverations earlier in the conflict and a tacit admission that the unionists were in a decided minority—"control the work of reorganization and reformation absolutely." Restoration, reorganization, reformation: like the modern interpreter, Johnson was groping for a suitable word to express the transition to peacetime; but "reconstruction" he eschewed, out of a basic conviction that the southern states had never departed the Union.

Have done with all this pussyfooting, said the governor. "The salvation of the country is now the only business which concerns the patriot." Extirpate the rebellion "because it is war against democracy." Shame on Tennesseans, "higgling about negros," and on midwesterners, warring "upon the Government out of regard to slavery!" They might as well be in the enemy camp. And looking toward the hour of reunion, he saw some unfinished business south of the border. The European nations, "anxious for our overthrow," had condoned the establishment of a monarchy in

2. Exchange with Daniel Clark, March 27, 1860, *Johnson Papers*, III, 493-94.

Mexico; putting down "this French concern . . . would be a sort of recreation to the brave soldiers who are now fighting the battles of the Union."

How should this collection of odds and ends, undoubtedly "off the cuff" but likely gotten by rote, be assessed? In part, it was merely a reiteration of opinions expressed at various times during the long struggle: a fixed belief in the indissolubility of the Union, an abhorrence of privilege, a southern white yeoman prejudice, an apothegm that punishment must follow crime. Of more recent vintage were the endorsement of emancipation, the advocacy of sequestration, the invitation to immigrants, the moral injunction to the freedmen, and the dogma that none but the loyal should undertake restoration. Novel, for Johnson at least, was the note of defiance to the Old World. Whether his auditors took literally the pronouncement that the office had sought the man is impossible to say; other contemporaries did not, and historians are skeptical. Whether his northern coadjutors accepted the proposition that the party, in nominating a Tennessean, was saying the South had never left the Union is exceedingly doubtful; it was a moot question thoroughly debated in war and Reconstruction. In its totality not a manifesto but more nearly an epitome of his views, this speech and the circumstances which prompted it may be seen as a harbinger of the future and a postlude to the past—the occasion symbolizing his reentry onto the larger national stage, the site serving as a reminder of his wartime focus on Tennessee.

By the fall of 1862 Andrew Johnson, brigadier general and military governor, was no stranger to the contradictions and ambiguities of the position which he had held since March—"a situation environed with difficulties, perplexities, and dangers of every kind." [3] Although caustic in his assessment, the editor of the Nashville *Press* spoke more truth than error when he asserted two years later:

> Military Governorship is an anomally [*sic*] in the United States of America. It is an office without a duty and a position which no rules govern, which no statute creates, which no law defines, which no court construes, and which lexicographers will hereafter explain by saying, the situation held by Andrew Johnson in Tennessee.[4]

The first and, as it turned out, longest incumbent of a military governorship, he early confronted the two-pronged responsibility of that post: to provide on a temporary basis civil government for a recently rescued—or conquered, depending on one's view—population living in the midst of a continuing war; and to restore loyalty to the Union as a necessary preliminary to the reestablishment of a "republican form of government." Lacking any written directive from his superiors in Washington—his brief appointment paper merely gave "authority to exercise and perform . . . all and singular, the powers, duties and functions pertaining to the office of Military Governor . . . until the loyal inhabitants of that state shall organize

3. Nashville *Times and True Union,* June 10, 1864.
4. Nashville *Press,* February 15, 1864.

a civil government" [5]— he spent a full year in "learning by doing," meeting each new situation and problem with pragmatic, *ad hoc* decisions and actions, before taking steps to get a more specific delineation of his power and position. We can speculate that the absence of recorded instructions had been offset by informal conversations with Lincoln and Stanton during the weeks before the senator left Washington; certain it is, the military governor regarded his as an executive mission and throughout his tenure brought his needs and concerns directly to the attention of the President and secretary of war. No intermediaries for him! And in this behavior he was given encouragement.

There is no evidence that the Tennessean paid any attention to the ineffectual efforts of Congress to get some voice in, or even information about, the management of recovered Confederate territory. These abortive efforts, harbingers of the ultimate struggle over Reconstruction in which the new military governor would be a central figure, proved to be premature; Johnson, Edward Stanly in North Carolina, and others would continue to function as "agents" of the President, appointed under his military power to operate, according to Senator John Carlile of Virginia, "as adjuncts to the Army, to mitigate, if possible, the rigors and the horrors and the severities of this war." [6]

Throughout his incumbency, Johnson would find the task of mitigating the horrors of war a never-ending challenge; the spectre of violence, raid, and destruction was never far distant from the populations for which he was responsible. In the state at large the march and countermarch of armies was a frequent occurrence; when armies departed, guerrillas, bushwhackers, and raiding parties remained; and where these military and paramilitary activities were absent, there persisted bitter rancor, the residue from the trauma of choosing between loyalties during the first year of war. These resentments and hatreds repeatedly erupted in personal and group vendettas, making security of person and property for many problematic at best. Daily the human anguish consequent upon the activities of armies, raiders, and vigilantes was brought to the governor for his amelioration, intercession, or adjudication.

All and singular, powers, duties, and functions: words with a proconsular ring; yet they do not adequately convey the challenge of Johnson's all-encompassing task. His was an assignment not fully understood—neither by Lincoln, who created the military governorships, nor by other contemporaries, who watched wartime developments in Tennessee. In early 1864 an old friend wrote apologetically: "I regret to have to tax your time with any personal matters, but Public Men are Public property, as well as public servants . . . having done the People a great Many favours you are expected

5. Appointment as Military Governor, March 3, 1862, *Johnson Papers,* V, 177.

6. *Cong. Globe,* 37 Cong., 2 Sess., 3146. It is worthy of note that Johnson alone among military governors had been confirmed in both office and rank by Senate action.

to do a great Many More."[7] It was a fitting homily for a stewardship beyond the capacity of one man; even the most casual examination of the Johnson corpus suggests the degree to which he had become "Public property." Plebeians, among them "aged men, from 50 to 70 years," confined for months without charge and their dependents left destitute, ask that action be forthcoming on their cases. Tidings that a house occupied by poor families—most of whom have husbands in blue—is to become a smallpox hospital, stir the governor's soul and belie the traditional image of an insensitive Johnson. "Would it not be as humane for persons to die with the small pox as for helpless women and children to perish in the street with hunger and cold?" Former First Lady Sarah Childress Polk, her loyalties put to the supreme test by the great crisis, intercedes to save the property of relatives gone South. Conditions in Old Fentress are desperate, writes "Tinker Dave" Beaty; "We need something here that will answer . . . for *bread* . . . . corn, flour, *crackers,* or anything that will sustain life." Union cavalrymen enjoy a three-hour sojourn at a unionist's home; "entered it with pistols drawn, and in a state of intoxication. . . Cursed my wife— entered my drawers, destroyed papers, took thirteen hundred and fifty dollars . . . drank whiskey, and played at cards, laid and rolled on my beds with their boots on," threatening to return "and hang me to the first lim." Calling Memphis "one of the worse Secess hole that I ever saw," a semiliterate physician warns that there are Tennesseans "who would cut your throught if they dare do it." Tennessee political prisoners incarcerated in Georgia become mudsills, beating dough and toting food, cleaning sinks and scrubbing floors, digging wells and mending fences—in short, "forced to do the most degrading part of the work." Did the great struggle represent a coming-out party for southern femininity? *"The truth is the women keep up this war,"* opines one of them; "Tomorrow were the men willing to lay down their arms they would not *dare* come home to their wives and daughters. . . . Break up their nests and the birds will fly." From "an Old Abolationist of the Chase, Hale, & Gidings stripe" comes inquiry about good farms in the Nashville area; this exporter of northern culture proposes to people them with "Union Republicans." For Prime & Company, Wall Street, it is business as usual: a minion asks "wether there is any prospects of paying Interest on your state debt as I have been anciously awaiting for several years."

Prime stuff for a great historical pageant: all Tennessee a stage and its borderlands the wings, a cast of thousands, a maze of Dickensian plots and subplots, the supreme tragedy of internecine war. The enemy without and within, the hairline between loyalty and disloyalty, the seductions of Dame Rumor, the ubiquitous uniform, the nether millstones of the contending armies, the destitute and the displaced, women suppliant and women

7. Letter from John W. Gorham, February 1, 1864.

defiant, northern emissaries and "observers," pettifoggers and philanthropists, entrepreneurs fascinating in their temerity and rogues picturesque intheir rascality—all these, and more, made up a scenario in which Johnson was continually "on the boards." Expediter, factotum, oracle, sounding board, eleemosynary institution, he found imposed upon him a bewildering variety of roles— his "multifariousness," an unimaginative biographer calls it. That he labored incessantly at his lines seems beyond question; that he would carry off each scene successfully is too much to expect.

His first five months in office had acquainted him with most of the larger problems associated with the assignment, though new situations constantly presented themselves, reminding him of the varied challenges accompanying an appointment unique in American history. By summer's end, he had confronted a number of issues with varying success. In the capital itself, the most outspoken voices of secession—a disloyal city council, embattled women and unrepentant clergymen, recalcitrant businessmen and aristocrats—had been reined in, if not necessarily muzzled; yet it was quite obvious that, contrary to his sanguine expectations, disunionist sentiment in Middle Tennessee remained the prevailing mood. The imposition of loyalty, always contingent upon the tides of war but conditioned by many other factors, had thus far proven fruitless; if it yielded any perceptible result, it was the increasing alienation of Tennesseans from Andrew Johnson. Yet there were those who approved of the governor and his policies, among them many who sought his aid: unionists languishing in southern prisons, captured Tennessee rebel soldiers held in the North, people searching for loved ones, the poor and abandoned of Nashville craving sustenance, and those suffering from the actions of the warring armies. He was laid under heavy siege by commission hunters and office seekers; a votary of the spoken word who disliked writing letters, he found himself perforce an active correspondent; a self-avowed man of peace, he must now deal with matters of war.

In the military realm *per se,* Federal forces held control of large parts of the state, yet the possibility of a major Confederate offensive against Nashville or other key points was still to be reckoned with, while rebel control of East Tennessee remained virtually unchallenged. Johnson's unceasing and oftimes injudicious efforts to arouse the authorities, in Washington or in the field, to greater activity in his adopted homeland, proved no more efficacious than had his earlier attempts as senator. Nor had the shadow of the gray been lifted elsewhere in the state. Confederate cavalry menaced the mid-state and border areas, intimidating local unionists, destroying property, and sometimes occupying cities and towns; Tennessee as a whole became a veritable laboratory in irregular warfare, whether conducted by guerrillas, home guards, scouts, bushwhackers, or individuals. Moreover, Governor Johnson had quickly discovered, if he had not surmised beforehand, the anomalous character of his appointment as it concerned his relationship with the military. Never in complete harmony with the shoulder strappers, bickering with major commanders and minor officers, prone to dispense gratuitous advice to the professional soldiers, impatient with military red tape, he had by late August reached a major confrontation with the commander of the Army of the Ohio.

His strong reservations about General Don Carlos Buell, resting upon what he would have considered cumulative evidence but directed toward a particular situation, the plight of Nashville, were made plain in a jeremiad to Lincoln on September 1, 1862. To the editor, sifting through Johnson's wartime correspondence, it is a twice-told tale: a Confederate threat, an irresolute and perhaps pusillanimous commander, a lamentation about East Tennessee, and withal, a sinister note of disloyalty. Braxton Bragg's Army of Tennessee was reported to be marching on the capital, and though Buell could "whip him with the greatest ease," he intended to take a defensive stance, leaving unionists east and south to the mercy of the rebels. If the general would only act with courage and dispatch, asserted this armchair strategist, he could repel the foe and even move forward into East Tennessee; but, "notwithstanding his fair promises to the President," he will never "redeem the Eastern portion of this State." Repel the enemy and move forward—why, this was a favorite *Lincoln* litany. Nor had the governor completed his declaration of grievances: General Buell "is very popular with the rebels, and the impression is . . .that he favors the establishment of the Southern Confederacy." The letter closed on an invocative note—"May God save my country from some of the Generals that have been conducting this war." [8] Obviously Johnson wanted Buell replaced. It was neither the first nor the last time that the Tennessean would lecture his Washington superiors about the shortcomings of their flag officers.

The governor, it turned out, had gotten himself into an unnecessary, if not altogether unproductive, dither. Bragg did not descend upon the capital but instead moved north into Kentucky. It was not Jehovah, but Lincoln, who intervened to "save my country" from Buell's ministrations. There were others who shared Johnson's opinion, and shared it for reasons which went beyond field generalship: Buell was a friend of McClellan, partaking not only of Little Napoleon's "slows," but likewise of his Democratic politics, and therefore doubly *non grata* to Republican critics of the war effort. Moreover, his policy with respect to Confederate civilians reflected the judicious rather than the Draconian, and hence directed suspicion to its author. In due time discontent with his command, climaxing with the controversial victory at Perryville, grew to the point where a Commission of Investigation was set up, before which the military governor testified in April, 1863, conveying the impression that he had persuaded a reluctant Buell to defend Nashville and to keep troops which

8. Letter to Abraham Lincoln, September 1, 1862.

he would fain have withdrawn.[9] By implication Andrew Johnson became the savior, a bias with which the commission's report tended to agree. Meanwhile Buell had been removed in October, 1862, to be succeeded by William S. Rosecrans. If the governor's strife with the generals was by no means over, Old Rosy was at least committed to the offense: "we have a man at the head of this army who will fight," Johnson assured the President.[10] And fight he did, albeit slowly, his victory at Murfreesboro in January precluding for the time being a major Confederate threat to Nashville and its periphery.

Yet the danger was by no means dissipated. Rebel spies and informers filtered through the lines, in and out of a capital heavily secessionist; guerrillas operated on the outskirts and in remote pockets of Middle Tennessee counties; and the Confederate cavalry, enjoying a numerical superiority over the Union horse, ranged over the vicinity, sometimes seemingly determined to take Nashville itself. The climax had come in October when the maneuvers of Bedford Forrest and John Hunt Morgan effectively isolated the city from the outside world for some two months. A New York *Herald* correspondent dramatized the situation: "No communications for a month . . . . Rations getting scarce. People getting uneasy. Hotels closed for want of supplies. . . . The cool and determined demeanor of Governor Johnson is the admiration of all."[11] At one juncture, it was the determined demeanor of the thespian. Watching the ramparts from the capitol in November when Forrest's troops attacking the city's outerworks appeared to have the upper hand, the governor allegedly declaimed: "I am no military man; but any one who talks of surrender I will shoot."[12] But softly! no call for his Tranter double-action; the hateful word remained unspoken and the attack was repelled.[13] Nashville seemed safe for the nonce and the Army of Tennessee retreated after Murfreesboro; but life, limb, and property in Middle Tennessee would be precarious for some time to come.

In the ensuing months Andrew Johnson continued to wage a double-action war—shooting at the enemy while skirmishing with the Union command. Writing in the spring of 1863, "Old Brains" Halleck delivered himself of a masterful understatement about the situation in Tennessee: "It is understood that there has been some conflict of authority between the military forces . . . and the civil government."[14] That Rosecrans had replaced Buell made no real difference. It did not take the governor long to perceive that the new commander was scarcely more manageable than his predecessor; or, to be precise, no more amenable to suggestion. On the

9. Deposition to the Buell Commission, April 22, 1863.

10. Telegram to Abraham Lincoln, November 18, 1862.

11. Samuel R. Glenn Diary, October 6, November 4, 1862, in New York *Herald,* April 24, 1865.

12. *Ibid.,* November 5, 1862.

13. For the governor's pistols, see *Johnson Papers,* V, 283-85.

14. Henry W. Halleck to William S. Rosecrans, March 20, 1863, *OR,* Ser. 3, III, 77.

surface, their relationship was not acrimonious but polite, certainly a testimonial to the restraint of two men whose stock in trade was tactlessness. Yet the accompanying correspondence in no way hides the dichotomy. The commander's primary mission was to defeat the enemy, the governor's to restore civil authority; but, "an eye to the general good"[15] notwithstanding, the one must inescapably intrude upon the domain of the other. To no small degree, it was a battle of prerogative. Rosecrans, like his fellow officers, was firm as regarded his sphere of command and solicitous of his authority; Johnson, a governor armed with a brigadier's commission, was inclined toward an increasingly broader view of his vaguely defined functions and prone to meddle in military matters. Moreover, the governor could, as he had in the past, go over the general's head to Washington.

It was the critical situation of Nashville which exacerbated this conflict between civil and military. By 1863, Tennessee's capital had become a bustling, overcrowded city in which space and privacy were at a premium: a major supply base and staging area for operations against the Confederacy, a gathering place for refugees, contrabands, and others of the displaced, a happy hunting ground for confidence men and for women who followed the drum, a listening post, a focus of intrigue and espionage. In the words of an army publicist, it was "one vast 'Southern Aid Society.' "[16] At once a city and a garrison, this conglomerate of soldiers and civilians badly needed governance. But from what source should it come: the commanding general or the military governor? Precisely how much authority should Rosecrans' representatives, the provost marshals in particular, have? The administration of justice in Nashville was further complicated by the existence, side by side, of civil courts, created earlier under the Johnson regime, and military commissions, an inevitability of the occupation. Just where was the line of jurisdiction to be drawn?

As long as the provosts followed the governor's orders, friction might be kept at a minimum. When they occasionally demurred, Johnson vociferously complained, not only to the commanding general but also to the secretary of war and even the President. That the governor stood totally dependent upon the regular army for enforcement of his authority, possessing no independent organization until 1863, was unquestionably a source of irritation, making him hypersensitive to uniformed subalterns. The dilemma was compounded by Rosecrans' efforts to eradicate traitors, spies, and illicit traders. Upon assuming command of the Army of the Cumberland, he had created a military police force; under an energetic and ruthless chief, "Colonel" William Truesdail, it displayed a zeal which angered both the governor and the citizenry. The resulting exchanges between Johnson and Rosecrans marked the nadir of their relationship.

15. *Ibid.*, 78.
16. John Fitch, *Annals of the Army of the Cumberland* (Philadelphia, 1864), 373.

Fortunately the governor's characterization of Truesdail as "a base and unmitigated jesuetical parasite"was not directed to the general, an ardent convert to Catholicism; unfortunately, Rosecrans heard that Johnson had reported the chief's trafficking in cotton—a speculation in which the commander was alleged to have a "personal interest."[17]

Eventually the Washington authorities took a hand in the larger contretemps. Dispatching Rosecrans some "views and instructions" in March, 1863, Halleck observed that "experience has proved that all matters of local policy should be left to the civil authorities"; marshals should be concerned only with military police duties and "their powers should be confined within narrow limits." In a postscript which may have been a trial balloon, a warning, or a clear choice of sides, the general-in-chief addressed the immediate issue: "the Secretary of War suggests that, as Governor Johnson is a brigadier-general of volunteers, it might be well to place him in command of the troops in Nashville, and thus harmonize the civil and military authorities there." [18] Denying knowledge of any conflict, Rosecrans countered with a *reductio ad absurdum* which the War Department received "with marked dissatisfaction." He would be agreeable to putting the governor in charge at Gallatin, averred this "first-rate epistolary controversialist," but "Nashville is too important a post for me to intrust to his command at this time."[19] Like most professional soldiers, Rosecrans subscribed to the dictum that fighting a war is serious business, of which the military must be in charge; let the politicians do the talking and the generals the commanding. Yet Rosecrans must deal with Johnson, and he undoubtedly knew beforehand that the latter was stubborn and outspoken, possessed a pipeline to Washington, and, in his triple role of governor, brigadier, and politician, altogether a hard case. Complicating matters was the general's far from harmonious relationship with the secretary of war. Writing to Halleck on April 4, Rosecrans was conciliatory but firm: "I have done, and will do, all in my power to give him aid and comfort; but Nashville is an inclosed garrison, and my grand depot." Aware that Johnson was at this very time in the national capital, he addressed the latter a note in care of Stanton, reiterating his intention of supporting the civil authorities and asking the governor to "communicate to me fully and freely all matters of conflict and complaint." [20]

Although *l'affaire Truesdail* passed, the basic civil-military conflict remained unresolved during Rosecrans' tenure and, for that matter, during the course of the war; instead, it was merely smoothed over. Yet the relationship between the general and the governor took a turn for the

17. Letter to Richard Smith, November 2, 1863; Clifton R. Hall, *Andrew Johnson: Military Governor of Tennessee* (Princeton, 1916), 82.

18. Halleck to Rosecrans, March 20, 1863, *OR,* Ser. 3, III, 78.

19. Rosecrans to Halleck, March 26, 1863, *ibid.,* Ser. 1, XXIII, Pt. II, 174; T. Harry Williams, *Lincoln and His Generals* (New York, 1952), 275.

20. Rosecrans to Halleck and to Johnson, both April 4, 1863, *OR,* Ser. 1, XXIII, Pt. II 208, 207.

better. Indeed, the dichotomy aside, they shared certain convictions about the conduct of the war. Old Rosy had a proven record as a fighter, and Johnson liked generals who would fight; Rosecrans' policy toward Confederate civilians was relatively harsh where Buell's had been comparatively mild, and Johnson had always taken a grim view of secessionists and the great undecided. Undoubtedly there was a personal touch to it; for the general gave the governor's faltering son Robert, colonel of a Tennessee regiment, some friendly advice—a gesture which must have touched the father deeply.[21] In September Rosecrans moved into lower East Tennessee, raising the possibility of regaining the "homeland"; and in early October, more than a month after the general had receded from the edge of glory and gotten himself bottled up in Chattanooga, the governor, perhaps prodded by Lincoln, asked whether there was anything he could do to "promote the interests of the Army of the Cumberland," adding that "your recent position is looked upon as a great victory and the nation will appreciate."[22]

So ended the Rosecrans chapter, but not Johnson's connections with the generals; from time to time, chiefly in communications to the President, he continued to voice opinions and make recommendations. Patently there were officers he liked, such as George H. Thomas, who "should be placed in independent command of the Department of the Cumberland"; Ambrose Burnside, who should be sent back to East Tennessee—"the people want him. He will inspire more Confidence than any other man"; Alvan C. Gillem, in charge of the Governor's Guard; and Lovell Rousseau, who would make an effective speaker at Union party rallies. Obviously there were officers he disliked: paramount among them was his old foil Don Carlos Buell, without a major command but, according to rumor, destined to take charge in East Tennessee; back in 1862, he had worked closely with General James S. Negley against Middle Tennessee secessionists; but by 1863, after Negley had commanded the post at Nashville for several months, the governor decided that the general was "a traitor" who should forthwith be removed.

Dramatic in its interplay of personalities and fundamental in its implications as was this game of epaulets, it reflected only one side of Johnson's involvement with things military. Ironically the plebeian Sartorius, who had cultivated the arts of peace and shown a pronounced aversion to the clangor of war, now found imposed upon him a variety of problems essentially military in nature. Some of these were of major importance and others quite routine, often insignificant; all in all, they were duties tiresome, duties never ending.

Of greatest importance was the governor's responsibility for law and order. Although the Federal armies were concerned with both war and

21. Telegram from William S. Rosecrans, April 12, 1863; Telegram to William S. Rosecrans, June 1, 1863.

22. Telegram to William S. Rosecrans, October 1, 1863.

pacification, they could scarcely be expected to keep the peace when the fortunes of war remained in doubt. Nor were they necessarily available in an emergency. How reckon with the sudden strikes of Confederate cavalry? How deal with enemy irregulars, self-appointed vigilantes, and marauding bands? To grant individuals the privilege of keeping and bearing arms, as Johnson occasionally did, would not suffice; not only had Tennessee's secessionist regime made heavy inroads on the citizenry's small arms, but there were serious reservations about the wisdom of allowing irresponsibles to carry weapons. Several other alternatives lay open.

Early in his tenure Johnson had learned that the military authorities were loath to detach units for the special service that he requested. Instead, he needed troops directly answerable to him; such an organization, he wrote much later, "might be exceedingly useful in sustaining and strengthening . . . the Civil Authorities, at the same tme rendering such military service. . . as might be required of them under proper authority." [23] These last are the key words; for General Johnson, like his professional counterparts, was quite proprietary of his men. It was not exactly a "state army," at least to the degree that some Confederate governors fancied—but men under his command, ready for action. There is, however, some ground for believing that Johnson envisioned such a body as a power instrument usable in ways which went beyond its immediate purpose. Provision had been made at the time of his appointment: he was advised that commanders operating in Tennessee were to detail troops for a "governor's guard" acting under his orders. A year went by and no guard materialized. Then, out of the general clarification of the governor's functions during the spring of 1863, Stanton issued orders detaching a unit of Tennessee troops from the general service and placing it under Johnson's command. Rosecrans complied grudgingly. Not only could he ill spare the regiment, but "a force located within the garrison of Nashville, but not subject to the orders of the garrison commander, would do little but breed discord." [24] By the summer of 1864 the guard, commanded by General Alvan C. Gillem, had been increased to brigade strength. Responding to repeated calls, among them an ominous communication from "Many Many Very Many Voters of Upper East Tenn.," Johnson dispatched much of the force to that region in August, with orders to "kill or drive out all bands of lawless persons." [25] The campaign, which opened auspiciously with an advance to Bull's Gap and the killing of John Morgan at Greeneville, seemed nothing short of redemption and atonement—final rescue of East Tenncssee from the hated foe, fitting revenge upon the scourge of Tennessee and the border areas. Subsequently, however, Gillem was routed and compelled to retreat. Despite its reorganization, the guard accomplished relatively little of consequence thereafter.

23. Letter to Lovell H. Rousseau, May 28, 1864.
24. Hall, *Military Governor,* 83.
25. *Tennessee Adjutant General's Report* (1866), 695.

In any case the problem of law and order was much too formidable to be solved by Andrew Johnson's personal army; rather, recourse must be had to local means of dealing with the chaos in great parts of the state. The most logical solution lay in the use of various types of irregulars. Should the state militia be armed? Yes, insisted various correspondents; its "enrollment" would not only provide a strike force against local enemies, but might likewise serve further to distinguish the loyal from the disloyal—an hypothesis reflecting the feverish political quest for unsullied, nonpareil unionists. What about "home guards?" Again, provision for such forces had been made in an act of July, 1862, appropriating arms to loyal citizens, a measure which Johnson himself had introduced in the Senate. During the ensuing months, these men, recruited for one-year enlistments, were both a source of support for the Johnson regime and of dispute with regular military personnel. The guards' preference for cavalry over infantry status, on the ground that guerrillas could be pursued only with horses, created problems of supply and equipment, even when animals belonging to secessionists were commandeered. Home levies also had certain innate shortcomings, a number of which were detailed by Colonel "Mitch" Edwards. Their activities invited rebel reprisal against unionists on a larger scale; they were careless, even indiscriminate, sometimes "robbing stealing and plundering both parties alike.... There is too great a risk of the system, however well intended, running into highway robbery and piracy." Such units should "be composed of men of advanced age and experience, and if young able bodied men wish to play soldier let them go into the army properly." [26] Despite such sound reservations, the home guards were in many parts of the state the only protection available to citizens, and they performed yeoman service in guarding the army's lines of communication.

Not least taxing of Johnson's military functions was what might be called an overseer's role. For Tennesseans in uniform, irrespective of their particular assignments, the governor was often the advisor, the expediter, the court of last resort. Not only did he hold the highest office in the state, but he was a seasoned veteran when it came to raising troops and dealing with their problems, and he had influence higher up. He directed recruitment for Tennessee, arranged for divers reorganizations, kept a weather eye on pay and bounties, scouted around for equipment, interceded with Federal authorities. But Johnson must also play nursemaid—harken to the eternal grousing, placate the prima donnas among the officers, do his best to mediate their frequent domestic jars.

Of all Union troops, the East Tennessean, his region longest under Confederate control, may well have been the most frustrated soldier of the war. What matter that he had donned the blue primarily to recapture his own fireside? Until the late stages of the conflict, he was more likely to be

26. Letter from Richard M. Edwards, September 30, 1863.

found elsewhere: across the Ohio River on a bootless errand; in some other part of Tennessee protecting the rebs and their property, as some correspondents claimed; or marking time in Kentucky, quarreling with his fellows while impatiently awaiting the signal for the Great Redemption. Shades of Xenophon *sans* the legendary heroics! Two East Tennessee regiments, part of a command which had evacuated Cumberland Gap and trekked for eighteen days "through a dry, sandy and wilderness country," found themselves holed up in the Ohio peninsula with the prospect of a further peregrination to Virginia; get us headed back to Tennessee, they besought their "greatest earthly Benefactor."[27] What a fratricidal spectacle in Louisville! Colonel Robert Johnson, the governor's own flesh and blood, arrested by Kentucky authorities, allegedly at the instance of his father's friend Mitch Edwards. What was all the fuss about? A sanguinary battle for the bodies of recruits. Some months later Edwards had trouble galore in his own regiment, unfolding a tale of conspiracy supposedly engineered by his officers. Even before Johnson had been appointed military governor, a storm of controversy had swirled around the "Carter Concern"—General Sam, Colonel Jim, and Preacher Bill[28]—a naval officer now a controversial brigadier, a conniver of a regimental commander, and a calculating civilian who had been the leading spirit in the notorious East Tennessee bridge-burnings of November, 1861. To read the mewlings of their comrades-in-arms is to imagine this troika the brothers Machiavel of the Civil War era.

Yet the easterners, nursing their refugee syndrome, enjoyed no monopoly on the trials, real or fancied, which beset Tennessee's Volunteers. William B. Stokes, erstwhile Whig politician and now colonel of the First Middle Tennessee Cavalry, proved himself a leading serial contributor to the Johnson papers. In December, 1862, Stokes was insisting that his men receive the bounty promised for enlisting; in January he sought Johnson's intercession to rid him of Lieutenant Henry Newberry, an inordinately influential junior officer who had been "denouncing the Regiment as Cowards, sais they run, & all such slanderous talk"; in February, shot by one of his own captains, he suffered "a wound . . . that will give me pain So long as I live"; the next month it was Newberry again, and "you are the only one that Can Cure the disease, or pest." To employ a euphemism of the day, Bill Stokes had "problems of command." Ironically, in the future Radical Congressman William B. Stokes would undertake to cure another "pest," voting for the impeachment of President Johnson.

Some of these tempests and flurries the greatest earthly benefactor could calm, some blew themselves out, others raged unabated. The lost legion quitted Ohio and, struggling through Kentucky 'mid snow and ice,

27. Letter from Robert Johnson, October 15, 1862; Memorial from East Tennessee Soldiers, October 17, 1862.

28. Samuel Powhatan, James Patton Taylor, and William Blount Carter.

reached Tennessee. "Little Bob" escaped house arrest within a day, but his troubles had scarcely begun. Like Poe's raven, the Carter concern had found a roost; as late as 1864, the governor was still trying to get shet of them.

Unsuccessful, but interesting in its implications, was another military maneuver conducted during the summer of 1863—an attempt to raise troops elsewhere for Tennessee service. Although King Andrew's *Île de France* had gradually expanded from Nashville and the mid-state region, the title "Military Governor of Tennessee" reflected aspiration rather than reality, since large areas remained under enemy threat or control. Aware that the state's manpower resources were inadequate for the challenge and impatient at the military's slow progress toward East Tennessee, Johnson obtained war department permission to recruit regiments "in any State where the Governor . . . will give his consent." Stanton stipulated, however, that "enrollment or enlistment should be for the service of the United States unconditionally and without qualification expressed or implied of any character whatsoever." Several agents went to work in the eastern and midwestern states. *An Appeal to the Citizens of New York for the Organization of the Andrew Johnson Cavalry, for Special Service in Eastern Tennessee,* featuring "brave 'old Andy' " as its centerpiece, enlarged upon the sufferings of the unionists in the South, emphasized the significance of Tennessee as a field of operations, called for the extermination of rebel guerrillas, and pictured East Tennessee with the adjoining Appalachian regions—likely to be "the final theatre of the war"—as "peculiarly adapted to successful cavalry operations." For the soldier-immigrant, the brochure painted a glowing picture of fertile lands awaiting the settler, a region "rich in mining products," and Tennesseans ready to extend "a cordial welcome." Two regiments were raised in New York and two companies in Pennsylvania; but western governors, unlike their eastern counterparts, demurred: one declining to surrender his rights "in *raising* & *officering* all Troops" and another preferring "to fill up the old Regts now in the field." Finally Stanton, always opposed in principle to recruitment for a specified location, revoked the authorization. In its military objective a fiasco, the venture invoked a miniscule war of prerogative, not only among the states but between the states and the Federal government; but for brave old Andy, always a fervent believer in the virtues of advertising, it was not altogether a failure.

As the actual fighting receded and portions of the mid-state returned to relative peace, Johnson found himself embroiled in the everlasting disputes among the three groups into which the populace divided: unionists, secessionists, and transitionists, the latter *in transitu* from an earlier adjustment to Confederate rule to an accommodation to Federal occupation. Responding to the first two was relatively simple—unionists were to be assisted and rewarded, secessionists, punished or exiled—but what of those "who are 'pig to day & pork to-morrow.' Union when the Federals are about & Secessions [*sic*] when the Confederates are nearby,"[29] who now claimed a dubious, perhaps spurious, loyalty? Johnson was assailed from all sides with complaints that current protestations of devotion to the Union masked ineradicable secesh proclivities, that loyal men were being mistreated and exploited by Federal troops, while notorious rebel sympathizers were being coddled and protected by these same misguided troops. What made this uncertainty over loyalties so compelling an issue was the feeling that recovery of the state could be accomplished only if many who had been "innocently" caught in Confederate Tennessee—a condition brought on, according to Johnson, by the perfidy of Governor Isham G. Harris and other traitorous leaders—were encouraged to recant their "enforced" secessionism and reembrace their never-extinguished, only temporarily in abeyance, devotion to the Old Constitution. Perhaps one way to clarify the situation would be through subscribing to a loyalty oath. But here again there were problems. Who should prescribe it? Who should be required to take it? What should be its nature? Men who had openly, and at great personal loss and hardship, proclaimed their union commitment from the start, who had stayed and suffered, or gone into exile to suffer in a different way, protested that taking the oath was both superfluous and insulting. At the same time, they pointed out that now that the jig was up, secessionists and transitionists with no real commitment to the Union would not scruple to take such an oath, the better to protect themselves and their property. Then when guerrillas, bushwhackers, and raiders were about, they would willingly provide them succor and assistance, oath or no oath.

For the first year and a half of Johnson's service in Tennessee, the revalidation of loyalty among former Confederate soldiers and notoriously overt civilian proponents of secession was a pressing question. As prisoners were taken or as deserters returned home and were apprehended by the Federals, they were sent to Camp Chase in Columbus, Ohio, to other points of detention beyond the Ohio River, or placed in the prison at Nashville. Many of these men and their families, with solemn assurances that they would ever after eschew all contact with the rebellion, pressed for the privilege of taking the oath of allegiance and returning to their homes. But not all were so minded, reasoning that "having . . .taken an oath to support the So. Confederacy, if they now take the oath of Allegiance to the genl. government it would be 'cross-swearing,' "[30] an action regarded by one of the governor's correspondents as "not consistent with my Sense of Honor," a behavior which would result in "forfeiting the respect of my fellow citizens."[31] For such men, the parole offered an acceptable avenue to coexistence with Union conquest. The parolee pledged "his honor . . .

29. Letter from Edward J. Read, March 19, 1864.
30. Letter from Connally F. Trigg, April 1, 1862, *Johnson Papers,* V, 264.
31. Letter from Thomas M. Jones, June 14, 1862, *ibid.,* 474.

that he will not take up arms against the United States or give aid or comfort or furnish information directly or indirectly" to persons in rebellion, nor would he "write or speak against said Government." [32] Somewhat later, after Confederate authorities had conscripted sizeable numbers of young men, the governor was besieged with appeals from those who, according to their stories, having been forced into service, had deserted and turned themselves in, only to be banished north of the Ohio on pain of death should they return to Tennessee. Pleading unimpeachable "Union Sentiments"—"I with other Union men were, persecuted, and driven from home"—claiming impressment into the Confederate forces—"I was hunted down . . . was tied, and handcuffed and in irons carried to Port Hudson"—and vividly describing his desperate decision to desert—"with a determination to sooner face death than to fight for their Cause, I left knowing if I was captured it would be death" [33]—a young Bradley countian complained that he was in exile while men who had volunteered in the rebel army had been allowed to return to their homes. But how much could the governor believe? How could he ensure that justice be done and at the same time the public safety protected?

Meantime, the reliability of the civilian population was a perpetual concern. After early attempts to woo back the wavering by offering amnesty in exchange for the traditional oath of allegiance, Johnson, in the light of widespread refusal and continuing secessionist support and behavior, turned to more exacting demands, especially on those with prominence and property, always in his eyes the most suspect group. During the fall of 1862 the governor and William S. Rosecrans, the new commander of the Department of the Cumberland, devised a plan to reward with a "guarantee of protection" [34] those *"true and steadfast citizens* of the United States" who signed a bond agreeing to forfeit a specified sum of money or amount of property if the signer did not "keep the peace," deny aid and comfort to the enemy, and refrain from going "beyond the lines of the Federal Armies . . . into any section of the country in possession of the enemy, without permission of the Authorities of the United States." As the editor of the Nashville *Union* pontificated: "It draws the line of distinction broadly and deeply between rebels and patriots, and proclaims the sound doctrine that the enemies of the Government shall not enjoy its blessings, while abundant security and compensation shall be given to its friends." [35] Perhaps the reality that the Federal Government during the subsequent months was unable to provide that security and often seemed as ruthless as the rebels in depriving the loyal of their property did much to reduce the effectiveness of the "guarantee" as a means of winning Tennesseans to the Union cause.

32. Parole Order for Reuben Ford, October 9, 1862.
33. Letter from James Hilderbrand, May 7, 1864.
34. Guarantee of Protection, November 28, 1862.
35. Nashville *Union,* November 29, 1862.

As 1863 wore on, the slow progress of restoring civilian participation in government through election of officers and legislators focused new attention on the importance of pure-D loyalty. Repeatedly the governor was warned that unrepentant secessionists did not scruple to take the oath of allegiance and yet give aid to the rebellion whenever opportunity offered; moreover, that many were taking the oath only to be able to file claims with the Federal government for damages sustained during the war. [36] To counter this backwash of disloyalty, Johnson, when ordering general elections late in January, 1864, announced the terms under which Tennesseans might have the privilege of voting. In addition to being a free white man, twenty-one years of age, a citizen both of the United States and, for six months preceding election day, of the county where he proposed to vote, as well as qualifying as a court witness and being guiltless of various crimes, like bribery, larceny and other offenses, the voter was required to take a special oath before the judges of the election. Not content with the conventional oath of allegiance, nor yet with Lincoln's December 8 oath of amnesty which required acceptance of recent laws and proclamations affecting slaves and slavery, Johnson's franchise oath called not merely for abjuring the rebellion, but, beyond that, for a commitment actively to work to destroy the Confederacy: "that I ardently desire the suppression of the present insurrection and rebellion against the Government of the United States, the success of its armies and the defeat of all those who oppose them . . . that I will hereafter heartily aid and assist all loyal people in the accomplishment of these results." Obviously, "all the judges, officers and persons holding the election" were obliged to subscribe to the same. [37]

The governor's "ardently desire" oath at once became a thorn of controversy, attacked by both the undeviatingly loyal and the expediently acquiescing secessionist. The former was insulted by having to subscribe so unqualifiedly to a loyalty he had never abandoned; the latter demurred at being asked both to repudiate so categorically a recent affiliation and to be so sweepingly and actively obligated to destroy a once cherished loyalty. But, as an opposition paper insinuated, for the governor to settle for the President's oath "would not answer his purpose of disfranchising the great majority of loyal men in the State." [38] Yet how could Johnson "in the midst of so much disloyalty and hostility . . . and in order to secure the votes of its friends and exclude those of its enemies," [39] set any lesser hurdle for the franchise? To one class alone was the governor willing to give the ballot without test or amnesty oath—an East Tennessee soldier in the Federal service, "prima-facia evidence that he was a loyal Citizen And therefore ought to vote without regard to any Oath." [40] Truth to tell, the problem of

36. Letter from William A. Sorrells, June 23, 1864.
37. Proclamation Ordering Elections, January 26, 1864.
38. Nashville *Press,* January 30, 1864.
39. Proclamation Ordering Elections, January 26, 1864.
40. Letter to James T. Shelley, March 29, 1864.

discovering what lay in the heart of an applicant for the franchise was insoluble. For Johnson and "every real union man" Lincoln's amnesty oath was palpably inadequate to screen out the undependable elements—"as it now operates its main tendency is to keep alive the rebel spirit in fact reconciling none"—hence the governor's controversial oath. With a view to elevating further the barrier, not merely for voting but also for the more basic restoration of civil rights and property, Johnson, anticipating the Reconstruction policy with which he would be so indelibly associated, proposed in May of 1864 that his state be made an exception, that all "pardons granted to Tennesseans be upon the application of those desiring it directly to the President. . . . they will feel a much greater obligation to the Government." Failure thus to except Tennessee would be "seriously detrimental in reorganizing the state government," since too many unrepentant secessionists were taking the amnesty oath and being returned to active economic and political life.[41]

There is no question but that Johnson's stringent stipulations—his "Damnesty oath" as many would call it—unpalatable to many moderate unionists as well as to luke-warm secessionists, contributed significantly to the fiasco of the local elections of March, 1864, when a small vote, obviously not reflecting popular sentiment because of intimidation, resentment, and the inclusion in the electorate of non-resident soldiers and other outsiders, provided Federal authorities with the excuse to install hardline unionists in town and county offices. "The whole affair brought no credit to its instigators and placed the government in a weak and equivocal position before the people."[42] More than a year earlier, at the end of December, 1862, the Union element of West Tennessee had experienced a similar humiliation when, after much backing and filling by governor and military commander, an election was scheduled for the Ninth and Tenth Congressional districts only to be, in effect, aborted by the resurgence of military activity, so massive as to prevent opening the polls in much of the area. The resulting election, patently unrepresentative, was rejected by the House of Representatives, even though the "victor," Alvin Hawkins, was an unimpeachable unionist. Insofar as the presence of elected officers was an index of the return to civil government, Johnson's administration of the state had been palpably unsuccessful as the summer of 1864 began. No progress had been made to restore a legislature; the limited effort to choose congressmen had ended in frustration; and even those local officeholders engaged in discharging their duties were under the cloud of having attained their positions by appointment or through rigged or unrepresentative elections.

But were unreliable loyalty and Confederate guerrilla and military activity the only explanations for Johnson's failure to carry out his mission

41. Letter to Abraham Lincoln, May 17, 1864.
42. Hall, *Military Governor,* 123.

to reestablish civil government in Tennessee? At least one contemporary observer saw a personal, calculating, even self-serving, consideration as a major factor in the governor's reluctance to restore the state's political life. With the presidency as the next step in his upward march, Johnson's hope for the Republican nomination depended on making himself attractive to the Radical wing of that party, a faction critical of and frequently at odds with Lincoln. To achieve this end, it was essential not only that the governor espouse emancipation, a position which he had begun to embrace during the early months of 1863, but also that he demonstrate both his commitment and his political skill by bringing about the abolition of the peculiar institution in Tennessee. The resumption of self-rule must, according to this observer, "wait until the emancipationists are thoroughly drilled— speeches delivered—tracts disseminated—documents distributed—newspapers circulated—and the organization of the party perfected, and the morals of the people lifted up to the comprehension of the grand and great idea of the abolishment of the institution of slavery in the State." [43] Who is to say that a man of Johnson's ambition, if he shared this somewhat Machiavellian view of the advantages of delayed civil government, was impervious to its appeal, permitting the ever visible perils of military insecurity and undependable citizenry to postpone relinquishing power to elected bodies and officials; meanwhile, by moving Tennessee toward emancipation, he improved his own posture vis-á-vis a presidential nomination? Undeniably, as 1863 drew to a close and during the early months of 1864, his voice became increasingly strident, urging Tennesseans to accept the demise of slavery as both inescapable and desirable and to proceed in an orderly fashion to remove it from their constitution.

Yet these strictures on the governor's motives may be too harsh. As long as large portions of the state were outside Federal control, it was impractical to expect to elect a state-wide civil government which would have an accepted claim to legitimacy. The most that could be hoped for was to hold elections in those congressional districts where Federal authority was reasonably effective. When in December, 1862, such a condition seemed to exist in West Tennessee, Johnson issued writs of election for the Ninth and Tenth districts, only to have a resurgence of military activity prevent a sizeable turnout at the polls, thereby vitiating the election results. When, as a consequence of the actions of the "Union State Convention" [44] meeting in Nashville in July, 1863, the governor was asked to order legislative elections to be held on the usual first Thursday in August, he took no action. True, much of the state outside of East Tennessee was by mid-July in Federal hands, and the proposal did not call for a state-wide gubernatorial election, only a district-by-district vote where the Federals held sway; however, on the basis of previous experience Johnson felt that "no ade-

43. "Republican" to the editor, November 5, 1863, Nashville *Press,* November 6, 1863.

44. Resolutions from Union State Convention, July 13, 1863.

quate Union strength could be developed in the state while the guerrillas remained to menace the inhabitants and East Tennessee was unredeemed."[45] With the seizure of Knoxville early in September and the heady prospect—destined to be thwarted—of having Federal control of all three parts of the state in the immediate future, he assured Stanton's representative, Charles A. Dana, that he planned to call for a general election for the first week in October— "A Governor and other State officers, Legislature, and members of Congress will then be elected." [46] Three days later, perhaps reflecting Dana's despatch, the President urged Johnson to forge ahead on the organization of a civil government. Unexpectedly, the ensuing months saw a renewal of the military struggle throughout the eastern part of the state, not only in Knoxville and upper East Tennessee, but equally so, and even more alarmingly, in the lower counties, around Chattanooga. This was no time for the state-wide elections contemplated in the governor's sanguine assurance to Dana.

Lincoln's ten percent plan, enunciated early in December, injected a new ingredient into the situation; for the first time, the specific conditions under which civil government was to be restored were spelled out. Now loyal citizens could, and did, prod the governor to take the necessary steps—to administer the prescribed oath, register the approved voters, and conduct an election for a convention to revise the state constitution in conformity to the President's December 8 proclamation. These steps "might all go on simultaneously." [47] Moving with somewhat greater caution, the governor on January 26, 1864, issued a proclamation ordering that elections for county officers be held the first Saturday in March. And when in some counties, "from various causes no election was held" on the designated day, the governor subsequently offered to appoint suitable persons to hold elections "at such times as the same can be conveniently held." [48] Johnson evidently felt that while county elections could be effectively guarded against infiltration by the disloyal, choosing a dependable state convention to remove slavery from the constitution was a more risky venture. Although he would speak vigorously during the coming months in favor of calling such an assemblage,[49] it is a striking coincidence that the convention did not meet until January of the following year, on the eve of the departure of the vice-president-elect, who would no longer be able to keep a steadying hand on the Tennessee ship of state.

In some ways, more important to the everyday life of Tennesseans of all persuasions than popularly elected officers or a revised state constitution was access to courts and their services. With the return of Federal sway

45. Hall, *Military Governor,* 99.
46. Charles A. Dana to Edwin M. Stanton, September 8, 1863, *OR,* Ser. 1, XXX, Pt. I, 182.
47. Letter from Citizens of Memphis, December 26, 1863.
48. Proclamation re County Elections, April 4, 1864.
49. Speech at Shelbyville, April 2, 1864; Speech at Knoxville, April 16, 1864.

came calls for "Judicial organization," for the practical reason that merchants were losing money as claims daily were being outlawed "for want of opportunity to begin suit" and as "Secesh" removed their assets beyond the reach of their stymied creditors.[50] Yet there was another side to this coin. In a city like Memphis, where merchants "owe debts North, and have debts due them South," the restoration of civil courts would make them liable to suits requiring payment "North," while continued hostilities made it impossible for them to collect debts "South," i.e., from Mississippi.[51]

Even before Johnson reached Nashville in the early spring of 1862, the military had reestablished certain civil courts in Middle Tennessee where Federal authority had been restored. Conflict of jurisdiction between these and parallel military courts provided one of the ingredients in the friction between the military governor and the generals during the following fall and winter, an issue addressed by General-in-chief Halleck in March, 1863, when, prompted by Johnson's lobbying activities in Washington, he attempted to delineate the line between civil and military courts. Stressing that the civil authorities were to be respected in their proper sphere, he assured that army personnel "will not interfere with the authority and jurisdiction of the loyal officers of the State government, except in case of urgent and pressing necessity." He went on to direct that "To the provisional State government . . . must therefore be left the trial and adjudication of all civil and criminal cases cognizable under the laws of that State, and to the courts of the United States, reestablished there, must be left all cases which belong to their jurisdiction under the laws of the United States."[52] But it was one thing to have such "official" clarification and quite another to get "loyal" courts reestablished. Not until early 1864, after Rosecrans' departure from the Tennessee scene, were the military courts in the Nashville area effectively removed as competitors with civilian tribunals for criminal and civil cases covered under Tennessee law.[53]

Even more dire was the plight of West Tennessee where Union control was far less evident than in the state's central counties. Throughout 1863 the governor's correspondents in that region repeatedly urged upon him the necessity of appointing judges and opening the courts. By so doing, "you will do more to bring back the people to their loyalty than all the military power of the Country."[54] Judges who, until the advent of Union forces had been holding courts, had fled to the rebels or, if remaining, "utterly refuse to hold their Court." Further, in many instances there was "total destruction of the Records and papers in the clerks offices of the Western District."[55] During spring the commanding general in Memphis

50. Letter from Washington Union Club of Memphis, December 19, 1862.
51. Letter from Benjamin D. Nabers, February 5, 1863.
52. Halleck to Rosecrans, March 20, 1863, *OR*, Ser. 3, III, 77.
53. Peter Maslowski, *Treason Must Be Made Odious* (Millwood, N. Y., 1978), 65.
54. Jeremiah C. Sullivan to Johnson, February 16, 1863, Johnson Papers, LC.
55. Letter from Thomas L. Sullivan, February 16, 1863.

set up a three-judge civil commission to hear suits for the collection of debts, but this arrangement, more costly than traditional litigation, was regarded by most citizens as merely a makeshift, since it exercised no jurisdiction over real estates and provided for no system of juries—"if we had our old courts established and the Code of Tenn resumed—we would be much better off than as we now are."[56] It would be March of 1864 before the Federal courts of West Tennessee would be open in Memphis and not until fall was a grand jury empaneled.[57]

Throughout his incumbency, the governor grappled with the perplexing problems arising from the disintegration of slavery and the concomitant transition of the blacks to freedom. Always ready to do battle with the slave aristocracy, Johnson had, nonetheless, steadfastly defended the peculiar institution. He had vigorously argued that its protection and preservation would best be achieved by remaining within the Union; at the same time, he predicted its decline and eventual demise if the South seceded. These months were to see both the advent of conditions destructive of the institution and, at the same time, a major change in his own attitude. The dislocations of war were gradually undermining the master-slave relationship. At first there were complaints that chattels were being carried off,[58] or, if runaways held in prison, released by Federal troops.[59] Then, as blacks discovered that contrabands—captured Confederate slaves—worked for daily hire, they began to abandon their loyalist owners, who thereupon lodged loud protests with the governor.[60] Simultaneously, the exigencies of war during the summer and fall of 1862 led to the use of Negroes on the Nashville fortifications, with a consequent debate over "whether the earnings are to be paid to the negroes or to their masters"—an especially troublesome issue, inasmuch as the disbursing officer often had only the worker's word as to the owner's loyalty or disloyalty; and worker and putative owner were often in disagreement about the black's actual status.[61]

Meantime, throughout these months of upheaval and dislocation, Johnson, if we are to believe a contemporary co-worker, revealed his humane concern not only for fellow white southerners coping with the crisis but also for the far less competent and even more drastically uprooted and helpless slaves. Sent by soldiers and civilians alike, "they flocked to his office by scores."

> His patience never wearied in listening to their simple stories; kindness never tired in giving them aid or advice; he explained to them, with cheerful and encouraging words, and in a plain and simple manner, so that their poor understandings could comprehend his ideas, the new relation they occupied, their rights, their duties, their wants . . . that the Government would help

56. Letter from Benjamin D. Nabers, June 15, 1863.
57. Memphis *Bulletin,* March 6, 1864.
58. Letter from Citizens of Madrid Bend, May 9, 1862, *Johnson Papers,* V, 37.
59. Letter from Alexander P. Smith, June 27, 1862, *ibid.,* 510-11.
60. Letter from R. J. Wood, August 21, 1862, *ibid.,* 627-28.
61. Letter from James St. C. Morton, December 5, 1863.

them, but it could not support them in ease . . . that they should learn to depend on themselves, learn to read and write.[62]

Similar, if somewhat more restrained, testimony asserted that "He listened to the poorest slave who fled from his rebel master, and bade him work for himself, and was assailed as a transgressor of the black code, and a dangerous radical." [63] Nor did he confine his efforts to instruction, advice, and admonition. Concrete help came in the form of jobs with the army and in business houses, use of empty houses belonging to secessionists, a committee to provide emergency foodstuffs and clothing, and assistance in moving North when such seemed feasible. That he similarly, according to this account, dealt with white refugees suggests that Johnson's personal response to human need knew no color line; yet this man could and did approach the peculiar institution with virtual indifference to its moral or ethical implications and totally in the context of its social and political impact, purportedly saying on one occasion "Damn the negroes! I am fighting those traitorous aristocrats, their masters!" [64] He is reported to have had qualms during the early months of 1863 about the wisdom of Lincoln's emancipation proclamation, observing "that the Administration made a sad mistake in touching the Negro," because it "hurt us in Tenn. & Ky. & everywhere else," [65] a reference to the proclamation's adverse effect on those slaveholders who might otherwise have been weary of the war and ready to return to their old loyalty.

During these same months a new ingredient—the decision to use Negroes as soldiers—was introduced into the confusions swirling about the peculiar institution. Over the protest of those who argued that behind the lines blacks were performing vital services which would have to be undertaken by others if they were recruited, the military authorities pushed ahead, enlisting Negroes under white officers, defending the action as a move which would keep the uprooted and undisciplined from mischief-making and destitution: not only were they "without employment," but "in their present condition are a festering sore upon the body politic. . . . they are terribly imposed upon; many of them being carried back to their traitor-masters to be most cruelly & inhumanly punished." [66]

Originally opposed to arming blacks, Johnson was drawn by Lincoln's deft flattery into supporting their recruitment. Informed that "you have at least *thought* of raising a negro military force," the President, observing that the "colored population is the great *available,* and yet *unavailed* of, force, for restoring the Union," assured the governor that the country needed "no specific thing so much as some men of your ability, and

62. John A. Martin in Nashville *Times and True Union,* January 7, 1865 [See Appendix].

63. *Ibid.,* June 10, 1864.

64. George T. Palmer, *A Conscientious Turncoat: The Story of John M. Palmer, 1817-1900* (New Haven, 1941), 90.

65. Aaron Goodrich to Henry S. Sanford, March 13, 1863, Henry S. Sanford Papers, Tennessee State Library and Archives, Nashville.

66. Letter from John Carper, July 17, 1863.

position, to go to this work." If Johnson, "an eminent citizen of a slave-state, and himself a slave-holder" has "been thinking of it please do not dismiss the thought." [67] It may be assumed that this letter, written while the governor was in Washington in the early spring of 1863, was supplemented by conversations with Lincoln and others in the administration. Upon his return to Tennessee, Johnson reluctantly sanctioned and encouraged the enlisting of black companies, only to find during the summer that the New England abolitionist George Stearns and "a number of persons running in from the other states" under direct authority from Secretary Stanton, were vigorously—too vigorously—enlisting Tennessee blacks in competition with recruiters authorized by the governor. Not only were Stearns's agents outsiders, but their sole goal was to make soldiers out of the recruits, placing them in camps "where they in fact remain idle[.] This will to a very great Extent impede the progress of the works & diminish the number of hands Employed. all the Negroes will quit work when they Can go into Camp & do nothing." [68] In cooperation with Rosecrans the governor aimed to "organize and employ all the Negroes in Tennessee upon the public works or as soldiers." [69] Such dual use loomed large in Johnson's plans.

Yet it would appear that he was not averse to suggesting a way to facilitate black enlistment. A week after his complaint about Stearns, Johnson, in the hope of making it more palatable to unionist owners, suggested offering a bounty of $300 for each slave who enlisted, a step which "would be an entering wedge to emancipation and for the time paralize much opposition to recruiting slaves in Tennessee[.] The slave to receive all other pay & his freedom at the expiration of term of service." [70] Ten days later, when General Orders No. 329—"considered confidential at the time of its issue" [71]—set forth the terms for recruiting colored troops in Maryland, Missouri, and Tennessee, the essence of Johnson's $300 payment, appropriately hedged about with proofs of ownership and documents of manumission, was one of its provisions.[72] The precise influences which produced this presidential action are not known, but we may speculate that the Great Emancipator was not indifferent to the advice of "his man" in the "trenches" of Nashville.

If the President played a role in Johnson's decision to use slaves as soldiers, he was similarly a factor in the Tennessean's conversion to emancipation as a pragmatic step essential to preserving the Union. In his

67. Letter from Abraham Lincoln, March 26, 1863.
68. Telegram to Edwin M. Stanton, September 17, 1863.
69. Telegram to William S. Rosecrans, September 17, 1863.
70. Telegram to Abraham Lincoln, September 23, 1863.
71. *OR,* Ser. 3, III, 861n.
72. In practice, most enlistees were slaves who had abandoned their masters or been enticed away by ambitious whites who saw in the formation of Negro companies an opportunity to improve their own status, often thereby advancing from non-com, or even private, to a commission. Letter from Three Illinois Soldiers, May 22, 1863; Letter from Three Iowa Privates, May 27, 1863.

efforts to prevent southern withdrawal, Johnson had vigorously contended that remaining under the Constitution was the only way to sustain slavery, that the demise of the institution was inherent in secession.[73] Yet as early as the summer of 1862, even as he warned his Nashville audience that "the Union is the only protection of slavery—its sole guarantee," he in the same breath declared that, faced with a choice, he would respond, "Give me my Government, and let the negroes go!" [74] It would be another fourteen months, and once again at the state's capital, before he took a decisive public stand. But decisive it was, and widely reported in the nation's press; from this time forth, there could be no doubt in any quarter that he was "a thorough going emancipationist" who "urged the immediate and entire abolition of slavery in Tennessee and elsewhere." [75] Condemning slavery as "baleful to the nation by arraying itself against the institutions and interests of the people," as the "cause of our domestic dissensions and this bloody civil war," and no less than "a cancer on our society," he urged that "the scalpel of the statesman . . . be used not simply to pare away the exterior and leave the roots to propagate the disease anew, but to remove it altogether." Favoring immediate, but willing to settle, if necessary, for gradual emancipation, "He avowed himself unequivocally for the removal of slavery; the sooner it can be effected the better." [76]

The statesman's reward came some two weeks later, when the President, spurring him on to reinaugurate a loyal state government, observed, "I see that you have declared in favor of emancipation in Tennessee, for which, may God bless you. Get emancipation into your new State government—Constitution—and there will be no such word as fail for your case." [77] Thereafter, the military governor would be found espousing in letter and speech the destruction of slavery—not for the sake of the slave, but rather for the sake of the white man and the early restoration of the Union. Johnson undoubtedly reflected the racism of his age; his stance with respect to the peculiar institution was determined not by moral or ethical considerations, but rather by hardheaded, pragmatic judgment of the way it affected those beacons which guided his life—the Constitution, the Union, the common man, and the democratic process. When preservation of the Union was best served by persuading southerners to eschew secession as the first step in the decline of slavery, he found it both comfortable and expedient to support slavery. When the master-slave relationship had so disintegrated as to loose on society a body of irresponsi-

73. Speech on the Seceding States, February 5-6, 1861, *Johnson Papers,* IV, 238.

74. Speech at Nashville, July 4, 1862, *ibid.,* V, 536. The identical sentiment—"if negroes are in the way, I say *let THEM GO!*"—is found in the Speech to the Ohio Legislature, March 3, 1863.

75. Chicago *Tribune,* September 10, 1863.

76. Speech at Nashville, August 29, 1863.

77. Letter from Abraham Lincoln, September 11, 1863; for similar flattering encouragement, see Letter from Salmon P. Chase, September 12, 1863.

ble, unmanageable blacks, he advised his countrymen to abandon efforts to recover the unrecoverable—"The institution of slavery is turned into a traveling institution, and goes just where it pleases" [78]—and find ways to employ the self-freed Negro, even as he had done with his slaves. And when he saw insistence on slavery as a major obstacle to ending the war, he fervently embraced emancipation. For Johnson a paramount principle was at stake—the well-being of his beloved nation and its white citizens. Who could doubt the wisdom of giving up slavery, if by so doing we could retain a government "based on and ruled by industrious, free white citizens?" [79] Let us dispose of the question, and thereby emancipate the white man.[80] The Negroes have gone off—"this institution is dead." Recognize the fact that this cancer "must be rooted out before perfect health can be restored." Only thus can we restore the harmony of our government.[81]

By spring of 1864, the former defender of slavery, having found at a recent Shelbyville meeting that "Indications on the part of the people were much better than I anticipated in regard to the emancipation of Slavery," not only looked to an early state convention to resolve the question "definitely and finely," but expressed the hope that Congress would propose a constitutional amendment, "the sooner it is done, the better—" [82] Is it cynical to wonder whether the impending nominating convention contributed to the governor's vigorous espousal of a course so popular among leading Republicans? Yet it would be inaccurate to conclude, as some of his political enemies asserted, that Johnson had joined the ranks of the "nigger-loving abolitionists." Far from it! His emancipated black would ideally be transported "to Mexico, or some other country congenial to his nature"; but failing that happy solution, the governor looked with equanimity on the Negro's being "compelled to fall back upon his own resources, as all other human beings are. . . . Political freedom means liberty to work . . . and if he can rise by his own energies, in the name of God let him rise." However, in the midst of this paean to opportunity, Johnson made it clear that he was not arguing "that the negro race is equal to the Anglo-Saxon—not at all. . . . If the negro is better fitted for the inferior condition of society, the laws of nature will assign him there." [83] Here was no paternalistic emancipationist! Moreover, freedom was not to be equated with citizenship, as was vividly revealed in the governor's response to the rumor that a black man had been elected to office in Wilson County. Demanding that an inquiry be made and the poll books secured, he ordered the arrest and forwarding to Nashville under guard of "all the parties in any manner

78. Speech on Restoration of State Government, January 21, 1864.
79. Speech at Franklin, August 22, 1863.
80. Speech at Knoxville, April 12, 1864.
81. Speech on Slavery and State Suicide, January 8, 1864.
82. Letter to Abraham Lincoln, April 5, 1864.
83. Speech on Restoration of State Government, January 21, 1864.

connected with this expression of contempt for the Government and its efforts to restore civil law in Tennessee."[84] He could with clear conscience, even enthusiastic zeal, contemplate Negro freedom, but not Negro enfranchisement or office holding, both of which would interfere with "a white man's government" controlled by "a free, intelligent, white constituency."[85] And neither persuasion nor threat would move him from this position during the ensuing years.

The Negro question remained a persistent problem, indeed an unpleasant, inescapable burden. But there were other assignments which Johnson as a longtime politician eagerly welcomed, nay even solicited. One of his most indispensable assets as a public man had been his ability to captivate the crowds which, as was the wont of the age, came together to be entertained, aroused, and informed on the "issues of the day." This talent, the cornerstone of his success on the Tennessee hustings, had until the early months of 1863 been but little demonstrated to the outside world. True, in the first flush of national notoriety following his union speeches in the Senate, he had received numerous invitations—"Choose your own subject, & either write your lecture, or give us a talk, as you would talk to your own loved citizens of Tennessee. We want to hear the man that the people would delight to honor"[86]—from city councils, civic groups, and mechanics' organizations, especially in the northeast, but he had rejected all of them "from the great pressure of public business, and the uncertainty of my future movements, in consequence of the alarming state of affairs in that section of the country to which I belong."[87] Occasionally, when traveling to and from the nation's capital, he had been prevailed upon to speak in Kentucky, often where Tennesseans in exile were found, and in Cincinnati and Columbus; further, he had several times spoken to groups assembled outside his Washington hotel; but not until the second year of his military governorship did large numbers of northerners have a chance to hear him talk as he would to his "own loved citizens of Tennessee."

Late in February, 1863, urged by political friends to lend his influence to offset disaffection with the war and to strengthen the work of the new Loyal Leagues, he embarked upon what proved to be an extended speaking tour of the North, beginning in Indianapolis, ending in Washington, and including as major stops, Columbus, Harrisburg, Philadelphia, New York, and Baltimore. Since Johnson was not in the habit of writing out his speeches and such notes as survive are unidentified and fragmentary at best, we are dependent for the substance of these addresses on the unpredictable recording of newspapermen. Usually at the onset of speaking he disclaimed being prepared, a gambit patently untrue and designed to win

84. Letter to Manson M. Brien, May 15, 1864.
85. Speech at Franklin, August 22, 1863.
86. Letter from Daniel S. Heffron (Utica Mechanics Association), July 31, 1861, *Johnson Papers,* IV, 653.
87. Letter to André Froment, August 20, 1861, *ibid.,* 686.

an audience's indulgence; he made no such excuses on this tour. Instead, he used the equally tried and true tactic of self-deprecation, minimizing his speaking talents, urging his auditors to divest themselves of any expectation that the evening would bring them an oratorical treat, advising them to "let yourselves down,"a phrase sure to get a laugh. Thereafter, master that he was at manipulating the common man, he moved directly into the serious questions of the day: the need to support the Lincoln administration to the bitter end in its struggle to reestablish the Constitution's sway throughout the land; an angry and unequivocal rejection of all talk of compromise; a tried and true formula for detecting Copperheads—"if you want to find out traitors . . . shake a writ of *habeas corpus*";[88] the positive identification of the conspirators who brought on the war—the southern aristocracy; the wisdom and success of the President's leadership, defending him against those who charged him with subverting the Constitution in order to preserve the Union; warning of the need to avoid the currently divisive and basically irrelevant debate on slavery—"I am for the Government of my fathers with negroes. I am for it without negroes";[89] and the arraignment of traditional partisan feuding, proclaiming that there were now only two parties, "one for the government and one against it, one of patriots, the other of cravens." [90]

While these themes and topics were the staples of all of these Union rallies, the emphases and even the arguments varied, depending on the character of the audience. In Indianapolis and Columbus, where nascent Copperheadism posed a threat to the war effort, the governor's attack on those who were critical of Lincoln, his treatment of the South, and of dissident voices North was especially virulent. Tracing the slavocracy's perennial effort to undermine constitutional government—"the palladium of our liberties"—he justified harsh measures—"What rights have rebels?"—urging his listeners not to be diverted from the pressing business of restoring the Constitution over all the land. In the eastern cities, where Loyal and Union leagues were being inaugurated to counter war weariness and to marshal support for continued sacrifice, he coupled his attacks on southern perfidy and pleas for support of Lincoln with fulsome discussion of the historical bases for the present struggle, invoking the names of the nation's heroes, and especially of that compleat patriot, with whom the speaker was so often compared, Andrew Jackson. The record of southern infamy was further highlighted by detailed examination of more recent history, i.e., a rehashing of the months following Lincoln's election. In the final two appearances, at Baltimore March 20 and at Washington eleven days later, Johnson seems to have gone out of his way to identify with and defend the President, justifying the suspension of habeas corpus

88. Speech to the Loyal League, New York City, March 14, 1863.
89. Speech at Indianapolis, February 26, 1863.
90. Speech to the Ohio Legislature, March 3, 1863.

and urging a willingness to abide by the recent Emancipation Proclamation, in both speeches quoting Lincoln to an extent he usually reserved for the long-dead. That, as a consequence of his sojourn in Washington, he had been having personal interviews with Lincoln and his cohorts during the weeks before these appearances may well account for this coloration. Certainly considerations of courtesy, and even of political expediency, affected the content and tone of the final effort—a speech in the Chamber of the House of Representatives on the occasion of a marathon Union rally featuring a series of addresses in both chambers simultaneously—inasmuch as the President and members of his cabinet were in the audience. It seems likely that this was the only time, except for the shared term in Congress two decades earlier, that Lincoln had heard Johnson speak in public. Is it possible that the governor's performance on this occasion played a part in Abe's subsequent assessment of Andy's vice-presidential potential? There can be no question but that this 1863 "swing around the circle," unlike its successor three years later, contributed significantly to Johnson's growing national reputation. Everywhere he was heard by huge crowds—nearly thirty thousand at Indianapolis—greeted with warm enthusiasm and favorable press reports. Although he had been known earlier to labor reformers, partisan Democrats, and grateful Union politicians, his broader-based recognition, cutting across class and party lines, was quite a recent phenomenon greatly enhanced by this tour.

Following his return to Nashville at the end of May, the governor appears to have had but little recourse to the stump during the remainder of the year. Yet one of those occasions, the jollification consequent upon the reported fall of Sumter, garnered an unusually wide press coverage in the North. Although pleading indisposition, Johnson responded to the appeals of a rollicking crowd on his doorstep late in the evening of August 29. In what might well be called "the heart of the masses" speech, for the phrase appeared in all the accounts, the Plebeian declared that "the heart of the masses of the people beat strongly for freedom," condemned slavery as "baleful to the nation," and announced that "the time had clearly come when means should be devised for its total eradication from Tennessee." No compromise with evil! "Emancipation at all events." No wonder the New York *Times* headed its column: "Slavery in Tennessee. An Important Speech by Gov. Johnson" and the Chicago *Tribune* proclaimed "Andrew Johnson an Abolitionist." [91] No longer was he merely a southern unionist demanding harsh punishment for traitors; another dimension—radical on slavery—had been added to the evolving portrait of Andrew Johnson, a southern man with northern principles!

Virtual silence for the rest of 1863 may well reflect the tense military situation which developed in Tennessee during these months. But the triumph of Union arms at Chattanooga and declining Confederate fortunes

91. New York *Times,* September 6, 1863; Chicago *Tribune,* September 10, 1863.

in the remainder of East Tennessee, together with Lincoln's December 8 proclamation of amnesty and reconstruction, brought a fresh impetus to the restoration of civil government in the state. As a consequence, the succeeding months would witness a resurgence of speechmaking as the governor sought to shepherd his compatriots safely through the brambles of restoration. Two speeches in January, one on the observance of the ever-popular anniversary of New Orleans, the other to an assemblage meeting "to take initiatory steps to restore civil government in Tennessee," set the tone of this campaign. Limning Old Hickory at New Orleans with "the goddess of liberty hovering over him . . . until victory perched on the stars and stripes," he launched into his familiar eulogy of the Constitution and government thereunder, with his by now cavalier dismissal of slavery as dead and only awaiting "the funeral obsequies . . . to dispose of this great question." But if an institution like slavery can die, not so the nation under the Constitution. Denying that a state can commit suicide, i.e., detach itself from the Union, he declared, "We are parts of a great whole, working at present somewhat inharmoniously, but as soon as the Government puts down the rebellion, and the machinery be again put in running order . . . the State will stand firm." If a state cannot destroy itself, surely the United States cannot destroy a state; therefore restoration, not reconstruction, lies ahead, as soon as the rebellion is suppressed. No territorial status! Thus he reassured his fellows and pointed them toward reanimating civil government.

They needed little prodding. Two weeks later a Union convention in the Hall of Representatives heard Johnson, ostensibly unprepared, retrace in a two-hour discourse the argument that Tennesseans, far from being "supplicants in reference to the restoration of the powers of State government . . . stand in the attitude of demanding—claiming at the hands of the Federal Government the guarantee of a republican form of government." Thence a description of the steps he proposed to take: election in March of local officials by loyal voters, so certified by their taking a state-prescribed, as well as the presidential, oath; assembling of a popularly elected convention to revise the state constitution in conformity with the outcome of the rebellion, declaring null and void acts of the Confederate legislature and abolishing slavery. Waxing eloquent in his attack on the peculiar institution and those who sought to preserve it, he implied that the rebellion might have been God's way of getting rid of "this great sin," thundering, "I say, then, remove the evil, obey the laws of Heaven." Castigating those who had brought on the rebellion, he closed his oration with the assertion, not unappealing to a loyal crowd, that he trusted the time would come "when the Union men who have been oppressed, and the loyal heirs of those who have perished on the battle field, or starved in the mountains, will . . . be remunerated out of the property of those who betrayed and tried to destroy their country." This rousing, forward-looking address, full of ringing phrases and exhortation, was destined for wide circulation. It was one of only three speeches during the military governorship which saw publication as a pamphlet, presumably for consumption within the state, although in a somewhat bowdlerized version it became part of a publication designed to win support for the Union ticket in the fall election.

Unlike the preceding year, the governor's late winter trip to Washington produced no public appearances. Undoubtedly he was "laying pipe," but it was evidently of a subterranean variety and would not be best advanced by speaking engagements. Moreover, conditions were dramatically different this March, as the tide showed signs of turning in favor of the Union; Johnson would have little to offer in the current political climate. But such an assessment did not hold in Tennessee. There, as he would discover upon his return in late March, his presence and his voice were sorely needed. The reactions of East Tennessee unionists to emancipation and amnesty, both associated with the Lincoln administration, were creating problems which threatened the movement toward civil government. On the issue of the status of slavery the Republicans were increasingly pressing for immediate and uncompensated freedom, a solution resisted by conservative Tennesseans, whether of longstanding or recent unionist persuasion. A second source of discontent, especially among those whose loyalty had brought them suffering and property loss, arose from the way Lincoln's recent amnesty offer seemed to threaten the process of restoration. It appeared that "repentant Rebels," by taking the oath, would be able "to get the control of the various departments of the State."[92] The governor's effort to stiffen the terms for voting had not quelled their fears, and the March local elections had done nothing to reassure them on this score. Thus, a call had gone out for a Knoxville meeting, ostensibly a reconvening of the prewar Greeneville-Knoxville Union conventions, to discuss both the restoration of civil government and separate statehood for East Tennessee. The majority resolutions emanating from committee failed to endorse Johnson's administration and were critical of the Lincoln government's refusal to seek a compromise solution to the conflict. In the ensuing struggle on the floor, the minority supportive of both Johnson and Lincoln found that the best they could manage was an adjournment *sine die,* proposed by the governor's crony, Sam Milligan. Latent sentiment for divorcing East Tennessee from the remainder of the state, on the recent pattern of West Virginia, seems never to have crystalized but was ever in the background as a threat to Johnson's goal of a restored Tennessee in which deserving unionists, perhaps with a preponderance of East Tennesseans whose fortitude under persecution had certified their loyalty, would govern the entire state.

In response to Parson Brownlow's urgent "come by all means," and Chattanooga editor James Hood's reminder that "it is important to fore-

92. Nashville *Dispatch,* January 21, 1864.

stall indescreet men at Knoxville on the 12th," [93] the governor traveled to East Tennessee, arriving at three o'clock in the morning as a consequence of an accident at Athens—a misfortune on which he capitalized by addressing the crowd which assembled when word of his presence got about. During the four-day convention, Johnson appears to have kept a low profile inside the hall; both of his speeches were to large crowds on the outside. The first, on the day of his arrival, was part of ceremonies connected with dedicating a "liberty pole" and flag which early in the war had been torn down by Texas Rangers passing through the city. One of his typical long harangues, it was only partially reported; we have no adequate record of the first part during which he addressed the topic of separate statehood. Apparently not rejecting such a move out of hand, he later told a reporter that "he made a bare allusion" to it, arguing "that the time had not come for decided action on a question so vital"; other more pressing matters "demanding immediate action on our part were upon us." [94] Thus he avoided public repudiation of a tactic with which on two previous occasions he had been associated. In the "not more than a fourth part" of the speech reported in some detail, the governor reminded his audience that "traitors must be punished," that slavery had caused the war, that the prosperity of Tennessee lagged behind that of northern states because of slavery, and that freeing the slave really meant emancipating the white man. Nor is it surprising that in this, his first major public appearance in his home section since 1861, the peroration was an emotional and extended eulogy of East Tennessee, its long-suffering people, his own great love for the region, and his not inconsiderable personal sacrifice on behalf of his countrymen.

Four days later, upon adjournment of the impotent convention whose members, according to the New York *Tribune* correspondent, "did not represent the opinions of the people at the present time," [95] Johnson and his supporters sought to salvage some advantage. To accomplish this end, resolutions were drafted—rumor had it by the governor himself—and presented to "the people, in grand mass meeting assembled" in front of the courthouse. A "forcible speech" by Parson Brownlow preceded Oliver P. Temple's reading of resolutions—later, after Johnson's address, unanimously approved—which condemned Tennessee's participation in the rebellion brought on by slavery, endorsed the early calling of a popularly elected convention to amend the state constitution, including the abolition of slavery, expressed "full confidence in the integrity and patriotism" of the military governor, and pledged support to "the Administration and war policy of President Lincoln." One resolution seems worthy of separate notice as an effort to reassure the crowd that emancipation did

93. Brownlow to Johnson, April 6, 1864; James R. Hood to Johnson, April 6, 1864, Johnson Papers, LC.

94. Cincinnati *Gazette,* April 19, 1864.

95. New York *Tribune,* April 30, 1864.

not mean equality. While asserting that the abolition of slavery will forever secure the nation against another rebellion, the principle was laid down that the Federal and state governments "are the Governments of the free white man, and to be controlled and administered by him, and the negro must assume that status to which the laws of an enlightened, moral, and high-toned civilization shall assign him." If this document was the handiwork of the governor, those abolitionists who were soon to welcome him as the Union party's vice-presidential nominee were destined for a rude awakening.

Johnson's speech followed well-trod paths, indicting those who had brought on the rebellion, stressing the need to legalize the overthrow of slavery, and urging that steps be taken to return the state to a "republican form" of government. But there were some distinctive emphases and arguments, especially designed to rebut his political opponents. Support the calling of a people's sovereign convention to dispose of slavery, rather than acting through the legislature as many conservatives were advocating, for the latter device opens the way for a lengthy delay, since according to the constitution, "the Legislature cannot emancipate without the consent of the owners." Not only were slaves "free already," but this freedom was beneficial to society. Moreover, a convention which wipes out slavery paves the way for admission of the state's representatives to Congress. Defending the wisdom and justice of his much criticized "ardently desire" oath, he launched an impassioned attack on Tennesseans who had cast their lot with the rebellion, dwelling on the harshness with which they had treated loyal East Tennesseans and, while conceding that the truly contrite who were willing to follow the lead of staunch unionists might be permitted to return home, inveighed against giving them full political rights at once and recommended that for some "the time was come for them to take up their beds and walk" out of the state. Throughout the discourse he sought to put the President in a favorable light, first painting him as the benign leader responsible for helping Tennessee resume her position within the Union and later denying his responsibility for the abuses wrought by Federal soldiers—"He had seen the President and the officers of his Cabinet almost in tears over these outrages." All in all, this second Knoxville appearance seems to have been one of Johnson's more successful efforts. Taken in conjunction with the resolutions so resoundingly approved, his speaking not only offset the convention's legacy of division and disaffection but metamorphosed the mass meeting into what E. S. of the *Tribune* applauded as "a triumph for Freedom in Tennessee."

By the time the governor made another major speech, he was the vice-presidential nominee of the Republican party, thinly disguised as the Union party. No matter the name, the party was committed to a policy with which the Tennessean, if contemporaries were to believe his speeches, was in full agreement—vigorous prosecution of the war under the Lincoln administration to an unequivocal victory over the Confederacy, condign punishment of the miscreant leaders of the rebellion, and immediate abolition of the "infernal and damnable system of slavery." [96] The fit had not always been so snug. A reader of his speeches would have long been aware that when northern criticism of the President threatened efforts to restore the seceding states, Johnson, while still in the Senate during the first summer of the rebellion, had placed himself firmly with those who defended Lincoln's war policies.[97] His determination that the South must be brought back into the old Union, that there be no compromise with treason, became the more stubborn as the struggle wore on. As for the leaders of this heresy, his vitriolic condemnation of slave-holding traitors had since the beginning been a staple of his public appearances; after all, they had brought on the war, against the wishes of the majority, the Union-loving common men of the South. It was on the question of slavery that the most dramatic change had occurred during the preceding two years. His speeches revealed his conversion to emancipation, putting him, it appeared, comfortably in the camp of the administration and its supporters. But what his political bedfellows overlooked, yet it was clearly expressed in those speeches, was Johnson's deep-seated racism. He never deviated from a lifelong commitment to a white man's government and an equally strong aversion to the idea of racial equality.

If support for emancipation was new in Johnson's speeches, so too was the dark hint that the property of aristocratic traitors might be used to compensate loyal citizens for their losses during the conflict, a suggestion which seemed further to confirm the Tennessean's radicalism. However, just as his position on blacks could be misread, so too could be his potential for harshness toward the defeated. But if Johnson observers might have been misled on these issues, there was no chance to misinterpret his view of the constitutional issue. Repeatedly the governor assured his listeners that Tennessee had never been, could never be, out of the Federal union; that restoration, not reconstruction, was the task in which he and the people of the state were engaged. That they had to move slowly was, at least in part, forced upon them by the need to prevent unregenerate rebels from taking over the revived civil government, reinstituting the old order, and persecuting loyal men. Yet even on this issue, the vice-presidential nominee was not at odds with his political partners—more precisely with his partner: the President's ten percent plan actually spelled out restoration, not reconstruction. In sum, the Tennessean, speaking both in-state and on his major northern tour, during the twenty-two months before the Baltimore convention had fully set forth his theories, prejudices, opinions, antipathies, and panaceas. That these speeches were widely applauded by enthusiastic

96. Speech at Johnsonville, May 19, 1864.

97. Speech in Support of Presidential War Program, July 27, 1861, *Johnson Papers,* IV, 606ff.

crowds who heard them, that they were ignored by Confederates and rejected or condemned by many moderates North, that they contributed to his selection at the Union party convention, and that they would constitute an ingredient in the bitter disappointment and savage recrimination which greeted Johnson's subsequent behavior, all seem valid statements.

Not least of the controversies associated with Andrew Johnson's war, and indeed with his career, was his nomination for the vice-presidency—"an inscrutable dispensation of Providence," Henry Dawes pontificated some thirty years later.[98] Why the choice of a candidate from the rebel states, a diehard unionist but a longtime southern Democrat engrafted on the ticket of a fundamentally northern party? Can one suppose that the Republicans, their attention riveted on their precarious position, conducted more than a passing examination of the Tennessean's background? A War Democrat who shared many of their convictions, the Johnson of record was nevertheless a controversial figure: a man generally uncompromising and sometimes intractable, a maverick never comfortable in any party harness, a sworn enemy of "the interests" irrespective of time or place, a provincial *southern* in almost everything but secession. Is it possible that the "Union party" failed to ponder the critical significance of a post sometimes obscure, often derided, and allegedly in a state of decline,[99] yet so proximate to the White House? Had the elders forgotten Whiggery's experience with His Accidency John Tyler? Or did the selection represent inexorable logic, given Johnson's heroic stand during the secession winter—"faithful among the faithless"—his tenure with the Committee on the Conduct of the War—"the only Democratic member of the Senate to take a prominent part" [100]—his demand for the relentless prosecution of the struggle—"Let the last life be lost, the last dollar spent, and the last drop of blood be spilled, but do not let us compromise" [101]—his increasingly radical rhetoric—"the leaders, the instigators, the conscious, intelligent traitors, they ought to be hung" [102]—and above all, his attractiveness as a loyal southern border-state Democrat? That the infighting among eastern Republicans accrued to his benefit, there can be little doubt; but the exact role played by the Sumner-Fessenden imbroglio and the Seward-Dickinson impasse remains unclear. Did these feuds make "unavailable" the two most likely contenders, Vice-President Hannibal Hamlin of Maine and Daniel Dickinson of New York? That the groundswell of popular approval had something to do with his selection seems plausible; but, in the absence of such latter-day barometers as the opinion poll and the state primary, who could effectively take the pulse of the electorate? Yet, as early as four months before the Baltimore

98. Henry L. Dawes, "Two Vice-Presidents," *Century Magazine,* L (1895), 466.

99. See Irving G. Williams, *The Rise of the Vice-Presidency* (Washington, 1956), 32, 51.

100. Harry Williams, "Andrew Johnson as a Member of the Committee on the Conduct of the War," ETHS *Publications,* No. 12 (1940), 71.

101. Speech to the Loyal League, New York City, March 14, 1863.

102. Speech on Restoration of State Government, January 21, 1864.

convention, the Kansas legislature had proposed a Lincoln-Johnson ticket, and throughout the preceding year numerous individuals had expressed confidence in the Tennessean's presidential prospects, often touting him for the pinnacle position. Twenty years after the fact a Republican congressman would aver that his nomination, "like that of Mr. Lincoln, seemed to have been preordained by the people, while the intelligent, sober men . . . who lamented the fact, were not prepared to oppose the popular will." [103] An inscrutable dispensation of Providence? Better to call it a scrutable dispensation of Abraham Lincoln; or better still, to ascribe it to a combination of factors, of which the President's will was by far the most important. Finally, did the office, as the governor contended in his "acceptance speech," seek the man? Our noble Cincinnatus, his hand on the Tennessee plow, responding to another imperative?

Contemporaries, their memories colored by the trauma of the Johnson presidency, shaped by the dictates of convenience, or clouded by the passing years, speculated at great length about the nomination. Now and then some of the drama's lesser actors titillated the audience with "revelations" which stirred anew the embers of controversy. Modern interpreters, displaying somewhat greater objectivity, have added considerable research and not a little hypothesizing, without, however, contributing much of anything novel. Three decades ago, a scholar reiterated the dubious Hamlin proposition that Lincoln did not dictate the choice.[104] Out of this amalgam of truth and conjecture—a worthy challenge for the historiographer—one reality is unassailable: neither the records of the railsplitter nor the tailor cast appreciable light on the subject. The Lincoln manuscripts are mute, the Johnson remnants disappointing. Given the fact that their relationship was partly expressed through personal conversations and through intermediaries like Horace Maynard or Daniel Sickles, it is quite possible that no written clues exist; but again, given the penchant for protecting historical reputations, it may be that such evidence was destroyed by accident or by design. Despite the dearth of documentation from these personal papers, a consideration of the larger setting and an examination of other sources suggest a logical explanation for the verdict at Baltimore.

The early months of 1864 ushered in what promised to be another trying year. That the Union had the upper hand seemed obvious enough, but when would the conflict end? Long casualty lists notwithstanding, there were no Gettysburgs or Chattanoogas; Grant seemed bogged down in the East, Sherman's march could not even be imagined. The mood North was kaleidoscopic: a war weariness accompanied by a growing war

103. George W. Julian, *Political Recollections 1840 to 1872* (Miami,1969 [1884]), 243.

104. James F. Glonek, "Lincoln, Johnson, and the Baltimore Ticket," *Abraham Lincoln Quarterly,* VI (1951), 255-71; see also Charles E. Hamlin, *Life and Times of Hannibal Hamlin* (Cambridge, 1899).

psychosis; a substantial peace sentiment, dramatized by the spread of Copperheadism but possessing a much broader base; and withal, a grim determination to carry the struggle to a successful conclusion.

The incumbent party, abounding in factional disputes but held together by the common threads of patriotism and the instinct for self-preservation, mirrored the troublous times. Embarrassed by their sectional label, the Republicans had long since begun a process designed to change an essentially northern organization into a Union party which transcended geographical limits. The elections of 1862 had sounded a warning: a narrowed Republican majority in the House of Representatives and Democratic control of six northern states. Who would be the standard-bearers in 1864? To the modern student, heavily armed with hindsight, Lincoln is inescapable; to the contemporary, deeply immersed in the crucible, there was no such certainty. Dissatisfaction with the President and his policies was widespread, not only among the Radicals and even some of the Conservatives but also among some War Democrats. There were two other main possibilities: the "bespattered hero" [105] John C. Frémont, party candidate in 1856 and darling of the Radicals, lurked in the background, while the ambitious Salmon P. Chase, treasury secretary, waited expectantly in the wings. Yet there remained a powerful popular undercurrent in Lincoln's favor, a consensus that there was no satisfactory alternative, a manifest unwillingness to change horses. In the long run, intraparty differences were subordinated to the common goal.

Despite this rallying 'round the Railsplitter, there was no assurance that the Republicans would prevail. Just how substantial was the "Union party?" Could it live up to its name, transcending political and sectional lines? Would the War Democrats, broadly supportive of administration policies but hardly Republican regulars, endorse the ticket and platform? How many would the prospective McClellan candidacy attract? Under these circumstances, the choice of Lincoln's running mate assumed a significance far out of proportion to the low esteem in which the vice-presidency was usually held. What about nominating a War Democrat? Might not the second office in the land serve as a means of repairing the sectional conflict?

There were numerous availables. The incumbent, a former Democrat turned Republican, wanted a second term; but Hannibal Hamlin had become a Radical, impatient with Lincoln's slow progress toward emancipation, his reluctance to raise Negro troops, his aversion to confiscation.[106] In terms of sectional reconciliation, Hamlin would add no great strength to the ticket. Daniel S. Dickinson, a steadfast supporter of presi-

105. A sobriquet attributed to Lincoln. Allan Nevins, *The War for the Union* (4 vols., New York, 1959-71), IV, 73.

106. H. Draper Hunt, *Hannibal Hamlin of Maine: Lincoln's First Vice-President* (Syracuse, 1969), 159-61, 163.

dential policies, had a considerable following in his home state of New York; General John A. Dix, another Yorker, commanded much attention in the party at large; Simon Cameron, Pennsylvania political hack and ex-secretary of war, was by no means unwilling to fill the post. The pundits mulled the possibility of General Benjamin F. Butler, possessed of both a military record and a Democratic background. There was "talk" about Judge Advocate General Joseph Holt of Kentucky, another War Democrat.

Except for Holt, these men were northerners and could not qualify as "unionizers." But there was also much ado about Tennessee's war governor—had been, in fact, since the flush of enthusiasm which followed his course during the secession winter and its aftermath led correspondents to predict greater things for him: "booked for the 'White House,' " with a " 'through ticket,' " wrote one.[107] By 1863 it had become obvious that Johnson boasted a popular following which went much beyond the spontaneous reaction of the few. Although individuals continued to express themselves, his potentialities increasingly attracted public recognition. It is difficult, and perhaps significant only for the chronicler, to ascertain precisely when he was first "ticketed." In March, Memphis *Bulletin* readers were presented with a most unlikely tandem of McClellan and Johnson, mounted by an enthusiastic but unrealistic private of the "West Tennessee Cavalry." [108] In September, the *Missouri Democrat,* looking toward Reconstruction, penned an intriguing editorial about the task which lay ahead. Denouncing Lincoln's "irresolute, fickle border slave State policy, or rather no-policy," and hailing Johnson's "repudiation of *gradual emancipation,*" the writer opined that the next chief executive should be "a man who thoroughly understands the disposition of the Southern people, and how to deal with them." In this respect, who was "better qualified" than the governor?[109] At year's end the Union League of Nashville endorsed him as Lincoln's running mate, and the Kansas legislature's concurrent resolution of February 2, 1864, called for their nomination "by general acclamation, without the formality of a national convention." [110] That same month the London *Times,* while calling such announcements "premature," reported that "Mr. Hamlin has been omitted from the lists . . . and Mr. Lincoln's friends are nominating a variety of persons for the minor office to run with their favourite, among others Governor Andrew Johnson." [111] The plaudits and endorsements from around the Union, the inevitable comparisons with Jackson, his designation as the right man for the "Herculean" task of Reconstruction—these and other expressions of opinion suggest strongly that Johnson had become a major prospect.

107. Richard K. Anderson to Johnson, December 27, 1860, Johnson Papers, LC.

108. Memphis *Bulletin,* March 6, 1863.

109. *Missouri Democrat* (St. Louis), September [14], 1863.

110. Chicago *Tribune,* January 7, 1864; J. G. Randall and Richard N. Current, *Lincoln, the President* (4 vols., New York, 1945-55), IV, 122.

111. London *Times,* February 4, 1864.

It can scarcely be supposed that such prognostications and pronouncements were etched upon a tabula rasa. On the contrary, they must have struck the recipient as further confirmation of a longstanding personal conviction. Just when the Plebeian first saw himself as presidential or vice-presidential timber is impossible to say, but the record demonstrates, albeit sometimes unclearly, a keen interest in both the major and "minor" offices. That his own steady ascent in politics invoked the legendary ladder with its metaphoric rungs appears obvious enough. His first gubernatorial address, the product of a soaring imagination, had pictured "Democracy progressive" and the "Church Militant" advancing in "converging lines" toward theocracy; by implication, at least, Andrew Johnson was of the lay priesthood presiding over this syncretism.[112] Heralded as an *"independent Land Reform Democratic"* candidate in 1856 and covetous of a favorite-son role at the Cincinnati convention,[113] he nevertheless recognized that he must perforce continue the climb rung by rung, biding his time. Indeed, speaking on the Senate floor in 1859, he professed to be content with the status quo and to decry higher ambition, asserting that the presidency "is not worthy of the aspirations of a man who believes in doing good, and is in a position to serve his country by popularizing her free institutions"; yet it was obvious that he would not frown upon initiatives in his behalf.[114] That he viewed himself as a presidential possibility in 1860, the Johnson papers make clear; but perhaps pessimistic about the main chance and looking to a salvage operation, he observed privately that "There could be no safer positin to Secure the first place four years hence than Second place on the ticket now." [115] As it turned out his immediate hopes for either post were in vain, but the prospects remained bright—enhanced by his response to the challenges of secession and war.

Although the Tennessean's aspirations and the public's receptivity are well documented, evidence concerning his wartime pursuit of higher office—or, conversely, its pursuit of him—remains fragmentary, conjectural, often a matter of inference. His surviving letters and papers do no more than lend themselves to surmise. Was there a larger import in the senator's swing around the circle in Kentucky and Ohio during the fall of 1861 when he sounded the tocsin of preparedness against the foe? Can one read "pinnacle strategy" into the governor's midwestern and eastern speechmaking tour during the spring of 1863, a jaunt designed to combat Copperheadism and steel northern resolve to see the conflict through? For that matter, can Johnson's literary executors, knowing full well his towering ambition, resist the temptation to see "the presidency" in many of his wartime addresses?

112. First Inaugural Address, October 17, 1853, *Johnson Papers,* II, 176.
113. *Ibid.,* xxvii.
114. Speech on Transcontinental Railroads, January 25, 1859, *ibid.,* III, 243.
115. Letter to Robert Johnson, April 22, 1860, *ibid.,* 573.

Just as tantalizing and fully as elusive are the gleanings from contemporaries. How should his extended visit to the national capital during the winter of 1864 be evaluated? A correspondent for the *Missouri Republican* reported that "Andy Johnson, is . . . here on his way to Washington, to lay pipe for himself for the next Presidency." [116] If so, just how did he go about it? We know that he conferred with Lincoln, but his other activities during what was essentially a private rather than a public trip are obscure. This, the last face-to-face meeting before the Baltimore convention, not only provided Johnson with a chance for further endorsement of his controversial test oath, but it also gave Lincoln "the opportunity to look the Tennessean over himself, to question, to evaluate, and to measure." [117] By spring, the Plebeian had evidently set his sights on "the minor office." A New York *Commercial Advertiser* dispatch, noting the presence of Johnson and Simon Cameron in the capital, observed that "Both . . . are understood to have placed themselves in the hands of their respective friends." [118] It is quite possible that the governor had been laying pipe for some time, utilizing such conduits as Horace Maynard, state attorney general but still a Tennessee congressman; James Bingham, editor of the Memphis *Bulletin;* John Forney, publisher, politician, and would-be kingmaker; and general newspaper publicity.

Despite the President's tête-à-tête with the governor, it seems improbable that he had fully made up his mind about the other half of the ticket. In March he sent Cameron to Fortress Monroe to sound out Ben Butler; but the general, evidently hoping for a presidential nomination under Radical auspices, recalled later that he had pointedly declined the proffer of second place.[119] Nor, if one considers the implications of the still mysterious Sickles "mission," was Lincoln yet satisfied with Johnson. In the course of that spring he dispatched Major General Daniel Sickles on a tour of the South via Cairo, New Orleans, the Gulf and Atlantic coasts, with stops at designated cities and "such intermediate points as you may think important"; the objective was to secure information about Reconstruction and the condition of the blacks.[120] With respect to one of the "intermediate points," however, the President may have had other motives. Sickles, who had known Johnson in Congress, conferred with him at the Hermitage in early May and presumably made his report to Lincoln.[121] Writing some three decades later, when the controversy over Johnson's nomination had been revived, the general denied that his Nashville sojourn had

116. Nashville *Press,* December 22, 1863.

117. Edwin M. Hardison, In the Toils of War: Andrew Johnson and the Federal Occupation of Tennessee (Ph.D. dissertation, University of Tennessee, 1982), 328.

118. Memphis *Bulletin,* March 6, 1864.

119. Benjamin F. Butler, *Butler's Book* (Boston, 1892), 634; see also Hans L. Trefousse, *Ben Butler: The South Called Him Beast* (New York, 1957), 158-60.

120. Edgcumb Pinchon, *Dan Sickles* (Garden City, N.Y., 1945), 208.

121. Letter from Daniel Sickles, [May, 1864].

anything to do with the vice-presidency; instead, "It was more of a diplomatic mission." Since Johnson's administration "was very severe . . . of a character which seemed to Mr. Lincoln too harsh," the purpose was to see whether he "could be tactfully checked so that his government would conform with Lincoln's conciliatory policy toward defeated peoples." [122] There is a certain logic here. Given Johnson's "treason is a crime and must be punished" syndrome, his apparent swing toward radicalism, and his superimposition of the "damnesty oath" upon Lincoln's proclamation of December, 1863, his policies must have seemed proscriptive. But Benjamin C. Truman, the governor's confidant, recalled a different version. Encountering in Nashville an old friend, a special correspondent of the New York *Herald* traveling with Sickles, he learned that the general had been sent "to look after Johnson. To see what he is doing. To look into his habits. The President wants Johnson on the ticket with him if his habits will permit." [123] What habits? The wicked ways of tyranny? Or frequent communion with spirits? Back in September, 1863, Assistant Secretary of War Charles A. Dana, then in Tennessee to observe Rosecrans' operations against Bragg, visited Johnson, noticing "that the Governor took more whisky than most gentlemen would have done, and I concluded that he took it pretty often." [124] Can such talk have reached Lincoln's ears? Whatever may be said about excessive drinking as an American cultural trait, it represented something of a liability to a prospective ticket in a canvass whose eventual outcome was by no means certain. Nor did there appear to be any certainty about the vice-presidential choice as the Republicans gathered at Baltimore.

In one sense, it is ironic that the only Union party convention ever held met in a southern metropolis of divided loyalties. Baltimore, "with its preference for free labor and its mercantile pragmatism" writes a twentieth century historian, "was imbedded in a state founded on the economy of tobacco and slavery." [125] It was an ambivalence sharpened and dramatized by the crisis: not only had the Monumental City been the scene of bloodshed when local secesh bearded northern troops in 1861, but its strategic location left open the threat of invasion. In other ways, however, this site for the foray of '64 seemed highly appropriate: not only had Baltimore witnessed the dissolution of the archrival Democracy four years earlier, but Maryland was a border slave state representing that larger constituency so vital to the *raison d'être* of a party masquerading under a more pretentious name. Administration policy toward the peculiar institution in these loyal borderlands had been under critical review for some time; moreover,

122. New York *Times,* July 10, 1891; W. A. Swanberg, *Sickles the Incredible* (New York, 1956), 261.

123. Benjamin C. Truman, "Anecdotes of Andrew Johnson," *Century Magazine,* LXXXV (1913), 437.

124. Charles A. Dana, *Recollections of the Civil War* (New York, 1902), 106.

125. Sherry H. Olson, *Baltimore: The Building of an American City* (Baltimore, 1980), 144.

delegates from Tennessee and other states in rebellion presented themselves, seeking recognition; and one of the leading second-place hopefuls hailed from this great middle region.

The intimate story of the convention—the almost inevitable June heat, the "crowd of sharp faced, keen, greedy politicians" (in Adam Gurowski's bitter words),[126] the hangers-on, hawkers, and manipulators, the unique expedition of the business at hand—lies outside this discussion; it is more appropriate here to consider the circumstances which led to Johnson's triumph.[127] That Lincoln would head the ticket no one seriously doubted: his agents had busied themselves in the state conventions, rounding up votes sufficient to ensure his renomination.[128] But the contemporary record provides no conclusive evidence that the second office was foreordained. Some of the faithful assumed that the incumbent, ipso facto, would be retained; as it turned out, Lincoln's horse-in-the-middle-of-the-stream metaphor applied only to the presidency. Nor, insofar as the states are concerned, can one find any such prearrangement for Johnson. The Tennesseans excepted, no state was pledged to him—and these loyal Volunteers had not been formally admitted. That there was a decided border-state and midwestern sentiment in his favor is hard to document, though his earlier advocacy of homestead legislation, his war record, and particularly his "swings" in 1861 and 1863 had evoked an enthusiastic response. On the surface of things, sentiment at Baltimore seemed to reflect a regional or state bias: New England, it was thought, stood behind Hamlin; New York leaned toward Dickinson; and there were various favorite sons. Most speculative of all is the proposition, suggested by hindsight but yet to be demonstrated by research, that Johnson shared with Lincoln a popular appeal which cut across all party, state, and sectional lines.

The vice-presidency was last on the agenda. Preceding it were several major tasks, one of which faced the Committee on Credentials: the admission of delegates from the "freshly reconstructed states" of Tennessee, Virginia, South Carolina, Florida, Louisiana, and Arkansas, as well as from several western territories. If Tennessee were denied, how could its governor be chosen? In reality, the "bayonet states" and the vice-presidency, issues patently inseparable, were being considered simultaneously. On the morning of June 7, before the convention opened at noon, Ohio reportedly caucused in Johnson's favor.[129] How, then, could it stand against Tennessee? That evening an ancient adversary become an ally in a union of convenience gave the tailor some further impetus. Styling himself "one of the old apostles" and complaining that he was "sick, sick,

126. Quoted in William Frank Zornow, *Lincoln & The Party Divided* (Norman, 1954), 91.

127. See *ibid.*, Ch. 7, and Zornow, "The Union Party Convention at Baltimore in 1864," *Maryland Historical Magazine*, XLV (1950), 176-200.

128. David Donald, *Lincoln Reconsidered* (New York, 1956), 77.

129. James G. Smart, ed., *A Radical View: The "Agate" Dispatches of Whitelaw Reid* (2 vols., Memphis, 1976), II, 167-68.

sick," Parson Brownlow delivered an impromptu statement devoid of superlatives. Do not reject the Tennessee delegates, for "we may take it into our heads . . . to present a candidate from that State," he pleaded. "We have a man down there whom it has been my good luck and bad fortune to fight untiringly for the last twenty-five years. I mean Andrew Johnson . . . . For the first time in the Providence of God, three years ago, we got together on the same platform, and we are now fighting the devil, Tom Walker and Jeff. Davis side by side." [130] Ailing but by no means superannuated, the old apostle had been specially chosen: a contemporary asserted that Brownlow and Maynard had come to Baltimore at the behest of Lincoln and Johnson, and that the Parson consulted with the governor the night before he departed Nashville.[131] When the Volunteer State was admitted, 300 to 151, the decisiveness of the vote must have struck the assemblage as "a marked indication of the preference for Andrew Johnson." [132] In this wise Tennessee might be viewed as a curtain raiser—not merely for the remaining rebel delegations, but, by inference, for the convention's will as registered on the first vice-presidential ballot. There is an interesting broad analogy between the state's role at Baltimore and its place in presidential strategy during the early winter of 1865-66, when the admission of Tennessee's representatives to the House was expected to set a precedent for other Confederate states reconstructed under the Johnson plan.

When it comes to state decisions about the vice-presidential rivals, the record is occluded, the surviving evidence not altogether dependable, the interpreters at loggerheads. It may be that Lincoln, operating through Simon Cameron, Alexander McClure, and others, influenced Pennsylvania to go for Johnson; if so, the choice was made over the opposition of Thaddeus Stevens of "the cold gray eye," who allegedly snorted, "Can't you find a candidate for Vice President without going down into a d----d rebel province?" [133] It is quite likely that Seward's friends in New York, notably Thurlow Weed and Henry J. Raymond, interpreting the Dickinson candidacy as a plot to force him out of the cabinet, prevailed upon the state's delegation to turn a plurality for the Tennessean; more doubtful is Seward's later contention that he had "dug Johnson out and had made him governor first and afterward Vice President"—though the secretary may have had a hand in both.[134] It remains debatable whether Charles Sumner, an enemy of both Seward and Senator William P. Fessenden of Maine, masterminded the withdrawal of Massachusetts from the New England "bloc" in the expectation that Hamlin's support would collapse

130. Philadelphia *Evening Bulletin,* June 8, 1864.

131. Benjamin C. Truman, in Erwin S. Bradley, *Simon Cameron: Lincoln's Secretary of War* (Philadelphia, 1966), 241.

132. Zornow, *Lincoln & The Party Divided,* 93.

133. Quoted in Fawn Brodie, *Thaddeus Stevens: Scourge of the South* (New York, 1959), 220.

134. See Glyndon G. Van Deusen, *William Henry Seward* (New York, 1967), 433.

and that, rejected by the convention, he would likely stand against Fessenden. For Sumner's latest biographer at least, the thesis lacks "reliable proof" and "is entirely out of character." [135]

In any case the first ballot, taken June 8, gave Johnson 200 votes, Hamlin 150, and Dickinson 108—not a majority but nonetheless a strong showing. The governor's name had been placed in nomination by Daniel Mace, an Indiana friend of the "Homestead" years,[136] but the coup was delivered by Horace Maynard, Massachusetts native, former East Tennessee University professor, and longtime Whig. Tall, thin, and ramrod straight, dark of feature and high of cheekbone, "the Narragansett Indian" strongly resembled one's image of a Civil War guerrilla, and he yielded to no one where political infighting was concerned. Regrettably, no detailed text of his address remains: we must rely upon remembrances, newspaper summaries, and the pallid *Proceedings* issued long afterward and not inconceivably watered down because of the Republican ordeal with President Johnson.[137] Maynard had spoken for Tennessee the previous day; spoken so emotionally, we are told, that the tears coursed down his cheeks and the audience sobbed along with him.[138] Now he lauded a man "known, honored, distinguished" who "had stood in the furnace of treason," a martyr mobbed, hanged, and burned in effigy for his courageous stand, a patriot whose "determined and undying hostility to this Rebellion that now ravages the land has been so well known that it is a part of the household knowledge of every loyal family in the country." Johnson would abide by the platform, pledged Maynard: "adhere to those sentiments, and to the doctrines of those resolutions as long as his reason remains unimpaired, and as long as breath is given him by his God." [139] Why this redundancy about unmistakable opinions and everlasting fidelity? Was it a premonition?

Like a thunderbolt on a hot summer afternoon, the speech electrified a staid, almost stultifying conclave; more significantly, it swayed the delegates toward Johnson. Phrases from contemporaries like "decisive effect," "a stampede," and "defeated Hamlin" suggest the impact of Maynard's histrionics. How fortunate for the governor's cause, the presence of this clear, dynamic speaker in his camp! How unfortunate for the historical researcher, the marked degeneration of the speaker's clear handwriting during the Civil War era! When the second ballot was taken, Johnson's "car of state" began to roll as first Kentucky, then Oregon and Kansas, enlisted on his side; Pennsylvania cast her fifty-two votes in his

135. David Donald, *Charles Sumner and the Rights of Man* (New York, 1970), 173.

136. See Letter from Daniel Mace, June 14, 1864.

137. *Proceedings of the First Three Republican National Conventions* (Minneapolis, 1893), 237.

138. George Fort Milton, *The Age of Hate: Andrew Johnson and the Radicals* (Hamden, Conn., 1965 [1930]), 51.

139. *Proceedings*, 237.

favor, even Maine abandoned Hamlin. By the time the tally was completed, the Tennessean had captured 494 of the 521 votes cast, and his selection was then made unanimous.

So ended what the locals saw as "the tamest and most spiritless Convention ever held in the city." [140] So began the nagging question still unanswered more than a century later, and perhaps unanswerable: *did* Lincoln intervene? "Impressive and suggestive evidence can be cited to show that the President picked the Tennessean—or that he favored someone else entirely," observes one Lincoln scholar.[141] Yet the war of interpretation drags on, still producing an occasional salvo. A latter-day cannoneer denies that the President engineered the outcome: "it was, instead, the product of curiously interrelated forces." While disenchanted with Hamlin, "he did not work to bring about the vice-president's defeat. On the contrary, even when a deadlocked convention sought his advise [*sic*], Lincoln remained consistently noncommittal." [142] A latter-day biographer pronounces the case dismissed: "He didn't care whom they chose as Vice-President." [143] A noncommital Lincoln, an indifferent Lincoln! Are these perceptions consistent with the President known to posterity? Not if we discriminate between the public and the private man. On the one hand, an innocent abroad—"You know I never was a contriver; I don't know much about how things are done in politics"—and an impartial observer—"Wish not to interfere about V. P. . . . Convention must judge for itself"; [144] on the other, Herndon's "enigma . . . incommunicative—silent—reticent—secretive—having profound policies—and well laid—deeply studied plans." [145] Was the Executive who "didn't care" the same onlooker who scrutinized so closely the nearby doings that the convention might, with some exaggeration, be considered an official chapter in his administration? Was a Republican victory so certain that the "minor office" made no difference? That "V.P." disclaimer: did it not, in reality, convey an unmistakable message? Do such hands-off tactics square with Lincoln's view of the presidency? Indeed it may be submitted that his interest in the governor may have gone beyond the obvious advantages to party and ticket: was it not preferable to have this potential rival in his own camp? As with the Radical Butler, so with the War Democrat Johnson—for all practical purposes, a defusing process.

As might have been expected, the decision at Baltimore elicited widespread approbation in the Republican press, which generally viewed the

140. New York *Times,* June 9, 1864.

141. Donald, *Lincoln Reconsidered,* 67-68.

142. Glonek, "Lincoln, Johnson, and the Baltimore Ticket," 270-71.

143. Stephen B. Oates, *With Malice Toward None: The Life of Abraham Lincoln* (New York, 1977), 388.

144. Roy P. Basler, ed., *The Collected Works of Abraham Lincoln* (9 vols., New Brunswick, N.J., 1953-55), VII, 376.

145. Quoted in Donald, *Lincoln Reconsidered,* 67.

Tennessean as adding strength to the ticket but also offered more specific evaluations. In selecting a War Democrat, observed the New York *Times,* the convention had shown "that it recognized no party test but that of faithful and constant devotion to the war against rebellion"; in naming a southerner, the Union party had lived up to its name, confirming itself to be "a party without sectional prejudice, ever ready to give the grasp of fellowship to every loyal man." [146] For Horace Greeley's New York *Tribune,* it represented an assurance to southern unionists "that they, at least, are not deemed outcasts from the pale of our Nationality. . . . that their long-suffering and devotion to the National cause is appreciated, and will not be forgotten." Other journals regarded the choice as symbolic of a new direction. Lauding Lincoln's renomination "on a truly Radical platform," the *Missouri Democrat* remarked that "The name of Andy Johnson is a synonym for both Radicalism and patriotism" and added that "A radical reconstruction of the Cabinet on a radical basis, and a radical prosecution of the war to a radically righteous issue, are results for which the people have long prayed." Taking note of the governor's recent enlistment in the crusade against slavery, the Philadelphia *North American* declared that "The humblest mudsill in the South may look up to him with a proud satisfaction, and hail him as his friend and champion."

Predictable, too, were encomiums about "Old Andy's" career, celebrating not only his identification with the people, but also his successful struggle against poverty and illiteracy, his ascension of the political ladder, his steadfast loyalty to the old flag. From William Cullen Bryant's New York *Post* came a contribution to the log-cabin myth: "Born in the midst of an aristocratic society—an orphan who was apprenticed to a trade by the Poorhouse Commissioners," Johnson "could not read until after he was married, and was then taught by his wife by the light of pine-knots"—a worthy companion piece to Young Abe's cyphering on a shovel by firelight. Calling the Tennessean "a moral hero," the Chicago *Journal* composed a catechism of the superlative:

> Who leaped to the rescue of the flag with an ardor and affection more fiery than his? None. Who confronted the conspirators with more eloquence—who heaped upon them more scorn, derision, and invective than he? None. Who has been more unselfishly or more untiringly devoted to the service of the imperiled Republic than he? None. . . . Who has shown more vigor, ability and success in the administration of the civil affairs entrusted to him than he? None. Who of the nation's servants . . . has more securely intrenched himself in the grateful hearts of the people than he? None. . . . Who of the people would the people more delight to honor and reward than he? None. Who could have brought more respect and strength and stamina to the ticket than he? None. Who of all the people's favorites could have been more certainly the people's choice for Vice-President than he? None.

146. Unless otherwise noted, these undated newspaper comments are taken from the Nashville *Times, and True Union,* June 14, 1864; they were collected by Johnson's "man," editor Sam Mercer.

To be sure, there were dissenting newspaper voices. Rebel organs naturally considered Johnson a traitor to the South, and treated him accordingly. The Democratic opposition North was no less caustic. Lamenting the low estate to which the Republicans had descended, the Copperhead New York *World* derided "a rail splitting buffoon and a boorish tailor," [147] while the Washington *Constitutionalist,* denouncing Johnson as "one of the most consummate demagogues living," told a sordid story of filial neglect: the Plebeian, boasting of his humble origin but now "rolling in wealth," suffered his aged mother to prowl the streets of Philadelphia peddling meat, "that she may buy bread to keep her poor old soul and body together." [148] A curious twist of history! Polly Johnson, southern rustic, howling tripe in a northern city.

Individual reactions, expressed at the time or later, also varied sharply. Insofar as the record is concerned, Lincoln said nothing directly; but one of his close friends wrote Johnson that "I was with the President ten minutes after receiving the intelligence. . . . I need not tell you of the satisfaction felt and *expressed* by him at the result!" Dickinson's defeat notwithstanding, New Yorkers were satisfied, "while outsiders are better pleased with your present locality in view of your political record & your sympathies and labors in the cause." [149] The vanquished Hannibal, addressing a ratification meeting in Bangor, endorsed the victor. "He knew him well," Hamlin was quoted as saying, "a purer patriot did not live in the land"; and, speaking more prophetically and ironically than he could have imagined, pronounced the nominee "eminently fitted to discharge the duties of President, should he in the Providence of God, be called to do so." [150] Apparently harboring no suspicion of presidential connivance and blaming his defeat upon the convention, he later spoke of having been "unceremoniously 'whistled down the wind.'" [151] The torrent of indignation from the Hamlin camp was not to flow until after his death.

Several correspondents, though enthusiastic about Johnson, expressed some dissatisfaction with the ticket. Writing in anticipation, Eli Thayer of "Beecher's Bibles" fame assured the governor that "if you were candidate for President I would vote & work for you with all my heart. . . . But to be Vice President is to be a cypher as we all know & I am sorry to see you lose the power for good you now have by being the shadow of a man who opposes your views at every point." [152] Another Bay State visionary opined that "if any thing can reconcile me to the renomination of Abraham

147. Quoted in Washington *Daily Morning Chronicle,* June 20, 1864.

148. Cincinnati *Enquirer,* n.d., reprinted in Nashville *Union,* June 18, 1864. It may safely be assumed that Mary McDonough Johnson managed to keep body and soul together until her death at Greeneville in 1856.

149. Letter from S. Newton Pettis, June 10, 1864.

150. Unidentified clipping, [June 10, 1864], Appls., Surveyors of Customs, N.Y., A.G. Johnson, RG56, NA.

151. Hunt, *Hannibal Hamlin,* 178.

152. Letter from Eli Thayer, June 6, 1864.

Lincoln, it is the association of your name on the same ticket" and from Pittsburgh came an echoing note: "Oh how I wish it had been for the Presidency.... I am sorry very sorry that you have not been associated with a better man than Lincoln." [153] Perceiving a different reason for reversing candidates, Johnson's financial agent declared that "what we want in the next administration is the real old Jackson democracy, which I fear but few, if any old line Whigs have." [154] Still another insight was offered by a writer who termed the choice

> a very masterly stroke ... for without your name and your great popularity I have my doubts whether Mr. Lincoln's Ticket could have secured the majority of the people. Now however I consider the votes of the great conservative masses secure ... which would not have been the case if one of those rabid and all grasping radicals had been put upon the Ticket in your stead.[155]

That some Republicans remained uneasy about *"Border State influence"* a New Yorker made clear in urging that Johnson's letter of acceptance, "of more importance that [*sic*] Mr. Lincoln's—just at this time," set forth "as clearly and as firmly as your *judgement* and your *conscience* will allow your *anti slavey policy."* [156]

Mingled with the voice of approbation were those of skepticism, of worry, of lingering doubt—misgivings about the propriety, the wisdom, the inferences to be drawn, and indeed the constitutionality, of choosing a nominee from an "incoming free state," as the jargoneers were wont to call those rebel entities now supposedly reconstructed. Was Tennessee in the Union? Yes, Johnson insisted over and over, she had never left the fold; and in his "acceptance speech," he asserted that the convention, in selecting him, had endorsed this point of view. Editor James Bingham, the governor's West Tennessee "fluence man," set him straight.

> It was your known patriotism and fidelity, in the darkest hour of the country's history, and your unswerving support of the government since the inauguration of the war, and not any recognition of the Southern States as in the Union, which placed you on the ticket. This I know from personal observation and from the declaration of those who voted for you in Convention.[157]

Indeed, had the nominee perused the *Congressional Globe* only a few days after the Baltimore proceedings, he would have noted that Charles Sumner, during a debate over the admission of senators from "reconstructed" Arkansas, theorized that Tennessee had forfeited "her ancient rights in the Union." Johnson's nomination was no argument to the contrary, said Sumner; and, pursuing his own war against the states, he proclaimed that "it is not necessary even that a candidate for President or Vice

153. Letter from George L. Stearns, June 9, 1864; Letter from Nathaniel P. Sawyer, June 10, 1864.

154. Letter from Enoch T. Carson, June 9, 1864.

155. Johann P. M. Epping to Johnson, June 12, 1864. Johnson Papers, LC.

156. Letter from George B. Lincoln, June 11, 1864.

157. Letter from James B. Bingham, June 26, 1864.

President should belong to a State. . . . It is enough, under the Constitution, that he is a 'citizen of the United States.' "[158]

Whether the governor responded to Bingham or read his Sumner is not of record. It seems beyond reasonable doubt that one innately inflexible, thoroughly persuaded of his own rectitude, and now flushed with his latest success, would have conceded the case. It taxes the imagination to believe that a southerner, his constitutional sanctions firmly anchored in the state rights-strict construction niche, would have held with Hamiltonianism as expounded by Charles Sumner—least of all the Andrew Johnson who would one day veto the fourteenth amendment, citizenship clause and all. One can do no more than speculate about the Tennessean's reaction had he seen other commentaries offered then or later: the blessing from "Beast" Butler, of ambitions unfulfilled—"Hurrah for Lincoln and Johnson! That's the ticket! This country has more vitality than any other on earth if it can stand this sort of administration for another four years"; the retrospective from George Julian—"I knew he did not believe in the principles embodied in the platform. . . . he was, at heart, as decided a hater of the negro and of everything savoring of abolitionism, as the rebels from whom he had separated"; and the verdict handed down by the historian James Ford Rhodes, sitting in olympian judgment—"A severe scrutiny of Johnson's personal character would have prevented this nomination, and either of his competitors was fitter for the place, but the ballot for Vice President was a rush to the rising man."[159] For the nonce, the other half of Lincoln's ticket was to be spared such animadversions from the party of the Union; the Johnson "slandered and vilified" by the Republicans and the press (as historian Harry Truman saw it)[160] belongs essentially, if not wholly, to the Reconstruction period.

What shall one say of the nominee and the larger context for the Baltimore decision? Consummate demagogue or glorious old Roman, paragon of consistency or "new light" politician, synonym for radicalism or symbol of conservatism, Moses of the mudsill or oracle of the common white, foreordained or accidental, severe scrutiny or practical politics, damned rebel provinces or incoming free states, restoration or reconstruction: phraseology of the day, a mixture of fact and fiction, seemingly polar opposites yet curiously interrelated and therefore proper fodder for the contrapuntalist, these assessments of the man chosen, of considerations affecting that choice, and of the broader settings for one of the most fateful decisions in American history, remind us of the disadvantages under which contemporaries labor. Sharing in the historical process, they are handi-

158. *Cong. Globe,* 38 Cong., 1 Sess., 896.

159. Benjamin F. Butler to Wife, June 11, 1864, in *Private and Official Correspondence . . . during the Period of the Civil War* (5 vols., Norwood, Mass., 1917), IV, 337; Julian, *Political Recollections,* 243; James Ford Rhodes, *History of the United States from the Compromise of 1850* (9 vols., New York, 1893-1928), IV, 470.

160. Quoted in Ralph W. Haskins, "Andrew Johnson and the Preservation of the Union," ETHS *Publications,* No. 33 (1961), 58.

capped by propinquity; involved in the current scene, they tend to oversimplify. Members of the governor's larger constituency saw various Johnsons—patriot, turncoat, avenger, radical, conservative, democrat, apotheosis of the self-made man. Viewed in perspective, his nomination was due to a fusing of elements, some of which contemporaries perceived: the need for sectional reconciliation, the appeal to the masses, the practicality of enlisting a friend of labor, the propaganda value overseas for a war waged by this democracy "of the people, by the people, and for the people," the fiat of Abraham Lincoln, and, in short, the response to the anxieties of a beleaguered party. Whatever the stereotype or the reality might have been, Johnson boasted undeniable assets which no rival could match. In the long run, some of these assets would become liabilities, but for the moment the dross lay partially concealed by the gilt. Like the party's nomination of the Railsplitter four years earlier, its selection of the tailor, in a way, represented the triumph of availability.

Undoubtedly the great conflict left an enduring imprint upon those who lived through its agonies; but the Johnson of the war years remained outwardly unchanged albeit somewhat grimmer, a testimonial to his grave responsibilities. Of medium height, stocky build, prominent nose and aggressive chin, small but sparkling black eyes and penetrating gaze—"great determination of appearance," as Dana described him[161]—he possessed a natural dignity enhanced by neat, almost fastidious tailoring. Judging from the evidence at hand, he seems to have kept a reasonably good state of health, though troubled at times by indispsitions of one kind or another: occasional pain from an arm broken in the prewar period, a "violent bilious attack" in August, 1863, a recurring "severe sickness" during the course of that late summer. Nevertheless his commitment was as firm as ever. His intimates (about whom we know disappointingly little), the few visitors who left written accounts, and the journalists of the time, testify to his dedication, his long hours, his numerous audiences with people irrespective of color or conviction, sex or station. Fundamentally, Johnson's life centered around his stewardship and his political ambitions, even though he might now and then relax with confidant or caller, possibly enjoying a sip of peach brandy but more likely worrying down a draught of "the ardent"—a potion not inappropriate to the cares of the governorship.

Largely unchanged too, the war notwithstanding, were the Johnson family circumstances, a source of distress to a devoted husband and father. The health of his wife Eliza, a consumptive, remained precarious, a condition scarcely improved by her experiences under the Confederate occupation of East Tennessee. Crossing the lines with other family members, she reached Nashville in October, 1862, departing two months later for the Indiana springs and returning to Tennessee the following May, her condition much the same. Concern for wife and children was the main burden of

161. Dana, *Recollections of the Civil War,* 105.

a letter Andrew wrote her from Washington in the spring of 1863. "I am kept in suspence all the time in reference to Some one of the family," he began. Expressing the hope that "you are gain[in]g strength and some flesh," he noted that he had had no communication from Charles and Robert since leaving Nashville, and despaired of seeing Martha and her children again. He trusted that there was nothing seriously wrong with Mary (whose husband Daniel Stover was dangerously ill) and urged that she "devote much of her time and attention to the instruction and train[in]g of her children." As for his youngest son, "You must tell Andrew that his father's hopes rest upon him now and that he must make a man of himself, he can do it if he will and I expect it of him— If he will only educate himself he has a destiny of no ordinry character." [162]

There may well have been occasions when Johnson felt that no news from the older sons was good news. The vicissitudes of Charles and Robert, perennial disappointments to their parents, continued into the war period. Charles, reputed to have been his mother's favorite son, was commissioned by his father assistant surgeon in the 1st Tennessee Infantry; but he died of a mysterious fall from a horse in April, 1863, when most of the family were away. Colonel Robert of the 1st Tennessee, a unit eventually converted to horse, engaged in field maneuvers but saw no battle action. Like his brother, he had long since turned to the bottle for solace—so much so as "to become a subject of remark every where,"as Rosecrans warned Johnson in the spring of 1863; "told him I wanted him to stop and he promised me he would." [163] It was a promise not kept; and, increasingly depressed, Robert eventually resigned his commission. To his father he wrote that "perhaps, I can in some other field of duty, make amends for the past, and gain that Character that I deserve, *and which I will win,* at all hazards." In a realistic yet compassionate letter, the likes of which he had penned in times past, Johnson replied that "I feared you would be dismissed from the Army unless you reformed and . . . give some evidence of a determination to Serve the country as a sober upright and honorable man." Alluding to one of Robert's remarks, he added, "I do most sincerely wish that my will was the law in regard to your future Course—I would be willing this night [to] resign my existence into the hands of him who gave it." Assigned to the governor's staff, the son assured his father that *"the intoxicating bowl goes to my lips no more,"* reporting later that "my system I think is thoroughly cleansed and I am a new man." [164] His subsequent course, however, would disclose that he was still disturbed, still at loose ends, the same old Robert of the bowl.

162. Letter to Eliza Johnson, March 27, 1863.
163. Telegram from William S. Rosecrans, April 12, 1863.
164. Letters from Robert Johnson, November 17, 1863, February 14, March 6, 1864; Letter to Robert Johnson, November 21, 1863.

Of family tribulations and the tragedies of war, there seemed to be no end; yet there was a less forbidding Johnson, one seldom seen by contemporaries who did not know him. Some of his grimness was actual, some rhetorical. He could be firm, even inflexible; but he had a soft side where the helpless, the uprooted, the distressed, were concerned—and he was particularly vulnerable to the feminine sex regardless of whether they wore blue or gray. Elizabeth Harding, wife of a wealthy secessionist sent north by the governor, was quite successful in persuading him to afford her property some protection against the occupying forces. And a charming vignette, apparently not all of it apocryphal, gives further credence to a gentle, understanding Johnson. One day in 1862 the post commander brought to the governor's office Laura Carter, a twenty-year-old girl arrested for spitting on Union officers from the porch of the St. Cloud Hotel, of which her father was the proprietor. "When I told her that she ought to behave herself while you were a guest at the hotel, she defied you, and said she would yet dance on your grave." According to the account, Johnson replied jocularly: "Oh, you mustn't mind these little rebels. There is no harm in Laura. Dance on my grave, will she? She will plant flowers instead. I'll take care of her. Let her go." [165] Later in the conflict the repentant Laura, now wed to Lieutenant Junius B. Holloway, a Federal officer of dubious serviceability and debatable loyalty, pleaded with the governor in his behalf. Eventually the little rebel bore out Johnson's prophecy when, after his death, she strewed flowers on his tomb. Nor was the story yet ended: years later, evidently planning a biography of her friend and benefactor, she came to the Greeneville homestead to collect material—to dance on his literary remains, one might say.

In sum, despite his temperamental shortcomings, his quarreling with military commanders, his mixture of harshness and compassion—the latter attribute often concealed from public view—and his truculent rhetoric, Andrew Johnson would ultimately prove to be Lincoln's most successful military governor.[166] Yet it must be conceded that, more than two years after arriving in Nashville, the President's new running mate had not achieved his principal goal of restoring a republican form of government. Basic to his lack of success was the failure of Federal forces to establish undisputed control of the state. So long as Confederates, whether army, guerrillas, bushwhackers, or raiders, might appear at any time, or, as in the case of East Tennessee, were for long periods in control of the country, it would be impossible to set up a conventional civil government over any sizeable area. By the spring of 1864, when much of the state had finally been secured to the Union, the knotty problems of discriminating between

165. Truman, "Anecdotes," 436.
166. Hardison, In the Toils of War, Ch. 7, *passim*.

dependable and spurious loyalty, of ensuring acquiescence in the wiping out of slavery, of keeping the apparatus of government from falling into the hands of its enemies, deterred a speedy reorganization of political institutions. As one correspondent reminded: "You will incur the heaviest responsibility of your public life if . . . you *permit* a *rickety* State organization, such only as could be effected now, to take control of affairs." [167] Thus, to achieve one goal—the maintenance of trustworthy Federal authority wherever possible—Johnson delayed the accomplishment of another—the reactivation of a citizen-based political life, the while undertaking himself to meet the day-to-day needs of a state literally and figuratively ravaged by internal divisions and external incursions. As would later be the case, faced by a task of incredible complexity and difficulty, the East Tennessee tailor sturdily trudged through the round of daily anxieties, confounding decisions, unending irritations, periodic crises, and perennial frustrations in an effort to accomplish the impossible; and in so doing, brought his beloved Tennessee through the rapids of rebellion to what would prove to be the no less turbulent shoals of a Radical Reconstruction. Meanwhile, for a "rising man" bent on "doing good," the vice presidency might provide a comfortable way-station on the road to the summit.

THIS VOLUME

Beginning with Andrew Johnson in extremis—presiding over a citadel virtually under siege, confronted by a sullen populace of butternut hue, embroiled with the military about strategy and general policy, agonizing over the plight of East Tennessee, troubled by the gloomy prospects for civil government, wondering whether Washington would stand behind him—this volume ends with Johnson in excelsis—nominated for the vice-presidency, enjoying Washington's support vis-à-vis the military, gratified by an East Tennessee redeemed and the likelihood of a state government restored. Between these antipodes lie twenty-two months of trial and error, travail and accomplishment.

The decision to calendar several addresses, delivered during a speaking tour in which the governor traversed the same forensic ground, has made it possible to include rather more letters and miscellaneous documents than in most previous volumes. Of the total correspondence, Johnson's letters (130) comprise twenty percent; in addition, assorted gubernatorial items, such as proclamations and public notices, guarantees of protection, and authorizations for raising troops, account for twenty-eight entries. Occasional lists of bonds and gold deposits, together with several letters, provide at least some clue to his material interests during these years. As with earlier volumes, the bulk of the text consists of more than five hundred

167. Letter from Allen A. Hall, January 19, 1864.

communications addressed to the governor, including seven memorials and petitions. While a dialogue with a wealthy secessionist is somewhat out of the ordinary, the most remarkable document—an item unique in the Johnson corpus—is the only extant letter to Eliza McCardle Johnson from her husband.

What aspects of the central war years are illuminated herein? The disintegration of slavery in Tennessee, the thin line between loyalty and disloyalty, the hazards of life and property in a beleaguered city and a divided state, the tribulations of the displaced, the plight of prisoners of war, and the difficulties attendant upon the restoration of a civil regime—all appear, sometimes in pleas for assistance, sometimes in representations and protests, often in flattering and self-seeking letters, now and then in essays of advice or information, most frequently in day-to-day correspondence.

As for the protagonist himself, the lights and shadows of the portrait persist—the power seeker, the redoubtable stump speaker, the implacable fighter, the dedicated unionist, the untiring East Tennessee sectionalist, all are further limned; the behind-the-scenes politico, the grim but merciful proconsul, the harassed administrator, the paterfamilias, are still in chiaroscuro. For every contour sharply defined, another remains indistinct. We learn much about his rising reputation on the national scene, but little about his vice-presidential nomination. That Lincoln had great confidence in Johnson becomes clear beyond peradventure, but we have no record of their conversations in Washington. There is ample evidence of his orientation toward radicalism, but little about his break with conservative Tennessee unionists. The reader finds much to substantiate Johnson's image as stern war governor, rather less to show his adaptability. Documentation of his relationships with Washington and the higher authorities abounds, while virtually nothing about his day-to-day experiences in Nashville appears. Johnson, arbiter and father figure to Tennessee troops, is revealed in great detail; less clearly delineated are his maneuvers to restore civil government. Of his interest in East and Middle Tennessee there can be no doubt; yet relatively little about his attitude toward West Tennessee emerges. Pervasive throughout is the dilemma of a civil governor whose vaguely defined functions overlapped those of the military. Once again, as in the past, we find a plethora of material on the public figure, a paucity about the private man.

Lacunae aside, the documents here printed offer a panorama of the wartime experience of one who found himself, perforce, in a variety of roles: viceroy in a recovered province, paragon of southern loyalty and champion of Tennessee unionists, scourge of unrepentant secessionists, renegade in the eyes of former Democratic friends, bedfellow of erstwhile political foes, umpire among contending individuals and factions, jouster with the military brass and their minions, factotum for all and sundry who saw him as a court of last resort. Perhaps the most intriguing aspect of these years is his gradual abandonment of the peculiar institution, an act which demonstrates that at this critical juncture Andrew Johnson was prepared to play the practical politician, to accept and rationalize the realities of life. That he could do so represented both a personal and political triumph; that he could not similarly respond to the realities of Reconstruction would be both a personal and national tragedy.

ACKNOWLEDGMENTS

Our debt to many individuals and institutions continues to be great; trite though it may sound, the preparation of this volume would have been impossible without their generous assistance. The following have contributed significantly to this volume: Frank E. Burke, Executive Secretary of the National Historical Publications and Records Commission, and members of his staff, especially Mary Giunta, Sara Dunlap Jackson, Ann Harris Henry; Robert Bassett, Olive Branch, John Dobson, Robert E. Harrison, Jill Keally, and their respective staffs at the University of Tennessee Library; Jean B. Waggener and staff of the Tennessee State Library and Archives; William J. MacArthur and staff of the McClung Collection, Knoxville-Knox County Public Library; Mary Glenn Hearne, The Nashville Room, The Public Library of Nashville and Davidson County; Dan Pomeroy, Tennessee State Museum; Stephen M. Findlay, Librarian, Memphis/Shelby County Public Library; Charles Isetts and William G. Myers of the Ohio State Historical Society, Columbus; and W. Neil Franklin and Hope Holdcamper, formerly of the National Archives.

It is inconceivable that a project of this scope could be successfully accomplished without the professional skills and hard work of a dedicated staff. This we have had. Under the efficient and benign supervision of Associate Editor Patricia Clark, a number of people have made a variety of contributions: John Cimprich, National Historical Publications and Records Commission Fellow; Marion O. Smith, research associate; C. James Taylor, research assistant; Kent R. Cave and Mark Wetherington, graduate assistants; Janet Hickman, secretary; Rita Boyland, Sherry Hardison, Beth Holt McCurdy, Ruby Manns, work-study students. Our overall understanding of the context in which Johnson functioned has been enhanced by the researches of Edwin Hardison presented in his dissertation, In the Toils of War: Andrew Johnson and the Federal Occupation of Tennessee.

We are most grateful to those repositories (see Editorial Method, Symbols List A) whose holdings are represented herein. To Mrs. Margaret Johnson Patterson Bartlett of Greeneville, Mrs. Betsy Bachman Carrier of Bluff City, and Jack Reynolds of Smyrna, Georgia, we are especially indebted for items from their private collections.

The three agencies most significantly involved in support of the Andrew Johnson Papers are the University of Tennessee, Knoxville, which provides housing for the Project, released time for the editors, and the services of its Press; the National Historical Publications and Records Commission which makes available generous annual grants and a publication subsidy; and the Tennessee Historical Commission, which annually contributes toward editorial costs, as well as publication assistance. For their continued support we are most appreciative.

As the decades pass, gratitude to our wives for their willingness to share us with Andrew Johnson remains paramount.

LeRoy P. Graf
Ralph W. Haskins

Knoxville, Tennessee
August 15, 1981

Editorial Method

The Library of Congress, the National Archives, and the Tennessee State Library and Archives provide most of the documents in this volume, the remainder coming from other repositories, private collections, and newspapers. All significant correspondence, both letters and telegrams, as well as reported speeches, appear here, either in full or calendared. Omitted have been repetitious and routine items, among the latter, requests for commissions, recommendations for office, release of prisoners, information about kinfolk in Tennessee, permits to move about, military appointments, military supplies, permission to take loyalty oaths, and invitations to speak, letters of introduction, authorization to raise troops, and other military minutia. Even so, at least one example of each of these has been printed; often an item not formally included will be found paraphrased, quoted, or even printed in full in a footnote.

Where there are multiple copies, the recipient's is used with the sender's date if, as may be the case with telegrams, there is a disparity. When recipient's copy is not available, a draft of the telegram or letter is used in preference to the *War of the Rebellion* version. A letter all in one hand is presumed to be an ALS, unless there is clear evidence to the contrary. As a rule, sources of footnotes are indicated. Absence of annotation may mean that the subject is a matter of general knowledge, that the person or event has been previously identified (as a check with the Index will show), or that information is unavailable. Reference to extended identifications found in the first five volumes is provided in the footnotes. Most city and business directories are from the microform collection produced by New Haven Research Publications, Inc.

In transcribing, the editors have sought to combine fidelity to the original with consideration for the reader. Thus, orthography is reproduced without change, except where confusion might occur; in such instances bracketed letters and words or *sic* are inserted to clarify the meaning. Elaborate stationery and telegraph headings have in most instances been omitted, an exception being made for official documents. In an effort to conserve space, the arrangement of dateline headings, addresses, salutations, and complimentary closings has been standardized, but nothing omitted. Unless otherwise noted, *Webster's Third International* is the authority for spelling, definition, and usage. Aside from the insertion of bracketed periods or question marks, original punctuation is retained; repetitious words or phrases, obviously slips of the pen, have been eliminated. Although information added by the editors is bracketed, exceptions are made when a correspondent's location or the date of a document are beyond doubt. Normally cities and towns without a state designation are in Tennessee.

SYMBOLS

A. Repositories

CLU — University of California, Los Angeles, California
CSmH — Henry E. Huntington Library, San Marino, California
DLC — Library of Congress, Washington, D.C.
DNA — National Archives, Washington, D.C.

RECORD GROUPS USED

RG15 Records of the Veterans Administration
RG21 Records of District Courts of the United States
RG36 Records of the Bureau of Customs
RG45 Naval Records Collection of the Office of Naval Record and Library
RG56 General Records of the Department of the Treasury
RG58 Records of the Internal Revenue Service
RG59 General Records of the Department of State
RG77 Records of the Office of the Chief of Engineers
RG92 Records of the Office of the Quartermaster General
RG94 Records of the Adjutant General's Office, 1780's-191
RG105 Records of the Bureau of Refugees, Freedmen, an Abandoned Lands
RG107 Records of the Office of the Secretary of War
RG109 War Department Collection of Confederate Records
RG153 Records of the Office of the Judge Advocate General (Army)
RG156 Records of the Office of the Chief of Ordnance
RG217 Records of the United States General Accounting Office
RG249 Records of the Commissary General of Prisoners
RG366 Records of Civil War Special Agencies of the Treasury Department
RG393 Records of United States Army Comtinental Commands, 1821-1920

MHi — Massachusetts Historical Society, Boston
NcU — University of North Carolina, Chapel Hill, North Carolina
NHi — New-York Historical Society, New York
NN — New York Public Library, New York
NNPM — Pierpont Morgan Library, New York, New York
NRU — University of Rochester, Rochester, New York
OClWHi — Western Reserve Historical Society, Cleveland, Ohio
PHi — Historical Society of Pennsylvania, Philadelphia
RPB — Brown University, Providence, Rhode Island
T — Tennessee State Library and Archives, Nashville
  RG21, Adjutant General's Papers
  Military Governor's Papers

T-MsD	Tennessee State Library and Archives, Manuscript Division
TKL	Knoxville-Knox County Public Library, Knoxville
TU	University of Tennessee, Knoxville
WHi-Ar	State Historical Society of Wisconsin, Archives Division, Madison, Wisconsin

B. Manuscripts

ALS	Autograph Letter Signed
ALS draft	Autograph Letter Signed draft
AL draft	Autograph Letter draft
ANS	Autograph Note Signed
Copy	Copy not by writer
D	Document
DS	Document Signed
L	Letter
L draft	Letter draft
LB copy	Letter Book copy
LB copy S	Letter Book copy, Signed
LS	Letter Signed
Mem	Memorial
PC	Printed Copy
Pet	Petition
PL	Printed Letter
Tel	Telegram
Tel draft	Telegram draft
Tel copy	Telegram copy

ABBREVIATIONS

GENERAL

A.; App.	Appendix
ACP Branch	Appointment, Commission, and Personal Branch
Appl.	Application
b.	born
c, ca.	about
Col.	Collection
Corres.	Correspondence
CSA	Confederate States of America
CSR	Compiled Service Records
Dist.	District
Div.	Division
Ex.	Executive
fl	flourishing
Gen. Let. Bk.	General Letter Book

l, ll.	line, lines
LC	Library of Congress
Lets. Recd.	Letters Received
Lets. Sent	Letters Sent
Mil. B.	Military Books
Mil. Gov's	Military Governor's
NA	National Archives
RR	Railroad
Recs. & Appts.	Recommendations and Appointments
Sec.	Secretary, section
Ser.	Series
Sess.	Session
st.	stanza
Subdiv.	Subdivision
Supp., supps.	Supplement, supplements
Tel., tels.	Telegram, telegraph, telegrams
Tels. Recd.	Telegrams Received
v.	versus

MILITARY

Adj. Gen.	Adjutant General
Arty.	Artillery
Bde.	Brigade
Btn.	Battalion
Bty.	Battery
Capt.	Captain
Cav.	Cavalry
Cld.	Colored
Co.	Company
Col.	Colonel
CSA	Confederate States of America (Army)
Dept.	Department
Gen.	General
Inf.	Infantry
Lgt.	Light [Lgt. Arty.]
Lt.	Lieutenant
Mid. Tenn.	Middle Tennessee
Mtd.	Mounted
Rgt.	Regiment
USA	United States of America (Army)
Vol.	Volunteer

SHORT TITLES

Acklen, *Tenn. Records*	Jeanette T. Acklen, comp., *Tennessee Records* (2 vols., Nashville, 1933).

American Annual Cyclopaedia	*American Annual Cyclopaedia and Register of Important Events* (42 vols. in 3 series, New York, 1862-1903).
Appleton's Cyclopaedia	James G. Wilson and John Fiske, eds., *Appleton's Cyclopaedia of American Biography* (6 vols., New York, 1887-89).
Basler, *Works of Lincoln*	Roy P. Basler, ed., *The Collected Works of Abraham Lincoln* (9 vols., New Brunswick, N. J., 1953-55).
BDAC	*Biographical Directory of the American Congress, 1774-1961 . . . (House Document* No. 442, 85 Congress, 2 Session, Washington, 1961).
Boatner, *Civil War Dictionary*	Mark M. Boatner, *The Civil War Dictionary* (New York, 1959).
Carter, *First Tenn. Cav.*	William R. Carter, *History of the First Regiment of Tennessee Volunteer Cavalry* (Knoxville, 1902).
1860 [1870, 1880, 1900] Census, Tenn., Greene [other states and counties]	U.S. Bureau of the Census, Eighth Census 1860, Population [state, county, post office, district or ward] (original schedules on microfilm).
1890 Special Census, Union Veterans and Widows	U.S. Bureau of the Census, Special Schedules of the Eleventh Census (1890) enumerating Union Veterans and Widows of Union Veterans of the Civil War [state, county, post office, district or ward] (original schedules on microfilm).
Cimprich, Slavery Amidst Civil War	John V. Cimprich, Slavery Amidst Civil War in Tennessee: The Death of an Institution (Ph.D. dissertation, Ohio State University, 1977).
Clayton, *Davidson County*	W. Woodford Clayton, *History of Davidson County, Tennessee* (Philadelphia, 1880).
Cong. Globe	U.S. Congress, *The Congressional Globe* (23 Congress to 42 Congress, Washington, 1834-73).
DAB	Allen Johnson and Dumas Malone, eds., *Dictionary of American Biography* (20 vols., supps., and index, New York, 1928-).

ETHS *Publications*	East Tennessee Historical Society's *Publications*.
Ex. Record Book (1862-63)	Record Book, Executive Office, Nashville, Tennessee, 1862-1863, Johnson Papers, Series 4C, Library of Congress.
Fitch, *Annals*	John Fitch, *Annals of the Army of the Cumberland* (Philadelphia, 1864).
Futrell, Federal Trade	Robert F. Futrell, Federal Trade with the Confederate States, 1861-1865: A Study of Governmental Policy (Ph.D. dissertation, Vanderbilt University, 1950).
Goodspeed's East Tennessee *Goodspeed's Bedford* [and other counties]	Goodspeed Publishing Company, *History of Tennessee, from the Earliest Time to the Present* . . . (Chicago, 1886-87).
Hall, *Military Governor*	Clifton R. Hall, *Andrew Johnson: Military Governor of Tennessee* (Princeton, 1916).
Heitman, *Register*	Francis B. Heitman, *Historical Register and Dictionary of the United States Army, from Its Organization, September 29, 1789 to March 2, 1903* (2 vols., Washington, 1903).
Hesseltine, *Civil War Prisons*	William B. Hesseltine, *Civil War Prisons: A Study in War Psychology* (New York, 1964 [1930]).
Hooper, Memphis	Ernest W. Hooper, Memphis, Tennessee: Federal Occupation and Reconstruction, 1862-70 (Ph.D. dissertation, University of North Carolina, 1957).
House Ex. Doc.	*House Executive Document*.
JP	Andrew Johnson Papers, Library of Congress. JP refers to the first series only; JP2, etc., to succeeding series.
Johnson Papers	LeRoy P. Graf and Ralph W. Haskins, eds., *The Papers of Andrew Johnson* (5 vols., Knoxville, 1967-).
Johnson-Bartlett Col.	Andrew Johnson materials in possession of Mrs. Margaret Johnson Patterson Bartlett, Greeneville, Tennessee.

Keating, *Memphis*	John M. Keating, *History of the City of Memphis, Tennessee* (Syracuse, 1888).
Long, *Civil War Almanac*	E. B. Long, with Barbara Long, *The Civil War Day by Day: An Almanac, 1861-1865* (New York, 1971).
McBride and Robison, *Biographical Directory*	Robert M. McBride and Dan M. Robison, comps., *Biographical Directory of the Tennessee General Assembly* (2 vols., Nashville, 1975-).
Maslowski, *Treason Must be Made Odious*	Peter Maslowski, *Treason Must Be Made Odious: Military Occupation and Wartime Reconstruction in Nashville, Tennessee, 1862-65* (Millwood, New York, 1978).
Mathews, *Americanisms*	Mitford M. Mathews, ed., *A Dictionary of Americanisms on Historical Principles* (2 vols., Chicago, 1951).
Mt. Olivet Cemetery Records, II	Mt. Olivet Cemetery Records, Interment Book, II, 1855-1891 (microfilm, Public Library of Nashville and Davidson County).
Nashville Bus. Dir. (1855-56)	John P. Campbell, comp., *Nashville City and Business Directory, 1855-56* (Nashville, 1855).
Nashville Bus. Dir. (1860-61)	L. P. Williams & Co., *Nashville City and Business Directory, 1860-61* (Nashville, 1860).
Nashville City Cemetery Index	*Index to Interments in the Nashville City Cemetery, 1846-1962* (Nashville, 1964).
NCAB	*National Cyclopaedia of American Biography . . .* (54 vols., New York, 1967-73 [1893-]).
NUC	Library of Congress, *The National Union Catalog: Pre-1956 Imprints* (754 vols., London, 1968-).
OED	James A. H. Murray and others, eds., *The Oxford English Dictionary* (13 vols., Oxford, 1933).
Official Army Register: Volunteers	Adjutant General's Office, *Official Army Register of the Volunteer Force of the United States Army for the*

	Years 1861, 1862, 1863, 1864, 1865 (8 vols., Washington, 1865-67).
Official Army Register (1863)	Adjutant General's Office, *Register of the Army of the United States for 1863* ([Washington, 1863]).
OR; OR-Atlas	*War of the Rebellion: A Compilation of the Official Records of the Union and Confederate Armies* (70 vols. in 128, Washington, 1880-1901).
OR-Navy	*Official Records of the Union and Confederate Navies in the War of the Rebellion* (30 vols., Washington, 1894-1927).
Porch, *1850 Census, Davidson*	Deane Porch, tr., *Davidson County, Tennessee, 1850 Census* (Fort Worth, 1969).
Powell *Army List*	William H. Powell, *List of Officers of the United States from 1779 to 1900* (Detroit, 1967 [1900]).
Reynolds, *Greene County Cemeteries*	Buford Reynolds, *Greene County Cemeteries* ([Greeneville], 1971).
Senate Misc. Doc.	*Senate Miscellaneous Document*
Senate Ex. Doc.	*Senate Executive Document*
Sistler, *1850 Tenn. Census*	Byron and Barbara Sistler, trs., *1850 Census, Tennessee* (8 vols., Evanston, Ill., 1974-76).
Sistler, *1890 Tenn. Veterans Census*	Byron and Barbara Sistler, trs., *1890 Civil War Veterans Census, Tennessee* (Evanston, Ill., 1978).
Speer, *Prominent Tennesseans*	William S. Speer, *Sketches of Prominent Tennesseans* (Nashville, 1888).
Temple, *East Tennessee*	Oliver P. Temple, *East Tennessee and the Civil War* (Cincinnati, 1899).
Temple, *Notable Men*	Oliver P. Temple, *Notable Men of Tennessee from 1833 to 1875* (New York, 1912).
Tenn. Acts, 1861-62	*Acts of the State of Tennessee,* 1861-62
Tenn. Adj. Gen. Report 1866	*Report of the Adjutant General of the State of Tennessee on the Military Forces of the State from 1861 to 1866* (Nashville, 1866).
Tenn. Hist. Quar.	*Tennessee Historical Quarterly.*
Tenn. House Journal	*Tennessee House Journal.*
Tenn. Senate Journal	*Tennessee Senate Journal.*

Tennesseans in the Civil War	Civil War Centennial Commission, *Tennesseans in the Civil War: A Military History of Confederate and Union Units with Available Rosters of Personnel* (2 pts., Nashville, 1964).
U.S. Official Register	*Register of the Officers and Agents, Civil, Military and Naval in the Service of the United States . . .* (Washington, 1851-).
U.S. Statutes	*United States Statutes at Large.*
Warner, *Generals in Blue*	Ezra J. Warner, *Generals in Blue* (Baton Rouge, 1964).
Warner, *Generals in Gray*	Ezra J. Warner, *Generals in Gray* (Baton Rouge, 1959).
Webster's Third International	*Webster's Third New Internatinal Dictionary of the English Language, Unabridged* (Springfield, Mass., 1968).
West Point Register (1970)	The West Point Alumni Foundation, Inc., *Register of Graduates and Former Cadets of the United States Military Academy: Cullum Memorial Edition* (West Point, 1970).
West Tenn. Hist. Soc. *Papers*	West Tennessee Historical Society *Papers.*
Wooldridge, *Nashville*	John Wooldridge, ed., *History of Nashville* (Nashville, 1890).
WPA	U.S. Works Project Administration, Historical Records Survey (Nashville, 1936-41).

Chronology

1808, December 29	Born at Raleigh, North Carolina
1812, January 4	Death of father Jacob Johnson
1822, February 18	Bound as tailor's apprentice
1826, September	Arrives in Greeneville, Tennessee
1827, May 17	Marries Eliza McCardle
1828, October 25	Birth of daughter Martha
1829-35	Alderman, then mayor
1830, February 19	Birth of son Charles
1832, May 8	Birth of daughter Mary
1834, February 22	Birth of son Robert
1835-37, 1839-41	State representative
1841-43	State senator
1843-53	Congressman, first district
1852, August 5	Birth of son Andrew, Jr.
1853-57	Governor of Tennessee
1857, October 8	Elected to Senate
1860, May-June	Presidential aspirant, Charleston
1860, December 18-19	Speech on Secession
1862, March 3	Appointed military governor
1862, December 10	Greeneville property sequestered
1863, February 26-March 31	Speeches in Midwest and East
1863, April 4	Death of son Charles
1863, May 30	Remarks at Nashville
1863, August 23	Speech at Franklin
1863, August 29	Speech at Nashville
1863, November 23	Testimony before Freedmen's Inquiry
1864, January 8	Speech on Slavery and State Suicide
1864, January 21	Speech on State Restoration
1864, January 26	Prescribes "Ardently Desire" Oath
1864, April 12, 16	Speeches in Knoxville
1864, June 8	Nominated for Vice President
1864, June 9	Speech on Vice-Presidential Nomination
1864, November 8	Elected Vice President
1865, April 15	Succeeds to Presidency
1866, August 28-September 15	"Swing around the circle"
1868, February 24	Impeachment by House
1868, May 16, 26	Acquittal by Senate

1869, March	Returns to Greeneville
1869, October 22	Defeated for Senate
1872, November 5	Defeated for congressman-at-large
1875, January 26	Elected to Senate
1875, March 5-24	Serves in extra session
1875, July 31	Dies at Stover home, Carter County

THE PAPERS OF

Andrew Johnson

1862

From Elizabeth M. Harding[1]

[Belle Meade, September, 1862][2]

Gov Johnson,
Sir,

If amidst the cares of office with which you are environed you may remember, I promised I would go in town to day, to hear your decision upon the proposition I made to you, to allow my husband to execute a bond, to any amount satisfactory to you, and come home, look around, upon the condition of his property, & of the country so that he may understandingly determine whether or not he will adhere to his present views, or after seeing the condition of things at home, make up his mind, as to what he will do, for the future.[3] I urged this plan of a bond, upon you, simply because, to me at least, it seemed, that in taking the oath prescribed for a parole, he would be in effect taking the Oath of allegiance to the United States, without any limitation of time. Of course, with the explanation, which you were kind enough to make to me, and the understanding that Gen Harding, will have the privilege of surrendering his parole, at any time, & leave him in the same condition as he was before taking it—but it seems to me that the Oath prescribed on the parole seems to be without limitation, and the fear that I will not be able to explain the matter satisfactorily to Gen H. induces me to press upon your kind attention, the idea I mentioned to you, that he might be permitted to give his bond, & return home, & there with all the lights before him, & the explanations of yourself, he would be better able to determine as to his future conduct. Indisposition alone has prevented me from visiting you to day, & hearing your decision upon a matter of, *to me* more importance than any thing else in the world beside. Allow me to say here, & surely you will pardon in me this womans argument, that in Gen Harding you have had a friend & a constituent, more devoted in times past, than any other person that I have known; you were not only his political champion, but his friend whom he delighted to honor, & notwithstanding your difference of political sentiments & feeling, I am sure that he entertains the highest opinion of your integrity & honesty, however much he may differ as to the true interests of the South, in this most unhappy war. I can only say for him that were your relative positions changed, I have no earthly doubt but that he would grant to you the favor, which I ask for him; this is, you may think, a womans argument, but it is drawn from the heart, & to me is conclusive, being in fact the golden rule, "As ye would that others should do unto you, do ye even so to them."—

Should you determine to grant my request, you will please fix the amount of the bond & I hope I can have it satisfactorily signed[.]

With sentiments of high respect—
Mrs Wm. G. Harding.—

ALS, DLC-JP.

1. See *Johnson Papers*, V, 634*n*.

2. Inasmuch as William G. Harding was paroled during the last days of September, it may be assumed that this missive (dated 1864 by the Library of Congress) was sent several weeks earlier. For Harding, see *ibid.*, 366*n*; Ridley Wills, II, ed., "Letters from Nashville: A Portrait of Belle Meade," *Tenn. Hist. Quar.*, XXXIII (1974), 82.

3. After his parole and release from Fort Mackinac, Harding returned to Belle Meade, where he remained for the duration of the war. *Ibid.;* Herschel Gower, "Belle Meade: A Queen of Plantations," *ibid.*, XXII (1963), 215.

To Abraham Lincoln[1]

Nashville, Sept 1st 1862.

His Excellency Abraham Lincoln
Washington City

On two occasions I have stated to the President that Genl. Buell[2] would never enter and redeem the Eastern portion of this State.[3] I do not believe he ever intended to, notwithstanding his fair promises to the President and others that he would.

A portion of the rebel troops, it is stated under the command of Bragg[4] have crossed the Tennessee River about Chattanooga and are marching in the direction of Nashville. His force is variously estimated from 12 to 50.000. My own opinion is that it cannot exceed ten or 15.000.[5] General Buell and his forces are in his front, ranging from Decherds on Rail Road to McMinnville & Sparta, and in my opinion, with such Generals as he has under his command could meet Bragg and whip him with the greatest ease, entering lower East Tennessee, and turn the rear of the force said to be now before Morgan[6] at Cumberland Gap, leaving Morgan to march into East Tennessee & take possession of the Rail Road, at once segregating and destroying the unity of their Territory and that too in the midst of a population that is loyal & will stand by the Government.

The forces which have passed Cumberland Gap on Morgan's right, under command of Kirby Smith,[7] entering Kentucky in Morgan's rear, can and will be met by forces coming in the direction of Lexington & Nicholasville and whipped & driven back.

I am now compelled to state, though with deep regret, what I know and believe General Buell's policy to be. Instead of meeting and whipping Bragg where he is, it is his intention to occupy a defensive position & is now, according to best evidence I can obtain, concentrating all his forces upon Nashville, giving up all the country which we have had possession of South & East of this place, leaving the Union sentiment & Union men, who took a stand for the Gov., to be crushed out & utterly ruined by the Rebels, who will all be in arms upon the retreat, of our Army. It seems to me that General Buell fears his own personal safety, and has concluded to gather the whole army at this point as a kind of body guard to protect and defend him without reference to the Union men who have been induced to speak out, believing that the Govt. would defend them.

General Buell is very popular with the Rebels, and the impression is that he is more partial to them than to Union men and that he favors the establishment of the Southern Confederacy.[8]

I will not assume that General Buell desires the establishment of a Southern Confederacy & a surrender of Tennessee to the Rebels, but will give it as my opinion, that, if he had designed to do so, he could not have laid down or pursued a policy that would have been more successful in the accomplishment of both these objects.

Notwithstanding the untoward events which have transpired since I reached Nashville, I feel & believe that much good had been done in preparing the public mind in being reconciled to the Govt. but if the policy which I have indicated is carried out by Genl. Buell, all will be thrown away without the most distant idea, if ever, when we shall recover our lost ground. East Tennessee seems doomed. There is scarcely a hope left of her redemption, if ever, no one now can tell. May God save my country from some of the Generals that have been conducting this War.

[Andrew Johnson]

L draft, Johnson-Bartlett Col.; also in Philadelphia *Press*, November 15, 1862.

1. There is some reason to question whether Lincoln ever saw this letter, except perhaps after it was printed in several northern papers. No copy is to be found among the Lincoln papers and only a draft among Johnson's. We can only speculate about the circumstances of its publication. In his November 9 dispatch from Nashville, Ben Truman of the Philadelphia *Press*, printed it in full, although he claimed to "transmit . . . extracts" from Johnson's letter "criticising the course pursued by Gen. Buell while in command of the Army of the Ohio." Explaining that the letter would have been sent at the time it was written, except that "the guerrilla Morgan cut off all communication with the North," he nonetheless gives no clue as to the precise date of transmittal. Did the military governor intentionally "leak" this communication in an effort to arouse public support for recovery of East Tennessee? Were Truman and his employer, the editor-politician John Forney, trying to strengthen the case against Buell? Philadelphia *Press*, November 15, 1862.

2. For Don Carlos Buell, see *Johnson Papers*, V, 33*n*.

3. These doubts had been expressed in conversations during the fall of 1861. See Letter to Abraham Lincoln, July 10, 1862, *ibid.*, 550.

4. Braxton Bragg (1817-1876), one of the Confederacy's most controversial generals, was born at Warrenton, North Carolina, graduated from West Point (1837), fought in the Seminole and Mexican wars, and attained a lieutenant colonelcy by 1856 when he retired to a Louisiana plantation. Appointed brigadier early in 1861, he commanded the coast from Pensacola to Mobile and led the II Corps at Shiloh, becoming in June, 1862, commander of the Army of Tennessee which he led in the unsuccessful Kentucky invasion and at Murfreesboro, Chickamauga, and Chattanooga. Relinquishing command in December, 1863, he became military adviser to President Davis. Subsequently a civil engineer at Mobile and later in Texas, he died suddenly in Galveston. *DAB*, II, 585-87;

Warner, *Generals in Gray*, 30-31; see also Grady McWhiney, *Braxton Bragg and Confederate Defeat: Field Command* (New York, 1969).

5. The *Tribune* version reads: "His force is variously estimated at from 20,000 to 50,000. My own opinion is that it cannot exceed 20,000." A modern biographer, pointing out that it is impossible to determine exact strength because effectives varied from day to day, estimates Bragg's army at 27,000 a short time before its departure from Chattanooga. *Ibid.*, 275-78.

6. For George Morgan, see *Johnson Papers*, V, 299*n*.

7. For Edmund Kirby Smith, see *ibid.*, 358*n*.

8. That the general, first as commander of the Army of the Ohio and currently of the Army of the Cumberland, was inclined toward leniency with southern civilians, had become a matter of some dispute. Witnesses before the Buell Commission, a military inquiry conducted in 1864, testified that this "leniency" secured the allegiance of thousands of Middle Tennesseans; his biographer called the policy "Machiavellian in the effectiveness with which it won Confederate sympathizers . . . and prevented guerrilla uprisings," adds that Buell "gained an immense respect and popularity in the South and among Democrats and conservatives in the North." Yet his conciliatory tactics caused some Federal officers to impugn his loyalty and also drew the wrath of politicians—particularly those of radical persuasion. Johnson's statement is patently an exaggeration which must be read not only in the light of the governor's growing difficulties with the military in general, and with Buell in particular, but also in view of an increasing conviction that his own handling of secessionists had been too lenient. *OR*, Ser. 1, XVI, Pt. I, 134-35, 697-98; James P. Chumney, Jr., Don Carlos Buell: Gentleman General (Ph. D. dissertation, Rice University, 1964), 131-32, 201.

Petition from Workhouse Prisoners[1]

Nashville Sept 2/62.

To His Exelency,
Andrew Johnson, Gov &c.

The undersigned, petitioners, most respectfully Show your Honor, That they are now confined in the workhouse of the City of Nashville as political prisoners, caused to be taken and imprisoned, by the order and direction of General Johnson.[2] They are informed that they have been turned over to Your Exelency for examination and trial.

Therefore by virtue of the powers in you vested, and relying upon your known clemany & mercy, and in pursuant to your powers of parden, to those that have errd, we appeal in mercy, those of us that have errd, upon our returning to loyalty, to parden and set us at liberty, upon our taking the usual oath, & giving such bond as may be requred, which we are ready to do. some of us are already loyal & have done nothing to our knowledg to warrant our confinement, supose we were arrested under a supposed State of fact, but which in fact are erroneous. we subjoin a Statement of facts which are true & which we defy refutation. The Statement marked Exhibit A & made apart of this petition[.][3]

Will you please have us brought out as, conveant, and examined, and if found wirthy dischagd upon such terms, as in your wisdom & mercy may see fit, to-day if you please.

As in duty bound they will ever pray &c.

Pet, DLC-JP.

1. Thirty-two signers, mostly Middle Tennesseans, and their attorney, Manson M. Brien.

2. During the preceding month, in the course of scouring certain Middle Tennessee areas for enemy cavalry, Richard W. Johnson had rounded up these secessionist sympathizers. *OR*, Ser. I, XVI, Pt. I, 265. For General Johnson, see *Johnson Papers*, V, 619*n*.

3. Not found.

From William H. Seward

Department of State,
Washington, 5th. Septr., 1862.

Honble. Andrew Johnson,
Military Governor of Tennessee,
Nashville, Tennessee.
Sir:

I have the honor to enclose the copy of a Memorandum from the British Chargé d' Affaires here,[1] relative to the refusal of passes to John Martin[2] and other British subjects to leave Nashville, because they would not take a certain oath, and to request that you will inform me what that oath was.[3]

I have the honor to be, Sir,
Your obedient servant,
William H. Seward.

ALS, DLC-JP; DNA-RG59, Domestic Letters, Vol. 58.

1. William Stuart (1824-1896), Cambridge-educated career diplomat who supported Confederate recognition, was in the midst of a two-year assignment at Washington (November, 1861-October, 1863). His memorandum, dated September 4, read: "John Martin is stated to be a British Subject, and to have been refused a Pass to leave Nashville, Tennessee, because he would not take the Oath, and other British Subjects in Nashville are said to have been treated in the same way." Frederic Boase, *Modern English Biography* (6 vols., New York, 1965 [1892-1921]), III, 812-13; Ephraim D. Adams, *Great Britain and the American Civil War* (2 vols., London, 1925), II, 37; Johnson Papers, LC.

2. Possibly John Martin (b. *c*1820), English-born carpenter living in the household of John W. Martin, a Davidson County farmer. 1860 Census, Tenn. , Davidson, Nashville, 4th Ward, 119.

3. For copy of oath, see E. Culverhouse to Her Britannic Majesty's Minister at Washington, August 15, 1862, Johnson Papers, LC.

From George W. Blackburn[1]

Nashville Ten.—Sept. 8th. 1862.

Gov. Johnson,
My Dear Sir,

I take the liberty of addressing to you the following lines to ascertain whether or not you can place me in possession of a certain amount of money at the expense of the friends of the rebellion.

The facts which I wish to lay before you are about as follows.

My place of residence is Hampshire, Maury County, Ten. Because of my uncompromising hostility to Secession, its friends ruined my business and made it nearly impossible for me to support my family.

Eventually—about three weeks since—a squad of Guerrillas—Captains "Dunk." Cooper[2] & Anderson's[3] Companies—came to my house and took the only horse I had—my wife telling them it was our only horse, and earnestly requesting them not to take him.

Some of my townsmen told me that if I did not slip off I would be hung.

I left. Went to Columbia and told Genl. Negley[4] that I wanted him to pay me out of money collected by fines from rebels, $255. for the horse & Bridle, & to make the Secessionists refund it. The Genl, advanced to me $150. in uncurrent Southern Paper, & said as soon as he collected more money by fining the rebels in my neighborhood that he would pay the bill. I come on her and Genl. Negley has left Columbia.

The paper I rec'd I could not use— I exchanged it for Union Bank, at 30 percent discount— Sent nearly all to my wife— I am now here nearly out of money— Can't go home— am too infirm to go into the army— Have not been able to get into business, & perhaps can not.

Now Gov. Johnson if you have the means to do anything for me at the expense of the freinds of those who have despoiled me of my property and driven me from my home—my wife and two little daughters, I, as an uncompromising Union man, who have performed my whole duty to my country at all times, ask you to do so. I would not, however, receive one cent unless it is at the expense, as above.

I called at your house this evening—being advised by Mr. East,[5] Secretary of State, to do so, with the enclosed lines from Mr. Ellis as a recommendation[6]—to see you—

Was informed by the lady of the house[7] that perhaps it would be best to call later in the evning, and being anxious to place this matter before you as soon as I prudently can I thus introduce it.

Wishing that you may soon be in good health and that you may live to see the end of this most ungodly revolution and enjoy many happy years in the glorious Era that will follow.

I am your friend with all due respect,

G. W. Blackburn[8]

ALS, DLC-JP.

1. George W. Blackburn (*c*1817-*fl*1881), Tennessee native, who went to California during the gold rush, was by 1860 teaching school in Maury County. Becoming state comptroller (1866-70), he was by the late 1870's U.S. deputy collector of internal revenue. 1860 Census, Tenn., Maury, 16th Dist., 230; (1880), 9th Dist., 11; Maury County Historical Society, *Frank H. Smith's History of Maury County, Tennessee* ([Columbia], 1969), 64; *Tenn. Official Manual* (1890), 172; *U. S. Official Register* (1879), I, 95; (1881), I, 135.

2. Duncan B. Cooper (1844-1922), half-brother of Edmund Cooper, had just been exchanged at Vicksburg, having been captured at Donelson as a member of the 51st Tenn. Inf., CSA. Organizing a company of partisan rangers, he was authorized by Gen. Gideon

Pillow in 1863 to raise a cavalry regiment inside Union lines; when he was captured in Lewis County in February, 1864, his command was broken up and distributed to other organizations. Subsequently he engaged in various business enterprises at Columbia and Nashville, serving also as clerk and master of chancery court, Columbia (1871-80) and in the Tennessee house (1881-83) and senate (1895-97). McBride and Robison, *Biographical Directory,* II, 189; *Tennesseans in the Civil War,* I, 108; Jill K. Garrett, ed., *Confederate Soldiers and Patriots of Maury County, Tennessee* (Columbia, 1970), 67.

3. John G. Anderson (b. *c*1838) was captain, Co. B, 2nd (Bate's) Tenn. Inf., CSA, until the reorganization of the regiment in April, 1862. On May 13 he obtained permission from General Beauregard to organize a partisan company to operate within enemy lines. *Ibid.,* 14; CSR, RG109, NA.

4. For James S. Negley, see *Johnson Papers*, V, 349*n.*

5. For Edward H. East, see *ibid.*, 245*n.*

6. Not found.

7. Perhaps Mrs. Anna M. Cone, with whom Johnson boarded from May to November, 1862, who had been Anna M. Roache (b. *c*1837), a "practical operator," until her marriage to Edward P. Cone, "sewing machinist," special mail agent (1864), and later (1865) clerk of the Tennessee senate and treasurer of the Republican state committee. 1860 Census, Tenn., Davidson, Nashville, 3rd Ward, 67; Receipt from Annie Cone, October 8, 1862, Johnson Papers, Series 10, LC; *Tenn. House Journal, 1870-71,* App., 785-87; *Tenn. Senate Journal,* 1865, p. 8; *King's Nashville City Directory* (1866), 137; Nashville *Times and True Union*, March 14, 1864.

8. A week later Blackburn once again reminded the governor of his plight and requested that he be paid "the balance due me on the property of which I was robbed = $147. in Tenn. money or its equivalent in any other kind of paper." He further suggested that if Johnson gave him an audience he "probably could give you some items &c in relation to men and matters in Maury—I know many men there who 'used to be' your friends enthusiastically, but who of late have been humbugged into the regions of all that is bad." Blackburn to Johnson, September 16, 1862, Johnson Papers, LC.

From Robert S. Northcott[1]

Beverly Va Sep 13th 1862.

Gov. Andrew Johnson
Dear Sir

I have this day started G.H. Connelley[2] who represents that he is a *deserter* from the rebel army, to you. He resides, or says he resides near Lebanon, Tenn. I am not exactly satisfied with him, being rather suspicious that he is playing the spy, but the evidence is not sufficiently strong against him to warrant his detention. I further have him escorted to the B. & O. R. R. so if he should be a spy I will have him in a position in which he cannot do much harm. He has given me an obligation to report himself to you and has taken the oath of allegiance.[3]

Most Truly Your Friend and Obt Servt
R. S. Northcott Lieut. Col.
12th Regt. V V I.

ALS, DLC-JP.

1. See *Johnson Papers*, V, 161*n.*

2. George W. Connelly (b. *c*1826), a Wilson County carpenter with personal property worth $250 in 1860, was a private in Co. K, 7th Tenn. Inf., CSA, from which he deserted August 18, 1862. 1860 Census, Tenn., Wilson, 10th Dist., 165; CSR, RG109, NA.

3. On this same date, Connelly pledged his "sacred honor" to report to Andrew Johnson, obey his orders, and "bear true allegiance to the United States" under penalty of death. Johnson Papers, LC.

From Elizabeth M. Harding

Belle Meade, Sept. 14th, 1862.

To Gov. Andrew Johnson.

As Military Governor of the State and the last refuge of an oppressed citizen—the link which unites the civil and military authority of the State—I address you this appeal.

There has been removed already from this place five hundred, or five hundred waggon loads of hay, corn, oats, wheat, etc. etc., for the use of the Government for which not even a semblance of receipt has been given. If you will make inquiry of Col. Stokes[1] he will inform you that I have in addition to this sent to his command at least sixty tons of hay—for which I hold the receipts of his Forage Master Quinn.[2]

The Government has made a requisition upon me for horses for the use of the Cavalry and have taken every suitable horse I had except my carriage horses. The soldiers have entered the lawns and killed before my eyes and carried away every head of poultry upon the place not only my own but the negroes also.

They broke my dairy and removed therefrom every onion, potatoes, and winter vegetables which I had provided for the use of a family of 150 persons. They have taken from me without even giving me a receipt therefor every negro man—able-bodied—on this place 22 in number, and have not left me wagoners enough to run the waggons and carry hay to Col. Stokes Cavalry.

On yesterday a squad of pillagers came out and entered the rear of the place and stole 9 of the finest mules on the place.

A soldier demanded the key of my meat house from my Niece[3] who is staying with me and upon her refusal seized an axe and threatened to dash her brains out with it. Another chased a negro girl into my own bed room and when my eldest daughter[4] attempted to close the door against him he stabbed at her with his bayonet and run it in to prevent the closing of the door. No negro woman on this place is safe in her house from the licentious soldiery and when they leave their houses and fly to me for protection their houses are entered and robbed. One woman had a gold chain stolen from her and all the silver money she had. They come and demand of the servants to give them all the milk and butter on the place on penalty of having their brains blown out if they refuse.

Night before last a Captain's company of 100 men came out here at midnight and wantonly shot without the least provocation my favorite man servant Bob.[5]

They have taken from me every grain of corn on the place and I am now buying corn to bread my family. They have not left me oats for seed. They have wantonly shot—without even eating them—two Cashmere goats which you yourself know cost my Husband $1000 apiece.[6]

Three weeks ago we had 100 deer, and a herd of twelve or fourteen buffaloes, now we have about 40 deer left and not one buffalo. There is not a fowl left on the place. And now, at this moment while I am writing a sweet potato patch of about 4 acres of potatoes not one fourth grown are being dug by at least fifty soldiers without even a non commissioned officer at their head, while the grounds around the house and every negro cabin on the premise is literally swarming with soldiers who are wandering all over the place plundering at will. At the same time there are thirty-seven wagons standing on the pike getting ready to load up with the small amount of hay and oats left on the place; and enstead of going through the gates they are knocking down the fences and opening the whole plantation to the inroads of stock.

On yesterday a whole Captain's company marched out here and when I asked them their business, they said they had come out to get a fine Stallion belonging to Gen.H., worth at least $1500. I remonstrated with them and told them that this was too fine a stock horse to use as a Cavalry horse, and they replied that they did not intend to use him as a cavalry horse but intended him as a *present* to one of their field officers. I told them that if the horse was as they alleged confiscated to the United States government that no one man had the right to take a horse of that value and appropriate him to his own use to be shot at. I showed them a protection from Gen. Thomas[7] but nothing but the presence of a guard of soldiers saved him from being seized and taken by those men who did not even pretend that they had an order for his removal.

As I once before assured your Excellency if allowed to keep my husband's fine stock I will keep them here subject to whatever decision the Government may make in reference to them, but surely no one man ought to be allowed until they are fairly and legally confiscated to come and take them without even the order of a commissioned officer given therefor. As a citizen living under your government as Governor of the State I ask your protection as well as that of Gen. Thomas to whom I am under obligations which I can never repay for his kindness in preserving my life and a shelter over me and my children—by sending me a guard of four men to protect my person from violence.

There has already been taken from this place as I before remarked four or five waggon loads of forage and what I am to do next winter God only knows with 150 mouths to feed and nothing to feed them with. They have torn down my stone fences and the whole plantation is now at the mercy of the stock of the neighborhood and this too when there were gates in less than twenty steps of the place where the fence was thrown down.

In short, your Excellency—either some remedy must be found for this evil or the citizens who desire to live in peace and quiet will have to leave their homes and leave the country an uninhabited waste. Our nearest neighbor, old Maj. Graham and his wife[8] have fared but little better than myself. A lot of marauders came to the house in the absence of Major Graham and on being remonstrated with on account of their pillaging they threatened to turn her out of doors and burn the house.

I am sure that these acts do not meet with your approbation, and it is to inform you of these things, that I have again trespassed so unreasonably upon your time and patience. So far as I myself am concerned—I promise to send in to any place that may be designated, all the forage on this place if they will allow me the use of my teams and drivers. And I have already made an arrangement with Col. Stokes to this effect, and, if allowed to do so I could haul to him all the forage on the place and not be subjected every hour in the day not only to insult but actual danger of my life and that of my servants.

You may suppose that this picture is overdrawn but if you will ask Col. Stokes you will find every word verified.

If your Excellency could use your influence to strictly enforce the order of Gen. Halleck that no foraging shall be done except under the command of a commissioned officer, and that the waggon guard will not be permitted under any pretense to break ranks. They make an excuse for water or some other, and break ranks and then pillage all they can find.

There are men that come here every day who have not a single *commissioned*—no not even a non commissioned officer with them. This fact can be proven by every guard detailed to protect the lives of families on this road.

With the hope that your Excellency will be able to do something to mitigate this monstrous evil.

I remain, your Excellency, Dear Sir,

Mrs. W. G. Harding

Typescript, TU-Fay W. Brabson Col., Box 1.

1. For William B. Stokes, colonel, 1st Middle (later 5th) Tenn. Cav., USA, recruiting in the Nashville area during the summer of 1862, see *Johnson Papers*, IV, 406*n*; *Tennesseans in the Civil War*, I, 329-30.

2. Martin E. Quin (b. *c*1843), Virginia printer, was corporal, Co. A, 5th Tenn. (July, 1862-February, 1865). CSR, RG94, NA.

3. Probably Mary Ellen Ewing, wife of Mrs. Harding's nephew James Randal McGavock Ewing, who was assisting in the management of Belle Meade. Wills, "Portrait of Belle Meade," 75.

4. Selene Harding (1846-1892), soon to be sent to Philadelphia for safety and schooling, later became Mrs. William H. Jackson and inherited Belle Meade. Margaret L. Warden, *The Belle Meade Plantation* (Nashville, 1979), 6, 21; Speer, *Prominent Tennesseans*, 4, 448.

5. Bob Green, a favorite groom, recovered and remained at Belle Meade after the war. *Ibid.*, 89n.

6. Of Harding's prize goats, one Union observer wrote: "The goats were ruthlessly taken 'in the wool.' " About a year after Harding's release from Fort Mackinac, he placed

a $32,000 claim against the Federal government for damages and was awarded $27,617. Warden, *Belle Meade,* 10; Fitch, *Annals,* 637.

7. For George H. Thomas, see *Johnson Papers*, V, 32*n*.

8. Daniel Graham (b. *c*1789), a North Carolinian married to Virginia-born Maria (b. *c*1812) and possessing before the war an estate worth $77,000, had been associated with Harding in the Richland Turnpike Company. He was reported to have taken the oath in the summer of 1862 for the protection it afforded his property. 1860 Census, Tenn., Davidson, 11th Dist., 12; Wills, "Portrait of Belle Meade," 75, 81-82.

To Don Carlos Buell

Nashville, Sept. 14th 1862

Maj Genl. Buell,
Comd'g &c Dist. of the Ohio.
General:

It is all important that Maj Genl. Thomas and his forces as now assigned should remain at Nashville. There is the utmost confidence in his bravery, and capacity to defend Nashville against any odds. I am advised that, including your Division of the Army, there are not less than Seventy Five Thousand men in Kentucky, and the number increasing, so that you will be enabled to meet Smith & Bragg successfully.

I was reliably informed on yesterday that a portion of Bragg's forces were lingering about Carthage & the Cumberland River—Bragg, no doubt, with them, daily informed as to the number of our forces passing into Ky and the force left here. If our strength is much reduced at this point, he will be induced to attack Nashville as a matter of course.

In conclusion I express the strong and earnest hope that the present assignment of forces under Genl. Thomas for the defense of Nashville may not be disturbed.

Very Respectfully Your Obt. Sert.
Andrew Johnson
Mil: Governor.

L, DNA-RG94, Gens. Papers, D. C. Buell; DLC-JP.

From Zachariah Chandler[1]

Detroit Sept 17th 1862

Hon Andrew Johnson
My Dear Sir

You once told me you would come to Michigan & make a speech upon the vigorous prosecution of the War. Can & will you come during the Month of Oct. You must need rest & recuperation. Come & spend a week or two with me. It will do us both good. Please write me when you will come & Oblige[.][2]

Truly yrs Z. Chandler

PS I pay all expenses[.]

ALS, DLC-JP.

1. For Chandler, Michigan senator, see *Johnson Papers*, III, 439*n*.

2. No reply has been found; Johnson did not go.

From William Hoffman[1]

Office of Commissary General of Prisoners,
Detroit, Mich., Septm. 25th, 1862.

Brig. Genl. Andrew Johnson
Military Governor of Temessee
Nashville, Tenn.
General

By directions of the Secretary of War, I have this day discharged from Custody, Joseph C. Guild[2] of Gallatin, Tenn, and William G. Harding of Davidson County Tenn. the first having complied with the Conditions prescribed in your letter of the lst. of August, and the latter with those prescribed in your letter of the 24th of August last, addressed to the Commanding officer of Fort Mackinaw,[3] and I have the honor to inclose herewith the oath of allegiance, bond, and parole in the Case of Judge Guild,[4] and the parole and bond in the Case of Genl. Harding.

Verry respectfully Your Obedt Servt. W. Hoffman
Col 3rd Infy Comy Genl of Pris.

ALS, DLC-JP.

1. William Hoffman (1807-1884), New York-born West Pointer (1829) who served in the Black Hawk and Mexican wars, was by October, 1860, lieutenant colonel, 8th Inf., USA. Now colonel, 3rd Inf., he served as commissary general of prisoners throughout the war, retiring as brevet major general in 1870. *Appleton's Cyclopaedia,* III, 228; Powell, *Army List,* 376.

2. For Josephus C. Guild, wealthy secessionist, see *Johnson Papers*, IV, 581*n*.

3. Grover S. Wormer (*c*1822-*fl*1881), a New York native and Detroit merchant and stave dealer, had raised in April the Stanton Guard, a company detailed to watch over Guild, Harding, and Washington Barrow at Fort Mackinac and disbanded September 25 upon their release. During the remainder of the war he served in various Michigan units, attaining brevet brigadier by June, 1865; subsequently he and his sons operated the Michigan Machinery Depot in Detroit. 1860 Census, Mich., Wayne, Detroit, 1st Ward, 57; John Robertson, comp., *Michigan in the War* (Lansing, 1882), 486, 688, 744; Heitman, *Register,* I, 1060; Detroit city directories (1859-81), *passim.*

4. See Parole Oath and Bond of Josephus C. Guild, August 1, 1862, *Johnson Papers,* V, 587-89.

From Payne, James & Co.[1]

Nashville 27. Sept. 1862

To Gov. Andrew Johnston

One case *Old, Knoxville Peach Brandy,* of the distallation of 1848 with the respects of

Payne James &Co

ALS, DLC-JP2.

1. Payne, James & Company, "Wholesale grocers, Commission Merchants & dealers in foreign and domestic liquor, tobacco, cigars, etc." at No. 4 Market Street, was formed in 1861 by Buckner H. Payne, John D. James, and Robert A. Barnes; subsequently it became R. A. Barnes & Co., located in 1866 at the corner of Church and College streets. Nashville *Union and American,* September 4, 1861; Nashville *Dispatch,* October 28, 1863; *Nashville City Directory* (1866), 91, 258; (1874), 93, 212.

From Anonymous

Private & *Confidential* Nashville Oct '62

To His Excellency
Gov Andrew Johnson

Dear Sir A gentleman who knows you well remarked to me not long since that you had kinder feelings towards the people than any one exercising military authority in Nash[.] I am also informed that you are opposed to soldiers going about through the country *pillaging* & *plundering* the people. War is horrid enough when viewed in any light, but when waged with savage cruelty, it is unworthy a civilized or Christian people. As a friend of the people—I appeal to you to do every thing in your power as Brigadar General and Military *Governor* to mitigate their sufferings. Your object is I believe to put down the rebellion and restore Tennessee to her former position in the Union—but in doing this you do not wish to heap injustice and wrong upon the people. The late foraging expeditions from the city—have caused a great deal of sufferings—

Federal soldiers sent out to get forage & provisions—have entered *private houses* and robbed *peaceable—unoffending* citizens of their clothing—bed clothing Household furniture etc— in numbers of instances—Women have been insulted, and some robbed of their Jewelry— I know one man who voted the Union ticket 9 Feb. 1861, who says he did *not vote* for seperation or secession June 8/61, and who has all along remained a quiet *good* citizen— He has *fed* hundreds of federal soldiers— although he has a protection he has been robbed of hundred of dollars in provisions—his wife insulted—& He has borne it with the patience of Job— I advised him to go to you—and that *you would have him protected.* This wholesale plundering and pillaging through the country while it causes great suffering among the people drives thousands to desperation, and causes a great many to enter the southern army—will also greatly *demoralize* the Federal soldiers—

I fully concur with you in your sentiments that "the soul of *liberty* is the love of *law*"[.][1] I also endorse the sentiment in your speech in Dec '60 "I believe the continuance of slavery—depends upon the preservation of this Union, and a compliance with all the guarantees of the Constitution"—[2] Thousands who went into secession for lost rights in the Territories, may now exclaim what has become of my rights in the states— Secession was the worst remedy that could have been resorted to—& thousands now see their error[.] I was in Tenn—most of the time during the progress of the revolution (for all must *now be* satisfied that peaceable secession was a humbug)—and I know that thousands and tens of thousands voted for secession or revolution, through error of judgment, They did not intend to do wrong—but were carried away by the *excitement* and *madness* of the *hour*. I appeal to you in *behalf* of this class of *people[.] Save them* from the consequences of their own folly or *madness*—if you *please*— Has it not occurred to you, in the last *18* months or 2 *years,* that for *one crazy man* in a *Lunatic asylum*—there are a hundreds if not *thousands running* at *large*— There can be a species of Secession or *proslavery* madness as well as abolition fanaticism[.] The madness of *Sumner, Phillips* Lovejoy—Greely and others in the North have enabled the Keitts, the *Rhetts* and *Yancey* & others to make thousands of *madmen* of otherwise good citizens in the South— Thousands of men who delighted to elevate you to power and office—have been led to their own *ruin*—a good deal through their sympathies for the south, and from error of judgment—

You concede in your speech of Dec' 1860, that the South had *her grievances*— I concur with you that the remedy for Tennessee and other southern states was to have adhered to the resolutions adopted by the convention in East Tenn. just after the Presidential election and *quoted* in *your speech[.]* To you as a statesman and a patriot I appeal in behalf of a people who desiring to do right have been led into error. I ask you as a friend of those who have in the past elevated you to high places of trust and power—to *overlook* their *faults*—and with true greatness of soul do all in your power to save them from *ruin*— *Do this* and *thousands* who now heap curses on you, may yet live to do you honor. I ask you as the people's friend to do all in your power to stop this wholesale *plundering* & *pillaging*— Of course the soldiers must have food for themselves and forage for their horses—but can't you put a stop to this robbing *houses* & citizens[?] To enter a man's house and rob him of everything—is the very way to drive him to desperation[.] The people here are not responsible for the railroad being torn up between here & Louisville—[3]

If private citizens are protected in their rights, and believe that the government does not wish to oppress them they will after a while stop and think over the evils of the present hour, and they may be won back to *loyalty* but *unkindness* and *cruelty only drives freemen* to *desperation*— If a man violates law, let him suffer the penalty—but let it be done *Lawfully*— We are all frail-erring creatures—and if we were volumed [*sic*] in the scales of even handed justice we would all suffer more or less— "Blessed are the merciful for they shall obtain mercy"— Mercy "is an attribute to *God* himself; And earthly power doth then show likest God's When mercy seasons justice"—[4] *Gov:* Johnson— I *ask of* you a *personal* favor.— Turner S. Foster—once befriended me in a personal difficulty and was instrumental in preventing me from doing an act, that I would have regretted with sorrow and anguish the balance of my days— Mr. Foster is a delicate man & has suffered dreadfully with inflammatory rheumatism— if he remains in a northern prison this winter it will kill him— I ask you to release him—[5] Let me appeal to you Gov. in the beautiful words of Jeannie Deans to Queen Caroline in behalf of her erring sister,[6] "Alas! it is not when we *sleep soft* and wake merrily ourselves that we *think* on *other people's sufferings,* & our hearts are waxed light within us then, and we are for righting our own wrongs and fighting our own battles[.] But when *trouble comes* to the *mind* or *body*—and when the hour of *death* comes, to high and low, &c—then it isn't *what we have done for oursells, but what we have done for others that we think on most pleasantly. And* the thought that you have intervened to spare" (poor *Fosters life*)—(for imprisonment if continued will *surely kill him)"*— "will be *sweeter* in *that hour* (of *death*) *Come* when it may"— than if a word of your *mouth* could have every rebel in the land— You know what it is to be separated from one's family— Therefore partly overcome your own *evils* by *doing good* to *others*. I almost daily read the following from 3d chapter of *Proverbs,* "Trust in the Lord with all thine heart; and lean not unto thine own understanding. In all the ways acknowledge him and he shall direct thy paths. Be not wise in thine own eyes, fear the Lord, and depart from evil"— I entreat you to restore Foster to liberty—and thereby do a great favor to the friend of *Truth Justice* & *Mercy*—[7]

Private & Confidential

My handwriting is so bad I fear Governor you will find it difficult to decipher what I have written. Among the houses pillaged I will mention Mr. Stumps[8] & others on the Charlotte Pike. I also learn that the Federal soldiers have pillaged & plundered a good deal along the Gallatin & other Pikes also in Neiley bend[9] & other neighborhoods— I noticed this morning a number of loads of Cedar rails brought into the city. A good prospect for the destruction of all the fences in the vicinity of the city. The rails soon burn up—and are of immense value for fences— If the fences are all destroyed nothing can be raised next year[.]

If this kind of warfare is continued the amount of suffering & want this winter will be fearful to contemplate. I know from the manner in which you discharged your duties while 4 year Governor of the state, you condemn all this— As Brigadier General & Military Governor, I suppose your authority is paramount to any other officer in the state. If I remember correctly you said in a letter to R G Payne & others in 1853. That the man who stands by the people, the people will stand by *him*—[10] Come then to the rescue of the people, Governor and save them from *utter ruin*[.] If I know *my heart,* the feeling that prompts me to write this letter is my sympathy for the people— The great Christianity virtue—called *charity,* is only *another name* for *love*— Love *God* supremely & thy neighbor as thyself are to the great commandments— Once more Governor be the people's *friend*[.] I have had to battle against poverty & trials & know what suffering is—[11]

ALS, DLC-JP.

1. Not found.

2. In his Speech on Secession, December 18-19, 1860, the senator had declared, "if I were an Abolitionist, and wanted to accomplish the overthrow and abolition of the institution of slavery . . . the first step that I would take would be to break the bonds of this Union, and dissolve this Government," adding that "I believe an interference with it [slavery] will break up the Union; and I believe a dissolution of the Union will, in the end, though it may be some time to come, overthrow the institution of slavery." *Johnson Papers,* IV, 33.

3. Both prior to and during the Confederate invasion of Kentucky in August, considerable damage was done to the railroads, especially the main line of the Louisville and Nashville and its branches; the company reported a loss of $108,690, chiefly from the destruction of bridges. In July Morgan had raided in the vicinity of Lebanon, Kentucky, and in August obstructed the tunnel near Gallatin, Tennessee; while in September the main Confederate forces destroyed numerous other bridges, including those over the Green and Salt rivers. Kincaid A. Herr, *Louisville & Nashville Railroad, 1850-1963* (Louisville, 1964), 34-36.

4. Shakespeare, *The Merchant of Venice*, Act IV, sc. 1.

5. A Nashville lawyer and one of the civilians incarcerated at Camp Chase, Foster was paroled in November. See *Johnson Papers*, V, 577*n*.

6. Jeanie's half-sister Effie Deans had been accused of murdering her illegitimate child. Walter Scott, *The Heart of Midlothian*, John Henry Raleigh, ed. (Boston, 1966), 366.

7. Along the margin: "Excuse haste bad writing & disconnected sentences—"

8. Probably Phillip Stump (b. *c*1813), Tennessee-born farmer, who possessed real and personal property worth $58,000. 1860 Census, Tenn., Davidson, 13th Dist., 153.

9. Neely's Bend is on the Cumberland, northeast of Nashville, at the juncture with Stone's River.

10. A sentiment expressed in To the Democracy of Maury County, Columbia, September [18?], 1853, *Johnson Papers*, II, 171.

11. Johnson endorsed this letter: "To be preserved—in reference to the people &c—"

Proclamation Appointing Nashville City Administration[1]

[October 1, 1862]

By virtue of the power and authority in me vested, as Military Governor of the State of Tennessee, I do hereby appoint the following persons to hold and exercise the functions, of the respective offices attached to this and their names, and to perform the duties thereof according to law, to wit:

First Ward.

John Carper, Alderman. James Turner and Wm. Roberts, Councilmen.

Second Ward.

Jos. J. Robb, Alderman. G. M. Southgate and A. Myers Councilmen.

Third Ward.

Ed Mulloy, Alderman. Andrew Anderson and Alex. McDaniel, Councilmen.

Fourth Ward.

H. G. Scovel, Alderman. L. B. Huff and Charles Sayers, Councilmen.

Fifth Ward.

W. S. Cheatham, Alderman. J. D. [B.] Knowles and W. A. McClelland, Councilmen,

Sixth Ward.

M. M. Brien, Alderman. T. J. Yarbrough and Wm. Driver, Councilmen.

Seventh Ward.

M. G. L. Claiborne, Alderman. Wm. Stewart and Thos. [J. W.] Cready, Councilmen.

Eighth Ward.

Jos. Smith, Alderman. Wm. Hail[e]y and Wm. Sanborn, Councilmen.

In Testimony Whereof, I have hereunto set my hand and caused the Great Seal of the State to be affixed, at Nashville, this October 1st 1862

Andrew Johnson, Governor.

Edward H. East, Secretary of State.

Nashville *Union*, November 12, 1862.

1. After replacing Nashville's pro-Confederate officials with unionists on April 7, 1862, the governor designated a new city administration each fall at the normal time for elections. The April and October appointees differed from their predecessors in having less experience in government, lower economic status, fewer southern-born members, and fewer Democrats. *Johnson Papers*, V, 278-79; Maslowski, *Treason Must Be Made Odious*, 122; Stanley F. Rose, Nashville and Its Leadership Elite, 1861-69 (M. A. thesis, University of Virginia, 1965), 17-24.

From Robert A. Bennett[1]

Military Prison Nashville
Oct 2th 1862

Gov Andrew Johnson

The reception I Recved at your hands on yesterday warrants me in addressing this letter. if circumstances have made us national enemies you have evidenced to me personal kindness for which I feel deeply and sensibly. I am labouring under the greatest mental agony in regard to the rumors I hear of my brothers being wounded perhaps mortally.[2] you can appreciate those natural ties[.] I would like to be paroled to see him—and will immediately return [to] the City. Gov Johnson I am met this morning again with the charge that I was taken a prisoner at Pulaski when Morgan passed through there last spring and after this had a battle at Lebanon— you remember your self that I was at Nashville making efforts to secure Yater's[3] release[.] Gov Campbell[4] came to Gallatin[.] I visited him at the

La[wrence?] and invited him to my house, the soldier has come to my room and makes these charges[.] Hon Baily Peyton[5] knows I was at home and never left until about the 1st of July[.] The soldiers say, I was shot in the breast and thus Identifies me and knows I am the man. Great God what charges how untrue, I can prove by every union man in Gallatin where I was[.] what predejuces will be raised against me by the soldiery[.] I would Respectfully ask an enterview with you[.] will [you] see that I can have it[?] I appeal to you for justice in my behalf [.]

Respectfully Your friend
R A Bennett

I want to send for witnesses and also my family[.] will you see that my freind will have a passport out of the lines if I cannot get a Parol[.] The charge made is that I commanded a company in Morgans command and was released as Captain upon Parol[.] I as heaven is my witness I never had the command of companies in Morgans command in my life—

ALS, DLC-JP.

1. Robert A. Bennett (1822-1875), native of Campbell County, Virginia, and Gallatin lawyer with property valued at $11,400, served as a captain in the Mexican War, representative in the state legislature (1859-61), and captain, 9th Tenn. Cav., CSA. He was captured by a detachment under the command of William B. Stokes on September 2, in a skirmish on the Dickerson Pike near Nashville. 1860 Census, Tenn., Sumner, 11th Dist., 1; McBride and Robison, *Biographical Directory,* I, 42; *OR,* Ser. 1, XVI, Pt. I, 954; *Tennesseans in the Civil War,* I, 74; *Sumner County Examiner,* November 12, 1875.

2. James D. Bennett (1816-1862), Sumner County merchant and farmer with an estate of $53,600, was colonel, 9th Tenn. Cav. Rgt., CSA, when he died December 23, in consequence of wounds received in the Dickerson Pike engagement. 1860 Census, Tenn., Sumner, 1st Dist., 93; R. R. Hancock, *Hancock's Diary* (Nashville, 1887), 576-77; *Tennesseans in the Civil War,* I, 28-29, 74-75; *OR,* Ser. 1, XVI, Pt. I, 954.

3. Wilkinson H. Yater (*c*1825-1903), native Kentuckian and "railroad omnibus line and Adams Express agent" at Gallatin, now in Nashville city prison, had been arrested in April, probably on charges of spying. Presumably he was cleared; in due time he "was employed in the commissary department of the Federal Government, being placed in charge of a steamboat in conveying supplies." Subsequently he became Nashville chief of police (1873-83) and later markethouse inspector. 1860 Census, Tenn., Sumner, 5th Dist., 16; *Mitchell's Tenn. Gazetteer* (1860-61), 71; *Rogers' Nashville Directory* (1881), 515; R. A. Bennett to Johnson and D. R. Haggard to Johnson, April 12; W. H. Yater to Johnson, May 24, 1862, Johnson Papers, LC; Nashville *Banner,* September 21, 1903.

4. For former governor William B. Campbell, see *Johnson Papers*, I, 367*n*.

5. For Balie Peyton, former Whig congressman, see *ibid.*, III, 443*n*.

From David M. Nelson[1]

Madison Ga Oct. 5th 1862

Hon Andrew Johnson
Dear Sir

I write under very peculiar circumstances. My Self and 92 other East Tennesseeans are confined here as political prisoners, With no hope of a release only through the instrumentality of the Federal Goverment[.] We have I may say two dreadful allternatives left us, and they are take the oath

Join their army or remain in prison[.] For my self I have refused Liberty on such degrading terms and shall continue to do so[.] I claim protection from you and the Goverment[.] The cartel[2] as I understand it includes Political prisoners[.] Gov I ask you in the name of God of crushed oppressed and downtrodden Freeman to make some effort to have us released.[3] We are fed on corn bread & rotten bacon[.] Hoping you will reccolect us

I remain Yours Resp
David M Nelson

ALS, DLC-JP.

1. During the preceding summer David M. Nelson (1845-1881), son of Tennessee congressman Thomas A. R. Nelson, had attempted to lead a group of seventy men through the Confederate lines to join Union forces at Cumberland Gap; caught and imprisoned, he was released in mid-October and made his way from Richmond to relatives in New Jersey. By November, 1863, he had become 1st lieutenant, Bty. B, 1st Tenn. Lgt. Arty., USA, remaining in service until July, 1864, when he resigned as a consequence of "a murderous assault" upon a civilian. After the war he practiced law at Cleveland. In a gunfight at Knoxville, September 27, 1871, he killed ex-Confederate general James H. Clanton, for which he was tried and acquitted in May, 1873. 1880 Census, Tenn., Bradley, 6th Dist., 4; CSR, RG94, NA; Thomas Alexander, *T. A. R. Nelson of East Tennessee* (Nashville, 1956), 18, 102-3, 112-13, 152, 154, 166; Cleveland *Banner*, December 16, 1881.

2. Article 3 of the cartel (July 22, 1862) providing for a prisoner-of-war exchange specified that civilians be exchanged for civilians. Hesseltine, *Civil War Prisons*, 32-33; *American Annual Cyclopaedia* (1862), 713-14.

3. By early November, when Johnson received this appeal carried north by an exchanged prisoner, Nelson had been released by southern authorities, apparently in an effort to bind his father closer to the Confederacy, and had written the President for assistance in entering the Federal service. Robert Porter to Johnson, November 1, 1862, Johnson Papers, LC; Nelson to Lincoln, October 22, 1862, Basler, *Works of Lincoln*, V, 484; see Telegram from Abraham Lincoln, October 31, 1862.

Parole Order for Reuben Ford[1]

October 9, 1862

I do hereby parole Rev. Reuben Ford of Davidson County Tennessee and upon his acceptance of this Parole he solemnly pledges his honor without any mental reservation or evasion that he will not take up arms against the United States or give aid or comfort or furnish information directly or indirectly to any person or persons belonging to any of the so-styled Confederate States who are now or may be in rebellion against the Government of the United States that he will not write or speak against said Government and holds himself subject to all the pains and penalties consequent upon a violation of this his solemn parole of honor and that he will report himself to this office within twenty days after his acceptance of this parole when and where terms of his release are to be arranged[.]

This Parole to be good must be endorsed by the party within his own proper name[.]

Andrew Johnson
Military Governor Tenn

Executive Office
Nashville Oct. 9th 1862

The above parole is accepted by me this 23rd day of October 1862[.]
Reuben Ford

D, DLC-JP; DNA-RG94, "Unfilables," Reuben Ford.

1. Although the governor sent the Reverend Mr. Ford's parole and bond to the commanding officer at "Johnson's Island Near Sandusky Ohio," the completed bond indicates that the prisoner was at Camp Chase in Columbus when he subscribed to it on the twenty-third. On the same date, three other "Political Prisoners from Tennessee"—William H. Wharton, William D. F. Sawrie, and Samuel D. Baldwin, also Nashville ministers whom the governor had sent North—were released, giving "their Parole of honor and individual Bond Each in the Sum of Five thousand Dollars." "Unfilables," Reuben Ford, RG94, NA; Peter Zinn to Johnson, October 24, 1862, Johnson Papers, LC; for Ford, see *Johnson Papers*, V, 489*n*.

From James Whitworth[1]

Nashville Oct 11th 1862

To His Excellency Gov Johnson
Dr Sir
In obedience to Your requisition upon me of the 8 inst, I herewith submit to you a report of the names of such persons as have paid money into my hands, under an order of yours on them so to do of the 18 August 62[2] which is as followis—to wit—

Amt paid by	Byrd Douglas	500.00	-	$2000
" " "	Jacob McGavock	300.00		$1000
" " "	Aris Brown	50.00		$500
" " "	R. S. Hollins & Co	200.00		$1000
" " "	W W Woolfolk	150.00		$2000
" " "	Gardner & Co	300 00		
" " "	R C Foster	100 00		
" " "	A C & A B Beach	150 00		
" " "	Danl F Carter	150 00		
" " "	James M Hamilton	100 00		
" " "	A W Vanlier	200 00		
" " "	And J Duncan	100 00		
" " "	L F Beech	100 00		
" " "	R C McNairy	250 00		
" " "	F R Cheatham	100 00		
" " "		$2,750.00—		

All of which is respectively submitted

James Whitworth

ALS, DLC-JP.

1. See *Johnson Papers*, V, 625*n*.

2. Circular Assessing Confederate Sympathizers, August 18, 1862, *ibid.*, 623-25.

From Charles Johnson

[Murfreesboro, October 12, 1862]

We reached this place Friday evening[1] at nine o'clock in a cold rain—got out of the cars—found no hotel in the place—and nearly all the private houses full—no place to put baggage, no hacks, no servants. . . . We wandered about the town for an hour or two and finally succeeded after pleading, entreating, begging in getting in a house to sleep on the floor without any fire. . . . At six o'clock Saturday morning General Forrest[2] sent a deputation of soldiers for us to appear before him immediately. We appeared before him. He would not see our passports—informed us that Jesus Christ could not cross his lines and that we should immediately return by the seven o'clock train—that the War Department had no control of his lines. . . .[3] We were now known in the town and not a soul would let us in his house. We were annoyed by taunts and jeers of a rabble soldiery. . . . Finally we got a room in a vacant house. . . . We put the women and children in this room where they stayed all night, we men laying in the cars by courtesy of the baggage master. . . .

Fay W. Brabson, *Andrew Johnson: A Life in Pursuit of the Right Course, 1808-1875* (Durham, 1972), 87.

1. Leaving Greeneville on October 8, the party—consisting of Mrs. Johnson, Charles, Mary Johnson Stover, her husband Daniel, and their three children—reached Murfreesboro on the tenth. For a discussion of Mrs. Johnson's treatment by the Confederates, see *Johnson Papers,* V, 352n.

2. For Gen. Nathan Bedford Forrest, see *ibid.*, 562*n*.

3. Although Forrest sounds unsympathetic in Charles's report, he was apparently amenable to persuasion, for that very day Governor Isham G. Harris, also in Murfreesboro, informed Mrs. Johnson that the general "sends a flag of truce to Nashville tomorrow morning and he wishes you and your party to make your arrangements to go down with the flag at 7 Oclock A M to morrow. The Genl. regrets that he has no transportation for you[.] He will send a two horse wagon to cary your bagage &c. By remaining until to morrow you can go the direct route to Nashville, by going previous to that time the route would be necessarily circuitous." Harris to Mrs. Andrew Johnson, October 12, 1862, Henry E. Huntington Library, San Marino, California.

From Jeremiah T. Boyle[1]

Head-Quarters Louisville, Kentucky,
Louisville, Oct 14th 1862

Gov Andrew Johnson
Nashville Tenn.

Your messenger, Mr. Riley[2] came through and delivered your verbal messages. I telegraphed the President that you were urgent for re-enforcements and for an other commander. The dispatch to President was referred to Gen Halleck[3] who dispatched me, without saying what he would do. He has not answered though I have mentioned subject except to say that he could not tell where or what re-enforcements to send until he heard from Buells army and results of his Campaign. McCooks army corps,[4] or two divisions of it whipped the whole rebel army at Chaplain Hills near Perryville Boyle Co on Wednesday 9th inst. There has been no battle since—Some heavy skirmishing Buell pressing the rebels on their retreat. They fell back to Camp Dick Robinson— Geo Owsley telegraphs Gov Robinson[5] that rebels are retreating on Lancaster turnpike southward and that Buells army is in motion from Danville for pursuit. I think they will yet give battle. The loss at battle of Chaplain Hills was severe on our side and probably greater on rebel side— Gen Jackson, Gen Terrill Col Webster, Lt Col Jouett & Maj Campbell were killed[6]—loss probably 2000 on our side, and as great if not greater on rebel side. We captured over 2000 prisoners, and large amt of arms and ammunition. If rebels retreat it will be by the Gaps, as they can hardly escape by Somerset— I fear we are only driving them back to desolate Tennessee, and may be to capture your city— I trust we will pursue them so that they can not rest in your state, and drive every sympathiser with them— We can not get along and leave them behind to do this work over.

I hope to be in communication with you in few days— If any important matter turns up, I will send courier to you— You can send courier hereafter to Col Bruce[7] at Bowling Green who will advise me.

Resptly & Truly Yr Friend
J. T. Boyle Maj Genl

ALS, DLC-JP.

1. For Boyle, see *Johnson Papers*, V, 337*n*.

2. Possibly John Riley (b. *c*1834), an Irish-born Nashville day laborer. When captured by Morgan later in October, "Mr. Riley" escaped to Murfreesboro where, convincing Gen. John C. Breckinridge of his southern sympathies, he was permitted to carry through the lines to Johnson a package of letters directed to Nashville Confederates. This same Riley was later a courier between Nashville and Louisville for the journalist Benjamin C. Truman. 1860 Census, Tenn., Davidson, Nashville, 1st Ward, 3; Philadelphia *Press*, January 5, 1863.

3. For Henry W. Halleck, see *Johnson Papers*, V, 63*n*.

4. Alexander McD. McCook (1831-1903), one of the "Fighting McCooks" of Ohio, commanded the I Corps at Perryville. A West Pointer (1852) who had served in the 3rd U. S. Inf. and as tactical instructor at the Academy, he was commissioned colonel, 1st Ohio Inf., in April, 1861, rose to major general by July a year later, and saw action at Shiloh, Corinth, and Chickamauga. Subjected, at his own request, to a court of inquiry for his part in the latter battle, he was exonerated but not returned to command. After the war he served on the frontier and as aide to William T. Sherman, retiring in 1895. *DAB,* XI, 600-601; Warner, *Generals in Blue,* 294-95.

5. George Owsley has not been identified. James F. Robinson (1800-1892), Scott County, Kentucky, lawyer and state senator (1851, 1861-62), had become governor on August 18, two days after Beriah Magoffin's resignation. Upon leaving office in 1863, he settled on his estate "Cardome" where he farmed and practiced law in Georgetown. *NCAB,* XIII, 9; Richard H. Collins, "Civil War Annals," *Filson Club History Quarterly,* XXXV (1961), 248-49.

6. For James S. Jackson, see *Johnson Papers*, V, 619*n*. William R. Terrill (1834-1862), a Virginian who graduated from West Point (1853), served in Kansas and with the U. S. Coast and Geodetic Survey until 1861, when he was promoted to captain, 5th U. S. Arty.; he was commissioned brigadier of volunteers in the Army of the Ohio on September 9, 1862. George Webster (*c*1822-1862), Ohio native and Mexican War veteran, practiced law in Jefferson County until the war. At the time of his death he commanded the 34th Bde., 14th Div., McCook's Corps. George P. Jouett (1813-1862), lieutenant colonel of the 15th Ky. Inf., USA, and son of Kentucky portraitist Matthew H. Jouett, was a graduate of Transylvania medical school who had practiced medicine and law and, since 1841, had owned and operated several steamboats. William P. Campbell (*c*1826-1862), Louisville tobacco dealer, was major, 15th Ky. Inf. *NCAB*, IX, 485; Warner, *Generals in Blue*, 496-97; *OR*, Ser. 1, XVI, Pt. I, 1031; Louisville *Journal*, October 14, 1862; Haskell M. Monroe and James T. McIntosh, eds., *The Papers of Jefferson Davis* (2 vols., Baton Rouge, 1971-), I, 451*n*; *Official Army Register: Volunteers*, IV, 1264; *Tanner's Louisville Directory* (1859-60), 46; CSR (William P. Campbell), RG94, NA.

7. Sanders D. Bruce, commanding the almost isolated Union forces at Bowling Green, was proving "a terror to the rebels and a source of security to the loyal." Louisville *Journal*, October 14, 1862; for Bruce, see *Johnson Papers*, IV, 531*n*.

From Benjamin F. C. Brooks[1]

Memphis Tenn Oct 14th 1862

Hon Andrew Johnson

Dear Sir. I wrote you a few days since relative to the Commissions for two Judges in this City.[2] The importance of such appointments yea the imparitive necessity for their appointment induces me to write you again and will be of sufficient excuse for my trespassing thus upon your time and patience.

That there are some who would be displeased to See our Civil Machinery at work again, there is no doubt. There are various reason for this opposition. Many, especially among the Seceshionest are greatly indebted to Northern and other Merchants whose whole aim in secceding to was to get clear of these debts[.] with such anything but a reorganization of our courts would be a desired object.

The injustice done the poor and Union creditors is not thought of[.] 1st[.] They never thinks or rather never seem to think that honest claims are in danger of being hopelessly lost by the Mere opperations of the "statute of limitations" alone, and by the by I wish to call your attention to this fact, that when that statute begins to arise, no subsequent disability, can suspend its opperation. Hence there being no courts in which proceedings can be instituted, many a poor mans claim will be lost, and all from a failure on the part of the federal or state authorities to afford the facilities to secure them in time.

2nd. The Federal authorities are daily seising the property of disloyal men, which property if we had courts would be held to repay loyal creditors many of whom have been reduced to abject want by the withholding from them the just reward of their labor or the return of their hard earned money. Thus it will be seen that for the want of these courts many who have had to look to the Goverment for protection, are compell by this neglect to sit by and see the property which should be secured to him, pass into the courts of confiscation, and themselves driven to a Court of Claims at Washington and its dirty thieving lobbys[.]

3rd. Again, if the courts of Tennessee were established another good effect would be the brining back from "Dixie," many who are now aiding and comforting the rebellion, Who does not know that if Honest Claims or bills from those who have honest Claims, were filed in a court and publication made in due form of law—that many of those pseudo patriots would return. How many Confederate officers would discard their official plumes can scarsely be defined, but one thing is certain, many would be the number who would return to arrange their debts for the purpose of securing their property[.]

4th. An other important fact which seems to present itself in favor of a thorough organization of the Civil Machinery is the confidence it would evince in the power and determination of the Government to restore to the people their rights under the Constitution[.]

5th. Will we not find it indespensable before a congressional representation is sent to Washington that we should have "a *home* organization" else we should be in the condition of a North Carolinia Congressman ("invited to take a seat out doors untill our home folks had a house in which to lodge")[.][3] All know that many, if not all Secessionests are perfectly anxious to have Tennessee represented in Congress before the first of January 1863 and in order to get such would readily cooperate in a thorough Civil organization serving to make a virtue of necessity.

6 The property holders of Memphis are chiefly Secessionest, so that this abeyance of our Courts is a positive benefit to them and to the extent that it leaves money in their hands that should be paid to others, loyal citizens, acts as an auxellery to the rebllion. This money enables them to do many things which the fear of Loss alone would prevent and which would be turned to the saving of their property instead of the distruction of our government— There are other reasons which present themselves which demand that you should give us courts not only here but throughout the state, where such a thing is possible. I have, for instance, as I really have, several wards to whom money is due and has been for some time[.] I have been unable to collect and if things remain as they now are I cannot untill it will be too late[.] You see at a glance what is the result—innumerable Law suits and loss to the innocent[.]

I have said enough, your good judgement will see at once the importance of the movement which we so much desire[.] Hoping that you will, at the earliest date possible, furnish us with courts, and order an Election for county and state officers together with an election for member to Congress I have the Honor to Remain

Your personal & political friend
B F C Brooks M.D.

ALS, DLC-JP.

1. Benjamin F. C. Brooks (1823-1903), Alabama-born physician and editor, advertised in 1855 that he "continues to treat, exclusively, those diseases peculiar to females and the lungs" and that "his practice is strictly *Botanic* and *Hydropathic*"; in 1856-57 he was part owner of the *Lamp Post,* an independent family and agricultural newspaper. His behavior during the first year of the war seems open to debate. According to a Johnson correspondent urging Brooks's appointment as Memphis postmaster, "He is one of the 'indomitable five' that voted the Union ticket here on the eighth of last June when the State was scared out by the terrors of the mob, and for that patriotic act it was with difficulty that he escaped their demon-like vengeance and the desires of their infernal rage." Yet in the late summer of 1861 he is to be found on the roster of the "Gayoso Guards," subsequently mustered into the Confederate army. The following June he organized the first public Union meeting in Memphis in which he attacked Mayor John Parks's loyalty; but shortly thereafter his own allegiance came under fire. After serving as alderman from the third ward (1862-63, 1864-65) and briefly as editor of two Republican newspapers—the Memphis *Daily Review* (1865) and the *Daily Republican* (1866), he started *The Workingman* which he moved to Nashville in 1869 and published until 1879, when he began *The National Flag,* a Greenback weekly. Nashville *Banner,* March 21, 1903; *Rainey's Memphis City Directory* (1855), 101, 231; Hooper, Memphis, 40, 42; *Tennesseans in the Civil War,* II, 57; Clayton, *Davidson County,* 245; Keating, *Memphis,* II, 30, 93, 225, 226.

2. Not found.

3. Undoubtedly a reference to the rump election of Charles Henry Foster, following Union occupation of the Hatteras area. Elected first on November 28, 1861, and again on the ensuing January 30—both times by a minuscule count—he was condemned as a "charlatan and cheat" by North Carolina loyalists, who felt that he was "taking advantage of the peculiar condition of public affairs, without having been chosen by any number of citizens anywhere to represent them." In a hearing June 5, 1862, a House committee discounted the election and the claims of the Hatteras government and denied him a seat. Norman C. Delaney, "Charles Henry Foster and the Unionists of Eastern North Carolina," *North Carolina Historical Review,* XXXVII (1960), 348-66; *House Report* No. 118, 37 Cong., 2 Sess.

From Richard M. Edwards[1]

Portland Ohio Oct 14th 1862

Hon Andrew Johnson
Dear friend

You are reported to be surrounded and likely to be captured,[2] but we hope the latter event may never occur. The Tennesseeans are doing all they can to get permission to go to your relief. We have been surrounded but we came out of the trap without the loss of a man, but with great loss of character I fear.[3]

I am progressing slowly with my cavalry Regiment but am receiving recruits from East Tennessee at this point[.] Twenty two joined me 4 days ago direct from East Tennessee who report that all East Tennessee is on the move. I have sent back some men into Kentucky to look after them and bring them on to my Regt.

Maj Pickens[4] & myself united our influence to raise a Regt, but I soon found he was of no use to me and I let him slide. We telegraphed to you to change our positions giving him the first & myself the the second place but you perhaps did not get the dispatch; at any rate I heard no more of it and am glad the matter stopped there for he is not the man to have charge of a

Regt. He is entirely too much devoted to the bottle and cards to be of any use any where. Now the matter has gone on till the accounts for clothing equipments &c have all been fixed up through my name and except by resignation or death there is no way [of] changing it.
At any rate we can not run the same machine together and the men will not go with him no how and so the thing will just have to go so for the present at any rate.

I hope the Blockade will be removed from round you in a few days and we can again communicate as in days of old[.]

Your devoted friend R. M. Edwards

ALS, DLC-JP.

1. For Edwards, Bradley County lawyer, see *Johnson Papers*, IV, 120*n*.

2. From mid-September until Rosecrans' arrival two months later, Nashville was a city under siege. By September 30 all "communication with the outer world" was "cut off"—to such a degree that on October 21, New York *Herald* reporter Samuel R. Glenn observed that "our supplies become exhausted." Meantime, Johnson had let it be known that rather than surrender, he would put the capital to the torch—thus "the enemy, if they should capture the city, will achieve an empty triumph amid blackened and crumbling ruins." John Savage, *The Life and Public Services of Andrew Johnson* (New York, 1866), 274-78.

3. Apparently a criticism of Gen. George W. Morgan's evacuation of Cumberland Gap and retreat to Greenup, Kentucky, on the Ohio River (September 17-October 3). Others, including his immediate superior Halleck, would be critical of Morgan's conduct. Despite a preliminary investigation which concluded that the general could not have come to any other decision, Halleck pointed out that just before the retreat, Morgan had reported having "several weeks' supplies" and a determination "under no circumstances" to abandon his post. *OR*, Ser. 1, XVI, Pt. I, 990-99.

4. William C. Pickens (1825-1872), son of Sevier County state senator Francis S. Pickens, had been county sheriff (1851-52) and was leader of those East Tennesseans who destroyed the Holston River bridge at Strawberry Plains in 1861. Unlike his father, William escaped capture and imprisonment; commissioned major, 6th Tenn. Inf., USA, in April, 1862, he resigned four months later. He and Edwards then began raising a cavalry regiment, but had a falling out, Edwards calling him a "d---nd scoundrel." Under Johnson's authorization Pickens recruited the 3rd Tenn. Cav., of which he was colonel until his discharge in November, 1863. After the war he lived for some years near Maryville, serving as Blount County clerk and master (1864-67), before returning to Sevier. Nellie P. Anderson, *The John Pickens Family* (Rockford, Tenn., 1951), 136-37; Temple, *East Tennessee,* 381-83, 404; *Tenn. Adj. Gen. Report* (1866), 119, 354; *Tennesseans in the Civil War,* I, 324; *Official Army Register: Volunteers,* IV, 1177; Letter from Richard M. Edwards, November 24, 1862.

From Robert Johnson

Camp Spears Near Portland Ohio
Octo' 15th 1862.

Dear Father,

After a toilsome March of 18 Days from Cumberland Gap, through a dry, sandy and wilderness country, we arrived at this place on the 5th ins't, and are now encamped without tents, clothes or anything else, our men being naked, Hatless and Shoeless—

I have the proud satisfaction of knowing that I, now, although in the State of Ohio, hundreds of miles from home, have the best and largest Regiment in this Division of the Army— the men, without exception, love and respect me, and will follow wherever I lead, and will have no other commander, and what I say for them to do—they will do, with cheerfulness, but will not submit to any other officer, which being the case, it is almost impossible for me to leave the Regiment, for even an hour, and I therefore make it my duty to be always with the Reg't— On the march from the Gap, I never slept in a house, but with one blanket under me and one to cover me, I staid at the Head of the Reg't, and was never found from my post— I lost everything at the Gap the order being to destroy all tents, property &c— I am now here with my Reg't and that is all—

It is reported here that we have been ordered to North Western Virginia— In the name of all that is good and Holy intercede immediately in our behalf and do not let us go to that section—but have us sent either to central Ky, or Tennessee, and especially my Regiment, to some point, where I can arm and equip my men as cavalry, as I never received my Official Order to chang my Reg't from Infantry to cavalry, and cannot be recognized as Cavalry until received— I have Telegraphed for a copy of the Order but have not received it— I wish you would Telegraph for them to be sent to the Commander of this Department[.]

Before leaving the Gap, I heard from home. All was going on well, except Judge Patterson[1] had to leave home from fear of being rode on a *rail,* Bob Crawford's[2] having been the day before— Mothers health was improving, she being at Col Stovers—his family all well— The people of East Tennessee are in a desperate condition— the country a waste and ruin, desolation and misery mark the steps of the ruthless invader—still the cry, do not hang and shoot traitors— In the name of God do we expect to put down this rebellion by merely taking traitors prisoners and then turning them loose to fight us over— If this policy is to be continued, I for one, am in favor of closing the war at once—for the rebels cannot be conquered but in one way, and that is to punish by *death, traitors*— I have seen rebels taken, fed, clothed, furnished with horses, while they vilified and abused us and then under a flag of truce, taken to the enemies lines and turned loose by parole— my doctrine would have been to have hung them or confined them until some future day & then dispose of their case[.]

Give my respects to Browning & other friends[.]

I will write in a day or two and let you know where we go[.]

Your Son Robert Johnson

ALS, DLC-JP.

1. For David T. Patterson, Johnson's son-in-law, paroled by the Confederates and now holding circuit court in the first district, see *Johnson Papers*, I, 110*n*; V, 114n.

2. For Robert A. Crawford, Greeneville attorney, see *ibid.*, IV, 190*n*.

Memorial from East Tennessee Soldiers[1]

Portland Ohio
17th Oct 1862

Honorable Andrew Johnson Governor &c of Tenn
Nashville Tennessee
We your friends and memorialits E Tennesseeans would respectfully say to you that is now fourteen months since circumstancies wholly beyond our power to controle drove us from our homes and families without the slightest chance for protection yet impeled by pure devotion to the Government of our Fathers we unhesitatingly staked every thing upon the Alter of our Countrys Salvation; and after suffering indescribably to get into Ky. where we expected to receive armes and suchor for bleeding E Tennessee[.]

It is now 12 months since we left Camp Dick Robinson in high hopes that we were on our way [to] the homes of our wives, fathers mothers & little ones; but who can discribe our disappointment and mortification from time to time marched from point to point every time flattering ourselves that it was preparatory to getting [to] Tenn[.] after wading through mud snow and ice from Somerset to Cumberland Gap & there in anxious expectation suffering extream privation from points on the Cumberland River about the 10th June with buoyant hopes we took up our march for Tenn. and never did men and officers evince more anxious devotion and determination to prosecute and accomplish on that march the consumation of which was so appalling to the enemy that they fled in confusion. But after taking possession of Cumberland Gap and inspiring the loyalist throughout Tenn with hopes of deliverance from the most withering oppression and making the strongest and most beautiful position perhapse in the United States and the Richest Magazine perhaps agreeable to age and fashion.

But on the 17 of Sept 1862 the deep and harsh sound was heared from the highest authority[.] this night all the Stores, Camp and Garrison Equipage are to be distroyed[.] officers & men are to burn all but a small amount of their Clothing &c &c which was obeyed[.] that dark still night we reluctantly took up the line of march; and after marching day and night through mountain cuting roads and cleaning out Rebel Blockades on the 8 of Oct we arrived at Sciotaville Ohio a distance of near 200 miles[.] officers and men almost starved and worn out[.] Many men bearfooted and without the name of a shirt in fact almost naked. It is now understood that our destination is the Canaway Valley[2] to which we are all opposed. We are yet destitute of money and Clothing[.]

and as Tennesseeans as a last resort looking to you as greatest earthly Benefactor the 1st & 2nd Regts, in own name & in the name of Suffering & defenceless women & children most earnestly & humbly ask you if in your power to have us relieved the doom of being sent more remote from our home & destitute families[.]

We are willing to encounter privations and dangers of any kind if we can be permited to move in the direction of Nashville or any point in Tennessee East of that[.]

But it is extremely repugnant to our feelings & the great majority of all the Tennesseeans to be ordered to Canaway. Not knowing the entire extent of your power we for ourselves & all Loyal Tennesseeans humbly ask your prompt attention with all your-power-& influence to make some[where] in Tennessee (by way of any point needing our assistance in Kentucky) be our destination[.]

G W Keith[3] Lt & Q.M 2nd Reg.

In order to facilitate this effort Capt. Langley[4] has procured the names of all the Officers present on a separate shheet[.]

Please answer as early as practicable[.]

Yours Very Respectfully
G W Keith

Mem, DLC-JP.

1. The forty-nine petitioners were commissioned and non-commissioned officers of the 1st and 2nd Tenn. Inf., USA, regiments raised in East Tennessee and organized at Camp Dick Robinson in August and September, 1861.

2. Although these units remained briefly in the Kanawha Valley, Virginia (now West Virginia), they were ordered on November 14, largely due to Johnson's intercession, to proceed via Bowling Green, Kentucky, to report to General Rosecrans at Nashville; on December 19 they were assigned to the 1st Bde., 2nd Div., XIV Corps, Department of the Cumberland. *Tennesseans in the Civil War,* I, 376; Tenn. Adj. Gen. Report (1866), 56; Telegrams to Abraham Lincoln, October 29, November 8, 1862; Lincoln to Johnson, November 14, 1862, Brown University Library.

3. For George W. Keith, prominent Morgan County citizen, see *Johnson Papers*, IV, 561*n*.

4. Ephraim Langley (b. *c*1826), native North Carolinian and for a time Campbell County farmer, became a merchant and postmaster (1855-65) at Sagefield, Morgan County. Delegate to the Knoxville and Greeneville conventions, he was commissioned captain, Co. F, 1st Tenn. Inf., USA, in August, 1861, and served three years. 1850 Census, Tenn., Campbell, 17th Subdiv., 598; (1860), Morgan, 8th Dist., 85; *U. S. Official Register* (1855-65), *passim*; *OR*, Ser. 1, LII, Pt. I, 150, 169; *Tenn. Adj. Gen. Report* (1866), 28; *Official Army Register: Volunteers*, IV, 1195.

From Leonidas C. Houk[1] *and Robert Johnson*

Camp Near Portland Ohio
October 18th 1862.

Hon Andrew Johnson,
Military Governor Tennessee,
Dear Sir,

On the 20th February last, I had (866) eight hundred and sixty six men! In the terrible service, and the various skirmishes, and battles, through which the 3rd has passed, leaves me, with about three hundred men! These are ordered to the Kanawah, with the remainder of Morgan's Division of the Army. This places me in a hopeless condition, so far as recruiting my Regt is concerned! If I was with Buell's army, I could soon have another Regt— But, my command being so far exhausted, and no prospect of Recruiting it, under existing circumstances, I feel certain the best thing that could be done, would be to change my Regt into Cavalry. If this can be done, I can consolidate with some other Regts—either Cook, Edwards, or your son Robert—

Indeed Gov, I think the best thing that could be done, would be to authorize myself, and Col Johnson, to raise a *legieon* of Cavalry[.] This we can do, without doubt if permitted, but if we have to go to this Hell of Kanawah, what few men I already have will leave me.

Hoping that this communication will find you in good health and better hopes in regard to the war, I remain

Your True Friend L. C. Houk
Col Comd'y 3d Regt E T Vols US army

I endorse all of the above in regard to Col Hawk's Regiment and most cheerfully and heartly agree with his proposition, and believe the public service would be greatly benefitted by it— I have been in the service with Col Hawk for several months and our intercourse has been of such a character as to unite closely together in friendship our two Regiments, and to unite Col Hawk and myself in a *"Legion"* of Cavalry would give general satisfaction to our men, and would afford a pleasure to me[.]

I received yesterday the instructions mailed by you to me on the 12th August, and have sent them to Gen'l Wright[2] for instructions as to where I shall be equipped &c[.]

Your Son Robt Johnson
Col 4th Regt Tenn Vols

ALS, DLC-JP.

1. For Houk, see *Johnson Papers*, V, 42*n*.

2. Apparently the order, "Changing your Regt to Cavalry, with full instructions," had just come to hand. Johnson to Robert Johnson, August 12, 1862, Johnson Papers, LC; for Horatio G. Wright, commander, District of Western Kentucky and Department of the Ohio, see *Johnson Papers,* III, 644*n*.

To James S. Negley

State of Tennessee,
Executive Department.
Nashville, Octo. 20th 1862

Brig Genl. Negley,
Commanding &c Nashville, Tenn.
General:

I enclose herewith copies of my commission as Military Governor of Tennessee, Telegram from Sect'y of War under date of March 22nd 1862, Telegram from Sect'y of War under date of July 12th 1862, and Extract from Special Orders No. 12,[1] Head Quarters Army of Ohio, to which I respectfully ask your attention. My object in transmitting these papers is to advise you of the power and authority vested in me as Military Governor, and to avoid any conflict that might arise from a misunderstanding of the authority under which I, as Military Governor of the State of Tennessee, may assume to act. In this connection, I must be permitted to state that from the increasing diversity of opinion as to the administration of military and civil affairs in this City and vicinity, conflicts as to the exercise of authority might possibly ensue, and it is with the view of coming to a right understanding of the powers respectively conferred upon us, and securing concert of action that I ask an interview with you at such time as you may designate.

In regard to the enclosed copy of extract of special orders No. 111 War Department I have to note that the officer therein referred to having been ordered to report to me, was appointed Provost Marshal by Genl. Buell, at my suggestion,[2] thus obviating for the time being the necessity of exercising the power specially conferred altho' it was intended, whenever the condition of affairs justified such action, to appoint a Provost Marshal for the State of Tennessee.

Very Resp'y Your Obt Svt.
Andrew Johnson Mil. Gov'r.

Copy, DLC-JP.

1. Buell's Special Orders No. 12, dated March 26, 1862, directed officers commanding in Tennessee to "execute within their respective limits any requisitions that may be made on them by the Military *Governor*, to enforce his authority as such," and further, that the provost marshal in Nashville should "comply with such requisitions made directly upon him by [Johnson]." Johnson Papers, LC. See also Telegrams from Edwin M. Stanton, March 22 and July 12, 1862, *Johnson Papers*, V, 222, 555.

2. Paragraph 11 of Special Orders No. 111, issued by Adj. Gen. Lorenzo Thomas on May 19, read: "Captain *Alvan C. Gillem,* of the Quartermaster's Department, has leave of absence until further orders, to take command of the Governor's Guard at Nashville, Tennessee." Regimental Books, War Dept. Special Orders 111, RG94, NA.

From Abraham Lincoln

Executive Mansion
Washington, Oct. 21., 1862.

Major General Grant,
Governor Johnson, &
all having military,
naval, and civil authority
under the United States
within the State of Tennessee.

The bearer of this, Thomas R. Smith,[1] a citizen of Tennessee, goes to that state, seeking to have such of the people thereof as desire to avoid the unsatisfactory prospect before them, and to have peace again upon the old terms under the constitution of the United States, to manifest such desire by elections of members to the Congress of the United States particularly, and perhaps a legislature, State officers, and a United States' Senator, friendly to their object. I shall be glad for you and each of you to aid him, & all others acting for this object, as much as possible. In all available ways give the people a chance to express their wishes at these elections. Follow law, and forms of law as far as convenient; but at all events get the expression of the largest number of the people possible. All see how such action will connect with, and affect the proclamation of Sept. 22nd.[2] Of course the men elected should be gentlemen of character, willing to swear support to the constitution as of old, & known to be above reasonable suspicion of duplicity.

Yours vey Respectfully
A. Lincoln.

ALS, NNPM; Basler, *Works of Lincoln*, V, 470-71.

1. Thomas R. Smith (1830-1872), Maine native and graduate of Bowdoin College, had settled in Bolivar, where he became a lawyer. Moving to Memphis in 1862, he served as judge of the Law Court (1866) and president of the board of education for city schools (1869-70). Keating, *Memphis*, II, 83, 151.

2. The Emancipation Proclamation which, effective January 1, 1863, freed all slaves in areas of rebellion. Basler, *Works of Lincoln*, V, 433-36.

From William P. Jones[1]

Nashville October 22 1862

Gov Johnson
Dr. Sir

Since the Government has taken possession of my place with a view to fortifying for the protection of Nashville, my Barn, stables, Negro houses, Smoke-house, Carriage-house, saddle-house, Bee house, woodhouse &c together with 100 feet of my residence (that is) two fifty feet wings) have been torn down to the ground. The remaining portion of my house is unroofed; Pillars of the front porch torn off, doors, windows and sash, together with the mantles, paper, shelving, mouldings, venetian blinds etc etc torn off, taken away or consumed. My fences, of pickett, plank and rails, have been utterly and entirely destroyed or taken away: and much of stone walls removed & worked into fortifications. The forest trees—the growth of ages—have been entirely cut from 20 or 25 acres around and near my house, and the wood is being hauled away[.] The ornamental shrubbery, vines, roses, etc, are cut to the ground. In addition to which, I have lost about 300 select fruit trees including Pears peach Cherry plum &c., most of them I selected with care & planted 5 or 6 years ago. They too have been leveled with the ground.

My barn was of Cedar, 20 by 60 feet, with new roof rafters etc[.]
Negro houses, were Cedar, with Shingle roof [.]

Carriage house, Bee house, Saddle house, & stable were frame structures weather boarded & shingle roofs[.]
The Smoke & wood houses were of brick[.]
The One Hundred feet of my residence which was torn down to the ground was also of brick and not a vestige of all these remain except the brick in massive piles & the stone foundations upturned in various directions[.]
I have neglected to speak of the gates, one of which, with Posts cost me $25. and Books which cost me more than $500. These are gone. The books were taken from one of the rooms of the wing of the house which contained a great many other things valuable to me, they were & had been stored there for some time for safe keeping, & contin[u]ed by permission of Eng Morton.[2]

Beside these I lost my Bees, hot house, &c &c and my grounds are trenched in various directions to suit military taste.
The house and 40 acres of land, cost me 8 years ago, Twenty two thousand four Hundred Dollars since which time, I have expended, from three, to four thousand $ upon it.
I have been thus minute, & explicit, in order to elicit from you, at yr earliest leisure, such statements in regard to my loyalty & this property as may at a proper time, facilitate recovery of damages in a Court of Claims. Cherishing grateful remembrance and appreciation of favours already extended by Yr Excellency

I have the honor to be verry truly
Your friend W. P. Jones

P.S I trust you will pardon this innovation [*sic*] upon yr official duties etc. I lost, by Buckners Invasion of Kentucky, & destruction of the Locks & dams on Green River $12000,[3] and have no hope of realizing 5 cents to the dollar upon the property in its present or prospective condition: that loss, together with this—if it should prove a loss, would bring me and my family pretty nearly, or quite to a pennyless condition[.]

Yrs with respect W. P. Jones

ALS, DLC-JP.

1. For Jones, superintendent of the Hospital for the Insane, see *Johnson Papers*, V, 187*n*.

2. James St. Clair Morton (1829-1864), Pennsylvanian, West Point graduate, and author of treatises on fortification, was chief engineer of the Army of the Ohio, superintending the construction of Nashville defenses (June 9-October 27). Following service at Stone River, in the Chattanooga area, and as assistant to the chief engineer in Washington, he was killed at Petersburg. *DAB*, XIII, 256; Warner, *Generals in Blue*, 336-37; Stanley F. Horn, "Nashville During the Civil War," *Tenn. Hist. Quar.*, IV (1945), 13-14.

3. Described by the Louisville *Journal* of September 24, 1861, as "one of the most important and valuable internal improvements ever made in Kentucky," these facilities were blown up the night of September 21 by the "renegade Kentuckian who brings an army for the conquest of his native State"; five days later Buckner destroyed the lock at the mouth of the Muddy River where it flows into the Green at Rochester. *OR*, Ser. 1, IV, 201; Arndt M. Stickles, *Simon Bolivar Buckner: Borderland Knight* (Chapel Hill, 1940), 99-100, 106-7.

Deposition of James M. Layne[1]

October 23, 1862

To the Governor of the State of Tennessee

The undersigned James M. Lane is a citizen of Independent Hill in the County of Rutherford & State of Tennessee & has been, for several years a merchant in that place & so continued until about three weeks ago. About six weeks ago some 80 or 100 *guerillas* appeared at his store & seized about $1500 worth of dry goods, consisting of clothing, shoes, boots, prints, calicos, hats, flannels &c—took them off & converted them to their own use, by a sale thereof, in Marshal County & a division of the proceeds among themselves. At the time his goods were taken, they also took the undersigned a prisoner—carried him to Marshal County *Tenn* & kept him over 24 hours under a strict guard. They took him first to John Jordan's[2] in Williamson County about ten miles, where they got breakfast. a large portion of them said Jordan seemed to know them all—was very familiar with them—knew they had his goods—approved of their conduct,—encouraged them in their proceedings & urged them to go on in their warfare.

Two weeks ago last friday, two other soldiers or guerillas came to his house & took from him $4,000 in money, partly in gold, say $180 or $185. One of these men was named William Thomas[3] & was, as he learns, a regular guerilla.

He is now & has always been a loyal citizen of the United States & for his loyalty, these depredations upon his liberty & property were committed. He supposes that this case comes within the provisions of your recent proclamation in regard to violations of the rights of Union men. Two thirds of his neighbors are secessionists or disloyal to the Government of the United States. He prays for such relief in the premises as you may deem him entitled.[4]

James M. Layne

DS, DLC-JP.

1. James M. Layne (b. *c*1832), a Tennessee native, was merchant, school commissioner, trustee (1860-61), and postmaster (1855-65) at Independent Hill. 1860 Census, Tenn., Rutherford, 4th Dist., 44; *U. S. Official Register* (1855), *243; (1865), 346*; *Mitchell's Tenn. Gazetteer* (1860-61), 88.

2. Probably John A. Jordan (b. *c*1824), a Triune merchant who owned a large brick home (the old Thomas D. Porter residence and Female Academy) and a "large, two-story brick store" on the Nolensville Pike. His stepdaughter Mary Overall, active with a nest of spies and scouts operating out of Flat Rock near Nolensville, was imprisoned in the Nashville penitentiary but released for lack of evidence. 1860 Census, Tenn., Williamson, E. Div., 119; Virginia M. Bowman, *Historic Williamson County: Old Houses and Sites* (Nashville, 1971), 16-17.

3. William Thomas (b. *c*1831), an uneducated Wilson County farmer born in Illinois, rode with Confederate guerrillas under David Bond from October, 1862, until early 1863, when he testified against one of his comrades in a murder trial and subsequently scouted for

the Federals. In April, 1865, a civil court convicted him on a second-degree murder charge stemming from his guerrilla days; sentenced to twenty years in the Tennessee penitentiary, he served until 1870 when he inexplicably disappeared from the prison rolls. Proceedings of a Military Commission . . . in the Case of William Thomas (Civilian), June 16-17, 1863, Court Martial Case Files, RG153, NA; Nashville *Press,* April 7-9, 1865; Nashville *Dispatch,* April 8, 1865; *Tenn. Senate Journal,* 1865-66, App. following 112; *ibid.,* 1869-70, App. 191; see also Telegram to William S. Rosecrans, June 16, 1863.

4. In the same hand as Layne's deposition, but under date of November 10, William O. Rickman gave testimony substantiating the petition (although identifying the "host" as John Holt, rather than John Jordan) and supplied names of the raiders, including Capt. Moses Swim, Lt. Frank Rainey, James Swim, and others, all of whom lived "within a few miles of Chapel Hill in Marshal County." William O. Rickman affidavit, November 10, 1862, Johnson Papers, LC.

From William H. Sidell[1]

Head-Quarters District of the Ohio,
Nashville 24th October 1862

His Excellency Andrew Johnson
Governor of Tennessee Nashville
Governor

I take the liberty to call your attention to the leading article of the "Union" this morning which asserts that there was an obstinate conflict of opinion between you and General Buell in regard to holding Nashville.[2] I think the article objectionable on this point, even if there be no misrepresentation of fact, for the reason that it informs the enemy of divided councils—and for the further reason that publications of this nature tend to check free conference. In consultations such as would seem to have been held, each person present should be suffered to bring forward unrestrained all the arguments that may be urged in favor of any course of proceeding whether they be in accordance with his own conclusion, or simply for discussion and refutation. The fear of publications like that of the "Union" this morning might restrain some persons from a full expression of their views, and therefore I say they tend to check free conference, to the serious detriment of the great cause.

I suggest with deference that your advice and influence might be potent in restraining the future publication of similar articles, if your views coincide with mine expressed herein.

I have the honor to be Governor

Your Obt Servt W H Sidell
Maj 15th US Infy AAAG

ALS, DLC-JP.

1. See *Johnson Papers*, V, 580*n*.

2. In discussing General Beauregard's recently intercepted letters which were being printed, the editor observed: "It will be seen how terribly disastrous to the Federal cause would have been the evacuation of Nashville, which was urged with such obstinacy by General Buell, and resisted with greater obstinacy, and fortunately with success by Governor Johnson." Nashville *Union,* October 24, 1862.

From Henry L. Newberry[1]

Nashville Tenn Oct 25th 1862.

Sir

A few days since, I enclosed some papers to you. I now enclose two more letters I have received from Col. W. B. Stokes[.][2]

I have this Statement to make, that after I had closed up my business as Qr. Master 2nd Tenn. Regt. you came to me of your own accord, and asked me if there was any thing you could do for me, you would do so with pleasure. I said to you there was positions in the Cavalry Regiment that was not filled and there was one or two business Positions in the Regiment that I would like. You said if there was I could have it and for me to see Col. Stokes about the matter and let you know[.] I saw Col. Stokes at the fair Grounds and repeated to him what you said to me[.] he said he would see you. Next morning he done so and told me I could have the position of Commissary. I was immediately Commissioned by you. Col. Stokes then said to me as the Qr Master was drunk[3] I would have to go up to his office and do his business. I done so for two days then you sent for me and in presence of Col. Stokes, in your Room, you said to me I want you to bring up your Commission[.] I want to give you a Commission as Qr. Master. I done so, and you immediatly gave it to me. Now, I wish you to be informed if the enclosed is not a true Statement of the facts and as Col. Stokes has branded me a liar, I wish you to do so.

I have done my duty faithfully in every respect[.] on the 30th Sept Col. Stokes said to me, I think I shall want you to resign as you are not a Tennessean that he wanted to make it a Tennessee Regiment[.] I said to him if he wished me to go back into the line I would do so. he said it would do if the men would like it[.] on the morning of Oct 16, I went to his quarters on business[.] he very angrily & abruptly said to me I want you to resign your Commission in my Regiment[.] I asked him for what reason[.] he said for inefficiency[.] I said it was the first time any man had ever said I was so[.] he then said I should resign[.] he would make me. I should not stay in the Service and get my living off the Government[.] I said to him, I pointedly now tell you I will not resign[.] if you have charges to prefer against me you can do so! I think you can find out all you wish to know how Col. Stokes has conducted himself by Enquiry of the following Persons Lt. Bowen Mr. Carter Lt. S. Waters Co B, Capt. Gilbreath Co. C and his two Lieutenants Lt. Henry Co. D Capt Smith & Lt. Hornback & Spencer of Co E. Capt Fleming of Co F and Capt. Clift Co. G[4] who will each and every one of them will say to you that they consider Col Stokes incompetent and do not wish him to command the Regiment[.] they will also say to you that *Every Man* in the whole 6. Companies will sign a petition to you for him to not Command them[.] You can send for any one simply if you chose and I know they will tell you as I do. I do not consider the fault Entirely Col. Stokes[.] it is the influence he is under, in having the adjutant[5] he has. he entirely controls him and the regiment. and just as sure as time flies, there will be such an outbreak of indignation that will reach you that you will be obliged to notice it, and I would advise you to send for any one of the Persons I have spoken of so that you can stop the feeling before it is to late[.][6]

I am Sir very Respectfully Your obt Servant.
Henry L Newberry
1st Lt & R Q M, 1st Middle Tenn Cavalry

To Gov. Andrew Johnson
Military Governor

ALS, DLC-JP.

1. Henry L. Newberry (*c*1821-1866), Michigan native and Detroit woodyard operator, became 1st lieutenant and quartermaster, Co. B, 5th Tenn. (also called 1st Mid. Tenn.), Cav., USA. On detached service at General Rosecrans' headquarters as chief of courier lines early in 1863, he resigned in April at the general's request and returned to Detroit. CSR, RG94, NA; Pension file, RG15, NA; Detroit city directories (1859-65), *passim*.

2. Stokes had written Newberry the previous day: "You know very well that when you were made Quarter Master that you were to resign at any time when you failed to do your duty or did not suit me. Now Sir I have charges against you but prefer that you resign as a Gentleman ought to do." This very day Stokes had reiterated his ultimatum: "You shall not stay if I remain at its Head. So the sooner you resign the better for you & myself." Johnson Papers, LC.

3. Probably Carlton D. Brien (*c*1829-1867), native Tennessean, lawyer, and former Davidson County chancery court clerk (1853-58), who served as 2nd lieutenant, Co. A, 5th Tenn. Cav., USA, from July, 1862, to June, 1863. 1860 Census, Tenn., Davidson, 9th Dist., 141; CSR, RG94, NA; Clayton, *Davidson County*, 95; Special Requisition No. 40, August 4, 1862, Johnson Papers, LC; Mt. Olivet Cemetery Records, II, 19.

4. Lt. Edward H. Gowen and Shelah Waters, Co. B; Mr. Carter is unidentified; Robert Galbraith and possibly Lts. James W. Mallard and Robert Shepard, Co. C; Lt. John R. Henry, Jr., Co. D; Capt. David D. Smith, Lts. Joseph H. Hornbach and Thomas J. Spencer, Co. E; Capt. Eli G. Fleming, Co. F; and Capt. William J. Clift, Co. G. *Tennesseans in the Civil War*, I, 329; *Tenn. Adj. Gen. Report* (1866), 78, 421-23, 426; William S. Hoole, *Alabama Tories:The First Alabama Cavalry, USA, 1862-1865* (Tuscaloosa, 1960), 84, 87, 119, 121.

5. Probably John Murphy.

6. It would appear that Stokes had other leadership problems, even to the point of being shot by Eli G. Fleming, a disgruntled captain, early in 1863. Admittedly the source may be considered somewhat biased and certainly recorded long after the fact, but in 1887 Rosecrans, supporting a pension for Fleming, observed that his "experience and observation warrant distrust of Col. Stokes' carefulness and fidelity to truth and justice in dealing with his officers and men." The general recalled cautioning Stokes for a "spirit of harshness and tyranny" which produced "heart-burnings and hatreds" and expressing the hope that he would "be on his guard against this fault in future." Stokes was allegedly "a Yankee hater" who "bore malice towards Fleming . . . a northern man by birth." Rosecrans to George E. Lemon, October 12, 1887; John Raum to F. C. Ainsworth, November 13, 1890, Pension file (Fleming), RG15, NA.

From William H. Sidell

Head-Quarters District of the Ohio,
Nashville 25th October 1862

To His Excy. Andrew Johnson,
Governor of Tennessee Nashville
Governor

A case has come before me, in my capacity as U. S. Mustering & Disbursing officer, of a claim for payment of certain accounts which, after deliberation, I conclude should be disposed of by civil authority; and I therefore respectfully submit to you, to the end that there may be such judicious action as will dispose of the case properly.

I state it thus: Alexr. S. Thurneck[1] late Major of 1st Mid. Tenn. Infy, was discharged from the service of the United States on 27th September by acceptance of his resignation. At or about that time he presented to me for payment a bill to the amount of $618. 95/100 for expenses incurred in raising the regiment. This bill is made out as due to himself and contains seven items, each item being supported by a sub-voucher or receipted account of the party to whom the amount is assumed to have been paid. The seven subvouchers are as follows, viz:

1 Bill of John B. Bender[2] for boarding & lodging recruits, the time when the several parties of recruits were entertained being specified. This is alleged to be fraudulent in gross and in detail. It can probably be proven by Lt. Col. Foster,[3] of the same regiment, and by others and by documentary testimony, that the recruits were quartered and subsisted at public expense during the time covered by the bill; moreover that the items are incorrectly made, more days being charged for in some cases than the dates indicate. If this account be fraudulent it necessarily involves Bender as in conspiracy with Thurneck, who certifies the account, to defraud the government. The bill is endorsed "Voucher No. 1"

2 "Voucher No 2" is bill of Fritz Tauber for rent of a recruiting office certified by Thurneck. Another bill for the same thing has been, since the above, presented to me by another party which has greater probability of correctness & if correct "Voucher No 2" would be fraudulent and Tauber probably be implicated[.]

3d, 4th, 5th, & 6th Endorsed Voucher No. 3-4-5-6 are for printing & posting bills and are perhaps correct, excepting the last.

7th "Voucher No 7" Bill of Phil Decker is asserted to be an overcharge and falsification of the original bill. The account is said to be made out in the name of a party different from the one who furnished the articles——

I have not paid any part of Thurneck's account having been advised of the probability of fraud in time to suspend the payment. Hearing that Thurneck was about to leave the city, I wrote to the Provost Marshal, Col. Gillem,[4] requesting his arrest at the same time stating the circumstances. Col. Gillem informed me to day that he had arrested Thurneck. I find however by reference to DeHart[5] on military law page 35 it is laid down as a principle that if a person be "once lawfully discharged the service he cannot afterwards be arrested or held amenable to trial by a Military Court for a military offence committed during the period of his military service" From this it might seem that Thurneck's arrest by Col. Gillem is illegal; but as he did not arrest him in his capacity as Colonel of the regiment to which Thurneck lately belonged for a military offence committed while a member of the regiment, but in his capacity as Provost Marshal, on a charge of attempted fraud, it is probably not the case contemplated in the quotation.

I enclose all the bills presented by Thurneck a schedule of which is given below[.]

I have the honor to be Governor

Your Obt Servt W H Sidell
Maj 15 U S Infy AAAG
& Mustering & Disbg. Officer

ALS, DLC-JP; DNA-RG393, Dept. of the Cumberland, Lets. Sent, Vol. I (1862).

1. For Alexander S. Thurneck, see *Johnson Papers*, V, 503*n*.

2. Inasmuch as Messrs. Bender, Tauber, and Decker do not appear in Nashville and Davidson County sources, it might be inferred that they were birds of passage, profiteering from wartime activities in the area; on the other hand, their absence from the major city directories suggests that they were fictions created by Thurneck as part of his swindling apparatus.

3. Frank T. Foster (b. 1826), Philadelphia native raised in the South, would appear to be a questionable witness for any wrongdoing. Serving as sergeant, 2nd Pa. Inf., in the Mexican War, he was later a civilian employee of the quartermaster department at Ft. Bridger, Wyoming, as well as in Texas and Kansas (1857-60). His war record was an extended sequence of brief stints, usually terminating in dismissal or resignation under suspicion. CSR, RG94, NA.

4. Alvan C. Gillem, *Johnson Papers*, IV, 680*n*.

5. William C. DeHart (1800-1848), *Observations on Military Law and the Constitution and Practice of Courts Martial* (New York, 1846).

To James St. C. Morton

Nashville, Oct. 27th 1862

Capt. Jas. St. C. Morton
Chief Engineer Army of the Ohio
Nashville Tenn
Captain

I was not aware that it was designed to change the names of the defenses constructed under your supervision, in and about Nashville from those acquired by their locations until a copy of your letter to General Negley upon that subject was forwarded to me[.] That letter is as follows

Nashville Tenn
October 17th, 1862

General J. S. Negley
Comdg U. S. Forces Nashville Tenn
General

In accordance with your communication of this date I have the honor to state that I have named the principal detached works that strengthen the entrenched lines around this city as follows viz:

The Fort on St. Cloud Hill— Fort Negley
The Fort on Capitol Hill— Fort And'w Johnson
The Fort on Currey's Hill— Fort Confiscation
The Fort on Terry's Hill— Fort Casino

I am General Very Respectfully Your ob't serv't
Jas. St. C. Morton
Chf. Engr. Army of the Ohio

In running over the list of names I find the fortifications or defenses of the Capitol have been out of compliment. I infer, to myself named "Fort Andrew Johnson"

As the skillful, talented and efficient officer under whom the military defenses of Nashville have been so well and energetically constructed, has from his innate modesty, no doubt, declined affixing his own name to any of them, I must be permitted to say that, while thankfully acknowledging the compliment implied, I doubt the propriety, under all the circumstances, of having my name bestowed upon this important stronghold. I am sure as a citizen, and public man, I do not desire it. My adopted State has conferred upon me every honor that a state can confer upon one of her citizens, and in this the measure of my ambition has been filled[.]

I certainly am not entitled to it for any military service or prowess, and such compliments should be awarded only to those who are entitled to them. I had rather an inquiring public would ask why my name was *not* given than to ask why it was. It is not safe at all times, and in all instances, to name children, cities, Forts &c after the living, for the bestowal, is often regretted, And repented.

There are names of Tennessee's illustrious dead, now resting within the protection of your works, far better and more appropriate, from patriotic and inspiring associations, for the defenses of the Capitol, than that of one whose merits have not passed through that trial in which all the living are to be tested.

The names of Jackson the champion of the "Federal Union" in one of the darkest hours of its peril, and of Polk, who stood by him during his mighty struggle for the preservation of the Government, and who during his own administration extended the boundaries of the Union and thereby the area of freedom would, it seems to me, inspire the hearts of our soldiers to make such a stronghold impregnable though assailed by fearful odds.

It may be that in the shock of battle some devoted one, now unknown, may yet pour out his heart's blood upon the massive altar-stones of our Capitol, as a libation to the sacred cause of Liberty and Union, and history will proclaim *that* man, officer or private, entitled to the honor which you have assigned me.

I have never sought honors in a military point of view, nor is it my desire to do so now.

War is not the natural element of my mind. I have always endeavoured to cultivate the arts of peace, and have therefore not pursued a military life. For my part I would rather wear upon my garments the dust of the field, and the dinge of the Shop, as badges of the pursuits of peace, than all the insignia of honorable and glorious war[.][1]

My heart would swell with joy to see the sword and bayonet laid aside and the soldier restored to his peaceful avocations— Heaven grant that ere long peace and good-will may be restored to a misguided and divided people[.]

In conclusion I will state that I feel more than flattered at the compliment conferred, but a consciousness of duty performed is my present remuneration, and the only reward I ask in the future is the lowly inscription of my name with those who loved and toiled for the people[.]

Accept assurances of my high esteem and sincere respect
Andrew Johnson

L, PHi.

1. The governor had first delivered himself of these sentiments in the Speech on the Seceding States, February 5-6, 1861, *Johnson Papers*, IV, 222.

Appointment of Deputy Superintendent of Fair Grounds

October 27, 1862, Nashville; D, DNA-RG15, Pension file, War of 1812 (Jas. Jackson), [Tenn. Vols. Capt. Hill].

Designating James Jackson as responsible for all property, but particularly for "the trees growing upon said grounds," the governor authorizes him to "warn off all persons, citizens and soldiers trespassing or committing depredations thereon" and to call upon "the nearest Military Commandant for adequate military forces to arrest" non-compliants. In such cases Johnson wishes to be informed, "thus securing a rigid enforcement of the law."

From Emerson Etheridge[1]

Washington D C October 29 1862.

Govr. Andrew Johnson
Nashville Tenn—
Dear Sir:

When the enclosed letter[2] was written, it was in contemplation to send it by a private messenger; but as mail communication is now open, I shall risk it in the mail bags.

I will offer no comment upon the President's letter which explains itself— I will only venture this suggestion; West Tennessee, especially the 9th and 10th Congressional Districts, being wholly under Federal control, the people will gladly avail themselves of the opportunity of electing members of Congress, in the event of your issuing a proclamation, fixing a day and directing the Sheriffs to hold the elections—

The elections, being in the nature of those for *filling vacancies,* might, if necessary, be held at different times; and as the Districts I have named are free from rebels, elections might be held there, without waiting on other portions of the State which may be under rebel rule. I will send a copy of the letter to Genl. Grant at Jackson and to Genl. Sherman at Memphis.

Very truly yours,
E M: Etheridge

ALS, DLC-JP.

1. For Congressman Etheridge, see *Johnson Papers*, III, 88*n*.

2. See Letter from Abraham Lincoln, October 21, 1862.

To Abraham Lincoln

Nashville Tenn Oct 29 1862
By courier to Louisville

Prest Lincoln

General Morgans entire command ought to be sent to Tennessee and if not all the Tennessee regts should be sent. They are the troops we need here[.][1] press the importance of sending these regts to Tennessee upon Genl Halleck. I know if his attention is called to it he will not hesitate one moment[.] Let them come and will redeem East Tennessee before Christmas. East Tennessee must be redeemed. I have much to say upon this subject at the proper time[.] Let sufficient forces be sent to Nashville, it must and can be held. I will communicate fully all that has transpired as soon as mail facilities are restored[.]

Very Truly &c
Andrew Johnson

Tel, DNA-RG94, Gens. Papers, H. W. Halleck, Tels. Recd., Vol. 11.

1. Unbeknownst to Johnson, George W. Morgan's unit, which arrived in Portland, Ohio, October 9, following its retreat from Cumberland Gap, was in process of being reorganized.

From Leonidas C. Houk

October 30, 1862, Gallipolis, Ohio; ALS, DLC-JP.

Reporting "a vast amount of dissatisfaction among the East Tennessee Troops," asks the governor's intervention with Stanton, "or the President himself," to alter plans to send them up the Kanawha Valley and instead return them to the Tennessee-Kentucky arena. "If we are kept in Western Va. this winter, the glory of the East Tennessee Regiments will have faded—departed forever, I fear!"

From Abraham Lincoln

Washington City D. C.
Oct. 31. 1862

Gov. Andrew Johnson
Nashville, Tenn. via Louisville, Ky

Yours of the 29th received. I shall take it to Gen. Halleck; but I already know it will be very inconvenient to take Gen. Morgan's command from where it now is. I am glad to hear you speak hopefully for Tennessee— I sincerely hope Rosecrans[1] may find it possible to do something for her—

"David Nelson" son of the M. C. of your state, regrets his father's final defection, and asks me for a situation— Do you know him? Could he be of service to you, or to Tennessee, in any capacity in which I could send him?[2]

A. Lincoln

Tel draft, RPB-McLellan Lincoln Col.; fragment, DLC-JP.

1. Gen. William S. Rosecrans had just been appointed commander of the Army of the Cumberland, replacing Don Carlos Buell. For Rosecrans, see *Johnson Papers*, V, 63*n*.

2. There is no evidence that Johnson replied to this inquiry; however, early in the spring of 1863, young Nelson turned up as 1st lieutenant, Co. B, 1st Tenn. Lgt. Arty., raised by Capt. Robert C. Crawford from among East Tennessee refugees in Lexington, Kentucky. *Tennesseans in the Civil War*, I, 364.

From Gordonsville Women[1]

Gordonsville Tenn. Nov [1862]

Hon Andrew Johnson
Sir,

We the undersigned offer our services for the purpose of aiding to put down the rebellion and will be very much obliged if you will supply us with arms and if you will accept us please send them immediately. if not we will arm ourselves and bushwhack it.

Pet, DLC-JP.

1. Most of the fifty-four signers were Tennessee natives and came from farm families. Those identified ranged from nine to sixty, many being young single women, and including a number of mother-daughter, as well as sister, combinations; a few were substantial property holders. 1860 Census, Tenn., Smith, *passim;* Sistler, *1850 Tenn. Census, passim.*

From William B. Campbell

Louisville Kentucky
Novr. 2 1862

Governor A Johnson
Dear Sir

On my arrival here after visiting the varous prisons and attending to the duty assigned me to do by you, I found it almost impossible to proceed further on my way to Nashville,—and my health having become much deteriorated by an old chronic complaint[1] which has seriously affected me for many years past, and finding here a physician of much reputation who professed to cure such diseases, I placed myself under his charge, and believe I am improving decidedly & hope in two weeks more to be relieved. I shall at least remain here a few weeks longer in hopes of a full restoration to health.— I am extremely anxious to be in Nashville, and sincerely hope that under the administration of Genl Rosecrans we shall have a more vigorous & successful prosecution of the war. Nothing but a very decided policy against the rebel citizens will avail any thing. Mildness has been tried without effecting any changes. The Presidents last proclamation[2] has had a very injurious effect in this state & doubtless in the Northern States also, and may yet produce most serious difficulties, and embarrass the suppression of the rebelion. I believe there will be great danger of revolt in the Army when it shall be attempted to carry the proclamation into full operation. The Kentucky battalions as well as a large number from the north are not disposed to sustain it. I have seen an order of a Kentucky Col.[3] published in the papers here, in which he states that all slaves in his Regiment shall be promptly given up to *loyal* as well as *rebel* owners. This is evidently a feeler & ominous of a determination to resist the proclamation. I feel sure the politicians in this state sympathize strongly with that position. I wish much to see you & will return to Nashville as soon as my health will allow me to do so. Bragg's army could have easily been destroyed while in this state, but I tell you I am decidedly of the opinion that there was no intention but to allow him to get out of the state unmolested. Nothing but a mere *demonstration* of *pursuit* was made. This opinion obtains with a large portion of the truly loyal men in this state. This city is as full of rebels as your city of Nashville & they exercise to much influence in the affairs of the army. Too many disloyal men are connected with the army, particularly as contractors sutlers & traders, and the enemy has been constantly supplied with necessaries & information through these sources. There should be more strictness in giving permission to persons to trade—to take goods into Tennessee. None but undoubted loyal union and honorable men should have the permission to take goods in to our state. But for the *contraband* trade that has been carrid on all the past year the rebels would have been naked & starved out & without medicine for the sick. Large amounts of drugs have been smuggled through by persons who had the authority to trade under the belief of their loyalty.— Trade should not be allowed with any portion of the country remaining disloyal & it will bring them to their senses sooner than an "army with banners." [4]

your friend W B Campbell

I may say further on this subject—that contraband trade will be carried on to an enormous extent & to the supply of the rebels & the rebel army, unless some different system is adopted granting *permits* to *traders*. So far as the trade to Tennessee is concerned, there ought to be some one of most reliable character & inteligence to superintend it and to grant the *permits*. It should be a department, and if managed properly will do as much as the army towards putting down the rebelion. It does not matter if the whole population should be made to suffer for in that way can they be brought to their senses and submit to the U. S. Govt.

There is now great preparations making here to carry good and supplies of every kind to Ten. on the return of the federal army & the *sutlers* to the army will carry a large amount of articles which will be sold to the rebel population & from thence be taken to supply the wants of the rebel soldiers. Sugar coffee & many articles will be carried in & sold to the rebels, which are almost necessaries of life & they are relieved from their suffering by the U. S. sutlers.— It is well worthy of consideration how far the selling of goods & necessaries to the rebel population ought to be allowed—

W B C

ALS, DLC-JP.

1. Campbell probably suffered from dysentery or a similar intestinal ailment. Beginning in June, 1851, he had remained bedridden for a month, missing much of that year's gubernatorial canvass, and experienced a similar illness during the summer of 1854 after returning from a trip to New Orleans. Nashville *True Whig,* June 28, 1851; Bell to Campbell, August 10, 1854, "Letters of John Bell to William B. Campbell," *Tennessee Historical Magazine,* III (1917), 224.

2. Lincoln's September 22 announcement of impending emancipation.

3. Col. John H. McHenry, Jr. (1832-1893) of Owensboro, who placed the special order, dated October 27, in the Louisville *Journal* of October 30, had spent three years at West Point before completing the law course at the University of Louisville in 1857. Recruiting the 17th Ky. Inf., USA, in 1861, he led his men at Donelson and Shiloh; but, becoming disenchanted after Lincoln announced the Emancipation Proclamation, he returned to practice law at Owensboro. H. Levin, ed., *Lawyers and Lawmakers of Kentucky* (Chicago, 1897), 339-40.

4. "Terrible as an army with banners." Song of Sol. 6:4, 10.

From Andrew J. Clements

November 3, 1862, Bowling Green, Ky.; ALS, DLC-JP.

Kentucky congressman seeks authorization "to establish a camp on Cumberland river near Carthage or Gainesboro to raise some [twelve-month] volunteers for the protection of the upper counties of the State." Inasmuch as the people of that area "have furnished a large number of volunteers," he doubts that many more can be raised for three years' service, but "if allowed to volunteer and go into camp to protect their homes" a number "sufficient to protect the country from the Cumberland river to the mountains" could be raised. Stanton has indicated that Clements "would have to get the authority from you as Governor of the State."

Order for Protection of a Widow

State of Tennessee,
Executive Department.
Nashville, Novr. 6th 1862

No person citizen or soldier will interfere with or molest the premises of Mrs. Knapp[1] (No. 113 South Cherry St. Nashville) without written orders from this office or from the Post Headquarters and any violation of this order will subject the offender to all the penalties of a violation of the laws, both civil and military, of the United States[.]

Andrew Johnson
Military Govr.

D, DLC-JP.

1. Probably Martha D. Knapp (*c*1819-1873), South Carolina-born widow, whose household was composed of three daughters, aged 24, 18, and 14, and a son, 20. *Nashville City Cemetery Index,* 46; 1860 Census, Tenn. , Davidson, Nashville, 7th Ward, 86.

To John M. Hale, Nashville

November 8, 1862, Nashville; L, DLC-JP.

In response to inquiry concerning the amount of fuel allowed the governor, the assistant quartermaster notes:

Self	4	Cords
Servts	1/2	"
	4 1/2	Cords Wood
	or 135	Bush Coal[.]

To Abraham Lincoln

Nashville Tennessee November 8th 1862

His Excellency Abraham Lincoln
President of the United States
Washington D. C.

More than a week ago, I repeated a former dispatch in regard to Genl Geo. W. Morgan's Division being ordered to Virginia.[1] The Courier who took it from this place has been arrested by the Enemy & the inference is that he has been hung. I must again press the propriety justice & humanity of sending that portion of Genl. Morgans command composed of the East Tennessee troops to Tennessee for the purpose of redeeming the Eastern part of the state & avenging the intolerable wrongs which have been inflicted upon her by heartless & relentless Traitors. It would be cruel in the Extreme to tear the East Tennessee Regiments away from their homes and defence of their families when they are willing & more than anxious to restore the government & at the same time protect their wives & children against insult robbery murder & inhumane oppression. I ask in the name of all that is right magnaminous & patriotic that these regiments be permitted to return. There are many things that I will advise you of in a short time. Since my location here we have had numerous Commanders placed at this post[.] some of them have been tolerable others intolerable but the one now in command Genl Negley who was left here by Genl Buell in his disgraceful retreat from Alabama & Tennessee has done us more harm than all others & is wholly unfitted for the place[.][2] under all the disadvantageous circumstances I have succeeded in raising one Regiment of Cavalry under Command of Col Wm. B Stokes which has rendered good service[3] also one fine Regt. of Infantry under Command of Col Alvin C. Gillet[4] now acting as Provost Guard of this City. Col Gillet is an officer of the Regular Army transferred by the War Dept. to command the 1st Middle Tenn. Infy. he is an intelligent & efficient officer & will make a good Brigadier General. I recommend & ask that he be appointed at once as Such[.]

He will fight, a quality very much needed by many of our officers. There are some Brigades here without Brig Genls & as soon as our army can move forward we will form [a] Brigade of Middle Tennessee. I hope you will lay this dispatch before the Secretary of War & General Halleck.[5] This dispatch will be sent through by Benj O. Truman[6] who leaves here with it & will see you in Washn.

Andrew Johnson
Mil. Govr.

Tel, DNA-RG107, Tels. Recd., U.S. Mil. Tel., Vol. 32 (1862).

1. See Telegram to Abraham Lincoln, October 29, 1862.

2. Apparently the difficulties between Johnson and Negley were of some months' standing; as far back as early October Gen. Jeremiah Boyle conveyed to Lincoln the governor's "earnest request" that Negley be removed. The most recent "incident" concerned a dispute in which the provost marshal, acting under the general's orders, denied that the civil court could try a suit already disposed of by the military—thus, in effect, overriding the municipal authorities. Boyle to Lincoln, October 7, 1862, *OR*, Ser. 1, XVI, Pt. II, 583; Maslowski, *Treason Must Be Made Odious*, 65.

3. Five days later Johnson telegraphed Stanton expressing the hope that Stokes would be mustered into the Federal service and explaining that his regiment "has eight (8) companies complete and has in fact been rendering invaluable service from the organization of the first company." Johnson to Stanton, November 13, 1862, E. M. Stanton Papers, LC.

4. Alvan C. Gillem.

5. Johnson's wire of November 4 "about returning troops from Western Virginia to Tennessee" had been referred to Halleck. Halleck to Johnson, November 11, 1862, Johnson Papers, LC.

6. In an accompanying letter of introduction, Johnson described Benjamin C. Truman as "a gentleman of intelligence and character, who has been in Nashville since my arrival," and assured the President that Truman was "perfectly familiar with the condition of things

here. . . . Whatsoever statement he may make can be implicitly relied upon." Johnson to Lincoln, November 8, 1862, in Nashville *Press,* June 27, 1863. For Truman, see *Johnson Papers,* V, 178*n*.

From John L. Williamson[1]

Trenton Octr [Nov.] 10, 1862—

Gov. A. Johnson,

Dear Sir, Enclosed find a Copy of the proceedings of a meeting of the people of Gibson County,[2] held for the purpose of considering the propriety of securing a member to the Federal Congress. Similar meetings have been held in Carrol and Henderson Counties, adopting in substance the same Resolutions. Weakly County I believe has had no meeting as yet, but concurs heartily in the same, I am satisfied other Counties of this Congressional District will vote for a member— The people are very anxious to hear from you and to have you issue a writ of election at as early a day as possible. Enclosed you will also find several petitions numerously signed by citizens of this county of all political creeds asking for an election, Some of whom have heretofore been the most violent of rebels.[3] If time permitted and it was thought necessary numerous other names could be procured. Those we have would have been forwarded sooner, but for the difficulty in the way of communication with you—

I think there is little or no doubt, but that a decided majority of the voters of the 9th Congressional District will go for Representation. We are exceedingly anxious to try the experiment at any rate, I suppose the new Districts created by the *Bogus* Legislature of 61-2 will not be regarded at all—[4]

The people hope to hear from you soon. In the mean time those of us who favor Representation will not be idle, but will do all we can in aid of any project having for its end the restoration of the authority of the Federal Union upon which hang all our hopes.

With sentiments of respect

I am yours &c, J. L. Williamson

ALS, DLC-JP.

1. John L. Williamson (b. *c*1833) was a Gibson County lawyer who claimed $500 real and $500 personal property prior to the war. 1860 Census, Tenn., Gibson, Trenton, 154.

2. Report of meeting at Trenton, November 3, 1862, Johnson Papers, LC.

3. In an October 19 petition, 125 citizens of Gibson County and the ninth congressional district, "being anxious to restore the federal authority, and put an end to this unnatural war," asked the governor "to issue writs of election for members of Congress to the United States Government." Similar requests came from Lauderdale, Tipton, and Haywood counties. William T. Strickland to Johnson, November 12, 1862, Johnson Papers, LC.

4. In October, 1861, the Confederate assembly had passed house bill No. 28, redistricting the state. Gibson remained in the ninth. *Tenn. House Journal*, 1861-62, pp. 50-52, 65; *Tenn. Acts*, 1861-62, Ch. XII.

From Calvin Goddard

November 12, 1862, Nashville; LB copy, DNA-RG393, Dept. of the Cumberland, Endorsements, Vol. 33 (1861-62).

Asserting that "no prisoner arrested by Military Authority should be released except by the same authority," Rosecrans' acting adjutant general asks with reference to a Mr. Brown whether the governor has been exercising such prerogative, "and if so under what orders."

From Stephen A. Hurlbut[1]

Head Quarters Dist of Jackson
Jackson Tennessee
12th November 1862.

His Excy Andrew Johnson
Governor of Tenn.
Sir

Communication being now opened with Nashville, I think it advisable to lay before you some suggestions in relation to the state of affairs in this part of the country. Recent successes of our arms and the advance of our troops have quieted apparently the spirit of resistence and I think the General feeling west of the Tennessee is to submit to the constitution and the law, to discourage guerilla warfare and to come as rapidly as possible under the administration of organized civil Law. There is a strong feeling in favor of an election of Representatives to Congress. This I submit if done must be done by proclamation from you.

Judge Williams attempted to hold a court but as I learned he was not commissioned by you I closed the court.[2] many of the sheriffs now in office are not reliable, but can only be removed and others appointed through you.

I take the liberty of recommending that you proceed as soon as practicable to organize the several Departments of state authority so that the people as speedily as may be may come under the customary course of law and settle down into regular habits.

This will be a work of extreme delicacy and should be confided to some person of undoubted loyalty and high personal character. Any protection if required from the military power within my District will always be ready for carrying out such measures as your Knowledge of the men and the country may dictate.

I have the honor to be Your most obedt servant
Major General Comdg. Dist of Jackson

LB copy, DNA-RG393, Dist. of West Tenn. and Successor Commands, 4th Div., Lets. Sent, Vol. 85-16AC.

1. Stephen A. Hurlbut (1815-1882), native of Charleston, South Carolina, was admitted to the bar (1837) before moving to Illinois in 1845, where he became politically prominent and eventually a Republican legislator. Brigadier general of volunteers in 1861 and major general the following year, he served at Shiloh and Corinth, commanded the garrison at Memphis, and was later assigned (1864) to the Department of the Gulf. Although involved in corrupt practices, he was allowed to be "honorably mustered out" in June, 1865. Returning to Illinois, he became the first commander-in-chief of the Grand Army of the Republic (1866-72), minister to Colombia (1869-72), congressman (1873-77), and minister to Peru (1881-82), meanwhile being periodically charged with malfeasance. Warner, *Generals in Blue,* 244-45; *BDAC,* 1100.

2. For Samuel Williams, whom Johnson did not commission judge of the 16th circuit until December 6, see *Johnson Papers*, III, 686*n*.

To Robert Johnson

Nashville, Nov'r 14th 1862

Col. Robt. Johnson,
Burnett House, Cincinnatti.

Charles has an opportunity to act here as Surgeon if he will.[1] Your Mother, Stover & family are here. Your Mother's health is bad. I think they will be in Cincinnati in a short time.[2] I will let you know in advance. You ought to be careful to get good horses. Cavalry horses soon break down unless they are durable.

Andrew Johnson
Mil: Gov'r.

Tel draft, DNA-RG393, Dept. of the Cumberland, Tels. Sent (1862).

1. With a back-dating of enlistment and muster date to September 15, Charles Johnson became an assistant surgeon in the 10th Tenn. Inf. Rgt., a rank he held until his accidental death, April 5, 1863, as the result of being thrown from a horse. *Tenn. Adj. Gen. Report* (1866), 160.

2. Eliza had hoped to go immediately on to the Queen City when they came through the lines in mid-October, but the enemy's threat to Nashville and the insecurity of roads by virtue of guerrilla activity had made it impossible for her to hasten on to see "*once* more" her second son Robert from whom she had been separated for more than a year and who, she feared, she might never see again. Mary Stover to Robert Johnson, November 10, 1862, Johnson Papers, LC.

From "A Peace Democrat"[1]

(Private & *Confidential)*

Nashville Nov 17/62

To His Excellency Gov Andrew Johnson
Dear Sir

I heard with regret a few days since that you would probably resign your office of Military Gov and resume your seat in the senate[2] Satisfied as I am that you will act more justly & leniently towards the *people* of *Tenn* than any successor likely to be appointed— You *can never forget your obligations* to *the Democratic party* of *Tenn* who have *made you what you are*— But Gov whether you remain as Military Gov or return to the senate I think the time has arrived when you should come forward as a *pasificator* or *peacemaker,* and I was much gratified at the remarks in your letter a few days since [to] Capt Morton[3] saying you prefered the dust of the field, and dinge of the shop to the clangor of war— Have we not had *bloodshed enough* already? Can we never have an honorable peace? My *hope* is that the *Conservative National Democratic party* will come to the rescue—otherwise I fear *Constitutional government is at an end*— Your Proclamation of 18th March '62,[4] I believe contains *your true sentiments*. You are in favor of *maintaining* a *Republican government* in the *state*. You say "To the people themselves, the protection of the Government is extended. *All their rights will be respected*—" You allso say it is your intention as Gov "as speedily as may be to restore her (state of Tenn) government to the same condition as before the existing rebellion—" You further endorse the Crittenden resolutions passed almost unanimously by Congress in July 1861—which says the "war is not waged" in any spirit of *oppression,* nor for any purpose of conquest or *subjugation,* nor purpose of *overthrowing* or *interfering with the rights* or *established institutions* of these STATES, but to *defend* and *maintain* the *supremacy* of the CONSTITUTION and to *preserve* the *Union* with all the *dignity, equality,* and *rights* of the *several states unimpaired:* —" But alas Gov—human nature is so frail. When the same Congress has turned right around in the teeth of their own resolution, and have done eveything in their power to violate it— The President has also issued an Emancipation Proclamation—[5] I suppose on the ground of military necessity—(Just so some of the fire eaters said they must *secede* to put down Abolitionism— So the Abolitionists, the Secessionist and the President are all appealing to a higher law than the Constitution which they have *Sworn* to support— The President—so manfully in the removal of *Cameron* & *Freemont*[6] that I had vainly hoped he would stand by the Constitution to the end—which he had sworn to *support, protect,* and *defend*—That Constitution saying "That The powers not delegated to the *United States* by the *Constitution,* nor—*prohibited* by it to the states, are reserved to the states respectively or to the people—" Where is the authority either express or implied—delegating to the President or Congress—the power to emancipate slaves— This *Proclamation* too in the teeth of the Crittenden resolutions—of July 1861—I beleive only 4 votes against them.[7]

Again—It is the duty of Congress to suppress insurrections—and enforce the laws of the Union. Congress while trying to suppress an insurrection among the white people of the South should do nothing to encourage an insurrection among slaves. The President *however* by his proclamation in trying to put down an insurrection or rebellion among whites does everything in his power to incite the slaves to servile insurrection— Secession was wrong in principle & policy—but to put it down neither the President or Congress have a right to violate the Constitution— Are you then astonished Governor at the tremendous popular revolution going on in the North[.] The Democracy of the North are rising in their might and declare they are for the *Constitution as it is,* and the Union as it was—[8] Just as you declare in your Proclamation of 18 March last. those who believe secession wrong & unconstitutional—must not themselves violate the Constitution, as two wrongs can never make one right— If we wish to maintain the Constitution we must be sure not to violate it, in order to maintain it—But waiving all Constitutional objections—and for the sake of argument suppose the President has the power to emancipate slaves. After he has emancipated the slaves will he not be in the situation of the man who drew an elephant as a *Lottery prize*[?] What will he do with Sambo after he frees him— Gov Johnson you are a practical statesman—and if the President had had your iron *will*—he would not have yielded to the Abolitionists. Do you not see the *hand-writing on the wall*[?] the *conservative people of the Country* are getting tired of *Abolitionism.* Senator Bigler's late letter[9] shows very conclusively that the Republican party in Congress were responsible for the defeat of the *Crittendon Compromise*—as it requires two thirds of Congress to recommend Amendments to the Constitution and the Republican party stood in solid phalanx in the senate against the Crittenden Compromise. Mr. *Cameron's* course not dictated entirely by policy—he is at *heart* an Abolitionist[.] Still the Gulph states ought to have made the fight on the Constitution *inside* of the *Union* but as secession was wrong—and not the remedy for evils—which the South justly complained of. And as the Republican party are bent upon the downfall of *Constitutional government* and the establishment of a military despotism The question presents itself doubtless to your sagacious mind—*what is my duty*— I do not *possess your intellect*—but it seems to me the time has come when you should take a *strong stand* for *peace*— Can we not have an armistice of 60 or 90 days and see if the difficulties between the north & south cannot be settled without a further *effusion* of *blood*[.]

If all your efforts for peace should fail and the war continue—Then I ask should it not be carried on according to *law* and *the constitution*— Should this *wholesale plundering* & *thieving* that has been so *prevalent* in Nashville & vicinity (which disgusts all good citizens and injures the Union cause) continue? Should the President & Congress continue to ignore the Constitution? If they expect to make Secessionists submit to law & the Constitution, they must not themselves violate both. If the Republican party are determined to overthrow the Constitution in their efforts to put down secession. Can you not rally to the gallant Democracy of the *North,* and conduct the war if it must go on according to law & the Constitution? If you pursue the right course, you may be the next President. But one thing is *true* the Republican is a doomed party— The people are heartily sick of *Republican rule.* The Democratic party must come to the rescue or the *Constitution* is a *thing* of the *past. The Democracy* carried through the

Compromise measures in 1850 and sustained Fillmore in his patriotic determination to maintain the Constitution & the Union. In an evil hour the Missouri compromise was repealed. the Kansas Nebraska bill was construed one way north, and another South. We were all caught in the trap. Slavery however in the Territories was pretty much an abstraction, and squatter soverignty was a thousand times better than *secession* & *anarchy*. The mischief has been done— The past cannot be recalled. "Things without remedy should be without regard. What is done, is done—" [10] The question now is, what can be done for the present and to provide against future evils— We must not shut our eyes to public sentiment in the South. So *much blood has been shed* that *patriots* & *statesman* must begin to view the *war* in the *light* of *humanity*— You may say the people are *insane*— *be it so, then* but as Tennesseans we must keep before our eyes the fact that Tennessee went into this rebellion by a majority of about 60,000.[11] I wish to call your attention to my observation of the state of public sentiment before the war. For several years before the fall of Fort of Sumter, I had traveled a good deal in Alabama Mississippi Virginia, part of No Cirolina, and met with a number of citizens from S. Carolina, Georgia, Florida—Louisiana & Arkansas, and from the sentiments generally expressed, I was satisfied that if *a Black Republican* was elected *President* that the Gulph states would immediately secede and try to drag the middle & border slave states with them[.] Tens of thousands of people in the south believe that a state has the *Consitutional right* to *secede* when her rights or equality in the Union *are denied* her. They think as New York & Virginia both passed resolutions[12] when ratifying the Constitution declaring whenever the government of the U.S. is *perverted* to their injury or oppression—The powers delegated can be resumed by the states— forgetting that the U S Constitution & laws made in pursuance thereof are the supreme laws of the land. Thousands regard the Constitution as a League or a compact and not a national government which it certainly is having the power of enforcing its authority. This very numerous class of people—*beleive honestly beleived* when *Lincoln* was *elected* that the *Republican party intended* to *overthrow* the *Constitution, subjugate them,* and *emancipate their slaves,* and the recent *acts* of *Congress* and *emancipation proclamation* of the *President* only *confirms* them in that opinion.

The confiscation act and the Presidents proclamation—have also driven thousands of hitherto strong union men to side with the rebellion, where now are Hons T. A. R. Nelson N. G. Taylor[13] & others. They trusted in the Crittenden Resolutions of July 1861— I concur with you if the States had stood firm in the *Union* we would have overthrown the Republican party during Lincolns administration consequently I regard secession as the wrong remedy for our grievances— The past cannot be recalled and we must deal with questions practically[.] I may be mistaken, but I believe the confederate army & a large portion of the people of the so called Confederate states will suffer annihilation unless their *Constitutional* rights are secured to them. Slavery in the Territories as I have said is pretty much an abstraction, but the principle of the *Constitutional rights* and *equality* of the states is involved— And unless the North will agree to the Crittenden or some other *Compromise*—or acknowledge the Independence of the Confederacy—I see no end to this rebellion for sometime to come—if ever. There is a great difference in the mere military possession, and permanent government of a country. If the people think the object of the government is to enslave and subjugate, and not n[u]rture a Constitutional government, they will sacri[fice] life, property, everything before they will yield. Fanatics and Demagogues brought these troubles upon the Country, (together with the great prevalence of sin, crime, contrainess, dissipation and general depravity),— The bitter national hatred and passions of the North and South are thoroughly aroused— And the question presents itself to all honest, *just statesman,* shall we if we can *exterminate* the *Southern people,* or concede them what they regard as their Constitutional rights—

Again Will the Conservative Democracy of the North sanction a war of *extermination* & *servile insurrection*[?] Will not the *Northern* Democracy—say while you are putting down an insurrection or rebellion—of the whites, you must do nothing to incite a Servile insurrection—thereby violating the Constitution & humanity both. If slavery is unprofitable it will never be permanently established in the territories at all. Although you & I may regard the question of slavery as an abstraction, in the territories, yet I assure you there are thousands and tens of thousands in the South who will pour out their hearts blood in defence of a *principle* (or *abstraction* if you prefer), that is or may never be of any practical importance whatever.

You may take this truth for what it is worth. The *rights* and *equality* of the *Southern States,* in the *Union* must be acknowledged or a *large portion* of the *Southern people* will suffer extermination before they will ground their arms, and thousands are so phrenzied that they will have nothing short of Independence— When you talk to them about the Republican party not intending to *interfere with their rights*—they tell you—it is a mere *trap* to *deceive* them. They say in *defence* of *slavery*—that it was a curse pronounced against *Ham* and his *descendants*.[14] They refer you to the 25th Chapter of the Book of Leviticus—which shows the distinction between hired & bond servants, where bond servants were to be inherited as a *possession* and to remain *bondmen forever*—[15] They also refer you to the teachings of Christ & his apostles on slavery especially Pauls epistle to the Colossians also 6th Chap 1st Timothy[.] [16] you may call it fanaticism or what you please, but they believe Slavery is a Divine institution sanctioned by the Bible[.]

They also bleive that the Constitution sustains the institution, and that both the *Constitution* & the *Bible* are ignored by the *Republican party,* and the Higher law, the irrepressible Conflict and the Chicago Platform,[17] are the principles the Republican intended to substitute for the Constitution and the Bible— These opinions thousands honestly entertain, and I repeat the late acts of Congress, and the Presidents proclamation only confirm this opinion. I submit *these* facts to you as a patriot and statesman of great sagacity— My object in writing this letter is to try and do something as an humble individual to end this horrid war.[18] I appeal to you, knowing that you have far more influence with the Northern people & the President than any *man* in the South. The people of Tennessee have made you—what you are and I appeal to you to save them from further bloodshed. Some weeks since I sent you a Sermon by Bishop Pierce on the death of Bishop Capers.[19] I have often thought Gov Johnson if you were only a *christian* how much *more good* you could do for your fellowmen. You have deep sympathy for the people who have honored you and for mankind generally, but you *lack* the *crowning virtue* of *christianity.*— *Religion* is *the one thing needful. What is a man profited* if *he should gain* the *whole world and lose his own soul?"*[20] or what will a *man not give in exchange for his soul*[?] We *must all die* and *after death* comes the judgment. If we are *not prepared* for *death, dreadful* will be *our fate.* If the *righteous* are *scarcely saved where shall* the sinner and the ungodly appear. I have experienced in my own heart the reality of the Christian religion— Your head, your heart, your immortal Soul, your very existence—everything in nature proclaim that there is a *God*[.] As there is a *God* it is natural he should *reveal* some *law* by which his *creatures* should be *governed.* The Bible is the best law I have found. Until I find a better, I must take the Bible to be *God's law.* "It is no cunningly devised fable,"[21] but proclaims peace on *earth, good will* toward *men* and *happiness beyond* the *grave.* The *Bible* is *God's book.* No mere mortal man could have written it. The finger of *God* is traced on all its pages— *Read* the *Bible. "read, bleive* & *live*—" Repentance for sin, and *faith in God's love* & *mercy, must possess your heart* to give you *saving grace* to *bleive*— Read, 3rd Proverbs. 5,6 & 7th Chapters of Matthew, 12th Romans, 13. of 1st Corinthians 14 & 15 of St John, 1 Chap 2 epistle of Peter, 1st 19, 23, 42, 46, 51, & 103 Psalms. Read the entire Bible. Bleive its sacred truths. It contains many mysteries which no man can understand but remember how little you know, of your own nature. One thing you know you *have* a "*Soul* to be *lost* or *saved*— Therefore *Search* the *scriptures.* Feel that you are a *poor lost sinner*—a *poor worm* of the *dust,* a *helpless, undone, miserable sinner*— *Cast all your burden* on the *Lord,* and you will be *happy* in *time* & *eternity*— You are now *military Governor* have heretofore been highly *honored.* You may yet be *President*—but these earthly honors—are *trash* compared with your *souls salvation*— God has endowed you with great talents. You will *have to render* a *strict account* of your *stewardship*—(Did you *preach war*—when you should have *whispered Peace* & compromise?) Do your duty but above all, if you would be *happy*—be an *humble Christian.* Remember the Lords prayer, "Forgive us *our trespasses* as we *forgive those who trespass against us?* The *people* of *Tennessee* are *in* a *miserable condition.* Pray God to enable you to be *instrumental* in *rescuing them*—(I will also pray for you)— "Blessed are the *merciful for they* shall *obtain mercy*. "Blessed are the *Peace Makers* for they shall be called the *Children* of *God*"— My object is to do *good* for my *fellowmen*—and to be *merciful* & *Charitable*—[22]

In haste "A *Peace Democrat*"

Excuse haste & bad writing—

ALS, DLC-JP.

1. Although not identified, this correspondent would seem to be the person who wrote as "Mercy," May 28, 1864.

2. Throughout the summer and fall of 1862 Johnson remained at odds with the military leaders in Tennessee. He was especially displeased with General Buell, whose apparent lack of concern for Nashville put the capital in danger during October and November. Under the circumstances, Johnson may have considered resigning, but there is no evidence, contemporary or subsequent, to this effect.

3. See Letter to James St. C. Morton, October 27, 1862.

4. See Appeal to the People of Tennessee, March 18, 1862, *Johnson Papers*, V, 209-12.

5. The preliminary Emancipation Proclamation, dated September 22.

6. In his annual report of December, 1861, Secretary of War Simon Cameron had suggested arming the slaves from captured territories, and Gen. John C. Frémont, as commander of the Department of the West, had issued an unauthorized proclamation (August 30, 1861), freeing the slaves of Missouri Confederates. However, the dismissal of the secretary resulted more from his inefficient and corrupt administration than from his attitudes toward slavery as suggested here, and Frémont's removal was prompted as much by his general intractability and political incompetence, as by his proclamation. Allan Nevins, *The War for the Union* (4 vols., New York, 1959-71), I, 331-40, 400-403, 408; for Cameron and Frémont see *Johnson Papers,* I, 508*n*; V, 83*n*.

7. On July 22, 1861, Congressman John J. Crittenden presented a resolution intended clearly to define Federal war aims, declaring that "civil war has been forced upon the country by the disunionists of the southern States" and "that this war is not waged . . . for . . . overthrowing or interfering with the rights or established institutions of those States, but to defend and maintain the *supremacy* of the Constitution, and to preserve the Union with all the dignity, equality, and rights of the several States unimpaired; and that as soon as these objects are accomplished the war ought to cease." The resolution was divided: the "war guilt" clause passed 122 to 2; the remainder 117 to 2. It is not without interest that two days later Senator Johnson introduced an identical resolution which passed, 30 to 5, on the twenty-fifth. The coincidence in both timing and phrasing suggests collaboration between these staunch southern unionists; indeed, Wood Gray calls them "authors" of the resolutions. Firm evidence, however, is lacking. *Cong. Globe*, 37 Cong., 1 Sess., 222-23, 258-65; Wood Gray, *The Hidden Civil War: The Story of the Copperheads* (New York, 1942), 74; *Johnson Papers*, IV, 597-99.

8. Paraphrasing Daniel Webster's famous credo of 1830, "I go for the Constitution as it is, and the Union as it is," this slogan had been adopted for the recent congressional elections by northern conservative Democrats opposed to the implementation of more radical war aims, as exemplified by the Emancipation Proclamation. *Register of Debates in Congress,* VI, Pt. 1 (1829/30), 62; Christopher Dell, *Lincoln and the War Democrats* (Cranbury, N. J., 1975), 141-45.

9. In a lengthy letter, dated November 1, to S. D. Anderson of Philadelphia, ex-Senator William Bigler had written, "It might be interesting . . . to unveil the hypocrisy of a certain school of politicians who have clamored so zealously about the war for the Union. It is . . . apparent . . . they do not intend that the Union shall exist hereafter on the terms of the Constitution, if it is to embrace all the States. The ratio of slave representation, and the rendition of fugitive slaves, are features of the Constitution which they condemn and abhor. Between the maintenance of these and the recognition of the Southern Confederacy, many of them . . . would prefer the latter." Cincinnati *Enquirer*, November 20, 1862.

10. Shakespeare, *Macbeth*, Act III, sc. 2.

11. Tennessee's June 8, 1861, referendum on separation showed a secessionist majority of 57,675. Mary R. Campbell, *The Attitudes of Tennesseans Toward the Union, 1847-1861* (New York, 1961), 294.

12. "Peace Democrat" was mistaken concerning the resolutions passed at the New York and Virginia ratifying conventions. In New York, an Anti-Federalist proposed that the state reserve the right to withdraw from the Union if amendments to guard state rights and individual liberties were not adopted. The proposal was abandoned and the amendments accompanying New York's ratification were merely suggestions. Ratification in Virginia, passing by a narrow margin, was contingent upon the subsequent adoption of amendments to the new constitution. Despite these provisos, neither state reserved the right to withdraw if injured or oppressed by the Federal government. Alexander C. Flick, ed., *History of the State of New York* (10 vols., New York, 1934), V, 60; Catherine Drinker Bowen, *Miracle at Philadelphia* (Boston, 1966), 301-4.

13. For Thomas A. R. Nelson and Nathaniel G. Taylor, originally unionists and now acquiescing in Confederate rule, see *Johnson Papers*, I, 159*n*; II, 229*n*.

14. According to proslavery apologists, Negroes were the descendents of Ham's son Canaan, and thus marked for slavery—"a servant of servants shall he be unto his brethren"—under the curse which Noah placed on them because Ham looked upon his father's (Noah's) nakedness. Gen. 9:21-25.

15. Lev. 25:39-55.

16. In Col. 3:22, reviewing the three basic superior-inferior relationships—God to man, husband to wife, and master to servant—Paul counselled servants to "obey in all things your masters according to the flesh; not with eyeservice, as manpleasers, but in singleness of heart, fearing God." In 1 Tim. 6:1, he admonished servants to "count their own masters worthy of all honor, that the name of God and *his* doctrine be not blasphemed."

17. The Republican platform of 1860 condemned any attempt at disunion and, while leaving the legal status of slavery to the discretion of the states, insisted that the territories must be free. Donald P. Johnson and Kirk H. Porter, comps., *National Party Platforms, 1840-1972* (Urbana, 1973), 32-33.

18. A marginal note declares, "I have written what I believe to be the sentiments of a large majority of the Northern people."

19. At the May, 1856, Nashville meeting of Methodist bishops, George Foster Pierce delivered a sermon, later published, on the death of William Capers (1790-1855), a South Carolina divine best known for his mission work with plantation Negroes. Pierce (1811-1884), a Georgia native who abandoned the law for the ministry, served mainly in Georgia, ascending to the presidencies of Georgia Female College (now Wesleyan) in Macon (1838-40) and Emory College (1848-54), before his episcopal election. Supporting secession, he spent the war years raising food for the army. *DAB*, III, 483-84; XIV, 580; George Smith, *The Life and Times of George Foster Pierce* (Sparta, Ga., 1888), 271.

20. Mark 8:36.

21. "For we have not followed cunningly devised fables, when we made known unto you the power and coming of our Lord Jesus Christ, but were eyewitnesses of his majesty." 2 Peter 1:16.

22. This extended homily may have totally missed its mark; the envelope endorsement reads, "To be read when an opportunity affords."

From Benjamin C. Truman

Washington D. C. Nov. 17, [1862]

My dear friend, Governor Johnson,

Of course, you know I have got through safe. Well, I had a long conversation with Mr. Forney,[1] and gave him a detailed account of matters and things in Nashville. I told him how your authority had been put to nought by everybody. I have written a severe article against deceased Stevenson and his thieves.[2] Mr. Forney says Negley is a "d---d fool."[3] I quote his expression. No person has seen even the outside of my letters except Mr. Forney, and in order to give him a chance to write an article. We went to see the President to day. At first he seem to be disposed to be more than indifferent, when Mr. Forney jumped up and told him that any request of yours should be promptly acceded to. Mr. Lincoln, himself then took the envelopes, endorsed them, and wrote me a letter to Mr. Stanton, and Gen Halleck. Before leaving Mr. Lincoln told me that he had already attended to the East Tennessee troops, and that Halleck promised him that they should be subject to your wishes.[4]

Mr. Forney is doing all in his power for Col. Gillem, although the President says there are too many generals, but at last left it to the discretion of Halleck & Stanton.

Mr. Forney & the President had quite a talk about your position, Mr. Forney urging that you should have the full control of everything.

I had a long talk with Stanton. Mr. Forney was not with me, but gave me a letter to him. He tells me to call again Wednesday.

Mr. Forney went with me to see Gen Halleck, and I presented the endorsed papers, which read thus:

"Please give the enclosed papers and the statements of the bearer immediate notice. Gov. Johnson is our great reliance in Tennessee."

I call for an answer to morrow morning.

Mr. Forney is writing a splendid article[5] upon your position, authority, &c.

In the course of conversation with Halleck Mr. Forney told him that you was head and shoulders above all other men, and should never have to ask for anything the seond time.

Mr. Forney tells me to write an editorial for the "Press" [6] after the tenor of his in the "Chronicle"[.]

Mr. Forney is very well pleased with me, and tells me that I am his best correspondent. Tells me I can go with Banks[7] to Texas, or to Florida, but desires me to go to East Tennessee. Therefore I accept the latter.

If I had not seen Mr. Forney, I would have made out bad with the President.

Mr. Forney told me that Stanton was gruff, &c, but told me to [be] brief, and touch on all subjects, and in a semi-authoritative manner. I did so, and he and Tucker[8] treated me well. I made a good story for Col. Gillem, & I hope for the best.

The President wouldn't listen to me about the railroad.[9]

Thanking you for your confidence, &c.

I remain yours truly
B. C. Truman

ALS, DLC-JP.

1. For John W. Forney, editor of the Philadelphia *Press* for which Truman was correspondent, see *Johnson Papers*, II, 32*n*.

2. In his dispatch, dated November 11, Truman described the late Capt. Richard Stevenson of Indiana as "extraordinarily fast upon a small salary," sporting around on

"blooded horses," driving an "eighteen hundred dollar team," giving "suppers," and indulging "in many other evils, which need not be mentioned." This same assistant quartermaster had "Upon several occasions . . . turned poor Union people out of their homes" which Johnson had provided them and "delivered up the houses to rebel owners [whose acquaintance he had cultivated], treating, at all times, the letters of censure sent him by the Governor with silence." Dying of typhoid at the home of a "notorious rebel," Stevenson was rumored to be "short some sixty thousand dollars" in his accounts. Philadelphia *Press,* November 17, 1862.

3. A private opinion which may or may not have been related to the quarrel between the general and the governor.

4. This message had been transmitted to Johnson some days earlier in separate but identical telegrams from the President and Halleck. Halleck to Johnson, November 11, 1862, Johnson Papers, LC; Lincoln to Johnson, November 14, 1862, Brown University Library (also in *OR,* Ser. 1, XX, Pt. II, 50; Basler, *Works of Lincoln,* V, 497).

5. An unsigned column appeared in the *Chronicle* the next day strongly supporting Johnson's efforts: "He has saved Tennessee to the Union. Fearless and self-sacrificing as he was in the Senate . . . he has been a thousand times more fearless and self-sacrificing in Tennessee. . . . let Andrew Johnson be sustained and strengthened by the Administration." Washington *Morning Chronicle,* November 18, 1862.

6. Apparently this editorial was not written.

7. For Nathaniel Banks who succeeded General Butler as head of the Department of the Gulf in late October, 1862, see *Johnson Papers*, V, 336*n*.

8. John Tucker (b. *c*1812), Philadelphia resident and longtime president of the Philadelphia and Reading Railroad Company (1844-56), was named second assistant secretary of war early in 1862 to supervise contracts and charter steamers, transports, and craft for army use. 1860 Census, Pa., Philadelphia, 8th Ward, 129; Frank A. Flower, *Edwin McMasters Stanton* (Akron, Ohio, 1905), 127; Nicholas B. Wainwright, ed., *A Philadelphia Perspective: The Diary of Sidney George Fisher* (Philadelphia, 1969), 212, 232, 416.

9. While still in the Senate, Johnson had advocated a railroad to link the "loyal portions of Tennessee and North Carolina with Kentucky," and the President had recommended such construction. During the fall of 1862 the difficulty experienced in supplying General Morgan by mule train over one hundred thirty miles of nearly impassable road had buttressed Johnson's case. As Brownlow suggested in a December letter in the Philadelphia *Press:* "The amount thus lost [in munitions, supplies, and animals] would have built the road. . . . Had the Kentucky politicians pressed the construction of the road it would have been built, and if built, it would have prevented the late destructive invasion of their state by Bragg's army. Had this road been constructed, it would have enabled the Federal army to take possession of the Virginia and Tennessee road"—the "*back-bone* of the rebellion"—and "cut off the supplies of the rebels." The proposed railroad "should go from Nicholasville to Cumberland Gap, and thence to Morristown" and there meet a road which connected Asheville with South Carolina. *Johnson Papers*, IV, 549, 711-12; Philadelphia *Press*, December 12, 1862.

To James S. Negley

November 17, 1862, Nashville; L draft, DLC-JP.

In order to adjudicate the claims of Maury countians for losses sustained at the hands of secessionists, the governor asks that he be provided with the names of "the disloyal citizens" of that county "from whom monies have been collected and to whom disbursements have been made, with the amount set opposite."

From William S. Rosecrans[1]

Head-Quarters Fourteenth Army Corps,
Department of the Cumberland.
Nashville Tuesday evening Nov 18, 1862

My dear Governor

I have just learned that the information given by the Nashville correspondent to the Louisville press of the movements of my troops[2] came from Mr Mercer[3] of the Union and pretending to have your approval—

Such information is the very worst injury that a spy could inflict. I would give a thousand dollars to know as much of the rebels. For Gods sake stop that— If Mr M. dont know—well, but if he does, he had better join Breckinridge or go to Alton[4] at once.

Very Truly Yours W. S. Rosecrans
Maj General.

Gov Andrew Johnson,
Nashville

LS, DLC-JP.

1. Rosecrans succeeding Buell in command, had arrived in Nashville on November 11.

2. Dispatches between October 31 and November 10, over the signatures of "Peregrine" and "Kentucky," though generally datelined Bowling Green, may have been the offending communications, inasmuch as they provided information about the disposition of various units of Rosecrans' Army of the Cumberland. This "Nashville correspondent" was probably the Philadelphia *Press* reporter, Benjamin C. Truman.

3. Samuel C. Mercer (*c*1831-1914), Pennsylvania-born Kentuckian and co-owner (1855-61) of the Know-Nothing Hopkinsville *Patriot* (later the *Mercury*), was brought to Nashville in 1862 to start the *Daily Union,* an administration organ which received the government patronage. In late 1863 he parted company with the paper and its publishers and the next February began the *Times and True Union* as a rival organ. Following the Brownlow regime, he returned to Hopkinsville to write "on current topics," was occasionally "connected with the press," and published two volumes of poetry, one called *The Star of Empire; or, Blue and Gray* (1884). 1860 Census, Ky., Christian, Hopkinsville, 138; Charles M. Meacham, *A History of Christian County, Kentucky* (Nashville, 1930), 97-98, 101, 118; Linda Joyce Redden, A Historical Study and Content Analysis of Nashville Newspapers, 1860-1865 (M. A. thesis, University of Tennessee, 1975), 37-39, 47-50; Nashville city directories (1867-70), *passim;* see also *Johnson Papers,* V, lvi, 314n.

4. That is, Mercer should either join Confederate troops under John C. Breckinridge, currently in Middle Tennessee, or face punishment appropriate for a traitor—a term in the Federal prison at Alton, Illinois.

From Peter Zinn[1]

Headquarters, Camp Chase,
November 18th 1862

Andrew Johnson
Military Governor
Tennessee, Nashville
Sir

Pursuant to orders received from the Secretary of War of the 14th inst. I have this day released the following 8 political Tennessee prisoners, on the terms and conditions, specified on bonds and forwarded by you through Special Commissioner Saml. Galloway[2] at this camp, viz.

1	E. F. Lytle	Parole to	Nashville, &	Bond	$1000.
2	D. M. Freeman	"	"	"	$1000.
3	Hazekiah Hill	"	"	"	$2000.
4	J. P. Rogers	"	"	"	$1000.
5	W H Ballard	"	"	"	$2000.
6	James Cain	"	"	"	$2000.
7	Henry Frazier	"	"	"	$2000.
8	C D Elliott	"	"	"	$5000.

G.W. Bogart the 9th name in the orders being too ill to go out at present, is retained till able.[3]

I have taken the paroles of each in Duplicate, in accordance with the terms expressed on the Bonds, and here inclose to you duplicates of their Bonds.

I am Sir very respectfully Your obedient servant
Peter Zinn Major Comdy Post

Wm J Holmes Mil. Secy.

L, DLC-JP.

1. Peter Zinn (1819-1880), Franklin County, Ohio, native, moved to Cincinnati (1837) where he was a printer and newspaper publisher before becoming a lawyer. Twice state representative (1850-51, 1862-63), he was major, 85th Ohio Inf., June through September, 1862, then major, 1st Btn., Governor's Guard (88th Inf.), Ohio Vols., commanding the prison at Camp Chase until his resignation December 29, 1862, in order to return to the legislature. Henry A. and Kate B. Ford, comps., *History of Cincinnati, Ohio* (Cleveland, 1881), 319, 424-25; CSR, RG94, NA; Frederick Dyer, *A Compendium of the War of the Rebellion* (Des Moines, Iowa, 1908), 1535-36.

2. Samuel Galloway (1811-1872), Gettysburg, Pennsylvania, native, and cousin of President James Buchanan, moved with his family to Greenfield, Ohio, in 1830. Graduating in 1833 from Miami University, he taught school (1836-40) before becoming a lawyer in 1843, serving as the Ohio secretary of state (1844-50) and later as a Republican congressman (1855-57). Appointed by Lincoln judge advocate at Camp Chase to examine southern sympathizers and prisoners, he was sent South by Johnson during Reconstruction to investigate conditions, *BDAC,* 925-26; *NCAB,* XXIII, 198.

3. Bogart signed his parole oath at Camp Chase a week later and his $2,000 bond early in December in Nashville. Bogart to Zinn, November 26; Parole Bond, December 8, 1862, Johnson Papers, LC.

To Robert Johnson, Cincinnati, Ohio

Nashville Nov 18 1862

To Col Robert Johnson
B.H.[1]

Your mother Colonel Stover & family left here this morning. they will be in Cincinnati on thursday evening[.][2]

Andrew Johnson

Tel, Johnson-Bartlett Col.

1. Burnet House.

2. This trip, evidently expected to take two full days, proved to be the first leg of a journey to safety and quiet which ended at Vevay in southern Indiana a month later.

To Abraham Lincoln

Nashville Tenn. Nov 18. 1862

His Excellency A Lincoln

I hope my telegram of 8th Sent by Courier[1] in regard to ordering Tennessee Regiments here & requesting the appointment of Col Alvan C. Gillem of the army Commanding 1st Middle Tenn Infy as Br Genl has been rec'd & favorably acted upon. I understand that Wm. B Carter of Tenn & others are making an effort to have Brig Genl Carter made a Major General[.] It would be much better to send him back to his Rank in the navy. This W B Carter procured some $20,000 from the War Dept. to aid in burning Bridges in East Tenn.[2] many of the men employed lost their lives and sacrificed large amts. of property[.] their families have rec'd not one cent from this fund[.] This matter should be looked into[.] I wish we were clear of the whole "Carter Concern." I feel in strong hopes that things will go well in a few days as we have a man at the head of this army who will fight.[3] I some time ago advised you that Buell would never redeem East Tenn.[4] & stated substantially what he has since proved himself to be.

Andrew Johnson
Mil. Gov Tenn

Tel, NHi-Lincoln Papers; DNA-RG92, Consolidated File, Nashville.

1. This was not a telegram but rather a dispatch carried by Benjamin C. Truman. See Letter to Abraham Lincoln, November 8, 1862.

2. See Letter from George A. Gowin, December 21, 1861, *Johnson Papers*, V, 75n; for Carter, see *ibid.*, IV, 670*n*.

3. Rosecrans, who had succeeded Buell on October 24.

4. See *Johnson Papers*, V, 549-50, and Letter to Abraham Lincoln, September 1, 1862.

From E. E. Platt, Jr.[1]

Memphis, Tenn. No. 20, '62

Hon Andrew Johnson,
Milty Gov of Tenn.
Dr Sir.

I embrace the first opportunity after hearing that communication is open with Nashville to inform you of my where-abouts. Shortly after arriving here I managed to get together between fifty and sixty men who wanted to enlist, provided I could guarentee them their Bounty &c in advance.[2] About that time some one in Genl Sherman's Division was paying the bounty down on enlistment. I immediately made inquiries with reference to that subject, and ascertained from Major Terrell[3] Pay Master at this place, that on the receipt of more money, he would advance to each and every new recruit his first month's pay. I had posters put up about the city to that effect, expecting the money every day so that I might muster the men into service. The money not coming, I was obliged to defer the men from time to time. They shortly commenced falling off until finally I had not a man left, when I determined it was useless to undertake to recruit any further without a fund to pay at least incidentory expenses, as I had laid out all my own money in furnishing subsistance to the men, which I was obliged to do because Genl Sherman would not approve a requisition for provisions even after he had admitted to me my right to draw them, but on the contrary he promised me every thing if I would recruit for his division. I saw it was useless to attempt doing any thing further, and was compelled to look after my own living. As I received my Commission from you on Genl Order No 75 from the War Dept, which says it will be revoked in case the Recruiting Officer does not secure an organized company, and as I have not one recruit left, I would respectfully beg to return the Commission, which I will do as soon as I learn that the mail route is regularly opened, at the same time thanking you for all past favors.[4]
I have drawn no pay, clothing nor subsistance, and have incurred no expense, except that of advertising, for which I paid as far as my means went. The remainder is due Mess Clark, Norton & Co[5] for printing of Posters, and I receipted to them for the same.
I have the honor to be Governor

Very Respectfully Your Obdt Servt
E. E. Platt Jr

ALS, DLC-JP.

1. Johnson's Executive Book for August 23, 1862, has the following entry: "appointed & commissioned E. Edward Platt, Jr. of Davidson Co. 2nd Lieut. 1st Regt. Mid Tenn Cav'y[.]" Although Platt does not appear in any Tennessee records, it is possible that he is Edward Erastus Platt (d. 1890), son of Erastus Edward (1809-1869), a Pennsylvanian who was captain of Co. G, 84th Pa. (1862-63), member of the veterans reserve corps, and

later subcommissioner of the Freedmen's Bureau. CSR (Erastus E. Platt), RG94, NA; Pension file, RG15, NA; Charles Platt, *Platt Genealogy in America* (New Hope, Pa., 1963), 108.

2. From his headquarters at No. 25 Front Row, under the enticing head, "A Good Opportunity to Make Money," and the alluring "probability that the war will end in less than six months," Platt offered potential cavalry recruits $13 per month, a $100 bounty, and 160 acres of land. Memphis *Bulletin,* October 1, 1862.

3. William G. Terrell (*c*1829-1900), Indiana native, was an "additional paymaster of volunteers" throughout the war and afterwards resided in the nation's capital. *U. S. Official Register* (1863), 187; Pension file, RG15, NA; Memphis *Bulletin,* September 30, November 28, 1862.

4. See Platt to Johnson, November 22, 1862, Johnson Papers, LC.

5. Isaac S. Clark, a job printer with R. S. Saunders at the "old Bulletin office," and Edward J. Norton, after the war a printer with the *Public Ledger*. Memphis *Bulletin*, September 11, 1862; Memphis City directories (1866-70), *passim*.

From Tennessee Union Citizens[1]

November 22, 1862

State of Tennessee

His Excellency, Andrew Johnson,
Military Governor of Tennessee.

The undersigned would respectfully, as Union Citizens of Tennessee, request you to enforce your Proclamation of May last,[2] and arrest or cause to be arrested ten rebels, or some such number, for each loyal Citizen of Tennessee now under arrest, or who may hereafter be arrested by the rebels, or under their authority, to be treated in all things as the loyal citizen may be treated by them. Such arrests, as far as practicable to be from the neighborhood of the loyal Citizen so arrested. The undersigned, in making the above request, are satisfed that they represent the Union sentiment of Tennessee and by pursuing the policy of the Proclamation, hundreds of loyal citizens, now confined in loathsome prisons will soon be released and at home with their families and others can remain at home in security. If the aid of the Military is necessary for the purpose, they would respectfully suggest that the aid of the gallant Rosecrans be invoked.

Respectfully your fellow Citizens,

Nov. 22, 1862.

Pet, DLC-JP.

1. One hundred thirty-two signatures, largely from East Tennessee, and including Brownlow, Maynard, East, Wm. J. Clift, and A. B. Shankland, make this a rather impressive petition.

2. See Proclamation Concerning Guerrilla Raids, May 9, 1862, *Johnson Papers*, V, 374-75.

To Enoch T. Carson[1]

Nashville, Tenn., Nov'r 22nd 1862

Enoch T. Carson Surveyor &c
Cincinnati

Grant no permits except upon recommendation dated after this date.[2]

Andrew Johnson
Mil: Gov'r.

Tel draft, DNA-RG393, Dept. of the Cumberland, Tels. Sent (1862).

1. See *Johnson Papers*, V, 368*n*.

2. Trade regulations worked out during Johnson's first eight months as governor had been scuttled when Bragg's offensive swept northward from Chattanooga in the fall of 1862. As a result, permits in most Federal areas in Kentucky and Tennessee were being issued only upon post commanders' recommendations. Although the Confederate drive was stopped at Perryville, Kentucky, on October 8, trade restrictions were not eased until the following year. Futrell, Federal Trade, 71-72.

From Richard M. Edwards

Louisville Ky Nov 24th 1862

Gov Johnson,

The blockade being now removed[1] (I hope forever,) I trouble you with another letter as a kind of report of progress under the authority you gave me to raise a *Battallion or Regt of Cavalry*[.]

Soon after obtaining the authority you also authorized Cook[2] a Kentuckian to raise a Regt together with Ray[3] who is a North Carolinian but has lived a while in East Tenn. These men being as unscrupulous as the Devil could wish them fearing that I would stand the best chance recruiting from East Tennessee, sent out runners in every direction with the lie in their mouths that I was a *Secessionist!* Aside from this they have learned that I was a Democrat and upon the principle that because Democrats inaugurated the rebellion there could be no good loyal men of that persuasion, they have injured my prospects vastly. Add to this Bill Pickens got in with me and then acted the Scoundrel secretly and slily to injure the Regiment—tried to get the men to leave me and go to Cook & Ray so as to secure him a position there & kept up a system [of] low underhand trickery to destroy the prospects of the Regt. Finally you gave him authority to raise a Regt & he succeeded in taking 48 men from me who after leaving tried to get back but could not get across the river. This occurred at Cincinnatti. I don't speak of your giving him authority to raise a Regt reprovingly or in bad humor for you like myself were deceived in the man. You will find yet that he is a d--nd Scoundrel as he has proved himself often heretofore. But let him go ahead. I am rid of him now and shall go on soberly and slowly to fill up my Regt and when I get it I hope I shall be able to give a good account of myself

& men, All my men will go with me to the death, because they are men of sense fighting for principle and are anxious to try their hand with the rebels. I have no drawback in my way now except to work against the Slanderous tongues of Cook & Ray's concern which I think I can manage. Unfortunately they are both d--m'd cowards and our East Tennessee friends therein will stand a poor chance to distinguish themselves. I would not say this on paper to you if I had not before told both of them the same thing.

I am going to arm my men here and get horses for them & then come on to Nashville—

If any effort is made at Nashville to obtain recruits for me (which will be done I think) I hope you will see to the matter that they obtain subsistence.

Hoping to be able to take you by the hand in a few days and greet you as in days of old

I am Very truly Your friend
R. M. Edwards

ALS, DLC-JP.

1. During Bragg's invasion of Kentucky in September and October, Nashville, held at Johnson's insistence, was left by General Buell to fend for itself. Contacts with the outside world were broken and the 12,000-man garrison under General Negley was frequently harassed by the Confederate forces of Forrest, Morgan, and Breckinridge. Communications were restored on November 14 with the return of Rosecrans' Army of the Cumberland. Hall, *Military Governor*, 62-63, 67; Robert Selph Henry, *"First with the Most" Forrest* (Indianapolis, 1944), 102, 104-6; Savage, *Life of Johnson*, 274-77.

2. For William R. Cook, see *Johnson Papers*, V, 494*n*.

3. For Daniel M. Ray, see *ibid*.

From Robert Johnson

Cincinnati Nov 24th 1862

To Gov Andrew Johnson

My equipments & horses all complete except Saddle & arms[.] they will be ready I understand this week[.] Mother is quite feeble[.] what will be the number of Stovers Regiment[?][1] I muster him in to day as Colonel[.]

Robt Johnson
Col 4 Tenn

Tel, DLC-JP.

1. Daniel Stover's commission was as colonel of the 4th Tenn. Vol. Inf. Rgt., USA, inasmuch as Robert Johnson, formerly so designated, had just (*ca.* November 1) transformed his infantry into the 1st Tenn. Cav. Like his brother-in-law, Stover never commanded his unit—recruited during the spring of 1863—in a military engagement, for he became seriously ill at summer's end and died a year later. *Tennesseans in the Civil War,* I, 318-19, 383; *Tenn. Adj. Gen. Report* (1866), 75.

From Robert L. Stanford[1]

Louisville Ky. Nov. 24th 1862

Hon A. Johnson Military Gov. and
Brig. Genl. U.S.V.
Dear Sir:

It has been a long time since I wrote you[2] & you may think that I have forgotten you, but not so, I have the same sentiments of high regard for you now that I have so often expressed for you both publickly & privately. And I to day desire to renew my sentiments of esteem & regard for you as both a public & private benefactor[.]

I can but state that so long as I live I shall ever be found ready to give my willing might to promote your interest, while, we are both permitted to dwell upon earth. Gov. I never can forget past favours and I constantly wish for an opportunity to requite such kindness, goodness & special favours as I have recieved at your hands. Pardon me & don't think that I attempt to exibit any other than the real sentiments of my heart, & reflect any other than the genuine aspirations of thousands, when, I tell you that I have not a revolving doubt but what you will be put in nomination for the next presidencey. I have conversed with hundreds of prominent, & I may say distinguished men upon this subject, and I have never found but one man who did not desire that you should recieve the nomination and he was for Abraham Lincon for President & for you for vice Presidint, this man is Maj. Bababer[3] one of the paymasters from Ohio, a good man & a strong Linconite & as strong for Gov. A Johnson of Tennessee for vice President. My opportunities for seeing prominent men all over the loyal states has been uncommonly good. General Morgans Division had many prominent visitors from many of the states North. I was Medical Director of his division for months & being at head quarters at all times gave me many opportunities to make important acquaintances, & believe me that I made use of my chances to learn the feeling of the people. You may think that I should rather spend all my energies in puting down the rebellion & then talk about who is to be the next President & it may be that it would be best, yet I am for you to fill that office during the four years following Lincolns term, & whether the rebellion is crushed out before then or not, the people will when the time comes make a president. I served after the first of August last up until the 17th of Sept. last in charge of Genl. hospital at Barbourville Ky. Then with Genl. Morgans Division while making its exit out of Kentucky. I was then assigned to duty in charge of Genl Hospital No. 12 in this City, & here I have had fine opportunities to bring before prominent men from all parts of the loyal states your claims for the next President. I find that you are spoken of before any other. All point to you as the man[.] Your speeches have made for you a world wide fame. Your stand & labours for the Union will make you President. Mark the assertion—I will not say prediction for I think it is a moral certainy. I should like very much to see you and talk matters & things over. I shall commense in a very short time to publish a series of articles under the title of the war policy of the nation, in which each actor will be seen as he is & has been since the commencement of the rebellion. I shall write over the signature of *Bona Fide.*[4] These articles may be interesting to some, while, they will be any thing else to others[.] I intend to make the fur fly off of many men[5] who have taken part in both politics & military opperations, while, I will brighten the mettle of which genuine men are made. Gov, There are hundreds of officials who need showing up. I have been no mean observer of matters, men & things since I entered the army, & I think but few men have had better opportunities to look into the characters of men. I have made numerous acquaintances all over the loyal states. I have had thousands under my charge at different points, these, have acquaintances all over the country many of whom come into hospital to see their friends[.] I suffer no opportunity to escape when I meet with a man of talent & standing to learn the feeling & sentiments of the people touching the character & prospects of certain men for the Presidency[.] Gov. will you believe me when I tell you that at least 9 out of 10 are strait out for you for the next presidency.

Pardon me for speaking out so plainly to you, for you have known me long enough to be satisfied that there is no flattery in me, & that when I am for a man I am for him with my whole soul.

Continue as you have in well doing & you will find your reward in being promoted to the highest office within the gift of the people of the U. S.

With respect I am your obt Servt
R L Stanford Surg. U. S. V.
In Charge of Hospital No. 12

I have written the foregoing in great haste without time to revise or even read it over for correction.

ALS, DLC-JP.

1. See *Johnson Papers,* IV, 603*n*.

2. Lengthy letters on December 13 and 31, 1861, had preceded a one-page epistle of February 14, the most recent Stanford letter preserved in the Johnson Papers, LC.

3. For Richard P. L. Baber, see *Johnson Papers,* V, 564*n*.

4. A search of Louisville, Cincinnati, and Nashville newspapers has not revealed any *"Bona Fide"* articles during the next two months. For an earlier letter under that *nom de plume,* see *Johnson Papers,* V, 144, 145*n*.

5. To attack successfully. Eric Partridge, *A Dictionary of Historical Slang* (Harmondsworth, England, 1972), 334.

To Abraham Lincoln

Nashville, Tenn., Nov'r 24 1862

His Excellency Abraham Lincoln
Washington City

We are of opinion that the appointment of Colonel A. C. Gillem of 1st Middle Tennessee Regiment as Brigadier General will be a good one and ought to be made.[1] He would render valuable service in connection with Tennessee forces. Moreover he will fight, a quality much needed by our Generals. He is a native Tennessean & 12 years Army officer.

W. G. Brownlow
Horace Maynard[2]
Andrew Johnson Mil: Gov'r.

Tel draft, DNA-RG393, Dept. of the Cumberland, Tels. Sent (1862).

1. Gillem was by this time clearly established as a Johnson protégé. It would, however, be August, 1863, before this promotion was achieved. Warner, *Generals in Blue,* 175.

2. For William G. Brownlow, Knoxville editor, and Horace Maynard, East Tennessee's one remaining Congressman, see *Johnson Papers,* I, 130*n*; III, 286*n*.

From E. M. Reynolds[1]

Springfield Tenn
Nov. 25th 1862

Gov. Andrew Johnson

Our Citizens arrested yesterday three Men, one professing to be Morgans Men but are nothing moore or less than thieves travling through the Country Committing depredations upon quiet Citizens[.] The Citizens of Our place have placed them in jail and request that you will send a Guard (it will not require Moore than Ten Men) and have them Taken To Head Quarters and dealt with as they deserve[.] two of Men are named McCool and live near Buena Vista Ferry[.] the other is named Marcum lives in Coffee County.[2] Your immediate attention is requested— Please give the Messenger Mr. Asa Harper[3] a letter So that he can get a pass to riturn to Springfield[.][4]

Most Respectfully E. M Reynolds.

ALS, CLU.

1. See *Johnson Papers,* V 506*n*.

2. James V. (b. *c*1833) and John McCool (b. *c*1841), residents of Davidson County and privates in Co. G, 2nd (Robinson's) Tenn. Inf., CSA, were listed in February, 1862, as "Absent within the enemy's lines." On November 24, in company with a Markham or Marcum, who has not been identified, they caused considerable alarm east of Springfield by taking mules belonging to Mrs. Martha M. Fort and others and by being "very boisterous and threatening rude and profane in their talk and deportment." 1860 Census,

Tenn., Davidson, 23rd Dist., 136; CSR, RG109, NA; Testimony relative to John and J. V. McCool and Markham, Johnson Papers, LC.

3. Asa Harper (*c*1834-*fl*1880) was a Robertson County farmer and blacksmith with $2,140 real and $1,500 personal property on the eve of the war. 1860 Census, Tenn., Robertson, 9th Dist., 15; (1880), 38.

4. In forwarding the letter to Rosecrans, Johnson observed: "Mr. Reynolds, the writer of the within, is a strong Union man, and his statements are entitled to the fullest credit."

Receipt from Enoch T. Carson

Office U. S. Depositary
Cincinati Nov. 25/62

Gov. Andrew Johnson, by Col. Johnson has deposited in the Vault in this office 1 sealed package of papers marked Gov. Andrew Johnson of Tennessee— Also one sealed bag of *gold* said to contain $1800. both packages subject to the *order* of Gov. Andrew Johnson of Tennessee,

Enoch T. Carson
U. S. Depositary

The Eighteen Hundred dollars in gold returned, to Governor Johnston January 1864.[1]

E. T. Carson

ADS, DLC-JP.

1. There is a similar endorsement across the face.

List of State and Railroad Bonds[1]

[November 25, 1862]

Statement of Bonds Deposited in the United States Depository at Cincinnati Ohio Nov 25 1862, by Col Robt Johnson for Gov Andrew Johnson of Tennessee

10 Regular Tennessee State Bonds

To Wit—

1 No	536—	Date	1st	Jany	1860
2 "	9048	"	1	"	1859
3 "	533	"	1	"	1860
4 "	9861	"	1	"	1859
5	10086	"	1	"	"
6	9860	"	1	"	"
7	9047	"	1	"	"
8	517	"	1	"	1860
9	535	"	1	"	"
10	534	"	1	"	"

19 Endorsed Bonds Nashville & Chattanooga Rail Road, Viz

1	No 321—	Date	of Bond 1st Jany 1854—	Endorsed	28 Feby 1854	
2	" 484	"	" " " "	"	20 "	"
3	" 650	"	" " " "	"	15— "	"
4	307	"	" " " "	"	28 "	"
5	304	"	" " " "	"	" "	"
6	194	"	" " " "	"	" "	"
7	310	"	" " " "	"	" "	"
8	295	"	" " " "	"	" "	"
9	306	"	" " " "	"	" "	"
10—	324	"	" " " "	"	" "	"
11—	317	"	" " " "	"	" "	"
12—	263	"	" " " "	"	" "	"
13—	330	"	" " " "	"	" "	"
14—	258	"	" " " "	"	" "	"
15—	312	"	" " " "	"	" "	"
16—	172	"	" " " "	"	" "	"
17—	109	"	" " " "	"	" "	"
18	287	"	" " " "	"	" "	"
19	275	"	" 1st July 1852	"	May 5th 1853	

1 Endorsed Bonds of East Tennessee & Virginia Rail-Road
No 94—issued May 1st 1856—endorsed 2nd June 1856

29	coupons	due	1st	July	1861
2	"	"	1st	May	1861

31 aggrgate—

Robt. Johnson
Daniel. Stover

D, DLC-JP18.

1. Some, possibly all, of these bonds had been returned to Johnson a year earlier by the East Tennessee and Virginia Railroad which had held them briefly on loan. *Johnson Papers,* III, 197-99; Robert Johnson memorandum, June 28, 1861, Series 18, Johnson Papers, LC.

From John A. Hamilton[1]

Sparta Illinois
Nov—26—1862

Hon. Andrew Johnson:—

Sir: I wish hereby to lay before you the condition of my Union friends in Middle Tennessee, hoping that you will be able and disposed to do something for them. They live in Lincoln Co. 8 to 10 miles west and north—west of Fayetteville, on the waters of Swan Creek. I have some friends too in Marshall & Bedford Counties. About 3 months ago a young brother of mine came from there,—run away by gangs of Guerrillas that infested their neighborhood,—and enlisted in 111th Illinois, raised at Salem Ill. & is now in the army.[2] A few days ago an older brother came—with a rebel conscript officer after him; but he made good his escape—reaching the union lines in West Tennessee & coming north, via Columbus Ky. He states that there were many union men—mostly young men, who were in great trouble, the rebel officers having conscripted them & told them they would send a guard or company of armed men after them. Some talked of hiding, others of resisting. He thought his only chance to escape being pressed into the rebel service, was to flee. He left his family, property—all.

Now I wish to say that I & your other Tennessee friends in this place & in Salem, Ill. hope you will use your power, as our army advances, to look after the safety of these and other union citizens. William Wyatt is one of the leading union men—a man of property & influence. Tates, Carey's, Blair's Taylor's & others are union. I have an Aunt Hamilton living two miles west of Fayetteville, who, with all her sons are rebels. My mother & brothers live ten miles west of Fayetteville on the waters of swan Creek.[3] I mention names & places, that the authorities may retaliate on their the union citizens rebel neighbors if they have committed outrages on the peaceful union citizens of those localities[.] Thomas Montgomery & brothers[4] in Marshall & Bedford Counties are personal friends & strong union men. Hoping you will have the power & *will use it* to protect all union citizens in Middle Tennessee, I remain yours for the Union, the Constitution & the Enforcement of the laws,[5]

John A. Hamilton.

P.S. I hope in the name of heaven, you will run all rebels south out of Tennessee. Many of our friends there have lost property by the rebels—*they should be paid out of rebel—property.*

Respectfully J. A. H.

ALS, DLC-JP.

1. John A. Hamilton (b. *c*1832), Lincoln County native and teacher, was in charge of Lewisburg Male Academy at the opening of the war. A silent unionist until the election of June 8, 1861, he became more outspoken and was obliged to leave Tennessee in mid-August. Hamilton to Johnson, August 30, 1861, November 28, 1862, Johnson Papers, LC; Sistler, *1850 Tenn. Census,* III, 95.

2. Probably his brother James (b. *c*1838) who, as J. H. Hamilton, enlisted in Co. A on August 12, serving until June 6, 1865. *Ibid.; Report of the Adjutant General of the State of Illinois, 1861-1866* (8 vols., Springfield, 1886), VI, 125.

3. Hamilton obviously wished to distinguish his immediate family from his disloyal relatives. His mother Elizabeth Morton Hamilton (b. *c*1793) might have been mistaken for his Aunt Elizabeth Hamilton (b. *c*1807). The similarity was further reinforced by the fact that each of the Hamilton widows had sons named David, James, John, and William living in Lincoln County. Sistler, *1850 Tenn. Census,* III, 95; 1860 Census, Tenn., Lincoln, 11th Dist., 151.

4. Robert S. (1829-*fl*1886) and Thomas S. Montgomery (1843-*fl*1886), both born in South Carolina, were sons of Thomas Montgomery (b. 1808). In 1855 Robert began a dry-goods business at Palmetto in partnership with Samuel Carpenter, often being aided

by his teen-age brother who served as clerk. After the war Thomas engaged in mercantile business at Farmington (1868-74) before returning to Palmetto to purchase Carpenter's share in Robert's business. *Goodspeed's Bedford,* 1164.

5. Two days later, without any mention of his recent letter, although reminding the governor that he had written "from Salem Illinois, last spring & summer, making application for an appointment under you," Hamilton renewed his request for a place, "either in the civil or military service." He gave as references the Montgomery brothers who had presented his case to Johnson during the previous summer and Charles A. French, Fayetteville postmaster and editor of the *Lincoln Journal,* the latter "if not a rebel. . . . I have not been able to learn certainly how he stands at this time." Hamilton to Johnson, November 28, 1862, Johnson Papers, LC.

To William D. McLelland[1]

Nashville, Tenn., Nov'r 28th 1862

W. D. McLelland
Burnet House Cincinnati

We can authorize the raising of no more Cavalry until the regiments now forming are filled. So many commissioned at once have caused conflict & defeated in fact the raising of some Regiments. I would like to gratify you and him,[2] and will do so as soon as it is consistent with the public service. I was more than gratified to learn that you and Holtsinger[3] had reached and united with East Tennesseans. and hope ere long to see you all at this place on your way to East Tennessee.

Accept the best wishes of my heart.
Andrew Johnson Mil: Gov'r.

(If not at Burnet House—send to Camp Dennison, O.)

Tel draft, DNA-RG393, Dept. of the Cumberland, Tels. Sent (1862).

1. The preceding day McLelland had inquired about a petition forwarded to the governor through Horace Maynard asking that Capt. Alfred J. Lane "be commissioned as Col with authority to raise a Regt of Loyal Tennessee[.]" Would Johnson telegraph his reply: "we are very anxious that he Sould have it & repair immediately to Green & Cocke Counties & get our friends out[.] he is the man to do it[.]" McLelland to Johnson, November 27, 1862, Johnson Papers, LC. For McLelland, a former tailor and Greeneville friend, see *Johnson Papers*, III 454*n*. A center of controversy over his recruiting for Robert Johnson's regiment, he nevertheless became captain of Co. H. CSR, RG94, NA.

2. Alfred J. Lane (*c*1825-1863), Jefferson County-born farmer with $2,100 real and $1,200 personal property, after serving as private and sergeant, 2nd Tenn. Inf., USA, transferred in April, 1862, to Co. D, 1st Tenn. Cav. Although denied the authority he sought, he was subsequently given detached duty in East Tennessee, recruiting for a regiment of infantry under Johnson's authority, when he was killed in a skirmish near Cumberland Gap on July 1, 1863. 1860 Census, Tenn., Greene, 19th Dist., 180; CSR, RG94, NA; Carter, *First Tenn. Cav.,* 288.

3. For John P. Holtsinger (1813-1875), Greeneville's Cumberland Presbyterian minister, who served as a chaplain throughout the war, being mustered out as "Supernumery," April 18, 1865, see *Johnson Papers*, III, 647*n*; Reynolds, *Greene County Cemeteries*, 94; *Tenn. Adj. Gen. Report* (1866), 303.

Guarantee of Protection[1]

[Nashville, *ca.*November 28, 1862]

This is to certify, That the citizen named in the within Bond,[2] having properly executed the same, with approved surety, he is entitled from henceforth, to the full protection and support of the Government of the United States and which is hereby pledged to him. All persons military as well as civil, are hereby commanded to respect him, as a good and loyal citizen, in the full enjoyment of his property, both real and personal. All foraging is hereby forbidden, upon his premises unless actually necessary, for the support and well-being of the Federal Armies, in which case all possible care shall be exercised, and full receipt given by the officer in charge, which shall be duly recognized, and the property paid for by the United States Government. Officers in command of foraging expeditions will be held to the strictest accountability for the protection herein guaranteed.

W. S. Rosecrans,
Maj.-Gen. Comd'g Dep. of the Cumberland
Andrew Johnson,
Military Governor of the State of Tenn.

Nashville *Union,* November 29, 1862.

1. In the "authoritative explanation" which accompanied this document and the sample bond in the Nashville *Dispatch*, November 29, it was pointed out that Rosecrans and Johnson, after "full examination and consultation with many of the prominent citizens of Nashville of various previous views," had drawn up the guarantee in terms "unobjectionable, in sentiment or phraseology, to all truly wise and conservative men, who desire the speedy return of peace and harmony." Everyone in Nashville, the state, and ultimately the South is urged to subscribe and receive the protection offered, because "By giving this bond the people become surety and hostages, one for another. By all giving it, there is no odious distinction made, and no one class of our people is set up in judgment against another."

2. Four days later the first sentence had been altered to read: "This is to certify that the citizen, within named, having taken the oath of allegiance, and having properly executed a Bond for the faithful observance of the peace, with approved surety, he is. . . ." Nashville *Union,* December 3, 1862.

From Isaac R. Hawkins[1]

Head Quarters 2d West Tenn Cavalry
Trenton Tenn. Nov. 29th 1862

Hon Andrew Johnson
Governor of the state of Ten

Dear sir As I now have what I regard as a safe and reliable opportunity, of sending you a small package, I embrace it to inform you of the fact I received your communication inclosing my commission as colonel of the 2d regiment of West Ten Cavalry— prior to the time of the receipt there of we had holden an election for Maj & Lieut col, at which election I was elected Lieut Col without opposition and T A Smith[2] was elected Maj and we had been accordingly musterd— It was however a matter of no small gratification to me to receive so decided an evidence of your confidence as the commission and I hope that you may never regret that you confered it[.] While I am pleased at the distinction thus confered upon me I regret to inform you that in point of arms, horses & horse equipments we are in the same bad condition in which we were when I last wrote you not having recd up to this date more than two saddles 14 halters & less than half a dozen bridles but even this does not dishearten my men, we have had the pleasure of learning the men who would trample our government and liberties under foot, that they must be as careful as we have been forced to be, and we think, let the fate of other states be as it may that Tennessee can never be a part of the Southern confederacy.

Col Jacob Fry[3] is now the commander of the forces at this place and Humboldt, and is pursuing a mild and conciliatory course and I think it is being attended with happy results.

On Monday the people will hold a convention at this place for the purpose of nominating a candidate for congress, and I have but little doubt but that a large vote will be polled[.][4]

War as you are well aware, is at all times attended with great inconvenience, among which, the least is not the great uncertainty attendant. And much to my regret there has been issued an order by the Gen' commanding this district suspending civil authority[.] however well this may have been atoned [intended?], I doubt the policy. It has been my opinion that the true policy was to set in motion at the earliest practicable moment all the machinery of the state government, believing as I do that the people can and will be much easier induced to respect civil than military authority, and I earnestly hope that your excellency may be able to devise some means consistent with the safety of the country by which the courts in this section may at an early day be reestablished[.]

You will find in my friend Judge Samuel Williams a true exponent of the Union Sentiment in this section, and a man in whoom the Union men have the utmost confidence—and he will be able to lay before you a more correct statement of the true condition of public affairs in this section than I could in a note of this character and I hope you may find it convenient, & compatible with your feeling, as I am shure it will be with the public interest to hear him[.]

Isaac R. Hawkins

LS, DLC-JP.

1. Isaac R. Hawkins (1818-1880), Maury County native and lawyer, was a resident of Carroll County with $10,150 real and $15,116 personal property in 1860. A lieutenant during the Mexican War and a delegate to the Washington Peace Conference in 1861, he was a circuit court judge the following year before becoming lieutenant colonel, 7th Tenn. Cav., USA. Twice captured by Forrest's command, he survived the war to become a

Republican congressman (1866-71). 1860 Census, Tenn., Carroll, 12th Dist., 215; *BDAC,* 1027; *Tennesseans in the Civil War,* I, 336-38.

2. Thomas A. Smith (b. *c*1817), North Carolina-born Henderson County farmer with $700 real and $450 personal property, served as captain, Co. A, and major, 7th Tenn. Cav., USA. Captured at Union City in March, 1864, he was imprisoned near Charleston, South Carolina, paroled, and discharged from the service nine months later. 1860 Census, Tenn., Henderson, 12th Dist., 172; CSR, RG94, NA.

3. Jacob Fry (*c*1800-1881) of Greene County, Illinois, was sheriff, colonel in the Black Hawk War, a major general of state militia, and for many years after 1827 one of Illinois' and Michigan's canal commissioners. Temporarily living in California, he represented Placer County in the state senate (1851) and in 1856 became collector of customs at Chicago. While colonel of the 61st Ill. Inf. during the war, he contracted a disease which led to the loss of eyesight and retirement to his farm near Carrollton, Illinois. Charles Bradshaw, "Greene County: Born 100 Years Ago," *Journal of the Illinois State Historical Society,* XIII (1920), 218; New York *Times,* February 5, 1881.

4. In the ninth congressional district convention held at Trenton December 1, Isaac's brother Alvin, the later governor, was nominated. Memphis *Bulletin,* December 13, 1862.

From Pitser Miller

November 29, 1862, Bolivar; ALS, DLC-JP.

Hardeman County leader, now at Cairo, Illinois, reports that "it is the wish of a good many good men that you Issue Writs of Eliction for a Congress Man from our District & we will try and return you a good man." Worried by the difficulties of reorganization, including the "want of Confidence that the Confederates can be kept away," he avers that "4/5' of my County are and have been opposed to the breaking up of the Union," but because of violence have been afraid to oppose the rebel faction. In a postscript: "the Enemy burnt the trusling on the RR 8 ms. this Side Holly Spring" which will retard the movement of the Union army.

To Jeremiah T. Boyle

Nashville, Tenn., Nov'r 29, 1862

Brig Genl. Boyle,
Louisville, Ky

D. T. McGavock[1] has just sent me your telegram. He states that the mulatto boy Watson in service of Dr. Swartzwelder[2] surgeon 1st Ohio artillery, is a free man of color. Mr. McGavock is a reliable man.

Andrew Johnson
Mil: Gov'r.

Tel draft, DNA-RG393, Dept. of the Cumberland, Tels. Sent (1862).

1. David T. McGavock (1813-1866), Davidson County native, was a wealthy farmer and businessman who, having studied medicine, was often referred to as Dr. McGavock, despite the fact that he did not practice. Immediately before the war he was believed to be worth one million dollars, although the census records only $550,000. 1860 Census, Tenn., Davidson, 13th Dist., 158; Nashville *Union and American,* January 11, 1866.

2. Adam C. Swartzwelder (b. *c*1821), Pennsylvania-born physician, resided at Ironton, Ohio, where he claimed $2,000 real and $500 personal property in 1860. Serving as a surgeon in the 18th Ohio Inf. (May-August, 1861), later in Bty. A, 1st Ohio Lgt. Arty., he was discharged December 5, 1862. Chief surgeon of the Freedmen's Bureau in Tennessee (November, 1865-July, 1867), he later functioned in the same capacity in Louisiana. Despite charges of graft and corruption at his New Orleans headquarters, no

action was taken. 1860 Census, Ohio, Lawrence, Ironton, 46; CSR, RG94, NA; Paul D. Phillips, A History of the Freedmen's Bureau in Tennessee (Ph.D. dissertation, Vanderbilt University, 1964), 92-94.

From J. L. Briese[1]

[Nashville, December, 1862]

To His Excelency Andrew Johnson
Mil. Gov. State of Tennessee
Sir

Being one of those persons who has lived in Dr. T R Jennings[2] House for the last Six months and having been informed that a false and malicious rumor has been brought to your notice that the occupants of the Said House were moving out and carring off the furniture belonging to Dr. Jennings. And being desiruous to correct and conterdict all Such Statements I have taken this method of informing you that no furniture of any discription has been moved or taken out of the House—or abused in any maner whatsoever Since I have been one of its inmates. But on the contrary each of the occupants have paid from Ten to Twelve Dollars pr Week to the Servants of Dr Jennings which has enable them to get Something to live on—and keep the House in good order which I understand was in accordance with the wishes of Dr. Jennings. Hoping this will Satisfy you—that no wrong was done—and no harm intinded

I am most Respectfully Your Obt Sevt
J. L. Briese

ALS, DLC-JP.

1. Not identified.

2. Thomas R. Jennings, Nashville physician, was head of physiology in the University of Nashville medical department. McBride and Robison, *Biographical Directory*, I, 405; see also *Johnson Papers*, I, 57*n*.

From Horace Maynard

Washington Dec 1, 1862

Dr. Sir

I entered the city yesterday. This morning I called on the Ordnance officer, who informed me that only 500 carbines had been sent for Stokes' Cavalry that the supply had not allowed them to provide more than 400 or 500 to each regt.[1]

I learn that Gov. Harris, I. G. in a recent conversation with a party he supposed to be a Secessionist, said in Substance "When we catch Andy Johnson, we are going to flog him alive, & then tan his skin into leather," not understood as speaking figuratively, but literally & in earnest.

I have seen the Secretary of War, but do not learn that any Genrl. from Tennessee has been nominated.

Supplies for a Union Outpost.
Courtesy Tennessee State Library and Archives.

Great interest is manifested in the condition of our affairs at Nashville & many questions asked.

I am very Truly Yours
Horace Maynard

His Excy Andrew Johnson

ALS, DLC-JP.

1. For months Johnson had been trying to secure additional carbines. On November 15 he wired Col. Thomas Swords, chief quartermaster at Louisville, asking "if a lot of carbines five-hundred (500) sent from Washington to my address some time ago have been forwarded"; four days later Capt. Walworth Jenkins responded that "these arms it appears have not been received." On the twenty-second Johnson reminded Gen. James W. Ripley, chief of ordnance, that the second consignment of five hundred carbines promised the previous July had not been received and asked that they "be sent forward without delay." Ripley replied that "A large supply of arms for the mounted troops in Tennessee has been sent to Gen Rosecrans[.] You will have to look to him to arm the ballance of the first Tenn Cavalry as the War Dept can spare no more carbines for the present[.]" Johnson to Swords, November 15, 1862; Jenkins to Johnson, November 19, 1862; Johnson to Ripley, November 22, 1862, Tels. Recd., Vol. 33, U. S. Mil. Tel., RG107, NA; Ripley to Johnson, December 1, 1862, Johnson Papers, LC.

From Leonidas C. Houk

Head Quarters 3rd Regt E Ten Vols
Camp near Nashville Tenn.
Decr 2nd 1862

Hon Andrew Johnson
Military Gov. Tenn.
Dear Sir

I make you a present of the horse I send you by Boy.

You will please accept him as a token of the regard I have for your patriotism![1]

I desire you to ride him in your triumphal return home to our beloved East Tennessee.

He will carry you six miles an hour and never go out of a walk. Try him, by paying us a visit.

I am truly Your Friend
L. C. Houk Col.
3rd Regt E Tenn Vols U.S. Army.

ALS, DLC-JP.

1. There is no evidence to indicate whether the governor, with his exaggerated sense of probity, accepted this present. As President he would consistently decline similar proffers.

From Robert Johnson

Burnett House Cincinnati
Dec 3 1862

To Hon Andrew Johnson

Mother is very low[.] had I better take her to the country[?] too much noise here[.][1]

Robt Johnson

Tel, DLC-JP.

1. A week later he reported: "Mother better[.]" Robert to Johnson, December 10, 1862, Johnson Papers, LC.

From William Truesdail[1]

Head-Quarters Fourteenth Army Corps,
Department of the Cumberland
Nashville, Dec 3d—1862.

Gov A Johnson

Sir— Mr John F. Fletcher[2] is under arrest, upon charge of being a spy. The evidence is strong, and accumulating. Maj Gen Rosecrans has appointed a Commission to try his & other spy cases. Any delay in his trial is not to be laid to the charge of this office, but to circumstances beyond our control. I will try to bring forward the case, tomorrow.[3]

Yours, very Respectfully
Wm Truesdail
Chief Army Police.

ALS, DLC-JP.

1. William Truesdail (1815-1867), born in Chautauqua County, New York, engaged in a variety of business enterprises in the vicinity of Erie, Pennsylvania, before becoming a railroad contractor in Panama (1849-50) and later in the Mississippi Valley and Texas. Appointed military superintendent of the Northern Missouri Railroad in 1861, he soon contracted to supply Grant's forces with beef, and subsequently was in charge of the army police and secret service under Generals Pope and Rosecrans. Although called "colonel," he was a civilian. That Johnson did not like Truesdail is evident in his correspondence; further, in September, 1863, the governor was charging that he had been "deep in all kinds of plunder, and has kept the army inactive to enable his accomplices and himself to become rich by jobs and contracts." By then, Rosecrans, according to the friendly *Press,* had relieved Truesdail "of his arduous duties," following his earlier offer to resign. C. A. Dana to E. M. Stanton, September 8, 1863, *OR,* Ser. 1, XXX, Pt. I, 183; Fitch, *Annals,* 346-51; Nashville *Press,* August 25, 1863; Nashville *Republican Banner,* November 30, 1867.

2. Fletcher emerges from the shroud of history only as an accused spy. Although referred to as a Davidson County resident, he appears neither in the census nor in Nashville directories. Nor is the precise nature of his treasonable activities revealed by the available evidence. Arrested on November 26, given a hearing early in January, he was "ordered to be sent to Alton Ill. Military Prison, there to be held until his trial can be had, in accordance with military usage." Appearing there on a "Roll of Citizens of Tennessee now in Confinement," dated April 9, 1863, he was evidently returned to Nashville for trial, for in January, 1864, while in that city's penitentiary, he was ordered "North of the Army lines,

not to return during the present rebellion, except by permission from this Head Quarters," presumably as a result of the trial "in accordance with military usage." He may be the John Fletcher, "an aged man, in poor health from Tennessee, where he was once in prosperous circumstances," who sought permission in December, 1864, to move from St. Louis to Chicago. Citizens File, RG109, NA; W. A. Browning memorandum, April 9, 1863; William Truesdail to Johnson, January 10, 1863, Johnson Papers, LC.

3. Provost Judge John Fitch called up Fletcher's case the following day. That Johnson was especially interested in Fletcher's case seems clear; however, no explanation for such concern has been discovered. The present letter was obviously in response to an inquiry from the governor; a subsequent "note of Jan. 8th," elicited a reply from Truesdail two days later; and an April 8 memorandum in the hand of the governor's secretary, William A. Browning, lists the charges against Fletcher and two others, information obtained presumably at Johnson's request, from Col. William Hoffman, U. S. commissary general of prisoners. Fitch to Johnson, December 4, 1862, *ibid.*

To James W. Ripley[1]

Nashville, Tenn., Dec'r 3d, 1862

Brig Genl. Ripley,
Ch'f of Ordnance
Washington City.
General:

I have to acknowledge the receipt of your communication of the 26th. Ult'o, enclosing circular from War Dep't, under date of 15th. Oct'o last, calling for a list of the different Regiments of Infantry, Cavalry, and Artillery in the service of the United States from the State of Tennessee. The communications on this subject, of prior date, to which you allude, have not yet been received.[2]

I regret to state that, owing to the peculiar condition of affairs in this State, and the almost entire withdrawal of Federal forces from that portion of the State which was supposed to be restored to Federal control, it has been impossible for us to organize anything like a military system, with the view of proceeding under the respective calls of the President for troops. Notwithstanding the great difficulties under which we have labored, we have succeeded in organizing, under authority of the Secretary of War, and in conformity with act of Congress approved July 22, 1861, for the service of the United States, the following forces, to wit:

Eastern Division

1st.	Regt.	East	Tennessee	Infantry—	Col.	R. K. Bird
2nd.	"	"	"	"	"	J. P. T. Carter
3rd.	"	"	"	"	"	L. C. Houk
4th.	"	"	"	"	"	Robt Johnson
5th.	"	"	"	"	"	J.T. Shelley
6th.	"	"	"	"	"	J.A. Cooper
7th.	"	"	"	"	"	Wm Clift
1st.	"	"	"	Cavalry	"	Robt Johnson
2nd.	"	"	"	"	"	Wm R. Cook

The 4th E. T. Inf'y has been changed to 1st. E. T. Cav'y, Col Robt. Johnson, Comd'g; the 3d. E. T. Cavalry, Col R. M. Edwards, and the 8th & 9th E. T. Inf'y are now organizing, and will soon be mustered in.

Middle Division.

1st.	Middle	Tennessee	Infantry	Col	A. C. Gillem
1st.	"	"	Cavalry	"	Wm B. Stokes
Battery	"A."	Tennessee	Artillery	Capt.	E. P. Abbott.[3]

Western Division.

1st.	Regiment	West	Tennessee	Cavalry.	Col	Fielding Hurst
2nd.	"	"	"	"	"	I R. Hawkins
1st.	"	"	"	Infantry	"	J. A. Rodgers

The foregoing list embraces all the troops from the State of Tennessee in the service of the United States at the present time.

Authority has been granted various persons of influence in the several Divisions of the State to recruit Regiments, and, as soon as the Army of the Cumberland moves forward, extending our lines so as to embrace the whole State, Tennessee will, beyond all doubt, furnish her quota of troops. Since my entrance upon the discharge of duty as Military Governor of Tennessee, there has been no time at which we could favorably proceed to effect a State military organization. We have not, in that respect, proceeded so far as to appoint an Adjutant General of the State,—hence the incompleteness of our military record.

Circumstances now favoring such action, a proper military organization will be promptly effected, and we shall be happy to furnish your office with such information in regard to our operation as you may, from time, require.

Very Resp'y Your Obt. Servt.
Andrew Johnson Mil Gov'r.

Copy, T-Mil. Gov's Papers, 1862-65, Corres. of Andrew Johnson.

1. See *Johnson Papers*, IV, 588*n*.

2. Inasmuch as Nashville, due to Confederate activity, was largely cut off from the outside during October and the first half of November, it is quite probable that the previous requests, dated October 15 and 30, "miscarried," as Ripley grudgingly suggests in his of November 26. Ripley to Johnson, November 26, 1862, Mil. Gov's Papers, Tennessee State Library and Archives.

3. Ephraim P. Abbott (b. *c*1833), native Ohioan and surveyor at Zanesville, enlisted at Nashville in September, 1862, and was dismissed in March, 1864, for absence without leave. 1860 Census, Ohio, Muskingum, Zanesville, 2nd Ward, 134; CSR, RG94, NA.

From William S. Rosecrans

December 4, 1862, Nashville; LS, DLC-JP.

Requests that Johnson appoint commissioners "in the various counties of the State, where it is practical or politic to do so, for the purpose of administering the oath of allegiance or noncombatant parole, and taking the necessary bonds—"and that he designate a commissioner to accompany Rosecrans' army to do the same for "all persons, falling into our hands, who are desirous of taking either."

Petition to the President[1]

State of Tennessee,
Executive Department,
Nashville, Decr. 4th 1862

To His Excellency Abraham Lincoln
President of the United States
Dear Sir:

The undersigned citizens, of the state of Tennessee and loyal citizens of the United States respectfully but most earnestly request that should you issue a proclamation on the first of January 1863 designating the states and parts of states that may be deemed by you to be in rebellion against the Government in pursuance of your proclamation of the 22nd of Sept. 1862 the State of Tennessee be not included[.]

We enter into no discussion of the validity or constitutionality of such proclamation[.] But aside from any such discussion we are assured that sound policy as well as strict justice to our people demands the exemption of Tennessee[.]

We have had but one fair vote on the question of secession in the state and that was held on the 9th of February 1861 which resulted in favor of the Union by a majority of more than sixty four thousand votes. The vote of the 8th of June 1861 for separation and representation was invalid unfair and not a true expression of the real feelings and wishes of the people of the state. That vote was taken under circumstances well known to the country and they will not be again repeated[.]

We earnestly desire another fair and unbiased vote and in the present condition of our state it is impossible for such vote to be taken. The whole of East Tennessee portions of West Tennessee and all of Middle Tennessee excepting a few miles around our Capitol are in possession of the rebel army and where it is not in possession, the Union army is in occupation[.] The state is almost entirely a military camp[.] This thing must be changed —these rebel forces expelled and dispersed and the minds of the people quieted before we can possibly have anything like a fair expression of the wishes of the people. We most anxiously desire this result and as speedily as possible believing as we do that at the earliest opportunity Tennessee will place herself on the list of the loyal states of the Union[.] As we have stated we are encompassed by the military and all the functions of the civil government of the state are practically suspended and it will be impossible for us to take the vote of the state until the Government shall have expelled the rebel forces from her limits[.]

In view of these facts we repeat the request that Tennessee be not embraced in any proclamation of the character specified. We have not the slightest hesitation or doubt as to the expediency wisdom and justice of the course we have indicated and we trust that you will be able to agree with us in our views and to take such action as will inevitably redound to the good of our common country[.]

Very Respectfully
Russell Houston[2] Nashville Ten
Jordan Stokes Lebanon
Allen A. Hall Nashville, Ten.
W B Stokes DeKalb Co.
W B Campbell Wilson County
Andrew Johnson
Alvan C Gillem
Manson M Brien, President of the board of Aldermen[3]

Pet, DLC-Lincoln Papers.

1. William B. Campbell and Jordan Stokes seem to have led the way in organizing this appeal to the President. Johnson's role is less clear. That the memorial was written on executive department stationery suggests his full endorsement; however, that his name appears well down the list of signatories might be interpreted as less than enthusiastic support. The governor's ingrained proslavery convictions and his contention that Tennessee, never having left the Union, should be able to regulate its own domestic institutions would seem to align him with the petitioners. But his public conversion to emancipation was less than a year in the future! Although contemporary papers cited Johnson among those urging Tennessee's exemption from the pending proclamation and historians have generally alluded to his purported influence on the President's decision, the latter have offered no conclusive documentation. Cimprich, Slavery Amidst Civil War, 231-32; James S. Jones, *Life of Andrew Johnson: Seventeenth President of the United States* (Greeneville, Tenn., 1901), 88; William B. Campbell and Jordan Stokes to Emerson Etheridge, December 16, 1862, Lincoln Papers, LC; Hall, *Military Governor,* 91n; Washington *National Intelligencer,* December 25, 1862; New York *World,* January 14, 1863.

2. Russell Houston (1810-1895), Nashville lawyer and state representative (1851-53), had been nominated to the proposed secession convention of 1861. A veteran of the Second Seminole War, Houston later served as judge of the Tennessee Supreme Court (1865) and, after moving to Kentucky, as attorney-in-chief and later president of the Louisville and Nashville Railroad. McBride and Robison, *Biographical Directory* I, 382.

3. Thirty-two additional signatures appear on the petition, which was presented to the President by clerk of the House Emerson Etheridge on December 23. Cimprich, Slavery Amidst Civil War, 232.

From Ogilvie Byron Young[1]

[Nashville, *ca.*Dec. 6, 1862]

To His Excellency Gov. Andrew Johnson—
My Dear Governor:

In the early part of last week, two gentlemen from abroad, entire strangers to me, sought my acquaintance and claimed confidence for the subjoined reasons and purposes as here stated by them.

The one (Dr. Russell[2] by name) represented himself to me as a paroled prisoner from the State of Texas, belonging to the medical staff of Gen. Sterling Price. He said that he was captured at Iuka and was brought here by Gen. Rosencrans and put on his parole of honor, which he immediately discovered to me he but little respected.

The other gentleman (Hailey[3] by name) said he was immediately from the city of St. Louis, and was here collecting moneys from sutlers here for some firm in St. Louis—the name of which I do not now remember.

The conduct of the gentlemen were so mysterious and inexplicable, and their statements so strange and contradictory, as to excite my forebodings that all was not right.

It soon became apparent to my mind, on last Saturday evening, that these men were one of two things—either Government detectives or confederate spies. These men supposed I was heart and soul for the confederacy, and plied their artillery accordingly. Amused at their raillery and riled at their impudence, I determined to mislead them. I agreed with them in all—smoked, drank, laughed and talked to suit them. After this I determined to hand them over to the authorities, stating what part I had acted and the motives that incited me to act. If these men should turn out to be Government detectives they may not have perceived that I was acting for the purpose of detecting them, and they may attempt to give me some trouble. This has impelled me to present them and an explanation to your Excellency.

Those who know my history know that I owe no gratitude or allegiance to either Jeff Davis or the Southern confederacy. I came here a fugitive from confederate bondage, an unfriended stranger, yet resting under the imputation of disloyalty to the Government. You received me back into the fold and gave me the liberty of the city—pardoned my past errors and bade me sin no more. I never did, and so help me God, I never will raise a paricidal arm against my Government, let come what will.

I have designed this to importune you, and have said this much to prepare you for the report which the above gentlemen may make against me if they are detectives. I may have acted indiscretly in dissembling to them, yet I did it from the best of motives—to detect their designs. I may be frequently reported by these new comers, who do not know my real sentiments, yet know and believe me always true to the State and Andrew Johnson.

Ogilvie Byron Young.

ALS, DLC-JP.

1. For the frustrated researcher, Ogilvie Byron Young (*fl*1870) has no beginning and no end. Described variously as "an unimportant adventurer," a "graceless scamp, rich in blood but poor in purse" who was "Wildly imaginative, but immensely impractical," he eludes detection prior to the secession crisis. According to Benjamin C. Truman, Young had been a Douglas supporter, the correspondent of a New Orleans journal (1860), and a member of Beauregard's staff at Sumter. Surfacing in Missouri as "Dr. Young," candidate for a seat in the state secession convention, he was soon after arrested at Cincinnati as a spy in the fall of 1861 and acquitted after a celebrated trial. The next spring he was apprehended under an assumed name in Covington, Kentucky, and paroled, only to reappear in Nashville the following November, operating as a smuggler and spy. Caught by counteragents in an attempt to spirit Confederate papers out of the capital in a "hollow heeled boot," he and the bootmaker were sent to Alton. When returned for trial in the summer of 1863, Young was once more acquitted, remaining in Nashville to practice law. By late 1864 he was importuning Johnson for assistance in obtaining employment as a secret agent to break up Confederate conspiracies in Canada. Foiled in this endeavor, he left Nashville for "some more friendly Region," apparently finding it in St. Louis where he was an attorney in 1870—presumably having made the transition from "operator" to practitioner. John Bakeless, *Spies of the Confederacy* (Philadelphia, 1970), 214; Fitch, *Annals,* 498-500; Washington *Morning Chronicle,* December 20, 1862; Nashville *Dispatch,* December 9, 1862, September 1, 1863; Nashville *Union,* April 27, 1864; Nashville *Press,* August 31, 1863; Young to Johnson, November 3, 5, 29, 1864, Johnson Papers, LC; *Edwards' St. Louis Directory* (1870), 946.

2. Dr. W. J. P. Russell of Jonesboro, Illinois, otherwise unidentified, came to Tennessee in October, 1862, and worked as an undercover agent for Police Chief Truesdail until the following March. Becoming a cotton trader, he was arrested for fraud but exonerated in mid-1863. According to Army of the Cumberland's publicist, John Fitch, he introduced himself to Young as being a "hostage for the return of certain loyal Mississippians captured at Iuka." Fitch, *Annals*, 499-500; Proceedings of the Military Commission in the case of Elisha H. Forsythe, RG153, NA.

3. Hailey eludes identification.

From West T. Belisle[1]

Bethel-Station Tennessee
December 7th 1862

Gov Andrew Johnson

Sir I have Been in the Recruiting Service ever since I left Nashville or at best the most of the Time[.] The Tennessee and Cumberland Rivers having fallen and the CeCesh gurellas having got in middle Tennessee it was Impossable for me to reach Nashvill so I was advised by Col Adams[2] of Hamburgh Tenn to Recruit for Col Hurst[3] Reg at Bethel who was making up a Reg by your orders[.] so good many of my recruits are in his Regment[.] I have nearly a company formed now and will have the company completed by christmast if I can but at the present time my hands are tied. During the time I was Recruiting I captured some negroes who had been throwing up breast works for the CeCesh and had been working on a cecesh gun-boat[.] I captured them and turned them over to the government authoraties And a good many Horses a large amount of salt &c which enraged the cecesh against me Tremendeously so They put out Rewards for me from $500 to $1,000[.] So on 2nd day of Nov. while alone on a reconnorting expedition I was captured by a band of Gurellas on the Tenessee River[.] I then without mercy or Humanity was drged in irons to Columbia Jail where I was striped of my Clothing and hung up three times by the neck, Thence I was Draged to Murphyesborough in Thirty miles of Nashvill and thurst in a cell without any thing to protect myself from the severity of the wether[.] in that dismal cell I had to walk the floor all the times of nights to or I should have chilled to death[.] I thought my time was come[.] striped naked of my warm clothing and shoes and had to die at last in Jail by the severity of wether Awful indeed[.] Inability seized my mortal frame[.] I was taken out of Jail and Brought before the provost martial to have the sentence of death pronounced against me[.] I was hailed by soldiers as entered the court house as Thief a rober and Scoundrel[.] Shoot the damed Rascal says one, get out of the way many voices cries[.] Ile shoot Ile shoot[.] god dam his soul hes tured traitor to country and joined the yankees[.] Kill, Kill him[.] They were tumultous[.] The Excite was quelled by the officers but with great Difficulty[.] I was brough in the court house[.] The charges against me were mad out by one Mr. Cox[4] guerella Captain formerly of Lindon Tennessee a pettifogger lawyer; the charges was as follows. Dr. W. T. Belisle guilty Negro steeling Horse steeling salt steeling and infact a great enemy to the southern confederacy a[nd] verry Dangerous to the confedratee cause[.] therefore you will keep him well secured for he is as slick as an eel. but owing to my disability I was ordered back in Jail for Three days to be kept by the fire in warm room untill I would Recruit a little under a strong guard which was done. I being Released from cell in prison I soon got acquainted with one Mr. Johnson[5] also a prisoner for aiding you (he so informed me) to organize a Union Meeting in that vicinity. we had Joyful time of it[.] Ile assure you I was glad to see him[.] we conversed nearly all day[.] I found him to be a good union man and a verry enteligent one; one that loved his country and appeared to sempathize with me verry much but they seeing such an intimacy existing Between us he was moved to Chattinooga and I was left alone to deplore my awful condition[.] But god would have it on the Seccond Night I was guarded by some North Carolinians who were good Union men Conscriped in service who were Careless about me and who petted [pitied] me very much and told me they Thought I would [be] Shot or hanged[.] I then Thought it was once or never for me to make my Escape so about 2'O Clock before day when Slumber had taken deep possession of all the guards but one I Broak out two nail above a window sash, Raised the sash and made my escape between the Camp fires into the cedar woods. Though I was barefoot and nearly Naked and the rain was pouring down on me I was happy to Happy to thinke I had escaped a mighty foe; one that sought to take my life because I loved my Country[.] Shivering with cold surrounded with an unfeeling enemy a dark and gloomy night I set out to try to find Nashvill; I traveled till day and found my self in side and surrounded by the CeCesh picketts so I was compelled to lay up all day and being unaquainted with country I traveled three nights trying to pass the picketts and get in to Nashvill[.] Hunger and cold had nearly appointed my end so one morning early I found my self surrounded by the picketts who took me and brought me before Gen. Wheeler[6] at lavern [Lavergne][.] I knew then I would have to do quick work or go up for ninety days so I told Gen. Wheeler that I bliongd to that company I came to Nashville with[.] I told him I belonged Comp C 1st Tennessee Cav and he believed me and perolled but would not let me report at Nashvill but put out of the lines withe orders if I was in his lines any more I was to be shot[.][7] This please me verry much And Skedaddled for Bethel Knowing when they found out the trick the perole woul do me no good[.] so got out of the way[.] So I have stated My Condition to you as it really is[.] I had to tell them that belonged to the army or else death would have been my portion[.] I soon found out Being in the Recruiting service would not release me[.] So you know I was only in the recruiting service as I received the authority from you on the 4th day of June last. So You see my condition at this time And I wish you to write to me what to do so soon as this comes to hand and you will oblige your obediant Servent

W. T. Belisle MD

Direct your letter to Bethel Tennessee in Care of Provo Martial

ALS, DLC-JP.

1. Probably West T. Belisle, or Belile (b. *c*1827), a farmer living in Stewart County in 1850, who, after enrolling at Savannah in Hardin County, had been a private in Co. F, 10th Tenn. Inf., USA, until the previous June, when he "deserted" at Nashville two days after Johnson authorized him to recruit for Tennessee regiments; whether he was on detached service is not clear. Evidence for a medical title has not been found. CSR, RG94, NA; Sistler, *1850 Tenn. Census,* I, 111.

2. Robert N. Adams (1835-1914), lieutenant colonel, 81st Ohio Inf., had been stationed at Hamburg guarding stores, before moving into Mississippi during the fall. After participation in the Atlanta campaign—the basis for his book on *The Battle and Capture of Atlanta* (1898)—he was breveted brigadier, March 13, 1865. CSR, RG94, NA; Charles Wright, *Experiences in the Ranks of Company G, 81st Ohio Vol. Infantry* (Philadelphia, 1887), 49.

3. For Fielding Hurst, see *Johnson Papers*, V, 568*n*.

4. Nicholas N. Cox (1837-1912), Bedford County native raised in Arkansas and Texas, was a Texas ranger before studying law at Lebanon and beginning practice in Linden, Perry County, in 1858. Originally captain, Co. C, 2nd Tenn. Cav. Btn., CSA, he later was major in Cox's Cav. Btn. (1862). Captured at Parker's Crossroads (December 31, 1862), he became colonel, 10th Tenn. Cav. upon his release, serving through the battle of Chickamauga and subsequently following Forrest to Mississippi and West Tennessee. Settling in Franklin at war's end, he resumed law practice and subsequently spent five terms in Congress (1891-1901). John Allison, ed., *Notable Men of Tennessee* (2

vols., Atlanta, 1905), I, 127-29; *BDAC*, 745; *Tennesseans in the Civil War*, I, 22-23, 39, 76-77; Nashville *Dispatch*, December 6, 1862.

5. Not identified.

6. Joseph Wheeler (1836-1906), Georgia-born West Pointer (1859), resigned in April, 1861, to join the Confederate army. Initially a first lieutenant of artillery, he served as colonel, 19th Ala. Inf., (September, 1861-July, 1862) before becoming chief of cavalry for the Armies of Mississippi and Tennessee (1862-65), rising to lieutenant general. After the war he was a commission merchant in New Orleans (1865-68) before becoming a planter and lawyer at Wheeler, Alabama. For many years a congressman (1881-1900), he was appointed major general in 1898 and commanded a cavalry division in Cuba and a brigade in the Philippines (1898-1900). Warner, *Generals in Gray*, 332-33; *DAB*, XX, 50-52; *BDAC*, 1799; see also John P. Dyer, *"Fightin' Joe" Wheeler* (University, La., 1941).

7. Belisle's parole at Lavergne, Tennessee, had occurred two weeks earlier, on November 22. CSR, RG94, NA.

To Abraham Lincoln

Nashville Dec 8th 1862

A. Lincoln

I know strickland well[.][1] unless he is greatly improved he is no manner of account[.] there are more persons here desiring to raise regiments who are known to the people than it is prudent to authorize at this time. If strickland is in the service let him stay where he is[.] If the army here should move forward & drive before it or disperse the rebels letting us into east Tenn we could then raise a strong force. As it is we have done very well. I will send you a statement in a few days[.] at Hartsville some forty miles east of this place Jno Morgan on yesterday captured & took prisoners some four regiments under command of Col Moore.[2] I suppose every body was asleep & taken by surprise as usual[.][3]

Andrew Johnson

Tel, DLC-Lincoln Papers; DNA-RG107, Tels. Recd., Halleck, Vol. 5 (1862).

1. The President had wired: "Jesse H Strickland is here asking authority to raise a Regt of Tennesseans[.] would you advise that the authority be given[?]" Lincoln to Johnson, December 8, 1862, Johnson Papers, LC. For Jesse Hartley Strickland, son of the architect of the state capitol and earlier incorrectly identified as John, see *Johnson Papers*, II, 447*n*; V, 282*n*; Basler, *Works of Lincoln*, V, 546.

2. Absalom B. Moore (*c*1827-1879), New Jersey native, moved to LaSalle County, Illinois, where he preached for the Methodist Church, worked for the Illinois Central Railroad, and became clerk of the circuit court (1860). Colonel, 104th Ill. Inf. (August, 1862-September, 1863), he resigned and resumed his duties as clerk, later moving to Chicago where he held a minor Federal appointment. 1860 Census, Ill., LaSalle, City of LaSalle, 517; William W. Calkins, *The History of the One Hundred and Fourth Regiment of Illinois Volunteer Infantry: War of the Great Rebellion, 1862-1865* (Chicago, 1895), 366.

3. Early on the morning of December 7, Morgan caught Moore's command almost totally unaware and unprepared for battle. Overrun in less than two hours, the Union force surrendered with the loss of 2,096 men killed, wounded, or captured. Conflicting reports of events before and during the battle largely condemn Moore for inadequate preparations and inability to respond to the emergency. Although Halleck, with Stanton's approval, recommended that Moore be dismissed for neglect of duty, he was allowed to resign, effective September 9, 1863, on account of disability. *OR*, Ser. 1, XX, Pt. I, 43-45, 52-55; Pt. II, 136.

Writ of Election for Congressional Districts

December 8, 1862

Whereas, The State of Tennessee is now, and has been, without a full representation in the XXXVIIth Congress of the United States of America; and whereas it is believed, upon information received,[1] that a large majority of the voters of the Ninth and Tenth Congressional Districts of this State, as apportioned by the Act passed February 20th, 1852, have given evidence of their loyalty and allegiance to the Constitution and laws of the United States.

Now, therefore I, ANDREW JOHNSON, Military Governor of the State of Tennessee, in order to secure to the loyal electors of these two Congressional Districts their constitutional representation in the House of Representatives of the United States of America, have deemed it proper to issue this my proclamation, appointing and ordering elections to be held on the twenty-ninth day of December, 1862,[2] to fill the vacancies in the XXXVIIth Congress of the United States of America in the following Districts, to wit: The Ninth Congressional District, composed of the counties of Henry, Weakly, Dyer, Obion, Lauderdale, Tipton, Gibson, Carroll and Henderson.

The Tenth Congressional District, composed of the counties of Madison, Haywood, Hardeman, Fayette, and Shelby.

Writs of election will be issued, and the election held at the places designated by law, and the proceedings under said writs returned to the office of the Secretary of State. The judges appointed to hold said elections, in addition to the oath prescribed by section 844 of the Code of Tennessee, shall further swear that they will permit no person to vote whom they believe to be disloyal to the Government of the United States.

And no person will be considered as an elector qualified to vote, who, in addition to the other qualifications required by law, does not give satisfactory evidence to the judges holding said election of his loyalty to the Government of the United States.

In testimony whereof, I, ANDREW JOHNSON, Governor of the State of Tennessee, and Commander-in-Chief of the forces thereof, have hereunto set my hand and caused the great seal of the State to be affixed at the Department in Nashville, on the 8th day of December, A.D. 1862.

By the Governor:
ANDREW JOHNSON.

Edward H. East,
Secretary of State.

Nashville *Union,* December 9, 1862.

1. The governor was acutely aware of the activity of unionists in the recently "liberated" counties of West Tennessee, having that very day received a wire dated the Planters' House, St. Louis, from Dr. A[bner] Benton of Dyer County reporting that "The union Congressional Convention for the Ninth Dist nominated A[lvin] Hawkins of Carroll & named the thirteenth 13th Inst for Election unless otherwise derected." Benton to Johnson, December 8, 1862, Johnson Papers, LC.

2. Rejecting December 13, the date selected by the ninth district unionists, Johnson was in turn to have his own date nullified as a consequence of Forrest's raid into West Tennessee during the last days of the month. Resetting the election for January 20, he would once again be obliged, this time by Grant's intercession, to postpone until March, what actually turned out to be so fragmented an election as to be worthless, largely repudiated by all parties and factions. Maslowski, *Treason Must Be Made Odious,* 79.

From E. Peter Follis[1]

Headquarters Camp Dec 9th 1862

Gov Johnston
Sir

About the first of September the Guerrillas came to my house and took forceable possesion of one Bay Horse valued by my neighbors at Onehundred and Seventy five Dollars—and about the fifteenth of October they took one fine mule from me valued at $200-00 Two hundred Dollars[.] Also the Same lawless band took from me 2 other mules—valued at $100-00 Each (One hundred Dollars each) = $200.00[.] they also took from me three Rifle Guns—that cost me $75—Dollars and Shot Gun [that cost me] $20—Dollars[.] They also took one shot Gun and one Rifle from my Son Wm Fallis worth $20—Dollars each = $40—Dollars[.] they also took two Guns from James Fallis—worth Ea $20— = $40—[.] they took from me Amunitions Flasks &C worth $8—Dollars[.] they took my Overcoat worth $15—

[E. P. Follis][2]

L, DLC-JP.

1. Tennessee-born E. Peter Follis (b. *c*1815), a Robertson County farmer with $4,880 real and $2,000 personal property in 1860, had two sons, William (b. *c*1839) and James (b. *c*1844). 1850 Census, Tenn., Robertson, 13th Dist., 229; (1860), W. Div., 6.

2. An endorsement with three signatures (J. J. Felts, J. F.[?] Reeves, and T. W. Bradley) certifies that the "above mentioned Articles . . . taken by force of Arms" were worth the amounts claimed, and that Follis is and always has been "a Loyal citizen of the State of Tennessee."

From William B. Watson

December 9, 1862, Peoria, Ill.; ALS, DLC-JP.

Former mason and stonecutter on the Memphis and Charleston Railroad—"a good Union man"—captured, imprisoned, and released by the Confederates, asks advice about obtaining back pay of $260 from railroad. Having refused payment in Confederate state bonds, he inquires about Federal reimbursement.

From Robert Reeve[1]

Frank Town Nevada Try
Decm 10th 1862.

Esteemed Friend Andrew Johnston

I used to live in Carter County Tennessee and with my brothers had iron works at the mouth of Doe River below Elizabethton. We were then opposed in politicks and you may not recollect me. Now however I am pleased to find, we both stand upon one great platform, The Union. I was somewhere about the years 25, or 26, engineering with Col S. H Long,[2] & other government engineers, to find a rout for a road from Pikevill kentucky, through Tennessee, and on to Morganton in North Carolina. I crossed through the mountains from Pikevill into Tennessee four times, & was the commissioner on the part of Tennessee.[3] It is about one hundred miles from Pikevill to where the rail road runing east & west through Virginnia & Tennessee, crosses the Whatauga. Divided about in this way, say from Pikevill to the sounding Gap in the Cumber Lan mountain, 35 miles, thence to Mockaqueson Gap in the Clinch mountain, 40 miles, from there to the railroad 25 miles, you will find Col Longs reports, one a reconnaisance and the other a survey in the office at Washington. You will perceive what I am after—To releive the Union men of Tennessee by this route. The Big Sandy is navigable for light steamboats, during the winter & spring months[.] Collect an army in the state of Ohio, oposite the mouth of Sandy, strong enough to effect the object, and keep that object a profound secret, send forward part of this force immediate and fortify at Pike Vill, and at the same time, forward every thing required for the experdition to that point, or to the mouth of Shelby creek, a few miles above. As soon as the weather would permit in the spring, bring up the whole force, and in ten days from Pike Vill the army and baggage could be at the rail road. Of course you would have to go down the country, say at the junction of the Beans Station road, with the rail road, to find a country that could suport an army. There I would have a Manasses. There is no way so short and cheap, as this in my opinion, to reach Tennessee, and the communication could be kept open by fortafications at the Sounding Gap, Mocqueson Gap, & at the Whatauga. The Sounding Gap is a good Gap, and Mocqueson Gap, I suppose you are acquainted with, a perfect water gap. I respectfuly submit these views to your consideration and would like to hear from you.

Respectfully your friend
Robert Reeve

If you write please direct to Carson Citty Nevada Teritory[.]

ALS, DLC-JP.

1. Robert Reeve (b. *c*1806), with his brothers Casper W. and Jobe W. and father Mark, started "a rolling mill, forge, furnace, and nail factory near Elizabethton" in 1826. WPA, Minutes of the Court of Pleas and Quarter Sessions of Carter County, Vol. 3 (1821-26), 202; Raymond F. Hunt, Jr., "The Pactolus Ironworks," *Tenn. Hist. Quar.*, XXV (1966), 193.

2. Stephen H. Long (1784-1864), New Hampshire-born explorer and Dartmouth graduate (1809), became a second lieutenant of engineers in 1814, and, after two years as a West Point instructor in mathematics, was permanently transferred to the topographical engineers. Sent to explore the upper Mississippi Valley (1817), the Rocky Mountains (1820), and three years later the Minnesota River area, he subsequently helped select routes for various eastern roads and railroads, including the Baltimore and Ohio, the Western and Atlantic, and the "National Road leading from Portsmouth in the State of Ohio, through Kentucky, Virginia, Tennessee, and North Carolina" herein mentioned. He was made major in 1838 and chief of the corps and colonel at the outbreak of the Civil War. *DAB*, XI, 380; see also Richard G. Wood, *Stephen Harriman Long, 1784-1864: Army Engineer, Explorer, Inventor* (Glendale, Calif., 1966).

3. Reeve served in this capacity in 1831. *Ibid.*, 151.

CSA v. Estate of Andrew Johnson

[Knoxville], December 10, 1862

Confederate States of America
vs
The Estate of Andrew Johnson
an Alien Enemy

Petition lst. Receiver District.

In this case appeared M. T. Haynes[1] Receiver for the 1st District of East Tennessee, and moved that the said Andrew Johnson be declared an alien Enemy to the Confederate States of America, and the Court directed that the matter be submitted to a Jury—thereupon came the traverse jury,[2] who had been summoned by the Marshal, and duly elected, empanelled and sworn to try all causes and matters civil and criminal in the Eastern District of Tennessee to be submitted to them during the present term of the Court to wit: Robert Cravens, James Montgomery, John Bise, Joel Bowling, John G. King, Carrick W. Crozier, Samuel P. Ivins, William S. Kennedy, William B. Smith, William Ray, E. W. Marsh and J. S. Blackwell, and the said jury having heard the testimony and the charge of the Court, upon their oaths do say, that the said Andrew Johnson is an alien Enemy to said Confederate States of America. It is therefore decreed by the Court that said Johnson is an alien enemy and all the property, rights and credits belonging to him either at law or in equity, are sequestrated under the acts of Congress, and the Receiver for said District is directed to proceed to dispose of the same as provided by law.

Court adjourned until to-morrow—morning at 10 O'clock.

W. H Humphrey J.[3]

Copy, DNA-RG21, East Dist. of Tenn., Confederate District Court, Knoxville, Minute Book, 98.

1. Matthew T. Haynes (1826-1863), Blountsville lawyer with $4,300 real and $5,500 personal property, was a brother of Confederate Senator Landon C. Haynes. 1860 Census, Tenn., Sullivan, 5th Dist., 82; Worth S. Ray, *Tennessee Cousins: A History of Tennessee People* (Austin, 1950), 173.

2. A trial jury impaneled to try a civil or criminal case.

3. For Judge West H. Humphreys, see *Johnson Papers*, II, 387*n*; for previous action against Johnson's property, see Notice of Sequestration Proceedings, November 27, 1861, *ibid.*, V, 37.

From Robert Johnson

Cincinnati [December] 11th 1862

To Gov Andrew Johnson
Nashville Tenn

Mother and Sister left today for vevay[1] to remain[.] My arms received today[.] will report to you for duty by Thursday eighteenth (18th) Inst[.]

Robt Johnson Col

Tel, DLC-JP.

1. Vevay, the county seat of Switzerland County, Indiana, "beautifully situated on the Ohio river, 70 miles below Cincinnati," had a population of 1,198 in 1860. Thomas Baldwin and J. Thomas, *A New and Complete Gazetteer of the United States* (Philadelphia, 1854), 1210; Joseph C. G. Kennedy, comp., *Population of the United States in 1860 . . . The Eighth Census* (Washington, 1864), 126.

From James Worthen

December 11, 1862, Paducah, Ky.; ALS, DLC-JP.

Noting that Johnson was about to "issue Writs of Election to the several Sheriffs to hold an Election for a member of Congress from our District," explains that Henry County "is without a Sheriff." Inasmuch as the chairman of the county court is a "strong secessionist," Worthen doubts "his taking any action" unless the governor had "the power to move him in the matter." Considering eight or ten members of the court loyal, he mentions that "one or two have been elected and perhaps sworn in under the Law requiring the oath to the Confederate States," that the court "has neglected to qualify the Civil Officers in the county," and that "our Bridges & Roads have become almost impassible, and everything of a public nature in the County has been neglected for the past year."

From William B. Stokes

December 12, 1862, Camp near Lebanon; ALS, DNA-RG107, Lets. Recd., Sec. of War, File T816(114).

Colonel of lst Mid. Tenn. Cav. reminds Johnson of the promise of bounty at the mustering of his regiment, made up of "union refugees" who "have left their families destitute and Suffering"; hopes that all of his men, including those enlisting since August 22, can be paid "$25.00 advance bounty" which "would very materially alleviate their [families'] Condition, as our army is now moving toward the part of the State from which they fled."

To William S. Rosecrans, Nashville

Nashville, Tenn., Dec 13th 1862

Maj Gen Rosecrans
Sir

We have positive information this morning, that the Confederates are hauling Salt and large quantities of Provision from Clarksville, by way of Charlotte Dixon County, and that a Company of Guerrillas are forming in Cheatham County near the Narrows of Harpeth[.]

Yours &c Andrew Johnson
Mil. Govr.

L, DNA-RG393, Dept. of the Cumberland, Lets. Recd., File T-54 (1862).

Assessment for Relief of the Poor[1]

State of Tennessee, Executive Office,
Nashville, Dec. 13, 1862.

Whereas, There are many helpless widows, wives and children in the city of Nashville and county of Davidson, who have been reduced to poverty and wretchedness in consequence of their husbands, sons and fathers having been forced into the armies of this unholy and nefarious rebellion, and their necessities having become great and manifest, and their wants for the necessaries of life so urgent, that all the laws of justice and humanity would be grossly violated unless something was done to relieve their destitute and suffering condition: The following assessment is ordered in behalf of these suffering families from those who have contributed directly or indirectly in bringing about this unfortunate state of affairs.[2] The amount annexed to each name may be paid in five months, the first payment to be made on or before the 20th December, 1862.[3] All persons called upon in this notice[4] will pay the amount required to the Comptroller of the State, and it will be applied in such manner as may be prescribed to the purposes for which it was collected:[5]

John Overton	$2,500	Evans & Co.	$500
John M. Bass	1,500	A. F. Goff	500
W. W. Berry	1,500	Dr. J. W. Hoggatt	500
Henry Frazier	1,250	Michael Vaughn	500
Macey & Hamilton	1,000	W. H. Lucas	500
W. W. Woodfolk	1,000	Dyer Pearl & Co.	500
W. G. Harding	1,000	Mrs. John R. Wilson	500
M. R. Cockrill	1,000	J. A. S. Acklin	500
A. W. Vanleer	1,000	W. R. Elliston	500
A. L. P. Green	750	D. F. Carter	500
Enoch Ensley	750	R. C. McNairy	500
L. B. Fite	750	J. W. Horton	500
J. M. Hill	500	J. H. Williams	500
Ed. Childress, Sr.	500	Morgan & Co.	500
Andy Hamilton	500	W. B. Walton	500
Wash. Barrow	500	Dunn & Co., Bankers	500
Niell S. Brown	500	Mrs. Luzinka Brown	500
David McGavock	500	R. H. Gardner	250
Granville P. Smith	500	Wm. Ewing	250
A. C. Carter	500	W. H. Hagan	250
C. E. Hillman	500	W. D. Phillips	250
James Cockrill	500	Phil. Shute	250
Anth. W. Johnson	500	G. M. Fogg	250
Allison, Andrsn & Co	500	W. K. Bowling	250
John Thompson	500	Wm. L. Murfree	250
Hiram Vaughn	500	Thos. McCampbell	250
Wilo. Williams	500	Wm. E. Watkins	250
L. F. Beech	500	Wm. Lawrence	250
A. B. Montgomery	500	W. H. Calhoun	250
Felix Demoville	500	James Webb	250
Byrd Douglas	500	Dr. W. A. Cheatham	250
Hollins & Co.	500	Isaac Paul	250
J. B. Craighead	500	Archer Cheatham	250
W. P. Bryan	500	John Johns	250
John M. Lea	500	Wm. Stockell	250
Mac. Ridley	500	Jo. Woods	250
John Harding, jr.	500	T. Fanning	250
T. O. Harris	500	A. J. Duncan	250

G. W. Donnegan	500	Frank McGavock	250
Stokeley Donelson	500	A. C. & A. B. Beech	250
John Lawrence	500	J. W. Hamilton	250
John O. Hadley	500	G. W. Hendershott	250

By the Governor:
Andrew Johnson,

Edward H. East,
Secretary of State.

Nashville *Dispatch*, December 14, 1862.

1. In keeping with his desire to tax those wealthy secessionists who had made substantial monetary contributions to the Confederacy, Johnson levied this second assessment on an expanded list of persons and at considerably higher sums than the order of August 18.

2. The list includes Nashville's most affluent citizenry, with John Overton, prominent Confederate, at its head. Not to be overlooked are former Governor Neill S. Brown, since June ostensibly a spokesman for the Union, and Lizinka Brown, Johnson's old friend of former days, now gone South.

3. Of the eighty-four individuals and companies assessed, fifty-five were cited the following February as delinquent on both installments, only "three or four" having paid the second. Nashville *Union*, February 7, 1863.

4. Omitted here, but included in the Nashville *Union's* list of the same date, was the name of W. S. Whiteman.

5. Late in February the governor's "Assessment of the Rebels" was given teeth in Special Order No. 53, issued "at the request of Gov. Andrew Johnson," by Brig. Gen. Robert B. Mitchell, commanding at Nashville. Lt. James W. Scully and Col. Alvan Gillem, both of the 10th Tenn. Inf., were assigned "to enforce the payment of the unpaid assessment under the levy . . . for the support of the destitute of this city." Even so, of the potential yield of $33,700 (the sum of the amounts listed in this assessment), only $18,824.31 had been collected by late spring, 1865. New York *Times*, March 8, 1863; *Tenn. House Journal*, 1865, App. 35.

From William F. Bradford[1]

Trenton Tenn Decr 15th 1862

To his Exelency Gov Johnson
Nashville Ten
Dear Sir—

Understanding that in view of the late order of Gen Grant prohibiting all civil officers exercising the functions of their offices without recommission, that there is an attempt makeing to have Judge Williams[2] recommissioned as said Judge—And as the charge and speech made by him that provoked this order was made at the Court he attempted to hold at my town Troy Obion County Ten, I thought it proper to forward to you the resolutions adopted at a convention of the loyal men of that County who heard his charge and public speech and perhaps are the most proper persons to judge of his loyalty[.][3]

The resolutions were under stood to apply to him in particular and were acted on in that view. I thought it due the convention to forward you the resolutions before you acted on the application for recommission[.]

In Judge Williams charge he stated that they had only to enforce state laws and had nothing to do with either the Federal or confederate Governments and he almost if not entirely ignored the authority of the Federal Govt. in regard to said court and stated many other things that was obnoxious to union men both in his speech and charge[.] Whilst in a charge he delivered some time ago when the state was under confederate rule he charged as I understand that it was treasen to the Southern Confederacy to give the enemy (meaning the Federal soldiers) an[y] meals vituals lodgeing a drink of warter or directions on his way, Judge Williams is regarded by many Union men of that county and I think of other counties of his district as disloyal[.]

I make these statements in Justice to the Convention thinking that he at least ought not to be recommissioned unless reelected[.] I think these statements can be abundantly proven by reliable union men in Obion County[.] at least I think he ought not to be recommissioned without the takening of the proof. However not knowing your policy I respectfully refer the facts[.]

Yours Truely &c
W. F. Bradford Troy Ten

P.S. Gov Johnson will please hand over to publisher of Nashville union the procederings of the meeting[.][4]

ALS, DLC-JP.

1. William F. Bradford (*c*1832-1864), native Tennessee lawyer with $1,250 personal property, recruited and became major in December, 1863, of the 13th Tenn. Cav., USA. Captured by Forrest at Fort Pillow the following April, he escaped only to be recaptured and murdered by his guards a few days later. 1860 Census, Tenn., Obion, 6th Dist., 275; *Tennesseans in the Civil War*, I, 353-54; John A. Wyeth, *Life of General Nathan Bedford Forrest* (New York, 1959), 313, 323-24, 328.

2. Samuel Williams.

3. Chaired by Dr. Almon Case, William P. Cranford, and Thomas Dougherty, with W. H. Caldwell serving as secretary, the Obion County Union meeting, held at the Troy courthouse, November 27, was attended by "a large number" of citizens. Bradford's resolution to "earnestly petition his exelency Gov Andrew Johnson to early order an election not only for members of Congress but for the State Legislature juditial and county offices" was adopted and twenty men were appointed to represent the county in the District Convention at Trenton on the first Monday in December. Minutes of the Obion County Union meeting, November 27, 1862, enclosed with this letter, Johnson Papers, LC.

4. Not found.

From William McLean

December 15, 1862, Nashville; ALS, DLC-JP.

Convicted of larceny at Memphis in 1858 and sentenced to ten years in the state penitentiary, prisoner wants release, considering "the charge [steeling 4 segars] triffling and my sentence excessive."

From Hezekiah G. Scovel

December 16, 1862, Nashville; ALS, DLC-JP.

Praising Johnson's "Energy, fidelity, trustworthiness, firmness, frankness, courage, and unmitigated attachment to your country" and comparing him to the undaunted pilot who stood fast at the helm "while the civil, political and religious world has been in commotion, and the 'ship of state,' heaving and plunging as though all would be lost," a Nashville realtor offers him "a beautiful building lot in 'Walnut Grove' on Ophelia Avenue, which is 100 feet wide; of 50 feet front, 150 feet deep,—opposite to which a lot was sold in 1856 at $30.00 pr. foot."

From Mason Brayman[1]

Head Quarters Bolivar, Tenn.
Dec. 17th, 1862

His Exclcy Andrew Johnson
Mil. Gov. Tenn:—
Sir:—

Your Proclamation, ordering an Election in the 9th & 10th Districts on the 29th came last night.[2] I have had it printed and will circulate it in both districts. I enclose copies. I also enclose copies of Maj. Genl. Grants order on the same subject,[3] which yours supercedes.

I deem it proper to furnish you also, a copy of the Proceedings of a convention held in this place on Monday the 15th, the reading of which will explain the object.[4]

I have also sent copies to the President, to Genl. Grant, and to Genl. Sullivan[5] commanding this District. I have expressed to each of those gentlemen, and respectfully repeat to you, my apprehension, that the resolutions *fall short* of that loyal and patriotic declaration, which the occasion fitly required. I have doubts whether the object of the President, in inviting, and of yourself, in directing, a representation in Congress from Tennessee, will be answered, by the presence of delegates whose scope of duty is defined by these resolutions.

I think you will soon learn that another candidate has taken the field, upon a safer platform.[6]

Respectfully Yours &c
M. Brayman
Brig. Genl. Comg.

ALS, DLC-JP.

1. Mason Brayman (1813-1895), New York-born editor of the Buffalo *Bulletin* (1835), moved first to Michigan and then to Illinois (1842) where he practiced law and was general solicitor for the Illinois Central Railroad. Commissioned major, 29th Ill. Inf. in 1861, he advanced to brigadier general of volunteers (September 24, 1862), commanding Bolivar, Tennessee (until June, 1863), Camp Dennison, Ohio, and Natchez, Mississippi. Returning to civilian life he resided variously in Missouri, Arkansas, Illinois,

Idaho (as territorial governor, 1876-78), and Wisconsin. Warner, *Generals in Blue*, 43-44; *NCAB*, XXI, 348-49.

2. See Writ of Election for Congressional Districts, December 8, 1862. Several days later General Hurlbut postponed the election until January 20. Memphis *Bulletin*, December 27, 1862.

3. On December 9, Grant, unaware of Johnson's proclamation of the preceding day, announced that an election would be held in the eighth, ninth, and tenth congressional districts on December 24. He stipulated that his announcement was subject to the governor's approval and would be null and void if Johnson issued a call for an election. Memphis *Bulletin*, December 23, 1862.

4. Chaired by John Thompson of Fayette, with Thomas R. Smith of Hardeman as secretary and delegates from Haywood, Hardeman, and Fayette counties, the meeting chose Thomas G. Smith of Haywood as the candidate. The resolutions favored an "honorable and speedy peace, and a reconstruction of the union on the old terms of the Constitution," and instructed their prospective congressmen "to oppose the Emancipation Proclamation . . . and to endeavor to procure the passage of some Law which will enable masters to recover their Fugitive Slaves and which will enable loyal citizens to receive full payment for all losses inflicted on them by the Federal Army, including the loss of Slaves." Proceedings of Convention, Johnson Papers, LC.

5. Jeremiah C. Sullivan (1830-1890), Madison, Indiana, native, was a midshipman (1848-54) before studying law. Rising to brigadier general of Indiana volunteers, he commanded in 1862 a brigade in Rosecrans' Army of the Mississippi and that fall was put in charge of the District of Jackson. Following staff duty with Grant and McPherson, he was transferred to the Department of West Virginia. Subsequently he lived in Maryland and California, working in minor clerical jobs. Warner, *Generals in Blue*, 487-88.

6. Ultimately three men—Thomas G. Smith, Benjamin D. Nabers, and James M. Tomeny—were in the canvass; however, all had declared prior to this time. Apparently no other candidate announced.

From Washington Union Club of Memphis[1]

Memphis Dec 19, 1862.

Hon Andrew Johnson
Sir.

Our Union Club passed unanimously the following resolution

Resolved—that this Club respectfully represent to His Excellency Governor Andrew Johnson, the great want of this County & Judicial District for appointments to fill the vacant Judicial Offices— And that he be urgently requested to oblige us by providing for such vacancies, according to Law.

Resolved, that the Secretary be requested to transmit a copy of this resolution to Governor Johnson.

Sir— In pursuance of above instruction I send you the resolution— and will add that we think you labor under wrong impressions as to our actual state— All kinds of business is in uninterrupted operation— There is not the slightest hope or chance for Secesh ever regaining position here— they feel it and are daily, gradually dropping into the new order of things— What we chiefly need is Judicial organization— Claims, merchants open accounts are daily outlawing for want of opportunity to begin suit—[2] We hope you will be pleased to consider this matter and act at once.— Every days delay please Secesh—and they are constantly removing their effects[.]

Another matter—Our Union Club has arranged to celebrate the 8th Jany[3]—and the Committee have extended an invitation to you, to visit us, address us, and celebrate with us— You may not receive the invitation sent by mail, Hence I repeat it by Express— We have no good talent for such an occasion— Genl Hawkins & Col Sullivan[4] who are "*bloods*"[5] at this business & were to address us, are to take the field & go to Vicksburg & will disappoint us— If you cannot come could you not send either Mr Campbell, Polk[6] or some other able men who will aid us and the cause on that occasion—

Respuy Yr Obt St
P. F. Schliecker[7] Secy

I enclose a letter of recommendation to you, from Judge Gale of Wisconsin,[8] in reference to the qualifications of Mr Kitchum,[9] who called upon you some time since, bearing a Petition from many of our citizens, soliciting his appointment to the Vacant Judgeship of the Common Law & Chancery Court of Memphis— I add a newspaper extract[10] to show Judge Gales position[.]

ALS, DLC-JP.

1. Organized at Memphis in July, 1862, with Joseph Tagg as president and Peter F. Schliecker as secretary, the club at its zenith had a membership of 1,600; but after a year, according to the *Bulletin*, dissolved because the "secret association within the club for regulating purposes . . . exploded." Joseph Tagg and Peter F. Schliecker to Johnson, July 28, November 13, 14, 1862, Johnson Papers, LC; Memphis *Bulletin*, September 22, 1864.

2. The last session of the Memphis circuit court had been held in October; thereafter various military commissions were charged with many of the civil and criminal functions of the state courts. In April, 1863, Gen. James C. Veatch appointed a commission "to hear and determine all complaints and suits instituted by loyal citizens of the United States for the collection of debts, the enforcement of contracts, the prevention of frauds, and the recovery of possession of property." Hooper, Memphis, 86-87; Hall, *Military Governor*, 132.

3. A Democratic, as well as a Tennessee, holiday commemorating Andrew Jackson's victory at New Orleans in 1815.

4. Probably Col. John P. Hawkins and Gen. Jeremiah C. Sullivan. Hawkins (1830-1914), Indianapolis-born West Point graduate (1852), served on the northwestern frontier until 1861. Transferred to the commissary department and stationed in St. Louis, he eventually became chief commissary of the Army of the Tennessee, commander of the District of Northeastern Louisiana (April, 1863-February, 1864), and a participant in the capture of Mobile (April, 1865). At war's end, he reentered the regular army, eventually becoming commissary general of subsistence. Warner, *Generals in Blue*, 218-19; Powell, *Army List*, 363.

5. A fresh, youthful, and vigorous party member. *OED*, I, 930.

6. William B. Campbell and William H. Polk. The latter had died three days earlier.

7. Peter F. Schliecker (*c*1814-*fl*1866), Maryland native, was a Norfolk, Virginia, merchant who returned there after 1863. His commitment to the Union cause would appear to have been of comparatively recent vintage. Although appointed in early December to attend the district congressional nominating convention, he had just one year earlier proffered, and had accepted as a Confederate government transport, his steamboat which had previously plied between Cairo and Columbus, Kentucky. 1860 Census, Va., Norfolk City, 233; *Norfolk City and Business Directory* (1867), 99; Memphis *Bulletin*, December 7, 1862; Memphis *Appeal*, December 21, 1861.

8. George Gale (1816-1868), Vermont-born lawyer, moved to Elkhorn, Walworth County, Wisconsin, in the early 1840's, thereafter holding several local offices before

becoming state senator (1849-51) and brigadier general of militia (1851). Founding Galesville and its "university" in 1854, he removed to LaCrosse where he became judge of Chippewa County and of the 6th judicial circuit (1857-63). His health partially failed in 1862 and he spent the next three winters in the south and east, usually on behalf of the sanitary and Christian commissions. Interested in the aboriginal history of the northwestern states, he wrote *The Upper Mississippi: or Historical Sketches of the Introduction of Civilization in the Northwest* (1867). Daniel S. Durrie, "Memoir of George Gale," *Wisconsin Historical Collections*, VII (1876), 422-25. See also Gale to Johnson, December 19, 1862, Johnson Papers, LC.

9. For Asa C. Ketchum who had studied law in Gale's Elkhorn office, see *Johnson Papers*, V, 573*n*.

10. Not found.

To William S. Rosecrans, Nashville

Nashville, Tenn., Dec 21st 1862

Maj General W S Rosecrans
Comdy 14 Army Corps
Dept of the Cumberland
General

Mrs Payne and sister[1] desire a short interview in regard to her return to this place. From her statement she has been treated very unceremoniously and desires to seek redress and protection from General Rosecrans. I hope therefore that her statement will be heard and such action had as the nature of the case seems to require.[2]

Very Respectfully
Andrew Johnson
Mil Governor
B.[3]

L, DLC-JP.

1. Maria Ryan (Mrs. Edwin D.) Payne (1825-1885) and Mary (Molly) Ryan (Mrs. Napoleon B.) Hyde (b. *c*1839) were the Kentucky-born daughters of Moses (1796-1862) and Dulcina Ryan (1804-1854). Mrs. Payne and Mrs. Hyde, the latter "a young, ardent, handsome, and smart rebel lady, mother of two children . . . whose husband was in the rebel army," were arrested in April, 1863, and charged with spying. Mrs. Hyde, whose graciousness and favors to the Union troops permitted her to pass through the lines, "was the travelling member of the firm of spys," while her sister stayed at Nashville collecting intelligence which they passed on to Generals Bragg, Wheeler, Van Dorn, and Morgan. Apparently the more notorious of the two, Mrs. Hyde was imprisoned at Alton from May to July, 1863. Brooke Payne, *The Paynes of Virginia* (Richmond, 1937), 278, 306-7; 1860 Census, Tenn., Davidson, 23rd Dist., 133; Fitch, *Annals*, 602-5; T. Hendrickson to W. Hoffman, July 26, 1863, *OR*, Ser. 2, VI, 153.

2. An endorsement by Rosecrans' aide-de-camp reads "The commanding General directs me to say that he has every reason to believe that Mrs Payne is a spy. her Case is being investigated."

3. For William A. Browning, Johnson's military secretary, see *Johnson Papers*, IV, 422*n*.

From Thomas T. Crittenden[1]

Nashville Decr. 29th 1862

Govr. Andw. Johnson
Nashville Tenn
Sir

Early in October last we were released from prison at Madison, Georgia where together with some one hundred and twenty five East Tennesseeans we had been confined for some months—

Bad as was the treatment of the prisoners of war, the Tennesseeans were treated much worse—

For instance, they were compelled, at the point of the bayonet, to beat the dough which the negroes cooked for our use, to police the ground enclosing the prison, to clean the sinks, to dig and clear out the wells, to make and repair fences, to carry food for others to eat, to scrub floors; in other words they were forced to do the most degrading part of the work in and around the prison, while they actually suffered for want of blankets, clothing and food and gladly received from us the fragments of our scanty fare[.]

What I have stated I saw and know to be true—

Many of these Tennesseeans were men of wealth and character—

I have been told by one of them who was released about a month ago, that seventy five still remain in that prison—

I feel a deep interest in them knowing what they must suffer until released—

To you as their Governor in their name and behalf I appeal for relief—

It can be efficiently rendered in this way: arrest an equal number of the leading rebels of Nashville—set them to work in its streets—keep them at it—send a flag of truce to Genl. Bragg—tell what you have done & why—propose an exchange and my word for it you will shake hands with those loyal and true-hearted Tennesseeans in your Capitol within thirty days—

Your friend
T. T. Crittenden[2]

James Henry Near Knoxville
Daniel Kelly
Alex W Kelley—
Wm. Triplett
Wm. Looper

John A Thornhill
S. M. Milwer Knoxville
Henry Kelley Jonesborough—
I W King—
N B Geoghegan N Carolina

About 75 East Tennesseeans Left there Novr. 11—

ALS, DLS-JP; Louisville *Journal*, January 3, 1863.

1. Thomas T. Crittenden (1825-1905), born at Huntsville, Alabama, and reared in Texas, studied law at Transylvania, and began practice in Hannibal, Missouri. Following service in the Mexican War, he moved to Madison, Indiana, and in April, 1861, became

colonel, 6th Ind. Inf., being promoted brigadier general of volunteers a year later. Captured by Forrest at Murfreesboro in July, 1862, and imprisoned until October, he resigned the following May and settled in Washington, D.C., moving in 1885 to San Diego, where he was a real estate developer. Warner, *Generals in Blue*, 101-2.

2. The following names, listed by Crittenden on a separate page, appear to have been a sample of what the Louisville *Journal* of January 3, 1863, referred to as "some of these unfortunate East Tennesseans" still incarcerated at Madison.

1863

From William Truesdail

Office Chief Police [Nashville]
Jany. 2/63

To His Excellency
Gov Johnson

Sir The Case of Samuels[1] has not came into office[.] I understod He Had been arrested charged with the Murder of Poor Waggoner[.][2] We Have arrested a good many Persons on suspicion of being Parties to the murder[.] I Have as yet found but too Identified by Mrs Waggoner, as Parties to the Murder. Samuels I understod from the Mayor,[3] was suspected as one of the Parties. the Case is in the Hands of the City Authorities.[4]

Yours Respectfully Wm. Truesdail
Chief Police

ALS, DLC-JP.

1. It has not been possible to identify the accused man.
2. Thomas J. Waggoner (1807-1862), minister and farmer with $14,175 real and $9,600 personal property at the outbreak of war, was murdered December 20, 1862, by men pretending to be Confederate officers. 1860 Census, Tenn., Davidson, 21st Dist., 100; Porch, *1850 Census, Davidson*, 380; Nashville *Dispatch*, April 15, 16, 18, 1863.
3. For John Hugh Smith, see *Johnson Papers*, V, 317*n*.
4. By late December seven suspects, including four Nashville area residents and three men "connected with the army," had been arrested by civilian and military authorities. Samuels apparently was not indicted. Beverly (alias Bose) Haley was tried during April, 1863, but not convicted because the jury could not agree; he escaped from jail the following July. Nashville *Dispatch,* December 31, 1862, April 15, 16, 18, 1863; Nashville *Press,* July 28, 1863.

To William R. Cornelius,[1] *Nashville*

Nashville, January 2, 1863

Mr. Cornelius:
Sir

I will see that your accounts against Lieut. W. Beaty[2] for coffins furnished for Col Milligan and Lieut. Condett[3] are paid[.][4]

Respectfully Andrew Johnson
Mil. Gov.

L, Johnson-Bartlett Col.

1. William R. Cornelius (1824-1910), Lewisburg, Pennsylvania, native who came to Nashville in 1849, possessed $5,000 personal property on the eve of the war. Originally

associated with the firm of McComb & Carson, "leading cabinet makers and funeral directors," he had become by 1861 sole proprietor, altering the name to W. R. Cornelius & Co.; except for a thirteen-year (1866-79) involvement with milling and farming, he continued in the undertaking business until his death. During the war he had a government contract to bury soldiers who had died in service, operating branch houses at Murfreesboro, Tullahoma, Wartrace, Shelbyville, Chattanooga, and Stevenson, Alabama. 1860 Census, Tenn., Davidson, Nashville, 5th Ward, 162; Nashville *Banner*, February 21, 1910; *Nashville City Directory* (1875), 350; Nashville *Union*, November 6, 1863.

2. Possibly William T. Beatty (b. *c*1818), who enlisted in 1861 in the 2nd Ohio Inf., was captured at Chickamauga, confined at Richmond, paroled in September, 1864, and honorably discharged as major, November 10, 1864. Special Orders No. 244 (October 20, 1886), RG94, NA.

3. Both were killed December 31, 1862, during the battle of Murfreesboro. Minor Millikin (1834-1862), Butler County, Ohio, native, Miami University graduate, and editor (1857-59) of the Republican Hamilton *Intelligencer*, served as colonel, 1st Ohio Cav. Timothy L. Conditt (*c*1835-1862), a student in 1860, enlisted September 15, 1861, as sergeant in Co. L, 1st Ohio, becoming 2nd lieutenant May 29, 1862. *OR*, Ser. I, XX, Pt. I, 619; Lester J. Cappon, "'The Soldier's Creed,'" *Ohio Historical Quarterly*, LXIV (1955), 324-25; 1860 Census, Ohio, Washington, Marietta City, 3rd Ward, 94; W. L. Curry, comp., *Four Years in the Saddle: History of the First Regiment Ohio Volunteer Cavalry* (Columbus, 1898), 42.

4. On July 15, Cornelius endorsed the letter, "The within named Bills have Been paid."

To Jacob H. Smyser,[1] *Louisville, Ky.*

Nashville Jany 6 186[3]

To Ordnance officer

I hope you will have no hesitancy in Letting first East Tenn cavalry have Six hundred Pistols[.] Genl Rosecrans is now at Murrfreesboro[.] as Soon as Practicable I will procure an order from him or the war Dept & I will be responsible till order is Secured[.][2]

Andrew Johnson Mil Gov

Tel, DNA-RG156, Louisville Ordnance Dept., Ky., Tels. Recd. (1863).

1. Jacob H. Smyser (*c*1838-1885), Pennsylvania native and West Point graduate (1861), was 1st lieutenant, 5th U. S. Arty., before transferring to the ordnance department; at this time he commanded the depot at Louisville. *OR*, Ser. 1, LII, Pt. I, 302, 346-47; Heitman, *Register*, I, 905; *West Point Register* (1970), 255.

2. On the reverse Smyser wrote: "These pistols can be issued on this telegram as a requisition for State of Tenn. Govr Johnson will be held responsible for the receipt of the proper order to Close this Case."

To Robert Johnson, Louisville, Ky.

Nashville Jany 6 186[3]

To Col Robt Johnson

I have Just telegraphed ordnance officer at Louisville asking him to let your Regiment have the Pistols[.][1] Rosecrans is away[.] will secure order as soon as practicable[.] where is Col Edwards & what is he doing[?][2]

Andrew Johnson

Tel, DLC-JP.

1. Robert had telegraphed: "I need six hundred pistols which I can procure here on General Rosecrans order[.] send order by telegram immediately[.]" Robert Johnson to Johnson, January 5, 1863, Johnson Papers, LC.

2. Two days later Robert responded: "Edwards Here but ordered to Laxington, Stover here with one Hundred Men[.] I will leave Saturday for Nashville[.]" *Ibid.*

From Abraham Lincoln

Washington Jany 8th 1863

To Gov Johnson

A dispatch of yesterday from Nashville says the body of Capt Tod[1] of Sixth Ky brought in today[.] please tell me what was his Christian name & whether he was in our Service or that of the enemy[.] I Shall also be glad to have your impression as to the effect the late operations about Murfreesboro will have on the prospects of Tennessee[.][2]

A Lincoln

Tel, DLC-JP; RPB.

1. Charles S. Todd (1841-1862) of Shelby County, Kentucky, was a great-grandson of Thomas Todd, U. S. Supreme Court justice, and of Governor Isaac Shelby. Descended from the Virginia branch, he was not related to Mary Todd Lincoln, whose family belonged to the Pennsylvania Todds. Captain of Co. C, 6th Ky. Inf., USA, he was killed at Murfreesboro on December 31. *OR*, Ser. 1, XX, Pt. I, 555; *Official Army Register*, IV, 1251; "Todd-Shelby Family Bible," *Daughters of the American Revolution Magazine*, XCIV (1960), 299, 340-41; James R. Bentley (The Filson Club) to Andrew Johnson Project, June 18, 1975; Louisville *Journal*, January 29, 1863.

2. For Johnson's reply to this query, see Telegram to Abraham Lincoln, January 11, 1863.

To Abraham Lincoln

Nashville, Jany 8th 1863

His Excy Abraham Lincoln

Body of Capt Charles S Todd of Shelbyville Ky belonging to federals 6th Ky is here in metallic case awaiting transportation[.] Your order in regard thereto will be promptly attended to[.][1]

Andrew Johnson Mil Gov

Tel, DLC-Lincoln Papers.

1. Inasmuch as this Todd was not a kinsman, the President had no instructions. "I presume the remains . . . are in the hands of his family friends, & I wish to give no order on the subject." Lincoln to Johnson, January 10, 1863, Brown University Library, Providence, Rhode Island.

From John H. James[1]

Louisville January 9 1863

To Andw Johnson
Mil Gov

Gen Boyle[2] has placed under arrest Col Johnson for receiving into his Camp men from Edwards Regt who were originally enlisted for Johnsons regt. It was done through the influence of Edwards[.] Edwards nor his men have been mustered[.] transfer their men to Col Johnson & all will be right[.] Edwards has about three hundred 300 men[.] examine general order no seventy five 75 by which you will see that you have the absolute control of Edwards men[.][3]

Jno. H. James Q M

ALS, DLC-JP.

1. John H. James (*c*1830-1867), Canadian-born, was a Hamilton County farmer in 1860 with $600 real and $800 personal property. Becoming 1st lieutenant and regimental quartermaster, 1st Tenn. Cav., USA, in November, 1862, he was discharged in July, 1864, and appointed captain in the quartermaster department at Nashville, where he served as chief commissary of subsistence until mustered out in May, 1866. Carter, *First Tenn. Cav.*, 273; *Official Army Register*, IV, 1174; Heitman, *Register*, I. 570; *OR*, Ser. 1, LII, Pt. I, 635.

2. Jeremiah T. Boyle, commander of the District of Kentucky.

3. War Department General Orders No. 78, issued September 16, 1861, specified that "All persons having received authority from the War Department to raise volunteer regiments, batteries, or companies in the loyal States are, with their commands, hereby placed under the orders of the Governors of those States, to whom they will immediately report the present condition of their respective organizations. These troops will be organized, or reorganized, and prepared for service by the Governors of their respective States in the manner they may judge most advantageous for the interests of the General Government." *OR*, Ser. 3, I, 518-19. For a detailed explanation of the contretemps between Colonels Edwards and Johnson, see Letter from Daniel Stover, January 12, 1863.

From David Tod

Columbus Jan 10 1863

To John [*sic*] Andrew Johnson
is it advisable that I Send a Hospital boat to Nashville for Sick & wounded Ohio Soldiers[?][1]

David Tod

Tel, DLC-JP.

1. Ohio Governor Tod exhibited great solicitude for soldiers and their families, sending a hospital ship to remove the wounded to Cincinnati after Shiloh in April, 1862. In January, subsequent to this telegram, he dispatched similar aid—surgeons and supplies, as well as a boat to Nashville—to minister to the wounded after Stones River. Although Johnson's reply has not been found, the envelope indicates that he referred the inquiry to the surgeon general who responded on January 11 "that med. Director recommends sending of the boat." Richard H. Abbott, *Ohio's War Governors*, Ohio Civil War Centennial Commission *Publications* No. 11 (Columbus, 1962), 34-35. For Tod, see *Johnson Papers*, V, 218*n*.

To Edwin M. Stanton

Nashville, January 10th 1863.

Hon. E. M. Stanton,
Secretary of War,
Washington City.
Sir:

I have the honor to acknowledge the receipt of your communication of the 23d. ult'o,[1] in reply to the letter of Col W. B. Stokes, Comd'g 1st. Mid: Tenn Cavalry, in relation to the payment of certain bounties to the men of his Regiment, referred by this office to the War Department.

From the reply of your office, it appears that the main point of Col Stokes' letter, and an answer to which was had in view by its reference to your Department, has been overlooked, and I would therefore respectfully ask your attention again to said communication.

I will state in connection therewith, that the men were enlisted on the promise that they should receive the Advance Bounty of Twenty-Five dollars. The stoppage of payment of this Bounty was not known here on account of the blockade so successfully kept up here for months by the rebels, and this promise was made in good faith. The men of this Regiment are for the most part refugees;[2] they have left their families in a suffering condition, and in need of the money. I would therefore ask that the advance of Twenty-Five Dollars Bounty be paid to the men of this Regiment who enlisted after the 23rd. of August last, as well as to those who can draw the same without further orders from the War Department.

I am advised that the money for the payment of Bounties is here in the hands of the proper disbursing officers.

Very Respectfully Your Obt. Sert
Andrew Johnson Mil. Gov'r.

L, DNA-RG107, Lets. Recd., Sec. of War, File T209 (114), 1863.

1. Three weeks earlier Assistant Secretary Christopher P. Wolcott, writing for Stanton, reported that the department had "exhausted every means within its power to secure payment of the money due to soldiers; that it has promptly prepared and signed every paper needful to that end; but that the difficulty is in the Treasury Department which cannot, at present, supply the means to meet the requisitions of this Department for such payments." Wolcott to Johnson, December 23, 1862, Copies of Lets. Sent, Vol. 51B (1862), Mil. B, RG107, NA.

2. The 5th Tenn. Cav., sometimes called the 1st Mid. Tenn. Cav., had been raised by William B. Stokes under a commission from Johnson. Filled largely in Nashville during July, 1862, the regiment consisted mostly of "recruits coming in from various counties in squads, making their way generally by night through a country invested by guerrillas and rebels of the most desperate and brutal character." *Tenn. Adj. Gen. Report* (1866), 441.

Certification of Congressional Election[1]

[Trenton] January 10, 1863.

I, Calvin S. Ezell,[2] coroner of Gibson county, Tennessee, do hereby certify that I opened and held an election in said county on the 29th day of December, 1862, for the purpose of electing a representative to the Congress of the United States from the 9th congressional district, and that at said election Alvin Hawkins[3] received four hundred and ninety-six (496) votes, and W. W. Freeman[4] 5. I further certify that many more votes would have been polled but for the fact that the recent raid of Brigadier General Forrest threw the people into confusion, and the stringent, though necessary, picket regulations at Trenton, the county seat of said county, and other points along the railroad, prevented many persons from voting who were anxious so to do.[5] I am satisfied that more than three-fourths of the voting population would have gone to the polls and voted but for the raid of General Forrest. I also certify that I received the vote from one district in Dyer county, as follows: Hawkins, 58; Freeman, 16; Johnson,[6] 1. The balance of Dyer county was so infested with guerillas as to render the opening and holding of an election by the people dangerous.

An election would have been held in this county on the 20th of January, 1863, but General Hurlburt's order[7] appointing that day was construed not to embrace the 9th congressional district, but only some portion of the 10th.

Calvin S. Ezell,
Coroner of Gibson County.

Governor Andrew Johnson,
Nashville, Tennessee.

House Report No. 46, 37 Cong., 3 Sess., 6.

1. This document appears as part of a sympathetic, but ultimately negative report of the House committee on elections reviewing "the credentials of Alvin Hawkins, claiming to have been elected a Representative from the ninth congressional district in Tennessee." That only about one-tenth of the voters participated, in an area "at that very moment under the control and occupation of contending armies in battle array" made a valid election "an impossibility." *House Report* No. 46, 37 Cong., 3 Sess., 2.

2. Calvin Ezell (b. *c*1811), a Gibson County farmer. 1850 Census, Tenn., Gibson, 11th Dist., 586; (1860), 7th Dist., 125.

3. See *Johnson Papers*, V, 185*n*.

4. Probably William W. Freeman (*c*1826-*fl*1870), a Tennessee-born Gibson County farmer, whose possessions totaled $29,500 on the eve of the war. Subsequently he joined the Confederate ranks as 1st lieutenant, Co. G, 12th Cav. Sistler, *1850 Tenn. Census*, II, 286; 1860 Census, Tenn., Gibson, 7th Dist., Trenton, 121; (1870), 5th Dist., 2; CSR, RG109, NA.

5. There would appear to have been valid military consideration—creating a diversion in the rear of Grant's advance toward Vicksburg, thereby delaying or even halting the Federal threat to that city—which produced Forrest's movement into this area of West Tennessee. But, according to the credentials committee, when the Confederates learned of Johnson's order calling for the election, "in order to prevent the holding of this election, the rebel General Forrest made a raid into this district just before the 29th, and on the day of

the election occupied almost all of it." Henry, *Forrest*, 107-20; *House Report* No. 46, 37 Cong., 3 Sess., 2.

6. Nat Johnson may have been a Lauderdale County physician (b. *c*1832) with $1,200 real and $7,195 personal property, or a Gibson County farmer (b. *c*1805) with $5,000 real and $8,000 personal property. 1860 Census, Tenn., Lauderdale, 1st Dist., 3; Gibson, 3rd Dist., 48.

7. Gen. Stephen A. Hurlbut's December 24 proclamation listed Madison, Haywood, Hardeman, Fayette, and Shelby counties as the areas in which "a fair expression of the popular will cannot be had." The order did not specify that the postponement would be limited to that portion of the tenth district but was worded so ambiguously as to provide support for differing interpretations. Memphis *Bulletin*, December 27, 1862.

From Donn Piatt[1]

Private—Confidential

Louisville Jany 11th 1863

Governor Andrew Johnson
of Tennessee &c &c &c
Governor,

I telegraphed you yesterday[2] and write again to day— We are drawing our investigation to a close and I wish now for you.[3] I have Said nothing about having you as a witness and would rather pick you up accidentally while passing through here than get out a summons—

I have yet to prove that the plains of Tenn could sustain an army that had "pluck and energy" sufficient to help itself[.]

I would like to find some one who knew of the movements of Breckinridge at the time of the invasion.[4] Can you tell me of such a witness—

Hoping soon to see you

I have the honor to be governor
Yours respectfully Donn Piatt
Maj. & AAG. Judge Advocate

ALS, DLC-JP.

1. Donn Piatt (1819-1891), an Ohio native and newspaper editor, served as common pleas judge of Hamilton County (1852-53), secretary of legation at Paris (1853-55), captain, major, and lieutenant colonel of the 13th Ohio Inf., and later Robert C. Schenck's chief of staff. After one term in the Ohio legislature (1865), he removed in 1868 to the nation's capital where he was correspondent of the Cincinnati *Commercial*, and a founder and co-editor of the independent *Capital* (1871-80). In his later years he wrote a number of books about the Civil War, including a biography of Gen. George H. Thomas (1893). *DAB*, XIV, 555-56; Charles G. Miller, *Donn Piatt: His Work and His Ways* (Cincinnati, 1893).

2. Piatt wired on January 10, "We are waiting for you[.] when can you be here[?]" Johnson Papers, LC.

3. Largely in response to the sweeping charges of treasonable activities leveled by Governors Johnson of Tennessee and Oliver P. Morton of Indiana, a commission to investigate the military operations of Gen. Don Carlos Buell during the Tennessee and Kentucky campaign of 1862 was set up in November of that year, heard testimony between December 1 and May 10, and ultimately made no recommendations. Johnson never testified in person but did make a deposition at Washington in April. *OR*, Ser. 1, XVI, Pt. I, 67, 697-98, 724; Warner, *Generals in Blue*, 52; Miller, *Donn Piatt*, 159-61; see Deposition to the Buell Commission, April 22, 1863.

4. Fearing the imminent conjuncture of Bragg's and Breckinridge's forces, Buell cautiously kept his army some distance from the Confederates after the battle of Perryville. Piatt wanted to discredit this strategy through witnesses who knew at the time that Breckinridge had no such intentions. *OR*, Ser. 1, XVI, Pt. I, 51, 315-16, 321.

To Abraham Lincoln

Nashville Jany 11th 1863

His Excy A Lincoln

The battle at Murfreesboro has inspired much confidence with Union men of the ultimate success of the Govt & has greatly discouraged Rebels but increased their bitterness.[1] If the Rebel Army could be expelled from the State & Union sentiment developed without fear or restraint, I still think Tennessee will be brought back into the Union by decided majority of popular vote. Eastern portion of the State must be redeemed before confidence can be inspired with the mass of the people that the Govt has the power to assert & maintain its authority in Tennessee[.] Your proclamation of the 1st excepting Tennessee has disappointed & disarmed many who were complaining & denouncing it as unjust & unwise.[2] I think the Exception in favor of Tennessee will be worth much to us Especially when we can get to discuss it before the people[.] I ordered congressional Elections in ninth & tenth Districts[.][3] have received no returns yet. I shall order Election in this District in a few days. Governor Campbell[4] should have been placed in command of this post. Things are not working well at this post considering the operations of what is called a detective police[5] under charge of persons wholly incompetent if not corrupt in the grossest sense of the term is causing much ill feeling and doing us great harm. I am with great respect

Yours Andrew Johnson

Tel, NRU; DNA-RG107, Tels. Recd., Halleck, Vol. 6 (1862-63).

1. These comments were in response to Lincoln's request for Johnson's views, expressed not only in his telegram of January 8 but more urgently in a wire two days later, acknowledging the governor's earlier reply about young Todd: "But I do wish your opinion of the effects of the late battles about Murfreesboro, upon the prospects of Tennessee." Lincoln to Johnson, January 10, 1863, Basler, *Works of Lincoln*, VI, 53.

2. The Emancipation Proclamation had declared free all slaves within any state or portion of a state in rebellion against the United States; the accompanying list of such areas did not include Tennessee. *OR*, Ser. 3, III, 2; see also Petition to President, December 4, 1862.

3. Both were West Tennessee districts, the ninth to the north and the tenth to the south.

4. William B. Campbell.

5. Organized at Nashville in December, 1862, by civilian William Truesdail under Rosecrans' authority, the army detective police were intended to maintain order, detect violations of trade regulations, and institute a counter-espionage system. Its multifarious activities, its secrecy, and its interference with the daily life of the people aroused both fear and hostility. Johnson was a sharp critic of Truesdail and his organization. Hall, *Military Governor*, 78, 83; John S. Daniel, Jr., Special Warfare in Middle Tennessee and Surrounding Areas, 1861-62 (M. A. thesis, University of Tennessee, 1971), 256; Fitch, *Annals*, 349.

From Daniel Stover

Louisville Ky
January 12th 1863.

Gov. A. Johnson,
Gov.

It has become necessary for me to make a statement to you of Some facts which have occured within the last few days.

Within a few days after I came to this place and made my Head-Quarters: One of my recruiting officers came in with 25 Recruits.— those 25 men together some 12 others came over from Greene & Cocke Counties in Company with one Thomas Reaves[1]—Who reported to R. M. Edwards that he (Reaves) had recruited those men for his (Edwards) Regiment and bore their expenses to the Regiment. The men (25) say they never enlisted with Reaves—Never signed their own name—nor authorised him to do so— Furthermore Reaves did not pay the men expenses— the men paid their own expenses and $50.00 to a Pilate to pilate them through the mountains— Then they was met at Rock Castle River Ky—by James L. Carter[2] my Recruiting officer, who properly enlisted the men and then paid their expenses to Lexington Ky There procured transportation for the men to this place— After all this Edwards claimed them. Also some 10 or 12 men Came to my Camp from Edwards—and said they had never been enlisted— But had been told by Edwards' officers in his presents—when they Came into his Camp—That if they did not join his Regiment—they must be sent back among the rebels and would not be allowed to remain this side of the Union Lines—And they wanted to Come into my regiment— I would not enlist the men until I knew whether I was right or not— Consequently I went to Gen Boyle— and asked him if it would be proper for me to enlist those men. When he sent me to Col W. Seawell[3] the Superintendent of the Recruiting Service in Kentucky. I went that same day to see Col Seawell. But he was sick, and could not be seen— Next morning I went again to Col Seawell's Office—found him unwell and he did not give me but little satisfaction on the subject—And before I could get Back to my encampment R. M. Edwards had by misrepresentation procured an order from Capt Fassen[4] inspecter General of Cavalry— and also another order for Col Robt Johnson— Some of Edwards men had also gone to Robt Regt—and said Edwards had lied to them—or his officers in order to get them to go into his Regt—And they wanted to stay with Robts Regt— We was served with the orders and ordered to report ourselves at Col Seawell's office at 2 o clock. We went and the matter was refered to Maj Setgreaves[5]—And after making some statements Major Setgreaves decided that Edwards' men had not been propoerly enlisted And had the right to go where they pleased—until they was sworn into a

Regiment.— this Edwards had not done, nor had no right to do so.— until his regiment was full.— After the matter was settled I and Robt Returned to our respective camps. The next day we received orders from Gen Boyle which Edwards had got by misrepresentation to the General—Ordering us to return all the men in our Camps that belonged to Edwards who had Drawn Clothing from his regiment— I sent all the men in my camp that he (Edwards) claimed—(except the 25 heretofore spoken off being Recruited by Carter at Rock Castle River.) Col. Robt. did not send back the men called for. But wrote a letter to General Boyle—Stating that all the men that was now in his Camp; left there home in E. Tennessee to Join his (Robt's) Regiment—And had Come through the mountains for that purpose and with that intention—And if they had not thought they Could have Joined his (Robt's) Regt when they Come up with it. They never would have left their Homes in E Tennessee—But it having been represented to them by Edwards recruiting officers that Robt Regt was full and they Could not get into it—And to some of them that his Regt was in western Virginia—and they Could not get to him &c—

In the mean time Robt received another order from Gen Boyle to report himself at his (Boyle's) head Quarters the next day at 11 oclock[.] This was Thursday the 8th Inst— Robt and myself went to the General's head Quarters at the appointed time & Robt had a statement from those men; that they had come up from Edwards' Showing they left their homes to Join his Robt's Reg[.] when they came up to Edwards' Regt They was told by his officers that Robt's Regt was full and that there was no chance to get into his Regt. &c, &c. Gen Boyle read the letter that Robt. wrote and the statements of the men in our presents—And then remarked to Edwards his being present that those men was from Robt's County and adjoining Counties; and ought to belong to his Regt. and be with him.— Furthermore he remarked to Robt—that he would keep all the men he has—take a list of their names—And Robt Q. M. Receipt Edwards Q. M. for the Clothing which the men have drawn from Edwards Regt.— But he Robt—must not take any more of Edwards men— Then we come away from Gen. Boyle's H'd Qrs—thinking all was settled—And Robt was going along attending to the business of his Regiment— And on Friday 9th Inst; Gen Boyle sent out and had Robt. arrested.— he was taken to the Louisville Hotel—and ordered to stay in his Room— Robt remained in his Room until this morning when he was released— it is said that the Cause of Robt arrest was that Edwards had went and represented to Gen Boyle that Robt had taken about 125 of his men after Boyle had told him he must not take any more of E's men[.] the above is said to be the cause— I really dont know it to be so— I have been an eye witness to all the facts that I state—And whether it is right or wrong—I am satisfied that Robt and myself both have been misrepresented—And Great Injustice Done Robt—Also there is a strong feeling and prejudice here against Robt— Why this is I can not tell—

I fully believe that the object of some persons either here or else where—is to mortify the feelings of the family by taking or trying to take the advantage of Robt— I may be mistaken—But dont think I am.—

Also I have been informed by good authority that Some One has been reporting Col Robt to the War Department—in order to get him Discharged—or his command taken from him—to get his place—or for some other person to be placed in his stead— I would say to you that I think it nothing but justice to Col Robt and yourself that you Demand of the War Department the name—or person who has been reporting him— You will please act on your own Judgment on this matter— I think it is an important matter; and steps should be taken to trap the guilty individual— I will not make any direct charge against any one—But I am of opinion that it is some of the Carter's.—[6]

Gov. I know I have been somewhat tedious But I wanted to make myself understood—and therefore have Give you the details as well as I was able to do so.—

I have about 80 men all told— there is a rumor that 6 or 700 have started to Join my Regt—But whether they will come or not I can not tell— Since this last raid into E Tennessee By the Carters again[7]—the Tennesseans have quit Coming over—at least there is a check at the present time—

Respectfully Yours
Daniel Stover

LS, DLC-JP.

1. Thomas H. Reeves (1843-1926), North Carolina-born farmer and lawyer, rose from private to colonel of the 4th Tenn. Inf., USA. Admitted to the bar in 1866, he served in the regular army (1866-68) and as a justice of the peace, chairman of the Washington County court, county attorney, mayor of Jonesboro, assistant clerk of the Tennessee legislature, U. S. marshal for East Tennessee, and delegate to the 1876 Republican National Convention. *Goodspeed's East Tennessee*, 1281; Knoxville *Journal*, August 26, 1926.

2. James L. Carter (1823-1872), Greene County miller, served as 1st lieutenant and captain, Co. A, 4th Tenn. Inf., USA (1862-64). Resigning in May, 1864, because of sickness and a family "consisting of females," he was charged the following February with having earlier, in June and July, 1864, advised men of his former company "to desert . . . and take their arms and go home telling them that the Authorities could not punish them for it." CSR, RG94, NA; 1860 Census, Tenn., Greene, 12th Dist., 75; Reynolds, *Greene County Cemeteries*, 243.

3. Washington Seawell (1802-1888), Virginia native and West Pointer (1825), had risen to the rank of colonel by 1862. He served as chief mustering and disbursing officer in Kentucky (1862-63) and in the Department of the Pacific (1863), as well as acting assistant provost marshal at San Francisco (1865-66). *Appleton's Cyclopaedia*, V, 448; Heitman, *Register*, I, 872.

4. Belgian-born Julius Fasses served in the Union army (1862-65) as captain and later as assistant inspector of cavalry, District of Western Kentucky. Powell, *Army List*, 788; *U. S. Official Register* (1863), 174; *OR*, Ser. 1, XXIII, Pt. II, 270.

5. Lorenzo Sitgreaves (*c*1810-1888), at this time superintendent of volunteer recruiting, was a Pennsylvania career soldier who graduated from West Point in 1832 and prior to 1861 served as an engineer at various posts, as well as in Mexico, receiving the brevet of captain for gallant and meritorious conduct at Buena Vista. During the Civil War he was mustering officer at Albany, New York (1861-62), disbursing officer at Madison, Wisconsin

(1863-64), and inspector of the temporary defenses in Kansas and Nebraska (1864-65). Retiring in July, 1866, with the rank of lieutenant colonel, he spent the rest of his life in Washington. George W. Cullum, *Biographical Register of the United States Military Academy at West Point, New York* (2 vols., New York, 1868), I, 409; *West Point Register* (1970), 222; Commission Branch, RG94, NA.

6. For Gen. Samuel P. Carter and Col. James P. T. Carter, see *Johnson Papers*, IV, 659*n*, 518*n*.

7. From late December into early January, Gen. Samuel P. Carter led a small cavalry force from Manchester, Kentucky, to East Tennessee where he destroyed bridges and fought several skirmishes, including one at Perkins Mill on December 28. Long, *Civil War Almanac*, 301.

To William S. Rosecrans, Murfreesboro

Nashville, January 14th 1863

Maj. Genl. Rosecrans.
Commanding Dep't of the Cumberland.
General:

I would respectfully call your attention to a matter which, I think, on the mere suggestion, will receive your favorable action.

I do not write in any spirit of fault-finding, nor do I wish to be regarded as objecting to any proceedings, on the part of any person or persons claiming to act here by your authority, that have been in accordance with the requirements of civil and military law; but, General, since you left Nashville, the proceedings had by the Detective Police & "Provost Court", connected with the army (and who assume to act by your authority) have been of such character, I am constrained to say, that, in my opinion, they not only fail in what I suppose to have been the object had in view by their location at this Post, but have done and are still doing great damage to our cause, and the effect of their operations is most decidedly averse to a restoration of a correct public sentiment.

A detective police, properly organized, and conducted upon correct principles, might do some good in connection with the interests & movements of the army, but I am compelled to say that the Provost Court and Detective Police here, by the extensive jurisdiction assumed and the summary manner in which they undertake to dispose of the persons & property of citizens, have not only excited a feeling of indignation among the more conservative portion of the community, but have greatly impaired the confidence of the loyal men, that class to whom we look for active support, in the correct intentions of the Government, it being held responsible for the unjust acts of its reputed agents.

We have here a United States Court, a U S. Attorney, and a U. S. Marshal for the District of Middle Tennessee—all the machinery necessary for the execution of the laws of the United States in that portion of this District restored to Federal control. There are for the Government of this city a Mayor and Boards of Aldermen and Council, a city Police, and Recorder's court, efficiently performing their respective functions; while the Commandant of the Post, and a Provost Marshal are here to execute and carry out all proceedings by military authority.

If, notwithstanding these facts, the necessity for the continuance of the "Provost Court" and Army detective police at this post still exists, I do sincerely hope, General, that, for the single purpose of promoting the public good, and restoring, as far as we can, the law and the Constitution, they may be restricted, in their operations, to that which pertains exclusively to military affairs and is authorized by military law.

I believe that common justice to this community requires it, and in asking it, I but express the sentiments of the union men of this city & vicinity. Without undertaking to enumerate cases, I will state that the complaints against these parties have become so loud and so numerous that justice to them as well as to the public would seem to require that an examination into their proceedings should be ordered.

With great respect, Your Obt. Sert.
Andrew Johnson Mil. Gov'r.—

L, DNA-RG393, Dept. of the Cumberland, Lets. Recd., File 12-J-63; DLC-JP.

From Mary Clendining[1]

Fountain Head
Jan 15/63.

Gov Johnson

Dr Sir—please find inclosed the bill of damage[2] sustained by me (Mary Clendining) and I hope you will have the case investigated immediately for my situation is an awful one[.] Col Case[3] gave orders to all of my neighbors not to help me, consequently I am turned out of doors with eight helpless children and not a neighbor dared to turn a hand for me so you can well imagine my situation and for God's sake act immediately and let me know my fate[.][4] My neighbors are all willing to do what they can in my case when they are permitted[.]

Yours truly Mary Clendining

ALS, DLC-JP.

1. Probably Mary Clendening (b. *c*1815), wife of William Clendening, a Tennessee-born carpenter, who in 1860 had nine children, ranging in age from four to twenty-two. One son, twenty-four-year-old James C., was serving in Virginia as a Confederate soldier in Co. C, 7th Tenn. Inf. (1861-65). 1860 Census, Tenn., Sumner, 17th Dist., 66; *Tennesseans in the Civil War*, II, 93.

2. This included an eighteen by twenty-two foot frame dwelling house, $500; a sixteen by eighteen-foot log kitchen, $250; a twelve by fourteen-foot log smokehouse, $75; three feather beds and bed clothing, $40; one bedstead, $5; one kitchen table, $5; one looking glass, $2.50; books, $10; wearing apparel, $40; kitchen furniture, $10; and 500 pounds of bacon, $40; a total of $977.50. Johnson Papers, LC.

3. Henry Case (*c*1825-1884), a Connecticut native and a lawyer in Morgan and Scott counties, Illinois, was at this time colonel, 129th Ill. Inf. (1862-65). Described by a fellow officer as a "good orator," he was breveted brigadier March 16, before being mustered out June 8, 1865. CSR, RG94, NA; Heitman, *Register*, I, 288; Fritz Haskell, ed., "Diary of

Colonel William Camm, 1861-1865," *Journal of the Illinois State Historical Society*, XVIII (1926), 808.

4. Johnson endorsed the letter: "To be presented to the 'Board of Claims.' "

From Fanny Drane[1]

Scottville Ky January 15 [1863]

Govenor Johnson

Sir I have taken the liberty to write you a few lines in regard to my slaves that are running at large about Nashville; as a gentleman of our Town was on his way to the senate I got him to see General Boyle, for me, and he says you are the gentleman to attend to that and you ought to do it, and as I am as loyal a Lady as there is, and as strong for the constitution and union as any body in the state of Kentucky I think you ought to take measures to return my slaves to me. I never have uttered disloyal sentiments in my life, although I have two sons in the *rebel* army,[2] they was persuaded by others not by their Parents[.] nothing left undone on our parts to prevent their going, there are seven there and if you will be so kind as to send them to me or put them where I can get them, I will give you thier names, to wit Gerry, Ben, Julia, Mary Bettie and two children all of which have been gone a year, I called to see you before I left Nashville and you did not give me any satisfaction and now I remind you of it again[.] The reason that I am attending to this business myself is that my husband is in such bad health he is not able to do, it now[.] if you please attend to this and I will reward you some way, yours with respect

Franny Drane

ALS, DLC-JP.

1. Probably Frances (b. *c*1795), Kentucky-born wife of Antony Drane (b. *c*1795), a Nashville barkeeper with $8,000 personal and $15,000 real property. 1860 Census, Tenn., Davidson, 10th Dist., 73.

2. Perhaps J. R. Drane, 1st sergeant, Co. A, and Thomas Drane, private, Co. D, 1st Btn. (McNairy's), Tenn. Cav., CSA. CSR, RG109, NA.

From Daniel Stover

Louisville Jany 15th 1863

Andw. Johnson
Mil Gov
Mother & Mary anxious to return to Nashville[.][1] Mother quite feeble[.]

Danl Stover Col 4 Tenn

Tel, DLC-JP.

1. Eliza Johnson and her daughter had arrived in Louisville two days earlier. A week after this telegram Stover reported that Eliza's health had begun to improve; however, she was not able to travel until late May, reaching Nashville on the 30th. Stover to Johnson, January 13, 23, 24, 1863, Johnson Papers, LC; Nashville *Dispatch,* May 31, 1863.

From Ulysses S. Grant

Memphis, Tenn. Jan. 16. 1863

Gov. Andrew Johnson
Nashville, Tenn.

The Union men here deem it advisable not to hold an election in this District now, and ask that it be postponed until an election shall be ordered for Governor, members of Legislature and Representatives.

If you will postpone it notify me by telegraph.[1]

Signed U. S. Grant Maj. Genl.

LB copy, DNA-RG393, Dept. of the Tenn., Lets. Sent, Vol. I; DLC-U. S. Grant Papers.

1. Although Johnson's response has not been found, the elections, scheduled for January 20, were not held.

From William G. Brownlow

Confidential

Cincinnati, Jany 17, 1863

Gov. Johnson:

I have just returned from Louisville, too sick to proceed to Nashville, or I would have gone on. The Cavalry Regiment left the day before the storm,[1] and encamped the first night between Floyds' Fork and Salt River, and the latter was rising so fast that I doubt their being able to cross next morning. If, however, they should get over, they will have a hard time of it, and cant reach Nashville under two weeks.

That is a fine Regiment, and numbered 980 when they left, but they are on wild and fresh horses, not sufficiently drilled to go into battle. I think you ought to keep the Regiment at Nashville awhile, if you can so arrange with Gen. Rosecrans, that they may drill, and that you may regulate them.

Capt. McNish,[2] a very reliable man, who was in the late Carter expedition, and who used to be an Engineer on the Road between Knoxville and Bristol, tells me that that man *Maj Tracy* has a deep scheme laid to get my son to resign,[3] and then to impeach Col. Johnson, and himself suceede in the command. He cant use my son for any purpose. But I was sorry to find that a bad state of things existed, as between Edwards and the Cavalry Regiment. And from all I could gather, *Tracy* was keeping up the bad feeling. They are all East Tennesseans, and ought not to have any quarrels among them.

Saml. Hunt, brother of the Doctor,[4] has got in here, from Cleveland, having come through great tribulations. He says that your threat to send Rebel families out of Middle Tennessee, if other Union families were sent out of East Tennessee, put a stop to their removal of Union families.[5]

Thos. J. Campbell,[6] is confiscating the property of Union men who have come into Kentucky, and he shows no quarters to their families whatever. The Unionists are begging for an Army to be sent in to relieve them. From all I can learn there is an expedition[7] now fitting out now, for the work, to be commanded by *Gen. Garfield,*[8] who will start from here, *via* Lexington.

I am, &c, W. G. Brownlow

ALS, DLC-JP.

1. During its two-month stay at Camp Dennison, Ohio, Robert Johnson's 4th Tenn. Inf., James P. Brownlow, lieutenant colonel, had become the 1st Tenn. Cav. Arriving at Louisville on Christmas Day, 1862, it did scouting duty until January 13 when it started for Nashville, reaching Bardstown that night, camping in the fairground. During the night an unusually severe storm, according to the regiment's historian, dumped snow to the depth of twenty-six inches, compelling the unit to "lay up four or five days." By mid-day, January 27, the command reached the Tennessee line and shortly thereafter arrived in Nashville, having been "much impeded by bad roads and high waters." Carter, *First Tenn. Cav.,* 57, 59, 61-66; Robert Johnson to Andrew Johnson, January 18, 20, 1863, Johnson Papers, LC; Louisville *Journal,* January 14-17, 19, 1863; Nashville *Union,* January 29, 1863.

2. Thomas McNeish (b. *c*1834), a Knoxville and Sullivan County resident and prior to the war an engineer on the East Tennessee and Virginia Railroad, served as 1st lieutenant, Co. I, 81st Pa. Inf. (1861-62) and as captain, Co. B, 3rd Tenn. Inf. (1862-64). McNeish to Johnson, December 18, 1861, Johnson Papers, LC; 1860 Census, Tenn., Sullivan, 17th Dist., 55; CSR, RG94, NA.

3. Having resigned from the 2nd Tenn. Inf., USA, in June, 1862, because of difficulties with fellow officers, William R. Tracy reenlisted in the 1st Tenn. Cav. in October, and after a few months was again experiencing problems. In a letter to the "soldiers of the 1st East Tennessee Cavalry," June 18, 1863, Tracy announced that, by command of General Rosecrans, he apologized for his part in the occurrence of March 10—no details given—that he had not intended to insult the regiment or wound the feelings of anyone in it. The next day Col. James P. Brownlow wrote Col. Calvin Goddard, Rosecrans' assistant adjutant general, "The resignation of *fifteen* of my *best* officers have been tendered because Maj Tracys was not accepted before[.] They will not serve under or with him." CSR, RG94, NA; for Tracy, see *Johnson Papers*, V, 140*n*.

4. For Dr. William Hunt, Brownlow's brother-in-law, see *ibid*., 359*n*. Samuel Hunt (1826-1899), a Bradley County farmer with a $6,000 estate, was arrested for his unionist sympathies in late 1861 and imprisoned at Tuscaloosa. At the conclusion of the war he was on Governor Brownlow's staff as brigadier and inspector general, later serving as clerk of the county court (1866-70) and Cleveland postmaster. J. S. Hurlburt, *History of the Rebellion in Bradley County, East Tennessee* (Indianapolis, 1866), 113; 1860 Census, Tenn., Bradley, 6th Dist., 5; *U. S. Official Register* (1879), II, 339; *Goodspeed's East Tennessee,* 800; *Tenn. Adj. Gen. Report* (1866), 11; Ernest L. Ross, comp., *Historical Cemetery Records of Bradley County, Tennessee* (2 vols., Cleveland, 1973), II, 161.

5. Johnson's proclamation of May 9, 1862. See *Johnson Papers*, V, 374-75.

6. Thomas J. Campbell (1824-1885), McMinn County banker who moved to Cleveland in 1856, served as major, 5th (McClellan's) Tenn. Btn. Cav., CSA (1861-62), and as sequestration receiver for lower East Tennessee, migrating after the war to Paris, Texas. CSR, RG109, NA; Penelope Johnson Allen, "Leaves from the Family Tree," Chattanooga *Times*, February 24, 1935; *Goodspeed's East Tennessee*, 801.

7. The Parson's concern for East Tennessee apparently caused him to grasp at any straw; this rumor seems to have been premature at best. Eight months later, when Federal troops did march from Lexington to East Tennessee, they were commanded by Gen. Ambrose Burnside, rather than Garfield. Long, *Civil War Almanac,* 398.

8. James A. Garfield (1831-1881), of Ohio, former president of Hiram College (1857-61) and future President of the United States, had recently been named brigadier general and chief of staff, Army of the Cumberland. Before the end of the current year he left the army and began a long tenure in the House of Representatives (1863-80). *BDAC*,

929-30; *DAB*, VII, 145-50; Allan Peskin, *Garfield: A Biography* (Kent, Ohio, 1978), *passim*.

From William S. Rosecrans

Head-Quarters, Department of the Cumberland,
Murfreesboro, January 17, 1863.

His Excellency Andrew Johnson
Military Governor &c Nashville, Tenn.
Governor:—

I have the honor, to acknowledge the receipt of your letter of the 14th inst, relating to the Police system of my Army, at Nashville. I am obliged to you for the interest you express in the success of the cause in which I am engaged, and your suggestion as to the proper conduct of affairs at Nashville. I am aware that complaints have been made in regard to the Provost Court, but, so far as I am aware, they have generally come from smugglers and unscrupulous Jews,[1] who have been detected in contraband trade, and their property confiscated. If you will furnish me the names and circumstances in any case in which wrong has been done, the matter shall be thoroughly investigated, and justice done.

Renewing the expression of my thanks for your suggestions, I am,

Governor, very respectfully your obedient servant
W. S. Rosecrans Major Genl Comdg Depart.

LS, DLC-JP.

1. Probably an allusion to the breaking up, late in 1862, of smuggling operations at Nashville conducted by Shwab, Salzkotter, and H. Dreyfoos of the firm of Shwab & Co., and by a number of others, including Isaac, Mike, and Abraham Friedenberg, Soloman Guthman, A. Haas, and Leo Cohen. Fitch, *Annals,* 491-93, 496-97.

From William C. Pickens

January 19, 1863, Camp near Murfreesboro; LS, DLC-JP.

Commander of 3rd Tenn. Cav. asks Johnson "to keep myself and those under my command from being placed under a Northern Man, or any other person than an East Tennessean." Now attached, under the governor's order, to Gen. James G. Spears's brigade—"the Brigade we all very anxiously desire to be attached to"—Pickens wishes to "go as the army advances . . . if Consistent with the public service."

From William B. Stokes

Camp South of Murfreesboro,
January, 19th 1863.

Andrew Johnson
Military Gov. Tenn.
Dear friend:
I am again setting up. I can now walk about my cabin. I have had a severe spell,[1] but thank God I will be able to mount my horse again in a day or two.

I write this to get you to assist me in getting clear of this man Newburry,[2] who has managed to get himself on Genl. Rosecranse Staff as chief of Couriers. He has one company of mine, he sends out & orders me to send him *orderlies*. He is laughing in his sleeve,[3] Saying that he is at last over me. He has been denouncing the Regiment as Cowards, sais they run, & all such slanderous talk,
Now Sir to be disgraced, & humiliated by his being over me, I cannot submit to it, & before I will do it I will be compelled to resign. I want you to write to Genl. Rosecrans, & state his case in full, & also request Lt. Henry L. Newburry to resign as he agreed to do, in case he did not suit me, This Gov. I hope you will do for me. I dont want to Quit the service, but I will not submit to being ordered by such a man as Newburry. This can all be remedied by your writing a strong letter to the Genl,
Besides it is taking a commissiond officer out of the Regt. and I have none to spare as so many are sick, others have been mustered out. if N. wont resign let him report to me & do duty in the Regt. I hope to be able to come to your city before long.

Respectfully Your, Obt. Servt.
W. B. Stokes
Col. Comdg, 4th M. T. Cavalry

ALS, DLC-JP.

1. Evidently the rigors of Stones River had taken their toll of the nearly fifty-year-old soldier. "From the arduous labor and great exposure in the recent battle . . . the Colonel had been confined to his room." Nashville *Union,* February 1, 1863.

2. Lt. Henry L. Newberry.

3. An expression dating back at least to the sixteenth century and meaning, as the *Oxford English Dictionary*, VI, 103, quaintly puts it, "to nurse inward feelings of amusement."

From Robert Johnson

Mumfordsville Jan'y 20th 1863
Head Qrs 1st Tenn. Cav

Hon. Andy. Johnson
Military Governor of Tennessee.

I am crossing Green River, this morning with my entire Train.[1] most of the regiment is across. owing to the fact of there being but one ferry boat at this place I will be delayed untill near noon. but expect to reach Glasgow to night.

I have shipped by railroad from this point under charge of Marquis D. Lyles,[2] Quartermaster sergeant of the Regiment, all my tents and other Camp Equipage, and the sick direct to Nashville. you will please give Mr. Lyle all instructions necessary in regard to the disposal of the above equipage until my arrival at Nashville.

Any favor and accomodation to Mr. Lyles will be duly reciprocated by me and I hope you will give them all proper instructions.

Respectfully Your Obt Servt
Robert Johnson, Col. Comd Ten Cav

L, DLC-JP.

1. Having left Louisville on January 13 and being delayed two days at Bardstown due to snow, Robert anticipated that he would arrive in Nashville by the twenty-seventh. Robert Johnson to Johnson, January 18, 20, 1863, Johnson Papers, LC.

2. Marquis D. Lyles (*c*1841-*fl*1880), a Jefferson County farm laborer, currently quartermaster sergeant, Co. F, and later 1st lieutenant, Co. G, 1st Tenn. Cav., resigned because of disability in August, 1863. 1880 Census, Tenn., Jefferson, 7th Dist., 1; CSR, RG94, NA.

To Robert Johnson

Nashville Jan'y 20th 1863

To Col. Rob't. Johnson.

There has been and will be no disposition made of Edwards until you reach this place. Take time and see that all your men are provided for and horses taken care of. Do your duty and all will end right.[1]

Andrew Johnson

Tel, DLC-JP.

1. Already en route a week, Robert had wired from Munfordville, Kentucky, "Make no disposal of Edwards until I reach Nashville. . . . Answer immediately." The next day, despite his father's reassurance, he returned to the fray with the admonition: "Make no disposition of his men until I arrive as the men want to come to my Regt[.] Edwards is a scoundrel as facts will develope on my arrival[.]" Robert Johnson to Johnson, January 20, 21, 1863, Johnson Papers, LC.

To A. Henry Thurston, Nashville

January 20, 1863, Nashville; L (fragment), DLC-JP.

Sends assistant medical director at Nashville a letter of Hugh Douglas, merchant, who "Since receiving assurances from you that he might rest easy and open up his spring goods . . . has proceeded to do so." Inasmuch as Douglas has "a large stock on the way," Johnson hopes "it will be found consistent with the public interest and comfort of the sick & wounded," to relocate Dr. James M. Weaver, a surgeon with the 93rd Ohio, and "let Mr. Douglas continue in the possession of his property."

From William A. Rodgers and William M. Sawyers[1]

Camp near Murfreesborro Jan 22 1863

Govenor

You will see from the accompanieing statements[2] of the officers of this Regment what their opinions and feelings are with regard to the blending of the 3rd and sixth Regt. You will probaly bee astonished when I state to you that from what I can learn from the soldiers my honest opinion is that they will mutiny immediately after it is done. I sincerely wish it was stopped if for no other reason than to keep the men from disgraceing themselves. As to my position I know that it would not interfere with me for I am the Segnior Surgeon in the Brig. and the Regt would have to go on in the name of the 3rd thereby probaly securing all our officers their positions The fact is we havent got more officers than it would take for five Companies. The objection that the most of our men would make is to Cooper[3] himself[.] The officers and men are apprised or think they are that the thing is in contemplation to change the commander[.] they have no objection to a change but they do not want Cooper. They say Childs and Cross.[4] I would say Cross and Childs[.] The present commander sayes he will (or probaly has resigned)[.][5] at all events I think his health is such that if he does not resign the Regment would not care if he was relieved. If he is relieved and Cross and Childs given the command I feel confident this can be made a first rate Regt and some individuals in the Regment who have wanted authority to raise a Regment would be satisfied to stay in it and help resuscitate it[.] we are apprised that there has been things done that ought not to have been done and things left undone that ought to have been done[6] which can be remidied by the change above named[.] You will probaly want to know why the proposed union is so odious to us[.] There was great rivaldry at the time the Regt was making up and a great many hard things said on bowth sides. We think Cooper is not a man of fine feelings if he consents to take the command of this Regment after that especully when he could not make a Regt himself with Col and Gen Carter to help him all the time. Capt Sawyers is present and concurs in the above[.]

This is confidential[.]

Respectfully Your Obdt. Servt.
Wm. A Rodgers Surg 3rd Reg E T V
Wm. M. Sawyers Capt Co K 3" R. E. T. V

Andrew Johnston
Military Gov Ten

ALS (Rodgers), DLC-JP.

1. William A. Rodgers (1820-*fl*1890), Graveston (Knox County) physician, merchant, and farmer, was assistant surgeon, 1st Tenn. Inf. and subsequently surgeon, 3rd Tenn. William M. Sawyers (*c*1835-*fl*1870), Jefferson County farmer with $6,000 property, served as captain, Co. K, 3rd Tenn. Inf. (February, 1862-August, 1863) and thereafter as lieutenant colonel. After the war he was a deputy marshal. *Goodspeed's Knox*, 1035-36; 1860 Census, Tenn., Jefferson, 215; (1870), New Market P. O., 7th Dist., 20; *Tenn. Adj. Gen. Report* (1866), 57; Sistler, *1890 Tenn. Veterans Census*, 271.

2. A petition, signed by nineteen officers and the chaplain and dated January 22, protesting the proposal to "blend this Regment with the 6th (Cooper's)," was attached. Johnson Papers, LC.

3. For Joseph A. Cooper, colonel, 6th Tenn. Inf., see *Johnson Papers*, IV, 663*n*.

4. John C. Chiles (b. *c*1820), Anderson County farmer with $7,000 in realty and $7,500 in personalty, was lieutenant colonel, 3rd Tenn. from March, 1862, until his resignation in April a year later. 1860 Census, Tenn., Anderson, 38; *Tenn. Adj. Gen. Report* (1866), 57; for William Cross, see *Johnson Papers*, V, 43*n*.

5. Col. Leonidas C. Houk.

6. A paraphrase of the Morning Prayer in the *Book of Common Prayer*.

From Donn Piatt

Private Confidential

Louisville Jany 24th 1863

Hon Andrew Johnson
Military Governor of Tenn. &c &c &c
Governor.

I am sorry not to see you although I have determined not to call you as a witness. I think it better to leave this investigation to Military men altho' your opinion and knowledge of certain facts would have great weight with the Commission[.] But it is better to have your opinion sustained by the officers themselves under this general. I have found a document here strongly confirmatory of your opinion that our friend was fighting for a boundery and not "the Union as it was."[1] After the capture of Mumfordsville when he knew that Bragg's army was not more than 36000 strong and inferior to his own, he writes to Nelson.[2] Encouraging the panic in Louisville by the tone of his letter—and advising that General to fall back—evacuating Louisville and to either cross the river or retreat down the river to some point where he could form a conjunction with the army from Nashville. This sounds strangely in accordance with the opinion expressed to you that Nashville was a place of no Military importance and should have been evacuated long since.[3]

We adjourn from this to Cincinnati tomorrow where I hope to close in a few days.

I see by the press that in the Bureau of Military Justice about being added to the War Department there is to be an Asst Judge Advocate with the rank of Colonel[.] This is a position I would be desirous of holding[.] May I ask your help. I am well aware that our short personal acquaintance scarcely justifies this request. But I know also, that you require only a short time to make up a correct opinion of any man. I should not be called upon to solicit assistance in this, but for that my acting as Judge Advocate, in this investigation, has brought upon me the opposition of certain corrupt politicians, who have been cultivating this General for some unknown purpose of their own.

My education as a lawyer added to my experience as an officer peculiarly fits me for a position of this sort—and trusting that you may find time and inclination to write it to Mr. Stanton or the President I remain Governor

Yours respectfully Donn Piatt
Lt. Col. and Judge Adv.

ALS, DLC-JP.

1. Although the letter in question is not extant, other correspondence makes it clear that the governor entertained strong reservations about Buell's dedication to a victorious war—and, indeed, about his loyalty. Writing to the President in the fall of 1862, Johnson speculated about the general's "intention to occupy a defensive position" and his indifference to Tennessee unionists, adding that "Buell is very popular with the Rebels, and the impression is that he . . . favors the establishment of the Southern Confederacy." Ergo, "fighting for a boundery" would imply that the general was not averse to a negotiated peace instead of restoring "the Union as it was"—a slogan of the earlier war years. See Letter to Abraham Lincoln, September 1, 1862.

2. In his letter of the preceding September 22, Buell indicated that his movements depended on those of the Confederates. He advised Gen. William Nelson not to defend Louisville unless he was strongly entrenched, and "under no circumstances," to fight Bragg's main force. Nelson might, at his own discretion, either cross the Ohio or join Buell's army at the mouth of Salt River. *OR,* Ser. 1, XVI, Pt. I, 18-19; for Buell and Nelson, see *Johnson Papers,* V, 33*n*; IV, 549*n*.

3. Concerned over Nashville during the Confederate invasion of Kentucky in September, 1862, Johnson, in three interviews with Buell, had urged the necessity of holding the city. In the second exchange, according to the governor, Buell made the statement alluded to. Deposition to the Buell Commission, April 22, 1863; Hall, *Military Governor,* 63-65.

From Joseph E. Manlove[1]

White's Creek, January 28, /63.

To Genl. Gillem[2] or Gov. Johnson,
Dear Sir,

I trust I shall not be considered impertinent for obtruding upon your time and patience, a subject of the first importance to me; and in view of the relation I sustain to you, and the Government which you represent, hope you will readily appreciate the motives which prompt me in thus addressing you.

Without further preface,—I was informed on yesterday morning that I was again to be arrested, and sent to a northern prison. I was slow to credit it; but the information came through such a source as to leave no doubt upon my mind of its truth.

I need not remind you that I was arrested on the first day of October last, *not for any alledged political offence,* but as a hostage for Dr Moore.[3] I was retained for near a month in the State Prison—then paroled and sent south to obtain the Dr's absolution from his Oath of Allegiance to the Southern Confederacy. The Dr was released upon the expressed condition that I was not again to be molested for any "past offences". Upon my release the release was handed to Dr Moore, and Genl. Gillem told me, (as I doubt not he has not forgotten) in the Capitol that I was now free—the Dr & I occupying our original status. While under parole, I have no knowledge of violating it in word or deed— Shortly after my return from the Southern Army, I subscribed the Oath of allegiance to the government of the U. S. If I have violated it in any manner, I am unconscious of it. The Order, requiring the Citisens of Nashville and Davidson County to give bond[4] would have been obeyed before this—but for the difficulty of getting to Nashville— I have been to Nashville but twice each day rainy and very inclement, since the issuance of that order. If then under this state of facts, I am again to be deprived of my liberty,—forced away from a large and dependent family[5] I simply ask for what? can it be so? Either of you gentlemen can inform me, and I have confidence to believe you will. That I have a few, and I thank God, but few, enemies, some of whom, availing themselves of the deplorable state of our Country—Knowing how easy it is to prejudice and injure any man whom they happen to dislike, that may, by false statements for sinister objects, have, pointed me out as a fit subject for exile, and punishment, is, I think, probable.—provided my information be correct. I trust, however, it is not.

In this connexion, as I have no concealments and never will have, of my political antecedents, allow me very briefly to allude to my past political history—of no interest to any human being in the world but myself but, in some degree reflecting upon my present position. I claim to be, before the present distracted state of the Country one of the oldest, if not the *oldest* Whig in the County. my youthful political prejudices, I will not say opinions, were formed in 1824—Messrs Adams & Jackson being the only opposing Candidates for the presidency, voted for in the County of my nativity. For no reasons of my own, but a prejudice in favor of My Father's choice, Mr. Adams I became then, an Adam's man[.] with that party in its various names and phases I have always been associated. In 1860 I voted for Bell & Everett—with their short but significant platform.[6] I did, during that Canvass make some speeches in my homely phrases in which I warned the people of the consequences of the election of a sectional Candidate, dreading as much the fire eater of the South as the abolitionist of the North—believing that each intended to bring upon the Country the present disaster and horrors, if it were necessary to the accomplishment of their object.

After the result of the struggle was known, and "*Secession*" became the order of the day, I again, seeing these dangers by [*sic*] with which the Country was threatened) abandoned for a time, my only legitimate vocation, and labored publickly and privately, consienciously and zealously, to save Tennessee in the Union. By a majority unprecidented in any previous election in the State, at the February Election 1860 [*sic*], she proclaimed her attachment to the Union. Thus matters stood until the 14th April, when the President's proclamation calling for 75000, was issued. This fell upon the country like an electric spark in dry stubble. The stoughtest and strongest union men quailed, faultered and gave up all as lost[.] Secession was marvelously Strengthed and so intolerant that reflecting, Sober minded men, with conservative Union prclivities were not safe from taunt and insult. Blieving as I most honestly did, tho' it was painful to admit the belief, that a sectional struggle was inevitable,—in a word that civil war with all its horrors, which in my humble way, I had endeavored to avert would come upon the country, like the shipwrecked mariner, I began to cast about to see where I was to stand. My decision is known to you. Could I under the circumstances, had done otherwise? Certainly not without a sacrifice that few men are willing or have the moral courage to make, and yet I believe I have sacrificed more. I have been deprived of my liberty, I have lost thousands of Dollars worth of property— I have been denounced, insultingly denounced, as a traitor or rebel, & "secesh"[.] with due defference to your better judgments, I do not feel that I merit the inflictions put upon me. As to "Secession" as a cure for any of our troubles, I always and upon every occasion, denounced it as a damnable political herresy. That the leaders would better call it Revolution,—another name for civil war—to which as already stated I was as much opposed as you, and would never have sanctioned it, had not circumstances of an imperious character compeled me to do so.

I have thus, Sir, in a very hasty and imperfect manner given you a truthful sketch of my humble participation, in the present wretched condition of our Country hoping ardently and devoutly that some speedy and satisfactory adjustment will be arrived at[.] "Tis time to sheathe the sword and spare mankind." [7] This strife is unnatural— tis unholy— It has had its origin in fanatacism on the one hand, and disappointed political ambition on the other.

Where the future historian shall make up a jury to try the guilty parties, the verdict, in all probability will be, let them both die the death of Haman.[8] As an humble individual, whose opinions can effect but little any way, I may in conclusion, be permitted to say, that I am in favor of resorting to any reasonable means of stopping this war— That I am in favor of a reconstruction or restoration of the Union upon the Constitution— In other words, I am for the union as it was with the Constitution as it is— And for this I will go as far as my means and very limited ability will permit. I have never advocated more, nor can we be reasonably required to ask less. Now, Sir, you have in a tangible & authoritative form my position & my poor opinions. If you think the man entertaining them deserves expatriation and imprisonment, let him be ostracised if not, interpose your authority and influence to prevent it[.]

Very Respectfully
J. E. Manlove

N. B. I hope one or both of you gentlemen will respond to this communication, by the bearer—either verbally or otherwise: as, I confess, I shall not feel easy under existing circumstances, until I hear further on the subject. Should I be permitted to have an interview with either of you, I will give, at length, the reasons that determined me to trouble you with this tedious letter.

Yours &c J. E. M.

ALS, DLC-JP.

1. Joseph E. Manlove (1806-1870), Virginia-born Davidson County physician and Whig state legislator (1845-49), had real estate valued at $11,500 and personalty at $24,800 on the eve of war. 1860 Census, Tenn., Davidson, 23rd Dist., 136; McBride and Robison, *Biographical Directory,* I, 492-93.

2. Alvan C. Gillem, provost marshal.

3. Jo Moore (*c*1817-1864), a native Tennessean with property worth $24,000 when the war came, practiced in Davidson County. 1860 Census, Tenn., Davidson, 25th Dist., 164.

4. See Guarantee of Protection, *ca.*November 28, 1862.

5. He was the father of nine children ranging in age from four to twenty-three. *Ibid.*, 23rd Dist., 137.

6. The Constitutional Union party did not issue a formal platform but rather a statement of principles, the essence of which was "The Constitution of the Country, The Union of the States, and The Enforcement of the Laws." Johnson and Porter, *National Party Platforms* 30.

7. Addison, *Cato*, Act II, sc. 1.

8. That is, hanged on the gallows he had prepared for someone else. Esther 7:10.

From Nashville Union Club[1]

Nashville Tenn Jan. 31 1863.

To his Excellency Andrew Johnston
Military Govr of Tenn &c
Sir

At a meeting of the Nashville Union Club held on the 30th January 1863 We the undersigned were appointed a Committee to lay before your Excellency the following Resolutions which were unanimously adopted by that Body[.]

Resolved that we are opposed to the appointment of any man to any office in the State who is not and has not been Since the Comencement of the present Rebellion an unconditional Union Man[.]

Resolved that we unanimously recommend Geo J. Stubblefield Esqr[2] for the office of Attorney General of this Criminal Circuit[.]

Verry Respectfully Yours
G W Simpson
A W Moss } Committee[3]
E. D. Wheeler

ALS (Simpson), DLC-JP.

1. Three months later, when the club published a declaration of principles, putting itself on record as pro-Constitution and antislavery and urging other unionists across the state to form similar organizations, it claimed 272 members. Nashville *Union*, April 23, 1863.

2. George J. Stubblefield (1817-*fl*1887), a McMinnville lawyer who received the appointment, had served as state attorney general, 13th district (1851-60) and was later an Edgefield alderman (*c*1869). 1860 Census, Tenn., Warren, McMinnville, 212; Acklen, *Tenn. Records,* II, 207; Nashville *Union,* April 12, 1863; R. L. Polk and Co., comps., *Tennessee State Gazetteer and Business Directory* ([Nashville], 1887), 608.

3. George W. Simpson (*c*1825-*fl*1870), native of New Hampshire and merchant with $6,500 real and $15,000 personal property, resided in Tennessee for about ten years beginning in the 1850's. By March, 1866, he had returned to his native state, where he worked in a sawmill. 1860 Census, Tenn., Williamson, E. Subdiv., 55; (1870) N.H., Grafton, Rumney, 5; Simpson to Robert Johnson, March 7, 1866, Johnson Papers, LC; for Alexander W. Moss and E. D. Wheeler, see *Johnson Papers,* V, 345*n*, 334*n*.

From James S. Duncan

February 2, 1863, Nashville; ALS, DLC-JP.

Desiring to raise "A Battalion of mounted men," Major Duncan proposes "to act in Concert with the army and Report every 20 days, my progress." Seeking "The priveledge of Scouting the mountan Counties of E. Tennessee," he asserts: "I Flatter myself to Believe I can do A great Deal of good toward putting down this Rebellion and Besides protect A Large amount of Loyal Citizens[.]"

From Isaac T. Reneau

February 3, 1863, Tompkinsville, Ky.; ALS, DNA-RG393, Dept. of Tenn., Lets. Recd. (Mid. Tenn.), 1863-64.

Church of Christ minister reports company of four hundred rebels—"some say they [are] a part of Morgan's men, some again say they are Forest's"—at Albany, Clinton County, Kentucky. There since January 22, "They have stolen most of the using horses in that *downtroden,* oppressed, misused but *loyal* county," which deserves to be protected because "No other small co. in the state has as many brave sons in the Government sevice." Asks that his name "be kept secret—I should be killed if the *rebels* here knew that I had written to *you.*"

From William S. Rosecrans

Murfreesboro Feby 3rd 1863

To Gov Andrew Johnson
I desire that the paymasters may have the use of the Bank of Tenn for office purposes[.][1] It is the only place available for keeping funds[.] will you have the kindness to allow them to use[?]

W S Rosecrans Maj Genl

Tel, DLC-JP; DNA-RG393, Dept. of the Cumberland, Tels. Sent, Vol. 62 (1862-63).
1. The bank's main office at Nashville; Murfreesboro had no branch office.

From James W. Scully[1]

[Nashville, *ca.*February 3 1863]

Gov. A. Johnson
Dear Sir:

I have been considerably annoyed about that Girl belonging to Mrs. Eldridge—[2] I kept her up to this at the request of Mrs. Eldridge, and was about to discharge her this evening but would rather ask your advice what to do with her— I am sick in bed with *Neuralgia,* or I would go see you myself and explain the matter— The girl is no aquisition to me whatever— I agreed to pay Mrs. E. her wages on condition that she would clothe her— But instead of that Mrs. E. went to the Dress Maker, and took some clothes that were making there which my wife gave the Girl, so on that account I paid the Girl her own wages— Has Mr. Chumbley & Capt Dickerson[3] any authority to take the girl by force?[4]

Yours Respectfully
J. W. Scully

ALS, DLC-JP.
1. Irish-born James W. Scully (1838-1918), came with his family to Ulster County, New York, in 1840 and subsequently to Gallatin, Tennessee, returning to Ireland for schooling in Kilkenny (1848-51). After working as a surveyor, he enlisted in the U. S. army (1856-61), rising during the war from 1st lieutenant and regimental quartermaster (1862-63) to colonel of the 10th Tenn. Inf. Currently on Johnson's staff as acting assistant quartermaster for Tennessee troops, he was later assigned to guard the Northwestern Railroad from Nashville to the Tennessee River. In 1864 Johnson detailed him to East Tennessee as disbursing officer for Gen. Alvan C. Gillem. Returning to the regular army after the war, Scully rose to the rank of colonel before he retired to Atlanta in 1900. A sometime aide to President Johnson, he had outfitted Custer's forces in 1876 and commanded the transport service to Cuba during the Spanish-American War. CSR, RG94, NA; *NCAB,* XVII, 38-39; Heitman, *Register,* I, 871.
2. Not identified.
3. John Chumbly (1824-*fl*1887), a native of Virginia and currently city marshal of Nashville (*c*1859-68), later served as warden of the state penitentiary (*c*1868-73). John H. Dickerson (*c*1821-1872), an Ohio native appointed to West Point from Indiana (1843-47), saw service in the Mexican and Indian wars and on the frontier. Except for seven months (October, 1862-May, 1863) when he was in charge of the clothing depot at Cincinnati, he

was captain and chief quartermaster of the Department of the Ohio from May, 1861, until his resignation in March, 1864. 1860 Census, Tenn., Davidson, Nashville, 6th Ward, 98; Nashville *Dispatch,* April 15, 1862; *Goodspeed's East Tennessee,* 1107; Cullom, *Biographical Register,* II, 187; *Missouri Democrat* (St. Louis), March 6, 1872.

4. The governor responded that he had not ordered anyone to take charge of "The girl of color" and did "not know whether her Mistress is loyal or otherwise." Johnson to Scully, February 4, 1863, Johnson Papers, LC.

To William S. Rosecrans, [Murfreesboro]

Nashville Feby 4 1861 [1863]

To Gen Rosecrans

I have just learned that you have ordered that possession be taken of the warehouse of Mr H Douglas[1] on the public square of this city for ordnance purposes[.] two of Mr Douglas houses valuble & extensive in dimension have been already taken for Government purposes[.] There are other houses in the immediate vicinity that would answer all the purposes of Government as well as the property of Mr Douglas[.] this building was taken for hospital purposes and after considering the amount of property taken by the Govt from him for use it was deemed unjust to press the only building left him into the govt service & he had assurances that he might proceed with his business without further interference & in compliance with this assurance he has opened an extensive stock of goods and to take it now will result in great damage which must be remunerated by the Gov't[.] the persistence to occupy Mr Douglas house has resulted no doubt from envy and rivalry in business. Mr Hugh Douglas is a better union man & has rendered more service to sustain the government infinitely than those who are pursuing him[.] Captain Townsend[2] the ordnance officer here is not entirely unknown to me & I think I have something like a correct notion of the influence that have been brought to bear on him[.] the house of Morgan & Co[3] adjoining that of Douglas has been taken by the govt but has as yet been applied to no use[.] Morgan[4] is in the southern Cofederacy[.] it is well suited for the purpose[.] under all the circumstances I hope other property will be selected[.] this house of Douglas is not a warehouse but an extensive dry goods establishment expensively fitted up—[5]

Yours with great Respect
Andrew Johnson Mil Gov

Tel, DNA-RG393, Dept. of the Cumberland, Tels. Recd. (1861).

1. For Johnson's old friend, Nashville merchant Hugh Douglas, see *Johnson Papers*, I, 21*n*; for the governor's earlier concern about this matter, see Letter to A. Henry Thurston, January 20, 1863.

2. Edwin F. Townsend (*c*1833-1909), New York-born West Pointer (1854), became captain, 16th Inf., USA, in 1861, participating at Shiloh before being placed in charge of the Nashville ordnance depot (1862-65). Remaining in the military, he rose to colonel, 12th Inf., before his retirement in 1895. *West Point Register* (1970), 248; Heitman, *Register,* I, 967.

3. Morgan & Co., importers and jobbers in dry goods, located on the Public Square. *Nashville Bus. Dir.* (1860-61), 224.

4. Samuel D. Morgan (1798-1880), Virginia-born merchant's son, settled at Nashville in 1833 and became a partner in wholesale dry goods firms. Both before and after the war, he sought to establish new industries, including ventures in iron and textiles. Espousing the Confederate cause after Lincoln's call for troops, he helped to establish a factory for the manufacture of percussion caps, an activity which he moved south with the fall of the capital. After the war he returned to business in Nashville. Wooldridge, *Nashville*, 225, 627-31.

5. Rosecrans wired: "The situation of Mr Douglas building is such that it is necessary to take it for ordnance[.] if he is a proper person to receive it He Can be paid for its use[.]" Rosecrans to Johnson, February 5, 1863, Johnson Papers, LC.

From Benjamin D. Nabers[1]

Memphis Tenn Feb. 5 1863

His Excellency Gov Johnston
Nashville Tenn
Dear Sir:

Your valuable communication to me of the 27th Dec. last, has remained unanswered up to this date for the following reasons: First. I had been from home three weeks next preceeding the arrival of your letter—and Secondly. Since my return I have only had time to consult with union men. I enclose Mr Ketchum's explanations of the charges preferred against him.[2] I was careful however not to let him know that I was indebted to you for my knowledge of these charges[.] Should the vindication of Mr Kitchum not be regarded Satisfactorily there is a gentleman here pre-eminently quallifed for the office of either Judge of the Common law and Chancery Court, or of the Criminal Court. The individual to whom I refer is Lewis Selby.[3] Mr Selby was originally a Breckenridge democrat, but when the question of Secession was raised, he took decided ground for the union, and has maintained it all the time. Your old friend E W M. King would make an excellent Judge.[4]

The policy of organizing any court here except the criminal court is doubted by many. The reason urged is this. Many Citizens here owe debts North, and have debts due them South. Now if the Civil Courts were organized here, a merchant at New York Could Collect his debt from a Memphis Merchant but a Memphis Merchant Could not Collect a debt against a man in Mississippi for the reason that he could not reach him[.] There is one very important matter in making appointments here which Should be kept in view. It is this. *All important appointments Should be given to old Citizens in preference to Strangers.* Of Course the Citizen Should be a loyal man. Nothing is more discouraging to a people than to have *Strangers rule over them.*[5]
The progress of unionism here is not so rapid as could be wished. It is checked in part by the appointments made, and by the want of dicipline in the army. Loyal men are not, in many cases Sufficiently protected.

Owing to the presence of Confederate troops in this Congressional district it was thought better, by most of the union men not to hold election for Congressman. Some votes were however cast, on the 29th Dec—for T. G. Smith,[6] and Some for Mr Gager[7] on the 20th of January. I was a candidate awhile but for reasons already assigned withdrew[.][8]

No appointment has been made of Post-master here. At one time, I wrote in favor of B F C Brooks. I addressed you on the Subject—but *his appointment is not fit to be made*[.][9]

I never wanted office except it would promote our cause. If good policy suggests to you my appointment as Post-master or as Collector of the Internal Revenue or as Surveyor of this port, I would be glad to accept—otherwise not.[10]

I think, in fact know, a visit by you to this place would be highly gratifying to our people, and if you could be here the 22 of this month—it would [be] a very appropriate time, as we hope to celebrate Washington's birth day[.]

I am, very truly your friend
B. D. Nabers—

King will accept if you appoint him—B.D.N.

ALS, DLC-JP.

1. See *Johnson Papers*, IV, 290*n*.

2. Asa C. Ketchum, who some months earlier had asked Johnson for an army appointment, was accused of bigamy, of being "charged with forgery at Cincinnati," of having served in the Confederate army, of "selling town lots on paper plots, of a new city in Kansas" which "had no existence other than on paper," and was described as "a man utterly void of all moral honesty . . . entirely unworthy of a public position of trust, honor or profit[.]" Ketchum to Johnson, August 28, 1862; Milton Barnes to Johnson, n.d., Johnson Papers, LC.

3. Lewis Selby (*c*1812-*fl*1870), Virginia-born planter who had lived for some years in Louisiana and currently residing in Memphis, held real estate valued at $162,000 and personal property worth $263,000. 1860 Census, Tenn., Shelby, Memphis, 3rd Ward, 14; *Edwards' Memphis City Directory* (1870), 254.

4. For Ephraim W. M. King, Memphis criminal lawyer, banker, and jurist, see *Johnson Papers*, III, 427*n*; McBride and Robison, *Biographical Directory*, I, 430-31.

5. A comment almost prophetic in its anticipation of the southern experience during Reconstruction.

6. Thomas G. Smith (1820-1867), Virginia native and Brownsville lawyer since 1843, was a "stern, uncompromising unionist." After the war, he lived in Memphis, serving as judge of the law court (1866-67). Keating, *Memphis*, II, 70.

7. Possibly John Gager (b. *c*1835, New York-born Memphis lumber merchant and former alderman (1862). *Ibid.*, 47; 1860 Census, Tenn., Shelby, Memphis, 1st Ward, 19.

8. Johnson had originally slated December 29, 1862, as election day for the 10th district, but Confederate raids forced postponement in all but one county where Smith defeated Nabers in a meaningless contest. Rescheduled for January 20, the canvass attracted two additional candidates, John Gager and James M. Tomeny. Although some local politicos, eager for the reestablishment of civil government, actively supported the idea of an election, most Memphians were opposed or indifferent. In the name of the district's Union men, Grant unsuccessfully petitioned the governor to delay, pending a full statewide election. The balloting proved to be a farce; Nabers withdrew at the last moment and the remaining candidates shared an insignificant fraction of the eligible vote. Gager received the majority of ballots cast; but the January canvass, like that of December, was never recognized as official. Memphis *Bulletin*, January 9, 20, 21, 23, 1863.

9. Nabers would appear to have vacillated mightily on the choice of a postmaster. His letter on behalf of Benjamin F. C. Brooks, now so completely in disfavor, has not been

found; but six months earlier he had urged the merits of Reuel Hough, in whose appointment "nine tenths of the loyal men of this City concur." Nabers to Johnson, August 25, 1862, Johnson Papers, LC.

10. The writer's interest in the latter office dated back to the preceding summer. Assuring Johnson that the governor's presence in Memphis was "indispensable," Nabers also declared his "devotion to my country," modestly confiding that Jeptha Fowlkes and others "ask me to say another thing, which is to ask you to write to the Secretary of the Treasury . . . to have me appointed Surveyor of the Port at Memphis"; still later he averred, "I may truthfully say the people here wish that I be appointed Surveyor." Nabers to Johnson, July 25, August 25, 1862, *ibid.*

From B. F. Cloud Smith[1]

Gallatin Ten Febry 5th 1863

Gov Johnson
Dear Sir

I wrote you some days ago[2] relative to the raising a regiment of independent scouts for United States Service or rather State service; said regiment to be raised from the counties of Wilson, Smith, DeKalb, Macon & Putnam and participate in the war for the restoration of the Union and be confined *mainly* in their action to the locality from which raised. I desire to state in this communication in addition to what I have before said that there are now at least one thousand refugees from the five counties above named who desere & would take hold if they could be allowed to enter the service for a shorter term than the war & who would prove efficient in ridding the country of the gurrillas but who cold not be influenced to enter the service for the war. The state, allow me to suggests, needs the services of a large number of independent mounted men on the Guerilla order to meet & rid the Country of the robbers that infest it in the garb of confederate soldiers and who from their acquaintance with the country would be most efficient auxillaries to the main army[.] Such a corps as suggested would be of much benefit in enabling you to set to work the machinery of the civil department of the state and restoring law & order & aid us perhaps in being sooner reprisented [in] the congress of the United States. If permission would be given to some man properly vouched for to raise & organise such a corps as above suggested for a term of, say, nine months I think the thing can be done immediately and would be disposed to try. If in your judgment such a move would be practable & a commission granted for the purpose, please notify me of the fact. I would ask also if you concur in the proposition before stated that you write me at this place giving particulars &c or if desired I will come to Nashville at your suggestion. Give me an answer as soon as possible.

Respectfully your obt servt
B.F.C. Smith

ALS, DLC-JP.

1. B. F. Cloud Smith (1832-*fl*1887), Smith County native with $4,000 real and $4,075 personal property, attended Irving College in Warren County, began practicing

law (c1854), and served as county surveyor (1855-59). Briefly deputy U. S. commissioner during the war, he was later county court clerk (1870-74) and delegate to the Western Water Ways Convention in New Orleans (1884). 1860 Census, Tenn., Smith, 17th Dist., 56; (1880), New Middleton, 17; *Goodspeed's Smith*, 966.
2. The letter is not extant.

From Daniel Stover

Louisville, Ky.
February 8th 1863.

Gov,

In answer to your enquiry as to the number of men that, I have, I would say, I now have 125 all told, (with a prospect as I think of increasing that number in a short time.) Of this number I have sent back into East Tennessee nine Recruiting Officers; Some of whom have been gone 4 weeks, I think some of them will return this week. The Tennesseans are still Coming into Kentucky in Small Squads. But from the fact of their having to Come so far before they Can git an oppertunity to go into the Service, They become discouraged. And many of them return home again. While others hier to work on farms, and as teamsters.

Whereas if my Head Quarters was at Lexington or Nicholasville Ky. I think I Could Recruit much faster, than at this point.

Should the Army of the Cumberland move soon, with the prospect of Occupying Chattanooga. In that event would it not be best for me to come to Nashville, and follow up the Army to that place? Or would it be better for me to move my Head Quarters to Lexington.

I refere this matter to you, for your Consideration And whatever your decision may be, You will please instruct me, when I will act accordingly. I have made a Requisition upon Major Wm. H. Sidell the Superintendent of the recruiting Service in the State of Tennessee, For Certain articles for my Regiment.

You will please find the same enclosed,[1] and please see him at once, Asking him to give the matter his earliest Attention.

Mothers health has improved very much since she come to this place. Mary and the Children are well.

I hope to hear from you soon.

I have the honor to be your most obt Sevt,
Daniel Stover

To. Gov Andrew Johnson
Nashville Tennessee

LS, DLC-JP.
1. Not found.

To William S. Rosecrans

Nashville Feb 9 1863

To Maj Gen Rosecrans

The first East Tennessee cavalry have just returned from a hard expedition with Gen Davis.[1] Their horses are nearly all barefooted[.] time should be given them here to get their horses shod & to put the regiment on an effective footing. I have consulted with Genl Mitchell[2] & he concurs in this opinion[.] I hope that Capt Abbotts battery[3] now at Clarksville will [be] permitted to return here and join the rest of the Tennessee forces. I think I will come with Genl Mitchell[.] I hope a few days will be granted them at least[.][4]

Andrew Johnson
Mil Gov

Tel, DNA-RG393, Dept. of the Cumberland, Tels. Recd. (1863).

1. Jefferson C. Davis (1828-1879), Indianan, was an enlisted man in the 3rd Ind. Vols. during the Mexican War, lieutenant and captain in the 1st U. S. Arty. (1848-61), and brigadier general of Indiana Volunteers (1861-66). He is perhaps best remembered for having slain his superior officer, William Nelson, at Louisville's Galt House in September, 1862, after a quarrel—a deed for which he went unpunished, although afterwards passed over for promotion. Returning to the regular army at war's end, Davis was colonel of the 23rd Inf. until his death. Warner, *Generals in Blue,* 115-16; New York *Times*, December 2, 1879.

2. Robert B. Mitchell (1823-1882), Ohio native, lawyer, and Mexican War veteran, in 1856 moved to Kansas where he served in the territorial legislature. Commissioned colonel, 2nd Kans. Inf. (1861) and promoted to brigadier the next year, he was briefly stationed in Nashville (1862) as chief of cavalry for the Army of the Cumberland and subsequently commanded the districts of Nebraska and Kansas before the war's end. Johnson's appointee as governor of the New Mexico Territory in 1866, he resigned three years later and ultimately moved to Washington, D.C. Warner, *Generals in Blue,* 328-29.

3. Ephraim P. Abbott.

4. Whether in response to Johnson's plea or otherwise, the 1st Tenn. spent the latter part of February with Gen. James B. Steedman's division at Concord Church, southeast of Nashville. Carter, *First Tenn. Cav.*, 67-68.

From William M. Wiles[1]

Head Quarters Department of the Cumberland,
Office Provost Marshal General,
Murfreesboro, Feb'y 10, 1863.

Governor:

By direction of the General Commanding I send to you, Ethereld Philips,[2] rebel conscript agent; Wm. B Persley,[3] same; Paulding Anderson,[4] rebel state senator; Wm. L. Marten,[5] rebel representative (state);

and Ollison Wollard[6] rebel mail carrier, captured by our forces near Lebanon, a few days since, with request that they be tried before the U. S. Dist. Court on charge of treason against the Government of the U. S.[7]

I am, Governor, very resp'y your obt serv't,
Wm. M. Wiles Capt & P. M. G

Hon. Andrew Johnson,
Military Governor of Tennessee, Nashville.

LS, DLC-JP; DNA-RG393, Dept. of the Cumberland, Book Records, Vol. 118 (1863).

1. William M. Wiles (1836-1880), Columbus, Indiana, druggist, rose to lieutenant colonel, 22nd Ind. Inf., serving on Rosecrans' staff as aide-de-camp and provost marshal general (May, 1862-October, 1863). Wounded during the Atlanta campaign, he was mustered out early in 1865; subsequently he engaged in various business ventures in Indianapolis and served as U. S. revenue assessor, 6th district of Indiana (*c*1869-73). Fitch, *Annals*, 286-87; CSR, RG94, NA; Pension file, RG15, NA; *OR*, Ser. 1, XXX, Pt. I, 63; Indianapolis city directories (1868-73), *passim*.

2. Etheldred B. Phillips (1837-*fl*1900), Tennessee farmer, private, and conscript officer, Co. E, 3rd Tenn. Cav., CSA, captured by Federal cavalry at Cherry Valley, Wilson County, February 3, was sent to Camp Chase, Ohio, and exchanged March 28. 1880 Census, Tenn., Wilson, 16th Dist., 24; (1900), 146th Enum. Dist., 10A; CSR, RG109, NA.

3. William B. Pursley (*c*1837-*fl*1870), Kentucky-born carpenter residing in Wilson County, served as private, Co. K, 18th Tenn. Inf., CSA. Captured at Donelson in 1862 and again near Atlanta in 1864, he spent much of his time in Union prisons. He was released from Camp Chase April 3, 1865, after taking the oath of allegiance; his service record reveals nothing of his 1863 capture. *Ibid.*; 1860 Census, Tenn., Wilson, 4th Dist., 62; (1870), 9.

4. Paulding Anderson (1803-1882), Lebanon and Nashville merchant, owned Big Spring plantation in Wilson County and possessed $59,450 real and $82,185 personal property in 1860. Three times state senator (1837-41, 1851-53, 1861-63), he was a high-ranking militia officer, who held strong secession sentiments. Imprisoned in the penitentiary at Nashville until June 17, he was thereafter released on short-term paroles. After the war he served as chairman of the county Democratic executive committee and for a time resided in Arkansas. *Ibid.* (1860), 10th Dist., 167; McBride and Robison, *Biographical Directory*, I, 13-14; Nashville *Union and American*, August 1, 1872; Anderson Parole, October 15, 1863, Johnson Papers, LC; Dixon Merritt, ed., *The History of Wilson County* (Lebanon, Tenn., 1961), 228.

5. William L. Martin (1804-1865), Wilson County lawyer and ex-Whig state senator (1843-45), was an Opposition and Confederate member of the state house (1859-63) who claimed $24,900 real and $42,065 personal property on the eve of the war. Like Anderson he was briefly imprisoned, until freed on temporary paroles. *Ibid.*, 141-42, 148-49; 1860 Census, Tenn., Wilson, 10th Dist., 156; McBride and Robison, *Biographical Directory*, I, 503-4; Martin Parole, October 15, 1863, Johnson Papers, LC.

6. Ollison Woollard (*c*1810-*fl*1880) was a North Carolina-born farmer with eleven children still at home. 1860 Census, Tenn., Wilson, 5th Dist., 80; (1880), 3.

7. That these prisoners were tried is evident from their service records and paroles; but the precise nature of their treasonable activities is not clear, inasmuch as court records have not survived.

To Alfred H. Hicks[1]

Nashville Tenn Feby 10th 1863

A H Hics Esqr
Nashville Tenn

Sir When Jesse Thomas[2] Surveyor of the port of Nashville, handed over to John A. Fisher Cashier Bank of Tennessee,[3] the funds and assets in his hands belonging to The United States on the 30th day of Apl 1861 he delivered over among other assets

A H Hicks & others Bonds[4] for	368.84
" " " " "	376.80
" " " " "	153.60
" " " " "	144.96
" " " " "	387.84
Amounting to the Sum of	$1 432.04

You are hereby required to appear before Horace H. Harrison[5] Esq U S Commissioner within the next three days and to state on oath, who were the Securities on each of said bonds, if the same have been paid, when, & to whom paid.[6]

Very Respcfly
Andrew Johnson Mil Gov

Copy, DLC-JP.

1. Alfred H. Hicks (1814-1876), North Carolina-born Nashville china and queensware dealer, possessed $111,200 real and $100,000 personal property. After the war he continued the same business as a partner in the mercantile firm of Hicks, Houston & Co. 1860 Census, Tenn., Davidson, Nashville, 2nd Ward, 58; Nashville city directories (1860-76), *passim*; Acklen, *Tenn. Records*, I, 27.

2. For Thomas, see *Johnson Papers*, V, 367*n*.

3. John A. Fisher (*c*1830-1868), native Tennessean, was a Nashville grocer and commission merchant with $21,000 in real and $15,000 in personal property. After the fall of the city, he accompanied the bank to Georgia, where in May, 1865, he was allegedly involved in the disappearance of $50,000 in gold of the bank's assets. At war's end he settled in England. 1860 Census, Tenn., Davidson, 13th Dist., 120; *Nashville Bus. Dir.* (1860-61), 168; Report of the Joint Committee on School Fund Frauds, *Tenn. House Journal*, 1870-71, App. 291-326 *passim*; Nashville *Union and American*, November 26, 1868.

4. These bonds were guarantees that duties due the Federal government would be paid by the merchant, in this case Hicks. Such bonds were negotiable assets which the U. S. surveyor turned over as deposits; in due time the bank would collect the face sums, either from the merchant or his sureties.

5. Horace H. Harrison (1829-1885), Wilson County native, moved with his parents to McMinnville in 1841 and held minor county court positions before commencing law practice in 1857. Moving to Nashville two years later, he served as U. S. district attorney (1863-66, 1872-73), judge of the state supreme court (1867-68), Republican congressman (1873-75), and state representative (1880-81). *BDAC*, 1016; Clayton, *Davidson County*, 96.

6. Two days later, Hicks deposed that he could neither remember which of several sureties, "in the habit of endorsing for him," he had called upon, nor whether the bonds had been paid. Deposition of A. H. Hicks, February 12, 1863, Johnson Papers, LC.

From William A. Rodgers[1]

Camp near Murfreesboro Tenn.
February 13th 1863.

To his Excellency
Andrew Johnston
Military Govenor of Tenn.

The 1st. 2nd. 3rd. 5th. & 6th. Regments E. Tenn. Vols. are without the number of Medical Officers allowed[.] They have but one Assistant Surgeon when they are allowed two. The 3rd. Regt. has no Assistant as I am informed tho J. C. Everett[2] has been acting for some time as such and ought in my opinion to be appointed. All the Regts ought to have their compliment of Medical Officers. I am informed that the power to appoint and commission after a Regt is organised is with the Govenor of the State from which the Regt. comes[.] if this is so permit me to call your early attention to the above refurred to Regts.

Respectfully Your Obt. Servt.
Wm. A. Rodgers Surgeon 3rd.
Regt E Tenn Vols & Act. Brig.
Surg. 1st. Brig 2nd. Div 14th Army Corps

ALS, T-Mil. Gov's Papers, 1862-65, Petitions.

1. Rodgers was surgeon of the 3rd Tenn. Inf. from March, 1862, until his resignation on account of disability, July 10, 1864. *Tenn. Adj. Gen. Report* (1866), 57.

2. John C. Everett (b. *c*1829), Tennessee-born Meigs County physician, was assistant surgeon, 5th Tenn. Inf., USA (April, 1862-July 15, 1864). He resigned to serve as the elector for the 3rd congressional district (1864) and as clerk and master of Meigs County (1864-68). 1860 Census, Tenn., Meigs, Decatur, 4th Dist., 59; CSR, RG94, NA; *Goodspeed's East Tennessee*, 816.

From A. Henry Thurston[1]

Medical Director's Office
Feb. 12[13]th 1863—[2]

General.

The Surgeons & assistant Surgeons of the East Tennessee regiments, are temporarily only, detached from their regiments, to perform hospital duty—

They are regularly detailed by order of Major General Rosecrans, & if they are able to show you that detail, they are absent by authority, & with the full consent of the authorities—

very respectfully
Brig. Gen Andrew Johnson — A Henry Thurston
Mil. Governor — Surgeon Med Dir

ALS, T-Mil. Gov's Papers, 1862-65, Petitions.

1. Alfred Henry Thurston (1832-1865), Rhode Island native, was a New York City physician before becoming surgeon of volunteers in October, 1861. A member of Rosecrans' staff in the fall of 1862, he was assistant medical director at Nashville (1863-65) with headquarters at 24 Cherry Street. Heitman, *Register*, I, 960; *Trow's New York City Directory* (1858-59), 795; *OR*, Ser. 1, XVI, Pt. II, 655; Nashville *Union*, February 25, 1863; New York *Herald*, August 3, 1865.

2. The clerk's endorsement of this document as "Feb'y 13th" would seem to be more accurate than the clear "12th" of the letter's dateline, inasmuch as Thurston was apparently responding to Johnson's inquiry prompted by the complaint of the preceding correspondent.

From Isaac R. Hawkins

Camp Chase Ohio Feb 14th 1863

Hon Andrew Johnson,
Military gov of the state of Ten,
Dear sir, enclosed you will please find lists, or rolls of men captured and paroled on the 18th and 20th of December 1862 at Lexington & Trenton, belonging to the 2 West Tennessee Cavalry.[1] When the men & officers were captured they were sent to their homes in the adjacent counties, and some short time there after they were ordered to assemble at Jackson and Trenton, for the purpose of being sent to St Louis for exchange.[2] On reaching that place, I was ordered to this, the general orders making such a move necessary and we now report at this point officers and men two hundred and eighteen, four men were left at St Louis in hospital[.] you will see that the entire number captured have not reported although they still come in slowly— many of the men are poor and the desolating influences of War have been heavily felt in our section of country, and many of their families stand in need of their assistence every moment that they can be spared from the public service. And I would respectfully request, that if there is a probability of any considerable delay in the exchange, that the privates and non commissioned officers be sent to their homes, and I have no dout, but it would in many respects be better for the government. I have no doubt but the men could be assembled at any time within three days, and that they would go in to the service with renewed energy. I think that the men would be more healthy, and in every way better contented[.] The men belonging to Cos F D & G are twelve months men and enlisted in August Sept and Oct and are as good men as can be found in the service[.] The other cos are three years men— I find it much more difficult for men to be kept contented in a camp like this, than in active service. I have not yet discovered the evidences of such a feeling among my men as I learn prevails

among others; but wisdom I think suggests that I should proffit by the experience of others and avoid if possible their difficulties[.]
The camp here is in some respects very well arranged, while in other respects it is very uncomfortable, The mud is perfectly intolerable and quite a number of the men are complaining[.]
I think the fact, that the men will be required in their immediate neighbourhood, where the remainder of the regiment is lends additional force to my suggestions and I should be much pleased if you would use such influence as you may possess to secure us an early exchange and in the event that should fail, that then, the other course be addopted[.][3] I have the Hon to be very respectfully

your obedient servt Isaac R Hawkins
Col com 2 West Ten Cav

ALS, DNA-RG249, Lets. Recd., File 74M (1863).

1. The accompanying unsigned document, dated Huntington, Tennessee, December 26, 1862, listed Hawkins, fourteen officers, and a roster of 293 privates and noncommissioned officers, with an additional twenty-six names of men "subsequently captured." The main body had been taken "by Brig Genl. N. B. Forrest of the Confederate Army and by him paroled upon their pledge of honor not to take up arms give aid or information against the Confederate States until exchanged[.]"

2. In April, 1862, after Shiloh, the Confederates began paroling prisoners on the field to be returned to their lines, and ultimately to their homes, there to await exchange. In an effort to make capture by the enemy less attractive and in order to have such men restored soon to service, Stanton established camps of instruction—at Annapolis, Benton Barracks (St. Louis), and Camp Chase. Men so paroled and at home were periodically rounded up and forwarded to these camps from which they might be sent to fight the Indians if formal exchange did not permit their early return to the front. Hesseltine, *Civil War Prisons*, 74.

3. On March 1, Congressman Maynard transmitted Hawkins' letter and list to Col. William Hoffman, commissary general of prisoners, with Johnson's February 19 endorsement to the secretary of war: "The 2nd W. T. Cavalry has rendered valuable service. The men were recruited in West Tennessee; they are perfectly familiar with the country, and it is very desirable that they should be put in the field at the earliest possible date. It is hoped that they will be speedily exchanged."

From Thomas L. Sullivan[1]

Head-Quarters District of Jackson,
13th Army Corps, Department of the Tennessee,
Jackson, Tenn., Feby 16th 1863

His Excellency
Gov. Johnson

At the request of many of your personal and political friends I write you to inquire whether some steps cannot be taken, or, some plan devised, to reorganize and reestablish the Law Courts in West Tennessee.[2] The whole community, is suffering to an extent not readily understood by the mere looker on, in consequence of the failure of Courts of Justice and in many instances, the total destruction of the Records and papers in the clerks offices of the Western District. Complaints are daily made by good and loyal citizens to Genl. Sullivan[3] at this post to devise some plan of relief, but as military law is deficient in affording the necessary relief, we have all concluded to ask your advice in the premises; and if you think it advisable, to appoint Judges from among our Union Lawyers, who shall hold their offices, until such time as the Legislature of the State may convene, or an election may be held—

The Judges in this end of the State utterly refuse to hold their Court and some of them, have for more than a year past absented themselves from the State claiming in other States, the protection of the rebel forces, and rebel laws.

I would be glad to hear from you on this subject and receive your permission to read your reply to the Union Club at Memphis and at Jackson—[4]

You can address me at Jackson Care of my Brother Genl. Sullivan[5]

Respectfully Your friend
T L. Sullivan

ALS, DLC-JP.

1. Thomas L. Sullivan (b. *c*1825), native Indianan and Mexican War veteran, moved to Memphis in the late 1840's where he practiced law, accumulating $150,000 real and $5,000 personal property by war's beginning. 1860 Census, Tenn., Shelby, Memphis, 8th Ward, 135; Joseph H. Schauinger, "Jeremiah C. Sullivan, Hoosier Jurist," *Indiana Magazine of History*, XXXVII (1941), 227, 231-32, 234; Schauinger, "Some Letters of Judge Jeremiah C. Sullivan," *ibid.*, 264, 270.

2. Not until August, 1864, were state courts in the western district reestablished. Hooper, Memphis, 90.

3. Jeremiah C. Sullivan.

4. The Washington Union Club of Memphis established satellites in neighboring counties; the Jackson unit was probably an affiliate during Federal occupation from June, 1862, to June, 1863. Memphis *Bulletin*, September 22, 1864; Emma I. Williams, *Historic Madison* (Jackson, 1946), 164.

5. In a covering letter, General Sullivan assured the governor that his district was "entirely clear of all rebels, and the time is auspicious for inaugurating Civil Law," further observing that "By appointing judges, and opening the Courts, you will do more to bring back the people to their loyalty than all the military power of the Country." Sullivan to Johnson, February 16, 1863, Johnson Papers, LC.

Confiscation Proclamation[1]

February 20, 1863

Whereas, Many persons owning and possessing real and personal estate, situate in that portion of the State of Tennessee within the jurisdiction of the Government of the United States, come within the provisions of sections fifth and sixth of an act of Congress, approved July 17, 1862,[2] and have failed and refused to avail themselves of the provision of the fifth section within the sixty days, which expired under the Proclamation of the President of the United States on the 23d day of September, 1862; and, whereas many such persons are now within the so-called confederate States, having left such property in charge of agents, who collect the rents, issues, and profits thereof, and forward the same to the parties, or retain and invest it for their benefit, therefore, in pursuance of said Act of Congress, I, ANDREW JOHNSON, Military Governor of the State of Tennessee, do hereby warn all persons holding, renting, occupying, or using any such real or personal estates, or the rents, issues, and profits thereof, belonging to any such parties, as well as all agents, not to pay the same over to said parties or their agents, but to retain the same until some person suitable has been appointed in the name and behalf of the United States to receive the same, and hold it subject to the order of the said Government of the United States.

Andrew Johnson,
Military Governor of Tennessee.

February 20, 1863.

Ex. Record Book (1862-63), DLC-JP4C; Nashville *Union,* February 21, 1863.

1. This proclamation was one of a series of moves by Federal authorities to force the population to renew its allegiance. Four months later Johnson designated Charles Davis commissioner for this purpose. See Appointment of Commissioner of Abandoned Property, June 23, 1863.

2. Section 5 of the act "to suppress Insurrection, to punish Treason and Rebellion, to seize and confiscate the Property of Rebels, and for other Purposes" provided for "seizure of all the estate and property, money, stocks, credits, and effects" of Confederate military and civilian officers, no matter "whether such office or agency be national, state, or municipal in its name" and to "use . . . the proceeds thereof for the support of the army of the United States." Section 6 stipulated that the property of others in rebellion or aiding rebellion, who, "sixty days after public warning and proclamation" by the President, did not cease to aid such rebellion and return to allegiance, would also be liable to seizure. *U. S. Statutes,* XII, 589-91.

From Daniel P. Braden[1]

Springfield Robertson Co. Tenn.
Febuary 23rd. 1863

Govenor Johnston Dear Sir

I claim the privledge of adressing you, not onley as a citizen, but as one who has always Supported you in your canvass before the people uppon the Democratic platform, and now being over Sixty, have never voted any other Ticket.

Our villege was visited the other day (18 and 19 Inst) by a Squad of mounted caverly, Say Some 45 men Commanded by Capt. A. C. Graves belonging to the 105th Illinois volunteer lnfanty,[2] There was also a Capt. Johnston belonging to the 11th Kentucky Cavralty;[3] each Captins had a part of the fource under their seperate Command. When they arived in town Several of the men were highly intoxicated useing most profain and very indecent and vulgar language in stores and on the Streets. They Scoured the neighbourhood, and took horses or mules without giving any Script, also Pistols or guns; they took a Small squarrell rifle from a citizen, and offered to Sell it for five dollars, They took a horse from a certain man, but finally agreed to give the horse up to the man again if he would give them fifteen dollars which he did and So retained his horse.

A Sergent or corporal calling himself "Waymoc" and five others, went about a mile from Town where there was no one at home but the lady and two Sick children and Some Servants, four of them going to the house Drawing their Pistols, and leaving one at the gate to watch; Demanded to Search the house, the lady asked them by what authority and for what did they wish to Search for; they Said they had authority from the Captain, to Search for arms, She told them there was no arms there except a pistol which was her own property for her Own proctection that govnor Johnston had Sent amunition by Mr. Holman[4] for the People here to protect themselves against the Robrs that were often Prowling about, the men with Pistols in hand and Some Drew Daggers, Demanded her to produce the Pistol, She Drew it Out but Said She would not give it up; they then asked her if they attempted to force it from her if She would Shoot them, She said She would if they attempted to do So; at this time of the meele [melee] an old neighbor lady arives, while the men guarded the lady of the house, the other two men were Searching Drawes, trunks, beds Smoke house and kitchen, while this general Searching was going on the Famley Physion came in, The comander of the Squad desired the Doctor to interfear for him to get the pistol for he Said he was bound to have it.

They finally agreed that the Pistol Should be given to the Doctor, that he the Doctor Should hand the Pistol Over to Mr. D. D. Holman or to Mr. Tanner[5] who was filling Mr. Holmans Place in his absence and for him to Deside who Should have the pistol, but Captain A. C. Graves would not consent to the agreement and So took the Pistol[.]

While the Search was going on at the house the Lady was guarded So close She could not watch them well, So that a good many articels was missing even to Some germts [garments] belonging to her Sick child Sone 5 years old.

I could give you Other Particulars and Instances of Such rongs dond by Other troops but let the above Suffice[.]

I know that while Col. Williams of the 9th. Pensylvania Calvry[6] Stayed here, which was Some Several months, him his oficers and men, were treated kindley by the citizens, and were Often invited Out to Dinings, and a good feeling exhisted betwend the citizens and the Soldiers, Some of his Sick were left heare, and I know to a Certinty that the ladies of this place done a great deal for their comfort; and among the first and the foremost to attend to the 9th Pensylvanie Sick at this place, was the lady who has been So cruelly used and her mother.

How can a man who has taken an Oath to Suppoart and protect the Constitution of the united States of America; and all Laws made in Persuiance of the Same; look on in Silence at officers commissioned by the great Seal of the U. S. and See them Put Down the Freedom of the Press, the Freedom of Speach; the Right to bear arms; the Right to peaceably assemble for Petition or greavences &c. &c: I had rather See this continent Sunk and a wide Ocean remain whear it onst was than to See a millatary centeral Consolidated Despotism Spread over this Onst happy land of Washington[.] May God grant a better fate to my Dear Country and like tried gold may She come out of her fiaery furnace Pure and freed from all allow [alloy.]

May you be able like a Skillfull Concious and prudent Pilot, to keep the Ship of State from a total rect[.]

Very Truly Respectfull
D. P. Braden

ALS, DLC-JP.

1. For Braden, Robertson County farmer, see *Johnson Papers*, III, 375*n*.

2. Amos C. Graves (1825-1901), New York native and sheriff of DuPage County, Illinois, served as captain, Co. D, 105th Ill. Inf. from September, 1862, until his resignation because of "Chronic Nephritis" in March, 1865. During the fall of 1863 he was briefly division provost marshal on Gen. Robert S. Granger's staff. 1860 Census, Ill., DuPage, 65; CSR, RG94, NA; Pension file, RG15, NA.

3. James A. Johnson (*c*1823-1876), a Grant County, Kentucky, physician (1848-62) with $14,000 real and $10,700 personal property, was captain, Co. B, 11th Ky. Cav. (1862-64). Captured at Philadelphia, Tennessee, in October, 1863, and confined at Libby Prison, he resigned a few months after being released the following March. 1860 Census, Ky., Grant, 64; CSR, RG94, NA; Pension file, RG15, NA.

4. For Daniel D. Holman, proprietor of Cheatham House, a Springfield tavern, see *Johnson Papers*, II, 238*n*.

5. Possibly R. L. Tanner (*c*1839-*fl*1887), a Kentucky-born clerk, who, by the 1880's, with B. F. Hurt owned a Springfield drugstore. *Goodspeed's Robertson,* 841; 1860 Census, Tenn., Robertson, Springfield, 1.

6. Edward C. Williams (1820-1900), Philadelphia native, Harrisburg bookbinder, Mexican War veteran, and Dauphin County sheriff (1850-54), whose regiment was at Springfield from March to May, 1862, moved in 1871 to Chapman, Pennsylvania, where he became postmaster the next year, serving until his death. John W. Rowell, *Yankee Cavalrymen: Through the Civil War with the Ninth Pennsylvania Cavalry* (Knoxville, 1971), 19-20, 47; Dewey S. Herrold, "Brigadier-General Edward Charles Williams," *Snyder County Historical Society Bulletin,* IV (1941-42), 21, 24, 30-43 *passim*.

Speech at Indianapolis[1]

February 26, 1863

Fellow-citizens of the State of Indiana, and I think I have a right to call you fellow-citizens. Although an inhabitant of another State, I claim to be a citizen of the United States, and recognize each and every one of you as a fellow-citizen, who claims citizenship under the broad panoply of this Union of ours. In presenting myself to you, it is with no ordinary degree of embarrassment. I find an audience far beyond my capacity to address, so far as my voice is concerned, nor have I strength to present the subject as I wish. Another cause of embarrassment is that I appear before you in the midst of a civil war, a revolution, which is calculated to interest each one of you. If any had come expecting oratory they would be disappointed. For in presenting myself to this concourse of people, if I know my own mind, it will be for the purpose of making a lodgment in your hearts of the truth on the great questions which have agitated the nation, and involved it in civil war.

When we look around, what condition do we find the country in? Just the other day all was peaceful, happy and prosperous. All portions of the country vied with each other in their professions of their desire for the common good. The great contest seemed to be between the advocates of the various parties and creeds, in pronouncing eulogies on their several States. Each one uttered eulogies on the blessings which had flowed upon this people under the Constitution of the United States since the formation of the Government. What has transpired or taken place in so short a period of time, as to make it necessary for one portion of your countrymen to commence a war of disintegration in the nation?

It has been contended by some in high places, and some in places not so high, that one portion of our fellow citizens had been deprived of their rights. Let me ask this sea of upturned faces before me to lay aside their prejudices—to forget that they ever belonged to the respective parties of the country—let me ask them what rights have been lost in the United States since the formation of the Constitution? Has any right been given up, or any right been taken away? I care not what party any man belongs to, can he put his finger on any one constitutional right which has been lost. Why, then, this crusade on the Constitution and the institutions under it?

As I remarked on a former occasion, I do not appear here as a partizan; but I have not given up my political creed in the slightest degree. I have neither come here, or been elsewhere, to revoke a single political principle which I espoused at the commencement of my public life. I stand where I have always stood, an uncompromising Democrat. I stand to-day, as the advocate of the great Democratic principle of self-government, that the people are the great source of political power. In later years I have come to the conclusion that the Union of these States was a fixed principle of Democracy. Hence, we simply adhere to the principles of self-government, and of the people as the source of power, when we talk of the Constitution and of all laws enacted under it as obligatory on those who live under it. This is Democracy. This is where I stand. It is a true doctrine that the Government was made for the convenience of man, and not man for the Government; just as the shoe is made for the foot, not the foot for the shoe.

One of the first ideas I learned in connection with government was that the soul of liberty was the love of law. What liberty have you without the Constitution or laws? Take away law, and you have vice and anarchy rampant. With law we have liberty. It protects the weak against the strong, virtue against vice. This is a part of my Democracy.

But, my countrymen, what has brought this condition upon us? I will illustrate the question by reference to the history of party politics. We have been divided into political parties—Whig and Democratic—and, latterly, Republican and Democratic. Whichever party was dissatisfied with the result of an election appealed to the people. Whatever the issue, banks or tariffs, or latterly the issues between the Democratic and Republican parties, there was waving over all the stars and stripes. All parties vied in their fealty to the Constitution and devotion to the banner of our country. Let me ask my Republican friends and my Democratic friends whether the contest has not been as to which would best promote the prosperity of the Union and preserve its existence? On all public measures the contest was whether the policy of either party would best preserve the Union and prosperity of the States. All agreed in the supremacy of the Constitution and Union of States. What are we doing about this matter now? These defenders of the South profess to find reasons for the men for whom they sympathize.

At the last election Lincoln, Bell, Douglas and Breckinridge were candidates, and they all professed to be strongly devoted to the Union. I made speeches for John C. Breckinridge, for the same reason I would have spoken for Douglas, had I been living in a free State,[2] because he was the strongest man there, and by supporting him we hoped to beat the candidate of the Republican party. This is the truth, and I will not lie about it. We repudiated all idea that Breckinridge was a disunionist. Each party was especially devoted to the country. To satisfy my Democratic friends that he was a professed Unionist, I will read to you a few extracts from his speeches. We all know how parties divide, some going one way, some another, and we had as well admit it as honest men that thousands of them have their sympathies based on old party biases. If we were deceived is it any reason why we would turn traitors? He deceived me then—that was his fault. If he deceives me now it would be my fault. If God forgives me for advocating the claims of one who turned traitor, I pledge this assembly that I will never again be guilty of a like offense.[3]

Now, what has transpired since the Presidential election to make the Union so odious, and the Constitution so inefficient and illy calculated to benefit the country? What has been done to destroy the Union of the States? Can any one tell? Let me ask my Republican and Democratic friends, in the language of soberness and truth, to-day, do you believe if John C. Breckinridge had been elected, could we not have stood this Constitution and this Union at least four years longer? [Cries of "We do."]

The question resolves itself into this. One party was in power, and after the election it saw the sceptre of the Union had gone from it. For, even looking to the expiration of Lincoln's term of four years, there was, even if Mr. Lincoln was not re-elected, other organizations coming up to retain the power from them, and they knew it. Now, they said, is the time to strike and make the slavery question a pretext to unite the Southern States.[4] We see to-day in this terrible war, what it ended in. Let me ask this audience to-day, if we are to have a civil war after every election, because one party or the other is defeated, what are we coming to? Look at Mexico, torn with internal dissension, too feeble to resent foreign oppression. What is it to end in? Anarchy, loss of property, of life, and of national prosperity and honor.

What is our true policy? Because Mr Lincoln beat us, and was elected under the forms of law, he was entitled to come into power and try his policy, and if the country prospered we ought to submit to it like men. If it was a bad administration we could oppose as in the past we had that of others. That being so, let me ask every Democrat in the State of Indiana, and every Democrat in the Southern Confederacy, where was the danger of wrong when Mr. Lincoln came into power? Let me be heard on this point a few moments. On the 4th day of March, 1861, he came into power. A new Congress came in. In the House was a majority of Representatives against him. In the Senate there was a majority of six against him. There could be no danger from his administration. He must bring his Cabinet about him, whose nomination must be confirmed by the Senate. If he attempted to bring into power men opposed to the interests of any one section, they had the power to reject them. He could not make a Cabinet without their consent. We had it in our power to make the whole Cabinet to suit ourselves.— Where was the danger, then, from his administration? He could not send out a foreign minister without our consent. Every treaty he made must be submitted to us for ratification. Nor could he appoint Consuls. Nor draw his own salary unless we appropriated it for him. Hence, you see, there was on the part of these men a fixed determination to break and destroy the government. This is no new thing. I will read you one or two extracts from Southern papers, to show you how disunion has been going on from time to time. There was a determination to break up the government, and the great difficulty was making an excuse for it.

Governor Johnson then read from the Montgomery (Ala.) Daily Advertiser, which said that "It was no precipitate rebellion." They could have staid in the Union and arrested every unfriendly measure. One of their organs says "it has not been a precipitate revolution, but with coolness and deliberation has been thought of for forty years. For ten years this has been the all-absorbing question." [5] I will read nothing further to show that it was their design in 1860 that the Union should be broken up. I might introduce other authorities.

In proof of what I am now saying I may quote an extract from a letter of General Jackson on the disunion movement of South Carolina in 1832. Let me ask Jackson Democrats, if there are any here, to hear him speak on this occasion. He now sleeps in a tomb which was, but a short time since, in the Southern Confederacy. I was told that, when they took possession of that county, they marched out to his tomb and attempted to plant the stars and bars upon it. On that occasion an old Jackson Democrat remarked: "By the Eternal God, I expected to see Jackson jump out of his grave!" Though he now sleeps in the grave, if it were possible to communicate with the dead, and if he could foresee the condition of to-day, I have sometimes thought he would turn over in his tomb, burst it asunder, and, extending that long arm and that long finger, declare: "The Federal Union—it must be preserved!" [Immense applause.][6]

Have we not come to it? Is the Constitution changed? I think not. What rights have the South lost? ["None"] Who can tell? Do you not see that the establishment of a Southern Confederacy was their real object? Jackson's prophesy has been followed out to the very letter.

Who commenced the war—this damnable struggle to destroy the people's rights? The South. Who struck the first blow, fired the first gun, shed the first blood? It is a matter of history that a delegation from Virginia urged the attack upon the Federal forts at Charleston, as a spur for Virginia to revolt.[7] They knew that in fifteen days Anderson and his gallant band in Fort Sumter would be out of food. But so fearful were they that these men would not be starved to death, or into a surrender, they opened fire on Fort Sumter, on this wretched garrison, and kept it up for three days, so incessantly that they were compelled to fall on their faces and wet their blankets to keep from suffocation. The surrender was communicated to Jeff. Davis at Montgomery. He could not speak in response to the news, but his Secretary did. It was, in substance:

"The first blow has been struck. Who can tell where it will end? Before May the Confederate flag shall be floating on the Capitol at Washington and on Congress Hall at Philadelphia." [8]

They at once raised men and levied taxes. Mr. Lincoln came into power, administering the Constitution like an honest man, and, loving my country, I determined to sustain him. Because he called for men to defend the Constitution and the laws, he has been denounced as a usurper and a despot. If he had not called on you when your country was in peril would not the same armies have been raised by the South, and the revolution gone on? What sort of a Government would you have had to-day? Would it not have been a military despotism? You complain of the great wrong he has done, of arrest, &c. If I have any complaint to make, it is that President Lincoln has not done more to crush the rebellion. Has Lincoln violated the Constitution and trampled the law under foot? Who commenced the war? Did not the South?— Somehow these sympathizers forget that Davis and his piratical crew have violated the Constitution. They can see only the blunders of the party in power, but they have not a word of disapproval for the total annihilation of the Constitution at the South. They can't see any wrong there, but it is all here. They are attempting to build up a party on the blunders and the imputed crimes of the present Administration.[9] Let me say here, if you want to build up a party on the ruins of the Administration party, you build upon a foundation of sand, which will be washed from under it. You must re-establish the Democracy in power on the basis of the restoration of the Union and the enforcement of the laws. That is what I intend to do.

It has been called a high crime to subjugate a State and to enforce the laws. Without law you can have no legislature, no State. Has a State a right to secede? Settle the question, they say, by peaceable secession and reconstruction. This is impossible. This government cannot be divided without bloodshed. Where will you divide it? Where will you draw the line? Who shall have the territories? Such are the questions which arise when you attempt to divide the Union. It cannot be done. The framers of the Constitution designed that it should be perpetual.— That instrument contains principles which are fundamental to all government, immutable, emanating from Deity himself. We are engaged in a long war, but we shall come out triumphant. Neither this nor succeeding generations shall destroy our rights. They had their origin in a seven years' war, in which our fathers spent their treasure and offered up their lives.[10] So now, brave men of Indiana, your sorrows will return like bread cast upon the waters.[11]

Let the idea be kept in mind. We have civil war and revolution. Why not have sought their remedy in the mode pointed out in the Constitution? But no, that must be destroyed, and the destruction of this Government must go with it. They wanted a separation of the States, and then reconstruction. They knew that reconstruction could not follow separation. I hold to the theory that no State can secede. The Union was to be perpetual. Separation dissolves all bonds, and restores the Union in its original elements. What State, what Government, could stand this result? To illustrate: you form a State government, pass laws, and impose penalties for crime. Each man assents to it. But suppose some one commits murder, and is arraigned for it, and should then notify you that he had seceded, and was no longer bound by your laws. He was a sovereign. Do you not think the other sovereigns would punish him? A man builds a house in a city; it is his property and he burns it down, on the principle that he can dispose of his own property as he pleases, without regard to the rights of others, and so burn down a block, or the city. Recognize such a principle, and you have no government but anarchy, and I repudiate the doctrine, *in toto coelo*,[12] that a State has a right to secede, without reference to its effect on the other States. Hence I am for the Union. I intend to stand by the Union so long as I live, and shed my heart's blood, if needed, as a libation for its preservation.

There can be no government unless the laws are enforced. What is the language of the sympathizers with Southern rebels? "I am for the Constitution as it is, and the Union as it was." [13] They are giving the enemies of the Union aid and comfort by their clamor. When these cringing, fawning, sycophantic set of fellows, are talking about dividing the Union, a Northwestern Confederacy, peace, armistice, etc. , they laugh at you, and hold you in utter contempt. No terms will suit them better than the acknowledgment of their independence.

Let me ask the rebel sympathizers of Indiana, why you are sympathizing with them—why your bowels of compassion[14] yearn for them. Why, you forget the Union men, then? You will not sympathize with us, but you would compromise with traitors. [Never.] Union men of those sections of country, whose necks rest beneath the iron heel of power, ask you to carry out the Constitution. I do not demand it for them, as a privilege, but demand it of you as a right, that the traitors of this rebellion shall be put down. Why? Because "the United States SHALL—not *may*—guarantee to every State in the Union a republican form of government." I call on the sympathizors here, I demand, in the name of the Constitution as it is, protection and support, and the guaranty of a republican form of government, for the Union men of the South. And, pardon me for my remarks. I ask, in the name of the Constitution, for the relief of that portion of the people in my State east of the Cumberland mountains, who, not excepting yourselves, are the most loyal people of the Nation, because they have dared to be loyal in the face of death—while some of you have been loyal, because you have not dared to be otherwise. We are loyal in our principles, and we have dared to speak and maintain them. I demand of the sympathizers a morsel of their sympathy, for the Union men of the South. You answer, "Compromise." What will you do with your humble speaker, and those who have stood by him? I suppose these sympathizers, like the rebels, want to see me hung.

The redemption of that brave people has been postponed long enough. I notify the people of Indiana, that, if the effort is not made soon, I will come to Ohio, Indiana and Illinois, and plead with you for a chosen band of men to go with me and redeem East Tennessee. [Cheers.]

Talk about being tired of the war! I know it is terrible, and realize its horrors, but these are incidents of a civil war. The ruin that has come, the blood that has been shed, are upon the heads of those who precipitated this civil war, and not on ours. You who have brought on this war, have forced this ruin, set brother against brother, orphaned these children, widowed these wives, and filled the land with mourning—you have done all this,—and let me ask you rebel sympathizers to lift up your hands and see if they are not crimsoned with the blood of the victims of the rebellion? Whether it comes sooner or later, justice will come. The slower its pace, the surer is its blow.[15] It will come, if we live; and if not living, when we are dead. Sooner or later, justice will overtake those whose hands are crimsoned with blood.

Tired of an eighteen months' war? Your fathers fought for seven years to establish this government, and you are tired of fighting eighteen months to defend it. So far as I am concerned, I am ready to fight seven years, thirty years, and would not stop then. What is a war of thirty years, when you look at the vast results to flow from it down the sea of time, in laying the foundation of a government which will live in future ages, and revolutionize the governments of the world?—Nothing. You are laying the foundation of a government which will endure while the sun rises and sets. I say, to-day, not from impulse, but from cool reflection, if my life was spared 700 years, I would fight on and fight ever. I would war against this Southern aristocracy as long as the Moors did against the Spaniards 700 years ago.[16]

The effect of a compromise would give strength to the rebels. You have commenced the demoralization here. An armistice will increase it. When divided, one half contending against the other, they would turn their invading armies on us and conquer the North. The very state of the war indicates the speedy suppression of the rebellion. If we prosecute the war, with the advance of the armies of the Mississippi, it would soon be opened, East Tennessee occupied by Rosecrans, and the great railroad artery of the South cut by our armies; a close blockade of Galveston, Mobile, Charleston, and other ports— would confine the rebellion so narrowly that it would die in its own feeble struggles.

Why has not this been done? Lincoln has made some blunders, but that is no reason for attacking the government. He is not perfect, but I sustain him in putting down the infamous rebellion, and in every other measure which is right. We are not committed to his blunders. When the government is saved by the suppression of the rebellion, and we have a government to quarrel in, we can quarrel as to whether Lincoln is right or wrong. Let us save the government first.

An armistice! The constitution as it is, and the Union as it was! I assure you as Jackson did about the tariff, it is a mere pretext for giving up the rebellion. A compromise is the last thing they want. They want to divide, and then conquer the whole. What will you put in your compromise? That each State shall regulate its own domestic institutions? That is spurious coin. After Jeff Davis and other Senators had left Congress, Mr. Corwin, a Republican, proposed an amendment to the constitution providing that slavery should not be interfered with by any amendment to the constitution hereafter. It passed Congress by a two-thirds vote, and now waits adoption by the Legislatures of three-fourths of the States to become a part of the constitution.[17] If they wanted a compromise to secure slavery from legislation, why did they not accept it?

Has any slave State adopted the amendment? Why did not Jeff. Davis urge Mississippi to adopt the amendment? It is nearly two years since it passed Congress, and not a seceded State has adopted the guaranty. They did not want it, because they wanted to get their rights—Southern rights. Another case in point was the organization of the territories. In the acts organizing them, the territorial legislatures were prohibited from impairing the rights of the people. This prevented any action against slavery in all the territory, then unorganized, of the United States. This proves that they wanted to separate from the other States, or conquer them. They had no desire for compromise, and had lost faith in man's capability to govern himself, and desired to establish an aristocratic form of government.[18]

This piratical King, Jeff. Davis, to be my master? Isham G. Harris to be my master? Instead of being my master he should not be my slave.[19] The time has arrived in connection with the down-trodden people of the South, when the tyrant's rod should be broken and the captive set free. Though a Southern man I am a citizen of the United States, and because a man lives at the South is no reason why he should be opposed to any one at the North.

Born and raised in the South, I have been a slave owner, having owned ten slaves. I obtained my Southern rights. The rebels stole my negroes, turned my invalid wife and children into the street, and made my house a barracks for "Butternuts" to lie sick in. That's my Southern rights, and if such are the rights to be awarded us when the Southern Confederacy is extended over us, I pray to be relieved from such a fate.

Great ado has been made about negroes. Let that be as it may, is that any reason why we should oppose our Government, and go croaking about and appealing to a squeamish sympathy in the country. I have lived among negroes, all my life, and I am for this Government with slavery under the Constitution as it is, if the Government can be saved. I am for the Government without negroes, and the Constitution as it is.[20] I want to be understood on this question. I am for the government of my fathers, if it is being carried out according to the principles of the Constitution.

If, as the car of State moves along, the negroes get in the way let them be crushed. If they keep out of the way let them remain where they are. I am for the Government and all measures necessary to maintain it. Is not this Government, the giant embodiment of the principles of human liberty, worth more than the institution of slavery? It is but as the dust in the balance. Some persons in the free States have an idea that if King Cotton didn't rule, they cannot sell a mule or a bushel of corn, but this Government would go on were the cotton plant lost to the world. And when you come to think of it, that by raising a little more wool and flax and hemp—[cries of "that's what's wanted"]—you may withold the article of cotton from the markets of the world, and they would be supplied without a ripple upon commercial waters, they will go on with or without cotton, and whether cotton or negroes continue in the United States, the Government will continue to remain. I am for the Government of my fathers with negroes. I am for it without negroes. Before I would see this Government destroyed I would see every negro back in Africa, disintegrated and blotted out of space.

Then let us defend this great fabric of human liberty, and the time will come when this nation will be the great centre of the world, the great guiding star to other nations in government, religion, science and arts, the great centre from which an influence and principle will radiate. Is this not worth battling for? Let us go on with this great experiment of Democracy.

The time has come and is now upon us when we are assured by Southern leaders and their sympathizers that we have an institution that is more powerful than the government itself. When any institution, whether banks or the aristocracy of wealth, or any other combination of capital, asserts that the government has no right to agitate its claims, and shakes it to its centre, then the government must put it down. If the institution of slavery denies the government the right of agitation, and seeks to overthrow it, then the government has a clear right to destroy it.[21]

I look upon these principles of free government as the powerful means of elevating mankind to a higher state of civilization. I look upon our system of religion as advancing man in his spiritual nature. And when we go on, as it were, in these two parallel lines of progress, then we shall pass beyond the church and political systems, and we shall secure harmony, "peace on earth and good will to all men." [22]

I will hold to the government as the palladium of our liberties, and cling to it as the mariner clings to the last plank when the waves are surging over him. If the government is to be overthrown, I do not want to survive it. If the government is to be entombed in the tomb of nation, let me be buried with it. Let us stand together with those brave Indianians, some of whom are in hospitals, some in new made graves, and others battling in the field. Indiana has erected a monument for herself. Her reputation will be inscribed on the highest pinnacle of fame. Will you disgrace it by witholding your aid and encouragement?

Will you deny that your soldiers' blood has been shed in a glorious cause? If you do you are unworthy fathers and mothers. Who will turn his back upon his blood?[23] [Cries of "traitors!"] Yes, traitors, none but traitors. For him who sleeps in the grave, let him know that he has fallen in a glorious cause, and water his grave with tears, and, if need be, to crown the war with success, you should shed your own blood and spend your last dollar.[24]

Indianapolis *Journal*, February 27, 1863; New York *Times*, March 2, 1863; *The Great Union Meeting Held at Indianapolis, February 26th, 1863 . . .* (Indianapolis, 1863).

1. This "Great Union Meeting," grandiosely described by an Indianapolis reporter as "a broad, bold, noble assertion of the right of the nation to save itself" and having "no element of party in it"—but seen by a modern historian as a Republican reaction to the Democratic by-election successes of the preceding October, when the anti-war, Copperhead party increased its congressional seats from four to seven and gained control of the General Assembly—attracted a crowd conservatively estimated at 25,000. In response to Governor Oliver P. Morton's call for help in arousing popular support for administration policies and for a vigorous prosecution of the war, Johnson agreed to speak in Indianapolis as the first engagement in a month-long northern tour. Crowds had poured into the city the previous day—"Train after train swelled the vast assemblage," until "there was not a spare bed . . . in any hotel, nor in many private houses, and hundreds had to sit up all night in hotel parlors sleeping in chairs, or how they could, or not sleeping at all." The audience "filled the State House Yard and overflowed into the streets," and although "three stands were erected . . . even those were insufficient to bring the masses within hearing distance of the speakers." One observer marvelled at this quivering mass of humanity: "faces upturned to the stand, as if their bodies were one huge chunk on which faces had been glued, like shells on a fancy basket, as thickly as they could stick." Indianapolis *Journal*, February 27, 1863; Emma Lou Thornbrough, "The Race Issue in Indiana Politics during the Civil War," *Indiana Magazine of History,* XLVII (1951), 178, 182; O. P. Morton to Johnson, January 15, February 6; H. C. Newcomb to Johnson, February 14, 1863, Johnson Papers, LC; New York *Times,* March 2, 1863.

2. That he was addressing a northern, predominantly Democratic audience, probably accounts for this novel explanation for his support of Breckinridge.

3. Here the reporter interpolated, observing that the governor quoted passages from Breckinridge's prewar speeches "to prove him a devoted Union man" who had prophesied "that the execration of mankind would rest on any one who attempted to disrupt the Union."

4. This cryptic observation about fears concerning the shift of political power was more accurately and succinctly conveyed by the New York *Times* account: "When the Southern leaders saw the scepter of political power departing, and saw, when Mr. Lincoln's term expired, that other men would make their way into the confidence of the people over them, it was their time to strike." *Ibid.*

5. Montgomery *Advertiser*, n. d., quoted in unidentified clipping, Series 20, Johnson Papers, LC.

6. At this juncture, the speaker invoked once again Jackson's prophetic vision: just as Calhoun had made the protective tariff an excuse for nullification, the "next pretext" would be the slavery issue.

7. When, during the Sumter crisis, Virginia's secession convention appeared ready to keep the state in the Union, Congressman Roger A. Pryor was in Charleston attempting to persuade South Carolina to seize the fort. The attack may have helped to bring uncommitted Virginia delegates to a secessionist stance. See *Johnson Papers,* IV, 507n; V, 232.

8. For Confederate Secretary of War LeRoy P. Walker's speech, see *ibid.*, IV, 627.

9. A jibe at the emerging Peace Democrats who were using the general dissatisfaction associated with high prices, taxes, conscription, the Emancipation Proclamation, suspension of habeas corpus, and unrelenting prosecution of the war to turn sentiment against the Lincoln administration. Nevins, *War for the Union*, II, 321-22.

10. Once again, the *Times* reporter presents a more vivid and, we may presume, more accurate version: "They sacrificed life and property for it, labored in cabinet and field, slept on the cold ground, under an inclement sky, only to rise with the morrow to march with blood spouting from their shoes, and by their trials, sufferings and blood, cemented the fabric of Constitutional Government."

11. Here ensues a brief interpolation of the speaker's remarks on the flexibility of the Constitution, which, as the reporter expressed it, "could be adapted to any change in the condition of man."

12. *Toto caelo:* "by as much as the distance between the poles"; in short, total disagreement. *OED*, XI, 179.

13. A paraphrase of Daniel Webster. See Letter from a "Peace Democrat," November 17, 1862, note 9.

14. I John 3:17—"Shutteth up his bowels of compassion."

15. A favorite cliché, first found in his circular To the Freemen of the First Congressional District of Tennessee, October 15, 1845. *Johnson Papers*, I, 267, 275n.

16. Johnson's statement would have been more historically accurate had he likened his dedication and perseverance to that of the Spanish, since it was they who engaged in an eight-century *reconquista* against the Moors. Once again a reportorial interruption, in which Johnson admonishes the North to stand together, quoting John Paul Jones's "I am just getting ready to fight" and citing a Knoxville secesh editor's comment about the demoralizing effect which the "quasi-rebellious attitude" of the New York and New Jersey governors and their northwestern sympathizers had on various Union armies.

17. See *ibid.*, IV, 569, 573n, 614-15, 644n.

18. According to the *Journal* reporter, "Gov. Johnson referred to the Southern papers, the Richmond Examiner, DeBow's Review, and to the utterances of such men as Isham G. Harris, and the Rhetts and others."

19. The *Times* correspondent clarifies: "Instead of Harris being my master, I would not have him for my slave."

20. A reprise of his "Give me my Government, and let the negroes go!" Speech at Nashville, July 4, 1862, *Johnson Papers*, V, 536.

21. Johnson's import would seem to be more accurately conveyed in the *Times* account: "The time has come to teach both the North and the South that institutions cannot exist when opposed to the Government. If banks are in the way, put them down—if aristocracy of wealth, put it down—if unlawful combinations, put them down. How long is it since we had in the United States an institution we dare not question? Has Slavery the right to agitate the Government and Government no privilege to agitate Slavery? When institutions grow too great for Government, they must give way, and the Government stand. It is for the nation to determine the nature and character of its institutions."

22. This paragraph is reminiscent of an article of mystical faith enunciated much earlier in his circular To the Freemen of the First Congressional District of Tennessee, October 15, 1845, and First Inaugural Address, October 17, 1853. *Ibid.*, I, 240-41; II, 176-77.

23. A more eloquent rendering of what the speaker presumably said is found in the *Times:* "If enough life has not been sacrificed—enough blood shed—if enough patriots do not sleep in their graves—then I say to Him who is on high, name the price and it shall be

paid; and if need be, let that flag, borne upon every battle-field, be baptized in fire from the sun and bathed in the blood of the nation."

24. Concluding with his customary flourish to the ladies, Johnson drew an invidious comparison between the "unsexed" women of the South who had spurred their men on to rebellion and the noble women of the North who preferred "to be a brave soldier's widow than a coward's wife." He "then retired amid vociferous cheering."

Speech at Cincinnati[1]

February 27, 1863

Gov. Johnson soon made his appearance, and said that it was not his purpose in appearing before them to make a speech. It was not on account of his unwillingness to respond to their calls, but on account of his indisposition. He had spoken in the open air the day before for over three hours, to so large a crowd that it required him to exert his voice beyond its compass, and yesterday he was compelled to stop and speak for over one hour on his way to the city. He wished that those who were listening to him now had been at Indianapolis, and they would have seen the true spirit of devotion and patriotism that animates the hearts of Indianans[.] It would have carried conviction to every one of your hearts, that the Union must be preserved. There is one of Indiana's citizens here to-night, who considers himself a citizen of the United States, and who owes allegiance to it, without regard to particular locality.

I am constrained to say and believe that a great reaction is going on in the public mind, which will carry conviction to every heart, that this war must be suppressed and the rebels put down. I believe the spirit of patriotism now being kindled will speak in language to Northern sympathizers that will compel them to desist in their traitorous efforts to overthrow the Government.

I have some little respect for men in the South, who are compelled, from the force of circumstances that surround them, to apparently support the Southern Confederacy—some little excuse for them, but when I look to the North and Northwest and find traitors who sympathize with the rebels and who propose to destroy the Government, I say I have no respect for them whatever. Large portions of the South are betrayed by designing traitors, and through the reign of terror that is maintained, thousands are driven into the vortex of rebellion against their will.

Men living in the South have to dare to be loyal, while in the North they have to dare to be disloyal. It requires great moral courage to be a Union man in the South. We find that secret organizations have been got up here in the North— Knights of the Golden Circle—and when its members are called to depose, they refuse because it will criminate them. If we were in a country where we were deprived of our rights, our liberties and our privileges, there might be some excuse for such organizations; but when we have all our liberties and rights guaranteed and protected by the Government, and we find men plotting to destroy and overthrow that

Government, you have the right, and it is your duty to expel them from your midst, upon the same principle that if you had a family and some person got in and destroyed your domestic peace and quiet, that you should expel him. When the object of such organizations is not to give the people freedom and perpetuate laws, but to overthrow and subvert the government, and deprive them of their rights and liberties, then take the speediest means to expel them. When you find men thus engaged do not stop to consider the question of habeas corpus, but seize them, and put them where they will do no harm. When they do this they cease to be free men, and have lost their manhood[.] Instead of retaining their dimensions, they shrink into the dimensions of reptiles. I say, having so shrunk, they deserve to be trod upon like reptiles.

We all know that it is the intention and object of these men to change the condition of the Government. It is no new or recent idea, but one of long standing. There are a number of men in the South who are prepared to establish a monarchical form of government, that is to be based on Negro Slavery. This is to be its chief corner-stone. This is a kind of government I have been opposed to ever since I understood what government was. I am not in favor of any government that is based on farms, on property, negroes if you please, but upon the good will of the people. I am for an aristocracy and against an aristocracy. Aristocracy of money, aristocracy of family, aristocracy of land, aristocracy of negro have my utmost contempt; but elevated labor—an aristocracy of labor, of virtue, of intelligence, of integrity, of merit, have my approbation and respect. This is the kind of aristocracy I am in favor of, and this the basis on which free Government should rest.

This Government is based on the eternal principles of Democracy. I am a Democrat, not one of your new-fangled Democrats, however, who being opposed to some of the acts of the Administration have turned traitors to the Government. My Democracy was learned at the feet of him who stood by the Government in great peril.[2]

Your modern Democracy are every ready to cry out that we of the North are violating the Constitution and subverting the laws; but you never hear them charge Jeff. Davis or his associates with violating the Constitution. Oh, no! They have no charges to make against them; but everything Mr. Lincoln does is found fault with, because Mr. Lincoln makes an effort to defend and preserve the Union, I do not propose to stop and inquire how he is going to do it. I believe him to be honest, and I am going to sustain him.

The Democracy talk of compromises. Will you compromise with traitors with arms in their hands? with the bayonets at your breasts? When the rebellion is crushed, and the traitors are hung, then will be the time to talk about compromise, and not before.

A great deal has been said about the President's proclamation. You and I might not agree upon that. But is that any reason why we should not be in favor of putting down the rebellion. They appear to be deeply concerned about the negro, and want a compromise and an armistice, but they are not concerned for the Union men of the South, who are bound down to this accursed rebellion. Who shall we compromise with? With traitors? Suppose you do compromise, and the necks of the Union men of the South will be brought under the heels of the traitors.

Governor Johnson then referred at some length to the sufferings and trials of the people of East Tennessee, and charged that some of the officers in command of the armies which should have released East Tennessee were not above suspicion. (A voice in the crowd—"General Buell") I wont specify, and I wont contradict. What we have most to fear are the internal foes and enemies. I would rather have a Government and nothing else than to have everything and no Government. The Government must go even if some institutions have to be annihilated.

Let us stand united, and go on in the prosecution of this war—in every effort to put down this rebellion—and having crushed it, the Government will be placed on a stronger basis.

Memphis *Bulletin*, March 3, 1863.

1. Accompanied by Ex-Governor Joseph A. Wright of Indiana, Johnson had just arrived from Indianapolis, having spoken informally at a number of stations on the way in response to popular demand. An evening serenade by Menter's Band in front of the Burnet House drew a crowd which "called for Governor Johnson, and manifested great enthusiasm whenever his name was mentioned." Memphis *Bulletin*, March 3, 1863.

2. Andrew Jackson.

Speech to the Ohio Legislature

March 3, 1863, Columbus, Ohio; *Ohio State Journal* (Columbus), March 4, 1863.

This three-hour address, the second scheduled speech in a month's tour designed to further the cause and particularly to counter criticism of administration war policies, was the centerpiece of a "Great Union Rally" held in the chamber of the House of Representatives before an overflowing and wildly enthusiastic assemblage. Covering much the same ground as in his Indianapolis speech five days earlier—elevating the preservation of the Union and the Constitution above party differences, rationalizing his support of Breckinridge, minimizing the threat of Lincoln's election to the South, while pleading for a patriotic closing of ranks around the President—Johnson castigates Copperheadism and decries compromise sentiment North, pointing out the impossibility of coming to terms with southern traitors who had engaged in a long-standing conspiracy against the nation and were now waging a war for its destruction. As for the Emancipation Proclamation, "laws derived from the nature of things . . . will work out the same results, whether right or wrong"; inevitably, the continuance of the conflict will mean the end of slavery. A truce to murmurings about the constitutionality of invading the "rights of the South": for "What rights have rebels?" Denying that he favors prosecuting the conflict for the purpose of abolishing slavery, the governor nonetheless avers, "if negroes are in the way, I say *let* THEM GO!" Any institution which threatens the "perpetuity" of the Union must be put down. "I tell you there are but two parties now—one for the government and one against it; one of patriots, the other of cravens." In a modest peroration he proclaims: "we are in a civil war,—how to extricate ourselves is the great question. *We must crush the rebellion by the power of the Government.*— When this power is fully felt, the thing is done . . . Let us join, then, in the embrace of heart to heart around the altar of our country, and solemnly swear, by the Majesty of Heaven and that altar of our country, that the country itself must and shall be saved."

From William B. Stokes

Camp near Murfresboro,
March 5th 1863.

Gov. Andrew Johnson,
Sir:

I arrived in Camp on Sunday last, found the Health pretty good.

Our Regt. with others have had Several engagements with the Rebs, Since you left, & in every instance has been successful in driving them from their Camps, Capturing goods, & prisoners. I am expecting every day to be ordered to join Col. Crook[1] at Some point on the Cumberland, or Caney fork Rivers.

I am sorry to inform you that Leut. Henry L. Newbury[2] is Still operating against me, about Hd.Quarters. it is giving me a goodeal of trouble, and in fact, is operating against the Regt. Now, Sir, yourself & you alone can relieve us of this trouble, you well know that he was to resign when ordered to do So. you can demand that he Send up his Commission.

I dislike very much to trouble you, but knowing that you are the only one that Can Cure the disease, or pest, I appeal to you.

There are many things that I could allude to as reasons for desiring this, but it is not important at this time.

I was Commissioned by you to raise this Regt. you have aided me in every way & any time, for which, I shall ever feel grateful.

While I regret it, yet I feel that unless this difficulty, Can be Settled, & Newbury removed, I will be compelled to Send in my Resignation. To live, with & Serve the Federal Government and exposure to Cold, & the emimey in front, & a fire on me in the rear, I am not willing to Submit to, if it is posible to get out of it.

I am truly gratified to See that you have been doing So much good by your talk to those Coperheads.[3] I honestly believe that it will pave the way to destroy the party north.

A few days good weather, & I think there will be a forward movement.

I Close by Submitting this hole matter to you for your Consideration.

Respectfully your Obt. Servt.
W. B. Stokes
Col. 1st Mdle. Tenn. Cavaly

P. S. Since writing the forgoing, I learn there is being made a Strong appeal to President Lincon, to pardon, Capt. Fleming[4] who inflicted a wound upon me, that I fear that will give me pain So long as I live.

I write this that you may State the facts to him, which I am Satisfied if he knew, he would approve the Sentence of the Court. You know how Such outsides influence is some times brought to bear.[5]

With respect, I am truly yours,
W. B. Stokes Col. Comd'g

Confidential

P. S. Will you please see the Secretary of War in regard to the Bounty for my men.

W. B. S.

ALS, DLC-JP.

1. George Crook (1828-1890), Dayton, Ohio, native, and West Point graduate (1852), had served on the frontier. Colonel of the 36th Ohio Inf., serving in the Virginias through 1862, he became brigadier in January, 1863, and transferring to the Army of the Cumberland at Rosecrans' request, commanded a division headquartered from early March to early June at Carthage on the Cumberland before returning to Virginia in 1864. Remaining in the regular army where he eventually rose to major general, he became a prominent Indian fighter in Idaho and later in Arizona, Wyoming, and the Dakotas. *NCAB*, IV, 70-71; Warner, *Generals in Blue,* 102-4; *OR*, Ser. 1, XXIII, Pt. II, 110, 386; see also Dan L. Thrapp, *General Crook and the Sierra Madre Adventure* (Norman, [1972]).

2. See Letter from Henry L. Newberry, October 25, 1862.

3. A reference to Johnson's recent speeches in Indiana and Ohio where sizeable groups of anti-war Democrats were urging a negotiated peace.

4. Eli Fleming (*c*1827-1896), Pennsylvania-born Warren County farmer, enlisted as captain, Co. F, 5th Tenn. Cav., USA, in September, 1862. The following January, after an altercation over his candidacy for major in a regimental election and over charges of being absent without leave, he shot and wounded Stokes, was court-martialed, and sentenced to death. However, in view of Fleming's outstanding record for bravery and loyalty, Rosecrans, while endorsing the sentence, reduced it to dismissal from service but, before acting further, awaited Lincoln's approval, which came in October. Years later, when Fleming successfully applied for a pension, Rosecrans indicated regret that he had not negated the court-martial altogether, feeling that the "acrimonious partisan testimony against Fleming, whom the Colonel [Stokes] and his adherents had resolved to stamp out," resulted in a verdict extremely unfair to "one of the most daring, active and efficient officers in the Regiment." Both before and after his army service, Fleming was a scout and guide for Union commanders operating in Warren and adjacent counties. CSR, RG94, NA; File GCM, LL-77, RG153, NA; 1860 Census, Tenn., Warren, 20; *OR*, Ser. 1, XVI, Pt. I, 414; XXIII, Pt. I, 267; Nashville *Dispatch*, January 25, 1863.

5. Three days later, Stokes was "pained *indeed*" to learn that Rosecrans had changed Fleming's sentence from death to dismissal. Declaring "I am Compelled in justice to myself & Regiment to re-sign, which I have done," he observes in the next sentence that he may need the governor's help in getting "from under Genl. *R*." He actually remained in service until the end of the war. Stokes to Johnson, March 8, 1863, Johnson Papers, LC.

From William T. Steiger[1]

Washington, D. C. March 6th 1863.

His Excellency Andrew Johnson
Governor of Tennessee at Nashville.
Sir,

By the act of Congress, approved 2d July 1862 (Chap. CXXX Stat. at Large p. 503) Public land & Scrip are granted to the Loyal States for the endowment of Agricultural Colleges &c.[2]

Looking to the Agricultural and mechanical interests of the State of Tennessee I presume her Legislature, notwithstanding the temporary embarrassments which at present surround it, will not neglect to secure all the advantages, by promptly accepting this munificent grant, (amounting to about 300, 000 acres,) as required by the Act of Congress, which limits the time of acceptance to *two years*. On this supposition, I respectfully offer my services as your agent at Washington, for the adjustment of the grant, and the safe delivery of the Scrip, when issued, into your hands.

My employments in the General Land Office, in high positions, for 22 consecutive years, have given me much practical information, which I trust fits me in a special manner to discharge, the duties of an Agent. Besides, since my resignation in 1857, I have had charge here, of the large Rail Road grants for several States for which I have procured the evidence of title, and settled all conflicts to *Four and a half millions of acres*.

My charge for the services now offered, if accepted, would only be Broker's Commissions or 1/4 P/C on the amount obtained, reserving the chances of further employment by the State's assignees for the location of the Scrip, in which I could be of essential service to them, by designating the regions of good lands, and settling any conflicts which may arise before the Department. If preferred I would also receive Land Scrip, at its market value, in payment for my services.

As regards my Standing and Capacity, I beg leave to refer you to the enclosed testimonials,[3] marked A, B, from Maj. Genl. John A. Dix,[4] and other friends, and I have reason to know that my appointment would be very acceptable to all the Officers here, charged with the adjustment of the grant.

In reference to the appointment of an Agent, it is proper to state, that in the Adjustment of my Rail Road grants the Department ruled that it would deal direct with the *States* and not with the assignees, and I am satisfied that this rule will be enforced in relation to the College grant. Hence only the Governor or his Agent will be directly recognized in the adjustment and I respectfully suggest that suitable provision should be made in the state law of acceptance[.][5]

I have the honor to remain, Your Obt. Servt.
Wm. T. Steiger
Washington D. C.

N. B. Please acknowledge receipt of these papers.

W. T. S.

ALS, DLC-JP.

1. William T. Steiger (*c*1801-*fl*1875), Maryland native who had been a draftsman and surveying clerk in the land office during the early 1850's, was living at 16 Pennsylvania Avenue, claimed $35,000 real and $5,000 personal property, and by 1875 was listed as a railroad agent. 1860 Census, Dist. of Columbia, Washington, 1st Ward, 194; Washington city directories (1863-75), *passim; U. S. Official Register* (1851), 135; (1853), 132.

2. The Morrill Act gave public lands (30,000 acres for each senator and representative based on apportionment under the 1860 census) to loyal states and territories to provide for

agricultural and mechanical colleges; states lacking sufficient public lands within their boundaries were to receive from the secretary of the interior land scrip to make up their share. Money from the sale of land and scrip was to be invested in stocks to "constitute a perpetual fund" for "the endowment, support, and maintenance of at least one college." *U. S. Statutes,* XII, 503.

3. James M. Edmunds, commissioner of the general land office, wrote that Steiger had been employed by "States and Rail Road organizations in the adjustment of Land Grants pending before this office," and that he "enjoys a high reputation for integrity and efficiency." Postmaster General Montgomery Blair and Elisha Whittlesey, first comptroller of the treasury, endorsed Edmunds' assertions. General Dix's statement was similarly worded. Endorsement of William T. Steiger by J. M. Edmunds, October 11, and John A. Dix, October 27, 1862, Johnson Papers, LC; *U. S. Official Register* (1861), 15; (1863), 98, 283.

4. Dix was in charge of Fortress Monroe from May, 1862, until mid-July of the following year, when he was assigned to command the Department of the East with headquarters in New York City. After the war he served as minister to France (1866-69) and governor of New York (1872-74). Warner, *Generals in Blue,* 126; *DAB*; V, 326; see also *Johnson Papers*, II, 104*n*.

5. Complications stemming from the Civil War delayed implementation of the Morrill Act in Tennessee; not until February 1, 1868, did the state accept the grant, in the form of land scrip. Apparently Steiger was not involved in any of the ensuing transactions. Stanley J. Folmsbee, *East Tennessee University, 1840-1879,* in *University of Tennessee Record,* LXII (May, 1959), 56-57, 67-68.

Speech at Harrisburg, Pennsylvania

March 6, 1863, Harrisburg, Pa. ; Harrisburg *Evening Telegraph,* April 6, 1863.

Having been denied use of the state senate chamber, Johnson and Governor Joseph A. Wright of Indiana spoke at the city court house. The Tennessean prefaced his principal themes—the perfection and inevitable perpetuity of our government, a spirited defense of the Lincoln administration's vigorous prosecution of the war, a scathing attack on Copperheadism—with a series of personal disclaimers and complaints: although engaged in public speaking since entering public life, "I never had any passion for it"; "The disposition to seek public position, is not a part of my character"; he had not sought the post of military governor—indeed, had sacrificed by giving up his Senate seat; despite his having been appointed by Lincoln, he is not "controlled by his will"; throughout his career he has had the misfortune "to have a particular class of individuals snapping and snarling at my heels as I went."

Castigating the President's critics—"There is great sympathy gotten up for those violators of the Constitution at the South, while there is no sympathy for the Government in its efforts to vindicate the Constitution against those who thus attack it"—he pleads with his audience to rise above partisanship and embrace patriotism—"sympathy with the traitors of the South is what I call the half-way house to treason." While he had "always been a Democrat," he is, nonetheless, working with the Republican Lincoln because he stands ready to help anyone "engaged in this glorious work of trying to preserve this Government as a unity. [Enthusiastic and long continued Applause]." He climaxes the familiar review of past compromise efforts, especially those of Crittenden and Corwin, by trumpeting: "My compromise is the Constitution of the United States—the best compromise that can be devised. [Loud applause.]" Tackling the knotty issue of slavery and the President's recent proclamation, the Tennessean announces that he is not for emancipating the slaves "unless there be a necessity for it," but goes on to declare that insofar as that institution is in the way of putting down the rebellion, "I say, slavery has got to get out of the way. [Long continued applause]."

As for the future, the governor prophesies: "there is one thing clear and certain; if this war goes on, the friction of war itself, without regard to proclamations, will settle the negro question." Further, we should not divide among ourselves, but rather devote all energies to putting down the rebellion. "This Government must all go one way or the other. The rebels will conquer you, if you do not conquer them." Expatiating on the suffering of Union men in the South, including their murder by "Indian savages," he both reassures—"Let me tell you that there are more Union men throughout the South than you imagine"—and entreats—"I ask of the people of Pennsylvania to guarantee to Tennessee a 'republican form of government.'" Addressing "You who are so deeply concerned about the negro," he urges that they "first . . . emancipate the white men of the South, before you trouble yourself about negro emancipation." Penultimate to the perennial concluding eulogy of the ladies, their influence and their sacrifice, the speaker expresses both optimism that the Union can be restored and hope that the tribulations of the war will make men more appreciative of the blessings of government under the Constitution.

From Pitser Miller[1]

Bolivar Tene. March 7th 1863

Govr. Andrew Johnson
Nashville Tene.

Dr. Sir I wrote you in Dcr. in regard to our Congressional Election about which we had much confusion[.] our Head Generals And you ordering Elections & our Commanders of Post for bidding it[.] I dont know that you got it[.][2] Mr Montgomery[3] who lives at Gallatin tells me he will be in Nashville next week & I conclude to write you[.] We are in a deplorable Situation[.] when the Union Army Genl. Wallace[4] entered here 7th June 5/6 of the County were Union Men and opposed to Secession the 1/6 more active & had got ballance very quiet[.] Genl. Wallace foraged light gave clear recpts[.] when he left he was Succeded by Genl. Ross[5] who was much more Stringent gave recpts for a small part taken whilst the men plundered every thing they could lay their hands on whether they had any use for it or not Stole our Horses Mules negroes Waggons Buggies clothing arms &c[.] Sometimes when we could find them they were returned but oftener not[.] no distinction Scarcely made between Union & Secesh[.] We are now comparatively without negroe or Horse Power[.] Indeed Meat Grain &c is very scarce & the Rules for Importing any necessaries if we had the money are very stringent[.] we have had no Salt this winter to salt what few Hogs the Stragling Soldiers left us, on my Farm not a Blade of fodder 200 lb. Meat about 30 Bbls corn not a mule or Horse except what I have bought within 30 days to make a crop[.] I was deprived of my necessaries by both armies The Secesh taking 3/4[.] I cant think the authorities at Washington know that Qr. Masters are allowed to go out & take all the Corn Horses fodder &c & allow little or Nothing for it & I suppose charge the Governmt full prices[.] Even Colts Jacks Jennies &c are taken to the Public Carrills & fed[.]

one of the greatest Hardships we have is the derention [detention] of negroes fed by the U S Governmnt put in Carrills & die in a heavy ratio[.][6] they do no good to the U S but a heavy Cost & a great loss to the owners[.]

I drop you these lines as History on which you can rely, and I pray God for a Speedy Settlement of all our troubles & restore us to our former happy times[.]

Very truly your obt
Pitser Miller

ALS, DLC-JP.

1. See *Johnson Papers*, IV, 342*n*.

2. This letter is not extant. On December 8, Johnson had ordered elections in the 9th and 10th districts for the twenty-ninth; unaware of the governor's order, Grant had given notice on the eighth that an election would be held in the 8th, 9th, and 10th districts on the twenty-fourth, unless Johnson should issue a call. Partly because of Forrest's raid into West Tennessee, Gen. Stephen A. Hurlbut, commander at Memphis, postponed balloting until January 20, 1863, by which time the unionists conceded the process would be a farce, since only a small fraction of those who had taken the oath could be induced to go near the polls—whereupon Johnson postponed the election indefinitely. Nashville *Union*, December 9, 1862; Memphis *Bulletin*, December 23, 27, 1862, January 20, 21, 1863; Boatner, *Civil War Dictionary*, 291-92.

3. William Montgomery (*c*1805-*fl*1870), Miller's former partner, was a Scottish-born cotton manufacturer, who was seeking an interview with Johnson to obtain protection for his factory at Gallatin. 1870 Census, Tenn. , Sumner, Gallatin, 5th Dist., 32; William Montgomery to Johnson, June 7, 1869, Johnson Papers, LC.

4. For Lew Wallace, see *Johnson Papers*, V, 91*n*.

5. For Leonard F. Ross, see *ibid.*, 351*n*.

6. In November, 1862, Grant had attempted to solve the question of what to do with numerous slaves flocking to the Union army by establishing a camp at Grand Junction, Tennessee, "where they will be suitable cared for and organized into companies and set to work, picking, ginning and baling all cotton now outstanding in the fields." Although care was provided for the sick, "the want and destitution were appalling." One soldier wrote, "Our efforts to do anything for these people . . . often failed; they had become so completely broken down in spirit, through suffering, that it was almost impossible to arouse them." After the loss of Holly Springs, the contraband camp was moved to Memphis, and others established at such locations as Corinth, Mississippi, and Helena, Arkansas. As early as October, 1862, at least 2,000 contrabands from the Mississippi Valley had been sent by the military authorities to Cairo, Illinois, to prevent starvation. The Bolivar Camp, to which Miller refers, had been set up in January, 1863, and would be evacuated in June when the Federals abandoned the post. Meanwhile, the commanding general sought to meet the complaints of Miller and others by forbidding additional runaways from entering his line. John Eaton, *Grant, Lincoln and the Freedmen* (New York, 1907), 12, 15, 18-19, 26-28, 30-32; Memphis *Bulletin*, October 25, November 25, 1862; *Missouri Democrat* (St. Louis), November 5, 1862; Cimprich, Slavery Amidst Civil War, 104; Manson Brayman, General Order No. 10, March 19, 1863, Johnson Papers, LC.

From Fannie Howard[1]

Lebanon March 9 1863

Gov Johnson

For your kindness to me in allowing me the privilege of bringing medecine out of Nashville for my sick mother,[2] I feel under many obligations and if there is ever a time when in my humble way I can serve you I will prove that I *feel* what I say— Having known you so long, and knowing your great liberality and generosity I feel encouraged to call on you for another favor— At my mother's death, she left what property she had to Mary[3] & Me exclusively and feeling so desolate and lonely, we are most anxious to sell our dwelling house, and board— But we find it impossible to find a purchaser— I write to you to know if with your aid and influence we cannot *sell it to the Government*—and if not will not a few of your friends join you and buy it— With your ample means it would be but a trifle to you and to us a great kindness— The property is well improved and in good repair, and I will pledge you my word that it shall be well cared for— We come to you the Orphan children, and the sisters of warm, personal, and political friends, and I feel and believe that our appeal will not be in vain, and the Orphan's prayers and the blessings of the Orphan's God will be yours— Mr Milligan & Mr Safford[4] are the Executors of my Mother's will—both truly loyal men— If you can do anything for us please let me know and I will come down with Mr Safford and see you— when you have an opportunity—can you not offer some inducement to Mr Milligan to come to Nashville— When convenient please let me hear from you—

Yours Truly Fannie Howard

ALS, DLC-JP2.

1. Fannie Howard (b. *c*1837) was a daughter of Jacob Howard, a Greeneville, later Lebanon, merchant, and sister of John K. Howard, late Confederate colonel. 1850 Census, Tenn., Wilson, 10th Dist., 118; (1860), 167; Sam Milligan Memoir, 1863-1869 (microfilm, Tennessee State Library and Archives), 68; for Jacob and John K. Howard, see *Johnson Papers,* I, 215*n*; II, 263*n*.

2. Sarah R. Howard (1800-1863), eldest daughter of state senator John Kennedy. Acklen, *Tenn. Records*, I, 288; "In Memoriam of Jacob Howard," Milligan Memoir, 441.

3. Mary Howard (b. *c*1841), Jacob's youngest daughter. 1860 Census, Tenn., Wilson, 10th Dist., 167.

4. Sam Milligan and James M. Safford were Sarah's sons-in-law, the former having married Elizabeth Howard in 1849, before her parents moved from Greeneville, and the latter, Catherine K. Howard Owen (widow of Dr. Benjamin R. Owen) in 1853. Temple, *Notable Men,* 154; Speer, *Prominent Tennesseans,* 484; for Milligan and Safford, see *Johnson Papers,* I, 114*n*; III, 304*n*.

Speech at Philadelphia[1]

March 11, 1863

Fellow-Citizens—for I desire to call you such—feeling and believing that I am yet a citizen of the United States, [Applause] I venture at least to address you as my fellow citizens. I regret, at the same time, in addressing you as such, that I shall do so under unfavorable circumstances. There are many reasons why I should feel embarrassed on this occasion. I am suffering from an indisposition and hoarseness, which every one will perceive who hears my voice. Now, I notify you in advance, that if you have come here for the purpose of being highly entertained by me, by any display of rhetoric or oratory, you will be mistaken, and I advise you to "let yourselves down."[2] [Laughter.] In ancient times there were various kinds of speakers that were called forth to address the people. Cicero addressed his audiences, and never failed to please them by gesticulations, intonations of voice, and handsomely rounded periods. Such was the power of his eloquence, that we are told he was occasionally interrupted by cries of "That's good." "A splendid sentiment," and so on. The Grecians had orators of a different stamp, but who moved the people as forcibly and as universally. When Philip undertook to invade the Grecian States, Demosthenes addressed himself to their good understanding. His sentiments always secured a lodgment in the minds of his audience, who, as they retired, had their hearts filled with the patriotism that he inspired, and exclaimed, "let us fight Philip." [3] I trust in God's name, that when this audience shall have dispersed from here to-night each man will have his heart filled with the importance of the occasion, and his lips exclaiming, "we will fight Jeff Davis, and will put down the rebellion and all the rebel conspirators." [Applause] I shall, in addressing you to-night, use the language of soberness and truth. I feel that we are engaged in a great cause. I feel that that cause is just and ought to be sustained. [Applause.] What are the circumstances under which we assemble to-night? We are in the midst of a rebellion, to the wickedness and causelessness of which history can furnish no parallel. Strange as it may seem, this rebellion has been provided for in the Constitution of the United States. When we examine that instrument, we find that our fathers, in their wisdom, anticipated that there would be rebellions. They have provided for them. We find also, on examination of the Constitution, that the writ of habeas corpus may be suspended in time of rebellion when the public necessity requires it.[4] [Applause.] We find that the Constitution confers power upon the Government of the United States to suppress insurrections, and to repel invasions, domestic or foreign. Hence, our forefathers provided for a contingency, in which the life of the nation might be put to risk. Then, in coming before you to-night by invitation[5]—and I need not say that I should have done so by inclination—I do so not for the purpose of appealing in behalf of a down-trodden people. I do not come before you to enlist your sympathies for an oppressed nationality. I come in the name of the Constitution to uphold the Government, and to inspire you with hope for its final success. That Constitution provides that the United States shall guarantee to every State in this Union a republican form of government. [Applause.] Our forefathers saw the importance of such a provision as this in the National Constitution. We, therefore, must insist on carrying out this as we insist on carrying out every other provision of that Constitution. Proceeding in the idea that no State has a right to secede, and that no State has seceded, we are as good citizens called upon to re-establish a republican form of government in every State, where it has been overthrown. [Applause.] Certain bad men have attempted to carry out of the Union several States, in despite of the Constitution and the wishes of the people. A band of conspirators, guilty of a crime worse than that of Catiline appeared in the United States Senate, and boldly preached treason in the face of the nation. They clothed their treason in honeyed words, and argued that secession was a constitutional privilege, and in demanding it they were but asking for that to which they were entitled. Have you ever been struck with the great fallacy of this doctrine of secession? It is a doctrine destructive of all government. It is a sort of universal dissolvent, that neutralizes all it touches. When admitted as a principle, you admit a disintegrent. No Government can exist that tolerates such doctrine. It originated in the Garden of Eden with the devil and sin. Secession is no modern doctrine in American politics. I have the documents to prove that it took root in this country forty years ago. Disunion has not taken place because any particular political party has reached power. That event has been only the pretext for the execution of a project so long in contemplation. They now insist that the South shall be irrevocably separated from the North, and that two Confederacies shall exist for Americans. It is for the Government to answer the conspirators in unmistakable and emphatic terms.

In addressing this large, this intelligent, this respectable audience here to-night, I do not intend to deceive you. My whole course of life has been plain and blunt. I stand before you to-night a Democrat. [Applause.] I am a Democrat, as that term has been defined here to-night. I have, in the whole course of my public life, maintained man's capacity for self government. I have always taken the position that the world was my home, and every honest man my brother.[6] [Applause.]

I am a Democrat upon the principles of the Constitution. I know, and you know, there is too much intelligence here not to know that the designs of the South is to change the genius of the Government. I have fought the Southern conspirators with this apprehension. They contend for an aristocracy, and an aristocracy without brains has my contempt. [Applause.] I stand before you the advocate of an aristocracy of virtue, intelligence, and that dignity which flows from nature's God. I am for an aristocracy of labor, [applause,] and for the amelioration of those who perform it. My democracy I learned in the school of Thomas Jefferson. [Applause.] I learned it in that school which punished treason when Burr attempted to overthrow the Government. Burr complained that he was arrested without process. [Applause.]

I do not intend to say much of arbitrary arrests.[7] All I need say is, that there have not been enough of them. [Applause.] Does any loyal man complain of illegal arrests? We are told that the President has no power to make the arrests. It is said Congress only has the right. Now, it is clear that the right exists somewhere. In my estimation, the President has not only the power, but it is his duty to exercise that power. [Immense cheering.] When the battle of New Orleans was about to be fought, there were a few people there who were disloyal; Jackson had them arrested; Judge Hall issued a *habeas corpus*; and General Jackson arrested the Judge. [Applause.] Do you think that the country suffered much from this act? True, he was fined $1000; and it is the proudest act of my life that I made a speech to restore that fine.[8] [Applause.]

When I speak of a man so honored by the people of the United States as Jackson, I do it with great reverence. I hold in my hand the original paper written in the old man's handwriting, and I feel as if I had taken it from his coffin. [Sensation.] Were it possible that Jackson could now witness the sad scenes enacting from the doctrine that he attempted to bury forever, the old man would turn in his coffin. Were it possible to communicate intelligence to the dead, he would rise from the tomb and reiterate that immortal sentiment of his: "The Federal Union—it must and shall be preserved."

I understand that you to-night are inaugurating a National Union Club,[9] and to give it a corner stone I should like to present to you this letter of the immortal Jackson, that that letter should be the corner stone of your Club. [Applause.] Will you accept of this relic? [Cries "We will."] I present it to you, then; in the hope that you will make its sentiments the basis of your organization.[10] [Cheers.]

Gen. Jackson has told us that the disunionists of the South would one day use the negro question as a pretext for breaking up the Union. You are told, at this late day, that that pretext could have been removed. You were told that the Crittenden Compromise would have saved the country. Nothing could be more false. When that compromise was before the Senate Mr. Clark offered an amendment substantially offering the Constitution itself as a basis of settlement. If the South could have got the compromise there would have been peace. The amendment passed; the compromise was lost, but how? Six Southern men refused to record their votes. They wanted no compromise. In truth, they wanted the compromise defeated, and its defeat they could have made a pretext to go before their constituents. I said to Mr. Benjamin, "Vote like an honest man for this matter." [Applause] He told me he wanted no lecture from me, and insisted on retaining his vote to himself. Thomas Corwin, of Ohio, subsequently offered an amendment to the Constitution, so that Congress could never interfere with the system of slavery. What became of that amendment? Can anything be more permanent than that? It was lost. The South would not accept Mr. Corwin's amendment, but insisted on a separation, total and absolute.[11] Compromises are all in vain. We must meet the Southern conspirators as they meet us. We must not permit anything to be above the Government. I, for one, am for prosecuting the war to the knife. [Applause.] There is no way to compromise with the leaders, except to put them to the sword. [Applause.] I am for the Union and the Constitution. If bank monopolies or negroes get in the way of the Government, they must be overturned. [Great applause.] I am for the Government, with slavery; I am for it, without slavery; in either event, give me my Government, and let all other institutions go. What have we without government? What is property worth without the protection of a good Government? Though we may suffer in the prosecution of the war, let it go on. I would see all the negroes of the United States sent back to their fatherland, rather than this Government should not go on. I would rather see Africa distinct from this earth, as a planet, out of the world's orbit, rather than any injury should happen to the Government. [Laughter and applause.] It is bad enough for a man in the South to be a traitor and sympathizer; but for a man in the North, who scarcely knows that there is a war going on, there is no excuse. Were it not for Vallandigham and Bright[12] [hisses] our armies would have long since advanced to the heart of the rebellion. There was a time when treason was a thing to be shunned, as abominable and wicked. Bob Toombs said that when traitors became plenty, treason became respectable.[13] That is probably the doctrine of the sympathizers. But they must be informed that treason is despicable, and that only loyalty can be respectable. There is only one way to meet traitors, and that is to meet them at the threshold, and if nothing else will do, to throttle and hang them. [Applause.] The Government has passed through two great ordeals to obtain and retain its nationality. Those two ordeals exhibited a strength that gives assurance that the third will be successfully encountered. Though we have a large territory, we have not an inch to give up to traitors. Let traitors South be punished, and then traitors North. [Applause.] If the sacrifice to put down the rebellion has not been large enough, let the price be named, and it shall be paid. Are you willing to give up the Southern States to the traitors of the land? Shall you give up the graves of our forefathers to be desecrated by unworthy sons? Are you prepared to surrender up the tomb of him who was the first in war, first in peace, and first in the hearts of his countrymen?[14] Are you prepared to let Jackson sleep beneath the bars of the traitor Confederacy? Should we consent to such baseness, some Peter the Hermit[15] would rise up in our midst to redeem the graves of Jackson and Washington. We must sustain the Government. If the Administration falters, it is our duty to inspire it with the importance of its duty. I did not help to place Mr. Lincoln in power. But he is the lawful President, and must be supported and sustained. [Applause.] And let me say to the men who are trying to found a party upon the faults of the Administration, that when the winds come, and the storms descend, that that party will be swept away from the earth. This is no time for the formation of parties. If there is no Government, what is the use of party? When the war is over, it will be time to hold every one responsible for any faults committed. [Applause.] Let us have only one compromise—the Constitution of the United States. If the South fails some of the traitors must be hung; if the South succeeds some of you must be hung. [Laughter and applause.]

Let me, my friends, conclude, for there are other able speakers to address you. I have only to urge you to stand by the Government in adversity as in prosperity, and transmit this glorious Union to posterity with none of its glory tarnished, nor its influence lessened among the nations of the earth.

Philadelphia *Evening Bulletin*, March 12, 1863; OClWHi, *Immense Meeting in Favor of the Union* [Philadelphia, 1863].

1. Speaking in Musical Fund Hall at the inauguration of the Philadelphia National Union Club, Johnson addressed a crowd reportedly larger than any assembled in that city

since the outbreak of war. Other participants included Senator James R. Doolittle, Governor Andrew G. Curtin, and former Congressman Hendrick B. Wright. When the Tennessean appeared "the enthusiasm was unbounded, the audience rising to its feet and cheering him vociferously for several minutes while the band played 'Hail to the Chief.' " Traveling well-worn paths, this disquisition is composed largely of odds and ends taken from other addresses; hence it requires a minimum of annotation. Philadelphia *Evening Bulletin*, March 12, 1863; Pamphlet: *Immense Meeting In Favor of the Union* (n.d., n.p.), 1.

2. Apparently a popular expression of the day used earlier by Stephen A. Douglas in his Speech at Alton, October 15, 1858, during the famous Lincoln-Douglas debates. Paul M. Angle, ed., *Created Equal? The Complete Lincoln-Douglas Debates of 1858* (Chicago, 1958), 366.

3. In 350 B.C. the Athenian orator and statesman Demosthenes (384-322 B.C.) attempted to arouse his fellow citizens to the danger posed by the ambitions of Philip of Macedonia. The Athenians ignored these "philippics" and Attica was eventually conquered. N. G. L. Hammond, *History of Greece to 322 B.C.* (Oxford, 1959), 546-55.

4. U. S. Constitution, Art. I, sec. 9.

5. In addition to the usual formal invitations, Johnson had received a strong nudge from his friend, senate secretary and Philadelphia *Press* editor, John W. Forney. "You *must* go to Phila. to-morrow evening. For your own sake and for our country's sake do accept the invitation of our hosts of loyal men. You will be greeted as never you were greeted before. For God's sake go!" Forney to Johnson, March 10, 1863, Johnson Papers, LC.

6. A variant of "The world is my country, all mankind are my brethren." Thomas Paine, *Prospects on the Rubicon* (1787). Bartlett, *Quotations*, 271.

7. Lincoln's revocation of habeas corpus became a major constitutional and political issue which, along with discontent over the draft, economic problems, and the emancipation proclamation, cost the Republicans dearly in the 1862 fall elections, with the Indiana, Ohio, and Pennsylvania legislatures falling to the Democrats. When Philadelphia newspaperman Albert Boileau was arrested in January for the anti-Lincoln posture of his *Evening Journal*, the city's "greatest wartime protest against arbitrary government" ensued. Johnson's remarks concerning arbitrary arrest may have been prompted by the resulting furor. William Dusinberre, *Civil War Issues in Philadelphia, 1856-1865* (Philadelphia, 1965), 129, 154-56.

8. See *Johnson Papers*, IV, 611.

9. This club, which evolved into the National Union League, had been founded on the preceding November 22 and organized a month later by loyal men who hoped to restore and maintain patriotism during the darker days of the war. *Chronicle of the Union League of Philadelphia* (Philadelphia, 1902), 34-36.

10. Despite a reminder three days later, Johnson apparently retained the letter; there is no record of its having been deposited with the League. A. G. Curtin to Johnson, March 14, 1863, Johnson Papers, LC; Maxwell Whiteman (The Union League of Philadelphia) to Andrew Johnson Project, March 14, 1978.

11. Johnson often recalled the Corwin Amendment and its rejection by southern senators. See *Johnson Papers*, IV, 569, 614-15; V, 228.

12. For Clement L. Vallandigham and Jesse D. Bright, whom the governor considered as archetypal northern traitors, see *ibid.*, IV, 284*n*; I, 491*n*.

13. *See ibid.*, IV, 616, 644n; for Robert Toombs, see *ibid.*, I, 612*n*.

14. A close paraphrase of Richard Henry Lee's famous eulogy of George Washington. Bartlett, *Quotations*, 281.

15. See Speech in Support of Presidential War Program, July 27, 1861, *Johnson Papers*, IV, 640, 649n.

Speech to the Loyal League, New York City

March 14, 1863, New York; New York *Times*, March 15, 1863.

In response to a long-standing invitation, Johnson harangues a huge audience ("I did not . . . expect to meet all creation assembled here to night") gathered for the purpose of inaugurating a Loyal League. A veritable catalogue of the familiar, the speech is a patchwork of attitudes, assumptions, anecdotes, and admonitions previously presented in Tennessee, the Midwest, and most recently, Philadelphia. Its one all-pervading theme is compromise: a lost opportunity rejected over and over by southerners during the secession crisis, as attested by the fate of the Crittenden Resolutions and the Corwin Amendment; a siren song which now threatens to dash the ship of state onto the rocks of permanent dissolution. "Compromise! Armistice! . . . The very instant you talk about compromise, you repudiate the idea of preserving the existence of the Government." Laced throughout are such perennials as the threat posed by Lincoln's election, which the governor predictably discounts—"he came into power with his hands crossed; he could not make his Cabinet. . . . send a Minister abroad. . . . draw his $25,000 to furnish his house, and buy his meat and bread"; the furor over suspension of the writ—"if you want to find out traitors just look round, and shake a writ of *habeas corpus*"; the perpetuation of slavery as against the preservation of the Union, with Johnson "for the Government, as it was given to us by our fathers, with Slavery, or without Slavery"; and the canker of aristocracy, with the Plebeian castigating monopolies of any kind—"of money, of banks, of railroads," or "decayed family reputation"—while lauding "an aristocracy of virtue, of talent, of intelligence, of merit, of worth." The speaker, paying his accustomed tribute to "the tenderer portion of this audience. . . . the power behind the throne, greater than the throne itself," closes with the exhortation: "Let us take this Constitution . . . take it as the ark of our safety, as the palladium of our liberty. Let us stand by it, and join in one fraternal hug, and lay it on the altar of our country, and with animated faces swear by the Gods that our country shall be saved."

From Salmon P. Chase

March 16, 1863, Washington; ALS, DLC-JP.

Secretary of the treasury requests Johnson's "perusal" and "such suggestions, if any, as may occur to your own mind" for "correction and improvement" of new "Regulations of Trade & Intercourse between inhabitants of States declared in insurrection and of the other States."

From Loyal Citizens of Weakley County

March 20, 1863, Dresden; Mem, DLC-JP.

Ask commission for B. F. Ferrell, longtime guide, so that he may raise a company "to put down a class [of] Robbers thieves and marauders banded togeather and going over the country night and day robbing stealing money and horses from honest citizens; besides killing those who attempt to resist them." They offer to "arm ourselvs and serve in this capacity without expense to the State[.]"

Speech at Baltimore[1]

March 20 1863

Fellow-citizens: In presenting myself here tonight, by invitation, I come before you as a citizen of the United States—[applause]—and an inhabitant of the State of Tennessee—[applause]—[that is, I may be permitted to remark within brackets, when allowed to do so by treason and traitors.] In presenting myself before you on the present occasion, it is not without some embarrassments, but in reference to that I shall not consume much, if any, of your time. I fear, though, that on this occasion there will be too much expected, and especially so after the complimentary introduction I have received this evening from my friend, the presiding officer of the meeting, and who has just taken his seat. But in the very outset I will say, as I have said on previous occasions, that if you have come here, male and female, with the expectation of hearing from me one of those speeches that will edify—or, I might speak in other language, one of those rounding, sounding, bounding *ad captandum* speeches, dealing in tropes, figures, and hyperboles, or an attempt to display the rhetorician—I want to inform you now that you had better let yourselves down—[laughter]—for, if you expect me to come up to any such standard, you will be greatly disappointed. And I think there has been some little mismanagement in affairs here to-night, for, if I mistake not, there is an old rule (whether true or not) that the fore wheels are getting to be as large as the others.[2] Ordinarily, they always put the fore wheels before any others—the small wheels being first—but I think they have done precisely right to-night, and in the after part, when the great and distinguished (and I mean what I say, for I do not speak in hyperbole,) individuals, more eminent and able, address you, that expectation can be met. In appearing before you to-night, let that all pass for what it is worth.

Let us proceed to consider the momentous occasion under which we are assembled. Let us proceed to consider what is upon the country, and what issues are before us here to-night. We find our country imperilled, and not parties; and in this connection, perhaps, it would become me to remark that a distinguished individual, who is now here as the commandant of this post, is only absent from this meeting to-night through his sufferings from a wound that he received in the battle-field of his country.[3] [Applause] I would have been more than gratified could he have been here. He and you know that we have not assembled to-night to make a battle of one party against another—to discuss mere questions of expediency in reference to measures of Government—but we have assembled for the purpose of discussing the great issue, the existence of free Government, and whether we will have a monarchy or aristocracy. [Applause] The distinguished commandant of this post, who is now acting in a military capacity, has occupied a distinguished position in the councils of the nation, but has always differed with me in politics, as some others here have differed, while others have agreed with me. Notwithstanding he was announced and expected to be here, he is confined to his bed by a wound received in defence of the existence of the Government. In times gone by he and I differed, and my views were opposed to his on what are called party questions and party measures; but, thank God, we all stand here to-night finding party lines obliterated, and party lines ripped up. We stand to-night forgetting that we have ever been Whigs, Democrats, or Know-Nothings. We stand to-night as Americans only, upon the platform of the Union, contending for the existence of the Government, resolved to do our all in that important struggle[.] [Applause] You can recur (and I do not want to consume much of your time), to a few years ago, when we presented ourselves arrayed on different sides, when one was Whig, one was Democrat, and one something else, yet when these parties got upon the rostrum and discussed banks, tariffs, and internal improvements, when the appeal was made and you looked to the flag what did you see? Go back to the days of Whiggery and Democracy, and when you look back, what do you find? Then the Whig party came forward under the lead of Clay—[applause]—you would find there the glorious Stars and Stripes. [Applause.] When you turned around and saw the Democratic party coming forward in procession in olden times, under what banner did they come? Under the banner that was borne by our fathers of the Revolution and throughout 1812. [Applause] This is not the issue now. It is not now mere party measures or questions of expediency, but the question is your country and the existence of free government. That is the question to be considered, and let us make one strong resolve that the Government shall be preserved; and when we have put down treason, when we have made treason odious, when we have punished traitors—[applause]—then the time will have arrived that we have got a Government. We may then again talk about banks and tariffs, but let us never stop our efforts until the Government is placed upon a permanent basis.

In ancient times (and I intend to be rapid) there were various kinds of speakers that presented themselves before the people. I remark this simply for illustration, and to present my feelings on this as on other occasions. In ancient times they had their speakers. We might go back to Rome. Every school boy is familiar with the orations of Cicero. He used to appear before public assemblies as well as before the Roman Senate and make his speeches, and he has been laid down as a model orator and speaker for young men to follow. When he appeared he would always please and interest them, and the remark generally was, "how grand his gesticulation, the modulation of his voice, his measured sentences, his excellently rounded periods," and all that kind of thing; and always when he dismissed his audience they retired commenting upon the fine attitude, correct gesticulation, and modulation and intonation of his voice. At another period of time there was another description of speaker. We find that when Philip, that ambitious prince, was making his inroads upon the Grecian States, they had a kind of speaker, and he appeared in the character of Demosthenes. When he addressed the people he addressed himself to their good sense, to their understanding, and his intention was always to make a lodgment in the minds of those who would give him their attention. He admonished and reasoned with the people, and presented them with facts and arguments in reference to the inroads being made by that ambitious prince; and when he concluded his speeches what was the impression left? It was that Greece was endangered—that it required the people to come forward and unite themselves against these inroads; and when they retired from the stand and rostrum, every heart was filled and every arm was strong. They were not talking about handsome gesticulations and fine modulations of the voice and superb periods. No, but every man went forth from the meeting and from the stand with his heart filled with patriotism and his arm strong, exclaiming, "We will fight Philip to death and to the very last extreme." [Applause.] My obligation is here to-night, without regard to the distinguished men before you, and without regard to the speakers, to let every man and woman know whether their hearts are filled and their arms strong to fight Jeff. Davis. [Applause.]

Fellow-citizens of the State of Maryland, I feel like congratulating you upon the present occasion. You know it was announced at an early period of this rebellion that the war would be confined to Virginia, Maryland, and Ohio, and that the Gulf States would be exempt from the ravages of war. You remember this, and ought not you here to-night, yes, male and female, be upon your bended knees, with your faces turned toward Heaven, thanking Almighty God that the State of Maryland has been freed and delivered. [Applause.] You are a Border State. I live in a Border State, or rather next to a Border State—[laughter]—and if you would go out there and look at the consumed dwellings, the devastated farms, the destruction of property, the dead carcasses laying along the thoroughfares and highways, and look at the new made graves, the battle-fields and the camp-fires, and the pieces or parts of men left from the devastating influence of battle, you will begin to repeat your prayer, and thank God that Maryland has been delivered from the destroying spirit. [Applause]

But I intimated that I should allude, or rather started out with the proposition that this was a struggle for free government, and if you give me your attention for a short time, in my crude way I will beg to show the fact. I don't expect to make a speech to stir men's blood, but will address myself to your judgment, good sense and patriotism, and if I can make a lodgment there, I shall have accomplished my object. The President of the United States—[applause]—in one of his annual messages says:[4]

> This is essentially a people's contest. On the side of the Union it is a struggle for maintaining in the world that form and substance of government whose leading object is to elevate the condition of men; to lift artificial weights from all shoulders;

to clear the paths of laudable pursuit for all; to afford to all an unfettered start and a fair chance in the race of life[.] Yielding to partial and temporary departures from necessity, this is the leading object of the Government for whose existence we contend.

My countrymen, that is the issue to-night. It is a struggle for free government. This is the principle that underlies the whole. I know in party times we would call this demagoguery. It is sometimes intended to deceive and to please the mass, but the time has arrived when the great mass of the people, when the salt of society—not a decayed society on the one hand which lives upon the remembrances or a decayed family reputation, or a miserable lazaroni[5] on the other hand—but the time has arrived when the salt of the American people and nation must come up to their work, and determine for themselves whether they are capable of self-government or not. [Applause.] You know as well as I do that the contest now going on is for the establishment of an aristocracy. ["That's so."] I know what I say. Don't call that egotistical. I have been born and raised in a Southern State. I own negroes, procured by the product of my own hands, and the few that I own cost me more money perhaps and labor than some who have owned five hundred or one thousand. But in the process of this civil war, or rebellion, or this attempt to establish a monarchical form of government, by way of giving me my peculiar Southern rights—[laughter]—being a Southern man and Southern slaveholder, my negroes have been appropriated to their peculiar purposes. [Laughter.] If I had been disposed when this rebellion commenced to have joined this band of conspirators, with Jeff. Davis at their head—a conspiracy which has been, and is, more diabolical than that band led by Cataline when he attempted to overthrow the Roman Senate[6]—as humble as I am, and as few negroes as I own, I could have held any place they could have given me. [Applause.] I preferred my country. [Applause] They have taken my slaves and have appropriated them to their own use; they have turned my wife and children in the street, and taken my property, and I have been banished from their presence, and for what? What am I here before you to-night for? What wrong have I done? What crime have I committed? My crime is, then, because of an undying tenacity and unyielding devotion, that I intended to stand by the Stars and Stripes. [Applause.] Let them take my negroes; let them take my land; let them turn my wife and children in the street, and convert my house and home into a hospital and barracks for Butternuts, [applause] let them do all this, or banish, exile, or quarter he who now addresses you, but give me my country. [Great applause.]

I was talking something about an aristocracy—[laughter]—a doctrine that I learned at an early day—and my Democracy. I have got nothing to conceal. I am a Democrat. I expect to live and die one, but the chief corner-stone of my democracy has been the preservation of this Union and the supremacy of the Government. [Applause.] I learned my democracy in the school of Thomas Jefferson and Andrew Jackson. I learned my democracy from him who arrested and intended to hang Aaron Burr for treason. I learned my democracy from one who sleeps now in the confines of his adopted State, and who intended, in 1832, to hang (if not for the interference of kind friends) John C. Calhoun. [Applause.] That's the school in which I learned my democracy. It has matured with my advanced life. It has become a part of myself and I intend to go down to my grave with it, let the consequences be what they may.

But as I was going to say, in this school of democracy I was taught that the great mass of the people were capable of self-government—that the great mass of the people were virtuous—that they were intelligent, and they were competent to govern themselves. My democracy taught me that Government was made for the convenience and for the accommodation of the people, and not the people made for the Government; that a Government combining the will of the people in the shape of constitution and law, was the Government we were to have. When I talk about aristocracy I am free to say to you, that I am opposed to an aristocracy of banks, and of monopolies of any description whatever. I want labor, and the pursuits of life, so far as property is concerned, as equally divided as the nature and condition of the country will permit. But so far as an aristocracy of money, so far as an aristocracy of families, based upon some long line of ancestors that have wasted away, till the tail can scarcely remember or trace themselves back to the head[7]—[laughter]—a sort of aristocracy like the potato-plant, with the best part of it underground—[laughter]—without brains, without merit, without anything to commend themselves to a virtuous and intelligent community, has always, and will through my life, receive my utmost contempt. But then it might seem to some extent paradoxical. I am in favor of an aristocracy. That's strange, but it is nevertheless true. I am here to-night an advocate of aristocracy—an aristocracy of virtue, of intelligence, of the real and true dignity of nature—an aristocracy of labor. [Applause.] What is the aristocracy I have advocated since my advent into public life? It has been this, that upon the shoulders of the industrious producer and sustainer the Government should rest. [Applause]. What is the kind of aristocracy proposed to us? Shall I go back and call your attention to a long list of extracts from the Rebel papers and speakers? I shall do no such thing, for to an audience so well informed and intelligent as this it would be an unnecessary consumption of their time. But can any one look to their papers and speakers, and be deceived? Look to the Richmond Examiner, and what do you find? Look also to the Enquirer, and we find them going upon the idea that rather than submit to the "gross and vulgar Administration" of Abraham Lincoln, they would prefer to be subjects of the Constitutional and amiable lady, the Queen of Great Britain[.][8] [Laughter] I might even go to my own State, and what do we find advocated? When this rebellion was commencing and going on, even the papers in the city of Memphis, in the State of Tennessee—even in Jackson's State—advocated a dictatorship, and they went on and argued in reference to one

Isham G. Harris, now an itinerant Governor,[9] running about from place to place somewhere through this Southern rebellion; and in reference to him, the editor spoke of the times, the confusion, and chaotic condition that is now upon the country, and they say, "In times like these let Harris be King, and let Barr [Baugh],[10] the Mayor of the city of Memphis, be Despot. [Laughter.] Yes, Tennessee has assumed at once, through organs of this kind, and leaders like Harris and their Mayor, the position of despots and kings. Go on and divide this Government[.] Let each State become separated from this Union, and there will be a little set of kings, princes and despots throughout this whole land. I am against the whole concern, and especially against it in my own State. [Applause.] Think of a Mayor of Memphis, or a little Governor of Tennessee, (I have been Governor, and am acting as Governor now); think of Isham G. Harris—I wish the man could be in every mind here to-night—being king! [Laughter.] King of Tennessee! think of it. Humble as I am, and having started a boy from the ranks amid the plebians—and were it not for plebian blood and plebian association what would become of aristocracy! [Applause.] I would scorn to live upon the soil over which he held sway when inaugurated in his kingdom. Think of a little petty Governor foisted into power by a few usurpers and the military! Think of a such a man as that being king of a people: Isham G. Harris to be king of Tennessee! [Applause and laughter.] I look at my friends Horace Maynard and George W. Bridges[11] when I make that remark. Think of it. To be our king. [Laughter.] Isham G. Harris to be our king! Let me say to you to-night, that as humble as I am, standing in the full dimensions of a plebian as I am, Isham G. Harris could not be my slave—[applause]—king of Tennessee! [Laughter.] And this is what this rebellion is bringing upon you. Don't you see where we are travelling? No one can be deceived. A part of the people of the United States, and especially in the South, who have lost all confidence in the capacity and integrity of the people to govern themselves, have entertained this idea for a long time, and hence slavery and the negro question has been made a pretext to split the Union, and in its division to establish a Southern aristocracy, based upon what? Upon negro property. [Laughter.] We had as well talk about the thing plainly. Call it by proper names, and speak of it as it is. Who commenced this rebellion? Why, we are told, upon high authority, it was commenced forty years ago. This has been discussed from Maine to Louisiana and California for the last ten years. The negroes have been made the pretext, and are to constitute the basis of this Southern aristocracy. I am no Abolitionist. [Applause.] I am no Disunionist. I am no Consolidationist either, but I am for preserving this Government as handed down to us. I do not want to wound the feelings of any one, but we hear a good deal of talk now about Conservatives and Copperheads. If being a Radical is for preserving this Government, in root and branch, as handed down by Washington and his compeers, then I am a Radical. If Conservative means to preserve the Government as it was of old, then I am a

Conservative. Hence, I am for the Government of my fathers, and intend to stand by it come what will[.] I am free to say, without intending to wound the feelings of any (and I think the proposition susceptible of demonstration), that the Abolitionists and the Secessionists occupy just about the same position. [Applause] Why do I say so? The man that is for secession of course is for disunion. If he is for disunion, why he must be an Abolitionist. [Laughter.] Take even Mr. Greeley's remarks, for he says he is for letting his "wayward sisters go."[12] Thus we see that the Secessionist and Disunionist occupy the same platform, because if you dissolve the Union of these States you destroy slavery. A Disunionist must be an Abolitionist, and *vice versa*. It is a syllogism, in fact, and the one proves the other. I am no Abolitionist. I am no Disunionist. I am for standing by the Government, and by the Government as it has been founded by our fathers, but in this connection I must be permitted to remark, that while I am neither Abolition nor Secession, I shall stand by the Union and cling to it as the sheet-anchor of our civil and religious liberty. While I say this, I want to be understood. I am not in favor of any institution in this Government that rises above the Government itself. [Applause.] If you have a bank that sets up and assumes to be too strong for the Government, I say let the Government put it down and make it conform to the Government. If you have a set of stock-jobbers that by their combinations of wealth and influence assume to be too strong, let them be put down, and make them conform to the Government. [Applause] If you have monopolies of any kind that attempt to raise themselves above the Government, put them down, and make them conform to the genius and character of the Government. But is it not strange, in this connection, that while you may agitate the question of banks, protective tariffs, internal improvements, or the distribution of the proceeds of the public lands or any other important question that came up under Government, there is one question that you dare not agitate—in short, that you can agitate all other questions, but the Government must not agitate it. You hear about banks and tariffs and internal improvements and all that, but if ever you mention negroes the thing is at an end. [Laughter and applause.] Negroes must not be talked about; hence I say slavery must be placed upon the basis of all other institutions with reference to this Government, and must be in that attitude, always moving forward and onward, so that it can be talked about as well as any other institution. [Applause.] I am for the Government, and I am for this Government standing above and superior to all institutions that come up in it—[applause]—and whenever there is an institution that sets itself up to control the Government in its moving forward, I say to that institution, "get out of the way." [Applause] If not, let the Government run over it. [Applause.] I mean to say by that, this (and I do not want to be misunderstood before this polite and intelligent audience) that, without regard to your institutions, I care not of what character, I here to-night, in this great peril in this great struggle for the existence of the Government, declare that I am for the Government with slavery, and I am here to-night for the Government without slavery. [Applause.] And if, in sustaining this Government, slavery has to give way as an incident towards the supremacy of the Constitution and the enforcement of the law, I say, "let it go." [Applause.]

I am for the Government. I know that some men say in these croaking times and times of civil war, "Oh, but you have got a Black Republican Administration, and I am against the whole concern," and appeal to your party prejudices, with a view of forming a party upon them at this day. Let me tell you that are thus catering with your friends, you that have rolled this sweet morsel under your tongues, and think that you can form a party under your country's misfortunes, let me tell you that you have built your house upon a sandy foundation, [applause] and when the winds come and the storm descends, they will sweep and wash your building away, [applause] and you will exclaim with more withering agony that you have been deceived. Suppose the Government should (which it will) put down this rebellion, [applause] where will you go? What position will you take? Suppose, for instance (which is not a reasonable supposition) that this bastard, hermaphrodite, nefarious, hell-diabolic rebellion succeeds at the South. What position have they got for you? Will they take you down there? No. No, but they sneer at and feel contempt for all your profers of peace and compromise. Yes, and in the end you will be taught to exclaim, in language more mortifying and disappointed than that of poor Macbeth, when he had been taught to believe by the juggling fiends or hags that he was never to be overpowered or overcome by one of woman born, he went on with his murders, and suffered his remorse of conscience. (Have you who are trying to destroy this Government any conscience)? When the time arrived for his defeat, when he came in contact with Macduff, and was informed that he was not one of woman born, he saw the deception and treachery with which these hags had been working, and in the midst of his greatest disappointment and mortification, Macbeth was compelled to exclaim:

> Accursed be that tongue that tells me so,
> For it hath cow'd my better part of man!
> And be these juggling fiends no more believed
> That palter with us in a double sense;
> That keep the word of promise to our ear
> And break it to our hope.[13]

Your condition will be worse than this. Mark, the time is coming when traitors will be hung. [Applause.]

A Voice.—They ought to have begun that long ago.

Mr. Johnson.—That's a very sensible remark[.] If you had commenced it earlier you would not have had so much to do hereafter. I repeat again, in response to that remark, that treason must be met, that traitors must be banished and impoverished. [Applause.]

In traveling along with this subject, after having commenced the rebellion and shed blood and involved the country in this war, what is the song that we hear? Why, are you not for peace, for compromise? Have you no sympathy with our brethren down at the South?

A Voice.—No.

Mr. Johnson.—That's the right response; but I am asking the question now of peace and compromise. Let me call your attention to a few facts about peace and compromise. Who is it that knows whether this question can be compromised or not? You have heard great complaint in reference to the writ of *habeas corpus*. I will venture to say that some of those men that know whether the thing can be compromised or not are alarmed at the suspension of the writ of *habeas corpus*. What is the medium through which they communicate down South that they know so much about peace and compromise? I will venture the suggestion that these very men that you hear talking so much about peace and compromise are wonderfully opposed to the suspension of the writ of *habeas corpus,* and this cruel Administration —President, Cabinet officers and all—that has violated the Constitution and trampled it under foot. Oh! the rights of the country and the Constitution have been violated. Somebody has been arrested. Somebody has been deprived of personal liberty and can't get a trial. It is very clear to my mind, at least, that the writ of *habeas corpus* can be suspended under the Constitution, and when you come to look at this thing, I think the precise occasion has arrived when it should be suspended. [Applause] "The writ of *habeas corpus* shall not be suspended except in time of rebellion and the public safety may require it." We are in a rebellion, ain't we? That's most clear. There are traitors amongst us; that is equally clear. It is equally clear that somebody can exercise this power. You have not defined who shall exercise it; but there is a grant in the Constitution to the effect that it may be suspended in time of rebellion and the public peace and safety require it. Well, then, the exercise of the privilege of the suspension of the writ of *habeas corpus* is accorded. Is it not clear? And I expect that right in this city of Baltimore there are many arrests that ought to be made. [Applause and "that's so."]. When there is a member in your family who endangers its peace, its safety, its security, and its happiness, you have a right to eject that member from your midst and place him where he can do no harm. This is a great family. It is the American family, and here and there are men who are dangerous to public liberty; and it is as much the duty of a nation to tolerate no man who is unfriendly to the institutions, as it is to eject an offending member of your own family. And if Mr. Lincoln and his Cabinet are to blame in reference to this subject, it is not in what they have done, but if there is fault to find it is because they have not done more. [Applause] Whenever you hear one of these gentlemen talking about constitutional rights and the suspension of the writ of *habeas corpus,* now, look a little to him and you will find there are some lingerings, some desire for the overthrow of the Government, and great sympathy for the Southern Confederacy. It reminds me of the story of Lorenzo Dow,[14] who, I presume, is familiar, even at this day, to a large portion of the people of Maryland. He was a preacher and a very eccentric character. He was on his way one Sabbath to the meeting house, and as he went along he fell in with a man, who came up to him and said that last night his only axe had been stolen. "Very well," says the preacher, "I will settle that to-day at church." He went to the meeting house, advanced to the pulpit, opened his Bible, took his text, and preached a sermon; but in going to the meeting house he found a stone that weighed about a pound and a half. He took it in his hand, and whilst preaching, the stone was laid beside the Bible. On the conclusion of the sermon, he said, "that on coming to church this morning, a neighbor informed me that his axe was stolen last night," and picking up the stone, he says, "my intention is now, for I have my eye upon the man that stole the axe," and drawing himself back, and with a huge motion as if to throw the stone, he swept his eye round the congregation, and saw a fellow dodge down under the bench. [Laughter.] Says he, "that's the man that stole the axe." Whenever you want to scare up a traitor, just ask him about the suspension of the writ of *habeas corpus*. Are you afraid of being arrested? [Cries of "No."] The suspension of the writ of *habeas corpus* don't affect you. Who are they that complain of the laws that punish theft and murder? It is those that have either committed some of those offences themselves, or have a desire to commit them[.]

But compromise is now the word. That is the syren song that is sung. Compromise! "Yes, if we could have got Mr. Crittenden's Compromise, O yes, rebellion could have been avoided. All this shedding of blood would have been prevented." Will you hear me a few minutes upon the subject of compromise. I happened to be in the Senate of the United States when the Crittenden Compromise was before it. These men pretended that they wanted something. I was willing to go for anything that would satisfy their pretence, as it were. The measure was introduced, matured, and referred to committees and reported back, until it at length reached that point when the test question was to be had. Mr. Clark, of New Hampshire, offered an amendment in lieu of the compromise. The yeas and nays were ordered upon it. It was looked upon as the test question; now mark how it was received. They wanted compromise, it is said, and if they could have got it, all this peril and difficulty would have been saved. The yeas and nays were ordered upon the adoption of Mr. Clark's amendment, and it was adopted twenty-three to twenty-five—twenty-five Senators voting for it and twenty-three against it. Hence, Crittenden's proposition was lost, and hence, upon the wings of lightning a message was transmitted to all parts of the Union that "all hope is lost, now we must have war." Analyze this a little further. Who defeated the Crittenden Compromise, I asked of these Southern men? You say you are in earnest and sincere[.] Do you want the Crittenden Compromise? I say you did not. Compromise was the last thing you desired, but you wanted to avail of Mr. Lincoln's election to break up this Government. But back to the fact. Who defeated this compromise? Black Republicans, I suppose, and Abolitionists[.] Did they defeat it? Who in the Senate of of the United States was it that defeated the Crittenden Compromise? There was one, a Judah Benjamin, yes, whose early history is some clue to what his after life would be. He stood right before me in the Senate, and when his name was called, refused to vote. Said I to him, "why don't you vote." Turning around rather abruptly, he replied, "I will not consult you or any other Senator in reference to my vote." I said, "vote and comply with the Constitution, and obey the rules of the Senate, and show yourself an honest man[.]" But instead of voting, he sent over the telegraph wires to Louisiana and elsewhere, "that all hope was lost." Take John Slidell and others, running up to six Southern men, declaring they could not get their Southern rights while Abolitionists and Black Republicans were overturning and bearing down their Southern country. Six of them withheld their votes, and by withholding their votes, permitted Mr. Clark's amendment to be adopted[.] Add these six to the twenty-three and it makes twenty-nine. Take twenty-five from twenty-nine and the Crittenden Compromise was adopted by four votes. Who are responsible for its loss? Republicans, Abolitionists, or Southern men? I said then, as I said before, that our true place to fight the battle was in the Union, and not outside, and our true position was to remain there and stay in the Senate, and fight the battle in the Constitution and inside of the Union, and save the Government. [Applause] But they preferred rejecting the compromise and breaking up the Union. Compromise! compromise! Now there was one compromise. Who rejected it?

But let me call your attention to another important fact, while these men are now talking about compromise. At the same session of Congress before alluded to, Thomas Corwin, of the State of Ohio, offered an amendment to the Constitution of the United States in reference to the subject of slavery, to the effect that Congress would be prevented in all future time from interfering in relation to that issue, making it at the same time unamendable. Can we have anything more secure? Can you have a stronger guarantee than an unamendable portion of the Constitution upon the subject of slavery? Let me ask this intelligent audience—suppose you had come here to-night and sat down and prepared guarantees or amendments to the Constitution, can you have anything stronger or clearer to the Constitution in reference to the subject of slavery? The point to which I call and demand your attention is, that that amendment was passed by two-thirds of both Houses—the Senate and the House of Representatives—and was submitted to the States. Let me tell these croakers and compromisers that this proposition is now before the States, and if you say you are alarmed, why not take up that amendment and adopt it? You can do it. You can do it here in Maryland. Why don't these croakers call upon the Legislatures to adopt that amendment to the Constitution? Have they done it? Will they do it?

No, but they will complain of the Administration, of the war, of taxes, of this, that and the other thing. I repeat again, and I ask this audience why don't they come forward and adopt it as an amendment to the Constitution?

What more was done at the same Congress? There were three bills passed, covering every square inch of territory owned by the United States—Colorado, Nevada and Dacotah—making three Territorial Governments, covering every square inch of territory we have. In the sixth section power is given and conferred upon the Territorial Legislatures to legislate, and it further says, "that the Legislature shall have no control over the disposition of the public lands, nor shall the Territorial Legislature pass any law that impairs the right to private property, or tax one description of property higher than another of equal value."[15] Can you have anything more in the Territories? Are not slaves property, and so decided by the law courts, and in express language: "Nor shall the Territorial Legislature pass any law impairing the right of private property." Is there anything of this negro question left? We must come to the conclusion that this rebellion is but a pretext, based upon the slavery question. In the language of Andrew Jackson, it is disunion and the establishment of a Southern Confederacy, or, in other words, a Southern aristocracy. [Applause] I repeat, take the Crittenden Compromise and see how it was lost; take the amendments offered to the Constitution; take the three Territorial bills covering the whole slavery question, and is there even a plank left for these croakers and compromisers to stand on! [Applause] Compromise! Has not everything been offered that can be, and they refused all, which shows that separation and the establishment of a Southern Confederacy was their real object! Compromise; yes, compromise is their cry. Compromise over a bleeding and violated Constitution! Compromise with traitors who have arms in their hands! Compromise with traitors who stand with bayonets at your breasts and the sword at your throat! Will you compromise over the graves of your Revolutionary ancestors! Will you compromise over the graves of your brave men who now sleep in this Southern Confederacy! Compromise over the bones and mangled flesh of your bleeding children! Yes, compromise is the word, and peace, when they know there is no peace. The time to compromise is, and never before, is when they ground their arms and su[b]mit to the Constitution of their fathers and the enforcement of the law! [Great Applause.] Compromise! Why you can settle this question in forty-eight hours. How? How will you settle it? Ground your arms, obedience to the law, acknowledge the supremacy of the Constitution which was made by your fathers. [Applause] Yes, compromise. There are a great many sympathizers and compromisers. Which do you sympathize with? Go to the South. Who is there that stand by the glorious Stripes and Stars of ours? I may call your attention to my own State. Look out there where Union men are crushed and down-trodden, with the mailed heel of despotism upon their necks—yes, into the very depths of tyranny, but the time has arrived when the tyrant's grasp shall be broken, and the captives set free. [Applause] No compromise, then, until that people are delivered, until the galling yoke of tyranny is removed from their necks. Compromise with Jeff. Davis and his band of conspirators, and leave his mailed heel of power upon the necks of Union men who are dying for their country's cause! [Cries of "No."] What will you do with the Union men of the South when you talk about compromise? Do you want to take Jeff. Davis' neck from the halter and put in a good Union man's? That's the whole proposition. Compromise! Do you hear any sympathy for down-trodden Union men! Our sympathies with those endeavoring to break up and destroy the Government!

And to add to the croaking proclamations, Mr. Lincoln is now showing (what has been long intended) his hand. Suppose the proclamation was right or wrong, and suppose, too, that Mr. Lincoln and his Cabinet had violated the Constitution of the United States. We all know that if they have violated it, that violation has been for the purpose of preserving the Government of the United States[.] [Applause] I make no such admission, but I merely state the case in the strongest terms against it[.] If there has been a violation, it has been to preserve the Government of our fathers, which was founded upon their blood and sufferings. Do you ever hear any complaints about Jeff. Davis and his cabal having violated the Constitution? O, no; they can violate it with perfect impunity. That is all right. And suppose for instance, or admit for argument's sake, that the Constitution has been violated for the preservation of the Government, is it not more terrible than a violation for its overthrow? [Applause.] You will complain of violations here to save the Government, but there is no complaint of violations to destroy it. Turn to your Constitution and you find that these United States have guaranteed to every State in them a Republican form of government. You find, too, that no State shall enter into treaty or alliance with foreign States, or enter into or make any contract, save through properly accredited agents. Let me relate a single instance that occurred in my own State as early as May. Before the people voted in June, the Legislature appointed three Commissioners, who deliberately entered into a contract and bargain to sell a united and free people of a sovereign State (a million in population, negroes and all) to Jeff. Davis and the Southern Confederacy. When you talk about being free men and violations of the Constitution, look at this proceeding. Here are three men that enter into a bargain, sign the bond and seal it, and hand over a million of people to the Southern Confederacy without their consent. To talk about violations of the Constitution with such facts as these before your eyes, when every advance that this Southern rebellion has made, from its very incipient steps up to the present time, has been one of encroachment upon the Constitution of the United States.

But Lincoln's proclamation! I don't care a single thing about his proclamation. I can tell you that there are great laws at work in this rebellion, that there are great elements moving forward to the end, the settlement of this slavery question won't be varied one hair's breadth one way or the other on account of that proclamation. And suppose that neither you nor I would have issued that proclamation, are you prepared to turn against the Government and destroy the Constitution because a ruler has done something that you did not like. When you have a bad Administration, love your Government more—[applause]—and when your Government is imperilled, let your patriotism rise higher and higher. No matter what may be said about Mr. Lincoln, it is our duty, as lovers of the country, to stand around him and hold his arms up. They say Mr. Lincoln is a sort of laying about loose, and I heard him mentioned as having a striking resemblance to a pair of old winding blades, considerably loose in the crossings.[16] [Laughter.] I did not help, however, to elect Abraham Lincoln, but being in power, I intend to stand by the Government and sustain him in trying to preserve the Government. I wish to God that one-half of those who are complaining of him and his Cabinet had one tithe of the patriotism they have. [Applause] I have no favors to ask from his Administration, neither from you, more than to stand with me and I with you in a common cause for the preservation of this Government; and if my Government could be saved, I would be willing to-night to pour out for its preservation the life-blood that warms my existence. Compromise! Strike that word from our vocabulary until the rebellion is put down. Compromise! what do you do when you compromise? Don't you acknowledge the rebellion? Don't you set a precedent, and the first time that any small prince or potentate might get into a bad humor, there would be another rebellion and another compromise, and as soon as you compromise it, still another rebellion and still another compromise, and so on! The instant you acknowledge the rebellion your Government is overthrown. [Applause.] Compromise! who would have virtue to compromise with vice, right to compromise with wrong? Would you have truth to compromise with falsehood? Would you have Deity, who rules on high, when the rebellion, headed by his Satanic Majesty, broke out there, to compromise with one who presided over the infernal councils of pandemonium or would you have him kicked down to the lower regions, where he is? Let us, therefore, gag this rebellion. This is the great Eden of the world; it is the haven of nations, and all Rebels should be kicked out of it. Its principles are indestructible, and this rebellion can no more obliterate them than it can pluck the sun from the heavens. When this affair is all over, these Rebels will find that there will be a great deal of Government left after all. Compromise! Yes, compromise away your birthright; compromise away the last experiment of free government; compromise away principles that are indestructible and are capable and comprehensive enough, when we shall have filled our mission, not only to embrace thirty-six States, but extensive enough to embrace the nations of the earth. Compromise! No, never compromise until this rebellion is put down. Never compromise until the principles of the Constitution are acknowledged and the laws are enforced which have been passed in its compliance. [Applause]

Let us lift ourselves above parties. Let us go forward to this great work, and let those who are suffering and have been down-trodden have your sympathies, instead of the traitors and enemies of our country. Why, you here in the city of Baltimore are very close to Virginia, and have read, and perhaps seen much of this war, yet withal you scarcely know what is going on down there. Go to my own adopted home, and what do you find? Men have been taken from their homes and incarcerated in dungeons of the most loathsome character, with no response to their groans and sufferings but the crowding of the dungeon and the clanking of the chains that bind their limbs; and yet here we are talking about compromise. Compromise! Why thousands of these very Union men are hunted down and arrested in the gorges of the mountains as they are making their way through the lines of despotism toward those of the United States. Compromise until that, the most loyal people of the United States are redeemed! You are said to be the most loyal State. [Applause] I will make an issue with you, however. Look at the people out there in Tennessee, who, standing under the Constitution and the Union, are willing to perish beneath its ample folds, without any protection whatever, if by that means they can hasten the great end of your and their disenthralment. [Applause.] But I know that you are not willing to compromise this question until all such are redeemed and regenerated. [Applause] Yes, compromise! Never compromise until the supremacy of the law and the Constitution is acknowledged. I am asked, and have been asked, "Are you not for peace?" O yes, I am. "Are you not for compromise?" Yes, I am. "What sort of a compromise are you for?" The Constitution of the United States is my compromise, the laws made in its pursuance is my compromise, and never ground our arms, or permit our flag to trail in the dust until its supremacy is acknowledged in every State throughout the country. [Applause] Let this war go on until the rebellion is put down, and the farther South you can keep the war the greater protection you will have. Get it once there, and we will help you to drive it further and further, until, like the swine possessed of the devil,[17] we will drown it in the Gulf. [Applause.] It is not worth while to mince this question. There is but one way to get along with rebellion and traitors, and that is to meet them at the threshold, and make them feel the law and submit to it! Compromise! Yes, will you compromise over the grave of Washington? Will you compromise over the grave of Jackson? A story was related to me by an old friend of General Jackson's, which I will tell you. When the Secessionists had that portion of the State under their control in which his remains lie buried, they even went so far, by way of expressing their contempt for his failure to hang John C. Calhoun, as to plant their stars and bars at the head of his tomb. William Donaldson[18] (not Andrew J.) related this incident to me with the tears trickling down his cheeks. He is now nearly seventy years of age, and putting an oath to it by way of being emphatic, not profane, he said, "By the eternal, when they struck the flag staff down, I expected to see the old man turn out of his grave;" and were it possible to communicate intelligence to the dead, and that old man could be made aware and understand what is going on, I sometime think he would turn over in his coffin; that he would arise and shake off the habiliments of the tomb, and extending that proud and lofty form of his, and in his own significant language, exclaim, "The Federal Union, it must and shall be preserved." [Applause]

Then why shall we despair? Because our arms here and there have met with a defeat or repulse, and seeming victories have been postponed for a time, why should we despair? We are a complaining people generally. If we fight twenty battles and win nineteen, we talk all the time about the battle we lost, and never about the nineteen we won. When we look over the field of this war, although it may not have been conducted in every particular as we would have desired, yet there has been a great deal accomplished since its commencement. You to-day have 140,000 square miles—making nearly four States as large as the State of Tennessee—more in your possession than when it commenced. The Mississippi is nearly open. We have got a complete blockade; we have got the rebellion encircled. If we will only complete, as it were, the opening of the Mississippi, and make the blockade of Galveston close, Texas and Arkansas are cut off, and of course they will conquer themselves. Make the blockade of Charleston and Mobile close, and you need not even penetrate the land. Then intercept the Weldon road, and let your army march into Eastern Tennessee and occupy Chattanooga.[19] Hold it, and let the Government plant itself there, and this boa-constrictor, as it is sometimes called, will gag itself to death. They are already bringing their last man into the field, and consuming their last resources.

Knowing that you will be addressed by those who can interest you more then I, I will bring my remarks to a close by paying my respects to the fairer portion of our audience who have honored us with their presence here to-night. The presence of females inspires an audience with respect. And let me say to them in a few words, that they occupy a very important position in this Government, because they can exercise a wonderful influence now as they have in times gone by, and as they have especially done in the Southern country to break up this Government. Woman! Union should be the instinct of her nature and life, and instead of trying to separate and dissolve the Union of States she should comply with the instincts of her nature and cling to the Union, especially so to a Union that has resulted in so much good for her. [Applause.] Woman can exert here, as they have done there, a powerful influence; and let me say to the women, or the ladies North of this combination and this conspiracy now against the Union of these States, if you will but give us your influence, extending through all these States, there will be no difficulty found in the putting down of this rebellion. You have it in your power to do much. We may need men and more money, but permit me to remark, that without regard to the cost as to men and money, this great Government must be preserved. [Applause.] Yes, we have not paid the price yet, but let it be named by the Ruler on High what that price is, and it shall be paid. [Applause.] Let the Government be saved, and in saving it, I ask your every power and influence; and though men may be called for, let me say to the wife (for even your husband might be called on, and you have a power that controls him), just whisper in his ear—you know there is a power behind the throne greater than the throne itself—that the country calls, that the Union of the States is endangered, and urge him to go then and obey his country's call. [Applause.][20]

Let me say in addition to this to her that has no husband, but who has one of whom she is fond, that when he comes to pay you a visit, say to him that his country needs his service, and if he won't obey your call, but would rather stay at home lingering about you, let me tell you, that if you form an union with him when the peril comes he will never defend it. [Laughter and applause.] Sweetheart, tell your lover to go and serve his country, and let the wife say to the husband, "go and serve your country, for I would rather stay at home and be a soldier's widow than a coward's wife. [Applause]. Remember the example of the Greek mother. When Greece was invaded, when the existence of the Government was imperilled, the Greek mother had a lovely and promising son, upon whom all her affections rested. She went out and bought a sword, and brought it home with her, and when her son returned she handed the sword to him and said, "take that my son, and go forth to battle, but never return until victory perches upon the standard of your country, or your dead body is brought home upon that sword." The young man took the sword, and handling it as if trying its elasticity, with perhaps some little doubt rankling in his mind as to his success, he said, "Mother, this sword is too short." "Never mind that, my son. Take that sword and go forward to battle, and when you come in contact with the enemy, if your sword is too short, just advance one step closer to the foe, and your sword will be long enough". [Applause]

Then give us your sympathies and your influence, and the day is not distant when the Constitution and the laws will be supreme, when this reign of fire and blood will be chased away and be superseded by the star of peace. Then shall we have good will on earth. Let us go forward with one heart, with one determination, and if the price is not yet paid, let us pay it at once. Let us take that flag and place it in the hands of stalwart and patriotic men. Let them go forward bearing it aloft, and if need be, bathe in it a Nation's blood and baptize it in fire.

Here to-night, in conclusion, let us stand upon the altar of our country, forgetting that we have ever been divided into parties, but that now we are for our country only, and, when we have got a country hereafter, let us stand around the common altar and join in one fraternal hug, each impulse beating forward and connecting peacefully around this grand circle[.] Let us resolve here to-night that this nation shall stand regenerated and redeemed. Let me say to you that your countrymen appeal to you for help. Shall you let that appeal go unheeded? Shall the wail of the oppressed and down-trodden be unresponded to? Go to my poor adopted home and see that suffering people fleeing from the dungeons of tyranny by hiding themselves in the gorges and caverns of the mountains. Look at their blood, look at their oppression, look at their embarrassment. Look at their blood like that of sacrificing Abel, crying even from the bowels and caverns of the earth to the American people for succor and assistance. Shall they appeal in vain? Let me ask you, have you got homes, wives, sisters, children that you love? You have. Have you got nature in you? If you have, I know my people will not appeal in vain. You will respond to their cries, and the time will come when you with us will mingle your blood in the same battle-field for the redemption and restoration of the Constitution of our country. [Applause.] Some of you I know personally, others by reputation, but a stranger to most of you, I must be permitted to say that I have no favors to ask; you have none to ask of me. If we can stand together upon the great idea of preserving this Government, it is well; and, though we may be strangers, if we agree upon the great principle that is running all through this struggle then we are brothers, and stand united here to-night. I stand upon those great principles. Yes, here to-night. I acknowledge the world is my home and every honest man my brother without regard to his creed. [Applause.]

In conclusion, ladies and gentlemen, accept my unfeigned thanks for the kind attention that you have given me here to-night, and the manifestations of your approbation which you have shown. [Great applause.][21]

Baltimore *American,* March 23, 1863.

1. At a great Union rally in the Hall of the Maryland Institute—Johnson as honored guest and other dignitaries, including Salmon P. Chase, Montgomery Blair, Gen. Ambrose Burnside, and Horace Maynard in attendance—Chairman D. H. Hooper introduced the governor as "one . . . of the distinguished patriots of the West," praising him for his "bold and uncompromising" defense of the Union in the face of great personal risk. Baltimore *American,* March 23, 1863.

2. A somewhat confusing allusion to the transition currently under way in the construction of wheeled vehicles. The age-old design with smaller fore wheels was gradually being replaced by equi-sized wheels, regardless of the number needed, a change perhaps most visible in the evolving design of railway locomotives.

3. Robert C. Schenck, former congressman and brigadier general of volunteers (1861-63), had been disabled for field duty by a wound in the right wrist at Second Bull Run and was now assigned at Baltimore, where he served until his resignation in December to return to the House. *BDAC*, 1567; Boatner, *Civil War Dictionary*, 725; *DAB*, XVI, 428; see also *Johnson Papers*, I, 347*n*.

4. From Lincoln's message to the special session of Congress, July 4, 1861. Basler, *Works of Lincoln*, IV, 438.

5. Beggars or people living in wretched poverty. *OED*, VI, 136.

6. For examples of Johnson's earlier Catilinarian references, see *Johnson Papers*, IV, 488, 642.

7. A figure apparently inspired by popular speculations on origins and evolution.

8. A reiteration of the South's alleged monarchical syndrome, to which Johnson had earlier referred. See *ibid.*, 618-19; V, 19, 230.

9. The Confederate legislature, fleeing with the governor to Memphis, February 20, 1862, adjourned *sine die* a month later. Thereafter, the government was "in the saddle," as

Harris refugeed with the army until war's end. James W. Patton, *Unionism and Reconstruction in Tennessee, 1860-1869* (Chapel Hill, 1934), 29.

10. For earlier mention of "King" Harris and Mayor Richard D. Baugh, see Speech in Support of Presidential War Program, July 27, 1861, *Johnson Papers*, IV, 620; for Baugh, see *ibid.*, 645*n*.

11. For Representative George W. Bridges of Athens, who escaped the Confederates and finally reached Washington nine days before Congress adjourned on March 3, see *ibid.*, III, 295*n*; IV, 690n.

12. Although Horace Greeley in editorials during November and December, 1860, suggested letting the "erring sisters" go in peace, it was Gen. Winfield Scott who coined the phrase "Wayward Sisters, let them go in peace" in a letter to Seward the following March 3. Don C. Seitz, *Horace Greeley: Founder of the New York Tribune* (Indianapolis, 1926), 191, 195.

13. Shakespeare, *Macbeth*, Act V, sc. 8.

14. Lorenzo Dow (1777-1834), Connecticut native and roving Methodist evangelist who gained the sobriquet "Crazy Dow," began preaching in 1794, covering circuits in New York, Georgia, Alabama, Tennessee, Virginia, and the Carolinas, as well as undertaking three trips to England and Ireland to preach to Catholics. After 1820 he lived on his Connecticut farm where he wrote more and preached less, issuing a flood of egotistical pamphlets. *DAB*, V, 410; *NCAB*, X, 472-73; see also Charles C. Sellers, *Lorenzo Dow: The Bearer of the Word* (New York, 1928).

15. A somewhat inexact rendering of this section from the Colorado, Nevada, and Dakota territorial bills; Johnson had made the point in earlier speeches. See Speech in Support of Presidential War Program, July 27, 1861, *Johnson Papers*, IV, 615-16; Speech at Columbus, October 4, 1861, *ibid.*, V, 18; *U. S. Statutes*, XII, 174, 211, 241.

16. For earlier use of this figure drawn from the blades of a winder and swift used in spinning, see Letter to Blackston McDannel, January, 1845, *Johnson Papers*, I, 185.

17. An allusion to Christ's driving the unclean spirits out of a man and into swine which then "ran violently down a steep place into the sea." Mark 5:13.

18. William Donelson (1795-1864), first cousin and brother-in-law of Andrew Jackson Donelson and veteran of the Creek War, was a Tennessee-born farmer and slaveowner with an estate valued at $90,000 on the eve of secession. 1860 Census, Tenn., Davidson, 4th Dist., 33; *ibid.*, Slave Schedule, 11-12; Sam B. Smith and Harriet C. Owsley, eds., *The Papers of Andrew Jackson* (1 vol., Knoxville, 1980-), I, 419; Pauline W. Burke, *Emily Donelson of Tennessee* (2 vols., Richmond, 1941), I, 34, 45; II, Addendum (Family Chart).

19. A favorite "grand design" of Johnson, first proposed while a member of the Joint Committee on the Conduct of the War, the idea was to cut Richmond, the head of the Confederacy, away from the body of southern territory by severing the railroads which linked them together. One of these arteries ran through Knoxville and Chattanooga, another through Weldon and Wilmington, North Carolina. Once the roads were sliced and the Union blockade complete, the Confederacy would be doomed. *OR-Atlas*, II, plate CLXII; *Johnson Papers*, V, xxviii.

20. According to the reporter: "At this part of the proceedings General Burnside entered the hall and made his way to a seat on the platform, amid deafening applause. On its conclusion, Mr. Johnson continued his remarks[.]"

21. A week later, the governor attended a "complimentary supper" for himself and others. Among those present were Generals Ambrose E. Burnside, Orlando B. Willcox, and William H. Morris, Postmaster General Montgomery Blair, Treasury Secretary Salmon P. Chase, Congressmen Horace Maynard and Henry Winter Davis, ex-Congressmen Samuel Galloway and Lewis D. Campbell, and former mayor Thomas Swann. After a number of speeches had been made, Johnson—"considerately excused by the company after his great effort at the Institute—consented to say a few words." Alluding again to Schenck's wound, "he said they could not shake right hands, but they could the left as a pledge of forgetfulness of merely political or party differences in the future, and thereupon gracefully stepping forward for the purpose, these old partisan antagonists grasped hands, closing the proceedings of the evening." Nashville *Union*, April 2, 1863.

To Lorenzo Thomas

Washington City D.C.
March 23, 1863.

General L. Thomas,
Adjt Genl. U. S. A.
General:

It does not appear from the records of your office that the acceptance of my commission as Brigadier General of Volunteers has been formally acknowledged by me. Upon receiving the Commission from you in person on the 6th March 1862, I immediately started for Nashville, Tenn, (where I had been assigned duty,) and have been constantly engaged ever since in the performance of duties growing out of my appointment.

Your delivery of the Commission to me in person and my performance of duties incidental to said appointment, I consider a virtual acceptance thereof, and therefore most respectfully request that the acceptance of the commission may bear date March 6th, 1862, the date of its delivery.[1]

Very Respectfully, Your Obt. Sevt.
Andrew Johnson.

When appointed—age 54,—Residence Greenville, Tenn. Born in Raleigh North Carolina.

L, DNA-RG94, ACP Branch, Lets. Recd., File J87.

1. Attached was his oath of office as brigadier general, dated March 25, 1863, "to be of the same force from the date of the receipt of my commission, to wit: the 6th day of March 1862," and sworn before R. W. Ferguson, justice of the peace for the county of Washington & District of Columbia.

From Abraham Lincoln

Private Washington, March 26, 1863.

Hon. Andrew Johnson
My dear Sir:

I am told you have at least *thought* of raising a negro military force.[1] In my opinion the country now needs no specific thing so much as some man of your ability, and position, to go to this work. When I speak of your position, I mean that of an eminent citizen of a slave-state, and himself a slave-holder. The colored population is the great *available,* and yet *unavailed* of, force, for restoring the Union. The bare sight of fifty thousand armed, and drilled black soldiers upon the banks of the Mississippi, would end the rebellion at once. And who doubts that we can present that sight, if we but take hold in earnest? If you *have* been thinking of it please do not dismiss the thought.

Yours truly A. Lincoln

ALS, NNPM; DLC-JP2; DLC-Lincoln Papers.

1. There is no record of Johnson's reply to this proposal, nor is there any evidence that the governor himself had been inclined to enlist black recruits. However, one may speculate that Lincoln, in his wisdom, was planting the seed which would flower six months later in the emancipation rhetoric which poured forth from the Tennessean.

To Eliza Johnson [Louisville, Ky.][1]

Washington City
March 27th 1863—

My dear Eliza,

It is so difficult for me to write[2] I am almost detered from now trying after having commenced— I desire to know how your health is— I am kept in suspence all the time in reference to Some one of the family— Col Stover telegraphed that your health is about the same and that Mary is not well—[3] I have heard nothing from Robert & Charles since I left Nashville —[4] I hope all is right with them— Martha and children I fear I shall never see them again—[5] I feel sometimes like giv[in]g all up in dispare! but this will not do[.] we must hold out to the end, this rebelion is wrong and must be put down let cost what it may in the life and treasure— I intend to appropriate the remainder of my life to the redemption of my a[d]opted home East Tennessee and you & Mary must not be weary, it is our fate and we Should be willing to bear it cheerfully— Impatience and dissatisfaction will not better it or shorten the time of our suffering— I expected to have been back some time ago, but have been detaind here by the Govmt—[6] In the event Genls Rosecrans & Burnside fails to redeem East Tennessee this spring or summer I [am] making arragements to have a force raised to go there this fall— My matters are now nearly arranged and will leave in day or so for Louisville— Things do not look in Tennessee at this time as would like to see them; but must take them as they are— I would like to see the confederate Army driven back before you and Mary goes to Nashville, but by the time I reach there we will see more about it— You have no doubt seen that there are more troops being sent into Ky and the intention is to send them from there into Tennessee unless they are beaten back by the Rebels which I do not think will be the case— However we must wait and See the result— Washington is about as usual as far as I have seen, nothing more than common— The weather since I left you has been uninterruptedly bad— I have scarcely had a well day since reaching the north; aboniable cold, with horseness, sore throat and a bad cough— I have been speaking and exposed to some extent which has kept it up— I hope you are gain[in]g strength and some flesh— I trust there is nothing serious the matter with Mary and that she will soon be well again— Tell Mary she must devote much of her time and attention to the instruction and train[in]g of her children[7] and say to them that the're grand father thinks of them evey day and prays for their future happiness— You must tell Andrew that his father's hopes rest upon him now

Washington City
March 27th 1863–

My dear Eliza,

It is so difficult for me to write I am almost deterred from [illegible] trying after having [illegible]. I desire to know how you are [illegible]. I am kept in suspense all the time in reference to some one of the family. Col Stover telegraphs that your health is about the same and that Mary is not well. I have heard nothing from Robert & Charles since I left Nashville. I hope all is right with them. Martha and children I fear I shall never see them again. I feel some[illegible] giving all up in [illegible] If he will [illegible] [illegible] and become as he [illegible] there is nothing that he wants that I can procure for him, but what he shall have. Say to Col Stover that I received his despatch and will try and have it attended to &c. I hope he is filling up his Regiment.

Give my love to all and accept for yourself the best wishes of a devoted husband's heart–

Andrew Johnson

The only surviving example of "a devoted husband's heart—"
Courtesy Library of Congress.

and that he must make a man of himself, he can do it if he will and I expect it of him— If he will only educate himself he has a destiny of no ordinry character— when I get to Louisville I shall expect to find that he has made considerable progress in writing as well as in his books— If he will be a good boy and learn as he can there is nothing that he wants that I can procure for him but what he shall have— Say to Col Stover that I receivd his despatch and will try and have it attend to &c—[8] I hope he is filling up his Regiment—

Give my love to all and accept for yourself the best wishes of a devoted husband's heart—

Andrew Johnson

ALS, DLC-JP.

1. Addressed to "Mrs. Andrew Johnson care of Col D. Stover Louisville, Ky—"

2. Probably the combination of his now chronic arm problem and his current indisposition made letter writing a chore.

3. Johnson's son-in-law had been keeping him informed about the health of his wife and daughter Mary (Stover's wife) since their arrival in Louisville on January 13. In early February Stover wrote, "Mothers health has improved very much since she come to this place. Mary and the children are well." Stover to Johnson, February 8, 1863, Johnson Papers, LC.

4. The governor had left Nashville for Indianapolis, by way of Louisville, Monday morning, February 23.

5. Martha Patterson and her children, Andrew J. (1857-1932) and Mary Belle (1859-1891), were in Confederate-controlled Greeneville.

6. Summoned to appear in March before the Buell Commission, the governor finally gave his deposition on April 22. He was discovering that a month-long northern trip designed to combine speaking on behalf of vigorous prosecution of the war and consulting with Lincoln and Stanton about Tennessee conditions required more time than anticipated. See Donn Piatt to Johnson, March 18, 30, 1863, Misc. Lets. Recd., Dept. of the Ohio, RG393, NA; Tels. Recd., Vol. 42 (1863), Sec. of War, U. S. Mil. Tel., RG107, NA; Telegram from Donn Piatt, January 11, 1863; Deposition to the Buell Commission, April 22, 1863.

7. Lillie M. (1855-1892), Susan Drake (1857-1886), and Andrew Johnson Stover (1860-1923).

8. Not found.

To Abraham Lincoln

Washington City
March 27th. 1863.

Sir:

We desire to call the attention of your Excellency to the enclosed Resolutions passed on the 5th. inst at a meeting of prominent citizens of East Tennessee, now in the Military service of the Government.[1] The sentiments expressed you may be assured, are their own, and they may be taken as fair representation of the Union people in that part of our State. So far as they assume to state facts, you may rely upon their accuracy.

May we not embrace this opportunity again to ask whether such a people are not entitled to claim and to receive all the power of the Government for their protection?

We have the honor to be

Your Excellency's Obt Serts
Andrew Johnson
Horace Maynard
Allen A. Hall[2]

His Excellency
The President of the United States.

L, DLC-Lincoln Papers.

1. This letter and its enclosure take their place in the unending campaign of pressure and cajolery in which Johnson and his cohorts had engaged for years. At a meeting of East Tennessee officers and soldiers, held in camp near Murfreesboro on March 5, Brig. Gen. James G. Spears presiding, a committee chaired by Daniel C. Trewhitt drafted fourteen resolutions. Calling for a vigorous prosecution of the war, a "permanent march" of the Union army into East Tennessee, support of the Emancipation Proclamation, condemnation of the Copperheads as "enemies, cowards and the basest of men," establishment of U.S. courts in East Tennessee, and a request that Brownlow set up his *Whig* in Nashville, the resolutions were sent to the Parson who had them printed in the Cincinnati *Gazette* on March 23. Nashville *Union,* March 26, 1863; newspaper clippings with this letter and with that of W. G. Brownlow to Lincoln, March 27, 1863, Lincoln Papers, LC.

2. For Hall, see *Johnson Papers*, IV, 461*n*.

Authorization to Raise Troops[1]

War Department Washington City,
March 28th 1863.

Ordered

1 That Brigadier General Andrew Johnson Military Governor of Tennessee, be and he is hereby authorized to raise troops for the United States service to rendezvous at such place or places in Tennessee[2] as may be designated by him or the Secretary of War, Infantry Cavalry and Artillery, to be organized according to the rules and regulations of the service; the number to be ten Regiments of Infantry, ten of Cavalry, and ten Batteries of Artillery.

2 Governor Johnson will nominate the Officers who will be commissioned by the Department; they will be mustered into the service of the United States by Governor Johnson. The troops will be enlisted for the term of three years or during the war.

3d. Quartermasters and Commissaries will issue supplies to the troops so raised upon the requisition of General Johnson, and whenever required by him.

4th. That Governor Johnson be also authorized to raise and muster into the service of the United States, such force as he may deem adequate, not exceeding one Brigade, for the purpose of a Governor's Guard,[3] which force shall be under his exclusive orders, and not to be withdrawn from his service or otherwise employed without his consent.

Edwin M Stanton
Secretary of War.

Tel, DLC-JP; DNA-RG107, Mil. B.: Copies of Lets. Sent, Vol. 52 (1863).

1. A brief order, incorporating the essence of the first two paragraphs, had been drafted as early as March 19. Stanton Papers, LC.

2. Some three weeks later Stanton extended the governor's authority to "enlist recruits from other States, by and with the consent of the State Executive." Stanton to Johnson, April 15, 1863, Johnson Papers, LC.

3. When appointed, Johnson had been advised by the war department that commanders operating in Tennessee were to detail an adequate force for a "governor's guard" to act under his orders. But after a year this was still unrealized. Upon receiving this renewed authority, Johnson moved to create the guard, obtaining on May 3 the nominal transfer of the 10th Tenn. Inf. from the general service to his personal command to serve as the nucleus. It was not, however, until the late spring of 1864 that the change was actually made; by summer the guard, commanded by Brig. Gen. Alvan C. Gillem, had been increased to brigade strength by the addition of the 8th, 9th, and 13th Tenn. Cav. Rgts. and Btys. E and G of the 1st Tenn. Lgt. Arty. Responding to a call from Brownlow and others, Johnson sent the guard (except the 10th Inf.) to East Tennessee in August, 1864, "to kill or drive out all marauders." Meeting with considerable success, they pushed north to Bull's Gap, killing Gen. John H. Morgan at Greeneville. Subsequently, Gillem fell into an ambush near Morristown on November 13, was routed, and compelled to retreat to Knoxville. Although he reorganized the guard, it never again operated independently. Hall, *Military Governor*, 42, 83, 186; *OR*, Ser. 1, XXXIX, Pt. II, 325; *Tennesseans in the Civil War*, I, 342-44, 352-53, 395.

From Catherine M. Melville

March 29, 1863, Washington; ALS, DLC-JP.

Enclosing a "pocket companion" and an "Extract . . . from the pen of an old man, whom you know well—Frank Preston Blair," an acquaintance of long-standing eulogizes Johnson's course "during these last years of great trial. From that hour, when, in the Senate Chamber, you called Traitors by their right name and in the *teeth of their superciliousness thundered* forth words which made these would be Aristocrats *tremble!* From that hour to this, I, as well as *many friends,* have watched your course, with the closest and deepest interest and thanked God that your unwavering march has been onwards and upwards!"

To Salmon P. Chase

Washingon City March 29th, 1863.

Hon S. P. Chase,
Secretary of the Treasury,
Sir:

I have the honor to acknowledge the receipt of your communication of the 26th. ins't, transmitting certain "Regulations of Trade & Intercourse between inhabitants of states in insurrection and of the other states" &c,[1] and requesting that I should make such suggestions "for their correction or improvement" as might occur to me.

In reply I have to state that I have examined them with some care, and think they are judiciously prepared and well calculated to carry out the designs of the Treasury Department in confining the trade and commerce in the rebellious states within proper limits. I have suggested some few alterations in the details, not very material, which Mr. Mellen[2] of your Dep't has no doubt submitted to your consideration. I would respectfully suggest however, for your consideration, the policy of making some provision to enable loyal families residing in many portions of the Valley of the Cumberland and Tennessee Rivers, and living at no great distance from those rivers, to procure the needful supplies of the prime necessaries of life. I know the furnishing of supplies in such cases will require great care to guard against abuse; but if entrusted to a person of inflexible integrity and patriotism, the supplies can be safely furnished without danger.

If it should be your determination to adopt such policy, I would suggest that Allen A. Hall Esq of Nashville, Tennessee, might, with entire safety and advantage to the public interests be allowed to furnish supplies in the cases above referred to. It is believed that he might at the same time be able to render service to the Treasury and War Department by reporting all irregularities of trade, and violations of established regulations.

Very Respy, Your Obt. Sevt.
Andrew Johnson

Copy, DLC-Salmon P. Chase Papers, Vol. 73.

1. See Letter from Salmon P. Chase, March 16, 1863.
2. For William P. Mellen, special treasury agent, see *Johnson Papers*, V, 267*n*.

Speech to Washington Union Meeting[1]

March 31, 1863

As has been very correctly and forcibly remarked by my friend and colleague from Tennessee[2]—for we have been colleagues—this is one of the most fitting places in the United States in which to hold a meeting like this—a Union meeting—a meeting in which our feelings and sentiments may be reflected in regard to the preservation of the Union which was established by Washington and his confreres. This city, founded by him and bearing his name, is the most fitting place for a meeting of this kind. Many meetings have been held in other places, and I must say that I regret this, thinking that Washington should have been the first city in which a meeting assembled to give expression to sentiments in favor of the Union.

As it is not my habit in making speeches to give a long exordium, I shall on this occasion march directly up to the discussion of the subject now under consideration; that is, the preservation of the Union of these States and the form of Government under which we live. And perhaps I may as well commence with a text.

It has been stated here to-night that more than two years ago I proclaimed in the Senate a design to break up this Union and establish a

Southern monarchy and a Southern aristocracy, giving such facts and reasons as were then at my command for so believing.[3] This declaration of mine was denounced, was not met in answer, but merely denounced as being the outpourings of a demagogue; of one who, wanting the people's favor, pandered to their taste without regard to principle. I am free to say here, as I have said on other occasions, I am one of those who have always advocated popular government—that form of government which recognises to the utmost the capability of man for self-government. This has been one of the principal tenets in the doctrines that I have always attempted to inculcate.

Before I proceed, it may not be out of place to state that I am a Democrat in the proper acceptation of that term. I am one of those who believe that the people are capable of self-government. I look upon our Government itself as being the representative of democracy. We have the combined will of the people in the shape of the Constitution; and when the will of the people is reflected according to law and through the Constitution, I look upon that will as being paramount, and it should be obeyed by the public rulers. But my democracy does not consist in what has turned out to be the democracy of some. But a short time since we had the spectacle of men calling themselves Democrats, and who proclaimed and contended for what they called Democratic sentiments, abandoning their seats in the Senate and their Government, and taking up their abode in the traitorous camp. ["That's true."] I am a Democrat, and the fundamental principle of my democracy is the preservation of the Union. [Applause] I learned my democracy in the school of Thomas Jefferson. He was my early teacher. His democracy was the preservation of the Union of these States; and when individuals entered into conspiracies to overthrow the Government he arrested them and tried them for treason [Cheers.] That was his democracy when Aaron Burr plotted treason and attempted to destroy the Government.

The present struggle is emphatically a struggle for free Government, as you have been told here to-night, and I will take a single paragraph from the President's message of 1861, as my text on this occasion—not promising to stick very closely to it, or to pursue an argument directly from it, but to have it a point to which I can return in the desultory remarks I shall make.

In the President's message to which I refer the following remark occurs:

> This is especially a people's contest. On the one side of the Union it is a struggle for maintaining in the world that form and substance of government whose leading object is to elevate the condition of men, to lift artificial weights from all shoulders, to clear the path of laudable pursuits to all, and to afford an unfettered start and a fair chance in the race of life.[4]

That single paragraph illustrates the contest in which the country is now engaged. [Cheers.] It is a struggle for free government. It is a contest of the many on the one hand and of the few on the other: shift it and mystify it as we may, this is the plain naked issue, and the query is whether we will maintain and perpetuate a free Government! [Cheers.]

I know it is said by some that this is a Republican war, and that it has been brought about by the Administration. Let us look at the facts. We know who struck the first blow, who fired the first gun at Sumter. We know where the war commenced, and we know, too, when the Administration made the first move to crush the rebellion. When the President called out a force to protect the Capital and the Government from traitors, it was denounced as a usurpation and violation of law and the Constitution.

Now, I have a few words to say to the people of the District of Columbia. When this war commenced, many of you sympathized with the South and went there. What did you go for? While you were here the Capital of the Government was in your possession. I am now talking to a man who belongs to the District of Columbia, and if he has a thimbleful of brains I want him to understand me. [Cheers.] You went to the South to join Jeff. Davis—to do what? To take Washington, the Capital of the Government? While you were here you had it; it was in your possession; it was under your control. The Government was free, and you had a Constitution. But you, for the purpose of getting your rights and carrying out Southern principles, gave up that which you had, and went South for the purpose of fighting to get it back again. That is the sense of the whole proposition; and because the President took steps to prevent the capture of the seat of government and its overthrow, he has been denounced. He called out men, as it was his duty to do, and if I have any objections to urge against him it is not that he did so much, but that he did not do more. If four hundred thousand men under the first call would have put down the rebellion, I would have said call them out instead of seventy-five thousand. [Cheers.]

When the rebellion was fairly initiated, certain persons remained in our midst whose sympathies should have led them into the enemy's camp. They staid with us, and did us more harm than if they had arms in their hands. They were dangerous to the existence of the Government and inimical to peace and all its interests. Because some few of these men have been arrested, the cry has been raised the Constitution has been violated, and that the Government is at an end. Because the writ of habeas corpus has been suspended, they say civil liberty has been violated. I am not going to argue this question from a legal point of view, even if I were capable, but I am going to argue from a common-sense point of view. [Cheers.]

There is one thing clear, and that is that in a time of rebellion the writ of habeas corpus can be suspended; that is clear—every body admits it. There has been some question as to who should suspend it—whether Congress or the President. It being clear that it can be suspended, there is another proposition equally clear—that since this rebellion, in the city of Washington and other places there are a number of traitors who are making war upon the Government clandestinely and secretly. Now, the question arises whether, when such men are discovered, it is not the duty of somebody to arrest them and put them where they will not endanger the Government. Shall we lose this power because a question is got up as to who should exercise it? Must we hesitate to put traitors out of the way because there is some doubt as to who has the power to suspend the writ of habeas corpus? I say that Congress not having passed a law on the subject, it was the duty of the President to suspend that writ; and the only fault I have to find with him is that he has not arrested more of these traitors.

Governor Johnson then proceeded to show that this cry of a violation of the Constitution was raised by croakers and peace men who desired to compromise. Any compromise, as was known by every one who read the newspapers of the day, was impossible, and a proposition for one would have been treated with contempt by the rebels. He reviewed the Crittenden compromise, and showed how it was defeated by Benjamin, Slidell, and the Southern men in Congress at that time, as were all other propositions looking to a peaceful settlement of the difficulty. He continued:

Since we have got into this rebellion blood has been shed, life sacrificed, the very existence of the nation been perilled, yet we find a party springing up in our midst with the cry of peace upon their lips. They want us to compromise. Compromise with whom? With our brethren of the South. Talk to me about my brother when he stands with arms in his hand, with his bayonet against my bosom, and his sword pointed to my throat! Call him my brother? Yes, I believe Abel had a brother, too. Such a brother they ask us to compromise with. Shall we compromise with traitors? They are in the wrong; they are attacking the best and purest Government the world ever saw, and we are called upon to compromise. We are right and they are wrong. Compromise! Would you have truth to compromise with falsehood? Would you have right to compromise with wrong? Would you have virtue to compromise with vice? Would you have the Deity, with rules in the celestial regions, to have compromised with his satanic majesty when he rebelled in Heaven? Would you have him to have compromised with the devil instead of kicking him from Heaven to the nether regions? I say the simile is just. [Applause.] This has been the heaven of nations, and when they ask us to compromise with rebels who have raised their hands against it, they might as well ask the Deity to compromise with the devil. [Cheers.]

Gov. Johnson drew a vivid picture of the sufferings of the loyal men of the South, and asked whether we were willing to make a compromise which would leave them at the mercy of the rebels to hang on gibbets and rot in loathsome dungeons. [Cries of "never"] He intimated that at no distant day the loyal men of Eastern Tennessee might appeal to the citizens of the District and those of other States to organize bands and come to their rescue. [Cheers.] He was in favor of but one sort of compromise, and that was the Constitution of the United States. Let the rebels lay down their arms, disband their legions, recognise the supremacy of the laws of their country, and then he would compromise and not before. If any attempt was made to settle the question short of implicit obedience to the Constitution, the rebellion would be acknowledged, and at the same time the impotency, the inefficiency, and the weakness of the Government and its inability to protect itself. Acknowledge this rebellion, and it will not be a month or six weeks before some portion of the country will become disaffected, and we will have another rebellion. Another compromise will be necessary and another rebellion will follow; and so we will go on until we are all compromised away. [Laughter and applause.]

Governor Johnson then proceeded to comment on the despair and despondency manifested by some of the friends of the Union. He regarded the signs of the times as hopeful. We had already repossessed fourteen thousand square miles of territory since the war commenced. Let us open the Mississippi, make the blockade at Galveston, Mobile, and Charleston close, hold them at bay before Richmond, and send forces into Eastern Tennessee. He could not help talking about Eastern Tennessee. [Cheers.] They were the most loyal people in the United States. In most places people did not dare to be *disloyal,* but there men had dared to be *loyal.* What he desired to advise was that forces should be sent to Chattanooga or Knoxville. Establish a Union force there, and you segregated the Southern Confederacy; you destroyed the unity of their territory; and if, following this, you cut the Weldon road in two, you will have a grip on the rebellion under which it will soon kick itself to death.[5]

Governor Johnson then endorsed and ardently argued in favor of the President's emancipation proclamation, and showed that it had in no way disadvantageously affected our cause in this war. He wanted it to be understood that he was for this Government with slavery or without slavery. If slavery has to go as an incident to the preservation of the Government, he said in the name of God, let it go.

In conclusion, he made a most eloquent appeal to the ladies, to encourage their husbands, fathers, and sweethearts to buckle on armor, enter the field, and continue in it until the Constitution was vindicated, the supremacy of the laws acknowledged, and the Government established on a firmer basis than ever. [Cheers.]

Washington *National Intelligencer,* April 2, 1863.

1. This speech was one of a number made in the two main halls of the Capitol during a mass meeting sponsored by the Washington municipal government. A large crowd filled the candlelit building to overflowing. Lincoln and several cabinet members attended the oratory in the House chamber, where Johnson spoke following "prolonged applause." Washington *National Intelligencer,* April 2, 1863; New York *Tribune,* April 1, 1863.

2. Horace Maynard had preceded Johnson in the speaking.

3. See Speeches of December 18-19, 1860, and February 5-6, 1861, *Johnson Papers*, IV, 36-38, 209, 217.

4. Basler, *Works of Lincoln*, IV, 438.

5. See Speech at Baltimore, March 23, 1863, note 19.

From Edwin M. Stanton[1]

War Department, Washington City
April 2nd 1863.

Governor,

Under your authority and commission as Military Governor, you are authorized in your discretion to exercise among others, the following powers:

lst To impose taxes for the support of the poor, for police purposes, and purposes of your government generally.

2nd To impose exactions upon all disloyal persons for the support of the wives and children of those who may have been expelled from the country or who may be in the rebel service.

3d To impose exactions upon all who have contributed to the rebel service by money, by property, or by the use of their slaves, the amount of exaction to be determined by the discretion of the Governor, or by a Board, whom he may appoint for that puppose.

4th The power also to extend to the taking possession of property and collecting rents for property or hire of slaves owned by persons who are within the rebel lines.

Very Respectfully, Your Obedient Servant
Edwin M. Stanton
Secretary of War.

Brigadier General A. Johnson,
Military Governor of Tennessee.

L, DLC-JP; NNPM; DNA-RG107, Mil. B.: Copies Lets. Sent, Vol. 52 (1863).

1. This represents the second in a series of statements clarifying and defining the military governor's powers and authority which Johnson secured as a result of his visit to Washington in March and April. A marginal note indicates that this communication was enclosed in Stanton to Johnson, April 15, 1863.

From William S. Rosecrans

Hd Qrs Dept Cumb Murfreesboro
April 4th 1863

To His Excellency Andrew Johnson
Military Gov of Tenn

I have heard that one of your officers has stated that Truesdail & Co or parties connected with them had been using an exclusive privilege of purchasing cotton & that you had written authority from Brig Genl Davies[1] for saying that I was personally interested in such an association—[2] No such privilege ever has been or will be given by me to any person or persons whatever and no interest direct or indirect to the value of a penny have I ever had or do I ever expect or mean to have in trade or speculation of any sort carried on in or under my command during this war[.] I therefore call upon you as a man of standing and honor and one whom I believe to be my friend as an act of justice to myself and the country to inform me of all that you know touching this matter and also to vindicate me in the broadest manner possible from even a shade of suspicion of contact with any such corruption[.][3]

W S Rosecrans Maj Genl

Tel, DLC-JP.

1. Johnson's "officer" remains unidentified; similarly, the "written authority" has apparently not been preserved. While the brigadier in question may have been Jefferson C. Davis—two other references to the man use Davis—it seems equally plausible that the informant was Thomas A. Davies (1809-1899), at this time commander of the District of Columbus, Kentucky. One of Rosecrans' subordinates in the Army of the Mississippi, Davies had been excoriated by the general for retreating during the Battle of Corinth. A West Point graduate (1829), he served on the frontier for two years before resigning to work as a civil engineer and become a New York City merchant. Returning to the army at the outbreak of the war, he served as colonel of the 16th N. Y. before a promotion to brigadier in March, 1862. After the war he wrote and published books on numerous topics, including *Cosmogony: or Mysteries of Creation, Genesis Disclosed,* and *How to Make Money, and How to Keep It.* Warner, *Generals in Blue,* 113-14.

2. The relationship between General Rosecrans and William Truesdail, chief of military police, remains clouded. The latter appears to have been corrupt yet efficient, and Rosecrans, needing assistance in ridding his command of enemy agents, seems to have overlooked the chief's indiscretions. Johnson, however, had to deal with a civil population outraged by Truesdail's machinations. As early as January, 1863, the governor called vainly on Rosecrans to investigate "loud and numerous complaints." Truesdail's reputation grew until it reached Washington, where Secretary Stanton ordered the appointment of a commission to look into the Nashville police, an investigation which never materialized; but when criticism became personally offensive to Rosecrans, he finally initiated an inquiry headed by Capt. Temple Clark, formerly of his staff and temporarily assigned to Gen. Richard W. Johnson. Clark's findings, published June 2, 1863, exonerated Truesdail and recommended that the army police be continued. Subsequent to this apparent whitewash, Truesdail continued to use Rosecrans' name in efforts to profit from the Middle Tennessee cotton trade. *OR*, Ser. 1, XXIII, Pt. II, 524; Fitch, *Annals*, 353; Hall, *Military Governor*, 83, 203; see also Telegram to Abraham Lincoln, January 11, 1863, note 5; Telegram to William S. Rosecrans, January 4, 1863.

3. For Johnson's response, see Telegram to William S. Rosecrans, June 1, 1863. Although privately expressing his regard for the general "as a patriot at heart and not a damn traitor like his predecessor [Buell]," Johnson seems never to have issued a public statement. Charles A. Dana to Stanton, September 8, 1863, *OR,* Ser. 1, XXX, Pt. I, 183.

To William Hoffman

April 4, 1863, Washington; L, DNA-RG249, Lets. Recd., File J-1863.

Three East Tennesseans "captured by the Rebels in Virginia in their attempt to leave the Confederacy, and recently released from Richmond prisons" had not been regularly mustered in before they were apprehended. "As they are anxious to return to Tennessee for the purpose of joining an East Tenn Reg't," the governor asks "that they may be permitted so to do, and . . . that transportation be furnished them."

From Robert Johnson

Nashville Apl 7th [1863]

Gov. Andrew Johnson

Charles' Funeral today was very large[.][1] he was embalmed & placed in a vault[.] I have placed all of articles in his room[.] the Keys I leave with East.[2]

Robt. Johnson
Col. 1st Regt

Tel. DNA-RG107, Tels. Recd., U. S. Mil. Tel., Vol. 44 (1863).

1. In an accident, the particulars of which remain obscure, the governor's oldest son, Charles Johnson, assistant surgeon, 10th Tenn. Inf., was killed April 4, in a fall from his horse at a military camp outside Nashville. The funeral procession from the governor's residence to Mt. Olivet Cemetery included Col. Alvan C. Gillem's 10th Tenn. Rgt. and part of Col. Robert Johnson's cavalry. His father, absent in Washington, could not attend. Nashville *Union,* April 7, 1863; *Official Army Register: Volunteers,* IV, 1214; Nashville *Dispatch,* April 5, 1863.

2. Edward H. East, secretary of state, who had called Robert to Nashville. East to Robert Johnson, April 5, 1863, Series 2, Johnson Papers, LC.

From Lorenzo Thomas

Helena, Ark, April 7, 1863

His Excellency
A. Johnson Governor of Tennessee,
Dear Sir

Mr. R. V. Montague[1] of Louisiana, a gentleman of intelligence and worth, residing on his plantation not many miles from General Grants Head Quarters has been a staunch Union man from the commencement of the rebellion. He is confided in by that General[2] and I have received valuable information from him. He succeeded, from time to time, in getting his sons[3] north, where they all now are, the last one Mr. M. L. Montague[4] only escaping very recently. He is thirty years of age, well educated, having been a cadet at West Point some three years. He is exceedingly anxious to enter our army and has gone to Washington to obtain a commission, but I have stated to his Father, that you might feel at liberty to authorize him to raise a regiment in Tennessee, from Union refugees from your state or from Alabama and Mississippi, as the refugees from those states naturally seek your protection. I feel that I can recommend him from what I learn of his character and unflinching devotion to the government, which I do most cheerfully.

I have the honor to be
Very Respy your obt srvt
L Thomas Adj't. Genl.

Charles Johnson (1830-1863).
Courtesy Margaret Johnson Patterson Bartlett.

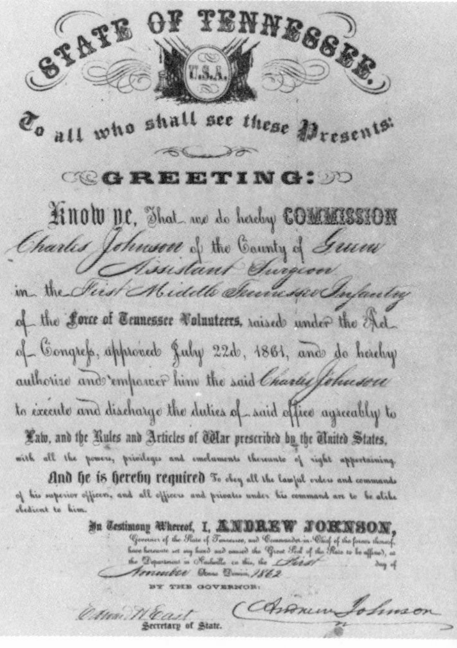

STATE OF TENNESSEE.

U.S.A.

To all who shall see these Presents:

GREETING:

Know ye, That we do hereby COMMISSION Charles Johnson of the County of Green Assistant Surgeon in the First Middle Tennessee Infantry of the Force of Tennessee Volunteers, raised under the Act of Congress, approved July 22d, 1861, and do hereby authorize and empower him the said Charles Johnson to execute and discharge the duties of said office agreeably to Law, and the Rules and Articles of War prescribed by the United States, with all the powers, privileges and emoluments thereunto of right appertaining.

And he is hereby required To obey all the lawful orders and commands of his superior officers, and all officers and privates under his command are to be alike obedient to him.

In Testimony Whereof, I, ANDREW JOHNSON, Governor of the State of Tennessee, and Commander-in-Chief of the forces thereof, have hereunto set my hand and caused the Great Seal of the State to be affixed, at the Department in Nashville on this, the First day of November Anno Domini 1862

BY THE GOVERNOR:

Edw. H. East
Secretary of State.

Andrew Johnson

A son's commission.
Courtesy Pierpont Morgan Library.

LB copy, DNA-RG94, Gens' Papers, Lorenzo Thomas.

1. Robert V. Montague (b. *c*1802), a Virginia-born planter and commission merchant, had $270,000 real and $15,000 personal property in 1860. 1860 Census, La., Madison Parish, 35; Peyton McCrary, *Abraham Lincoln and Reconstruction: The Louisiana Experiment* (Princeton, 1978), 248.

2. Three weeks earlier Grant had approved Montague's shipment of cotton to Memphis "on his own account" and endorsed him as "a Southern man of known loyalty." Grant to George W. Graham, March 19; Grant to Unknown, March 22, 1863, John Y. Simon, ed., *The Papers of Ulysses S. Grant* (10 vols., Carbondale, Ill., 1967-), 544-45.

3. The younger sons were the planter De Sha (b. *c*1837), the law student R. Vaughn (b. *c*1839), Robert (b. *c*1840), and Henry Clay (b. *c*1845), all born in Alabama. 1860 Census, La., Madison Parish, 35-36.

4. Mickelborough L. Montague (b. *c*1832), Robert's eldest son, who was admitted to West Point in 1851, had operated a plantation of his own near his father's. *Ibid.*, 30; *West Point Register* (1870), 249.

To William S. Rosecrans

Washington, April 8, 1863

Major-General Rosecrans:

Your telegram of 5th, through War Department, has been received.[1] I will be in Nashville in a few days, and will immediately thereafter meet you at any point that may be indicated, for the purpose of conferring with you fully and freely upon the subject and matter of your telegram. This, I think, will be more satisfactory to both. There has been nothing, there will be nothing desired by me but harmony and concert of action to put down this rebellion and restore to the people of Tennessee all their legal and constitutional rights; of this you know I have given assurance both in action and words.

Andrew Johnson.

OR, Ser. 1, XXIII, Pt. II, 220.

1. Addressed to Secretary Stanton "for And Johnson" and dated "Murfreesboro Apr 4th 1863," the telegram read: "From letters from the War Dept. there seems to be an impression that there has been some conflict between your authority and the millitary power here. You know very well how often I have assured you I would do all I could to build up and support civil authority and aid you every way in my power. Please communicate to me fully and freely all matters of conflict and complaint, and be assured I will rectify or show you decisive public reasons for not doing so[.]" Below Rosecrans' signature was a note, "Please open and communicate if *Gov Johnson* is not in Washington[.]" Rosecrans to Stanton, April 4, 1863, Tels. Sent, Vol. 63 (1862-63), Dept. of the Cumberland, RG393, NA; *OR*, Ser. 1, XXIII, Pt. II, 207.

Johnson's Federal Bonds

[April 10, 1863]

List of U. States Bonds deposited in the safe of the Secretary of the Senate for safe keeping by Hon Andrew Johnson of Tennessee.

7.30's[1] $50 each: Nos. 63043

[Eighty serial numbers follow]

Dated Oct. 1st. 1861—

81 Bonds $50 each $4050.00

Also the following 6 per cent Bonds ("5.20s")[2] of $1000 each: dated May 1, 1862.

No. 31.601—31.602—31.603—

31.604—31.605 = 5 Bonds		$1000 each	$5.000
Brought over—[3] 81	"	$50. "	*4.050
Package Contains			$9.050

*(Four thousand and fifty dollars)

Washington City S. J. Bowen[4]
April 10th1863 Financial Clerk

The Package to be Kept till called for by Gov. Johnson, or (in the event of his death) by a member of his family.

S. J. Bowen

D, DLC-JP18.

1. These twenty-year bonds at 7%, authorized by the loan bills of July and August, 1861, could also be sold in $50 short-term three-year notes at 7.3%. Davis R. Dewey, *Financial History of the United States* (New York, 1931), 277; Margaret G. Myers, *A Financial History of the United States* (New York, 1970), 150.

2. With a wartime treasury facing a tremendous financial burden, Secretary Chase requested, and was granted, authority in February, 1862, to raise $500 million by issuing 5-20's—bonds "callable in 5 and redeemable in 20 years" at 6% interest. When the sale of these bonds moved slowly, Chase turned to financier Jay Cooke, who, serving as the treasury's agent, flooded the country with advertising, appealing to small investors rather than to banks and lending institutions. By the end of 1863 this issue had been oversubscribed. *Ibid.*, 161-62; Dewey, *Financial History*, 280-84.

3. A reference to the tabulation of bond numbers on the reverse side of the statement.

4. Sayles J. Bowen (1813-1896), a New York native, came to Washington in 1845 as a Democrat to become a government clerk. Losing his position because of antislavery opinions, he successfully turned his hand to business ventures. An early convert to the new Republican party, he was rewarded with a string of political appointments in the national capital: financial clerk to the Senate's secretary (1861-63), police commissioner (1861-63), collector of internal revenue (1862-63), and postmaster (1863-68). He served one controversial term as mayor of Washington (1868-70), after which his political and financial fortunes collapsed. William Tindall, "A Sketch of Mayor Sayles J. Bowen," Columbia Historical Society *Records*, XVIII (1915), 25-43.

To William S. Rosecrans

Washington, April 11, 1863

Major-General Rosecrans:

I am informed that the four cavalry regiments from East Tennessee were to form a brigade, and be placed under the command of Col. Robert Johnson.[1] His regiment (the First East Tennessee Cavalry) is the largest in the service. Can this be done and promote the public interest? If so, it would be gratifying to me as well as others. I shall proceed at once to raise 25,000 troops, cavalry and infantry.[2]

Andrew Johnson.

OR, Ser. 1, XXIII, Pt. II, 228.

1. Three days later, wiring Edward H. East in Nashville, Johnson injected the verb "desires," which rather alters the original message. "I dispatched Rosecrans that the east Tennessee cavalry desires to be formed into Brigade & placed under command of Colonel Robert Johnson[.]" Johnson to East, April 14, 1863, Johnson Papers, LC.

2. The governor's efforts were unavailing.

From William S. Rosecrans

Murfreesboro Apl 12th 1863

Gov And. Johnson
Nashville

Robert has been drinking so as to become a subject of remark everywhere.[1] I sent for him told him I wanted him to stop and he promised me he would. If he keeps his word I will do all I can for him, but he is Junior to several other Colonels. It depends on himself for he can distinguish himself if he will[.]

W. S. Rosecrans Maj Genl

LB copy, DNA-RG393, Dept. of the Cumberland, Tels. Sent, Vol. 63 (1862-63).

1. It might be noted that this behavior, while not altogether unknown in the past, comes close upon the heels of the death of his older-by-four-years brother Charles.

From Edwin M. Stanton

War Department Washington City,
April 15th 1863.

Brig. General Johnson
General.

Under the authority given you by this Department, you may, if opportunity offers, enlist recruits from other States,[1] by and with the consent of the State Executive. And for the troops so enlisted, the respective States to which they belong, will be entitled to, and shall receive a credit in any draft that may be ordered.

Yours Truly Edwin M Stanton
Secretary of War

L, DLC-JP; DNA-RG107, Mil. B.: Copies Lets. Sent, Vol. 52 (1863).

1. On the reverse side of a copy of this order is the notation: "Colonel [Thomas B. W.] Stockton authorized to raise in N.Y. Ill, Ohio & Michigan 4 Regts Infy—dated June 1st 1863." Johnson Papers, LC.

From Edwin M. Stanton

War Department Washington City,
April 18th, 1863.

General,

First: You will establish your headquarters as Military Governor of the State of Tennessee at the City of Nashville,[1] and as such officer, you will take possession of all the public buildings belonging to the State of Tennessee, holding them in your charge and under your control for the public purposes for which they were designed, and in which you have occasion to employ them.

Second: You will appropriate such of the buildings for the civil officers, executive, legislative and judicial, as may be required for the performance of their respective functions, and you will employ such force of the military or civil police as you may deem necessary for the security and proper care of such buildings, and all other public property in the City of Nashville.

Third: All the public commons and public property in the City of Nashville, and elsewhere in the State, will be in your charge as Military Governor, and so far as possible you will exercise control over them, your authority and jurisdiction over all such public property being as exclusive and absolute as was exercised by the State of Tennessee, subject only to such military occupation and use, as may in the course of the war, be authorized and directed by the General commanding the Department.

Fourth: You will also take possession of, and occupy, all vacant and abandoned buildings and property within the City of Nashville possessed or owned by persons engaged in the rebellion, and will apply them to such uses as you may deem appropriate. You will[2] exercise, also, the same powers throughout the State of Tennessee.

Fifth: You will also take possession of all abandoned lands and plantations that may come within your power, and lease them for occupation and cultivation, upon such terms as you deem proper, keeping an account of the products, and registering the name of the former proprietor and of the person and terms upon which they are leased, reporting the same to this Department.

Sixth: You will also take in charge all abandoned slaves, or colored persons, who have been held in bondage, and whose masters have been, or are now engaged in rebellion, and provide for their useful employment and subsistence in such manner as may be best adapted to their necessities, and the circumstances in which you find them, having reference to the Acts of Congress relating to this class of persons, and be governed by their provisions.

Seventh: You will cause all such persons to be enrolled upon a descriptive roll, setting forth their names, their age, their sex, with any other remarks that may be useful in defining their capacity for usefulness, or as descriptive of their persons, and transmit a copy of it to this Department.[3] Such of them as are able bodied, and can be usefully employed, upon the fortifications, or other public works, you will so employ, securing and causing to be paid to them reasonable wages for their labor;[4] also taking measures to secure employment and reasonable compensation for the labor of all others of whatever age or sex, making from time to time report to this Department.

Eighth: Such as may be sick, or otherwise helpless from age or infirmity, you will have provided with suitable hospital care and attendance.

Ninth: You will also furnish from the Quartermasters and Commissary stores, such clothing and subsistence as may be necessary for the decent clothing and support of those who are poor or destitute, keeping a distinct account of all such appropriations.

Tenth.[5] As a general instruction to guide your administration you are authorized to exercise such powers as may be necessary and proper to carry into full and fair effect the 4th Section of the 4th Article of the Constitution of the United States which declares "the United States shall guarantee to every State in this Union a republican form of Government and shall protect each of them against invasion and domestic violence"; and whatever power may be necessary in restoring to the people of Tennessee their civil and political rights under the Constitution of the United States and the Constitution of the State of Tennessee and the laws made in pursuance thereof.

Very respectfully, Your Obedient Servant
Edwin M. Stanton
Secretary of War

Brigadier General Andrew Johnson
Military Governor of Tennessee.

LS, CSmH, Misc. #8222; DLC-E. M. Stanton Papers; DNA-RG107, Mil. B.: Copies Lets. Sent, Vol. 52 (1863).

1. Although he had operated for over a year without specific instructions from the administration, Johnson needed a clear directive which finally came as a consequence of his extended stay in Washington during the spring of 1863.

2. In the War Department version the verb is "may."

3. During Johnson's stay in Washington, Lincoln and Stanton tried to persuade him to use contrabands in the war effort, something the governor was reluctant to do, fearing its harmful effect on slavery. Except in cases of enlistment or government employment, Federal officials in Tennessee rarely kept descriptive rolls of escaped slaves. Letter from Abraham Lincoln, March 26, 1863; Cimprich, Slavery Amidst Civil War, 78, 235.

4. Article 7 of the War Department version ends here, with article 8 beginning: "You will also take measures to secure employment . . . ."

5. Only one of the three copies of this document—that in the Stanton Papers—contains this article, which appears as a separate addendum with accompanying endorsement:

"Gov. Johnson thinks it would be well to have the within added to his letter of instruction — If the Secretary of War sees no objection I see none. A. Lincoln April 25. 1863." Apparently Johnson, upon receipt of the original communication, sought out the President and persuaded him that there should be an explicit statement looking toward the restoration of civil government. The governor undoubtedly saw this article as assisting his effort to win over wavering Tennesseans and as an assurance to those hardy unionists under attack from guerrillas and Confederate troops. Edwin M. Stanton Papers, LC.

From Catherine M. Melville

Washington April 20/63

Gov Johnson,
Dear Sir,

To return to our conversation of this morning. Had Miss Gay[1] and myself been able to retain our house in Washington, we should at once have proposed that Mrs. J. & your son with Mary & her children should have boarded with us, & it would have given us pleasure to have directed Frank's education,[2] & seen that his Teachers did their duty. As it is, we have been compelled, since last Sept. to live in one room, teach a little &c. and unless we can get the assurance of work *given out* to us as Copyists, or something equivalent—sufficient to support us, we shall in all probability go to California next July.[3] So you see, we are altogether uncertain as to *our* future plans, & can only trust that the good God may direct our days to come, even as he has done the past.

I shall bear your dear boy's case on my memory & heart; and feel assured that some means can at once be found to advance that which you so earnestly wish, the education and best moral welfare of your son.

It would not do to seperate Frank from Mrs. Johnson during these times of terror. I trust her health will soon be restored. Present me kindly to her and to Mary, when you see them or write to them.

I cannot recommend Washington Schools, any more than Washn. Boardig Houses,[4] & I cannot believe that the health of either Mrs. Johnson or your children—would be benefitted by a sojourn in this City.

I mentioned this morning a school in Pena. in a beautiful & healthy region of Country which I cannot help thinking may be just such a place as would suit.[5] I enclose you the Advertisement & I shall write to the Principal & find out all about it; &, if, there is near the school, either a furnished house which your wife and daughter could occupy, & with whom Frank could spend all his time out of school, or a good boarding house which would be pretty much the same thing & less trouble. When I get all necessary information, I shall forward it to you without delay.

That region of country is exceedingly beautiful & *healthy*, and as *Centrical* as any other can be to *you*—during these awful times.

I hear the school & commun[ity] highly spoken of by all who know any thing about the place & whether it meets your needs or not, it will do no harm for me to make all enquiries.

If there is any thing that either Miss Gay or I can do for you, or any of our noble Union friends of East Tennessee Command us.

Respectfully, Yrs.
C. M. Melville

ALS, DLC-JP.

1. For Eliza Jane Gay, see *Johnson Papers*, V, 549*n*.

2. The object of all this concern was Johnson's youngest son, Andrew, Jr., who would be eleven in August and who must have had minimal and irregular schooling during the preceding two years.

3. They did not leave Washington. Before the year was out, Miss Melville became a clerk in the quartermaster general's office and after the war held a similar position in the treasury department. *U. S. Official Register* (1863), 130; *Boyd's Washington and Georgetown Directory* (1870), 267.

4. A contemporary journalist who frequented the capital observed: "Washington is a city of boarding houses, and of all cities which charge extraordinary prices for very ordinary board, it bears the palm." Frank G. Carpenter, *Carp's Washington*, Frances Carpenter, ed. (New York, 1960), 1.

5. In the absence of the advertisement to which Miss Melville refers, it has not been possible to determine which of several Pennsylvania schools she suggested.

Deposition to the Buell Commission[1]

[Washington, D.C.]
April 22, 1863.

Hon. ANDREW JOHNSON, Military Governor of Tennessee and brigadier-general U. S. Volunteers, being duly sworn, responds to the questions submitted by the judge-advocate of the Commission called to investigate the operations of the Army of the Ohio and the cross-interrogatories of Major-General Buell, as follows:

By the JUDGE-ADVOCATE:

Question. State your name, present address, and position in the service of the United States.

Andrew Johnson; Nashville, Tenn. I was brigadier-general in the volunteer service and Military Governor of Tennessee.

Question. State what you know of Major-General Buell proposing to evacuate Nashville in the summer of 1862 on the approach of the rebel forces under Bragg.

In September, 1862, General Buell, on his retrograde move with his army from Huntsville, Ala., Decherd and Battle Creek, Tenn., reached Nashville. Upon General Buell's arrival in Nashville I sought and had an interview with him in regard to the army falling back and giving up the country we had once been in possession of. With the retreat of the army the rumor came, and it was repeated by the rebels, that Nashville would be evacuated and surrendered to the enemy in the same condition we had received it. It was also understood that a number of prominent persons who had formerly resided in Nashville, in Tennessee, were returning with

Bragg and in the retreat of General Buell's army, with the understanding that Nashville was to be surrendered. These rumors caused me to be exceedingly solicitous as to what was to be done. In the first interview with General Buell, after some conversation in regard to the policy of a retreat, I asked him the question directly whether Nashville was to be given up to the enemy or evacuated without making resistance. I urged at some length and with much earnestness the great importance of holding Nashville at all hazards, and in end, rather than it should be retaken and held by the enemy, that it should be destroyed. This interview ended and another was had, in which the same arguments were repeated and urged as to the propriety of holding Nashville. General Buell replied with some little warmth that he was indifferent as to the criticism that might be made in regard to his policy or manner of conducting the campaign. He should rely upon his own judgment and convictions, without regard to consequences. The holding of Nashville in a military point of view was of no very great importance; that in fact upon military principles Nashville should have been abandoned or evacuated three months ago. In the third interview with General Buell, after repeating and urging again the importance of holding Nashville, he then stated that he had come to the conclusion to leave a force for the defense of Nashville, in answer to which I expressed my gratification and thanked him sincerely for doing so. He stated, though, in leaving a force for the defense of Nashville that he did not do it so much from military as from political considerations which had been pressed with so much earnestness upon him. We then separated. I think this was on Wednesday. On Thursday he left in pursuit of the army, which was then advancing toward Bowling Green, Ky.; on Friday a courier returned with a dispatch to General Thomas, who had been left in command of the forces for the defense of Nashville, notifying him to be in readiness to march with his division and General Palmer's[2] on Sunday morning. Another dispatch was received from General Buell by General Thomas to march unless a certain portion of Bragg's army should be in striking distance of Nashville, and in that event he (General Thomas), in his discretion, to leave General Palmer with his command, which he did. It was understood, though, at this time that Bragg's army had passed into Kentucky. General Thomas, notwithstanding Bragg had passed with his forces, upon my earnest solicitation left General Palmer with his division and marched with his own in compliance with General Buell's dispatch. With the courier returning to General Buell on Sunday morning I forwarded a letter, in which I urged and pressed the importance of General Thomas remaining at Nashville or his being returned in the event he marched before the letter reached him; but General Thomas and his command did not return. There was much said *pro* and *con* by General Buell and myself in regard to the evacuation of Nashville which is deemed immaterial in this deposition. This deposition has been made in the absence of dispatches and letters which would be important to refer to as to date and days, which are not remembered by me at this moment.

ANDREW JOHNSON
Military Governor and Brigadier-General of Tennessee.

OR, Ser. 1, XVI, Pt. I, 697-98.

1. Wiring from Cincinnati a month earlier, Lt. Col. Donn Piatt, judge advocate, had summoned Johnson, then in Washington, to appear before the Buell Commission in Baltimore on March 23. Some two weeks later, still in Cincinnati, Piatt telegraphed: "Your testimony is required. If you cannot attend here in person your deposition will be taken at Hon J Holts office tomorrow March 31st 1863[.] answer[.]" It would be another three weeks before the deposition was finally read to the commission on April 24. Piatt to Johnson, March 18, 1863, RG393, Dept. of the Ohio, Misc. Lets. Recd. (1862-68), NA; Piatt to Johnson, March 30, 1863, Tels. Recd., Sec. of War, RG107, NA.

2. John M. Palmer (1817-1900), Kentucky-born Illinois lawyer, had been state senator (1851-54, 1855-56) and delegate to the Washington Peace Conference (1861). Colonel of the 14th Ill. Inf. (May, 1861) and promoted major general (November, 1862), he served under Pope at Corinth and under Crittenden at Murfreesboro. Commander of the XIV Corps at Chattanooga, he was relieved from duty with Sherman in August, 1864, but the following February was in command of the Department of Kentucky. His postwar career included terms as Illinois governor (1869-73) and U. S. senator (1891-97). *BDAC*, 1422-23; Warner, *Generals in Blue*, 358-59.

From George W. Ansley[1]

Cleveland Apr 27 1863

to Gov Andey Johnson

Sir i have take the liberty of writing to you with regardes to the troopes that you are about to rais which the News papers state to bee about 25,000 in all and that you expected to get a portion of them from northen states as diferrent Govenors had signified their desposition to do and that Gov Johnson will not be curious as to the Collar of his soldiers[.][2] Now if this be true that Colard will answer your purpose i would rais you a battrie of Artillery or for som other Branch of the sirves[.] We have not meney blacks in this part of the state and sum of them have gon to Masschusets to inlist[.][3] i write this suposing that if you got eny soldiers from this state that you would have to ortherise the rasing of them as in all cases hear to fore. Gov tod has opposed or refuesed to rais eny such trupes but i due not know how he standes with regardes to raising troopes for you[.] With regardes to referance as to my qualities and character i think that i can give satisfactory[.] i Will hear state that i am white and of [*sic*] expect that all the officers will de white in any Companay that i should rais[.] if this should meat with your Aproval write me or iff yo want [*sic*] not like to Authorixe the raising in any other state than your one let me know as some other plan might be adopted[.]

Yours With Respect George. W. Ansley
Cleveland Ohio

ALS, T-Mil. Gov's Papers, 1863-65, Petitions.

1. George W. Ansley or Ensley (b. *c*1837) was a Canadian-born tinsmith with property worth $500. 1860 Census, Ohio, Cuyahoga, Cleveland, 5th Ward, 57; *Williston's Cleveland Directory* (1861-62), 12.

2. In an April 25, 1863, article on Johnson's authorization to raise 25,000 new troops, the Washington *National Intelligencer* claimed that he "will not be curious as to the complexion of his soldiers."

3. The 54th Massachusetts, a Negro regiment commanded by Col. Robert G. Shaw, recruited throughout the midwest. Dudley Cornish, *The Sable Arm: Negro Troops in the Union Army, 1861-1865* (New York, 1956), 110.

To Joseph S. Fowler,[1] Nashville

Washington April 29th 1863

To Jos S Fowler
Comptroller
Robert[2] whom I left in Charge of the House opposite the Capital you will please pay Same wages & tell him he must keep the property Safe[.] I will be back Soon[.] can you meet us in Cincinnati on Sunday or Monday[?] is there anything of interest going on in your vicinity[?]

Andrew Johnson

ALS, NcU, Southern Historical Col., Joseph S. Fowler Papers.

1. See *Johnson Papers*, IV, 323*n*.

2. Robert was one of three servants—Thomas and Martha the other two—who were with Johnson April-July, 1863. Of the three, only Robert had been with the governor the previous year. Pay Vouchers for Johnson and servants, March, 1862-March, 1863, April-July, 1863, Series 10, Johnson Papers, LC.

Authorization for Raising Troops[1]

Executive Department
Nashville, Tennessee.[2]
April 29, 1863

To Whom it May Concern:

By virtue of the authority conferred upon me by the Secretary of War under orders of the War Department dated March 28th 1863., "to raise troops for the United States service" &c (a copy of which is hereunto attached), I do hereby authorize Colonel Jesse E. Peyton[3] of Philadelphia, State of Pennsylvania, to recruit in the States of New Jersey, Pennsylvania, Delaware, and Maryland, (provided the consent of the respective Executives thereof shall have been previously obtained),[4] two Regiments of Volunteer Infantry, two of Cavalry and one Battery of Artillery for said service to serve for the term of three years or during the war, and to rendezvous at such place or places in Tennessee as may be hereafter indicated.

These forces will be armed and equipped by the Government, and horses will be furnished the Cavalry at the place of rendezvous. When two or more Companies are organized transportation will be furnished by the Government to the place of rendezvous.

Volunteers raised under this authority will, it is understood, be first engaged in an expedition for the redemption of Tennessee and especially the eastern portion thereof, and will thereafter be employed at such places and in such manner as the Government may direct.

Colonel Peyton is further authorized to muster said volunteers into the service of the United States.

Given under my hand this
Twenty-ninth day of April A.D. 1863.
Andrew Johnson
Brig. Genl. & Mil. Gov'r of Tennessee.

DS, DLC-JP.

1. Having been encouraged by Stanton to authorize recruiting in other states for Tennessee service, "if opportunity offers," the governor was now implementing the power previously granted him. Letter from Edwin M. Stanton, April 15, 1863.

2. The Nashville dateline belies the fact that this letter was issued in Washington and perhaps handed to the recipient.

3. Peyton (1815-1897), a Kentucky native, operated a Philadelphia dry goods establishment (1841-54) and was later in the western Virginia coal business. Helping to recruit Pennsylvania cavalry regiments during 1861, he had been empowered the following year to enlist a regiment for special service in Kentucky. Denied an extension, he was now attempting to raise troops under Johnson's aegis, only to be frustrated once again by Stanton's rescinding the governor's authority in June. An agent for the East Tennessee Relief Association (1865), he subsequently became a key organizer of the 1876 centennial celebration. Jesse E. Peyton, *Reminiscences of the Past* (Philadelphia, 1895), *passim; NUC,* CCCCLIV, 124; Letter from Jesse E. Peyton, June 12, 1863; Thomas W. Humes, *Report to the East Tennessee Relief Association at Knoxville* (Knoxville, 1865), 25.

4. In support of Peyton's efforts, Johnson wrote letters to the governors of these states and of New York, introducing Horace Maynard, "whom I have delegated to confer with you in reference to the organization of a military force, affecting . . . the interest of your respective States, but especially that State the loyal parties of which Mr. Maynard had the honor of representing in the last Congress." Johnson to "Sirs," April 30, 1863, Johnson Papers, LC.

From Ephraim W. M. King

St. Charles Hotel,
Washington, D. C. May 5th, 1863.[1]

Permit me to present to you my friend Mr. E. Cheek,[2] who will hand you this letter.[3] His home is Mound City on the west bank of the Mississippi, five miles above Memphis. He is an extraordinary man for Intelligence, Industry, Punctuality, and Perserverance.— He selected the location where he lives, the best for all purposes in the country, about 15 years ago, which was many years after the nabobs of Memphis[4] thought they owned all that was worth having. He had large means— He saw that was the only suitable place for a Town, on the west bank of the Mississippi for many miles above and below Memphis, and the point where all the travel east and west must cross the Mississippi eventually, as it was the only point for more than twenty miles above and below, where the high lands in all directions came together at the river where there was a good landing at all stages of the water, and it saved five miles travel to and from Memphis— The nabobs of Memphis, Overton & Co., who you know well, located where Memphis is built many years before, and for about three miles on the west bank in Arkansas. They claimed the exclusive Ferry privilege across the river— Cheek examined their title, discovered it was worthless, attacked their Ferrying by running a Ferry from Mound City to Memphis.— After five years law in the State and Federal Courts of Tennessee, he was fully sustained, and he had purchased the exclusive right of Ferrying from the legal owners and enjoyed it unmolested up to the time the Federals took Memphis.—[5] He consequently became better acquainted with the roads and people of Arkansas than any one else. He built up a pretty little town, named it Mound City, in opposition to Hopefield,[6] which belonged to the nabobs of Memphis and their hirelings— he broke it down as he did their Ferry, and because he avowed himself determined to aid his best with his boats and his negroes, in crushing this unrighteous Rebellion, and re-establishing the Union; the Rebel Traitors at Hopefield burned one of his Steamboats, burned all his Houses at Mound City, 22 in number, worth over $50,000, and he and his negroes barely escaped with life.—[7] He visits Washington with a petition to the President to try and get the Military Authorities to interpose and aid him in getting Restitution. You may rely fully and certainly upon what Cheek agrees to do, if possible for a man to do it. Give him any aid you can in getting the President to hear him and examine his petition.[8] It will be duly appreciated by him and confer a favor on

Your friend, E. W. M. King.

Broadside, DLC-Lincoln Papers.

1. This communication was obviously written several weeks earlier, inasmuch as Johnson's endorsement commending King to the President is dated April 11. This letterhead and dateline relate to its publication as a broadside.

2. Elijah Cheek (*c*1798-1864), a Virginia native, resided in Shelby County before moving to Mound City, Arkansas, in 1851. With his son, George W. he established the first Mound City Ferry, later investing in steamboats, toll bridges, and the Memphis and St. Francis Plank Road Company; by 1860 his personal property and real estate was worth $67,000. Arrested by the Federal authorities in 1862, he was charged with aiding the enemy. 1860 Census, Ark., Crittenden, Mound City, 10; *OR*, Ser. 2, II, 1552-53; R. B. Baker (Arkansas History Commission) to Andrew Johnson Project, July 14, 1976.

3. Evidently Cheek, through the good services of Memphis friends Jeptha Fowkes and Benjamin D. Nabers, as the accompanying endorsements show, brought his case to King's attention. This document is not the original letter but rather a "Synopsis of Judge King's letter to Hon. A. Johnston."

4. The early nineteenth century proprietors and their heirs were known as the "Memphis Nabobs." In 1794 Judge John Overton purchased a 5,000-acre tract from the heirs of John Rice, the original owner, and subsequently conveyed portions to Generals Andrew Jackson and James Winchester. These men began to promote the city's settlement after the Chickasaws' title to West Tennessee was extinguished in 1818. The second generation of nabobs included John Overton, Jr., and Marcus Winchester, both of whom had an interest in the ferry between Memphis and Hopefield, Arkansas. John P. Young, ed., *Standard History of Memphis, Tennessee* (Knoxville, 1912), 59-60; James E. Roper,

"Marcus B. Winchester: First Mayor of Memphis His Later Years," West Tenn. Hist. Soc. *Papers*, XIII (1959), 11-36 *passim*; Roper, "Marcus Winchester and the Earliest Years of Memphis," *Tenn. Hist. Quar.*, XXI (1962), 328.

5. In October, 1851, the Cheeks, with the permission of the Shelby County Court, began to ply the waters between Memphis and Mound City. Their ferry was an immediate success because the nabobs' ferry rights had been leased to two men who were providing unsatisfactory service. The Tennessee Supreme Court in 1855 decided the contest for control of Memphis ferry rights in favor of the Cheeks. Roper, "Marcus B. Winchester: Mayor," 28-36.

6. Hopefield, in Crittenden County, about five miles south of Mound City and directly across from Memphis, was largely owned by several wealthy Memphians as part of the Memphis and Hopefield Real Estate Company. Under the circumstances, the struggle for control of the ferry rights became a contest between promoters of the two potential Arkansas ports. Both settlements survived the Civil War, but Hopefield eventually succumbed to the encroaching waters of the Mississippi. *Ibid.*, 26; Allen W. Jones and Virginia Ann Buttry, "Military Events in Arkansas During the Civil War, 1861-1865," *Arkansas Historical Quarterly*, XXII (1963), 147.

7. The evidence concerning the attack does not support the contention that Hopefield rebels were responsible. Rather, the Cheek family was suspected of being in sympathy with the Confederates, and on January 13, 1863, the U. S. gunboat *Linden* shelled the area, troops landed, took several local citizens prisoner, and burned numerous buildings—many of them belonging to Elijah Cheek. *OR*, Ser. 1, XXII, Pt. I, 230-33; *OR-Navy*, Ser. 1, XXIV, 135.

8. Insisting that because he was loyal his slaves should be returned, Cheek the next day addressed a letter to the attorney general, who forwarded it to the President. Cheek to Edward Bates, May 6, 1863, Lincoln Papers, LC.

From Harriet Alexander[1]

17 East 19 St
New York, May 6th/63

Gov Johnson.
Dear Friend.

I have just recieved a letter from my long absent husband. he says that he waited 48 hours in Nashville to see you but had not the pleasure of seeing you at last, he is anxious to see me but says he cannot send for me unless he is stationed at or near Nashville. Will you not see in to his case, tell him what you can do for him, and see that he gets a leave to visit you again. Oh I do want to see you my self[.] I think I might do something to help him along[.] Please arrange it so that he can go to Nashville and then I will be there immediately[.]

I hope you will write to my husband, address him

Capt. J. H. Alexander
7th Regt Ky Cavalry
Franklin, Tenn

I am quite well, hope you are well and safe at home[.] Will you be kind enough to write me immeadiately what the prospects is of me meeting my husband soon in Nashville[.][2] I will surely go if he gets a place under your directions[.]

With kind reguards believe me
Affectionately Yours
Mrs Alexander

P S Please address
Mrs Alexander
No 17 East 19 St New York

ALS, DLC-JP.

1. Harriet Alexander (*c*1830-*fl*1881), Virginia-born, importuned Johnson on two other occasions for a position for her husband, Julius H. Alexander; in July, 1865, requesting a marshal's appointment, either in Florida or South Carolina, and in May, 1868, asking help in obtaining some unspecified post. Alexander (*c*1820-*c*1870), a Polish-born New York merchant and at this time provost marshal in Franklin, was discharged in February, 1864. 1860 Census, N.Y., New York City, 15th Ward, 65; New York city directories (1859-81), *passim*; *OR*, Ser. 1. XXIII, Pt. II, 425; *Official Army Register: Volunteers*, IV, 1226; Mrs. Alexander to Johnson, July 31, 1865, May 31, 1868, Johnson Papers, LC.

2. Evidently the governor did not respond. Six weeks later she was reminding him to "see my husband and do all you can for him. You toled me at Washington if I would come to your city you thought you could give me a place where I could make my self useful in careing for the sick and wounded[.]" Mrs. Alexander to Johnson, June 23, 1863, *ibid.*

From Bezaleel P. Wells

May 8, 1863, Camp Chase, Ohio; ALS, T-Mil. Gov's Papers, 1862-65, Petitions.

Captain of 2nd Mich. Cav. requests commission to raise a "Regiment of Colored [Cavalry] Troops Officered by white Officers of nearly Two years Experiance in the field, Some of them native born Tennisseeans.... There can be large numbers of Recruits raised in this State and Indiana and Illinois the main portion from the Contraband Camps of Corinth Grand Juction and Island, No 10."

From Joseph J. Lewis[1]

Treasury Department,
Office of Internal Revenue,
Washington, May 12th 1863

Sir:

It is represented by the Collector of Internal Revenue at Russellville, Ky.,[2] that large quantities of spirits are distilled in Robertson Co., Tenn., and that dissatisfaction and complaint exists among the distillers in his district, because they are obliged to compete with the distillers of Tennessee, on whose liquors no Excise duty has been collected. There seems to be no good reason why the Excise Laws of the United States should not again be enforced in so much of the State of Tennessee as is under the protection of the Government, and it is proposed to appoint a Collector and Assessor for the district comprising all that part of Tennessee east of the Tennessee River. Among the recommendations on file in this office, are those of Messrs. Q. C. DeGrove[3] for the office of Collector, and Wm. Driver and W. R. Horley[4] for the office of Assessor. As some time has elapsed since the date of their recommendations, I have thought it prudent to consult you, before advising any appointments.

Any suggestion from you upon this subject will receive immediate consideration.[5]

Yours Respectfully, Joseph J Lewis,
Commissioner

Hon. Andrew Johnson,
Military Governor, &c.,
Nashville, Tenn.

LS, DLC-JP; DNA-RG58, Office of the Commissioner, Press Copies, Misc. Lets. Sent, Vol. 8.

1. Joseph J. Lewis (1801-1883), a native Pennsylvanian and West Chester lawyer, went to Washington to serve as commissioner of internal revenue (1863-65), returning to private practice until his retirement in 1878. Throughout his career, Lewis actively participated in politics as Whig, Antislavery Democrat, and finally Republican. *NCAB*, XXVII, 413.

2. The *U. S. Official Register* (1863), 35-41, lists no collector at Russellville. The reference may have been to George Blakesby, located at nearby Bowling Green.

3. Quincy C. DeGrove (*c*1828-1905), Tennessee native and Davidson County revenue collector, moved to New York City in 1860, became a stockbroker, member of the New York Stock Exchange, and conducted business continuously until a week before his death. *Nashville Bus. Dir.* (1860-61), 154; *Trow's New York City Directory* (1861), 216; New York *Times*, August 23, 1905.

4. William Driver (1803-1886), of Salem, Massachusetts, retired as a sea captain and moved to Nashville in 1837 because of his wife's poor health. He had gained lasting fame when, in September, 1831, he carried the surviving Pitcairners from their temporary home in Tahiti back to their native island aboard the whaler *Charles Doggett*. Employed variously as salesman, driver, and claims agent, he remained an unflinching unionist, and upon the arrival of Federal troops, his flag, "Old Glory," was the first flown over the capitol. In March, 1863, he was one of three commissioners appointed by Rosecrans to report upon "the amount of damage sustained by citizens from the occupation or destruction of their property by the forces of the United States." Jill K. Garrett and Iris H. McClain, *Old City Cemetery, Nashville, Tennessee: Tombstone Inscriptions* ([Columbia, Tenn., 1971]), 31; Porch, *1850 Census, Davidson*, 359; Robert B. Nicolson, *The Pitcairners* (Sydney, 1965), 105-6; Maslowski, *Treason Must Be Made Odious*, 89-90. For William R. Hurley, see *Johnson Papers*, IV, 75*n*.

5. According to the endorsement, Johnson replied by telegram on June 1, asking that no appointment be made until he could write Lewis, to which the latter replied: "Please address Secretary Chase on all matters relating to appointments hereafter." Lewis to Johnson, June 3, 1863, Johnson Papers, LC.

From M. Elizabeth Young[1]

[Nashville] May 12, 1863

Gov Johnson
My dear Sir

If Mrs. [P-ane?][2] comes to you to keep this house for her oblige me *personally* by refusing— she has had a Prisoner in the house nearly the whole time since you have been gone—and altogether our situation has been intolerable— I have defered making a change until I see you— be so kind as to call as soon as possible— I must make some change—as anoyance & insults are added to other things after all I have done for them.

I send this to Robert to give to you as soon as you arrive—[3] Be so kind as to attend to it immediately—

Yours truley
M E Young

Tuesday, May 12"/63/
I should think you could find some Union family that would be glad to have it— if you give it up she will then get the Military to hold it— either she must go out o[r] I will— Mrs Washington[4] the owner is very anxious for me to have it— excuse my troubling you—but I been more anoyed than I can express[.] compeling her to pay rent would soon make her decamp— she has been receiving 30$ per week for this woman—that is confined here—and obliging evey one in the house to submit to the constant presence and tramping in and out of Gaurds— I write this in Aunts name—

M E Young

ALS, DLC-JP.
1. M. Elizabeth [Lizzie] Young (*c*1815-*fl*1895), daughter of John and Caroline Somerville Young, had been one of Johnson's fellow-boarders at the St. Cloud during the civil governorship and on the eve of the war resided with her aunt, Martha Somerville (*c*1803-*fl*1877), in the household of Nashville editor Allen A. Hall. Subsequently she sought through the President's intercession a job in the treasury office or a trading permit for Chattanooga and Atlanta and a pension for her aunt, who had lost two brothers "in the service of their country." 1860 Census, Tenn., Davidson, Nashville, 3rd Ward, 89; *Nashville Directory* (1877), 336, 390; Jane H. Thomas, *Old Days in Nashville* (Nashville, 1897), 41, 100-101; WPA, Davidson Marriage Book I (1789-1837), 50; Young to Johnson, April 13, 1868, January 17, 1869, Johnson Papers, LC.
2. Not identified.
3. Robert Johnson was in Nashville awaiting his father's return from Washington.
4. Possibly Mary (b. *c*1803), widow of Nashville attorney Thomas Washington. 1850 Census, Tenn., Davidson, Nashville, 241; Nashville city directories (1861-66), *passim*.

From John S. Brien[1]

Nashville May 13 1863

To Gov Johnson
[Washington]
Dr. Cheatham & wife[2] are ordered to Alton prison tomorrow morning[.] It is of the utmost importance to your plans here that he be not sent off until after your return[.][3] telegraph Gen Rosecrans at Murfreesboro to Suspend the order until you can get home— your presence here is very important[.]

yours truly John S Brien

ALS, DLC-JP.
1. For Brien, Nashville lawyer and former judge, see *Johnson Papers*, V, 247*n*.
2. Dr. William A. Cheatham, former physician of the Tennessee insane asylum, and his wife, the sister-in-law of Gen. John H. Morgan, were arrested for passing information through a Confederate spy (actually an employee of Federal police chief Truesdail) and were shipped north as far as Louisville, where Mrs. Cheatham's health prohibited their

continuing on to Alton. *OR*, Ser. 2, V, 709-10; Tels. Recd., Vol. 48, U. S. Mil. Tel., RG107, NA; M. Goldsmith to Col. Mundy, May 20, 1863, Johnson Papers, LC; for Cheatham, see *Johnson Papers*, V, 508*n*.

3. Presumably, the testimony of the Cheathams would assist in Johnson's campaign against Truesdail and his cohorts. Detained in Louisville by his wife's illness, the governor two weeks later asked Judge Advocate General Joseph Holt to intercede, holding the pair in Louisville pending orders from Rosecrans. A month later, by joint order of Rosecrans and Truesdail, the Cheathams were released both from arrest and exile. William P. Mellen to Salmon P. Chase, May 15, 1863, Special Agent's Reports, RG36, NA; Nashville *Press*, June 20, 1863.

From Edward H. East

Nashville, Tenn., May 13, 1863

Govenor Johnson

Two young men, named Reuben S Smith and E P Smith[1] were sent as Prisoners of war from this City to Louisville. After they had left we were inform'ed that they had deserted from the rebel Army and came to the Camp of Gen Hazen[2] and then conducted him to a detached Camp of rebels, whom he captured. I saw Col Martin[3] the Provost Marshal and he agrees with me that they should not be exchanged, as an infamous punishment would be inflicted upon them. They desire to be released and stay North. Will you please Call the attention of Col Mundy[4] or Gen Boyle to this.

I am Edward H East

ALS, DNA-RG109, CSR (Richard S. Smith).

1. Richard S. (b. *c*1837), 3rd sergeant, Co. G, and Elias P. Smith (b. *c*1843), private, two Cincinnati brothers living in Nashville, enlisted in the 11th Tenn. Inf., CSA, in May, 1861. The following May, upon reorganization of the regiment, they were both privates in Co. B. Captured in June, Richard escaped from Sandusky in November and rejoined the unit on the eve of the battle of Stones River, the regiment's first major engagement. On the retreat they deserted at Shelbyville in March, 1863, were captured, sent to Louisville, and in May transferred to Camp Chase where they were discharged upon taking the oath. CSR, RG109; John B. Lindsley, ed., *The Military Annals of Tennessee, Confederate* (Nashville, 1886), 295; *Tennesseans in the Civil War*, II, 370.

2. William B. Hazen (1830-1887), a West Pointer (1855) who had served on the frontier, in the Pacific Northwest, and in Texas, became colonel of the 41st Ohio in October, 1861, and was with Buell at Shiloh. Promoted brigadier in April, 1863, he took part in Rosecrans' campaigns and battles in Tennessee and was with Sherman at Atlanta and on his "March to the Sea." Appointed colonel of the 38th Inf. in regular service in 1866, he saw duty on the western frontier until appointed chief signal officer with the rank of brigadier in 1880. Warner, *Generals in Blue*, 225-26.

3. John A. Martin (1839-1889), Pennsylvania-born editor of the Atchison (Kansas) *Champion* (1858-89), was a Republican who served as secretary of the Wyandotte constitutional convention and as senator in the first state legislature (1861), before resigning to become lieutenant colonel, 8th Kans. Inf. in October. Provost marshal of Nashville and after Chickamauga a brigade commander, he was mustered out of service in November, 1864, returning to his newspaper and Kansas politics. A prohibitionist, he established a temperance policy for the party and state while serving as governor (1885-89), and he pioneered in legal and penal reform and in settling labor disputes by arbitration. *DAB*, XII, 341-42.

4. For Marcellus Mundy, see *Johnson Papers*, V, 323*n*.

From Edward R. S. Canby[1]

War Department Washington City,
May 14 1863

His Excellency. A. Johnson
Mil. governor &c. Nashville, Tenn.
Sir

I am instructed by the Secretary of War to say that it is seen in the authority given Colonel Stockton, of Michigan,[2] to raise a Brigade that the condition of service in Tennessee is indicated or at least implied for these troops.[3] Although it is the intention of the War Department to give them this destination the enrollment or enlistment should be for the service of the United States unconditionally and without qualification expressed or implied of any character whatever.[4] It will, in his judgment be exceedingly unwise to make any promises or hold out any inducements as the exigencies of the service may prevent their being realized, and this would lead to embarrassments of the gravest character.[5]

I have the honor to be

Very Respectfully, Sir, Your Obdt. Servt.
Ed. R. S. Canby
Brig. Genl & A.A.G.

Copy, DLC-E. M. Stanton Papers, Vol. 12.

1. See *Johnson Papers*, V, 217*n*.

2. Thomas B. W. Stockton (1805-1890), New York native and West Point graduate (1827), served as a lieutenant, until his resignation nine years later to become a civil engineer (1836-46). Colonel of Michigan regiments in the Mexican and Civil wars (1861-63), he was held prisoner at Richmond from June to August, 1862. In his May 18 letter of resignation he explained that he was "accepting the position that Gov. Andrew Johnson of Tennessee has given me, to raise *three* Regiments to Serve under him in Redeeming that State from Rebeldom." After the war he had a "forwarding and commission business" until he retired in 1872. CSR, RG94, NA; Heitman, *Register*, I, 927; *West Point Register* (1970), 217; Buffalo (N. Y.) *Commercial Advertiser Directory* (1861), 77, 132, 264; Flint *Daily News*, December 9, 1890.

3. Citing War Department Orders of March 28, 1863, Johnson's authorization addressed "To whom it may concern" and dated May 4, provided for raising three regiments of three-year enlistees from New York, Michigan, and Illinois: "Volunteers so raised, will, it is understood, be first engaged in an expedition for the redemption of Tennessee, and especially the eastern portion thereof." Johnson Papers, LC.

4. War Department General Order 15, February 15, 1862, prohibited enlistments conditioned upon the place of service. *OR*, Ser. 3, I, 889.

5. Johnson's subsequent correspondence with Washington did not contest Stanton's decision but instead called for more troops for the expedition which Gen. Ambrose E. Burnside, commander of the Army of the Ohio, promised the governor would be prepared for the liberation of East Tennessee. Letter from Ambrose E. Burnside, May 16, 1863; Letter to Abraham Lincoln, May 29, 1863.

From Jacob S. Maurer[1]

Genl. Hospital No 12[2]
Nashville Tenn. May 15" 1863.

His Excellency Governor Johnson
of the State of Tennessee.
Sir.

I have the honor to Send you a list of the names of Soldiers from the State of Tennessee who have died in this Hospital.[3] Their Captains have either neglected to send a list of the effects or something has prevented them from being sent for by the heirs.

As there is a list of every man from your state, in the Adjutant General's Office, you could oblige me very greatly and assist the friends of the deceased in getting these effects, by having sent to me at this Hospital the residence of each one as far as can be ascertained. Also please inform them that to procure such effects it is necessary to send a Duplicate Receipt and a Power of Attorney, which is generally made out for the surgeon in charge. I have the honor of remaining

Your Most Obet. Servt, J S Maurer
A. A. Surg. U. S. A in charge

LS, T-Mil. Gov's Papers, 1862-65, Corres. to Andrew Johnson.

1. Jacob S. Maurer (b. 1837), Hagerstown, Maryland, native, lived in Chambersburg, Pennsylvania, before graduating from the Jefferson Medical College of Philadelphia (1859). Having entered the 77th Pa. Vols. as assistant surgeon (1861), he resigned in November, 1862, and early the next February took a contract to work with the sick and wounded at Nashville. Executive officer of Hospital No. 16 until April 21, he was put in charge of Hospital No. 12 until September, 1863, when at his request his contract was cancelled. He then became acting assistant surgeon and medical purveyor for the XVIII and XXV Army Corps in Virginia, serving until March, 1865. Medical Officers and Physicians, 1861-1865, RG94, NA.

2. The Broadway Hotel, corner of Broad and Cherry streets, was Hospital No. 12 at this time. Nashville *Union*, May 12, 1863.

3. The following twenty-two names appear: "Wm. Lane, Alex. Cambell, H. Bart, William Rodgers, Abraham Feltis, F. Farner, S. Whitney, W. W. Colwell, Jesse Davis, John M. Davis, M. V. Thornton, Patrick Clasky, Jos. M. Roberts, Andrew Steward, James A. Riggs, Wm. R. Love, James R. Esbo, H. Dyke, Elijah Staunton, Gideon Knoblett, J. W. Robinson, J. R. P. Snelling."

From Ambrose E. Burnside[1]

Cincinnati May 16 1863

To Gov Andy Johnson

Your dispatch received[.] I have no contention of abandoning the movement into East Tenn[.] in fact I am determined to inaugurate it at the earliest possible moment[.] I am very much gratified that you approve of my statement to the Court[.][2]

A E Burnside Maj Gen

Tel, DLC-JP.

1. See *Johnson Papers*, V, 139*n*.

2. On April 13, Burnside, commander of the Department of the Ohio, had issued General Orders No. 38 to the effect that all persons found within Union lines committing "acts for the benefit of the enemies of our country will be tried as spies," including those in the "habit of declaring sympathies for the enemy." Meantime, Democratic congressmen made speeches encouraging resistance to the draft; Clement L. Vallandigham, addressing an audience at Mt. Vernon, Ohio, on May 1, contended that Lincoln was a tyrant, reminding his hearers that "resistance to tyrants is obedience to God." Arrested by Burnside's order, he was arraigned before a military commission in Cincinnati. On May 11, having learned that application had been made for a writ of habeas corpus, Burnside made a statement in opposition, asserting that with the nation in a state of civil war, he had a duty to keep his department "in the best possible condition." While he and the troops had a duty "to avoid saying anything that would weaken the army," it was "equally the duty of every citizen to avoid the same evil," the greater responsibility falling "upon the public men and upon the public press," behooving "them to be careful as to what they say. They must not use license and plead that they are exercising liberty." Ben: Perley Poore, *The Life and Public Services of Ambrose E. Burnside: Soldier, Citizen, Statesman* (Providence, 1882), 203-9; Louisville *Journal*, May 13, 1863.

To Edwin M. Stanton

Louisville[1] May 17 1863.

Hon E. M. Stanton
Secy of War

It is important that the investigation of Operations of the Army police at Nashville should be commenced at once[.] The Character of the Govt. demands it[.] The abuses are enormous and should be arrested[.] I would respectfully suggest that the appointment of Genl Casey,[2] Hon Horace Maynard and Judge Jno S Bryen[3] of Nashville as the Commission[.] Please advise me of your action[.][4]

Andrew Johnson

Tel, DNA-RG107, Tels. Recd., Sec. of War, Vol. 28 (1863).

1. The governor was detained in Louisville on his way back from Washington to Nashville by the illness of his wife. William P. Mellen to Salmon P. Chase, May 15, 1863, Special Agents Reports, RG36, NA.

2. Silas Casey (1807-1882), Rhode Island native and West Point graduate (1826), participated in the Mexican War, served many years on the Pacific coast, and in 1855 attained the rank of lieutenant colonel. Appointed brigadier general of volunteers in

August, 1861, he saw active field service in the Peninsular campaign, commanded a provisional brigade in the Washington defenses, and was president of a board to examine candidates for officers of Negro troops. After the war he reverted to the regular rank of colonel, retiring in 1868. *Infantry Tactics*, which he had compiled and edited, was adopted by the government in 1862. Warner, *Generals in Blue*, 74-75.

3. John S. Brien.

4. Apparently this commission was never organized; however, Rosecrans appointed Captain Temple Clark of Gen. Richard W. Johnson's staff to investigate charges against William Truesdail and the army police. Clark, in a June 2 report, recommended "that the army police be continued." Fitch, *Annals*, 353-56.

From Three Illinois Soldiers[1]

In Camp Near Murfreesboro May 22d *1863*

Maj-Gen-Johnson
Govenor of Tenn

Sir I find in the papers that you are about to raise some negro regiments and supposeing you want some good men and men that can give good Reccomendation if nessary—to officer then and men that has seen service—and being as we would like to do a little more for our country than we are doing now we have come to the conclusion to offer our services to you and asking the faver of you to try us— we have been in the army two years the first of next month—and we have had a good many skermishes with the enemy and Some pretty good Battles—

we was enrolled in St Louis Mo—the lst of June—1861 and we took a tour through Mo—to Rolla where we spent our first winter and in Feb—(1862) we marched on Price[2] at Springfield Mo—where on our approach fled by night[.] we chase'd him into Ark—and there he was reinforced by Vandorn[3] and gave Battle on the 6 7 and 8th of March (the Battle of Pea ridge)—[4] that was our first— then we next came to Corinth and around through Mississippi and Tenn after Bragg into Ky.—and at louisville we was all organized over with new troops and with Maj Gen Buel at our head we set out on the lst of Oct 1862 after Bragg again[.] we overtook him at Chaplin hill[5]—and had a few Rounds and he fled again— then on our road to Nashville we had another skirmish and then at nolensville[6] our Divis (1*st* Divis 20th A—Corps—under Gen Jeff. C. Davis) had a contest of about two hours and again he left— then the last was the Battle of Stones river—where we lost our gallant col—T. D. Williams[7] 25th Ills—and a good number of men but I have come off through all without a scratch— and thinking there will be a chance for us in your comand we take the oppertunity to drop you a line and hope you will drop us a line and let us know if there is a chance for us within your command— you can Direct to Either one of us— there is 3 of us[.] we will officer one company or we would do as you would think best but hopeing there is a show for us we will close by giveing you our address— we can give good Reccomendation if you want—and I think if some of us was examined we would be able to fill something more than a co-office— I would beg an answer to let us know—what we can hope at least—while we remain your most obedient—

Hiram. J. Ward
Sergt. Jerman Ingalls,
Henry. W. Robinson

P.S. direct to
Co G, 25th Ills Vols
3d Brig—1st Divis 20th A—C—
Murfreesboro Tenn

LS, T-Mil. Gov's Papers, 1862-65, Petitions.

1. Hiram J. Ward (*c*1841-1901), Jerman (German) Ingalls (1842-1930), and Henry W. Robinson (*c*1837-1864) were all originally privates, with Ingalls becoming 5th sergeant May 1, 1863, and Robinson, corporal January 1, 1864. Ward and Ingalls completed their enlistment and were mustered out at Springfield, Illinois, on September 1, 1864, but Robinson, a farmer and Seneca County, Ohio, native, was wounded at Chickamauga and Peachtree Creek, dying August 10, 1864, in a Chattanooga hospital. CSR, RG94, NA; Pension files (Ward, Ingalls), RG15, NA.

2. For Gen. Sterling Price, see *Johnson Papers*, V, 261*n*.

3. Earl Van Dorn (1820-1863), Mississippi-born West Point graduate (1842), fought in the Mexican and Seminole wars before serving on the frontier as an Indian fighter. Resigning his major's commission in January, 1861, he was immediately named major general of Mississippi forces and soon after a major general in the Confederate army. He briefly led a division in Virginia before commanding the Trans-Mississippi Department (January-May, 1862) and subsequently the Department of Mississippi with headquarters at Vicksburg. Defeated at Corinth, he was transferred to a cavalry command which he led successfully at Holly Springs in December, 1862, and Thompson's Station, Tennessee, in March. He was killed early in May, 1863, at Spring Hill, by Dr. George Peters, a personal enemy who claimed that Van Dorn had "violated the sanctity of his home." Warner, *Generals in Gray*, 314-15; Robert G. Hartje, *Van Dorn: The Life and Times of a Confederate General* (Nashville, 1967).

4. Price spent the winter of 1861-62 at Springfield. When Gen. Samuel Curtis moved against him in February with 12,000 men and forty cannon, he retreated into the Boston Mountains of northern Arkansas, joining forces with Generals Ben McCullough, James McIntosh, and Albert Pike. Van Dorn, as commander of the Trans-Mississippi Department, took personal charge and ordered an attack on Curtis, who had taken up a defensive position at Pea Ridge. After three days' fighting, Van Dorn was obliged to retreat to the Arkansas River. Robert E. Shalhope, *Sterling Price: Portrait of a Southerner* (Columbia, Mo., 1971), 198-99; Boatner, *Civil War Dictionary*, 530, 533, 627-28.

5. Chaplin Hills was an alternate name for the battle of Perryville, Kentucky, October 8, 1862. *Ibid.*, 642.

6. Nolensville was one of the preliminary actions during the Murfreesboro campaign. On December 6, 1862, Gen. Jefferson C. Davis' three brigades advanced upon the town (northwest of Murfreesboro) and dislodged the enemy. Two miles beyond Nolensville they encountered more resistance, with the gray line occupying a range of high, rocky hills through which the Nolensville and Triune Pike passed at Knob Gap. Two hours of fighting resulted in the Confederates' again being forced back, after which the Federals bivouacked for the night. *OR*, Ser. 1, XX, Pt. I, 262-63, 269.

7. Thomas D. Williams (*c*1827-1863) served as captain, Co. G, and as colonel, 25th Ill. Inf. (1862-63), dying January 6 of a wound received at Murfreesboro. CSR, RG94, NA.

Order to Robert Johnson

State of Tennessee
Executive Department
Nashville May 22. 1863.[1]

Whereas: By an order of the Secretary of War, Robert Johnson—Colonel, first Regiment, Tennessee Cavalry, is authorized to raise in the S[t]ate of Tennessee, under the direction of Andrew Johnson, Military Governor of the State, one Brigade of Cavalry, and by special Field Order No. 136—Extract VIII—Department of the Cumberland, date at Murfreesboro, May 19th 1863, the said Col. Robert Johnson was temporarily relieved from duty with his Regiment to carry out the order of the Secretary of War.

Now therefore, I Andrew Johnson, Military, Governor of the State of Tennessee, do order, that the said Col. Robert Johnson, report himself to these Head Quarters without delay, and establish his Head Quarters in the City of Nashville—until farther order.[2]

Andrew Johnson
Mil Gov & B Genl

DS, DLC-JP.

1. Inasmuch as Johnson at this date was in Louisville on his way home from Washington, it is presumed that this order was written by a secretary and signed upon the governor's return to Nashville at month's end.

2. This wrote finis to Robert's active military career. Mustered in at Camp Dennison in February, 1862, for three-years' service, he became colonel of the 1st Tenn. Cav. in October. As of May 19,1863, he was placed on detached duty, first to raise a brigade, in which he was unsuccessful, and then for unspecified activities at Nashville until May, 1864, when he resigned, explaining that he had been "solicited to undertake and perform" non-military duties and "in view of all the Surrounding facts, and circumstances," had "come to the conclusion, that the public Service, and the interests of my Regiment, will be promoted by my retiring." He subsequently became private secretary to his father. CSR, RG94, NA; Robert Johnson to Gen. W. D. Whipple, May 4, 1864, in *ibid.*

From Lewis S. Wilson[1]

Jackson Tenn May 26 1863

Gov. Johnson

I have one hundred & ninety five men aggregate present[.] authorities doubt your having the right to order the Regt from this place[.] the matter is being investigated[.] your orders have been referred to Genl Grant[.] have had no chance to bring the men to Camp although I have made every effort[.] I wish for full time to get the men together[.]

L. S. Wilson Lt Col

ALS, T-Mil. Gov's Papers, 1862-65, Petitions.

1. Possibly Lewis Wilson (d. *c*1895), Ohio native and Cincinnati chief of police on the eve of the war, who was originally colonel, 2nd Ohio Vols., becoming a captain, 19th U. S. Inf., until his resignation in July, 1864. He returned to Cincinnati after the war. This rather cryptic message may be seen as an evidence of the governor's reactivated campaign to assemble troops for the recovery of East Tennessee. CSR, RG94, NA; ACP Branch, RG94, NA; Powell, *Army List*, 681; Cincinnati city directories (1858-66), *passim*.

From William B. Campbell

Nashville May 27 1863

Govr. A. Johnson
Dear Sir

Genl P. Anderson[1] now a prisoner on *parole* in this city, is in very bad health and I think no injury to the public service will be done by giving him a *parole* for *twenty* or *thirty* days to return to his home, that he may recruit his health. Mr East is not willing to grant the *parole* unless directed by you, and I earnestly hope you will write to Mr East giving him the authority to *parole* him for 30 days.— I would also state that the wife of Col Wm. L Martin[2] is in very bad health, and I ask for him the same *parole* which I ask for Genl Anderson. Will you be pleased to write to Mr East on the subject. I would not make the request until your arrival here,[3] but the cases need immediate action[.]

I am confident no injury can result from paroling them, and it will be an act of kindness and humanity to them which I know they with their friends will duly appreciate.

Your attention to this matter will be appreciated by your friend & Obt Svt

W B Campbell

Mrs Anderson is here attending on her husband, and requests me to say to you that she was the wife of Robert M Burton[4]—and that she *is now* & *has been your friend* and she begs that you will *parole* her husband—

WBC—

ALS, DLC-JP.

1. Paulding Anderson.

2. Mrs. Mary L. Barry Martin (b. *c*1802), William Martin's third wife, was a native Tennessean. 1860 Census, Tenn., Wilson, 10th Dist., 156; McBride and Robison, *Biographical Directory*, I, 504.

3. For over three months Johnson had been away from Nashville, not returning until May 30. Nashville *Dispatch*, May 31, 1863.

4. Virginia-born Martha H. Donelson (b. *c*1809) had married Robert M. Burton (1800-1843) in 1826. A native of Granville County, North Carolina, he began law practice at Lebanon, Tennessee, in 1823, served in the General Assembly (1827-29), attended the 1834 constitutional convention, and was an unsuccessful Democratic candidate for Congress in 1839. A widow for nearly twenty years, Mrs. Burton had been married to Paulding Anderson for less than two years. McBride and Robison, *Biographical Directory*, I, 104-5; Sistler, *1850 Tenn. Census*, I, 246; Daughters of the American Revolution, Marriage Record Book I, Davidson County, 1789-1837 (Nashville, 1952), 92.

From Three Iowa Privates

May 27, 1863, Ford Donelson; ALS, T-Mil. Gov's Papers, 1862-65, Petitions.

James S. Young, Porter D. Williams, and C. W. Brawers of Co. H, 5th Iowa Cav., aware of the plan to create Tennessee Negro regiments, inquire whether it is possible for privates to obtain commissions to raise companies. There are "a great many blacks here that is willing to engage in the service of their country. We ask to be permitted to recruit a company and we think that we could raise several companies[.]"

To Abraham Lincoln

Louisville[1] May 29 1863.

His Excellency
Abraham Lincoln

It is beleived that the third Division of ninth (9) Army Corps at Suffolk Genl Getty Comdg[2] had better be added to Burnside's Command— We hope this can be done as it will enable him to prosecute with success the Expedition into East Tenn[.][3] This part of the State should be entered— The oppressions & inhumanity daily inflicted are indescribable & must be redressed[.] if the Govt does not give that protection guaranteed by the Constitution the Tenn forces should be massed & permitted to enter East Tenn[.] This they will do though they to a man perish in the attempt[.] This summer should not pass without protection being extended[.] Genl Burnside is in high spirits & confident of being able to enter the State[.] I have received much encouragement in getting up forces & think I shall succeed[.][4]

Andrew Johnson

Tel, DLC-Lincoln Papers.

1. Still detained in Louisville by his wife's illness, the governor would travel to Nashville on the next day.

2. George W. Getty (1819-1901), Georgetown, D. C., native and West Point graduate (1840), served in Mexico, Florida, and Kansas before the war. He commanded four batteries during the Peninsular campaign and was Burnside's acting chief of artillery at Antietam. Promoted to brigadier general of volunteers in September, 1862, he commanded the 3rd division of the IX Corps, was acting inspector general of the Army of the Potomac in early 1864, and led a division of the VI Corps at the Wilderness where he was wounded. After the war he commanded the districts of Texas and New Mexico and for six years the artillery school at Fortress Monroe, retiring in 1883. Warner, *Generals in Blue*, 170-71; *NCAB*, XII, 259-60.

3. This direct appeal to the President comes as the culmination of Burnside's unsuccessful efforts to persuade General-in-Chief Henry Halleck to assign Getty's division to the Tennessee theatre. *OR*, Ser. 1, XXIII, Pt. II, 338, 355.

4. Lincoln responded that Getty's division could not be spared at that time. Lincoln to Johnson, May 28, 1863, Johnson Papers, LC.

Remarks at Nashville[1]

May 30, 1863

Gov. Johnson said he had no speech to make at this time. He would merely tender his sincere thanks to citizens and soldiers for the kind reception they had given him. As he said, when he came more than a year ago, *he returned to them with the olive branch of peace, the Constitution, and the laws.* [Cries of "Good!" "That's the talk, Governor!"] There can be no peace, except by obedience to the Constitution and the Laws. You who have prospered and been happy under the Constitution and the Laws of your country, ought to submit now, and be happy once more. ["God bless Governor Johnson!" shouted some one, possessed of a clear, ringing voice. "Amen!" called out another.] "I am come to ameliorate the condition of my fellow-citizens. [Cheers.] I have a responsible duty to perform to you, and to my country, and God willing, that duty will be faithfully performed, as far as my humble ability extends. Did I ever deceive you? [Never, never.] Never, nor do I wish or intend to do so now. I wish to retain that confidence. Shall I have it? [Yes! you shall!"] I will not flatter you. I will not deceive you. This is my adopted State; in it are all that I hold dearly. Here are my wife and family, my property, my all; and I desire to free the State from treason and rebellion. Be true to yourselves, to your country, and to her laws, and all will be well. In conclusion, Governor Johnson said he was not fond of making speeches; he seldom made one unless he was obliged to do so. Some other day he would lay before his fellow-citizens the policy of the United States Government toward his adopted State, and address them on the absorbing topics of the day.[2]

Nashville *Press*, June 1, 1863.

1. On the evening of May 30 Johnson, his wife Eliza, daughter Mary Stover and her children, and William A. Browning returned to Nashville, the governor and his aide having been in Washington and the family's having been in Louisville. Met at the depot by many citizens, Gillem's 10th Tenn. Inf., the Post band, and a portion of the 1st Tenn. Cav., the governor's entourage immediately entered two open carriages and proceeded via College and Cedar streets to Johnson's residence, with the band playing "Hail Columbia" and the party "repeatedly cheered on the way." Upon arrival at their destination, "loud calls were made for a speech." Nashville *Press*, June 1, 1863.

2. Although not delivered in the capital, this promised discourse came nearly three months later in the Speech at Franklin, August 22, 1863.

From David P. and James W. Bullock

[June, 1863, Gallatin]; ALS, DLC-JP.

Citizens complain that they are to be sent by Gen. Eleazer A. Paine, commander at Gallatin, "from our homes . . . into an enemys Country against our concent"; they "protest against the injustice done us and our families," concluding with "there has been no duty required of us by the Federal authorities that we have not been willing to perform." [Endorsement: "Rec'd Executive office June 4th 1863"]

To William S. Rosecrans

Nashville June lst 1863

Gen'l Rosecrans

Your telegram of April 4th has Just been received[.] I was expected to return to Nashville long before I did[.] it was therefore not forwarded. the principal portion is new to me[.] Gen'l *Davis* has never furnished me with any information touching or affecting your character as a citizen or soldier in the slightest degree[.] My opinion of *Truesdail* and his establishment was communicated sometime since.[1] it was predicated upon fact entirely satisfactory to my mind and it has undergone no change. You state in your telegram that you consider me your friend. You are right in this and no one will go further than I in vindication of your character. I have never believed & do not now believe that you have fully understood the character & extent of the proceedings under *Truesdail* direction. it will afford me much pleasure to visit you in person[2] in a few days or at such time as you designate for the purpose of confering freely & fully on the policy to be pursued in the State of Tenn. in restoring the law and putting down treason and traitors. please send a pass indicating when it will suit for me to visit you. I fear that some designing persons have been trying to make an impression intended to disturb that good feeling which was understood to exist between us while you were here. if so it will all be dispersed— please accept my thanks for the gentle admonition you gave my son and the kind manner in which it was done[.][3]

Andrew Johnson
Mil Governor

Tel, DNA-RG393, Dept. of the Cumberland, Tels. Recd., Vol. 67 (1863).

1. See Telegram to William S. Rosecrans, January 14, 1863.
2. Rosecrans was then headquartered at Murfreesboro. *OR*, Ser. I, XXIII, Pt. I, 8-9.
3. See Telegram from William S. Rosecrans, April 12, 1863.

Authorization to Raise Troops

State of Tennessee Executive Department.
Nashville June 1 1863

Col Joseph Parsons[1]
John B. Brownlow[2]

By virtue of the authority confered upon me by the Secretary of War, under order of the War Department, dated March 28th 1863 to raise troops for the United States service &c; I do hereby authorize Joseph Parsons and John B. Brownlow of the County of Knox State of Tennessee, to recruit men for a regiment of Cavalry for said service, to serve for the term of three years or during the War, and to rendezvous at such place and places as may be hereafter designated. Clothing, subsistence and transportation will be furnished by U. S. Quarter Masters and Commissaries, upon application of said parties or either of them. The authority[3] herein confered upon the said Joseph Parsons and John B. Brownlow is to expire on the 1st September A.D. 1863[.]

Andrew Johnson
Brig Genl. & Mil Gov Tenn

Tel copy, T-RG21, Adj. Gen's Papers.

1. Joseph H. Parsons (b. *c*1823), a Blount and Knox County lawyer and former state representative (1849-51), had served as colonel, 9th Tenn. Cav., USA (1863-65) until dispatched on recruiting service in East Tennessee. In July, 1865, he was court-martialed for the murder of Capt. John A. Thornhill of Company B and sentenced to hang, but in "consideration of high social & military standing . . . & as he was actuated by no malice or hatred but simply by a sincere though mistaken idea that the fatal act was necessary for the safety of himself and friends" was released. CSR, RG94, NA; *OR,* Ser. 1, XXX, Pt. IV, 25; Chattanooga *Gazette,* August 24, 1865; *Goodspeed's Blount,* 830; McBride and Robison, *Biographical Directory,* I, 573; *Knoxville City Directory* (1888), 293.

2. See *Johnson Papers*, IV, 518*n*.

3. Similar authorizations to George W. and John L. Kirk, May 3, 1864, and R. Clay Crawford, June 17, 1864, have been found.

From George L. Marr[1]

Penitentiary, 2nd June 1863

His Excellency Gov Andrew Johnson
Dr Sir

I have been confined in prison nearly four months having been arrested on the 4th of Feb below Clarksville[.] I was sent from there to Louisville after which I was sent to this place as I learned by your order[.] The firs charge against me was acting in the capacity of Conscript officer[.] This however has been withdrawn as a despach I received from the Provost Marshall at Clarksville[2] in answer to one I sent my Brother[3] which informs me that he has no evidence of my having acted in that capacity[.] I am also charged with dealing in Salt Petre[.] The facts are as follows Two years ago I had a surplus of negro labor[.] I worked them in Salt Peter Cave in East Tenn for their support[.] The product of the labor I sold to the person paying the highest price for it[.][4]

Finding this unprofitable I moved my negroes to Miss[.] Last winter I returned to Tennessee to get some provisions for them not coming however within the Federall lines but was taken by a Federal Scouting Party. I think I am not asking too much in requesting you to grant me a trial before convicting me of Crime and I make this request of you knowing that you will see that Justice is done[.] If there are any other charges against me they are without the shadow of foundation[.] hoping this may receive your favorable attention I am with great respect your obedient Servant

G L Marr[5]

ALS, DLC-JP.

1. George L. Marr (*c*1834-1877) of Montgomery County, possessing $4,000 in personal property, briefly served in the "Home Guard of Minute Men (Confederate)." 1860 Census, Tenn., Montgomery, N & E of Cumberland River, 168; William P. Titus, ed., *Picturesque Clarksville: Past and Present* (Clarksville, 1887), App. 46; Clarksville *Chronicle*, October 27, 1877.

2. James Andy Wallace (*c*1840-1893), 2nd lieutenant, 70th Ind. Inf., was the provost marshal at Clarksville. In March, 1864, he became 1st lieutenant and regimental quartermaster of the 10th Ind. Cav. Deputy to his father, the sheriff of Indianapolis, before entering service in 1862, he was a clerk and bookkeeper after the war. CSR, RG94, NA; Pension file, RG15, NA; Indianapolis city directories (1862-70), *passim.*

3. Marr had three brothers: John (b. *c*1824), Duncan M. (*c*1827-*fl*1880), and William M. (b. *c*1833). John and Duncan were farmers, with the latter possessing $42,900 real and $39,700 personal property on the eve of the war; by 1859 Duncan was also a stove dealer in Clarksville. Like George, John and Duncan were in the Home Guard of Minute Men (1861), while William, captain of Co. D, 10th Tenn. Inf., CSA, escaped from Fort Donelson and joined another command. Ann E. Alley and Ursula S. Beach, trans., *1850 Federal Census of Montgomery County, Tennessee* (Clarksville, 1971), 125; 1860 Census, Tenn., Montgomery, N & E of Cumberland River, 48; (1880), Clarksville, 13th Dist., 1; Titus, *Picturesque Clarksville,* 138-39; *Tennesseans in the Civil War,* I, 194; II, 260; *Williams' Clarksville Directory* (1859-60), 56.

4. Marr had not only hired out his slaves for labor in the caves and sold saltpetre to the Confederates, but also had sold mules, wagons, and harness "For use at Chattanooga Potash Works." Confederate Papers Relating to Citizens or Business Firms, RG109, NA.

5. On June 9 Col. John A. Martin, Nashville provost marshal, endorsed Marr's letter to the effect that the charges against him were correctly stated, adding that Marr "is, however, a violent, uncompromising rebel, and his influence, even in the Penitentiary, is constantly exerted against the Government. He should be kept in Prison until the war is over, or he reforms." In July, with three other prisoners, the resourceful Marr made good his escape, using "an opening in the roof... through which they passed by means of a rope made of bed clothing." Because they had been so "stealthy" in getting away, "no suspicion was aroused, and their escape was not known until too late to hope that they will be recaptured." Nashville *Press,* July 10, 1863.

From J. D. Tracy

June 2, 1863, [Nashville]; ALS, DLC-JP.

Sumner County physician complains that on April 27, four days after receiving an order from Gen. Eleazer A. Paine "to go South within ten days," he was arrested and put in jail when "a personal difficulty arose between myself and a Lieutenant boarding at my house. The cause of which I would rather state to you in person." Recently transferred to the penitentiary, Tracy asks Johnson to have his case investigated; a June 9 endorsement indicates that he is to be sent "South of the Federal lines[.]"

From Mildred A. Hall[1]

[Nashville], June 5th 63

To his Excellency Governor Johnson
Dear Sir,

Let me beg of you Govenor, to give me protection in collecting what is due me & my children. Judge McConnico,[2] Mr. A. W. Pyles,[3] Mr. John Chumbly & others refuse to pay me their just indebtedness to Dr. Hall on acct of your proclamation[4] made three months ago.—

We have endured privations and economized in the strictest sense to live—. I am now in great need of money—to pay debts & make necessary purchases— will you please set this matter right—as I am well assured you never included me in that Proclamation—& no *honest* man would have taken advantage of it. Judge McConnico owes me 87$00 eighty seven dollars.—

I have opened my house for the reception of boarders but do not make *table* expenses—as yet—not having enough boarders to pay.— My sisters[5] being arrested & imprisoned increases my family to six more persons and of course my expenses are heavy.

I get quite discouraged & know not what to do— My resources were cut off from our little farm last year by the soldiers and again this Spring by sending my tenant to Alton jail.[6]

Respectfully Mrs. Dr. Hall

ALS, DLC-JP.

1. Mildred (Malinda) Ann Ryan (1822-1896), Kentucky-born wife of Dr. Barton Warren Hall (1808-1875), a penitentiary inspector during the 1850's, was living at 26 Cherry Street, Nashville, which she probably rented from Ben Clark. Dr. Hall had been arrested on June 21, 1862, for parole violation and sent to Louisville. Faced with surgery which might "tirminate fatally," Mrs. Hall importuned Johnson for the doctor's return, but there is no evidence that he was released. After the war, the Halls lived in Sumner County; following his death she returned to Nashville and once again operated a boarding house. 1860 Census, Tenn., Davidson, Edgefield Dist., 15; (1870), Sumner, Gallatin, 42; Mt. Olivet Cemetery tombstone inscriptions; Letters from Mildred A. Hall, July 14, December 28, 1863; Mrs. Hall to Johnson, July 14, 1862; B. W. Hall to Johnson, July 17, 1862, Johnson Papers, LC; D. C. Payne, "A Political Prisoner," *Confederate Veteran,* XXVII (1919), 17; *Johnson Papers,* II, 360n; *Marshall & Bruce Nashville Directory* (1880), 251.

2. Lemuel B. McConnico (b. *c*1800), Nashville lawyer, had been Williamson County court clerk and judge. 1870 Census,Tenn., Davidson, Nashville, 7th Ward, 51; McConnico to Johnson, February 17, 1865, Johnson Papers, LC.

3. Alexander W. Pyle (*c*1812-*fl*1892), Virginia-born Nashville carriage maker with only $200 worth of personal property on the eve of the war, continued to ply his trade with Tarpley & Co. after that conflict. 1860 Census, Tenn., Davidson, Nashville, 6th Ward, 128; (1880), 8th Ward, 2nd Div., 16; Nashville city directories (1866-92), *passim.*

4. Confiscation Proclamation, February 20, 1863.

5. With three daughters and a son of her own, Mrs. Hall was now responsible for the two daughters of her sister, Mrs. Maria Payne, inasmuch as the latter and Mrs. Molly Hyde had been arrested in April.

6. Polish-born Joseph Rymarkieswicz (*c*1834-*fl*1900), a merchant with $3,000 in personalty in 1860, was apparently living on the Halls's Goodlettsville property in the

Edgefield District. Arrested by Truesdail on April 26 for smuggling and spying, Rymarkieswicz was held in the county jail and state penitentiary before being shipped to Alton. That he had had ample opportunity to connive with the Confederates is revealed by the series of passes issued by Union officials—February 19 to Chattanooga and return, March 27 "at will until further orders," March 28 to Tullahoma, April 1 and 5 to Shelbyville, April 8 to an illegible destination. 1860 Census, Davidson, Nashville, 4th Ward, 137; *Nashville City Directory* (1900), 1030; Rymarkieswicz to Johnson, June 2, 1863; passes in Series 18, Johnson Papers, LC.

From Richard M. Edwards

Nashville Tenn June 6th 1863

Gov Johnson
Sir:

You to day mentioned the fact that you had been trying to get the facts in reference to the organization of my Regiment, and I therefore take the liberty of making a further statement. I will say nothing in reference to myself. For the present I shall only say that so far as the 1st Major is concerned, I think and feel that Thornburg ought to have the place, for several reasons[1]

1st He has given his assistance in recruiting the Regiment to its present status from the beginning—has borrowed and used his own & the means of others in recruiting. He also had a fine horse which cost him $175.00 which was captured from him by the rebels. He has to some extent a Military education especially in cavalry tactics. He & his father's[2] family have suffered severely from Rebel cruelty & he ought to have a position that would pay him something for past losses.

As for Capt Stephens,[3] he is a good infantry officer & will make a good captain of cavalry, but he has been paid for every thing he has ever done, and is now on pay; whilst Thornburg has done more service in the field than he has.

In order that you may understand precisely how things stand,I must notify you that Beard[4] & Stephens have made a sort of bargain to this effect. Stephens is to be for the present 1st Major. Beard Lt. Col. When mustered in they will take complete control of the Regiment and expel Thornburg & me from camp then go on to complete the Regiment. When completed Stephens is to be elected col and thus make room in the first Battallion for some one of the captains whose company is bought for that purpose.

Thus you see that bribery and hopes of promotion are made to have a powerful influence in the scale towards breaking me down in the istimation of the men,[5] & the same means & influences have their effect in the case of Thornburg.

Now I propose to test Col Beard with this proposition to wit: that if he will recruit two companies for the Regiment he may be the Lieutenant Col. Make that proposition to him & he will refuse it & why because he will not risk a dollar to make the Regiment.

I make these statements in order that you may know the influences that are being used against Thornburg & me; knowing that you will not endorse men who will not risk any thing for the cause in which we are engaged.

Thornburg having been elected in the 1st Battallion ought to have his place.

Respy R. M. Edwards

ALS, DLC-JP.

1. Jacob M. Thornburgh (1837-1890), Jefferson County native, was educated at Holston Seminary, read law, and was admitted to the bar (1861). Leaving Tennessee in 1862, he helped Edwards recruit the 4th Tenn. Cav., USA, at Cumberland Gap. Commissioned lieutenant colonel, July 11, 1863, he commanded the regiment and often the brigade of which it was a part through the rest of the war. Later district attorney of the 3rd judicial circuit (1866-71) and congressman (1873-79), he concluded his career practicing law in Knoxville. A year after this letter Edwards would express concern about Thornburgh's replacing him. Alexander Eckel, *History of the Fourth Tennessee Cavalry, U.S.A.* (n. p., 1929), 25, 106-7, 113; *BDAC*, 1713; Edwards to Johnson, June 4, 1864, Johnson Papers, LC.

2. For Montgomery Thornburgh, see *Johnson Papers*, IV, 190*n*.

3. Meshack Stephens (1828-*c*1911), a lifelong resident of Morgan County, Mexican War Veteran, and former sheriff (1858-60), was captain, Co. A, and shortly to be major of the 4th Tenn. Cav. USA. Subsequently he served as a state legislator (1869-71) and justice of the peace (1876-87). 1900 Census, Tenn., Morgan, 106th Enum. Dist., 4B; Eckel, *Fourth Tenn. Cav.,* 108; McBride and Robison, *Biographical Directory,* II, 863-64.

4. For Stephen Beard, see *Johnson Papers*, V, 572*n*.

5. This very day fifteen officers of the 4th Tenn., including Captain Stephens, signed a petition asserting that they had "but little confidence in the patriotism, honor & integrity, of R. M. Edwards" and requesting that someone "not obnoxious to the charge of Sympathizing with Valandigham Copperheadism" be put in command. According to the historian of the regiment, Edwards had endorsed a speech of Ohio representative Samuel S. ("Sunset") Cox and the sentiments of others who were in open opposition to the war, thereby casting suspicion on his loyalty. Edwards' recent squabble with Robert Johnson over recruitment possibly had an influence on the Governor's decision not to commission him colonel. Lately Thomas, *The First President Johnson* (New York, 1968), 253; Eckel, *Fourth Tenn. Cav.,* 27; Officers of Fourth Tenn. Cav. to Johnson, June 5, 1863, Johnson Papers, LC.

General Order No. 3

State of Tennessee.
Adjutant General's Office,
Nashville, Tenn., June 6, 1863.

Notice is hereby given to all Tennesseans desiring to volunteer in any of the Tennessee Regiments, in the service of the United States, or now forming in or about Nashville for said service, that transportation will be furnished them to this place upon application to any officer doing duty in the Quartermaster's Department.

All Quartermasters are respectfully requested to furnish transportation to this place to all Tennesseans desiring to enter said service, and to report to this office the names of persons to whom transportation has been furnished, and all persons receiving transportation are requested to report to the Adjutant General at the State Capitol.

By order of Brig. Gen. Andrew Johnson,
Military Governor

Alvan C. Gillem, Col. and Adjt. Genl.

Nashville *Press,* June 8, 1863.

From Frank H. Hamilton[1]

Nashville, Tenn June 9th 1863.

Dear Sir:

Enclosed you will find a copy of a portion of my monthly report[2] to the Medical Inspector General & to Major Genl. Rosecrans, which will inform you as to the results of my inspection in the regiments under your immediate command.[3]

What is needed especially, you will observe, is a more abundant supply of fresh vegetables, especially potatoes, lime juice & pickled cabbage—and more attention to camp police.—

The supplies of fresh vegetables, being now furnished by government, are wholly inadequate to the immediate wants of these regiments.

Their circumstances are peculiar, the men being more scorbutic[4] than those of most other regiments now on the field.—

I trust therefore, you will be able to find some means by which these extra supplies may be promptly furnished.

Very respectfully Yours
Frank H. Hamilton
Medical Inspector U. S. Army.

A. Johnson
Mil. Gov. St. of Tenn.

ALS, DLC-JP.

1. Frank H. Hamilton (1813-1886), Vermont native, was a well-known surgeon and professor of surgery in upstate New York, teaching at the Geneva Medical School (1840-44), and helping to found the medical department of the University of Buffalo (1846-58), before moving to New York where he worked in Long Island College Hospital (1858-61) and Bellevue Hospital Medical College (1861). Surgeon, 31st N. Y. Inf. (June-September, 1861), U. S. medical director (1861-63), and medical inspector, Department of the Cumberland (February-August, 1863), he rose to the rank of lieutenant colonel. The author of numerous articles, including a *Treatise on Military Surgery and Hygiene* (1862), he taught after the war at Bellevue (1868-75) and was consulting physician to President Garfield when he was shot. *DAB,* VIII, 185; *Official Army Register: Volunteers,* II, 467; Powell, *Army List,* 793.

2. Hamilton's fairly detailed report described the 4th Tenn. Inf. as "nearly 800 strong" and "composed almost entirely of refugees from Eastern Tenn." with "one Surgeon & one Asst Surgeon. The police of the Camp is not very good, and there is among the men a large amount of sickness, chiefly diarrhea. . . . They need especially waterproof blankets & fresh vegetables. The number sick in field hospital is eight with seventy four sick in quarters!" The regiment, "until very recently," had not had any fresh vegetables. The 10th Tenn. Inf. (1st Mid. Tenn. Inf.) had "790 men; one Surgeon & one Asst. Surgeon . . . Have been

in no battles & have not done much marching. Men recruited mostly from Nashville & the vicinity. 16 sick in field hospital; 17 in quarters. Police excellent. . . . Have had very few fresh vegetables since they have been in the service." The 3rd Tenn. Cav. had "472 men. One Surgeon, no Assistants. Police not good. 7 sick in field hospital, 44 in quarters. About 48 or 49 have died since the regiment was organized. (Jan. 27th, 1863.) Lost none in battle," while the 4th Tenn. Cav. had "600 men. One Contract Surgeon" and "Up to the first of April last, they had received almost no fresh vegetables. Since the 1st of April about one ration of potatoes every two weeks." Attached report, Hamilton to Johnson, June 9, 1863, Johnson Papers, LC.

3. They were the Tennessee troops, under Col. Alvan C. Gillem at Camp Spears near Nashville. *Ibid.; OR*, Ser. 1, XXIII, Pt. I, 417.

4. Scorbutic refers to scurvey, caused by a dietary deficiency of ascorbic acid, and characterized by spongy gums, loosening of the teeth, and a tendency to bleed into the skin and mucous membranes.

From Theophilus Fiske

June 10, 1863, New York; ALS, T-Mil. Gov's Papers, 1862-65, Petitions.

Desiring appointment as commissioner of deeds in Tennessee, he concludes: "I still cherish the one great hope of my life, that of seeing you the President of the *United* States—to realize which I shall task my energies to their fullest extent."

To Thomas M. Vincent[1]

Nashville June 10 [1863]

Maj Thos. Vincent

The authority conferred upon Jesse E. Peyton to raise troops has been revoked agreably to your telegraph of this date—[2] No one has been authorized by me to command— The instructions of the Secy of War have been strictly complied with[.] to withdraw authority from all others who have been authorized to raise troops will work a great hardship upon them & operate injuriously to volunteering[.] They have proceeded to raise troops in accordance with the authority and are Succeeding well & I have assurance of the most reliable character from various quarters that the forces can be raised without conflict or any great difficulty if I am permitted to exercise the authority conferred by the Secy of War[.] Most Tennesseans in the service entered in Ky after having escaped from rebel rule[.] It is hoped that the authority given me by the Secy will remain as it is[.] If so the volunteering can be made to work well[.][3]

Andrew Johnson Mil Gov

Tel, DNA-RG107, Tels. Recd., U. S. Mil. Tel., Vol. 50 (1863); DLC-JP.

1. Thomas M. Vincent (1832-1909), an Ohioan and West Pointer (1853), served as lieutenant and captain, 2nd U. S. Arty. (1853-61) before transferring to the adjutant general's department. Promoted to major during the war, he eventually became colonel (1890) before retiring in 1896. Powell, *Army List*, 647; *Who Was Who in America*, I, 1279.

2. On June 9, by instructions from Stanton, both Vincent and provost Marshal General James B. Fry directed Johnson to revoke all powers conferred upon Peyton to raise and command troops, Fry observing, "From experience, the War Department has no confidence in his fitness for said duties." Johnson this day revoked Peyton's authority. Fry to

Johnson and Vincent to Johnson, June 9, 1863; Johnson to Jesse Peyton, June 10, 1863, Johnson Papers, LC; see also Authorization to Raise Troops, April 29, 1863.

3. A week later, in response to this telegram, Fry wired that Stanton declined to change the revocation of June 9. Fry to Johnson, June 17, 1863, Johnson Papers, LC.

From Robert A. Crawford[1]

London, Ky. June 11th 1863.

Gov. Johnson:
Dr. Sir:

I came to this place on yesterday evening leaving Lexington on the 8 Inst. on the road from Lexington to this place I met at least 200 men all from East Tennessee & mostly from Washington Greene Hawkins & Jefferson Counties. They all say that the people of East Tennessee are allmost ready to give up. that robery, theft and murder is of daily occurrence. that the men over forty five yeas of age of the Secession party have organized themselves into home Guard Companies[2] and are prowling over the County serching the Houses of the Union men examining their letters and private papers and taking off such things as they need. The Indians are scattered over Greene & Jefferson Counties, doing the work of Treason, Hell & secession.[3]

The families of the men that are now in the Federal army, are being striped of every thing they have by a set of cowardly scoundrals such as Bill Girdner[4] at Cedar Creek, Sam Davis,[5] Bill Oliphant[6] Old Charles Hays[7] and a host of other such infernal rascals heading companies of Home Guards as they term themselves.

From the best and most reliable information I can get, as late as the 5 Inst. is that the secession forces have nearly all gone to Braggs army. I am assured by men that live close to the E. T. & Va. R. R. that there are not 2000 men between Bristol & Knoxville. There are at Cumberland Gap 1500—men under Genl. Gracy[.][8] at Beans station there are 1200 men under Col. Hillyard, known as Hillyards Legion.[9] besides these forces there are not 500 men in East Tenn. East of Knoxville— The Great Genl. A. E. Jackson[10] of Jonesboro, has left with his forces for the west probably Chatanooga. I am also credibly informed that, Genl. Pegram[11] has not exceeding 3000 men. he is at Clinton & Big Creek Gap. How easy East Tenn. could be taken. It, is also certain, that, the only two large Guns at Cumberland Gap, have been removed and taken to Loudon Bridge. it is certain they are removed from the Gap. I have seen two men who saw the Guns on the road ten miles beyond the Gap.

They are out of provisions at the Gap. get meat once a week. these are facts that you may rely upon. how easy! Could the Country be taken, but who is to do it! There are no forces here. about 350 near this place, none beyond this and few between here and Lexington. they have all been sent somewhere else God only knows. 5000 men could go into East Tenn. distroy the Salt works & the Rail Road from Abingdon to Loudon[12] & hold the Country until reinforcements could be had[.] with what little trouble all this could be done!

The wheat crop is better than it has been for five years before. are the damed Rebels to have this wheat crop! if they are the few remaining loyal men will give it up that, this Government is a failure.
The Confederate authorities, are prepairing to call into the field, all able bodied men, from 18 yeas to 55 yeas.[13] if this is done before East Tenn is invaded the Tennesseeans now in the Federal army, will never get to their homes until they first slaughter men as loyal as themselves because, on the battle field we cannot tell our friends from our enimies. The Secessionists say they will force all the Union men into the army and therefore they will check the Tennesseeans who have left and gone into the Federal army, as they will be compeled to fight against men as loyal to the Lincoln abolition Government as they are who have gone to it before they can ever get the Country.
I find it all most impossible to get the East Tennesseeans to go to Nashville. they come here tired and worn out and discouraged at seeing no army here. The most of them out of money and nothing to be had for them to eat unless they pay for it for at least fifty miles beyond this place hense they join the first Regiment, they come to. some fifty are here now who will go to Col. Stokes I suppose. James Galbraith & David Jewell[14] came here last night[.] they will come to Nashville. I will leave here in a few days & I think I will come to Nashville. if there is no advance to be made into East Tenn. I need not stay here. I have done what I was sent to do,[15] and it is all of no use as no forces are here to go across the Mountains. there is nothing to hinder the forces at Cumberland Gap from taking this whole Country and many persons are fearing it will be done.
You must excuse this hasty and badly written letter, as it is done under circumstances that cannot be avoided at this time in a crowded room with a mean pen ink & paper. Judge Patterson & family are all well[.]

Yours Truly
Robt. A. Crawford

ALS, DLC-JP.

1. A Greeneville attorney with combined property worth $7,500 in 1860, Crawford became General Burnside's chief of secret police in November, 1863, and subsequently practiced for many years in Washington. 1860 Census, Tenn., Greene, 10th Dist., 90; Washington city directories (1867-81), *passim;* see also *Johnson Papers*, IV, 190*n; OR,* Ser. 1, XXXI, Pt. III, 111-12.

2. At this time men over forty-five, not liable to conscription into the regular Confederate service, were often organized for local defense. Several companies were currently being organized in Washington and Hawkins counties under 1st Lt. W. W. Blair, Capt. J. B. McLin, and Capt. Jacob Miller. Lowell E. Harrison, "Conscription in the Confederacy," *Civil War Times,* IX (July, 1970), 14; *Tennesseans in the Civil War,* I, 312.

3. Four companies of Cherokees were in Col. William H. Thomas' Legion (officially the 69th N. C. Inf.) which made up part of Gen. Alfred E. "Mudwall" Jackson's Brigade of Buckner's Army of East Tennessee. *OR,* Ser. 1, XXIII, Pt. II, 711, 946; Michael Frome, *Strangers in High Places* (Garden City, N. Y., 1966), 124-25.

4. William Girdner (1803-1889), Tennessee-born physician, possessed $6,000 real and $27,300 personal property. Two years earlier Blackston McDannel had complained about a "damned secession traitor at Cedar Creek, a Post master by the name Girdner." 1860 Census, Tenn., Greene, 18th Dist., 41; Reynolds, *Greene County Cemeteries*, 388; *Johnson Papers*, IV, 404, 405*n*.

5. For Samuel W. Davis, see *Johnson Papers*, V, 531*n*.

6. William S. Oliphant (b. *c*1829) was a farmer with combined property worth $12,510. 1860 Census, Tenn., Greene, 14th Dist., 94.

7. Charles Hays (*c*1800-1873), native Tennessean, was a farmer with $2,500 real and $2,200 personal property. A southern sympathizer with several sons in the Confederate army, he, sometime during the war, was called to the door of his house and shot by bushwackers. *Ibid.,* 17th Dist., 68; Carl N. Hayes, "Neighbor Against Neighbor, Brother Against Brother: Greene County in the Civil War" (mimeographed copy), University of Tennessee Library, 4.

8. Archibald Gracie, Jr. (1832-1864), New York native and West Point graduate (1854), served two years as a lieutenant, 4th Inf., before resigning to enter business with his father at Mobile. Beginning as a captain, 3rd. Ala. Inf., CSA, he became brigadier in November, 1862, and saw service in East Tennessee and at Chickamauga. Transferred to Virginia in 1864, he was killed in the Petersburg trenches. Warner, *Generals in Gray,* 113-14; *OR,* Ser. 1, XXIII, Pt. II, 864-65; Powell, *Army List,* 336.

9. Organized at Montgomery, Alabama, June, 1862, this unit originally consisted of five battalions under Col. Henry W. Hilliard. It spent nearly a year in East Tennessee, fought as part of Gracie's brigade at Chickamauga, returning to East Tennessee to be dissolved November 25, 1863. Clement Evans, ed., *Confederate Military History* (12 vols., Atlanta, 1899), VII, 234; *OR,* Ser. 1, XXIII, Pt. II, 792, 946; Carlton Jackson, "Alabama's Hilliard: A Nationalistic Rebel of the Old South," *Alabama Historical Quarterly,* XXXI (1969), 204; for Hilliard, former Confederate commissioner to Tennessee, see *Johnson Papers*, I, 396*n*; IV, 498n.

10. Alfred E. Jackson (1807-1889), a Davidson County native educated at Washington and Greeneville colleges, farmed on the Nolichucky River and later became a well-known trader. A major on Zollicoffer's staff in 1861, he was made a brigadier in East Tennessee in February, 1863. Participating in a number of minor engagements, he won the sobriquet "Mudwall" by capturing the 100th Ohio Inf. at Telford's Station on September 8. Impoverished by the war, he rented land in Washington County, Virginia, in 1866, received a special presidential pardon for kindness shown Johnson's family during the conflict, and gradually reclaimed his Tennessee estate, residing in Jonesboro at the time of his death. Warner, *Generals in Gray*, 148-49.

11. John Pegram (1832-1865), Virginia-born West Pointer (1854), was a lieutenant, 2nd Dragoons, until he joined the Confederacy in 1861. On the staffs of Beauregard, Bragg, and Kirby Smith, before being promoted brigadier in November, 1862, he served at Murfreesboro and Chickamauga, as well as in East Tennessee. Transferred to the Army of Northern Virginia, he was wounded at the Wilderness in May, 1864, and killed at Hatcher's Run. *Ibid.,* 231-32; Powell, *Army List,* 524.

12. The most important salt works in the South were at Saltville, Smyth County, Virginia, only a short distance from the Tennessee line. A branch led to it from the Virginia and Tennessee Railroad. The East Tennessee and Virginia and East Tennessee and Georgia railroads controlled the line from Abingdon, Virginia, to Loudon, Tennessee. John F. Stover, *The Railroads of the South, 1865-1900* (Chapel Hill, 1955), 9; *OR-Atlas,* Plate CXLII; William Davis, "The Massacre at Saltville," *Civil War Times,* IX (February, 1971), 4.

13. Crawford was mistaken about the imminence of a change in the age limit. The Confederate conscription act of September, 1862, had extended to 45 the upper draft age of all white men not legally exempt. In February, 1864, the age was broadened to include 17 to 50-year-olds, the theory being that the boys and 46-50 year-olds would be used for guard and other detail duties and for local defense against raids. Harrison, "Conscription in the Confederacy," 11, 14; Wilfred Buck Yearns, *The Confederate Congress* (Athens, Ga., 1960), 65, 77-78.

14. For James A. Galbraith, see *Johnson Papers*, V, 298*n*. David R. Jewell (1839-1913), Tennessee-born clerk, who lived in Galbraith's house prior to the war, subse-

quently became a farmer. 1860 Census, Tenn., Greene, 10th Dist., 82; (1880), 13th Dist., 27; Reynolds, *Greene County Cemeteries*, 266.

15. Under Burnside's direction, Crawford was attempting to establish a line of couriers to gather from loyal men in East Tennessee information about conditions and rebel activity there. See James A. Galbraith to Johnson, June 29, 1863, Johnson Papers, LC.

To William S. Rosecrans

Nashville June 11 1863

To Maj Gen Rosecrans

W H Grummet[1] recommended to me as reliable man wishes to visit Gen Rosecrans for the purpose of making an arrangement to transfer a large amount of forage to the Government. It is about 15 miles north east of Murfreesboro. He fears it will be taken by the rebels as much of his property has already been used by them— He desires a pass to Murfreesboro for this purpose[.][2]

Andrew Johnson
Mil Governor

Tel, DNA-RG393, Dept. of the Cumberland, Tels. Sent, Vol. 63 (1863).

1. William Harvey Grimmett (1815-1888), Sevier County native, spent most of his life in Wilson County as a farmer and Baptist preacher. Licensed in 1839 and ordained to full ministry nine years later, he preached at Greenvale until declining health forced his retirement. He represented Wilson County in the state legislature (1865-67) and was one of the founders of Union University at Murfreesboro. McBride and Robison, *Biographical Directory,* II, 361.

2. The following day Johnson telegraphed: "Q M Hodges thinks he [Grimmett] should at once go to Murfreesboro on acct of the valuable information he can give in reference [to] forage in his immediate neighborhood[.]" Tels. Sent, Dept. of the Cumberland, RG393, NA.

From William P. Mellen

June 12, 1863, Cincinnati, Ohio; ALS, DLC-JP.

Supervisor of special treasury agents requests governor promptly to nominate for assessor and collector of internal revenue, Nashville district, "men of such unquestioned probity, business capacity, firmness and force of character" as to "insure a prompt and efficient execution of their duties" and "inspire the respect and confidance of *all* those interested either as payors or otherwise"; also advises that "steps will be taken very soon" to "protect citizens from unwarrantable seizures of their property."

From Jesse E. Peyton

Philadelphia Penna.
June 12, 1863

His Excellency Andrew Johnson
Brig. Gen. & Mil. Governor, Tennessee
Nashville, Tennessee
Dear Sir

In reply to your telegram of the 10th inst, please find enclosed the Authority delegated to me to recruit men for the United States service under your command in Tennessee! for which evidence of confidence and respect, accept my very sincere thanks.

The order had been previously revoked by a dispatch direct from the Honorable Secretary of War, who seems to have a very poor opinion of my abilities or a very tender regard for my life, as I am entirely ignorant of the cause of his remarkable conduct, I know not which to attribute it to. There is evidently a manifest desire among the nine months men to become attached to this branch of the Federal service.[1]
Governor Parker[2] of New Jersey would be pleased, I think, to furnish the entire Brigade from his state, if requested by the President or Secretary of War to do so, first, from the fact, that he sympathizes with the Union men of your state, Second, its healthy locality and the Military service being preferred and as New Jersey is an agracultrical state, cut up into small Farms, chiefly occupied by Tenants, he thinks their condition would be eventualy benefited, by becoming citizens of your State.

He assured me that he would be glad to fill any order that might be made upon him to aid in the redemption of Tennessee. I may say the same of the Executives of Pennsylvania and Delaware,[3] with whom I have had personal interviews.

With sincere Friendship and Respect for yourself personally, and a regard for those assotiated with you in the noble cause, I remain, Respectfully

Your Obedient Servant
J. E. Peyton

P. S. Can you give me the reason assigned by the Secretary of War, for the revocation of this authority—[4]

LS, DLC-JP.

1. A potential reservoir of recruits for duty in Tennessee were those who had responded to the war department's order of August 4, 1862—pursuant to authority given the President by the Act of July 17—calling out the militia for a period not to exceed nine months. Fred A. Shannon, *The Organization and Administration of the Union Army* (2 vols., Gloucester, Mass., 1965 [1928]), I, 276-77.

2. Joel Parker (1816-1888), graduate of New Jersey College (Rutgers, 1839) and Freehold lawyer, saw service as Democratic state assemblyman (1847) and Monmouth County prosecutor (1852-57); during this same period he reorganized the local militia,

rising to the rank of major general. Twice elected governor (1863-65, 1872-74), he ended his career as a state supreme court justice (1880-88). *DAB*, XIV, 232.

3. For Andrew G. Curtin, governor of Pennsylvania, see *Johnson Papers*, IV, 510*n*. William Cannon (1809-1865), Delaware native with only an elementary education, became a wealthy merchant, fruit grower, and large landholder. Elected as a Democrat to the state legislature (1844, 1846), he served as a delegate to the Washington Peace Convention (1861), thereafter coming out firmly for the Union and winning the governorship on that party's ticket. During his term (1863-65) he had several sharp clashes with the Democratic majority in the legislature over war-related issues. *DAB*, III, 478.

4. Peyton's own hypothesis—that the secretary disliked him—may well have been accurate. Earlier in the year, for what he cryptically termed "good & valid reason," Stanton had refused a presidential request to allow the Pennsylvanian additional time to raise a regiment. But, personal considerations aside, the secretary was in principle opposed to recruitment for service in a specified location. A month earlier he had revoked a similar authorization issued by Johnson to Thomas B. W. Stockton, because enrollments were conditioned upon service in East Tennessee. Basler, *Works of Lincoln*, VI, 44, 50; Letter from Edward R. S. Canby, May 14, 1863; Johnson to Peyton, April 29; Johnson to Stockton, May 4, 1863, Johnson Papers, LC; *OR*, Ser. 3, I, 889.

To James B. Fry[1]

Nashville June 13 [1863]

Col J B Fry P M G

Are all men who volunteer for three years or during the war entitled to the premium one months pay in advance & twenty five dollars bounty on being mustered into the U S Service[?][2]

Andrew Johnson Mil Govr

Tel, DNA-RG107, Tels. Recd., U. S. Mil. Tel., Vol. 50 (1863).

1. James B. Fry (1827-1894), West Pointer (1847) from Illinois, spent his entire career in staff service. Chief of staff for Gen. Irvin McDowell during the Manassas campaign and subsequently under Buell in the Army and Department of the Ohio, he was appointed provost marshal general, March 17, 1863, holding that position until his commission expired in 1866, at which time he was assigned to the adjutant general's office until his retirement in 1881. A prolific writer on military subjects, he produced pamphlets and reminiscences, as well as a lengthy study on *The History and Legal Effect of Brevets in the Armies of Great Britain and the United States* . . . (1877). Warner, *Generals in Blue*, 162-63; Powell, *Army List*, 320.

2. Although the governor seems never to have received an answer from Fry, his question had been answered in the affirmative by War Department General Orders No. 163 dated June 4 which reconfirmed payment of the two-dollar premium, a month's pay in advance, and twenty-five dollars of the one-hundred-dollar bounty. *OR*, Ser. 3, III, 250-51.

From Laura C. Holloway[1]

Nashville June 15 1863.
Monday Morning.

Gov Johnson
Dear Sir.

At the request of my Husband who is under arrest[2] I write this note thanking you for the kind interest you have taken in him, and for your uniform gentle kindness to myself. Your acts have not been unappreciated, and your deeds not thrown away. In the hearts of your people you will live Gov Johnson long after present struggles are over, and in the affections of Tennesseeans you memory will be cherished. Again we both join to thank you, and hope the time may yet come when we may in a measure return all you have done. My Husband would write himself but he is not allowed the privilege. If you can spare a few moments, Gov, will you come down and see him? He is very unhappy about this unfounded arrest and wishes to see you. If you could leave your buisness for a few moments, you will confer a very great favor.

I remain always, Your friend & well wisher,
Laura C. Holloway

St Cloud Hotel, City

ALS, DLC-JP.

1. Laura (*c*1843-*fl*1922), daughter of St. Cloud Hotel proprietor Samuel J. Carter with whom Johnson had boarded in 1856 while civil governor, married Kentucky-born Lt. Junius B. Holloway, son of a Richmond dry-goods merchant, on June 18, 1862. The ceremony was conducted by the Rev. Dr. R. B. C. Howell, one of a number of "secesh" clergymen with whom the governor had an acrimonious interview that same day. Eventually Laura had enough of her Brutus, writing the governor in 1871 that "the very name I bear is not my own and I despise it"; in 1890 she married Col. Edward L. Langford, a Brooklyn politician and businessman. She had removed to Brooklyn after the war, serving for twelve years as associate editor of the *Daily Eagle* and—resolved "to carve a name in history"— producing a potpourri of works with such titles as *The Ladies of the White House, or In the Home of the Presidents; The Woman's Story, as told by Twenty American Women; The Authorship of the Plays of Shakespeare; Chinese Gordon, the Uncrowned King;* and *The Buddhist Diet-Book.* Planning a biography of the President, Mrs. Langford visited Greeneville twice during the last decade of the century and was given access to the Johnson papers, then in the possession of Mrs. Martha Patterson, his elder daughter. 1860 Census, Tenn., Davidson, Nashville, 5th Ward, 156; Acklen, *Tenn. Records*, II, 10; Nashville *Press*, May 21, 1863; Heitman, *Register*, I, 538; *OR*, Ser. 1, LII, Pt. I, 227; Laura C. Holloway to Johnson, May 10, 1871, Johnson Papers, LC; *NUC*, CCCXV, 197-98; LC, *Index to the Andrew Johnson Papers* (Washington, 1963), vii; *Who Was Who in America*, IV, 554; New York *Times*, July 26, 1902.

2. Holloway (*c*1842-*fl*1905) had been appointed 2nd lieutenant, 2nd U. S. Cav. in May, 1861, and later transferred to the 5th Cav., Army of the Ohio. His vicissitudes began during the fall of 1861. Over a period of months extending into the following year, he was visited almost regularly with various physical complaints—a foot wound caused by the accidental discharge of a pistol and aggravated by erysipelas, and typhoid fever, worsened by "Chronic Diarrhoea." Invariable accompaniments to this "long spell of sickness" were requests for leave or extension of leave, maneuvers which proved uniformly successful. Meanwhile Holloway, rapidly becoming a controversial figure, sought alternatives to the cavalry, inquiring of the governor about a possible appointment to West Point, getting temporarily assigned to Buell's headquarters as acting adjutant general, and, with the endorsement of Johnson and other officials, seeking reassignment to the quartermaster corps. Having exhausted the possibilities, he was enroute to rejoin his regiment in September, 1862, when captured by the enemy in Kentucky. Paroled by General Forrest in November, he requested service in Tennessee or Kentucky until exchanged; but, having been absent without leave since August, *Captain* Holloway was dismissed from the service effective December 6. Nor were his troubles over: arrested the same month by Federal forces operating in West Tennessee, he was accused of acting as a Confederate guide (though a rebel officer wrote that he had done so under duress) and of disloyalty; one of Samuel Carter's slaves later deposed that Holloway not only had said that he would "rather go South and join the Southern Army" than take the loyalty oath but also that he had spoken of Union officers as "Abolition Sons of Bitches." If Holloway was not actually a Confederate sympathizer, he would appear to have been a "hermaphrodite" of flexible

principle. He was released late in June, 1863; apparently no further action followed, though his dismissal from the service stood. Subsequently he became House of Representatives clerk concerned with Civil War claims (1881-1905). 1860 Census, Ky., Madison, Richmond, 151; Holloway to Johnson, March 31, 1862, Johnson Papers, Ser. 2, LC; Johnson to Stanton, July 30, 1862 (File H1011C.B.1863); W. S. Rosecrans to Lorenzo Thomas, June 28, 1863, with statement of Harrison Reynolds (File C339C.B.1863), Lets. Recd., ACP Branch, RG94, NA; Holloway to Thomas, December 31, 1861 (File 917H1861); January 31, 1862 (File 65H1862); J. H. Whittlesey to Thomas, April 14,1862 (File 357W1862); Ezekiel F. Holloway to Adj. Gen., May 26, 1862 (File 424H1862); J. B. Holloway to Adj. Gen., June 30, 1862 (File 576H1862); Johnson to Stanton, January 31, 1863 (File 397T1863), Lets. Recd., Main Series, RG94, NA; Holloway to Adj. Gen., September 10, November 11, 1862, with parole copy from N. B. Forrest, November, 1862 (File 53H1862), RG249, NA; R. V. Richardson to "Sir," December 22, 1862, Union Provost Citizens File, RG109, NA; War Dept. Special Orders No. 176, RG94, NA; *OR,* Ser. 1, XX, Pt. II, 25; *U. S. Official Register* (1881-1905), *passim.*

From John M. James[1]

Memphis Tenn 15 June 63

Hon A Johnson
Dear Sir

You will please excuse me for troubling you with a letter on buisness that is of no importence to you, but of deep interest to myself & your being the only acquaintence that I felt that I [could] address on this subject[.] According to late Regulations of trade to this City we are allowed $125,000 worth of goods pr month[.][2] this amt has been lavished out to a few Persons many as Loyal men as there are in the state not being allowed one cents worth. I amongst those who did not get any[.] Can you not get me a permit to ship goods to this Place for sale! I can if required establish my Loyalty beyond a doubt[.] Hon E M Ethridge will vouch for me. All I ask is equal Rights with other men in buisness. My Father[3] sends his Respects with myself[.]

I am Very Respectfully Yours &c
J M James formerly of Paris Tenn

P S Let me hear from you at once[.]

ALS, DLC-JP.

1. John M. James (1824-1900), Tennessee-born merchant, resided in Henry County until the war when he moved to Memphis. Associated for several years with Keel and Company, he began his own wholesale grocery business, *ca.*1870, and was joined by his sons, Charles and William, during the decade to form the J. M. James and Sons Wholesale firm, a family business superceded in 1880 by J. H. McDavitt and Company. Memphis *Commercial Appeal,* March 11, 1900; Memphis city directories (1866-81), *passim.*

2. Soon after Memphis fell under Union control it became a smuggler's and speculator's paradise; contraband goods, especially cotton, poured through the river city. Military and treasury officials in charge of regulating commerce were faced with the problem of restricting illegal trade without seriously disrupting the regular and necessary flow. In April, 1863, special treasury agents, collectors and surveyors in the Mississippi Valley meeting in Cincinnati agreed that the residents in restricted areas, such as Memphis, should be supplied according to the total population based on the 1860 census. Although Shelby, Fayette, and Tipton counties were to receive goods through Memphis at a monthly rate of $2.00 worth per person, the actual rate varied from $1.25 to $5.00 with numerous

exemptions which permitted the value of goods imported far to exceed the per capitation limit. Futrell, Federal Trade, 246-50; Joseph H. Parks, "A Confederate Trade Center Under Federal Occupation: Memphis 1862 to 1865," *Journal of Southern History,* VII (1941), 304-5.

3. Probably Amos James (b. *c*1795), former Henry County merchant with $5,000 real and $3,000 personal property. 1860 Census, Tenn., Henry, 1st Dist., 14.

From Benjamin D. Nabers

Memphis Tenne June 15 1863

His Excellency Andrew Johnston
Military Gov of Tennessee
Sir—

Many of your friends here are anxious that you appoint—E. W. M. King Judge of the Common law and Chancery courts of this City. He is well known to you as an able lawyer and honest man. He is too—thoroughly loyal—has taken the oath of allegiance.

There has been a civil commission appointed here by Brig. Genl. Veatch[1]—before which Suits are brought for the collection of debts. This commission is composed of three Judges—one of whom is A. C. Ketchum[2] (you refused to appoint him Judge) Williams[3] and Lewis.[4] This commission is self sustaining—the Judges being paid from bills of cost—taxed on each case[.] And such bills were never heard of before in this county! The average cost in each case is not less than $35. or $40!

This court does not exercise any jurisdiction over real estate, nor are there any Juries empaneled to try Suits. Now, it appears to me that if we had our old courts established and the Code of Tenn resumed—we would be much better off than as we now are.

No better man for Judge than E. W. M. King can be found, and if it were thought necessary the names of all the union men in Memphis could be had to a petition for his appointment.

Judge King will accept the appointment if you tender it to him[.] This I *know,* and he would make application directly to you if necessary[.]

Yours respectfully
B. D. Nabers

ALS, DLC-JP.

1. James C. Veatch (1819-1895), Indiana native and Rockport lawyer, was elected to the state legislature in 1861. Entering the army as colonel of the 25th Ind. Inf., he led his men at Donelson, Shiloh, and Corinth, before commanding the District of Memphis throughout 1863, and later a division of the XIII Corps during the capture of Mobile. Brevetted major general of volunteers in 1865, he returned after the war to Indiana where he was collector of internal revenue for his district (1870-83). Warner, *Generals in Blue,* 525-26.

2. Despite Johnson's apparent refusal of a commission, Ketchum, whom Veatch had appointed in April, remained in Memphis, serving in 1864 as colonel of a local militia regiment. See Letter from Benjamin D. Nabers, February 5, 1863, note 2.

3. Joseph Williams (1801-1871), Pennsylvania-born lawyer, served as associate justice, Iowa territorial supreme court (1838-45), chief justice after statehood (1845), district judge in Kansas (1857), and judge of the circuit court in Tennessee. Returning to the

North after the war, he ended his career in Kansas. *NCAB*, XII, 342; *Memphis City Directory* (1866), 193; see Letter from James M. Tomeny and James B. Bingham, September 17, 1863.

4. Barbour Lewis (1818-1893), Vermont native and graduate of both Illinois College (1846) and Harvard Law School, was captain, Co. G, 1st Mo. Cav. before appointed to the Memphis Court. Mustered out of service in November, 1864, when he began the practice of law in the river city, he remained active in politics, being elected president of the Shelby County commissioners (1867-69), and congressman (1873-75). Moving first to St. Louis and then to Salt Lake City, he eventually settled in Washington Territory as a farmer and stockman. 1870 Census, Tenn., Shelby, Memphis, 4th Ward, 43; Walter J. Fraser, Jr., "John Eaton, Jr., Radical Republican," *Tenn. Hist. Quar.*, XXV (1966), 242; *BDAC*, 1214.

From Thomas T. Smiley[1]

Nashville June 15th 1863

To Hon: Andrew Johnson
Military Governor of Tennessee:
Dear Sir:

Mr Silas Norris,[2] a Citizen of this County, was arrested a few months Since, on a Charge of "Kidnapping negroes," tried and Condemned to the Military Prison at Alton Ill: there to remain during the present War. At the request of his family and Some of his friends, your attention is respectfully Called to the Consideration of his Case, knowing, that if Consistent with justice and the interests of the Goverment, you would Cheerfully lend your aid to relieve him from his present unhappy Condition—

To learn the Charges against Mr Norris I made application to the Police department, for a Copy of the proceedings, and received a reply from Col Truesdail, which I herewith enclose—[3]

Mr Norris admits that he was employed with some other person,[4] by one Mr McFerrin[5] to assist in removing his Slaves to the State of Alabama or Georgia[.]

It has been a matter of Common occurrence, for owners of Slaves to remove them from here to some Southern state, and was not in violation of any law of Ten. how it would be regarded by the Military author[it]ies, I am not prepared to Say. It Certainly, in no Sense, Could be regarded a Crime of So high a grade as "kidnapping". I am assured by Mr Ns friends that if he had known it was against any Civil or Military rule he would not have Consented to act as employee of Mr McFerrin—

As to the allegation of having Sold the negroes or any of them he wholly denies and says the Charge is without any foundation; and not being the owner of any Slave himself he had none to sell. Many of our best Citizens will Cheerfully testify that Mr Norris has always been a quiet, good industrious man, and especially in his domestic relations, as a husband and Father his deportment has been unexceptionable—

His friends feel it their duty, further to say that the family have limited means, and were entirely dependant on his exertions for Support and maintenance.

They confedently Commend his Case to your high Sense of justice and humanity.

With Sentiments of respect
I have the honor to be Yr Obdt Servt
Tho. T. Smiley

ALS, WHi-Ar-Thomas T. Smiley Papers.

1. For Smiley, Nashville lawyer handling a number of civilian claims and military petitions, see *Johnson Papers*, II, 321*n*.

2. Silas Norris (*c*1828-*fl*1870), Tennessee-born resident of Edgefield and a carpenter by trade, had served for several years as a constable. Sent to Alton in January, 1863, he was still languishing there nine months later. After the war he plied his trade in Robertson County. 1860 Census, Tenn., Davidson, Edgefield, 27; (1870), Robertson, 9th Dist., 39; Fitch, *Annals*, 541-42.

3. Denouncing Norris' deed as "vile, dirty & unholy," Truesdail conceded that Johnson had "manifested some interest in the case favorable to the prisoner." William Truesdail to Smiley, June 9, 1863, Thomas T. Smiley Papers, Archives, State Historical Society of Wisconsin.

4. James Stewart, an Edgefield shoe and boot maker. See Norris' statement, January 15, 1863, Johnson Papers, LC.

5. John B. McFerrin, ardently supported Tennessee's secession and was a chaplain with the state troops. The impending capture of Nashville in early 1862 forced him to move behind Confederate lines and eventually to Alabama. He later insisted that he had made no attempt to have his slaves brought to him or sold. Returning to Nashville in May, 1865, he found his estate ruined. *NCAB*, VIII, 267-68; Oscar P. Fitzgerald, *John B. McFerrin: A Biography* (Nashville, 1889), 267-87; see also *Johnson Papers*, V, 306*n*.

From James B. Williams[1]

[Nashville], June the 15th 1863

To the Honourable Andrew Johnston
Govenour of the State of Tennessee

Honoured Sir Permit me in the language of Cinciarity of purpose and duty and affection for my self my Country and my Brother Lewis Williams.[2] permit me *Govenour Johnston* to ask you vary Respectfully to Read these few lines in behalf and relating to my *Brother Lewis Williams* who is now in his *Seventy seventh* year of his *Age* Borned in the State of *North Carolina* and Emigrated to the State of Tennessee in the year Eighteen hundred and three and have bean a Citizen of Davidson County and the State of Tennessee Ever since[.] He has ever beane a Peacable truthfull and a *Loyal* Citizen of Davidson County and the *State* of *Tennessee*[.] Our farther, *Francis Williams*[3] Stood by Our Beloved *Washington* and under his Guideance gained the Power to make our *American* Constitution the Goodness of heart and integrity of our Venerateed *Washington* for his fellow man was never Excelled and rearley Ever Equled in this *World* in regard to the Protection of *Human* Liberty and their *Constitutional*

Rights[.] *This Legacy* of Constitutional Liberty and the Protection of *Constitutional* Rights is a *Priceless* Legacy Beyond Human Conception— The *American Constitution* is the Onley One Lewis Williams Ever k[n]ew and now knows No other[.] and to Shew the Evidence of his *devotion* to Our *Constitution* he Risked his life *often times* For it on the Plaines of *Neworleans*[.] Lewis Williams was a *Volunteer* under Genl *Carroll*[4] in the latter part of the year Eighteen hundred and fourteen and went to Neworleans under the Command of Genl *Carroll*[.] he was one of his life *Guard* and then under the Command and *Guidance* of our Devoteed Patriot *Andrew Jackson* Lewis Williams Displayed his part as *a Patriot* and *Gallant Soldier* that wont be forgotten[.] When the *unhappy Revolution* took place and *Tennessee* was Invaded by the Federal Army and *Nashville* Capitulateed, afterwards the Presment of *Negroes* Took place[.] not long after Presment *commenced* The *Negroes* commenced leaving their homes in the Country and going to Nashville as a place of Protection.[5] Lewis Williams had *thirty odd Negroes* To leave him Two old Negro women the Ballance women and children which Lewis Williams have Raised[.] In Regard the Number of thirty odd there was fifteen of them young Negroes most of them *children* And most all these Negroes was Influenced *to leave* their Master Lewis Williams, who was one of *Kindest* Masters in the *world* and *Animateed* by the *Spirit* of Humanity and Common Justice[.] I *am satisfyed* the *Negroes had Rather* be at home with their *Old Master* Lewis Williams who is now *Seventy Seven years* old and correctly wait on him as he has *waited* on them and Raised nearly Every one of them— The time is now becoming vary sickley in *Nashville* and maney of them must sicken and *die* As all readey some four of them is dead onley one of that number a grown Negro the Blance of them Children[.] My Brother Lewis Williams believing it to be his duty to try and get his Negroes *back again* at *Home* If it is posible to do so, and honestly I believe it is Which In deed it would be best for the great cause of *suffering hummanity* and Common Justice— Both in the sight of *God* and man and the Cympatheys and wishes that the Negroes Realey wishes to be at home again with their Old *Master Lewis Williams, Again*—

Govenour Johnston I do hope and trust you will Favour the *Designes* and wishes of my *Brother Lewis Williams* to get his Negroes home again— Whear I am Certain they will live and do much Better than Whear they are and it will be the Cause and Meanes of salving the lives of maney of Them[.] *situated* as they are they must *Die* From the unhealthy condition they are in[.] *nothing* can be more truer—

My Brother Lewis Williams have Given his Bond and Security in the sum of *five thousand Dollars* To the Federal Government under *President Lyncoln's Administration* and nothing can be more truer than he will [discharge] his Obligations Respecting his Country[.] the cincearity and Solem and feeling Integrity and true Devotion to his beloved Country In the Remnant and Noons tide and *sunset of life* [can] never be *unjustly questioned*[.]

In Regard to the facts contained in this *dockument* I solemley make Oath to them before *Alexander McDanel*[6] an Acting Justice of the Peace For Davidson County State of Tennessee[.]

Truley and Cincearly your friend
James Blanton Williams
For his Brother Lewis Williams

Sworn to and subscribed
Befor me an Acting
Justice of the Peace
for Davidson County this
17th June 1863[.]
Alexr. McDaniel J.P.

ALS, DLC-JP.

1. James B. Williams (b. *c*1799) was a North Carolina-born farmer living in Nashville's third ward. 1860 Census, Tenn., Davidson, Nashville, 3rd Ward, 92.

2. Lewis Williams (b. *c*1787), a Davidson County farmer, reported $6,000 real and $2,000 personal property in the prewar census, but the latter figure is patently incorrect, since he also owned thirty-three slaves. Porch, *1850 Census, Davidson,* 390; 1860 Census, Tenn., Davidson, 23rd Dist., 131; *ibid.*, Slave Schedule, Davidson, 23rd Dist., 43.

3. Probably the Francis Williams who died in Davidson County, *ca.*1809. WPA, Davidson County Wills and Inventories, Books 4-6(1808-16), 61.

4. For William H. Carroll, see *Johnson Papers*, I, 57*n*.

5. The impressment of black laborers, initiated by the military for work on the fortifications during the summer and fall of 1862 and continued by civil authorities for "scavenger duty" in 1863, augmented a migration which had begun with Federal occupation. Despite the horrible living conditions and the fact that some Federal commanders permitted their recapture and return to the plantation, many Middle Tennessee slaves fled to the city, considering it a refuge from slavery and the Federal army as their liberators. Maslowski, *Treason Must Be Made Odious*, 100-101; Hall, *Military Governor*, 207-8.

6. Alexander McDaniel (*c*1789-*c*1869), Virginia-born carpenter with $1,000 personal property, had run a grocery store in the 1850's, while his wife, Sarah, kept a boarding house. During the war he was a justice of the peace and city councilman. 1860 Census, Tenn., Davidson, Nashville, 3rd Ward, 87; Nashville city directories (1855-68), *passim;* Clayton, *Davidson County,* 90.

To William P. Mellen

[Nashville, June 15, 1863]

W. P. Mellen
Supervising Agent of Treasury
Memphis, Tenn

Is it to be understood, from the local rules Article 3d. that Cotton, Tobacco &c South of the Cumberland & East of the Tennessee River, are considered as abandoned property, and no shipments in the name of the loyal owner permitted. There is no Cotton north of the Cumberland River, but some south, which ought to be permitted to go into markit—

Andrew Johnson

Sent above June 15 to Cincinnati Ohio[1]

LS, NNPM.

1. This inked notation is not in Johnson's hand.

From William P. Mellen

Cincinnati June 16, 1863

Hon. Andrew Johnson
Nashville

Dr Sir: I have just received your telegram[.]

At *present* no licenses can be granted for the shipment of cotton or other merchandize from Tenn. raised south of the Cumberland & East of the Tenn. I am just starting for Washington and think some arrangement will be made under which our *friends* who have *raised* the cotton &c may be permitted to ship it North from all places within our lines.[1]

I shall be in Washington only a day or two and hope to find your recommendation as to assessor & collector *here* on my return[.]

I am truly &c Wm. P. Mellen
Supervising Sp. Agt Treas Dept

ALS, DLC-JP.

1. New, comprehensive treasure regulations, notably less stringent, promulgated by Secretary Chase on September 11, probably reflected Mellen's influence; this change, in conjunction with Rosecrans' lenient attitude toward commerce, permitted a temporary easing of restrictions in the region of Middle Tennessee south of Nashville. In the long run, however, laxity yielded to the demands of military security. "Trade Regulations . . . for . . . Limited Commercial Intercourse . . . September 11, 1863," in *House Ex. Doc.* No. 3, 38 Cong., 1 Sess., 408-27; Futrell, Federal Trade, 242-43, 262-64.

To William S. Rosecrans

Nashville June 16th 1863

To Maj Gen Rosecrans

I have been informed that there is a man in prison in Murfreesboro named Thomas[1] who is the man that murdered Geo Sloan[2] some time since near this place[.] I understand he wishes to be exchanged as a prisoner of war[.] if he is there you will take steps to have him identified & he should [be] tried for murder[.][3]

Andrew Johnson Mil Gov

Tel, DNA-RG393, Dept. of the Cumberland, Tels. Sent, Vol. 63 (1863).

1. For William Thomas, see Deposition of James M. Layne, October 23, 1862.

2. George L. Sloan (*c*1806-1862), a Connecticut-born farmer and former coach maker, was shot by guerrillas while returning to his home in Nashville from a trip into the country. 1850 Census, Tenn., Davidson, Nashville, 312; (1860), 2nd Ward, 56; Jill K. Garrett and Iris H. McClain, *Old City Cemetery, Nashville, Tennessee: Tombstone Inscriptions* (Columbia, 1971), 87; Nashville *Union,* October 1, 1862.

3. Rosecrans responded promptly but inaccurately that Thomas was being tried by a military commission for the murder in mid-January, 1863, of Thomas G. Scarber of Wilson County and asked that Johnson send on at once any evidence that he might have

against the defendant. Actually, Thomas was found guilty only of "Shooting at with the intent to Kill" Scarber. In September, 1862, Thomas did kill Sloan, and two years later a civil court convicted him of second-degree murder. Rosecrans to Johnson, June 16, 1863, Johnson Papers, LC; Court Martial Case Files, William Thomas (Civilian), RG153, NA; Nashville *Press,* April 7-9, 1863.

To William S. Rosecrans

Nashville June 16th 1863[1]

To Maj Gen Rosecrans

If the commission fail to find Thomas guilty of murder of Scarber[2] would it not be better to have a trial for the murder of Sloan in this place near where the witnesses resides[.] it will take some little time to get them together[.][3]

Andrew Johnson Mil Govr

Tel, DNA-RG393, Dept. of the Cumberland, Tels. Sent, Vol. 63 (1863).

1. Bearing the time notation of 6 P.M., as compared with 11:20 A.M. of the preceding document, this wire obviously represents an afterthought.
2. Thomas G. Scarber (*c*1807-*fl*1870) was a native Tennessee farmer. 1870 Census, Tenn., Wilson, 4th Dist., 2.
3. For Thomas' fate, see note 3 of the preceding document.

From Daniel H. Kelly[1]

Castle Thunder Richmond Va.
June 17th/63

Gov. A. Johnson
my der Sir.

I will inform you of my self & Son with several of our east tennessee friends that are in prison at this place. Some of us enlisted in the Servis of the United states and some citizens[.] all the prisoners in prison at this place at this time is 23 from East tennessee[.] the names of the enlisted are D. H. Kelly A. W. Kelly N B Gahagan William Keller William Triplett Lemuel Mcgee Gilbert Hacksey A J Coggburn R B Darling under Capt David Fry[2] 2 tennessee F Co Regt Carters brig and was on our way to Join said Reg. when captured on the 22nd day of March 1862 and have been confined in prison ever since[.] our capt was captured when we was[.] we ware captured in lee county Va and seperated at Knoxvill and have not Seen our capt since[.] Now the exchange has bee going on ever since we came here.[3] we cannot see why we are not excanged for we wore Sworn in to the Servises of the united States[.] we wish you to see that we get out of prison by having some of the most prominent cessation [secessionists] held till we are exchanged[.] the Civilians names are H Walker C Walker George Baty David Pain Thos. Catoon William Bauman Andrew Johnson Junr[4] L H Beard E Fortner D Ledger J C Guy J H Hicks John Brown A. Roe all of us from east tennessee and still clings to the union all though we have suffered anough to have kiled us several times[.] now do all you can to get us out of prison for we are allmost worn out[.] with Sentiments of the Highest Respect I remain

your most obedient Servant
D. H. Kelly

ALS, DLC-JP.

1. Daniel H. Kelly (*c*1815-1863) and his son Alexander W. (1843-1924) were Tennessee-born Greene County farmers and privates in Co. F, 2nd Tenn. Inf., USA. Daniel died in prison a month before his son and the other prisoners captured in Lee County, Virginia, were paroled (December 28, 1863). Johnson did not receive this letter until the latter half of October, when it was forwarded to him by Chaplain D. C. Eberhard, who had been in Castle Thunder. 1860 Census, Tenn., Greene, 18th Dist., 47; CSR, RG94, NA; Reynolds, *Greene County Cemeteries,* 267; Eberhard to Johnson, October 19 [11?], 1863, Johnson Papers, LC.

2. David Fry (*c*1826-1872), Greene County miller and captain, Co. F, 2nd Tenn. Inf., USA (1861-63), was detailed to aid William B. Carter in the November, 1861, East Tennessee bridge-burning enterprise, which was to be coordinated with a Federal military expedition. Unaware that the expedition had been countermanded, Fry's company burned the bridge over Lick Creek, Greene County. Remaining in East Tennessee through the winter, Fry, according to one source, kept a force together and fought a number of skirmishes with the Confederates, deciding in March to fight his way to the Federal lines. Attacked by a large force near Jonesboro, he was defeated, and his men scattered. A few days later, on March 22, 1862, he and a small group of recruits and refugees were captured in Lee County, Virginia, and carried to Knoxville. Tried for bridge-burning and sentenced to be hanged, Fry was transferred to Atlanta in June, 1862. In October he escaped and succeeded in reaching East Tennessee through North Carolina, rejoining his company at Murfreesboro in February, 1863. 1860 Census, Tenn., Greene, 2nd Dist., 23; CSR, RG94, NA; Temple, *East Tennessee,* 379, 384, 399-400; William Pittenger, *Daring and Suffering: A History of the Andrews Railroad Raid into Georgia in 1862* (New York, 1887), 274-75, suppl. 5.

3. Kelly's company was taken to Richmond in late March, 1863. Although exchanges and paroles in the field were not uncommon, the Lincoln administration for some time withheld approval of a general exchange, fearing it would imply recognition of Confederate sovereignty; not until July, 1862, was the first formal agreement for a regular prisoner-of-war exchange completed. It specified two exchange points, Aiken's Landing, Virginia, and Vicksburg, Mississippi, with the first prisoners repatriated August 3 at the former site. Kelly's reasoning indicates that the southern authorities may have briefly considered the members of "F" Company civilian, rather than military, prisoners, a status which would have made exchange under the July 22 agreement impossible. Hesseltine, *Civil War Prisons,* 7-33, 69-113 *passim.*

4. Andrew Johnson, Jr. (1836-1897), Tennessee-born son of Johnson's brother William, had returned from Texas shortly before the war. Arrested "as a Union man" by a "company of Confederate Partizan Rangers" in November, 1862, he was sent to Castle Thunder where he remained until December when he was exchanged for a civilian, Daniel T. Chandler. In January, 1864, he became a treasury aide at Nashville, the following year penitentiary agent, and later a tax commissioner (1866-68?). In the 1870's he was farming near Goodlettsville and serving as a mail agent. 1880 Census, Tenn., Davidson, 20th Dist., Goodlettsville, 11; "Examination of Andrew Johnson Jr," July 30, 1863, File C484, Lets. Recd., 1861-1865, RG109, NA; William P. Mellen to Nathan Sargent, June 28, 1864, Lets. Recd., Office of the Commissioner of Customs, Misc. Record, RG366, NA; Andrew Johnson, Jr., to Johnson, December 23, 1865, August 20, September 20, 1866, June 24, 1868, June 22, 1872, Johnson Papers, LC; *U. S. Official Register* (1877-83), *passim.*

From Richard M. Edwards

Camp 4th E Tenn Cavalry
Camp Spears June 18th 1863

Brig Gen Johnson Mil. Gov. &c
Dear Sir

As I told you when you showed me that celebrated petition[1] that I was willing to leave the question to the men, and have waited patiently for you the proper authority to order an election until I learned that Capt Stephens was about to receive his commission as Major & not knowing what else might be done on the strength of that Bogus election, on yesterday I read a copy of that petition to the men without however exposing the names of any of the signers; in order that the men might have an opportunity to endorse or refute the statement. The result was that in every company a large majority have emphatically denied the statement. Enclosed you will find the petitions from the different companies.[2] Capt Easly & Lt. Baskit in Co. B[3] stand solitary & alone in their glory[.]

I am as ever Your friend
R. M. Edwards

ALS, DLC-JP.

1. See Letter from Richard M. Edwards, June 6, 1863; 4th Tenn. Cav. officers to Johnson, June 5, 1863, Johnson Papers, LC.

2. Directed to "Gov Johnson," the virtually identical seven petitions, with a total of 363 signatures, read: "We the undersigned Recruits for the 4th E Tenn Cavalry having confidence in the Patriotism honor and integrity of R. M. Edwards respectfully request that he be put in command of this Regiment at the earliest date practicable[.]" Petitions, 4th E. Tenn. Cav., June 17, 1863, Johnson Papers, LC.

3. Thomas H. Easley (1825-*fl*1900), a Sullivan County farmer and cabinetmaker with $1,500 real and $1,400 personal property, served as captain, Co. B, 4th Tenn. Cav., USA (1862-65). George W. Basket (1840-1920), a Greene County farmer, was 2nd lieutenant in the company for the same period. *Official Army Register: Volunteers,* IV, 1178; Eckel, *Fourth Tenn. Cav.,* 144; 1860 Census, Tenn., Sullivan, 15th Dist., 7; (1900), 10B; Reynolds, *Greene County Cemeteries,* 157; CSR, RG94, NA; 1890 Special Census, Union Veterans and Widows, Tenn., Sullivan, 15th Dist., 1.

From James L. Fullilove[1]

near the big spring Hardin County Kentucky
June 18, 1863.

hon A Johnson Govennir of Tennessee
Dear Sir

permitt me to say to you that last Augt. my Son W. E. Fullilove[2] left home and on the 2d day after he left me he was taken a prisonner and Sent to Johnson Island near Sendusky Ohio and last December was Exchanged at Vicksborough and it was said belonged to Genl. Vandorns Command. I got a letter from him dated 24 of april passed in which he stated that he was a prisoner in the pennetinery at Nashville having been taken on 18 of Aprail on Comberland River near Charlotte[.] he alson wrote me on 28 and 6 of May— in all of the letters he spook of wishing to take the oath and Come home[.] in one of his letters he said at as soon as govennor Johnson got back to Nashville he would know if he could be released— I went to Louisville was thare abought 14 of may[.] I then wrote to my Son and also Sent a request that my Son be Sent to Louisville if agreeable to the Department at Nashville[.] this letter to my Son & my letter to Genl Boyle was forwored by the Department of Louisville, to Nashville as I understood.

I saw it stated in the papers that you Govennor arrived in Nashville on 30 of may and on the Tuesday after that 10 prisoners had been released from the pinnetinary on taking the oath & I then hoped that my Son was one of the 10 named. I have not heard a word from my Son Since his letter 6 of May tho I have written him 2 letters. Govennor Johnson I accknowlledge that it is prosuming on my part that I take the liberty to write to you on the Subject, but I have known you by name & station for years. I feel sure you can for give me when I say I have great disere to know what is the facts relative to my poor boy who is young only 18 the passed Febuary, and when with me was a kind boy. through excitment he left home which I have and do regret. I do hope that from you I can learn if my Son has been released or is he exchanged & gone in to the rebel armay again. (I hope not) or is he yet in Nashville sick or will[?] if he is in Nashville sick or will can I be permited to Furnish him some mony if he nead any— my disere and pray to allmighty god is that he in Mercy be pleased to give the rullers of this nation wisdom, that all thier councils & acts tend to the restroration of peace on earth & good will to men North South East & West.

I am Sir your humble servant
J L Fullilove

my post office is Big Spring
Hardin County Kentucky
Jas. L. Fullilove.[3]

ALS, DLC-JP.

1. James L. Fullilove (b. *c*1800) was a Virginia-born Hardin County, Kentucky, farmer with $5,100 real and $2,500 personal property. 1860 Census, Ky., Hardin, 2nd Dist., Big Springs, 43.

2. William E. Fullilove (b. *c*1845), private, Co. E, 2nd Ky. Cav., CSA, appears to have been undependable as a soldier and unreliable, if exceedingly creative, as a petitioner. According to his service record, he enlisted on August 14 and was reported "absent without leave" from November, 1862, through the following February. If we are to believe his father, this dereliction arose from his capture and confinement by the Federals. The record shows that he deserted on two subsequent occasions—at Columbia, Tennessee, on April 15, 1863, and in Middle Tennessee, in September, 1864—the first of these, apparently, the result of his current incarceration. Not knowing that his father would appeal to Johnson, Fullilove concocted a sanitized and sentimentalized version of his plight—"a poor Boy who has bin led of from the path of duty"—which he sent to the governor on June 2. Stressing his "youth and inexperience," saying naught of his earlier capture and imprisonment, and pulling on the heartstrings with allusion to "a poor old

Widowed Mother at home and Some little Brothers and Sisters who have to depend upon there daily work to obtain a liveing," he assured Johnson that in response to the latter's appeal to Confederate soldiers, he had laid down his arms and "give my Self up to the Uninted States Cavelry[.]" Fullilove to Johnson, June 2, 1863, Johnson Papers, LC; CSR, RG109, NA.

3. Under date of June 19 Fullilove adds an apology for having mailed some other "paper" in the envelope addressed to Johnson and sent the previous day.

From John G. Eve[1]

Mt. Vernon Ky June 19, 1863

Gov A. Johnson

We are sold, I am afraid. A Rail Road is to be made right away, as I learn, from Nicholasville via Danville to Somerset and without having the Cumbd. Gap route surveyed. Your interest is identified with ours. You well know that we have the best and cheapest route for a Rail Road and that no better base of military operations can be had than Cumbd. Mountains with a concentrating and diverging point at Cumbd. Gap. Aside then from any personal preferences we might have ought not the Road to be made that way. ought they not at least to give us a Survey. Will you not look after this matter. Let us by all means have a Road to Cumbd. Gap. You put the thing on foot.[2] Will you not now complete it?

Very Truly Yours
John G. Eve

ALS, DLC-JP.

1. See *Johnson Papers*, IV, 549*n*.

2. For over two years Eve had been urging as a military necessity a rail route through Cumberland Gap to Morristown, there to connect with the East Tennessee and Virginia Railroad. Such a line would perforce pass near or through his home town of Barbourville, whereas the alternate route through Danville and Somerset, Kentucky, with Chattanooga as its destination, would bypass Eve's part of the state. Johnson's efforts, before leaving the Senate, to get approval of a road connecting Kentucky, East Tennessee, and western North Carolina had been unsuccessful. See Letters from John G. Eve, July 7, 1861, January 1, 1862, *Johnson Papers,* IV, 549; V, 89; also *ibid.,* IV, 711.

From Thomas B. W. Stockton

Columbus Ohio June 20th 1863.

Brig. Genl. Andrew Johnson
Mili. Govr. of Tennessee
Govr.

Since I last wrote you, enclosing you a copy of Govr Seymour's[1] consent to my raising one Regt. of Infantry in New York State, I have personally appling to Governors Blair & Yates[2] for their consent, but in both instances failed in obtaining it—

I wrote you the result of my interview with Govr Todd, & expected to have heard from him before now— not doing so, I came here to day to see him again, but found he was absent— he will return to night & I shall stay over to see him & will write you what he finally determines upon.

The late movements of the Rebels under Genl. Lee, which has induced the recent call for an 100,000 men; 30,000 of whom are to come from Ohio, will, I fear, cause the Govr to refuse any out side recruiting at the present.

Govr Blair's objection was "that he wanted to fill up the old Regts. now in the field and therefore did not want any thing to interfere with that[.]"

Gov Yates objected "in toto", to yielding up his perogative in *raising* & *officering* all Troops sent out from Illinois—but even if he had consented, I much doubt whether recruits (Volunteers) could be got from that State under the *present political aspects,* at *this time*— In fact he said distinctly that "he objected to any *Volunteers* being taken, *because* none but good *Union Men* would volunteer & *that* would just so much weaken *that party*"![3]

I regret to say that affairs look gloomy indeed— It is Evident that "*volunteering*", (unless, as now, the Rebels bring the war home to them) seems to have been played out—and if the "Conscript Law" be resisted, as it seems it has in some localities, I see no way that we can recruit our Armies except by an Armed force like the Rebels have done—[4]

And the sooner this is done, I think the sooner this War will be Ended.

From what I can learn I now believe that I might recruit a Regt. from East of the States of Wisconsin & Iowa or Minasota were you willing to let me try—

I shall, unless you otherwise direct, go on with the Regt. from New York— perhaps in a short time, one, or all of the Executives who *now refuse,* may yield their consents for troops to be raised[.]

Gov Blair informs me he should visit Tennessee this or next week—[5] You will see him & may induce him to consent *at once*[.]

If so, please inform me— Could not these Regiments be *mounted*?— They would be far more efficient, & could be much more *rapidly* recruited— An Early response is solicited directed to "Buffalo, N.Y."—

Very respectfully
T. B. W. Stockton

ALS, DLC-JP.

1. For Horatio Seymour, see *Johnson Papers*, III, 317*n*.

2. Austin Blair (1818-1894), New York-born lawyer and Union College alumnus (1837), moved to Michigan in 1841, where he served in the lower house (1845) and senate (1854) before becoming war governor (1861-65) and congressman (1867-73). A Republican, he supported Johnson's impeachment and upon leaving Congress resumed law practice. *BDAC,* 560-61; for Richard Yates, governor of Illinois, see *Johnson Papers,* V, 272*n*.

3. Yates was battling the anti-administration, anti-war Democrats in Illinois. The previous fall's election having been a Democratic landslide, largely due to the volunteer system which brought the enthusiasts into the army while leaving the dissidents at home, he was now unwilling to take any chance of further weakening Union support in the state. E. L. Kimball, "Richard Yates, His record as Civil War Governor of Illinois," *Journal of the Illinois State Historical Society*, XXIII (1930-31), 55.

4. The Confederate conscription system, hampered by exemptions and cumbersomely administered through state enrollment officers, had been so slow in filling depleted ranks that commanders, using a January 8, 1863, circular permitting recruitment in the field, set up military details to round up men of military age, including stragglers and deserters. Gen. Gideon Pillow, designated "superintendent of Volunteer and Conscript Bureau," initially for Bragg's, later Johnston's, army, strongly believed that compulsory "obedience," not "moral obligation" inadequately propped up by "enrollment and orders," was necessary. Credited with more than 12,000 recruits the first month, Pillow's armed details, numbering at one time about 2,000 men, were "not unfrequently . . . compared to the press gang, sweeping through the country with little deference either to law or the regulations," overruling exemptions and in many cases overpowering the legally established conscript boards. Failing to gain the sanction of the secretary of war, this military conscript bureau ultimately collapsed in December, 1863. *OR,* Ser. 4, II, 359-62, 403-4, 449-50, 675-76, 680-81, 748-49, 859, 868-69, 1063-64; Albert B. Moore, *Conscription and Conflict in the Confederacy* (New York, 1924), 191-95, 208-15.

5. On the evening of June 25, Blair, accompanied by his adjutant and quartermaster generals as well as other dignitaries, arrived in Nashville to inspect the various Michigan regiments there and at Murfreesboro, "for the purpose of ascertaining their condition and wants, if any." Nashville *Union,* June 27, 1863; *Missouri Republican* (St. Louis), July 1, 1863; Nashville *Dispatch,* July 3, 1863.

From Thomas B. W. Stockton

Columbus Ohio June 21, 1863

Brigr. Genl. Andrew Johnson
Mil. Gvr. of Tenne.

Genl. I wrote you yesterday of my arrival here & of the result of my applications to the Executives of New [York] Michigan & Illinois.

I have had interview to day with Govr. Todd— He informed me that he had written to you and the Secy. of War,[1] as he said he would do on my first application to him, but that he had not recd. any answer from Either—that he now, as then felt willing to furnish Troops in the manner he proposed—but that *now,* whilst called upon by the Genl. Govt. to furnish 30,000 men immediately for the protection of his own borders,[2] he could not, under any Circumstances, consent to any recruiting in the State for other purposes— As soon as this emergency was over, he would do all he could—

As I stated in my letter yesterday, I see no chance, *at present* & as affairs now stand, of recruiting in either of these States (Ohio, Michigan & Illinois)[.]

I will ascertain what can be done in Wisconsin, Iowa & Minnesota, if you will authorise me to do so—& in the mean time use every means to get up the Regt. from New York— All of the Governors agree that Troops raised in the manner proposed, would *not* be entitled to the *State* bounties—if so can not one be promised from the State of Tennessee?— If a liberal state bounty could be given, it would help much to induce men to prefer that service to any other—

I would also suggest that *each* Company as soon as filled, might be ordered on to the place of rendezvous instead of waiting for any other— The sooner men are got away from home & their old associations the better, & the fewer desertions will occur—

What success are others, who, are authorized by you, meeting with?— I am satisfied that Cavalry & Artillery Troops can be much sooner raised than Infantry—for men are charmed with the idea of having a horse to ride— If therefore you could and would authorize me to raise these Regiments as "*Mounted* Infantry," I could the more easily enlist men—and I am fully satisfied that for *frontier* duty *all Infantry should be Mounted*—so as to make rapid moves either to reconnoiter or attack—

I leave here by first Train for Buffalo N.Y. where I shall hope to receive your reply[.]

Very respectfully— T. B. W. Stockton

ALS, DLC-JP.

1. Tod's letter to Johnson and Stanton has not been located.

2. As Lee advanced north and threatened Ohio's eastern border, the President called 100,000 militia from Pennsylvania, Ohio, Maryland, and West Virginia into the U. S. service. Tod had learned on June 15 that Ohio's quota was 30,000. *OR*, Ser. 1, XXVII, Pt. III, 140, 144, 364; Ser. 3, III, 360.

From R. Clay Crawford

June 23, 1863, Somerset, Ky.; ALS, T-Mil. Gov's Papers, 1862-65, Petitions.

Captain of Co. B, 1st Tenn. Lgt, Arty. Bty., having "laboured faithfully" to bring his command up to "the standard of disciplined troops," and now authorized "to recruit further," wants command of the regiment or battalion; because of his sixteen years in the service (with López in Cuba and Walker in Nicaragua), he is not "willing to place myself under the command of one unacquainted with military science." He has "laboured for the Government since the fall of sumpter . . . except when laying on my bed from wounds received in action or when in a southern prison as a prisoner of war."

From Richard M. Edwards

Wellers[1] Nashville June 23rd 1863

General A Johnson Mil Gov &c,
Nashville
Dear Sir;

Feeling a proud consciousness of having done my duty in the attempt to organize a Regiment by your authority, as well as my limited judgment warranted; I have so far shrank from no investigation of my conduct, & now would infinitely prefer an open fair investigation to this detestable secret plotting and conspiring policy adopted by the officers of my Regiment. The fact that you have appeared impatient at all times when I would seek to talk with you freely and frankly, has been a source of painful regret to me, and causes me now for the last time to attempt a plain unvarnished statement of facts, which have transpired, (not so much for my justification, for until a tangible charge is made I hope no such thing will be deemed necessary) but rather that you may have the facts, & decide for yourself. As I told you or wrote you once before I have had my difficulties during the entire time since I commenced organizing my Regiment. These difficulties mostly seem to have sprung out of the fact that I had held office in the Legislature of 1861-2[.] Those who began to cry me down on that subject Ray, Cook, & Pickens,[2] have long since got ashamed of it & quit it & now profess friendship for me personally, & neither of them doubts my loyalty, for a moment. They did not doubt my loyalty in the beginning, but they saw they could make a point against me in the recruiting business & they did it on that score. I felt that to some extent I deserved censure, and for fourteen months have served the Government without pay as a kind of penance for whatever of dereliction of duty might have been involved in that act. Now I think I have done enough. I am unwilling to be any longer made the football[3] & sport of every little selfish upstart who cares more for his own advancement than the good of his country.

When these efforts were being made by other parties not connected with the Regiment, the line officers now in the Regiment were ready on all occasions to fight my battles & vindicate my character. Especially in my presence they were my devoted friends, and of course won my unbounded confidence by their oft repeated expressions of Sympathy and friendship. To some of them I loaned money for which I owe to day to aid them in getting up companies. Thus stood matters when your telegram was received at Louisville ordering me to report without delay to you. I lost not a moments time in obeying that order. On my arrival here it became necessary to organize the men into companies & have them mustered into service. There were but two companies that had the requisite number for mustering in Easly's Co (B.) & Meadors Co (C)[.][4]

There were eight others in course of formation, no one of which half full. But some kind of organization was absolutely necessary. I issued an order that the different squads should try to consolidate in some way so as to be agreeable all round. One week was consumed by them and no understanding or arrangement was made. Although sick and very weak I got lists of their names & consolidated the different squads and so arranged as to give the offices round to the heads of the various parts of companies. Thus you see I did for those officers what they could not do for themselves, I helped them to positions which I am sorry to find they are so poorly qualified to fill. During all this time these officers were whispering into the ears of the men the important fact that you would not issue a commission to me; and at the same time expressing in my presence great displeasure towards you in consequence. This was a part of a design which I did not dream of then, but clearly understand now. It was for the purpose of getting the men's minds turned to another as a leader. That being accomplished half the work was done, towards my downfall, as they supposed.

They even had the report in camp that you had stated that you would not commission me, and while leaning upon me for support to positions were very loud in their denunciations of you for the supposed injustice you were going to do me. So long as their personal interest could be subserved by being friendly with me they were most devotedly friendly. When I had helped them as high as I could without surrendering the place designed for myself, they turn round and conspire to force me to give up that position in order that they may rise a little higher. After the most bitter condemnation of you for what they pretended to believe you were going to do, by which they got my confidence & their positions, they now turn round with the hope of helping each other still a little higher and petition you to do that which they condemned.[5]

In their petition they accuse me or rather express a want of confidence in my patriotism honor & integrity. In the presence of these same officers I read their petition and demanded a specification of some act leading to such conclusion & they failed to show or attempt to show a single thing.

Seeing that they had been caught in signing a falsehood for a large majority of the men signed petitions denying the allegations of their officers, they send off post haste to Col Gillam[6] the additional falsehood that I am trying to get up a mutiny in camp. These men because they happen to be officers can say & do any and every thing against me the prospective head of the Regiment and that is all right, no insubordination in that. But if the men petition for me to be put in command these *officers* consider that insubordination, because it may interfere with their prospects for promotion.

Being determined on carrying a point they talk of resigning if I am put in command. Thus saying to you in effect, that it makes no difference whether the men are pleased or not, if you don't please us we will resign! Perhaps this is the kind of *Patriotism* they refer to in their celebrated petition. If so the petition is nearer correct than I had supposed, for I do not lay claim to much patriotism no how & especially that kind of patriotism.

Again they complain to Col Gillam that I struck the Dr.[7] &c. Now the facts stand thus. One of the recruits was lying in one of those hot tents suffering terribly & the recruiting officer desired him sent to the hospital & I made out his descriptive list & prepared to send him. The old Dr. refused to let the ambulance go to take him & Stephens[8] backed him in the same. I went to the old fellow & asked him politely to let the ambulance go & he refused & insulted me grossly.

I retorted in harsh language no doubt, he hunted a stick & in presence of Stephens *struck me!*

Maj Stephens stood by & uttered not a word while the old fool was striking me with a stick, but when I walked up to the Dr. & pulled him out of his tent & slashed him against the ground, Stephens all at once became greatly indignant & seized me rudely & pretended that I had done something terribly bad & talked very insulting hoping to get me to strike *him,* for which he certainly would have some holt on me. Seeing what he & his pimps were after I held my temper & submitted to gross insults from those who had positions that shielded them from danger. I suppose Stephens made complaint to Col Gillam about that.

And why did I interfere with the Doctor's business? Because he is wholly incompetent. He permitted one case of smallpox to lie in the tent three days without knowing what it, was. He permitted one man in Co (C) to lie in the hot tent & die rather than send him to the Hospital[.] Several of the men are seriously injured some with deafness and one with insanity by mistreatment.

Under such circumstances I felt it my duty, to interfere to save life. The men looked to me for it & I did what I believed to be my duty & am now better convinced than ever that I did right. You perhaps may take a different view of it but I cannot believe that any officer does his duty who fails to look after the health of their men. Because I do this, and because I have on all occasions treated men like they were human beings & have not affected a superiority where none existed, & because I have frequently expended the last cent out of my pocket to purchase something for the men to eat when they had nothing I now have the good will of the men and because those who have been with me so long still adhere to me particularly Co. B. & C. (nearly every man of whom signed petitions for my appointment), these officers pretend that I am trying [to] get up insubordination. Such shallow pretences are disgusting.

Now you have been told that the men did not sign those petitions as I am informed. There is a way to test this matter. You go to the Regiment at the earliest possible moment, & I will stay away myself, make all those officers who have signed that petition get outside of the lines call the men together & talk the matter over with them & ask them if what I have said is true, & then tell all who are in favor of me being their commander to form line, & those opposed to form another & see how the matter stands. The men have all the time expected you to do that ever since you did them the honor to make them a speech at the other camp,[9] in which you told them you would respect their preference.

I deemed this statement necessary for the vindication of the men the humblest one of whom has just as good a right to say he will not serve under certain officers as the oldest captain in the Regiment.

I am staying at the Weller house because Maj Stephens has taken my tent & left me no place to stay in camp.

This last act of brutality and usurpation is sanctioned by Col Gillam, because he has been informed thus & so!!!

Whoever heard of any Military man passing sentence without trial or evidence?

But Col Gillam takes it upon himself to uphold Maj Stephens in the most outrageous violations of all military law and Regulations, and if I complain, he says he has been informed of this and that &c. Now why not have the matter investigated and give me a chance. Because they dare not give me a fair showing, & hence they work secretly & Col Gillam pretends to believe all they say altho he knows I have proved them false. He would deprive me of a hearing entirely. You gave me authority to draw a tent in which to live while discharging the duties you had assigned to me. He gives another permission to force that tent out of my possession for which I had receipted thus virtually usurping your authority or directly trampling it under foot. Am I to be thus treated and not complain.

The desk & other public property in which I had many private papers of value was by Maj Stephens forced open in my absence & papers searched & examined *secretly*. Thus I am treated & when I ask this paragon of Military Science to correct the irregularity of the officer, he replies "I have been informed so & so!" & refuses.

The truth is it is a deep laid scheme which Col Gillam in my opinion is privy to, to destry me for the promotion of these officers & what else I know not.

Will you order the tents returned to me or endorse the outrageous conduct of those who never have been your friends & thereby sacrifice one who never was your enemy, without a hearing although asking the investigation?

To conclude.

They alledge to Col Gillam that I am trying to get up mutiny in camp. Go ask the men who are not *interested* by the hopes of office & they will deny it.

They alledge that a majority of the men dislike me. Four-fifths give a contrary statement.

They say they will resign if I am placed in command, & the men say they will disband if I am not. It is all right for them to resign out of the Service but all wrong for the poor soldier to express even a wish for me to be commander. You as Governor of the State endorse my application for Quarter Master stores, & they by force take them out of my possession, thus defying your authority[.] One day they denounce you for what they pretend to think you are going to do, & the next day they petition you to do that same thing!! One day Lieut Blackman[10] denounces you on account of your democracy & says you never did a public act from patriotic motives, but to promote your own private aims; also that you had taken your position as a Union man from purely selfish motives[.]

The next day he becomes a supplicant at your feet & speaks as falsely of me as he formerly did of you.

I confess to you that I am ashamed of having pleaded his cause before you. It only proves however that I was not engaged as he was in trying to promote or pull down any one on account of former political associations[.]

It will be a nice story to go back to Dixie, that after a years service I am dismissed without thanks because I once was a Democrat.

Your friend as ever
R. M. Edwards

ALS, DLC-JP.

1. The Weller House, 29 S. Cherry Street, was owned by Ben S. Weller, Sr. (*c*1800-1873), a Kentucky-born tin- and coppersmith with $25,000 real and $8,000 personal property. 1860 Census, Tenn., Davidson, Nashville, 3rd Ward, 71; *Singleton's Nashville Business Directory* (1865), 243; *Nashville City Cemetery Index,* 83.

2. Daniel M. Ray, William R. Cook, and William C. Pickens.

3. A reference to the embryonic American game of football, a blend of rugby and association football or soccer. With no established rules, the play was crude and rough, consisting of "kicking, pushing, slugging, and getting angry." By 1860 football was organized in the secondary schools around Boston, but it was not until 1869 that the first intercollegiate game was played between Rutgers and Princeton. *Encyclopedia Americana* (1963 ed.), XI, 455-56; Allison Danzig, *History of American Football* (Englewood Cliffs, N. J., 1956), 6-7.

4. Thomas H. Easley and Daniel Meador. Meador (*c*1830-1863), a Campbell County farmer and captain, Co. C, 4th Tenn. Cav., USA, drowned while bathing in the Cumberland River near Nashville, August 8, 1863. *Tenn. Adj. Gen. Report* (1866), 395; CSR, RG94, NA; 1860 Census, Tenn., Campbell, 6th Dist., 47.

5. See 4th Tenn. Cav. officers to Johnson, June 5, 1863, Johnson Papers, LC.

6. Alvan C. Gillem. For notice of the petitions, see Letter from Richard M. Edwards, June 18, 1863, note 2. The regiment, reorganized in January, 1863, as 4th Tenn. Cav., was assigned to Gillem's command. *Tennesseans in the Civil War,* I, 327.

7. Possibly John S. Jones (b. *c*1820), a surgeon who mustered into the 1st East Tenn. (Edwards' original regiment), December 31, 1862, and resigned June 9, 1863. *Tenn. Adj. Gen. Report* (1866), 303.

8. Meshack Stephens.

9. Now located "north of the city on the Buena Vista pike," the 4th, upon arrival from Kentucky early in February, had pitched their tents "a little west of where the old penitentiary stood." It can be assumed that the governor addressed them at the latter site. Eckel, *Fourth Tenn. Cav.,* 25.

10. Luther M. Blackman (1834-1919), a northerner who moved to Knoxville in 1855, engaged in the marble business before the war. He served as 1st lieutenant and major, 4th Tenn. Cav., USA (1862-65), state representative (1865-69), assistant district internal revenue assessor (1869-70), special revenue commissioner (1870-74), and editor of a Clinton newspaper before retiring to a farm in Monroe County. McBride and Robison, *Biographical Directory,* II, 67-68; CSR, RG94, NA; Eckel, *Fourth Tenn. Cav.,* 109-11.

From Henry Kaldemorgen[1]

Cincinnati June 23th/63
Columbia street No. 6
bet main & state street

His Excelency Johnson Governor

With this letter I send a letter to Parson Brownlow but as I am afraid that my letter might not come to his hand I take the liberty to write to you too.—

The conscript law is here now in force[.][2] I am with all my heart willing to obey any law of the U. S. and you know that I have risked my life for it and suffered for it in the Jail at Knoxville—with Parson Brownlow and others, I was realised [released] from the Jail *On Honor* and had to give security[.] Dr Gates[3] gave the necessarry security for me.

Mr. Brownlow knows all of it that I had to leave every thing, my little brewery, even got my pockets robbed[.] if I was in the U. S. army again and happened to be war prisoner from the South I would be shot imeadately. You will therefore please to send me the necessary paper to be exempt from the conscript Law—as the Laws of the U. S. provided.[4] You will remember I spoke about my case at the Burnet house at this City— I refer to Mr. Brownlow for the truth of my statement.

I remain with great respect
Your obedient servant
Henry Kaldemorgen
Knoxville E. Tenn.

ALS, DLC-JP.

1. In view of his having managed to reach adulthood without leaving any trace for the assiduous searcher, it is not surprising that Henry Kaldemorgen avoided the draft, as he remained in Cincinnati through 1868, operating a saloon and boarding house during most of that time. *Williams' Cincinnati Directory* (1863-68), *passim*.

2. The Conscription Act of 1863 made all able-bodied men between the ages of twenty and forty-five liable to be drafted into military service. *U. S. Statutes*, XII, 731-37.

3. Probably Dr. Edward O. Goetz (1816-1876), who had immigrated to Wartburg in Morgan County after supporting the Revolution of 1848 in Baden, Germany. Moving his medical practice first to Kingston and then to Knoxville, he served as a major and surgeon in the U. S. Hospital Corps during the war. Hobart S. Cooper, German and Swiss Colonization in Morgan County, Tennessee (M. A. thesis, University of Tennessee, 1925), 62-63, 101; WPA, Knox County Tombstone Records: Old Gray Cemetery, 141.

4. The act does not specifically mention exemptions for civilians paroled from imprisonment by Confederates.

From Samuel Watson

June 23, 1863, Sycamore Mills, Tenn.; ALS, DLC-JP.

Samuel Watson, a manufacturer, requests compensation for B. F. Binkley's services taking loyalty oaths and bonds in their native Cheatham County. Reports that "in Cheatham County on our side of the Cumberland, Union feeling is decidedly in the ascendency. Your kindness toward many of our Citizens has won for you a strong feeling of esteem & attachment & I *know* that it has made many true & devoted Union Men & amongst them some of our most substantial Citizens."

To Ernest M. Bement[1]

Nashville, June 23 1863.

Major Ernest M. Bement,
New York City.

Will Governor Seymour, under the circumstances, turn over to me the men you have raised[2] and place them under your charge, or had they better be turned over to him. If such arrangement as will effect the object of their enrolment cannot be made, would it not be better to release them.

Perhaps it would be best under all the circumstances to release them in New York & Pennsylvania. They will be very acceptable if they will come to Tennessee as emigrants. You will please tender to Governor Seymour my sincere thanks for the manner in which he has favored the attempt to raise troops in N. Y. for the purpose of reclaiming Tennessee & putting down this Rebellion.

You will exercise your best judgment in disposing of the men recruited and then come to Nashville and I will do the best I can for you.

Andrew Johnson Mil. Gov'r

Copy, Johnson-Bartlett Col.

1. Ernest M. Bement (b. *c*1834), New York native and Detroit produce and commission merchant, served briefly as major, 3rd Pa. Cav. (1861-62). During May and June, before his authority was revoked by the secretary of war, he recruited (at 167 Broadway, New York City) the "Andrew Johnson Cavalry" for special service in Tennessee. Arriving in Nashville in August, he founded the Nashville Wood Company and helped supply the inhabitants with fuel during the next winter, severing his ties with that firm in mid-May, 1864. After the war he lived in New York City. 1860 Census, Mich., Wayne, Detroit, 1st Ward, 22; Detroit city directories (1855-59), *passim; Official Army Register: Volunteers*, III, 763; Bement to Johnson, August 5, October 8, 1863, January 15, 1864, Johnson Papers, LC; Nashville *Union*, August 11, 1863, May 20, 1864; *Trow's New York City Directory* (1867), 79; (1868) 79; (1869), 82.

2. The preceding day Bement had reported: "Two full companies in Penna four hundred good men here enrolled part mustered." Bement to Johnson, June 22, 1863, Johnson Papers, LC.

Appointment of Commissioner of Abandoned Property[1]

State of Tennessee
Executive Department.
Nashville, June 23d 1863.

Charles Davis Esq[2]
Nashville, Tenn.
Sir:

By virtue of the authority conferred upon me by the Secretary of War under orders of the War Department dated respectively April 2d & April 18th 1863, you are hereby appointed Commissioner to take possession of property, and collect rents for property, within the City of Nashville and County of Davidson, "possessed or owned by persons engaged in the rebellion",[3] and rent or lease them upon such terms as you think proper, subject however to the approval of this office.

You will keep a Book of Registry in which you will enter what property you have taken in charge, the name of the former proprietor or owner, and keep therein an accurate account of the rents or products of the same, the name of the party to whom the same is rented or leased, and the terms thereof.

You will execute to all parties with whom you officially contract in the premises, such vouchers, receipts or other papers, as may be necessary, in your official name as "Commissioner of abandoned property."

You will receive all monies, services, or products due upon contracts so made, and hold the same subject to the orders of the Government of the

United States, of which you will be informed through this Department.

In all cases of doubt or embarrassment, you will report the fact fully to this Department, and receive instructions in regard to the same.

You will report your action in the premises from time to time to this Department.

For your services you will receive $ per day to be agreed upon so soon as the extent of your duties and field of labor can be ascertained.

Mil: Gov'r of Tenn.

Draft, DLC-JP.

1. This action belatedly implements the governor's Confiscation Proclamation, February 20, 1863.

2. A few days later Charles Davis (b. *c*1824), Maryland-born clerk living in the first ward, published a notice requiring "all persens having in their possession, or acting as agents for the same, any property" owned by rebels, "to hand in a list . . . in the 3d story of the Bookstore of W. T. Berry & Co, Public Square, between now and the 10th of July." 1860 Census, Tenn., Davidson, Nashville, 1st Ward, 1; Nashville *Press*, July 7, 1863.

3. The following day Johnson issued him an additional authority, also based on the February 20 proclamation, "to take charge of property in the City of Nashville 'owned by persons who are within the rebel lines.' " Johnson to Davis, June 24, 1863, Johnson Papers, LC.

From James A. Galbraith

Cincinnati Ohio June 24th 1863

Gov. Andrew Johnson
Nashville Tenn
Dear Sir

I wrote you at London Ky 14 inst on my way up intending to mail at Richmond or Lexington but mislaid the letter.

I am here, as hundreds of other E Tennesseans are from home a refugee from Cruel Oppression. The land of our homes and of my nativity is not now the land of the *free* & the home of the brave.[1] The Iron heel of tyrany has, ground them, until freemen no longer dwell there: every *loyal* Man is a serf regardless of age or condition[.] Unhappy people! Miserable destiny. Women are insulted maltreated in inumerable instances & ways robbed of good name, & sustenace, & God only knows the extent of insult & injury imposed upon the most truly loyal body of people on the Continent. They show their faith & allegiance, thousands of them, in leaving their homes their Parents, their Wives & children, subjected and exposed to Outrages of the merciless pitiless mob, and flying through the perils of the difficult Mountain passes to join the army of their Country to battle for the right, to fight for their Country, their homes & their dearest friends[.] They must steal away as the culprit in the silent dark hours of the night with light footfall & silent tongue but heavy heart— They come hoping to return soon to redeem their land from tyranys despotic sway—to relieve their best friends from oppression & outrage. To meet in joy those loved ones left behind— But it seems they are doomed to sad disapointment and a long weary existence in Camp—fighting for those who will not fight for themselves. I believed before leaving home that the people of the Northern States did not feel the effects of this war sufficiently to induce or force them to go to the field & fight to bring it to a close. I am now satisfied of it and I sometimes fear the very carelessness or indifference manifested by the citizens—indicates too plainly, Success to the rebellion. If there is not, more active interest taken in the cause of Sustaining the best government God ever gave to men. If there are not more sacrifices made for it by the most concerned, the *citizens* the government is gone irremediably irretrievably gone. And a wicked Scheme at least apparently so, a causeless rebellion, Succeeds in rending in twain a great & good nation & establishing itself upon its wreck—

Your good & fast friends of East Tenn are pining away, litterally dying, from effects of Oppression & disapointment. They have longed and looked for the coming of the Fedl army, (as their deliverers) with as great faith & hope as ever the Jews of old did for the Coming of their great King & ruler— Still one unwelcome disapointment treads upon the heels of another through months and years. The good Lady friends are imploring releif, deliverance from their sorrows, bereavements & trials, which are by no means light. Their Fathers, husbands, brothers & friends are torn from them by a ruthless mob & forced to battle, against their honest convictions of right, against their Country & liberty—& still the Fedl govenment will allow them to endure it all— They treat no other friends so ill, as before said there is not more loyalty embraced in the Sentiments & acts of any people on the Continent male & female3—but their patience is wearing out tis threadbare and not much wonder— The females urged me If I might be able to reach this side and to accomplish *anything* that would tend to relieve them, their frinds & Country, to act promptly & earnestly[.] But my God, Governor, I am not more than a gnat on the horn of the ox— So many others of more influence, higher position in name & fame have been at work, *If honestly*, in behalf of our homes—that I see nothing for me to do, my efforts would be as chaff before the tempest.[2]

But I am here, a wanderer a way-farer among Strangers in, I may say, a strange land.[3] & While it is Gods will I shall live I must do something to sustain myself—and If you can put me in a position or way to gain a position—where I can make some or meet expenses, I shall be very gratefull to you.

When I left home I expected to join R. A. Crawford Esqr in raising a regiment of Cavalry, but the phase of military affairs changed his intentions and also my own. Since Seeing & learning what we have on this Side as affairs stand at present I prefer not to be fastned Securely to the army. I had thought ever since coming across, of making application for Commission to raise a sufficient No. of men to organize An Artillery Company to man a light battery of 6 or 8 pcs. for E. T. don't know whether I could obtain the Commission, and If no attention is to be paid to E. T. I Shall care very little about a place as a soldier in the army. I am under obligation to my wife & children *first* to give them my attention & care, and to do so properly will endeavor to have them passed to this side the line in the course of the next 3 mos, and then my presence with them will be necessary to their enjoyment & comfort of body & mind: I love my Country. I have a strong passion for that old flag, emblem of liberty.— But when a vast majority of our people stand carlessly by & see its greatness & glory passing away and will not raise a hand to help sustain it aye and render it more powerfull & more honord, I dont feel like throwing my body before the wheels of the great car of rebellion that rolls along our Southern border that It may be crushed and mangled and life extinguished for no purpose. The circumstances that surround me forbid that I should do so. If I were a Single man I would long since have been in the field— There are men & means abundant in command of the executive to crush the infernal rebelion *Speedily* and why, can any one imagine, in the name of God, is it not done— why this temperizing? this disastrous delay! If it is the intention not to do it then at once the sacrifice of life the flow of blood & the Squandering of treasure should cease & the rebelious parties be acknowledged independent. If the Constitution is nothing more than a rope of sand, If institutions are greater more powerfull than governments or nations then to use the Vulgar phrase "just let her rip[.]"[4]

Traitorous, Swindling, Speculative, money loving Spirits pervade the Sentiments & aims of too many of our Officers & leaders to a ruinous extent. love of place of honor & selfaggrandizement is first in their hearts and vastly outweighs their patriotism[.]

If the draft would be rigidly executed & the men, honestly & effectively commanded I would have no fears of the result.

If however every newspaper Editor & every demagoging politician & stump speaker and whippersnapper[5] lawyer is to be allowed to write and speak dissention & discord & mob law is to rule down & terify officers from the just and right excution of the laws of the land—then farewell to our Old Govenment. its gone forever gone.

There is such thing as too much liberty under certain circumstances—and we are now in my humble opinion in a condition when rights & priveliges should be restricted, whenever & wherever necessary. The Stability of the govenment & the eventual welfare of the people demand it. If Jeff Davis & Co had not resorted to the despotism now exercised over the southern states, the rebelion would long since have been crushed out—

But I am tresspassing upon your time & patience[.] I *would be glad to see you* but from what I can learn I am almost afraid to go to Nashville now lest I should not be able to *get away* soon[.]

It would have been a God send to the good citizens of E. T. If a Fedl force could have been thrown into that section that they might have been able to secure the fine crop of wheat grown this season. And also to prevent the further extension of the draft or conscription which will I think soon be made to 45[.] it is too bad that we must of necessity shed the blood of so many of our friends, good loyal citizens, to reach our homes[.]

How many firesides will be made desolate how many hearts filled with grief & sorrow, by friends—Fathers arrayed against son, brother against brother—by force[.]

Would to God relief could *soon* be sent to that Criminally neglected & opressed people[.]

If convenient will you please write me at your earlist opportunity at this place and anything you can do to give me or my young frind Davd Jewell, who is with me occupation or employment—will be most favorably rememberd.

Very Respectfully Yr friend
James A. Galbraith

If the raid now making into E. T. should prove a success[6] It should be immediately followed by a considerable force with the object and for the purpose of permanent occupation of the country—or those unfortunate people will be again castigated for the foolish tresspases upon southern rights[.]

But we will patiently wait & earnestly hope for favors shown to our region[.][7]

I have Some Union Bk. Planters Bank, & State Tennessee Bk notes I cannot use here only at a discount of 13 to 15%[.] Could I do any better with it in Nashville for U. S. Treasury notes?

Yours Very Truly
J. A. Galbraith

ALS, DLC-JP.

1. A phrase less trite in 1863 than in the twentieth century. Although written a half century earlier, the "Star Spangled Banner" had not been widely popular until the Civil War when it began to be played and sung frequently in the North. P. W. Filby and Edward G. Howard, *Star Spangled Books* (Baltimore, 1972), 37-38.

2. A common Biblical figure to be found several places in Psalms and elsewhere.

3. A variant of "I have been a stranger in a strange land." Exod. 2:22.

4. A slang expression, probably of nineteenth-century American origin, meaning "to rush along with . . . great speed" and "damn the consequences." *OED*, VIII, 702; Partridge, *Historical Slang*, 532.

5. From seventeenth-century English usage, a contemptuous term to describe a precocious but impertinent youth. *OED*, XII, 56.

6. To pave the way for the invasion of East Tennessee, General Burnside had recently sent 1,500 cavalry under Col. William P. Sanders to wreck bridges and communications south of Cumberland Gap. Leaving Mt. Vernon, Kentucky, June 14, Sanders went via Huntsville, Tennessee, to Lenoir's Station where he captured the artillery garrison and crippled telegraph lines and part of the railroad to Knoxville. On the twentieth he actually entered that town but after an artillery duel withdrew north toward Strawberry Plains, destroying several bridges, the most important being the one over the Holston River.

Abandoning his artillery and crossing Clinch Mountain at Smith's Gap, he was back in Kentucky by the twenty-fourth. Having captured and paroled 461 prisoners, he had lost only 2 killed, 4 wounded, and 13 missing. *OR*, Ser. 1, XXIII, Pt. I, 385-89; Digby G. Seymour, *Divided Loyalties* (Knoxville, 1963), 77-78.

7. On June 29 Galbraith wrote the governor that he had been offered a very remunerative position scouting for General Burnside in East Tennessee, but wondered if Johnson had a less dangerous job "that will pay me as well, or If better no objection of course."

To Henry C. Hodges[1]

State of Tennessee
Executive Department,
Nashville, June 24 1863.

Capt. H. C. Hodges
A. Q. M. Nashville Tenn
Captain:

The bearer, Michael Gurnard,[2] represents that he and his family are in great trouble and want from having their house and place of residence seized and occupied by the military.[3]

If you can procure the release of Mr. Gurnard's property it would be a great favor to him and one no doubt that he deserves[.]

Very Respectfully Yr Ob't. Servt.
Andrew Johnson Mil: Gov'r

L, DLC-JP.

1. Henry C. Hodges (*c*1831-1917), Vermonter and West Point graduate (1851), served as lieutenant on the frontier at Fort Vancouver in Oregon and with the McClellan Expedition making surveys for the Pacific railroad. Earlier in the war he had been on duty in New York City; currently quartermaster of the post at Nashville, he was about to become chief quartermaster, Dept. of the Cumberland. He retired with the rank of colonel in 1895. ACP Branch, RG94, NA; *West Point Register* (1970), 244; *U. S. Official Register* (1863), 147; Louisville *Journal*, September 4, 1863.

2. Michael Gurnard (b. *c*1812), a French-born carpenter and groceryman with $6,500 real and $500 personal property, lived on Market Street. 1860 Census, Tenn., Davidson, Nashville, 2nd Ward, 52; *Nashville City and Business Directory* (1859), 72; *King's Nashville City Directory* (1870), 131.

3. Assistant Quartermaster Simon Perkins, Jr., responding to Hodges' request for information, indicated that the house was being used by Lt. Irwin, A. A. Q. M., "as Quarters for Mechanics in his employ." Explaining that the ownership had been erroneously attributed to a Mr. Mitchell, he reported that "The House is entered on my reports at $16.00 per month Rent due from Mar. 1st." Endorsements by Hodges and Perkins.

From Francis M. Farmer[1]

Loveland Ohio June 25th 1863

Will your Honour please to inform me whether I am subject to conscription or draft or not. Here is my case. I am an East. Tenn. 14 months ago I left home to join the *Union Army*[.] in crossing the Lines I was captured as a citizen, to remain a prisoner during the war. so having no protiction from the U. S., I took an oath not to fight, against them. (Rather then to remain a prisoner) gave Bond $2000. Dollars. Since I crossed the Lines rather than go to the Rebel *Army*, I have also got my family here, with me[.] My home was once in Greeneville Tenn. I was a printer in the Democrat office,[2] in /54 &c &c[.]

I hope to have your opinion soon[.]

Your Friend F. M. Farmer

ALS, DLC-JP.

1. Probably Francis M. Farmer (b. *c*1834), who subsequently worked as a painter in Cincinnati. Sistler, *1850 Tenn. Census*, II, 238; *Williams' Cincinnati Directory* (1864), 131.

2. Established in the fall of 1858 by H. G. Robertson and edited by him and Samuel S. Turner, the Greeneville *Democrat* by late 1860 had become the Greeneville *Banner*. A radical, pro-southern paper, it was issued until Federal occupation in 1863, functioning for the last few weeks as a small tri-weekly. *Goodspeed's East Tennessee*, 889; Greeneville *Democrat*, April 17, 1860.

To Salmon P. Chase

June 27, 1863, Nashville; L, DLC-JP.

In conformity with the July 1, 1862, act "to provide Internal Revenue," Johnson recommends that Davidson, Robertson, Cheatham, Montgomery, and Stewart counties constitute District No. 1, and Sumner, Macon, Smith, Jackson, and Wilson, District No. 2; also endorses John W. Bowen of Smith for assessor, 2nd District.

To George Harrington[1]

Nashville, June 27th 1863.

Hon George Harrington,
Ass't Secretary of Treasury,
Washington City D. C.
Sir:

I have the honor to acknowledge the receipt of your communication of the 20th ins't[2] in regard to the appointment of Surveyor of the Port of Nashville, and enclosing copy of Petition of Wm. G. Brownlow and others recommending H. A. Cooper Esq[3] for the position.

In reply thereto I have to state that my attention has been for some time directed to the subject of this appointment, and I think that William B. Wallace Esq[4] of this city, whom I have determined to recommend to the Secretary, will fill the position with greater satisfaction to the public and the Department than any other person named in connection therewith.

He is and has always been an uncompromising Union man, of thorough business capacity, and I earnestly recommend him for appointment as Surveyor.

Mr. Cooper, the party recommended, is now employed as a clerk in the Post office, and, in my opinion, better qualified for that position than the one for which he is recommended.

It is desirable that the appointment shall be made without delay, and I shall be highly gratified if my recommendation should receive the approval of the Secretary.

I have the honor to be,
Very Respectfully, Your Obt. Sert.
Andrew Johnson Mil: Governor.

L. DNA-RG56, Appl. and Recom., Box 15, Tenn., William Wallace; DLC-JP.

1. See *Johnson Papers*, IV, 422*n*.

2. According to this communication, the vacancy in the Nashville surveyorship resulted from the rebel capture of J. R. Dillin, the former incumbent. Besides Brownlow, the signers were Horace Maynard, Samuel C. Mercer, Joseph S. Fowler, Jordan Stokes, Adrian V. S. Lindsley, John Catron, and John A. Campbell. Harrington to Johnson, June 20, 1863, Johnson Papers, LC.

3. Henry A. Cooper (*c*1828-*fl*1889), a New York-born postal clerk, tinner, and plumber with $4,300 personal property, lived at 172 South Summer Street. 1860 Census, Tenn., Davidson, Nashville, 8th Ward, 19; *Nashville Bus. Dir.* (1860-61), 148; *Nashville City Directory* (1889), 212; *U. S. Official Register* (1863), 718.

4. William B. Wallace (b. *c*1834), native Tennessee clerk, whose appointment was approved July 7, became a cotton weigher after the war. 1860 Census, Tenn., Davidson, Nashville, 2nd Ward, 57; *King's Nashville City Directory* (1867), 279.

From Benjamin W. Sharp[1]

Memphis Tenn June 28th 1863.

Gov Andrew Johnsen
Nashville Tenn

Dr Sir Many Causes conspire to urge the people of this Section of the State to an effort to re-organize the State, by the election of members of the Legislature, of Congress the Judiciary &c and to effect which a proposition has been made to hold a *Convention* at Nashville sometime during the Month of July or Aug.

It is believed that such a course would have the tendency to relieve the people from the ma[n]y embarrisments which now oppress them.

Our State is regarded and treated as *disloyal*, while it is known to the World to be as truly Loyal to the Constitution and Laws of the United States, *and to* the *Administration* as the states of *Indiana* or Illinois. Our City is made to suffer much in Commercial relations in consequence of the Status which is imputed to the State, by denominating it "Insurrectionary" &c. I submit to your better Judgment *as the Constant* and devoted friend of the State—and ever Loyal to the U. S. Government; if a remedy can not be provided by the Call of a Convention, in which the people of our State, m[a]y, at an early day, repeal the *ordinance* of *Secession*, order elections to be held in conformity to Law, and so thoroughly reorganize the State; as to place our Gallant old State, in her proper position in the Union of L[o]yal States.

Not being personally acquated with you I feel some delicacy in thus addressing you, but a Sense of duty, and the frequent solicitations of our

Mutual friends impels me to respectfully ask your opini[on] touching this matter, hoping to hear from you at your earliest convenience

I am very truly &c your friend
B. W. Sharp

I take pleasure in referring to Hon John Catron & Judge C. F. Trigg

ALS, DLC-JP.

1. Benjamin W. Sharp (*c*1821-*fl*1883), Pennsylvania-born lawyer, was mayor of Columbus, Kentucky, in 1861. After a brief fraternization with the Confederacy, he moved to Memphis where he was employed as engineer and superintendent of the Memphis and Ohio Railroad before being appointed U. S. commissioner for the West District of Tennessee in the fall of 1862. Remaining in Memphis through the late 1860's, he appears to have moved to Red Bud, Illinois, where he continued as commissioner. 1860 Census, Ky., Hickman, Columbus, 37; *OR*, Ser. 1, XVII, Pt. II, 865; LII, Pt. I, 260; Pt. II, 89; Sharp to Johnson, October 11, 1862, Johnson Papers, LC; *Halpin's Memphis City Directory* (1867-68), 223; 1880 Census, Ill., Randolph, Red Bud, 15; *U. S. Official Register* (1883), I, 681.

From William P. Innes[1]

Hd. Quarters 1st Michigan Engineers
Murfreesboro Tenn 29th June /63

Hon Andrew Johnson
Nashville
Governor.

I leave here in about an hour for the front to put the Rail road in order to Talahoma and will not probably See you in some little time— I find the opposition to my taking charge of these roads Still continues. Gov Blair[2] has agreed to do what he can for me, but cant tell what Success he may have.

I would respectfully Suggest that you at once write to Washington to the Secty of War, and get *his* consent to the appointment of a Receiver by you or consent to your appointing a Suitable person to run the Roads upon the Same terms and conditions as the Louisville and Nashville Road is run— I think you can do it and that will avoid any dificulty— I am confident they are determined to keep the Roads from you and make *you* trouble if you undertake to push it— You ought to ask for the Roads as a necesity for *your* power for doing good in the State; at the Same time ask that my Regiment be detailed to report to you, as they now do all the Mechanical work. I would also respectfully Suggest you get the indorsement of Secty of War to your appointing an Agent for abandoned property So that these Military men *cant* interfere with your plans. Hoping Soon to hear from you and with high regards.

I remain Governor Your Obd. Servt.
Wm. P. Innes
Col Comg 1st Mich Engineers

ALS, DLC-JP.

1. William P. Innes (*c*1827-1893), New York native and Grand Rapids civil engineer, was superintendent of the Amboy, Lansing, & Traverse Bay Railroad. Colonel, 1st Mich. Engineers (1861-64), he was in charge of rebuilding bridges along the Nashville and Chattanooga Railroad during 1862-63, becoming in mid-August military superintendent of railroads under Rosecrans and serving until the latter's dismissal in the fall. In March, 1865, he was brevetted brigadier of volunteers for gallant and efficient service. After the war he was a real estate and insurance agent in Grand Rapids. 1860 Census, Mich., Kent, Grand Rapids, 2nd Ward, 90; *Williams' Grand Rapids City Directory* (1859-60), 70; (1873-74), 178; Fitch, *Annals*, 196; Heitman, *Register*, I, 563; *House Report* No. 34 (Affairs of Southern Railroads), 39 Cong., 2 Sess., 287, 288.

2. Michigan governor Austin Blair, at this time in Murfreesboro visiting the troops from his state, was expected in Nashville for the Fourth of July. Nashville *Dispatch*, July 3, 1863.

From Ernest M. Bement

New York Head-Quarters,
Andrew Johnson Cavalry,
For Special Service in Eastern Tennessee.
167 Broadway, New York, June 30th 1863.

Brig: Gen: Andrew Johnson,
Military Governor &c
Nashville, Tenn.

General: Upon the receipt of your telegram of the 23rd inst.[1] I proceeded to Albany and laid its subject matter before Gov: Seymour, at the same time thanking him in your name for the manner in which he had favored your plan for the redemption of Tennessee. Gov: Seymour expressed his sincere regrets that your humane enterprise should have failed, and by *such means*.[2] You could have his entire state for the cause if the general government would permit. The Governor told me that any disposition of my recruits which I saw fit to make would be perfectly satisfactory to him. He advised me to secure them all and take them with me if I could. I have been disposed to follow Gov. Seymour's advice, and think I shall manage to secure some of the men. Owing to the recent and still pending scare in Pennsylvania I have been obliged to give up the recruits I had in that State.[3] The accompanying copy of a late order from the War Department will do me no good[4]—it may disarrange all my plans: but I shall not give up your interests here until the last moment. I shall probably determine whether to relinquish all claim to recruits—or I shall have all business settled here by the last of this week, and then go directly to Nashville. My failure here has been a sad blow to me: but I trust the "Andrew Johnson Cavalry" will yet live and make its mark in Tennessee. If I could take a Squadron or so with me, I might induce emigrants sufficient to join in Tennessee.[5] I will do the best I can.

In conclusion I must thank you for the kind offer you have made me. I shall endeavor to merit a continuance of your good opinion.

I am, General, Very respectfully
Your obt Servant Ernest M. Bement.

ALS, DLC-JP.

1. See Telegram to Ernest M. Bement, June 23, 1863.

2. At this point the failure could be blamed on the war department which revoked Johnson's authority to appoint recruiters for out-of-state regiments. See James B. Fry to Johnson, June 9, Johnson to Bement, June 17, Bement to Johnson, June 19, 1863, Johnson Papers, LC; Telegram to Thomas M. Vincent, June 10, 1863.

3. Bement realized his recruiting in Pennsylvania was over. The Confederates' second invasion of the North, which had begun in early June, resulted in the capture of York (June 27) and a general panic at Harrisburg, and would culminate at Gettysburg. Long, *Civil War Almanac*, 367, 370, 372; Bement to Johnson, June 22, 1863, Johnson Papers, LC.

4. Not found.

5. After the war department put the kibosh on Johnson's out-of-state recruiting, the governor had suggested that men already enlisted in the "Andrew Johnson Cavalry" might wish to come to the Volunteer State as "emigrants" and thus avoid Stanton's prohibition. Bement had already addressed himself to the task of attracting outsiders, publishing on June 1 a pamphlet in which he described the state's attractions. Two months later, having himself come to Tennessee, he returned to the fray with an open letter "To the Gentlemen who were connected with me in the City and State of New York in recruiting for the 'Andrew Johnson Cavalry,' " in which he spoke rapturously of Nashville: "The climate is unsurpassed. There is no handsomer city in the whole country. . . . All mercantile pursuits are very prosperous here. Whoever engages in them must succeed. . . . No man who comes here will be disappointed. This is a land of patriots, of poets, painters, honest men and beautiful women." And lest his audience be leery of casting their lot with a traditionally southern society, he assured that "The noble head of government here. . . will bring the State into the Union—not in the condition she was three years ago; but it will be emphatically a *white State*. Copperheads have no business here—they will not be welcome." Ernest M. Bement, *An Appeal to the Citizens of New York for the Organization of the Andrew Johnson Cavalry* (New York, 1863); Nashville *Union*, September 1, 1863; see Telegram to Ernest M. Bement, June 23, 1863.

From William Smith[1]

Tennessee Penitentiary
Nashville July 1863.

Gov Johnson:

Hon Sir. I hope you will not consider these few lines in the light of an intrusion upon Your Valuable time and patience. But will consider it in the light of an humble and earnest appeal to Your Excellency for that Justice and Mercy which I consider has been denied me elsewhere.

Upon the 20th of February 1859 I was arrested in Memphis Tenn upon a Charge of obtaining Money under false pretences.[2] The grounds of the Charge and prosecution seemed to be that a stock drover from Alabama stated that I in company with another man had approached him upon the platform of the Memphis & Charleston Rail Road Depot and wished him to give us change for a $20 gold piece. He complied and after we had departed he found that it was not a $20 gold piece but a New York City Hall Medal.

This is substantially the evidence he gave in before the Court against me.

I was arrested and kept in Jail 10 months, was tried and convicted here for 6 Years. I have been in here 3 years last December. A List of Names was made out last Winter by the Inspectors and Agent of the Prison here of all the Old men and those who had been Confined here a long time. My health being poor and being nearly 50 years old my name was in the list but having no friend to press the matter I was left while many others were turned out. I have a family of female children and a forlorn and hopeless wife in Niagara County, New York,[3] (of which State I am a native) who no doubt Mourn me as one dead, and from whom I have not heard since I have been in Prison. Now Gov Johnson this is My Situation. Before high Heaven I am entirely innocent of this Charge although the Circumstance of my being here would seem to discredit my assertion.

I have been in Prison nearly 5 years have suffered severe privations, and much suspense and uneasiness and much more Remains in store for me unless you kindly stretch forth the helping hand to my rescue. I most Respectfully refer you to Mr Cavert[4] and all the officers with whom I have had to do, for a recommendation Concerning my behavior and Character since I have been here.

Hoping you will Consider these lines as an humble petition to you as the fountain-head of Justice and Power, in Tennessee, and will give them that Consideration & weight you may think is right

I remain with great Respect Yours
William Smith

ALS, DLC-JP.

1. William Smith (b. *c*1815), New York-born farmer and laborer who worked as a harness or wagon maker while in prison, was ultimately released on August 5, 1865. 1860 Census, Tenn., Davidson, 10th Dist., 60; *Tenn. House Journal*, 1865, App. table opposite page 112.

2. On February 24, 1859, the Memphis grand jury found bills against Smith and Charles J. Roberts (b. *c*1817) bogus gold coin operators. Roberts, tried immediately, was found guilty of obtaining money under false pretences by passing valueless coins and sentenced to seven years imprisonment. Smith's trial was postponed; not until December 15 was he convicted of larceny and sentenced. 1860 Census, Tenn., Davidson, 10th Dist., 61; Memphis *Appeal*, February 25, 27, March 1, October 26, December 17, 1859.

3. Probably Sarah Smith (b. *c*1828), an English-born milliner with a household containing two daughters, aged three and one, and a thirty-year-old Irish domestic. 1860 Census, N. Y., Niagara, Lockport, 13.

4. James Cavert (*c*1821-1872), Pennsylvania cabinetmaker with $20,000 real and $10,000 personal property on the eve of the war, came to Nashville from Kentucky in the early 1850's, served as penitentiary agent from June 2, 1862, to January 2, 1864, and as revenue collector the following year. 1860 Census, Tenn., Davidson, Nashville, 8th Ward, 52; *Nashville City Cemetery Index*, 14; *Tenn. House Journal*, 1865, App. 41-42; *Singleton's Nashville Directory* (1865), 165.

To James A. Garfield, Tullahoma

Nashville July 1st 1863

To Gen Garfield
Chf [of] Staff
There are a number of Rebel Prisoners here many of them conscripts who desire to Enter the service [of] US[.] will they be permitted to do so[?][1]

Andrew Johnson Mil Gov

Tel, DNA-RG393, Dept. of the Cumberland, Lets. Recd. (1862-65), File 519-T-1863; T-RG21, Adj. Gen's Papers.

1. Garfield replied that Johnson is "permitted to enlist into the service . . . all prisoners now in our hands or hereafter captured" who may be deemed "trustworthy and loyal men." Garfield to Johnson, July 2, 1863, Lets. Sent, Vol. 7 (1863), Dept. of the Cumberland, RG393, NA.

From David Fry

July 2, 1863, Camp near Somerset, Ky.; ALS, DLC-JP.

Claiming to know of 900 potential volunteers in Confederate-held Tennessee, who are "just waiting for some one . . . they can trust to pilot them through out of Dixie," captain of Co. F, 2nd E. Tenn. Rgt. requests authority to raise a regiment which could be organized "within thirty days after receiving the recruiting papers." If the governor fails to accept the proposal, Fry, anxious to "get out from under the Carter boys," wants "very much to be detached from this Regt. and attached to Genl. [*sic*] Robert Johnson Brigade."

From John Gormley[1]

Washington D. C. July 4th 1863.

To His Excellency Andrew Johnson Governor of Tennessee—

Dear Sir: I was taken prisoner by the Rebels on the 11th of July, 1861. I was held a prisoner 8 months at Richmond Va. Raleigh and Salisbury N.C. I escaped from the Rebel Prison at Salisbury NC. on Feby 2nd 1862 and after travelling over a rough mountainous country for nearly 200 miles I arrived in Carter Co. East Tennessee[.] I remained amongst the kind and loyal people of that county for nearly 5 months stopping a portion of the time with my good friend Col. Stover (Your Son-in-law) on the Watauga River[.] Sometime in July 1862 two mountain guides (belonging to Col. Houck's 3rd Reg of Tennessee Infantry penetrated their way across the mountains into Sullivan Co, Tennessee, with these guides I started accompanied by several young men from Carter Co; After 7 days travelling on the mountains only, we arrived 24 above Cumberland Gap Kentucky[.] After arriving home in Philadelphia, I had a long account in the Philadelphia Washington and New York papers[.][2] I only remained at home a few days when I rejoined my Regiment and participated in the Battle of Antietam[.] a few days after the struggle General Howard[3] gave me a meritorious furloagh for 30 days[.] While at home on this furloagh I was taken ill with Chronic Diarrhoe and small-pox, from these diseases I suffered some months[.] I have now received my discharge from the U. S. Service[.]

It is my desire to make application to Gov Curtin of Pennsylvania for promotion[.] If your Excellency would deem it proper I should be happy to receive a recommendation from you directed to me and addressed to Governor Curtin for promotion[.] I have other recommendations to present but would consider yours of greater value.

My Respects to Your wife Charles & Frank Col Stover wife & Family. If Col Stover has run the Blockade I should be very happy to receive a letter from him[.] If your Excellency would not consider it too much trouble I should be happy to receive Parson Carter's[4] directions[.] I wrote several letters to the young men who accompanied me from Carter Co but never received no answer[.]

Hoping that your Excellency will give my case early and favorable consideration I remain Your Obt Servt.

John Gormley
No 389 H Street Washington D C.
In Care J B Abbott Esq—[5]

ALS,DLC-JP.

1. John Gormley (b. *c*1843), native Philadelphia printer, was a private, Co. E, 71st Pa. Inf. (Baker's "California" Infantry). There is no record of the hazardous escape here chronicled. Service records indicate that, although captured at Hampton, Virginia, he actually deserted at Fortress Monroe "on account of bad treatment," delivered himself into the hands of the southern army, was told that he would be released and sent home if he took an oath not to bear arms against the Confederacy, but the Confederate secretary of war would not release him on these terms. On May 23, 1863, Gormley received a disability discharge because of "Hypertrophy of the heart, and indolent ulcers of left leg." CSR, RG94, NA; Philadelphia *Inquirer*, August 20, 1862.

2. The headline read: "Local Intelligence. Statement of An Escaped Union Soldier, from North Carolina. Interesting Details." *Ibid.*

3. Oliver O. Howard (1830-1909), native of Leeds, Maine, West Point graduate (1854), and assistant professor of mathematics, resigned his regular commission in 1861 when he was elected colonel of the 3rd Maine Inf. A brigade commander at First Bull Run and on the Peninsula, he lost his right arm at Fair Oaks. Promoted major general in November, 1862, he commanded a corps at Chancellorsville and Gettysburg, was transferred to the West where he saw service in the Atlanta campaign and in the Carolinas. Appointed a brigadier in the regular army at the close of the war, he served in the West, as superintendent of West Point, and as commander of the Division of the East, becoming major general in 1886 and retiring in 1894. Deeply concerned for the welfare of the Negro, he was the first commissioner of the Freedmen's Bureau and helped establish Howard University. Warner, *Generals in Blue*, 237-39; William S. McFeeley, *Yankee Stepfather: General O. O. Howard and the Freedmen* (New Haven, 1968).

4. William B. Carter.

5. Chief assistant in the Special Relief Department of the U. S. Sanitary Commission. *Boyd's Washington and Georgetown Directory* (1856), 101, 121.

From Eleazer A. Paine

July 6, 1863, Gallatin; ALS, DLC-JP.

Union commander at Gallatin, responding to Johnson's inquiry of the previous day that former slaves working for Paine be enrolled as soldiers, declares that he "cannot . . . spare our black teamsters, cooks, waiters &c as they are just as good to us as so many of our own men in the ranks." However, "there are a number of colored men here who are ready and willing to enlist."

From George W. Tyler

July 6, 1863, Louisville, Ky.; Tel, DLC-JP.

New York Associated Press agent relays cryptic telegraph messages about the military situation in the vicinity of Gettysburg, noting that the "enemy retired under cover night & heavy rain in direction Cashtown," that it was expected their retreat would be "cut off," and that dispatches captured from Jefferson Davis "reveal objects of Lees campaign & Cause of his failure," as well as rebel casualty figures. In addition, reports "Rumored Engagement progressing thirtieth between Johnstons advance & Grants rear" in Mississippi.

To Thomas M. Vincent

Nashville July 6th 1863.

Maj. T. M. Vincent

Can the Tennessee Prisoners of war & especially the conscripts be permitted to join the Tennessee regts. through agents of the Military Prisoners for that purpose[?][1] they ought not to be forced into regiments from other states— I hope the Secy. of war will give this matter his early attention.

Andrew Johnson Mil. Gov.

Tel, DNA-RG107, Tels. Recd., Provost Marshal General, Vol. 1 (1863).

1. The war department's response did not directly answer Johnson's question regarding enlistment in Tennessee regiments but stated that "rebel prisoners of war, who have been impressed into the rebel service, and wish to join our Army in good faith, may be permitted to do so on taking the oath of allegiance." In August Stanton prohibited such enlistments without his approval in each individual case but subsequently made a temporary exception to the rule for enlistments authorized by Rosecrans and Johnson within the Department of the Cumberland. James B. Fry to Johnson, July 10, 1863, Johnson Papers, LC; *OR*, Ser. 3, III, 722, 735, 737-38.

From William S. Rosecrans

Tullahoma July 7 1863

Gov Andrew Johnson
Nashville

I have the pleasure to tell you that the Secry of War telegraphs they have official Information of the Surrender of Vicksburg to Genl. Grant on the 4th of July. on the 1st 2nd 3rd July Lees army was beaten in battle[.][1] on the 2nd of July, Bragg left this his last Strong hold in Middle Tennessee, and on the 4th the rear of his Infantry was over the Cumberland mountains. We may thank God and Congratulate ourselves that the idea[2] of July were auspicious for freedom, and for our own army that we have accomplished a great work without bloodshed, and were prevented only by the unprecedented rains from giving the Coup de grace to Braggs army[.] Come up if you can.

W. S. Rosecrans Maj Genl.

LB copy, DNA-RG393, Dept. of the Cumberland, Tels. Sent, Vol. 63 (1863).

1. At Gettysburg.

2. Possibly "ides"; if so, a testimonial to the general's confusion about the Roman calendar.

From Maury County Refugees

July 8, 1863, Franklin; Pet, DLC-JP.

Driven from their homes "by a lawless band of rebel ruffians because we refused to fight in their unholy cause," twenty-one Maury countians petition for guns and ammunition to "do our whole duty in freeing Tennessee of these out-laws."

To George Burroughs[1]

Nashville, July 8, 1863.

Lieut. Burroughs
Superintending Fortifications Nashville Tenn
Dear Sir

I send you with this note[2] eleven negro men and four negro women to be employed by you in constructing the works under your direction. Their names are Jo, Rafe, George Lewis, Ephraim, Tony, Newton, Green, Pleasant, Russell, William, Milly, Betsy Lucinda Ellen. Please return receipt for them.

I would be pleased to see you at this office at your earliest convenience. I have some instructions from the Secretary of War that I desire to show you[.][3]

Very Respectfully Yr ob't. Serv't.
Andrew Johnson Mil: Govr.

L, DNA-RG77, Claims (1862-92), No. 175.

1. George Burroughs (*c*1841-1870), New Jersey native and West Point graduate (1862), served as a lieutenant and captain (1862-65) with the U. S. Corps of Engineers in the Department of the Cumberland and was currently assisting Capt. James St. Clair Morton in constructing Nashville's defences. Powell, *Army List*, 223; *West Point Register* (1970), 257; *OR*, Ser. 1, XX, Pt. II, 215; XXX, Pt. III, 285; XLIX, Pt. II, 776.

2. A week earlier, in response to the governor's query, "Can you give employment to Negro boys &c," Burroughs had replied, "as many such boys as you may see proper to send us." Burroughs to Johnson, July 1, 1863, Johnson Papers, LC.

3. Possibly Letter from Edwin M. Stanton, April 18, 1863, which instructed Johnson to take charge of contrabands and "provide for their useful employment and subsistence." For later correspondence regarding this matter, see Letter from George Burroughs, October 8, 1863, and Letter from James St. C. Morton, December 5, 1863.

From William F. Stowell[1]

Camp at University Springs[2]
July 9th 1863

Gov Johnson

Sir we have halted here for the night and as it is not dark yet I have concluded to write you a few lines[.] I hope you will pardon my boldness in thus addressing you but Sir the subject I hope will be a sufficient excuse[.] Sir I have thought that there should be some action taken in regard to the vast numbers of Tennesseeans who are leaveing the Southern Army haveing received their rights[.] I have conversed with many of them and they seem willing to do almost any thing rather than to be forced back again into the Southern Army by an exchange of Prisoners[.] there are many of them who will not come into our camps for this reason[.]

Now Sir

I believe that there could be a whole Briggade formed in a short time of these men who would garrison the Forts and States thus relieving our troops and I would humbly sugest that you consider the matter and acct accordinly[.]

Could I do any thing to assist in the matter I would willingly do so[.] for Refference in regard to my self I would refer you to Leit Watterman and Let A L Cole[3] of Gen Morgan Staff also to Col Bradley[4] of Gen Sheriden Div[.]

Sergt. W. F. Stowell
Co K 51st Regt Ill. Vols.
Sheriden Division

Excuse all as I am writting upon an old stump with a poor pencil in hast[.]
W F S

ALS, T-Mil. Gov's Papers, 1862-65, Petitions.

1. William F. Stowell (b. *c*1835), a private and sergeant, Co. K, 51st Ill. Inf. (1861-65), was detailed as a telegraph line repairer at Knoxville in 1864. CSR, RG94, NA.

2. The spring at the Unversity of the South, Sewanee, in Franklin County. One Union soldier wrote that it was "a very large spring of the clearest and finest water I ever drank." Edgar L. Pennington, "The Battle of Sewanee," *Tenn. Hist. Quar.*, IX (1950), 241.

3. George I. Waterman (*c*1836-1884) and Osman L. Cole (1834-1915) of the 51st Ill. Inf. Waterman, 1st lieutenant, Co. B (1862-64) and captain, Co. F (1864-65), was detached to serve as an aide to Gen. James D. Morgan (1862-64). Wounded at Spring Hill, he was mustered out June 16, 1865, subsequently becoming a Chicago lawyer. Cole, a minister and Charlotte, Vermont, native, rose from private to lst lieutenant, Co. H (1861-65). Wounded and captured at Chickamauga, he was not released until March 1, 1865. After the war he lived in New York state. CSR, RG94, NA; Pension files, RGl5, NA; *Bailey & Edwards' Chicago Directory* (1868), 704,934.

4. Luther P. Bradley (1822-1910) of Connecticut moved in 1855 to Chicago where he was a bookkeeper, salesman, and militia officer. Entering the Union army as lieutenant colonel, 51st Ill. Inf.,and promoted to colonel (October, 1862) and brigadier (July, 1864), he was wounded at Chickamauga and Franklin. After the war he remained in the army, advancing to colonel, 27th U. S. Inf., before retiring in 1886, to Tacoma, Washington. Warner, *Generals in Blue*, 40-41; New York *Times*, March 15, 1910.

From John C. West[1]

Provost Marshal's Office,
Bowling Green, Ky., July 13th 1863.

Govr. Andrew Johnson
Gen

I send as requested by you two men charged with stealing Horses or mules. I have no charges nor eveidence in their cases, but I presume they are very hard cases. they have been forwarded to this post from Russellville Ky. They Live in Edgesfield Ten[.] their names is Thos Humpherys & James Humpherys[.][2] There is every Reason to believe them noted Thiefs, although I have no proof to Convict them.[3]

I am Gen Your Obt Servt
J. C. West Lieut & Provost Marshal

ALS, DLC-JP.

1. John C. West (b. *c*1834) enrolled at Hartford, Kentucky, on September 1, 1861, as 1st sergeant, Co. B, 26th Ky. Inf. and was promoted to lieutenant in June of the following year. From February, 1863, until his resignation in February, 1864, he was provost marshal at Bowling Green. CSR, RG94, NA.

2. Thomas (b. *c*1846) and James (b. *c*1847) Humphries (Humphreys) were illiterate sons of Harriet Humphries Hutcherson. After posting a $500 bond, they appeared before Johnson on July 20, and the case was continued to July 27. There is no evidence concerning the outcome. After the war Thomas returned to Edgefield and became a saddletree maker. 1860 Census, Tenn., Davidson, Edgefield, 17; (1880), Nashville, 11th Ward, 2nd Div., 13; Thomas and James Humphries to Johnson, July 14, 1863, Johnson Papers, LC.

3. The same day Felix Robb and James Fleming wrote that the Humphrieses' "character for honesty has always been good" and, until their arrest, "had not heard their honesty questioned." Robb and Fleming to Johnson, July 13, 1863, *ibid.*

Resolutions from Union State Convention[1]

Nashville, Tenn. July 13 1863.

Gov Johnson

I have the honor to enclose to you a copy of the resolutions reported by a Committee and adopted by the Convention or Meeting of Union men recently assembled in this City.

Very respy Your Obt Servt
Horace H. Harrison Secretary

RESOLUTIONS

July 3, 6, 1863.[2]

Resolved that all laws ordinances and resolutions passed by the Legislature of Tennessee since April 12, 1861, intended to affect constitutional changes in the government of the State and to Seperate it from the Federal Union, are unauthorized, the work of usurpation, and therefore void.

Resolved that in view of these circumstances and the condition of the State resulting from such pretended legislation, it is of vital importance to the people to elect a Legislature to meet at the capitol, on the 1st Monday of Oct next or as soon thereafter as practicable.

Resolved that as the overthrow by treason of the civil powers of the State has demanded the exercise of the power granted to the Federal Government to guarantee to every State a republican form of government—that this convention Cordially approves the action of the President in the appointment of Andrew Johnson Military Governor of Tennessee.

Resolved that we request Gov Andrew Johnson to issue writs of Election, and appoint such agents as may be nescessary to hold Elections for members of the Legislature on the 1st Thursday in August next or as soon thereafter as may be expedient, and that he provide Such agents with the means of carrying out the purpose, of such appointment.

Resolved that we fully approve the course of policy of Gov Johnson as Military Governor of the State and pledge to him our hearty co-operation and support, in whatever measures may be requisite for the restoration of Tennessee and her people to their Civil and Federal relations[.]

ALS (Horace H. Harrison), DLC-JP.

1. In June a notice signed by Horace Maynard, William G. Brownlow, and twelve others appeared in the Nashville papers suggesting to "fellow citizens who desire to maintain the State Government in connection with the Federal Union as it stood prior to the rebellion and the war to meet in convention . . . in Nashville, on Wednesday the 1st day of July." Accordingly, over "two hundred duly accredited delegates" from forty-three counties met in the Representatives Hall of the capitol, July 1-3, 6-7. William B. Lewis of Davidson was selected as president; William Spence of Rutherford, William C. Pickens of Sevier, and Robert Crawford of Greene, vice presidents; and Samuel C. Mercer and Horace H. Harrison of Davidson, secretaries, with Crawford actually presiding at most sessions. After extended debate about establishing a loyal state government, the attached resolutions, reported by the Federal relations committee (W. G. Brownlow, chairman, Russell Houston, James G. Spears, W. Bosson, and Joseph S. Fowler), were adopted. Nashville *Press,* June 30, July 2-4, 7-9, 1863.

2. The first three resolutions were approved on the third; the last two on the sixth. Nashville *Dispatch,* July 4, 7, 1863.

From Franklin Businessmen

Franklin Tennessee
July 14th 1863

Gov. Andrew Johnson
Dear Sir

On the 4th of June 1863 certain persons hostile to the Government of the United States from three to five hundred in number banded together as Rebel Soldiers led by Forrest Starnes[1] &c entered the town of Franklin

Irregulars in action near Nashville.
From John Fitch, ANNALS OF THE ARMY OF THE CUMBERLAND (Philadelphia, 1864).

Tenn—and robbed the undersigned of ten thousand and seven hundred dollars worth of Goods, Wares and merchandise[.] That is to say they robbed Sinclair and Moss[2] of eight thousand dollars. H C Sinclair being the looser of three thousand dollars individually, S. H. Bailey[3] twelve hundred dollars and John B. Cliffe[4] fifteen hundred dollars worth. Now as we upon honor believe that the above depredations were committed upon us for and in consideration of the fact that we were known by the leading depredators (many of whom we were acquainted with as citizens of Williamson County prior to the rebellion) to be loyal to the Government of the United States. We most respectfully present these our grievances to your Excellency with the earnest desire that you will inforce in our behalf your Excellencies Proclamation issued at Nashville May 9th 1862.[5]

Yours truly,

Also at the same time and in the same manner they took from J. B Lilly[6] a fine horse worth two hundred dollars. He being personally known to them to be a union man and a friend to the Government of the United States[.]

Sinclair & Moss
by A W Moss
John B. Cliffe
J. B. Lilly

S H Bailey
H. C. Sinclair

ALS (John B. Cliffe), DLC-JP.

1. Attacking Franklin on June 4, Gen. Nathan Bedford Forrest and Col. James W. Starnes drove the Federals out and occupied the town. For Forrest and Starnes, see *Johnson Papers*, V, 562*n*, 370*n*.

2. Henry C. Sinclair (1821-1874), native Alabamian with $4,200 real and $19,300 personal property, and Alexander W. Moss were apparently partners in a tailoring business. 1860 Census, Tenn., Williamson, 1st Dist., 151; *Goodspeed's Williamson*, 803; Williamson County Historical Society, *Directory Williamson County, Tennessee, Burials* (2 vols., n. p., 1973), I, 269.

3. Schuyler H. Bailey (*c*1811-*fl*1880), a Virginia-born grocer with $5,000 real and $10,000 personal property, later made his living by farming. *Goodspeed's Williamson*, 803; Williamson County Historical Society, tr., *1850 Census of Williamson County* (Franklin, 1970), 69; 1860 Census, Tenn., Williamson, 1st Dist., 19; (1880), 9th Dist., 13.

4. John B. (b. *c*1845) was the son of Dr. Daniel B. Cliffe, a Confederate surgeon who turned unionist. Bowman, *Historic Williamson County*, 106; 1860 Census, Tenn., Williamson, E. Subdiv., 8.

5. For the Proclamation Concerning Guerrilla Raids, May 9, 1862, see *Johnson Papers*, V, 374. Under its terms Johnson could force Confederate sympathizers in the neighborhood to indemnify unionist victims.

6. Joshua B. Lillie (1828-1908), born near Watertown, New York, moved to Tennessee in 1855, became a carpenter and joiner, and engaged in the saw mill business (1864-69) before buying and improving Franklin Flouring Mills. *Goodspeed's Williamson*, 994; WPA, Williamson County, Tennessee, Bible, Family and Tombstone Inscriptions, 57.

From Mildred A. Hall

[Nashville] July 14th 63.

To His Excellency
Govenor Johnson.

Have you ever thought of the difficulties that surround & embarrass me—"a poor, lone, defenceless, woman"? brought on too, *some of them,* by your own Proclamation?[1] Will you not release me? My Creditors & especially *Ben Clarke*[2] are persecuting me. I am sick in bed, my boarders are leaving me in consequence of my sickness—& if you do not send for *Garret* & *Gower*[3]—both Constables— & give them orders to collect for me—& release me from the Clark suits & persecutions—then Govenor—you had just as well put me in the Penitentiary & be done with it. I have paid this year's house rent—& Clark has sued me for last year—or rather the balance on last year—

Garret has had at least a thousand dollars worth of my accts ever since March and the cowardly man has not brought me a dollar.

There is a hackman in the city, *Jerry Stoddard,*[4] that owes me one hundred dollars & the scamp wont so much as let me ride in his hack. He owns two hacks & is rich— how can I make him pay— he has boys too—that might be hired out.

Please tell me Govenor, what to do? I have bought no clothing this year.

Respectfully Mrs. Dr. Hall.

ALS, DLC-JP.

1. See Confiscation Proclamation, February 20, 1863.

2. Probably Benjamin Clark (b. *c*1822), native Tennessean and steamboat clerk, who lived on Franklin Pike and was the son of the state supreme court clerk James Clark. Porch, *1850 Census, Davidson,* 250; 1860 Census, Tenn., Davidson, 10th Dist., 76; *Nashville Bus. Dir.* (1860-61), 144.

3. John D. Gower (b. *c*1826), a Tennessee native and former merchant, and John E. Newman (*c*1823-1867), a Tennessean, former clerk, and alderman, were the constables at this time. Mrs. Hall may have mistakenly thought that William W. Garrett (*c*1824-1883), a farmer then serving as a county magistrate, was a constable. Nashville *Union,* July 9, 1863; 1860 Census, Tenn., Davidson, Nashville, 2nd Ward, 54; 4th Ward, 147; 24th Dist., 150; Nashville *Press and Times,* July 9, 1867; Mt. Olivet Cemetery Records, II, 135; Clayton, *Davidson County,* 91; Wooldridge, *Nashville,* 123-24.

4. Jerry Stothard (*c*1816-1866), a Tennessee-born mulatto, had a hack service located on Cherry Street. Although Stothard could scarcely be called "rich," he did admit on the eve of the war to $2,000 in personal property. 1860 Census, Tenn., Davidson, Nashville, 4th Ward, 147; *Nashville Bus. Dir.* (1855-56), 113; *Nashville City Cemetery Index,* 77.

Petition of F. M. Carter[1]

[Nashville] July 16, 1863

To His Excelency Andrew Johnson
Govenor &c

Your petitioner, F M Carter, a resident of Dixon County Tennessee, a true Loyal union Citzen of the United States, and ever have been true & faithful.[2] But is a man in quite Humble circumstance.

That about the midle of April last there came a small band of men calling them selves southern soldiers, to his house and arrested petitioner, and carrid him a way from his little helpless family, and took and carrid away his only nag he had to mak a crop with a mare worth about 125$. carrid him to a place calld Kinderhook[3] about 40 miles from hom, where he suceded in making his escape, they kept his mare. He was arrestd & carrid off & his mare taken for nothing only he was & had been all the time a union man. He is satisfied he was pointed out & causd to be arrestd & thus tried by some of his neighbors who are strong *Secesh* and been aiding & abetting the rebellion and those gurellers, towit, Plumer Williams[4] where they stayed the over night, before he was arrestd erly next moring, Ben Robinson Henry Steuart,[5] & prberly others. Robinson heped them one night & went with them to Williams.

In consequence of this treetment he lost his mare & crop & was therein greatly damege. Petition is adv[i]s[e]d this comes within your proclamation of May 9th 1862.

Therefore, if it can be done, he prays to be remuneratd, & such steps had & may seem right. Williams Robinson & Steuart are now in the City.

as in duty bond &c. F M Carter
by M. M. Brien[6]

July 16th 1863

Pet (M. M. Brien), DLC-JP.

1. F. M. Carter (b. *c*1820), Tennessee native, was an impecunious farmer with only $88 in property in 1860. Deane Porch, tr., *Dickson County, 1850 Census* (Nashville, 1970), 55; 1860 Census, Tenn., Dickson, Mid. Div., 173.

2. An endorsement subscribed to by five signatories attested to his being "a true Loyal union man & a man of verasity." It is interesting to note, however, that in mid-August an F. M. Carter pleaded guilty to the charge of impersonating a policeman and was fined $10.00. Nashville *Dispatch,* August 21, 1863.

3. Kinderhook is in Lincoln County.

4. Plummer Williams (*c*1802-*fl*1870), a farmer and neighbor of Carter, claimed $4,100 real and $16,207 personal property on the eve of the war. 1860 Census, Tenn., Dickson, Mid. Div., 173; (1870), 7th Dist., 2.

5. Arrested, confined in Nashville, and tried on a conspiracy charge of "aiding and establishing guerrilla bands," Robertson was fined $50,000 (later reduced to $10,000) and sent to Johnson's Island. In poor health, he died in Nashville in January, 1864, "released by the authorities at Washington, only a short time before the mandate of a higher power released him from all earthly cares." Henry Stewart, or Stuart (*c*1808-*fl*1870), a Pennsylvania-born brickmason and farmer, in 1860 possessed $5,000 real and $6,807 personal property which dwindled to $4,000 and $1,000 a decade later. Nashville *Press,*

January 23, 1864; see also J. E. Bailey, Jno. F. House, and D. N. Kennedy to Johnson, August 8, 1863, Duke University Library; 1860 Census, Tenn., Dickson, Mid. Div., 153; (1870), 7th Dist., 4; for Benjamin C. Robertson, see *Johnson Papers,* V, 244*n*.

6. For attorney Manson M. Brien, see *ibid.*, 186*n*.

From John Carper

July 17, 1863, Nashville; Pet, T-Mil. Gov's Papers, 1862-65, Petitions.

Nashville citizen petitions for a commission to raise a Negro regiment: "our city is infested with a large number of contrabands, many of whom are without employment & in their present condition are a festering sore upon the body politic. . . . they are terribly imposed upon; many of them being carried back to their traitor-masters to be most cruelly & inhumanly punished." Moreover, "The value of a negro as a soldier, & especially as a cavalry solder is too well known to require any comment— With a body of negro cavaly it appears to me Tennessee could soon be cleared of guerillas & robbers."

From Samuel Morrow[1]

Burnet House, Cin O.
July 18, 1863

Hon. Andrew Johnson,
Brig. Genl and Military Governor of Tenn.
Nashville Tenn.
Sir.

I have been very anxious to visit you at Nashville but events transpiring here have been of more importance for East Tennessee than anything in Middle Tennessee.

Bob Crawford[2] stated to Maj. Chas. Inman[3] that you had telegraphed President Lincoln that no move should be made on East Tennessee before October.[4] I pronounced it false and assured East Tennesseeans that you were now as you had been all the time for the earliest, speediest redemption of East Tennessee—

Isham G Harris has ordered out all of our men from 45 to 55 for defense of homes.[5] If East Tennessee is not relieved before our wheat crop, (which is very fine) is seized by the Rebels, our people *will suffer*—

I send you the Commercial containing an article headed 'Chivalry of Knoxville,' this is from the pen of Fleming and may be called 'fiction founded on fact.'[6] I should like to have it copied in the Nashville Union, with request 'Chattanooga Rebel' and Richmond Examiner "please copy one time and send bill to Union office"[7] Always concealing Fleming's name—

I am very Respy Yr Obedient Servant
S. Morrow

LS, DLC-JP.

1. For Knoxville banker Morrow, see *Johnson Papers,* IV, 281*n*.
2. Robert A. Crawford.

3. Charles Inman (1810-1899), Tennessee-born Sevier County farmer with a large family, attended the Greeneville Convention and briefly served as major, 2nd Tenn. Cav., USA, before resigning in March, 1863. Subsequently, while provost marshal in East Tennessee, he was captured and imprisoned (November, 1863-February, 1865); later he was a state representative (1865-69). McBride and Robison, *Biographical Directory,* II, 451-52; CSR, RG94, NA.

4. No such telegram has been found and it is unlikely that one was ever sent; actually, Johnson was enthusiastically urging Burnside to move into East Tennessee before the summer ended. See Telegram to Abraham Lincoln, May 29, 1863.

5. When Jefferson Davis, under provisions of "An act to provide for local defence and special service," made a requisition upon Tennessee for 6,000 troops for a term of six months from August 1, 1863, the governor, in a June 22 proclamation, announced that the troops would be mustered into Confederate service, "but held for the defence of their own homes and in no event will they be ordered beyond the limits of their State." To be composed of men over forty, the force if not raised by August 1, was to be formed by "a draft upon that part of the militia between the ages of forty and fifty-five." Davis meanwhile ordered the conscription of persons forty to forty-five into the regular Confederate army, an action which caused Harris on July 22 to modify his proclamation to include men between the ages of forty-five and fifty-five. Chattanooga *Rebel,* July 23, 1863.

6. Written by John M. Fleming, former editor of the Knoxville *Register* and now presumably in exile in Cincinnati, the "Chivalry of Knoxville" was a satirical article, amusing from a unionist's point of view, about incidents that supposedly occurred during Col. William P. Sanders' June raid on that city:

> Knoxville is, and has been for the last two years . . . infested by a clique of intolerant secession leaders. . . . They have all the while been furious war men—"last ditchers," "the Yankees could only enter Knoxville over their dead bodies," &c, &c,—but fortunately, until recently their courage had never been tried. Our informant gives us an account of this test. . . . It *seems* that when Colonel Saunders (supposed at the time to be Gen. Carter) approached Knoxville, and turned his artillery toward the town, the courage of the chivalrous knights began to ooze out at their fingers' ends, and . . . they fled in every direction, (except toward Col. S.). . . . Crozier . . . is reported to have precipitately paddled himself across the Holston River, "a straddle" a pine log, while Sperry, the Uriah Heep of the *Register* . . . unwilling to abide the tardy motions of the ferryboat, which chanced to be on the opposite side, plunged frantically into the stream with his half emptied bottle in his hand . . . and . . . soon found himself stranded on the friendly rocks of a dam a short distance below the ferry. The ferryman . . . relieved him from his perilous predicament and landed him, all dripping on the southern shore. . . . Sneed . . . finding his line of retreat cut off, incontinently subsided into a cellar, and, when called for by a servant, who opened the cellar door some two hours after our troops had left, arose from his hiding-place and with eyes dilated, heroically exclaimed: "*Don't fire, General Carter! My name's SNEED, the Hon. WM. H. SNEED, late of the United States Congress. In the language of General Buckner, Sir, I SURRENDER!*". . . . Captain Kain . . . known about Knoxville as "Claib Kain"—was in the town at the time of Col. Saunders' approach, and being a Captain of Artillery was ordered into a battery by the Colonel commanding. But the said Claib, never having enlisted with any idea of going into such a dangerous place as that, is said to have procured his detail as Judge Advocate, and urged furthermore that his company was at Cumberland Gap, that it would never do for an officer to expose his life as a private, etc., etc., but all to no avail. He was peremptorily ordered into the Summit battery. Seeing a Lieutenant pointing a gun toward our forces, the valiant Captain rushed forward exclaiming:—"*For God's sake, Lieutenant, don't fire that gun—the enemy will find out where we are*!"
>
> But the melo-drama of the whole affair is said to have been witnessed in the Branch Bank of Tennessee. That institution is presided over by Dr. J. G. M. Ramsey. . . . When our troops were reported at Lenoir's the Doctor is said to have been quite valerous, but at a later hour, it was ascertained they had reached the Tazewell Road, nervousness got the better part of his courage. . . . He turned to his bank and his first impulse was to secrete himself within the vault; but then the thought of "plundering vandals" drove all idea of security from his mind and he sat down in despair. Calling his Cashier, he said: "Sir, I shall probably not survive this conflict. Should I fall, let the

simple inscription on my monument be "*He died a true son of Mechlenburgh.*" At this instant a shell exploded in a vacant lot near by. The Doctor was overcome. Seizing a copy of "Ramsey's Annals" and clasping it to his bosom he fell back into his chair crying, "*Bury me thus!*"

Nashville *Union*, July 22, 1863; for Fleming, see *Johnson Papers*, IV, 296*n*.

7. Not surprisingly, the Confederate papers failed to respond to Morrow's taunting invitation.

From Charles L. Pascal[1]

Philada July 19—63
No 8. South 6th St

Dear Govenor,

I have just returned from the Battlefields at Gettysburg Pa, where I devoted two weeks hard Labor, among the wounded & dieing Soldiers of both Armeys as a delegate of the U. S. Christian Commission,[2] Among the number was a conscript, your Nephew James M Burchette[3] Co K, 8. Va Reg—with left leg off above the knee, His case to me was very interesting. I cared for him as best I could, He is doing very well, but the chances are against his recovery. Amputation 7 days after the fight.

We washed him, put clean shirt & draw[er]s on him & left him doing very well.

Very Respectfully
C. L. Pascal

P. S. It may be interesting to you to know that he has prepared, through one of our delegates a History of his capture[4] with others on their way to Kentucky & sent as Prisoners to Richmond & from there sent in the Rebel army & a more Loyal Man can't be found.

Very Respectfuly C. L. P.

ALS, DLC-JP.

1. Charles L. Pascal (*c*1820-*c*1878), native Pennsylvanian, carried on a hat business at 8 South 6th Street, Philadelphia, and claimed $4,000 in personal property in 1860. After the war he remained in business at the same address in partnership with James Sullender. 1860 Census, Pa., Philadelphia, 7th Precinct, 24th Ward, 100; Philadelphia city directories (1857-79), *passim*.

2. Organized by the Young Men's Christian Association in November, 1861, and lasting until February, 1866, the commission was a civilian agency dedicated to improving the moral welfare of soldiers by preaching sermons and distributing religious literature. It also encouraged them to communicate with their families and send goodly amounts of their pay home. It assisted medical and hospital personnel both in the field and in hospitals by helping to make the sick and wounded more comfortable and by purchasing and distributing foods unavailable through the military kitchens. During the war it commissioned some 5,000 agents and expended over $6,000,000 to perform benevolent services. James O. Henry, "The United States Christian Commission in the Civil War," *Civil War History*, VI (1960), 374-88; Frank H. Taylor, *Philadelphia in the Civil War* (Philadelphia, 1913), 264-65.

3. James M. Burchett (b. *c*1843), a native Virginian, was a farm laborer from Johnson County, Tennessee. Wounded and captured at Gettysburg, he was paroled from a Baltimore hospital on November 12 and furloughed from Richmond's Chimborazo Hospital in late November. It has not been possible to establish any family connection with Johnson. 1860 Census, Tenn., Johnson, 1st Dist., 11; CSR, RG109, NA.

4. As told to M--h, an agent of the Christian Commission, Burchett, in company with ninety-four others, attempted to escape from East Tennessee to Kentucky to join the Union army late in August, 1862. En route they were surrounded by Confederates near Lucy Cove Seminary in Powell Valley, Lee County, Virginia, where forty, including Burchett, were captured on September 10. Imprisoned at Richmond for a few days, they were then sent to Staunton where they were conscripted into the 8th Va. Inf., CSA (September 29). Nashville *Union,* August 8, 1863.

To James A. Garfield

Nashville, July 21st 1863.

Brig. Gen. Garfield
Chief of Staff—Nashville Tenn
General:

Enclosed please find a statement in regard to a horse taken from Mr. Gower.[1] He has made every effort to secure his horse or obtain the pay for him. He has been sent from one to another for redress since the fourth of June last, but So far has failed[.]

The endorsement upon the enclosed paper by Wm. Truesdail Chief of Army Police[2] states that the horse was turned over to the Quartermaster Lt. Irwin[3] of this place. I am advised that Lt. Irwin has no recollection whatever of the horse being turned over to him. John Riddle[4] in charge of the stable of the police, whose statement please read, asserts that the horse was not turned over to Lt. Irwin, but was taken from the police stable by Capt. Thelan[5] who had the stable in charge.

Will Gen. Garfield be kind enough to call the attention of General Rosecrans to this case so that Mr. Gower may obtain that redress which he is entitled to[?][6]

Very Respectfully Yr Ob't. Serv't.
Andrew Johnson Mil: Govr.

L, DLC-JP.

1. William T. Gower (b. *c*1812) may be the native Tennessean listed as a farmer in the 12th district with $1,250 real and $700 personal property. On May 1, 1863, his "Dark Bay Horse between five and six years old about fifteen hands high" was seized by a squad of the 4th Tenn. Cav., USA, under Capt. John F. Kinchelow. 1860 Census, Tenn., Davidson, 12th Dist., 32; W. T. Gower to Robert S. Granger, June 5, 1863, Johnson Papers, LC; *Tennesseans in the Civil War,* II, 538.

2. Truesdail's observations are on the back of a June 4 letter from Alvan C. Gillem to Robert S. Granger, attesting to the fact that on May 2 his men had given the horse in question to the "Detective Police . . . Since which time nothing can be heard of said horse." Johnson Papers, LC.

3. Charles H. Irvin (*c*1833-*fl*1881), English-born resident of Detroit, served as 1st lieutenant, 9th Mich. Inf. (1861-63), becoming captain and assistant quartermaster of volunteers in July, 1863. During the preceding year he had been quartermaster at Nashville. Brevetted colonel of volunteers in May, 1865, and mustered out two years later in March, he remained in Nashville until appointed a customs collector at Port Huron, Michigan (1873-81). CSR, RG94, NA; Heitman, *Register,* I, 564; *King's Nashville City Directory* (1868), 235; (1869), 264; *U. S. Official Register* (1873-81), *passim.*

4. Not identified.

5. George Thelan, whose title seems to have been honorary, is otherwise unidentified. Affidavit of John Riddle, July 21, 1863, Johnson Papers, LC.

6. An endorsement, "By Command of Maj Gen Rosecrans" and dated July 26, directed that Kinchelow "furnish a proper receipt" to Gower. Actually what the latter needed in order to be reimbursed for his horse was a receipt from Truesdail's office. Nashville *Press,* May 11, 1864.

To William S. Rosecrans

Nashville, July 23 1863.

Maj. Genl. Rosecrans,
Comd'g Dep't of the Cumberland
General:

There are a number of citizens throughout this section of country whose loyalty and devotion to the Gov't is unquestioned, who are in danger every night and day of being robbed and murdered by marauding bands engaged only in plundering &c. Many of these citizens are daily applying here for the privilege of keeping and bearing arms for the purpose of defending themselves against such bands.

I have on various occasions granted this privilege, as contemplated under the Constitution of this State and the United States. The form enclosed herewith,[1] in granting the privilege, has been adopted. I have thought proper to call your attention to it, and ask your advice upon the subject, as to its propriety or impropriety.

I would be glad to see you, in regard to other matters which have been referred to,[2] whenever it will suit your convenience.

In reference to persons keeping and bearing arms, I would be glad to have an early reply, as there are a number here this morning who desire the privilege granted them.

Very Resp'y Your Obt. Sert.
Andrew Johnson Mil Gov'r.

L, DNA-RG393, Dept. of the Cumberland, Lets. Recd. (1862-65) File T-583.

1. The permit reads: "Whereas the Constitution of the State of Tennessee in the declaration of rights Article. I. Section 26 declares that the loyal citizens of this state have a right to keep and bear arms for their common defense, and whereas the Constitution of the United States Article II, Amendments to the Constitution provides as follows, 'A well regulated militia being necessary to the security of a free state the right of the people to keep and bear arms shall not be infringed'.

Therefore ___________ a loyal citizen, of ___________county, is authorized to keep firearms necessary for the defense of himself and family against the marauding bands of guerrillas now infesting the country[.]"

2. In the absence of correspondence explicitly setting forth the "other matters," we can only speculate that at least one of them related to efforts currently being made to remove Col. George Spalding as provost marshal in Nashville. Spalding to Johnson, July 10; Calvin Goddard to Johnson, July 11, 1863, Johnson Papers, LC.

From James M. Tomeny[1]

Memphis July 24, 1863

Gov Andrew Johnson
Nashville
Dear Sir

I take the liberty of calling your attention to the enclosed article, published in the Bulletin this morning, upon the subject of arming our State malitia.[2] The question is one of vital importance, and the present condition of West Tennessee makes the plan entirely feasible. In an interview with General Veatch,[3] soon after my return from Nashville, the first question he asked, was: "Why does not Governor Johnson organize and arm the malitia of the State, for the purpose of clearing it of guerillas?" Next to the enlistment of troops for the regular service, it seems to me, the malitia, properly enrolled and armed, would be the most powerful auxiliary towards the restoration of peace, law and order in this State. Isolated as we are, from the Capitol, we are comparatively uninformed of your official action in this, as well as, in almost every other respect. If any thing has been done with the view of arming the malitia, it has not come to our knowledge. When in Nashville recently, I learned many interesting facts about what has been quietly accomplished in the few brief months of your administration, but on this particular point I learned nothing.

Persons direct from Richardson's Camp,[4] bring the information that he has only about fifty or a hundred men; and yet he is able, with this squad, to conscript every man for fifty miles round him. Thirty or forty have made their escape, and come to Memphis, within the past few days. Those in Command here, say it is useless for them to send a force after him, for his men will scatter in every direction and it would be impossible to find them. Genl. Veatch thinks it advisable to wait till he gathers up several hundred conscripts, and then send a sufficient force to capture them. But in the mean time the farmers can raise no cotton or other produce for market, and the energies of this portion of the State are prostrated. All accounts from the interior indicate that the people are heartily tired of this state of affairs and desirous of ridding the country of this dead incubus. The recent Union triumphs have had a *charming* effect.[5] The capture of a few more Confederate armies would ensure a *general* return to loyalty on the part of the people in this section. 'Tis wonderful how the success of our armies in the field, modifies opinions of our *sympathizing* population. Such of our Union men, with whom I have conversed since my return, appear to be greatly pleased with our report of the condition of things in other parts of the State. Not the least agreeable news to them was the fact that you are not at all indifferent to the interests of this region, and that you will soon be with them to listen to their suggestions, and give them your own views, as to the best and speediest means of restoring the State to her place in the Union. All are sincerely desirous of seeing you and hearing what you have done for the State, and what you still intend doing. I trust you will not disappoint this reasonable hope; especially as you have added to it a new impulse, by promising, or at least indicating your purpose, to come to Memphis very soon. When will you come? Let us know a few days before hand, and I promise you, you shall have an appropriate welcome. Men of all the old political parties; men who have differed in politics with you all their lives, are loud in their praises of your incomparable devotion to the Union.

Very respectfully Yours
J. M. Tomeny

ALS, DLC-JP.

1. James M. Tomeny (*c*1838-1878), Pennsylvania-born lawyer, came to Memphis in 1857, becoming bookkeeper and later secretary-treasurer of the Memphis and Ohio Railroad. A strong loyalist, he had recently attended a Union convention in Nashville directed toward persuading Lincoln to reorganize the state as soon as possible and to remove trade restrictions. In the spring of 1864 he was named a special treasury agent and, although elected the following year to the legislature, did not serve, becoming instead collector of customs at Mobile (1865) and later U. S. marshal for West Tennessee (1869-78). McBride and Robison, *Biographical Directory,* II, 914; 1870 Census, Tenn., Shelby, Memphis, 7th Ward, 72; Hooper, Memphis, 70, 85, 102; *Memphis City Directory* (1859), 164; *Williams' Memphis Directory* (1860), 324; Memphis *Appeal,* October 9, 1878.

2. Concern over guerrilla activity in Middle and West Tennessee brought demands from harassed unionists for the governor's action on this matter. Given the fact that arms for home guards and regular troops were in short supply, it was not until October that Johnson could report any success in organizing such companies for local use. Maslowski, *Treason Must Be Made Odious,* 42-43; see also Letters to Rosecrans, October 12, to Thomas, October 25, 1863.

3. James C. Veatch, commander at Memphis.

4. Robert V. Richardson (1820-1870), North Carolina native, moved early to West Tennessee, was admitted to the bar, and began practice in Memphis (1847). For a time editor of the *Appeal* and business associate of Nathan B. Forrest and Gideon J. Pillow, he served under the latter early in the war and during February, 1863, raised the 1st Tenn. Partisan Rangers (12th Tenn. Cav., CSA) within Union lines. Despite a conflict with Richmond officials about his authority, Richardson operated in West Tennessee until August, "marauding the country, and conscripting for the rebel army." After the war he went abroad for awhile, returning to Memphis to engage in levee and railroad building, again in association with Forrest, before being killed by an assassin at Clarkston, Missouri. Warner, *Generals in Gray*, 256; *Tennesseans in the Civil War*, I, 80-81; *OR*, Ser. 1, XXIII, Pt. II, 65; Thomas H. Baker, "The Early Newspapers of Memphis, Tennessee, 1827-1860," West Tenn. Hist. Soc. *Papers,* XVII (1963), 31.

5. Tomeny was no doubt referring to Gettysburg, Vicksburg, and Port Hudson, Louisiana (July 9).

From William M. Wiles

Nashville July 24, 63

Hon Andrew Johnson
Mil Governor Tenn

Examining condition of prisoners at the penitentiary I find, it necessary if possible to have some more room, and would like very much to occupy Wing No 1., which is now nonoccupied. It will not interfere in the least with prisoners, and will vacate at any time you desire, if permitted to use it. Will you have the kindness to give me the authority to occupy[?][1]

Very Respy Wm M. Wiles
Maj & P. M. G

LB Copy S, DNA-RG393, Dept. of the Cumberland, Book Records, Vol. 118 (1863).

1. No reply has been found; however, for Johnson's views about the prison, see endorsement on Letter from William S. Rosecrans, July 27, 1863.

From Manson M. Brien

[Nashville] July 25, 1863

To His Excelency Andrew Johnson
Governor &c
Governor

I am induced to make this application, In behalf of one A. Markewys[1] who was on last Tuesday morning, sent off, some where to be exchanged.

From the facts in this case, I do not [think] his is a proper case to be exchanged, Therefore hope you will here the facts and consider this application.

Markewys, was a merchant about 11½ miles from Nashville, on the Mufreesbrough pike. last November he packed up his goods and Started to Nashville to get inside the federal lines. But before he got to Nashville, was arrested by the pickets & conscripted in the reble army, where he was keped for several months. One day he was sent to a neighbors home for some milk & he found out they were Union people So the first chance he met with, he deserted went to this hose, where they consealled him for some 7 weeks, and untill he got the chance to get to the Federal lines, which he did. That is he Deserted & went & volentarly give himself up to a Fedl Capt. who sent him here last week, with a Cirtificate, showing the fact that he deserted & give himself up. This He sent in to Col Spaulding[2] & prayed to be permited to take the oath & remain here a loyal Citzin, but for some cause, he was overtaken & sent off. If he is exchanged and sent back he will be shot as a diserter. There is no charge against him, the provo marshal has the Cirtificate, before refered to.

I was very well acquainted with Mr. Markewys, before he moved out on the Pike. I regarded him as a very clever nice man, but never knew whether or not he was a union man. I am informed here by good Loyal authority, that he Markewys, has always been true & loyal so I take it to be so from his conduct.

I hope you may intersed for him.

Resptfully M M. Brien
for A. Markewys

July 25/63

ALS, DLC-JP.

1. Adolph Markowiez (*fl*1876), a Nashville cigar manufacturer who claimed to have been captured by Forrest and conscripted into the Confederate army before escaping—or deserting—was harbored for thirty-five days by a woman with Union sympathies. Subsequently "robbed" by a Federal soldier when attempting to take the oath, he was arrested and confined in Camp Chase until Secretary Stanton ordered his release. CSR, RG109, NA; Fedora S. Frank, *Beginnings on Market Street: Nashville and Her Jewry, 1861-1901* (Nashville, 1976), 40; Nashville city directories (1855-61), *passim;* (1876), 202.

2. George Spalding (1836-1915), Scottish native and on the eve of the war a school teacher at Monroe, Michigan, rose from private to lieutenant colonel in the 4th and 18th Mich. Inf. Regts. Appointed provost marshal of Nashville in early June, 1863, he transferred the following February to the 12th Tenn. Cav., USA, becoming its colonel in August. After the war he served as postmaster of Monroe (1866-70, 1899-1907), special treasury agent (1871-75), and congressman (1895-99). *BDAC,* 1634; CSR, RG94, NA; Nashville *Dispatch,* June 7, 1863.

From Stephen E. Jones[1]

Head-Quarters District of Kentucky,
Louisville, July 27th 1863.

Genl. Andrew Johnson,
Military Gov. of Tenn:

By instruction of Genl. Boyle, I have paroled R. F. Powers,[2] formerly 2d Lieut. Co. "I", 4th Tenn. (Rebel,) to report to you. He is an applicant for permission to take the Oath of Allegiance; was sent here by order of Genl. Rosecrans with other prisoners. The General desires me to suggest to you, for the good of the service, the economy of public Money, and as a matter of justice to individuals, the desirability of having arrangements made to Examine prisoners, especially political prisoners, not under sentence of Court Martial, and deserters, at Nashville, and dispose of their cases there, instead of sending them to Louisville with instructions to turn them loose in Kentucky.[3] If they are fit subjects for release on oath and bond, Tennessee, where they are known and where a surveillance could be exercised over them, would seem the proper place for their release. If it would be dangerous to the interests of the service to release them in Tennessee, it would also be dangerous in Kentucky, Similarly situated in so many respects to Tennessee.

I have the honor to be,
Very Respectfully Your Obdt. Servt.
Stephen E. Jones Capt & A.D.C.

One Copy sent by the party

ALS, DLC-JP.

1. Stephen E. Jones (1833-*fl*1897), native Kentuckian and a graduate of Transylvania Law School, served (1862-65) successively as aide-de-camp, provost marshal, and commissary general of prisoners on the staffs of Generals William Nelson, George H. Thomas, Jeremiah T. Boyle, and Stephen G. Burbridge. After the war he stayed in Louisville where he was a government tobacco inspector, an assignee in bankruptcy, and president of the Kentucky Wagon Manufacturing Company. Louisville city directories (1866-81), *passim;* Thomas Speed, *et al, The Union Regiments of Kentucky* (Louisville, 1897), 83.

2. Robert F. Powers (b. *c*1832), a 2nd lieutenant, 34th (4th) Tenn. Inf., CSA, mustered at Camp Sneed, Knoxville, in August, 1861, had recently been captured near Manchester. Paroled at Lousville, he was returned to Nashville, given "freedom of the city limits," and ordered to report daily to the provost marshal. CSR, RG109, NA; Nashville *Press,* August 12, 1863.

3. The military prison at Louisville had become the collecting point for both military and political prisoners from Tennessee, beginning with those captured at Henry and Donelson in February, 1862, who were then sent on to Camp Chase or Fort Warren. Jones had earlier complained about Louisville's being used as a dispatching point—men retained "only long enough to have their rolls made out, when they are forwarded for exchange or to more permanent depots" or, in the case of deserters and political prisoners, upon taking the oath, released outright. Johnson had been sending troublesome dissidents, notably the secesh clergymen, there since the summer of 1862. Jones to William Hoffman, April 30, 1863, *OR,* Ser. 2, V, 543; *Johnson Papers,* V, 576.

From William S. Rosecrans

Head-Quarters Dept. of the Cumberland.
Nashville July 27/63

My Dear Govenor

The City Prison here is a disgrace to humanity— there is no place where the prisners can be put, without you will allow us to use one wing of the Penitentiary— Will you do it?[1]

Vry Respectfully
W. S. Rosecrans Maj' Genl

ALS, DNA-RG393, Dept. of the Cumberland, Lets. Recd. (1862-65), File R-334-1863.

1. Johnson returned Rosecrans' letter with the following near incoherent penciled endorsement: "Any portion of the prison will be occupiaed necsiary for the putting it under Genl Rosecrans directions." Rosecrans immediately ordered that "the prisoners be transferred from the City Jail to that place." J. A. Garfield to R. Granger, July 27, 1863, Lets. Sent, Vol. 6, Dept. of the Cumberland, RG393, NA.

From Ogilvie Byron Young

July 30th 1863

His Excellency—Andrew Johnson—
Military Governor of Tenne—

Your solicitor—Ogilvie Byron Young—a native of Hampton Virginia A resident of New Orleans La—now a Prisoner of War in The Military Prison at Alton Illn, would most respectfully represent, to your Excellency—

That—He was arrested in the City of Nashville—State of Tenne—on, or about the 1st of Nov. 1862 by order of one so-called Col. Throusdale—Chief of the Detective Police Corps, in said City and State—

That—said arrest was made upon the *base* allegations of an *infamous,* and *disreputable man*—One so-called Dr. Russel,[1] *Alias Hailey—alias Black Hawk* "A *Hireling Informer and paid Detective*" of said Trousdale's Corps—who has since expiated his monstrous crimes by a violent death, which he had *prepared,* and *intended* for another of his victims.

That he—your Solicitor, was hurried off to Alton Military Prison, in a most summary and illegal manner, from the District and State, where the offence was alledged to have been committed, without a tryal or the mere semblance of an investigation upon false and insufficient charges, preferred by said disreputable Personage—said charges having neither specifications, or evidence to sustain them. And this too contrary to that Provision of the Constitution, which declares That "*In all criminal prosecutions, the accused* shall enjoy the right of a speedy, *and public trial, by an impartial jury of the State and District wherein the crime was committed*"—[2]

And It further provides that "No person shall be held to answer for a capital or otherwise infamous crime, unless on a presentment or indictment of a grand Jury." [3]. . . . . That His Excellency—The Secty of War, speaking through the General in Chief Halleck to Maj. Genl. Curtis,[4] at St. Louis, and other District Commanders *enjoins Commands* and enforces the observance of this Constitutional provision in the subjoined letter of May the 11th 1863—which I here transcribe and to which I respectfully invite your notice:—

[Young extracts from Commissary General Hoffman's instructions to Curtis that, because of the arrest and detention of many persons on charges which "*had neither Specifications nor evidence to sustain them,*" the "General-in-Chief," has ordered that those apprehended and charged with spying "or the Commission of any specific offense" must have a trial and "an *immediate investigation must be had before a Military Tribunal at the place where the offence was committed, and where the witnesses are within reach.*"]

That when the General in chief penned the above letter, he had in his mind's eye just such cases, as your solicitor's— I was arrested upon a specific charge, and without a trial, and the merest semblance of an investigation, I was ferretted off in the night, out of the limits of the State, and District where the offence was said to be committed, and lodged in Alton Military Prison, where I have been an inmate for the last *Nine Months,* upon *a base charge,* unsustained by corroborative evidence.

Was this well done? Was it in accordance with written Instructions? Has either the Constitutional provision been observed, or the orders of "the Genleral-in-chief" respected in this case? No! It is wholy at variance with the one,—and in direct violation of the other.

Your Solicitor would further represent—That, at the time of his arrest, and imprisonment, that he *was*—and had been for a period of *Ten* months, on a "Parole of Honor" to the Government of the United States—Also a Parole of Honor, with Bond to your Excellency—on behalf of the State of Tenne.

That said Paroles were taken under these circumstances, and for the following purposes—

That when "the Federal Army of occupation" was "en route" from Bowling Green, to the City of Nashville, they found me at a wayside Inn cofined to my bed by extreme illness. They placed a Guard around the Hotel, and when I was convalescent I was ordered to report to General Buel, at Nashville Tenn That my political affinities and public course during the presidential Campaign, and subsequently, at the Gulf State Conventions,[5] was such as to have rendered me an object of interest to some and of apprehension to others— That my *then* radical course was rather the result of an ardent temperament and pathetic mental organization than an evil heart or mischievous purpose. That I reported, by order of Maj. Genl. Buel to Col. Stanley Mathiews—the *then* Provost Marshal of Nashville— That Col. Mathews, after consultation with Genl. Buel Col. Lew Campbell[6]—Major Grosvenor[7]—and by advise from Washington, deemed it advisable to circumscribe my limits, and *restrain* my *future* actions— *That the Government did not purpose, nor did it wish to oppress and endanger my life by close confinement and long continued incarceration in a gloomy Prison.*

That, the Government knew,—that an "*irreconcilable* animosity" existed with President Davis against me, in consequence of my opposition to,—and denunciation of him in a series of letters, and speeches, uttered during the *disintegration* of the Gulf State Dynasty.[8] That President Davis is known to be a man, who never forgets, nor forgives either a personal, or political opponent— That he, *never,* merges personal motives or hates into patriotic considerations and intentions. That he would not appoint to a military station a personal enemy, or political opponent even if he knew him to be endowed with the superhuman virtues and heroic abilities of "*the Imperial Four*"—Caesar—Hanibal—*Charlemagne* and *Napoleon*—

That where he has found such a man in position he has rather *superceded* him by some "*Old field*" Colonel or "Broom-Sedge" Major[9] than preferred his claims to higher appointment— That the appointments of

McCullough—Van Dorn—and old Holmes[10] over the gallant Price—Of Tilghman—over Aldcorn of Mississippi[11]—of the inebriate—Old Morgan, of Fort Jackson notoriety[12]—Old Mitchell of the Louisiana who blew up his Armada without firing a gun[13]—Of the "Forty Dollar Ingineer"—Lovell to command the New Orleans Army;[14] and Pemberton from a 1st Lieut— to a Lieut General—[15] All these are brilliant examples in point. The Government of the United States rightly concieved, that under the reign of such a man—my personal and political foe, I could make no calculations of good— I could expect no preferment, and would not likely accept a subaltern position under his *miserable mediocres*. The Government correctly construed my intentions—That though I might have accepted civil office over which he had no control—I would never enter the military service of the Regular Confederate Army in which he would be constantly annoying, and embarrassing me with his petty hates, and his ignorant and incompetent appointments over me—That in view of these things—The Government deemed it sufficient, *merely* to circumscribe my *whereabouts,* and restrain my future actions— For this purpose, I was placed upon my Parole of Honor"—allowed and enjoyed the largest liberty within my prescribed limits.

That I remained uninterrupted, until the establishment of the Provisional Government under the auspices of your Excellency— You then ordered me before you, and after some consideration you put me upon an additional Parole, and Bond to the State of Tenne—Not at all abridging my privileges, or altering my former Covenant with the General Government—That—I continued for upwards of Eleven months under your immediate eye, and the Governmental official in the City of Nashville—*known* and *noted* by all, mingling freely, openly and above board with officers and citizens among whom I had many warm and attached friends—observed by all—*Known by all and subjected to the constant and rigid scrutiny* of many federal officers, who were well acquainted with my *antecedents* and who would not have spared me, had I deviated in the least from my written agreement, with the Government— Yet, not one of these ever, by *word, deed* or *inuendo,* accused me of having infringed my Covenant with the Government— On the contrary every consecutive Provost Marshal and Commander of Nashville, up to the advent of Genl. Rosecrans *endorsed* and *approved* it. After the establishment of Trousdale's Detective Corps an *instrument* was found, in the person of one of his attaches[16] mean enough to prefer the *base preposterous* and untenable charge—of a Spy,—which bears the blush of falsehood entraced upon every line. This disreputable personage was in the employ of my personal enemies, and worked for a reward. Now Sir, for, and in consideration of these premises well and truly set forth as your Excellency well knows and can attest, your Solicitor begs and prays your Excellency, either to restore him to his former status and agreement with the Government by placing him back, on his former Parole, and Bond and allow him to return to Nashville, and resume the practice of his profession—(the Law) or if this should not meet with your Excellencys concurrence, then, that you would grant him such *relief, alteration,* or *amelioration* of his present unhappy condition, as your Excellency's Government may deem consonant to Justice, and honorable to him. And he promises, your Excellency, to observe to the *letter* and the *spirit* any Covenant that he may sign.

With Sentiments of high consideration and distinguished respect

I am Your Excellency's
Very humble and obdt Servt
Ogilvie Byron Young

To Gov. Andrew Johnson
Military Governor of Tenne at Nashville

ALS, DLC-JP.

1. See Letter from Ogilvie Byron Young, December 6, 1862, note 2.
2. Sixth Amendment.
3. Fifth Amendment.
4. Samuel R. Curtis (1805-1866), New York native, moved to Ohio, graduated from West Point (1831), and worked as an engineer, studying law in his free time. Following service as a colonel in the Ohio infantry during the Mexican War, he settled in Keokuk, Iowa, where he practiced law, engaged in engineering, and served as mayor (1856). A Republican Congressman (1857-61), he resigned to become brigadier general of volunteers. Defeating the Confederates at Pea Ridge, Arkansas, in March, 1862, he was promoted major general and thereafter commanded the departments of the Missouri, Kansas, and the Northwest. Warner, *Generals in Blue,* 107-8; *BDAC,* 767.
5. Texas, Louisiana, Mississippi, Alabama, and Florida held secession conventions between January 7 and February 11, 1861; there is no evidence of Young's attendance. Ralph A. Wooster, *The Secssion Conventions of the South* (Princeton, 1962), chaps. 3-5, 7-8.
6. For Col. Lewis D. Campbell, 69th Ohio Inf., appointed Nashville provost marshal, June 29, 1862, see *Johnson Papers,* V, 188*n*.
7. Charles H. Grosvenor (1833-1917), Connecticut-born Ohio lawyer (1857), served as major, 18th Ohio Inf. (1861-63) before rising to colonel and brevet brigadier general at war's end. Subsequently he was twice presidential elector and a legislator both in the Ohio house (1874-78) and in Congress (1885-91, 1893-1907). *BDAC,* 979; Heitman, *Register,* I, 481; *DAB,* VIII, 24.
8. Although not found in available St. Louis newspapers, these letters, according to a contemporary reporter, contrary to Young's assertion in this apologia, were strongly secessionist, with the intent of drawing Missouri out of the disintegrating Union. Fitch, *Annals,* 498.
9. A field formerly cultivated and now worn out; a species of the coarse grass of the genus *Andropogon*—in a word, Davis was allegedly appointing worn-out, incompetent, or inexperienced officers to positions of major responsibility. Mathews, *Americanisms,* I, 193; II, 1156.
10. The reference is to Earl Van Dorn and Sterling Price; for Benjamin McCulloch, see *Johnson Papers,* IV, 647*n*. Theophilus H. Holmes (1804-1880), North Carolinian and West Pointer (1829), had attained the rank of major at war's beginning. Named brigadier general by Davis, his academy classmate and intimate friend, he rose by October, 1862, to lieutenant general and commander of the Trans-Mississippi Department. Unequal to this high rank, oppressed with his responsibility, he sought to be relieved the following February, ultimately being transferred to North Carolina (1864) where he was in charge of the reserves. *DAB,* IX, 176; Warner, *Generals in Gray,* 141.
11. Lloyd Tilghman (1816-1863), Marylander and West Point alumnus (1836), resigned early to become a construction engineer, returning as a captain in the Mexican War. Having taken up residence at Paducah, Kentucky, he entered the Confederate army in 1861, commanded at Fort Henry when it fell in February, 1862, was exchanged the next

fall, and was killed at Champion's Hill, Mississippi. James L. Alcorn (1816-1894), Illinois-born, Kentucky-reared planter of Coahoma County, Mississippi, was a Whig who served in the legislature (1846-57) and in the state convention of 1861 where he led the opposition to secession. Yielding to the majority, he was appointed a brigadier general of state troops. Although he served under Buckner in Kentucky and Polk in Mississippi, his main contribution was in recruiting and training soldiers. Having raised and enlisted his own command in 1862, he was later, at his request, relieved and succeeded by Tilghman. After the war he joined the Republican party, becoming governor (1870-71) and senator (1871-77). *Ibid.,* 306; *NCAB,* XIII, 421, 493; Evans, *Confederate Military History,* VII, 236; Percy Lee Rainwater, *Mississippi: Storm Center of Secession, 1856-1861* (Baton Rouge, 1936), 208, 212.

12. Not identified.

13. John K. Mitchell (1811-*fl*1880), North Carolinian and former commander in the U. S. Navy, received the same rank South and was in charge of the Confederate ships at the fall of New Orleans, ordering the destruction of the unfinished ironclad *Louisiana* a few days after his flotilla was scattered. Imprisoned, he was exchanged in August, 1862, and made chief of the bureau of orders and detail until appointed commander of the James River Squadron in May, 1864. He stayed on in Richmond after the war. *Register of Officers of the Confederate States Navy, 1861-1865* (Washington, 1931), 136; *OR,* Ser. 1, VI, 611, 614; William N. Still, Jr., *Iron Afloat* (Nashville, 1971), 172, 186; 1880 Census, Va., Henrico, Richmond, 77th Enum. Dist., 81.

14. Mansfield Lovell (1822-1884), born in the District of Columbia, graduated from the Military Academy (1842), and saw service in Texas and Mexico before resigning in 1854 to become a New York City businessman. At war's start he went south and was soon assigned to command at New Orleans which he was compelled to yield to the Federals early in 1862. After Corinth in October, he held no further responsible command. Returning to New York after the war, he worked as a civil engineer and surveyor. The source of the condescending sobriquet has not been found. NCAB, IV, 352; Warner, *Generals in Gray,* 194.

15. John C. Pemberton (1814-1881), native Philadelphian and West Point graduate (1837), rose to the rank of captain by the Civil War, having seen action in Mexico as an aide to Gen. Daniel Worth. Married to a southern woman, he joined the Confederacy in April, 1861, and by October of the following year was a lieutenant general in command of the Department of Mississippi and East Louisiana where he unsuccessfully managed the defense of Vicksburg, later (1864) serving under Lee. After the war he lived on a farm in Virginia before returning to Pennsylvania in 1876. *Ibid.*, 232; *NCAB*, X, 241; John C. Pemberton, *Pemberton: Defender of Vicksburg* (Chapel Hill, 1942).

16. Not positively identified but very possibly the "Dr. Russel" previously alluded to.

From Amanda M. Simons[1]

Nashville Tennessee
July 31st 1863.

His Excellency Andr. Johnson.
Military Govenor &C.
Sir:

My husband Simon W. Simmons[2] & my brother in law W. V. Dalton[3] are now confined as prisioners at Johnson's Island. They both reside in Macon County in this State and about the 22d. day of May last they were arrested at their homes by a body of Federal Cavalry carried to Bowling Green, Ky, & from there Sent to Johnson's Island. They had been soldiers in the rebel army, but they had abandoned the service some three or four months before their arrest, with fixed determination not to return to the army again. They did not have any connection with the rebel service in any way from the time of their return home to the day of their arrest, & hence there could not have been any charge against them further than that of being once in the rebel service. They are very anxious to be permitted to take the oath & come home as will be seen by the two letters from them herewith filed,[4] & I make this application in their behalf to induce & invoke your active interference in their favor. I can state with absolute conviction that they will in my opinion keep faithfully any oath they may take. They are in very moderate circumstances & are greatly needed in their families. Your interference in their favor will bring them & their families under a lasting debt of gratitude.[5]

Very respectfully Your friend
Amanda M. Simons

LS, DLC-JP.

1. Amanda Butler Simons, or Simmons (b. *c*1841), only recently married, seems to have been the daughter of Macon County farmer Elijah Butler. In drafting her petition, she had enlisted the help of attorney Jordan Stokes, both as scrivener and as writer of an appended supporting letter. Deane Porch, tr., *Macon County, Tennessee, 1860 Census* (Franklin, Tenn., 1975), 36; 1860 Census, Tenn., Macon, Lafayette, 31; Stokes to Johnson, August 1, 1863, Johnson Papers, LC.

2. Simon W. Simons, or Simmons (b. *c*1837) of Macon County was conscripted in November, 1862, into Co. A, 1st Tenn. Cav., CSA. According to his service record, he had "Always been a Union man[.] Was sick & sent into country by Co. officer to get well, but escaped home & was captured." Sent by the Federal authorities to Louisville, he was incarcerated at Johnson's Island by mid-June, 1863, and was "released on oath" September 23 of the same year. CSR, RG109, NA.

3. William V. Dalton (b. *c*1835), Macon County farmer, had married Amanda's sister Martha several years before the war. Enlisting as a private, Co. F, 20th Tenn. Inf., CSA, June 1, 1861, he deserted January 1, 1863, "went home and remained there in bad health" until May, 1863, when, claiming he had "always been a Union man . . . persuaded into the Rebel army by a clergyman," he reported at Bowling Green, Kentucky, with his father-in-law to take the oath. He was transferred from Johnson's Island to Point Lookout, Maryland, the following November; his records are not clear as to when and how he was released. After the war he lived in Sumner County. 1860 Census, Tenn., Macon, Lafayette, 29; (1870), Sumner, 6th Dist., 21; CSR, RG109, NA.

4. Earlier in the month, Dalton and Simons had urged that a petition, signed by the provost marshal, county clerk, Governor Johnson, and "a boute fifteen or twenty good loyal union men," be prepared and sent to Johnson's Island in order to effect their release. William V. Dalton and S. W. Simons to "familey," July 8, 13, 1863, Johnson Papers, LC.

5. An endorsement, also in Stokes's hand but signed by W. H. Garding, testifies "that Mrs. Simmons correctly sets forth in the above letter their connection with the rebel service & their character as honest men. They would in my opinion keep any oath they may take, & make quiet peaceable citizens."

From John H. Townsend[1]

August the 3d 1863
Manchester Coffee County Tenn,

To his Excellency—Governor Andrew Johnson of Tenn

Dear Sir if it will not be too great a trespass upon your time I desire you to inform me of the proper mode of getting Duplicates against the united States Government for private property taken for public uses by unauthorized persons in the Service of the united States from peaceable Citizens[.] there is quite a number of Such cases in Coffee County[.] the people has been Severely robed in my neighborhood of their Stock and provision and in a majority of cases by unauthorized persons that could not give receipts without criminating themselves[.] the people of this Country is generally poor there being but few Slave holders in it and they are generally all loyal to the old government[.] I can Speak with certainty in regard to my own district[.] there is 45 voters in it and 44 of them is union men and as Sutch they expect and ask the federal Authorities for the benefit of that paragraph in the Constitution of the united States that expressly Says that private property Shall not be taken for public use without Just Compensation[.] I will Say to you that my Neighbors and fellow Citizens has put Several thousand Dollars Of Sutch claims in to my hands for collection and I want to know how to proceed to get them adjusted and the Commanding General at Manchester[2] though & excellent Man Cannot give me the desired information as to who will be entitled to pay nor what kind of a tribunal will adjust Sutch claims but Sent Some of my papers up to General Rosencrantz but they have not returned and I concluded you could inform me on the Subject[.] I will inform you that the people is all willing to give the government a Set off for their war tax when they have been robed of their property[.] I petition your excellency to write to me what Certificates of Indebtedness[3] against the united States Government can be negotiated at in current funds groceries or provisions in Nashville[.] As early & answer as practicable is desired from your excellency[.] by Complying with the above requests you will Confer a great favor upon the under Singned and many good loyal Citazens of Coffee County who will ever feel grateful to your excellency for So kind a favor[.]

I remain your most Obedient and humble Servant
John H. Townsend esqr

To his excellency Governor,
Andrew Johnson.

ALS, DLC-JP.

1. John H. Townsend (b. *c*1828), Tennessee-born wagonmaker and justice of the peace with property worth $2,000, had as recently as July 28 chaired a Mount Pleasant unionist meeting which passed a resolution requesting that "by the first Thursday in August next," Johnson order an election to restore Tennessee to the Union. 1860 Census,

Tenn., Coffee, 8th Dist., 173; Nashville *Union,* August 6, 1863; Dorothy Williams Porter, tr., *Marriage Books A and C, 1853-1870, Coffee County, Tennessee* ([Manchester], 1973), 32-33, 39.

2. During the absence of Gen. Thomas L. Crittenden, who had gone to Kentucky to see his dying father, John M. Palmer was temporarily in command of the XXI Corps at Manchester. Nashville *Union,* July 23, August 6, 1863.

3. The military authorities, without much attention to the allegiance of the owner, appropriated private property in each theater throughout the conflict. When food, fuel, and livestock were seized, the owners were given receipts or vouchers for later payment. The jurisdiction of the Court of Claims, which reimbursed citizens for such property, was modified and extended both during and after the war until, by an act of March 3, 1871, loyalists in the seceded states became eligible for payment. Kenneth W. Munden and Henry P. Beers, *Guide to Federal Archives Relating to the Civil War* (Washington, 1962), 125-26; *OR,* Ser. 3, III, 152; Frank W. Klingberg, *The Southern Claims Commission* (Los Angeles, 1955), 90-91.

From William M. Wiles

Winchester Aug. 3, 63

Hon Andrew Johnson
Nashville Tenn

By direction of the Maj Genl Commanding the Dept, I have to enclose general passes[1] for yourself, *Mess. East* & *Fowler* & families[.]

Similar passes will be furnished the officers of State, if you will have the Kindness to furnish me their names[.]

I am Governor ect
Wm M. Wiles Maj & P. M. G.

LB copy S, DNA-RG393, Dept. of the Cumberland, Book Records, Vol. 118 (1863).

1. Passes for public personages and their families were normal courtesies, even in times of peace. That the matter came up at this time was in consequence of Johnson's intended visit to Memphis early in the month, a trip postponed because of a "violent bilious attack." Nashville *Union,* August 4, 1863.

From William S. Rosecrans

August 4, 1863, Winchester; Tel, DLC-JP.

In Giles, Lincoln, and adjacent counties "Some of the Citizens wish to organize . . . against Guerrillas," while others "want an election to enable the people to return to their allegiance." According to Col. Eli Long, 4,300 "have taken the oath at Fayetteville[.] would it not be well for you to come down here tomorrow or next day[?]"

Memorial of Jacob Bloomstein[1]

[Nashville, August 5, 1863]

MEMORIAL

To His Excellency,
Andrew Johnson
Military Governor of Tennessee

I—your memorialist—Jacob Bloomstein—a citizen of Nashville, Tenne—merchant—by profession, would most respectfully represent to your Excellency . . . .

That, I was arrested by order of one socalled Col. Truesdail, on the 5th of May 1863— That I was "*Balled* and *Chained*" by order of the Said Truesdail, and incarserated in the Nashville Peniteniary— That I remained in said Penitentiary four weeks, without a *trial, enquiry, or investigation* into the facts of my arrest, and confinement— That during said confinement, at Nashville, several Waggons were driven up to my place of Business, and loaded with my Goods—mostly staple Dry Goods purchased, in Nashville— These Goods were taken, and carried off by order of said Truesdail— That, a few day anterior to the removal of the Goods Truesdail's officers went to my Store, and seize and carried off all my Bills, Invoices and Receipts of said Goods—

That, at the expiration of said four weeks, I was transferred from the Nashville Prison to Alton Military Prison, where I now am and have been for the last *two months*— That the value of the Goods taken as above stated including *Three* Thousand pounds of Cotton, taken since my imprisonment here, is about six Thousand Dollars ($6000.00) worth. That these lawless acts,—and the sending me out of the District, and State, where my offense (if any) was alledged to have been committed were in utter violation of every precedent of law—totally at variance with Constitutional provision, and in direct conflict, and disregard of the Instructions of the Secty. of War—issued in a letter baring date, May 11th 1863.

That said letter was addressed by the General-in-Chief—Maj. Genl. Halleck—to Genl. Curtis[2] and other District Commanders. To said letter, and the Constitutional Provision, upon which it is based, I would most respectfully invite your distinguished attention, and consideration.

[The letter, in exerpted form identical to that found in the Ogilvie Byron Young letter of July 30, ensues.]

Did not "the General in Chief" have just such cases, as mine in view, when he penned this letter of Instructions to his District Commanders, as a guide and Rule, by which they should be governed? Has not this letter, as well as the more sacred provisions of the Constitution been grossly violated in my Case? Arrested and imprisoned without cause—I appealed to them for a trial—well knowing, that, if I could get an impartial trial, that, I could establish my innocence beyond the possibility of a reasonable doubt? did they grant my prayer?— They responded by seizing my Goods and chattles, and appropriating them to their own use! They then sent me beyond the limits of the District and State where they alledged the offense was committed. Was this well done? Was it done in accordance with Law—with the Constitution, or this Letter of Instructions—Sequestration and Spoliation Sentence and Imprisonment without trial or conviction Investigation, or the merest enquiry into the facts in the Case.

In view of these premises well and truly made and set forth, your Memorialist begs and prays your Excellency to interpose your Executive prerogative and relieve him from this foul injustice and most cruel wrong. That you will either release him with out farther endurance, or that you will cause him to be returned to the City and state from whence he has been so unlawfully ferretted off, and that you will cause him to be brought immediately before some Competent Military Tribunal in order that he may, and will prove his innocence of these most foul and unjust charges. And this he prays, and asks of you, as the Guardian of the people of the State, whose Rights and Liberties have been entrusted to you.[3]

With sentiments of high consideration and distinguished respect I am Governor

Your Very humble and Obdt Servt
Jacob Bloomstein

Mem, DLC-JP.

1. Jacob Bloomstein (1828-1891), Polish-born grocer who came to Nashville in the early 1850's, had by mid-war apparently gone over to dry goods. Engaging in the variety store business after the war, he was, by 1870, reputedly Nashville's wealthiest Jew with property worth $74,000. Frank, *Beginnings on Market Street,* 105, 129, 154.

2. Samuel R. Curtis.

3. Two months earlier Bloomstein's wife Mary and brother Louis, a cigar maker, declared that "the said charges . . . are untrue from beginning to end, that he never Smugled one dollars worth of goods through the lines, directly nor indirectly, nor did he at any time know of aid or in any maner assist or Countinance the doing of the same[.]" They further denied his having "in any maner" given "any information to the Rebel army or any soldier of [or] Sympathizer," and as a final argument averred that he has a wife "who is and has been for a considerable time in bad health and six Small children to take care of, that his presents at home is indispensable to there care & support." To all of this Provost Marshal Wiles replied: "Ample evidence is on file . . . to convict Bloomstein. . . . His case will be brought before a Military Commission as soon as the Exigences of the service will permit." Incarcerated in Nashville and later at Alton, he was released some four months later, probably on Johnson's intercession. Petition from Mary and Louis Bloomstein to Johnson, June 5, 1863, Johnson Papers, LC; Frank, *Beginnings on Market Street,* 105; Annie Somers Gilchrist, *Some Representative Women of Tennessee* (Nashville, 1902), 74.

From George W. Keith

Camp Near Danville Ky 7th Aug 1863

His Excellency Andrew Johnson
Gov. & Commader Tenn &c
Sir

In order to get your attention a moment I would refer you to the Stand upon which you & Col. Trigg stood which I prepared & the Flag made by my wife which floated over you & the Sentiment[1] which I pulled off the Oak at your backs (which compared with this hand you would know) and handed you as you left the Stand at Montgomery in July 1861 then furnished Friend Langley[2] a horse to convey one of you to Kingston Roane Count your next appointment[.] because I had to fill my own appointment [in] Scott Cty. could not go with you to Kingston[.] I also refer to Recommendation to President for Clerks appointment Signed by every Officer who saw it and Sent you at Office Nashville for approval[.][3] I would also refer you to a brief interview with you at Camp Dick Robinson where you told me you would endeavor to procure me the privilege of a *Scouting Force* for the relief of *E. Tenn* but being engaged much longer on your Mission North[4] than you expected I to[ok] Regtl. Q. M. appointment under J P T Carter who is down upon you & Maynard & all Democracy & whom I esteem as a Nabob & a Tyrant[.] He sent his Reg. after Morgan[.] I went a step or two further than those who did not giveout of the 2nd Tenn. I Saw the Villia John Morgan surrender 3 ms North of Salineville[5] Columbiana County O. which he had done with the 1030 which we captured at 8 mile Island 2½ mi. below Cheshire 7 days before but findng out that we had not men enough present to form a ring guard around, about 1700 men in the dark (it was then night) he with over 500 of his favorites & best mounted thieves sliped out & pursued them upwards of 300 miles[.][6]

Col J P T Carter & Brother[7] are determined to Stand preeminent to none in E Tenn or keep every thing cloged & confused in order to defeat the organization of the 1st Brig in 1st Div. 23rd U C[.] there is a general effort being made to authorize the Col. to make & command a legion & defeat R K Byrd Col. 1st T Reg[.]

Gov I would rejoice at pivilege from you to take a Majors Davis[8] Battalion & make it a Regiment, & prevent going into Carters legion[.] Please excuse me & accept my sincere regard[.]

G W Keith Lt & Q M
2nd Reg E T U S

To his Excellency Andrew Johnson Governor &c
Nashville Tenn

ALS, DLC-JP.

1. In an effort to save the state for the Union, Johnson and Trigg, along with T. A. R. Nelson, had canvassed East Tennessee in June, 1861, prior to the June 8 vote on separation. On June 6 they spoke in Montgomery, Morgan County. See Letter from George W. Keith, July 12, 1861, *Johnson Papers,* IV, 561, 562n.

2. Ephraim Langley, postmaster at Sagefield, Morgan County.

3. Not found.

4. During the summer of 1861 Senator Johnson tried to get arms for the citizens and arrange for an army to be sent into East Tennessee. *Johnson Papers,* IV, xxii; Nashville *Patriot,* June 22, 1861.

5. Morgan had been captured on July 26.

6. The pursuit of Morgan from Buffington Island, July 19-26, covered at least 230 miles. Allan Keller, "... A 'Thunderbolt' Out of the South," *Civil War Times Illustrated,* II (June, 1963), 37.

7. Samuel P. Carter.

8. Probably Reuben A. Davis (1833-*fl*1890), native Tennessee cattle buyer, who represented Roane County in the Knoxville convention in May, 1861, and later became lieutenant colonel, 11th Tenn. Cav., USA. Escaping a short time after being captured in February, 1864, at Wyerman's Mill near Cumberland Gap, he was discharged in September for incompetence. Ethel Freytag and Glena Kreis Ott, *A History of Morgan County, Tennessee* (Wartburg, 1961), 112; Sistler, *1890 Tenn. Veterans Census,* 80; CSR, RG94, NA; *OR,* Ser. 1, LII, Pt. I, 150; XXXII, Pt. I, 411; Pt. III, 73-74.

From Robert L. Stanford

Hospital No. 12, Louisville Ky.
August 7th 1863

Dear Sir:

I write to inform you that all things in this city are moving on quietly.

The election is over. Bramlet elected Gov.[1] and old *ear biter* (Wickliff)[2] disgracefully beaten. The whole, *no-men—no-money* party[3] are beaten & disgraced. I wish you could see their faces. Their mouths and noses, their chins & foreheads, are parted, a space lying betwen, almost as wide as one of the streets of this City. Oh! heavens, how ghastly they look.

All hope has left their trator souls, except, the Sting of hells bitterest pangs, which they are now permitted to antidate.

The *hind quarters* of *bad luck* is no comparison to the wild consternation which now sits upon their evry feature, designating them as the defeated emisaries of the arch-trator Jeff Davis, not, to say of hell. My blood boils when I think how villians like these have tortured our people of East Tennessee. I cant help but desire to have the oppertunity to girt on the sword & take active duty in the field.

I desire to spend and be spent in more active service than that which now engages my time although my position is an honorable one & in it I can do good upon a large scale. Yet, whilst my own beloved East Tennessee is bleeding from head to foot from the Cumberland mountains to the Unaca:

Oh! what son of hers can tollerate the idea of being prevented from taking a *fighting* part in her redemption. I would glory in having the oppertunity to meet them upon the field that tries mens souls[4] and there

inflict that sort of castigation which would tell upon them through all coming time; but enough of this[.]
I think the orb of political day is now fully above the dark horisen of this long & bloody rebellion. Upwards may he rise untill his full orbed splendor arriving at the zenith shall flash the light of political redemption and liberty from pole to pole, from the Atlantic to the Pacific and if need be over all Urope.

I have the honor to be
Yours sincerely R L Stanford

Gov. A. Johnson
Brig. General
P. S.
Please pardon me for troubling you. I have some items which I think will be interesting to you which I will communicate when I see you[.]

Not having a nature to forget past favors I am now & I hope ever be your devoted friend

R. L. S.

Gov. A. J. Brig. Gen'l

ALS, DLC-JP.

1. Thomas E. Bramlette (1817-1875), native Kentuckian, active as lawyer, state representative, and judge before the war, raised the 3rd Ky. Inf., USA, in violation of the state's "neutrality," and served as its colonel. Resigning in 1862, he was a U. S. district attorney before becoming governor (1863-67). A Union Democrat and at first a strong supporter of the war effort, he became within a year one of Lincoln's most bitter critics. He spent his last years in Louisville in the practice of law. *DAB*, II, 595-96; Boatner, *Civil War Dictionary*, 80.

2. Charles A. Wickliffe, ending a half-century of public service which began in the legislature in 1812 and ended with a term as Union Whig congressman (1861-63), had just been defeated in a gubernatorial bid as a Peace Democrat. According to the Louisville *Journal* of July 29: "He first brought himself into notice half a century ago by eating off a gentleman's ear." *DAB*, XX, 182; see also *Johnson Papers*, I, 109*n*.

3. The Union Democrats derided their opponents' conciliatory stance toward the South and the continuation of the war by tagging them "the no-more-men and no-more-money seccessionists." For an example of this usage, see Bramlette to Editors, Louisville *Journal*, July 17, 1863.

4. An echo from Thomas Paine's "These are the times that try men's souls" which appeared in *The Crisis: Introduction*, December, 1776. Burton Stevenson, ed., *The Macmillan Book of Proverbs, Maxims, and Famous Phrases* (New York, 1948), 2331.

From Robert A. Crawford

Cincinnati Aug. 8th 1863.

Gov Johnson!
Dr. Sir!

Mr. Morrow[1] handed me your Telegram yesterday requesting me to report immediately to Genl. Burnside. *I have done so*— when I left Nashville, I came direct to this City[.] I got here on Sunday[.] on Tuesday morning I went to General Burnsides head quarters. I was there informed by his orderly, or subalterns, that I could not see the Genl. that he was too much engaged. I retired but left special word that I would call the next day at 10 oclock A. M. I did so, and met with the same answer that the Genl was too much engaged. so I again retired and went back on friday with other Gentlemen, but owing to the press of business none of us got to see him. I was then unwell and was confined to my Room four days with sore throat. I went up to Hillsborough wednesday evening & returned yesterday morning. as Thursday was set apart for fasting & prayer, I did not return until friday.

I went to see Genl. Burnside last night, and told him just what I have herein stated only more in detail. He said he was so engaged about the Morgan capture and the Raid of Pegram & Scott[2] that he had forgotten. So I still Stand "rectus in Curia." [3] I merely make this statement to you that you may see that there has been no deriliction of duty on my part[.]
I will say to you Confidentially what Genl. Burnside, said & intimated to me last night. He will start in a few days to East Tennessee, does think the Country will be immediately held. He will distroy the Rail Road, from Abingdon to Knoxville, distroy the Saltworks & the Country Generally, as I understand his move is to be a big Raid, distroy the Country so that the Rebels will abandon the Country & give it up—
I will leave here on Monday, for Barbursville &c &c[.] the Ninth Army Corps, is not yet come[.] it is daily looked for. the force that will move upon Cumberland Gap & East Tenn are about five thousand men.
an immediate attact will be made upon the Gap, a force will be sent above & below the Gap.

I have just learned from Col. Bird, who has just come from Ky. that a large force of Rebels is thought to be entering Ky. by way of Cumberland Gap. as to the how true the report is the Col. does not know, it is merely a report said to be from 12000 to 15000 men.[4]

If this expedition to East Tennessee fails, I want you to let me get up a Brigade of Negroes. I feel confident they will make the best fighters and can kill a d--d Rebel better & deader than any man North of Mason & Dickson line.
I have been offered 400 Negroes at this place. the Negroes can be easily got. I think the Slaves would make better fighters than the free Negroes, as they will fight more understandingly.[5]

Yours Truly
Robt. A. Crawford.

ALS, DLC-JP.

1. Samuel Morrow.

2. On July 25, Col. John S. Scott's cavalry brigade passed through Big Creek Gap on a raid into Kentucky to disrupt communications, capture horses, mules, and cattle, and, incidentally, to make a diversion in favor of Morgan. They moved via Williamsburg and London toward Richmond where on the 28th they encountered and drove back 1,200 men under Col. William P. Sanders. Learning of Morgan's capture, they started back south, capturing 150 prisoners, two cannon, and 600 Enfield rifles near Irvine on the 30th. But soon the Union forces, concentrated by rail, pressed them and converted Scott's success

into a partial disaster, obliging his retreat back into Tennessee by August 6. Gen. John Pegram's cavalry brigade was headquartered at Ebenezer, Knox County, during this time and did not participate in the raid. *OR*, Ser. 1, XXIII, Pt. I, 839-42; Pt. II, 946.

3. "Upright in the court"—exonerated, so to speak.

4. There seems to have been no basis for this rumor; Scott's raid was the only significant Confederate invasion of Kentucky at this time.

5. According to a contemporary view, the slave, conditioned to accept autocratic authority and strict discipline, would respond more readily to a military regimen—an assumption not always borne out. It might be argued that as the destruction of slavery increasingly became a goal of the conflict, who, more than the chattels, would understand and support the effort? Cornish, *The Sable Arm*, 71, 76; T. W. Higginson, "Leaves from an Officer's Journal," *Atlantic Monthly*, XIV (1864), 526; see Cimprich, Slavery Amidst Civil War, 197-98.

From Thomas B. Johnson[1]

Nashville Aug 8th 1863

Hon Andw Johnson
Military Gov of Tennessee
My Dear Sir

Personally I have but a slight acquaintance with you— suppose you have some know[l]edge of me—as the Neighbour of your Friend Felix R. Rains[2]—by whom I had the honour of an introduction to you & as the Treasurer of the Tennessee Agricultural Bureau—I have seen & had short conversations with you at your Office— But there are so many Johnsons—I mention this to Identify myself before you—

And now for my purpose—in an humble & unpretending position before the military authorities—I need your cooperation to help me to the injoyment of the undoubted rights of every faithful & Loyal Citizen of the *united States* & that you may understand my Rights & wishes fully (I must pray you—to bear with my long letter, which is required to make myself understood)[.]

Near a year sine 3 of my Negroe men were impressed to work on the fortifications at this place[.] I found they had left the work & runing at will & missing some valuable property from my Farm suspected one of them— laid a plan for his arrest & detection—which proved successful & after geting my property—& punishing the thief I applied to Genl Robt S Granger to know what I should do with him & allso to know if I could not recover a lot of women & children which he had incited to run off from my Son James P.[3] living 6 mls south of Franklin on Collumbia Pike to whom I had loaned them[.] After discribing the Negroes & advising the Genl. that two of them was in the Pest house with small Pox he said they being a pest he could order them taken to the Country by their owner as soon as the Surgeon in charge would pronounce them well Enough— this order I presented to the Surgeon who says one of them is now well & ready to go but the other will not be for a few ds yet—& further remarked to me—that the childrens mother & some others assumeing to take some interest for them objected to my geting them— he said he would consult with you &

then answer me further & I left the order with him— to return to my application to Brig. Genl. Granger he advised to turn the Bad negroe & other of the men I could get hold of over to the Government & take Receipt for them which I done with two of them that being all I can as yet get holt of— upon mentioning to the Genl—that the Pro Marshal had scolded me for trying to get some of the small negroes—& said to me that they had been ordered here from Franklin by Maj Gel Granger as the property of my Rebel son—he Brig Genl Granger said I must go & see the Maj Genl which I did & upon his being satisfied not only of my own Loyalty but my Sons also—he also advised the men be passed over to the Government but said I might take the women & Children home if I could get them & gave me a pass for them nameing them all— but Sir when I found one of them *Vina* the mother of these little Boys spoken of as having small Pox as allso the mother of one little girl I have at home & got her into my family carriage I was met by officers & soldiers in force the woman forced from my carriage or rather the door forced open & her permitted to go free I Myself ordered by Col Spalding to the Penitentiary for dareing to take my own negroe home—of which so soon as Maj Genl G Granger obtained the facts which was but a few hours he ordered my release—now Gov I pray your cooperation—not only to secure the privilege of taking the little Negroes home but the women also— I dont ask the military authorities to assist me—but with your advise I will ask for a protection against being molested—in the Exercise of what is not only my legal right, but sir as you well know a duty for if I suffer my Negroes to run at will in the City I am under the civil Law liable in every case to Indictment & fine—& sir I ask if I am not as a faithful Citizen of these *United States* having worked for the means & bought my Negroes not only under the sanction of our State but the *Constitution* & *Laws* of the *United States* & there not having been any Law of Congress or Proclamation of the President—to deprive me of them as much entitled to the controll & injoyment of them as you or I am to our Horses & Cattle & Houses— to say that I may take my negroes home if they wish to go or may controll them if they [are] willing I should—is to say that slavery ceases to exist except at the will of the slave[.] I dont understand this to be the purpose of the Government or that it assumes any such power— If you can write me a response I shall be verry thankful[.] if not will you be so kind as to signify to me the earliest period & the place when I can have a personal interview with you—

Respectfully &c Thos. B. Johnson
Box 53 PO Nashville

ALS, DLC-JP.

1. Thomas B. Johnson (1808-1874), Kentucky-born farmer and stock raiser, possessed $40,000 real and $17,035 personal property and was the superintendent of the Nolensville Turnpike Company on the eve of the war. 1860 Census, Tenn., Davidson, 9th Dist., 141; *Goodspeed's Williamson*, 990-91; Nashville *Union and American*, July 28, 1874; Nashville *Patriot*, April 6, 1861.

2. For Rains, Davidson County farmer, see *Johnson Papers*, III, 446*n*.

3. Kentucky-born James P. Johnson (*c*1832-*fl*1886), Thomas' eldest son, was also a Williamson County farmer and stock raiser. Porch, *1850 Census, Davidson*, 122; *Goodspeed's Williamson*, 991.

From Joseph Ramsey[1]

Shelbyville August 8th 1863

Dear sir

In Reference to those Abandoned Houses in this Place I have spoken to Mr. Thos Coldwell[2] the Gentleman whom I Called your Attention[.] he will If you Desire It, take charge of such property of that character as you may di[r]ect[.] My Judgement is he will make as suitabl a person as you can obtain for that purpose.

The Large Flouring Mills Also spoken of is still Idle[.][3] If General Rosencrans has Made no Disposition of Same, Instructions to Mr E Cooper[4] who was up at Winchester a day or so Ago and is as I understand now in Nashville and I am in hopes, he will Call on you and call your Attention to It. Mr McCroy[5] the Bearer is a practical Miller and would Attend to It[.] we have a Considerable quantity of Wheat now Ready for Market and the citizens of Bedford Mar[s]hal & Lincoln Counties would like to have a Market for their wheat and Should the Govermet conclude to purchase wheat & Run the Mill I have a good clerk and would Like to purchase wheat for the Mills— Should the Govrmt conclude to Run It you can Enquire of Mess Cooper Wisener,[6] or any other Loyal Citizens[.] the Mill is somewhat out of ordr[.] will Require some Expense for Repairs. as soon as the Business of your Respective Duties will permit I would Like to hear from you upon the subject[.]

Yours Respectfully Joseph Ramsey

ALS, DLC-JP.

1. For Bedford County unionist Ramsey, see *Johnson Papers*, V, 300*n* [there incorrectly Ramsay].

2. Thomas H. Coldwell (1822-1891), Bedford County lawyer and unionist, had been a delegate to the Nashville Convention of 1850. Claiming $25,000 real and $2,500 personal property on the eve of the war, he was briefly chancellor of the 4th chancery division of Tennessee (1864) before being commissioned state attorney general and reporter of the supreme court in October, 1865. A Republican after the war, he was presidential elector (1878) and a director of several corporations and institutions. 1860 Census, Tenn., Bedford, W. Div., 7th Dist., 27; Nashville *Union*, May 10, 1850; Shelbyville *Times-Gazette (Sesqui-Centennial Historical Edition)*, October 7, 1969, p. 34.

3. Possibly either Steele and Holt or Steele and Hammond, both milling operations in Shelbyville. *Mitchell's Tenn. State Gazetteer and Business Directory* (1860-61), 288; *OR*, Ser. 1, XXIII, Pt. I, 559.

4. For Edmund Cooper, see *Johnson Papers*, IV, 270*n*.

5. Abram McCroy (b. *c*1827), Tennessee-born miller with $500 worth of personal property. 1860 Census, Tenn., Bedford, Shelbyville, 57.

6. For William H. Wisener, Bedford County unionist, see *Johnson Papers*, IV, 279*n*.

To Joseph S. Fowler

Executive Office, Nashville, Tenn.
Aug't 8th, 1863.

Joseph S. Fowler Esq
U. S. Disbursing Agent &c
Sir:

You will please pay to Ernest M. Bement, out of the Government funds in your hands for disbursement, the sum of Seven Hundred and Thirty seven Dollars and eighty three cents, the amount of the foregoing account, which is just and proper—rendered so by the following circumstances:—

Ernest M. Bement was authorized by me to raise a Regiment of Cavalry in the States of New York, Pennsylvania, and Ohio (provided the consent of the respective Executives thereof should have been previously obtained) to serve for the term of three years or during the war—said authority being based upon orders of the War Department dated March 28th, 1863. The said Bement was engaged in recruiting said Regiment, and did recruit in New York State, with the consent of the Governor thereof, about four hundred men, when through the office of the Quarter Master General under date of June 17th, 1863, he was notified "that the authority under which Governor Johnson acted, has been revoked by the Secretary of War, so far as States other than Tennessee are concerned."

This account is for monies actually and necessarily expended by him in such recruiting.

Andrew Johnson Mil. Gov'r.

The United States,

1863	No of Voucher		To Ernest M. Bement	Dr.
June 16	1	For	railroad travel,	126.14
July 16	2	"	Clerk time,	75.
"	3	"	Postage,	15.
June 11	4	"	Printing,	50.
May 19	5	"	"	5.25
26	6	"	Advertising,	10.80
June 2	7	"	"	6.12
16	8	"	Printing,	4.25
May 25	9	"	Advertising,	8.10
July 16	10	"	Telegraphing.	15.17
"	11	"	Services as Recruiting Officer,	422.
				$737.83

I certify on honor that the above account is accurate and just, and that no part of the same has been paid.

Ernest M. Bement Recruiting officer.

Approved
Andrew Johnson Mil. Gov'r.

L, NcU-Joseph S. Fowler Papers, Southern Historical Col.

From David A. Briggs and James P. Brownlow

August 9, 1863, Fayetteville; Pet, DLC-JP.

Advising that Lincoln County "is infested by a considerable body of Guerillas and for their suppression it is indispensible that a force should be organized of resident Citizens," Union officers of the 2nd Ind. Cav. and 1st Tenn. Cav., USA, respectively, recommend William French, "a firm—uncompromising Union man as the proper person to be permitted to Effect an organization of the Union forces . . . and to be appointed their leader."

From Isaac R. Hawkins

Head Quarters 2 west Ten Cav
Saulsbury Ten Aug the 9th 1863

Andrew Johnson Military Gov of the state of Ten

sir: I address you a few lines at the request of some of the Union men of Henderson county, for the purpose of obtaining information if it is possible as to the best course to be addopted under exhisting circumstances and that you may be able to Judge inteligibly, I think it would be better that you have the facts before you, After the withdrawal of the Union forces from Jackson the confederates began to assemble in the western district, Capt Newsom[1] crossed the Ten River with a small force but sufficient to controll an unarmed people; Soon Biffle[2] came, with a Reg'[.] Then Col Jesse Forest[3] with a Reg'[.] Richardson[4] made his appearance in Haywood & Fayett[.] first they arrested and forced into arms all the men they could Get who had been in the confederate Army and who had taken the oath, Then they commenced conscripting and calling for volunters[.] I suppose from the best information, that Richardson raised about five hundred men, Newsom about the same[.] what number has been raised by Forrest and Biffle I am not advised; Numbers of small parties under their leaders are patrolling the country and the Union men are out in the woods or refugees at some Union post, So soon as I reached my reg' I asked to be allowed to take my men to the rescue of our friends, promising to resign if I did not hold the country, but up to this time I have failed to get leave. other troops have twice since been sent there but still I guard this road. The Loyal men of that section desire to know if there is *any way* in which they can be organised so that they can defend their own homes and they think quite a force could be raised for that purpose, There are many things that I can not comprehend, and as you would of course be better advised and consequently better enabled to interpret I think much good would result from a visit by you to this section of the state[.] I hope you will reply at the earliest practicable moment[.]

Isaac R Hawkins
Col 2d West Ten Cav

P S I sent a co to Ripley Mis about four days since[.] no enemy there that day[.] Ruggles[5] 12 miles below 200 strong[.]

I R H

ALS, DLC-JP.

1. John F. Newsom (1827-1884), native Tennessean and resident of Madison County, had $6,500 real and $9,000 personal property. Enlisting as captain, Co. F, 6th Tenn. Inf., CSA, he later commanded an irregular regiment before becoming colonel, 18th Tenn. Cav., under Forrest in May, 1864. During the preceding summer he, Col. Jacob B. Biffle, Col. Jesse A. Forrest, and others were operating in Henderson, Madison, and McNairy counties, "recruiting, conscripting, and organizing." After the war he was a farmer and lawyer. 1860 Census, Tenn., Madison, 8th Dist., 144; (1870), 29; (1880), 6; Mid-West Tennessee Genealogical Society, *Riverside Cemetery Inscriptions, 1830-1875* (Jackson, Tenn., 1975), 56; *OR*, Ser. 1, XXIV, Pt. III, 434, 526; *Tennesseans in the Civil War,* I, 93-94, 187.

2. Jacob B. Biffle (*c*1830-1877), a well-to-do Wayne County farmer, reporting $15,000 real and $25,575 personal property in 1860, entered the war as lieutenant colonel, 2nd (Biffle's) Tenn. Cav. Btn., CSA, later becoming colonel of the 19th (9th) Tenn. Cav., serving alternately under Forrest and Wheeler. After the war he lived in Mississippi (or Alabama?) before moving to Texas, where he was fatally shot during an argument. *Ibid.*, 66, 95-96; 1860 Census, Tenn., Wayne, 5th Dist., 13; CSR, RG109, NA; OR, Ser. 1, XXIV, Pt. II, 666; Jill K. Garrett and Marise P. Lightfoot, *The Civil War in Maury County, Tennessee* ([Columbia, Tenn.], 1966), 212.

3. Jesse A. Forrest (1834-1889), brother of Nathan B. and a Memphis slave trader before becoming a cavalryman in the 21st (Wilson's) Tenn. Cav., CSA, was seriously wounded at Athens, Alabama, in September, 1864, but recovered before the Selma campaign. Returning to Memphis after the war, he was a farmer, a livestock dealer, and a contractor. 1870 Census, Tenn., Shelby, Memphis, 7th Ward, 56; Memphis *Appeal*, December 16, 1889; *Williams' Memphis City Directory* (1860), 164; *Tennesseans in the Civil War*, I, 99.

4. Col. Robert V. Richardson of the 12th Tenn. Cav., CSA.

5. Daniel Ruggles (1810-1897), Massachusetts native and West Point graduate (1833), served in Florida and Mexico before his resignation to join the Confederacy. At first assigned to Virginia state forces, he was promoted brigadier and transferred west. Leading a division at Shiloh, he became mainly an administrator in district and departmental commands, though he was often without an assignment, and in March, 1865, was named commissary general of prisoners. After the war he lived, except for four years, in Fredericksburg, Virginia. Warner, *Generals in Gray*, 265-66; *Appleton's Cyclopaedia*, V, 343.

To Abraham Lincoln

Nashville Tenn. Aug 9th 1863.

His Excellency A. Lincoln
Prest U. S.

Three hundred men of 2nd West Tennessee Cavalry who were captured by Forrest[1] & paroled have been at Camp Chase since December last 1862. They are good soldiers and are anxious to join their Reg'ts[.][2] Numbers of other troops have been exchanged since they were sent to Camp Chase and I hope steps will be taken to have these released. Now is the time for an entrance into East Tennessee. If you will let us mass the entire Tennessee force we will enter take and hold the Country without regard to transportation which has always seemed to be an obstacle that could not be overcome[.]

Andrew Johnson Mil Governor

Tel, DLC-Lincoln Papers; DNA-RG107, Tels. Recd., President, Vol. I (1863-64); *OR*, Ser. 1, Vol. XXIII, Pt. II, 603.

1. These men had been captured at Trenton December 20, 1862, during Forrest's first West Tennessee raid. *Tennesseans in the Civil War*, I, 337; Wyeth, *Forrest*, 101, 118; *OR*, Ser. I, XVII, Pt. I, 561-62, 593.

2. Because of the expense and burden of maintaining prisoners, the Confederates frequently paroled captured Union troops with the proviso that the parolees were to remain noncombatants until they had been officially exchanged. The Union command feared that some troops were surrendering in order to obtain the paroles and relief from duty. In June, 1862, the war department established three regional camps of instruction—at Annapolis, Camp Chase, and Benton Barracks, Missouri—to which all paroled Union soliders were ordered to report, those from regiments raised in Virginia, Tennessee, Kentucky, Ohio, Indiana, and Michigan being assigned to Camp Chase. *OR*, Ser. 2, IV, 94; Hesseltine, *Civil War Prisons*, 74-83.

From James B. Bingham[1]

PRIVATE AND CONFIDENTIAL

Bulletin Office,
Memphis, August 11, 1863.

Hon. Andrew Johnson,
Governor of Tennessee:

Dear Sir: In accordance with your request to keep you posted with reference to movements in this section of the state, I drop you these few lines, for your own private eye:

I understand that E. Etheridge has been in constant correspondence with certain of his friends here, and in Western Tennessee, since our late state convention adjourned, the object being to divine some scheme by which to thwart *you* and your plans. I have learned enough to know that they design, whenever you appoint an election for members of the legislature, to vote for a candidate for Governor also, they contending that if a majority of the votes cast in any one county should be for *their* candidate, he will be duly elected Governor, and you displaced. Ex. Gov. Wm. B. Campbell is the man fixed upon as the Etheridge candidate. I *know* that this is their plan, for Etheridge has recently written a letter to his friends here on the subject. I have had no means as yet to learn how many, and who compose the Etheridge party here, but I incline to the belief that they are confined to a few leaders and managers thus far. They have induced the military authorities to permit them to issue a paper to be called the *Journal*, which is to be edited by Etheridge's friend, Rolfe S. Saunders[2] and others equally opposed to you. Saunders, I understand, has lost some negroes by the Proclamation, and I happen to know has been advised to appeal to you in the matter. I suppose that S. P. Walker,[3] B. D. Naber's, the Farringtons,[4] and a few others compose the Etheridge party. I am certain they have no hold as yet on the great mass of the people, nor do I believe they will have.

I have not heard a word from *you* in reference to your policy in re-inaugurating law and order in the state. I would be glad if you would communicate to *me*, if only for my own guidance, your plans and purposes, in this matter, as I expect to co-operate with you most cordially in that matter. I want the state added to the union as soon as it can be done without detriment to the public interest, and I wish to aid in defeating the schemes of wily demagogues, who appear incapable of taking any view of public matters that does not promise to promote their individual aggrandisement. The people at this end of the state feel a deep interest in the question of reconstruction, and I can communicate nothing.

When I left Nashville you promised to come to Memphis in *ten* days and authorized me so to announce. I did so, and had the mortification of knowing that you did not come, and failed to send a word of explanation. I have lately seen that you had been sick,[5] and I have placed it to that account. Can you not come and see us before long? And make us a speech? And let our people have an opportunity to do you honor? The Union League, composed of true men, would especially be pleased to have you as their guest.

On a calm review of the condition of affairs in West Tennessee, I would recommend that you authorize the enrollment of the militia of the state. Let all who are for the South be sent away, and those for the Union be enrolled and armed, and required, as occasion calls for it, to perform military and police duty. In this way, guerrillas, marauders and thieves would be expelled and punished, and civil law be re-established in every county. The plan has worked well in Missouri,[6] and in my own opinion, it is the only one which will be *safe* for Union men for some time to come. By arming the militia, if there were any who turned traitor, they could be shot under military law, and a few wholesome examples would not be without benefit.[7] In the foregoing suggestion I am strengthened by Generals Veatch and Hurlbut, who regard it as the very plan needed in our present exigencies.

I delivered your message to Gen. Hurlbut, but he did not receive it very kindly, saying that he had written to you several times,[8] but had received no answer, and would not receive a verbal message on the subject. He also expressed the opinion that you were not coming to Memphis at all, and did not care for that part of Tennessee this side of Tennessee river. Still, if you will come on here, I think it will change his views and *feelings* toward you amazingly. Hurlbut's command has been recently enlarged, but he is not yet in command of a *Department*.

I have ordered the Bulletin to be sent to you daily, and from it you will learn all that it is politic to make public of affairs in this quarter. I never get the *Union*. The *Press* and *Dispatch* come occasionally.[9]

I hope you will write me fully and freely in reference to all matters of public interest, and at your earliest convenience, and believe me, as ever,

Yours, truly,
James B. Bingham

ALS, DLC-JP.

1. Virginia-born James B. Bingham (*c*1830-*fl*1881), having purchased the Memphis *Bulletin* with P. B. Wills in May, 1861, edited the unionist sheet alone during Federal occupation, though Wills returned to the paper afterward. Following the demise of the *Bulletin*, Bingham briefly edited the *Sun* in the early 1870's and later owned and edited the Memphis *Herald*. 1870 Census, Tenn., Shelby, Memphis, 7th Ward, 75; (1880), Memphis, 148th Enum. Dist., 26; *Goodspeed's Shelby*, 905; *Sholes' Memphis Directory* (1881), 167.

2. Rolfe S. Saunders (*fl*1889), originally of Davidson County, a Whig journalist since 1850 and more recently editor of the Memphis *Bulletin*, had been appointed postmaster in 1861, but "never qualified." Associated after the war with the Memphis *Commercial* until Johnson appointed him collector of internal revenue (1866-70), he was at the same time a partner with Daniel C. and James R. Jones, printers. From 1880 to 1882 Saunders lived in Richmond, Virginia, editing *The Southern Planter*; in the late 1880's he moved to Birmingham. Saunders to Benjamin Harrison, January 26, 1889, Harrison Papers, LC; Memphis city directories (1866-70), *passim*; "Virginia Newspapers in Public Libraries," *Virginia Magazine of History and Biography*, IX (1901), 5-6.

3. Samuel P. Walker (1824-1870), Maury County native who went to Memphis before 1850 and was a cotton merchant, served as alderman (1850-54), president of Citizens Bank of Memphis and Nashville (1853), and director of the Memphis and Charleston Railroad. After the war he was briefly in the legislature as a conservative before resigning in 1866. Hooper, Memphis, 198; McBride and Robison, *Biographical Directory*, II, 946-47.

4. William M., John C., and Madison J. Farrington, all native Tennesseans. William M. (b. *c*1830), wholesale grocer and commission merchant who reported $15,000 real and $10,000 personal property in 1860, was the son-in-law of Robertson Topp. After the war he was president of the DeSoto Insurance and Trust Company, Memphis City Railroad Co., and the Union and Planters Bank, and for twenty years vice president of the Louisville & Nashville RR. Madison J. (b. *c*1828) was a lawyer and real estate dealer. 1860 Census, Tenn., Shelby, Memphis, 4th Ward, 38; *Memphis City Directory* (1859), 77; (1866), 112; Memphis city directories (1867-73), *passim; American Ancestry* (12 vols., Albany, N.Y., 1895), X, 171; for John C. Farrington, see *Johnson Papers*, II, 251*n*.

5. The Nashville *Union* of August 4, reported that Johnson "has been detained for some days past by a violent bilious attack," which postponed an intended visit to Memphis.

6. In Missouri, as elsewhere, people suspected of southern sympathies had been either imprisoned or exiled to some northern state. Gen. Samuel R. Curtis, commander of the Department of the Missouri (1862-63), stepped up the banishments, but sent many south to join their Confederate friends, allowing families to take $1,000 and single persons $300, any property remaining to be confiscated for the Union cause. Meantime Gen. John M. Schofield, in charge of the Missouri militia, on July 22, 1862, issued General Orders No. 19 which required every able-bodied man in the state to enroll, even those who had aided or supported the South. The latter were to surrender their arms and be allowed to return home and remain as long as they attended to their legitimate business. After the District of the Border, composed of counties south of the Missouri River, was created in May, 1863, Brig. Gen. Thomas E. Ewing, Jr., its commander, in August issued General Orders No. 10 which attempted to rid the state of those willfully aiding bushwhackers. Their wives and families were ordered to leave the state immediately; should they be derelict, the military would escort them to Kansas City for shipment south. William C. Quantrill's destructive raid on Lawrence, Kansas, three days later prompted Ewing to issue a more severe order—that citizens of Jackson, Cass, Bates, and the northern portion of Vernon County were to leave their homes, regardless of innocence or guilt in aiding the guerrillas. Ann Davis Niepman, "General Orders No. 11 and Border War During the Civil War," *Missouri Historical Review*, LXVI (1972), 185-94 *passim*; James L. McDonough, *Schofield: Union General in the Civil War and Reconstruction* (Tallahassee, 1972), 36, 42, 54; William E. Parrish, *Turbulent Partnership: Missouri and the Union, 1861-1865* (Columbia, Mo., 1963), 95, 110.

7. Not until September 13, 1864, did the governor finally order the enrollment of all able-bodied men between the ages of eighteen and fifty into the militia. Nashville *Press*, September 15, 1864.

8. The Hurlbut letter nearest to this date had urged Johnson to reopen the courts in West Tennessee. Hurlbut to Johnson, February 21, 1863, Johnson Papers, LC.

9. All four were unionist during the war. The *Bulletin*, a Constitutional Unionist paper before the war, had ceased publication in May, 1861; shortly after the Federal occupation, Benjamin D. Nabers and Reuel Hough revived it. In the past April, James B. Bingham had taken over the editorship. Samuel C. Mercer edited the *Union* from its birth shortly after the capture of Nashville until December, 1863, after which a workingmen's cooperative managed it. Benjamin C. Truman founded the *Press* in May, 1863, as a conservative alternative to the *Union*, with Edwin Paschal as editor during most of its existence. The *Dispatch*, founded in April, 1862, under John M. McKee's direction, rarely printed any editorials of its own during the war. Except for the neutral *Dispatch*, these papers firmly supported Johnson until the *Press* turned hostile in late 1863. Keating *Memphis*, II, 218; Memphis *Bulletin*, July 3, 1862, April 27, 1863; Redden, Nashville Newspapers, 38-48, 52-53.

From David J. Temple and William H. Herron

August 11, 1863, Fort Pillow; ALS, T-Mil. Gov's Papers, 1862-65, Petitions.

Lieutenants of Co. E, 32nd Ind. Inf., want to raise a battalion of Tennessee fugitives, "hundreds" of whom are "sku[l]king in the woods—in the Counties of Lauderdale—Dyer—Tipton, and Haywood—ready and eager—to go in the service under our command—"

From Samuel Morrow

Confidential

Cincinnatti Ohio
August 14 1863

Honl Andrew Johnson
Military Governor of Tenn
Nashville Tenn
Sir

I recd. a telegram from Genl Burnside notifying me to be at Hickmans Bridge[1] by tomorrow morning, unwell as I am, shall be there, and able will share the fate of the expedition[.][2]

I expect much trouble in East Tennessee not only from the Union & secesh parties, but from the *revival* of old party predujices. I left home known as an "Andy Johnson Democrat[.]" If able I return a better one than when I left. My position in Knoxville has been won against the predujices of "*the first families*"[.] amongst the Common people I stand the equal of any one.[3] for this influence I have been *patronized*. it has been used modestly and as I think wisely[.]

Untill you have just cause to doubt my proffessions of devotion to you, I ask your fullest confidence[.]

Many things have transpird here that tend to confirm my suspicions of old party feuds breaking out in E T. when we are relievd from Rebel rule. *Jno Baxter[4] who has never taking* the oath of allegiance to C S A (& never will) will stand by you, if I should not be able to stand the trip across the mountains,[5] will return here and join you[.]

You will pardon the freedom in which I have written and believe me to be truly & respectfully

Your friend S. Morrow

ALS, DLC-JP.

1. Spanning the Kentucky River, between Bryantsville and Nicholasville, about eight miles north of Camp Dick Robinson. *OR-Atlas*, II, plate CL; *OR*, Ser 1, XXIII, Pt. I, 165-66.

2. Leaving Camp Nelson, Kentucky, August 16, with an expedition of 18,000 men, Burnside captured Knoxville on September 2 and Cumberland Gap a week later. Long, *Civil War Almanac*, 397-98, 403, 407; Poore, *Burnside*, 213-15.

3. Morrow was undoubtedly referring to prominent Knoxville secessionists—a group which included Dr. J. G. M. Ramsey and his son John Crozier, former congressman William H. Sneed, Judge William G. Swan, Tennessee branch bank president John H. Crozier, former postmaster Charles W. Charlton, and *Register* editor J. Austin Sperry. It would appear that Morrow, like Johnson, of humble birth, had smarted under the condescension of these local notables. *Knoxville Whig and Rebel Ventilator*, January 9, April 9, 1864; *Williams' Knoxville Directory* (1859-60), 35, 45, 71, 76, 78; William B. Hesseltine, *Dr. J. G. M. Ramsey: Autobiography and Letters* (Nashville, 1954), 123, 240.

4. For Baxter, who, though a unionist, ran unsuccessfully for the Confederate Congress, see *Johnson Papers*, IV, 195*n*.

5. Whether Morrow returned with the expedition or not, he was in Knoxville in November. *OR*, Ser. 1, XXXI, Pt. III, 157.

From Frank P. Dougherty

August 15, 1863, Memphis; ALS, DLC-JP.

Inasmuch as there are neither notaries nor a county court to appoint same—"all the records &c having been carried away by the Confederate Authorities"—inquires as to the possibility of Johnson's granting "Commissions in view of 'Military necessity' "; if governor lacks authority to appoint notaries, would like his petition returned to forward to President Lincoln.

To William Hoffman

Nashville Tenn Aug 16 [1863]

Col W. Hoffman
C. G. P.

I have reliable information that my nephew Andrew Johnson is now confined in Castle Thunder & subjected to horrible treatment. He has been imprisoned over ten months. His case is peculiarly hard. I do hope that immediate steps will be taken to secure his release or exchange. The attention of the authorities has been several times called to this case but it seems nothing has been done for him[.] Your attention to this matter will be regarded as a personal favor[.]

Andw. Johnson Mil Gov

Tel, DNA-RG249, Lets. Recd., 1862-67, File 848M(1863); DNA-RG107, Tels. Recd., U. S. Mil. Tel., Vol. 59 (1863).

To William S. Rosecrans

Nashville, August 18, 1863

Major-General Rosecrans:

This is a favorable time to commence work on the Northwestern Railroad. The Government, no doubt, will replace the iron belonging to the road which it has used. The force necessary is a guard. Its construction need not be large. The labor and money necessary can be readily obtained. Your authority for its construction, whatever agent you may select, is all that is necessary.[1]

Andrew Johnson, Military Governor.

OR, Ser. 1, XXX, Pt. III, 67.

1. The next day one of Rosecrans' staff wrote Johnson: "The General Comdg authorizes & directs the construction of the North Western RR as soon as possible[.] Maj Gen Granger has had orders to clear that country & furnish guards." Calvin Goddard to Johnson, August 19, 1863, Johnson Papers, LC; see also Letter from William S. Rosecrans, August 27, 1863. It might be noted that on this same day, for the third time in as many weeks, Rosecrans sought unsuccessfully to persuade the governor to come to confer with him, topic undesignated, at Winchester. Four days later he was still persisting: "I telegraphed you a few days ago asking you to join me[.] when may I expect you[?]" Rosecrans to Johnson, August 5, 8 (2 telegrams), 18, 22 (2 telegrams), 1863, Tels. Sent, Vol. 63, Dept. of the Cumberland, RG393, NA; Johnson Papers, LC.

From Isaac P. Knight and Vincent Meyers[1]

Mount Vernon Ky
Aug 19th 1863

Gov Johnson
Dear Sir
I am almost forced to report Some very unpleasant circumstances to you. I and Lt Myres went in with Capt Crawford[2] to recruit the 1st E Tenn Battary which is organized & bin paid twice[.] Wee have bin legally mustard in as Officers of this Battory and bin paid as Such and we want to know of you what is the reasin Our Commissions have not bin Isued[.] if the facts has not bin reported to you, you can obtain them from Capt Casey[.][3] Capt Crawford Says you have no authority to commision a man[.] he says Heel get our commissions from the War Department. when asked about them, He curses you for evry d-- rashal he can think of[.]

And he is gilty of the following charges[4] 1st he abuses his men by Strikeing them with his Saber drawing his Pistol and Swareing he will Shoot their d-- braines Out[.] 2n Giving his Lts. orders to Shoot them if they volate an order[.] He has got Negroes & Privates to bring Horses to his Camp & then converted them to his own benifit[.] He allows men under his command to Take horses from Citizens and keep them as their Property. He uses the Goverment Ambulance for the transportation of

Whores in the Place of the Sick Soldier riding in it, And many other things of miner importance. He and Lt Childress[5] gave orders and Childress profered to treat on wine if Some men under their command would Steal Some Goverment Axes.—which they did[.] Gov. there is a great deal of dissatisfation in this command[.] I can Speak for 3 Lts and 2/3 of the men and if you will Put a gentleman Over us for a Commander you will Oblige us or Submit it to the men for then to Chooze one from the Lts[.] Gov there is a report here that Capt Crawford has bin in Some State Prison[.][6] if you know any thing of that pleas let us know the facts in the case (this is confidential)[.] thoze charges wee are able to Proove, wee believe that wee are not the kind of men Capt Crawford wants in his Battary is the Reason wee have not bin Commissioned[.] wee want to know the facts about the Prizon Soon and if he is the Best wee can get wee can quit[.]

Yours Resptly and in Haist
Lt I. P. Knight
Lt Vincin Myres

ALS (Isaac P. Knight), DLC-JP.

1. Isaac P. Knight (b. *c*1834), native Tennessean, was a Meigs County "farm hand" who served as a 2nd lieutenant in Bty. B, 1st Tenn. Lgt. Arty. Btn., USA (1863-64) until his resignation in September. In asking for a leave of absence in April, 1864, he wrote that three brothers had been killed in Federal service and his father murdered by guerrillas. 1860 Census, Tenn., Meigs, 7th Dist., 95; CSR, RG94, NA. For Meyers, see *Johnson Papers*, V, 406*n*.

2. Robert C. Crawford, Jr. (1825-1907), who signed himself R. Clay, was born in Hawkins County. There is much about his career which remains conjectural. According to his own testimony, "I come from a Soldier Race": his father served in the War of 1812, his grandfather was a colonel in the Continental Army, his mother a sister of Commodore Perry. That he served in the Mexican War, on Johnson's recommendation attended West Point (1850) until dismissed for "deficiency in studies," and worked as a surveyor in Utah (1858-61) are authenticated; still subject to documentation are his association with Narciso López in Cuba, William Walker in Nicaragua, and in the 1880's, with General "Chinese" Gordon. Captain of a company of West Tennesseans enlisted as Missouri troops early in the war, he was wounded and captured at Shiloh. Following his release in October, 1862, he joined the 5th Tenn. Inf. and soon after became active in the recruiting which elicited this letter. Ever the controversial figure, he was arrested in late June, 1864, on charges brought by Meyers, for personal use of bank notes belonging to the Rogersville branch of the Bank of Tennessee, was court-martialed and dismissed the service in November. Meanwhile, Crawford had been appointed colonel by Governor Johnson (who probably was unaware of his impending court-martial) and commissioned to raise a regiment of colored artillery, but appears to have been unsuccessful. Undoubtedly this scion of "a Soldier Race," was the prototypical soldier of fortune, attracted to enterprises reckless and daring, prone to have his way. U. S. Military Academy, Appl. Papers (1849-67), RG94, NA; CSR, RG94, NA; Pension file, Mexican War, RG15, NA; *OR*, Ser. 1, XXXI, Pt. III, 265; *Tenn Adj. Gen. Report* (1866), 102, 655; *Tennesseans in the Civil War*, I, 363; Crawford to Johnson, February 22, 1863, Petitions, Mil. Gov's Papers, Tennessee State Library and Archives; Nashville *American*, February 24, 1883; death date supplied by Eileen M. Hickey, U. S. Veterans Administration Center Library, Hampton, Va.

3. Probably Daniel Casey, captain, 29th Ind. Inf., who had been wounded at Shiloh, fought at Stone's River, and was currently serving as commander of the "Consolidated Convalescent Camps at Nashville." File C1478C.B.1864, ACP Branch, RG94, NA.

4. Although Crawford seems not to have been arraigned on this catalogue of infamy, his court-martial the following year on "some twenty charges & specifications" was undoubtedly prompted by continuing behavior of this sort. Penning an apologia from New York's

Astor House in January, 1865, he characterized the proceeding as "a cowardly and contemptible scheme of [Gen. Lovell] Rousseau to punish me in revenge for my strictures on his conduct," and further exonerated himself by declaring that neither of the two specifications of which he was found guilty, even "if fully proved sustain any charge made[.]" Crawford to Johnson, January 29, 1865, Johnson Papers, LC.

5. James A. Childress (b. *c*1842), native Tennessean from Roane County, was 2nd lieutenant, Bty. B, 1st Tenn. Lgt. Arty. Btn., USA (1863-64), resigning February 7, "on account of dissatisfaction amongst the officers of the command." 1860 Census, Tenn., Roane, 1st Dist., 7; CSR, RG94, NA.

6. No evidence of this allegation has been found.

From Thomas Rusellon

August 19, 1863, Lebanon, Ky.; Tel, DLC-JP.

A free Negro youth, "indicted here for enticing Slave from Master" and facing "trial tomorrow for Penitentiary," wants Johnson to notify his father of his immediate need for money to hire a lawyer.

Dialogue with William G. Harding[1]

ca. August 20, 1863

Gen. Harding introduced the conversation by asking an explanation from the Governor of the course to be pursued by the Federal Government with reference to enlisting negroes in Tennessee. He added:

I have a daughter now in the North,[2] and if it is the intention of the Federal authorities to employ negro soldiers, I shall let her remain there, rather than bring her back to a State which will become the theatre of indiscriminate violence, robbery, rape, bloodshed and every species of outrage perpetrated by negro soldiers, who will have no regard for the lives, and property of citizens, or the chastity of women.

GOVERNOR. Before you inveigh against the policy of the Federal Government, which you claim the privilege of criticising, you ought to ask yourself, who brought this state of things upon the country and who was responsible for it? You talk of outrages and the violation of female chastity, when your Confederate Government has Indian savages employed in hunting Tennessee loyalists to their hiding places in the mountains, and when your rebel cavalrymen are now engaged in seizing and stripping women in the mountains, under pretext of ascertaining whether they are men disguised in female garments to escape Conscription.[3] These brutalities are perpetrated daily by your friends and you are silent.

GEN. HARDING. But, Governor, I do not approve of these things at all; I am opposed to them.

GOV. Of course you are opposed to them now; because you dare not express yourself otherwise. But you helped to set on foot the rebellion, which is the parent of all these crimes and sufferings. You boasted[4] that you had circulated $5,000,000 to promote the rebellion, in the once quiet and happy State of Tennessee. Sir, if I had done what you have done, my hands and every thread of my garments would seem to blush with the blood of my murdered countrymen. You are responsible for the murder of the flower of the youth of Tennessee, and the desolation of her households. You are one of the conspirators who delivered them over to an untimely and ignominious death, in battle against their country, in order that you might hold to your negro property. You and your guilty comrades are red and dripping with the blood of your deluded victims.

GEN. H. I obeyed the dictates of my conscience in all that I did, as I did when I held office under you, in years past.[5] Did you not once consider me worthy of trust?

GOV. Yes, I did. Once you were considered an honorable man. Benedict Arnold was once a faithful soldier, and fought bravely for his country, but he turned traitor and endeavored to sell her to the enemy, and he died in disgrace. Aaron Burr was once deemed an honorable man, and a brave soldier, but he too died a universally detested traitor.

GEN. H. Do you compare me to Arnold and Burr?

GOV. Yes. I consider you a traitor, an enemy of your country. If you regret your misconduct why do you not make amends for it, by openly espousing the cause of the country against the rebellion, instead of carping at and censuring the policy of the Government?

GEN. H. I am under bonds at present.[6]

GOV. And why are you under bonds, except that you are an unrepentant enemy of your State and country? You have stirred up mutiny, insurrection, and anarchy in this State, and instead of helping us to put the rebellion down, you are here denouncing the inhumanity and brutality of the Federal Government, and the barbarism of the Northern people, at the very time you are keeping your own daughter among these very Northern people for quiet and protection! Be assured, sir, that the Government is determined to put down this rebellion in any way, and by any means it may choose to select, without regard to the fault-finding and objections of rebels and malcontents. And it is equally determined to bring all traitors to a strict and terrible accountability. Wealth and position shall not shield a traitor from the avenging justice of the people.

Nashville *Union*, August 22, 1863.

1. The accuracy of this confrontation is highly debatable: it smacks too much of the moralistic propaganda pieces with which loyal editors sought to arouse indignation over rebel arrogance while extolling the patriotism and dedication of Union leaders. On the other hand, it should be observed that Johnson was sometimes wont for political purposes to assume a harsh public posture, while entertaining somewhat less draconian private views. Edwin T. Hardison, In the Toils of War: Andrew Johnson and the Federal Occupation of Tennessee (Ph. D. dissertation, University of Tennessee, 1981), *passim*.

2. Selene Harding was enrolled in Madame Masse's private French school in Philadelphia. Speer, *Prominent Tennesseans*, 4.

3. Two companies of William H. Thomas' 69th N.C. Inf. were composed of Cherokees; after one of their lieutenants was killed in East Tennessee in September, 1862, they scalped several of the Union dead and wounded. Nothing has been found to substantiate Johnson's other accusations. John G. Barrett, *The Civil War in North Carolina* (Chapel Hill, 1963), 196.

4. Harding had been a member of Tennessee's three-man military and financial board which by October, 1861, had spent over $4,600,000 to arm the state, with the total expected to "fall little if any short of $5,000,000." *OR*, Ser. 1, LII, Pt. II, 160.

5. Sometime before the war, Harding had been brigadier general of the state militia; nominated by Johnson in 1856 as a penitentiary inspector, he was not confirmed. Wooldridge, *Nashville*, 608; see also *Johnson Papers*, II, 518.

6. Presumably Harding's parole was like that given at about the same time to Reuben Ford, one of the imprisoned Nashville ministers, which stipulates that "he will not write or speak against said Government." Ford also had to post a $5,000 bond. Speers, *Prominent Tennesseans*, 3; see Parole for Reuben Ford, October 9, 1862.

From Samuel Hays

August 21, 1863, Danville, Pa.; ALS, DLC-JP.

Member of state Union Central Committee and long-time admirer wants a statement of "your Views in extenso of the present condition of our country—the encouragement which the present affords—the duties of every citizen in the State of Penna." and "such other suggestions as will tend to promote the success of the cause in this fall's election— I *know* an exhortation from *you* would be attended with the happiest result."

From Robert A. Crawford

London Ky Aug 22nd 1863

Gov. Johnson
Dr Sir!

I am just in from Cumberland River & Barbersville, where I was sent by Genl. Burnside.

The General will be here to day, so will the army— From the best and most reliable information I could get the force in Cumberland Gap was from three to six hundred—the force at Big Creek Gap was from three to four hundred[.] this I think is reliable. I saw two men who left Knoxville last Sunday. they say there are not over 600 Troops at that place and but very few East of there.

I feel certain that by Sunday morning we will all be in East Tenn—[1]

5000 Cavelry & two Batteries will pass here to day for the Gap.

I have no doubt but Cumberland & Big Creek Gaps will be evacuated and East Tennessee will go up without the fire of a gun.[2] This little Town is full of men women and children to see the army[.]

excuse this hasty scraul[.]

Yours Truly
Robt. A. Crawford

ALS, DLC-JP.

1. Burnside, having left Camp Nelson on the 16th, moved south through London and, maintaining a rapid march of twenty-miles per day, arrived in Knoxville on Wednesday, September 2, thereby conforming to the optimistic pace predicted by Crawford. Seymour, *Divided Loyalties*, 83-85; Poore, *Burnside*, 215-16; *OR*, Ser 1, XXX, Pt. II, 26; Pt. IV, 560.

2. Bypassing both gaps—the only sizeable Confederate force was at Cumberland—the advancing Union army faced no organized opposition, though there were occasional skirmishes. The Cumberland garrison surrendered September 9. Seymour, *Divided Loyalties*, 84; *OR*, Ser. 1, XXX, Pt. II, 621-22.

Speech at Franklin[1]

August 22, 1863

I am here to-day, my fellow citizens, for the purpose of noticing your own deliberations and action, and of intermingling and reasoning familiarly with you, rather than to make a set speech. A great question forces itself upon the minds of all: "What has involved the land in this fearful peril? The peril is upon us, and there must be some cause, for there can be no effect without a cause. There has been an effort on the part of a portion of the people of Tennessee, and of other Southern States, to break up the Government; there has been a nefarious plot to destroy the greatest, best, and most benign institutions which the world ever knew. Now, when we examine the basis of the Government, if we comprehend its principles, we must conclude that it cannot be broken up. Try to destroy the principles of freedom? as well might you try to lock up the winds of heaven, or bind the billows of the ocean. It is sacrilege to attempt it. You have made the trial, and assailed this glorious Government and the trial has recoiled upon yourselves. You have been crushed and disgraced in the attempt to destroy it. The building of free government still stands erect, while you are covered with shame. This Government will live, for it is indestructible. Go back to old articles of the first American Confederation, and their idea was durability. The States were to be united forever. The idea of unity and freedom was a divine one, recorded in the beginning, and the Government was to be perpetual. After we had put down British tyranny, we began in 1787 to make the Government more perfect still. We find in the beginning of the Federal Constitution that its purpose was, "To form a more perfect Union." As an emblem of the Union the thirteen Stars and Stripes were chosen a symbol of its divine mission which all earth and hell, although combined, can never destroy. And this Union, planned and constructed with admirable wisdom, was cemented with the hardships, patriotism and bloodshed of a seven years' war. Our fathers who thus suffered and toiled for our benefit, and founded a nation with so great labor, expected rebellions at some future day, and provided for them in the Federal Constitution, and in it gave power to repel invasion and suppress rebellion. This is just what the loyal people are carrying out to-day. This is not a war of the North against the South, nor of the South against the North. It is a wicked rebellion on the one hand, and a just and constitutional war for its suppression on the other. The Government is suppressing a rebellion—an injunction of our fathers, as written in the Constitution. And while doing this, if a State Government should be paralyzed or disappear what shall be done? The idea has been cunningly circulated that after the rebellion has been suppressed, that the North will not let us back into the Union, nor let us have a State Government! What shallow humbuggery and deception! Some think we must petition the Government to get back into the Union. I deny the doctrine of secession wholly, absolutely, *toto celo*. Tennessee is not out of the Union, never has been and never will be out. The bonds of the constitution and the Federal power will always prevent that. This government is perpetual; provision is made for reforming the Government, and amending the Constitution, and admitting States *into* the Union; not for letting them *out* of it. The ever-changing condition and wants of the people require the improvement not destruction of the government. Our State government lies dormant, and civil government suspended in this convulsion. What shall be done? I come, not with the sword in the one hand and the torch in the other,[2] but with the olive-branch of peace, and urge you to the work of restoration. It is a noble work. The beauty and wisdom of the Constitution are unequaled for its grouping of principles, seems like an emanation of divine wisdom. It guarantees a republican government to all the States. When the rebellion overthrew your State government, the United States guaranteed you a republican government still. This is its simple duty and obligation. It is a government of many States and there must be harmony between all parts of the machinery; there must not be clashing between the different wheels of our political system. Where are we now? There is a rebellion; this was anticipated, as I said. The rebel army is driven back. Here lies your State, a sick man in his bed, emaciated and exhausted, paralyzed in all his powers and unable to walk alone. The physician comes[.] Don't quarrel about antecedents, but administer to his wants, and cure him as quickly as possible. The United States sends an agent, or a Military Governor, which ever you please to call him, to aid you in restoring your government. Whenever you desire, in good faith, to restore civil authority you can do so. Manifest a desire to do so, and a proclamation for an election will be issued as speedily as it is practicable to hold one. One by one all the agencies of your State government will be set in motion. A legislature will be elected. Judges will be appointed temporarily, until you can elect them at the polls; and so of Sheriffs, County Court Judges, Justices and other officers; until the way is fairly open for the people, and all the parts of civil government resume their ordinary functions. This is no nice, intricate metaphysical question. It is a plain common sense matter and there is nothing in the way, but obstinacy. Do you want Government or rebellion, chaos, anarchy, and guerrilla warfare and rapine? It is with you, fellow-citizens, to choose; which will you have? You used to contend stoutly for man's capability for self-government. Have you been so deluded that you have lost faith in this doctrine? My countrymen, if I know my heart, the best energies of my life have been devoted to the defence of this great principle. I ever honestly sought to elevate my fellow-men. I did it openly; I waged no guerrilla warfare, nor lurked in any ambush, and I advocate now the same great principles which I ever did. We make the issue to you directly—WILL YOU HAVE FREE, CIVIL GOVERNMENT? I tell you people of Franklin and Williamson, not in the spirit of menace, nor with a forked tongue for the purpose of deception,[3] that the Government will put down the rebellion, and govern you, either through your own instrumentality, or through its appointed agents. You talk about the bugbear of coercion: Coerce a State! Coerce individuals! Why, the first political truth I ever learned was that the soul of liberty was the love of law. Let burglars and assassins cry out against coercion and the execution of the laws. There can be no government without power to enforce the laws and coerce transgressors. The man who clamors against coercion is either a charlatan or a knave. This people must have government; take your choice—either your own government, free and uncontaminated, or a military government which does not stop to argue. These bayonets are pointed arguments. These leaden messengers, which fly on wings of fire, are rather hard to answer! My soldier friends know that I intend no reflection upon them. They are doing a glorious work in putting down rebellion. Now it is for you, my fellow-citizens, to say what shall be the end. You struck the first blow and precipitated the rebellion. Is it not for you to endeavor to make amends for this offence? Ah, you say you "have done [illegible] you were nearly all Union men once, but you went astray. I had a sharp argument on this very point the other day. There is a turning point in the career of every criminal. Benedict Arnold was once a brave soldier, and was highly esteemed by his countrymen, but he turned traitor. So was Aaron Burr once esteemed a soldier and a patriot; and was elected Vice-President of the United States, but he turned traitor, and became universally abhorred. It is not worth while to mince phrases in this matter, for fear of hurting somebody's feelings. It is better to speak plainly; treason is nothing but treason; so that constitution calls it, under which you attained a greatness unrivalled by any other nation on the earth. It provides for the punishment of traitors. I want the leaders of the rebellion punished, and just penalties meted out to their treason. Treason must be made odious and traitors must be punished and improverished. If this be not done, that government cannot stand. Many humble men, the peasantry and yeomanry of the South, who have been decoyed, or perhaps driven into the rebellion, may look forward with reasonable hope, for an amnesty. But the intelligent and influential leaders must suffer. The tall poppies must be struck down.[4] Therefore the confiscation act was demanded [Prolonged applause.] What did the Government do that we should lift our hands against it? Point to one law, or act by which our rights were taken away. Yet after wading for over two years in blood and carnage, and filling the land with desolation, these rebels when whipped turn about and talk of a compromise! I have no compromise to offer, save the Constitution and the laws. Obey these and the difficulty will be settled in forty-eight hours. Can you make a better compromise? Call on us to compromise? We have been stripped and plundered, derided and persecuted. Compromise, when the rebel stands with a bayonet at your breast! Compromise! Will you have virtue compromise with vice? Whenever such a compromise is made is not virtue ever the loser? Will you have right compromise with wrong? Whenever such a compromise is made does not the wrong gain the advantage? Will you have Truth compromise with Falsehood? Whenever that occurs will not Falsehood be the conqueror? If the people of Tennessee had come forward one year ago and given their hearty support to the Union they could have obtained their own terms. Now they can't. I told the people, when engaged in a heated debate with Gentry in yon grove, in 1855,[5] and a bitter war was made against me, on this slavery question, that slavery had no protection but the Constitution. Slavery is now become an itinerant institution, and uses its legs to walk off.[6] When I was in the Legislature, years ago, and urged the passage of a law distributing our Congressional representation among the districts according to their white population, not questioning the three-fifths apportionment as respected the State, many of you cried out: "Oh he is a d--d abolitionist!" I believed the white basis of representation to be most just and most in accordance with the spirit of our institutions. I was then, as I am now, for a white man's government, and for a free, intelligent, white constituency, instead of a negro aristocracy. Intelligent freemen constitute a State, not wealth, or negro property. I am for a Commonwealth composed of enlightened and industrious freemen, and not one based upon slavery as in the pseudo-Southern Confederacy—a monarchy based upon slave property, where no more whites are wanted than are necessary to form a negro police. The time once was when we could discuss all questions, political or theological, *except slavery*. Fellow-citizens, whenever you cannot discuss any institution of a State, then liberty is gone. You said slavery was above the Government, and in seeking to confirm this your plot recoiled. If in this recoil slavery must go, I say, let it go! I am for my Government with or without slavery; but if either the Government or slavery must perish, I say give me the Government and let the negroes go. I believe if they do go, that in less than ten years they will be more productive than they are now. We have sat here cursing the North. Look at Ohio, Indiana and Illinois, how far ahead they are of us. Here, if a man goes to farming it takes $1000 to buy a negro, and then the negro's hand must be directed by the supervision of a white man.

In Ohio, or Indiana, the man himself goes to work, his $1000 is invested in something productive, which will not run away, and the whole commonwealth moves onward. Cotton and negroes have ruled here in the South; they are rulers no longer. How long has it been since cotton became an article of general use? Herodotus speaks of *the cotton tree* as a curiosity.[7] The world got along very well for 4000 years without being aware of the existence of King Cotton. It has been in general use for some ninety years, and some people think that without it the sun would cease rising and the world be ruined. A little more silk, flax, and wool will displace it effectually.

The government is above cotton and negroes. Rather than have it destroyed I would send every negro back to Africa, and see Africa itself swept beyond the line where gravitation ceases to act. I intend to deceive no man. I am for a government based on and ruled by industrious, free white citizens, and conducted in conformity with their wants, and not a slave aristocracy; and come weal or woe by such a government I will stand. You cry out against coercion. What has happened beyond your own mountains? A people pure and free as their own mountain streams, met in Convention, and asked you to let them stay in the Union. But in a few weeks, in response to their petition, the rebel cavalry rode through their country, imprisoning, outraging and murdering the freemen who asked the privelege of being allowed to stay under the old government. That was what I call practice versus theory. The time has come when the tyrant's rod shall be broken and the oppressed shall go free. Did that people bring on this contest? No; their skirts are free from the crime. How many of you in this audience, have been instrumental in inducing others into the ranks of the rebel army, while you clung to your "niggers" at home? Where is that noble looking boy the pride of his father, and the love of his fond mother? Alas, he sleeps in yon new made grave with no coffin or winding sheet save his bloody blanket. Father, ask yourself who is answerable for this unnatural deed, this untimely slaughter of the flower of the State. Conscience cries: "Yes, I loved my negroes better than I did my own son, the offspring of my own loins, the fruit of my own body!" You thrust your child to death that you might hold on to your miserable slaves; and look at the sad recompense.

> Justice divine, to punish sin moves slow,
> The slower is her step, the surer is her blow.

Let me ask these mothers, whom I have seen in Nashville robed in mourning, what have you been doing? And what have these young ladies been doing who in thoughtless excitement sent away their lovers to the battle-field that they might return Napoleons! Alas! poor fellows, they now moulder in unmarked graves, in all the stages of loathsome decomposition. I ask all who have engaged in this fearful work to help us restore the Government. Will you do it? Will you have a Government of your own, or the bayonet? for one of these two you must have. Just as the people indicate the wish we will have free government; there is no intention to withhold it. I know nothing about "reconstruction," as some call it; all that is necessary is to restore your government.[8] Let me say to the ladies in no unkind spirit, the female sex have done much to get up this rebellion. We know how very much you can do now to restore prosperity and happiness. Help to chase away this malignant planet of fire and blood which is now in the ascendant. There is a power behind the throne. Set about to work for your country, as patriot women did in olden time[.] You have a glorious government, and if your sons fall in its defence, they fall in a glorious cause. Which do you prefer, that they perish in its defence, or in the vain attempt to destroy it? Remember the story of Cornelia, the mother of Gaius and Tiberius Grachii. When some of the Roman nations [matrons] were sitting around her exhibiting their rich and costly jewels, Cornelia called her sons to her side, and clasping them to her bosom, as they leaned upon her, all flushed, and buoyant with the vigor of youth, she exclaimed, "These are my jewels!" Your sons are your most precious jewels; consecrate them to your country.

Let us all join in the work of restoration, and when this shall be accomplished, I would be willing to be led to an altar and pour out my blood as a last libation to freedom. I love peace. I have no affinity in my nature for war; it is not my natural element. I would rather wear upon my garments the dust of the workshop than bear upon my person all the glittering insignia of war. Still this war is necessary, and must be waged until the overthrow of the rebellion. I welcome these soldiers who are present to-day, as fellow-citizens of the same country, and as protectors and defenders. You are engaged, my friends, in a just, a righteous, and an honorable cause. Accept, ladies and gentlemen, soldiers and citizens, one and all, my thanks for your very patient attention.

Nashville *Union*, August 25, 1863; newspaper clipping, Johnson-Bartlett Col.

1. On this Saturday, a Union meeting—"for the purpose of devising measures for the reorganization of the State government, with a view to the restoration of the loyal people of Tennessee to their rights and benefits as citizens of the United States"—was held at the courthouse, which was filled to overflowing. William G. Brownlow began with a fiery speech, at the conclusion of which the committee on resolutions made its report. At this juncture Governor Johnson, who had just arrived on a special train, entered the room and spoke. Subsequent speeches by Judge John S. Brien, Col. Richard M. Edwards, and Col. Leonidas C. Houk were interspersed with music from the brass band of the 14th Mich. Inf. Nashville *Press*, August 24, 1863; Nashville *Union*, August 23, 25, 26, 1863; undated and unidentified clipping, Johnson-Bartlett Col.

2. A frequently used figure. Eight months earlier, Samuel Mercer, editor of the *Union*, had written "Let the work of destruction go on, and let the torch and sword of war complete their work." In May the governor had used the same phrase. Nashville *Union*, December 24, 1862; Remarks at Nashville, May 30, 1863.

3. Reflecting North American Indian speech to mean a lying or false tongue. Mathews, *Americanisms*, I, 647.

4. An allusion to Charles Sumner's Senate speech of May 19, 1862: "But the tallest poppies must drop. For the conspirators, who organized this great crime and let slip the dogs of war, there can be no penalty too great." *Cong. Globe*, 37 Cong., 2 Sess., 2196.

5. Johnson and Meredith P. Gentry, former Whig congressman, had stumped the state in the gubernatorial canvass of that year.

6. Large numbers of slaves were abandoning their former masters.

7. Judged to be "the first Western mention of cotton," Herodotus' *History*, III, 106, in describing the flora of India observes: "And further, there are trees which grow wild there, the fruit whereof is a wool exceeding in beauty and goodness that of sheep. The natives make their clothes of this tree-wool." W. W. How and J. Wells, *A Commentary on Herodotus* (2 vols., London, 1912), I, 290; A. J. Grant, *Herodotus: The Text of Canon Rawlinson's Translation* (2 vols., London, 1897), I, 303.

8. As President, Johnson would hold that secession had not destroyed states; it had merely suspended the legitimate operation of their governmental functions. In his opinion, the Federal government should not attempt to reconstruct what already existed but should simply restore these states to their status as of old. Eric L. McKitrick, *Andrew Johnson and Reconstruction* (Chicago, 1960), 91-92.

From Robert P. Shapard[1]

Shelbyville Augt 23 1863

Gov A Johnson
Sir

Nine days since I was Caught by a band of Robbers, 11 miles beyond Fayetteville and my money saddle & hat taken from me[.] a few days after the Citizens geathirn their squirrel guns and went in persuit of the Robbers Captured the horse of the Chief and one of his men— last accounts a have the same Citizens are in persuit of some horse thieves— if the Citizens should Come a cross a federal force I fear they will be takin for bushwhackers[.] I have advised them to adopt some badge and let it be known to the Union Armey and Citizens[.] The Citizens are becoming aroused and feele a determination to put down bushwhackers & thieves if some plan Can be adopted[.] Cant you advise some plan and put it in Opperation[.]

The Citizens with a little help can do the work more affectually than the armey[.] if you do not recollect me enquire of Thos. A. Kerchival[2] Esq at the Provost Office in the Capital[.]

I am anxious to hear from you on this subject and will do all I can to advance the object named[.] hopeing to hear from you soon I Remain

Yours Truly R. P. Shapard

ALS, DLC-JP.

1. For Shapard, Shelbyville wholesale grocer with two sons in the Confederate forces, see *Johnson Papers*, V, 511*n*. Late in 1863 he moved to Louisville, Kentucky, returning sometime after April, 1864, to continue in business until his death in 1871. Louisville *Journal*, December 30, 1863-April 20, 1864, *passim*.

2. Thomas A. Kercheval (1837-1915), Maury County-born lawyer and subsequently a Radical Republican who served in the Nashville provost marshal's office (1862-64), was later state representative (1865-67, 1869-71) and senator (1885-87), as well as Nashville mayor (1872-73, 1875-83, 1886-87). McBride and Robison, *Biographical Directory*, II, 493-94; Nashville *Union and American*, September 1, 1872.

To William S. Rosecrans

Nashville, August 23, 1863

General Rosecrans:

Arms for cavalry are needed. The ordnance officers refuse to furnish them without an order from you or the Secretary of War. Will General Rosecrans please give such order by telegraph, as we are trying to equip the men as fast as possible.[1]

Andrew Johnson,
Military Governor.

OR, Ser. 1, XXX, Pt. III, 131.

1. Rosecrans apparently forwarded the request to Gen. James W. Ripley, chief of ordnance, who replied: "Four thousand sets of horse equipments will be forwarded to the

ordnance depot Nashville, as fast as possible." Ripley to Rosecrans, August 23, 1863, *OR*, Ser. 1, XXX, Pt. III, 131.

From Robert M. Pettey[1]

Oak Hill Seminary Coffee Co Tenn
August 24th 1863

Dear sir

I wrote to you some 5 or 6 weeks since but probabley you never reced it, consequently I write to you again, hoping you will receve it as a token of friendship. I reced a fall from a horse the week after the U. S. troops came into this section, & have been confined to my house & mostly to my bed ever since until the last week[.] I am now able to walk a little on my crutches & I hope ere long I shall be able to get about some to attend to my local affairs. I wrote to you concerning the destitution of the country as to provisions & I do not think that our crops of corn will yield more than a third as much as usual & as to hogs for pork there is scarcley any[.] The troops took nearly every thing that was to eat, we had left from the impressment of the Southern troops or rebels, consequently unless we get aid from some source we will suffer. true there [are] some who have drawed rations from the goverment, but it has been quite limited[.] I hope it [will] not be stopped for the amout we have drawn has been of great benefit. There was no respecter of persons both rebs and union men joined alike in devastation[.] I suppose that the troops were obleeged to have something to eat as there provision trains were left behind & could not get up or keep up with them. you know that I have stood on the same platform with you & W. B. Stokes & others stand & do yet notwithstanding I am now destitute of all most every thing, except my wife & children.[2] 9 of my negros went off at once, they are now in Tullahoma[.] My wife & son overtook them at the pickett line & went in & informed Genl R. W. Johnston[3] who was commander of the Post. I also wrote to him cocening the matter 10 days before the event, believing from every thing I observed that the negros would go, as almost every day some of the soldirs were here talking to them & persuading [them] to leave. Genl Johnston give orders for the picketts not to let them inside & for the negros to go home[.] I will here give you a copy of a paper he sent me & which is now in [my] possession viz

Head 2d Div. 20 Cav Corps
Tullahoma Tennessee
August 15t 1863

The Bearer hereof Mrs Pettey came in and reported to me that her sevants had all left her; and were at my pickett line, asking to get in. Knowing that she & her husband were both Loyal I orderd the pickets not to allow them to come inside[.] The order sent was misconstrued and the negros were pass[ed] inside. They are now here and I do not know how she is to get possession of them. The whole subject is a difficult one to settle[.] she has 9 negros inside of my lines aged as follows, sarah 36, Mary 34, Henry 11, Jane 8, Gerge 8, Hariett 6, Elias 5, Mia 2 John 4[.]

R. W. Johnson
Brg Gnl Vols Comd Post

Comment is unnecessary for me. I should be pleased for you to give me some information of the subject, if compatible with your station & if there has ever such a case come under your knowledge[.] As to the negros I have no use for them unless they could be made to know their proper place & obey my commands, but still I do not know how it is or by what process I am deprivd of them or their value[.] My father[4] is in a similar situation[.] every one of his negros 3 went last summer & 8 this & the old man is now nearly 77 years of age & has no one to cut or haul a stick of wood for him. I hope you will be kind enough to answer this soon & give me all the information you can on the subjects I have written upon for I am anxious to know my fate[.]

If I cannot get assistance I do not know how I am to live[.] several of my neighbors have valued my damages aside from the negrose at $489.00[.] will I be remunerated & how & when are questions you will please give me information[.] Hoping that you will correspond with me soon & often I remain

yours &c Respectley
R. M. Pettey

Direct to Tullahoma Tennessee[.] the bearer hereof is personally acquanted with me & has been for several years[.]

R. M P.

ALS, DLC-JP.

1. Robert M. Pettey (b. *c*1813), North Carolina native, farmer with $5,000 real and $7,000 personal property, and earlier a resident of Franklin County, whose oldest son (James Pettey, private, Co. E, 28th Tenn. Inf.) was conscripted into the Confederate army, lost by his own estimate property valued at nine or ten thousand dollars during the war. Mrs. V. K. Carpenter, tr., *1850 Franklin County, Tennessee, Census* (Huntsville, Ark., 1970), 69; 1860 Census, Tenn., Coffee, 6th Dist., 119; R. M. Pettey to Johnson, November 21, 1864, Johnson Papers, LC.

2. Wife Elizabeth (b. *c*1819) and sons James (b. *c*1845), Robert (b. *c*1847), Thomas (b. *c*1849), William (b. *c*1856), and Charles (b. *c*1858). 1860 Census, Tenn., Coffee, 6th Dist., 119.

3. Richard W. Johnson.

4. Probably Eli Pettey, or Petty, Patty (b. 1786), North Carolina-born farmer with $7,000 real and $9,900 personal property on the eve of the war, who had settled in Coffee County by 1840, moving to Franklin County before 1850. Carpenter, *1850 Census, Franklin*, 69; Dorothy W. Potter and Betty M. Majors, "1840 Federal Census of Coffee County, Tennessee," *Coffee County Historical Society Quarterly*, I (Fall-Winter, 1970), 30; 1860 Census, Tenn., Franklin, 8th Dist., 184; WPA, Tennessee, Coffee County: Bible, Family and Tombstone Records, 2.

From Jeremiah T. Boyle

August 27, 1863, Louisville, Ky.; ALS, DLC-JP.

Commander of the District of Kentucky, forwarding a letter from Mrs. Henry (Mary) Rowland of Sumner County, reports that her husband's farm had been "taken and turned over to another person, while she was absent temporarily at Lebanon"; asks "what is the policy pursued in such cases, and whether Mrs Rowland can be restored to the possession of her farm—" Expresses regret that "it has not been left to you to devise and fix the terms on which the rebellious people of Tennessee could assume their citizenship . . . and to inaugurate a policy for complete restoration of your state—"

From William S. Rosecrans

Head-Quarters Department of the Cumberland,
Stevenson Ala Aug 27 1863.

Governor:

If consistent with your orders from the President, I wish to place under your orders the building of the North Western Railroad— Maj. Genl. Gordon Granger, will receive instructions, to furnish on your requisition, such military force as may be required for the protection of the road— You can also have the services of Brig. Gen. Gillem, and such part of the Tennessee troops, as shall be mustered into the service, as you may need, including Gillem's Regiment. Your requisitions for the necessary funds will be sent to the Dept. Chief Quarter Master, who will be directed to make requisition for, and supply what you need. The Chief Commissary will in like manner, be directed to supply subsistence for the troops and men employed in construction of the road. He will give directions to the Post Commissary, how requisitions are to be made. Col. Innis[1] Military Supt. of Rail-roads, will detail the requisite number of engineers, and furnish rolling stock necessary to carry on the work.[2]

It is probable we can spare Col. Thompson,[3] and the 1st and 2d. Reg't Colored Troops, to be employed on the line.

Ask President Lincoln if he cannot send you some Colored, or Engineer troops, from Genl. Grant's Department, for the same purpose, the whole to be under your Command.[4]

As a matter of course, I shall desire to have reports from you, of the progress of the work.[5]

Very Respectfully Your Ob't Servt.
W. S Rosecrans Maj. Genl. Comd'g

Brig. Gen. A. Johnson
Mil'ty Govr. of Tennessee.

LS, T-Mil. Gov's Papers, 1862-65, Corres. to Andrew Johnson; DLC-JP; DNA-RG393, Dept. of the Cumberland, Lets. Sent, Vol. 7 (1863).

1. William P. Innes.

2. In a special order dated October 22, 1863, Stanton placed the construction of the railroad under Johnson's authority, allowing him to hire an engineer and requisition all necessary materials. Grant was to provide troops to protect the railroad and laborers. Edwin Stanton, Special Order, October 22, 1863, Vol. 29, Orders and Circulars, 34-35, RG94, NA.

3. Charles R. Thompson (1840-1894), Maine native and St. Louis clothing salesman, enlisted in October, 1861, as a private in the Engineer Regiment of the West, Mo. Vols., becoming a first lieutenant the following month. Appointed ordnance officer of the Army of the Mississippi the following August, he became an aide-de-camp to General Rosecrans and by the end of the war had been breveted brigadier general. Fitch, *Annals*, 53-54; *St. Louis City Directory* (1859), 321, 467; Heitman, *Register*, I, 956.

4. No such request has been found.

5. A week later Johnson wired: "I have taken steps to execute, and will proceed to have it finished without delay. Will write you in a few days upon the subject." Johnson to Rosecrans, September 2, 1863, *OR*, Ser. 1, XXX, Pt. III, 297.

Speech at Nashville[1]

August 29, 1863

Governor Johnson said that the heart of the masses of the people beat strongly for freedom, that the system of negro slavery had proved baleful to the nation by arraying itself against the institutions and interests of the people, and that the time had clearly come when means should be devised for its total eradication from Tennessee. Slavery was a cancer on our society and the scalpel of the statesman should be used not simply to pare away the exterior and leave the roots to propagate the disease anew, but to remove it altogether. Let us destroy the cause of our domestic dissensions and this bloody civil war. It is neither wise nor just to compromise with an evil so gigantic. He avowed himself unequivocally for the removal of slavery; the sooner it can be effected the better. Some inconveniences might, most likely would follow, temporarily, but these would be more than compensated, by the grand impulse given to all our interests by the substitution of free for slave labor. He was for immediate emancipation, if he could get it, if this could not be obtained he was for gradual emancipation; but emancipation at all events. He thought that the benefits of gradual emancipation, were a good deal like the benefits conferred on the dog in the fable, whose tail was cut off an inch at a time by a humane surgeon, whose kindness of heart would not permit him to remove it at one stroke. He believed slavery was a curse and he wanted to see it wiped out without delay. We would be stronger, richer, happier and more prosperous, as soon as this was done.

He invoked the people to cast off the slavish fear which had hitherto sealed their lips on this question, and speak and act henceforth as freemen should. The slave aristocracy had long held its foot upon their necks, and exacted heavy tribute from them, even to robbing them of free speech. Let the era of freedom be henceforth proclaimed to the non-slaveholders of Tennessee![2]

Nashville *Union*, September 1, 1863.

1. During the evening, a large crowd of unionists, having heard a rumor of Sumter's fall, paraded through the streets, held a rally in the capitol building, and later gathered in

front of the governor's house, calling upon him for a speech. This two-hour impromptu address which represented a new departure—an unconditional advocacy of emancipation in Tennessee—was widely noticed in the northern press, contributing to the growth of Johnson's emerging reputation as a radical on the slavery question.

2. This contention that emancipation would free nonslaveholders from tyranny—a new application of his oft-used tactic of appealing to class antagonisms—appeared frequently hereafter in his speeches. Cimprich, Slavery Admidst Civil War, 5-7.

From Edwin M. Stanton

August 30, 1863, Washington; ALS, DLC-JP.

Introduces Charles A. Dana, assistant secretary of war, visiting Tennessee to confer "upon such matters relative to the public interests that you may desire to have brought before this Department for its action"; asks Johnson to afford Dana "every facility for becoming acquainted with the state of affairs within your command, and explain to him fully any matters which you think it important to bring to the notice of this Department."

To Samuel J. Carter[1]

Nashville Ten August 30th 1863

Mr Samuel Carter— If you have any pure Simple whiskey that is good send me some of it— I have enough that is not fit for any one to drink, yet it is called [good] by some—

Andrew Johnson

ANS-NN, Harkness Col.

1. For Carter, Nashville hotel proprietor, see *Johnson Papers*, II, 437*n*.

From William W. Reed[1]

Colligе Greene Barracks
Annappolis Maryland
August 31st/63

Govenor. Johnson.

by request of your Niphew Andrew Johnson that is now a prisoner in the Confederacy I take this opportunity[.] I was in the same prison with him three months and he requested me to let you know how he was treated as well as a number of loyal Southern born men thats with him[.] they are confined in Castle Thunder Richmond Va in a very small room and that is in the very comb of the castle in the fourth story and nobody is allowed to speak to them[.] they are not allowed out of their room on no pretense whatever and living on such rashions as would sicken any man to think of that never experienced any such thing and then they dont get quarter enuph of that[.] they are in a manner on starvation and naked besides[.] I dont know what in the world they will do this winter[.] they must frees and starve to deth if they are not aided in some way now[.] Cant they be got out of there[?] there is about two hundred Union Sitisens and Soldiers there and must they lay and rot and die off in such prisons[?] men that belongs to the strongest nation on Earth yes lay and die in hopeliss Dispare and thus (the Rebel) prisoners wallos in luxuries such as they never knew untill they was prisoners[.] I have confidence enuph in the Goverment to think those men could be brought out of there if the thing was rightly seen to— I was a prisoner over Seven months and just arrived here yesterday. Now Govenor in the name of God and humanity try [to] do all in your power to get the men in question released[.]

I would propose to put the same number of their men in the fix feed them the Same and notify the authorities at Richmond of it. But you Know best what to do for them and I hope you will loose no time for the men feels sensible every hour thats lost.[2]

No more at present Yours Very Respectfuly
Wm W Reed Paroled Prisoner

ALS, DNA-RG249, Lets. Recd., File 237T(1863), Andrew Johnson, Jr.

1. Not identified.

2. Johnson forwarded this complaint to General Hoffman, commissary general of prisoners, with the comment that he earnestly hoped "the government will take some action in regard to the confinement in the Richmond prisons of these unfortunate men that will procure their liberation," for they "deserve this, having shown a devoted loyalty to the Government under the most dreadful persecutions and sufferings." Johnson to Hoffman, September 5, 1863, File 237T(1863), Lets. Recd., RG249, NA.

From Jeremiah Clemens[1]

[Huntsville, Ala., September, 1863]

To his Exellency Andrew Johnson,

Gen Jas. Hickman[2] has requested me to make a statement of facts within my knowledge in relation to his conduct, during the existing troubles between the North & the South. Gen. Hickman was an original Union man, but after the state seceded he was understood to acquiese in its action— early in the contest he proposed raising a Co. for the Con. service. He was also engaged after that in trying to raise a Brigade. Both of these things fell through— in April 1862 Gen. Mitchell[3] occupied this place. Notwithstanding the two enterprises above alluded to, Hickman was still regarded as a Union man, and very soon after Gen. Mitchell's occupation of this place, he commenced trading in cotton, bacon & other things, under permits from different U. S. officers. In the libel exhibited against him in the District Court of Tenn.[4] I observe that he is charged with being engaged in armed rebellion against the U. S. both in Ala. & Tenn. on the 2nd July 1862[.] at that time, Huntsville was occupied by U. S. troops— Hickman was here and completely in their power— he could not have been engaged in any such rebellion without immediate arrest. In all his trading he had the sanction of & I believe the written permission of the U. S. officer then in command. Huntsville was evacuated on the 31st of

Aug. 1862 about 4 o clk. in the the morning— On the same day it was entered by two company's of Con. Cavalry who arrested Hickman on the charge of disloyalty to the Confederacy. He was subsequently discharged, but was arrested again on the same charge about the 1st Dec 1862 and carried to Gen. Forrests head quarters at Columbia—[5] From thence he was sent to Gen. Bragg near Murfresboro who dismissed him upon the ground that he was properly amenable to the civil rather than the military law. After the battle of Murfresboro Gen. Bragg changed his opinion & sent an order for his re-arrest & transportation—to Chattanooga— Hickman sued out a writ of habeas corpus & was discharged by the Probate Judge[6] of this co. but the Con. Grand Jury presented a true bill against him for treason & he was confined in jail until the next session of the Court, when he was finally acquitted by a Petit Jury.[7]

Both prior and subsequent to his trial Hickman has been regarded here as a decided Union man, & has been so treated by the U. S. officers and soldiers who have at different times occupied or passed through Huntsville— He has never been engaged in armed rebellion any where, nor am I aware of his ever having furnished provisions or supplies to any body of troops— He was engaged in an extensive trade, but I thought the supplies he brought were for the use of citizens not soldiers & I am still of that opinion. I know I purchased from him a considerable amount of bacon and salt— I know that other citizens did the same, & I never heard of his selling any thing for the use of either army. Within the time specified in the libel, it is certain he could not have been engaged in armed rebellion or rebellion of any kind against the U. S. Government, and it is certain that if he had been at any time engaged in such rebellion the fact would have been known to the community and must have come to my knowledge— So far from any such opinion prevailing here, it was almost universally believed that all his opinions & feelings were against the Confederacy & in favor of the U. S. I make this statement because Gen. Hickman requests it and knowing it to be true, I do not feel at liberty to withhold the evidence he requires. I was not his counsel & have not the slightest interest in his affairs & but perform an act of justice in making the statement he desires.

Very respectfully Yours
Jere: Clemens

ALS, DLC-JP.

1. Jeremiah Clemens (1814-1865), Huntsville lawyer and state legislator (1839-41), fought in Texas (1842) and in the Mexican War, retiring as a colonel and serving as a Democrat in the Senate (1849-53). His political career in eclipse, he turned to writing novels: *Bernard Lile* (1856), *Mustang Gray* (1858), and *The Rivals: A Tale of the Times of Aaron Burr and Alexander Hamilton* (1860). Briefly editor of the Memphis *Eagle and Enquirer* (1858-59), he was a leader of the cooperationists in the Alabama secession convention, although he signed the ordinance when the fight was lost. In 1862 he moved to Philadelphia, conducting a pamphlet campaign against the South and for Lincoln's reelection, returning in early May, 1865, to Huntsville, where he died on May 21. *DAB*, IV, 191-92.

2. James Hickman (1810-1894), native Tennessean and general of volunteers in the Mexican War, had been a Negro trader and hotel proprietor in Huntsville, with $20,000

real and $10,000 personal property on the eve of the war. After brief Confederate service, which included two arrests and acquittals for disloyalty, he moved in February, 1864, to Nashville where he operated a dry goods store for a year before turning to real estate. 1860 Census, Ala., Madison, Huntsville, 47; Anonymous to E. M. Stanton, June 3, 1864, Lets. Recd., File M1545 (May 20, 1864), RG107, NA; Nashville *Dispatch*, January 27, 1863, February 7, 1865; Nashville *American*, March 13, 1894; Nashville city directories (1865-92), *passim*.

3. For Ormsby M. Mitchel, see *Johnson Papers*, V, 63*n*.

4. After re-occupying Huntsville in late summer, 1863, the Federals, "At the instance of William Bibb," seized both Hickman's money and cotton, and were still holding them in June, 1864. U. S. proceedings were apparently brought because Hickman, in his earlier Confederate trial, had testified that he sympathized and cooperated with the South. Anonymous to E. M. Stanton, June 3, 1864; Nashville *Republican Banner*, March 8, 1870.

5. In 1862, during the Union occupation of Huntsville, Hickman purchased cotton from the surrounding counties to sell to northern buyers and also guided a detachment of the 3rd Ohio Inf. to Jackson County to repel bushwhackers. For the latter act, after the withdrawal of the Union forces late in August, he "was indicted for treason to the Confederate government." By the time he was sent on to Columbia, Forrest, who had occupied that place since December 4, was preparing his men for a raid into West Tennessee. Anonymous to E. M. Stanton, June 3, 1864; Thomas Jordan and J. P. Pryor, *The Campaigns of Lieut. Gen. N. B. Forrest* (New Orleans, 1868), 192; Andrew N. Lytle, *Nathan Bedford Forrest and His Critter Company* (New York, 1931), 114.

6. James H. Scruggs (b. *c*1820), Alabama native possessing $6,000 real and $9,500 personal property, was probate judge. 1860 Census, Ala., Madison, Madison Station, Northwestern Div, 25.

7. After five months' imprisonment in the Huntsville jail, Hickman was discharged "because the proof requisite for his conviction could not be procured." Anonymous to E. M. Stanton, June 3, 1864.

From William Truesdail

Head Quarters Army Cumbld
Office Chief Army Police
Stevenston[1] Sept 1/63

Gov. A. Johnson,

Sir, Mr Jackson[2] of Nashville called upon me yesterday with a view of obtaining some information in regard to parties now in possession of the Sewanee Coal and Mining Co.[3] & desired me to write to you, the information and facts we had in regard to the parties & property— After the Army came to Winchester I learned that this great and valuable property had been marked for supplying the Confederate Authorities with Coal, & that they had run off much of the Machinery belonging to the Co.— That the managers were mostly in the Confederate Service; that Mr McGee,[4] of Winchester, who professed to have been strongly identified with the success of the Rebellion claimed to be the real & principle owner! that he had taken the *Oath*, & was now for the Union, Believed the Rebellion would be crushed & wanted to start the Mining & bringing out of Coal for the use & benefit of the Federal Army, and has I believe Associated parties with him, to this end. Learning that after the Rebellion had broken out, the property had been sold, for a very small sum of money & bought in by McGee, I took the statements of several citicens in regard to the original

Stockholders & owners of the property, I found that all the *Records* in regard to the Sale of their property were at Jasper. I found the Deputy Sheriff who sold the property, all the information we obtained seemed to show, that there had been great injustice done in the Judgment & Sale, to the Real Stockholders & owners, most of whom resided in New York; that the Hon Geo. Law[5] & Wm. B. Astor[6] and others of New York were heavy Stockholders.— I forwarded a statement of such facts as we had obtained to Mr Law. We were unable to see the Records, and the only information obtained was from citicens who may have not in all particulars been correct.— Mr McGee professed to be an Union man now, I was a little amused at a remark he made to me a few days since.— I stated to him that I feared the enemy would attack and burn their cars and other property.— He remarked that he intended to ride through the neighborhood & prevent such an event by seeing those who might do so."— I have no doubt but Mr McGee feel that it is to his interest to be a loyal man, and will so act, as all will do under a liberal policy of Government, in regard to Laws of Trade & Commerce,

Respectfully Wm. Truesdail

N.B.

Col. Ashburn[7] who is well acquainted with the facts in relation to this Co. will be in Nashville in a day or two, and can inform you, as to facts, more fully—

W T

ALS, DLC-JP.

1. Stevenson, Alabama.

2. Probably Joseph (James) Jackson (b. *c*1820), English-born moulder, or founder, in the Brennan Iron Foundry. 1860 Census, Tenn., Davidson, Nashville, 7th Ward, 70; *Nashville City Business Directory* (1859), 87.

3. Organized in January, 1854, with Samuel F. Tracy as president, the Sewanee Mining Company by 1858 had built a spur line from Cowan up the Cumberland Plateau to Tracy City. The following year the company faced serious financial problems in paying Ben F. McGhee and Company of Winchester, the road contractors, whose lawyer, Arthur S. Colyar, obtained a court order that the property be sold to them to satisfy their claims. At about the same time, in April, 1859, other creditors secured a court order that the property be sold. On May 15, 1860, Thomas Richardson of Tennessee became the purchaser, selling it a month later to John Cryder of New York. In the fall of 1861 Colyar, McGhee, and others were reported as buying the company. After the Confederates had been driven from the area in the summer of 1863, M. F. Howard leased the mines from McGhee and shipped coal to the military authorities in Nashville. Subsequently Colyar succeeded in acquiring control and by 1876, under the name Tennessee Coal & Railroad Company, was operating the enterprise which consisted of 25,000 acres, five locomotives and 149 cars, and a working force of 405 persons, including 210 convicts. James M. Safford, *A Geological Reconnaissance of the State of Tennessee* (Nashville, 1856), 95, 98; Clyde L. Ball, "The Public Career of Colonel A. S. Colyar," *Tenn. Hist. Quar.*, XII (1953), 25, 39; Isabel Howell, "John Armfield of Beersheba Springs," *ibid.*, III (1944), 160; J. B. Killebrew, *Report of the Bureau of Agriculture, Statistics, and Mines for 1876* (Nashville, 1877), 136-37, 140; Nashville *Union*, September 4, 1863; Nashville *Republican Banner*, October 2, 1861.

4. Ben F. McGhee (*c*1816-*fl*1870) was a native North Carolina farmer with $27,000 real and $14,800 personal property. 1860 Census, Tenn., Franklin, 1st Dist., 6; (1870), 31.

5. During the two decades before the war, George Law (1806-1881), New York-born contractor and transportation promoter, built several street railroads in New York City and established a steamship route to Havana. *DAB*, XI, 39.

6. William B. Astor (1792-1875), New York city native and son of John Jacob, was, at his father's death in 1848, the richest man in the United States. Buying real estate in New York City south of 59th Street between 4th and 7th avenues, he came to be called the "landlord of New York." *Ibid.*, I, 401.

7. Probably George W. Ashburn, a Georgia unionist refugeeing in Murfreesboro and serving as a scout for the Army of the Cumberland. See *Johnson Papers*, V, 334*n*.

From William M. Wiles

Stevenson, Septr 1st 63

And. Johnson, Mil. Gov. Tenn.
Nashville.
Governor.

The bearer of this, is my brother *Robert J. Wiles*,[1] formerly of the firm of *Forsyth & Co.* at Murfreesboro', Tenn., and now, of the firm of Shine & McKinney.[2]

A telegram from you to *Maj. Gen. D. S. Stanley*, President Mil. Cotton Commission,[3] stating, that he and Forsyth were charged with fraud,[4] was referred to me, and he now appears to answer all charges against him.

He has been unfortunate in being connected with parties, who upon investigation have been proven to be scoundrels, but nothing has appeared, during the military investigations against him. If charged as stated, give him a fair and impartial hearing (which I am satisfied, you will do) and I know, that he will not only show to your entire satisfaction, that he is not guilty of fraud either directly or indirectly, but will show a record for honesty, general integrity and fair dealing in all transactions, which any person of his age might well feel proud of.[5]

Wm M. Wiles
Lt. Col. & P. M. Gen.

LB copy, DNA-RG393, Dept. of the Cumberland, Book Records, Vol. 118 (1863).

1. Robert J. Wiles (*c*1837-*fl*1894), native Indianian with $600 personal property, served as sutler for the 22nd Ind. Inf. (1861-65). Moving to Atlanta in the mid-1870's, he was a traveling agent with a sewing machine company and later a dealer with Herring Safe Company. 1860 Census, Ind., Bartholomew, Columbus, 175; Pension file, RG15, NA; Atlanta directories (1874-80), *passim.*

2. Forsythe & Co., a partnership between Elisha H. Forsythe (*c*1819-1886) and Robert J. Wiles, dealt in cotton trading and probably also in sutlers' goods. It and several other businesses, including those of the otherwise unidentified Eugene Shine and D. H. McKinney, merged into the Union Cotton Co. (here called Shine & McKinney) in an effort to monopolize cotton purchasing in the Murfreesboro area. 1870 Census, Tenn., Davidson, Nashville, 2nd Ward, 31; Proceedings of the Military Commission in the case of Elisha H. Forsythe, September 16-October 2, 1863, RG153, NA; Mt. Olivet Cemetery Records, II, 173.

3. Johnson's telegram to C. Goddard, August 25, 1863, is in the Army of the Cumberland Endorsement Book, Vol. 36, RG393, NA. David S. Stanley (1828-1902), Ohio-born West Pointer (1852), served in the West until the commencement of the war. Participating in the Missouri campaign of 1861, he became brigadier of volunteers in September and was at New Madrid, Island No. 10, and Corinth the next year. Promoted to

major general, he was chief of cavalry, Army of the Cumberland, from November, 1862, to September of the following year. During August, 1863, he headed a military commission investigating alleged swindles by cotton traders. Commander of the IV Corps in the Chattanooga and Atlanta campaigns, he was wounded in the battle of Franklin, thereby ending his active participation in the war. Returning subsequently to the regular army, he again served on the frontier and attained the rank of brigadier before his retirement in 1892. Warner, *Generals in Blue*, 470-71; Chicago *Tribune*, August 31, 1863.

4. A military court tried Forsythe for 1) passing counterfeit money, 2) theft, 3) unlawfully collecting government revenue, 4) obtaining money under fraudulent pretenses, and 5) conspiring to bribe military officials. Although the record doesn't show it, Wiles was probably tried for similar offenses. Proceedings in Case of Elisha H. Forsythe.

5. Forsythe was convicted of only the last two counts in the list of charges against him. *Ibid.*

From Alfred H. Hicks

Nashville Sept 2nd 1863

To His Excelency Gov A Johnson
Sir

I beg personally to call your attention to the fact, that my Store House #3 on the Public Square, is still occupied by the state Troops, under your orders to my serious injury. In the spring or summer of 1862—under the impression that I must look to the Quarter Masters of the Army of the Cumberland for Rent—having no help at my place of business, nor knowing to whom I should apply for redress, I employd Judge Jno S Bryan[1] to aid me in getting the matter in proper form for payment, not doubting that I would be paid full rents for all the time it was occupied for the use of the Army. After some months investigation, the judge returned me the papers, stating, that the whole matter was under your entire Contraul, and that you had declined to acknowledge my right to any Compensation whatever. I felt this decision to be a very great injustice, if you understood the *facts* in the case, And at the suggestion of friends C A Fuller & John P White[2] I made a plain & truthfull statemt of the facts to them & they to you, in my behalf. They stated to me after this interview with you that you would consider the case, and *do me justice*. Since that time I have been awaiting to hear from you most patiently, but have not as yet, and as my affairs are urgent & Complicated, I desire to ask your special attention to the matter, feeling Confident that you will do full justice, to one who professes to be a true & faithful Citizen of the United States & Claims to be entitled to all the privaleges, while he is under all the obligations appertaing to such Citizenship[.]

My House was rented to the Confederates for an ordinance store by my Tenants—Fite Shepherd & Co[3]—under protest by me, and at my instance made to pay *extra*—premiums, on all the policies—to the amount of Seven Hundred Dollars, before they were permitted to use it for that purpose. The property reverted back to me the first day of January last—1863—by termination of lease. It has been greatly damaged by present occupants, nevertheless, I could *easily* rent it at four Thousand dollars per annum, now, was it at my disposal. I do not think it right, that I should be made to suffer for the Sins of others. Besides the property is incumberd by lien to the Mechanics, and I am bound to pay $3,000 annually ground rent, besides Taxes Insurance & and I have no other means of releving it from this incumbrance & other expenses except by the rent. Your kind, just & prompt Consideration and disposal of this case Sir, will greatly oblg your most obt svt

A. H. Hicks

P.S.

Should you desire it I shall be glad to have a personal interview with you at any time *this* week, desiring as I do to go East next week—

A. H. Hicks

ALS, DLC-JP.

1. For Brien, see *Johnson Papers,* V, 247*n*.

2. Charles A. Fuller (1816-1868), native New Yorker, resident of Edgefield, and Hicks's brother-in-law, had been treasurer of the Nashville Savings Institution and Building Association. On Johnson's recommendation he was appointed assistant special treasury agent in November, 1863. For White, a member of Irby Morgan & Co. and later a partner in a wholesale clothing concern, see *Johnson Papers,* IV, 299*n*; Charles A. Snodgrass, *The History of Freemasonry in Tennessee, 1789-1943* (Nashville, 1944), 156; 1860 Census, Tenn., Davidson, Edgefield, 3; *Nashville Bus. Dir.* (1860-61), 172; Acklen, *Tenn. Records,* II, 3,4; Futrell, Federal Trade, 264-65, 386-87.

3. A wholesale dry-goods, clothing, and varieties store with Thomas D. (*c*1826-1907) and Leonard B. (1811-*fl*1880) Fite and Frederick A. Shepherd (*c*1828-*fl*1880) as proprietors, the firm had moved in early 1860 to "No. 3 Hicks' Building, North side of the Public Square." On the eve of the war the Fite brothers' wealth totaled $210,800. *Nashville Bus. Dir.* (1860-61), 168, 256; Clayton, *Davidson County,* 432; Nashville *Patriot,* March 1, 1860; 1860 Census, Tenn., Davidson, Nashville, 5th Ward, 159,166; (1880), 1st Div., 3rd Ward, 16; William Waller, *Nashville 1900-1910* (Nashville, 1972), 346.

From James Trimble[1]

Nashville Sept 2nd. 1863

To His Excellency Hon: Andrew Johnson
Military Governor of Tennessee
Sir

It is respectfully desired that you would consider the following statement of facts & act in the premises as you think best. The facts are these. Oone Mary Alloway,[2] free woman of color, rented a certain house on Line St. no 8 from one Mr. Larkin[3] for the year 1863. Mary Alloway on the 1st. of Jan. 1863 subrented one room of said house to Jesse Porterfield[4] (colored) for the entire year, on condition that he pay $6 every month in advance, with which contract he has ever since fully complied. And on or about the first of April 1863 one Adam Smith[5] (colored) rented another room of the said house from Mary Alloway on the same terms as above specified & has also entirely complied with his contract. Sept 1st Jesse Porterfield obtained an order from your Excellency to the effect that he could remain in said rooms, until further orders from your office. An order issued from your

Excellency on yesterday referring the matter to Recorder Shane.[6] It seems to be a matter over which the Recorder has no Jirisdiction & he has consequently failed to take any action upon it. It can be proved by satisfactory evidence that the said Mary Alloway has all along been using the hous for the purposes of prostitution, & now in violation of her contract, wishes to turn Jesse Porterfield & Adam Smith out, in order to let in some lewd white women (notorious prostitutes) because they will pay higher rent. The neighborhood is a respectable one & the neighbors all are scandalized. All the above facts can be proven if necessary & it is earnestly desired that the said Mary Alloway may be made either to vacate the house or keep a decent one, or at all events that she not be allowed to violate her contract—[7]

James Trimble Attorney

ALS, DLC-JP.

1. James Trimble (b. *c*1838), a Gallatin lawyer and John Bell man, had joined the Tennessee Provisional Army "with the express stipulation I should not go out of Tennessee, and never serve Jeff Davis or any of his crew," only to find himself "nolens volens" in the Confederate service. Procuring a discharge, he was currently practicing in Nashville prior to embarking on the recruitment of colored troops, a venture foiled when Stanton refused to muster him into service because he "had been in the rebel army, and had made secession speeches." 1860 Census, Tenn., Sumner, Gallatin, 11th Dist., 2; Nashville *Union,* February 21, 1864.

2. Mary Alloway, who had subleased these rooms in a dwelling rented by a Mrs. Ament, was also charged with "keeping a bawdy house." Nashville *Dispatch,* September 4, 1863.

3. Larkin, unidentified, was possibly serving as Mrs. Ament's agent.

4. Porterfield—technically still a slave, although lawyer Trimble argued that, with his master in Confederate service, he should be considered a free man—claimed without producing evidence that he had Governor Johnson's authorization to use the premises. *Ibid.*

5. Adam Smith (*c*1818-1867) was also a contraband. *Ibid.; Nashville City Cemetery Index,* 73.

6. William Shane (*c*1835-*fl*1879), native Tennessean, Nashville attorney, and former councilman (*c*1859-62), was city recorder (1862-64). In the late 1870's he practiced his profession in St. Paul, Minnesota. 1860 Census, Tenn., Davidson, Nashville, 3rd Ward, 72; Wooldridge, *Nashville,* 118, 123; *R. L. Polk's and A. C. Danser's St. Paul Directory* (1879-80), 425.

7. Shane ruled in favor of Mary Alloway: Trimble's clients, Porterford and Smith, were assessed costs and ordered to vacate the house within a week; the bawdy-house charge was dismissed. Nashville *Dispatch,* September 4, 5, 1863.

From Henry R. Mizner[1]

Columbia Tenn Sept 3rd 1863

To Brig Gen Andrew Johnson
Mil Gov—

Col Cypert[2] left this morning with nearly two hundred men[.] I sent advance guard to protect him to Franklin[.] I shall earnestly cooperate in furnishing Negroes for North western Road unless directed by Genl Comdg to do otherwise[.] I have suggested to officers here recruiting for Negro Regiments that they Return to Nashville & Report to Maj Stearns[.][3]

Henry R Mizner[4] Col Comdg

Tel, DLC-JP.

1. Henry R. Mizner (*c*1827-1915), a native New Yorker, was a Detroit land and tax agent and lawyer before becoming captain, 18th U. S. Inf., in May, 1861. Transferring to the volunteer service, he became colonel, 14th Mich. Inf. (1862-65) and brevet brigadier (March, 1865). After the war he rose to colonel in the regular army before his retirement in 1891. New York *Times,* January 6, 1915; Heitman, *Register,* I, 718; Detroit city directories (1855-59), *passim.*

2. Probably Thomas J. Cypert (1828-1901), a Wayne County farmer with $200 real and $1,100 personal property in 1860, who became captain, Co. A, 2nd Tenn. Mtd. Inf., USA. Captured in his home county on April 17, 1864, he escaped from prison and returned to duty less than two months later. Subsequently, he served in the state senate (1865-67, 1889-91). 1860 Census, Tenn., Wayne, 13th Dist., 73; CSR, RG94, NA; *OR,* Ser. 1, XXXI, Pt. I, 593; McBride and Robison, *Biographical Directory,* II, 214-15.

3. George L. Stearns (1809-1867), a Massachusetts-born ship chandler and manufacturer of lead pipe, became increasingly involved in the antislavery crusade after 1840. A leader of the movement that put Charles Sumner in the Senate and a financial "angel" of John Brown's raid, he early organized recruiting activities for Negroes, first for Governor John A. Andrew of Massachusetts and then for the war department. Designated by Stanton in June, 1863, as recruiting commissioner for colored troops with the rank of major, he had his headquarters in Philadelphia before being ordered to the Department of the Cumberland in September. His arrival in Tennessee precipitated a conflict between those who favored the traditional use of blacks as unenlisted military laborers and those who saw them as a source of fighting power as enlisted and drilled soldiers. Mizner held the former view, as would be revealed later in the fall when he refused to let recruiters talk to the contraband military laborers under his jurisdiction. In spite of the practice of impressment for work details and a confused recruiting situation, Stearns raised six regiments in Tennessee. However, his advocacy of bounties for black recruits made him unpopular with Stanton, and his objections to impressment and large-scale use of Negro soldiers for fatigue duty made him unpopular with field officers, leading to his resignation, March 30, 1864. The next year he established a radical Republican paper, the *Right Way,* in Boston. *DAB,* XVII, 543-44; Cornish, *Sable Arm,* 103, 235-37; Heitman, *Register,* I, 918; Henry Romeyn, *With Colored Troops in the Army of the Cumberland* (n. p., 1904), 8.

4. Before the end of the month, the colonel once again would share with the governor his sense of the dilemma which they faced. Reporting that he was sending sixty able-bodied Negroes to Nashville "for soldiers," he went on to query: "which course is best[?] to raise soldiers or put the Negroes on the road[?]" Mizner to Johnson, September 29, 1863, Adj. Gen's Papers, RG21, Tennessee State Library and Archives.

From Caleb W. Sewell[1]

Louisville, Ky, Sept, 3, 1863.

Gov. Andrew Johnson.
Dear Sir.

Through the kindness of General Boyle, I have procured the release, several weeks ago, of a Southern conscript, by the name of John. W. Carver,[2] whose father, Mr. Archibald Carver,[3] is living near Lebanon, in Wilson county, Tenn.

He was released, after cheerfully taking the oath, on condition that he should keep himself North of the Ohio River until he could get permission to return home to his father's, in Tennessee.

It was stated in his bond that this permission sohould be given only by yourself.

The young man was conscripted only a few days after he was married, and he has learned, by a communication from his father, that his wife *particularly* needs his presence at home now.

He belongs to a good family. His father has taken the oath, and is anxious to have his son at home.

The only acquaintances I have in Nashville, so far as I now remember, to whom I could refer you, to convince you of my veracity, are P. S. Fall,[4] Pastor of the Christian Church, and Mr Church Anderson.[5] I am known in Lebanon, and also by Mr Scoby,[6] between Nashville & Lebanon, and by many others in Wilson Co.

The young man, for whom I write you this petition, is now in Jeffersonville, Indiana. If you can give him permission to go home, just address the letter to me in Louisville, or to himself, in Jeffersonville, Ia.

By granting our request,[7] you will not only greatly oblige the young man, but many friends, as well as your humble servant,

C. W. Sewell.

P. S. I forgot to state that the young man deserted from the rebel army the first chance he had after he was conscripted.

C. W. S.

ALS, DLC-JP.

1. Caleb W. Sewell (*c*1828-*fl*1880), Overton County native and pastor of Louisville's Second Christian Church, was later a teacher and an agent for the Domestic Sewing Machine Company. Sistler, *1850 Tenn. Census,* VI, 41; *Louisville's Directory and Business Advertiser* (1859-60), 209, 311; Louisville city directories (1874-80), *passim.*

2. John W. Carver (b. *c*1843), a private in Co. F, 28th Tenn. Inf., CSA (1861-63), had deserted at Cowan, Tennessee, on July 4, was forwarded to Louisville ten days later, and discharged August 1. CSR, RG109, NA. His oath dated September 3, 1863, is in Johnson Papers, LC.

3. Archibald Carver (b. *c*1810), was a Tennessee-born farmer possessing $9,000 real and $11,894 personal property. 1860 Census, Tenn., Wilson, 22nd Dist., 147.

4. Philip S. Fall (1798-1890), English-born minister and educator, came to Nashville from Louisville in 1825 to teach in the female academy and become pastor of the First Baptist Church. Sympathizing with the doctrines of Alexander Campbell, Fall was largely responsible for establishing the First Christian Church, of which he was pastor until 1831 when he opened a "female academy" near Frankfort, Kentucky. Called back to the Nashville church (1858-77), he operated a private academy during the war and spent his last years in Frankfort. Earl I. West, *The Search for the Ancient Order* (2 vols., Nashville, 1974 [1874], 1950), I, 236-40; W. H. Perrin, *et al, Kentucky: A History of the State* (5th ed., Easley, S. C., 1979 [1887]), 785.

5. Church Anderson (1818-1878), a Wilson County native, was a wholesale grocer and commission merchant on College Street. *Nashville Bus. Dir.* (1860-61), 120; Nashville *American,* August 22, 1878.

6. Possibly Robert C. Scoby (*c*1828-*fl*1880), a Tennessee-born farmer, who on the eve of the war held property valued at $23,510. 1860 Census, Tenn., Wilson, Lebanon, 21st Dist., 84; (1880), 4.

7. Eleven days later Johnson endorsed Carver's oath: "It is hereby ordered that the said John W. Carver be permitted to return to Nashville & report, immediately after his arrival at this office; provided the consent of Brig Genl Boyle Comd'g &c Louisville Ky shall have been previously obtained." Endorsement, September 14, on Carver's Oath of Allegiance, September 3, 1863, Johnson Papers, LC.

From Calvin Goddard[1]

Hd. Qrs Dept Cumbd. Sept 4th 1863

To Brig Gen Andrew Johnson
The Genl Comdg directs me to Say that Mr Worley[2] of Jasper who has been in our employ for Some months past has occupied the house of Mrs Freeman wife of Thomas Freeman[3] on Spruce Street Nashville— Freeman & his wife are now in Texas[.] his two Sons are in the Rebel Army[.] his Son-in-law who occupied the house left on the occupation of Nashville by the U S Army & is now in Richmond as a clerk[.] the Genl trusts you will protect Mr Worley in the possession of the house an agent of the owner having Served a write of Ejectment upon him & Commenced Suit for Back Rent— if there is no other way he thinks the property Should be libelled[.] it is Said the title is in Mrs Freeman[.]

Very Respectfully Your Obt Servt
C Goddard A A G

Tel. DLC-JP.

1. Calvin Goddard (1838-1892), native of Norwich, Connecticut, in 1851 moved to Cleveland, Ohio, where he was a bookkeeper. Commissioned lst lieutenant, 12th Ohio Inf., he was detailed as aide to General Rosecrans in western Virginia, eventually becoming his assistant adjutant general, with the rank of lieutenant colonel, before resigning November 27, 1863. After the war he served as an officer of the Wells Fargo & Company in New York City and was later president of the Chicago and South Side Rapid Transit Company. Fitch, *Annals,* 47; *J. B. Williston's Directory of the City of Cleveland* (1859-60), 90; CSR, RG94, NA; New York *Tribune,* April 6, 1892.

2. Possibly William Worley (b. *c*1802), South Carolina-born railroad contractor with $3,500 real and $2,000 personal estate. 1860 Census, Tenn., Marion, 7th Dist., Town of Jasper, 79.

3. Mary A. Freeman (b. *c*1818), a Delaware native dealing in "millinery and fancy goods" at 22 North Cherry St. on the eve of the war, and her Virginia-born husband Thomas (b. *c*1810 or 1816), a framer by profession, had come to Tennessee in the early 1840's. Although not found in rosters of Tennessee Confederate troops, their sons appear to have been Clement (b. *c*1838) and Senelin [?] (b. *c*1841), both born in Pennsylvania. 1850 Census, Tenn., Davidson, Nashville, 282; (1860), 5th Ward, 172; *Nashville Bus. Dir.* (1860-61), 172.

To Salmon P. Chase

Nashville, September 4th 1863

Hon S. P Chase
Secretary of the Treasury,
Washington City
Sir:

It is with pleasure that we bear testimony to the earnest efforts being made by the loyal merchants of Nashville for the restoration of trade and commerce, and state that we believe them, as a body, fully entitled to the confidence and protection of the Government of the United States.

Their memorial[1] is most respectfully recommended to your favorable consideration.

We have the honor to be,
Very Respectfully &c &c

Jos R Dillin Surveyor of Customs
Andrew Johnson, Mil. Gov'r.
Gordon Granger Maj Genl
W. G. Brownlow
Comdg Dist. Cumberland.
Ast Sp. Ag. Tr. Dept.

LS, DNA-RG56, Misc. Lets. Recd., K Series, Vol 4 (1863).

1. It asked the treasury to modify regulations so as to allow Nashville merchants to engage in the wholesale trade. Nashville *Union,* September 3, 4, 1863.

From Milsom & Wand[1]

Nashville Sept. 7th 1863

Hon. Andrew Johnson

Sir we Sent you a Demijohn of Robinson [Robertson?] Co Whiskey[.] Hopeing it will meet with your approval

we remain Yours
Milsom & Wand
Cor. of Deaderick & Cherry St

ALS, DLC-JP.

1. In 1861 the saloon on this site belonged to Patrick Walsh who, seven years later, reappeared as partner in Milsom and Walsh. In the meantime, at war's end, J. O. and T. C. Milsom were the principals in Milsom & Bro. saloon at the same location. The current operators would appear to have been one of the brothers and either J. C. Wands, a postwar grocer, or one of several Wards engaged at various times in the same business. Nashville city directories (1860-68), *passim.*

From Daniel W. Nye[1]

Cheatham Co Sept 7" 1863

To his Excellency
Andrew Johnson

I was at Clarksville on the 4th Inst and had a conversation with *J O Shackleford* Esq.[2] who authorised me to use his name in this communication— On the 26th July Whitehead and Cornelious Peacher[3] *assassinated* a man by the name of Rawson[4] in Robertson County. It was said Mr Shackleford "the most diabolical act that I ever heard of "[.] Whitehead was arristed and tried before the military court. What the court have decided is unknown as their finding has been forwarded to the Commanding Genl.[5] but Whitehead was placed in Jail on the morning of the 4th Inst[.]

Peacher has fled from the north side of the Cumberland and as I am informed & believe has joined a band of robers. Mr Shackleford is of opinion that the Jail in Clarksville is not a safe place for Whitehead. He is in a room with common prisoners unironed. I am further authorised by Mr

Shackleford to advise Your Excellency to offer a reward for Cornelious Peacher. The foregoing remarks embrace the substance of my conversation with Mr Shackleford who was prosecuting attorney in the case of Whitehead but I beg your Excelency to weigh well the following suggestions of my own which are made not only in my capacity of Loyal citizen but as *agent of Police,* for this section of country, by the appointment of Col. Bruce[.][6]

Clarksville is not a safe place for Whitehead because the Garrison is weak— the murderers have many influential frinds in Montgomery & Robertson Counties—as well as amongst the organized bands of Robers in the section of country north & west of the Cumerland and in the vicinity of Clarksville amongst whom the said Peacher is a man of influence— the murderers are *free masons* as is their counsel (*your friend* & *my friend* D Holeman[7] Esq of Springfield) and by a combination of the friends of the assassins on the north side of the Cumberland the robers on the south side led by Peacher, any roving band of Confederates who may be induced to join the enterprise for the purpose of taking the Clarksville post and sacking the place. the misterious aid of the free masons and money judiciously applied. I apprehend the liberation of Whitehead & the Capture of Clarksville.

A reward ought to be offered for Peacher.—Because he is a most unmitigated assassin, has influence with unmitigated Scoundrals, is deeply interested, in feeling, for his co-assassin and is of a character *so desperate that Detectives will not exert themselves for his capture, for ordinary considerations*[.] This will be handed you by B F Binkly Esq[8] who I think will endorse all I have said in the foregoing[.]

I have been authorised by Col Bruce, as agent of Police, to organize a force of thirty or more men—not to fight Rebels because we would be too weak for that purpose—but to detect and bring to justice Robers, assassins & marauders.

The force can be made up, if we can procure arms & ammunition, and could be greatly augmented if we could procure horses from the Federal authorities. My frend & neighbour Mr Binkly will be glad to confer with you in regard to these things and to bring back with him a small supply of army or navy Pistoles, guns & ammunition.

Some of those who contemplate joining the Company would like to have the opinion of Your Excellency in regard to the probable treatment, by the Confederates, of those who may be so unfortunate as to be captured by them[.]

They would like to be satisfied whether, citizens organized and acting under federal authority for their own defence, if captured by the Confederates, would be entitled to the priveleges of prisners of war? Or would be considered spies[?]

Very respectfully
D W Nye

ALS, DLC-JP.

1. Daniel W. Nye (1825-*fl*1880), formerly of Sumner and Cheatham counties but during the war a partner in the Nashville grocery firm of Ben M. Noel and Company, had been recommended for a collectorship of internal revenue in Middle Tennessee. Failing to receive the appointment, he settled briefly in Clarksville where he served as recorder in 1865, subsequently returning to Cheatham as a farmer. 1880 Census, Tenn., Cheatham, 14th Dist., 36; *Nashville Bus. Dir.* (1860-61), 236; *Goodspeed's Montgomery,* 771, 814; S. Watson and others to Johnson, August 12, 1863, Johnson Papers, LC.

2. For James O. Shackelford, Clarksville lawyer, see *Johnson Papers,* V, 431*n*.

3. George H. Whitehead (1820-*fl*1886), Robertson County native and farmer, was tried in August, 1863, released in October, only to be rearrested the following July, found guilty, and sent under a five-year sentence to Alton and later to the penitentiary at Jefferson City, Missouri. Cornelius E. Peacher (1832-1877), also a Tennessean, a "Tobacconist," and captain, Co. F, 2nd Ky. Cav., CSA, was captured the following March and forwarded to Nashville where he was tried for murder and other crimes. Although sentenced to be hanged, he was exchanged in March, 1865. *Goodspeed's Robertson,* 1201-2; Alley and Beach, *1850 Census, Montgomery,* 18; 1860 Census, Tenn., Montgomery, N. & E. of the Cumberland River, 132; Acklen, *Tenn. Records,* II, 262; WPA, Montgomery County, Tennessee, Bible and Family Records, Tombstone Inscriptions, 54; Union Provost Marshal's File/Citizens, RG109, NA; Nashville *Union,* April 2, 1864; CSR (Peacher), RG109, NA.

4. John S. Rosson (*c*1829-1863), Tennessee-born farmer. Porch, *1850 Census, Robertson,* 96.

5. William S. Rosecrans.

6. Sanders D. Bruce.

7. Daniel D. Holman.

8. Probably Blackstone F. Binkley (1804-1863), Tennessee-born Christian minister living in Cheatham with property worth $8,100 on the eve of the war. A justice of the peace in Davidson (1839-40), he became one of Ashland City's first residents (1856) and Cheatham County's first magistrates (1856-60). Binkley was slain by Confederate guerrillas in November. 1860 Census, Tenn., Cheatham, 1st & 2nd Dists., 20; WPA, Davidson County Marriages, Books 2 & 3 (1838-49), 16, 26; WPA, Cheatham Marriage Licenses (1856-97), 3-21; *Goodspeed's Cheatham,* 964, 1363; Nashville *Press,* July 9, 1864.

From Ambrose E. Burnside

Cumberland Gap Sept 9th 1863

To Gov Johnson

I arrived at this place from Knoxville this morning[.] The place surrendered this afternoon *unconditionally* with over two thousand prisoners & small arms & fourteen pieces artillery[.] We have been elegantly received by the whole of East Tenn. The whole people are crazy to see you doctor Brownlow Mr Maynard Mr Fleming Judge Trigg[1] & in fact all refugees[.]

A E Burnside

Tel. T-RG21, Adj. Gen's Papers.

1. For John M. Fleming and Connally F. Trigg, see *Johnson Papers,* IV, 296*n*, 562*n*.

From William J. Kelly[1]

Jasper Tennessee sept 9th/63

Governor Andrew Johnson
Dear sir

Knowing that you are better informed as to what will be the result of the institution of slavery than any other man in our state, we wish your advice as to what is best for us to do with our negroes. My Brother, A. Kelly[2] and family and my own have about 40 negroes.[3] they are nearly all at home yet, but their services are worthless[.] they are almost in a state of confusion. I dont think they will leave us without our consent, but we can make no calculations as to how long they will stay while the armies are so near us, and they are eating up our substance when we are already nearly bear of provisions, but we do not like to turn them loose without some provision for their welfare being made. they have nearly all been raised in our families and we feel a great-deal of sympathy for them, we suppose from the tone of the army that they will all be freed and they are persuading all ages and sexes of negroes to go with them when they have no provision for their comfort or protection from exposure, now we would rather if we have to give them up that you would take them, with their families united so that they would be made comfortable and provided for in some manner, and not turned out homeless and without an object to accomplish as all the negroes who go with the army are at present; (they are a drain upon the supplies of the army and no essential service to it;) and pay us for them whatever the Government price may be. As to our loyalty every union man of this county can testify[.] I suppose we would have no difficulty in establishing it. It will be several years at best, even if the institution of slavery is preserved in our state, before it can be again reduced to system and profit, and if the negroes are ever to be emancipated now is the best time that ever will occur to do it, and let it be done effectually and speedily so that when we emerge from this chaos we may enter upon the life we will have to live, without any dread of future disturbancey[.] I hope there will be an election held immediately for members to a convention and our state placed back in the union as it was.

Please write me what to do with our negroes, and if you can, consistently, take them and let us have our means in something else that will be of more service to us and render us more comfortable and easy.

Your Obt Servt W. J. Kelly

ALS, DLC-JP.

1. William J. Kelly (1823-1900), a Tennessee-born civil and military engineer with $5,000 real and $4,500 personal property, subsequently served in the legislature (1869-71). McBride and Robison, *Biographical Directory*, II, 487-88; 1860 Census, Tenn., Marion, 7th Dist., 58; (1880), 29.

2. Alexander Kelly (*c*1804-*c*1878), native Tennessee farmer, ferry operator, and sometime storekeeper, had a combined estate of $37,000. *Ibid.* (1860), 57; J. Leonard Raulston and James W. Livingood, *Sequatchie* (Knoxville, 1974), 240.

3. According to the slave census of 1860, the writer possessed two adult slaves with five children, his brother Alexander had eight adults and fourteen under 18 years of age, while their sister, who lived with the latter, owned one adult and three children, for a total of thirty-three. 1860 Census, Slave Schedule, Tenn., Marion, 7th Dist., 3.

From James M. Tomeny

Memphis Sept. 9, 1863

Dear Sir:

I wrote you on the 24th July, upon the subject of arming the malitia of the State. I believe the people, throughout those portions of the State that have been harassed by rebel guerrillas, would hail the measure as a blessing.

The people in this end of the State have been neglected so long that many of them refuse to look to Nashville for aid. Last week two prominent Union men from Brownsville (James P Wood formerly Pres't of the Mem & Ohio RR and Mr. Bond his brother-in-law)[1] came to Memphis to obtain authority to raise a battalion or regiment in Haywood county for the purpose of local protection and to drive out the accredited thieves of the "Confederacy". Mr. Bingham and myself, with these gentlemen, called upon Gen. Veatch Commanding this post to get his views and suggestions. After discussing the matter fully with this officer we proceeded to Genl. Hurlbut's headquarters to get the necessary orders and authorization, but failed that evening to obtain an interview. The next day Mr. Bingham and Mr. Bond made a similar fruitless effort to see the General, after having informed him of their business by letter. Messrs Wood and Bond were obliged to return home, and left the matter with us.

The day after they left, I was fortunate enough to get into the presence of the General, and explained to him that a number of Union men in Haywood County desired that one or two companies of Cavalry be sent to Brownsville for the purpose of protecting them while organizing a force for service in Haywood and the surrounding counties; and that he would authorize J. H. Morton[2] to commence the entlistment of volunteers for such service, and also give an order on the Commander at Fort Pillow for the necessary arms. He promised to issue orders in accordance with these requests, detailing two companies of Illinois Cavalry for this specific duty, and directed me to call the next day for the papers. I called but they were not ready, I called again, and was informed that the papers were not prepared, but "that all the irregular bands of rebel cavalry had disappeared from that country" "Well" said I, "General the means these gentlemen propose are the best that could be devised to keep them out; and I think that all who are willing to fight on our side should be allowed and encouraged to do so, I hope you will make the order." He again promised to issue the order and send it out by the cavalry. I intend to visit him every day until I am satisfied he has fulfilled his promise, or will not do so.

I relate these facts to illustrate two points: the spirit of the Union men in the interior, and the indifference of the General Commanding the 16th Army Corps. Some general system, arming the malitia of the State, emenating from you, would remedy this indifference and develope a good deal more of the same sort of spirit. One thing is certain, that very little real progress in the work of reorganization, can be made in this region, until the people, sustained by authority of law, are encouraged to defend themselves and wage a war of extermination against the murderous bands with which the country is infested. Persons from Haywood with whom I have conversed, consider Capt Hale[3] a totally inefficient officer, but his company in other respects is a very good one.

I regard the arming of volunteers for local defence as by far the most important work to be accomplished at this time, especially as the people appear anxious for it, and hence would like very much to know what you have done, and what you purpose doing for the disinthrallment of this portion of the State from guerrilla terrorism. I hope we shall have the pleasure of greeting you in Memphis, before this letter reaches Nashville, but fearing that you will be again prevented from coming, I send it.

Present my regards to Mr. East and believe me
Very truly yours
J M Tomeny

Hon Andrew Johnson
Military Gov. &c Nashville Tenn.

ALS, DLC-JP.

1. James P. Wood (*c*1821-*fl*1870) and William P. Bond (1813-1894) were North Carolina natives. Wood, a farmer and Brownsville merchant, was active in railroad promotion, holding offices in several companies, while Bond, a lawyer, served before the war in the legislature (1843-45) and afterwards as 14th district circuit judge (1867-70). Carpenter, *1850 Census, Franklin,* 9; 1860 Census, Tenn., Haywood, Brownsville, 37, 46; (1870), 21, 53; (1880), 12; *Williams' Memphis Directory* (1860), 33; *Goodspeed's Haywood,* 823; McBride and Robison, *Biographical Directory,* II, 1025.

2. Joseph H. Morton (*c*1822-*fl*1880) was a native Tennessee farmer living near Brownsville. 1860 Census, Tenn., Haywood, 6th Dist., 62; (1880), 38.

3. Unidentified, but probably in the home guard or militia.

From Abraham Lincoln

Private

Executive Mansion,
Washington, September 11, 1863.

Hon. Andrew Johnson,
My dear Sir:

All Tennessee is now clear of armed insurrectionists.[1] You need not to be reminded that it is the nick of time for re-inaugurating a loyal State government. Not a moment should be lost. You, and the co-operating friends there, can better judge of the ways and means, than can be judged by any here. I only offer a few suggestions. The re-inauguration must not be such as to give control of the State, and its representation in Congress, to the enemies of the Union, driving it's friends there into political exile. The whole struggle for Tennessee will have been profitless to both State and Nation, if it so ends that Gov. Johnson is put down, and Gov. Harris is put up. It must not be so. You must have it otherwise— Let the reconstruction be the work of such men only as can be trusted for the Union. Exclude all others, and trust that your government, so organized, will be recognized here, as being the one of republican form, to be guaranteed to the state, and to be protected against invasion and domestic violence.

It is something on the question of *time*, to remember that it cannot be known who is next to occupy the position I now hold, nor what he will do—

I see that you have declared in favor of emancipation in Tennessee,[2] for which, may God bless you. Get emancipation into your new State government—Constitution—and there will be no such word as fail for your case.

The raising of colored troops I think will greatly help every way.

Yours very truly
A. Lincoln

ALS, NNPM; DLC-Lincoln Papers; Basler, *Works of Lincoln*, VI, 440-41.

1. For the moment Tennessee was, indeed, clear of all regular Confederate military forces—a condition which gave armies and civilians a brief respite until November 4, when Bragg sent Longstreet's corps back from Georgia into East Tennessee. Long, *Civil War Almanac*, 403, 407, 430.

2. Only three days before, Charles A. Dana, assistant secretary of war, informed Stanton: "I have had this morning a prolonged conversation with Governor Johnson. . . . Slavery he says is destroyed in fact, but must be abolished legally. He is thoroughly in favor of immediate emancipation, both as a matter of moral right and as the indispensable condition of that large immigration of industrious freemen which is necessary to repeople and regenerate the State. He has already declared himself publicly in behalf of unconditional abolition, and will recommend it emphatically to the Legislature when it assembles." Dana to Stanton, September 8, 1863, *OR*, Ser. 1, XXX, Pt. I, 182-83; see also Speech at Nashville, August 29, 1863.

From Daniel Tyler[1]

Head Quarters Del. Department
Wilmington Del Sept 11th 1863

My dear Governor

I see you are moving for immediate emancipation in Tennessee. God speed you[.] I am no political abolitionest, but I am perfectly willing to stand still and see the slavocracy carry emancipation through in spite of themselves. John P. King[2] told the people of Georgia in April 1861 that if secession prevailed, in five years there would not be a slave out the Gulf states and in ten years there would not be one in[.] His chronology did not keep up with the facts and emancipation is making a faster gait than he imagined[.]

My notions for the settlement with the seceeded states are simple if they are crude. Now as applicable to Tennessee, by way of example I would have your people, the loyal people settle among themselves as follows

1. . . . . The Slavery question
2. . . . . All rights to property which should include all confiscations (which should be applied only to recompence loyal persons who may have been despoiled of their Property)[.] I would have all confiscations made by the *people* of the States and not by the General Government
3. . . . . Settle the question of public debt justly owed by the people of Tennessee
4. . . . . Remodle your state constitution to meet the altered state of things; elect your Senators and Representatives and send them to Washington

Now my dear Governor this is a crude and may be an impracticable plan, but *some States* must start with a plan and demand to come back into the Union and I beleive you can engineer Tennessee through in the right way and God speed you in doing it.

Faithfully your friend
Dan Tyler Brg Genl

His Excellency Andrew Johnson
Nashville Tenn.

LS, DLC-JP.

1. Daniel Tyler (1799-1882), Connecticut-born West Pointer (1819), who studied at the artillery school in Metz, resigned his commission in 1834 and became a successful businessman, president of the Macon & Western Railroad in Georgia at the outbreak of the war. Commissioned colonel of the 1st Conn. Inf. and later brigadier of volunteers, he was mustered out August 11, 1861, after he had exceeded his orders and provided undistinguished leadership at First Manassas. Appointed a brigadier general of U. S. Volunteers the following March, he commanded the posts of Harper's Ferry, Baltimore, and the district of Delaware before resigning in April, 1864. Founding the town of Anniston, Alabama (1870), Tyler later invested in Texas land and served as president of an Alabama railroad. Warner, *Generals in Blue*, 514-15.

2, John P. King (1799-1888), Kentucky native, moved to Augusta, Georgia (1815), where he practiced law and had business interests in textiles, railroads, and banking. Serving as a judge of the court of common pleas (1831), U. S. senator (1833-37), and president of the Georgia Railroad and Banking Company (1841-78), he dedicated his efforts to furthering the Confederate cause and, in consequence, suffered a personal loss of approximately three million dollars. *BDAC*, 1167; *DAB*, X, 395.

From Salmon P. Chase

Washington, Sep. 12. 1863

Dear Sir

Let me congratulate you that Rebellion is driven from East Tennessee, your home.

The President read me yesterday the letter he addressed to you touching reorganization. It is a noble letter and I hope all its aims will find a cordial response in you.

God offers men opportunities: those who wisely use them are great. To you is now offered an opportunity to established the renovated institutions of Tennessee on the basis of Free Labor. God grant that you may take it boldly. Prompt courage in this matter is indeed the highest wisdom. Difficulties vanish before stout will.

A few months—a very few months will decide the position of Tennessee. Let her not act so as to leave the festering sore to break out anew.

Your friend S P Chase

Hon Andrew Johnson.

ALS, DLC-JP2.

From William Ledbetter[1]

Murfreesboro 12th Sept 1863

Gov. Andrew Johnson,
Sir,

My health having been much impaired prior to last Fall, I was advised by the most eminent physicians of the country, it was indispensible to my recovery that I should live quietly and maintain an equable temperament. I was therefore contemplating a removal to some place (probably my former residence in Stewart County) where I would be more likely to be relieved of the liability to excitement produced by the presence of large armies. About that time, and under date the 24th of Novr. 1862, I received a letter from Ed. Cooper Esq of Shelbyville, who had recently had an interview with you, and who wrote as follows "Gov. Johnson authorized me to write to you that if the Federal lines extended over Murfreesboro, and you remain there, you should not be *molested*; that your parol being indefinite, knowing you to be a gentleman, would not be abridged or interfered with." I need not say I was gratified at the receipt of this assurance. It determined me to remain here. Since I was embraced by the Federal lines, I believe I have, as I did before, complied with the terms of my parol, and feel sure there is no charge of my having violated it.

My health has continued to decline, and I am satisfied from the opinions of Federal as well as local physicians, that I ought last Fall, to have changed my abode. It might now, be unnecessary, and in the absence of any special cause of annoyance, I might do as well here as elsewhere, if I could have the benefit of recreation, occasional change of air, scenery, society &c which the medical faculty recommend as necessary, and which I had until recently. But I am now subjected to a special annoyance which grows out of a late order of the commanding General here, a copy of which you will find enclosed and to which I beg leave to refer.[2]

It has since been so far modified as to allow me the privilege of the area within the picket lines, which are about co-extensive with the corporation limits[.]

I should regard this order as a serious *molestation* at any time, and at present it is a most grievous one. I need not speak of the hardship of holding me, with a half dozen others, responsible for the damages done to the Rail Road from Nashville to Chattanooga,[3] or even for a few miles in extent, while we are imprisoned in an area of a mile in diameter and can have no more control over the matter, for good or evil, than if we were beyond the Atlantic. In this connection I have only to say I am ready to abide whatever may be properly required of me, But when my health, it may be my life, is involved, surely I may say I am "molested" by the order, and to appeal to you to relieve me, in pursuance of the assurance so kindly conveyed me through Mr Cooper.

Very Respectfully
Wm Ledbetter

LS, DLC-JP.

1. Although proof positive has not been found, the evidence suggests that this is William Ledbetter, the prominent Whig banker, identified in *Johnson Papers*, II, 160*n*, where his death date appears as 1862. Available sources provide no exact date or place of death.

2. Issued by the local provost marshal, this document placed Ledbetter under arrest, ordered him to remain at home except for reporting twice daily to headquarters, and warned that he would "be held responsible for the safety of the R. R." James B. Steedman to Ledbetter, September 9, 1863, Johnson Papers, LC; for Ledbetter's 1862 arrest, see *Johnson Papers*, V, 387n.

3. The Nashville and Chattanooga Railroad, vital supply and communications link for Rosecrans as he advanced southeast against Bragg, had just been rebuilt following Wheeler's raid in April. Murfreesboro was a supply depot for Federal operations. Long, *Civil War Almanac*, 336, 418; *OR*, Ser. 1, XXIII, Pt. I, 215-21; Carter, *First Tenn. Cav.*, 83.

From William L. Pope[1]

Penitentiary Sept 13th/63

Gov A. Johnson,

Dear Sir. I wish to have a private interview with you. I think I can make known Something that would be of much advantage to the government in the future, and to the Army. I am the man who originated the oath of Allegiance among the prisoners at Camp Morton last year, and, drew up the petitions therefor.[2] You probably have the documents at present. I allowed myself to be arrested for certain reasons which I will explain when I See you,[3] and which will no doubt meet your hearty approval. I would be pleased to hear from you at your own convenience.

Very Respectfully Your Obdt. Servt.
Wm. L Pope

P.S.

Mrs Bynum wife of Mr C. P. Bynum,[4] refugees from Columbia, Now in the City, can tell you a little in regard to a conversation I had with her some time ago.

W. L. P.

ALS, DLC-JP.

1. For Pope, Maury County surgeon, who had been captured at Columbia two days before, see *Johnson Papers*, V, 505*n*.

2. In June, 1862, confronted with the threat of being "exchanged and returned to the Southern Army," Pope had been one of the leaders urging that the prisoners be given the opportunity "to return to our former allegiance." Letter from William L. Pope, June 24, 1862, *ibid.*, 504-5.

3. Conceivably, fearing for his life at the hands of Confederate sympathizers, Pope may have been seeking protection from the advancing Union troops.

4. Mary D. Bynum (b. *c*1808) was the Virginia-born wife of Chesley P. Bynum (b. *c*1808), a staunchly unionist Columbia editor and printer, whose elder son, a Confederate soldier, had been killed a year earlier at Perryville. Deane Porch, tr., *1850 Census, Maury, Tennessee* (Nashville, 1966), 169; 1860 Census, Tenn., Maury, 9th Dist., 8; Jill K. Garrett, *Maury County, Tennessee, Historical Sketches* (Columbia, Tenn., 1967), 47, 100.

From C. G. Jameson[1]

Union City Tenn Sept 14th/63

Hon A Johnson Nashville
Gov Tenn
Excelent Sir

My object in writing to you was to get permission to raise an Independent Company for *Home Guards* in Carroll Henry & Weakley Counties West Tenn for the purpose of putting down Bushwhackers & Gurrillas for if we do not do Something the loyal Citizens will have to leave that part of the State[.] it is so at present that a truly loyal man dare not stay at home— thare has been severl of them shot by bushwhackers at there own homes—and we want permission to raise a Co for to protect our homes and some way to arm & equip ourselves— if we have to levy a Tax on the dis-loyal Citizens (who are harboring those Bush whackers)—for the purpose of arming ourselves[.] please let us hear from you Soon as this matter requires *immediate action*. It is true we get a Scouting party about once a month but they only drive the Gurrillas to the Bush untill they are gon when they come out again as thick as ever[.]
Since the evacuation of Jackson Trenton Humbolt & Ft Heiman[2] by our soldiers we have been without any protection, and we are willing to protect ourselves if we can only get permission to arm & organise ourselves as State or Home Guards[.] please let us here from you immediately[.]

I am your most Obdt Servt &c
C G Jameson
Union City Tenn

ALS, DLC-JP.

1. Except for evidence of a marriage to Margaret Connell in 1861, C. G. Jameson eludes identification.

2. In early June Federal forces at Jackson and adjacent areas in West Tennessee were ordered by General Grant to abandon their positions and move to the line of the Charleston and Memphis Railroad, in order to allow other troops to join Grant in besieging Vicksburg. Fort Heiman, Kentucky, located two miles south of Fort Henry on the opposite side of the Tennessee River, was evacuated in mid-July. *OR*, Ser. 1, XXIV, Pt. III, 364, 368-69, 381, 382; LII, Pt. I, 121; *OR-Navy*, Ser. 1, XXV, 304.

From Stephen A. Hurlbut

Head Quarters 16. A. Corps
Memphis Sept. 15, 1863

His Excy Andrew Johnston
Mil Governor of Tenn.
I am satisfied from pretty thorough acquaintance with West Tennessee, that it is advisable that your Excy should visit this part of the State as soon as practicable.

There are many subjects on which I desire full conference with you and I think your presence at an early day would have a beneficial effect upon public sentiment. The Country is now in that plastic state that it can readily be moulded into shape fitting for an honorable return into the Union.

The Militia of the State too requires attention. I inclose you an order[1] issued by me on the subject of Home Guards.

I believe the people of West Tennessee can be trusted to put down the Guerillas— against regular & organized force I must of course protect them.

My judgment is that as soon as it becomes apparent that the enemy have definitely abandoned East & Middle Tennessee it will be advisable to issue writs of Election for the Legislature to reorganize the State, Call a Convention, repeal the slave features of the Constitution & place Tennessee as a free State.

This will be more popular than it appears. There is a weariness of Slave property. So too I am satisfied that by repealing the act of Secession a large portion of Tenn. Soldiers now in C. S. Army will return.

Your obt Servt
S A Hurlbut. Maj Genl

ALS, DLC-JP.

1. Dated Memphis, September 14, and signed by Henry Binmore, A A G, Order No. 129 directed division commanders in Kentucky and Tennessee to encourage the formation of home guards under the militia laws of each state. Johnson Papers, LC.

Authorization to Recruit Union Guards

September [15?], 1863

WHEREAS, a portion of the people of Tennessee are engaged in open rebellion against the Government of the United States, and have resorted to any and all means for the overthrow of the same—such, for instance, as organizing themselves into marauding gangs of freebooters, commonly denominated guerrillas; and, whereas, life, liberty and property have been rendered insecure wherever they have been found. Now, therefore, ________________, of ________ county, ________ hereby authorized to recruit and organize a company of mounted men to be denominated Union Guards, the object of which shall be to operate offensively and defensively in the suppression of the rebellion, and all freebooting and marauding combinations which have been, or may hereafter be found in this State.

This company, when organized, shall be mustered into the service of the State of Tennessee, and of the United States, and shall continue in service for a period of twelve months, unless sooner discharged, and be subject to the rules and articles of war as prescribed by the Government of the United States, and shall be entitled to the same pay, rations, clothing, &c., that is now paid per month by the United States for the volunteer service, and shall be under the control and direction, while in the service of the State, of Andrew Johnson, Military Governor, or his successors in office.

This company, when formed, will be reported, officers and men in full, to this office, when its organization will be perfected.

Given under my hand at the Executive office at Nashville, Tenn., this ______ day of ______ 1863.

Nashville *Union*, September 26, 1863.

From Horace Maynard

Attorney General's Office[1]
September 17, 1863.

Sir,

The memorials in behalf of Thos. W. Bradford,[2] referred to me for examination & [r]eport, have been considered.

It appears from a transcript of a record in the Clerk's Office of the Supreme Court, that at the March Session of the Circuit Court of Franklin County 1861, said Bradford was tried for the murder of one Charles Vaughn.[3] He was convicted of murder in the first degree; but the jury having found mitigating circumstances in the case, Judge Marchbanks,[4] presiding commuted the punishment from death by hanging to imprisonment for life in the penitentiary. From this judgment he appealed to the Supreme Court. As that court has had no session since to try the appeal, he remains in the county jail of Davidson[.]

A bill of exceptions contains the proceedings at the trial & the evidence upon which the verdict was based. The murder was committed, at a county election, in March 1860, upon the body of a man totally un[con]-scious with liquor, & incapable either of offence or defence by stabbing in the bowels with a knife, so that his entrails protruded, causing death the next day. It was a cruel homicide & wholly unprovoked.

The evidence shows that the prisoner gave the fatal blow under the following circumstances, "Vaughn was standing in the yard, Def[endan]t. walked up to him, Vaughn pushed him back & Said he did not want any fuss with him—then Bradford walked up to him again. Vaughn pushed him back a second time & told him he did not want any fuss with him. Bradford then walked up to him again: when he walked up to him I saw the blade of knife in his right hand, He motioned at Vaughn two or three times, and then drew his hand back & motioned it towards Vaughn. Vaughn turned off and lay down by the gate. Bradford had the blade of his knife sticking out in his hand. At the time he made the lunge at Vaughn he was in the reach of him." This is the language of a son-in-law[5] of the prisoner, shown to have been sober & his character is unimpeached.

An attempt was made to throw the guilt upon Ephraim Bradford,[6] an illegitimate nephew of the prisoner. It failed & after carefully examining the record, I think properly. Several members of the jury, after the trial, were introduced, who stated that the "mitigating circumstances" were the drunkenness of the parties & the possibility that Ephraim Bradford, not the prisoner, might have struck the blow. Their leniency has saved the prisoner's life, as the case is represented in this record.

The prisoner's good conduct since he has been here in jail, is abundantly shown by the officers having him in charge; showing a great reformation, since the killing of the deceased. Prior to that time, it appears incidentally that he was a bad man.

As the time draws nigh for the sitting of the Supreme Court, I deem it my duty to advise your Excellency to take no action in the case.[7] An atrocious crime has been committed beyond doubt; & there is scarcely less doubt, that it was done by the hand of the prisoner.

I am very Respectfully your obt. sevt.
Horace Maynard

His Excy Andrew Johnson
Governor &c. &c.

ALS, DLC-JP.

1. His congressional term ended, Maynard had returned to Tennessee and in late August accepted Johnson's appointment as state attorney general. Nashville *Union*, August 28, 1863.

2. Not only the memorials—apparently presented to the governor and by him to his attorney general for an opinion—but even the defendant himself have disappeared from the pages and archives of history leaving no trace.

3. Not identified.

4. Andrew J. Marchbanks (1804-1867), a McMinnville lawyer, served in the state senate (1835-37) and was judge of the 13th circuit from 1837 to the outbreak of the war. By August, 1864, he had "gone South." McBride and Robison, *Biographical Directory*, I, 495-96.

5. Not identified.

6. Ephraim Bradford (*c*1837-1863), Franklin County native and a farm hand before joining Co. I, 41st Tenn. Inf., CSA, as a private, was killed at Chickamauga two days after this letter was written. According to "a young man from near Mr Bradford's home," Ephraim confessed, but not to authorities, that he, and not his uncle, killed Vaughn "and in Self defence turned States evidence against Bradford." 1860 Census, Tenn., Franklin, 11th Dist., 228; CSR, RG109, NA; John M. McGinnis to E. H. East, September 12, 1863, Johnson Papers, LC.

7. Whether Johnson intervened or not, Bradford was no longer a prisoner by 1865. In a memo in the Johnson Papers, all the principal Franklin office holders were noted as either

"gone South" or "dead in Virginia." *Tenn. House Journal*, 1865, App. 47-89 *passim*; memo: "In the case of T Bradford at Winchester," [August, 1864], Johnson Papers, LC.

From James M. Tomeny and James B. Bingham

(Confidential)

Memphis Sept 17. 1863

Dear Sir:

We learn with much regret of your severe illness,[1] rendering you unable to attend to official duties, and depriving your friends here for a still longer time of the pleasure of seeing and hearing you. We have not written to you upon many matters of special local interest, because we have been expecting you to visit Memphis, when an opportunity would be afforded you of obtaining more accurate and minute information by consultations with many of our Union men, in relation to their wants and wishes. There is one subject upon which, however, we think there exists little or no division of opinion and upon which we may therefore, venture to speak with some degree of freedom and certainty. All loyal men here, so far as we know, are agreed that the appointment of Judges and the re-establishment of our Courts, is of immediate necessity and great importance. It would be a work of supererogation to attempt to point out to you the evils incident to a state of society, in such a populous district as this, where no adequate judicial tribunals exist for the punishment of crime the enforcement of claims against delinquent debtors, and the general administration of justice and civil law.

If these evils are apparent to the common citizen, they need not be named to the great Statesman. Brig Gen. Veatch commanding this post from a laudable desire to remedy these evils, constituted in April last Judge Williams of Iowa, A. C. Ketchum of Memphis and Captain Barbour Lewis 1st Mo. Cavalry a "Civil Commission" "to hear and determine all complaints and suits instituted by loyal citizens of the United States for the collection of debts, the enforcement of Contracts, the prevention of frauds, the recovery of the possession of property, real or personal, and generally to perform such duties and exercise such powers as can be done by a court deriving its powers from military authority." To illustrate the defects of this tribunal we may mention that the only evidence of loyalty required by it is a simple oath of allegiance to the U. S. Under this ruling a rebel may drop his gun, come to Memphis, take an oath of allegiance, successfully prosecute a suit and collect a claim against a really loyal man, return with money thus collected and renew his efforts to subvert the Government. Judge Williams, the principal Commissioner, was not identified with the Unionists of Missouri where he resided before he came to Memphis. Those who knew him intimately in Missouri do not hesitate to class him with the secessionists of that State. We invited him in June last to make a public speech here, and told him that the resolutions to be offered endorsed and sustained the Administration and not then knowing his views, we requested that his address would harmonize with the resolutions. In the course of his remarks he did not permit a word to fall from him upon that vital subject. Besides many grave personal objections to Messrs Williams and Ketchum, the action of the Commission in the assessment of costs has occasioned almost universal complaint. The Commission was to be self-sustaining; that is, it was not to put the Government to any expense. This was reasonable; but it was not, we apprehend, contemplated to enrich the Commissioners, (all but one of whom are non-residents of the State and not identified with its people) or to endow them with princely salaries. The Commissioners, however, think otherwise, and their assessments for costs in the determination of suits, have been exorbitant and oppressive. We will cite but one instance. In an appeal from the judgment of a justice of the peace, involving only thirty eight dollars, the assessment and costs in confirming the decision of the justice amounted to more than forty dollars. To show that this is not an isolated case, we may state that the fees collected during the first three months of its sittings, after paying the subordinate officers and all expenses, netted the Commissioners about *fifteen hundred dollars* each, or six thousand dollars per annum; equal to the salary of the associate justices of the Supreme Court of the United States. From the recital of these facts we come to the conclusion that justice needs *cheapening* (not to say that it ought to fall) in Memphis and he who effectuates a reform will deserve well of her loyal citizens. We are informed by attorneys practicing before this Commission, (and here again the oath of allegiance is the only proof of loyalty required from lawyers wishing to practice before it) that its decisions are so vacillating, and inconsistent with established precedents, that they have fallen into contempt among the ablest members of the bar.

No appeal is allowed, no plea to the jurisdiction and the stay laws of the State, for the time being are absolutely swept away. Personal property is levied upon and sold in three days after execution issues. The Commission is not authorized to order the *sale* of real estate, but the rents and profits of such property is subject to sequestration in satisfaction of judgments.

Although the Commission was intended as a remedy, we hazard nothing in asserting that "the remedy is worse than the disease." [2]

It is certainly but a very miserable substitute for our regular Courts. Hence, we would respectfully urge upon you the propriety of exercising the power vested in you by the President, in appointing suitable persons judges in this district, with authority to organize and open Courts and proceed to administer the law, according to the forms of our State Constitution. The question here arises, who and where are the suitable persons; and, perhaps you would rather be satisfied upon that point than as to the expediency or necessity of making the appointments. This is really the great difficulty in the case, and we are free to confess that we know of no one in Memphis, who would accept the position, to whom there are not insuperable objections. E. W. M. King is spoken of, and will probably be recommended by certain persons of loose morals and doubtful loyalty, (for that is the character of his own) and possibly by some few good Union men, whose knowledge of the man is extremely limited. Mr. Ketchum, who in 1861 commanded a company recruited from the chain gang, will also, doubtless, be a candidate. We don't hesitate to affirm that neither of these men are at all qualified to fill the position of Judge; nor could either secure the respect which should attach to the person and acts of an able upright jurist. When Mr. Woods and Mr. Bond of Brownsville were here recently to consult with the military authorities in reference to the enlistment, organization and arming of loyal men in Haywood County for purposes of local defense, we discussed this matter with them, and asked them to name some thorough going Union man of their County who would accept the office of Judge here. They assured us that the loyal men of their district would be unanimous in recommending Thomas G. Smith Esq of Brownsville, a very fine lawyer, and who is now a fugitive from his home, on account of his devotion to our cause. We know Mr. Smith personally and regard him as a man of eminent ability, extensive legal attainments and unimpeachable integrity.

The only objection that could be urged to his appointment is that he is not a resident of this County. His residence is, however, embraced in our Congressional district. As there must be some irregularity attending almost every step in the progress of re-organization, we do not attach much importance to this objection; and if the people of Haywood, (than whom there is not a more loyal people in West or Middle Tennessee) shall endorse Mr. Smith as unanimously as we think they will, we will as soon as we are assured of that fact, forward to you a petition signed by loyal men here, asking his appointment. We deem it of the first importance that no one but a man of unsullied character, acknowledge ability, and with the clearest record should occupy the position of Judge at this time under the sanction of your authority.——

As the liberation and occupation of East Tennessee has now become an accomplished fact, we presume that an election for members of the Legislature will soon be ordered. From various causes and especially from the course pursued by our military commanders, Union sentiment has made little, if any, progress in this city during the past nine months. Wealthy secessionists have managed some how or other to get nearly every privilege for which they have applied, including that of passing our lines at will; and very often the best union men have been refused favors which they knew had been granted to their disloyal neighbors. This course naturally engendered indifference or hostility toward the officers making such unjust discriminations. Learning this these officers feel themselves obliged to declare that there are no loyal men here. Not more than three days ago a gentleman wearing two stars[3] declared to a semi-secessionist that he did not believe there was a loyal man in Memphis. This, too, very shortly after having attended by invitation an ovation to Gen. Grant by loyal citizens of Memphis and making a speech on that occasion.[4] It is not, in our opinion consistent to accept the hospitalities of friends, as such, and then attempt to falsify their professions of loyalty to their country; but "such is life"—in Memphis. We have no hesitancy in saying that the conduct of those high in authority here, has weighed like an incubus upon the Union Cause, and instead of reclaiming the disloyal it has encouraged them to persist in their opposition to the Government, while it has actually repelled and discouraged the truly loyal. The most extravagant professions and promises have been followed by the most miserable performances. One of the bitterest rebels received a letter saying that he would be exempted from taking the oath of allegiance under order 65 on the ground of "high moral character";[5] and it is notorious that this same "moral" individual does not and will not pay his honest debts. But he is only one of a class; and we mention the case simply for illustration; and we describe this state of things for the purpose of impressing upon you the great importance, in the first election, of throwing around the ballot box such restrictions as will effectually prevent the polling of disloyal votes. In Kentucky a special act of the Legislature authorizing persons who have forfeited their rights to the elective franchise, by participating in this rebellion, is necessary before they can resume its exercise.[6] Similar laws will likely be passed in this State as soon as a Legislature convenes, but in the meantime very rigid regulations should be made, to guard against the indiscriminate voting of public enemies. No man who is against the Union on any pretext should be permitted to vote in the approaching election. If this rule is not adopted and adequate precautions taken to enforce it no unconditional Union man can be elected in Memphis. In the interior it would probably be different, but here such a result would be inevitable. The Union men do not claim to have a majority here now; that is, if all who have taken the oath of allegiance can vote. Under order 65 thousands took the oath of allegiance, who are still, at heart disloyal. The oath of allegiance will not do as a test of loyalty, nor should it qualify a man in that respect, to vote. Some retrospective test would be better,[7] but the whole question is one requiring the most mature reflection and judgment, and with these suggestions we leave it with you, feeling confident that whatever plan you may adopt will be peculiarly adapted to the accomplishment of the object.

By way of parentheses, we may add that all who are not unconditionally for the government are politically your enemies as well as of the cause which you represent.

We write thus freely and confidentially to you upon these matters of public interest, and while we would not shrink from the responsibility of every word we write, yet we do not think it necessary that we should be involved in any personal controversy with the parties named or alluded to in this letter.

Reiterating the hope that your health and official duties will, ere long, allow you to fulfill your promise to us, and that we shall have the pleasure of welcoming you to our city, we remain

Very truly Yours
J. M. Tomeny
James B. Bingham

To Hon Andrew Johnson
Nashville Tenn

ALS (Tomeny), DLC-JP.

1. A week earlier a Nashville paper, reporting that the governor was "again suffering from severe indisposition" and had been "confined to his bed for two or three days," assured its readers that "there are no apprehensions of his protracted absence from his pressing duties." Nashville *Press*, September 9, 1863.

2. From "there are some remedies worse than the disease." Pubius Syrus: *Maxim* 301, Bartlett, *Quotations*, 110.

3. The writers were probably referring to Maj. Gen. Stephen A. Hurlbut, commander of the XVI Corps at Memphis, who, although a Republican commissioned from Illinois, was a native South Carolinian. Warner, *Generals in Blue*, 244-45.

4. On the evening of August 27, Hurlbut had attended a supper at the Gayoso House honoring Grant. Memphis *Appeal*, September 4, 1863.

5. Hurlbut's May 26 General Order No. 65 required all citizens over eighteen to subscribe to a loyalty oath or be considered undesirable aliens. On July 29 the order was relaxed to exempt certain persons—namely widows, orphans, those over fifty, and those employed as manual or mechanical laborers. Hooper, Memphis, 58-59; Memphis *Bulletin*, May 27, August 4, 1863.

6. On October 1, 1861, the legislature decreed that any Kentuckian who invaded the state was guilty of a felony and punishable by one to ten years' imprisonment; also that persons persuading a Kentuckian to enlist in the rebel army and those so enlisting were guilty of a high misdemeanor, punishable by a fine up to $1,000 or imprisonment up to six months. A few months later, March 11, 1862, a stronger law expatriated any Kentuckian who aided the Confederacy in any capacity, his citizenship not to be restored except by permission of the legislature. E. Merton Coulter, *The Civil War and Readjustment in Kentucky* (Chapel Hill, 1926), 139-40. See also Edward McPherson, *The Political History of the United States of America During the Great Rebellion* (Washington, 1865), 312-13.

7. When Johnson finally called an election for county officers in March, 1864, he prescribed a test oath which demanded more than a simple pledge of allegiance. By no means the "retrospective test" employed widely elsewhere, it nonetheless required the voter to swear that "I ardently desire the suppression of the present insurrection . . . [that] all laws and proclamations . . . may be speedily and permanently established and enforced over all the people . . . and further, that I will hereafter heartily aid and assist all loyal people in the accomplishment of these results." Nashville *Union*, January 27, 1864.

To Samuel C. Mercer

[September 17, 1863]

Mr Mercer will please say in his editorial[1] that the Military will giv protection where ever they can in the organization of these companies.

Run your eye over the order of Genl Hulburt in reference to the organization Home Guard[.] You will send the order back by the bearer—

Most respectfully
Andrew Johnson

ANS, DLC-JP.

1. Nashville *Union*, September 26, 1863.

To Edwin M. Stanton

Nashville September 17th 1863.

Hon E. M. Stanton.

I have made the acquaintance &c. of Maj. Stearns Asst. Adj't Genl. U.S. vols. who is here with authority to raise negro troops in the Dep't of the Cumberland.[1] We have been taking steps in that direction & have organized the men with a double purpose first to Employ them on the Gov't works where needed & then Convert them into soldiers & have so far succeeded well. we need more laborers now than Can be obtained for the prosecution of works that are indispensable to sustain the Rear of Genl Rosecrans army. Maj Stearns proposes to organize & place them in Camp where they in fact remain idle[.] This will to a very great Extent impede the progress of the works & diminish the number of hands Employed. all the Negroes will quit work when they Can go into Camp & do nothing. We must Contract[2] them for both purposes. I must be frank in stating my opinion that Maj Stearns mission with his notions will give us no aid in organization [of] negro Reg'ts in Tennessee. There are a number of persons running in from the other states who are anxious to raise such Reg'ts for the simple purpose of holding the offices without regard to the Condition of the Negro or the suppression of the rebellion. I must further state that we Can organize Reg'ts in Tennessee as well as we Can others[3] & that we can find more men in Tennessee ready & willing to Command than we can raise Reg'ts to Command in Tennessee. Answer will raise Negro troops[4] & lead them to battle it will have much better influence upon the public mind. We are just now beginning to organize & put the state facility [fairly] in motion. It is Exceedingly important for this question to be handled in such way as will do the least injury in forming a Correct public Judgement at this time[.] We hope therefore that the organization of Negro Reg'ts in Tennessee will be left to the Gen'l Comd'g this Dept. & military Governor. I would respectfully ask that the President may be furnished a Copy of this telegram[.] an early answer is respectfully asked.

Andrew Johnson

Tel, DNA-RG107, Tels. Recd., Sec. of War, Vol. 31 (1863); DLC-JP.

1. This wire, in all likelihood, was prompted by the way in which Stearns and his associates were beginning their recruiting of Negro troops. We have no evidence that the governor had yet received a copy of Stanton's telegram of the previous day which Stearns was directed to provide for both Johnson and Rosecrans. In that document, sent in response to the major's inquiry of the twelfth, the secretary of war, "directed by the President," stipulated that enlistees would be free at the expiration of their term, that in due time non-commissioned officers of colored regiments would receive the same pay as their counterparts elsewhere, that slaves belonging to loyal citizens could be enlisted with their masters' consent, and that, if Johnson and Rosecrans deemed it necessary, the slaves of loyal citizens might be enlisted "without" their masters' consent. Stanton to Stearns, September 16, 1863, Johnson Papers, LC.

2. The official copy of this telegram, retained in Johnson's files, reads "control" rather than "contract"—the first of several aberrations of the telegrapher's art found in the recipient's copy.

3. The Johnson version is more precise: "we can organize Negro Regiments in Tennessee as well as we can the white. . . ."

4. This incomprehensible clause becomes clear only if the word "answer" is removed and we use the sender's copy: "If Tennesseans will raise negro Regiments. . . ."

To William S. Rosecrans

Nashville Sept 17th 1863

Maj. Genl. Rosecrans,
Chattanooga.

I have just sent a telegram to the President[1] in regard to Major Stearns[2] mission to your Department. I have expressed the opinion to him fully and freely that the Comd'g General of the Dep't of the Cmrld [Cumberland] and Military Governor of Tennessee can organize and employ all the Negroes in Tennessee upon the public works or as soldiers as well without as with the aid of Major Stearns. At this time, General, while we are just verging upon a reorganization of the State it is important that this question should be handled with care, and we must have your aid and assistance. We are doing all we can to keep every thing right in your rear. There have been some improper and injurious steps taken by those who have been recruiting negro forces,[3] of which I will apprise more fully. I shall be with you in a few days [4] when I can confer with you fully in regard to the thorough organization of the state—

Andrew Johnson Mil. Gov'r.

Tel copy, DLC-JP.

1. See preceding telegram to Edwin M. Stanton.

2. George L. Stearns.

3. The recruiting of Negro troops by Stearns and others was regarded as both "improper and injurious," because it placed former slaves in camp where they were idle, thereby reducing the manpower available to sustain the rear of Rosecrans' army.

4. Johnson's plans to travel to the Chattanooga vicinity during this time were interrupted by the battle of Chickamauga, September 19-20.

To Abraham Lincoln

Nashville Sept 17 1863

Abm Lincoln

I have just recd your letter[1] which gives me pleasure & encouragements. It remind me of calling your attention while in Washington to the 4th Section of the Constitution & the propriety under that Section of authorizing the military govt to exercise all power necessary & proper to secure to the people of Tennessee a republican form of govt[.] you will perhaps remember that I showed you a paper which was drawn up containing the whole proposition which you endorsed & referred to the Secy of war[.] Such authority emanating from the Prest under the clause above referred would exert much influence on the public mind here[.] I desire it directed from the President. I have taken decided ground for Emancipation for immediate emancipation from gradual emancipation[.] now is the time for settlement of this question[.] Hence I am for immediate emancipation[.]

A Johnson Mil Gov

Tel, DLC-Lincoln Papers.

1. See Letter from Abraham Lincoln, September 11, 1863.

From Abraham Lincoln

Washington Sept 18th 1863

To Gov. A. Johnson

Despatch of yesterday Just received. I shall try to find the paper you mention and carefully consider it.[1]

In the mean time let me urge that you do your utmost to get every man you can black and white under arms at the very earliest moment, to guard Roads bridges and trains allowing all the better trained soldiers to go forward to Genl Rosecrans. Of course I mean for you to act in cooperation with and not independently of the military authorities.

A. Lincoln

Tel (in cipher), DLC-JP; *OR*, Ser. 3, III, 823.

1. For Johnson's proposal referred on April 25 to Stanton, together with the latter's changes in wording, see Basler, *Works of Lincoln*, VI, 187.

From Edwin M. Stanton

Washington Sept 18 1863

To Brig Gen Andrew Johnson
Mil Gov

Your telegraph just received. Major Stearns was sent to Nashville to aid in the organization of colored troops under your directions & the directions of Gen Rosecrans[.] to prevent any possible misunderstanding he was directed to report to you & the commanding Genl[.] he is while in your state your subordinate bound to follow your directions & may be relieved by you whenever his actions is deemed by you prejudicial[.] upon your judgement in matters relating to the state of which you are Governor The Department relies in respect to whatever relates to the people whether white or Black bond or free. No officers of colored troops will be appointed but in accordance with your views as Chief of state Executive[.] If Maj Stearns can be of no aid & his presence is obnoxious he will of course be removed whether relieved by you or not[.][1]

Edwin M Stanton
Secy of War

Tel, DLC-JP; DNA-RG107, Tels. Sent, Vol. 20 (1863).

1. Actually, Stanton two days earlier had admonished Stearns, "You will not act contrary to the wishes of Gov. Johnson in relation to enlistments without express authority for so doing from this Dept.," and on September 19, he would be even more emphatic: "If any difference of opinion exists or shall arise . . . respecting the Organization and Employment of Colored men in the State of Tennessee, He being the State Executor you will conform your action to his views[.] all disention is to be avoided and if there is any want of harmony between you, you had better leave Nashville and proceed to Cairo to await orders." Johnson learned of these directives some time after the twenty-second. Stanton to Stearns, September 16, 19, 1863, Johnson Papers, LC.

From Abraham Lincoln

Private

Executive Mansion,
Washington, D.C., Sept. 19, 1863.

Hon. Andrew Johnson.
My dear Sir:

Herewith I send you a paper,[1] substantially the same as the one drawn up by yourself, and mentioned in your despatch, but slightly changed in two particulars.— First, yours was so drawn as that I authorized you to carry into effect the fourth Section,[2] &c. whereas I so modify it as to authorize you to so act as to require the United States to carry into effect that Section. Secondly, you had a clause committing me, in some sort, to the State Constitution of Tennessee, which I feared might embarrass you in making a new Constitution, if you desire— So I dropped that clause.

Yours very truly
A. Lincoln.

LS, NNPM; DLC-Lincoln Papers.

1. Lincoln's "paper" appears as the following document; the governor's earlier proposal, mentioned in his Telegram to Abraham Lincoln, September 17, has not been found. Basler, *Works of Lincoln*, VI, 469n.

2. That section of the Constitution which guarantees to each state a republican form of government.

From Abraham Lincoln[1]

Executive Mansion,
Washington, D.C. Septr. 19, 1863.

Hon. Andrew Johnson,
Military Governor of Tennessee

In addition to the matters contained in the orders and instructions given you by the Secretary of War, you are hereby authorized to exercise such powers as may be necessary and proper to enable the loyal people of Tennessee to present such a republican form of State government as will entitle the State to the guaranty of the United States therefore, and to be protected under such State government, by the United States, against invasion and domestic violence—all according to the fourth Section of the fourth Article of the Constitution of the United States.

Abraham Lincoln

LS, NNPM; DLC-Lincoln Papers.

1. An enclosure in the preceding document. Basler, *Works of Lincoln*, VI, 469.

From Ellen M. Dunnington[1]

Columbia Sep. 20th [1863]

Gov Johnson
Dear Sir

I received a letter yesterday stating my husband had been quite sick for five or six weeks which has made me very uneasy and anxious to be with him. When in Nashville last spring you kindly promised me if I still insisted on visiting him to assist me in procuring a pass[.] not being able to visit Nashville, and having no one to apply for me, my great anxiety to go to him has determined me to call upon you for a fulfilment of your promise. I would like a pass to Tuscumbia Ala. to *go* & *return*[.] I say *return* as I have children & much prefer being in my own house[.] I complied with Gen Shermans order viz that Non Combatants could remain at home unmolested by taking the Oath of a Non Combatant and giving bond, all of which I have complied with and none can say I have ever violated it. My home is *my own* bought with my individual means given to myself & children[.] I gave a bond of twenty thousand dollars. I give you these facts that I may more readily procure a pass to *go* & *return*. Mr Lander[2] & family occupy the house with me and will remain during the war[.]
Mr Dunnington is in very delicate health, has been for several years and as he has never been in the army, I would like very much to have permission to take home one full set of warm under cloathing if you can grant it or obtain it for me.

As I will go by the way of Florance Alla and not *pass through either* army I hope I will have no difficulty in obtaining a pass for myself & children & protection for my baggage & conveyance & horses. I will have the baggage examined and approved by the military here, and sealed before leaving. Hoping to hear from you soon and believing knowing my anxiety you will grant my request[3]

I remain Respectfully
Mrs E Dunnington

To His Excelency Gov Johnson
Nashville Tenn

ALS, DLC-JP.

1. Ellen McEwing (*c*1832-*fl*1908), a native Kentuckian, was the wife of wealthy lawyer and printer Francis C. Dunnington, sometime Johnson supporter, who became a strong advocate of secession. 1860 Census, Tenn., Maury, 9th Dist., 70; Nashville *Banner*, November 10, 1908. For Dunnington, see *Johnson Papers*, III, 8*n*.

2. Russel B. (b. *c*1812) and Elizabeth (Dunnington) Lander (b. *c*1820), Kentucky-born brother-in-law and sister of Frank Dunnington, were Hopkinsville grocers with three daughters and a son as the war began. 1860 Census, Ky., Christian, Hopkinsville, 45; *Goodspeed's Maury*, 936.

3. Not found.

From H. A. Parr[1]

Jersey City New Jersey
Sept. 21, 1863

Gov Johnson

Sir I write you these few lines begging leaf of you to Permit me to return to Nashville[.] I am a poor boy who has got no Father and a helpless Mother. I hav had to work hard for my living ever since I was 10 years old[.] I was borned in Canada and raised in Tennsee[.] I am now in my 19 year old[.] I did allways contend for the Union untill I was compelled to hush by the rebels. I was in Nashville during the rebel campaign there and never thought of enlisting in Such a caus, and I would not even drill with the Malitia, but one night during last January I was led off by bad company and maid use of Language which was not right,[2] and now I feel Sorry that I did so and am willing to make aney apology you may think propper for So doing[.] Gov I would like to return Soon for my monny has most gone and I am destitute of a grate many things which I realy need for cold wether is now Setting in[.]

N.B. During the riot in N. Y. C it was thought that there would be Some trubble over here[.] So I in company with others went to the Station house where we got Some guns and intended to stop it at the risk of our lives, but Bishop Kelly Saved us that trubble[.][3]

I hav told my condittion to Some of the Citizens here and they told me to write to you and ask you to Pardon me and they will vouch for my good behavior here after[.]

Pleas donot lay this one Side unnoticed but give it an answer for the others who was Sent off when I was has returned[.]

I remain your most Obeident Servant
H. A. Parr Jersey City N. J

I was sent off by the order of Gen Mitchel[.][4]

ALS, DLC-JP.

1. Probably the H. H. Parr (b.*c*1843) who was listed as a New York-born apprentice living in the household of Jacob Sharp, a "Coach Smith" in Columbia on the eve of the war. 1860 Census, Tenn., Maury, Columbia, 9th Dist., 55.

2. Arrested by Truesdail in late 1862 for Confederate sympathies, Parr had spent several months in a Nashville jail before being paroled to remain North during the war. Several weeks later he again requested permission to return to Tennessee. Parr to Johnson, October 10, 1863, Johnson Papers, LC.

3. The 1863 Federal draft law prompted several riots around the country during July. The most destructive outbreak occurred in New York City where, for six days beginning on July 11, mob action resulted in hundreds of deaths and extensive property loss. The crowds, composed primarily of Irish workers, directed much of their hostility toward the city's black population. Similar violence threatened to erupt in Jersey City. On the night of July 14 a few hundred persons, mostly boys, assembled, but persuaded by Father John Kelly, Hudson County Sheriff Bernard McAnally, and Chief of Police Edward D. Reily, they refrained from violence, "further than hunting negroes." Kelly (1801-1866), an Irish native who served as a missionary in Liberia in the early 1840's, was for twenty-three

years pastor of St. Peter's Roman Catholic Church in Jersey City. New York *Times*, July 16, 1863; Joseph Butsch, "Negro Catholics in the United States," *Catholic Historical Review*, III (1917), 40; New York *Tribune*, April 30, 1866; see also Adrian Cook, *The Armies of the Streets* (Lexington, Ky., 1974).

4. Robert B. Mitchell. A second postscript in another hand reads "None So far from home as those who hav no home[.] Quoted to G. A. Henry Edgefield"

From John Thompson[1]

La Grange Tenn Sept 21/63

Gov. Andrew Johnson
Nashville Tenn
Dear Sir—

I have lived in this place Since Sept 1839, now twenty four years. Came from Nashville to this place lived there while then a youth with the Misses Nichol', Mr. Wm. Nichol[2] being the principal, who has always been a fast friend of mine, will always remember his kindness with gratitude while quite poor, with only the Small pittance of $3,000 Saved from my salery he gave me a letter on which I could buy more goods than I could have paid the freights on & Mr James L Meigs[3] late of our place as professor in a College[4] we had here in prosperity before vile & Infamous Secession was *forced* on the people which is now abandoned and surrounded by breast works, and now of Nashville a most noble & true man, he was one of the very few men when he left us that I Could Communicate with and Express my true Sentiments and feelings—(Enough of all this)[.]
My object in Commencing this letter was to take the liberty of Expressing to you my approval and gratitude for the very firm, Manly and Patriotic Course you have taken in the hour of our beloved Country's greatest peril— their is no man living a greater admirer of the great Henry Clay than the writer, and as a Matter of Course you will know that I always opposed you, and that with all the Energy and decided Character that I possess, but Sir when you arose in the Senate of the U S. in reply to Infamous Wigfall & Jo Lane[5] I forgave you all your political Sins, you there & then struck treason a blow that was felt throughout our whole Country, the best Evidence of the fact is the manner in which you have been hunted down and abused, and my further object in addressing you was to offer to you my Cooperation in any [way] in my power to restore our bleeding & devastated State, to its once happy & prosperous Condition— I have been absent from home with the whole of my family for the last five months, and I have taken a house in Phil—where my children can get the benifits of good Schools, and have that quiet & protection always gave, and always would have been given the South. Sir—I am an unconditional Union Man. Nothing in my opinion should Stand in the way of the perpetuity of this great Nation—

Yours Very Truly and Sincerely
Jno Thompson

Things are fast reaching that point to which you Said they must go in your Speech at Nashville July 4 1862,[6] Treason must be made odious & traitors impoverised[.]

JT

ALS, DLC-JP.

1. Probably John Thompson (b. *c*1820), Irish native and LaGrange merchant who claimed $8,000 real and $40,000 personal property just prior to the war. 1860 Census, Tenn., Fayette, 13th Dist., 179.

2. William Nichol (1800-1878), born in Abingdon, Virginia, was a longtime Nashville businessman who served as mayor (1835-36), president of the Bank of Tennessee (1838-47), and as a commissioner to superintend the construction of the capitol (1844). In 1860 he reported $180,000 real and $120,000 personal property. The Misses Nichol were probably William's sisters—Jane, Henrietta, and Mary E.—who lived with their widowed mother in the 1840's. *Ibid.*, Davidson, Nashville, 5th Ward, 163; Clayton, *Davidson County*, 198-A; Clayton B. Dekle, "The Tennessee State Capitol," *Tenn. Hist. Quar.*, XXV (1966), 218; Nashville *American*, November 23, 1878; Jane H. Thomas, *Old Days in Nashville, Tennessee: Reminiscences* (Nashville, 1897), 41-42.

3. James L. Meigs (*c*1827-*fl*1891), Tennessean with $3,600 real and $500 personal estate, was professor of mathematics at LaGrange Synodical College (1860) and superintendent of Nashville schools (1861-62). 1860 Census, Tenn., Fayette, 13th Dist., LaGrange, 188; Clayton, *Davidson County*, 253; Washington *Evening Star*, October 20, 1891; John H. DeBerry, "LaGrange—LaBelle Village," *Tenn. Hist. Quar.*, XXX (1971), 145.

4. Offering a curriculum of ancient languages, natural philosophy, chemistry, mathematics, astronomy, and civil engineering, with lectures in physiology and international law, the LaGrange Synodical College for men, Dr. John H. Waddell, president, opened October 1, 1857. The only graduating class was that of '61. Following Federal occupation in June, 1862, the college was used first as a hospital and later as a prison. *Ibid.*, 145-46.

5. Speech on the Seceding States, February 5-6, 1861, *Johnson Papers*, IV, 218*ff*.

6. Speaking in the capitol, Johnson had thundered: "*The time has arrived, when treason must be made odious and traitors impoverished . . . and their property should be taken from them to defray the expenses of the war.*" *Ibid.*, V, 538.

From William B. Stokes

Tracy City Sept 22 1863

To Gov Andrew Johnson

Sir. I have just received information of the treatment of my family by Tom Murray[1] with a band of three hundred men is now in my section of County has taken all my stock insulted & fired a pistol over my wifes head & attempted to burn my house & are doing all sorts of mischief to the Union mens families[.] now governor I want you to intercede with Genl Rosecrans to let me return with my Regt & guard & protect people[.] you know I have served faithfully for fifteen months[.] aid me if you please in this matter at once[.]

Respy. W B Stokes Col Comdg

Tel, DLC-JP.

1. Thomas B. Murray (*c*1829-1878), Tennessee-born lawyer and attorney general of the Sparta district (1854), had been lieutenant colonel, 16th Tenn. Inf., CSA, becoming major, 22nd Inf. Btn., in January, 1863. Detached in July for recruiting and mounting the battalion, he subsequently commanded a guerrilla force "prowling around" in DeKalb, Warren, Smith, White, and Wilson counties, "committing depredations upon Union families." Captured in Putnam County, February, 1864, he was paroled at Morganton,

North Carolina, in May, 1865. After the war he practiced in McMinnville and served on the Democratic state committee. McMinnville *New Era*, January 24, 1878; CSR, RG109, NA; *OR*, Ser. I, XXX, Pt. III, 900; Louisville *Journal*, February 23, 1864; see also *Johnson Papers*, II, 235n; IV, 127*n*.

To Abraham Lincoln

Nashville Sept 23 1863

His Excellency
A Lincoln

If we were authorized to offer three hundred ($300) dollars in addition to the present bounty[1] to Loyal Masters consenting to their slaves entering the service of the U. S. It would be an entering wedge to emancipation and for the time paralize much opposition to recruiting slaves in Tennessee[.] The slave to receive all other pay & his freedom at the expiration of term of service[.] If a white man pays his three hundred dollars for his substitute he need not care whether he is white or black. This would relieve the loyal owners & punish the rebels & traitors for as to his slaves we should ask no questions nor make any promises[.]

Andrew Johnson Mil Gov

Tel, DLC-Lincoln Papers; DNA-RG107, Tels. Recd., President, Vol. 1(1863-64).

1. The current bounty for a new recruit was $100. Thus Johnson's proposal contemplates a $400 return to the slaveowner who gives up his slave. On October 3, the war department issued a general order authorizing the payment of up to $300 to loyal slaveholders for each of their slaves who enlisted. Rowell, *Yankee Cavalrymen*, 15; *OR*, Ser. 3, III, 861.

From Wilberforce Nevin[1]

Head-Quarters United States Forces,
Nashville, Tenn., Sept. 24th 1863.

Hon. Andrew Johnson
Mil. Gov. of Tennessee
Sir.

I am directed by the General Comd'g to forward to you the enclosed complaints regarding the conduct of the board of Trade at Gallatin Tenn.[2] The statements made therein are borne out by verbal Report and complaints from Citizens of this and that locality. It seems to be a matter pecurliarly within the jurisdication of the civil Authorities. The Suggestion of Mr. Dillon[3] is impractiable at present. There are not troops anough at Gallatin to enforce any custom house regulations by a line of Pickets, and the whole matter must be confided to the discretion and competency of the Board of Trade.

I have the Honor to be Sir
Your Most Obdt. Servt. W. Nevin
Capt. and A A. G.

ALS, DLC-JP.

1. Wilberforce Nevin (*c*1836-1899), Lancaster County, Pennsylvania, lawyer, was 1st lieutenant and captain, 79th Pa. Inf. (1861-63), before serving as captain and assistant adjutant general, U. S. Vols. (1863-65). 1860 Census, Pa., Lancaster, Lancaster Township, 7; J. I. Mombert, *An Authenic History of Lancaster County, in the State of Pennsylvania* (Lancaster, 1869), 327, 434; Heitman, *Register,* I, 744.

2. By authorization from Secretary Chase in April, 1862, Johnson had appointed boards in Nashville, Memphis, and other cities to regulate trade by permit, limiting the patronage to those of proven loyalty. Complaints against the Gallatin board emanated from the Nashville surveyor of customs over the issuance of trade permits for contraband articles— medicine, salt, and leather—except for family use and in quantities sufficient only for a two-month supply; cotton cards, except to those of proven loyalty; and liquor, prohibited entirely. *Johnson Papers,* V, 267n; Futrell, Federal Trade, 62-63, 66-67; Joseph R. Dillin to R. S. Granger, September 18, 1863 (two letters), Johnson Papers, LC.

3. Joseph R. Dillin (*c*1832-1889), Warren County, Kentucky, native who moved in 1850 to Tennessee where he became a planter, was a hardware salesman at the Nashville firm of Fall & Cunningham when appointed special agent and acting surveyor of customs in Nashville (April 9, 1863); in this capacity he instructed the Sumner County board of trade concerning "articles which they Should not permit only in very Small quantities," so that the "country Should not be Stocked with . . . articles as would aid the enemy Should they fall into their hands." Captured and temporarily imprisoned by Confederates in June, 1863, he became an attorney after the war and alternately made his home in Davidson and Rutherford counties, serving as state representative (1865, 1869-71), assistant U. S. district attorney (1882-86), and chairman of the Republican state committee. McBride and Robison, *Biographical Directory,* II, 234-35; *Nashville Bus. Dir.* (1860-61), 154, 164; William G. Brownlow to S. P. Chase, June 10; George Harrington to Johnson, June 20, 1863; Dillin to Johnson, December 7, 1864, Johnson Papers, LC; Dillin to Benjamin Harrison, June 15, 1889, Harrison Papers, LC; Nashville *Times and True Union,* April 3, 1865.

From J. G. Sams[1]

Dechard Sep 24 1863

To Brig Gen Andrew Johnson
Mil Govr

Sir we have met & Captured a part of Col Holmans[2] freebooters 9 privates & four Commanding officers[.] Holman himself one of the prisoners[.] will you receive them under the Civil law or what shall be done with them[?] Captured by the third Ohio Cavalry Comdg by Maj Howland[.][3]

J G Sams
Capt union State Guards

Tel. DLC-JP.

1. J. G. Sams, otherwise unidentified, had been sent to Franklin County to organize troops to suppress marauding. Three weeks later, having enrolled 71 men, Sams expressed the hope that he could raise enough for a company and would report to Johnson "for the perfecting of the organiz[at]ion." Apparently he never did. Sams to William S. Rosecrans, September 17, 1863, Johnson Papers, LC; Sams to Johnson, October 11, 1863, Petitions, Mil. Gov's Papers, 1862-65, Tennessee State Library and Archives.

2. James H. Holman (1836-1910), Lincoln County native, was 2nd lieutenant, 1st U. S. Inf. (1857-61) before resigning to become lieutenant colonel, 1st Tenn. (Turney's) Inf., CSA (1861-62). After staff duty with the armies of Kirby Smith and Bragg, he was promoted to colonel and ordered into Tennessee to gather up soldiers cut off by Bragg's retreat. Captured near Winchester, he was eventually imprisoned at Johnson's Island until

October, 1864, when he was sent to Richmond on parole. The following January, at the expiration of his parole, he was attached to John B. Magruder's Texas command. Returning to Tennessee, he became a lawyer and later attorney general, 6th judicial circuit (1870-77). Speer, *Prominent Tennesseans,* 45-47; *Goodspeed's Lincoln,* 894-95; Nashville *Banner,* March 28, 1910.

3. Horace N. Howland (1826-1895), Ohio-born, rose from captain to colonel in the 3rd Ohio Cav. (1861-65), becoming brevet brigadier of volunteers in March, 1865. After the Atlanta campaign, he was at war's end again in Georgia with Gen. James H. Wilson's army. Subsequently he dealt in real estate in Toledo before moving to Morgan County, Missouri, in 1886. Toledo *Blade,* June 26, 1895; *OR,* Ser. 1, XXX, Pt. IV, 88; XLIX, Pt. I, 380; Heitman, *Register,* I, 549; Toledo city directories (1872-76), *passim.*

From Ethan A. Hitchcock[1]

Washington City D.C.
Sept 28, 1863

To His Excelly. And. Johnson
Mily. Govr. of Tenn:
Sir

There is, in prison at this place, a civilian of the State of Maryland, who was arrested in attempting to cross our lines to go South.[2] He has proposed to go South on a parole of honor to effect the release of a *Colonel* in exchange for himself, or to return. On hearing of this proposal this morning it has been determined to send him south; but, under obligations to obtain the release of your nephew, or to return to prison here—no alternative being allowed him; and his wife, now in Baltimore, is not to be allowed to accompany him, but he is to be informed that if he shall effect the release of your nephew, his wife will be sent across the lines.

I beg you to feel assured that your claims in behalf of your nephew have been fully admitted and appreciated from the first, but there has appeared no way of inducing the enemy to deliver him up until now. It is hoped that he will soon be among us.

Very respectfully Yr. Obt. Servt.
E A Hitchcock Maj Genl Vol.
Commr for Exch. of Pris:

P.S. The above course has been taken at the suggestion of Col. Hoffman, the Commy. Genl. of Pris.

ALS, DLC-JP.

1. Ethan Allen Hitchcock (1798-1870), Vermont-born and West Point graduate (1817), served at the Academy, on the frontier, and in Florida and Mexico before his resignation in 1855. Appointed major general of volunteers in February, 1862, he became commissioner for the exchange of prisoners in November. Mustered out in October, 1867, he spent the remainder of his life in Charleston, South Carolina, and Sparta, Georgia. Warner, *Generals in Blue,* 230-31; *DAB,* IX, 73-74.

2. Daniel T. Chandler (*c*1820-1877), a Washington native, was commissioned 2nd lieutenant in 1838, rising to colonel before he resigned in December, 1862. Arrested in early 1863 by Federal authorities as he tried to make his way South, he was incarcerated in Washington's Old Capitol prison until exchanged for Johnson's nephew, Andrew Johnson, Jr. The trade was effected in October, young Johnson arriving in Washington in early December. Commissioned lieutenant colonel, CSA, Chandler served as an assistant adju-

tant general, later residing in Baltimore as "Librarian, Law Library." Heitman, *Register,* I, 294; W. Hoffman to S. A. Meredith, October 6; Hoffman to J. H. Martindale, October 22; Hoffman to E. A. Hitchcock, December 3, 1863, Lets. Sent, Vol. 6, RG249, NA; Endorsements on Lets. Recd., Vol. 22B, Office of the Agent for Exchange of Prisoners, RG109, NA; Baltimore city directories (1868-77), *passim.*

From Horace Maynard

Cincinnati, Sept. 28, 1863.

Dr Sir,

I enclose you a letter from Mr. Coldwell[1] of Shelbyville touching the Agency for abandoned property.[2] You see he regards it as important that one be appointed. Suppose you let them get up a petition by the union men, to avoid the perplexity that suggested itself?

My family arrived yesterday & I have considered our movements with reference to two points,—

1. I am satisfied we are going to hold East Tennessee And in that point of view I think it important, that more of us go there as soon as practicable.

2. I am satisfied that Rosecrans will not make any further movements for several weeks & until he does that, very little can be done towards civil administration.[3]

In this state of affairs, I think I had better take my family to Knoxville, & make some temporary provision for them before returning to Nashville[.]

So you may expect me in the latter half of October[.]

Brownlow is prepared to start his paper.[4] We will have three cardinal points.

1. To sustain your administration

2. To urge a vigorous policy towards the known rebels. We are fearful that Sam Carter's course will be influenced by a too gentle regard for his rebel Kin—[5]

3. The "Divin Institution" Incidental matters will attach—[6]

After looking over the whole ground with all my present lights, I am satisfied this is the most effective line of action for the present.

You will receive this before I can get away, & if you dissent from conclusion please telegraph—

Would you not do well to appoint Judges for East Tennessee? How would these do[?] Saml Milligan, Sup. Court, James P. Swan, 2nd C. Ct, E. T. Hall 3d[.][7]

I am very Truly Yours
Horace Maynard

To His Excy. Andrew Johnson
Governor &c.

ALS, DLC-JP.

1. A week earlier Thomas H. Coldwell had declined appointment as receiver of abandoned property in Bedford County, expressing the hope that "you will make an appointment at once & one who will account to the Government for ever[y] cent & *pay over*

promptly." The next day Coldwell recommended James P. Moore for the position. Coldwell to Maynard, September 22, 23, 1863, Johnson Papers, LC.

2. Under acts of July 17, 1862, March 3, 1863, and July 2, 1864, special treasury agents were responsible for receiving and collecting abandoned, captured, or confiscable property. At first agents were appointed but assigned no definite areas. Later five agencies were created, each given a specific geographical jurisdiction; subsequently, a supervising general agent was designated and the existing jurisdictions redefined to form seven, each having local special agents to keep records of permits, certificates, and bonds. Munden and Beers, *Civil War Archives*, 233-34.

3. Following the sanguinary battle of Chickamauga, September 19-20, Rosecrans had retired to Chattanooga, now in a virtual state of siege. Obviously, the further extension of civil government into eastern Tennessee would have to await a turn in the fortunes of war.

4. Returning to Knoxville soon after its occupation by Burnside, Brownlow was currently making preparations to revive the *Whig*. In his first issue the Parson observed: "With the highest regard for friends, a decent respect for honorable enemies, and the lowest contempt for the leaders in the Rebellion, this Journal, with whatever of talents its editor can muster, launches upon the troubled sea of life!" E. Merton Coulter, *William G. Brownlow: Fighting Parson of the Southern Highlands* (Chapel Hill, 1937), 250-51; Knoxville *Whig and Rebel Ventilator*, November 11, 1863.

5. Samuel Carter, appointed provost marshal general of East Tennessee, and his brothers were members of a sprawling clan that had intermarried over three generations with other prominent southern families. The "rebel kin" may have included any of several families. The Taylors and Rheas each had members in the Confederate service. Carter's Taylor cousins from his own county, Nathaniel M., George D., and Henry H., as well as his Rhea nephews from Sullivan County, William, John H., and James T., actively supported the southern war effort. In addition, Confederate General Alfred E. Jackson and Colonels James T. Carter and William Caswell were Carter kin. Octavia Zollicoffer Bond, *Family Chronicle and Kinship Book* (Nashville, 1928), 536-37, 557, 558, 572; Sistler, *1850 Tenn. Census*, V, 197.

6. The "divine institution" was almost certainly slavery. Brownlow had carried on a vociferous proslavery campaign before the war, employing the Bible, from both the podium and the press, to demonstrate its providential origin and righteousness. Yet in the first number of his *Ventilator*, the Parson announced for emancipation, insisting that slavery was a dying institution which the southern masses opposed. Coulter, *Brownlow*, 94-95, 102; Steve Humphrey, *"That D----d Brownlow"* (Boone, N. C., 1978), 264; Knoxville *Whig and Rebel Ventilator*, November 11, 1863.

7. In due time Johnson appointed his old friend Sam Milligan to the state supreme court (1865) where he served until 1868. James P. Swann (b. *c*1820), Jefferson County lawyer, attended the Greeneville Union convention (June, 1861), was judge of the 2nd circuit (1865-69), and continued in practice until about 1882. Elijah T. Hall (1827-1896), Knoxville attorney, served as judge of the 3rd judicial circuit (1864-77) and of the state supreme court (*c*1884). *Goodspeed's Jefferson*, 858; Temple, *Notable Men*, 52, 103; *Tenn. Official Manual* (1890), 182; WPA, Tennessee, Knox County, Tombstone Records: Old Gray Cemetery, 12; *Knoxville Directory* (1882), 207; (1884), 187.

Proclamation Appointing Nashville Municipal Officers

September 28, 1863

By virtue of the power and authority in me vested, as Military Governor of the State of Tennessee, I do hereby appoint the following persons to hold and exercise the functions of the respective offices in the Municipal Corporation, of the city of Nashville, to which [t]his and their names are respectively attached

1st Ward—Alderman—John E. Newman.

Councilmen—James Turner and John Carper.

2d Ward—Alderman—Joseph J Robb
Councilmen—G. M. Southgate and A. Myers.
3d Ward—Alderman—G. A. J. Mayfield.
Councilmen—Andrew Anderson and A. McDaniel.
4th Ward—Alderman—H. G. Scovel
Councilmen—L. B. Huff and Charles Sayers.
5th Ward—Alderman—J. B. Knowles.
Councilmen—E. R. Glascock and W. S. Cheatham
6th Ward—Alderman—M. M. Brien.
Councilmen—T. J. Yarbrough and Wm. Driver
7th Ward—Alderman—M. G. L. Claiborne.
Councilmen—J. W. McCready and J. E. Rust
8th Ward—Alderman—Joseph Smith.
Councilmen—L. D. Wheeler and Wm. Haily.

IN TESTIMONY WHEREOF, I have hereunto set my hand and caused the great seal of the State to be affixed at Nashville, this the 28th day of September, 1863.

By the Governor,

ANDREW JOHNSON

Edward H. East,
Secretary of State.

Nashville *Union*, September 29, 1863.

From George L. Stearns

September 29, 1863, Nashville; ALS DLC-JP.

Assistant adjutant-general and commissioner for organization of U. S. Colored troops asks that Adam Young, a Negro who "is furnishing meals to Colored recruits for me," be given "necessary papers to Exempt him from impressment."

From Richard M. Edwards

Chattanooga Tenn Sept 30th 1863

Gov A Johnson;
Dear Sir;

The recruiting business for three years service is greatly retarded here in consequence of hopes entertained by many that you have or will authorize the raising of twelve months troops for state defence and also that you are authorizing the raising and arming of "home guards" &c. Not knowing how the facts are whether their hopes in these respects are well founded or not, I venture to address you on the subject as much for the information of the citizen as my own.

A word or two on the subject of home guards I hope will not be deemed obtrusive. When we were at Cumberland Gap in 62 Genl. Morgan distributed a large amount of arms to home guard companies in Kentucky.[1] They took the guns & ammunition and went to their homes.

When the rebel army got into Kentucky, we left the Gap and all that country exposed to their depredations. In a few instances the home guards bushwhacked & killed a few rebels. The result was that a larger number of citizens were picked up indiscriminately and murdered by the rebels than would cover their loss.[2] The guns were hunted up and taken south and became the most effective weapons in rebel hands to fight us with. The idea of home guards has been a good one in times gone by, when our fathers contended with small bands of Indians. An army in those days scarcely ever exceeded a thousand or fifteen hundred men. A thousand Indians was quite a large force for any tribe to assemble; consequently home guards might successfully contend with them. Now however less than twenty or thirty thousand is rarely relied on for any offensive operation. Home guards can hardly be relied on to resist such forces. But a more serious objection still exists and facts are rapidly occurring which call loudly for the disbanding of the companies already formed on Cumberland Mountain or a corrective applied that will keep them in bounds. The fact as detailed to me by undoubted loyal men and men of good standing, are that one company under Capt Bricksey on Cumberland Mountain & another whose captain I do not remember are robbing stealing and plundering both parties alike and have been burning houses and committing outrages that are truly shocking.[3]

I am informed that Capt Bricksey and the other captain both obtained their authority from Genl. Rosecrans. The facts have been made known to him, & I only speak of them in this connection to exemplify the results of home guards so far. There is too great a risk of the system, however well intended, running into highway robbery and piracy.

If home guards are to be established let them be composed of men of advanced age and experience; and if young able bodied men wish to play soldier let them go into the army properly; because there is the true place to be effective. Another item in reference to those companies already formed is that they are composed mainly of *deserters from Bragg's army*.[4] The citizens are perfectly at their mercy and are actually afraid to complain, & in fact they seem not to know who to appeal to. I am sorry to say also that even the soldiers are disgracing their profession by a wholesale destruction and waste of property of Union men. Of this complaint should be made to Genl. Rosecrans. But on the subject of home guards or even twelve months men I hope you will not call such into service nor authorize their formation until the Regiments being formed for three years are more nearly completed. I have the arrangements made that promise a speedy completion of my Regiment in any event; and only have written so much on this subject as I deemed necessary to give notice to you as Governor of the state, of the condition of things here in East Tennessee knowing that you take great interest in the welfare of this people. The facts are that Union men are being forced now to leave homes where but a few days ago they had plenty, and go North to get subsistence for themselves and families— You will see them passing through Nashville and they will endorse my statement that they are forced to this, not by the rebels, but by the wanton waste and destruction of our own soldiers & camp followers, and irresponsible pretended home guards. If we do not protect loyal men it were as well to have left them in Rebel hands & gone down to Alabama after niggers & cotton.

These are stubborn facts and as an american citizen on behalf of other loyal American citizens, entitled to protection of law and order I make it known to you; hoping that you will take pleasure in extending protection to them.

I am very Respy your friend
R. M. Edwards

ALS, DLC-JP.

1. In anticipation of a move upon Knoxville, Gen. George Morgan had a surplus of arms for "six additional regiments of Patriotic Tennesseans." Although no order authorizing him to do so has been uncovered, it is more than likely that Morgan did distribute arms to the Kentucky Home Guard, among many Union elements. Large numbers of refugees were passing through and Morgan had asked for instructions in regard to "troops taken from other States, formerly officers and soldiers of the Home Guard and rebel army" who desired to take the oath of allegiance. *OR,* Ser 1, XVI, Pt. I, 1001, 1010, Pt. II, 81.

2. In the wake of the Federal evacuation of Cumberland Gap and retreat to the Ohio River, Kentucky home guard units, usually at a disadvantage, contested the invaders in a number of counties, including Knox, Carter, Clinton, Henry, and Bracken. Because of the lack of records, it is difficult to determine the extent of citizens' being "indiscrimately" murdered. Richard Collins, *History of Kentucky* (2 vols., Covington, 1874), I, 112-13; Louisville *Journal,* September 27, 29, October 6, 1862.

3. Calvin Brixey (*c*1839-*c*1864), Coffee County "Artist," served for a time in Co. C, 16th Tenn. Inf., CSA, before deserting and returning to his home area to become an infamous bushwhacker, preying alike on Union and rebel sympathizers. Transferring his nominal loyalty to the Union and becoming 2nd lieutenant and later captain, Co. D, 1st Ala. and Tenn. Vedette Cav., USA, Brixey during the last part of 1863 and the first months of 1864, continued his depredations in Grundy and adjacent southern Tennessee counties. In January his company was reported to be "without discipline and a lawless set of men," which had been "plundering families whose loyalty is undoubted." Six months later Governor Johnson ordered him arrested and sent to Nashville "for trial for his long continued offences," but within a few weeks he obtained his release and began recruiting another company. Captured by Wheeler's cavalry near Dechard in early September, he was presumably executed. The other captain has not been identified, although in the spring of 1864 two more officers of the Vedette Cavalry, a Captain Hampton and Lt. C. B. Ainsworth, had been arrested for "playing Guerrilla." 1860 Census, Tenn., Coffee, Manchester, 100; *Tennesseans in the Civil War,* II, 56; CSR, RG94, NA; J. W. Brixey to Johnson, September 27, 1864, Johnson Papers, LC; Sistler, *1890 Tenn. Veterans Census,* 35; C. B. Ainsworth to Johnson, July 5, September 6, 1864, Johnson Papers, LC.

4. Desertion, a constant problem with Civil War armies, was particularly troublesome for the Confederacy. Bragg, reported by the northern press to be "fiercely hated by his Kentucky and Tennessee soldiers" and to hold his army together "almost wholly by the terror his name inspires," daily lost men. Although there is no documentation, it seems plausible that since Brixey was himself a deserter, he would attract others of like stripe to his band, especially inasmuch as he operated on the Cumberland plateau, an area with many places of concealment. Nashville *Union,* August 15, 1863.

From J. Wilson Johnston[1]

Office of United States Depositary.
Cincinnati, Sep 30 1863

Hon Andrew Johnson
Nashville Ten.
Sir

I telegraphed you yesterday[2] of the sale of your gold which I effected at full rates (40¢)[.] The reports today indicate a temporary flurry in the New York Market but the price seems to be receding to the old Mark[.]

I regret to say that the coin counts out Ten dollars short. Mr. Carson is not at home and the writer knows but little of the circumstances connected with the deposit, the bag was sealed and the seal unbroken[.]

Very Respectfully
E. T. Carson U S Depy
by J Wilson Johnston

ALS, DLC-JP.

1. J. Wilson Johnston (*c*1818-*fl*1881), Pennsylvania-born bookkeeper with $500 personal property and currently deputy surveyor of customs, was after the war a member of George L. Johnston & Co., "Forwarding Merchants and Steamboat Agents," and secretary of the Commercial Insurance Company of Cincinnati. 1860 Census, Ohio, Hamilton, Cincinnati, East Half 15th Ward, 39; Cincinnati city directories (1862-66, 1869-81), *passim.*

2. Johnston had wired two days earlier that he did not "know anything about the Gold," but would telegraph Enoch Carson in New York. On the thirtieth Carson notified the governor that he had "sold gold at forty." It is interesting to observe that this was a good price when compared with the year's low of 23½¢ reached in July; however, had he waited two weeks the rate would have been 54¢. Johnston to Johnson, September 28; Carson to Johnson, September 30, 1863, Johnson Papers, LC; Albert S. Bolles, *Financial History of the United States, from 1861 to 1885* (New York, 1894), 141n.

From Edward A. Thomas and James W. Shaw[1]

College Green Barracks[2]
Annapolis Maryland
September 30, 1863

Hon. Andrew J Johnson
Governor of Tennessee
Sir

Owing to the peculiar and distressing condition of the citizens, whose names you will find here enclosed and a promise made, while prisoners with them on Bell Isle,[3] at Richmond Va. Will be our excuse for troubling you with this Letter.

These *Gentlemen* have been prisoners over *Eighteen Months,* confined most of the time in the *Libby* and *Castle Thunder.*[4]

A few weeks ago they were removed to Bell Isle, which gave them strong hopes of soon being exchanged; Such hopes have proved but vain illusions. Squad after squad has been paroled and sent through, They instead of being paroled, Have been ordered back into camp, "And told to *Lie there until they Rotted*" Being nothing but G-D-n Tennesseeans[.]

It is their desire that you as their Governor, bring their situation before the U. S. Government, feeling assured that the government will not allow them to suffer when once aware of their unhappy condition.

Tennessee and her *Governor* may well *be proud* of the band of Patriots that are to night suffering on Bell Island. Notwithstanding their long imprisonment and presant suffering condition; not a word derogatery to the Government is ever heard to escape them. On the contrary it is the *Union,* forever *one* and *inseparable.*

They have repeatly refused offers of Liberty, when based on the condition of returning to their homes and remaining *Neutral.* They have preferred impisonment rather than to falter in their allegiance to what they call (and rightly too) the best Government the sun ever shone upon. The Rebels may well desire the death of such men for they are to be feared in a righteous cause[.]

Now Governor being well acquainted with your well known energy of purpose in all that appertains to Tennessee and her citizens, we feel assured that these men will through your influence obtain a successful hearing, and the Goverment will give them that protection that [is] due to all such patriotic men[.]

We remain with respect Your Obedient Servants
Ed A. Thomas, Sergt. Maj 2 Reg
Jas W. Shaw Ord Sergt 34 Reg O

List of Prisoners on Bell Isle.
Tennesseeanes

Mr.	Gilbert Woolsey,	Co.	F.	2nd	Reg	Tenn.
"	D. H. Kelley	"	"	"	"	"
"	A. H. Kelley	"	"	"	"	"
"	R. B. Darling	"	"	"	"	"
"	W. R. Triplet	"	"	"	"	"
"	J. H. Cogburn	"	"	"	"	"
"	Wm. Keller	"	"	"	"	"
"	A English	"	"	"	"	"
"	L. McGee	"	"	"	"	"
"	N. B. Galligain	"	"	"	"	"
"	J. C. Hicks			3rd	Reg	Tenn.
"	J. C. Guy			"	"	
"	D Lidger			"	"	

ALS (Thomas?), DLC-JP.

1. Edward A. Thomas (b. *c*1834), an 1861 three months volunteer in Co. E, 18th Ohio Inf., who mustered out in August of that year, would appear to have reenlisted, although his service record does not show it. James W. Shaw (*c*1838-1893), a carpenter mustered in as sergeant, Co. I, 34th Ohio Inf., in 1861, was captured in July, 1863, confined in Richmond, and paroled in September. Discharged the following year, he reenlisted in Co.

G, 78th Ohio; after the war he lived in Ohio and Dakota Territory. CSR, RG94, NA; Pension file (Shaw), RG 15, NA.

2. College Green Barracks was one of three "camps of instruction" where Union soldiers paroled from southern prisons spent time before returning to their homes or other military duties.

3. Belle Isle, in the James River, served as a Confederate prison camp for enlisted men and was occupied continuously after First Bull Run. In 1864, after the prison became the target of several cavalry raids and a burden on the city's food supply, the inmates were transferred to Andersonville, Georgia. Hesseltine, *Civil War Prisons,* 114, 129-32; Boatner, *Civil War Dictionary,* 57.

4. Constructed in 1845 by Luther Libby, a ship chandler, the structure known as Libby Prison had been a grocery and tobacco warehouse before the war. It housed Union officers until May, 1864, when most inmates were transferred to Macon, Georgia, serving thereafter as a temporary shelter. At the fall of Richmond it became a prison for captured Confederates, subsequently reverting to use as a warehouse. Bought in 1887 by Chicago businessmen, it was dismantled, shipped by rail, and reconstructed to house a Civil War museum—a project roundly criticized by those who believed that renewed attention to the prison could not but rekindle old atrocity stories better left forgotten. Opening in September, 1889, the museum became a profitable attraction during the 1893 World's Fair. Although torn down six years later, much of Libby was perpetuated—some of its bricks, together with the doors and shutters—forming one wall of the Chicago Historical Society's Civil War room, and its timbers—some with initials and names carved by prisoners—appropriated for a large cattle barn built by state senator Charles Danielson in LaPorte County, Indiana. Although two Confederate prisons, one at Petersburg and the other at Richmond, were called Castle Thunder, this reference patently is to the latter, also a converted tobacco warehouse, which frequently held political prisoners, spies, and criminals charged with treason. It had an unsavory reputation; after the war Captain George W. Alexander, one of its commanders, was accused of harshness, inhumanity, tyranny, and dishonesty. Subsequently it housed Confederates charged with war crimes. *Ibid.,* 131, 483; Hesseltine, *Civil War Prisons,* 246-47; Frank L. Byrne, "Libby Prison: A Study in Emotions," *Journal of Southern History,* XXIV (1958), 441-43; Chicago Historical Society, Reference Report on Libby Prison, n. d.; Chicago *Tribune,* January 8, 1899; January 3, 4, 5, 1954.

From William P. Jones

October, [1863], Nashville; ALS, DLC-JP.

Attending physician of Tennessee Hospital for the Insane, concerned about "pitiable condition" of the inmates for whom he has tried to get "clothes, bedding, Etc.," asks that Johnson discharge him from responsibility, if "relief Cannot be brought speedily to the patients."

From William F. Sturm[1]

Kirkland Clinton Co. Indiana
[October, 1863]

Gov Johnson—
Dr Sir—.

I take the privilege of writing you a line, hoping that I may-not tax your patience, last oct one year since I was conscripted in E Tenn together with 65 others who had formed ourselves into a combination to cross the mountains, so that we might be armed & help to rescue our Eastern portion of the state from the Tyranical despotism that then rigned, but we were betrayed & guarded from there to Vicksburg Miss. though formed as we were into a Regiment. at Black River Bridge[2] 30 of the Company surrendered on the field and most of them joined the Federal service, the ballance were Payrorolled & returned to E Tenn[.]

Not one of the Company are now in the Confederate service nor will be during the war again. It was with difficulty that I reached home being accused of having acted treacherous to-wards the land that gave me birth. after reaching home, a Gurilla squad was sent after me and I got out of our town Rogersville Hawkins County with nothing but my person. My friends there or those at Knoxville who had fled there for safety advised me to stay away until the country would be free from raids & maroding bands. I had a letter of Recommendation from A. A. Kyle[3] of Hawkins— and Judge David T. Patterson to you, but was overhauled by a Drinking Scouting party and my Carpet-Bag was opened, & Coat taken out in which I had my letters of introduction together with a small amount of mony. My object now is to try & get some employment that will pay my expenses, until the above mentioned time arrives[.] if you can introduce me into such a channel it will be greatfully received, I would cheerfully go into the army but should I be captured at any time by confederate or Rebel forces, I would-not be treated as a prisner of war having done all within my power to weaken their forces before I was conscripted & afterwards, before the war my buisness was merchandising & was ample— hoping to hear from you at an early day I am

Very respectfully Wm. F. Sturm
Kirklin Clinton co Ind—

ALS, DLC-JP.

1. William F. Sturm (*c*1832-*fl*1880), Rogersville merchant and captain, Co. B 61st Tenn. Inf., CSA (September, 1862-July, 1863), was paroled at Vicksburg; after the war he was a dry goods merchant and farmer. 1860 Census, Tenn., Hawkins, 10th Dist., Rogersville, 6; (1870), 10th Dist., 5; (1880), 8th Dist., 19; CSR, RG109, NA.

2. During the night of May 16, 1863, after the defeat at Champion's Hill, most of Gen. John C. Pemberton's army retreated toward Vicksburg via the railroad bridge over the Big Black River west of Edwards. A 4000-man rear guard was posted east of the bridge to await the arrival of a missing division. Early on the 17th Grant opened fire on the entrenched Confederates, who retired in disorder, burning the bridge and losing 1,700 prisoners. "In this precipitate retreat," reported Pemberton, "but little order was observed": many swam the river, some drowned, "and others too timid to expose themselves to the fire of the enemy by an effort to escape, remained in the trenches and were made prisoners." Sturm and his fellows appear to have been among the latter. *OR*, Ser. 1, XXIV, Pt. I, 267-68; Boatner, *Civil War Dictionary*, 876; Long, *Civil War Almanac*, 354; Lindsley, *Military Annals*, 575.

3. Absalom A. Kyle (1818-1885), Hawkins County native and lawyer with $12,000 real and $10,000 personal property, was attorney general of the 1st judicial circuit (1847-53) and a member of the 1861 Greeneville Union convention. Quietly remaining in Rogersville until 1863, when he passed through the lines to practice law in Knoxville, he subsequently served as the U. S. direct tax commissioner for Tennessee (1866), as a Democratic elector in 1868, and as a member of the 1870 constitutional convention. 1860 Census, Tenn., Hawkins, 10th Dist., 2; Speer, *Prominent Tennesseans*, 431-32.

To James W. M. Grayson[1]

[October, 1863]

Col J W. Grayson
Knoxville Tennessee

I hope you will succeed in filling up the Regiment—[2] I cannot tell at this moment when I will be in Knoxville, but will be there as soon as it is practicable— Have any of the 4th Regiment captured at McMinnville[3] reached Knoxville yet— The parol will not be regarded as valid and the men should be organized at once—[4]

Is Judge Patterson in Knoxville— I received a dispatch from him on the 3d— I have sent two Telegrams to him since: but can get no answer— Judge Gaut[5] is here and is exceedingly anxious to send word to his family of his whereabouts— They live in Cleveland— Have word sent if it can be done—

Andrew Johnson

ALS draft, DLC-JP.

1. James W. M. Grayson (*c*1832-*c*1900), North Carolina-born Johnson County farmer with $3,725 real and $2,919 personal property, was lieutenant colonel, 4th Tenn. Inf., USA (1862-63). Relieved by Johnson in September, 1863, he was on recruiting duty before becoming major, 13th Tenn. Cav., from which he resigned the following April because of ill health. After the war he served a term in the legislature (1867-69) before moving to Grayson, North Carolina. 1860 Census, Tenn., Johnson, 9th Dist., 162; McBride and Robison, *Biographical Directory,* II, 353-54; Grayson to Johnson, October 9, 21, 1863, Johnson Papers, LC; *Tenn. Adj. Gen. Report* (1866), 75, 606.

2. It appears that Grayson was still recruiting for the 4th Tenn. Inf; on October 13 he telegraphed, "I have completed the old regiment with its quota of Companies." Grayson to Johnson, October 13, 1863, Johnson Papers, LC.

3. On September 9, 1863, the 4th Tenn., under the immediate command of Maj. Michael L. Patterson, marched to McMinnville, where, on October 3, after a two-hour fight with a large force of Confederate cavalry under Gen. Joseph Wheeler, it was captured and paroled. Patterson reported his total force at 270 men and 50 armed convalescents; he had lost 7 killed and 31 wounded or missing prior to the surrender. He and Capt. Thomas H. Reeves went to Nashville with forty men, while most of the remainder returned to their homes in East Tennessee, thus completely breaking up the regiment for the time being. *Tenn. Adj. Gen. Report* (1866), 98; *Tennesseans in the Civil War,* I, 383.

4. According to Rosecrans, the parole did not conform to General Order No. 207 (July 3, 1863): "all captures must be reduced to actual possession and all prisoners of war must be delivered at the places designated"; the "only exception allowed is the case of commanders of two opposing armies who are authorized to exchange prisoners or to release them on parole at other points mutually agreed upon." Neither Patterson nor Wheeler were commanders of opposing armies. Patterson was sent to Camp Nelson to reorganize his regiment. James A. Garfield to Johnson, October 12, 1863, Dept. & Div. Tenn. Book Records, RG393, NA; Hesseltine, *Civil War Prisons,* 99; *Tenn. Adj. Gen Report* (1866), 98.

5. For John C. Gaut, judge of the 4th Circuit Court, see *Johnson Papers,* II, 377*n*.

From Marius C. C. Church[1]

Corner of La fayette Place & 4th
New York Oct. 1 1863.

Hon Andrew Johnson
Dear Sir

It has been my purpose to write you now for some time, not only to express my sympathy with your recently expressed views in regard to the present duty of Tennessee,[2] but also to express to you Some plans of my own which you may be interested to know.

It is my purpose as soon as I can complete some business arrangements, and there seems to be an opening in Nashville for such an enterprize, to establish a paper there, the object of which will be to advocate those great cardinal principles first enunciated in the Declaration of Independence and afterwards elaborated by Jefferson, Jackson and that host of American patriots, not excluding yourself, who have labored for Liberty, and the Common Rights of Man. This first and primary.

Secondly. To advocate those measurers of *reconstruction* which must sooner or later in order to bring about a proper adjustment of relations, be adopted for the Common good, both of the white and black races.

If I can complete my arrangements, I shall have ample means to sustain such an enterprize, independent of any patronage it may receive at the hands of its friends— In this way it can be preserved in independence, and carry out the objects in which we feel a common interest. Of course as long as you hold your present representative position, your claims will be appreciated; and this independent of private relations or personal friendship.

My former connection with the press of Nashville, coupled with the experience I have obtained in a sojourn of five years in the North, in which I have been silently maturing my purposes, and fitting myself for this arduous and heavy responsibility, is some guaranty that I may not prove impracticable in what, if this is favorably received, I have to unfold in the future—

If I come it will not be to ask favors of any kind. I shall have sufficient means for my purposes. I shall stand in the freedom which God gives me and utter whatever of Truth, the times may demand— You need no word of commendation from me— Your own conscience bears you witness that nothing but true service to the best interests of *man, as man,* can yield permanent success. It is time the people should know the Truth on all questions affecting their interests; and that you will be faithful to this call, I believe and trust—

I am desirous of calling upon President Lincoln, when I go to Washington, which will be in the course of a week or ten days, and if it not asking too much, I would be glad to have a letter of introduction from yourself—[3] Please address me as above—

Very Truly Yours
M. C. C. Church.

P. S. It is proper to say that my acquaintance with men of the finer writing ability in the North, will enable me to bring together a corp of co-operative talent sufficient for all the purposes had in view. Your own experience has taught you the importance of preserving a press free in the expression of its thought— such will be my purpose if I can succeed in carrying out my plans—

ALS, DLC-JP.

1. Marius C. C. Church (1827-*fl*1880), native Tennessean and part owner of the Nashville *Union* during the 1850's, was a War Democrat and served as a correspondent of the New York *Tribune* during the war. He was not successful in his effort to establish the independent journal he envisioned. Subsequently moving to Parkersburg, he was a "transporter of oils" and also edited the *West Virginia State Journal*. In 1872, as chairman of the state Liberal Republican party, he represented West Virginia on the national committee. 1880 Census, W. Va., Wood, Parkersburg, 1st Dist., 40; Clayton, *Davidson County,* 239-40; Paul D. Casdorph, "The 1872 Liberal Republican Campaign in West Virginia," *West Virginia History,* XXIX (1967/68), 295-96, 298.

2. In an August speech Johnson had declared in favor of immediate emancipation in Tennessee. Speech at Nashville, August 29, 1863.

3. No such letter appears in the President's papers.

From Alvin Hawkins[1]

Paducah Ky Oct 1st 1863

Hon Andrew Johnson
Dear Sir

You are aware of the fact that the Loyal men of Carroll & Henderson Counties have volunteered, liberally to fight the battles of the union[.] Fathers and mothers gave up their sons wives their husbands and children their Fathers—for the sake of protection under the flag of the union and the Government of their Fathers,— For months the West Te soldiers in the union army have been guarding the Memphis & Charleston Rail Road and protecting the *persons, families* & *property* of Rebel sympathizers,—while their own homes, their own families and every thing they possessed have been exposed to the Ravages of Rebel Guerrillas and even now the homes of many of them have been plundered & made desolate, their families have been Robbed of every means of support—and still the work of desolation goes on,— again these marauding bands are not only engaged in the work of pillage,—they are enforcing the Rebel conscription, a few days ago a Rebel force crossed the Te River above Reynoldsburg with about 600 conscripts— a Federal force went from here after them but of course the Rebels were advised of the movement in time to escape but no sooner had the union forces turned back, than the Rebels were in their Rear, stealing, Robing & conscripting—and are again scattered all over that portion of Tennessee, engaged in their hellish work of Desolation & Ruin,—

Although it may seem strange tis nevertheless true that notwithstanding the union army has undisputed possession of that Country the Rebels & Rebel sympathizers are more secure and enjoy more protection there than the Loyal men,—or the families and property of union soldiers— Federal scouts from a distance can do no good,— The Rebels always apprised of the approach will hide untill the scout has passed,—and then they come from their hideing places and resume their *fiendish work* such as *plundering* the *families* of *union Soldiers chasing, Running down* & *catching union men with Blood hounds*— I do assure you that unless Relief can be given to that country soon, there will be nothing left worth living there for, tis even now a perfect Hell for the Loyal people there,— The *aged Fathers* and *Mothers, little Brothers* and *sisters,* the *wives* and *children* of *union soldiers will be reduced to beggary* and *compeled to flee the country for Bread*— But this can be prevented—only in my opinion in one way. Let a Regiment of Federal soldiers be stationed somewhere in that vicinity,— The Tennessee River is navigable at all seasons of the year to Rockport opposite the mouth of Duck River,—and a force stationed there will give protection, to Henderson & Carroll[.] something of this sort must be done speedily or our country is ruined—and I write to invoke your influence in *saveing* the *Loyal people* of that section,—

I am also well satisfied that if a force be stationed in that section for a while,—one or two more Regiments of union soldiers can and will be raised in West Tennessee[.] I know a sufficient force can be raised to protect all that portion of the state from the depredations of Guerrilla bands, and untill that be done it is idle to talk about reorganizing the state Government—or reestablishing civil authority,—Dont these Rebel Guerrillas know their "occupation is gone" when civil authority is reestablished, and a hadful of armed men in each county will be sufficient to prevent the people from doing any thing in that way— *The People* are clamorous for a restoration of Civil Law, the Reopening of the Court &c.

I would be glad to hear from you upon these subjects at your earliest convenience, address me at this place "care B. G. Brazelton Esq,—[2]

I am most respectfully
Your obt Servt—
Alvin Hawkins

ALS, DLC-JP.

1. For Hawkins, Carroll County lawyer, see *Johnson Papers,* V, 185*n*.
2. Not identified.

Whereas, A portion of the People of Tennessee are engaged in open Rebellion against the Government of the United States, and have resorted to any and all means for the overthrow of the same: such, for instance, as organizing themselves into marauding gangs of Freebooters, commonly denominated Guerrillas; AND, WHEREAS, life, liberty and property have been rendered insecure wherever they have been formed. NOW, THEREFORE,

Mathew J. J. Cagle

of Dickson County, is hereby authorized to **RECRUIT AND ORGANIZE A COMPANY OF MOUNTED MEN,** to be denominated UNION GUARDS, the object of which shall be to operate offensively and defensively in the suppression of the Rebellion, and all freebooting and marauding combinations, which have been, or may hereafter be, formed in this State.

This company, when organized, shall be mustered into the service of the State of Tennessee and of the United States, and shall continue in service for a period of Twelve Months, unless sooner discharged, and be subject to the Rules and Articles of War as prescribed by the Government of the United States, and shall be entitled to the same Pay, Rations, Clothing, &c., that is now paid per month by the United States for the Volunteer Service, and shall be under the control and direction, while in the service of the State, of Andrew Johnson, Military Governor, or his successors in office.

This Company, when formed, will be reported, officers and men, in full, to this office, when its organization will be perfected.

Given under my hand at the Executive Office,
at Nashville, Tenn., this First day of
October, 1863.

Edward H East
Secretary of State

Andrew Johnson
Mil Gov

Commission to raise Union Guards.
Courtesy Library of Congress.

To William S. Rosecrans

Nashville, Tenn.,
October 1, 1863

Major-General Rosecrans:

John Kelly[1] is hereby authorized to raise a company of mounted men to serve for twelve months,[2] which you will have mustered into service when organized upon the conditions which have this day been forwarded by mail.[3] Is there anything that I can do in your rear that will promote the interests of the Army of the Cumberland? If so, say what it is. The holding of your recent position is looked upon as a great victory and the nation will appreciate.[4]

Is there any service that General Gillem or myself can render you by being there in person?

We are making all possible progress with the Northwest railroad. We now realize its value to your army in the present crisis more than ever.

Andrew Johnson,
Military Governor.

OR, Ser. 1, XXX, Pt. IV, 10.

1. John Kelly (b *c*1832), Irish-born resident of Marion County, may be the John Kelly who joined the 12th Tenn. Cav., USA, as a sergeant (October 5, 1863) and served on detached service at Nashville before deserting on April 29, 1864. 1860 Census, Tenn., Marion, 12th Dist., 122; CSR, RG94, NA.

2. Four days earlier, in what must surely be a somewhat unusual action for a commanding general, Rosecrans had interceded for Kelly, wiring: "John Kelly, of Sequatchie Valley, desires to raise a company of mounted men for twelve months. Please send authority to organize and I will have it mustered into service." Rosecrans to Johnson, September 27, 1863, *OR,* Ser. 1, XXX, Pt. III, 892.

3. See Authorization to Recruit Union Guards, September [15?], 1863.

4. A view not shared by the press and high officials in Washington, where Rosecrans was being severely criticized for his failure at Chickamauga; his reputation sank daily, as more details were learned about the battle and his subsequent behavior. Extremely damaging was the fact that, in the belief that all was lost, he had left the field before the fighting stopped. Meanwhile, Undersecretary of War Charles A. Dana was sending Stanton daily and always devastating dispatches about the general. By early October, Lincoln, having lost confidence in Rosecrans, placed all departments and armies in the West under Grant, whom he directed to go to Chattanooga and inspect the situation there. Almost at once, Grant relieved Rosecrans and named George H. Thomas commander of the Army of the Cumberland. Bruce Catton, *Never Call Retreat* (New York, 1965), 251, 257-58; T. Harry Williams, *Lincoln and His Generals* (New York, 1952), 281-82, 284-85; William M. Lamers, *The Edge of Glory: A Biography of General William S. Rosecrans* (New York, 1961), 392.

From J. G. Sams and Horace N. Howland

Decherd Oct 3 1863

To Brig. Genl. A. Johnson Mil. Govr.
Sir.

I have now seventy one men enlisted as state Militia. You will please inform me what I shall do. Could I not put them in Maj. P. Howland Camps at this place & drill? I would like to bring them into a fight with vetran troops. I can draw fifty Horses out of the correll. Will you furnish arms and equipments immediately?

J. G. Sams

P.S. Respectfully approved & recommended.

Capt Sam's Company may be very useful as scouts to accompany our own[.] they having been recruited here are acquainted not only with the country but with many Guerrillas— We have plenty of room for said Company & if consistent would be pleased to have it attached to this command[.]

Horace Howland Maj 3 0 Cavy Comdg

Tel, T-RG21, Adj. Gen's Papers.

To Stephen A. Hurlbut

Nashville, October 3d 1863.

Maj. Genl. S. A. Hurlbut,
Comd'g &c Memphis, Tenn.
General:

I have the honor to acknowledge the receipt of your letter of the 15th Ult'o,[1] for which I tender my sincere thanks.

The flattering prospect of a speedy restoration of law and order in West Tennessee, and the success attending your administration of the Military Department are very gratifying.[2]

I have been for a long time endeavoring to arrange so that I might visit Memphis not only for the purpose of conferring with you as to the best policy to be pursued in the administration of affairs in West Tennessee but in order to give the people of that section, altho' remote from their Capital, a personal assurance that they should receive the same consideration that has been extended to the other Divisions of the State.[3]

So it is, I have not been able to leave here, but hope to visit you very soon. In regard to the organization of Home Guards I have to state that the subject has received my attention and action already had with the view of securing the services of loyal & trustworthy men in the several Counties in putting down home Guerrillas[.] To that end a plan such as the one enclosed[4] has been adopted. Under it, there have already been organized companies in several counties and I think it will be generally received with favor— There is great danger, however, that disloyal persons may become identified with or attached to such organizations with a view to injuring the cause, hence the necessity of confining the authority to organize to men of known character and loyalty willing to assume the responsibility of all that may be entrusted to them—

In the reorganization of the State authority, if practicabl, the Slavery question should be settled in this state definitely—and now in the reconstruction is the time it should be left out and no longer constitute an institution established by law— Practically I look upon the Emancipation of negroes in this state as having taken place, and the main thing now is to what status they shall occupy— This is a question I should like to confer upon with you freely as to how it can be best disposed of— As soon as we can have anything like a fair & full reflection of popular sentiment it should lead either in the election of a Legislature or a convention. This is a point to be maturely considered.

I will be in Memphis soon[5] and will be much gratified to have a free and full conference upon this and all other subjects pertaining to the restoration of the State Governmt.

I am pleased to see your proclamation order remunerating Union men for depredation committed by guerillas out of the property of rebel sympathizers.[6]

Very Truly Yours &cc

I have no doubt you have seen articles published in the memphis Argus in regard to the reorganization of the State—[7] There is an evident design on the part of some to produce a division of the Union party & the basis of that design no doubt is *disloyalty*[.] I would respectfully call your attention to an article taken from the nashville Union of this date a copy of which I enclose you—[8]

L draft, DLC-JP.

1. Hurlbut had written that it was "advisable" that Johnson visit West Tennessee "as soon as practicable"—that the "Country is now in that plastic state that it can readily be moulded into shape fitting for an honorable return into the Union." In addition to the governor's order on the subject of home guards, Hurlbut suggested: "as soon as it becomes apparent that the Enemy have definitely abandoned East & Middle Tennessee it will be advisable to issue Writs of Election for the Legislature to reorganize the State, call a Convention, repeal the slave features of the Constitution & place Tennessee as a free State." Hurlbut to Johnson, September 15, 1863, Johnson Papers, LC.

2. Here Johnson deleted the following sentence: "I most fully concur with you in the general views you present as to the policy to be pursued in the reorganization of the State."

3. The governor crossed out these lines: "They have been most cruelly wronged and oppressed. West Tennessee has been overridden by Guerrilla bands and her people most cruelly wronged & oppressed and it is time that they organ[ized]. The relief that they call for must proceed from themselves. It is they and they only."

4. For Johnson's home guard plan, see Authorization to Recruit Union Guards, September [15?], 1863.

5. Although "indisposition" cancelled this planned trip in September, there is no evidence that the visit was rescheduled or that Johnson travelled to Memphis at any other time during the war. Memphis *Bulletin,* September 5, 1863.

6. Hurlbut's order, dated September 10, directed commanders in Tennessee and Kentucky to "cause reprisals to be made for all violence done to Union men." The assessments, fifty percent over the actual loss, were to be levied "upon the most wealthy and notorious sympathizers with the rebellion." The excess was to be held for the use of Union refugees. *Ibid.*, September 22, 1863.

7. In early September the *Argus* printed two letters from "Amour Patrie," who "occupies a high official position, and is one of the leading men of the State." Arguing that neither national nor state constitution authorized Johnson to exercise civil powers and that only an elected governor could revive the state government by calling new elections, the correspondent claimed that Edmund Cooper had won a gubernatorial election held according to the state constitution in August (actually held in only a few counties and without official writs of election). Other politicians contended that William B. Campbell won it. Nashville *Press*, October 2, 7, 1863; Memphis *Bulletin*, September 15, 1863; Hall, *Military Governor*, 100-101.

8. Johnson apparently finished this letter the day after he began it as the clipping which commented upon the two *Argus* letters came from the October 4 issue of the paper.

From Salmon P. Chase

October 5, 1863, Washington; ALS, DLC-JP.

Introduces Delano T. Smith, "one of the Dist Tax Commissioners for Tennessee," and asks Johnson's "kind counsels," explaining that it "has been thought best that one of the Commissioners should come from without the State" with the "advantage of familiarity with business" in Washington. Inasmuch as the other two must be Tennesseans, hopes "that Gen Rogers and Mr. Wilkins already appointed may prove competent and faithful."

From Daniel Hillman[1]

Clarksville Oct 5 1863

To Gov Andy Johnson

I learn an order is here to press negroes in Dixon Co.[2] I have the Cumberland furnice in my charge as trustee for Kirkman heirs and have her in blast[.][3] If the negroes are taken the furnice has to stop[.] Genl Rosecrans who I spoke to about it advised the alowing in of this furnice and my furnice in Hickman Co[4] which is also going saying he would not need to press them[.] I saw him about it when I last saw you[.] If the furnices are stopped serious loss incur thereby[.] Please answer immediatly[.][5]

Danl Hillman

Tel, T-RG21, Adj. Gen's Papers.

1. Daniel Hillman, Jr. (1807-1885) was a wealthy iron manufacturer with plants in Kentucky, Tennessee, and Alabama. William H. Perrin, *Histories of Counties of Christian and Trigg, Kentucky* (Chicago, 1884), 258; Mt. Olivet Cemetery Records, II, 150.

2. The post commander at Clarksville had been ordered to impress enough slaves from the area to finish the Northwestern Railroad in sixty days. Alvan C. Gillem to A. A. Smith, October 1, 1863, Adj. Gen's Papers, RG21, Tennessee State Library and Archives.

3. The Cumberland furnace, built in the early 1790's by James Robertson in the northern part of Dickson County, had produced the cannon balls used by Jackson at the battle of New Orleans. Florence Kirkman (*c*1844-1905), married to a Federal officer, and her brother Van Leer Kirkman (1849-1911) were the heirs of Anthony W. Van Leer, a subsequent owner and business associate of Hillman. Jill K. Garrett, comp., *Historical Sketches of Dickson County, Tennessee* (Columbia, 1971), 121; Byrd Douglas, *Steam-*

boatin' on the Cumberland (Nashville, 1961), 73, 89; Van Leer Kirkman tombstone inscription, Mt. Olivet Cemetery.

4. The Aetna furnace, opened in 1836 in the southern portion of Hickman, was bought by Hillman and Bellfield Carter around 1848. Late in 1863 Federal troops halted the operation by confiscating the stock and liberating the slave laborers. W. Jerome D. and David L. Spence, *A History of Hickman County, Tennessee* (Nashville, 1900), 302, 310-11.

5. For some reason, possibly a refusal by Johnson to grant the requested exemptions, Cumberland furnace shut down during the latter part of the war. J. P. Drouillard to Clinton B. Fisk, July 16, 1865, Registered Lets. Recd. by Assistant Commissioner for Ky. and Tenn., RG105, NA.

From Alexander McDonald[1]

Mass. School for Idiotic and Feeble Minded Youth,[2]
Boston, October 5th 1863.

Dear Sir,

Before leaving Richmond, where I was confined in the same prison with your Nephew,[3] he supposing I would soon be released, requested that I would on regaining my freedom, write you regarding his condition.

He is confined in an attic room with some fifty or more civilians, mostly men from Kentucky, Tennessee & North Western Virginia; is looking quite as well as one could expect to find a person who had been so long confined. The main causes of complaint among these prisoners is regarding want of out-doors exercise & air, (which is denied them) also want of beds, being compelled to sleep on the floor with only a blanket between them and the boards, and a sameness of diet, no change being made in their food for months.

Mr. J. appeared to be in good spirits but very anxious for his release & wished me to urge that everything possible be done for his liberation.

With kind regards, I remain,

Respectfully Yours, Alex McDonald, M. D.

Direct your reply to
School for Idiots, Boston, Mass.

ALS, DLC-JP.

1. Alexander McDonald, teacher and superintendent of the school, was a physician with the U. S. Sanitary Commission. Captured in June, 1863, he was released from Libby as a noncombatant in September and continued with the commission. After the war he practiced in Boston. Boston city directories (1855-67), *passim; OR,* Ser. 2, VI, 315; William Q. Maxwell, *Lincoln's Fifth Wheel: The Political History of the United States Sanitary Comission* (New York, 1956), 210, 213, 257.

2. Founded by Dr. Samuel Gridley Howe in 1848, the institution opened in South Boston with 13 students; by 1885 it had about 128. *King's Hand Book of Boston* (Cambridge, 1885), 166.

3. Andrew Johnson, Jr.

From Horace Maynard

Cincinnati, Oct. 5, 1863.

Dr. Sir,

We start to-morrow southward— My orders will be to return to Nashville by the way of Chattanooga— I am truly glad you go to Memphis; you can do much by being there & speaking. By the time you return, I trust you will be able to come to East Tennessee & meet the people, at least at Athens, Knoxville & Sevierville. Telegraphic communication is now open to Knoxville & I will communicate with you after I arrive—
From all I can hear, I think your presence in East Tennessee just now would have a happy effect. I hear the same complaints that our people have made in other places, that they have little more protection than rebels— Of course, I do not pretend to guess how much foundation there is for them—

Mrs. Maynard requests compliments—

I am very Truly Yours
Horace Maynard

His Excy. Andrew Johnson

ALS, DLC-JP.

From Nancy L. Avent[1]

Murfreesboro, Oct. 6th. [1863]

Gov Johnson.
Sir.

I appeal to you for Justice. My daughter Mrs S. W. Morgan, left this place last fall, and went South with her husband.[2] She left about $350. worth of common furniture, includeing one cooking stove, for which I paid her. She also sold my daughter Mrs James. P. Childress[3] one carpet, and a box of common table ware, for which she received pay. The policemen here have assessed, with the intention *they say* of confiscation. I do not think it equity to do so. Knowing you to be a gentleman of influence, and judgement, I appeal to you for justice. I am willing to be governed by your decision. Please let me know.

respectfully. Mrs Dr. Avent.

ALS, DLC-JP.

1. Nancy Lytle (1816-*fl*1900), native Tennessean, was married since 1835 to Dr. Benjamin W. Avent, at this time in charge of the Confederate hospital at Kingston, Georgia. WPA, Rutherford Marriage Record, 1804-1837, p. 6; 1900 Census, Tenn., Shelby, 83rd Enum. Dist., 10B; Carleton C. Sims, ed., *A History of Rutherford County* (Murfreesboro, 1947), 136; *OR*, Ser. 1, XXX, Pt. IV, 738.

2. Mary Avent Morgan (*c*1836-*fl*1879) was the daughter of the Benjamin Avents and the niece of Mrs. James K. Polk. Her husband, Samuel W. Morgan (b. *c*1830), entered the army in August, 1861, and rose from a regimental quartermaster (23rd Tenn. Inf.) to

property quartermaster of Hardee's Corps, serving after March, 1863, as quartermaster for Pillow's volunteer and conscript bureau. Deane Porch, *1850 Census, Rutherford County, Tennessee* (Nashville, 1967), 371; *Sholes' Memphis Directory* (1879), 347; Anson and Fanny Nelson, *Memorials of Sarah Childress Polk* (New York, 1892), 176; CSR, RG109, NA.

3. Ellen Childress (1845-*fl*1900) had been widowed the previous year. 1900 Census, Tenn., Shelby, 83rd Enum. Dist., 10B; Speer, *Prominent Tennesseans*, 26-27.

From David W. Knight[1]

Nashville Oct 6th 1863.

To his Excellency
Governor Andrew Johnson,
Sir.

On the 9th of May 1862 you issued your Proclamation regarding the taking and destroying of the property of Union citizens by Guerrillas. Since then I have lost by that class of men five horses, one saddle several bridles and a large quantity of forage and provision which was fed away on my Farm, 12 miles below Nashville in this county and on Cumberland River. I have now proof that the loss of two of my horses and a considerable amount of forage was caused by one M S. Royce[2] then commanding a Guerrilla company as the accompanying proof will show.[3] Royce has now funds sufficient, deposited in the hands of H Eelbeck[4] to more than equal the damages I have sustained by him and I urge as a special request, that you issue the requisite Order, to enforce the payment of these damages, they being at a low estimate four hundred dollars. Royce having caused the taking of the property, I would suggest the payment of a sum equivalent from the above funds referred to if sufficient or any other he may have rather than the enforcement of a collection from the Rebel citizens as your Proclamation declares.

Respectfully D W Knight.

ALS, DLC-JP.

1. Probably David Knight (b. *c*1826), New York native and Davidson County farmer who possessed $500 in real and $1,050 in personal property on the eve of the war and who was a U. S. secret service agent at Murfreesboro in 1863. 1860 Census, Tenn., Davidson, 12th Dist., 33; Proceedings of the Military Commission in the Case of Elisha H. Forsythe, RG153, NA.

2. Moses S. Royce (*c*1825-1873), Episcopalian minister and Vermont native, moved to Greeneville in the 1850's. Later residing at Franklin, he was pastor of St. Paul's Church and bookkeeper of the Tennessee and Alabama Railroad. A member of Captain James W. Starnes' Escort, he was captured and confined in the Nashville penitentiary in 1864. Returning to the ministry he served as rector of Nashville's Church of the Holy Trinity (1869-73) before succumbing to cholera. 1860 Census, Tenn., Williamson, E. Subdiv., 136; Nashville *Republican Banner*, June 10, 1873; *Nashville Bus. Dir.* (1860-61), 250; Clayton, *Davidson County*, 338; *Tennesseans in the Civil War*, II, 351; *OR*, Ser. 2, VII, 19.

3. Ben S. Miles and Churchill Hooper made statements in support of Knight's claims. Miles had been conscripted into Royce's outfit, but when he "learned . . . that he was nothing more than a roving Guerrilla . . . left him." While under Royce's command, Miles was one of three men ordered to take from Knight a gray horse and a mare, the former being either traded or sold to an artillery company at Spring Hill. Hooper "saw the horses but a short time before they were taken and the damages . . . sustained by their loss would be

estimated low at four hundred dollars." Statements of B. S. Miles and Churchill Hooper, October 6, 1863, Johnson Papers, LC.

4. Probably Henry Eelbeck (*c*1795-*fl*1880), North Carolina-born Williamson County coach factory operator with $4,000 real and $8,000 personal property. 1860 Census, Tenn., Williamson, E. Subdiv., 1; (1880), 9th Dist., Franklin, 22.

To George L. Stearns

Nashville, Octo. 6th 1863.

Maj. Geo. L. Stearns,
Ass't Adj't Genl. U. S. Vol's.
Major:

I have just been informed that a Lieutenant, under your direction, visited the rendezvous of colored laborers and took away some three hundred hands (cold.), who had volunteered for present service on the North Western Rail Road.

I addresse this note for the purpose of ascertaining the reason of their being taken away and all the facts connected therewith.[1]

Very Resp'y &c
Andrew Johnson Mil. Gov.

L, DNA-RG393, Dept. of the Cumberland, Div. and Dept. of Tenn., Records of R. D. Mussey and George L. Stearns.

1. In the developing quarrel over the enlistment of Negro soldiers at the expense of the laboring force available for building the railroad, there is no evidence that Stearns responded to the governor's query. Instead, three days later he imperviously, or, if one chooses to interpret it as such, defiantly fired off two letters, the one asking Johnson's approval to establish recruiting stations for colored soldiers at "Fort. Donaldson," Clarksville, Franklin, and Columbia, and the other complaining that a few 30-day labor volunteers had refused to work and asking permission "to have them arrested and sent to the North Western R Rd. for work." It seems unlikely that he expected the latter request to mollify the governor's obvious irritation over his enlistment program. Stearns to Johnson, October 9, 1863 (2 letters), Johnson Papers, LC.

To Abraham Lincoln

Nashville Oct 7th 1863

His Excellency A. Lincoln

Nothing definite from the front.[1] Our hopes are strong that all will come out right. the damage on the R. R. is being rapidly repaired.[2] Telegraph wire will be up tonight. Chattanooga must be held.

Andw. Johnson Mil Gov

Tel, DLC-Lincoln Papers; DNA-RG107, Tels. Recd., President, Vol. 1(1863-64); *OR*, Ser. 1, XXX, Pt. IV, 150.

1. The President had inquired by telegraph earlier that day, "What news have you from Rosecrans army or in that direction beyond Nashville[?]" Lincoln to Johnson, October 7, 1863, Johnson Papers, LC.

2. Gen. Joseph Wheeler's cavalry, after the destruction of Rosecrans' supply train in the Sequatchie Valley and the capture of McMinnville (October 2-3), moved toward Murfreesboro, destroying at least three miles of track and all bridges on the Nashville and Chattanooga Railroad between there and Wartrace, including the one over Stone's River

(October 4-5). The damage had been repaired by the ninth. John W. Dubose, *General Joseph Wheeler and The Army of Tennessee* (New York, 1912), 211; *OR*, Ser. 1, XXX, Pt. II, 724; Pt. IV, 174-75.

To Edwin M. Stanton

Nashville Oct 7 1863

Hon. E M. Stanton:

Arms are much needed to supply the troops that have been raised under your order for the regular service also for a number of companies of union guard which have been organized & are being organized for twelve months & mustered into the service of the U. S. this organization will render great & efficient service in Genl. Rosecrans rear in putting down guerrillas, guarding the Rail Roads & in co-operating with the various military posts[.] Some of the companies are here organized ready to enter the service[.] the arms are here but are withheld without instructions from you to issue[.] if the instructions are given I hope they will be explicit to ordnance officers & Quarter master to furnish the necessary supplies.[1]

Andrew Johnson Mil. Gov.

Tel, DNA-RG107, Tels. Recd., Sec. of War, Vol. 32 (1863-64); *OR*, Ser. 1, XXX, Pt. IV, 150.

1. See Telegram from Edwin M. Stanton, October 8, 1863.

From Ernest M. Bement

New York Head-Quarters,
Andrew Johnson Cavalry,
For Special Service in Eastern Tennessee.
Nashville, October 8th 1863.

Brig: Gen: Andrew Johnson.
Military Governor of Tennessee.

Governor: I beg respectfully to submit the following for your consideration and advice.

I am credibly informed that parties of this city and vicinity—among them "Gen'l" Harding[1]—are holding wood at sixteen dollars per cord, with every prospect of an advance to twenty dollars. Poor people must suffer at such prices for so important and essential a commodity, and something ought to be done—something can be done to lie extortioners on the shelf, and allay the suffering that must come with the winter unless something *is* done.

I have a plan in my head in regard to this matter upon which I crave the privilege of asking your advice, and if it should look feasible to you, I would be very glad of the assistance you could render to enable me to carry it out. I have certainly two objects in view in connection with this subject. I am again out of funds, and am about to begin to run my face[2] once more like a trollop unless dame Fortune deigns to smile on me very speedily. It is plain that I must have employment. Active brains very often get out of order when not in use. It is dangerous to be idle—it is demoralizing, it is unchristianlike.

If I can obtain the requisite permit and a guarantee against impressment, I have the means, the inclination and the will to furnish the people of Nashville with a full supply of wood the approaching winter, and at a reasonable price. I purpose to purchase of loyal citizens wood in the tree, and cut and deliver in the city at a small advance over actual cost, or I would take the property of disloyal parties on appraisal, by and with the consent of the Government. If I can be fortified with the necessary protection, I can command means sufficient to insure the entire success of the proposed enterprise so far as the supply of wood is concerned, and, as I would control the business myself, it might be relied upon as a fixed fact that exorbitant prices would not be entertained.

I do not now see how I can benefit the people—*I being one of them*—more than by successfully carrying out the proposed undertaking. I therefore take the liberty of asking you to aid me with the proper authority—if you can consistently do so. I should prefer to have my wants supplied from Washington: but if that cannot be some one of the lesser lights of the Cumberland would answer the purpose, I presume.

I write this because I cannot get to converse with you as I would like.

I have the honor to be, Governor,

Very respectfully, Your obt: servant,
Ernest M. Bement

ALS, DLC-JP.

1. William G. Harding.

2. A comparatively recent (1840) slang expression meaning "to depend altogether on one's looks for favors or credit." Used in conjunction with trollop, whether referring to a woman of ill-repute or to Mrs. Frances Trollope, associated with business failure and indebtedness, it conveys clearly the precarious, nay dire, state of the writer's finances. Mathews, *Americanisms*, I, 575.

From George Burroughs

Engineer Depnt. Army of the Cumberland—
Nashville Tenn. Oct. 8th 1863—

Hon. Andrew Johnson—
Military Governor—Tennessee—
Sir

Yrs. of today recd. I have the honor to state for your information that I have in my possession thirty thousand dollars for payment of negro laborers in Engineer Depnt. to April 1st 1863— They will be paid as soon as practicable. I have just arrived from the front with a view to liquidating as far as may be these and other Engineer Claims. I anticipate a surplus from the above thirty thousand dollars with which I propose to pay for negro labor since April 1st to the extent of the surplus. Should additional funds be needed I shall include them in my estimates for Washington— The above payment would have been made before this had decisions requested from Washington as to payment of slaves or owners been given. No definite decision has as yet been sent. The case has however been practically settled by an order from Capt. Merrill[1] Corps of Engrs. (given when Chf. Engr.) directing me to pay the negroes themselves— This order has date of Sept. 1st 1863— Since then until within a few days I have been on active service in the front— I have besides this payment a large amount of other business to attend to— I had the honor in a personal interview in the early part of last July to state to you the above facts as far as developed at that time. I would also respectfully add that the Engr. Depnt. has been in the habit of providing with coffins & of burying negroes dying in camp & (on application) also those employed in the Depnt. who may die in town or vicinity. In many instances coffins have been on application furnished to negroes employed in the Depnt. on the occurrence of deaths in their families— The latter (although hardly an authorized expenditure) was done on account of the circumstances under which the negroes were placed—

I am Very Respectfully Your Obedient Servant—
George Burroughs—
Lieut. Engineers—

ALS, DLC-JP.

1. William E. Merrill (*c*1837-1891), Wisconsin native, graduated from West Point (1859) and was commissioned in the engineers. Serving in Virginia, Tennessee, and Georgia, he reached the regular rank of captain, the volunteer rank of colonel (1st U. S. Veteran Vol. Eng.), and, remaining in the army, eventually became lieutenant colonel. Powell, *Army List,* 479; *West Point Register* (1970), 252.

From Andrew G. Curtin

Pennsylvania, Executive Chamber,
Harrisburg, Pa. October 8th 1863—

My Dear Sir—

Mrs. Holstein[1] a benevolent lady who resides at Gettysburg and who has done much for the relief of our wounded men writes to Mrs. Curtin[2] under date of Sept. 29th, 1863—as follows

In my walks to day around the Camp I chanced to meet in a Rebel tent a nephew of that noble Union man Gov Andrew Johnston of Tenn. his name is James M. Burchett, Co. K. 8th Virginia Regt & his history if you have not previously heard is—briefly this he was caught with 45 others while endeavoring to make his way into our lines and thus forced into the Rebel ranks— his Father[3] lives in Johnson Co Tenn.— his property he says nearly all confiscated. his purpose is to go to Tenn. for that reason he is afraid to take the oath of allegiance fearful that he may lose all and be in still greater danger on returning— he is a good Union man—has lost his left leg above the knee—the left arm disabled permanently, by a shot which passed through the shoulder and the arm, near the joint[.] he can use his hand freely, but has no power to raise the arm— he wishes to go to Philadelphia instead of being sent elsewhere[.]

I thought it proper to advise you in order that something may be done for the young man in case his statements are correct which you will of course know—

I am in the midst of an exciting political contest[4] which occupies every moment of my time or I should like to write you more fully—

I am Very Truly Yours
A. G. Curtin

Governor Andrew Johnston

LS, DLC-JP.

1. Anna Morris Ellis (Mrs. William H.) Holstein (*fl*1892), of Montgomery County, Pennsylvania, was a Civil War nurse and, with her husband, tended sick and wounded on major battlefields in Pennsylvania, Maryland, and Virginia (1862-66), including Gettysburg, where she was matron-in-chief at the hospital until November, 1863. She chronicled her experiences in *Three Years in Field Hospitals in the Army of the Potomac* (Philadelphia, 1867). Linus Brockett, *Women's Work in the Civil War* (Philadelphia, 1867), 251-59; Anna M. Holstein, *Swedish Holsteins in America* (Norristown, Pa., 1892), 113-15.

2. Catherine Wilson (*c*1819-1903), a Pennsylvania native, married Andrew G. Curtin in 1844. New York *Times*, December 8, 1903; *NCAB*, XXIV, 413.

3. The relationship of James Burchett (b. *c*1817), Virginia-born farm laborer with personal property worth $1,000, and his son to the governor has not been established. According to Mrs. Holstein, young Burchett, a "free-spoken Union man," had been intentionally placed by the rebels in the "front ranks," hence his serious wounds. 1860 Census, Tenn., Johnson, 1st Dist., 11; Holstein, *Field Hospitals*, 45.

4. In the election held five days later, Curtin emerged the victor by a margin of 15,325, out of 523,667, votes over his Democratic challenger, George W. Woodward. *American Annual Cyclopaedia* (1863), 739-40.

From Edwin M. Stanton

Washington Oct 8 1863

To Brig Gen Andrew Johnson
Mil Gov

You are hereby authorized to make requisition upon the Ordnance officers and quartermaster at Nashville for arms ammunitions equipments & military supplies for all the white & colored troops raised by you in Tennessee[.] the said officers are hereby directed to fill your requisitions promptly If they have supplies on hand & if not they make application to have them immediately furnished[.] A copy of this telegram will be regarded of [*sic*] formal instructions to the officers to whom it is presented[.] You will please promptly report to this dept any neglect or delay in furnishing supplies[.]

E M Stanton
Secy War

Tel, DLC-JP.

From Wilberforce Nevin

October 10, 1863, Nashville; LS, DLC-JP.

Adjutant on Brig. Gen. Robert S. Granger's staff reports that a Tennessee regiment, "not under orders from these Head Quarters," had been "drawing ordnance and storing it in such a place and manner as to endanger the City." Noting that a guard had been placed over it, he requests "prompt action in the matter."

From Michael L. Patterson[1]

Nashville Tenn. Oct. 12, 1863

Brig Genl. Andrew Johnson
Mil Gov. State of Tenn
Genl.

I have the honor to submit the following report relative to the surrender of the Post of McMinnville Tenn.

In compliance with an order issued by Maj Genl. G. Granger I moved my command from Nashville Tenn on the 9th day of Sept and arrived at McMinnville on Tuesday the 10th Sept. reported to Maj. A. B. Bracket,[2] 5th Iowa Cav. then in Command of the Post.

On Saturday the 26th Sept. Maj Bracket, left the Post under orders as I understand placing myself in command of the Post[.]

Immediately upon assuming command of the Post I made a thorough examination of the town and means of defence in case of an attack.— I found several long Rifle Pits on the East and South west sides of the town at about the distance of ½ mile from the centre or Court House.

They had undoubtedly been prepared for a large force, Brigade or Division. I only having about 400 effective men Infty I could not see that they would be of any use to me, or that I could use them in any way to my advantage whatever with so small a force, as I had 7 different roads to Picket the Q.M. and Commissary Stores to guard as well as a Provost Guard which in all took 130 men daily on duty also a Rail Road Bridge with a Guard of 1 Commissioned officer 1 Sergt and 15 men.

Immediately upon assuming Command of the Post I sent a Telegram to Gov Johnson asking him to send me the 3rd Tenn Cav.— he replied that he could not spare them from Nashville.—[3] On the 28th inst. I Telegraphed to the commander of the Post at Murfreesboro[4] to send me two Hundred (200) Cavalry,— he replied he had no Cavalry to send. On the 30th Sept or 1st. Oct. I Telegraphed Brig Genl R. S. Granger for Cavalry and he replied that he had no Cavalry to send, and for me to impress horses and mount men for scouts being all the time threatened by Guerillas.

On the 2d of Oct. I issued an order and impressed between 40 & 50 horses mounted a like number of men and sent out two scouting parties of 20 men each. One under Lieut Farnsworth[5] on the Sparta Road to go 6 or 7 miles and the other under Lieut Allen[6] on the Pikeville Road to go the same distance[.] both Lieuts reported to me at about 11 o'clock P. M. that they had executed their orders and that there was no enemy in front.

However in the meantime a large number of Citizens came into McMinnville Tenn direct from Sequachie Valley among whom was Judge John C. Gaut of Cleveland Tenn who reported the enemy to have crossed the Tennessee River above Washington[7] in force from 5,000 to 10,000 and moving down the valley. Considering the reports of these citizens reliable I concluded to burn the Q. M. & Commissary Stores and evacuate the place on the morning of the 3rd.

About sun down on the same evening Captain Blackburn[8] with Co "A" Stokes Cav. came in and reported he had just come on the road from Tracy City to McMinnville and stated most positively that there were no enemy in force this side of Tenn. River[.] upon being interrogated he stated the same again & again.— Again at 8 o'clock in the evening Judge Gaut came into my room and I sent for Captain Blackburn and Lieut Heath.[9] Capt. Blackburn could not come but sent Lieut. Heath. Judge Gaut on one side of the table stating that the Rebels had crossed the Tenn River in force,—Lieut Heath upon the other stating most positively that there was no enemy in force on this side of Tenn River and offered to pledge his right arm that there was none.

Deeming it most proper to take the statement of Commissioned officers in preference to that of citizens I came to the conclusion not to burn the Q. M & Commissary Stores but remain quiet and await further information.

On the 29th or 30th inst I ascertained how many men Surgeon S. J. W. Mintzer[10] in charge of Gen'l. Hospt'l. had for duty. I had what old arms were at the post repaired and armed 50 of them and gave them ammunition and on the morning of the fight sent a commissioned officer to take charge of them.— On the morning of the 3rd at 8 o'clock I sent out a scout of 24 men under Lieut Farnsworth on the Pikeville Road with orders to go 10 or 12 miles— Himself and command were cut off and failed to give me any information.

At 10½ o'clock I ordered out Lt. Allen with 20 men on the same Road[.] he had passed my Pickets between ¼ & ½ mile and returned reporting the enemy in force.

I immediately drew up my command consisting of about 270 men together with 50 Convalescents whom I had armed.— This 50 men were ordered to guard two roads leading by the Hospital to the center of Town.

Companies B, D & G. were thrown to the immediate front in the Suburbs of Town. Company "C" ordered to go on the Sparta Road entering town. Co's "E" & "A" were placed so as to guard the Manchester and Woodbury Roads and also held as a reserve in case the enemy should succeed in making their way into the center of town to hold them in check until the whole force could be rallied together when it was my intention to put the men in houses and fight them in that position. While in this position we were attacked by their advance and Skirmished with them 1¼ hours. while skirmishing they moved a heavy force to the right and left of the town surrounding us and put their Artillery in position (8 pieces)[.] They then sent in a Flag of Truce demanding the immediate and unconditional surrender verbaly of the place which I refused and sent the Flag back stating I would not surrender until the demand was properly made and not then until I was compelled to do so.— In about ½ an hour the Flag again returned borne by Col Hodge[11] Com'dg. Ky Brigade, with an order or demand in writing for the immediate and unconditional surrender of the Post with the entire Garrison. I herewith give a copy of the order—

Hd Qrs. in the Field of Maj Genl. Forrests
Forces of Cav. & Arty, Oct. 3rd, 1863

Maj. M. L. Patterson
Commanding at McMinnville
Major,

I have the honor of stating to you that we are here in Force with Four Divisions of Cav. and Arty and demand the immediate and unconditional surrender of the Post of McMinnville with the entire Garrison.

Respectfully Yours &c.
[Signed] Jos. Wheeler
Maj Genl. C S. A

Seeing that I was surrounded by a greatly superior force and the enemies Artilley in position after a conference with a portion of my officers all deeming it useless to contend longer with so large a force and in order to save life and the effusion of blood I surrendered the post asking protection for my officers and men both in person and private property the same being agreed to, we made a formal surrender to Maj Gen Wheeler C. S. A.

I lost 7 men killed and 31 wounded and missing. The enemy admit a loss of 23 killed and about twice that number wounded.

From a personal examination of the defences around and about McMinnville I could not see in what way the rifle pits would be of any service to me with so small a force. neither could I see in what way I could improve the defences of the place.

I have managed this affair to the best of my ability and done what I believed to be best under existing circumstances.[12]

I am General Very Respectfully
Your Obdt Servt M. L. Patterson
Maj 4th Tenn Infty

ALS, DLC-JP.

1. See *Johnson Papers,* III, 388*n*.

2. Alfred B. Brackett (*c*1824-*fl*1881), New Hampshire native, became major in February, 1862, and later raised troops for frontier service (Brackett's Btn., Minn. Cav.), which participated in Gen. Alfred Sully's expedition against the Sioux in 1864. Following the war he lived in St. Paul, serving as a detective and deputy U. S. marshal. 1880 Census, Minn., Ramsey, St. Paul, 10th Enum. Dist., 11; *Official Army Register: Volunteers,* VII,

235, 305; George W. Northrup, "The Information Bureau," *Minnesota History Bulletin,* V (1923), 292; Theodore E. Potter, "Captain Potter's Recollections of Minnesota Experiences," *ibid.,* I (1916), 492; St. Paul city directories (1874-82), *passim.*

3. Late in September Patterson had wired: "There is a considerable quantity of Quartermaster stores and Commissary at this place & am informed by Major Brackett & other Reliable persons that there are guerrillas force in Vicinity[.] Must have Some Cavalry[.] Send Col Pickins Cavalry immediately." Johnson's reply does not appear to be extant. Patterson to Johnson, September 25, 1863, Johnson Papers, LC.

4. Probably William L. Utley (1814-*fl*1879), Massachusetts native, who was a legislator (1850-52, 1860) and adjutant general of Wisconsin (1852, 1861) before becoming colonel, 22nd Wis. Inf. (1862-64). After the war he edited the Racine *Journal* and served as the town postmaster. *OR,* Ser. 1, XXX, Pt. II, 697, 701; Pt. III, 273, 329, 636; *Official Army Register: Volunteers,* VII, 196; Stuart M. Rich, "John E. Holmes: An Early Wisconsin Leader," *Wisconsin Magazine of History,* LVI (Winter, 1972-73), 137; Willeshire Butterfield, *The History of Racine and Kenosha Counties Wisconsin* (Chicago, 1879), 613.

5. Joseph A. Farnsworth (1835-1871), native Tennessean, Greeneville hotelkeeper, and first lieutenant, Co. F, 4th Tenn. Inf., USA (1863-64), was dishonorably discharged the following September, "for absence without leave, conduct unbecoming an officer and a gentleman, and desertion." CSR, RG94, NA; 1860 Census, Tenn., Greene, 10th Dist., 89; Reynolds, *Greene County Cemeteries,* 29.

6. William C. Allen (1837-1918), Greene countian and farmer, was first lieutenant and captain, Co. A, 4th Tenn. Inf., USA (1863-65). *Ibid.,* 320; CSR, RG94, NA; 1880 Census, Tenn., Greene, 17th Dist., 12.

7. Located about forty miles above Chattanooga, Washington was the seat of Rhea County during the nineteenth century.

8. Joseph H. Blackburn (1842-1913), native Tennessean and resident of Liberty, DeKalb County, resigned from the 5th Tenn. Cav., USA, in June, 1864, because of dissatisfaction with the regiment and "partiality of my superior officers." A year later, while lieutenant colonel, 4th Tenn. Mtd. Inf., he cleared the counties of White, Putnam, DeKalb, and Jackson of guerrillas by capturing Champ Ferguson. In August, 1865, Blackburn created a sensation in Nashville by attacking ex-Confederate General Joseph Wheeler with a cane. Subsequently he was a delegate to the 1870 constitutional convention and U. S. marshal for the middle district of Tennessee. CSR, RG94, NA; Will T. Hale, *History of DeKalb County, Tennessee* (Nashville, 1915), 194-96; Nashville *Press and Times,* August 27, 29, September 2, 1865.

9. Probably Philip N. Heath of the 6th Ky. Cav., which was with Colonel McCook's 1st Cavalry during this campaign against Wheeler. Mustered in December 24, 1861, as a 2nd sergeant, Co. E, Heath (b. *c*1837) was promoted to 1st lieutenant in October, 1862, and separated from the service at the end of his three-year enlistment. CSR, RG94, NA; *OR,* Ser. 1, XXX, Pt. II, 675; *Official Army Register: Volunteers,* IV, 1224.

10. St. John W. Mintzer (d. 1894), Philadelphia physician and manufacturer of porcelain teeth, served as surgeon, 26th Pa. Inf. (1861-63) and later of the U. S. Volunteers, with the rank of major (1863-67), returning to Philadelphia to practice medicine. Heitman, *Register,* I, 715; Philadelphia city directories (1861-80), *passim;* Philadelphia *Inquirer,* December 29, 1894.

11. George B. Hodge (1828-1892), native Kentuckian and Annapolis graduate (1845), resigned in 1851 to study law. Kentucky legislator (1859) and Breckinridge elector (1860), he became a Confederate congressman and army officer, spending the majority of his time with the army as acting adjutant general on Breckinridge's staff (1862-63) and as captain and colonel, before commanding cavalry under Generals Preston and Wheeler. Promoted brigadier in August, 1864, he commanded the District of Southwest Mississippi and East Louisiana. After the war he practiced law, was a Greeley elector (1872), and Kentucky state senator (1873-77), before moving to Longwood, Florida. Ezra J. Warner and W. Buck Yearns, *Biographical Register of the Confederate Congress* (Baton Rouge, 1975), 121-22; Louisville *Courier-Journal,* August 15, 1892.

12. On October 20 Gen. Gordon Granger endorsed his copy of Patterson's report: "Orders were given for the evacuation of McMinnville in time to have saved the garrison. The explanation herein given for not obeying it is not satisfactory." *OR,* Ser. 1, XXX, Pt. II, 709.

To William S. Rosecrans

Nashville Tenn Octo. 12th 1863

Maj. Gen'l. W. S. Rosecrans
Chattanooga Tenn
Gen'l.

Will the parole of the 4th Infantry Tennessee Volunteers at McMinnville be regarded as valid— If not, I desire to reorganize the Regiment as soon as possible—[1] most of the parole men were sent in the direction of Sparta, and from there they have gone into East Tennessee— There are some fifty of them at this place.

I think Maj Patterson who was in command at McMinnville, done all that could have been done under the circumstances— He had only four Hundred men, and fought the enemy One hour and a quarter, which were thousands, while his were hundreds, and that too without a single piece of Artillery— Hence, when his exposed condition was known, there was but one opinion and that was, he would be annihilated or captured—unless he was ordered to fall back upon Murfreesboro.

Major Patterson is a worthy man, and a good citizen, and if permitted will do good service yet[.][2]

The Colonel of the Regiment is lying prostrate in a Sick bed, his recovery doubtful—[3] The L't Colonel[4] is now in Eastern Tennessee, raising men to fill out the Regiment, and with your consent, will send the fragment here with Maj Patterson to unite with them in East Tennessee[.]

I have succeeded so far very well in organizing companies to fight guerellas in your rear— Two full companies will be equipped this week at this place— The men have come in from the country where the guerellas are most numerous, and understand how to meet them— There are many others nearly ready to be equipped— We are getting along very well with the North Western Rail Road, especially so, when we consider all that has transpired since its commencement— We have started this morning a full Regiment of Negroes, armed and equipped to the North Western Rail Road, to work and fight. As they passed through the town, they looked and behaved well—[5] The work is going on.

May the protecting arm of a just and almighty God, be suspended over you and your gallant army, and pass you through in triumph, as it did the Children of Israel through the red Sea[.]

Andrew Johnson
Mil. Gov. &'c

Tel copy, DLC-JP; *OR*, Ser. 1, XXX, Pt. IV, 308.

1. Rosecrans' response, over the signature of his chief of staff, was prompt and unequivocal: "The paroles of the McMinnville prisoners are not valid and will not be recognized. The General Commanding desires the men to be reorganized at once." James A. Garfield

to Johnson, October 12, 1863, Tels. Sent, Vol. 63, Dept. of the Cumberland, RG393, NA.

2. Suggesting that Patterson should ask for a court of inquiry concerning the surrender, Garfield guardedly observed: "His case may be all satisfactory. We hope so." At a court of inquiry the next month in Chattanooga, the major was exonerated. *Ibid.*; *OR,* Ser. 1, XXX, Pt. II, 712.

3. Daniel Stover, Johnson's son-in-law, who died in December, 1864.

4. James W. M. Grayson.

5. Circumstantial evidence indicates that this was the 13th [2nd] U. S. Colored Infantry. On October 7, at Nashville, Stearns had "six full companies of the 2nd U. S. Col. Vols . . . of one hundred men each with a lt. Col. and an commissioned officer to each company. If I receive the order for them to move in the morning they will be ready in the following morning." Twelve days later Lt. Col. Theodore Trauernicht reported the 13th encamped on the Northwestern Railroad thirty miles from Nashville. Stearns to William P. Innes, October 7, 1863, Johnson Papers, LC; *OR,* Ser. 1, XXX, Pt. IV, 482.

From James J. Wilson[1]

General Hospital No. 1.
Ward No. 10, Vicksburg Miss.
October 13th 1863.—

To Gov. Andrew Johnson.
Dear and Hon Sir:
It gives me much pleasure to remember you; and know at the head of affairs in my native State. Especially, has it rejoiced me to see the candid, and noble stand; and bearing which you have maintained in our present National difficulties.— It used to be my pleasure to hear you speak in the Towns of Huntingdon and Paris Tenn.
I am a native of Tennessee. Born there, and principally raised in Henry County; in the former neighborhood and Town of Isham G. Harris.

I commenced my career in life, for myself, in the Paris Post Office, where I staid four and a half years; principally, for self improvement, feeling within myself; that perhaps, I was casting "Bread upon the waters which I should find many days hence." After this, I clerked in Stores. And marrying, I alternately farmed and Taught School.— Being poor, and Landless, I moved nearly four years ago to Randolph County in Arkansas to get a home. I got one in the woods. The Presidential Election passed, excitement and tumults began. You Gov, may perhaps remember, that I then, wrote to you at Washington[2] to aid me in getting to be Register of the Land Office at Batesville Ark. Gloom, Terror and Violence became rife in our midst. A few of us held union meetings, untill at length we were compelled to leave our Families and our Homes, to save our selves from Guerrilla assassination. We come out for help soon to return. We could not get it, and I Volunteered as a private in the 31st Mo Regiment. I Have now been from Home fifteen months and fourteen months a Union Soldier with no means of communicating with my Family. My Regiment was in the Chickasaw Charge, and we were in the Arkansas Post fight. On the Greenville Miss. Expedition. Also in the Expedition around from Milliken's Bend La. to Grand Gulf, from thence also through Raymond Miss to Jackson Miss. From Here we marched upon Vicksburg. Here, we were engaged in the siege of this place. And again sent on an expedition to Yazoo City. We returned to Vicksburg. on the return I was exhausted, and was prostrated with Pneumonia and Pleurisy, and afterwards with Flux and Diarrhoea. I have been in the Hospital about four months[.] I am about to be turned into the invalid Corps, and not wishing to go into it, Gov, My Desire is to go right straight to Nashville the Capitol of my native state and under your Direction perform some Clerkship service there. It would be the highest source of gratification to me, to be an amanuensis for you. And Gov, I solicit you to give me some Position as a Clerk in your City or state. If possible some position in your immediate presence, by *Detail* or *Promotion* or into the Post Office Dept. or mail arrangements in which I Have had much Experience or into some Commissary, Sanitary, Quarter Master's Dept. or Hospital Clerk. I am, I think able for any such like Position. But Gov if Possible, and first of all Let me be an Amanuensis for you. I wish to be there under your charge and Tuition.

I refer you to my Col Thos. C. Fletcher,[3] or to any Old Citizen of Paris Tenn. who is not a Rebel. Please answer me soon and Direct to

James J. Wilson,
General Hospital No. 1. Ward No 10.
Vicksburgh Miss.

ALS, DLC-JP.

1. James J. Wilson (*c*1829-1900), Tennessee-born farmer and school teacher who migrated to Randolph County, Arkansas, enlisted as a private, Co. D, 31st Mo. Inf., in August, 1862, and transferred in April, 1864, to Co. I, 23rd Rgt., Veterans Reserve Corps. CSR, RG94, NA; Pension file, RG15, NA.

2. See Letter from James J. Wilson, March 2, 1861, *Johnson Papers,* IV, 352.

3. Thomas C. Fletcher (1827-1899), native Missouri lawyer, was appointed assistant provost marshal with headquarters at St. Louis in 1861, before raising and becoming colonel of the 31st Mo. Inf. the following year. Wounded and captured at Chickasaw Bayou, he was exchanged in May, 1863, and took part in the Vicksburg, Chattanooga, and Atlanta campaigns before illness forced his return to Missouri where he raised two more regiments and was instrumental in thwarting General Price's advance toward St. Louis. Serving two terms as Republican governor (1865-69), he resumed private practice in St. Louis and later in Washington. *DAB,* VI, 468; *NCAB,* XII, 306.

From David T. Patterson

Greenville Tenn Oct 15 1863

To A Johnson

We will leave for Nashville next week[.][1] I will make arrangements to send all of our Negroes forward[.] They are not willing to remain[.] our forces occupy Blontville[.]

David T Patterson

Tel, Johnson Papers, LC.

1. Burnside reportedly furnished Patterson with two ambulances to transport family—himself, Martha, and children, Andrew J. and Mary Belle—to Nashville. Traveling by

way of Louisville, they took the train to Nashville, arriving in November. Speer, *Prominent Tennesseans,* 531.

From James R. Hood

October 16, 1863, Washington; ALS, DLC-JP.

Having recently received through Johnson's "partiality" the appointment as postmaster at Chattanooga, former editor of the *Gazette* asks "whether it is in consonance with your own feelings . . . that I should be the editor of the paper and have charge of the post office." Determined to participate in the reorganization of the state, he queries, "Where else would I go, but to that place where the traitors whom I know have been humbled?"

From William H. Wisener[1]

Shelbyville, Oct 16th 1863.

Governor Andrew Johnson.
Nashville,
Dear Sir:

On yesterday afternoon I received your Telegram of the 12th.[2] inquiring whether I had "declined the office of Tax Commissioner for Tennessee." It came to Lt. Col Galbrath[3] by courier from Wartrace. I immediately answered & handed it to him to be forwarded by Telegraph from Wartrace & to be sent thru, if opportunity offered. My answer was "I have received no official information of my appointment & have therefore neither accepted or declined." [4]

I now write more full upon the subject[.] The only information I have ever received in regard to it except talk of citizens & friends, was a Telegram from Washington published in the Louisville Journal in July 1862— giving the names of persons appointed in the different states. This Telegram read "For Tennessee—O. P. Temple, John B. Rogers[5] & Wm. A. Wisner". Genl Rogers wrote me a few weeks afterwards that I was one. This is all the information I have received. I have therefore had no opportunity of accepting or declining. When in Nashville a few [days] since I heard that Genl Rogers was in Memphis collecting taxes & that he had appointed his son, clerk, of the board.[6] Whether this was correct or not I do not know. Since then I saw in the press that some gentleman from E. T.[7] had been appointed in place of Mr Temple (I supposed) & that Genl John B. Rogers & myself constituted the board, but it was understood that I declined. In a few days afterwards I saw that some gentleman of Washington[8] had been appointed & that the board was full & they would proceed to business. I have received no communication whatever from the department at Washington in regard to it, and the only knowledge I have is what is stated above. It was not my name in the Telegram in the Journal. I do not see how any person can decline before an office is tendered him nor how he can accept either. If I was the person appointed, it was conferred without my knowledge or application & I always thought it would have been indelicate in me to either write to the department accepting or declining until I should receive official information of the apointment & still think so.[9]

Respectfully Your friend
Wm. H. Wisener

ALS, DLC-JP.

1. For Wisener, Shelbyville lawyer, see *Johnson Papers,* IV, 279*n*.

2. Not extant.

3. Robert Galbraith (1836-1881), a Shelbyville merchant, was commissioned captain, 5th Tenn. Cav., in September, 1862, and promoted lieutenant colonel the following February. Resigning in March, 1864, he served in the Tennessee house of representatives (1867-69) and was a bookeeper. 1860 Census, Tenn., Bedford, W. Div., 7th Dist., 1; (1880), 7th Enum. Dist., 36; McBride and Robison, *Biographical Directory,* II, 319; CSR, RG94, NA; Pension file, RG15, NA.

4. Wisener to Johnson, October 15, 1862, Johnson Papers, LC.

5. For John B. Rodgers, Middle Tennessee lawyer, see *Johnson Papers,* V, 201*n*.

6. There is no evidence that one of Rodgers' four sons served in this capacity.

7. N. Wilkins, otherwise unidentified, briefly and unofficially served as commissioner with Rodgers. Memphis *Bulletin,* September 30, 1863.

8. Delano T. Smith, New York-born but Minnesota-appointed chief clerk of the 3rd auditor's office, had been designated. See Letter from Salmon P. Chase, October 5, 1863; *U. S. Official Register* (1863), 24.

9. Three days later Wisener delivered his answer in person, explaining to the governor that his refusal to serve was "not on account of any dissatisfaction with the administration but for other reasons." Johnson, in reporting this to Smith, observed: "I am more thoroughly satisfied than when you were here that new men should be appointed to act with you." Johnson to Smith, October 19, 1863, Salmon P. Chase Papers, LC.

To George L. Stearns

Nashville, Oct 16th 1863.

Major Steans

Dr Carter[1] who lives one the line of the N. W. R wishes to communicate some information to report conduct of some of the Colored troops under the Command of ________ [.] I hope you will give him a hearing in the premises— I hope that steps will be taken to correct the abuse complained and to prevent its future occurance—

I have the honor to most respectfully &—
Andrew Johnson

P. S. I prefer you haing it the correction made—[2]

A J

AL draft, DLC-JP.

1. Probably Dr. William J. Carter (1808-1878), whose family emigrated from North Carolina in 1816. He studied medicine under his brother Bellfield Carter and at Transylvania University, before moving to Cheatham County in 1831. At the time this complaint was lodged, he resided on the Harpeth River near Dog Creek about fifteen miles southwest of the state capital. Clayton, *Davidson County,* 432.

2. In an endorsement of the same date, Stearns replied that he had been apprised of the problem and that "five men were promptly punished for the offence[.]"

From William P. Innes

Office of Superintendent Military Railroad,
Department of the Cumberland,
Nashville, Tenn., 17th Octr 1863

Hon Andrew Johnson
Milty Gov &c,
Governor

I have the honor to request you to give Mr. M. P. Clark[1] an order to dispose of the Contrabands going out this A M. as I have told him that is to put them at work on Sects 29, 30 & 31. May I also request you to give him an order take charge of the 150 Contrabands that were sent out some few days ago and who were retained by order of Lt Col Skully[2] at Sullivans Branch for some reason not known to me—

With respect I am Gov. Your Obd. Sert.
Wm. P Innes Col & Mil Supt

ALS, DLC-JP.

1. Probably Morris P. Clark (*c*1823-*fl*1880), New York-born railroad contractor who moved to Tennessee about 1858 and was now helping with the construction of the Northwestern Railroad; he was also president of the Union League. 1870 Census, Tenn., Davidson, 13th Dist., 105; (1880), 89; Nashville *Press,* July 29, 1863.
2. James W. Scully.

From Arthur A. Smith[1]

Hd. Qr's U. S. Forces
Clarksville Oct. 17, 1863

Brig. Gen. Andrew Johnson
Mil. Gov.
Dr Sir,

Your Telegrams of the 15th & 17th are recd.[2] In regard to "Friendley"[3] it appears that Cagle went to his (F's) house in the night and told F. that he was a leader of a Guirrella band and wished to be piloted to some point where they could cross the River and also the names of Union Men.[4] Friendley appeared very glad to see them, got up and left a sick wife and told them he would take them to a Mr Davis[5] who was in the habbit of doing that kind of business and knew the *ropes* better than he did. he went with them to this man Davis' house[.] on the road he reported all the Union Men in that part of the Country, (Cagle among the rest) and said that he would do anything that he possibly could to assist them, and was sorry that he could do no more. this was done freely and willingly[.] As to J.T. Carney[6] the horse in question had been by his (C's) own admission in the Reble service for several Months. Carney had no permit for the gun and Cagle could not carry it and walk in[.] I had anticipated your instructions to Capt. Cagle. I feared that he might improve this opportunity to pay off old *grudges*. I have been annoyed a good deal by citizens complain'g of Cagle but find *as a rule* that they hate Cagle for the same reasons that the "Jews" hated Christ because he exposed their Sins.

I am not able to report Andrew Bent'ly[.][7]

I am vy Respecty Gen. your obet Sert,[8]
A. A. Smith
Col. Comg. Post

ALS, DLC-JP.

1. Arthur A. Smith (1829-1900), native of Batavia, Ohio, moved to Illinois in 1840, graduated from Knox College thirteen years later, and was admitted to the bar in 1855, practicing in Galesburg and serving in the legislature (1861-62). Lieutenant colonel, later colonel (1863), 83rd Ill., Inf., he commanded the Clarksville district and after the war practiced law briefly there, returning to Galesburg where he became judge of the 10th judicial circuit (1867-94). Galesburg *Daily Republican-Register,* September 22, 1900; Albert J. Perry, *History of Knox County, Illinois* (2 vols., Chicago, 1912), I, 59; John Clayton, *The Illinois Fact Book and Historical Almanac 1673-1968* (Carbondale, 1970), 223-24; Heitman, *Register,* I, 894; Arthur A. Smith to James A. Garfield, January 12, 1881, Garfield Papers, LC.

2. Not found.

3. William D. Frensley (variously Frendsley, Friendsley, Frenzz, Frenasey) (b. *c*1812), Virginia-born farmer, claimed $2,000 real and $1,050 personal property. 1860 Census, Tenn., Cheatham, 1st Dist., 10.

4. Evidently at Johnson's order, Mathew J. J. Cagle, pretending to be a Confederate guerrilla, was engaged in entrapping southern supporters in Cheatham County north of the Cumberland. Case of U. S. v. J. B. Frensley, John Daviss and William D. Frensley, October 22; Smith to Johnson, October 14, 20, 1863, Johnson Papers, LC; for Cagle, former Dickson County refugee, see *Johnson Papers,* IV, 533*n.*

5. John S. Davis (b. *c*1837), Tennessee-born farmer who was Frensley's neighbor. 1860 Census, Tenn., Cheatham, 1st Dist., 10.

6. Possibly J. T. Carney (b. *c*1808), another native Tennessee farmer, with $4,000 real and $8,000 personal property. *Ibid.,* 19.

7. Unidentified.

8. Nine days later Johnson ordered the release of Frensley and Davis provided they subscribed to the oath and gave bond, unless further proof against them could be forwarded to him. By that time Smith possessed sufficient evidence to warrant their being sent to Nashville at the end of the month. That Frensley may have taken advantage of the governor's offer is suggested by a printed form of the oath, found in Series 18 of the Johnson Papers, on which is written "Mr. Frendsley will take the oath before the Provost Marshal, and give bond in the sum of Twenty Five hundred Dollars. November 22, 1863. Andrew Johnson Mil—Gov[.] Form of Oath enclosed that is to be taken[.]" Case of U. S. v. J. B. Frensley, et al, October 22; Johnson to Smith, October 26; J. T. Morgan to Provost Marshal, October 28; Smith to Johnson, October 29, 1863, Johnson Papers, LC.

Remarks at Nashville[1]

[October 17, 1863]

His Excellency greatly interested his large and attentive auditory for more than an hour. He termed it a mere overflowing of his gratitude to the meeting for the attention bestowed and the honors intended, but the audience accepted the thank-offering as a very excellent speech.

In a sentence or two he scattered to the winds the idea that Slavery was necessary to the production of cotton. He had picked cotton in the cotton-fields near Raleigh, North Carolina; and he could pick more cotton than any black boy in the field.[2] It is only necessary to cut up Alabama and Mississippi into moderate sized farms, for industrious men to cultivate with their own hands, and there would not only be an increase of the cotton crop, but the production also of all the bread and meat necessary for those States.

The Governor uttered many interesting and important truths on the aristocracy of wealth, family, and position. He was in favor of an aristocracy of labor; of merit.

He expatiated on the resources of Tennessee—her soil and climate, her mines, minerals and timbers. He invited men of industry and economy to come and settle among them and develop her treasures.[3]

To the question, "What is to be done with the negro?" he uttered an important aphorism worthy a stereotyped position in every newspaper in the land: "In the pursuit of a correct principle you can never come to a wrong conclusion." He left his audience to make the application, simply adding that the "Slavery question will adjust itself, if we pursue the principles of truth and right."

No government can exist that has an institution within it more potent than the government itself. If Slavery is in the way of the harmonious working of the government, it must be destroyed. The train must move on, and Slavery must get out of the way.

Cincinnati *Gazette,* October 21, 1863.

1. Nashville unionists, gathered in the capitol to celebrate recent election victories in Ohio, Pennsylvania, and Iowa, greeted Johnson enthusiastically when he appeared. Before addressing the audience, however, the governor introduced a "Dr. Boyle or Bowan," a planter and "pro Slavery" man, who proceeded to blame the rebellion for the death of the institution. This spare account of the governor's observations was part of a letter sent to his paper by "Granite," the Nashville correspondent of the *Gazette*. Cincinnati *Gazette,* October 21, 1863.

2. Although North Carolina was not a cotton state during Johnson's youth, the staple was beginning to be cultivated; hence it is conceivable that Johnson demonstrated his prowess as claimed. Guion G. Johnson, *Ante-Bellum North Carolina* (Chapel Hill, 1937), 53.

3. This would appear to be the first (but not the last) time the governor had issued such an invitation. Although in the midst of war, he seems to be looking forward to the economic needs of the restored state.

From Wright Rives[1]

Head-Quarters, Eleventh & Twelfth Corps,
Army of the Cumberland.
Stevenson, Ala. Oct. 18th 1863

Sir

I wrote you a letter a few days since[2] in reference to the regt. I now find that I am not able to stand the fatigue of a campaign on account of my leg.[3] I have done but little duty since I have been here, but that little I have done, has caused my leg to swell and be painful. The doctor's forbid me to go to the field, but I could not remain at Pittsburgh and do nothing[.] I am perfectly willing to accept a position in your office, although I will lose rank by it, yet I am willing to do that and have something to do rather than keep my present rank and obtain a sick leave and remain absent. I feel confident that the first two or three days hard work will render me useless. I hope that you will reply by telegraph the day you receive this letter,[4] which will be (Wednesday) for in case that you do not now wish me I shall apply to go east and if not successful in that, will be compelled to resign from necessity[.] Gen. Hooker[5] is willing for me to come. If you consent telegraph to the Secy of War on the receipt of this and also to me. If I do not hear from you by Thursday, I shall consider that I am not needed[.]

Yours in haste
Wright Rives

Care Maj. Gen. Hooker
Stevenson Ala

ALS, DLC-JP.

1. Wright Rives (1838-1916), District of Columbia native and eldest son of Washington editor John C. Rives, graduated from West Point in 1861, was appointed 2nd lieutenant, 6th U. S. Inf., and the following June became captain and aide-de-camp to Gen. John McClernand. Breveted major and lieutenant colonel, March 13, 1865, he retired disabled in December, 1870. Throughout Johnson's presidency Rives served on his staff as assistant military secretary, with special responsibility "to attend all military cases." James R. Childs, *Reliques of the Rives* (Washington, 1929), 387; *West Point Register* (1970), 255; Rives to Johnson, June 10, 1862, and to James B. Jameson, September 6, 1865, Johnson Papers, LC; Exhibit "A," September 3, 1870, File R221-1870, ACP Branch, RG94, NA.

2. Probably his October 12 letter from Stevenson, Alabama, reporting that he had arrived the day before and "found that a telegram had been sent to . . . Nashville stating that there was no objection to my accepting the position" and that "if recommendations as to my fitness are needed I will send them in." Rives was apparently seeking a staff position with Johnson. See also Letter from Wright Rives, June 10, 1862, *Johnson Papers,* V, 463.

3. Subsequent to the winter of 1862-63 when he suffered a severe attack of typhoid fever, Rives was plagued with swelling of his limbs so much so that on the trip from Pittsburgh to Vicksburg during the spring of 1863 he was unable to wear shoes. Exhibit "A," September 3, 1870, File R221-1870, ACP Branch, RG94, NA.

4. Although Rives's commanding officer, McClernand, a week later was urging the governor to appoint him colonel of a Tennessee regiment, there is no record of Johnson's reply. Rives spent the remainder of the war in New York City on the staff of General John A. Dix. *Ibid.;* McClernand to Johnson, October 24, 1863, Johnson Papers, LC.

5. Joseph Hooker (1814-1879), Massachusetts native, West Point graduate (1837), and Mexican War veteran, resigned from the army in 1853 to try farming in Sonoma, California. Recommissioned in August, 1861, as brigadier general of volunteers, he served under several commanders in Virginia, earning the sobriquet "Fighting Joe Hooker." Assuming command of the Army of the Potomac in January, 1863, he lost the battle of Chancellorsville; removed from command on the eve of Gettysburg, he was sent to Tennessee in the fall and participated in the battle on Lookout Mountain. When a subordinate was promoted above him, Hooker asked to be relieved from field service and spent the rest of his career, until retirement in 1868, in various departmental commands. Warner, *Generals in Blue,* 233-35.

From Salmon P. Chase

Treasury Department,
Oct. 19, 1863

Dear Governor,

Thanks for the "Union" with its leader[1] & your autograph of approval.

He who recognizes the lesson of the day and acts on its teachings *bravely* is more than a benefactor of his country—he is a benefactor of the race. History will build the *monumet* which will bear their names; and high up among these future generations will read the name of Andrew Johnson.

Yours truly S P Chase

Hon. Andrew Johnson.

ALS, DLC-JP.

1. Undoubtedly, the "leader" was that of the October 11 issue, in which the *Union,* defending its position that Tennessee is currently too insecure, because of widespread guerrilla activity, to risk restoration of civil government, takes occasion to applaud Johnson's stance "in behalf of freedom and free labor," contrasting his position with that of the "pro-slavery" military governor of Missouri. Nashville *Union,* October 11, 1863.

From Thomas Cotton[1]

Nashville Oct 19th/63

To his Excellency Gov Andrew Johnson

Governor. The bearer Maria[2] Colored woman recently belonging to Wm. Cartright[3] residing about eight miles on the Murfreesboro Pike has represented her case to me as one of peculiar hardship and ill usage.

According to her statement her husband is a colored soldier in the regular service of the government, that while living with in the lines of this post her owner came and managed to steal her child away and convey it to his residence, being desirous of obtaining her clothes, and her other children she trusted the word of a Tennessee soldier who offered for five dollars to convey her safely to the residence of her master, obtain her children and clothing and insure her safe return within the lines, but this was a trap, as she alledges by which for the sum of thirty dollars the soldier or individual so representing himself had agreed to deliver her up to her master, who no sooner had her in his power than he locked her up for four days and inflicted upon her a most cruel beating, the marks of which she now carries on her person. a cruel beating was also inflicted on one of the children whose marks and scars was seen by one of the soldiers of the 129th Ill Reg. she now hopes to obtain from your excellency the necessary authority and help to obtain her clothing and two children. I have no doubt of the entire truthfulness of her statement, and I feel sure Govenor that your well known regard for righteousness and your sympathy for the weak and oppressed will prompt you to do what may be within your power to redress the wrongs of the suppliant who will present you with this humble document.[4]

I am Govenor with much esteem Yours most respectfully
Thos. Cotton
Chaplain 129th Reg Illinois Vols

ALS, DLC-JP.

1. Thomas Cotton (b. *c*1822), native Maine farmer living in Livingston County, Illinois, served as chaplain, 129th Ill. Inf., from September, 1862, until his resignation August 6, 1864. 1860 Census, Ill., Livingston, Broughtonville Township, 292; *Official Army Register: Volunteers,* VI, 395; CSR, RG94, NA.

2. Probably Mary Cartwright (b. *c*1830), a Mississippi-born mulatto who by 1880 was a laundress. 1880 Census, Tenn., Davidson, 5th Dist., 5.

3. William E. Cartwright (*c*1811-*fl*1870), Tennessee farmer with $3,000 real and $11,000 personal property, owned thirteen slaves on the eve of the war. *Ibid.* (1860), 82; *ibid.,* Slave Schedule, 5th dist., 26; (1870), 5th dist., 11.

4. Although the children were brought to the city for Johnson's decision, it is not clear whether they were returned to their mother. R. S. Granger to Johnson, October 27, 1863, Johnson Papers, LC.

Remarks at Nashville[1]

October 20, 1863

He proceeded to speak in warm terms of Gen. Grant's services to the nation, and to welcome him in behalf of the loyal men of Tennessee to his newly assigned field of labor.[2] The deeds of Gen. Grant would compare with those of Napoleon or of Caesar himself and endeared him to the friends of the Union. The Governor here attempted to retire, but the crowd was enthusiastic and hilarious and would not hear to it. They had the Star Spangled Banner fever, and insisted on being talked to; so the Governor proceeded. He dwelt with earnestness on the importance of the present war to the free institutions of the country. Every man present had a deep individual interest in it, for the men who were fighting against the Union were seeking to form a despotic Government, based upon a miserable slave aristocracy; an aristocracy not of virtue, intelligence, art, or refinement, but a degraded, selfish, soulless aristocracy of wealth. This was the motive power of the Southern rebellion, and every man should feel himself personally interested in opposing it. The nation was fighting to place the laws, the Constitution, and our free institutions on a secure basis; it was fighting the sacred battle of human rights against the encroachments of aristocracy. You know that there has been a reign of terror in Tennessee for many years, and people were not allowed to express their sentiments by this arrogant slave power. If a man dared to question its power he was tarred and feathered and rode upon a rail. Slavery could agitate the nation; that was all right; but it was a great offense for the nation to agitate slavery. Thus slavery, a mere species of property, actually set itself up as more powerful than the Government, and ruled it. Now, whatever is prejudicial to the safety of the Government, must go down in this contest. When we come to restore the State Government, and put all the various parts of the machinery together, if we find a part which does not harmonize with the whole let us leave it out. Let us have a Government freed from the element which has ruined its peace.

Some people asked what would become of the negroes if they should all be freed. Without answering this question in detail, he would say that if the principle of free government, on which we planted ourselves, was right, all incidental matters would accomodate themselves to it in the end. We never could go astray if we kept our eyes fixed upon the great principle. First see that the principle be correct, and then all incidental and collateral matters will be disposed of as they arise, in the right manner.[3]

Memphis *Bulletin,* October 30, 1863.

1. When Gen. Ulysses S. Grant, the object of a military serenade at the St. Cloud, "bowed and retired to his room," declining to make a speech—"an art," he declared, "which he was too old to acquire"—the governor responded to the "stentorian call" of a crowd, "in no humor to go home." Memphis *Bulletin,* October 30, 1863.

2. Basking in the glory of his July victory, "the hero of Vicksburg, who has captured more prisoners than any commander of modern times, and fought the most brilliant battles of the present war," had two days earlier at Louisville been placed in command of the armies of the Tennessee, the Ohio, and the Cumberland. *Ibid.;* McKinney, *Education in Violence,* 271.

3. At this juncture the reporter concluded with the observation: "The Governor continued in this strain for some time amid loud applause, and concluded amid calls from the crowd to go on."

From Sam Milligan

Confidential

Greeneville Tenn
Oct 21, 1863—

Dear Governor,

It has been a long time since I had the pleasure of writing to you, and many fearful events have swept over our once peaceful, happy, and prosperous country since I saw you. I have been compelled to bow like the tender osier,[1] before the pittiless storm; but thank God, my faith in the ultimate triumph of *truth,* and the power of the Government, tho. often blind, and without "the evidence of things seen",[2] has not for one moment failed me. I am still here as you left me—tho. broken in my profession, and nearly all my little means of life gone—*an unyielding Union man.* It is true, some of my opinions of the *policy* of the Government have under gone a change. Whether from unbiased convictions, or the stress of circumstances, I can not tell, but I now am convinced, that we can no longer hope for a permanent and prosperous peace, while the institution of slavery exists in a single state of the Federal Union. I am aware this doctrine is not palatable to many of the larger slaveholders even in E. Ten., and it must be much less so to those of middle and west Ten; but who that has studied its history as I have attempted to do since I saw you, from Abraham down even [to] Jeff Davis, can believe it is a permanent institution, and must not one day be abolished? Why not now assist the Almight in causing the wrath of the South to praise him, and at once and forever remove the cause of this horrible war? Our people by this institution are not *homogenious,* and if freedom is the true theory of Government, then individual liberty is the normal condidition of man. The negro will be the greatest sufferer. They like the Indian must was[t]e away, or sink into a state of miserable serfdom, attached to the soil upon which they are found. The white race are and will continue masters of this Country. But all this is better than continued strife.—All better than to tolerate an institution that contests the very power and authority of the Government itself. The one must yield to the other. They can not remain any longer, in my opinion, under the same government. The issue has been made, and an appeal to arms for a decision. It must be ended in permanent seperation, or permanent emancipation. Seperation ruins the North as well as the south, and therefore as the least evil I choose emancipation.

But I can not enlarge on this subject, and will drop it.

Judge Patterson can give you all our ups & downs, and the miserable triggering now going on here.

The campaign in E. Ten. begun well, but it has been bunglingly managed, and there is none of us that feels secure. We have had once to *"fall back",* and how soon that may again occur none of us knows. I am exceedingly anxious to remove my family out of the scene of war, but have nothing absolutely nothing to support them with any where else. I am no applicant for office of any sort, but if you could see any opening where you thought I could for eight or ten months, at any employment, sustain my family in a *safe place* I would take it as a great favor for you to advise me of it.[3] I have so often regretted [cut out] thing I had and go [cut out] that is now too late, [cut out] [spi]lt milk.

Well Johnson, I feel curious even while I write— It seems even yet contraband to mention your name, and I instinctively look round me to see if any Gray-back[4] is not watching me; but I still hope on for even better & brighter days than we now enjoy.

The last two years I have spent in reading & studying the Elementary Law-books, and tracing up the history of slavery, and think I shall write a Book on the latter subject which I will dedicate to *"Bell"* of martial memory near the African Church[.][5]

Tell Bob to write to me a long letter— Send it to Knoxville care of David Baker[6] Depot Agent at Knoxville— My Love to Mrs. Johnson Col Stover & all the family—

Your true friend
[Sam Milligan]

ALS, DLC-JP.

1. A willow whose tough pliant branches are used for basket-weaving. *OED,* VII, 219.

2. A corruption of Heb. 11:1: "Now faith is the substance of things hoped for, the evidence of things not seen."

3. Almost immediately, Johnson recommended Milligan as a direct tax commissioner and within the year would appoint him state supervisor of banks. Johnson to S. P. Chase, November 10, 1863, Appl. and Recomm., Direct Tax Commissioner, Dist. of the State of Tenn., RG58, NA; Nashville *Dispatch,* June 30, 1864.

4. A Confederate.

5. This allusion, apparently reflecting an earlier personally shared experience, has not been uncovered.

6. Probably D. L. Baker (b. *c*1831) who, on the eve of war, was a conductor living in the Lamar House in Knoxville. 1860 Census, Tenn., Knox, 1st Dist., 103.

From Edwin M. Stanton

War Department Washington City,
Oct 21 1863

To the Military Commandant at
Nashville, and to Brigadier General
Andrew Johnson Military Governor of
Tennessee and all other officers
in the Service of the United States.

The dwelling house on Spruce Street in the City of Nashville occupied heretofore by Wm. Berry[1] is hereby seized and appropriated to the Military Service of the United States and assigned for Quarters to Mrs John Harris[2] and such other humane and benevolent ladies as may under her direction be engaged in the care & attention of our wounded and sick soldiers under authority of the War Department, and you are hereby directed to protect and maintain them in the peaceable and undisturbed possession thereof and to prevent any hindrance or annoyance to them in such possession and if need be arrest and remove any person or persons who may interrupt or disturb Said ladies in the quiet & peaceable possession of said premises. All orders & safeguards to secure the possession of said premises to any other person than the ladies herein designated are annulled.

Edwin M Stanton
Secretary of War

Copy, DNA-RG94, Orders and Circulars, 1822-1871.

1. William Berry was a Nashville banker and drug wholesaler, whose Confederate sympathies placed him on Johnson's assessment list. His Franklin Pike residence had been occupied by Buell's army earlier in the war. See *Johnson Papers,* V, 347n.

2. Mrs. John Harris, wife of a physician and secretary of the Ladies Aid Society of Philadelphia, served as a nurse on nearly every major battlefield in Virginia, Maryland, Pennsylvania, and Tennessee. In early October, 1863, with assistants Miss Mary A. Tyson and a Mrs. Beck, she came to Nashville and stayed nearly two months, attending to the needs of refugees, before moving on to Chattanooga. Brockett, *Women's Work in the Civil War,* 149-60.

From Edwin M. Stanton

War Department Washington City
Oct. 21st 1863

Brig. Gen. Andrew Johnson Mil. Govr. of Tennessee
Major Stearns Supt of Raising, Organizing and Commanding Col Troops
Gentlemen:

You are authorized to appoint any persons whom you may deem suitable for Raising, Organizing and Commanding Colored Troops in the State of Tennessee whether such persons have passed Examination of the Board or not and upon your designating such persons to the proper Bureau at Washington proper commissions will be made out. This exception to the General Order on this subject is deemed essential to the service in your locality.

(Signed) Edwin M. Stanton
Sec. of War

Hd. Qrs. Comr Orgn U S Col Troops
Nashville Oct 25th 1863

Copy, DLC-JP; DNA-RG107, Mil. B.: Copies of Lets. Sent, Vol. 53A (1863); DNA-RG393, Dept. of the Cumberland, 1912-C-1863.

From John W. Geary[1]

Head-Quarters United States Forces,
Murfreesboro, Tenn., October 22nd 1863.

His Excellency, Andrew Johnston
Mil. Governor, Tenn.,
Governor.

As Mrs. Avent's letter was referred to me by you, I deem it proper to inform you that I have carefully examined the case of Mrs. Avent, concerning household furniture taken from her by the agents of the government.[2]

The facts are as follow, viz: It seems that, on the day of the evacuation of Murfreesboro by Gen. Bragg's army, Mrs. Samuel Morgan[3] went with it, and then transferred the furniture of her house to Mrs. Avent, Mrs. Childers, and Mrs. Beans,[4] and it does not appear that any consideration was given for it.

I have therefore decided that the property is properly taken by the U. S. Agent and that the aforesaid women have no legal title to it whatever.

With highest regard, I am, Very respectfully,
Your friend & Ob'd't servant, Jno. W. Geary
Brig. Gen. U. S. Vols., Comm'd'g

ALS, DLC-JP.

1. John W. Geary (1819-1873), Pennsylvania-born teacher, lawyer, and politician, served in the Mexican War, as the first mayor of San Francisco, and as territorial governor

of Kansas before becoming colonel, 28th Pa. Inf. in June, 1861. Promoted to brigadier, he was twice wounded at Cedar Mountain, returning to duty for Chancellorsville and Gettysburg. Transferred west in October, 1863, he participated in the Chattanooga battles and the March to the Sea. After the war he was governor of Pennsylvania (1867-73). Warner, *Generals in Blue,* 169-70.

2. See Letter from Nancy L. Avent, October 6, 1863.
3. Mary Avent Morgan.
4. Ellen Avent Childress and possibly Ellen Bean (b. *c*1837), a Virginia native. 1870 Census, Tenn., Rutherford, Murfreesboro, 5th Ward, 8.

From Joel W. Gordon[1]

Greenup County Greenupsburg Kentucky Oct 24th 1863

His Excellency Andrew Johnson
Military Governor of the State of Tennesse

Dear Sir— I desire to inform you that I am a citizen of the State of Kentucky, & that I have within a few days past landed at this place direct from the city of Richmond Virginia at which latter place & in the State of Virginia I have been confined as a prisoner for One year & six months previous to the 22nd day of Sept last, on which day I was released by the Rebel Authorities from Castle Thunder prison in the City of Richmond, I was captured and taken as a citizen Prisoner from the State of Ky by the Rebels & held that length of Time on account of my opinions being favorable to the Government of the united States & I finally obtained my release. I obtained it in this wise a Mr. Wm. L. Hurst[2] of Kentucky who had been kept a prisoner in the South a considerable length of Time & who had been exchanged knowing of my condition wrote to Mr. Green Adams,[3] of Ky (who is 6th clerk in the U. S. Treasury Department) and who now resides in Washington City—and Mr Adams presented my case to the U. S. Comr. of Exchange for prisoners then at City Point & the Comr. then demanded me from the Rebel Authorities at Richmond & I was soon after released and sent home by way of Washington City[.] I wish to say that the only the reason I have to offer for giving you a short account of the way & manner in which I obtained my release is only to let you know how such cases may be managed though unfortunately they are but seldom attended to— When I left Richmond a great many Citizens were there held in Prison for their union sentiments or their loyalty to the united states Government Probably five hundred or more & some of them have been in Prison nearly ever since the war began[.] they are suffering more cruelties than Civilized beings should be made to endure & when I left the Prison hundreds of them flocked to me & implored me to attend to obtaining their release after I should get once again in my Own Government Proper and among my own people and friends, which I assured them I would do & as god is my Judge I intend to use every energy I am Capable of using to obtain their release[.] some of said Prisoners are from Tennessee[.] they are mostly from Tennessee Virginia and Kentucky & a Tennessee or Kentucky union man stands no better chance in Dixie than a cat in H--l, without claws[.] among the number of Prisoners that I became acquainted with in Castle Thunder Prison in Richmond was a young man from Tennessee by the name of Andrew Johnson[.] he has been in prison for a considerable length of time as he informed me & he also informed me that he was a nephew of your Excellency, and he made me promise before I left him to drop you a letter concerning him as soon as I should arrive at home & I promised him I would do so—& he requested me to say to you that he wished you to have him released, if you should have to arrest every Rebel in Tennessee & hold them as hostages for him in order to procure his release for he said he would willingly die a dozen deaths if he had it in his power before he would consent to join the Southern Army or take the Oath of Allegiance to the Southern Confederacy[.] all the Union Prisoners I saw there are perfectly willing and anxious if they can get their release to join the union army as soon as they get out & fight till the end of the war & I think it would be much better to have them released & let them avenge themselves upon their enemies than to leave them to die in a dirty southern prison for if they shall not be released soon hundreds of them are bound to die before the end of the coming winter, for they will boath freeze & starve to death[.] It seems to me that our Government officials have up to this time been culpably & cruelly negligent in not trying to have these unfortunate beings released for their release can be obtained by a demand on the confederacy & the giving up of an equal number of Prisoners on our side which our Goverment holds of the Rebels[.] I have written to Mr. Green Adams in Washington City since I came home, asking him to use his exertions to get these men exchanged from the Southern Prisons and I hope you will give the subject your earnest & continued attention until the design shall be accomplished— I have no personal acquaintance with you but I presume it will not be considered improper in me to make known to you the subject that I have herein stated— hoping that you will do your full duty in the premises I will conclude by subscribing myself yours with high regard

Joel W. Gordon

ALS, DLC-JP.

1. Joel W. Gordon (b. *c*1811) was a Morgan County, Kentucky, farmer with $6,000 combined estate. 1860 Census, Ky., Morgan, 1st Dist., 88.

2. Probably the William L. Hurst who was a commissioner on the board of enrollment, 9th district, Kentucky (1863-65). *OR,* Ser. 3, V, 909.

3. For former Congressman Adams, see *Johnson Papers,* IV, 525*n*.

From Christopher C. Andrews[1]

Head Quarters, Post of Little Rock, Arkansas.
October 25 1863.

Gov. Andrew Johnson
Nashville Tenn.

I hear of you every little while and am happy to know you are alive and in good health. I trust you will live to enjoy as glorious a reward as the Lord gave to Caleb for his unwavering fidelity.[2] Every body acknowledges you to be one of the great heroes of this remarkable era. Every body also acknowledges that you could do much more for the cause if you had more power. Some day you will have it.

I was two months with my regiment in the heat of the summer near Vicksburg, participated in the capture of this place and have been in command of this Post since its capture. My command is now that of a brigade.

The union cause is quietly gaining ground here. There has been, indeed from first to last, an under current of loyal sentiment among the people. They however do not yet dare to come out publicly in an active demonstration, lest the guerrillas will someday wreak vengeance on them. It requires therefore that our forces extirpate these scourges of civilization as fast as possible. We are doing something at it. There is no large rebel force in the state. Price[3] had only 5000 men when we came here; and many of them have since deserted.

Our army numbers from 12,000 to 15,000. We have two points (Benton one) garrisoned west and north of here. Another also at Pine Bluff.

Sebastian[4] is living quietly a loyal man at Helena. Ex Gov. Conway[5] is here takes no active part. Albert Pike[6] is in some town west of here disgusted with Jeff Davis & Co. Underwood [7] lives north of here; what he is doing I don't know.

The best of order has prevailed here and matters move on pleasantly.

Hon. E. W. Gantt,[8] member elect of the U. S. congress when the war commenced but since a Brig. Gen. in confed. service has published an address renouncing the rebel cause. I will send you a copy.

Governor, there is I believe a fair show for my promotion before long. I feel sure of the recommendations of Gens. Grant, Steele, Hurlbut and several other officers; and of the support of my Congressional delegation. I know a few lines from you would exert a great influence. I will be glad therefore if you will address a note to the President *and inclose it to me* stating how I stood when in the service in your state and whether or not you consider me deserving of promotion. I believe you will take pleasure in promoting your true friends if they are industrious and painstaking.

My little book "Hints to Company officers"[9] is considered of so much benefit to the service that Gen. Kimball[10] Com'g a division in this army has ordered 600 copies for distribution. This ought to be of some help to me.

Regretting to trouble you on such a matter

I remain truly Your friend
C. C. Andrews.
Col. 3d Minn. Vols
Com'g Post of Little Rock

ALS, DLC-JP.

1. Christopher C. Andrews (1829-1922), New Hampshire native and lawyer, settled at St. Cloud, Minnesota, in 1857, two years later becoming a member of the state senate and subsequently rising from captain to colonel, 3rd Minn. Inf. (1861-63) before promotion to brigadier general of volunteers in January, 1864. Returning to Minnesota, he was active in local politics, edited a newspaper, and served as the state chief warden and forest commissioner. He was also minister to Sweden and Norway (1869-77) and consul general to Brazil. Warner, *Generals in Blue,* 8-9; see also Christopher C. Andrews, *Recollections, 1829-1922,* Alice E. Andrews, ed. (Cleveland, 1928).

2. Among the twelve sent to search out the promised land, Caleb and Joshua alone kept their faith in Jehovah, and they only, of all the grown men of Israel, were permitted to enter Canaan forty years later. As a reward for his fidelity, Caleb received the town of Hebron. *A Dictionary of the Holy Bible* (New York, 1859), 76.

3. Since April, 1863, Maj. Gen. Sterling Price had commanded a division in Arkansas and in early June assumed charge of Confederate forces in the northeastern part of the state. Albert Castel, *General Sterling Price* (Baton Rouge, 1968), 139, 142-43.

4. For former Senator William K. Sebastian, see *Johnson Papers,* III, 205*n.*

5. For Elias N. Conway, see *ibid.,* IV, 49*n.*

6. Albert Pike (1809-1891), Boston native and man of letters, lawyer, editor, and exponent of Freemasonry, became a Confederate brigadier general in August, 1861. A Mexican War veteran, avowed Whig, and anti-secessionist, he was a large landowner who joined the Confederacy to save his property. He convinced the Indians living west of the Arkansas River to fight with the Confederates at Pea Ridge (March, 1862), but their dubious conduct, which reflected on Pike, and his differences with superiors over Confederate Indian policy, brought about his resignation in November. Living in semi-retirement and regarded with suspicion by both sides during the remainder of the war and afterwards, he spent some years in Memphis before moving to Washington, D. C. Warner, *Generals in Gray,* 240-41; Walter L. Brown, "Albert Pike and the Pea Ridge Atrocities," *Arkansas Historical Quarterly,* XXXVIII (1979), 354; Frederick W. Allsopp, *Albert Pike: A Biography* (Little Rock, 1928).

7. Probably Q. K. Underwood (*c*1823-*fl*1870), Alabama-born editor and publisher of the Helena *Southern Shield,* who was recommended for the military governorship of Arkansas. Also a lawyer, he was county judge after the war. 1870 Census, Ark., Phillips, St. Francis Township, 6; Memphis *Bulletin,* December 16, 1863; Helena *Southern Shield,* January 28, 1860, February 8, 1862; Nashville *Dispatch,* December 10, 1863.

8. Edward W. Gantt (b. *c*1831), a Little Rock lawyer and a congressman-elect in 1860, after participating in the disasters at Donelson, New Madrid, and Island No. 10, was captured in the latter place; upon his exchange in August, 1862, he lived in retirement. The following June 11, surrendering himself to the Federal authorities, he issued an address to the people of Arkansas asking them to terminate the war and rejoin the Union. Pardoned by Lincoln, he led a self-appointed delegation in January, 1864, to Washington in an effort to achieve the restoration of the state. In 1870 he was Arkansas' prosecuting attorney. *OR,* Ser. 1, XXIV, Pt. I, 97; John L. Ferguson, *Arkansas and the Civil War* (Little Rock, 1964), 7, 15, 256, 263, 267; Margaret Ross, "Retaliation Against Arkansas Newspaper Editors During Reconstruction," *Arkansas Historical Quarterly,* XXXI (1972), 161.

9. Andrews' sixty-eight-page *Hints to Company Officers on Their Military Duties* was published in New York by D.Van Nostrand in 1863.

10. Nathan Kimball (1822-1898), Indianian, school teacher, medical doctor, and Mexican War captain, became colonel, 14th Ind. Inf. in June, 1861, and brigadier the following April. On duty in Virginia through 1862, he participated in the siege of Vicksburg, during 1863 was stationed on detached duty in Arkansas, and served in the 1864 Atlanta and Tennessee campaigns. His postwar career included two terms (1866-70) as Indiana state treasurer, one term (1872) in the legislature, service as surveyor general of Utah Territory (1873) and as Ogden postmaster. Warner, *Generals in Blue,* 267-68; *DAB,* X, 378.

From James W. Scully

Head Quarters, 1st Mid. Tenn. Infy.
Sullivan's Branch, Oct. 25. 63

Brig. Genl. A. Johnson,
Mil. Gov. of Tenn.
Governor:

I hope you will excuse this informality in my not sending this communication through the Adjutant General's Office, as a great part of the subject has nothing to do with that Office.

According to your written Orders I have mustered into the service of the United States ninety-nine colored men, being those sent from Gallatin, and under command of Sergt Thornton.[1] The men were *all* volunteers, and seemed highly elated at the prospect of soon getting *pay,* and arms to defend them selves *whilst working on the R. Road.* Immediately after muster, Capt. Thornton reported to me for instructions as to how the men should work, and who was to "Boss" them— I told him that I had as yet no instructions with regard to that matter from you, but stated that the proper way was for he (Capt Thornton) to furnish as many men as Mr. Clarke required, and if they were sperated during the day, to send a Non-commissioned officer with each party who would allow none of the men to leave the work. These men, I told him, were to be subject to the orders of the Working "Bosses", *while at work* but at no other time until instructions were received from Governor Johnson. To day I have been informed that there was no work done on yesterday by those men, and also that Messrs. Clark and Kelley[2] went to Nashville, for the purpose of reporting me to "the authority there."

Now Governor, I wish you to know that not one of the *Civil* Conductors or "Foremen" of this road has ever consulted me in any manner whatever, about Negroes, or the working of them on this road. If Mr. Clarke, or any one else of Col. Innes' *employees* hat come to me, I could probably have adjusted the matter of working them as a *Military Organization,* under civil superintendents. They say "what has Scully to do with them." They seem to lose sight of the fact that I have supplied about 400 with clothing, Camp & Garrison Equippage, and have not received receipts from any person for them; nor can I, except from an Officer of the Army. The public property which I am responsible for is now in a terrible condition, on account of the way it has been distributed to those Negroes at Nashville since I came down here, and were it not for my experience in the Quartermaster's Department I would have been ruined.

I have not to my knowledge, in any manner offended the Engineers Department except on one or two occasions refusing to comply with *extraordinary requests (sending a Guard to their Boarding house* a mile from camp) and that *I have suspected dishonesty*. Governor, You have been my friend, and I am resolved to let nothing slip that tends to injure you, without either *preventing* it, or making you aware that such a thing is on foot. *There is a clique at work trying their whole power to get the building of this road out of the hands of you and General Gillem*. Colonel Innes is at the bottom of it. He does not want this Regiment here, and is doing his best—through his employees—to find something to make a report about. Clarke has remarked to several persons that You and General Gillem were about starting for Chattanooga, but hearing of the Battle of Chickamauga, you postponed the trip, and imputed *cowardice* on the part of you both. You can now see on the corners of several streets in Nashville, the sentence: "Where were you General Gillem, at the battle of Chickamauga[?]"

There are only two places, Governor, that that sentence could or would emanate from—*One is this Railroad,* the other I will name to you when next I see you. The many kindnesses that I have received at your hands, *and nothing else,* prompt me to write you this letter. I do not ask you to believe all I say, but *I do* ask you to watch those men closely, and see for yourself—I suppose Gen. Gillem showed you my *unofficial* report of our little skirmish on Thursday— I know where they (the rebs.) are concentrated, and am impatiently awaiting the order to attack them. I am seizing all the horses (surplus) in this vicinity to prevent them from being used against me, as well as to mount a portion of my men. I have received no authority to do so, but am doing it in the *lawful* manner, giving receipts &c. I would have sent for authority, but it is so hard to communicate with you, when the cars dont run. I hope you will approve of my conduct in that matter— If not, I can easily turn them over again to their former owners. I have now forty two. I wish you would procure me "Enfield rifles" or any other *good* arm for my Regt. Those we have are almost worthless[.] We have a responsible duty to perform, and ought to have good weapons— Also, please try to procure me *one* 12. pound Howitzer to put in the Stockade guarding this bridge which is almost a mile long— There need be nothing but the *Gun and its Carriage*.

Now Governor, please send me instructions in relation to those Negroes, and how they stand with regard to the *Military* and *Civil* part of their duties— They report not having *half enough to eat,* and Capt. Feudge[3] has been foraging for provisions for them for the past week. Their rations had been drawn by the E. D. but we can't tell what had become of them. Please investigate it.

I am Governor Very Respectfully Your Obt. Servt
J. W. Scully Lt Col &c

ALS, DLC-JP.

1. Emanuel M. Thornton (1839-1907), Hamilton County farmer, served as private and commissary sergeant, 10th Tenn. Inf., USA (1862-63), and captain, Co. B, 40th U. S. Cld. Inf. (1863-66). Briefly living in Marion County after the war, he moved west and in 1874 settled in Cartersville, Missouri. CSR, RG94, NA; Pension file, RG15, NA.

2. Probably Morris P. Clark. Kelley is unidentified.

3. John Feudge (*c*1823-1902), Irish native who spent his youth in New York City, served in Texas as a private in the regular army (1855-60), before becoming a merchant in San Antonio. Refugeeing north, he acquired, at the instance of Alvan C. Gillem, a captaincy, 10th Tenn. Inf., USA (November, 1862), and later a lieutenant colonelcy (1864-65). For four years after the war he served as Indian agent in Arizona before becoming a farmer at San Bernardino, California. CSR, RG94, NA; Pension file, RG15, NA.

To George H. Thomas

Nashville, October 25 1863

Maj-Gen. George H Thomas
Chattanooga—

I have returned from Louisville, where I had, an interview with the Secretary of War in reference to the immediate completion of the Northwestern Rail Road. He has authorized, and instructed me, to proceed with it as rapidly as possible.[1] Col Ennis of the Engineer Corps, as you are aware, was selected by me, while acting as Military Superintendent of Railroads, to take charge of the general direction of the work. He has since been superseded by the appointment of Jno B Anderson[2] as Military Superintendent. I doubt this change, Col Ennis making a good and efficient officer, and was not under an influence in Louisville[3] operating to our injury[.] I desire Col Ennis and as many of his Companies as may be needed, continued on the Road. The work is under way, and progressing very well[.] We are defending it with the little force we have driving Guerrillas off, and some of them out of the country. We have a large number of hands at work, and could employ a great many more, if we had a small force to send, to the other end of the Road which would exert a good influence in driving the Guerrillas from that Section of the country, and to cut-off an intercourse carried on, by the Rebels, through that region of country. I am succeeding very well in organizing many companies to be employed in scouring the country, to expel and d[r]ive beyond our lines, rebels and Guerrillas. Gen Gillem will visit you in a few days for the purpose of communicating with you on this and other subjects, connected with the state.

Permit me to congratulate you upon your new position. It is the one, as you know, I have long desired, you should occupy[.][4] I trust and hope most sincerely that your efforts in the future, like those of the past, will be crowned with brilliant success[.]

Andrew Johnson Mil-Gov

Tel copy, DLC-JP.

1. Dated "Louisville Ky, Oct 22nd 1863," a Special Order placed the governor in charge, "with full power to provide material to employ a competent engineer and other officers agents & workmen necessary to complete . . . without delay" the road from Nashville to the Tennessee River at Reynoldsburg. Quartermaster and commissary personnel, as well as the general manager of military railways, were to respond to Johnson's request for needed provisions, supplies, and equipment. Upon completion the line was to be turned over to the general manager of government railways; in the meantime, Grant "will furnish such Military forces as may be necessary for protection of the Road and the working parties engaged thereon—" E. M. Stanton Papers, Vol. 18, LC.

2. John B. Anderson (b. *c*1820), former superintendent of the Pittsburg, Ft. Wayne and Chicago and later the Louisville and Nashville, was superintendent of railroads for the Department of the Cumberland (1862-63) and later general manager of railroads within the departments of the Cumberland, Ohio, and the Tennessee. Under criticism that he lacked initiative and that his organization was defective and inefficient. Anderson was relieved February 4, 1864. *OR*, Ser. 1, XVI, Pt. I, 297; XX, Pt. II, 5; George E. Turner, *Victory Rode the Rails* (Indianapolis, 1953), 323-24; Nashville *Patriot*, December 29, 1859; *Tanner's Louisville Directory* (1861), 20; 1860 Census, Ky., Jefferson, Louisville, 6th Ward, 103.

3. This "Louisville" reference reflects a growing conflict between the L & N officials and the military. Although the company's officers, principally President James Guthrie, had earlier exhibited prosouthern sympathies, it was more a case of economics than of personal loyalties which forced them into a position of moving private freight, often at the expense of supplying the army, in order to operate for the benefit of stockholders. As a result, on the eve of Chickamauga, with the movement of men and materiel paramount, General Rosecrans threatened to "press the whole road in the service . . . unless things are remedied." Anderson, as a former employee of the railroad, was suspected of favoring the company's policy. Maury Klein, *History of the Louisville and Nashville Railroad* (New York, 1972), 37-39; Rosecrans to Guthrie, September 16, 1863, *OR*, Ser. 1, XXX, Pt. III, 667.

4. Six days earlier the "Rock" had succeeded Rosecrans as commander of the Army of the Cumberland. The year before, when Buell was relieved, Johnson had urged Thomas' appointment. Freeman Cleaves, *Rock of Chickamauga: The Life of General George H. Thomas* (Norman, 1948), 182-83; see also Letter to George H. Thomas, August 16, 1862, *Johnson Papers,* V, 617.

From George H. Thomas

Chattanooga Oct 26 1863

To Gov A. Johnson

Dispatch of yesterday Recd[.] I deem it of vital importance that the N W R R be finished as soon as possible & will therefore cheerfully give you as many companies from the Michigan Engineers as can be spared. Gen Grant informed me that J B Anderson has been appointed by the War Dept. I sincerely hope the new arrangement will work. Col Innes is an energetic and intelligent officer[.] I shall be glad to see Gen Gillem & confer with him on the matters you mention in your dispatch[.] Nothing will give me more pleasure than to aid all in my power to restore tennessee to the Union[.]

Geo H. Thomas
Maj Gen Comdg

Tel, DLC-JP; DNA-RG393, Tels. Sent, Vol. 63 (1863).

To John Hugh Smith

Nashville, October 26th 1863

John H Smith
Mayor &c

Sir— As winter is coming, there must and will necessarily be much suffering from cold, among the poorer classes of society, In fact, the applications to this office are, thus early in the season, becoming numerous and pressing. If you have the power, to effect arrangements, for this class, I desire to make the following proposition. If you will procure the wood along the line of the North Western Railroad, I will have the same brought to Nashville free of transportation. If you have not the power you will please communicate this proposition to your Board[1] and have their actions upon the same, or upon any other proposition, relating to the matter. I would urgently press this matter upon your body, and will heartily second, any effort in this behalf as it is getting to be a matter of embarrassment and importance.

I am Andrew Johnson Mil-Gov

Copy, DLC-JP.

1. Board of aldermen.

From Delano T. Smith

October 27, 1863, Memphis; ALS, DLC-JP.

A tax commissioner for Tennessee, recently come to Memphis, writes, "I have become acquainted with several sound Union Men here; and find . . . matters in a better condition than I expected; Still treason lurks here abundantly and, I conclude, the city is full of secret secessionists—leaving a great work yet to be done—"

From Richard Smith[1]

Office of the Cincinnati Gazette
N. E. Corner Fourth and Vine Sts.
Cincinnati, Oct. 27 1863

His Excellency Gov. Johnson,
Dear Sir:

Some of the Eastern papers have made it their business, since Gen'l Rosecrans' removal from Command, to blacken the character of that officer. I enclose you a specimen brick from the Washington Chronicle, in which your name is frequently used, in connection with a man named Truesdale.[2] I would like to know whether there is any truth in the charges; but I do not presume to ask for an answer, unless you feel free to give it.

Truly Yours Rich'd Smith

ALS, DLC-JP.

1. Richard Smith (1823-1898), Irish native, came to the United States and settled in Cincinnati (1841), where for many years he was associated with the *Gazette* and later with the *Commercial*. Charles T. Greve, *Centennial History of Cincinnati and Representative Citizens* (2 vols., Chicago, 1904), II, 602-4.

2. In the *Morning Chronicle* of October 24, a column, headed "How Confidence in Rosecrans Was First Undermined" and probably written by Benjamin C. Truman, accused that general of countenancing numerous corrupt acts by Truesdail's military police, thus, by inference, impugning the general's reputation. Throughout the article, Johnson is depicted as remonstrating to Rosecrans concerning Truesdail's behavior, "but the general turned a deaf ear to his appeals."

From J. Warren Bell

October 28, 1863, St. Louis, Mo.; ALS, DLC-JP.

An old Greeneville friend, mustered out as colonel when his regiment was consolidated into three companies, avers that he "should be pleased to come to Tennessee" if Johnson can help him get something to do so that he can "make a support for my three young children now under my care." Wonders whether his father is still living and reminds the governor of "*my* promise to you should you be *President*—and you *will be*—"

From John Long[1]

Eddyville Ky Oct 28, 1863

To His Excellency
Gov. A Johnson

Sir— your note of the 19th ult is received, and contents duly noted.

The negro referred to by you was arrested and under the laws of the state of Kentucky, he was regularly committed to the Lyon County Jail as a runaway slave. It is true he then professed to be on his way to the city of Nashville, but I am satisfied he could never have reached there without being molested, if he had not been arrested here.

The negro being legally placed in my custody, I am obliged to hold him untill the law is complied with, which is, that unless he is identified and claimed by his owner in six months from the date of his committment, and the apprehension fee of $20.00 and his Jail fees paid he will be ordered by the Court to be sold to the Highest Bidder on a credit of three months, and on the other hand if so claimed and identified within that time and the above conditions duly complied with his owner can have him. Though his owner Mrs. Woods[2] has been informed of the fact of his being here and she has signified her intention to send an agent for him.

Respectfully John Long, Jailor
Lyon County

ALS, DLC-JP.

1. John Long (1791-*fl*1878), Virginia native who moved with his family to Nelson County, Kentucky, about 1797, was a volunteer in the War of 1812. Settling in Eddyville in 1815, he was jailor there during the early years of the war. J. H. Battle, *et al., Kentucky: A History of the State* (Louisville, 1885), 857; 1860 Census, Ky., Lyon, Eddyville, 109.

2. Not identified.

From John B. Garrett

October 29, 1863, Louisville, Ky.; ALS, DLC-JP.

Dyer County resident, drafted in November, 1861, and member of the 47th Tenn. Inf., CSA, writes, "To day I am compelled to make my choice; to go forward as a prisoner and be exchanged, or take the oath of allegiance and banish myself north of the Ohio River during the War. Of the two I have chosen the latter, with the firm hope that you will give me permission to return home as soon as you consistantly can."

From David Pinkerton[1]

Military Prison Nashville Octr. 29th, 1863

His Excellency
Gov. A. Johnson

Dear Sir I take the presant opportunity of adressing you a few lines in regard to Case, in discharging my duties by order of Captn. Fife[2] Chief of Poliece was arrested and Sent to Jail on the 9th July 1863 and on the 21st day of July was released & Sent under guard to R. R. to report to my Regt which was at Galiton at that time[.] I asked the guards to give me permission to go and get my Pistol which was taken from [me] at the Provost Marshall Office. that was denied me so I said no more about it. I reported to my A Q M for duty & Some time after that I sent an order by a friend to the Provost Marshall for my Pistol which was refused[.] the order then was returned to me on the 6th of Sept 63. I then got a leave of absence to Settle up Some business at Clarksville & Fort Donaldson[.] My pass was for 7 days[.] after getting my business Settled up I came back to Nashville, and Called on Col Spaulding P.M[3] for my Pistol. he gave me no Sattisfaction but told me I was released through a mistake, and took my leafe of absence from me & the order I gave for my pistol, and ordered me to the Military Prison[.] that was on the 11th of Septm. 63 and on my arrival at the prison my watch & Pocket knife was taken from me by the turn key Mr. Brown[4]—& Since I have ben here I learned the watch & knife was Stolen out of the office[.] it appears my property amounting to the Sum of $59.50 was taken by the authorities of this place and cannot be accounted for in any way, but a dead loss to me[.] if that is the way to treat Loyal Men—all is right. when I was released I did not hide or try to keep out of the way to avoid bringing any charges against [me] if they could. I call myself proof I have ben tried and true to cause which I can prove, and for this I have not ben in the north for Ten years untill the war broke out[.] then I left the South & came north in May 29th, 1861 and in November following 29th 1861 I Joined the Federal Army, & the Public can Say what I am. I can refer you to Capt Irvin[5] A. Q. M[.] he will remember me by the time Colo Mason[6] Serrendered Clarksville. I was Waggon Master at that time & transacted Business with Capt Irvin reparing Stables Shipping Forage and Horses &c[.] the last lot Shipped was on the 16th August 1862 and the Surrender was on the 18th August 1862[.] when I think what I have done for the Federal army in the dischage of my duty and Otherwise and now See the treatment I get, it makes my very blood run cold in my veins and if I could be made a rebel of I think this is the best plan could be taken. there is a number of Federal Sold[iers] and Citizens in this place[.] Just look at the Situation & treatment they receive and you will think as I do on the Subject & have Some hopes of reviving after getting out of this place. as I have been 61 days in prison and cannot hear from my case or get a trial I have written to Colo Spaulding and Captn. Goodwin[7] & can hear nothing from Either of them. my case I am informed by some Reformed Rebel is the person who had me arrested and if So the athority of this place must know that there is persons in this place would like to have all the Federals in prison if they could or Union men. all I want is justice which I ask at your hands[.]

Yours truly David Pinkerton
71st O. V. I.

ALS, DLC-JP.

1. David Pinkerton (b.*c*1826), Irish-born teamster who enlisted in November, 1861, was appointed wagon master, Co. C, 71st Ohio Inf. the following May. Languishing in military prison from September to December, 1863, for allegedly "insulting an aged lady & daughter," he was mustered from the service a year later. CSR, RG94, NA.

2. Not identified.

3. George Spalding.

4. Not identified.

5. Charles H. Irwin.

6. For Rodney Mason of the 71st Ohio Inf., who gave up the city on August 18, 1862, see *Johnson Papers,* V, 430*n*, 628n.

7. Robert M. Goodwin (b. 1836), Franklin County-born, Indiana lawyer, was 1st lieutenant and captain, 37th Ind. Inf. (1861-63) before being detailed as 2nd assistant provost marshal at Nashville in February, 1863. He resigned in May, 1865. CSR, RG94, NA; Fitch, *Annals,* 41, 287.

From Andrew G. W. Puckett and Others[1]

Hamilton County E Tenn
29th October 1863

Andrew Johnson Esqr
Military Gov of Tennessee

We have learned with regret that our neighbour and friend Thomas W Raulston[2] is now and has been for some time under arrest and now held in prisson upon a charge that he is a rebble which charge We are satisfied is untrue[.] We have known him from a child and his farther[3] and family and when we say we know them to be Loyal union men we speak the truth in Every particular, and that Thomas W. Raulston who is in prisson was while he remained at home an active union man aiding & assisting in Every Way in his power the oppressed union men in this East Tennessee[.] he was a conscript and compelled Either to go into Confederate service and fight against the Goverment of the united states to which he together with many others of his neighbourhood wer compled to hide themselves in the woods and keep concealed for many months untill an opportunity of a safe retreat through the Confederate into the federal Lines where they then could be free men and claim protiction under the flag of thier Country[.] T. W. Raulston when he Left carried several others with him amongs whome was his Brother and friends all of whome are now in the federal service[.] this we know to be true[.] now do you believe it can be possible that a man after doing all this *can be a rebel or Enemy to his country*— We are satisfied that he is not and Respectfully ask his release from prisson[.] you cannot Imagine how harrowing it is to his old farther who has done much for the union cause in E Tennessee to know that his son is held a prisner by the Verry Government he is working to save. if the goverment is not satisfied with this and requires a bond We his neighbours and friends will make it for him[.] we know the accusers and their standing in society here and are satisfied he is misrepresented. You may say you do not know us to be good and Loyal men[.] We refer you to John Newton[4] now living in Edgefield and Samuel A McKinzie[5] in the post office department at your place or to Genl J. G. Speers D C Trewitt[6] together with all the officers & privates of that brigade as to our Loyalty and our course since the commencement of this Wicked rebelion[.] We ask your Early attention to this simply that Justice may be done as we believe to an Inosent and Loyal man. Yours Respectfully

A G W Puckett
B. F. Clark
C. W. Vinson

N B Let us hear from [you] soon[.]

LS (Puckett), DLC-JP.

1. Andrew G. W. Puckett (*c*1811-*fl*1880), Virginia-born lawyer and railroad contractor with $10,000 real and $4,000 personal property in 1860, served as Hamilton County register (1840), circuit court clerk (*c*1850), and judge (1867-70). His co-signers were Benjamin F. Clark (b. *c*1813), teacher and physician, a native Tennessean with $21,000 real and $3,500 personal property (1860), and Charles W. Vinson (1830-*fl*1913), a Tennessean with $2,500 combined estate (1860), who was county court clerk (1860-64) and later circuit court clerk (1864-78). 1860 Census, Tenn., Hamilton, 7th Dist., 158; 15th Dist., 78; (1880), Chattanooga, 1st Ward, 53; Zella Armstrong, *The History of Hamilton County and Chattanooga, Tennessee* (2 vols., Chattanooga, 1931-40), I, 205, 228; *Goodspeed's Hamilton,* 831-34; Will T. Hale and Dixon L. Merritt, *A History of Tennessee and Tennesseans* (8 vols., Chicago, 1913), VIII, 2424.

2. Thomas W. Raulston (1838-*fl*1900) was a Hamilton County school teacher and bookkeeper. 1860 Census, Tenn., Hamilton, 2nd Dist., 254; (1870), Chattanooga, 1st Ward, 6.

3. William J. Raulston (*c*1807-*fl*1870), native Tennessee farmer with $1,500 real and $300 personal property on the eve of the war. *Ibid.* (1860), Hamilton, 2nd Dist., 254.

4. Not identified.

5. Samuel A. McKenzie (b. *c*1796), South Carolina-born carpenter, was a Nashville postal clerk (*c*1863-65). *Ibid.* (1850), 27th Dist., 197; *U. S. Official Register* (1865), 440.

6. For James G. Spears and Daniel C. Trewhitt, see *Johnson Papers,* V, 85*n*; IV, 159*n*.

To William L. Utley

Nashville, October 30th 1863.

To the Officer Com'ding at
Murfreesboro Tennessee
Sir,

With this Communication, I enclose to you a letter from Mrs James K Polk[.][1] As to whom Mrs Polk is, her high character &c I need not write to you, but trust you will give her letter, and the matters of which it treats such consideration as it deserves, coming from such respectable source, and relating to a matter of importance, to the parties concerned, and of equal importance to the Government, and National troops. Upon the suggestion of this case, I would respectfully call your attention, to the safe keeping and custody, of such property, as is, or may be considered "abandoned property" within the Acts of Congress.[2] It requires, before confiscation of such property, judicial action, and without this, great injustice would be done the Government, if the parties seizing uses the same it accrues to the benefit of such party, and the Government is deprived of the proceeds of the sale— All such property, should be carefully guarded and handed over, to the agent of the Treasury department, so that if upon investigation, it turns out that the property, is the subject of legitimate seizure, the Government will receive the benefit accruing[.]

I, am [Andrew Johnson]

Copy, DLC-JP.

1. For Sarah Childress Polk, widow of the President, see *Johnson Papers,* II, 260*n*.

2. According to Section 7 of the July 17, 1862, Act "to suppress Insurrection, to punish Treason and Rebellion, to seize and confiscate the Property of Rebels, and for other

Purposes," in order to secure condemnation and sale after seizure, proceedings had to be instituted in the name of the United States in any district or territorial court; if the property was "found to have belonged to a person engaged in rebellion . . . the same shall be condemned as enemies' property and become the property of the United States." *U. S. Statutes,* XII, 589-91.

From Edmund Cooper

Shelbyville Ten.
Novr. 1 1863.

To His Excellency
Govnr. Andrew Johnson
Dear Govnr.

I find published in the "Union" of Friday—the order of the War Department in relation to enlisting of soldiers of color—and I find one clause that includes if "necessary" the servants of loyal citizens—[1]
I do not object to the enforcement of the order, when the servants of the loyal citizen are willing to enlist—but I very much doubt the policy in those cases where the servants prefer staying with their masters—
But I write to you particularly to procure for me protection against the recruiting of my two servants Damascus and William—[2] Of course I mean their impressment or being compelled to go in the army. If they voluntarily go into the army—I would not say a word—but [it] is to guard them against being compelled to go that I write to you— they wish to stay with me.
The policy of the Administration in regard to the arming of colored persons is fixed—and therefore we cannot alter it—but these servants of mine, have stayed with me all the time during the troubles— they are faithful, honest, trustworthy—*absolutely necessary* for my comfort and convenience— if taken away I do not know how I would supply their place—and I would be compelled to break up Housekeeping— "Damascus" is my Hostler and Blacksmith—and William is my body servant and House man—

If in your power my Dear Governor, furnish me such protection as will free them from "involuntary service" in the army—at least until all the "colored servants" of the "Secesh" and their "sympathizers" have been exhausted.

The fear I have grows out of the fact that a "recruiting station" is located at our town—and the officer being desirous of speedily filling up the ranks—may take all the colored persons indiscriminately—
I do not wish to come in contact with the "Recruiting Officer" and therefore ask your aid—
If you have no power in the matter will you be kind enough to direct me to the proper authority—with such recommendations as will accomplish my wish.

It is the first application I have as yet made to the Goverment in regard to my own matters—other than the exchange so kindly procured for me when held as a prisoner by the Confederate Authorities—

Hoping to hear from you soon

I remain Govnr. Very Truly Yr friend
Edmund Cooper

ALS, DLC-JP.

1. The fifth clause of General Order No. 329 stipulated that "enlistments may be made of slaves without requiring the consent of their owners," if enough free Negroes, slaves of Confederates, or slaves with consent of their owners have not been mustered within thirty days. Nashville *Union,* October 30, 1863.

2. In 1860 Cooper's holdings showed two mature males, aged 45 and 38, and a 17-year old. Although ages do not match, Damascus Cooper (b. *c*1818), a free Negro blacksmith in 1870, is probably one of these. 1860 Census, Slave Schedule, Tenn., Bedford, Shelbyville, 17; (1870), 7th Dist., 17.

From William L. Utley

Head-Quarters United States Forces,
Murfreesboro, Tenn., November 2d, 1863.

Governor Andrew Johnson.

The bearer Mrs Johnson[1] has presented a case for my consideration, that has to many points for me. I have therefore taken the liberty to advise her to lay the case before you Excellency, believing you to be the only person in the State, competent to give her proper counsel in the matter. I have taken some pains to inquire into the case, and I learn from very reliable Union families in this place, that she is a very estimable Lady, and that what she relates about her situation is substantially true. While she has always been a *true* woman, and Loyal, her husband has been a Libertine and a Rebel, and is now living in a state of *adultery* within the Rebel lines, leaving her and her little ones to suffer the anguish, that necessarily follows such transactions. I look upon it as a dreadful thing for a pure minded woman, to be under the necessity of living with either a Libertine or a Rebel, but when the two great sins, become united in one person, it becomes positively insufferable, and will certainly admit of executive interferance. Mrs Johnson can tell you the situation of the Property, and in short, the whole story better than I can. I really hope something can be done for her, although I have no interest in the matter, any more than the natural sympathy, that ought to be found in every human breast, when the innocent are wronged. I have no acquaintance with the Lady and should not have known anything about the case except by the accident of my position at this time. Believing you to feel a lively interest in all that pertains to the citizens of Tennessee, is the only excuse I have to offer for this intrusion[.]

I am Sir Very Respectfully
Your Obedient Servant Wm L. Utley, Col.
Comd'g Post Murfreesboro Tenn—

Gov. Andrew Johnson Tennessee

ALS, DLC-JP.

1. There were at least eleven Mrs. Johnsons living in Rutherford County (1860), making accurate identification impossible. 1860 Census, Tenn., Rutherford, *passim.*

To Abraham Lincoln

Nashville Nov. 2 1863

His Excellency A Lincoln
President

Since your dispatch of the twenty eighth (28)[1] ulto I have been trying every way to start for Washington but it has been impossible to do so[.] I will be there the earliest moment practicable. No doubt you have seen the violent attack which has been made on me by the Louisville Journal.[2] It is under the absolute control of the disloyal portion of Kentucky & its entire influence is brought to bear upon us here[.]

The appointment of J. B. Anderson as Genl Manager of all the Railroads in the three Depts in my opinion is an unfortunate one & especially so for Tennessee. He is no doubt under the Louisville influence & he will be used to advance their interests[.]

Andrew Johnson Mil Gov

Tel., DLC-Lincoln Papers; DNA-RG107, Tels. Recd., President, Vol. I (1863-64).

1. Lincoln had wired: "If not too inconvenient please come at once and have a personal Consultation with me." Lincoln to Johnson, October 28, 1863, Johnson Papers, LC.

2. The long editorial of October 30, said in part: "The work of restoring Tennessee to her constitutional relations in the Union appears to be at a stand-still or to be going backward rather than forward. Unquestionably one of the principal causes . . . is the course which the so-called Military Governor has thought fit to pursue in relation to the domestic affairs of the State. . . . His simple task was to protect and second the people in reorganizing their local government as it *was* under their local constitution as it *is*. . . . But unhappily he has not confined himself to this task. He has departed from it. . . . He has called upon the people . . . not merely to resume their constitutional relations in the Union but forthwith to abolish slavery. . . . Without formally asserting the theory of Sumner and Whiting and Butler, he is vigorously carrying it out in practice. . . . What motive has prompted General Johnson to pursue this unwarrantable and unpatriotic course we know not. . . . It is conjectured very widely that Gen. Johnson has struck a bargain more or less informal with the abolition leaders of the North, according to which he is to receive the abolition nomination for the Presidency next year in consideration of his either restoring Tennessee to her place in the Union as a free State or not restoring her at all, and that his official course in Tennessee is simply the expression of a very conscientious determination to perform his part of the bargain. . . . There is a remedy. . . . The people of Tennessee in August last duly elected Wm. B. Campbell as the Governor of the State. . . . the inauguration of Governor Campbell will in less than ninety days restore Tennessee to her place in the Union under the Constitution as it is. And, when this shall be done, the people can dispose of slavery, and of all other domestic interests, according to their discretion under the constitution and laws of the State." Louisville *Journal,* October 30, 1863.

To Richard Smith

Private Nashville, Nov 2nd 1863

Richard Smith, Esqr
Cincinnati Ohio
Dear Sir,

Your note of 27th ult, calling my attention to an article recently published in the Washington "Chronicle", was been received—

In reply, I will state that I do not wish to be involved in any controversey that has, or may arise, in regard to Gen'l Rosecrans and Truesdail, Chief of the army police, in the Department of the Cumberland—

The removal of Gen'l Rosecrans, is a matter with which I had nothing to do, and knew nothing of it, until it had taken place, And Gen'l Thomas, appointed in his stead, and Major Gen'l Grant on his way to take command of the Three Departments—

In regard to Truesdail, who was denominated Chief of the Army Police, the man I presume, alluded to in your note, was understood, and believed by the best Union men in the Department, to be one of the worst, and most unprincipled of his kind, and a great misfortune to our cause, in this section of the country, that such a man should have ever been associated with Gen'l Rosecrans in any manner whatever—

From all that I know personally, and what I have learned from other sources, I am well satisfied in my own mind, that he is a base and unmitigated, jesuetical parasite, and should be denominated John A. Murrel,[1] second—

Since I have been discharging the duties of Executive of the State, I have refused and rejected the application for the release of Fifty convicts, confined in the cells of our State prisons, who are better, and more worthy men, than he is—

I have said this much as an indication of my Opinion of this man Truesdail—

Yours Truly Andrew Johnson.

L (Robert Johnson), NNPM-810; DLC-JP.

1. For John A. Murrell, Tennessee outlaw of an earlier time, see *Johnson Papers,* I, 275*n*.

From Joseph G. McKee and M. M. Brown[1]

Nashville Tenn Nov. 3. [1863]

To his Excellency Andrew Johnston, Governor of Tennessee

The Undersigned would respectfully represent, That the condition of the colored population in this city and especially of that portion of them whose condition has been changed by recent events, is such as to call for the serious consideration of all concerned. Their great and continually augmenting number renders it impossible for all to obtain remunerative employment in their accustomed sphere of labor or indeed in any other & thus many are thrown upon the charity of the citizens for their support & thus they have become a source of great & increasing annoyance, to say nothing of the burden, to the citizens. Or they must resort to crime for the means of subsistence, or perish. Neither of these alternatives is acceptable to any. They come also in competition with the white population, in part, for labor, thus inducing enmities & often actual collisions, unfavorable to the good order & good name of the city. They occupy old & decayed buildings, cellars & out-houses as dwellings & from the insuficiency of shelter & the scarcity & high price of fuel, suffering must ensue from their present condition. It is known also that in many cases, criminal connections are formed between the younger females & soldiers of the Federal army, who, in many cases, have decoyed them from their former homes & are now living in more or less intimate relations with them to the literal demoralization of both & the military demoralization of the latter. This fact can be well attested, if any doubt remains.

Thus various considerations—regard for the comfort of the citizens, for the peace & good order of the city, for the welfare & efficiency of the soldiers & of the country in whose service they are, a consideration of the claims of humanity in reference to the class in question, unite in pressing the consideration of the problem now presented for solution— What is to be done with them?

Is not one thing now probable if not evident, that the comfort and benefit of both races require their separation & yet that such connection with the source of power be maintained as shall secure this class from want & at the same time secure to them adequate protection? May we not add another consideration—that of placing them under such circumstances that they shall be easily & readily accessible to efforts for their intellectual & moral improvement? Such results appear to us worthy the enlightened consideration of the philanthopic & the powerful—the Statesman & the Christian.

To us it appears that while the plan we suggest is not devoid of mighty objections, yet, on the whole, offers the grea[te]st benefits with the least drawback. It is that of forming them into a camp or camps under suitable regulations & superintendence & removed from military control or interference, except so far as may be necessary for their protection & that of those having charge of them & bringing them under such intellectual & moral training as shall tend to fit them for greater efficiency in whatever sphere they may afterwards occupy, & render them safer members of society.

We, therefore, take the liberty of suggesting that whatever ultimate disposition may be made of them whether on plantations or otherwise, the interest of all parties, in the meantime, might be promoted by separating them from present corrupting influences, into a missionary camp, managed & taught by benevolent Christian enterprise & furnished in material support by the Government.

With 6 hours per day spent in school, half an hour, morning & evening in religious exercises & the remainder in cooking, washing & sewing under the direction of lady teachers, little time would be left for dissapation incident to a military camp. Thus many would acquire more correct ideas of self-respect and a taste for learning. From this camp they could be transferred from time to time as openings might be found for them on plantations & elsewhere until all are disposed of.

DETAILS. As we represent an association of Christian people, who contemplate merely the moral & religious improvement of this class wherever we might find them, we have not the means of furnishing anything to the material support of such an enterprise, except teachers & a portion of the clothing needed by the "Contrabands."

Should the Government furnish rations to the members of the corps of teachers & some salary to the General Superintendent (one of ourselves) in consideration of his being diverted from the specific work to which he was designated, it would enable us to employ a sufficient force of teachers to carry on the various branches of instruction.

We should have to look to the Government for the fitting the camp & furnishing camp equipage, for rations necessary for the people & teachers, & Supt. and a commissary agent for the distribution of the same & barracks for the accommodation of teachers agent &c if necessary.

Should the location for the camp be chosen on the Gallatin turnpike near the town of Edgefield, there is a large unoccupied church convenient, which with a little fitting up would answer for religious & school exercises.[2]

With these suggestions, we leave this matter to your judicious & benevolent consideration, not doubting that the result will be for the benefit of all concerned.[3]

With much respect, Yours
Joseph G. McKee
M. M. Brown

ALS (McKee), DLC-JP.

1. Joseph G. McKee (d. 1868) of Ohio, Irish-born Presbyterian minister, came to Nashville in the fall of 1863 as agent of the United Presbyterian Church and of the Western Freedmen's Association to open a mission school for black refugees. Frequently absent

North because of poor health, he resigned as Freedmen's Association agent, county school superintendent, and alderman shortly before his death in September, 1868. M. M. Brown, also from Ohio and a minister sent by the Synod of the West (UP Church), had just arrived in Nashville to help operate the school. Nashville *Press and Times*, October 3, 1868; United Presbyterian Church of America, *Historical Sketch of the Freedmen's Missions of the United Presbyterian Church* (Knoxville, 1904), 1-13; Wooldridge, *Nashville*, 125; Elvira J. Powers, *Hospital Pencillings . . . as Matron and Visitor* (Boston, 1866), 61.

2. McKee's first school, opened in the "Baptist [colored] Church, Northwest Nashville," was later moved to Capers Chapel. In 1865, McKee School was built on Ewing Street; at the time of his death it had 670 students. UP Church, *Sketch of Freedmen's Missions*, 1-7.

3. Johnson did not support these proposals. Testifying before the American Freedmen's Inquiry Commission (November 23), he flatly opposed the establishment of contraband camps and during that winter refused a request from McKee to issue tents to shelterless contrabands, saying "Anything that will tend to promote their comfort will increase the number flocking in and exasperate still more their haters and persecuters— thus increasing their misery." However, Major Stearns did use the abandoned chapel as a home for the unemployed members of recruits' families. Nashville did not get a full-scale camp until Adj. Gen. Lorenzo Thomas ordered one established in February, 1864. *Ibid.*, 14; R. D. Mussey to George L. Stearns, December 9, 1863, Lets. Sent by the Mustering Officer for U. S. C. T. in Nashville, Tenn., RG393, NA; Wooldridge, *Nashville*, 460; *Senate Ex. Doc.* No. 28, 38 Cong., 2 Sess., 1.

To William P. Mellen

Nashville, Nov 3rd 1863

Mr Wm. P. Mellen
Dear Sir,

The large store House of Douglas & Co.[1] having been taken possession of by the Government and failing to obtain one elsewhere, have been prevented from making Sale of a heavy Stock of goods— they now wish to ship them to New York, and feel that it is a great hardship now to be taxed, five per cent for that purpose— The Government having deprived them of selling their Stock in Nashville, and appeal to you, the Special Agent of the Treasury Department for relief— This does seem indeed to be a hard case[.][2]

Very respectfully Yours &c
Andrew Johnson Mil Gov

ALS, DLC-JP.

1. For brothers Byrd and Hu Douglas, see *Johnson Papers*, I, 21*n*; V, 591*n*.

2. Johnson's intercession was successful. Mellen agreed that if the Douglases had paid the tax upon bringing the goods into Tennessee, they might now return them "without the payment of 5.% on the shipment, and the production of this letter to Mr. Dillon [acting surveyor of customs in Nashville] will be his warrant for permitting the goods to New York[.]" Mellen to Johnson, November 10, 1863, Lets. Sent by Special Agent William P. Mellen, Vol. 41, RG366, NA.

From James B. Bingham

Bulletin Office,
Memphis, Tenn., Nov. 4th, 1863.

Hon. Andrew Johnson,
Governor of Tennessee:

My Dear Sir: I write to ask that you will perform the same service for the loyal men of Memphis, that you have lately performed for the same class in Nashville[1]—that is, to displace our present unworthy Mayor and Board of Aldermen,[2] and to give us an opportunity to put better men in their places. My reasons for this request I will briefly state, as follows:

1st. Last June, when the present Mayor and Board of Aldermen were elected, the men elected had the appointment of the Judges and Conductors of the election, and the men thus appointed permitted the grossest frauds on the elective franchise.[3] In wards where there were not over three hundred voters, over six hundred votes were polled. Bands of drunken and dissolute men went around the city voting in every ward, and many have since declared that they voted *four times* at each ward in the city. In one ward, the most shameful disregard of all law and usage was resorted to, the ticket of the unconditional Union men, composed of gentlemen, was defeated, and the most dissolute and unworthy men in the community placed in honorable positions. Before the election took place, we had the assurance of Gen. Hurlbut that he would set the election aside, but you will remember that about that time we commenced making efforts to restore Tennessee to the Union as a loyal member of the national sisterhood, and we thought, in view of that fact, that it would look bad to have *the military set aside even an illegal election*, and did not ask their displacement. We knew that enemies of the Union cause would take advantage of it, and make a great ado about it at Washington. Hence we concluded to submit. But since that time the Mayor and Board of Aldermen have entered upon a wholesale scheme of fraud, by which, we confidently believe, they hope to enrich themselves at the public expense.

2d. Immediately after this shameful election, they caused it to be published, in the St. Louis *Republican*, Chicago *Times*, Cincinnati *Enquirer*, and other Copperhead papers at the North,[4] that their election was a Democratic, anti-Administration triumph. It is true they made no such issue in the canvass, but they were but too anxious to have it appear abroad that Memphis was opposed to the government.

3d. The Mayor and Board of Aldermen are, for the most part, ignorant and unprincipled men, of low instants, without honor or social position, and capable of any act of meanness that will inure to their own personal aggrandizement. The Mayor was a rebel of the strongest character, as all his official acts show, and several of the members of the Board *are deserters from Jeff Davis' army.*[5]

4th. But the principal consideration by which I would urge their immediate displacement, in order that better men may be substituted is this, that *it will have the best possible effect upon the progress of the Union cause.* I can recommend to you names of undoubted loyal Union men, in whom all classes have confidence—men who will fill the positions with honor and fidelity. Their influence for our cause will be great in the community, and all parties except a few rebel sympathizing copperheads will applaud the act! Even the better class of the copperheads will approve it, for there is a general distrust of these agrarian[6] unprincipled men now in authority. But, besides these incidental advantages, the move I suggest will enable the unconditional Union men of Memphis to appoint just and fair men as election Judges in future elections, and by that means, whenever an election is held, either State or National, we shall triumph.

If you will signify your co-operation in this matter, I feel assured that whenever another election is held Unionism will triumph; if you should decline—which I hope you will not—the Union men are destined to suffer long and grievously with Copperheadism in Memphis.

Yours in the bonds of a common faith,

James B Bingham.

P.S. As the mail generally has so many interruptions, will you please notify me of your approval of my suggestion by telegraph,[7] and I will immediately have a meeting of our party friends, and select the men who should be appointed as Mayor and Board of Aldermen.

Yours, J B Bingham

The above has been submitted to me and I testify to the correctness of the facts, and most cordially approve of the suggestions and recommendations and hope Gov. Johnson will act upon them immediately[.]

Respectfully J. M. Tomeny

ALS, DLC-JP.

1. In keeping with the prewar practice of selecting councilmen and aldermen each fall, Johnson had appointed Nashville's new council and board on September 30, 1863. Maslowski, *Treason Must Be Made Odious*, 122-23.

2. The current office holders were Mayor John Park and aldermen John Donovan, Martin Kelly, John Glancy, W. Evans, S. T. Morgan, Gilbert D. Johnson, Louis Wunderman, L. Amis, A. P. Merrill, C. S. Stillman, Michael Mulholland, William W. Jones, Michael McEncroe, George W. Harvey, Henry T. Hulbert, and Hiram Vollentine. Memphis *Bulletin*, June 26, July 4, 1863.

3. Regarding the June 25 election, Bingham's *Bulletin* editorialized the next day: "There never was a greater farce of an election in Memphis. Notwithstanding the publication of the regulations by the sheriff, there never was such a shameless disregard of all law and precedent. Men who had landed at our wharf within a few days past, were . . . made to vote in favor of their persecuted friend [Park]! Nor were they satisfied with one vote. Some of them we learn, offered to vote as many as six times. There were great irregularities in the voting in all the wards. . . . but a few of that portion of our citizens who had recently become enfranchised by taking the oath, either failed or refused to participate in the election." Park won, with a majority of 985 votes (1,555 to 570) over his closest contender, Charles Kortrecht. *Ibid.*, June 26, 28, 1863.

4. The following appeared in the Chicago *Times* of June 29: "John Park, Democrat, is elected Mayor of this city [Memphis] over C. Kortrecht, administrationist, by 1,000 majority, and over Kortrecht and Ware 800. The entire democratic ticket is elected by a large majority."

5. As is the wont of the polemicist, Bingham exaggerated. These aldermen apparently had served with two Confederate units: the 3rd Btn. (Memphis) Tenn. Inf. and the 154th Senior Rgt. Tenn. Inf. The former, in which Johnson and Hulbert were privates, one in Co. D and the other in Co. E, was for local defense and disbanded upon surrender of the city. A John Donovan, possibly the alderman, had been a private, Co. C, 154th Inf., deserting May 20, 1862. *Tennesseans in the Civil War*, I, 165, 308-9; CSR, RG109, NA.

6. A pejorative term "sometimes applied to agitators accused of leveling tendencies or of hostile designs against the holders of property." Craigie and Hulbert, *Dictionary of American English*, I, 20.

7. The governor ignored the advice to "throw the rascals out," and the Park administration remained in power until Gen. Cadwallader C. Washburn replaced it with an appointed city government on July 1, 1864. Memphis *Bulletin*, July 2, 1864.

From Catherine M. Melville

Washington Q. M. Dept. Novr. 5th 63

Gov Johnson,

Dear Sir. I enclose a few *items* that may be interesting. We have not heard for a long time from either Mr. or Mrs Maynard, or indeed from any of our Tennessee friends. I send these *clippings* to you, & to him if near you.

Please send us a Nashville paper on receipt. Genl Roger's speech[1] has surprised us here for we thought him a Copperhead— I trust and pray that Tennessee may not go unrepresented by good & *thoroughly proved* Union men in this next Congress. Oh that I could do any thing for dear East Tennessee. My Greeneville & Jonesboro friends especially, are hardly ever out of my mind.

May the Almighty guide you in your arduous labors for the welfare of this great Republic!

If you or Mr. Maynard can suggest any thing that Miss G[2] or myself could do for the *good cause* here—say the word.—

Our prayers are for you all.— Remember me kindly to Mrs. Johnson & the rest. What about Frank?

Yours truly C. M. Melville

Excuse this hurried scribble, written at my desk in the Dept. where I work harder, & for less remuneration than I ever did before in my life as a teacher. There are plenty of idle ones around me— It is here as every where else—a *few* do the *work*—

ALS, DLC-JP.

1. In all probability, John B. Rodgers, Tennessee politician; evidence of the speech has not been found.

2. Eliza J. Gay, Melville's close friend.

From Henry F. Williams[1]

Office A. A. Q. M Nashville Tenn
Nov. 5th 1863.

General

I have the honor to acknowledge the receipt of your communication of today[2] and in reply would respectfully report that the colored laborers on line of N. & N. W. R. R. have always been supplied with the same rations in kind and quantity as our soldiers. Rations are drawn and issued every ten days. It has frequently happened that full rations could not be drawn, particularly of coffee and sugar. this was unavoidable, on account of the small amount on hand at the post. Once we were unable to procure a train for several days and those negroes at the farther end of the road *may* have been out of rations. this was last week when we waited from Sunday untill Friday for a train. This I hope will explain the matter satisfactory, as I assure you I have left nothing undone to provide all that was needed for the men and for the advancement of the work.

Hoping this will be satisfactory I remain General With Respect

Your Most Obt Svt Henry F. Williams,
1s Lieut Mich Engineers
& act. Asst. Q. M N & NW R R

Brig. Gen Johnson Mil. Gov.

ALS, DLC-JP.

1. Henry F. Williams (b. *c*1844) of Grand Rapids, was a private, sergeant major, and 1st lieutenant, 1st Mich. Engineers (1861-64), serving as regimental quartermaster and acting assistant quartermaster in charge of the Nashville and Northwestern. Fitch, *Annals*, 197; *Official Army Register: Volunteers*, V, 284; Johnson to Whom It May Concern, November 3, 1863, Johnson Papers, LC.

2. A document announcing Williams' appointment to the railroad post. "Lt. Williams will make weekly reports of the earnings . . . the amount rec'd for freight and passage and the amount of freight and passage furnished and charged to the United States." *Ibid.*

From Nellie H. Baird[1]

Winchester, Nov. 6th 1863.

Gov. Johnson—

Dear Sir,

You will remember *Mrs. A. J. Baird*? Our acquaintance was short, but very pleasant— *I introduce* a *friend* of mine, *Mrs Esely*,[2] who will return in a few days— could you assist her in getting a pass out, with some goods for her and myself? Any *favor* showed *her* will be very highly appreciated.

I wrote you last summer—asking, if you could grant me a *free pass* to my friends beyond Nashville, *to Clarksville*, that I might get *money* for getting some *Winter provisions*—but did not hear from you— thought it likely you did not get it[.] Now Winter draws near— The Federal army has taken all my corn, wheat, Barley &c that I had intended to turn into "*Green-Backs*" to get *supplies*. (I have plenty of "Confederate" money, but that does me no good within your lines—) So now, I must call again either, for this *free Pass* to my friends, or if you can not grant me *that*—I will ask you to lone me, (till some future day)—*one*, or two hun dollars ($200.00 cts) I will send you my *note*, till ready to pay.

Gov. I would not call upon one of so short an acquaintance—but feeling that you are ready and willing to sympathise with one situated just as I am—it will all be well—

I do not hear from my husband—as all communication with the South is cut off— I see no other way, than to get a pass to go to my friends, or get help— What the Army left us last summer, it is *consuming now*. What we in Franklin County are to do, we can not tell!

We have confidence in an *all-wise Providence* that *some way* will be *provided* but, *this* must be effected through *means*, what that means is to be, the future will develope.

There is a whole Brigade camping on my farm at this time—*Head quarters* in my office, where you stayed, Staff officers in my yard— So you may guess how I am situated useing up my *timber, the last thing left me*— there is no other chance for me than to suffer, or go to my friends; and it is the same case with many, many familys—

Remember me, with best regards to *Col. Browning*—[3] Yours very truly,

N. H. Baird

ALS, DLC-JP.

1. Nellie H. (*c*1826-1880), native Tennessean, was the wife of Pennsylvania-born Cumberland Presbyterian minister Andrew J. Baird (*c*1823-1884), a strong Confederate sympathizer, general manager of the government boot and shoe factory at Atlanta during the war, and later pastor of the First Cumberland Presbyterian Church in Nashville. 1860 Census, Tenn., Franklin, 1st Dist., 24; (1880), Davidson, 15th Dist., 13; Nashville *American*, October 14, 1880, June 16, 1884.

2. Possibly Martha (b. *c*1812), North Carolina-born wife of Henry Easley, a Franklin County farmer. 1860 Census, Tenn., Franklin, 7th Dist., 159.

3. William A. Browning.

To George L. Stearns

Nashville, Novr. 6th 1863

Maj. Geo. L. Stearns
A. A. G. & R. C. C. T[1]
Major:

Mrs. Rodes[2] has nine servants who have entered the service in one of the colored regiments. She desires to ascertain where they are, and as she is a lady of undoubted loyalty she wishes to procure the certificate that will entitle her to compensation for them. Will you please give her all the assistance you can in accomplishing her design?

Very Respectfully Yr ob't. Serv't.
Andrew Johnson mil: gov.

LS, DNA-RG109, Union Provost Marshals' File of Papers Relating to Two or More Civilians.

1. Assistant adjutant general and recruiting commissioner for colored troops.
2. Not identified.

To George H. Thomas

Nashville, Nov 6th 1863.

Maj. Genl. Thomas,
Commanding the Army of the Cumberland,
Sir,

Mr. William L. Murfree[1] will present to you a statement, accompanying this letter, explanatory of the purposes and objects of an application to be made by him for "Protection" to his farm &c which lies adjacent to the Military Works at Murfreesboro[.] Mr. Murfree also owned large possessions on the Mississippi River and his interests there have, by the inevitable results of war, suffered severely—in fact, I am informed about to the extent of total deprivation.

Mr. Murfree is a citizen of Nashville, well-known and highly esteemed —universally regarded as a man of honor—never held any public position—but as a private citizen used his influence in behalf of the Union in the earlier stages of our political troubles, having voted against the withdrawal of Tennessee from the Union even after the State of Mississippi, where his chief interests lay, had passed an ordinance of Secession. Subsequently Mr. Murfree, tho' in no particularly offensive or prominent way, identified himself with the majority which then unfortunately ruled this State, but he has since taken the oath of allegiance, and, upon assurances given me by those in whom I confide, I believe that he intends faithfully [to] keep it—not merely as a means of protection to himself and his property—but from a sense of duty to his country as a loyal citizen, who accepts the results of the war and is trying to reconcile his business to the new *status* of affairs.

I hope you will entertain the proposition of Mr. Murfree and grant to him any favor consistent with your sense of public duty.

Very respectfully

Copy, DLC-JP.

1. William L. Murfree (1817-1892), native Tennessean and University of Nashville graduate, was a lawyer, planter, and businessman, helping to establish the Second National Bank of Nashville (*c*1866). A writer, he later contributed articles to *Scribner's* and *Lippincott's*, in addition to publishing the *Central Law Journal*. Acklen, *Tenn. Records*, II, 21-22; Sims, *Rutherford County*, 38, 122; Clayton, *Davidson County*, 303; *Nashville Bus. Dir.* (1860-61), 226.

From Henry C. Gilbert[1]

Head Qrs. U. S. Forces
McMinnville Tenn Nov. 7, 1863

Gov. Andrew Johnson
Nashville
Sir;

I am stationed here with a single regt. of Infantry (19th Mich.) & have been engaged since my arrival in making such defences as will enable me to hold the place if attacked— The whole region East & North of me— Embracing the Counties of Van Buren White & DeKalb is dominated over by Champ Ferguson, Muncy,[2] Carter & other outlaws and Union men with their families are compelled to flee for their lives— murders are comitted by them daily— It is a disgrace to our Government that Union men cant live at home when their homes are 50 or 60 miles inside the lines of the Union Army— The Head Quarters of these guerillas is at Sparta & they cannot muster in the aggregate more than 600 to 800 men & I think that is a liberal Estimate— With 300 good cavalry I could clean them all out & I believe we could capture their leaders— I assure you there is a terrible state of things there— I haven't a mounted man under my control with the exception of a score of Home Guards who are not worth much — I cannot do much with infantry, except to hold our position here— I submit it to your better judgment if there ought not to be a cavalry force sent here long enough to do this little job— If you think there had I hope you will use your influence to have it sent to me— I promise you if I can have it & have the control of it—if they are any fighting men—that I will make it pay—

I send this by Mr. Berger[3] of Woodbury who will give you further information on this subject[.]

Very Respectfully Your Obt Servt
H C Gilbert Col 19th
Mich Regt. Camp Post

ALS, DLC-JP.

1. Henry C. Gilbert (*c*1818-1864), New York-born, well-to-do ($61,000 estate), Coldwater lawyer and colonel, 19th Mich. Inf., died the following May of wounds received at Resaca, Georgia. 1860 Census, Mich., Branch, Coldwater, 112; Robertson, *Michigan in the War*, 392, 394.

2. Evidently Thomas B. Murray.

3. Possibly Abraham Burger (b. *c*1807), Tennessee-born lawyer of modest means. 1860 Census, Tenn., Cannon, Woodbury, 211.

To William P. Innes

State of Tennessee
Executive Department
Nashville Novr. 7, 1863

Col. Wm. P. Innes
Nashville Tenn
Colonel

You are hereby appointed Engineer of the Nashville and North-Western Rail Road (as provided for under letters of instruction from the Secretary of War dated October 22, 1863)[1] and will have the exclusive control of the construction of said Road, the running of the trains repair the same and the management generally necessary to ensure the speedy completion and the efficient working thereof with power to appoint such officers and men to assist you as may be deemed necessary[.]

You are authorized to appoint a general book-keeper whose duty it shall be with such assistance as he may require to open a set of books for said Road keep an account of all freights and passengers forwarded and received: also an expense account keeping a correct [record?] of all purchases made for the benefit of the Road as well as monies received and paid out[.]

All monies received for freight, passage or from any other source will be paid into the hands of the General book-keeper who will report and pay over the same weekly to the Comptroller of the State. You will immediately by making application to the proper officer provide adequate officers for the use of the Rail-Road and will collect all papers, books, maps profiles &c belonging to the Road and take charge of the same. You will as soon as practicable commence the efficient working of that portion of the road now running and for this purpose you are authorized to establish such rates of tariff for freight and passengers as in your judgment will be for the best interests of the Government and the Road. All persons now employed on the Road will immediately report to you for duty and they will be assigned such positions as you may deem best. All colored troops and other laborers will also report to you and will be distributed along the line of the Road in such manner as may be deemed best to insure the early completion of the work[.]

Commanding officers of troops on the line of the road will give you all the assistance in their power when called upon for fatigue parties, guards for your working parties whether they be soldiers or civilians and will co-operate with you in all matters tending to the speedy completion of the road regarding always the best interests of the Government[.]

You will promptly report any officer or officers refusing to comply with these orders as well as any officer who permits his men to commit depredations along the line of the road without taking necessary steps to prevent the same. All appointments made under and by virtue of the authority herein conferred will be subject to approval[.]

Very Respectfully &c &c
Brig. Genl. & Mil: Govr. Tenn

Copy, DLC-JP.

1. See Telegram to George H. Thomas, October 25, 1863, note 1.

To Arthur A. Smith

Nashville, November 7 1863.

Col Smith
Com'ding at Clarksville.
Dr Sir.

The object of this communication is to call your attention to the case of Mr Dunning & Mrs Parrish, W H [Castner] & Warfield[1] of which I have just been informed. I desire, as far as possible, to re-inaugurate Civil Law and Civil proceedings, and to accustom the public mind again, to the courts, and necessity of same. There seems to be a matter of dispute between these parties, of a civil nature, arising out of Mercantile transactions. There is a United States Court now in session in this city and will continue to hold regular sessions, and as the parties are citizens of different states, the case can at once be adjudicated. The assets can be returned to court, and held subject to the judgment of the court. in this case, one of the parties or any third party can collect the uncollected assets and hold them subject to the order of the same.

I much desire that all these matters should be disposed of by the courts, and civil Law as much restored and as quick as possible. You will appreciate the policy of this, and also the necessity[.]

I am Respect
Andrew Johnson Mil Gov

L, DNA-RG109, Union Provost Marshal's File of Papers Relating to Two or More Civilians.

1. Although the records of this case have not been found, the principals appear to have been R. D. Dunning, a Clarksville dry-goods and produce merchant on the Public Square; Kentucky-born Lucy A. Parrish (b. *c*1823), recently widowed, her husband Charles D., formerly an agent for Dunning, having died in June; possibly Wilson J. Castner (1817-1864), a Pennsylvania-born Clarksville dentist; and George H. Warfield (1804-1870), wealthy farmer, a director of the Planters' Bank and president of the Union Wharf Company. *Clarksville City Directory* (1859-60), 46, 59; 1860 Census, Tenn., Montgomery, Clarksville, N & E of Cumberland River, 22, 25; WPA, Montgomery County

Bible and Family Records: Tombstone Inscriptions, 63; *Goodspeed's Montgomery*, 1112-13.

Military Pass[1]

Headquarters Mil. Div. of the Miss.
Nashville Tenn. Nov. 7, 1863

Permission is hereby given to Hon. Andrew Johnson, Military Governor, State of Tenn. to pass, with personal baggage, to any point within this Military Division, until further orders. Military Rail Roads and Chartered Steamers in Government Service will furnish Gov. Johnson free transportation.

By order of Maj. Genl. U. S. Grant.
W R Rowley[2] Major &
Provost Marshal General.

DS, DLC-JP.

1. As a measure of control over the civilian population, Gen. Robert Mitchell, commander at Nashville, inaugurated in January, 1863, a pass system, prohibiting all except "persons of known and undoubted loyalty" from leaving or entering the city. Maslowski, *Treason Must Be Made Odious*, 57.

2. William R. Rowley (1824-1886), New York native, moved by way of Ohio to Jo Daviess County, Illinois (1843), where he served as sheriff (1854-*c*56) and circuit clerk (*c*1856-76). Enlisting as 1st lieutenant, 45th Ill. Inf. in November, 1861, he became aide and military secretary on Grant's staff, rising to lieutenant colonel before his resignation in consequence of ill health in 1864. Returning to Illinois, he continued as circuit clerk and was elected county judge (1877). *The History of Jo Daviess County, Illinois* (Chicago, 1878), 649; CSR, RG94, NA; Heitman, *Register*, I, 849.

From Melinda Williams

November 8, 1863, Terre Haute, Ind.; ALS, DLC-JP.

Wife of an East Tennessean declares that her "husbands health is so precarious it is an absolute necessity I should see about my effects . . . in the neighborhood of Yazoo City" and not knowing if it was within Union lines, she felt the "safest plan" would be to get a pass from the governor. While in St. Louis she had heard "influential Tennesseans who were once opposed to you, say that they regarded Gov Johnson as their only protector."

From Henry H. Grindstaff[1]

Charleston Missouri
Novr. 9th 1863

Sir

In these days of distress and seperation You will not think it strange that I have rambled from East Tennessee here since the rebellion broke out, how many thousands of our fellow creatures have went further & faired worse.

In the spring of 1861 times got so hot on the subject of *Secession* that I was obliged to leave my home & business in East Tennessee and fly for safty to Cairo Ill. Having nothing but Southern funds, I could not pass my money, and was forced to come to this state, where Tennessee money was commanding from 25 to 55 cts pr dollar; this great waste has absorbed nearly all the meanes I was enabled to geather up previous to leaving home.

My health being verry bad, (confined to my room one half of the time) I have not been able to recruit my meanes[.] this, leaves me in a precarious Condition—

Having served in the Mexican War, and being an Invalid Pensioner on the Jonesborough Roll I made out my Papers, certified by the Proper officers, & forwarded them to the department and received the following officially from Commissioner Barrett—[2]

"All Pensioners on the agencies in the so-called seceded states, were suspended at the Commensement of the rebellion, and no arrangements can be made for their payment until order is restored, and a proper Government establised therein."

I have not made a draw for about four Years, at $96. pr Year this amounts to a sum sufficient to enable me to get home or elsewhere, so my health might be improved. It seems to me to be nothing but fair for the Government to pay Pensioners as well as other persons— the Government invites me to come from Tennessee here, & offers me Protection in person & property but when a Penniless—refugee—it refuses to pay me money it has owed for years. I was born and raised in the district which You represented in Congress. Knowing the great length of time you served in Congress the more than corresponding weight of Your influence I write to ask you if there might not be consistantly a act of congress covering my case which would enable me to draw my money before *Peace is made*, &c. If your influence could be obtained it does seem to me the matter could be satisfactorily arranged[.] I am told by some friends that Mr. Scott[3] of this district will also lend his influence but as I know nothing of his public character I would rather trust for success, a letter from you than a speech from him.

A man of your experience sir can Judge of my necesities under the circumstances and knowing you to Sympathise with honest poverty I almost feel assured of your interest[.] Please let me hear from you at your earliest convenience[.]

Verry respectfully
Henry H Grindstaff

Andrew Johnson Governor of Tennessee—

ALS, DLC-JP.

1. Henry H. Grindstaff (*c*1827-1888), Carter County native and Mexican War veteran, was a unionist who had fled the Confederate draft, moving to Missouri in 1861, and to Pulaski County, Illinois, in 1864. Pension file, Mexican War, RG15, NA.

2. Joseph H. Barrett (1824-1910), Vermonter and Middlebury College graduate (1845), was admitted to the bar in 1851. After service as a Vermont legislator (1851-53) and as secretary of the state senate (1853-55), he became editor of the Cincinnati *Gazette* (1857-61) before appointment as U. S. commissioner of pensions (1861-68). Returning to Cincinnati, he resumed editorial work. In 1860 he wrote campaign biographies of the Republican candidates. *NCAB*, XIII, 167.

3. Probably John G. Scott (1819-1892), Philadelphia-born civil engineer who moved to Missouri in 1842, becoming general manager of the Iron Mountain Company and establishing the Irondale Iron Company (1858). Defeated as a Democratic candidate for Congress in 1862, he was later elected to fill a vacancy, serving from December 7, 1863, to March 3, 1865. After the war he had a drug business in St. Louis before resuming mining; about 1880 he moved to East Tennessee and died at Oliver Springs, Roane County. *BDAC*, 1573.

From Cave Johnson

Clarksville Nov. 9th 1863

Dear Sir,

The accompaning petitions[1] were brought to me by the wives of the Prisoners who reside about Twenty miles from me. They urge me to enclose the petitions to you and ask your interference in their behalf.

Their only offence, I understand, consists in their having volunteered to defend their own County when Fort Donelson was attacked, which they believed a patriotic duty and never intended to engage further in the war. The old man Andrew J Dorr[2] was captured and after exchange was discharged on account of his age. The younger one[3] escaped & both remained peacably at home, within a few miles of Fort Donelson— recently a squad of Soldiers from Hopkinsville, came over & arrested them—took them to Hopkinsville & thence to Louisville, where, they have been some five or six weeks without any trial & without any charges ag[ains]t them so far as they know— they are both poor men, whose families are dependent on their own labor for a support and their presence for protection, which is the more important as they reside in a section of country more demoralized than any other portion of our State. They hope you will interfere in their behalf by sending their petition to the proper officer at Louisville where they are confined & perhaps lately sent to New Albany on the opposite side of the River[.]

They are excedingly anxious to learn whether you can with propriety do any thing in their behalf & what? and you will confer a very great [favor] on them by letting them know through me any steps you can with propriety take in their behalf. As their husbands had been active democrats all their lives—they look with more confidence for assistance from us.

I am very respectfully
yr. obdt. servt
C Johnson

Hon Andrew Johnson
Nashville Tenn.

ALS, DLC-JP.

1. Dated November 1, the two petitions, with thirty-four and sixty-four signatures respectively, were from "citizens and residents" of Stewart County asking the release of Andrew J. and G. W. Darr, former members of the Confederate army and now "quiet and peaceable" citizens. Petitions to Johnson, Johnson Papers, LC.

2. Andrew J. Darr (*c*1811-*fl*1870), native Tennessee farmer with $600 real and $800 personal property, had served as corporal, Co. F, 50th Tenn. Inf., CSA. Captured at Donelson and imprisoned at Camp Douglas, he was exchanged and released from duty October, 1862. Arrested by Federal authorities in August, 1863, he ultimately took the oath and was sent north of the Ohio River. 1860 Census, Tenn., Stewart, 1st Dist., 7; (1870), 3; CSR, RG109, NA.

3. George W. Darr (*c*1827-*fl*1880), Tennessee-born farmer with $1,000 real and $500 personal property, who had been a private in Co. F, was "sick at home on date of surrender of fort Donelson." Captured by the Federals in October, 1863, he, too, was "released on oath to go North Ohio River." 1860 Census, Tenn., Stewart, 1st Dist., 7; (1880), 2nd Dist., 21; CSR, RG109, NA.

From Hezekiah G. Scovel[1]

Nashville Nov. 10th 1863.

Hon. Andrew Johnson.
Military Gov. of Tenn.
Dear Sir

With pleasure I introduce to you the bearer Revd. Herman Eggers,[2] who is associated with the German Lutheran denomination, and has occupied the German Church on north College Street, for several years, from which building, he has recently been severed by the action of the methodistical portion of the church, in which the title to the property is vested.[3]

Mr. E. from an acquaintance with him of years has made the impression upon my mind, that he is a *gentleman*, influence by a *desire to do good*, and acting in the capacity he does, has, and is likely to accomplish much in the amelioration of the German people; this being considered, as well as the fact that that element has contributed largely to the extinguishment of this "cruel rebellion," and the supremacy of law, would not that people be greatly benefited, and the interests of our "Heaven blessed Govt." be much enhanced by the exercise of your influence in securing for him the position which he desires?[4]

Very Respectfully &c. &c.
H. G. Scovel.[5]

P.S. I will further state that Mr. E. has, so far as I have been able to learn, been *steadfast in his Union sentiments*.

H. G. S.

ALS, DNA-RG94, ACP Branch, Lets. Recd., File E243 (1863).

1. Hezekiah G. Scovel (*c*1818-*fl*1892) was a wealthy New York-born druggist, real estate agent, and loan broker, listing $208,300 real and $17,000 personal property as the war began. Early in the conflict he had been hailed before the Confederate court in Nashville, found guilty of "feelings and sentiments . . . hostile to the Confederate States," and obliged to post large sums of money as guarantee "for his good behavior during the

war." Appointed by Johnson as alderman for the fourth ward, he served three terms on the city council (1862-64). 1860 Census, Tenn., Davidson, Nashville, 4th Ward, 132; *Nashville City Directory* (1871), 202; *Davis' Nashville City Directory* (1892), 799; Nashville *Union and American*, November 5, 1861; Wooldridge, *Nashville*, 124.

2. Herman Eggers, formerly a professor at Western University, Pittsburgh, became pastor of the First Lutheran Church of Nashville in July, 1859, remaining until the fall of 1867. Clayton, *Davidson County*, 339; Joseph T. Macpherson, Jr., Nashville's German Element, 1850-1870 (M. A. thesis, Vanderbilt University, 1957), 101-2.

3. The German Lutherans had held services in the city courthouse until the advent of the Union army when the German Methodists, whose pastor Sebastian Barth had returned north at the beginning of the war, offered the use of their brick church on North College. The offer was accepted and the building used until the Methodists received a new minister and resumed worship in the fall of 1863. *Ibid.*, 102, 104.

4. Since this letter appears in his military commission file, Eggers was probably requesting a chaplaincy.

5. Johnson's endorsement averred that Scovel, "an original and uncompromising Union man," was "a gentleman of the highest character, perfectly reliable in every respect" whose "statements are entitled to the fullest credit."

Memorial from Union League Councils[1]

November 10, 1863

The Committee appointed by the Tennessee Union League" Council No. 1. to memorialize Gov. Andrew Johnson on the municipal affairs of the State, report the following Resolutions

Resolved 1st That the members of the different Union Leagues. of the City of Nashville and the State of Tennessee do most respectfully call the attention of Hon. Andrew Johnson Military Governor. to the civil and municipal affairs of the State. and earnestly request him to bring about a Reformation in the same. We ask that Hon. Andrew Johnson exercise to the fullest extent his power and authority as Military Governor of the State of Tennessee. by declaring null and void all Elections heretofore held in the State, and all appointments heretofore made in the State.

And that he declare all civil offices vacant and further we ask him to fill all offices thus made vacant by the appointment of Staunch Union Men whose record of unconditional Loyalty stands clear without a spot or blemish upon it. and we pledge ourselves to stand by him in sustaining the power of the Government of the United States and the integrity of our once prosperous and happy State of Tennessee.

Resolved 2nd We respectfully call his attention to the present County Clerk and Justices of the Peace. Sheriffs and Constables in Davidson County. Elected while under the rule of the so called Southern Confederacy.[2] We call his attention to the Common Council of the City of Nashville among whom are men who have been well known Rebel Sympathizers and among whose present appointments two thirds of the men appointed have been and perhaps still are active Sympathizers with the Rebellion.[3] We call his attention to the Fire Department[4] in the City of Nashville. which is made up mostly of men who have been in the Rebel Army. Men who have been connected with gangs of Rebel Marauders that have fired into Federal Steamers and committed other depredations against the cause of the Federal Government. such men are not to be trusted and should not be placed in positions of importance and trust to protect our private property. our lives and the Government Commissary and Ordnance Stores in the City of Nashville amounting to more than two Millions of Dollars.—

We make the above charges without fear of contradiction for all the above charges can be substantiated by the evidence of men who have always been true Union Men.—

Resolved 3rd That we depricate all Elections at the present time in the State of Tennessee. Either City Elections or County Elections. or a General State Election for state officers for although we hope and believe that the day is not far distant when an Election by the People may be held in our State. We do not believe it now advisable. nor do we believe that men of the right Character and unyielding Union principles could be chosen until the true and Loyal Citizens of East Tennessee can throw their glorious unconditional Loyalty into the scale.

Therefore be it Resolved 4th That having full confidence in the integrity, ability Fidelity and Judgement of Hon. Andrew Johnson and confidence in his full knowledge of the wants of the People of Tennessee. We ask him to fill all necessary offices by appointments from himself direct.—

Resolved 5th That we all stand on the broad Platform of our country. let our country be right or wrong. and representing as we do over sixty thousand (60.000) votes in the State we pray for the hearty co-operation of Governor Johnson in this great work of Reformation. believing that we ask nothing incompatable with the best interests of the State or his power as Military Governor.—

Committee
F F. Smith[5]
Andrew Joyce[6]
R. F. Bates[7]
Wm. R. Tracy[8] Chairman

The above Resolutions were unanimously adopted by Council No. 1 of the Union League of Tennessee[.][9]

F F Smith President
George W. Orr.[10] C. Secty.

Nashville Tennessee
Nov. 10th 1863

Mem, DLC-JP.

1. Although drafted early in November, this document did not reach the governor until the last weeks of December. See Extract of Minutes, Council No. 1, W. J. Cochran, secretary, December 14, 1863, Johnson Papers, LC.

2. Called by Confederate authorities, the last county election was held in the spring of 1862, just after the beginning of Federal occupation. It is certain that Sheriff James M. Hinton and County Clerk Philip L. Nichol were elected then; Justices of the Peace Herbert Townes and John Rucker, Constables John E. Newman and John D. Gower probably were also chosen. Nashville *Times*, March 4, 1862; Clayton, *Davidson County*, 91-92; Nashville *Dispatch*, April 17, 1862.

3. The Nashville aldermen for 1863 were: John E. Newman, Joseph J. Robb, George A. J. Mayfield, Hezekiah G. Scovel, Joseph B. Knowles, Manson M. Brien, Micajah G. L. Claiborne, and Joseph C. Smyth. The councilmen were: James Turner, John Carper, George M. Southgate, Abram Myers, Andrew Anderson, Alexander McDaniel, Charles Sayres, Lewis B. Huff, Edwin R. Glascock, William S. Cheatham, Thomas J. Yarbrough, William Driver, James E. Rust, J. W. Cready, Lorenzo D. Wheeler, and William Hailey. All had been in Nashville prior to 1863, eight in government service prior to 1861 and seven serving in the Confederate period. Among them only Driver, Scovel, and Cheatham were well-known unionists. With this council southern-born representation rose from eleven to thirteen and northern-born dropped from eleven to ten. Except for Brien, who served briefly in the Tennessee Confederate army, none had been in southern military service, although sons or namesakes may have been. Wooldridge, *Nashville*, 124; Maslowski, *Treason Must Be Made Odious*, 83; Rose, Nashville and Its Leadership Elite, 25-26, 65.

4. Chief engineer of the Nashville fire department, John M. Seabury, resigned October, 1863, and was succeeded by L. M. Freeman. Engineers for the three fire companies were Joseph Irwin, Richard Horn, and William H. Smith. The ruck and run of these "Rebel" firemen have not been identified. Wooldridge, *Nashville*, 149.

5. F. F. Smith, candidate for fire chief, is otherwise not identified. Nashville *Union*, October 9, 1863.

6. Andrew Joyce (*c*1828-*fl*1881), native Tennessee stonemason, had $800 real property (1860) and in the 1870's worked as an engineer on a steamboat and for the L & N Railroad. 1860 Census, Tenn., Davidson, Nashville, 7th Ward, 60; Nashville city directories (1871-81), *passim*.

7. Robert F. Bates (1815-1882) was an Irish-born shoemaker with $500 personal property. 1860 Census, Tenn., Davidson, Nashville, 1st Ward, 5; Garrett and McClain, *Old City Cemetery*, 9.

8. Tracy had recently resigned as major, 1st Tenn. Cav.

9. During the following weeks, the Memorial was endorsed by the following councils: No. 2 (Nashville); No. 5 (Edgefield); the State Grand Council; No. 3 (Shelbyville).

10. George W. Orr (b. *c*1820), a "Com Laborer" of Hardin County with only $100 personalty, had evidently been drawn to the city by the hazards of war. 1860 Census, Tenn., Hardin, 12th Dist., 192.

From Benjamin C. Truman

Washington Nov. 12, 1863

To Gov. Johnson:
My dear friend:
Governor:

I understand from various sources that a first class newspaper is to be established in Nashville, under the auspices of *the* "Union" portion[1] of the Nashville *Daily Union*.

Governor, there are attractions for me in that city, and I would like to return, if I can employ myself in my legitimate calling. Therefore, I would be anxious to secure the position on the new paper as general superintendent of the establishment, as I am thoroughly a practical man, and conversant with all the "ropes" of a modern printing office. There is no department in such a house that I am not familiar with, and as to my industry and tact, and natural capacity, I leave you to judge.

If such a position has been tendered to any one, I would accept the situation of news editor, a situation I know I can fill as well as any gentleman connected with the newspaper business.

You may consider this letter abrupt after so long a silence; but I have often feared that the little unpleasant episode[2] in the history of my tarry in Nashville, which occurred last summer, might have been the source of great displeasure to you, if, perhaps, it had not altogether impaired your confidence in and regard for me. Now, if I *had* been anything but an honest, straightforward clever fellow, I could have come out of the affair whole. But I was obstinately generous, and have pursued such a course all my life. When dozens of my most intimate friends turned from me, I made no retaliation. And I can assure you that I am too shrewd a journalist and have seen too much of the world to have been so completely capsized had I deemed it manly to have raked up the little indiscretions of my associates. Although I am compelled to say it myself, I give you my word, (and I could transmit you an abundance of proof,) that I am not the hero of a multiplicity of mean things. I think you, and Browning and others will bear me witness that I am a man who does not use my spare time in reciting the errors and failings of my neighbors, while I love to put in a good word for my friends. Although this is strictly confidential, I am candid, and ought not to be ashamed.

There is one thing, Governor, which I can say truly: I always stick to my friends, and am always willing to make my peace with whom I have quarrelled.

You have no doubt noticed that I have been particularly kind towards you in the columns of the Chronicle.[3] Of course I did it from high personal regard.

Located in Nashville, I could do you good service. Mr. Raymond,[4] of the Times is very friendly toward you and is equally inclined toward General Grant. It is his intention to hire a man to go into that department to watch matters of a political bearing. I should be only too happy were I near you to furnish "political opinions" for the *Chronicle*, Philada *Press* and New York *Times*.

I have been accused by "slow coaches"[5] and "bummers"[6] of being dishonest in the way of giving the public news. Now, Governor, although I often take great risks, I exercise due caution before preparing certain articles for the public print. After I left Nashville, Shanks of the Herald[7] devoted a half column to me in an article praising Buell. In it he said that I was a literary thief, and being trusted in your office went through your draws and picked up a great many things. He said that I was the author of the article which gave "your opinion of Buell," and says that I made it up from hearsay and scraps which I stole.[8] Now here are the facts: *First*, in all my dealings at the Capitol I never in any place or in any shape whispered what I had learned in private conversation. *Secondly*, even after I had been around for more than a year did I ever look over the backs of Browning or Lindsley[9] when they were writing: I never took up a letter or overhauled anything on the tables in my life, and never went to any of the draws or cases without asking Browning. This he will inform you. Good manners taught me different, and my conduct was often contrasted to that of Bent's[10] by Messrs. Browning and Lindsley. *Thirdly*, I did never take advantage of your kindness, and never made myself familiar by sitting in your room with my hat on or talking boisterously, most especially when any one was present not connected with your office. To sum up, as far as that article in relation to Buell was concerned, I heard it read, after the army had got into Kentucky, and begged Browning for it. He would not let me have it, but when I came on last fall he let me copy it to show to Mr. Forney. I did so, and he said that if you wrote it you wouldn't care if the whole world saw it, and subsequently published it.

Again Mercer accused me of stealing a despatch addressed to you, of mutilating it, and forging the initials of Col. Forney and publishing it as a Washington despatch to my paper.[11] Now, East showed me the despatch in question, Col. Martin[12] being in my company, and says I "I'll get out an extra." East says "well, change it, Truman, as this is a despatch from Stanton to the Governor." I did so. I changed it, dated it Washington, and signed it F. F is not the initials of John W Forney; and although I am willing to confess that I calculated to make the unsophisticated believe it came from Mr. Forney, I was too careful to employ the initials "J.W.F."

I could name other instances, but do not care to bore you on that subject longer. But as to my newspaper doings, I am as reliable as gossippy, and tell as few lies as others in the same profession.

You knew while I was editor of the Nashville Press, I slaughtered Bickham[13] stood up squarely for you, and refused all proposals, (which were to have been accompanied by pecuniary advantages) from Truesdail.[14] I have written letters and editorials for the *Chronicle* always favorable to you and Tennessee. I have given Truesdail his deserts in the *Chronicle* and showed him up also in the New York *Times*.

I have often thought of my career in the provost marshal's office, especially since you have provost marshals, provost marshal generals, boards of trade, collectors, surveyors, &c, and refer back to the time when I used to give (with assistance) all the passes for evywhere and permits for evrything. In all that time I believe I was reliable and honest, although, I will say that during the four months I was in that office not a single illegal offer was made me with the exception of that of the Federal surgeon in the case of old mother Barrow[15]—do you recollect it? I bet you recollect her.

If I was doing nothing, I would not apply to you, but as I hold one of the most elegant positions a man can, I do not address you as an itinerant.

I shall be most highly indebted to you, Governor, if you will favor me with a speedy answer, and if you do not deem it injudicious, please tender me a favorable reply.

As to my general knowledge of the best mode of getting up a modern line newspaper, I could refer you to ma[n]y, but I reckon you know me.

I will just add, Governor, that if you feel harshly disposed towards me, you are deceived— I am not a bad man.

Let me renew my assurances of esteem, for you and yours, and believe me, respectfully,

Yours to command,
Benj C. Truman

ALS, DLC-JP.

1. Truman may have heard rumors of friction between editor Samuel C. Mercer and his publishers. Ousted during December, 1863, Mercer started the Nashville *Times and True Union* several months later, with Truman as associate editor. Redden, Nashville Newspapers, 47-49.

2. Soon after Truman assumed the editorship of the Nashville *Press* on May 4, 1863, he was accused by the *Union* of being the author of the "L" letters (published in the Louisville *Journal*) which charged that *Union* editor Mercer and his publishers were abolitionists and rebels. Mercer maintained that Truman, meeting the Louisville editor at the St. Cloud Hotel, had supplied the information which appeared in the letters. Steadfastly denying the story, Truman nonetheless yielded to the storm, resigning July 1. Nashville *Press*, May 4, June 27, July 1, 1863; Nashville *Union*, June 23, 1863.

3. Truman was a correspondent for John W. Forney's Washington *Sunday Morning Chronicle*, founded in 1861 and converted to a daily in November of the following year. Presumably the writer was referring to the five entries laudatory of Johnson which appeared in the *Chronicle* between September 4 and October 11.

4. Henry J. Raymond (1820-1869), native New Yorker and University of Vermont graduate (1840), studied law and engaged in journalism, being connected with the *Tribune* (1841-43), the *Courier and Enquirer* (1848-50), and *Harper's Magazine*, before establishing the *Times* in 1851. His political career included membership in the state assembly (1849-51, 1862), service as a delegate to the Whig and Republican national conventions of 1852 and 1860, as lieutenant governor, and as congressmen (1865-67). He was a Johnson supporter until 1868 when he broke with him on financial issues. *DAB*, XV, 408-11; *BDAC*, 1501.

5. Anyone who thinks or moves slowly.

6. "An idler, or worthless fellow," the term during the Civil War "was applied to a camp follower or plundering straggler." *Century Dictionary* (1889), I, 719.

7. William F. G. Shanks (1837-1905), Kentucky-born journalist and currently a New York *Herald* war correspondent, later wrote for *Harper's Magazine* and was on the New York *Tribune* staff (city editor during the exposure of the Tweed Ring). In 1885 he organized the National Press Intelligence Company, "whose purpose is to read the papers of the world for busy individuals and corporations." *NCAB*, III, 459; New York *Times*, February 24, 1905.

8. The Sunday *Herald* of August 16 carried nearly two columns of Shanks's dispatches from northern Alabama, concluding with the charges to which Truman refers. Without naming the culprit, Shanks, citing General Gillem as his source, wrote: "It appears that one of Governor Johnson's aids, a correspondent of Forney's *Press*, found in the Governor's portfolio a number of memorandums, on separate slips of paper, in the Governor's handwriting, without address, date, signature or connection. These he dovetailed together into the letter purporting to be from Johnson to the President." Published in the *Press*, November 15, 1862, the letter "created so much feeling against Buell, and gave him the character he unjustly bore as a rebel sympathizer. . . . It is strange that Governor Johnson has never denied the authorship of the document; but it is very certain that he never sent, nor did the President ever receive, any such letter." See Letter to Abraham Lincoln, September 1, 1862.

9. James Lindsley (*c*1839-1875), Tennessee-born son of Nashville postmaster A. V. S. Lindsley and one of Johnson's aides, made his livelihood after the war as a lawyer and real estate agent. 1870 Census, Tenn., Davidson, 18th Dist., 12; Nashville city directories (1867-75), *passim*; Nashville *American*, December 2, 1875; receipts, courtesy Mrs. Betsy Carrier, Bluff City.

10. Probably C. H. W. Bent, an agent for the associated press and sometime clerk in both the provost marshal's and quartermaster's offices in Nashville, who had been a cashier in a Boston publishing house before moving to Nashville in 1859 where he was a teller and bookkeeper with the City Bank. Although Johnson recommended him to

Stanton for a paymaster position, there is no evidence that he received the appointment. Reported in the Confederate press as killed at Murfreesboro, he nevertheless was in Nashville until 1866, when he disappears from all directories. Nashville *Press*, September 17, 1864; *King's Nashville City Directory* (1866), 97; C. H. W. Bent, ACP Branch, 1863, RG94, NA; Memphis *Appeal*, January 27, 1863.

11. This adulterated dispatch has not been located. If Truman, as he suggests, published it as an extra, a copy has not found its way into extant files of the paper.

12. John A. Martin, Nashville provost marshal.

13. William D. Bickham (1827-1894), after several years of adventuring, even as far as California, returned to his native Cincinnati as a reporter for the *Commercial* and as correspondent of the New York *Tribune* on the side. Following service as a war correspondent, including a stint as a volunteer aide on Rosecrans' staff, he published in 1863 *Rosecrans' Campaign with the Fourteenth Army Corps, or the Army of the Cumberland* containing critical observations about Johnson, to which Truman reacted with a strong *Press* editorial in the governor's defense. Later Bickham was the owner of the Dayton (Ohio) *Journal* for over thirty years. Louis M. Starr, *Bohemian Brigade* (New York, 1954), 183; J. Cutler Andrews, *The North Reports the Civil War* (Pittsburgh, 1955), 63; Nashville *Press*, June 8, 1863; Frank Conover, ed., *Centennial Portrait and Biographical Record of the City of Dayton and of Montgomery County, Ohio* (Dayton, 1897), 403.

14. William Truesdail, chief of army police in Nashville.

15. Probably Ann M. Shelby Barrow (b. *c*1813), wife of Washington Barrow, whom Johnson had exiled to Fort Mackinaw in May, 1862. 1860 Census, Tenn., Davidson, Edgefield, 24; DAR, Davidson County Marriage Book I, 102.

From John C. Crane[1]

Quartermaster's Office,
Nashville, Tenn., November 13, 1863.

To his Excellency Andrew Johnson,
Military Governor, Tennessee:

Governor: The bearer (colored), Jane Woodall,[2] is my house-servant. She is a slave, claimed by Christopher Woodall,[3] a resident of Tennessee.

It is said that he is disloyal, and on a previous occasion the military authorities prevented him from taking her.

Has Mr. Woodall any right, under the President's proclamation and military law, to take this woman?

It strikes me not, as we have taken possession of rebel property without compensation.

Requesting your decision in the premises, I am, Governor, very respectfully, your obedient servant,[4]

John C. Crane,
Captain and Acting Quartermaster.

Philadelphia *Press*, November 24, 1863; Frank Moore, ed., *The Rebellion Record: A Diary of American Events* (11 vols. and supp., New York, 1861-68), VIII, Diary, 7.

1. John C. Crane (*fl*1880), native of New Jersey, joined the 1st Mo. Cav. in 1861. Captain, subsequently colonel, in the quartermaster corps, he was attached to the military railroad service at Nashville until late 1864. Accused of defrauding the government as early as January, 1862, he was court-martialed in the summer of 1865. Johnson endorsed him as "a very efficient officer" who "in the late political contest rendered no small degree of service in behalf of our cause," and ultimately in 1867 signed the order remitting the court-martial sentence. After the war, Crane lived in Ohio. Johnson to Zachariah Chandler, December 12, 1864, Chandler Papers, LC; E. M. Stanton to Johnson, January 29, 1867,

Mil. Books, Executive, RG107, NA; Crane to James A. Garfield, November 2, 1880, Garfield Papers, LC; CSR, RG94, NA; Court-martial, GCM-MM3216, RG153, NA.

2. It is impossible to ascertain which of the two female slaves in Woodall's family, one thirty-three, the other nineteen, was Jane. 1860 Census, Slave Schedule, Tenn., Robertson, 11th Dist., 26.

3. Christopher Woodall (b. *c*1779), a Virginia-born farmer, owned $15,978 worth of property in 1860, including six slaves. *Ibid.*; 1860 Census, Tenn., Robertson, 11th Dist., 109.

4. On the same day Johnson responded: "*Respectfully returned.* If the girl referred to within is *willing* to return with Mr. Woodall, she should be allowed to go; but, if not *willing*, she will not be compelled to go with him." Philadelphia *Press*, November 24, 1863.

From Calvin Goddard

Head Quarters Department of the Cumberland
Chattanooga Nov 13, 1863.

To Brig. Genl. A. Johnson

Respectfully returned to Brig Genl *Andrew Johnson* Military Governor of Tenn. If Dr. *Jones*[1] will cause accounts to be made out on Form 18 subsistence Depm't. (Revised Army Regulations 186) for each of the Patients as have Descriptive Rolls[2] the Commissary Department will pay them at once.— For those patients who have no Descriptive lists, the Gen'l Commanding will use every exertion to have the deficiency supplied, and to that end has already requested and received a list from Dr *Jones* embodying all the information he is able to give in regard to the matter and the regimental Commanders have been directed to forward descriptive rolls at once.— A General Order will also be published requiring all Comd'g Officers who have sent insane soldiers to the Tenn. Asylum to forward their names and description to these Head Quarters. An arrangement will be made, through Lieut Col. *Donalson*[3] Supervising Quartermaster at Nashville by which clothing can be issued to these men.— It is the wish of the General Commanding to have these men properly provided for and the a/cs against the Government promptly settled, and no effort on his part shall be wanting to place the matter on the proper footing.

By Order of Major General Thomas
C. Goddard
Lieut. Col & A. A. Genl.

LB copy, DNA-RG393, Dept. of the Cumberland, Endorsements, Vol. 36 (1863-64).

1. Dr. William P. Jones, superintendent of the state hospital for the insane.

2. The Federal army kept company descriptive books in which were recorded age, height, complexion, color of eyes and hair, birthplace, and occupation, as well as information about enlistment, including date, place, by whom, term, and sometimes general remarks. CSR, RG94, NA.

3. James L. Donaldson (1814-1885), Maryland-born West Pointer (1836) and Mexican War veteran, had served in Florida and Texas, rising to chief quartermaster of the Department of New Mexico (1858-62). Prior to his Nashville assignment (1863-65), he was stationed at Pittsburgh and Baltimore. He resigned from service in 1874. *NCAB*, XI, 518.

From I. L. Roark[1]

Prison, No, 2
Camp Chase Ohio Nov 13th, 1863

Gen Andrew Johnson

Dier Seer ther is a good many of the Tennessee Boyes and others that has all the time Been for the union and a good many of them that has been p[r]essed into the Rebel armey all of which are hear as pisioners; and has refused to go South for Exchange and has Sent out ther writton application to the Commander of the pision[2] to take the oath and be releast[.] Now I have applied to the Commander of this pision ('Viz) Col Paten; to know if I forme said Boyes into a Company of State or home guards for the State of Tennessee if we would be sent to Nashville to report to you; Which I have no dought as they have applied to take the oath as aforesaid that the priviledg asked for will be granted.

But I desire to know if you would receive us in the Service as above Stated if we was to Come and make application[.]

I was in the Rebel armey myself a fiew months, but Seeing my errow I left, and has been out and an Idle Spectator now for near two yeares. I am opposed to the rebelion and fuley endorses the policy of the administration, upon the Slave question to put down the rebelion, and I trust as the Rebelion goese down that the Institution of Slavery Will go down with it; Though you may not Concure with me upon the policy and principal above aluded to (but never the less it is my notion or principal upon the Subject) [.]

I can if I am admited to forme said Company and report to you, as State Troops or state guards, give to you referancies or proof not onley of Lawyel Citizens, but eaven from the lines of the Federal armey, as to my verasity and principals &c.

So all I aske of you, will you admit me to enter the Survice as above stated with said Company; I am a pisioner heare it is true, but I before being a pisioner voluntearley takened the oath. I have been a pisioner more than two monthes and have been enformed that ther is no Chargies against me onley for having been in the Rebel armey—

I would reaither joine said Survice and assist in putting down the desloye theaving and gurilor Bands and other Conduct that is and has so longe manist [menaced] and disturbed the pease and diginty of my State (towit) Tennessee &[.]

you will please reply in haste[3] and oblige your friend[.]

I. L. Roark

ALS, DLC-JP.

1. Possibly Iredell (or Israel) Linville Roark (1830-1914), Macon County native, who became a lawyer (1853) and was a Douglas presidential elector in 1860. Enlisting as a sergeant major in the 30th Tenn. Inf., CSA, he eluded capture at Fort Donelson but fell

Perquisites of office.

Courtesy Hugh Lawing, Andrew Johnson National Monument, Greeneville.

into Federal hands at Elizabethton, Kentucky, in 1863 while reportedly scouting for Morgan. After acquittal in a trial for spying, he was interned at Camp Chase and later at Rock Island. Paroled in 1864, he resumed his practice and served in the legislature (1879-81). CSR, RG109, NA; McBride and Robison, *Biographical Directory*, II, 773.

2. "Col. Paten" has not been identified; at this time the commander at Camp Chase was Col. William Wallace (b. *c*1828), 15th Ohio Inf. CSR, RG94, NA.

3. Uncertain about the governor's receipt of his communication, Roark wrote again six days later. Roark to Johnson, November 19, 1863, File 563R (1863), Lets. Recd., RG249, NA.

From Loyal Men of Nashville

November 13, 1863, Nashville; Nashville *Union*, November 17, 1863.

Committee presents governor with silver service inscribed "From the Loyal Men of Nashville, Tennessee, to Andrew Johnson, as a testimonial of their high regard for his patriotic labors in defence of the Constitution and the Union: and especially for his zealous and able defence of the Government, in the Senate of the United States, Dec. 18 and 19, 1860; and for his devotion to Tennessee, and invaluable services rendered in the preservation of her Capital."

From Edward E. Jones[1]

Nashville, Tenn., Nov. 14, 1863.

His Excellency Andrew Johnson
Mil. Gov. of Tennessee—

My dear Sir— Knowing your charitable disposition, and your universal kindness to the poor and those in distress, I write you without other apology on a subject which I know you will consider of vital importance—it is on behalf of poor orphans. There are in this City several orphan children, and others who have lost their mothers, and whose fathers belong to the Army of the Union. These fathers have no means of providing for the care of their children, and many of them are running about our streets, destitute and without friend or relative to look after them. The Rev. Father Kelly,[2] proposes to organize a Society among the Catholics of Nashville for the support and education of these orphans, and a number of us have resolved to apply to you for aid. All we want from you is a temporary home in which to place them, and we will do the rest. It has been suggested that perhaps you could give us permission to occupy the residence of Maj. Hyman,[3] northwest from the Capitol, or some other building. If you *can* aid us, my dear Governor, I am sure you will do so, and your Catholic fellow citizens will feel themselves under lasting obligations to you, and the orphans will ever pray for and bless you.

I have called to see you several times, but never found you at leisure, & my time is too fully occupied to wait long. If you will be kind enough to send me a line, I will take great pleasure in waiting upon you at any time, and explain more fully our objects and plans, and furnish you whatever information I am possessed of.[4]

Believe me, Sir, with great respect
Your humble servant,
E. E. Jones

Dispatch Office.

ALS, DLC-JP.

1. Edward E. Jones (*c*1814-*fl*1878), English-born Edgefield resident and member of the firm of Bell, Jones, & Co., publishers of the Nashville *Daily and Weekly Gazette* (1866), was later (1868-69) a printer in the *Union and American* office. 1870 Census, Tenn., Davidson, 17th Dist., Edgefield, 19; Nashville city directories (1866-78), *passim*.

2. Joseph A. Kelly (*c*1810-1885), Dublin-born cleric, came to the United States sometime after 1827, attended St. Mary's, Bardstown, Kentucky, and became a priest of the Order of St. Dominic. At this time administrator of the diocese of Nashville (1863-65), he was later assigned to St. Peter's in Memphis. 1880 Census, Tenn., Shelby, Memphis, 138th Enum. Dist., 18; George Flanigen, ed., *Catholicity in Tennessee* (Nashville, 1937), 74; D. A. Quinn, *Heroes and Heroines* (Providence, R. I., 1887), 34.

3. For Adolphus Heiman, Nashville architect and Confederate colonel who had died in late 1862, see *Johnson Papers*, V, 544*n*. The house, built in 1850, was located on Summer Street adjacent to the Catholic Cathedral. John G. French, "Adolphus Heiman: Architect and Soldier," *Tenn. Hist. Quar.*, V (1946), 45.

4. Either Johnson or the Reverend Kelly disapproved of Jones's proposal, inasmuch as five months later, after a number of fund-raising activities, the Catholic Orphan Association bought a building for its charges. Nashville *Dispatch*, April 17, 1864.

From James B. Bingham

Cairo, Nov. 15, 1863.

Hon. Andrew Johnson,
Governor of Tennessee.

Dear Sir: I wrote to you at length, in reference to our municipal affairs at Memphis, and urging you to turn out the motley set of officers now in authority, on the 4th instant. Business of importance, connected with my private affairs, calls me to Cincinnati, and may take me farther East. I shall return home in two weeks, and in the event you have acceded to our request, the absence of Mr. Tomeny, Mr. Hill,[1] and others, will necessarily delay the matter until I can return—

You wrote me that you would visit Memphis in the early part of October, and I made arrangements for such a reception as would have gratified you. I hope you will try and find it convenient to visit our section before you shall deem it proper to appoint an election for State officers, in which event I promise to do every thing in my power to make it pleasant, if profitable.

The Secretary of the Treasury[2] has numerous appointees down at Memphis, all whom are understood to be active in labors looking to his selection as the next candidate for the Presidency. *Favors* are granted with that object in view. Many of us prefer you, if there is any chance; if not, we are not perfectly satisfied that Lincoln will not do for a second term.

I am sick, and nothing but pressing private business takes me away from home at present. I shall be glad to hear from you whenever your onerous duties will permit you to drop me a line.

Yours, truly, J. B. Bingham

ALS, DLC-JP.

1. Ira M. Hill (1819-1888), New York-born and Vermont-reared, moved to Memphis in 1841 and became a member of the firm of Cossitt, Hill, & Talmadge, wholesale dry goods merchants, accumulating an estate of $50,000 real and $130,000 personal property, which had grown to $365,000 by 1870. Appointed councilman for the 4th ward by Gen. C. C.Washburn, he subsequently served in the state lower house (1877-79) and senate (1881-83). 1860 Census, Tenn., Shelby, Memphis, 4th Ward, 51; (1870), 20; McBride and Robison, *Biographical Directory*, II, 417.

2. Salmon P. Chase.

From John Wygle[1]

Nov 16th A D 1863

Mr Andrew Johnson,
Dear Sir

I had a son die in field hospital Stevenson Ala and seeing Mr Cornelius advertisement in the Nashville Union[2] I employd him to send his remains home. I sent him 97 dollars the sum required 18 days ago. We felt perfectly safe in sending because you endorsed him.[3] If you will see him and let me know why the body is not sent you will oblige an anxious father.

John Wygle
Ravenna Portage Co Ohio

ALS, DLC-JP.

1. John Wygle (b. *c*1816), Pennsylvania-born farmer with property valued at $3,860, may have lost either of his sons—Henry, aged twenty-one, or William, eighteen. 1860 Census, Ohio, Portage, Freedom Township, 31.

2. Government undertaker William R. Cornelius was advertising in the *Union* during fall, 1863, that he would "attend promptly to the transportation of bodies, or giving any information regarding deceased soldiers," with "all communications promptly answered." Nashville *Union*, October 20, 1863.

3. Johnson's endorsement affirmed that Cornelius "is a gentleman of integrity, and will perform all that he undertakes or promises." *Ibid.*

To George D. Ramsay

November 16, 1863, Nashville; DNA-RG107, Tels. Recd., U. S. Mil. Tel., Vol. 71 (1863).

Quoting in its entirety Stanton's October 8 telegram authorizing him to make requisitions for arms and military supplies on ordnance officers and quartermasters for troops raised in Tennessee, Johnson reports to the chief of army ordnance that appeals to Captain Townsend at Nashville have elicited the response that "no arms are issued until the troops are mustered into the service of the U. S"; even so, "we have a number of troops here without arms."

hours. We have a baggage waggon at the depot on the arrival of each train, North and South.
When you stop inquire for the "KEYSTONE."
Jan28 3m

W. R. CORNELIUS,

Government Undertaker,

DEALER IN ALL KINDS OF METALIC BURIAL CASES AND

Zinc Coffins.

Will attend promptly to the transportation of bodies, or giving any information regarding deceased Soldiers.

"Bodies Embalmed."

Having secured the services of Dr. E. H. LEWIS, of New York, (and more recently from the Army of the Potomac,) for embalming of the dead, by Dr. Holmes AMERICAN PROCESS, acknowledged to be the best, and only true process in the United States, will have bodies embalmed when desired.

Principal Office and Ware-Rooms, No. 49 Church Street, Nashville, Tennessee.

Branch houses at Murfreesboro', Tullahoma, Wartrace, Shelbyville, Chattanooga and Stevenson, Alabama.

All communications promptly answered.

Mr. W. R. CORNELIUS is authorized to refer to me. He is a gentleman of integrity, and will perform all that he undertakes or promises.

ANDREW JOHNSON,
Military Governor.

Jan 1—tf

HERMAN W. HASSLOCK,

EMPFIEHLT SEINEN

A meritorious undertaking.
From Nashville *Union,* March 15, 1864.

From Robert Johnson

Nashville Nov 17th 1863

To His Excellency, Gov. Johnson,
Gov,

Herewith enclosed please find my resignation as Colonel of the 1st Regiment Tenn Cavalry, which you will, I hope accept—as I understand *you* desire it—[1]

If necessary & desired by you, I will resign the position authorized by the Secretary of War, to raise and organize a Brigade of Cavalry, under your direction— And perhaps, I can in some other field of duty, make amends for the past, and gain that Character that I deserve, *and which I will win*, at all hazards[.]

Respectfully I am Yours &c
Robt Johnson

ALS, DLC-JP.

1. The formal letter of resignation, also dated November 17, traces Robert's affiliations, locations, and activities since mustering in as a colonel at Washington, D. C., on March 1, 1862, and notes that since May 19, 1863, he has been relieved from duty with his regiment "for the purpose of organizing a Brigade of Cavalry." Vaguely explaining his resignation as "In Consequence of reasons more of a personal nature than otherwise," he rationalizes, "not that I expect to remain long out of the Service, but the better to enable me to do more good in our glorious Cause—" Although father and son differed over the former's direct role in the resignation, it is clear that Robert's inability to handle alcohol was at the heart of the problem. It was this which had brought about General Rosecrans' "gentle admonition" of April and which undoubtedly contributed to Robert's difficulty in personal relations with fellow officers. Robert to Andrew Johnson, November 17, 1863, Johnson Papers, LC; see also Letter to Robert Johnson, November 21, 1863; Telegram from William S. Rosecrans, April 12 and Telegram to William S. Rosecrans, June 1, 1863.

From Thomas L. Yancey[1]

[Clarksville], Nov 17th 1863.

Gov- Johnson

Sir— I have the honor to address the following petition and statement of facts to your Excellency. In August of last year while Coln. Woodward[2] held Clarksville I acted as his Quarter master. By the orders of Woodward a lot of forty five bales of cotton laying on the bank of the river between Clarksville and Nashville was brought to Clarksville and Sold. The cotton has been shipped by Andy Hamilton[3] to parties in Cincinnatti and New York. Woodwards command was not accepted by the Confederate Government, and my Soldiering ceased. About the 1st of Oct following at Bowling green Ky. I took an oath of allegiance to the United States and gave a bond of five thousand dollars to keep the same. I have not violated that oath, nor have I been accused of doing so. The first of last March a Mr Miles[4] of Nashville and another gentleman came to my house and informed me that Coln. Bruce[5] wanted to See me in Clarksville, arriving there I was informed that I was a prisoner to Coln. Ashburn[6] of Nashville[.] I was in prison a week and with two others gave a bond of Twenty Thousand Dollars to be in Nashville in twenty days. We were in Nashville at the end of the twenty days in Ashburn's office. Coln. Ashburn Said the Cotton was his. He demanded Twelve Thousand Dollars of us for the cotton and made many threats of imprisonment and other punishments if we did not pay the money. I thought Ashburn *tyranical* and beleived he was to have a certain portion of what he extorted from me. At the time of Seizure the cotton was not worth a third of what was demanded. I encouraged Ashburn to think if I was at large I would get the money and pay it in twenty days. I failed to raise the money and would not voluntarily put myself in Ashburns power. Since the 1st of April last I have kept myself out of his reach. I am able and willing to Shoulder all the responsibilities I have incurred.

I am anxious to be with my family and ask for an exercise of your authority to protect me from Summary arrest and wrong. Had you been in Nashville when I was there a prisoner, I should have asked for and confidently expected your intercession. I ask to be permitted to Stay at home in peace with my family.

Yours Very Respectfully
Thos. L Yancey.

ALS, DLC-JP.

1. Thomas L. Yancey (b. *c*1828), native Tennessean, was a Montgomery County farmer and Clarksville lawyer with $3,000 real and $30,000 personal property, much of the latter in thirty-six slaves. 1860 Census, Tenn., Montgomery, N & E of Cumberland River, 68; *ibid.*, Slave Schedule, 35; Titus, *Picturesque Clarksville*, 24.

2. Thomas G. Woodward (*c*1827-1864), a Christian County lawyer, organized the Oak Grove Rangers for Kentucky state guard service in April, 1861, and eventually became colonel of the 1st Ky. Cav., CSA. After his capture of Clarksville in August, 1862, his command was scattered and dissolved in September. Reorganizing his unit as the 2nd Ky. Cav., he was killed at Hopkinsville in August, 1864. 1850 Census, Ky., Christian, Hopkinsville, 421; CSR, RG109, NA; Titus, *Picturesque Clarksville*, 129-32.

3. Possibly A. L. Hamilton (b. *c*1827), Virginia-born preacher, teacher, and former president of the Clarksville Female Academy (1856-61). 1860 Census, Tenn., Montgomery, N & E of the Cumberland River, 168; Titus, *Picturesque Clarksville*, 69; Nashville *Patriot*, June 23, 1863.

4. Perhaps John Miles (b. *c*1828), a Tennessee-born watchman with $6,500 real and $300 personal property. 1860 Census, Tenn., Davidson, 10th Dist., 83.

5. For Sanders D. Bruce, former commander of the post of Clarksville, see *Johnson Papers*, IV, 531*n*.

6. George W. Ashburn claimed to own thirty-eight of the cotton bales confiscated by Yancey and Woodward. He apparently used his power as the military customs house surveyor at Nashville to have Yancey arrested. G. W. Ashburn to Abraham Lincoln, June 18, 1864, Lincoln Papers, LC; Proceedings of the Military Commission in the Case of Elisha H. Forsythe, September 16-October 2, 1863, RG153, NA; for Ashburn, see *Johnson Papers*, V, 334*n*.

From Joseph Ramsey

Shelbyville Nov 18th 1863

Dear Sir—

Permit me to Call your Attention To the Subject of Property Abandoned By Rebels as I Suppose there is at least One Million of Dollars Worth in this Town & County which Doubtless is Forfeited To the United States and of Course will Be Confiscated at Least a Considerble portion of It. But as It Appears as yet no person has Authority To Take charge of It and It is Already Greatly Wasted by damage Unnecessarily & Wantingly Committed by the Solders & Even the Negroes feel Authorized & do Commit Most Wanton outrages upon Such property[.] They Seem not disposed to Look after Wood for Fires But continue To Haul in from the Fences of such Land and To Witness the destruction of the Houses thus Abandoned is Terrible[.] for Example Take the property of Dr. Barksdales[1] in this Town finely Ornamented dwelling and was placed by him in possession of a Citizen To Take charge of It[.]
General Grainger ordered that Citizen to deliver it up for Mr Cleaveland[2] A Loyal Man who was [n]ot in the Service of the Govertent at that Tim[e.] the Raid Came Along and Mr Cleavland did not Come to occupy It[.] the Soldiers was permitted To Enter not only the outer Temple (yard) with Horses which Litteatly devord [devoured] the Beautifully & Ornemted [Ornamented] Shrubbey while the new Family Parlour is made a Cook Room[.][3] this property Certainly is forfeited & propely Belongs to the Unted [States] and should Be protected as A Matter of Economy to the Govertment[.] Mr Cleavland the gentleman who was the Authority of General Graing will Enter & Take good care of It until sum Regulations Can Be obtained[.] Attend to this matter.

Your Resptfully Joseph Ramsey

P S Things are as usual in this place[.] J R

ALS, DLC-JP.

1. James G. Barksdale (1801-1885), Virginia-born physician, possessed $15,000 real and $7,000 personal property. 1860 Census, Tenn., Bedford, Shelbyville, 60; Helen Crawford Marsh and Timothy R. Marsh, *Cemetery Records of Bedford County, Tennessee* (Shelbyville, 1976), 264.

2. Quite probably Jeremiah Cleveland (1806-1878), a South Carolina merchant who moved to Bedford County *c*1833 and became a farmer and railroad investor, ultimately possessing some 1,500 acres of land on the Duck River, 3,000 acres on the Mississippi, and $50,000 stock in the Nashville and Chattanooga Railroad. It may be assumed that he qualified as "loyal," despite the fact that one of his sons, having recently served with John Hunt Morgan, was currently in a Federal prison. Deane Porch, tr., *1850 Census of Bedford County, Tennessee* (Nashville, 1968), 32; *Goodspeed's Bedford*, 1135.

3. That Barksdale's residence, "a large rambling, two-story frame" built in the 1830's, and located "in a setting of shade trees and informal plantings of flowers and flowering shrubs," was a showplace is confirmed by its use as an inn after 1872. It appears that Mrs. Barksdale, confronted by her husband's invalid condition during these postwar

years, was obliged to open "The Shelbyville Hotel," later designated as the "Barksdale House," which, after more than three decades of operation, burned early in the new century. Bedford County Historical Society, *Doors to the Past: Homes of Shelbyville and Bedford County* (Shelbyville, 1969), 87; Nashville *American*, February 25, 1885.

From Sarah B. Cooper[1]

Memphis Nov 20th 1863

Gov Johnson
Dear Sir—

I cannot fail to drop just a line, to assure you that although we have received your *refusal* in regard to the matter requested by our friend Mrs. Cameron,[2] yet we can but feel that a sense of duty and a devotion to principle have prompted your action in regard to it.

You will allow me to add that *I* am responsible for the request[.] Mr. Cooper discouraged me from so doing urging your multiplied cares. But I promised him to be brief—the *impracticability* of the scheme did not for a moment occur to me, as so many, both in civil and military office are thus doing. Our heavy, necessary expenditures—and the salary of $1500—out of which Mr. C—is compelled to furnish his office and provide fuel—were the *only motives* that prompted the request. I hope, Sir, you will pardon any trespass upon your valuable time—or addition to your multiplied cares. I have a high sense of the valuable service rendered to me in Washington in a very trying time to me, and I shall not cease to hold it in lively remembrance.

You may not appreciate the sense of gratitude felt under such circumstances—and I would not be remiss in giving proper expression to the same.

Wishing for you and for the great and noble cause in which you are so faithfully engaged, every blessing of Heaven—I will subscribe myself very gratefully & truly

Sarah B. Cooper

To His Excellency Gov. Johnson

ALS, DLC-JP.

1. Sarah B. Ingersoll Cooper (1835-1896), Cazenovia, New York, native, educated at the Cazenovia and Troy seminaries (1850-53, 1854), spent a year as a governess on a Georgia plantation before marrying in 1855 a Cazenovia classmate, Halsey Fenimore Cooper, editor of the Chattanooga *Advertiser*. Unionists, they returned to New York in 1861, moving to Memphis two years later when Cooper was appointed assessor of internal revenue. There she organized a Union soldiers' Bible class and became president of the Society for the Protection of Refugees. Ill from overwork, she spent 1867-69 in St. Paul for her health, moving in May, 1869, with her husband to San Francisco, where he eventually became deputy collector of internal revenue. She wrote book reviews and articles for the *Overland Monthly* and the San Francisco *Bulletin*, and prepared reports on California education for the U. S. commissioner of education, as well as lecturing and teaching a Bible class. After 1879 she was active in the formation of the Golden Gate Kindergarten Association and in support of women's suffrage. Her husband committed suicide in 1885, and she and her daughter were asphyxiated eleven years later when the latter deliberately turned on the gas. Edward T. James, ed., *Notable American Women, 1607-1950* (3 vols.,

Cambridge, Mass., 1971), I, 380-82; *U. S. Official Register* (1865), 57; *San Francisco Directory* (1875), 207.

2. Possibly Emma Alcock Cameron, an artist and wife of Scottish-born artist James Cameron whom she married in 1847. They lived in Washington, where Cameron was a portrait painter, until the early fifties when they came to Chattanooga. Arrested as a Union sympathizer during the fall of 1861, Cameron was apparently released soon after, for the couple spent the war years in Philadelphia, returning to Tennessee when hostilities ended. Finding much of their property in ruins and their attempts at business a failure, they migrated in 1870 to California where Cameron entered the Presbyterian ministry and died in Oakland in 1882, having been accidentally poisoned by his wife. According to Mrs. Cooper's earlier letter, Mrs. Cameron sought a personal interview with Johnson "upon the subject concerning which we earnestly desire your favorable consideration"—a request which may have been concerned with the Camerons' return to Chattanooga. S. Cooper to Johnson, November 5, 1863, Johnson Papers, LC; Penelope Johnson Allen, *Genealogy of a Branch of the Johnson Family and Connections* (Chattanooga, 1967), 413-19; New Orleans *Picayune,* November 19, 1861; Washington *National Intelligencer,* May 28, 1852.

From John Patterson[1]

Ramsey Ills Nov 21st 1863

Mr A Jonson
Nashville Ten

Dear sir Haveing some business to transact in your state and being uninformed with regard to matters there concluded to solicit information from you. the circumstances are as follows I have comeing to me some five thousand dollars all in Judgement and some against parties in the Confederate service[.] now what I want to know is whether or not I can collect my demands or not. the parties all did live in Murry & Marshall County's[.]

I left the state of Ten in 1860 and that time Had an Execution against T. C Miller[2] ex Representative of Marshall Co and Thos R Cane[.][3] Miller joined the Confederate army in the Capacity of Capt and if his propperty should have been Confisscated could I recover my demands in any way. I was born and raised in Marshall Co and have three sons in the Union Army[4] and Can produce any evidence that may be required of my own loyalty. Has any money been pd to the state Treasure for John Patterson[?] would you be so kind as to answer this and give me what information you Can[.]

Direct to Ramsey Ills John Patterson

Yours Respectfully John Patterson

ALS, DLC-JP.

1. Probably John Patterson (b. *c*1814), Tennessee-born Marshall County farmer with combined property worth $6,550. 1860 Census, Tenn., Marshall, 10th Dist., 11.

2. Thomas C. H. Miller (b. *c*1808), North Carolina native, was a well-to-do farmer at Chapel Hill, Marshall County, with $35,925 real and $48,090 personal property. A member of the Tennessee house (1843-49), he later served briefly as colonel, 17th Tenn. Inf., CSA (1862), before resigning to become captain, Co. C, 11th Tenn. Cav. (1862-65). *Ibid.,* 8th Dist., 125; McBride and Robison, *Biographical Directory,* I, 521.

3. Not identified.

4. Patterson in 1860 had five sons eligible for military service: Thompson, aged 24, Brown, 22, Van Buren, 18, Andrew J., 17, and James K. P., 15. None served in Tennessee units. 1860 Census, Tenn., Marshall, 10th Dist. 11.

To Robert Johnson

Nashville, Nov 21st 1863

My dear Son,

Your note of the 17th inst is now before me— My sources of grief and care have been enough without your adding to them at this time— I have been determined that no act of mine Should be an excuse for your recent course of Conduct and do not now intend to depart from it— You tender your resignation, predicated upon my wish for you to do so, and as I obtained the Commission for you have the right to require you to resign and therefore you do resign— I have not indicated to you by word or deed any desire or wish on my part, that you Should resign your Commission as Col of the regiment: but on the contrary have expressed myself in the most emphatic terms, that I would rather See you once more your Self again and at the head of your Regiment going to your own native home than be possessed of the highest honors which Could be conferred upon me— In this so far I have been doomed to deep disappointment— I have said and now repeat that I feared you would be dismissed from the Army unless you reformed and took Command of your Regiment and give Some evidence of determination to Serve the country as a sober upright and honorable man— I have also said further, that your own reputation and that of an exiled family, required one of two things, reformation in your habits and attention to business, or to withdraw from the Army—one or the other is due yourself, the Regiment and the Govnt— This is what I have Said, it is what I now feel and think— Though my son I feel that I am but discharging the duty of a father who has devoted his whole life to the elevation of those he expected to leave behind him—

In your letter you Say my will is the law with you in reference to the resignation— I do most sincerely wish that my will was the law in regard to your future Course— I would be willing this night [to] resign my existence into the hands of him who gave it—

Your devoted father
Andrew Johnson

ALS, CSmH, Misc. #8211.

From Cheatham County Citizens

November 22, 1863, Cheatham County; Pet, DLC-JP.

Observing that lack of a coroner prevents having "a legal *post mortem* examination when a fellow creature is found dead," D. W. Nye and three others report that the preceding day Federal soldiers of the 1st Tenn. Cav. arrested a William B. Demumbre on Sycamore Creek and subsequently shot him. Inasmuch as "this occurrence has created great alarm in the neighborhood," they ask Johnson to "cause the matter to be investigated."

From Andrew Johnson, Jr.

November 22, 1863, Castle Thunder, Richmond, Va.; ALS, DLC-JP.

"your Affec nephew" points out that the previous month he had asked Johnson "to send some influential man for my Exchange." Being "without money or clothing and as Winter is coming on," he wishes his uncle "would do something . . . if possible."

To Joseph J. Reynolds[1]

Nashville Nov. 22, 1863.

Maj. Genl. J.J. Reynolds
Chief of Staff

The grading on the *North Western R. R.* is progressing well & will be completed as rapidly as the iron can be laid[.]

Thirty three 33 miles of rail have been laid & is in running order. Iron has been contracted for sufficient to complete the road but has not yet been received. It is feared that the Superintendent of Military Railroads[2] will make some excuse for applying to some other purpose. The work would have been much further advanced if the Supt. had furnished two (2) engines & construction cars as required by Govenor *Johnson* who was authorized by the Sec'y of War & Genl. *Rosecrans* to make the requisitions necessary for the prompt completion of the work. If the requisitions had been complied with The work could have been commenced at both ends of the road which would have ensured its completion in half the time, as yet there has been but one engine to the interest of the road & please have nothing interfere with these as it is a matter of deep interest in the present position of public affairs. This iron is what is brought to replace the iron taken from the state by the Govt & hope not to be taken for any other purpose.

Andrew Johnson
Mil Gov & Brig. Genl.

Tel, DNA-RG393, Dept. of the Cumberland, Tels. Recd., Vol. 68 (1863).

1. Joseph J. Reynolds (1822-1899), a native Kentuckian and adopted Hoosier, graduated from West Point (1843) where he served as an instructor, resigning from service in 1857 to teach engineering at Washington University, St. Louis. Engaged also in a grocery business in Lafayette, Indiana, in 1861 he rejoined the army, rising from colonel of the 10th Ind. to brigadier. A division commander at Chickamauga and Thomas' chief of staff, he was placed in charge of the defenses at New Orleans in 1864, organized the campaign against Mobile, and ended the war as commander of the Department of Arkansas. Subsequently in charge of occupation forces in Texas, he was elected by the carpetbag legislature to the U. S. Senate, but the seat was successfully contested and he never served. In 1876, during an attack on the Sioux, he ordered a premature retreat and resigned soon after under the threat of a court-martial. Warner, *Generals in Blue,* 397-98.

2. John B. Anderson.

From Thomas H. Coldwell

November 23, 1863, Shelbyville; ALS, DLC-JP.

Asks that someone be appointed to take care of abandoned property in Bedford County as "There is a considerable amount of it here & some of it is being very badly abused for the want of some one to attend to it." Suggests former sheriff James Wortham for the position.

From Orin G. Rutter[1]

Nashville 23d No 1863

Gov A. Johnson
Dear Sir

as the winter is approching and supposing that you will levvy a kind of tax on the welthy citizen as you did last winter[2]—for the support of the poore. I take the liberty of Pointing out to you a man who is worth about 65000 dollars and who has done all he could to brake up this Goverment, by inducing young men to go in the army, he has sent clothing frequently to Murfreesboro before the Battle[.] he has a son now at Camp Chace, his name is John Beaty[3] on front st[.] he says you never shall leave Nashville after peace, alive[.] for the truth of the above I will refer you to Mr. Jno Carper,[4] an alderman, who knows him well, by pilfering & otherwise he has made 15000 dollars since this war. I point him to you, as you cannot know all[.]

Respectfuly Orin G Rutter

ALS, DLC-JP.

1. Not identified.
2. See Assessment for Relief of the Poor, December 13, 1862.
3. John Beaty (1790-1874), born in Dunganon, Ireland, immigrated to New York City (*c*1804) where he learned the trade of chandler. After spending several years in Lexington, Kentucky (*c*1818-23), he moved to Nashville and operated a soap and candle factory, accumulating $21,000 real and $1,000 personal property by the beginning of the war. There is no evidence that his son William (1832-1900), a physician, served in the Confederate army, though a businessman William T. Beaty (*c*1829-*fl*1881), was a lieutenant in the 10th Tenn. Inf. 1860 Census, Tenn., Davidson, Nashville, 1st Ward, 8; 7th Ward, 66; (1900), 97th Enum. Dist., 19B; Nashville *Republican Banner,* December 3, 1874, June 8, 1900; *Nashville Bus. Dir.* (1860-61), 126; (1881), 118; CSR, RG109, NA.
4. John Carper (*c*1803-*fl*1874), Virginia-born locksmith, with $5,000 real and $3,500 personal property, served as councilman (1863-64) from Nashville's first ward. 1860 Census, Tenn. Davidson, Nashville, 1st Ward, 6; *King's Nashville City Directory* (1868), 95; *Nashville City Directory* (1875), 105; Wooldridge, *Nashville,* 124.

To Robert Johnson

Nashville Tenn
Nov 23d 1863

My Son,

Your note was handed me by your Sister[1] and was read with pleasure— My heart more than rejoiced to find that you had detemend [to] reform your course and become a Sober man— when-ever you are sufficiently restored to do business it will be most gratifying to me to place you in the office or any where else within my Control— But must I add that promises do not amount to much, without performance— You have made the promise that is done, the next thing is compliance with it— You certainly can control your appetites until reason and self respect once more get the ascendency— I shall wait with anxious hope for the result—

Your affectionate father
Andrew Johnson

ALS, CSmH, Misc. #8212.

1. Presumably, Mary Stover was the personal bearer of Robert's assurance of reform, a missive which has not survived the ravages of time.

Testimony re Condition of Negroes[1]

Nashville, Tenn, Nov. 23d, 1863.

Testimony of Gov. Andrew Johnson

Q Suppose the slaves emancipated throughout the South, do you think they would be able to maintain their position, without any interference on the part of the Federal Gov't, to make up to them the disadvantages they have incurred in slavey, in the way of education & the capability of taking care of themselves?

A I dont think they will be in a condition to do it. There is a vast difference between the mass of the negroes in South Carolina, & the mass of negroes here. We have found that by undertaking to gather them into contraband camps, we got only the dross;[2] and instead of doing that, we now tell the masters that they ought to begin at once to give them employment and pay them for their work; and the moment that begins, the whole question is settled. No longer ago than week before last, there was a gentleman here[3] who wanted to go into the making of cotton quite extensively, with hired negro labor. Women & children come in here in great numbers, and say they need a house and something to eat, and some of them will say, "My husband is in the service"; and they expect the Gov't will support them. I tell them, "There are white women whose husbands are in the service, and they have to work. The idea of freedom is not to do nothing; you must go to work[.] We have not brought you away from your masters, but we are not going to send you back. You must go to work and depend upon yourselves, and live by your own industry. We will give you a few days rations, and you must go round and get work." And in most instances they have done so; and we find this plan works much better than getting them all together in that squallid, debased condition which we see in contraband camps. I have thought it was better to set these negroes to work, paying them wages, than to make soldiers of them, because a soldier's life is a lazy one; but by setting the negroes at work, we give them an idea of contracts, and when the rebellion is over, they will be in a better condition to take care of themselves than if they were put into camps. A good many will not go into the service, but will go to work, and so we are able to employ them in both capacities. The women are kept at work cooking & washing, so that all are employed. Our experience so far has proved that to be the best policy.

I think the negro population in this State can be better managed than in South Carolina or Georgia, if we can only go along and give them work. There are hundreds of thousands of negroes here who will stay here, and almost perish in the gutters, rather than colonize.[4] They will stay, unless there is some compulsory process to drive them away.

Q Should you consider it necessary that Superintendents should be appointed to take care of the women and children, put them on plantations, pay them wages, and reimburse the Gov't from the proceeds of their labor?

A We have been talking about that here, too. There will be a good deal of property confiscated, but it has not been yet. So far as we can carry out the policy, in pursuance of law, I think it had better be done; but I have thought it not best to take property until the whole thing is settled. While there are hundreds of thousands of white families perfectly destitute, because the Gov't has not given them that protection in time, which they ought to have, I should not be disposed to cut up the plantations and put the negro women and children upon them. Such a course would create a good deal of feeling.

Q You think, then, they should be left alone?

A I think it is better to leave things as they are than to commence the other system, because many are making contracts now, and in many instances, their owners are paying them wages.

The idea that cotton cannot be made by white men is all a mistake. I was born and raised in a slave State, and I can remember when I went into the cotton field and picked out cotton,[5] and I could do more than any negro boy I ever saw; and if all the Alabama country was taken, and cut up into reasonable sized farms, with a white population, and the negroes hired, at fair wages, they would make more cotton than they could with slave labor, and raise their own meat & bread. It is true, no one would raise so many bales as the large planters have raised, but the aggregate product would be as great. If the rebellion was all settled up, I think a large portion of the servants would go right back, if they were stimulated with the offer of fair wages for their work.

Q To what extent do you think the slaveholders of Tennessee fall into the plan of hiring negroes?

A I don't think I have sufficient data to approximate a conclusion. A good many, however, are looking to that, and some have made application and want to go into it. If we could have two or three instances that succeeded pretty well, a large proportion of the slave labor would be absorbed.

Q You think the best way is to let that thing work itself out as it is without Gov't interference?

A I think so.

Q Previous to the war, when negroes were hired out, what was the average price paid for them?

A In the last few years, I think they would average from $100 to $120.[6] The hand[s] about the iron works & the cotton plantations were hired for more than the others, and women, of course, for less. The person who hires is generally required to pay the taxes & furnish clothing. Let me give you one single illustration. There has been a great mistake about the wealth of the South. Here is a man who has five whites in his family, and it is with difficulty that he makes one year's end meet the other. He is looked upon as a very poor man. Right over there is a man with fifty, sixty or a hundred negroes, and at the end of the year, it is with difficulty that he can pay his debts. Now, he is just about as poor as the other man. My idea is, that with proper management, free labor can be made more profitable than slave, in a very few years. This will place the negroes upon & within the great Democratic rule; it will unfetter industry, & if they have the talents and enterprise in them to rise, let them come. In adjusting this thing, the object is, to make them take the best and most benefical relation to society. Now, here are the women and children, who are incapable of making contracts. Sometimes, the children have no parents at all, and have become a charge upon the community. Now, we have in the State statutes in reference to orphan children, and the question comes up if a large portion of this negro population might not be made to take a much better position in society through the means of orphan asylums & similar institutions. When everybody occupies the same position in reference to slavey, every body will be in favor of that system which will make their condition advantageous to society. There will be no squabbling when that takes place. There must be vagrant laws for the negroes, as there are for whites, and laws to prevent their congregating in improper assemblies. So we should go on, & the time would come when black boys, as well as white, would be put to apprenticeships. I was a regular indentured apprentice myself, and I don't think it would hurt them at all. And these things are just as much needed for a great many of the whites as for the blacks.

Q How is it about kidnapping in this State?

A There is very little of it in this State. There have been a great many negroes run off further South. I think some of the rebels, notwithstanding they were great Southern men, have stolen negroes sometimes, sold them, and put the money in their pockets. When we came here, we just cleaned out the slave pens & the workhouses of all negroes that were not put in for crime, and I have no doubt that had some influence. Do not understand me as speaking against anything being done. I mean, let us see the practical condition of things, & conform our action to that.

Q What do you consider the legal status of the slaves in Tennessee?

A So far as emancipating the negroes in Tennessee is concerned, I don't think you need to trouble yourself much about that. I think that is already settled.[7]

Q Have you any colored troops here?

A Oh, yes, we have three regiments here.

Q How have they acted?

A They have performed much better than I expected. I was very agreeably disappointed. The negro takes to discipline easier than white men, and there is more imitation about them than about white men. Then another thing: when the idea is in his mind, that the connection between him and his master is broken, and he has got white men to stand by him and give him encouragement, and a gov't which says, "There is freedom before you—put down the enemies of the country; and if you desert, there is death behind you," my impression is that, after a little while, he will fight. Of course, he must have some experience. The thing succeeded much better than I expected, and the recruiting is still going on.

I object to massing the colored people together, and think they should be scattered as much as possible among the whites, because the influence of the whites upon them is beneficial, whereas the influences that surround them when congregated together are not calculated to elevate or improve them.[8]

Copy, DNA-RG94, Lets. Recd., Freedmen's Inquiry Commission; also in John Y. Simon and Felix James, eds., "Andrew Johnson and the Freedmen," *Lincoln Herald,* LXXIX (1977), 71-74.

1. With a growing number of newly freed blacks becoming wards of the government, Secretary of War Stanton appointed a commission to study and report on the "condition of the colored population" and "what measures will best contribute to their protection and improvement." This commission, the American Freedmen's Inquiry Commission, consisting of Samuel G. Howe, Col. James McKaye, and Robert Dale Owen, interviewed persons of both races, including Johnson. Simon and James, "Andrew Johnson and the Freedmen." 71-72; *Sen. Ex. Doc.* No. 53, 38 Cong., 1 sess.

2. Johnson had not experimented in Nashville with contraband camps and there is no evidence that he had investigated those established elsewhere in Tennessee. Camps

particularly attracted the unemployed, who may have constituted "the dross," given the governor's firm belief in self-reliance and laissez-faire. Cimprich, Slavery Amidst Civil War, 101-6.

3. Not found.

4. The return of Negroes to Africa had long been considered by some Americans to be the best possible solution to the problem of race relations. Lincoln favored it during the early war years and endorsed an ill-fated colonization program during 1863-64 at Ile à Vache, Haiti, involving 453 Negroes from Washington and Hampton, Virginia. James M. McPherson, *The Negro's Civil War* (New York, 1965), 77, 89-97.

5. In a later speech Johnson reminisced: "When fifteen years old I could pick more cotton than any negro I ever saw." In these, his only references to this aspect of his past, he neglected to mention a location; however, some Alabamians believe that he lived at Mooresville, in a cotton-producing region, during part of his youth. Speech to the Union State Convention, January 12, 1865; Scottsboro (Alabama) *Jackson County Advertiser,* January 10, 1979.

6. These rates were for a year's service. Eugene D. Genovese, *Roll, Jordan, Roll: The World the Slaves Made* (New York, 1974), 391.

7. As slavery remained legally untouched in Tennessee (the Emancipation Proclamation had exempted the state), Johnson is probably referring to the fact that many slaves in federally occupied areas refused to act as slaves. Given his state rights convictions, he may also have intended to discourage any Federal legal action on the matter in Tennessee. See Letters to Stephen A. Hurlbut, October 3, and to Montgomery Blair, November 24, 1863.

8. Actually the exact opposite occurred, with runaway slaves concentrated in contraband camps and Negro ghettos near Federal garrisons. Cimprich, Slavery Amidst Civil War, 99-112.

To Montgomery Blair

Nashville Nov 24th 1863.

To Hon M. Blair
P M. G

Confidential. I hope that the Prest will not be committed [to] the proposition of states relapsing into Territories & sold as such[.][1] if he steers Clear of this extreme his election to the next Presidency is without a reasonable doubt[.] I expected to have been in Washington before this time when I could have conversed freely & fully in reference to the policy to be adopted by the Govt but it has been impossible for me to leave Nashville[.] I will be there soon. The institution of slavery is gone & there is no good reason now for destroying the states to bring about the destruction of slavery[.]

Andrew Johnson Mil Gov

Tel, DLC-Lincoln Papers.

1. A number of the more radical Republicans like Charles Sumner and Thaddeus Stevens held that secession amounted to state suicide, an abdication of all rights under the Constitution, and a reversion to territorial status. Herman Belz, *Reconstructing the Union: Theory and Policy During the Civil War* (Ithaca, 1969), 10-13, 45.

From Caroline Chase[1]

Platte Valley November 25 [1863]

Dear Friend

You will no doubt be somewhat suprised to recieve a letter from me after so long a silence, I have thought of you often if I have not written to you, This war has so completely changed the order of things that I hardly know what to say to you, I have a Son in the Union Army,[2] a private in the Michigan Fist Infantry, He has been there one year last April[.] He is eighteen years of age. When he enlisted, the recruiting offier told him that the war would end in three months and many other fine stories, He has been in six severe battels but has never been promoted[.] no boy alone as he is and a *Democrat* stands any chance of being promoted in *Our* Army, Now can you by any means either get him transfered to your own state or discharged entirely? So that he can come home, We are liveing away up in Nebraskia out of civilization nearly, driven here by political influence[.] Or at least Ned[3] was and of course I followed him——
We have got the gold feave now and shall I think start for Bannock City[4] as early as the first of May, I would be glad to have my boy to go with me there, Dear Friend when shall we meete again? Oh! how much I would like to see you. Are you going to Washington this winter? Or do your duties demand your attention at home, What do you think of our broken to peicies country? Should all the piecies ever be gathered up will our rulers ever be able to put them togather again so that they will stay, Alas I fear not, I have nearly done lamenting the war now[.] at first it did seem so hard that we should be fighting against ourselves[.] Now if you are not to much ocupied with your many duties will you write to me and tell me if you can do any thing for my boy— He is a good boy, (*like his Ma you know*) writes a good hand and would be of some use to you should you see fit to do any thing for him,

January 3rd 1864

Dear Friend

Since writeing the within I have been very sick, I am a little better now and will finish this poor apology for a letter by asking you to do all you can for that boy of mine[.] He is in the first regiment of Michigan Infantry Co H. His name is Samuel D Chase, Now good Bye God Bless You[.] If you write to me please direct to Platte Valley Post Office, Nebraskia and oblige[.][5]

Cara Chase

ALS, DLC-JP.

1. Caroline A. Chase (b. *c*1826), a New York native married to Edward R. Chase, former patent office clerk, knew Johnson when they were all living in Washington in 1858. 1870 Census, Nevada, Elk, Clover Valley, 87; *Boyd's Washington and Georgetown Directory* (1858), 66.

2. Throughout his military career a private, Co. H, 1st Mich. Inf., Samuel D. Chase (*c*1845-*fl*1913?), despite his mother's opposition, reenlisted after two years' service in March, 1864, only to be charged with desertion at "North Ann [*sic*], Va. in face of the enemy" on May 23. He claimed to have been captured and sent to Andersonville; but the army record, after noting that he was "reported to have taken oath of allegiance to Southern Confederacy," concluded that "the final record of this soldier is that of a deserter[.]" After the war he was a Nevada farmer. CSR, RG94, NA; 1870 Census, Nevada, Elk, Clover Valley, 87.

3. Her husband, Edward R. Chase (b. *c*1819), a New Yorker and an assistant examiner in the patent office in the late 1850's, was a lawyer in Austin, Nevada, in 1866, and by 1870 was a farmer. *Ibid.; Boyd's Washington and Georgetown Directory* (1858), 66; *Harrington's Directory of the City of Austin, Nevada* (1866), 71.

4. The first of Montana's several gold rushes occurred at Bannock City in the late summer of 1862, after three men found a rich placer deposit at Grasshopper Creek. The news spread and by October about four hundred people were at the site; by the end of the year the mines had produced gold worth approximately $600,000. The following May a richer deposit in Alder Gulch, some seventy miles east, attracted thousands of miners, resulting in several towns, including Virginia City and Nevada City. *Mineral Resources in the United States* (Washington, 1868), 46, 47, 51; Michael P. Malone and Richard B. Roeder, *The Montana Past: An Anthology* (Missoula, 1969), 68, 70, 98.

5. A month later, reminding the governor of "the pleasent times we used to have in Washington," she once again begged his intervention: "You can get his discharge, if you will[.]" Chase to Johnson, February 5, [1864], Johnson Papers, LC.

To Montgomery C. Meigs[1]

Nashville Tennessee
Nov. 26" 1863

Brig. Genl. M. C. Meigs
Quarter Master General.
Genl:

I have requested Col. Wm. P. Innes to visit you in person and talk over Nashville and North-Western Rail Road matters[.]

Under Orders from Maj Genl Rosecrans I desired Col. Innes, last September, through his Quarter Master of U. S. Mil. Rail Road to contract for the Iron necessary for the Road to replace that used by the U. S. Government, which he did, and the Iron is now on the way to this place. I request your Cooperation with me to make the necessary arrangements to have the Iron forwarded here as soon as possible, and would be obliged if you would order Col. Donaldson or Genl. Allen,[2] or whoever is the proper person, to aid me in Every way to forward the Iron, and also order them to pay for the same, and for other materials necessary, upon my requisition, as provided for in the Order of Oct. 19th 1863.

We are progressing very well indeed and have the work now in such position, that we can lay down the rail as fast as delivered, and in a very short time open Communication to the Tennessee River, thus giving us another and entirely independant base of supplies.

I dont think I over estimate the value of this new avenue, when I say the value to the Gov't. can not be computed: and I only regret that the Iron was permitted to be removed: had it not been removed, ere this time the work would have been much farther ahead, but I shall endeavor to make up for lost time with your cooperation.

Please furnish Col. Innes with every required document,

And Oblige, Your Obt. Servt.
Andrew Johnson
Mil. Gov. and Brig. Genl.

LS, DLC-JP.

1. See *Johnson Papers,* III, 179*n*.

2. James L. Donaldson and native Ohioan Robert Allen (1811-1886), West Point classmates (1836), had fought in the Mexican War. Both saw service in the quartermaster corps during the 1850's, the one in New Mexico, the other in the Pacific Division. Donaldson, as chief quartermaster of the Middle Department and the Department of the Cumberland, and Allen, as chief quartermaster for the Mississippi Valley, were both headquartered in Nashville. Boatner, *Civil War Dictionary,* 10, 243; Warner, *Generals in Blue,* 3-4.

From Edward R. S. Canby

War Department Washington City
November 27th 1863.

General:

The Secretary of War directs me to invite your attention to the accompanying orders and vouchers for transportation, purporting to be signed by yourself as Military Governor of Tennessee.

These accounts are not properly chargeable to the Quartermaster's Department, and, before giving an order for their payment out of any other fund, the Secretary desires you to report by what authority you have furnished orders for transportation to persons not traveling on military errands, and also to explain the evident forgery of your signature to one or the other of the orders.

You will please return the enclosures with your answer.[1]

Very Respectfully, Your Obedient Servant
Ed. R. S. Canby
Brig: Genl., A. A. G.

Brig: Genl. Andrew Johnson,
Military Govr: of Tennessee,
Nashville, Tenn.

LS, DLC-JP; DNA-RG107, Mil. B.: Copies Lets. Sent, Vol. 53B (1863-64).

1. The endorsement of the enclosed voucher, addressed to the "Ohio & Miss. RR" for $2.96 and signed for Johnson, reads: "The party transported [from Vincennes, Indiana, to St. Louis] was on civil business." Johnson Papers, LC.

To Maunsell B. Field[1]

Nashville Nov 29 [1863]

Hon. M. B. Field
Asst Secy Trery

The bonds to which you refer[2] were no doubt removed south by Gov. Harris when he fled south together with all the public records of the state & the assets of the state Bank at an early period of the rebellion. It was published in the papers that he had seized these bonds then in the hands of Jesse E Thomas who was then Surveyor of Customs at this place[.] The letter referred to in your telegram of a previous date was answered at the time by Mr Fowler the Comptroller of the state giving the information then desired on the subject[.][3]

Andrew Johnson Mil Gov

Tel, DNA-RG107, Tels. Recd., U. S. Mil. Tel., Vol. 72 (1863).

1. Maunsell B. Field (1822-1875), Yale graduate (1841), made several extensive European tours in the 1840's and 1850's, serving a year (1854-55) as secretary of legation to John Y. Mason, minister to France. Appointed U. S. deputy assistant treasurer at New York City in 1861, he was promoted to assistant secretary of the treasury in September, 1863. Resigning two years later, he subsequently served as collector of internal revenue for the 6th district of New York (1865-69) and judge, 2nd judicial district court, New York City (1873-75). His literary works included reminiscences, *Memories of Many Men and of Some Women,* and a small volume of poems (1869). *DAB,* VI, 368-69; *NCAB,* XXIII, 212.

2. The preceding day Field had inquired about "Bonds of State of Tennessee, amounting to $66.666.66. sent to Surveyor of Customs in 1855, referred to in a letter to you May 7, 1862, to which no reply was received." Field to Johnson, November 28, 1863, Lets. Sent, Vol. 2, p. 197, RG56, NA; Letter from George Harrington, May 7, 1862, *Johnson Papers,* V, 366-67.

3. Not extant.

To Stephen A. Hurlbut, Memphis

November 29, 1863, Nashville; L draft, DLC-JP.

Acknowledging receipt of Hurlbut's November 18 letter, observes that he has borne with "the incompetency of persons organizing Regiments in this State . . . for the purpose of having their influence in raising troops"; however, Colonels Hawkins and Hurst "were among the first in West Tennessee to engage in the work[.] And after having lost much time, running considerable risk, making considerable Sacrifice would now feel that they had been very harshly and unjustly treated now to be relieved from their commands without their consent." Assuring that he will place in command "those gentlemen alluded to in your letter," if they will undertake to raise regiments, the governor hopes to be soon in Memphis, "when we can consult freely and fully in regard to the policy to be pursued in the restoration of the civil authority of the state."

From John Hambright[1]

Bradley County December 1863

Dear Sir I Send you by Sterling a fur hat made by Andrew Carr[.][2] he Lives in Polk County and was at one time one of your friends and always voted for you[.] he Lives fourteen miles from Benton (the County Seat of Polk) Eight Miles from where the Ocoee River passes through the Chilhowee mountains near Silco Creek in a deep Revine of the mountain[.] I do not know what Carrs politicks now are as thare are many of your old friends who are now your bitter Enemies and many of your Old political foes are now your best friends[.] I do not write this beleiving it would be of any perticular Information to you but I would be glad for you to know that there is not a *Union* man in Lower East Tennessee but would vote for you for any office they Could prevail on you to Except[.] the Hat I send you I Caught the Raccoons in Bradley County (the Otter that the hat is napped with) was Caught in Chestua Creek in Polk County[.] So you See we have both the animals and the mechanicks, (although the war has devasted our Beautiful Homes and Country[.] Please Except my thanks for the favors you have done to Sterling[.] Sterling can tell you the news here, but I am proud to say that the Star Spangled Banner now Floats over the County of Bradley (Long may it wave)[.] God has hitherto Protected that Proud Flag and I beleive that God will Curse and Blight the Traitrous Hands that dare to Disacrate and tare it, while we live my dear Sir let us Live for our Country and if need be when we die let us go down in its defence, I Could write you about many other things that has been Rappidly Passing before my Eyes for the Last two years about the Negroes and their masters their feelings Two years ago their feelling now their actions Two years ago what they say now the great Change that appears to have Come over them how docile now how haughty Two years ago what I beleive has made the Change how S[l]aves are Ruled (Especially Slave Owners)[.] all this perhaps would not be Interesting to you but has made a deep Impression on my mind that will not be forgotten Soon[.] I Learn you Expect to visit East Tennessee Soon[.] I hope I will then See you and See once more Law and Order Restored here[.]

Yours Respet., John Hambright

To his Excelency A. Johnson
Nashville Tenn.

I would have been glad to have been about to have furnished trimings for the hat[.] you must Excuse me as there are no Such things in this Country[.]

J. H.

ALS, DLC-JP.

1. John Hambright (b. *c*1806), native Tennessee farmer with $33,000 real and $7,000 personal property. 1860 Census, Tenn., Bradley, 1st Dist., 188.

2. Sterling (b. *c*1840), Hambright's second son, joined the army in Nashville in August and ultimately advanced to major, 10th Tenn. Cav., USA (1863-65). Andrew Carr (b. *c*1805) was a Polk County farmer. *Ibid.; Tennesseans in the Civil War,* I, 344; II, 518; CSR, RG94, NA; 1870 Census, Tenn., Polk, 5th Dist., 6.

From William G. Brownlow

Cincinnati Dec 1 1863

To Gov Johnson
Some three to five thousand persons little & big came through the mountains and are between Lexington & Barboursville in a state of great destitution[.] Those who have money have such as will not pass[.][1] they are trying to get to their relations in Ind Ill. & O. It is sickening to the heart to see them pass & converse with them[.] can we do any thing for them[?] Transportation is wanting[.][2]

W. G Brownlow

Tel, DLC-JP.

1. Possibly a reference to Confederate currency.

2. It can be inferred from the Letter from Joseph Powell, December 6, 1863, that the governor was trying to meet the transportation needs of the refugees.

From Henry B. Carrington[1]

Indianapolis. Ind. Dec. 1. 1863.

Sir.
A steel die, purporting to be the first "Great Seal of the State of Tennessee, dated the year of the birth of the state was purchased by a Jew, with a lot of cannon axles and other valuable pieces of iron, hid by the rebels at Nashville, and taken upon our occupation of the city. A gentleman purchased several barrels of the iron & found this Seal among them. He has promised to send it to me to send you if it is of genuine worth. Please write me whether the Original seal is missing & whether it could be of interest to the state to receive this.

I am very Truly Your Obt. Servt.
Henry B Carrington
Col. 18th U. S. Infy. Brig. Genl. U. S. Vols.

His Excellency, Gov. Andrew Johnson
Nashville Tenn-

ALS, DLC-JP.

1. Henry B. Carrington (1824-1912), Connecticut native and Yale graduate (1845), studied law and in 1848 moved to Columbus, Ohio, where he practiced with William Dennison. His reorganization of the state militia in 1857 led to appointment as state adjutant general. Commissioned colonel, 18th U. S. Inf. in 1861, he became brigadier a year later and at Governor Morton's request superintended troop recruitment in Indiana, while "ruthlessly suppressing the disloyal Sons of Liberty." After the war he built Fort Phil Kearny in the Rocky Mountain District, participated in the Red Cloud War, "occupied a prominent position in Indian negotiations," taught military science at Wabash

College, and wrote a number of books, including *Battles of the American Revolution* (1876) and *Washington: The Soldier* (1898). *DAB,* III, 520-21; Warner, *Generals in Blue,* 72-73.

From Citizens in Nashville Military Prison[1]

December 1st 1863

To his Excelency Andrew Johnston
Millitary Governor of the State of Tenn
Respected Sir.

We the undersigned Citizens, at present Confined in the Millatary Prison at this place, would most respectfully and humbly call the attention of your Excelency to our Situation, hoping some action may be taken on our Cases, and the charges if any, against us investigated.

Many of us have been here severall months, have left our families destitute, and without any meens of support, and have made no preparation for the hardships of the coming winter, which will find our Families destitute of every Comfort.

Several of us are aged men, from 50 to 70 years of age, and are unable to endure the hardships of our imprisonment. Many of us are loyal Citizens of the "United States," and others are willing to take the Oath of allegiance to the United States Gov't, and some have already done so, while against the majority of us no charges exist whatever, and none are guilty of any crime of magnitude against the Gov't.

What we most earnestly wish, is that our cases may be investigated without delay, many of us having been here for some months, and have not had a hearing, and do not know of any charges against us.

Our Room is much crowded, to much so for comfort and helth, many of us are without bedding, and have only the Clothing we have on, and no meens of procuring any. So it is impossble to remain free from disease which to the aged confined here, deprived of the comforts of home, may prove fatal.

Trusting that we will be granted a hearing without delay and our cases disposed of,[2] and that you will use your influence to that end, we remain with much respect

Nashville Millitary Prison — Your Fellow Citizens

Pet, DLC-JP.

1. This petition was signed by forty-nine Tennesseans of scattered residence, all of whom would appear to fall in the plebeian class.

2. According to Provost Marshal Galloway's endorsement, "Most of the within named men have been before Capt Goodwin Asst Pro Mar Gen Dept of Cumb and are held by command of Maj Genl Thomas[.]"

From John Durand & Co.

December 1, 1863, New York City; PL, DLC-JP.

Publishers' circular, not "to be seen by any one but yourself," announces pending publication of "*THE DEFENDERS OF THE UNION*" and solicits photograph, autograph, and biographical information, as well as contributions "according to their ability," from "those living Heroes and Statesmen, whose portraits and biographies will adorn its pages."

From William Shane

December 1, 1863, Nashville; ALS, DLC-JP.

In response to Johnson's inquiry about cause and length of sentence for "Jim Sanders (colored)," the city recorder, citing mule-stealing as the offense, reports that Sanders went to his former owner's house "in the night & got the mule valued at $125.00 & sold him the next morning for $20.00[.]" Fined fifty dollars and sentenced to the workhouse, the culprit paid the fine and is currently incarcerated— "Will be released when his time comes. They accumulate so fast that we continuly release those in the long[est] time to make room for the new ones."

To Robert S. Granger[1]

Nashville, December 1st 1863

Brig Gen'l R. S. Granger
Comd'g Post Nashville
Gen'l,

There are a number of families occupying a building owned by Mr Whiteman—[2] I have been advised by Mrs Garvin[3] that Some person assuming to act under the authority of the Military, proposes to turn them into the Street, without providing them with other quarters— These families are poor and destitute—most of them have husbands in the Service of the United States as private Soldiers— If these families are disposessed, quarters should be provided elsewhere for them— If this is being done, by an order of the Military, I hope that Genl Granger will have it examined into, and prevent women and children from being thrown in the street at this inclement season of the year, to freeze to death.

If it is not being done in compliance with an order from your Department, please advise me of the Same, and I will without delay have it attended to[.][4]

Most respectfully
Andrew Johnson Mil Gov

L, DLC-JP.

1. Robert S. Granger (1816-1894), Zanesville, Ohio, native and West Point graduate (1838), served in the Seminole and Mexican wars, and as an instructor at the Point (1843-44). Captured in Texas during April, 1861, he was paroled—not to serve within Confederate lines. As brigadier general of U. S. volunteers after October 20, 1862, he

commanded successively at Bowling Green, Kentucky, Nashville and the District of Middle Tennessee, and the District of Northern Alabama. Breveted major general in March, 1865, and mustered out of the volunteer service the following January, he afterwards commanded various posts in Virginia, retiring as colonel of the 21st Inf. in 1873. *NCAB,* XII, 284; Warner, *Generals in Blue,* 182.

2. Probably William S. Whiteman (1808-1889), a Nashville paper manufacturer with real estate valued at $150,000 and personalty of $30,000, who, having supplied the Confederate state government with powder, fled the city after Donelson. It is not uninteresting, given the fact that these were unionist families, that Whiteman, a year and a half earlier, had promised to provide free housing for the families of Confederate recruits. 1860 Census, Tenn., Davidson, Nashville, 2nd Ward, 35; Clayton, *Davidson County,* 208; Garrett and McClain, *Old City Cemetery,* 99; *OR,* Ser. 1, LII, Pt. II, 163; New York *World,* June 18, 1862.

3. Not identified.

4. The same day Granger endorsed the letter: "Respy returned to Gov Johnson— This house is ordered to be taken for addition to small pox hospital— This is a military necessity consequent on the spread of this pestilential disease at this post"; to which Johnson responded a day later: "Respectfully returned to Gen. Granger Comdg. Post with the inquiry, have tenements been found for the women and children who were dispossessed of these houses[?] Would it not be as humane for persons to die with the small pox as for helpless women and children to perish in the street with hunger and cold?"

From James A. Galbraith

Lexington Ky Decr 2d 1863

Gov Andrew Johnson
Nashville Tenn
Dear Sir

Being from home and Short of funds I am Compelled to Call upon you to assist me a little If you please— Yourself & Son Col Robt owe me an a/c of 80$ and 20$ respectively, perhaps something over, = equal to 100$[.] Will you be so good as to Send it to me at *Cincinnati Per Express* Care of Mess Barwise & King[.][1]

What Chance for the position of Lt. Col. in the 4th Ten Inft.? I understand the place is vacant.[2]

Very Respectfully
James A. Galbraith

ALS, DLC-JP.

1. Johnson sent the money in care of Luther T. Barwise and Joseph King, merchant tailors and clothiers at 171 Main Street. Johnson to Galbraith, December 5, 1863, Johnson Papers, LC; *Williams' Cincinnati City Directory* (1861), 55; (1863), 61.

2. In September Johnson had removed Lt. Col. James W. M. Grayson. Galbraith did not get the appointment; instead, Maj. Michael L. Patterson was promoted in February, 1864. *Tenn. Adj. Gen. Report* (1866), 75.

From T. Hopkins Bunch[1]

Nashville, Dec. 3rd 1863

Andrew Johnso[n]
Military Gov Tenn
Genl.

I have the honor to state that the property that Mr Darden[2] reports to you that was taken from him by me are two mules & five Negroes, the above property that is the negros claimed protection from me and rode the mules to my Camps and claimed them as their property[.] one of the Mules has had its leg broken and the other is not any account. I do not think Gov. that I am responcible for property that negroes bring with them in to my Camp.[3] But am compelled to give the negroes protection[.]

I have the honor to be Yor Obt Svt
T. Hops Bunch
Capt Co "A" 9th Tenn Cavalry

ALS, DLC-JP.

1. Conscripted into the Confederate army in East Tennessee while trying to reach Federal lines, T. Hopkins Bunch (b. *c*1839) transferred after service in Mobile to Bragg's command and escaped during the latter's retreat from Tullahoma. Raising Co. A, 9th Tenn. Cav., USA, he served as its captain from August 13, 1863, until his resignation, for the "Good of the service," on June 8, 1864. That he "brought a woman from a House of ill fame and introduced her to a boarding house as his wife," that he was accused of shooting at several men, and that he had on occasion misrepresented his name and position may help to explain the circumstances of his departure from the service. CSR, RG94, NA; *Tennesseans in the Civil War,* I, 343.

2. John C. (b. 1826) and Virginia Darden (1829-*fl*1901), Tennessee natives, ran a boarding house in Nashville; Darden additionally worked as a grocer. Mrs. Darden owned six slaves, ranging in age from eight months to seventy years. 1860 Census, Davidson, Nashville, 3rd Ward, 83; *ibid.,* Slave Schedule, 1st-4th Wards, 11; *Nashville Bus. Dir.* (1860-61), 152; *Marshall and Bruce Nashville Directory* (1901), 372; 1900 Census, Tenn., Davidson, 84th Enum. Dist, 7A; James D. Richardson, *Tennessee Templars: A Register of Names* (Nashville, 1883), 48.

3. The somewhat contentious tone of this letter and the writer's subsequent history seem strangely at odds with the exuberantly favorable response of eighty-three citizens of Springfield less than two weeks later to his and his corps' presence. Describing in purple passages their plight—"anarchy resigned Supreme! . . . daily depredations of murderers, Thieves, marauders and robbers"—before Bunch's arrival, "instantaneous in its effects . . . light Seemed to spring up in The midst of darkness . . . our deliverance had been affected!" The gist of their message was a plea to permit this "best behaved set of men that has ever visited our Town" to remain; but, failing that, at least, "that *Capt. Bunch* should be retained in Command of the Post." Citizens of Springfield to Johnson, December 14, 1863, Johnson Papers, LC.

From John Hugh Smith

December 3, 1863, Nashville; ALS, DLC-JP.

On behalf of Mrs. Miller, "a true and loyal woman, raised in East Tennessee and respectably connected . . . a widow lady [who] resides in an old delapidated frame building" supporting "5 or 6 very small children . . . by her needle," the mayor requests Johnson's intercession to prevent threatened eviction by landlord Joshua Spain.

Gun Permit

State of Tennessee
Executive Department,
Nashville, Decr. 3rd 1863

Miss Maxwell[1] of Davidson County is authorized to keep a shot-gun and pistols for protection of herself and property[.]

Andrew Johnson Mil: Gov. Tenn

L, Travelers' Rest Historic House, Nashville.

1. Probably Mira [Myra?] L. Maxwell (b. *c*1797), a widow who was a farmer with $6,000 in real and $15,750 in personal estate. 1860 Census, Tenn., Davidson, 8th Dist., 135; Porch, *1850 Census, Davidson*, 181.

From Albany Committee of Army Relief Bazaar

December 5, 1863, Albany, N. Y.; PL, DLC-JP.

Circular letter with endorsement of New York Adjutant General John T. Sprague requests "fifty or less" of Johnson's "official signatures," to be sold with his photograph at a February 1, 1864, "Great Fair" to benefit the U. S. Sanitary Commission.

From Blackston McDannel[1]

Winnie House Cincinnatti Ohio
Saturday Dec. 5, 1863

Friend Johnson

I scarcely know whether to write you a short letter or a long one, as the former would be unsatisfactory and the latter might be intrusive; but upon the whole, I will be as brief as possible.

November 7, Saturday night, I had the honor of advancing backwards, from Greeneville, with Gen'l Wilcox.[2] About an hour before sundown one of his regiments of six months Indianians, marched through town toward Bulls Gap, singing "Rally to the Flag boys"[.] The other regiments, "horse, foot and dragoons" wagon trains and all, arrived in town by 9 Oclock, completely blocking up the whole town, giving us poor devils but a short time and a poor chance to make preparations and escape from the enemy, as they (the rebels) were supposed to be close at hand.[3] Some left on foot, some on horseback and others in Wagons. I took the Warrensburg road in company with Sheriff Jones[4] and others, passing through a bridge on fire, three miles below, and halted four miles from town for the night. Wilcox ordered all the trussel work and bridges, as far down as the R. R. Bridge at Lick creek, to be burned. So all was burned, except the Swan Pond trussel work and Lick Creek bridge. The guard at these places prevented their destruction that night. Well, on Sunday we arrived at McFarlands[5] in Jefferson county. Wilcox halted at Bulls Gap and commenced fortifying— Lawyer Jim Britton[6] and myself, on Wednesday, started for home, by the way of Bulls Gap. We made an attempt to get through the pickets, but were repulsed. So we fell back to Whitesburg. Next morning we succeeded in passing in, but the authorities told us we could not get to Greenville— So I left Wilcox fortifying and went to Knoxville on Friday. That day Woolford and Sanders were whip't, nine miles South of Knoxville, and fell back;[7] next day, whip't again and fell back; next day, (Sunday) they were fighting briskly about two miles, South, from town. That night Brownlow, Baxter and Temple[8] and others left town for one of the Cumberland mountain gaps. Burnsides with his main force was at Lenoirs, and no troops to defend Knoxville but the brigades of Woolford and Saunders.[9] On Saturday night Gen'l Carter[10] cried like a child at the prospects of having to abandon E. Ten. and arrangements were made to fire the depots and destroy shops and every thing that would benefit the rebels. So, seeing and knowing all these things, I concluded it would save a rope by taking possession of Big Creek Gap,[11] at which place I arrived on Tuesday evening in time to get across the mountain that night by 10 Oclock. Here a train of 30 wagons had halted, with a few soldiers— They kindly gave us our suppers, and the heads of some barrels to sleep upon in a wagon. We (brother Jo. and my brotherinlaw Thompson)[12] jogged along, with only one horse, until we arrived at London. Here we found that we had out run Brownlow and Baxter, they having halted for a few days at Barbersville, We finally arrived at Lexington where we took the Cars and came to this Stone coal city,[13] where we can live high every day and get drunk, provided we have the Greenbacks. Brownlow, Temple, Jno. Netherland, Monroe Meek, Swan of Dandridge, Jim Galbreath, his brother David, Jo. Powel, Bob. McKee and Mitch McKee, Jim Lyon[14] and many others are here, and many more on the road— Lawyer Jim Britton went back from Bulls gap and brought his family off. He is somewhere in the rear. Some of the boys are out of Greenbacks, but it is believed they can be supplied in some way or other, as those who can work, may find employment.

I called on A. C. Sands,[15] U. S. Marshal for the Southern Dist of Ohio. He gave much valuable information concerning Federal Court matters, and treated me kindly and gentlemanly. I brought no papers with me except my Commission.

Upon that I have applied for the amount of Salary due me, my identity being certified to by Judge Trigg, with a reccommendation that the amount be paid— But as the Rebels have my oath and Bond, executed on the 26th of May 1861 in their possession, and as I have no certified copies, I think it doubtful as to the salary being paid until I renew the oath and Bond, which I proposed to do here, but Trigg thought I could succeed without doing so. Patterson knows all about the Oath and Bond, and that it was all done in accordance with the instructions of Judge Humphreys, prior to the so called Secession of Tennessee. If I fail to get my salary, I may be under the necessity of calling on you and Patterson to assist me in drawing it.—[16] I have been sick two or three days, but am better now. Within the last two years, I have been reduced in flesh from 180 to 150 lbs.

I have a thousand things to say, but cannot now say more. Drop me a line, and let me know whether or not I can get back to Knoxville by the way of Chattanooga— We all want to go home as soon as possible, as the most of us left our families unsupplied for the winter. They are in a bad fix, and if Longstreet retreats to Virginia, they will be stripped of what little we left them. Could you find employment for some of our boys at Nashville?

Yours &c B. McDannel.

ALS, DLC-JP.

1. For Johnson's longtime friend McDannel, see *Johnson Papers,* I, 184*n*.

2. Orlando B. Willcox (1823-1907), Michigan-born West Pointer (1847), served in Mexico and along the southern and western frontiers before resigning in 1857 to practice law in Detroit. As colonel, 1st Mich. Inf., he commanded a brigade at First Bull Run where he was wounded and captured; released thirteen months later, he was made brigadier and commanded a division of the IX Corps during the remainder of the war. Mustered out in January, 1866, he was six months later commissioned colonel in the regulars, serving in Virginia, California, Arizona, and New York before retirement as brigadier general in 1887. Warner, *Generals in Blue,* 558-59; *DAB,* XX, 243.

3. Joining Burnside with reinforcements in early October, Willcox subsequently established his headquarters near Greeneville, advancing one brigade as far as Rheatown to support cavalry outposts at Kingsport, Blountville, and elsewhere. About November 1 these posts began to be drawn back to Rheatown. On the sixth Confederates from southwestern Virginia attacked and routed Federal forces at Rogersville, capturing about 850 prisoners and four cannon, the survivors retreating to Morristown; whereupon Burnside ordered Willcox to fall back to that place and defend it. Learning that the Confederates had not advanced past Rogersville, Willcox halted about fifteen miles west at Bull's Gap and started fortifying it. In succeeding weeks, until further orders from Burnside, he retreated westward to the vicinity of Cumberland Gap. *OR,* Ser. 1, XXXI, Pt. I, 402-3, 551, 555; Pt. III, 67.

4. James Jones (1821-1891) had been Greene County sheriff (1854-60). Reynolds, *Greene County Cemeteries,* 231; *Goodspeed's East Tennessee,* 890; see also *Johnson Papers,* II, 385*n*.

5. Possibly William McFarland (1821-1900), who was at the Knoxville Union Convention in 1861 and later served as circuit judge and congressman; or his brother Robert, Jr. (1832-1884), Tennessee supreme court judge (1871-84). McBride and Robison, *Biographical Directory* I, 477; *OR,* Ser 1, LII, Pt. I, 150; *BDAC,* 1297; John W. Green, *Lives of the Judges of the Supreme Court of Tennessee, 1796-1947* (Knoxville, 1947), 189-92.

6. For James Britton, see *Johnson Papers,* I, 497*n.*

7. His corps detached from Bragg's army at Chattanooga with instructions to capture Knoxville, Gen. James Longstreet on November 13 ordered Gen. Joseph Wheeler to ford the Little Tennessee and seize the heights overlooking the Holston (Tennessee) River south of Knoxville. During that night Wheeler dispersed a lone regiment of Col. Frank Wolford's brigade at Maryville and the next day pushed the balance of Wolford's command back to a position north of Stock Creek, about five miles from Knoxville. On the fifteenth Gen. William P. Sanders moved a force southward from Forts Dickerson and Stanley and met Wheeler, only to be defeated and forced back to the forts, many of his men crossing the pontoon bridge into Knoxville. Finding the bastions too formidable for direct assault, Wheeler withdrew to Stock Creek, returning the next morning to find that they had been reinforced. Ordered by Longstreet to join the main force, Wheeler withdrew again, crossing the Holston near Louisville on the seventeenth. Sanders (1833-1863), Kentucky native, grew up in Mississippi, graduated from West Point (1856), and served on the frontier and as captain of the 6th Cav., USA, in Virginia (1862). On sick leave in early 1863, he was reassigned to the 5th Ky. Cav. as colonel and chief of cavalry for the Department of the Ohio. Promoted brigadier, he was commanding the 1st Division, XXIII Corps at Knoxville, when mortally wounded on November 18 while checking Longstreet's advance. Seymour, *Divided Loyalties,* 105, 113-14, 119, 124-37; *OR,* Ser. 1, XXXI, Pt. I, 456, 540-42; Warner, *Generals in Blue,* 419-20; for Wolford, see *Johnson Papers,* V, 268*n.*

8. William G. Brownlow, John Baxter, and Oliver P. Temple. For Temple, see *ibid.,* IV, 195*n.*

9. To oppose Longstreet, Burnside had initially posted the bulk of his army—the IX Corps and 2nd Division, XXIII Corps—along the north bank of the Tennessee at Loudon. In order to draw Longstreet farther from his base and thereby make it more difficult for him to return to help Bragg, Burnside decided to abandon all territory south and west of Knoxville. By the fifteenth the Federal withdrawal had progressed as far as Lenoir City; thereupon, the opposing armies, moving by parallel roads, raced for the crossroads at Campbell's Station where Burnside's men won and fought a successful holding action on the sixteenth, allowing time for the wagon train to pass through and for Knoxville's defenses to be strengthened. Early the next morning the Union army reached Knoxville. Seymour, *Divided Loyalties,* 110-11, 126-37; Boatner, *Civil War Dictionary,* 117.

10. Samuel P. Carter, commanding the cavalry division of the XXIII Corps.

11. Five miles northeast of Jacksboro in Campbell County, Big Creek Gap is a route through the Cumberland Mountains. *OR-Atlas,* Plate CXLII.

12. Samuel S. Thompson (*c*1815-1911) of Knoxville, sometime carriage maker and more recently clerk, had married Mary McDannel. Laura E. Luttrell, comp., *United States 1850 Census for Knox County* (Knoxville, 1949), 54; 1860 Census, Tenn., Knox, Knoxville, 1st Dist., 40; WPA, Tenn., Knox: Old Gray Cemetery, 261; for Joseph C. S. McDannel, see *Johnson Papers,* IV, 102*n.*

13. Although now used to describe anthracite, this term, during these years, was broadly defined as "hard coal or mineral coal," evidently to differentiate it from charcoal. For years Cincinnati had been and would be notorious for the prevalence of coal smoke and smell: "It contaminates everything—air, earth, dwellings, and inhabitants." *Webster's Dictionary* (1856); *Webster's Third International;* George H. Twiss, ed., "Journal of Cyrus P. Bradley," *Ohio Archeological and Historical Society Publications,* XV (1906), 220; Willard Glazier, *Peculiarities of American Cities* (Philadelphia, 1886), 128.

14. Swann of Dandridge is James P., and the Galbraiths are James A. and David Jewell, who lived with his older brother. James Monroe Meek (1821-*fl*1899), Jefferson County lawyer who began practive at New Market in 1852, was twice a state representative (1855-57, 1861-63), the second time as a Union member. Arrested in April, 1862, for having assisted Union soldiers, he was imprisoned at Tuscaloosa, Montgomery, and Macon, before being released in July; his postwar career included service as attorney general for Tennessee's 2nd judicial circuit (1866-78), U. S. district attorney for eastern district of Tennessee (1883-87), and director of the East Tennessee and Georgia Railroad (1866-79). John M. McKee (b. *c*1840), a railroad agent, and his railroad postmaster brother Robert M., who subsequently became a lawyer, lived with their mother, a farmer, on the eve of the war. James B. R. Lyon (1825-1902), North Carolina-born printer and son-in-law of James Britton, was later the proprietor and editor of the Greeneville *Republi-*

can. McBride and Robison, *Biographical Directory,* I, 511; Speer, *Prominent Tennesseans,* 568-69; Temple, *East Tennessee,* 405; 1860 Census, Tenn., Greene, 10th Dist., 82; (1880), Greeneville, 7; *Goodspeed's East Tennessee,* 1251; Reynolds, *Greene County Cemeteries,* 268. For John Netherland, Joseph Powell, and Robert M. McKee, see *Johnson Papers,* III, 276*n*; IV, 297*n*, 190*n*.

15. Alexander C. Sands (b. *c*1832), a New York native and resident of Zaleski and Cincinnati, Ohio, was marshal (1861-65) and assessor of the 1st Ohio congressional district (1866). A powerful figure in the Republican party in southern Ohio, he was, according to a recent scholar, removed from office by Johnson in 1866 for his anti-Sherman activity at the time of the senator's reelection. 1860 Census, Ohio, Vinton, Madison Township, 78; *U. S. Official Register* (1861-67), *passim:* Felice A. Bonadio, *North of Reconstruction: Ohio Politics, 1865-70* (New York, 1970), 124-25, 130, 148.

16. Ultimately both Patterson and Johnson were obliged to intercede in McDannel's behalf, the former certifying to having administered the original oath and the latter early in 1864 personally conveying papers, including Patterson's statement, to the treasury department, receiving the response that "the evidence respecting the date when the oath of office was administered is deemed sufficient." In due time Blackston received his back salary. David T. Patterson Certification, January 13, 1864, Misc. Lets. Recd; R. W. Taylor to Johnson, March 3, 1864, Fair Copies of Misc. Lets. Sent, Office of First Comptroller, RG217, NA.

From James St. C. Morton

Nashville Tenn Dec 5th 1863

Hon. Andrew Johnson
Mil. Governor & Brig. General
Nashville Tenn.
Governor

I have the honour to acknowledge the receipt of your communication of the 3rd inst[1] relative to negroes employed on the Fortifications of Nashville since August 1862, and to state in reply that the sum of $30,000.00 which Lieut. Burroughs[2] received from me in May last for the purpose of paying their wages remains unexpended in his hands except $2,280.—which was paid by him through Major Stearns to volunteer negroes.

In regard to provision being made to pay the negroes, beyond the above amount, I have to state that all that is necessary is to estimate for the amount required, upon the "appropriation for contingencies of Fortification including Fieldworks," and that estimates for an aggregate of $23,800.—have been forwarded to Washington to the Engineer Bureau, by Lieut. Burroughs, for such purpose. Also, that additional estimates to cover the whole indebtedness of the U. S. on said account will undoubtedly be forwarded.

I respectfully state that the impediment which has mainly delayed the settlement with the negroes lies in the responsibility which attaches to the decision whether the earnings are to be paid to the negroes or to their masters—a responsibility which is too heavy for a disbursing officer to assume with safety. I will instance a case which occurred within a day or two viz that of Mr. Bowling Embry[3] of Nashville, whose bill against the U.S. for labour of his slaves on the fortifications was ordered to be paid by me, by an order from Department Head Quarters: had I paid said negroes the amount of their wages, I should have been obliged to pay Mr. Embry's bill out of my own pocket.

As many of the negroes employed are not known here, and their own account of their owners loyalty or disloyalty is the only one to be guided by, and as loyal owners may turn up for many who represent themselves as entitled to payment as formerly owned by rebels, it is evident that some higher authority than that of the superintending officer of the works is required to dispose satisfactorily of the question.

Beleiving that the enclosed copy of a communication I have made to Hon. R. D. Owen on this subject[4] comprises all the additional points I have to present in this connection, I respectfully submit it to you.[5]

I beg leave to say in conclusion that I have sought earnestly to bring about the payment of the hard earned wages of the faithful blacks, and that I should take sincere satisfaction in settling with them.

I am, Governor, very respy. your obed servt.

J StC Morton Captain

ALS, DLC-JP.

1. Not found.

2. George Burroughs.

3. For Embry, see *Johnson Papers,* IV, 547*n.*

4. Robert Dale Owen, reformer and former congressman, had been appointed by Stanton in 1863 to head a commission to investigate the conditions of the newly-freed blacks, the results of which study Owen published as *The Wrong of Slavery, the Right of Emancipation, and the Future of the African Race in the United States* (1864). *DAB,* XIV, 120; for Owen, see *Johnson Papers,* I, 273*n.*

5. Addressed to Capt. Reuben D. Mussey for the commission, rather than to Owen, the president, Morton's report gave further statistics as to the number of Negroes employed, their wages, conditions of employment, effectiveness, and loyalty. Morton to Mussey, December 4, 1863, Johnson Papers, LC.

To Ethan A. Hitchcock, Washington, D. C.

Nashville Dec 5 1863.

Maj Gen Hitchcock

Please accept my thanks for the interest you have taken in obtaining the release of Andrew Johnson[1] from Libby prison[.] Please have him furnished with transportation to this place or such other place as he may designate & money sufficient to bear his expenses. The officers attending to this will please dispatch the amount & I will remit it by Express[.]

Andrew Johnson Mil Gov

Tel, DLC-E. A. Hitchcock Papers.

1. Johnson's nephew, son of his brother William.

From Joseph Powell[1]

Cincinatti Ohio Dec 6th 1863

Gov. A. Johnson
Dear Sir

You will learn by this, that I am now in C----- directly from Greenville Tenn—with many others of your acquaintances from that Section After an unpleasant trip of four weeks by every kind of transportation except Baloon[.]

We left many Loyal Citizens in Kentucky nearly in a State of total destitution[.] I have not Language to describe the deploreable State of things that at this moment exist in East Tennessee— You however, are able to form Some correct idea how they are—

I arrived here utterly exausted physically But my Spirits are nothing the less and my opinions the Same. I have been driven out of two States[2] by the Rebels and I Shall still flee from their Rule and Insolence[.]

I design going through Indiana and Illinoise[.] I am a Stranger in those States[.] I wish that you would give me a letter of a general character in order that the Loyal People may know who I am— I have two letters from officers in the Army to Gent—in this City—from whom I have received the kindest & most polite attention—

Your Suggestion[3] to give us transportation from any Rail Road or Steam Boat in the employment of the Government is duly appreciated by all of your unfortunate friends—But we can find no one here authorized to grant or give the order—

But many are awaiting its benefits[.]

We do not know when we shall be able to return home and God knows what is to become of ours in the mean-time[.]

Please write immediately on receipt of this as the State of the finances with the most of us, will not admit of delay—[4]

I will be in Nashville on my return Home— The people of Cincinatti & all through Kentucky Sympathise with us *deeply* by charging us *exorbitant* prices for every thing[.]

Yours truly J Powell

Gov Johnson

ALS, DLC-JP.

1. See *Johnson Papers,* IV, 297*n*.

2. A thirty-year resident of Greenville, South Carolina, he became a refugee in Bristol, Tennessee, early in 1861, following his state's secession. Letter from Joseph Powell, February 16, 1861, *ibid.*

3. Evidently Johnson had reacted favorably to Brownlow's recent request for governmental assistance to East Tennessee refugees who lacked funds to reach midwestern relatives. See Letter from William G. Brownlow, December 1, 1863.

4. There is no evidence that the governor responded.

From Simon Cameron

Harrisburg, Pa Dec. 7, 1863.

Dear Governor,

May I beg your assistance for a distant relative of mine, in whose welfare, I feel much interest, who is now, in the Insane Asylum, at Nashville, put there, as I fear, by the officers of his regiment, at Chatanoga.

His name is A. J. Bostater,[1] Sergt in a regiment of Ohio vols. for whom I had obtained a commission as Lieut-Col. in one of the Louisiana regiments of Negroes. The commission has been returned to me and will be forwarded to you, if you find on examination, that he is sound mind. You will find him in Hospital No. 8.

He says in a letter which I have, that his attempt to expose frauds on the Govt. have brought him under the ban of his officers. He is a young man of good education & good connexions in Ohio.

Very truly yrs Simon Cameron

His Excellency Gov. Johnson

ALS, DLC-JP.

1. Andrew J. Bostater (*c*1836-1923), native Buckeye and on the eve of the war an Ohio Wesleyan College student, became a sergeant in Co. D, 38th Ohio Inf. in September, 1861. Paroled following capture near Decatur, Alabama, the following August, he secured an appointment as lieutenant colonel, 10th La. Vols. of African Descent (October, 1863), falling almost at once into violent dispute with other officers. Arrested and charged with insubordination and behavior "so eccentric as to give rise to the belief that he is partially insane," he was examined early in November by a board of medical officers who reported "that he is deranged & measures will be taken to have him forwarded to the Asylum at Nashville." In April, 1864, he was transferred to the asylum in Columbus, Ohio, where the records show he was "not disposed to violence, but very full of mischief." Mustered out of service in the fall of 1864, he subsequently practiced medicine in Defiance County. James L. Murphy (Ohio Historical Society) to Andrew Johnson Project, October 23, 1980; CSR, RG94, NA.

From J. J. Pickett[1]

Dickson County Tennessee
Dec the 8th 1863

Govr Andrew Johnson
Dear sir
I am sorry to trouble you with a letter of this kind but I know not who else to trouble & I feel impelled by duty to troble some one[.] If you are not the proper one please hand this over to the proper authority[.]
I have been most seriously agrieved by the soldiers & I feel it both my privilege & my duty to ask you for protection against such outrages & for redress of grievances[.] Some time in last september a squad of soldiers led by Lieutenant Henry Barr[2] who I have been informed lives or did live in Nashville but now belonges either to the third or the first Tennessee

regiment, came to my house in my absence & without any insult from my family or any one else on the place or that belonged to the place or was in any way connected with the place, set fire so my house & would not let the family remove any thing from it till the flames had so far advanced that they could save but little[.]

My dwelling house which was a large comfortable convenient house & well furnished was consumed with nearly all its contents[.] My smoke-house also with a fine lot of bacon lard &c was consumed & five other houses including my kitchen with its furniture negro house furniture & clothing also my blacksmith & farming tools with almost my entire crop of wheat & the pailings from the grave of the innocent dead making in all seven houses with nearly all their contents[.]

When my wife and daughters[3] begged the Lieutenant in the most imploring manner not to burn the house the only comfort they got was the harsh threaten that if they did not hush he would shoot them[.][4] When they asked why he burned the house he said the rebels shot one of his men & he intended to burn them up for it & burn them up he did[.] His iron heart could not be moved by female prayers nor female tears[.] It was too calous no tenter cord could be touched[.]

My wife told him that she had nothing to do with the soldiers that they did not visit her house & that she had no control over them & could not help what they did but it all did no good[.] burn he would[.]

The facts in the case are these[.] the Lieutenant was passing by my house & passed quietly by[.] soon after he had passed eight rebel soldiers came dashing by in pursuit of them & over took & captured two of them at the next house blow mine[.] The Lieutenant by this time had reached the second house below mine & halted[.]

The rebels wheeled & came back by my house with their prisoners & the Lieutenant in pursuit of them[.] Soon after they passed my house one of the prisoners made his escape from the rebels & fell back to his own command & when the Lieutenant came up with him he found him wounded in the arm & not being able to overtake & punish the rebels he determined to wreak his vengance on some one & he came back to my house to take vengance on my innocent helpless family & rudely rode his horse into my wife's room & sat there on him till his men fired the house[.]

I am now broken up literally ruined. My house furniture books tools to work with cloths & provisions have been burned[.] I was left without any thing to eat without any thing to eat off & without any thing to eat with[.] I am now old & feeble & unable to build again & the bleak winds & cold rains frosts & snows of winter are upon me[.] I may be too sensative but I can't help feeling that such treatment is cruel unjust & intolerable that it is a burning shame enough to make the cheek of civilization justice & mercy blush & that it should not be tolerated by a government that has any regard for Justice or that makes any pretensions to civilization[.]

Can we suppose that a God of justice & mercy approbates such conduct or do we say with David's fool there is no God[.][5] Suppose sir I were to steal your horse & run off with him & you could not catch & punish me for it would you be justifiable in punishing Lieutenant Barr for it or in punishing the Lieutenant's wife & daughters[?] Certainly not sir, but you would be equally as justifiable in killing Lieutenant Barr or in burning his house over the heads of his wife & daughters because I stold your horse as he was in burning my house because the rebels shot one of his men[.] The cases are annalagous[.]

The attack was made on the Lieutenant not only without my knowledge but contrary to my wishes[.] If I had shown disloyalty either by helping to vote the state out of the union by raising arms against the government or by making my house a home or a place of resort for guerrilla bands or marauders they would have had some excuse for burning my house but I did neither & they had not the shadow of an excuse[.] The act was purely gratuitous[.]

It was the out gushing & logitimate fruits of a deeply corrupt heart[.] The men for whose conduct my house was burned were mostly men from other states & were almost entire strangers to me[.] no intercourse or intimacy existed betwen us[.]

When we met in the road we met & passed as strangers[.] I dont recollect that I had ever had an introduction to either of them or a familiar conversation with either of them[.] I had not invited either of them to my house & they did not visit my house[.] I have taken no part in this rebellion[.] I am a quiet peaceable man[.] I stay at home & attend to my own business & do not meddle with governmental affairs & have always submitted quietly to the goverment & I think peaceable citizens should be protected by the government[.] It is senseless & unreasonable to say the state has gone out of the union & therefore her citizens cannot claim protection[.] Those citizens who did not vote out & have been peaceable are not accountable for what others did & should be protected[.] Although I have always submitted I have been unmercyfully & cruelly treated but the sin is on the shoulders of the government & not on mine[.] Although I have been crushed ruined & broken up & feel the rong as keenly as any man I am still determined to do right[.] I am determined to [do] right if the heavens fall[.] In conclusion I ask for protection & for redress[.] If it is not too much trouble please give me an answer & such advice as you think proper[.]

Yours truly J. J. Pickett

ALS, DLC-JP.

1. J. J. Pickett (*c*1817-*c*1895), native Tennessean, was a Dickson farmer and preacher. 1870 Census, Tenn., Dickson, 11th Dist., 12; WPA, Dickson County Will Book, Volume B (1856-1908), 169-70; *Goodspeed's Dickson,* 1353.

2. Henry W. Barr (b. *c*1842), a Nashvillian, formerly private, Co. C, 21st Ky. Inf., USA, and currently first lieutenant, Co. C, 3rd Tenn. Cav. (1863-65), served in a variety of capacities during these years. That he may earlier have exhibited questionable traits may be surmised from the response of Provost Marshal Gen. William Wiles to an inquiry from Rosecrans when Barr, in January, 1863, sought command of a scouting company to

operate in the Nashville vicinity. "Mr. Barr has been employed as he states [as officer and scout for Truesdail's army police], and (under close watching) he has rendered some valuable services. Still I can not recommend him to be placed in the position." Subsequently he was a Freedmen's Bureau agent (1867) and a Nashville policeman (1868-69). CSR, RG94, NA; *King's Nashville Directory* (1868), 51, 78; (1869), 50, 80; *OR,* Ser. 1, XL, Pt. II, 302; *U. S. Official Register* (1867), 198.

3. Jane May (*c*1817-1898), widow of Hartwell Slayden (d. 1845), had three daughters by the Reverend Mr. Pickett: Margaret Rebecca, Mary Jane, and Martha D. Presumably all were at home with her when these events occurred. 1870 Census, Tenn., Dickson, 11th Dist., 12; Jill K. Garrett and Iris H. McClain, *Dickson County, Tennessee, Cemetery Records* (Columbia, Tenn., 1967), 13; *Goodspeed's Dickson,* 1353.

4. For Barr's version of the story, see Letter from Henry W. Barr, January 19, 1864.

5. Ps. 14:1.

From James A. Galbraith

Cincinnati O Decr 9th 63

Gov Andrew Johnson
Nashville
Dear Sir

Your kind favor of the 3rd Ins't[1] covering 100$ on a/c of yourself & son Col. Robt Johnson is this day received[.] Many thanks to you for I assure it came in time of my need— I am sorry to hear of Illness in your family hope no fatal results may be consequent[.][2]

I have been quite unwell confined to my bed for a day or two since I came to this place— I left my wife in a critical state of health.

But this unGodly war knows no sympathy[.] the tenderest Chords are broken.

Weak & helpless Old age & wives and children are left to weep sad & lonely.

I am informed Lt. Col. Grayson has accepted the position of Maj. in the 12th Tenn. Cavalry. Thus it was I spoke of the Lt Colonelcy of the 4th[.][3]

Maj. Patterson[4] expressed his opinion to me however that I could not safely undergo the exposure & privation of a soldiers life in the Camp or field—& suggested to me that I ask your influence in my favor—as Post Q.M. at Greeneville but I don't know—That I desire the position or could get it If I did as I suppose some one regularly enlisted in the army would be most likely to have, the place— I made application through Maj. Gen'l Burnside for the Post Office at that place—[5]

Andrew Johnson Jr. arrived here yesterday is well—

The news from our section is pretty good but I fear it may be sometime yet before we of upper E T. can go home— hope not though I would like to return via Nashville If I knew when I could do So. I shall go from here to Paris Ill and thence home as circumstances may direct[.] I should be glad to hear from you when the way may be opened to Knoxville thence to Gv. via Nashville & Chattanooga by R. R. or Boat[.]

B. McDaniel & Bro.[6] W. G. Brownlow O. P. Temple Jn'o Netherland N G Taylor, and a host of other Tenn. are here still[.] Some of them are making arrangements to start for Knoxville first of next week.

Most Respectfully Yours
J. A. Galbraith

ALS, DLC-JP.

1. Johnson's remittance was dated December 5.

2. Probably a reference to son-in-law Daniel Stover, whose illness was such that two months earlier the governor had regarded "his recovery doubtful." Letter to William S. Rosecrans, October 12, 1863.

3. James W. M. Grayson, removed by Johnson as lieutenant colonel of the 4th Tenn. Inf. in September, had been mustered in as major of the 13th, not 12th, Tenn. Cav. on October 6.

4. Michael L. Patterson.

5. Apparently Galbraith got neither the quartermaster job nor the Greeneville postmastership. In January, on his way through Nashville, he informed Johnson that he "would like to investigate the Cotton growing question"; in October he was recruiting for the army in East Tennessee. Galbraith to Johnson, January 9, October 25, 1864, Johnson Papers, LC.

6. Blackston and Joseph C. S. McDannel.

From Abraham Lincoln

Washington Dec 10 1863

To Hon Andw. Johnson

I still desire very much to see you[.] can you not come[?][1]

A Lincoln

Tel, DLC-JP; Basler, *Works of Lincoln,* VII, 59.

1. Responding the following day with "I will come," Johnson left almost at once, reaching Louisville by the 15th. The purpose of the trip was variously assessed by newspaper correspondents: one sarcastically seeing it as "to lay pipe for himself for the next Presidency"; another more sympathetically suggesting that discussion of political affairs in Tennessee, especially the volatile issue of slavery, would provide the agenda. Lincoln Papers, LC; Nashville *Press,* December 22, 1863; Nashville *Dispatch,* December 27, 1863.

From William G. Brownlow

Cincinnati, Decr. 14, 1863.

Hon. A. Johnson:

I have been shown your dispatch to B. McDannel, in reference to Flemming.[1] He did not come here with us, but returned from Barboursville with Baxter and others. We all start back in the morning *via* Cumberland Gap, as our information is that the way is open.

You had better send Flemming his documents by some one going through *via* Chattanooga. If the way is open, I shall go from Knoxville to Chattanooga, to see about the opening of the trade there. Flemming needs the office, and if we can all keep him from drink, he will attend to it with some degree of pride and energy.

W. B. Carter and N. G. Taylor left here for Springfield, Ohio, on Friday, to commence their *joint labors in soliciting money for East Tennessee sufferers*. Nat solicited me to aid him, but I declined to take any part in the enterprise, as we all did. Carter consulted Temple on the subject and Temple told him he was opposed to the whole thing[.][2]

Carter asked me for a certificate, or rather *receipt* for the money he paid me, remarking that he expected a blow up with you, or words to that effect. He wrote me out a receipt, and I declined to sign it. I then wrote out one, and signed it, and he declined receiving it, and I put it in the fire. I had no other conversation with him.

While I think of it, I authorise you to show this hurried note to Maynard.

I understand that Parsons[3] is in the hands of the Rebels. He was sick, got well enough to go to his Mother's above town, in an Ambulance, and was there captured. His Regiment is full, numbering more than one thousand. My John recruited 600 of them at Knoxville. They were in the siege,[4] and did all that green hands could.

I am, &c, &c, W. G. Brownlow

ALS, DLC-JP.

1. Johnson's December 10 letter asked Blackston McDannel to tell John M. Fleming, if in Cincinnati, that the governor had the latter's commission as U. S. district attorney for East Tennessee. See McDannel to Johnson, December 12, 1863, Johnson Papers, LC.

2. Nathaniel G. Taylor was embarking upon an extensive and successful tour of the north to raise relief funds for East Tennessee unionists. Formed early in February to receive and disburse these contributions, the Knoxville East Tennessee Relief Association designated Taylor as its "agent abroad." He continued his efforts in Maine and other states before resigning July 1, 1865. Carter seems not to have participated to any great extent; he was back in Knoxville in April, 1864, as a representative to the re-convened Knoxville-Greenville Convention. O. P. Temple and Brownlow evidently reconsidered their position and served on the association's executive committee. Edward Everett, *Account of the Fund for the Relief of East Tennessee* (Boston, 1864), 7, 57; Humes, *Report to the East Tenn. Relief Association*, 3-4, 10, 23, 24; Humes, *Second Report to the East Tennessee Relief Association at Knoxville* (Knoxville, 1866), 7; Knoxville *Whig and Rebel Ventilator*, April 16, 1864.

3. Probably Joseph H. Parsons.

4. Beginning the siege of Knoxville on November 17, Longstreet unsuccessfully attempted to breach Burnside's defenses at Fort Sanders on the twenty-ninth. Meanwhile, Grant had defeated Bragg at Chattanooga and sent Generals William T. Sherman and Gordon Granger to aid Burnside. When Longstreet learned of the relief column's approach, he retreated toward Virginia, ending the siege on December 4. Seymour, *Divided Loyalties*, 138-213 *passim*.

From Alvin Hawkins

Green Castle Ind
Dec 14th 1863

Hon Andrew Johnson
Dear Sir

Since the 20th of Oct. I have been here with my family but intend to return to Tennessee as soon as I can be of service to our friends in that State[.]

I do not wish to be considered impertinent or troublesome but I feel that a sense of duty to loyal Tennesseans requires that I communicate to you as the Military Governor of that State that facts which have been for Several days and are now transpiring at Paducah, Ky. I am reliably informed that under the pretended authority of Gen. Hurlbuts' recent order, loyal Tennesseans who have fled to Paducah Some to protect themselves against personal violence at the hands of Rebels, others to avoid Rebel Conscription which has been going on for months in West Te. and others of whom there are not a few to Seek Shelter and Subsistence for their wives and children which had been denied them at home, are being Conscripted by the Federal Authorities at that place, whilst the citizens of Paducah are exempted from the operation of that order.[1] There may be some good reason for this discrimination by which it can be justified but it is unknown to Tennesseeans and they do not understand that Gen Hurlbuts' order makes any distinction or authorises any such discriminaton— They do not understand why under that order they should be forced into the army to protect Rebel sympathizers for which Paducah is notorious—whilst those sympathizers are permitted to remain at home—in a word, Tennesseeans feel that injustice is being done them, and that they are being made the victims of an unauthorized discrimination[.] if they be in error, it is for the want of information upon the Subject, and the objects and reasons of the policy should be explained to them—for I am also informed the effect of this treatment by Federal officers at Paducah has been to induce many to join the Rebel army—or rather to permit themselves to be conscripted into the service of the Rebellion— I trust you will see that the union men of West Te have justice done them and these evils be corrected so far as may be within your power.

I have the honor to be
Your Most Obt. Servt.
Alvin Hawkins

ALS, DLC-JP.

1. In his General Orders No. 157, promulgated at Memphis, November 15, 1863, Hurlbut, on the assumption that many men had come to Memphis to escape military service in their home communities, directed that "all officers commanding Districts, Divisions and detached Brigades of this Corps, will immediately proceed to impress into the service of the United States such able-bodied persons liable to military duty as may be required to fill up the existing Regiments and Batteries to their maximum[.]" It was undoubtedly the comprehensive language of this order which was used as the rationale for conscripting Tennesseans in Paducah. Memphis *Bulletin,* November 17, 1863.

From Timothy H. Williams[1]

Gallatin Tennessee
December 16th 1863.

General Andrew Johnson Govenor &c.
Dr Sir

I have determined to enter the Federal Service. General Payne[2] told me that he would give me a recommendation to you—which perhaps he has done or in the press of business forgotten. I feel that I owe this to my Government. You doubtless are aware that I was for a time a major in the Rebel service and this may cause you to doubt somewhat my integrity. You need not however—for I shall go my lenth and with a *hearty good will.* Jordon Stokes—(my Brother-in-Law) since last June was [*sic*]a year ago has known my sentiments[3]—So has John Williams[4] of Knoxville—who promised to speak to you for me. I think I can easily raise a Battallion of Cavalry in the Counties of Smith Jackson & Putnam—with which I can do effective service. I am thoroughly acquainted in several adjoining counties & could I raise a regiment I would be more than proud to command them[.] So I propose that you send me such authority as you may deem me worthy of & I will go to work at once. There is one company already made up (Capt Anderson's) another fairly on the way (Capt McKee's)[.][5] If I hear from you in time I will speak at Carthage on the 1st monday in January—and at other places.[6] Thereafter with the view to see what I can do— I have the pleasure of subscribing myself

Yours to Command
Tim H. Williams

P. S. Please send me such instructions as you may deem adviseable & they shall be Strictly complied with[.]

Yours &c T. H. W.

ALS, T-Mil. Gov's Papers, 1862-65, Petitions.

1. Timothy H. Williams (b. *c*1829), Smith County lawyer with $4,000 real and $14,000 personal property and at war's beginning attorney general for the 6th judicial circuit, served as major, 25th Tenn. Inf., CSA (August, 1861-May, 1862), failing to be reelected at the regiment's reorganization at Corinth. There is no evidence that he was commissioned by Johnson. 1860 Census, Tenn., Smith, 1st Dist., 8; CSR, RG109, NA; *Tennesseans in the Civil War,* I, 226; Nashville *Republican Banner,* July 2, 1861.

2. Eleazer A. Paine (1815-1882), Ohio-born attorney and West Point graduate (1839), served briefly in the Seminole wars, moved to Illinois about 1848, and became a friend of Lincoln. Appointed brigadier of volunteers in September, 1861, he held various commands in western Kentucky and Tennessee, resigning near the end of the war to resume his law practice in Monmouth, Illinois. Warner, *Generals in Blue,* 355-56.

3. Jordan Stokes's first wife, whom he married in 1840 and who died eleven months later, was Penelope C. Williams. Speer, *Prominent Tennesseans,* 467; for Stokes, see *Johnson Papers,* IV, 159*n*.

4. John Williams, an "uncompromising unionist," was influential in recruiting for the Union army. Later unsuccessful as a congressional candidate, he became a U. S. commissioner for East Tennessee. Knoxville *Chronicle,* April 26, 1881; McBride and Robison, *Biographical Directory,* I, 795; see *Johnson Papers,* II, 317*n*.

5. Francis M. Anderson (1827-*fl*1900), native Jackson County farmer and captain, Co. C, 1st Tenn. Mtd. Inf., USA, resigned June 30, 1864; Francis M. McKee (b. *c*1836), captain, Co. A, and subsequently major (1864-65), worked later as a carpenter in Smith County. Company C was mustered December 3, 1863, and Company A, January 21, 1864. 1870 Census, Tenn., Smith, 1st Dist., 7; Jackson, 10th Dist., 4; (1880), 9; (1900), DeKalb, 53rd Enum. Dist., 7B; CSR, RG94, NA; *Tennesseans in the Civil War,* I, 354.

6. Williams was as good as his word. While there is no evidence of his appearing at Carthage in January, 1864, a month later he was announced as speaking in the Nashville City Council Room "at early candle lighting. His subject will be the war. He has been a Major in the rebel army." And a full year later, on January 5, 1865, he presided at a Carthage meeting in which delegates to the upcoming Union convention in Nashville were appointed. Nashville *Press,* February 2, 1864; Nashville *Times and True Union,* January 10, 1865.

From John Harold[1]

Camp Nelson Ky Dec 18th 1863

Hon Andrew Johnson
Gov

I think it due to you to inform you as to persons & matters here amongst the Tennessee Troups. There are four Regiments here-to-wit. R. C. Crawfords, 1st Tenn Artillery John. K. Millers,[2] styled 12th Tenn Cavalry, Pattons[3] 10th Tenn. Cavalry, and our own the 4th Infantry[.] R. C. Crawford was appointed Brigade commander two weeks ago, but it has since been countermanded[.] he is a most intriguing person and a very bitter enemy of yours. he says that you offered him recruiting powers but he would not move a peg until he received authority from the Secretary of War, and that he does not recognize You as Governor or as having any authority over him. There is another person here of some note one R. R. Butler[4] appointed Lt Col in John K Millers Regt and a moving Image of hypocracy & deceit who is continually inveighing against you, and throwing every obstacle in his power in the way of reorganizing our Regt. calling us Johnson's Pets &c[.] The rest of the persons here are without much Note or influence. Lt Col Grayson has been mustered out of Our Regt and in as Maj in Millers Regt, as I understand by Order of Genl Burnside, so endeth the chapter in regard to him as far as we are concerned and heartily glad are we to get rid of him; hoping that you will commission a better man to fill his place. We have (200) two hundred men here and are expecting to start in a few days for E Tenn, where I think we can gather up the balance without much trouble as they are all anxious to return to the Regt. those that have been in E Tenn dont want to go back[.] they say they have enough of home. I think by the first of April we can fill the Regt to maximum number but you will have to give us another Field officer as there is too much for one to do[.]

With Much Respect I Remain
Your Obdt Servant
John Harold

ALS, DLC-JP.

1. John Harold entlisted as a private, Co. A, 4th Tenn. Inf. in August, 1862, becoming 1st lieutenant and regimental quartermaster, and in October, 1864, captain, Co. B, before being mustered out of service in August, 1865. CSR, RG94, NA; see also *Johnson Papers*, III, 200*n*.

2. John K. Miller (1828-1903), native Carter County farmer, was sheriff (1860-63), before becoming colonel, 13th Tenn. Cav., USA (1863-65). Subsequently he was a hotelkeeper in Washington County. 1860 Census, Tenn., Carter, Elizabethton, 7; (1880), Washington, 9th Dist., 13; CSR, RG94, NA; Orville T. Fields, *Cemeteries of Carter County, Tennessee* (n. p., 1976), 119.

3. For Samuel K. N. Patton, see *Johnson Papers*, III, 465*n*.

4. For Roderick R. Butler, who helped raise the 13th Tenn. Cav., USA, see *ibid.* IV, 169*n*.

Certificate of Loyalty

State of Tennessee,
Executive Department,
Nashville, December 18th 1863

It has been represented to me by undoubted Union authority, that Mrs. Ann Wilkinson[1] is a loyal lady, and in the occupancy of a house, the property of her son-in-law, *S. A. G. Noel*[2] who is absent from this City on account of the ill health of his wife, and who is represented by the same authority as a reliable Union man.

Andrew Johnson Mil. Gov'r.

DS, DNA-RG366, 1st Special Agency, Nashville District.

1. Ann Wilkinson (*c*1805-1873), a Kentucky native with $2,500 personal property, was living in her son-in-law's home on the eve of the war. 1860 Census, Davidson, Nashville, 8th Ward, 54; Mt. Olivet Cemetery Records, II, 48.

2. Simms A. G. Noel (*c*1823-1867), a Kentuckian with total assets of $42,000, had shifted his business involvement from a livery stable to a grocery just before the war. His wife Tennessee (*c*1830-1884) evidently recovered from this period of illness. *Ibid.*, 18, 147; 1850 Census, Tenn., Davidson, 21st Dist., 756; (1860), Nashville, 8th Ward, 54; *Nashville Bus. Dir.* (1855-56), 91.

From William A. Haun[1]

New Collumbia Illinois
Dec the 19th 1863

Mr Andrew Johnson military Gov of Tenn

Dear Sir I left East Tenn in Nov last for the purpos of looking at the contry of the north western states at the time that general wilcock's [2] left bulls Gap E. Tenn[.] I am not able to discharge soldiery servise from disability but dont ask a discharge[.] I am willing to serve my contry in some maner to doe the most good I can[.] I would like to have a commision to recruite for the servise of the state of Tenn as I live in East Tenn bulls gap[.] I profess to be a union man and want this sothern rebellion put down at all hazard[.] pleas answer me by return mail[.] I am here not able to

travel afoot and caint I travel by publick coneyance with out some showing[.]
I would like to recrute for Col A. J. Lanes[3] regm[.] pleas send me a comision as a Recruting officer for Tenn[.] if this request is not in accordence please pardon[.]

Yours Truly Wm. A. Haun
of Jefferson county bulls gap
but know in state of Illinois Massach county New Collumbia

ALS, T-Mil. Gov's Papers, 1862-65, Petitions.

1. William A. Haun (1825-1907), Tennessee-born farmer who moved to Greene County after the war, had represented Jefferson County at the 1861 Knoxville convention. 1900 Census,Tenn., Greene, 34th Enum. Dist., 2B; *OR*, Ser. 1, LII, Pt. I, 150; WPA, Hamblen County Tombstone Records, 29.

2. Orlando B. Willcox.

3. It is probable that the writer had not yet learned of Lane's death six months before.

From Asa C. Ketchum[1]

Civil Commission for the District of Memphis,
Memphis, Tenn., Dec 20th 1863.

Governor
Dear Sir

Beliving that you have the interest of the loyal People of Tenn at heart and ready to advance the Same on all occasions I have taken the liberty to address you and ask your influence in Securing the Passage of a Bill through Congress, legalizing the acts of the Civil Commission of the Dist of Memphis;[2] Established by Brig Genl Veatch in April last & to Supply a want of the State Courts in this part of the State. The commission has tried and decided between Seven and Eight hundred Cases, has been in continual Session Since its organization, with the exception of ten days, and has given general Satisfaction to the People of this City and of West Tenn— The Bill Sent to Hon Wm. Holman[3] of the house of Representatives from Indiania, he was here and prosecuted Some claims for parties residing in Cincinnati. It Simply Provides for the continuance of the Commission until the State Courts are restablished; The Bar now numbering about Seventy five members were nearly unanimous in Preparing the Bill and Recommending its Passage by Congress; I have the fullest confidence if you give the Bill your concurrence it will pass at once, which I have no doubt you will do, if Satisfied that it is for the Benefit of the loyal citizens of the State, and other States who have claims to collect here— Your *true* friends here were highly gratified at your Position in reference to Re-organization of the State upon a Basis, that would Secure Peace to the State for all time to come. We are still pleased that the President has adopted your plan for Reconstruction[4] and believe we can at no great distance, hold an Election and Set the Civil Government in operation— I shall be for one be ready when you as the great leader in this State, Proclaim the day has come, for an effort to establish the Civil Authority.

Trusting that you may look upon our efforts to Secure the People in this part of the State with favor

I am very Respectfully
Your most obedient Servant
A. C. Ketchum

ALS, DLC-JP.

1. See *Johnson Papers,* V, 573*n*.

2. The civil commission, charged with hearing cases involving debts, contracts, property ownership, and fraud, and presided over by Ketchum, Barbour Lewis, and Joseph Williams, had aroused much criticism and questions about its legality. Holman introduced the bill on January 11, 1864; however, the judiciary committee recommended against passage and it was tabled on June 6. Hooper, Memphis, 87-88; *Cong. Globe,* 38 Cong., 1 Sess., 149, 2773.

3. William S. Holman (1822-1897), a native Hoosier, attended Franklin College before becoming a lawyer. Filling various state offices, including a term in the legislature (1851-52), he subsequently served for many years as a Democrat in Congress (1859-65, 1867-77, 1881-95, 1897), where he became known as the "Watch Dog of the Treasury." *DAB,* IX, 158-59.

4. Although Johnson at this time had no unique or original "plan for reconstruction," he and Lincoln did agree on two important points in the President's amnesty and reconstruction proclamation of December 8, 1863: (1) secession destroyed only the legitimacy of a state's governmental administration, not its status in the Union, and (2) the Federal government, under its constitutional power to guarantee republican government in the states, could initiate the restoration of legitimate government. *Johnson Papers,* V, 210-11, 383; Basler, *Works of Lincoln,* IV, 439-40; VII, 55-56.

From John Cothran and James W. Garrett[1]

Head Quarters (Co. D)
56th New York Vols
Beaufort, S. C. Dec 22nd/63

To his excellency Andrew Johnston
millitary Gov of Tennessee
Honored & respected Sir.

I hope & trust you will forgive me for presuming to address these lines to you without communicating through my commanding officer, but I am here with James W. Garrett & know body knows that I am a deserter from Col. Stokes Regt. 1st Middle Tennessee Cavalry, Capt Galbraths Company.[2] I am also here under an assumed name Viz. James Ingham[.] my real name is Jno. Cothran, of "Bedford Co" Tenn. for further information you can get from Capt Davis[3] of Col. Stokes Regt. Comdg Co B. It is useless for me to enter into further details about how & when we came here. But we came away under the belief that our regt was captured & that we were to be tried as deserters, & further more came under the solicitation of a commissioned officer whom I will not name at present but one who had disgracefully been dismissed from our Regt. by yourself.[4] I am sorry I left & if you will reclaim me I am willing to suffer the penalty of a "deserter" if in accordance with your Views, & if returned to my Regt my future conduct will show how sincerly I have repented leaving my old & respected Commander. If you choose to have any thing to do with an unworthy youth as myself who has been led astray, by others older than myself You can adress my Captain.

Viz Capt. E. D. Wheeler[5] Comdg Co. D.
C. H. Van Wycks Regt[6] the 56 Regt. N. Y. S. Vols
Camp at, Beaufort South Carolina
Brig. R. Saxton[7] comdg "Post"

If you choose to reclaim us please do so as soon as possible as the Regts time will soon be expired. Our reasons for writing this are that we wish to return home without being arrested as deserters & wish to do duty in our Own state during the War & to suffer the punishment that you may see cause to inflict upon us.

We therefore remain

Your most obt. Servants
Jno Cothran (alias J. Ingham)
& James W Garrett (alias Wm. Garrett)[8]

ALS (Cothran), DLC-JP.

1. Probably John B. Cothran (b. *c*1843), Smith County machinist or merchant, who had joined Co. B, 5th Tenn. Cav., USA, as bugler July 23, 1862. According to his service record, he deserted January 5, 1863, returned March 15, was court-martialed, found absent without leave, and sentenced to forfeit four months pay. There is no evidence of the desertion he reports; on the contrary, the records show him "present" until mustered out at Fayetteville, Tennessee, on June 25, 1865. James W. Garrett (b. *c*1844) mustered as a private, Co. A, 5th Tenn., September 9, 1862, deserted December 26. Confirmation of their story would seem to lie in the fact that Privates James Ingham, aged twenty, and William F. Garrett, aged twenty-one, were mustered into Co. D, 56th New York Vol. Inf., at Tarrytown, New York, in October, 1863; the former was discharged at Beaufort, South Carolina, in July, 1864, and the latter deserted at Summerville, same state, in July, 1865. Porch, *1850 Census, Bedford,* 26; CSR, RG94, NA; *Tenn. Adj. Gen. Report* (1866), 419; Joel C. Fisk and William H. D. Blake, *A Condensed History of the 56th Regiment New York Veteran Volunteer Infantry* (Newburgh, 1906), 206, 209, 219.

2. William B. Stokes and Robert Galbraith.

3. Thomas C. Davis (b. *c*1831), Smith County-born farmer, was briefly captain, Co. B, 5th Tenn. Cav. (August 30-November 7, 1862) before resigning on account of disability. CSR, RG94, NA.

4. There is no evidence that Johnson dismissed any of the cashiered officers in Stokes's regiment.

5. Edward D. Wheeler, beginning as lieutenant in August, 1861, became captain a year later Co. D, 56th N. Y., serving until his resignation in March, 1864. CSR, RG94, NA; Fisk and Blake, *56th Regiment,* 217.

6. Charles H. Van Wyck (1824-1895), New York-born politician and Rutgers graduate (1843), served as Congressman (1859-63, 1867-69, 1870-71) before moving in 1874 to Nebraska where he was elected to the state (1876-80) and the U. S. senates (1881-87). He had become colonel of the 56th N. Y. Inf. in September, 1861. *BDAC,* 1751; Warner, *Generals in Blue,* 524.

7. Rufus Saxton (1824-1908), Massachusetts native and West Pointer (1849), commanded an artillery detachment at the St. Louis arsenal in 1861. Becoming a brigadier general of volunteers in April of the following year, he was briefly in charge of the Harper's Ferry defenses (1862) and held various commands near Beaufort, where his primary concern was the enlistment of Negroes. Mustered out of the volunteers early in 1866, he returned as a major, becoming colonel and assistant quartermaster general before his retirement in 1888. *Ibid.*, 420; Boatner, *Civil War Dictionary*, 722-23.

8. In a brief letter accompanying this joint representation, Garrett endorses Cothran's statements about their desertion, concluding "I think it is your duty as a Commander to reclaim us as deserters to be tried accordingly to deserts."

From James R. Hood[1]

Post Office Chattanooga Tennessee
December 22nd 1863

Gov. Andrew Johnson,
Sir,

Lieutenant Col Wiles,[2] Provost Marshal General of the Department of the Cumberland to day gave me verbal notice to send *all* citizens letters to him for inspection. I put the question to him whether he meant to include the letters of those few citizens here who have been true as steel from the commencement of the War. He answered, yes, and remarked that it was a military necessity.

You may imagine that I felt indignant that a number of subordinates should be permitted to have the disposal of the letters of men whose patriotic conduct entitles them to all the privileges of American citizens in any portion of the country.

I know nothing of Lt Col Wiles. He may be as pure a patriot as our country affords, and his object in giving this order may have been based on the conviction that the public service would be benefitted thereby. *But I do not believe it.* I believe him to have been governed by selfish motives in this matter.

Of course I did not argue the question with the Provost Marshal but immediately repaired to General Thomas' Head Quarters and protested against the examination by mere clerks of the mail matter of loyal citizens. I distinctly and emphatically disavowed any desire to protect Rebels or Rebel sympathizers, for the simple reason that I believe them fit subjects for punishment rather than the proper persons to be the recipients of Government favors. General Thomas treated me very kindly, and after a somewhat protracted conversation ordered me to deliver letters addressed to persons for whom I could vouch and send all others to the Dead Letter Office. I have, by the mail that brings this letter, communicated briefly the facts narrated above at some length to the Post Master General. It is my desire and intention to pay proper respect to all military orders by those in command in this vicinity, but at the same time I shall do all in my power to protect those noble spirits in this and adjoining counties who have stood the test of Rebel persecution for nearly three years, against unnecesary interferences and anoyances of upstarts who have nothing but their shoulder straps to recommend them. To this end I deemed it advisable to communicate with your Excellency, knowing you to fully appreciate their many sacrifices for the Union.

Please say to Mr. Maynard that those of the people who have read his letter to Mr. Spurlock[3] are highly pleased with its recommendations. Judge Gant[4] is here and warmly approves it.

Give my respects to Mr. Maynard, and Col Browning, and rest assured that I shall never forget your own uniform friendship for me.

I am, Sir, your Obt Servt
Jas. R. Hood

ALS, DLC-JP.

1. For Hood, Chattanooga editor and postmaster, see *Johnson Papers,* IV, 345*n.*
2. William M. Wiles.
3. Dated December 8 and published in the *Dispatch* a week later, Maynard's communication, responding to an inquiry about the reorganization of county government, indicated that the election would be held in March, and that the constitution and statutes prior to May, 1861, would be the guide. The addressee, John L. Spurlock (1829-1871), was probably the McMinnville lawyer. 1860 Census, Tenn., Warren, 181; Nashville *Dispatch,* December 14, 1863; Acklen, *Tenn. Records,* I, 149; *Goodspeed's Warren,* 819.
4. John C. Gaut.

From Jonathan W. Dolbear[1]

Nashville Dec 24th, 1863

Gov Andrew Johnson,
Sir

An honest aged colored man wishes a pass to allow him to remain in the city with the privilege of going back and forward through the lines of the Army to bing chips &c into the city in a one horse waggon. This man "Gid. Handy" [2] was ruptured while working on the fortification on capitol hill and is not fit for hard labor, but I understand he was by threats made to go to Gallitin to chop wood for that *rebel* wood contractor Witkowskie,[3] while his (Gids) wife was sick at home. It appears to me rather inhuman to make a man in his condition chop all day and then camp out at night.

If consistent with your views I hope you will grant him a pass.

Yours &c J. W. Dolbear

P S He is epected to return to the city tonight and wish to remain.

ALS, DLC-JP.

1. Jonathan W. Dolbear (c1815-1883), identified variously as an Englishman and as a Massachusetts native, taught stenography and penmanship and conducted a small Nashville "Commercial College" for many years, both prior to and after the war. 1860 Census, Tenn., Davidson, Nashville, 4th Ward, 137; (1880), 37th Enum. Dist., 28; Nashville city directories (1866, 1872, 1881), *passim;* Nashville *Banner,* September 15, 1883.

2. Unidentified.

3. Gustave Witkowski, a Nashville clothing merchant, had advertised for 500 woodchoppers at "*the best price paid*" and that he would "provide passes from pressing," i. e., protection for Negro laborers from being pressed into military work details. The charge that he was a rebel is debatable, inasmuch as he was hired by Union authorities. *Singleton's Nashville Business Directory* (1865), 245; Nashville *Union,* September 15, 1863; C. B. Comstock to Gen. Robert Granger, January 15, 1864, in CSR (William B. Stokes), RG94, NA.

From John McLaughlin

December 25, 1863, Penitentiary, Nashville; ALS, DLC-JP.

Prisoner who has served four years of a five-year sentence writes that he had "labored hard and faithfully for the State until 6 months ago" when he "gave out from over-exertion," and has since been confined in the hospital. Claiming that the charge of attempting to stab a man was his first offense, avers that he is "sometimes attacked with fits caused by neuralgia on the brain and I may die suddenly here at any time a thing which I hope your Excellency will prevent if possible by releasing me."

From Mary F. S. Pepper[1]

Springfield Dec 25, /63.

Gov Johnson
Dear Sir

Not forgetting the friendship that existed between yourself and my Husband I venture to address you a few lines. I have no one to advise or councel me, I know not what to do, and afraid to do any thing for fear of doing something wrong. You knew my Husband[.] You knew his history. You knew how he struggled through poverty and privations, he at last was brought to an untimely grave, through much mental labor and exposure, trying to make a little propety so that his children[2] would not have to contend with the privations that he did. Knowing all this I feel it my duty to save a little if there is any possable chance. I hate for his life to be spent for nought. We are fast becoming beggars[.] I have no one to look to, to educate my Dear little boys. Is there no protection for the Fatherless babes, their father died before the war broke out, had nothing to do with it[.] I never have given any thing nor aided in any way[.] Oh I have had Wars enough to contend with at home with bothering with the public, but what is the intention of the Federal Goverment towards the property of Orphan children[.] if there is no provision for such there ought to be for humanity sake[.] Our only means of support was a few Negroes[.][3] They are fas[t] leaving me[.] I have raised the most of them[.] They have been happy and contented untill that old Negro came here from Cincinnati[.][4] he is not only getting them off but taking my stock also. they are leaving us in a very helpless condition[.] I am in very poor health[.] I am not able to cook a day much less support myself and children and if it gets any worse with me I will like the Negroes go to Nashville to be fed and clothed and not have to work, but you know I would not do that, but it does not seem nothing but wright that if they will support my negroes they would the Widow and Fatherless. We have 5 Negroes there and a mule,[5] the Negroes are I suppose a clear loss but surely they will not deny me an old mule that I stand very much in need of[.] I understand that orders have been issued that contrabands comeing in with Stock they have a right to them, but I do not believe that there is any such orders. if there is every one will want to take a horse along to sell, Great God Sir to think of the relations friends and propety I once had around me, and now this christmas day sitting here alone no one even to whisper a kind word of consolation[.] I have lost what little mind I had and my little remaining strength is fast giving away. I see nothing before me but beggery and suffering[.] God knows why he has allowed this horrable War to afflict the country. May his wrath be appiesed and piece be restored[.] I feel that unknow[n] callamities are now suppended as if by a thread over the heads of the Wicked rulers of this land, that had to do in bringing it on, Who to carry out their own public and Private aim have filled the land with unutterable woe. They have decieved the people with lies[.] They have fanned ther zeal into fanitisism and made them mad. The wind they have sown has become a whirlwind before which they that have raised will be swept powerless to allay or resist. God help the innocent and helpless— If it had not been that you used your influance in my Fathers case[6] he I suppose would have died in the old Jail at Gallatin[.] he now has a street parole, for which I feel under many obligations to you. Mr Solomon is my Father. Oh how I wish it could be arrainged so that he could come to me[.] I have not seen him in a year and most a half[.] He cannot get a premit and I am not able to go to him. My brother that recently died in Calafornia[7] wrote to me to write to Gen Halleck as they were personal friends, but he is not in reach of me and I know that there is no one that would give me any advise sooner than you. if there is any way of getting my propety or the value you I know will let me know. I feel it my duty to make some exertions in my childrens behalf, and if there is no provisions made there ought to be, I can't tell what is to become of us. My oldest living child is only six and the other was born three months after the death of his Father. My Dear Sir have I not suffered enough[?] My two oldest was take[n] from me since the death of their Father[.] My oldest was ten years old. might they not let me pass. if either side had all

I possess on earth it would be a mere drop to them and of infinite value to me and my little ones[.] Excuse this long and hasty letter[.] I had no idea of writing but a few lines, but I have seen so much trouble I could write volunes.

With due respect Your friend
Mrs W W Pepper.[8]

To Gov Johnson
Nashville Tenn.

ALS, DLC-JP.

1. Mary F. Solomon (1832-1897) became Mrs. William W. Pepper in 1847, was widowed in 1861, and sometime after the war married her brother-in-law Thomas Pepper. 1860 Census, Tenn., Robertson, 9th Dist., 7; (1870), 8; (1880), 9; (1900), 52nd Enum. Dist., 1A; Sistler, *1850 Tenn. Census,* V, 103; McBride and Robison, *Biographical Directory,* I, 578; Mrs. Charles W. Durrell and Mrs. Richard A. Williams, comps., *Cemetery Records of Robertson County, Tennessee* (3 vols., Ashland City, Tenn., 1973-75), II, 47; for William W. Pepper, Johnson's old friend the "blacksmith" judge, see *Johnson Papers,* II, 216*n.*

2. At the time of his death, Judge Pepper still had at home Young (*c*1843-1873), son of his first wife, Pernecy Young Pepper; Bromie C. (1852-1861); a daughter designated in the census as S. F. (b. *c*1855); and William W., Jr. (1856-*fl*1906). 1860 Census, Tenn., Robertson, 9th Dist., 7; (1870), 8; (1900), 52nd Enum. Dist., 1A; Durrett and Williams, *Robertson County Cemetery Records,* II, 47; Young & Co.'s, *Business and Professional Directory . . . of Tennessee, 1906-07* (Atlanta, 1906), 484.

3. On the eve of the war, Pepper was credited with eighteen slaves—six females and twelve males, five of whom would have been of military age by 1863. 1860 Census, Slave Schedule, Tenn., Robertson, Springfield, 1-2.

4. That "old Negro" may have been one of the northern-born agents whom the Federal recruiting service used so effectively in Middle Tennessee. Cimprich, Slavery Amidst Civil War, 189.

5. Two weeks later Mrs. Pepper wrote, "I have four men in Nashville two of whom I know to be in the Service the other two have but recently left home, but I persume that they are employed for the Govement in some way." Pepper to Johnson, January 6, 1864, Johnson Papers, LC.

6. William H. Solomon (b. *c*1799) was a North Carolina-born Gallatin hatter with $3,000 real and $10,000 personal property. 1850 Census, Tenn., Sumner, 5th Dist., 328; (1860), 12.

7. Perrin L. Solomon (*c*1822-1863), born in Kentucky, served in Mexico as a lieutenant, 1st Tenn. Inf., before moving to California where he was U. S.marshal for the northern district with his residence in San Francisco. Deane Porch, tr., *Sumner County, Tennessee, 1850 Census* (Franklin, Tenn., 1972), 66; *Goodspeed's Sumner,* 811; *U. S. Official Register* (1859), 171; *San Francisco City Directory* (1861), 314.

8. Early in January Mrs. Pepper asked for whatever "bounty the Goverment sees fit to provide" for two of her hands, assuming that they were employed by the Nashville authorities, a request which Johnson, identifying the writer as "the widow of an Ex Judge of this state," referred "to Maj Stearns office for information[.]" Pepper to Johnson, January 6, 1864, Johnson Papers, LC.

From Williamson County Citizens

December 25, 1863, Brushwood; Pet, DLC-JP.

The petition, signed by twenty-four men, describes Benjamin Bond's ten-year sentence for "larcency and highway robery," as "a just measure of punishment." Fearing there might be "Some unfair and unjust influence presented for Your Executive Clemency to him," requests "that the Said Bond be regarded an unworthy object for Your Executive *pardon* and he be permitted to Serve out his allotted time in the State Prison, where his deeds of rascality have So justly Consigned him[.]"

From Citizens of Memphis

December 26, 1863, Memphis; Pet (Kortrecht), DLC-JP.

Seven Memphians, including Charles Kortrecht and Ira M. Hill, write concerning "reestablishment of the State Government of Tennessee" in accordance with Lincoln's ten percent plan. Asserting that "one half of the people remaining in this Congressional District desire such reestablishment," the signers, "anxious to see the machinery put in motion for the practical accomplishment of the proclamation," look to Johnson "to put us on the road to this practical outworking." Suggesting the appointment of county officers to supervise registration, they propose that the governor "immediately" call a convention to implement the plan. To expedite the reorganization of the state, they recommend that "the administration of the prescribed oath, the registration of those taking it, and the election, might all go on simultaneously; and the registration and election returns be made at the same time. If . . . the requisite number of votes appear to have been cast, the convention would proceed otherwise not." The petitioners "would be glad" to hear from Johnson in regard to reorganization. Kortrecht, in a postscript, reports that "We are considering the propriety of a meeting here sometime within two or three weeks to give expression to the views and wishes of the loyal people of Memphis."

From Elizabeth S. Grant[1]

Christiana Dec. 28th 1863.

To His Excellency
Gov Johnson

Although retaining myself a very agreeable impression of our interview on the cars, on our way to Shelbyville to attend the Union Convention:[2]—in the multiplicity of your arduous duties you may have forgotten it—the purport of our conversation, was the difficulties of our position here as Union people. Allow me to trespass for a short time on your valuable time.

Since the advance of the army and the occupation of this point by the troops—our farming operations are entirely destroyed for years to come. Our only resource left is our little country store, which has been kept up by my Father, Mr Sherbrooke,[3] who has been selling to loyal people and the soldiers—under the restrictions of the Provost Marshall here.

In bringing out his goods my Father has conformed to the law both civil and military as far as he understood them— Sent to Cincinnati for permits etc. etc. After the purchase of the Past bill of goods it came to his knowledge that this was not a trading Station.[4] for this his goods are now retained in Nashville.

Now Gov. what I hope and think you will do for us is to write a note to Mr Mellen furthering my Father's views in regard to making Christiana a trading station.

One consideration which weighs with me, is that the poor people who are willing to live under the old flag may have a chance to obtain the necessaries of life.

With considerations of high respect and esteem.

Mrs James H. Grant.

ALS, DLC-JP.

1. Elizabeth Sherbrooke (b *c*1828-*fl*1870), from Syracuse, New York, had been a French teacher at Soule College in Murfreesboro before her 1857 marriage to James H. Grant, third cousin to Ulysses S. Grant and resident engineer of the Nashville and Chattanooga Railroad. She and her husband remained staunch unionists and, although their home enjoyed Federal protection during the Murfreesboro campaigns, it was nevertheless "a haven for hungry and wounded Confederates." 1870 Census, Tenn., Rutherford, 20th Dist., 9; Mary B. Hughes, *Hearthstones: the Story of Historic Rutherford County Homes* (Murfreesboro, Tenn., 1942), 45, 54; Thomas N. Johns, Sr., "The Nashville and Chattanooga Railroad through Rutherford County, 1845-1872," *Rutherford County Historical Society Publication,* No. 5 (1975), 11.

2. On June 7, 1862, Johnson, William H. Wisener, and others spoke at a meeting held at the Fair Grounds; it was reported that "from three to four thousand persons, including many ladies, were present." Savage, *Life of Johnson,* 266.

3. Possibly Freeman Sherbrooke, commissioner of registration for Rutherford County in August, 1866. Sims, *Rutherford County,* 81.

4. Situated on the railroad, Christiana is in the southern portion of Rutherford County, about nine miles south of Murfreesboro.

From Mildred A. Hall

Dec 28th 1863—
No 26 Cherry St—

Govenor Johnson

I slept sweetly last night in the hope and belief that you would not permit me to be thrown into the streets— I have no place to go—have no where to store my furniture—and if you will only suspend that writ[1] till March — I can then go North—but fear to do so now on acct of my health— Oh Govenor—I hope I do not appeal to you in vain— I will pay the rent to any person you may appoint—Mr Fogg, Mr Houston, Mr Fowler[2] or any responsible person. Please do Govenor—send an orderly down with the order suspending the writ—& thus save me from exposure and a sacrifice of all I have.

A whole heart full of gratitude Govenor, will ever be yours—if you will extend this act of humanity to me— I have neither friends nor counsellors in the City— Will you assist me? This will be my last appeal—excuse me for troubling you—the unfortunate position in which I am placed I hope will be ample apology. Shall I come up, or will you not send an Orderly with the order—? [3]

Respectfully, Mrs. B. W. Hall

ALS, DLC-JP.

1. The impending order probably coincided with the expiration of her lease at the end of the month and reflected the landlord's anger at delays in the payment of part of her 1862 rent. Letter from Mildred A. Hall, July 14, 1863.

2. Probably Francis B. Fogg, Russell Houston, and Joseph S. Fowler. Fogg (1795-1880), native of Connecticut, was admitted to the bar prior to moving to Nashville in 1818 where he practiced law for the remainder of his life. A delegate to the constitutional convention of 1834, he also served in the senate (1851-53), on the local board of education (1856-63), and as a trustee of Cumberland College and its successor, the University of Nashville (1823-80). McBride and Robison, *Biographical Directory*, I, 253; Clayton, *Davidson County*, 115-16.

3. There is no evidence of the outcome.

From James F. Henderson[1]

Jeffersonville Indiania
Dec 28th 1863

To his Exellancy
Gov Andrew Johnson
Dear Sir

I have been a solder in the so called Confeddrate Armey for a little over twelve months under Capt Js Tyner[2] of Tyner St[a]tion Hamilton county Tenn[.] I have Ever benn opposed to a Disolution of this Greate govrnment[.] I voted a gainst it[.] that was all that I cold Do but after the conscript law was Passed & the law inforced I was compelled to go in as it was allmost imposible for me to get my familey a way[.] I have Lived in Hamilton County the most of my time for sixteen or seventeen years Ever since I was a beoy[.] I am a poor man[.] I had to Labor horde for the supporte of my familey[.] I was imployed on the R Road for six years a preavious to the War[.] I have not been with the Reg since the 26th of Sept[.] my familey has been Living at Chickamauga Depot Ever since I went in to armey[.] I was in 2 miles of home when the federals got posesion of the Villege where my family Lived[.] I then came home & gave my self up to Col Spuner[3] of the 83rd indiania Reg[.] I Remained at home for 8 Days and was not under arrest[.] I was advised by various men to go to Chattanooga & take the oath & that I cold Get transpotation for my familey but when I went to the provst Marchial at Chattanooga I Did not get the opertunity of stating to him my condition[.] he was buisey in talking to some sittozens[.] the Clearks promies me they wold have my case attended to but they Did not Do it[.] I was placed in the garde house where there was about Eighty or a hundred others[.] we was sent from there to Nashville where I taken the oath of allegiance[.] I was sent from there to Louisville Ky where I taken the oath again[.] it was all so aded to the oath to go immediatly North of the Ohio River & Remain untill further Orders[.] I am now Deprived of my familey or of hearing from them[.] will you assit me in getting my family where I can soporte or Do something for them at least[.] if you will I will promise you I will Ever Recolect you as my children is small & my wife very weakly[.] I am cutting corde wood near Jeffersonville[.] I will send you a copy of the oath[.][4]

J F Henderson

ALS, DLC-JP.

1. Possibly James Henderson (b. *c*1824), native Tennessean, who was a farmer with $12,000 real and $853 personal property after the war; or, more likely, James F. Henderson (b. *c*1831), Alabama-born farmer, a resident in 1850 of Walker County, Georgia. 1870 Census, Tenn., Hamilton, 11th Dist., 43rd Subdiv., 15; (1850), Ga., Walker, West Chickamauga Dist., 914.

2. J. S. Tyner (b. *c*1827), native Georgian, was a civil engineer with $5,000 real and $5,000 personal property on the eve of the war. In 1862 from the Harrison-Tyner Station-Ooltewah sections of Hamilton County, he recruited and was elected captain of a company which became Co. K, 1st Tenn. Cav., CSA. He was later transferred to the engineering department. 1860 Census, Tenn., Hamilton, 7th Dist., 145; Armstrong, *Hamilton County*, II, 297.

3. Benjamin J. Spooner (*c*1823-1881), Ohio-born Lawrenceburg, Indiana, attorney and Mexican War veteran, saw service as lieutenant colonel, 7th and 51st Ind. Inf., and colonel, 83rd Ind. Inf. Losing an arm at Kenesaw Mountain and resigning in April, 1865, he was later U. S. marshal of Indiana. *NCAB*, IV, 503; Heitman, *Register*, I, 911-12.

4. Henderson's holographed oath was attached.

From Joseph Ramsey

December 30, 1863, Shelbyville, Tenn.; ALS, DLC-JP.

Commissioner for deserted property in Bedford County, enclosing his performance bond of $5,000 and "A Slip Containing the Rents of some Houses & and an farm," reports his activities, and requests a ticket on the Nashville and Chattanooga Railroad, "so that I Can Communicate with you more fuly[.]"

1864

From James B. Bingham

Bulletin Printing Office,
Telegraph Building, Court Street.
Memphis, Tenn., Jan. 2d 1864

Gov. Andrew Johnson:

My Dear Sir: Owing to a protracted spell of sickness of the most disagreeable character, (diarrhoea and dysentery) I was not able to leave my room until day before yesterday, and consequently could not write to you as soon as I had promised and expected. Besides, I have a carbunkle on the instep of the left foot, and even up to this time, I am compelled to ride or hobble about very slowly and poorly.

As soon as I could leave my room, I waited upon Gen. Hurlbut, and after waiting at the door *two* hours lacking ten minutes, I succeeded in getting an audience. I found him *apparently* sober.[1] I presented him the documents relating to my commission, and when he had read them *all through*, I explained that I had taken occasion, sometime before the recent issue of his order, to recommend to the people of Tennessee to take measures for their own defence—that I had reference to the "Union Guards" operating under you, and that in consequence of my applications to you on the subject, I had received the commission which he saw before him.[2] I also stated, that inasmuch as he had issued orders of great stringency since that action had been taken, I was at a loss to know whether there was any thing *conflicting*, and had therefore waited upon him before making any move in the matter. I particularly asked him if any person now in the Home Guards, by his order, would be permitted, if so disposed, to join the companies which I was authorized to raise. He replied that any who desired to join my companies would be permitted to do so, inasmuch as that was *active* service, while the Home Guards he had organized would only be used in case of emergency. If he had to send all his troops away, he would put them on guard in the city. He added that Forrest was bold enough to make a raid into the city, and for his part he should not care much—for he owed Memphis a "grudge" and would like to have an opportunity to destroy all of it except the Fort. Of course I dissented from the justice of such a course, but the above spirit is no doubt sincerely entertained, since while *beastly* intoxicated, he told Major Norris[3] that he expected to be overruled in regard to his order, but if they did not let him have his way he would resign. He also said that he wanted our people to know that Memphis was "only a military post, and a d--d small one at that, and that if he had his way he would destroy all of it except the fort," or words of similar import.

Gen. Hurlbut was kind enough to say, that he could arm ten companies if formed, wished they were ready now, *he* could use them so efficiently, &c. but instructed me to correspond with you and learn how they were to be subsisted and mounted. This I promised to do before I moved further in the matter.

I ought perhaps to explain to you, that from some cause, there has been no attempt to carry out Hurlbut's order, except in a few individual cases. Instead of conscripting all who failed to enroll themselves into regiments in regular service, *all* such are *fined* from $500 to $10, according to supposed ability to pay. Only a few are fined as high as five hundred dollars. Thus, you see, that this order, like all others, is made a means of collecting money from the people. Gen. Thomas,[4] Adjt Gen., was here while I was in Nashville, and perhaps his influence was potent enough to induce a change in the programme.

So much for Hurlbut and his famous order. He informed me that there might have been some chance to get up the companies *before* Forrest's conscription in West Tennessee,[5] but he thought that men were very scarce in our Western section now. This brings me to remark, that after whipping Hurlbut's forces at Lafayette—news of which had reached Nashville before I left—Forrest went to Jackson, Tenn., where he concentrated his forces and operated at pleasure, conscripting every man he could find, stealing every horse, cow, wagon, and in short everything he could use. Some days before he left Jackson, Forrest sent two thousand Union men, captured in West Tennessee, *across* our lines, to Enterprise or Columbus, Miss. to be armed. After a great deal of preparation, Hurlbut sent *three* columns after Forrest at Jackson. Forrest, however, eluded them all, and camping three miles from Collierville last Sunday night, he again *crossed* our lines and went South last Monday, carrying with him about 1800 head of cattle, an abundance of horses and wagons, and in fact every thing he wanted. Whether such exploits evince Generalship or drunkenness, I leave you to determine.

It has been given out here that the Home Guards organized under Gen. Veatch's order are nothing but enrolled militia, and that *you* will be called upon to commission the officers. If such is the fact I beg you not to commission any of the three appointed by Gen. Veatch with Hurlbut's consent. If appears that Veatch, before making the appointments, did ask the advice of a few—say one or two—Union men, but he is said to have disregarded every recommendation which was made. The man appointed Colonel of the *first* regiment is John McDonald,[6] a resident of Memphis only a few months, and said to have been compelled to resign the position of Major in the 8th Missouri regiment on account of cowardice in face of the enemy. McDonald's brother[7] is Lt. Colonel. He is young, and possesses but little better qualifications, while Joseph Tagg,[8] an old citizen, and a

Union man, is made a Major under these young men; and I. M. Hill,[9] one of the soundest Union men that ever lived in Memphis, an old, intelligent and capable man is made quartermaster in the same regiment. The McDonalds are said to have been appointed by Hurlbut. In the second regiment, A. C. Ketchum,[10] who fought against "the flag" at Belmont as a rebel Colonel, is now appointed to the same position by Gen. Veatch, and to command gentlemen. Ketchum is the same man whom you refused to appoint Judge, a position assigned him in Veatch's corrupt civil commission. Ruel Hough[11] was appointed Lt. Colonel under Ketchum, without his knowledge or consent, and will not serve. Buttinghaus,[12] appointed Colonel of the third regiment, is a low-flung, dirty foreigner, who while in command of a Home Guard company in Confederate times, insisted on having his company sworn in to support the rebel cause, while those who refused to take the oath *then*—some of them gentlemen—have to serve under him. But time would fail me to go over in detail the moral and political delinquencies of the batch of officers appointed by Veatch. They have given much dissatisfaction to the real earnest Union men of Memphis, and if it be true that you will have to issue commissions for them, I beg you not to make any such appointments, but to acquaint the Executive Committee for this end of the state,[13] and we will take steps to recommend to you such as are worthy of your consideration, or to permit the regiments to elect, just as shall appear most expedient.

A few days before I got home, an informal meeting of some *five* gentlemen—two of them (Kortrecht and Bland)[14] aspirants for Congress—was held in reference to the President's proclamation and reconstruction, and a committee appointed to correspond with you on the subject. What the nature of their communication[15] I do not know, and only mention the subject to say, that I have induced all parties to wait until you could go to Washington and return, and make known to us your views. The members of the Executive Committee for this district have issued cards for a free and full conference to-night, among leading Union men, but anxious as some are to move *at once*, I apprehend I shall have no difficulty in inducing them to wait *two weeks*, until you can be heard from. But, in order that we may act understandingly,—for we wish to act in concert with you—I beg that you will write to me at your earliest convenience and let me know what will be your policy, and how fast we shall move, when you can be with us, &c. Also, your views as to the policy of making the canvass for reconstruction and reorganization on the plan presented by the President, or for Emancipation straight out. My own impression is, that we shall have more help, in this section, and attain the same result, in the President's plan, but I am anxious to know your views, feeling well assured that yours will be best for the present circumstances.

The report is, that Sherman and Hunter will be here next week, and that the latter will supersede Hurlbut.[16] It would be hailed with universal joy by all loyal people.

In regard to raising the companies, I wish you would inform me, for Hurlbut's benefit, how the men I shall enlist can be subsisted and mounted, and then I shall go to work at it and do what I can, his evil prognostications to the contrary notwithstanding.

Hoping to hear from you soon, I remain, with great respect,

Your ob't serv't,
James B. Bingham

ALS, T-Mil. Gov's Papers, 1862-65, Petitions.

1. Hurlbut had a notorious affection for the "ardent." He was reportedly drunk for a week after his appointment as brigadier in June, 1861, and was less than sober when he led his Zouave regiment off to the Missouri front. Nevins, *War for the Union*, I, 230; Warner, *Generals in Blue*, 245.

2. Bingham was engaged in what proved to be an abortive effort to recruit for West Tennessee a regiment of Johnson's "personal" army, designated as "Union Guards," to be used in recovering and securing Tennessee in the face of Confederate guerrilla activity. Signing of such twelve-months men obviously competed with Hurlbut's efforts to organize home guard units for the protection of Memphis. In pursuit of the latter goal, Hurlbut had issued General Order No. 157, November 15, 1863, providing for the impressment of all able-bodied men to fill up regiments depleted by casualties. Hooper, Memphis, 30; Memphis *Bulletin*, November 17, 1863.

3. Probably Maj. Basil Norris (d. 1895), Maryland surgeon at Vicksburg in mid-1863, who became physician to President Johnson's family and rose to the rank of colonel (1888) before retiring in 1892. Powell, *Army List*, 507; Johnson to Norris, July 12, 1870, Johnson Papers, LC.

4. Lorenzo Thomas.

5. His troops somewhat depleted in late 1863 and needing to be replenished with conscripts, Forrest came into West Tennessee and western Kentucky from his headquarters in northern Mississippi in November. Apparently owing to Hurlbut's inaction, the mission was successful with fifty to a hundred men recruited each day. Henry, *Forrest*, 204-6.

6. John McDonald (*fl*1876), of St. Louis, former major of the 8th Mo. Inf., which he helped raise, was a Mississippi riverman. Under court-martial charges during September, 1863, he apparently escaped further difficulty to become colonel of the 1st regiment of enrolled militia (Memphis). Remaining in Memphis after the war, he handled private claims against the government until his appointment in 1869 as supervisor of internal revenue for the Missouri department headquartered in St. Louis, where he was a prime organizer of the "whiskey ring," which collected half the taxes due the government by distillers, ostensibly as a campaign fund to reelect Grant. Indicted in 1875 and sentenced to three years, he served only a year before the President pardoned him. Simon, *Grant Papers*, VI, 91n; Ulysses S. Grant, III, *Ulysses S. Grant: Warrior and Statesman* (New York, 1969), 333-34; Lucius E. Guese, "St. Louis and the Grant Whiskey Ring," *Missouri Historical Review*, XXXVI (1941-42), 161-83.

7. Charles McDonald (1838-1864), New York-born captain of the 8th Mo. Inf. and currently engaged in the wholesale grocery business in Memphis, became lieutenant colonel, later colonel, of the 1st regiment of enrolled militia, and was killed when his horse fell and rolled on him December 12, 1864. Heitman, *Register*, I, 662; Memphis *Bulletin*, January 20, December 13, 15, 1864.

8. Joseph Tagg (1825-1901), English-born paint and wallpaper dealer who served as president of the Washington (Memphis) Union Club (1862), was appointed a provisional alderman in 1864. 1900 Census, Tenn., Shelby, 79th Enum. Dist., 3A; *OR*, Ser. 1, XVII, 869; *Memphis Directory* (1860), 209; (1901), 962; Keating, *Memphis*, II, 28-30.

9. Ira M. Hill.

10. Asa C. Ketchum had served as captain of Co. B, 15th Tenn. Inf., CSA.

11. Reuel Hough, a native of Maine, came to Memphis shortly before the war as general superintendent of the Mississippi and Tennessee Railroad office depot. He was owner of the *Bulletin* from 1862 until April, 1863, surveyor of the Port of Memphis, and internal revenue collector (1865). In 1868 he returned to the *Bulletin* staff. Hooper, Memphis, 100,

126; *U. S. Official Register* (1863), 41, 94; (1865) 61; *Memphis Directory* (1860), 198; (1868-69), 116.

12. Frederick W. Buttinghaus (*c*1824-*fl*1881), Prussian-born Memphis insurance agent and clerk, was captain of Co. F, 3rd Tenn. Inf. Btn., CSA, until he resigned in September, 1863, and converted to unionism. He then served with the enrolled militia until appointed city recorder in the provisional government. After the war he was a Memphis attorney. 1860 Census, Tenn., Shelby, Memphis, 7th Ward, 110; (1870), 9th Ward, 56; *Memphis Directory* (1860), 109; (1881), 191; *Tennesseans in the Civil War*, II, 70; Memphis *Bulletin*, September 21, 1864; Keating, *Memphis*, II, 28-29.

13. The members for West Tennessee were Bingham, James M. Tomeny, and William H. Fitch, Jr. Memphis *Bulletin*, December 30, 1863.

14. Charles Kortrecht (1822-1878), New York-born journeyman carpenter who read law under Judge John C. Humphreys, became a lawyer and city alderman (1858-62). Originally a Whig, he was elected chancellor of the 12th division in August, 1878, as a Republican, dying the following month in the yellow fever epidemic. Peter E. Bland (*fl*1881), a St. Louis lawyer, was colonel of the 6th Mo. Inf. until he left the service in December, 1862. After the war he resumed his law practice in St. Louis. Keating, *Memphis*, II, 71; St.Louis city directories (1860-81), *passim; Official Army Register: Volunteers,* VII, 87.

15. See From Citizens of Memphis, December 26, 1863.

16. It was not Gen. David Hunter but rather Gen. Ralph P. Buckland who became commander of the District of Memphis in January, 1864, serving one full year before resigning to become an Ohio congressman. Warner, *Generals in Blue*, 50.

From George L. Stearns

Boston Jany 2. 1864

To His Excellency Andrew Johnson
Nashville

Gov. We are in great want of men to fill the quotas of our Atlantic States against the coming draft for 300.000 men.[1]

Bounties offered by States of $300—and upwards fail to bring the required numbers, and we need them at home to keep our Machine Shops and other work necessary for the successful prosecution of the war[.][2]

Some of us have thought it would aid us, and also the destitute white families in your State, for our Agents to recruit in Tennessee and elsewhere. I mean that Agents from all Free States should have that liberty. Would it not work well to mix Tennessean's and Ohioans in the same Regt. Please give it your thought and advise Mr Stanton as you may think *best* I enclose printed circular,[3] Also extract from my report[.][4]

Your friend Geo L. Stearns

P. S. I hope to bring men and some Capital to cultivate abandoned lands this year.[5]

ALS, DLC-JP.

1. Lincoln's most recent call for troops, on October 17, 1863, had been for 300,000. However, the "coming" draft of February 1, 1864, was for 500,000. Shannon, *Organization of the Union Army*, II, 34; Basler, *Works of Lincoln*, VII, 164.

2. The draft posed a grave threat to the economy of Massachusetts, the most industrialized state in the country. This letter was part of an organized campaign to persuade Stanton to allow northern states to fill their quotas through recruiting in the South. Congress passed such a law in July but repealed it seven months later because of the

numerous abuses which resulted. Richard H. Abbott, "Massachusetts and the Recruitment of Southern Negroes, 1863-1865," *Civil War History*, XIV (1968), 197-210.

3. A broadside, No. 149, December 22, 1863, of the New England Loyal Publication Society, it offered arguments for filling northern quotas with poor whites and blacks. Loyal southerners would have the opportunity to escape the Confederacy, a "bounty of $725 would deplete the rebel army," and blacks might gain freedom. In consequence, northern armies would be filled and the southern military and economic system weakened.

4. Stearns justified recruiting in the South, especially Tennessee, as a means of lifting "the poorer classes white and black from their present destitute condition." Undated handwritten "Extract from report to Secy of War" attached to this letter.

5. Stearns, who had leased two farms near Murfreesboro in March, 1863, seems to have had only limited success in persuading others to follow his example, because of lack of safety and legal protection for northern capitalists and investments during the early postwar months. Boston *Daily Advertiser*, October 25, 1865; Lawrence N. Powell, *New Masters: Northern Planters During the Civil War and Reconstruction* (New Haven, 1980), 28.

From W. W. Bierce

January 4, 1864, Circleville, Ohio; ALS, DLC-JP.

A casual acquaintance, finding himself "out of business very suddenly," inquires about "prices of farming lands near Nashville and also as to the safety of taking a family there."

From Andrew J. Cropsey[1]

Hd. Qr's 129th Ill Vol
Nashville Tenn. Jan'y 6th 1864

Gov. Andrew Johnson

Sir— I was recently sent by Gen Grant, with 200 sharp shooters and two gunboats on a reconnoitering expedition up the Cumberland river.

And some of the officers of the Tenn Union Guards, whom I met and consulted up there were very anxious, that I should state some of the facts thus ascertained to you, thinking that they would be thus more likely to get relief.

And they were so urgent in this that I make this written statement in addition to what I told you verbaly— Much of the information was obtained from those officers in which they were confirmed by citizens— The country along the river is pretty much cleared of guerillas except Jackson County, But this County or rather that part of it on the South side of the river, is the head quarters of Hamilton Hughes,[2] Ferguson and other guerilla leaders, who by their robberies and murders, which are large and numerous, keep that region in perfect terror, and occasionaly make robbing raids into distant parts of the Country especialy up into Kentucky.

They can muster in all some two hundred and fifty *fighting* men, and twice that number for robbing excursions.

Capt. Abram E. Garret,[3] who went with us part of the time, seemed to have a complete knowledge of the country, and to have had considerable experience in guerilla warfare— He is now raising a battalion for especial service in that region, and is now very anxious for permission or an order to go into that region with the troops he has already enlisted for his battalion, something over two hundred,— he would problably succeed, but to insure success, should have some temporary assistance, which I was told there could be had from, the Kentucky troops at Columbia Burkesville and Creelsburg, as these fellows are now getting a large proportion of their plunder from K.Y.

By such a movement that entire region could be soon cleared, the navigation of the Cumberland made safe, hundreds of deserters from the rebel army protected from their conscription, in fact that entire region connected to the Union Cause— To make the work complete of course Maj. Garret or some other command would have to be stationed there for some time— He is now in the First Tenn Union Guards and for the present stationed at Carthage— If you could have time to inaugerate some movement in that region I think it would be of immense service to the Union Cause there—

Yours Respectfully A. J. Cropsey
Lt. Col. 129th Ill. Vol.

ALS, DLC-JP.

1. Andrew J. Cropsey (*c*1824-1896), New York-born Illinois farmer, was mustered in September, 1862, as major, field and staff, 129th Ill. Inf., rose to lieutenant colonel, and resigned in February, 1864, because of "Tubercular Deposition of the Superior Lobe of the right lung." After the war he lived in Nebraska (1868), Texas (1876), and finally Utah (*c*1890). 1860 Census, Ill., Livingston, Indian Grove Township, 226; Pension file, RG15, NA.

2. John M. Hughs (b. *c*1833), a Livingston hotelkeeper was sent by General Bragg with a small force to Middle Tennessee during the summer of 1863 to pick up stragglers and conscripts. Cut off behind Federal lines until the spring of 1864, he "created a considerable disturbance" before rejoining the Confederate army in Dalton, Georgia. 1860 Census, Tenn., Overton, Livingston, 1; *Tennesseans in the Civil War*, I, 227-28; for Oliver P. Hamilton and Champ Ferguson, see *Johnson Papers*, V, 259*n*.

3. Abraham E. Garrett (1830-1907), Livingston lawyer and farmer who saw service in Kentucky units before enlisting in December, 1863, was major, 1st Tenn. Mtd. Inf., and promoted lieutenant colonel the following March. After the war he served as a delegate to the state constitutional convention (1865), as a member of the Tennessee house (1865-66), and as a Democrat in Congress (1871-73), returning subsequently to his law practice in Carthage where he had moved before 1871. McBride and Robison, *Biographical Directory*, II, 327; Knoxville *Whig and Rebel Ventilator*, April 26, 1865.

From J. B. Meriwether

January 6, 1864, Jeffersonville, Ind.; ALS, DLC-JP.

A sympathetic provost marshal, wishing to aid Tennessee refugees whose "conditions are truly forlorn and pitiable," inquires about regulations governing their return home.

From Alvan C. Gillem[1]

Head-Quarters Camp Nelson,
Jessamine Co. Ky. January 7 1864.

Governor.

On my arrival at this camp I found the

8th	Tenn Cav	Strickland[2]	230	men
9	Tenn Cav	Col Parsons[3]	450	
10	" "	Col Patton[4]	437	
12	" "	Col Miller[5]	700	
16	" "	Col Elliot[6]	60	
17	" "	Col Doughty[7]	120	
1st	Artillery	*Col* Crawford[8]	389	
	Making a total in this camp		2386	

These men have come through from East Tennessee most of them in the most miserable condition—the distance to Knoxville from this place is one hundred and ninety miles—to take up these Regiments in order.

The 8th is Stricklands Regiment and was organized or at least mustered in at Lexington & this place. Strickland has never been with it but about 4 weeks. for absence without leave General Burnside dismissed him from the service subject to the approval of the Sec. of war. Strickland I understand has succeeded in having the order countermanded & is now safe back in his old quarters at *Cincinnatti*. the Regiment is here under Major Sawyers[9] a brave energetic (I speak from General report) Tennessean —the Lieut. Colonel was dismissed for cowardice in the recent operations in East Tenn. his name was Capps.[10] if this Regiment was at Nashville, you might prevent Strickland being mustered into service. some *one* or *two* of the officers of the Regiment have been mustered into the U. S. service & the Regiment is armed with Burnside Carbines, I think it would be a good idea to take this Regt to Nashville & thus get it beyond the control of Strickland and his friends, they have had nine companies & a half mustered into service but has but 230 at this place. Some have been Captured some have deserted as it is claimed by Major Sawyers on account of Stricklands conduct in *selling* the offices to men unknown to the Regt.

Parsons Regt the ninth (9th) had 389 men when I arrived here but to-day has 450 and they continue to arrive many having broken down on the road as they came on foot & the road was very bad. they have in that Regiment ten companies mustered in & number above 800. have no arms came here with such old arms as could be picked up. Parson's & his men are anxious to go [to] Nashville, would go any where beyond the limits of Kentucky[.] Parsons men are a good class of soldiers[.]

Col Miller of the 12th has just 700 present[.] six companies have been mustered in but not their Officers except the Colonel & Lieut Col. they

have drawn horses & saddles but no arms. they did have a few old captured arms but I saw all these piled up in their camp when I arrived here. these men claim that their agreement with Genl. Burnside was that they were to be placed under your orders. they now protest against being sent back to Knoxville half armed & disorganized. they are now under orders to go with General Fry[11] to Halls Gap six miles beyond Stanford. they came here I believe under a Colonel Casement[12] from Ohio who was detached to command the Tennessee troops[.] Casements own Regt. the 103 Ohio numbers I believe 175[.] he was authorized to *consolidate* & *organize* the Tennessee Regts.
The 10th Pattons, has not a single company full or mustered has ten *parts* of companies—numbering present 449. he desires to go to Nashville to organize & collect his men, & declares his men will never come to this place[.] I do not entertain a high opinion of his abilities but he has a good man with him & I believe will make a Regt. his Lieut Cols name is Brown[13] a young man I think of good ability.
Doughty has 120 men & I believe intends to consolidate with Miller. that would make Millers strength present 820. Doughty has given up all idea of raising a Regt.
An old Gentleman named Elliot has here sixty men[.] he is absent but will be here to-morrow[.] I will pursuade him to combine with some other Regt, he has also given up all hope of raising a Regiment.
Now for *Col. Clay Crawford.* he has here 390 men. this does not include his own company which by the [way] is all he was ever authorized to raise— he has his men are in better shape than any other at this place. by some means or another he manages to get more comforts for his men than any of the other officers and strange to say he is more anxious than anybody to go Nashville. that is he is louder in the expression of his desires more loudly than the others. but the plain truth is that *all* the officers & men are more than anxious to get into Tennessee anywhere. Nor do I blame them[.] they have tested Kentucky hospitality to their hearts content. the prejudice against them is too plain to be disguised[.] I was greeted by the senior officer here with pleasure as it would rid him of the trouble of settling their difficulties.

Governor the men now here certainly deserve some consideration. They are quiet, obedient & I have heard no complaints from them though they are here in Dog tents.[14] they were sent here on foot, half naked—armed with such old arms as had been thrown away by our own troops or captured from the enemy, many of them gave out on the road & were left on the route and now they arrive daily. I saw some of these brave fellows come in to-day their legs bound up in rags shoes tied together with strings a fragment of blanket around them—armed with an old gun useless save as an *ornament*, & the thermometer 7 degrees below zero. this is no fancy sketch, but is a daily occurrence[.] To turn such men into Dog tents & make them cut & pack their own wood is not just, to call it by gentlest name. I have not seen a more patient uncomplaining set of men. they look to you as their natural protector, & believe that it requires but a word from you to take them to any designated point.

I have been unable to see any reason Military or Political for the establishment of this tremendious Depôt[.] Why should several hundred wagons be employed in transporting supplies to the mouth of Big south Fork, when the same supplies can be delivered their by *Steamers*, nor am I aided in solving the difficulty by the fact that the greater part of the road is through, a country destitute of Forage & over the worst road in the world, you know its nature—

I have endeavored to give you a correct account of things at this point[.] if I have made this letter too long it was not intentional, for to write is extremely painful from the inflamation of my eyes.

I can not see any difficulty in the way of any of the troops going to Nashville except Millers Regt. they have their horses & saddles, but the ordnance officer declines issuing any arms to them until they are mustered. There are no arms here for them.

I am Governor Yours sincerely
Alvan C Gillem

Gov. Johnson Nashville.

ALS, T-Mil. Gov's Papers, 1862-65, Corres. to Andrew Johnson.

1. Appointed adjutant general in June, 1863, Gillem was currently carrying out Johnson's decision made late in December to reorganize the several Tennessee units. The governor had ordered unorganized recruits to Camp Nelson. Samuel W. Scott and Samuel P. Angel, *History of the Thirteenth Tennessee Volunteer Cavalry* (Philadelphia, 1903), 129.

2. Jesse H. Strickland, whose 8th Cav., formerly 5th East Tenn. Cav., was merged with Patton's 10th.

3. Joseph H. Parsons' 9th Cav., organized in the summer of 1863 and assigned to DeCourcy's brigade, was by October, 1863, unattached and largely unarmed; it was later attached to Miller's Brigade of Gillem's Division. *Tennesseans in the Civil War*, I, 343.

4. Samuel K. Patton, whose regiment was a consolidation of the 10th East Tenn. and 8th Tenn. Cav.

5. John K. Miller, colonel of the 13th Cav., originally the 12th.

6. John Elliott (b. *c*1809), whose enlistment would date from February, 1864, was unable to assemble a regiment; becoming a major, field and staff, 10th Cav., he was "cashiered Oct 4 64," apparently for desertion. *Tenn. Adj. Gen. Report* (1866), 554; CSR, RG94, NA.

7. James A. Doughty (*c*1823-*c*1896), Knox County native who was a farmer and merchant in Blount and Anderson before enlisting in August, 1861, as captain, Co. K, 1st Tenn. Inf., resigned in December, 1862, to raise, under Johnson's authorization, the 17th Cav., which, consolidating at this time with the 12th, became the 13th Cav. under Col. John Miller. Although afterwards commissioned to raise some artillery batteries, Doughty failed to attain another command. Elected as a Radical to the Tennessee house (1865-69), he practiced law in Clinton until 1873 and at Sneedville until 1883 when he moved to Knoxville. *Goodspeed's Knox*, 948; Scott and Angel, *13th Tenn. Cav.*, 124; Knoxville city directories (1891-97), *passim*.

8. R. Clay Crawford.

9. John M. Sawyers (*c*1825-*fl*1890), an Alabama native and Maynardville "Grocery Keeper" before the war, was commissioned in April, 1863, as major, 8th Tenn. Cav. After the war, he returned to Grainger County to farm. CSR, RG94, NA; 1860 Census, Tenn., Union, Maynardville, 3; (1880) Grainger, 1st Dist., 1; Sistler, *1890 Tenn. Veterans Census*, 278.

10. Thomas J. Capps (b. *c*1825) of Knoxville, a schoolteacher, originally mustered in as a captain, Co. F., 1st Tenn. Cav., resigned in December, 1862, and reenlisted as lieutenant colonel of Strickland's 5th East Tenn. Cav. In October he was on "detached service" until resigning in December, 1863, on disability. Subsequently he moved to San Diego, California. CSR, RG94, NA; Sistler, *1850 Tenn. Census*, I, 273; Luttrell, *1850 Census, Knox County*, 84; Carter, *First Tenn. Cav.*, 298.

11. Speed S. Fry (1817-1892), Kentucky native, lawyer, and Mexican War veteran, was judge of Boyle County (1857-61), becoming colonel, 4th Ky. Inf., USA, in 1861. Promoted brigadier general of volunteers the following year, he served without distinction in the Shiloh and Murfreesboro campaigns before commanding Camp Nelson, Kentucky. Mustered out in 1865, he was later supervisor of internal revenue for Kentucky. Warner, *Generals in Blue*, 163-64.

12. John Casement (*c*1829-1909), New York-born railroad contractor, was major of the 7th Ohio (1861-62), colonel of the 103rd Inf., and eventually brevet brigadier. Returning to Painesville, Ohio, he served in the state senate (1872-73) and continued to build railroads, including the laying of a portion of Union Pacific track. New York *Times*, December 14, 1909; Heitman, *Register*, I, 289; Harry J. Brown and Frederick D. Williams, eds., *The Diary of James A. Garfield* (3 vols., Ann Arbor, 1967-73), II, 343*n*.

13. Andrew J. Brown (1834-1901), Washington County lawyer and former Whig, was Jonesboro mayor when mustered into service. Lieutenant colonel of the 8th Cav., he moved his practice to Greene County after the war, serving as Republican state senator (1881-83) and as judge of the first circuit court (1886-94). McBride and Robison, *Biographical Directory*, II, 98.

14. Introduced for field use early in the war, the "dog" or pup tent, was a one-man shelter, four feet wide and six feet long, constructed of a serviceable weight cotton. Shannon, *Organization of the Union Army*, I, 200.

From Robert L. Stanford

Head Quarters Sup't Hospitals
Knoxville Tenn. Jan. 7th, 1864[1]

Governor:

Allow me to present for your concideration a few things, that to my mind are no small matters.

1st.— Much business could be done resulting in great good to the government as well as to individuals, if we had a Federal Court established here.

2nd.—I understand a judge, attorney, and martial have already been appointed, and the two latter ready to commence business in their offices at any time; but no judge is here.[2]

3rd.—If a clerk and commissioner were appointed and sworn—actions could be commenced; but no judge is here.

4th E. Tennessee has been occupied for more than four months; but no judge is here.

4.— If a clerk and Commissioner were appointed, actions could be brought, against persons for political offences.— Actions could be commensed for confiscation of property and for violations of the Regulations of the Treasury Department,—against Southern rebels by Northern creditors.

5. Unless a court is soon established, much of rebel property will be squandered by individuals, rebels, in the neighbourhood of its

abandonment, and lost to the government and Union citizens.

6. Multiplied thousands of dollars would go into the U. S. Treasury in a few brief months resulting from the establishment of a Federal Court at this place, but no judge is here. The country is full of contraband property; but no court to adjudicate any thing. Treasury Regulations are violated every day, Stores are closed by order of the custom officers, Israelites caugh smugling and their goods seized Stored away and locked up. The streets are often filled with wagons loaded with abandoned rebel property brought in from the country, this is stored away and locked up, and in fact, if the half of abandoned property was brought in to this city from this and the ajoining Counties the buildings of the place would not hold it; but there is no court to adjudicate any thing, and the authorities being averse to turning the inhabitants out of doors to make place for abandoned property, the result is that it still remains in the country[.]

In view of the facts which I have stated and many other things which I might state if I had space, can you not aid in having a Federal Court speedily established.

Governor permit me to suggest that your presence here for a few weeks would in the opinion of your friends here, (and they embrace nearly evry body,) would be most salutary. Do not concider me as complaining of military authority here, when I say altogether too much lenity has been extended to vile rebels whose conduct has been such, that they have forfieted their right to live, Yet, in hundreds of instances the *hellians* have been able to procure protection for their persons and property, whilst, the loyal men have been striped of evry thing they possess in this lower world, except, the suit of clothes upon their persons. And to day all the families of uper E. Tenn. are being robed of evry thing movable, which they possess in the world, while, rebels here are allowed to riot in the enjoyment of their fortunes. I don't complain of military authority but of its not being exercised with more rigor upon rebels, whilst, more protection should be thrown around loyal families[.]

Evry body express desire to see you here except rebels, and *one* or *two* others,[3] & I judge you could guess who they are.

I am of the opinion that your presence here would frighten the black and filthy souls out of some leading rebels here, and in the country around this city, and cause pale consternation to depict itself upon all of them.

I had a talk with Col. John Fleming a few nights ago, and he expressed his desires for the establishment of a Federal Court in the very strongest terms, and as you know he sees the necesity as well as the advantages of a court at a single glance. Col. John Fleming is one of the best men in the world, and knows not the end to his desire to punish rebels by Military authority as well as legally.— He is as you know, one of your warmest friends, and expressed to me his warm and earnest desire to see you here, in fact, his attachment to you in my opinion can never be diverted[.][4]

Governor; allow me in conclusion, to hope that you will use your influence to secure the early establishment of a Federal court here, and also, to express my earnest gratitude to you for past favours as well as to express my sincere conviction, that the greatest people of the greatest nation, are anxiously waiting an opportunity to bestow on you, the highest honors within their power to confer. Will you please answer and give your opinion as to when a court will be established, and state when you will be here[.]

I have the honor to be
Your obt servt
R L Stanford Surgeon
Supt Hospitals E Tenn.

Brig. Genl. A. Johnson
Military Governor of Tennessee

ALS, DLC-JP.

1. It was nearly a month before Stanford dispatched this letter, adding: "I intended to send this by samuel Morrow but did not get to see him when he started[.] Things have changed since this was written[.] our army then was at Mossy Creek & Dandrige now at Knoxville & Louden. Nashville. Feb. 4th 1864"

2. Although Connally F. Trigg had been appointed judge not only for East Tennessee but also for the other two grand divisions of the state, he had not yet returned from the north where he had been since 1862. John M. Fleming and Blackston McDannel, both of them on the ground, had been commissioned district attorney and marshal, respectively, for East Tennessee. Temple, *Notable Men*, 210; Letter from Blackston McDannel, December 5, 1863; *U. S. Official Register* (1863), 268-69.

3. It may be that Stanford was reflecting on old-line unionists, like John Baxter and T. A. R. Nelson, who had acquiesced in Confederate rule and were now critical of Lincoln's policies, particularly emancipation. Temple, *Notable Men*, 70-72, 173-77.

4. Although Fleming joined the conservative unionists in 1864, supporting McClellan and Pendleton over Lincoln and Johnson, his relationship with the latter seemed unaffected, inasmuch as President Johnson reappointed him Federal district attorney. *Ibid.*, 120; Mary U. Rothrock, ed., *The French Broad-Holston Country: A History of Knox County, Tennessee* (Knoxville, 1946), 417.

To Lovell H. Rousseau[1]

Nashville, January 7" 1864.

Maj Gen Rousseau
Condg at Nashvill
Dear Sir

There are a number of East Tennesseans here, in the Service of the United States, whose Families are in a state of destitution, all their subsistence having been taken by one or the other of the Armies passing through the county[.] These men are anxious, many of them, to be furloughed, for a short time for the purpose of visiting their Families and extending to them whatever relief they can, The Regiments, many of them are not yet complete, and might be furloughed by me, but as they are, in the service of the United States and under your command, I prefer it being done by you, or by your permission[.] I am satisfied that if something of this kind is not done, that a large number will desert and go to East Tennessee, at all hazards. If furloughed, I have no doubt, of their complying with its terms in good faith. I hope that steps will be taken for the Cavalry from East Tennessee to return.[2]

I am most Resp
Andrew Johnson

L. DLC-JP.

1. For General Rousseau, see *Johnson Papers*, IV, 560*n*.

2. The following day Rousseau's adjutant, B. H. Polk, returned this letter endorsed: "The General Comdg directs me to say that Gen Johnson will take such action in these cases as he deems best, if the troops are not regularly organized and mustered into the service—" It has not been possible to determine what action, if any, the governor took.

From Enoch T. Carson

Office U. S. Depository
Cincinnati Jany 8th 1864.

Dear Sir

On the 28th of September you Telegraphed me to sell $2000, gold which you had left on Special deposit with me, I was absent at the time in the City of New York. Mr Johnston my first clerk, followed your instructions, sold the gold at and realised 40 per cent premium, the highest rate that could be obtained at that time, he wrote you on the 30th of Sept[1] what he had done also advising you that upon counting the gold which was in a *sealed package* it was found to contain only $1990, $10 *short*, of this we have never had a word from you since in regard to it. My object in writing now is to ask you what disposition you wish me to make of the proceeds, it has been lying in my hands for three months yielding you nothing— If you are not going to use the money soon I would suggest that you deposit it with me on account of "Temporary Loan" [2] to the United States, by this means you will be getting 5 percent interest, and you can withdraw it at any time when you may want to use it. I enclose printed circular of conditions upon which I receive deposits on account of this Loan, or you can deposit with me to credit of Jay Cooke Co[3] who are authorized to deposit with me on account of 5 per ¢ interest bearing Legal Tender Notes and in due time you will receive these notes[.]

Account

Amount of Gold	$1.990
Gold Premium 40 per ¢	796
Total Amount in my hands to your credit	$2.786

If you wish to deposit on account of Temporary Loan I can only receive in even hundred dollars, so it would be either $2700 or $2800.

I would be glad to hear from you at your earliest convenience[.]

Truly Yours
E. T. Carson
(U S. Depositary)

Gov Andrew Johnson
Nashville. Tennessee

ALS, DLC-JP.

1. See Letter from J. Wilson Johnston, September 30, 1863.

2. By the act of February 25, 1862, which established the five-twenties (6% bonds redeemable after five years and payable at twenty), Congress also authorized the Federal depositaries to accept private and corporate deposits for thirty days or longer at 5% interest. These short-term certificates proved to be relatively popular and the ceiling on such deposits was advanced from $25,000,000 to $150,000,000 by war's end. Bolles, *Financial History*, 87-91.

3. Jay Cooke & Co., formed in 1861, was until 1873 one of the foremost banking institutions in the country. During the war Cooke acted as principal "fiscal agent" of the treasury. *DAB*, IV, 383-84; see also Ellis P. Oberholtzer, *Jay Cooke: Financier of the Civil War* (2 vols., New York, 1968 [1907]).

To James B. Bingham

Nashville, Jan. 8, 1864.

To James Bingham, Esq., Memphis.

Dear Sir—Enclosed you will find forms and commissions to persons to hold elections in such counties as are without county, court and loyal officers to hold the same. You will see some of our friends in the counties of Western Tennessee, and select suitable persons to hold these elections.[1] Send lists of them to me that I may know whom to look to for returns of the elections.[2]

I am, respectfully,
Andrew Johnson, Military Governor.

Chicago *Tribune*, February 12, 1864.

1. This sweeping authority would seem to establish clearly Bingham's role as Johnson's political lieutenant in West Tennessee.

2. For names of those whom Bingham selected, see Letters from James B. Bingham, February 7, 11, 16, 1864.

Speech on Slavery and State Suicide[1]

January 8, 1864

Ladies and gentlemen—I appear before you only to make an apology. I claim to be a practical worker, and constant attention to duty, combined with domestic troubles,[2] have prevented me from making such preparation as would enable me to do justice to you or to myself. We have met to celebrate the battle of New Orleans, an anniversary which ought to be commemorated by every one who reveres that great man who achieved that great victory. When we think of that distinguished man, every lover of freedom must feel his heart beat with pride and veneration. I revere him. Thank God, I can say that I respect any man, wherever born, who contributed to the establishment and perpetuation of our Government. My admiration of great and good men is not confined to particular localities or people; all who love freedom, and contribute to the support and perpetuation of democratic institutions, I revere. It is not my *forte*, if I have one, to pronounce eulogies on great men, and if I had tried to prepare myself for this occasion, you would be disappointed. I did not come before you to make a round and bounding speech which tickles the ear; I cannot do it, and will not try it. When memory goes back to the war of 1812, and I think of the sufferings of those brave and devoted patriots, fighting for our second independence; when I think of that great and good man, Andrew Jackson—God bless him and his name!—(cheers)—who led his men on to victory, who shared their toils and slept on the tented fields, who suspended the writ of *habeas corpus* and compelled the citizens to fall in the ranks and fight for their country; he who urged his men on to the stern encounter, the goddess of liberty hovering over him, as the battle waxed strong and fearful, until victory perched on the stars and stripes, when I think of him, and that he sleeps close by, almost within the sound of my voice, I think that were it possible to convey intelligence to the dead of what is now transpiring, he would turn over in his coffin, arise from his grave, extend his long bony finger, and exclaim—"By the Eternal God, this Union must and *shall* be preserved?" (Tremendous applause). Yes, he would be with us to-night, to aid us in the great work we are about. One thought just now occurs to me; it has always been my teaching, from early years, that the Government was made for the people, and not the people for the Government. The people made the Government, and it must remain under the control of the people. The Government being under the people, and the institutions under the Government, any institution antagonistic to the Government must necessarily give way for the preservation of the Government. Institutions must not rise above the Government. Institutions are tolerated, for a time; they are not fixed; they are subject to change, or they die out. Not so the Constitutionl Government, which is a fixed, a lasting institution of the people. We once had a United States Bank, and we had a Jackson who hated aristocracy in any shape, whether in slaves or money. He crushed it. All institutions must be subordinate to the Government of the United States. Before the rebellion, we could discuss all institutions, all subjects, all measures, except slavery. On that subject no one dared speak or write, or print, except on the side of the slave aristocracy. Now, thank God, the time has come when the press is unmuzzled, when the press can discuss this *and all other subjects*. The time has come when this institution is dead—when the chains are broken and the captive set free. (Applause). The institution is dead (applause), and slaves are not worth a quarter of a dollar a dozen. (Laughter). Being dead, let us, in a becoming manner, prepare for the funeral obsequies. Now is the time to dispose of this great question. It is a great question, and one which must be settled upon the great principle of human freedom; not by Abolitionists in the North, nor by Secessionists in the South, but by that great law of self-preservation which governs all men alike. Slavery is the cancer upon the body politic, which must be rooted out before perfect health can be restored. The great law I refer to is now at work, and negroes and all things else which may be in the way, to impede its course, must get out. Don't go to inventing, but find out the great principles of that law, and conform your actions thereto. I will go back to the subject of Institutions: I want no better League than the Constitution of the United States, and laws made in pursuance thereof. The Constitution, that palladium of civil and religious liberty, is my League; it is small enough for me, and large enough for all—*for the whole world*. No Institution must rise above it.[3] This is the people's Constitution—The people's Government. The voice of the people is the voice of God, and hence the purity, the beauty, the harmony of our Government. Go back to the articles of Confederation, which were designed to secure a *perpetual* union of the States; the Constitution was formed to secure a more *perfect* union. In it provision is made for its own amendment, for the admission of new States, for everything, but secession. Nowhere is there found provision for letting a State out. It provides means to repel invasion and suppress insurrection; it also guarantees to every State in the Union a republican form of government, and to protect them from domestic violence. This Government of ours was intended to be indestructible, to be perpetual. Like the Christian religion, the Constitution is comprehensive enough for the whole world. Away with the idea of State suicide! Away with the doctrine of secession, its twin brother! We are parts of a great whole, working at present somewhat inharmoniously, but as soon as the Government puts down the rebellion, and the machinery is again put in running order, leaving out whatever may have before prevented its running smoothly, the State will stand firm. Some of her institutions may be rubbed out, but the State stands. She is and will continue to be, a State, whether with or without slavery, and the Government will go on. I admit no such thing as reconstruction; the idea is as bad as secession. your legislature ran away; does that destroy the State? The Governor ran away; does that destroy the State? They took with them the bank funds and the school fund; but the State is here yet. The ordinary civil functions of the State have been for a time necessarily suspended,[4] but the United States is bound to secure to us a representative form of government. Does that look like secession—like reconstruction? The President posesses the necessary power, and *must* exercise it. Officers may be appointed to administer the law; any thing may be done, to secure a representative form of government. The rebellion being put down, the Legislature might be convened to-morrow. To admit that a State can be out of the Union, is virtually admitting the principle of secession. Nor can a State be put back to a territorial condition. It is contrary to the genius of our Government. The State cannot destroy herself, nor can the United States Government destroy a State. When you destroy a State you destroy the union of the States. Hold fast to your liberties under the Constitution. Destroy the rebellion, and let slavery go with it. (Cheers). Were it possible to destroy a State, I would almost be willing to see South Carolina destroyed; but I will not depart from my theory, from the truth, and will not have even *her* destroyed. The Union and the Constitution must be preserved intact. I have owned slaves—slaves that I bought with my own money—money earned by myself, a quarter of a dollar at a time. They were confiscated and sold; yet two of them ran away from the Rebel dominions and came here to me. I hired them—made a bargain with them for their labor, and thus recognized their freedom. And I find they do better than when they were slaves. Now if any of you are slave owners, I advise you to go and do likewise, while you have the chance. Hire your negroes to work for you, and you will find they will do better labor for you than when they were slaves. By this means you will do your part in this great transition to teach them self-reliance. The edict has gone forth, and all that remains to be done is to change the relation of master and slave. The day is not far distant when this nation will be the great centre of civilization, of the arts and sciences, and of true religion. Time was when the tide of emigration ran westward; the time will soon be when it will run southward. Let us go on with our mighty work. To talk about breaking up a Government like this for slavery! 'Tis madness. Let it go on with its great mission. I trust the time will soon come when the sword will be sheathed and peace reign throughout the land—when the dove will appear, and prosperity bless the people.[5] Officers and men, thrice welcome. You have come to aid us in establishing and perpetuating free government. Go forward, I say, until the flag of our country is planted in every State, at every cross-road, and on every court house in the country, (cheers) though the stars and stripe may be bathed in a nation's blood. The Governor here thanked the ladies for their attendance, and complimented them on the good they had accomplished in behalf of the Union. He alluded to the influence brought to bear in behalf of the rebellion by the ladies of Tennessee, and drawing a sad picture of the mangled bodies of sons, husbands and brothers, asked who caused this desolation, this woe, and exclaimed, "Oh! sister! oh! mother! what have you done!" He next alluded to the patriotism of the Greek mother, and called upon the ladies present to persevere. "Women control governments," he said; "they are the power behind the throne." Again thanking them, the Governor retired amid loud cheers.

Nashville *Dispatch*, January 10, 1864; Nashville *Union*, January 12, 1864.

1. The recently organized Union League of Nashville used the anniversary of New Orleans as the occasion for "a large rally of soldiers and others." Despite the "extremely cold" night, an enthusiastic crowd assembled in the Hall of Representatives, where prayer and patriotic airs, a statement of League goals, and a preliminary speech preceded the governor's appearance. Nashville *Dispatch*, January 9; Nashville *Union*, January 10, 1864.

2. Possibly his wife's precarious health or son Robert's current spell of heavy drinking.

3. These reflections upon the League would seem to place Johnson at some odds with the organizers of the rally.

4. This "state of suspended animation" theory, a description of the southern relationship to the Union, foreshadows Johnson's presidential course.

5. Here a reporter's interpolation: "the Governor alluded to scenes of his early years, in East Tennessee, (where he took the partner of his bosom, the mother of his children,) in words so full of pathos and sublime feeling, that we will make no attempt at reporting them. He alluded to the beauty of the country, the salubrious climate, the fertile soil, the magnificent mountains, the pellucid streams, the patriotism of the people, their long and severe sufferings, and said he hoped to see the stars and stripes floating upon the highest mountain peak, indicating the country from whence liberty took its last flight—they were the last to yield. 'They dared to be freemen!' said the Governor; 'they were born free and will die freemen.' "

From Alexander W. Moss and Henry C. Sinclair[1]

[Franklin] January 9, 1864

To his Excellency Andrew Johnson
Governor of the State of Tennessee
Sir

Upon testimony herewith submited and the current rumor of the country the undersigned H. C. Sinclair and A. W. Moss composing the firm of Sinclair & Moss would respectfully represent to your Excellency that on the 4th day of June A. D. 1863 a body of men composed of from three to five hundred in number banded together as rebel soldiers commanded by Forrest, Starnes &c entered the town of Franklin Tennessee and robbed the undersigned of Eight thousand dollars worth of Goods, Wares, Merchandise, etc. That is to say They robbed Sinclair & Moss of Five thousand dollars worth and H. C. Sinclair (upon his statement) of Three thousand dollars worth and furthermore From the caracter of the goods thus taken and the wanton manner in which the foul deed was perpetrated together with the malishious remarks that were made by officers and privates we are forced to the conclusion that the leading object of the Banditi was to injure and plunder union citizens whenever found[.]

The goods taken were composed principly of silk Dress goods, Boys & Childrens Readymade Clothing, Calicos, Delanos, Fingis[2] and a general assortment of Dress Trimmings, Muslins Linins, Etc that were unfit for soldiering altogether[.] They took a lot of Readymade Clothing that had been again and again picked over for goods suitable for Army purposes which doubtless many of the plunderers knew as many of them were well acquainted with us and the caracter of the goods we had. Our glass doors and shoe case and lites in the framework of the Post office were broken up and our Desk wantonly punched and split with their guns[.]

They plundered the stores of the most prominant union men and did not plunder those belonging to men less odious on account of their loyalty to Government of the united states[.] They were in town long enough to acertain the political Status of every Merchant then doing business here if they had been strangers but as many of them were residents of the county they doubtless knew without inquiry[.] Thus the avowed enemies of the Government of the United States have robbed us of our own heard earnings and just rights and malishously distryed them or appropriated them to the use of their Relatives Friends and Rebel sympathisers because we were *its Friends*[.]

Furthermore your petitioners would represent to your Excellency That but for the existing rebellion in which these plunderers were engaged against the Government of the united States and the Government of the state of Tennessee as an integral part therof That we could collect remuneration of the depredators themselves by virture of the Laws of the state of Tennessee and moreover By the Laws of the state of Tennessee your petitioners could convict several of the friends and sympathisers of this Rabble Bandit as Particeps criminis in said plundering as they were the recipients of our goods known to be thus obtained in defiance of the Laws of the state of Tennessee.

But we are estopped by the extraordinary troubles upon the country superinduced by the Rebellion against the Government of the united states and the thusfar successful defiance of the Laws of the State of Tennessee in which these plunderers were engaged and by which they are being shielded from the penalties due Burglers & Thieves under the Laws of the state of Tennessee[.]

Your petitioners are Bonafide citizens of the united states and have demeaned ourselves as such for which we have been maltreated[.] We think we come fully within the purview of your Excellencies Proclamation of May the 9th 1862[.][3] We therfore earnestly petition your Excellency to enforce said proclamation in our behalf to the end that such an amount be collected as your Excellency may think that we are intitled to from our own Statements, and Statements by others herewith submitted and cause the same to be paid to us that we may pay the Same to our creditors who had intrusted the goods to our hands for which we are still bound morally and legally and would have been paid long ago but for the losses brought upon us by the Rebellion For which your Excellencies consideration and kindness will ever be acknowledged.

State of Tennessee }
Williamson County } Personally appeared before me Alexr. Witherspoon[4]
Provost Marshall of Franklin Tennessee A W Moss who afirms and H C Sinclair who makes oath that the Statements made in the foregoing petition are true to the best of their knowledge & belief.

A W Moss
H C. Sinclair

Pet, DLC-JP.

1. This is the second complaint of these merchants, the first lodged six months earlier. See Letter from Franklin Businessmen, July 14, 1863.

2. A corruption of delaine, a lightweight dress wool, and fingram, a course serge. *Webster's Third International*; Stephen S. Marks, ed., *Fairchild's Dictionary of Textiles* (New York, 1959), 221.

3. Loyal citizens who had suffered at the hands of guerrillas were to be compensated from "the property of such rebels in the vicinity as have sympathized with . . . the parties committing such depredations." See Proclamation Concerning Guerrilla Raids, May 9, 1862, *Johnson Papers*, V, 374-75.

4. Alexander Witherspoon (*c*1837-1900) of Detroit joined the 14th Mich. as sergeant, Co. H in October, 1861, rising to 1st lieutenant in July, 1863. Wounded near Atlanta a year later in September and discharged for disability the following May, he returned to Detroit where he served in the customs house (*c*1873-85). CSR, RG94, NA; Pension file, RG15, NA; *U. S. Official Register* (1873-85), *passim*.

From George H. Thomas

Head Qrs. Dept. Cumberland
Chattanooga Tenn. Jany. 9, 1864

Gov. Andrew Johnson
Nashville

I believe you can reestablish civil authority throughout Tennessee and it is my earnest advice that you do so— Confidence will be restored and many people brought under the constitution who are afraid at this time to exhibit their real sentiments. I ordered *Col. Stokes* to Nashville some time since to reorganize his Regiment, and when his Regiment was completely reorganized it was my intention to send it to Sparta to operate against Furguson[1] and other guerrilas.

Please to let me know when the reorganization is completed. If you can do so I would advise a separation between *Stokes* and *Galbraith* making two Regiments.[2] They will be more efficient than they are at present. I understand that *General Rousseau* has ordered *Galbraith* to McMinnville. He had no authority for doing so. The order for him to go to Nashville expressly stating that it was for the purpose of reorganization. Please show *Rousseau* this telegram and say to him that I desire he will countermand his order.

Geo. H. Thomas
Maj. Genl. U.S.V.Comdg.

Tel, DNA-RG393, Tels. Recd., Dept. of the Cumberland, Vol. 64 (1864); RG393, Dept. of the Tenn. (Mid. Tenn.), Lets. Recd. (dated January 10).

1. For the notorious partisan cavalryman, Champ Ferguson, see *Johnson Papers*, V, 259*n*.

2. The Stokes-Galbraith brouhaha was not ended until Galbraith resigned a month and a half later in an effort "if possible to create harmony in the command [and] for the purpose of tranquilizing the affairs of this Regiment." The preceding December Robert Galbraith had complained that the reappointment of William B. Stokes to command had "caused confusion—officers and men publicly announcing that they would not serve under him," whereupon Stokes had offered to divide the regiment, with each then recruiting to reach full strength. An order to that effect was issued, but when Galbraith learned that his companies were still considered part of Stokes's command, he appealed the matter to Thomas and Grant. Robert Galbraith to W. D. Whipple, December 5, 1863; Galbraith's resignation of February 24, 1864, in CSR, RG94, NA.

To William D. Whipple[1]

Nashville Jany. 9th. 1864.

Gen W. D. Whipple

There are a number of Tennesseeans attached to regiments from other states which regiments have reenlisted as veterans. These men do not want to reenlist but wish to be assigned to some Tennessee regiment for the remainder of their enlistment[.] who will make the assignment of these men to Tenn Regts., as prescribed in paragraph 5 Gen Orders 376 War Dept.?[2]

Andrew Johnson
Mil. Gov. Tenn.

Tel, DNA-RG393, Dept. of the Cumberland, Tels. Recd., Vol. 69 (1864).

1. William D. Whipple (1826-1902), New York native and West Point graduate (1851), was chief of staff to Gen. George H. Thomas. After the war he served as assistant adjutant general in several military divisions before promotion to colonel in the adjutant general's department in 1887. Warner, *Generals in Blue*, 555; *NCAB*, IV, 339.

2. On the same date, Whipple telegraphed that these Tennesseans could be "transferred to the 6th or 10th Regts Tennessee by order from these Head Qrs. upon their names, rank, company and regiment being sent here, provided the regiments to which they now belong are serving within this Department and not of *Genl. Shermans* Army." Whipple to Johnson, January 9, 1864, Tels. Recd., Vol. 64, Dept. of the Cumberland RG393, NA.

From Citizens of Third Judicial Circuit

January 11, 1864, Knoxville; LS, DLC-JP.

Seventy-eight East Tennesseans, appealing for the organization of a circuit court "to meet the contempt which is being Shown for law and order," recommend Elijah T. Hall for judge and David K. Young for attorney general.

From James Erwin[1]

Sullivan's Branch Tennessee
January 11-th 1864.

Gov. Johnson—
Sir—

I hope your excellency will not scorn my intentions of addressing you these lines, since the subject of this letter is of vital importance to me and my family, while I am serving my Country in the Army. As a member of the 10th Tenn. Inftry, I deem it not improper to seek of your excellency such information requisite to put me in the right direction to obtain some remuneration for my effects, which the Rebels have taken and destroyed. I hope your excellency will condescend to impart to me the desired information.

The Rebels taken from me the following property to wit:

One brude mare worth	$150.00.
One Yoke oxen worth	75.00.
One Plantation wagon worth,	75.00.
800 Bu. corn $1. Per. Bu.	800.00.
30 Head fattening hogs worth Six dollars each,	180.00.
3 Milk cows—50 dols each,	150.00
3 Hiefers—25 dols. each,	50.00
12 Head Stock hogs worth	20.00
Agregate	$1500.00

Hoping that you will give me an early response I have the honor to be with very great respect your most obedient Servt—

James Erwin—Co. "I"

P. S. I live in Hamilton County 4th district &c—

ALS, DLC-JP.

1. James Erwin (b. *c*1824), enlisting as a wagoner in Co. I, 10th Tenn. Inf., at Nashville in April, 1863, served until June, 1865. CSR, RG94, NA; *Tenn. Adj. Gen. Report* (1866), 182.

From B. R. Peart[1]

Clarksville Tennessee, January 12th/ 864

Gov. Johnson

After my respects to you, pleas allow me to State to you a case in regard to which we wish to get your opinion. The case is simply this.

Mr J. T. Johnson[2] wishes to put an Iron Furnace in Blast. He is at a loss to Know How to procure the necessary labour for that purpose[.] He wishes to have your opinion of the propriety of hireing Contrabands for Such purpose (With or without the Consent of former Owners), his Furnace is near the Line between this County and that of Stewart County, He thinks that a Furnace may be put in Blast if such Labour is allowable, that is the Labour of the Blacks, it is in such an unsettled state, hence the wish to obtain your Opinion on the propriety and Justness of Employing such kind of Labour, if He will be Safe as a Citizen in that Branch of business.

Pleas give this your attention and answer at your Earliest Conveniance.[3]

Oblige your Friend and Humble Survant
B. R. Peart

ALS, DLC-JP.

1. For Peart, Clarksville mason and unionist, see *Johnson Papers*, V, 444*n*.

2. J. T. Johnson (b. *c*1828), blacksmith and wagonmaker, on the eve of the war had real and personal property worth $64,500. 1860 Census, Tenn., Montgomery, Clarksville, 13; *Mitchell's Tenn. Gazetteer* (1860-61), 39.

3. The envelope is endorsed: "Answered January 14 1864"

To Ulysses S. Grant

Nashville Tennessee
January 13th 1864

Major Genl U. S Grant
Comding U S Army Nashville
General

The facts of the case of the boy Anslem are these[.][1] Information was lodged in my Office in 1862, that he had committed an offence in the County of Montgomery, of which death was the penalty by the Laws of this S[t]ate. I gave the information of the Same to the Honorable Wm. K Turner[2] then Judge in the district (requireing him before exersiseing the priveliges of his Office to take the usual oath)[.] He went down to Clarksville organized a court appointed an Attorney General for the State and assigned for the Defendant, upon this trial he was convicted and sentenced to be hung[.] From this Judgement of the court by the advice of his counsel he applied to the next Term of the Supreme Court to be holden at Nashville, the boy was originally arrested by the Military authorities then Stationed in that County and had been held by them up to the time of this trial and after conviction was delivered to them for safe keeping as there was no civil Officers in the County, Some three weeks or more ago I requested the Commandant at Clarksville to forward him to Nashville for safe keeping.[3] In the course of two or three days he was forwarded and sent to the Penetentiary to await his fate on the appeal to the highest court of the State, and has been and is still held there.[4] The court trying him granted him the appeal, according to Law.

I have the honor, to be Respectfully
Andrew Johnson Mil Governor

Copy, DLC-JP.

1. Grant's enquiry about the slave Anselm Brown, accused of poisoning his master's family, may have been prompted by an angry editorial in the Nashville *Press* of December 31, critical of the Federal authorities for permitting the prisoner's enlistment. For Brown, see *Johnson Papers,* V, 287-88, 288*n*, 292.

2. For Turner, Clarksville criminal court judge (1848-62), see *ibid.,* 425*n*.

3. From the correspondence associated with the prisoner's transfer, safekeeping seems to have been but a minor consideration. "If you have no means of taking care of him, or it is troublesome or expensive to do so, if you will forward him to Nashville, he can be taken care of here, without expense to the state, and at the same time secure for himself a hearing before the proper Tribunals[.]" Edward H. East to Arthur A. Smith, December 5, 1863, Lets. Recd., Nashville Post, Dept. of the Tennessee, RG393, NA.

4. Brown sought relief from his confinement "in a small room 7 by 4 feet square" which "Clost confinement an the anxiety of my mind concerning my destiney is beginnig to tell on my constitution—" He also requested that, if a hearing was delayed, he be employed at some labor within the prison. A recruiting officer, writing for Brown, attested to his innocence and asserted that he was now an enlisted man in Co. C, 16th Cld. Rgt. His mother, a "Coloured woman of wealth," writing from Clarksville and "anxious to hear from my Son" and "whether he is kneedy of cloths or Anything of the Kind," spelled the name "Absolam." Brown to Johnson, January 13, 1864; C. B. Morse to Johnson, January 15, 1863 [1864]; Fillis Brown, February 12, 1864, Johnson Papers, LC.

To Horace Maynard, Washington

Nashville Jan 14 1864,

Horace Maynard
Care R J. Meigs[1]

In reference to the recent proclamation[2] before whom is the oath prescribed to be taken[?] Will persons who have been notoriously loyal have to take it in order to vote? The voters in March next should be put to the severest test. I am satisfied that a convention should be called which will put the state at once upon its legs for ever settle the slavery question[.] If it should be thought advisable two (2) Senators could be appointed now who are sound as regards the slavery question & the Union[.] will the Senate admit them[?] Public sentiment is becoming stronger every day for a restoration of the Government[.] I would give some of the fault finders to understand that the real union men will be for Lincoln for President[.] the war must be closed under his administration[.] I desire you to see the President in person & talk with him in regard to these matters[.] Steps should be taken at once in reference to the March Elections[.][3] when I receive your reply I will let you know when I'll be in Washington[.] I desire you to come to Nashville for I will need you.

Andrew Johnson Mil. Govr

Tel, DNA-RG107, Tels. Recd., Sec. of War, Vol. 34 (1864).

1. For Return J. Meigs, former state librarian and currently a war department clerk, see *Johnson Papers,* IV, 78-79*n*.

2. Lincoln's December 8, 1863, amnesty, restoring all rights and property, except slaves, to southerners who subscribed to the oath, a copy of which appeared in the proclamation. Basler, *Works of Lincoln,* VII, 53-56.

3. Johnson was planning his proclamation of January 26, setting elections of county officers for March 5. Maslowski, *Treason Must Be Made Odious,* 87-88.

From Ernest M. Bement

Office of The Nashville Wood Co.
Nashville, Tenn. Jany 15, 1864

Brig: Gen: Andrew Johnson,
Military Governor of Tennessee,

Governor— I have the honor to present you in the name of this company, with a load of Cannel Coal[1] out of a small lot lately received from the mines in Kentucky. Believing that you are well acquainted with the many virtues of this coal, I deem it unnecessary to utter a word in praise of them. That you will enjoy them, however, is the earnest wish of

Your obt: servant Ernest M. Bement Agt.

ALS, DLC-JP.

1. A type of bituminous, dull black in color but fine in texture and highly volatile. It may be inferred that this "gift" from the Nashville Coal Company represented an expression of appreciation for the governor's earlier support when the company was seeking approval to supply the city with coal. Simon, *Grant Papers*, IX, 631.

From John W. Bowen[1]

[Gordonsville, January *ca.*15, 1864]

To Andrew Johnson Military Gov. &c.

Permit me to call your special attention to that large district of country lying east of the Caney Fork river, and west of the Cumberland mountains; and south of the Cumberland river, and north of a line on which are the towns of Mcminnville & Sparta, including the counties of Jackson, Overton, Putnam and parts of Smith, White and Fentress in Tennessee, and Clinton, & Wayne in Kentucky. Much of this region is composed of fetile valeys, highly productive, of corn & other cereals—

It has been held by rebel bands during the rebelion, and is still so held, and has furnished large supplies to the rebel armies. It is believed considerable amounts of these are still there, as well [as] quite a number of horses, mules, &c, many of which have been stolen from the surrounding regions. This region has never been occupied by the national troops. The well known rebel chief Hamilton[2] still holds undisputed possession there, but it is believed with greatly reduced forces and means of defense.

I do not wish, as you know, to appear to dictate, or intermedle, but ask respectfully to sugest that, perhaps the opportune time for an expedition into that region has arrived. If you should so judge & determine, may I be permitted to ask, who so well qualified to lead such an expedition as Gen. Alvan C Gillem? It is his native region, and it could not fail to gratify him to be allowed to redeem his childhood's home, and his aged father & friends from rebel rule, and he well deserves the complement. It is unnecessary for me to say, that this is my own individual sugestion, not made at the instance, or with the knowledge of Gen Gillem. Asking from you only such considerations as my poor sugestion deserves, & knowing that you will take only such action in the premisis as your better judgement may dictate,[3] I am Governor

with much respect your friend & obt Servt
John W Bowen

ALS, DLC-JP.

1. John W. Bowen (1811-1892), native Tennessee minister and farmer, a Clinton College, Tennessee, graduate (1837), and a unionist during the war, was a state senator (1865-66) and later postmaster at Gordonsville (1876). 1860 Census, Tenn., Smith, 15th Dist., 37; McBride and Robison, *Biographical Directory,* II, 80.

2. Oliver P. Hamilton.

3. Col. William B. Stokes's cavalry was sent on an expedition against the Confederate cavalry units in late February. The foray scattered the rebels and Hamilton was captured. *OR,* Ser. 1, XXXII, Pt. I, 155-56, 416, 624.

From Frances G. Austin

January 16, 1864, Washington; ALS, DLC-JP.

A woman physician employed by the U. S. Sanitary Commission thanks Johnson for past favors and warns him of Tennesseans "who would cut your throught if they dare do it and Some of them who preten to think So much of you and get out why than talk in your back." Describing her experiences in Memphis—"one of the wourst Secess hole that I ever saw"—this staunch unionist observes that "the Rebels has a greate deal more privlige there than a Loyal man or woman."

From Nathaniel G. Taylor

Continental Hotel Pha.
Jany 16th 1864

Brigr-Gen. A. Johnson
Mily. Gov. of Tennessee

Dear Sir. Well aware of the warm interest you feel in the welfare of our beloved East Tennessee and her impoverished and suffering loyal population—and aware also of the great influence you possess with the Authorities as well as the people of the Nation—I will not regard it as presuming merely upon courtesy to address you freely upon subjects of special interest to East Tennessee as well as of general interest to the Country.

Seeing the destitution and suffering that the operations of large contending armies—and the depredations of robbers and rebel soldiers have brought to every door and into every house in our section of the State—and the impossibility of relief at the hands of the State, by reason of the absence of organized Civil Government— I came to the North with the view of endeavouring in the first place to secure some action of the Federal Government which would furnish prompt relief to the sufferers—and failing in that to appeal to the Magnanimity of the people & the Legislative assemblies of the North and West for that assistance without which famine and destitution will I fear, bring many of our women and children and old men to a miserable end. I went to Washington—visited the President and laid this matter before him—and talked of the matter with Some Members of Congress— All seemed to Sympathize with our people—and the President promised that every thing the Executive *could* do should be done to succor them. I am sure my, dear sir, your large acquaintance with the public men of the Country your great experience as a Statesman and your powerful influence with the President—with Congress—and with the country—give you a position which will command prompt and efficient action by the Govt. for the salvation of our people from the horross of Destitution which are even now assailing them. If Tennessee could act in the capacity of a State—and with and by the authority of her Legislature—she could procure and apply the needed supplies—but she cannot—we must therefore look elsewhere[.] You, Governor, possess the ear and the confidence of the Government—and I believe that government will listen attentively to your statements and act promptly upon your suggestions. My little experience of the tardiness of congressional action—led me to despair of prompt aid from that body—& I have therefore taken no measures, as yet to get the subject formally before that body. I venture to suggest to you the propriety and necessity of giving your great influence to such measure as your wisdom and experience may suggest—as best adapted to secure the promptest relief to East Tennessee.

My own humble efforts, though comparatively a stranger, are meeting with Some Success, and will I trust result in raising a considerable amount of means. These will be appropriated by the parties donating them, through agents of their own selection.

One of the greatest difficulties to be met is the transportation of relief supplies when obtained—. What can you do Governor, or suggest in the way of obviating these difficulties? Can they find transportation from Nashville—if the agents can get them there? And if so can the Government be induced to bear the expense of transportation?

This brings me to another matter that I wish to talk to you about—I mean the importance of inducing the Government to Construct immediately (I mean as fast as possible) the projected R Road from Camp Nelson to Knoxville. This Road, it seems to me is of more immediate and vital consequence to the Government—as well as to E. Tenn—than any to which public attention could be directed. I verily believe the losses incident to the recent occupation of E. Tennessee by our troops would have already amounted to more than the cost of the road. With that Road E Tenn. is forever safe & can be a convenient base of operations in every direction and on interior lines. Without it we are always insecure—always distant from supplies—always in danger of loosing the great gateways into Kentucky—The public mind here is alive already to the importance of making this Road, and I believe a word from you addressed to the proper quarters would go very far towards its speedy construction—. This subject derives greater importance from the probable fact that the last dying struggle of the rebellion will perhaps be made upon the Soil of E. Tennessee. If this should turn out to be so—who can estimate the value of the Road we are considering to the Nation.

A few words on politics Governor before I close. Having been "born a veteran" Whig, you know I did not like your Democracy, and I fought you on it always—but when old parties were submerged and the elements rose to the Surface and rearranged themselves—under the banners of the Union on one side and treason on the other—You and I were found standing together under the banner of the Nation upholding the flag staff of the Union—and there we shook hands over the struggles of the past. Since then I have been against every one who is against my country, and for every man that is for my country—and I am proud to know that your country & mine—my people and yours—the great masses of glorious East Tennessee—though more fiercely assailed, and more terribly tried than any other Section of the Union, have come forth faithful and true. East Tennessee has suffered every thing sacrificed every thing on the altar of our common Country—she has nothing left but "Poverty and patriotism" and her heroic children, and when asked for her jewels like the mother of the Gracchi, she points proudly to her loyal sons[1]—prominent among whom, at the head of the column stands the Military Governor of Tennessee Andrew Johnson, her adopted son—the next Vice President of the United States—*President elect of this great nation in 1868*. We of E. Tennessee Governor are very poor since the tide of desolation has swept over us—we have nothing but our lands & some of our humble houses left—but thank God, we are proud of our Country even in her desolation and ruin—proud because she has been true to humanity—true to civilization to Christianity and God—true to the Constitution and our Nationality—proud because her sublime record will illuminate and adorn perhaps *the brightest* page in all history. I would rather write my home East Tennessee ruined bleeding famishing fainting with hunger—as she is—but staunch to the last in her unyielding fidelity to the great cause of Nationality and human Liberty—than roll in the wealth and luxury of a Prince and know myself a traitor. So much by way of parenthesis. You will be nominated with President Lincoln as Vice President—a compliment—even had it been *first* on the ticket—East Tennessee, deserves—, a compliment richly merited by her distinguished Son—. I have closely watched the signs of the time and you may rest assured—without some miraculous change) that ticket will triumph—God grant the incumbents a peaceful and a glorious term.

Be kind enough dear, Sir to give me an early response, and a favorable consideration of the subjects I have offered to your notice & excuse the liberty I have taken of so freely addressing you.

I am your friend &c
N. G. Taylor

Address me at the
Continental Hotel Philadelphia

ALS, DLC-JP.

1. Cornelia, the "mother of the Gracchi," Tiberius and Caius Gracchus, when asked by a visitor about her jewels, sent for her sons, saying "These are my jewels." William Rose Benét, *The Reader's Encyclopedia* (New York, 1965), 243.

To Ulysses S. Grant

Nashville, January 16 1864

Maj Gen U S Grant
Comd U S Army
General

I herewith enclose to you papers relating to the case of Jno C Newman[1] & others now in Prison by order of Gen Rousseau. The facts as stated are taken from statement filed by each party before any action was taken. There have been many such suits brought, towards the close of last year and the beginning of this. The judgments of the Justices were disregarded in so many of such cases, by parties who happened to be in possession by contract or otherwise that it became oppressive, upon the owners[.] My Commission, authorizes me to establish Tribunals, and abolish existing Tribunals, and create offices and officers and in the exercise of this power. I thought this a proper case to exercise that power, as manifest injustice was being done, as I have done in several other cases of like nature, only though after a thorough examination of the case by .[2] I desire your interference in behalf of these men[.]

L draft, DLC-JP.

1. Perhaps Joseph C. Newman (1818-1870), Nashville physician and graduate of the University of Pennsylvania, who served in the Mexican War and as surgeon for the Provisional Army of Tennessee, CSA, as well as on General Leonidas Polk's staff. A week earlier he had been arrested in Alabama and returned to Nashville. After the war he continued his Nashville practice. Clayton, *Davidson County,* 284; Nashville *Union and American,* September 11, 1870; Nashville *Press,* January 11, 1864.

2. The word "disinterested" is crossed out.

From William H. H. Day[1]

Whiteside Tenn.
Jany 17, 1864.

To his Excellency
Gov Johnson,

Sir I take the liberty to thus address you, as I wish to be informed in what manner I or any other man must proceed to get possession so as to make it safe to work these coal mines at this station.[2]

If they are to be sold when, where, and at what place, And then Can an officer in the Army be the buyer, and as far as you know what will be the terms of sale, and probabilities as to the amount of, or worth of them[.][3]

Sir I am an "Indianian" and hold a Commission in the 30th Indiana Regiment. I see that by some little capital and good management that there can be some money made in this Country provided a man can be safe in making investments of which he wants to know before he does so to any extent. I find that there are inexhaustable quantities of Coal in these hills and the Caves are full of "Salt Petre" [4] also. Sir I appeal to you as a "Son" Should to a "Father" for information, And hope to receive it in the same good faith. My term of service will be out in about eight months and I wish to avail myself of some of these rare opportunities if such you could or would recommend. I like your Country and I like your Climate, and would bring my family into it to live if I could make a thing of that kind pay or sure, as far as the right of Soil and guarantee of protection[.] Any information you can give me on this Subject or any other whereby a Northern Man can do well, and be Safe to take his family will be thankfully received[.] N.B. Direct to the undersigned at Whiteside Tenn.

William H. H. Day
2d Lt. Comdy Co (G)

30th Regt Ind. Vol. Infy
3d Brigade 1st Division, 4th A.C.

ALS, DLC-JP.

1. William H. H. Day (1820-1899), Ohio-born editor of the Angola, Indiana, *Republican* and 2nd lieutenant, 30th Ind. Inf., resigned from service in March, 1864, returning to Angola to work as a house carpenter. Subsequently he settled in Randolph County, Missouri. 1860 Census, Ind., Steuben, Angola, 115; CSR, RG94, NA; Pension file, RG15, NA; *Hawes' Indiana State Gazetteer* (1860-61), 11.

2. Probably a reference to the Aetna mines opened in 1854 at Whiteside, Marion County, fourteen miles from Chattanooga on the Nashville and Chattanooga Railroad. Eastern capitalists were the original owners. The coal was limited in quantity, easily mined, and of good quality. At one time 367 cars per month were loaded; but by 1874, only 40 cars went out, and in 1881 the mines were in receivership. Joseph B. Killebrew, *Introduction to the Resources of Tennessee* (Spartanburg, S. C., 1974 [1874]), 193-95; Killebrew, *Iron and Coal of Tennessee* (Nashville, 1881), 164-65.

3. There is no indication that a sale of the mines was in the offing.

4. At least four Marion County caves have been mined for saltpetre. Two, Nickajack Cave and Battle Creek (now known as Monteagle Saltpetre) Cave, were extensively mined

during the war. Production at Nickajack was begun by Chattanooga manufacturer Robert Cravens and was taken over by the Confederate government the next year. Battle Creek Cave was being mined by October, 1862, and had "about 40" hoppers or leaching vats inside and "7 large furnace-kettles" outside the cave. Both operations were abandoned by the Confederates on the approach of Rosecrans' army and the remaining works were destroyed by the Federals. No statistics are available of saltpetre actually made at these sites, but a northern estimate that the Confederates "procured one thousand pounds per week" at Nickajack is probably an exaggeration. Robert Cravens to Samuel D. Morgan, May 24, 1861, Samuel D. Morgan Papers, Tennessee State Library and Archives; C. S. Nitre Service, Voucher No. 50 to G. L. Marr, November 30, 1862; Voucher No. 93 to James Scott, September 30, 1863, Confederate Papers Relating to Citizens or Business Firms, RG109, NA; *OR,* Ser. 1, XXX, Pt. III, 250; Ser. 4, II, 29; Louisville *Journal,* March 8, 1864.

From John A. Campbell[1]

Salem, Indiana, Jan. 18th 1864

Dear Sir:

I hesitate to trouble you with this communication, as I am well aware of your innumerable annoyances and onerous duties. The subject, however, which I will notice is of so much importance to the future of Tennessee & the Union of these states, I will venture these lines, although, I feel my incompetency to lay hold of the subject. I allude to the question of the annulling of slavery in Tenn. This is a matter of deep consern, especially, to us of Tenn. I have considered well of it for a long while and am fully satisfied that the Country can never have peace and harmony until this slave power is broken, therefore & for other reasons, I had entertained for twelve months the very views and subscribed to the very principles enunciated in your Speech of the 8th of January.[2] There is only one difficulty in my way, and that is, as to how we will attend its funeral obseques. Shall we ban it simply & only by the force & authority of the President's Proclamation? Or shall we at this time, or a future day, have a state Convention & dispose of slavery by its authority? The latter would seem to me advisable as it would stand as a bearer against objections to the authority of a proclamation. Indeed there could be no objection—no doubt as to the powers of a convention to emancipate or abolish slavery. But in reference to a convention an important question comes up. It is this. By whom shall the convention be composed & by the authority of what electors shall it meet? It seems to me the loyal & the legal only should act. Because it is by the loyal men of the nation—(of course Tenn included) that the rebel power and army is broken in the state. These loyal men at the sacrifice of blood & treasure are reclaiming the state—and taking it out of the hands of those who overthrew its Constitution and laws & declared it a foreign power.

In this illegal act they forfeited privileges the loyal enjoy. Therefore, the loyal have a right to determine—and haveing the right should have the nerve to determine what shall be the future *status* of the state. If the loyal put down the rebellion, they, upon the principle of self preservation *have a right and it is their duty, to put down the cause.* Then should we have a convention, would those be counted, loyal who have never cast their lot with the rebellion, but have acted as far as possible for the Union cause all the time. These of course would be counted loyal, because, they are so. But then there is a class, who have renounced the rebellion—some have joined our army. What shall we do with them? Can, or should we deny them the right to vote for members to the convention? It would seem they should vote. But suppose we are liberal in this particular. Is there not danger of a proslavery power & influence getting into the Convention, which would distract its councils and seek to pervert its object,—seek to get up a political howl in the state—to divide the Union party into hostile factisons. I think I see danger here, and the importance of the Union party dividing as little as possable, particularly, upon the slavery question.

I have every confidence in your patriotism and wisdom, and for this reason, feel gratified in the hope that the best plan and least objectionable mode for reorganising the civil authority will be adopted—and that the proper time for this action will be understood. As I have not been in Tenn since the Knoxville siege, I am not prepared to judge when we should move in this matter. I wish to live in Tenn., but do not see what inducement there would be to live there, after the war with the slave power ruleing the state with their usual impudence & notions of their high prerogatives.

You will excuse me for imposing, these lines on you. I write, because, I am a Tennesseean & desire you to have all the information, possable, as to the minds of those for whom you have the greatest consern, and whose interest & wellfare your position & influence wields so much[.]

Yours Truly John A. Campbell
Loudon East Tenn.

To Gov. Andrew Johnson
Nashville Tenn.

ALS, DLC-JP.

1. Although a prominent Roane countian who was a delegate to the Nashville reconstruction convention of January, 1865, John A. Campbell seems to have eluded the census takers and other contemporary record keepers. Marrying Abiah Gallaher in 1852, Campbell, an "old friend" of Robert Johnson, had left East Tennessee as a refugee in November, 1862. Nashville *Press,* January 13, 1865; Willis Hutcherson and Marilyn McCluen, *Marriage Records of Roane County, Tennessee, 1801-1855* ([Rockwood], 1973), 257; Campbell to Robert Johnson, December 16, 1862, Johnson Papers, LC.

2. See Speech on Slavery and State Suicide, January 8, 1864.

From Henry W. Barr

Headquarters District of Nashville,
Provost Marshal's Office,
Nashville, Tenn., Jan 19th 1864.

Gen
Dear Sir

As you wish me to Give you A Statement of the facks Concerning the burning the House of Mr. *J J Pickets*[1] of Dixon County State of Tenn I will do So with the best of my ability. I was Sent down there by Capt Nelson[2] then Commanding at Kingston Springs. And after arriving on yellow Creek And Infact before I Got theare I Learnt that yellow Creek was A place of resort for Guerellas[.] this I Got from nearley evry Citizen I met and was warned by Some Citizens bfore I Got theare that I wood find them at evry house that I Came to after arriveing on yellow Creek. And that I wood be bushedwacked from evry hill Side. And I Found it to be so When in About three fourth (¾) of A mile of Mr. Pickets house at Mrs Adams[3] my pickets Was driven in wile my men was eating Breakfast[.] I ordered them to mount And I proseed down yellow Creek And I had Not Gone more than About (400) four Hundred yards when I was fired upon from boath Sides of the road from the tops of hills that A man Wood have to wride about two (2) or three (3) miles [to] Get to them. I new that was no place for me if I wanted to Save my men so I ordered the Gallop and ran down yellow Creek And the first house I Came to was some widdow ladies And thare was Some Guerillas theare eating breakfast and Some walking about the yard[.] I chargd the house and captured two (2) or three (3) horces I have forgotten Witch. I Stoped theare about five (5) minutes and Just as I Was Going to leave I was fired upon again from the Hill Side[.] I then moved futher down yellow Creek And as I was pasing mr Pickets house my rear Gard was fired upon again[.] the wemming at mr Pickets house Came out on the porch and hollowed and laughing at my Command[.] I did not Care for that but keep on my way[.] after arriveing at the next house below Mr Pickets I heard fireing behind me so I halted my Command Gave the command Wright about and then the Command to Charge and as I was Charging back Mrs Picket Came out and herried the rebels off *Saying Kill them Kill them Kill them* and then Sed Get away with them yankeys for yonder comes some more And made some insulting remarks to the two (2) men belonging to my Command that the rebels had Captured. And as I Came up to the house the Same womming was Standing laughing[.] again I passed on by in persuit of the rebels and captured one of my men back and when tha saw that tha was going to Lose him tha Shot him the Ball Passing threw his left arm and Passing along the small of his back Cuting the Skin in several places[.] he Sed to me that them wemming was the Cause of him being Captured for tha Seen the rebels and new that tha was theare And that When tha Seen my Command Comeing back that tha Wanted the rebels to kill him and that he heard them tell the rebels foare or five times to Kill them after witch I went to the house and ast them Whether tha did Say or not Suth things and tha wood not say, Whether tha did or not So I thought it was Just and proper to burn the house witch I ordered done being as my man life was sought by them by trying to Get them (the rebels) to kill them (my men)[.] I think to the best of my Judgment that it was nothing but wright that the house was burnt And the Statement of mr Pickets Saying that I threnend to kill his wife and daughter is falce[.]

I Spoke no insulting langach to them—Gene[r]al—this Is the facks of the Case[.]

I remain your frend and obediant Servant
Henry. W. Barr
1 Lieut Co "C" 3d Tenn Vol Cav and
asst Provost Marshal Distrit of Nashville

ALS, DLC-JP.

1. See Letter from J. J. Pickett, December 8, 1863.

2. It has not been possible to determine which among several Nelsons held this post.

3. Probably Martha Adams (1839-*fl*1900), Tennessee-born wife of a farmer with property valued at $4,520 and living in the fourth house beyond the Picketts. Martha was about to become a widow, her husband, M. N., 3rd sergeant, Co. K, 50th Tenn. Inf., CSA, dying at Kingston, Georgia, January 22, from his wounds. 1860 Census, Tenn., Dickson, Middle Dist., 21; (1870), 11th Dist., 13; (1900), 12th Enum. Dist., 9B; CSR, RG109, NA.

From Francis P. Blair, Jr.[1]

Washington City
January 19, 64

Dear Governor

I send you herewith $86 $^{50}/_{100}$. in payment of the bills you so kindly settled for me in Nashville.[2] I did not anticipate that I should put you to any inconvenience of this kind as I did not suppose that my servants & horses would meet with so much delay. I am very much obliged to you for your kindness in this matter[.] My father & brother desire to be kindly remembered to you[.]

I am very Respectfully
Yr friend & obt Sert
Frank P Blair Jr

ALS, DLC-JP.

1. Francis P. Blair, Jr. (1821-1875), native Kentuckian and brother of Lincoln's postmaster general, Montgomery Blair, grew up in Washington, where his father, Francis P., Sr., was advisor to Andrew Jackson and editor of the *Globe*. Graduating from Princeton, he studied law at Transylvania and in 1842 opened a practice with his brother in St. Louis. State representative (1852-56), congressman (1857-59) and Democratic senator (1871-73), he became a brigadier general of volunteers in 1862, resigning three years later

to return to Missouri politics. An intimate of Johnson, who twice nominated him for Federal posts only to have him rejected by the Radical Senate, Blair was the Democratic candidate for vice president in 1868. Warner, *Generals in Blue*, 35-37; *BDAC*, 561.

2. The endorsement, indicating the total sum, further read: "Frank P Blair All bills paid"[.]

Petition of Robin Ewing[1]

[Nashville, January 19, 1864]

To His Excellency Andrew Johnson, Military Governor of Tennessee—

Your petitioner, Robin Ewing, Colored man, would show to your Excellency that last Sunday night, he, together with eight other Colored men, were engaged in playing cards in a little eating house, on Union Street, between Summer & High Streets, when three city policemen and two guards entered and arrested us all. We were then searched on the spot, to ascertain whether we had any weapons on our persons. A Mr. Ingall,[2] one of said City Policemen, searched me, &, in said search, took from me a knife, my watch, and my pocket book, the latter containing over $26. He handed back my watch, it being broken, remarking that he did not want that— The knife, not being worth more than thirty cents, he delivered up in the Police office— But the pocketbook & its contents he held on to, & still holds on to— These statements petitioner can prove by eight Colored witnesses. He has, however, no white witness, & can therefore effect nothing in a regular suit—[3] He submits the case to your Excellency, & invokes your extra ordinary powers to defeat a piece of unmitigated rascality, & to restore to him his hard earnings.[4]

Pet, DLC-JP.

1. Unidentified.

2. John F. Ingalls (*c*1833-1885), for the greater part of his life engaged in carriage-building—as a laborer before the war and as a manufacturer in the late 1870's, was during these years a policeman (1862-65) and for a time a sanitary policeman (1868-69). 1860 Census, Tenn., Davidson, Nashville, 2nd Ward, 53; Mt. Olivet Cemetery Records, II, 151; Nashville *Union,* July 9, 1862; Nashville city directories (1860-81), *passim.*

3. Negro testimony was not admissible in court against white witnesses. Return J. Meigs and William F. Cooper, comps., *Code of Tennessee* (Nashville, 1858), 687.

4. On January 20 Johnson referred the petition to Recorder William Shane, who replied that, "having examined the two policemen D. Lynch & James Miller . . . who were present at the time of the arrest and search," he finds "that the statement about the mony is faulce in evey res[p]ect. He had no mony at the time and so stated as proven by officers Miller & Lynch."

From Allen A. Hall[1]

Legation of the United States.
Cochabamba [Bolivia], January 19, 1864.

My dear Governor:

You keep "piling up" obligations upon me! Letters from Isabel and her Mother [2] inform me of your kind offer to render them, at any time, any service in your power. Your kindness has sunk deep into their hearts. The acquaintance of Mrs Johnson and Mrs Stover, Isabel writes me, has been a source of much gratification to her. My oldest daughter, Mary Lucy, has received highly encouraging expressions of opinion from some of the best educators in all New England in regard to her *book* in manuscript.[3] She is in Boston, among friends who love her dearly, and better in health, which had become alarmingly precarious, than she could have been had she remained in Tennessee. Boston was *the* place, I well knew, for the improvement of her health, the promotion of her happiness, and for *a fair start* in the career of authorship. She is now, there, as happy as she can be, with a promise of future usefulness. All this is owing to you. She could not have been *there,* had I not been *here.* A change of scene, too, I have long been satisfied, would be of great benefit to Isabel's health, and, if any thing could, such change would, work a thorough restoration of it. To *you* she is indebted for that change. You have been the means of my family's enjoying more happiness than you can imagine, or I express. I hope to live and to have it in my power to show by my *acts* my gratitude for all your kindness to me and mine.

I see by the papers that you have "taken the bull by the horns" and come out for the abolition of slavery in Tennessee. Right! It is the only sensible way of dealing with the "institution."

You know, that from the beginning, I never had one particle of faith in the possibility of a *healthy* State organization in Tennessee, for the present and that I was opposed to any present effort in that direction. From one or two copies of the Nashville *Union,* published in August, which have reached me, I see *completely verified* all that I had predicted in regard to the consequences that must inevitably result from any attempt to organize the State by *elections before the people.* Elections! *What* people! Governor! in your situation, I can well understand the repugnance you would naturally feel to being *thought* opposed to the *holding of elections* for all manner of State officers—members of Congress *Governor,* and members of the Legislature, who would elect *Senators* to Congress, &c. But the public good, the public safety, peremptorily *demand* of you, that from no "squeamishness," you should fail to put your face upon a course of policy, which *you know* as well as I do is fraught with great mischief. It is your right, and peculiar, duty, to see that the State shall suffer no detriment, which you can prevent. And you will incur the heaviest responsibility of your public life if you yield, through an unwillingness to *seem* to be opposed to trusting the *people* of Tennessee, at this revolutionary conjuncture, with all the power exercised by men under the constitution, in times of tranquility and domestic peace when all were loyal,—if, I say, yielding to *this* consideration, you *permit* a *rickety* State organization, such only as could be effected now, to take the control of affairs. I beseech you in the name of the public good, to allow of nothing of the sort. Stay where you are until the work appointed for you to do is finished, or until you clearly see that you can serve your country better in some wider sphere of action.

You will be glad to hear, I have no doubt, that I have had the good fortune to *draw from Washington* a most gratifying compliment by the address I delivered to the President of this Republic, on the occasion of presenting to him my letter of credence. This address was written under the most unpropitious circumstances imaginable. *I* thought the matter of it good—far better than the diction; but the complimentary reference to it in an official despatch from Washington, was a surprise to me—a gratifying one, nevertheless.

I had thought that *Chase* scarcely did me justice in his opinions; or supposed opinions, in regard to me—my ability to be useful, I mean.[4] You may judge of my surprise, then, when, on reaching Washington, on my way to this country, he expressed emphatically his regret at my leaving the United States, and told me if I would remain, I should have the best of the Government offices in Tennessee which pertained to his Department. This was in his office. He invited me to take dinner with him, and while at his house for that purpose, he renewed his expressions of regret, and the offer of the best office in Tennessee in his gift. He was evidently so in earnest, that it accorded me some embarrassment to say positively *no.* I said it, however, in the best manner by alluding to the situation of my family—the claims they had upon me—now to the fact, *which was fact,* that after the breaking out of the rebellion, I had voluntarily surrendered a similar office (which Mr Seward told me he had kept open for me) in order to go home, and stand by my union friends.

Concerning myself personally, I may briefly say to you, that on my ride over the Andes, and during my stay at La Paz and Oruro, I suffered greatly from the effects of the altitude—cold, rarefaction of the air &c. The prospect before me, if I were compelled to reside at either of these places (the Government was at Oruro), was gloomy indeed. There is no fixed seat of Government here. Wherever the Government goes, there, for the time being, is the capital; and in consequence of the revolution and state of the country, which has become *chronic,* the Government goes from City to City, as revolutionary exegencies require.[5] After suffering from a billious attack so severely in Oruro, that I had to be lifted on and off my horse, I followed the Government from that place to this, and *here* received a despatch from Washington leaving it wholly discretionary with me, under the peculiar circumstances of the case, to fix my residence where I thought proper. So I have concluded to establish my Head Quarters here. On the score of climate and beauty, this valley is unsurpassed *anywhere.*[6] It is near eight thousand feet above the level of the sea, and four thousand feet lower than the cities of La Paz and Oruro. The mercury in a thermometer hanging close by where I write hardly ever rises higher than 72 or falls lower than 68. The country adjacent to the city is fertile, and beautiful exceedingly—covered with vegetable gardens, fruit trees and fields of corn, wheat, barley, and a species of clover, of more luxuriant growth than our clover. This is a great *corn* country, the yield per acre being quite as much as in Illinois, and thousands of acres being devoted to its cultivation. But of the grain, the favorite liquor of the people is made—a sort of cross between whiskey and ale. It is called *chicha*—prounounced *chee-char*—and was found by the Spaniards to be in use here when they conquered this country, in 1532. The first process in the manufacture of it, is the *chewing* of the grain into meal by the Indians. Grinding or pounding will *not* do—they have been tried, and do not give the *peculiar* and *highly valued flavor,* which *chewing* does. It is chewed for so much a pound. A party of Indians, old and young, male and female, seat themselves round a trough, and chew and "throw in." It is then dried, mixed with water, allowed to ferment, and by and by, *chicha* is the product. Every body here who drinks liquor at all drinks *chicha*. The President, who was to see me the day before yesterday in some conversation we had about corn, asked me if I had tried *chicha*. I replied in the negative. He said it was a fine liquor. There is a great deal of drunkeness upon it among the Indians. But enough concerning *chicha*.

I spoke of the fruit trees just now, which are to be seen in this valley. There are peaches, apples, pears and figs in abundance. Besides them, we have lemons, oranges, pineapples, &c.

It is a country of wonderful natural resources. Bolivia is only a part of the former Peru, and the *richest part in mineral wealth*. It was from Potosi, now a city of Bolivia, that the great mass of silver was taken which made Spain, for a season, the most powerful nation in Europe. Next to Potosi in that respect, was Oruro, where I sojourned two months before coming to this place. More than nine-tenths of the mines worked by the Spaniards are now unworked, and full of water. I have not a doubt, that the same amount of intelligence and enterprise which has produced from forty to fifty millions of gold per annum in California, would produce a greater amount in this country, in silver chiefly, but with a good deal of gold. Many valuable mines before becoming exhausted of metal, became full of water, and there are not enterprise and intelligence enough in the country to draw the water out of those mines. There is but *one* steam engine applied to that purpose in all Bolivia, and *that* has just been brought out from the United States. It will make a fortune for the proprietors at a single mine when it has been successfully set to work.

This is a great day in Cochabamba. The military, cavalry and infantry, with fine bands of music, are parading—the streets are crowded with people—the balconies of one street are full of splendidly dressed and *fine-looking* women—the President with his military staff and a large number of citizens on horse-back have just passed by me as I stood in a door of that street—gone to meet a dozen stage coaches, all the way from Yankeedom, which have been brought to this country by "Norte Americans," as we are called, in order to be run on roads leading to and from this City. Do not laugh! It is really as great as the history of Bolivia—a day *to* be celebrated. Not another coach besides these was ever seen in this country. It may be the beginning of an era of internal improvement—so much needed, and the only thing needed, to make Bolivia one of the richest and most desirable countries in the world.

I am unspeakably annoyed at not being able to get my newspapers from the United States in any reasonable time. My latest reach down to the 21st of October. Through a Panama paper of the 8th of December, which I saw today, I learned of the fighting before Chattanooga on the 23rd and 24th of November; but nothing further. When I read of the disastrous battle of Chickamauga, in September last, I thought of a conversation which you and I once had respecting the merits, as Generals, of Rosecrans McCook and Crittenden; and I *distinctly recollect* that, without either of us having the slightest unkind feeling towards these Gentlemen, *we both* concurred in opinion that reasonable *grounds for apprehension* of serious disater to the army commanded by those Generals, *existed* solely on account of what *we feared* in them—a lack of high military capacity.

But I am inflicting a fatiguingly long letter upon you, in place of a short one. I sat down to write to thank you with my whole heart for your kindness to my family in my absence. Please present my kind respects to Mrs Johnson and Mrs Stover and believe me to be

ever, your obliged friend,
Allen A. Hall

Hon. Andrew Johnson
Nashville Tennessee.

ALS, DLC-JP.

1. For Hall, see *Johnson Papers,* IV, 461*n*.

2. Isabel (b. *c*1836) and Sophia M. (*c*1807-1863) were Hall's daughter and wife; because of slow communications, he had not heard of the latter's death late in November. *Nashville City Cemetery Index,* 33; 1860 Census, Davidson, Nashville, 3rd Ward, 89.

3. *Our World, or First Lessons in Geography* (1864) by Mary Lucy Hall (*c*1833-*fl*1889) lived up to her father's expectations, going through nineteen printings, to be followed by *Our World No. 11: A Second Series of Lessons in Geography* (1872) with six printings. *Ibid.*; *NUC,* CCXXVII, 399-400.

4. Chase had removed Hall from his position as special treasury agent because of the latter's drinking problems. *Johnson Papers,* V, 350n.

5. The Bolivian political scene was extremely unstable during the three-year (1861-64) rule of Gen. José Maria de Acha who came to power through a bloodless coup d'état and was ousted by one of his generals in a similar manner, Robert Barton, *A Short History of Bolivia* (La Paz, 1968), 192-94.

6. Cochabamba is located on the eastern face of the Andes in a valley cut by tributaries of the Rio Grande. *Ibid.,* 105-6.

From Edwin M. Stanton

War Department Washington City.
January 20th 1864.

To His Excellency Andrew Johnson
Military Governor of Tennessee
Nashville, Tennessee.
Governor:

Conflicts between the orders of General Grant and your orders under the telegram of the Secretary of War dated October 8. 1863,[1] in respect to arms and ammunition at the Ordnance Depot in Nashville, having arisen, which tend to embarrass the service and to perplex the officers in charge of Ordnance stores, it has become necessary to revoke the telegraphic order.

You will therefore please to make your requisitions upon the Ordnance department here, and the necessary instructions will be given to fill them as promptly as supplies can be obtained.

In making requisitions for Ordnance supplies let them be signed by the proper officers of the Company, Battalion, or Regiment for which they may be designed, and approved by yourself.

In any pressing emergency you can make requisitions by Telegraph.

Very Respectfully Your obedient Servant,
Edwin M Stanton
Secretary of War.

LS, DLC-JP; DNA-RG107, Mil. B: Copies Lets. Sent, Vol. 54A(1864).

1. Stanton's communiqué had announced: "You are hereby authorized to make requisition upon the ordnance officers and quartermaster at Nashville for arms ammunitions equipments & military supplies for all the white & colored troops raised by you in Tennessee." Johnson Papers, LC.

From Enoch T. Carson

Cincinnati January 21, 1864

Gov Andrew Johnson
My Dear Sir,

Your favor of the 18th *inst*, to hand to-day. And I hasten to reply and to correct an error which I made in my former letter.[1] I wrote then from recollection and mistated the account. This morning upon receipt of your letter I discovered my error. I made up your acct as $2000, $10. short when in fact it was $1800 $10. short—$1790, *net*. This was a mistake as you will see upon reference to my receipt which you hold which was for a sealed bag of gold marked and said to contain $1800.— Therefore the account was this

Amount of gold	1790
Prem. 40 pr. ¢, on Same	716
Total in my hands	$2506

I made up the statement to you without referring to Mr Johnstons[2] account of sale, he merely informed me that he had sold it at 40 pr¢ premium.

I have as you request deposited the proceeds less the odd $6. ($2500) on account of Temporary Loan to the U. S. bearing 5 pr¢ interest. I enclose you the *original receipt*,[3] the duplicate I send to Washington, in accordance with the regulations governing this Loan. Please cancel my receipt for the $1800, and return it to me.

I shall hope to see you when you come to Cincinnati when I will pay you the odd $6.

With many apologies for my blundering in this matter.

I am very Truly Yours,
E. T. Carson,
U. S. Depositary

LS, DLC-JP.

1. See Letter from Enoch T. Carson, January 8, 1864.
2. J. Wilson Johnston.
3. Not found.

Speech on Restoration of State Government[1]

January 21, 1864

Fellow-Citizens: In responding to the call that has been made upon me, I do so not for the purpose of making a speech, but simply to enter into a conversation, as it were, upon the subjects brought to your consideration here to-night in the resolutions just adopted.

The time has come when we should begin to consider the true policy to be adopted. I know in making speeches it is easy to make a flourish of trumpets or a display of fireworks, and entertain an audience for a time, but at present we should be practical. Our business now is to commence the restoration of our State government, and if I understand the resolutions adopted to night, I think they cover the whole ground.

Our object is to restore all the functions of State government. We have been involved, or, more properly, engaged, in a rebellion. Rebellions were anticipated by our forefathers, and their suppression provided for. And when a rebellion occurs it devolves upon the Government of the United States to suppress it. Admitting the functions of a State to be paralyzed for a time, it does not destroy the State, as has been correctly remarked. In the progress of the rebellion, the governor of a State may fly to seek protection in foreign climes, the Legislature may disappear, the civil magistrates may cease to act, but that does not destroy the State. Its functions have only been paralyzed—its powers are only remaining inactive.

In the 4th section of the 4th Article of the Constitution we find that the United States shall guarantee to each State in this Union a republican form of government. Instead of petitioning the President or the Congress of the United States—instead of assuming the attitude of suppliants in reference to the restoration of the powers of State government, we stand in the attitude of demanding—claiming at the hands of the Federal Government the guarantee of a republican form of government. We are no suppliants, no petitioners. We stand upon the broad platform of the Constitution, demanding our rights—that the guarantees in the Constitutition shall be secured to us—that is, to secure to us a republican form of government.

We find also in the Constitution of the United States that the President is required to take an oath of office. He is sworn to support the Constitution of the United States. He is bound to see that the laws are faithfully executed, and he, in the exercise of his constitutional obligations, may appear in the State of Tennessee in the person of an agent—I care not by what name, either military Governor, agent, or commissioner—but he can appear through his agent, and restore to the people of Tennessee, and to every other State in the Union, a republican form of government. He has been sending brave men and gallant officers to suppress this rebellion, and for a time the functions of government in this State have been suspended, we have no Governor, no Legislature, and but few Judges—and we have one of these here to-night, (Judge M. M. Brien), who has been discharging his duties in obedience to the principles I have been describing.

But in beginning to restore the Government—in carrying out the obligations of the Constitution, preserving and guaranteeing to the people a republican form of government, we must have justices of the peace, constables, etc. There are many here, no doubt, to-night, who are not citizens of Tennessee. Those who are, are familiar with our regulations. For instance, our State is divided into counties, then civil districts, each one of which elects two magistrates and one constable. There are provisions and exceptions made for different towns to have additional justices of the peace and constables. We will say, by way of illustration, that the first Saturday in March has been the usual time for the election of all county officers—justices of the peace, constables, trustees, sheriffs, clerks of the county and circuit courts—and when we come to the constitutional basis, would it not be clearly constitutional—would it not be carrying out the behests of the Constitution, and would the Executive be doing anything more than discharging his duty, to say to the people of this State on the first Saturday in March next: Go to the ballot-box and elect your constables, sheriffs, justices, county trustees and clerks. And when elected, let them be commissioned as they ordinarily are. The agent of the Government supplies the vacuum. Is there anything outside of the principles of the Constitution in that? Is there any usurpation in it? There must be a beginning somewhere.

In the absence of government there must be steps taken, though they may be irregular, for the purpose of bringing back order? Then we take a step without precedent, but clearly justifiable, and proceed to elect our officers as we have done heretofore. In looking over the various judicial districts of the State, we find them without judicial officers. In turning to the laws and Constitution of the State we find that when vacancies occur by death, resignation, or otherwise, the Executive shall make temporary appointments, and these appointees shall hold their places until their successors are elected and qualified.[2] Then we see how easy the process is. Begin at the foundation, elect the lower officers, and, step by step, put the government in motion. But it may be said this can't be done in all the counties throughout the State. But, if it is done in a half dozen counties, it is so much done, and that much done we can do more.

In this connection there comes up a very important question, and that is, who shall be allowed to vote? This is the touchstone. And let us talk about this in a plain, common sense way, and see if we can ascertain who ought, and who ought not to vote. I assume that an individual who has engaged in this rebellion, who has got his consent to give up the government of the United States, and with his person attach his fortunes to the Southern Confederacy, or to any other Government—I say he has been, by his own act, *expatriated*—at the very point of time at which he gets his consent to take up arms against the Government of the United States, he ceases to be a citizen of the United States. [Applause.] A man coming into the United States from Great Britain, Ireland, or elsewhere, does not become a citizen until he has filed his declaration and taken the oath of allegiance. We describe in our laws the process by which he may become a citizen. Renouncing his allegiance to all powers, kings and potentates, thus complying with our naturalization laws, he comes a citizen of the United States. We know that a great many who went into this rebellion, went into it under a reign of terror; we know a great many were conscripted, a great many went from interest and speculation; and others—the intelligent portion—went into it for the purpose of changing the Government and establishing an Aristocracy or negro oligarchy. [Laughter.] This we know; and now shall we act upon the doctrine that a man can't repent, or, upon the Christian principle, that a man can conscientiously acknowledge his error and once more become a citizen of the United States? This is the question. Shall we lay down a rule which prohibits all restoration, and by which all will be excluded from participating in the exercise of the elective franchise? Think: we are told that honest men sometimes do change their opinions. We are told upon pretty high authority that sinners sometimes repent, and honestly repent; and we are told that in this repentance there should be works meet for repentance—that there should be some evidence of it. That is the condition of the community. We want to restore the Government, and the restoring process is that you, the people, must go to the ballot-box and exercise the elective franchise in so doing. Now let us get at it practically. These three gentlemen sitting here to-night—[3] who are reporting, I presume, are judges of an election. We want to elect our squires, our constables, our county officers and our judges. I am speaking of things to be done before we get to convention, about which I have much to say before I conclude. What rule will you adopt, by which you can tell disloyal from loyal men? Over there I can point to a man who has been standing out like Saul of old, head and shoulders above the rest [4] for the Union, as everybody knows. Over there stands another who has been equally prominent on the other side. Of these two we can say at once that the one may vote and the other may not. But in this instance we have got two extremes—we have got a case which everybody or anybody can decide without difficulty. But is the whole community in this condition? You may discriminate for a while—these are union men, these are rebels—but after a while you approach a line where they have not been prominent, and then how many can tell which is which? Will you have no test? No rule? Will you confer the power upon these judges, to say that no person shall vote save those that be loyal? But they cannot tell; they may act correctly as far as their judgment goes. Then again, in addition, I tell you you are trusting a great deal, where you leave this matter to the discretion of judges. They may, in many instances, act right, and they may think they act right in all. Here sit the three judges; they look around the neighborhood and say: "Why, I do not like to discriminate in favor of one friend and against another—I hope he has done right, and if he has done wrong, I hope he has repented." Then what rule will you establish? We want some standard by which we can put he that has been a traitor to the test, though he has repented. Now what will it be? It is easy to talk that rebels shall not vote and Union men may, but it is difficult to practice this thing. What rule will you establish? I ask the question. I want information. I came up here to talk to you, and you to me.

I know it has been said by some Union men that we should not be placed in the attitude of culprits—of men asking for pardon. I do not feel that you, and you, should be required, for the sake of a vote, to ask for pardon. I am not a criminal—I have violated no law—I have not raised my arm against my government. Therefore, I do not want pardon. But in the election of officers who are to take charge of the government we want some test, at least, that the men who vote are loyal and will act with loyal men. In all the States of the Union there is a qualification attached to voters without regard to treason, traitors, or anything of the kind. And taking the State of Tennessee for an illustration, what is the qualification? We find that the person to vote must first be a citizen of the United States; next, he must be a free white man.[5] I want you to understand that although I am going to talk about negroes presently, I am for a white man's government, [cheers,] and in favor of free white qualified voters controlling this country, without regard to negroes. [Continued cheering.] Next, the voter must have been in the county six months immediately preceding the day of election. Then if we were to say in addition, before you can vote, you must take an oath something like the following:[6]

Is there any one, Union at heart, who can object to taking an oath like this? [A voice—"None."] Is there a solitary Union man who cannot take this oath? [Voices, "no, no."] Is there any Union man but what would take great pleasure in coming before the judges of election and take this oath to test him who has been warring against his country? You put him to the test, you don't come up asking pardon, but are only giving evidence of being a loyal and a qualified voter. These are simply the qualifications of a voter. On the other hand, if there is anybody in this large assembly of voters who needs and desires a pardon or amnesty, whether he seeks it in good faith or for the purpose of saving a little remnant of negro or any other property, I would say to him, "Go over there; there is an altar for you. There is President Lincoln's altar if you want pardon or amnesty—if petitioning to the President for executive clemency. If you want to escape the penalties you have incurred by violations of law and the constitution, go over there and get your pardon. We are not in need of it; we wish not to take that oath; that is the oath for him who has committed crime." Now, gentlemen, it seems to me this will be fair. We want a hard oath—a tight oath—as a qualification for everybody that votes. He that wants pardon must take the oath prescribed by the President of the United States;[7] and I am free to say that I think the President has been exceedingly lenient in permitting them to do that. If this will not do, will you suggest something that will be better? What standard will you erect? Don't stand here and find fault with my suggestions and say they will not do; but suggest others that are better and more acceptable. I am for a rule that will test a loyal man as against a disloyal one; that is the rule I am for. I am free to say to you that I believe there are many even in the Confederate army, many who have deserted, and even some captured, who I believe are honest and loyal to-day and regret that they have ever been involved in this infamous, diabolical and damnable rebellion. I have had men come before me who evinced, by their emotions and the tone of their voice, that they were as much opposed to the rebellion as I am. If this be so, and they are now willing to support the constitution, and fight in vindication of it, as far as I am concerned, I am willing to admit them and give them a fair chance to return. We cannot put all in prison; we can't suspend all upon the gallows. No, this is not a war of extermination, but a war for the restoration of Government; and while restoring the Government, if we reclaim honest men we have only done our duty.

If we want to restore the government we must start at the foundation. Having elected our squires, constables, sheriffs and other county officers, as we can get men to serve, we have got the goundwork laid. Then what will you do next? Now mark: under the 4th clause and IVth article of the Constitution of the United States we have a pledge to secure to the States a republican form of government. To carry out the spirit and letter of the Constitution, as the people are the rightful source of political power, I should say the executive would have the right to invite the people to have a convention to restore government to the people. Then, even looking to the Constitution of the United States, we have a right to call a convention, and have the convention as a means of flowing from the constitution to guarantee the restoration of a republican form of government. We find in the constitution of this State that you can amend the constitution by the legislature, but it takes about six years to amend it in that way.[8] But when we recur to the bill of rights, which is a paramount part of our State Constitution, we find that the sovereign people have the right to alter, amend or abolish their form of government whenever they think proper, and in their own way. This is perfectly consonant to the Constitution of the United States, and admits the great principle that all political power is inherent in the people.

I have unfortunately or fortunately, as the case may be, always been one of those who hold that all power is inherent in the people, and that the Government is made for the people instead of the people being made for the Government; as much so, at least, as the shoe is made for the foot, instead of the foot being made for the shoe. Government emanates from the people; and now, when your Government has been paralyzed or its functions suspended, is there any better way that can be adopted than to call a convention here? In other words: let us have the sovereign present in the shape of delegates; or, were it practicable, to appear in a large amphitheatre, and know what their opinions were in taking the steps to restore the workings of government, I would say let the people be convened in obedience to the Constitution of the United States and of the State, and in strict compliance with the fundamental principles of our Government, that power is inherent in the people. Who dares say the convention shall not assemble? Who dare say that the people shall not assemble in convention? I know there is a little croaking dissatisfaction among some that have been nominally Union men, and some that have been Rebels in this hell-born and hell-bound rebellion, who, now that they are subjugated, after having been instrumental in paralyzing to some extent the Government, and after having helped to produce the rebellion, hypocritically say: Oh! they don't want so much disturbance;—it will be too revolutionary to have a convention; it will not do to trust the people with the settlement of this great question. Let us think. Give me your attention, and I will show you that there is a cat in the meal.[9] They turn to the Constitution as it now stands, and say, let us get the Legislature back here; let us patch up things and have no fuss. They think of that little clause in our Constitution which provides that the Legislature shall not emancipate slaves without the consent of their owners.[10] Don't you see? Then if they get the Legislature back under the Constitution as it is, they think they can hold on to the little remnant of negroes that is left—the disturbing element that has produced all this war. [Applause.] I then say this: Bring the people forward in convention—the source of all power—they that made the Constitution, and let them act upon this important question and upon this momentous occasion. Let us have the people here, and when they assemble in convention—when the sovereign is present, he can do all that the Legislature can, and he can do a great deal more. Have a convention here, and it can put your State upon her legs in eight and forty hours. It could appoint these magistrates, these squires, these sheriffs, all the officers, and carry on the machinery of State to perfection in eight and forty hours. Let the people come forward and speak, and in speaking upon the negro question, my honest convictions are, that they will settle it, and settle it finally.

Now, my countrymen, it is not worth while to try to deceive each other, and thus play a hypocritical part as the soothsayers in olden times; while practicing their deceptions upon the people, when meeting, would always smile in each others faces.[11] I know there is going to be division in Tennessee; and I tell them now, politically speaking, that my sword is unsheathed, and it never is to be returned until I fall, or until this great principle of free government has triumphed. [Cheers.] Now is the time to settle it. This question of slavery has been the disturbing element in this Government, and the time has come now to settle it. The Rebels commenced the destruction of the Government for the preservation of slavery, and the Government is putting down the rebellion, and in the preservation of its own existence has put slavery down, justly and rightfully, and upon correct principles. It attempted to rise above the Government, and had it succeeded, negroes or their masters would have controlled the Government; but in making the attempt to control the Government, the mighty car of State has moved forward, and the institution has been crushed, and thank God for it. [Applause.]

But in this connection I have got a single word to say in reference to the brave and gallant men of Tennessee who have entered the service of their country. Is there any one who would like to deprive them of the elective franchise? [A voice—"No."] Mr. Lincoln has done no such thing. He will not require these fifteen thousand heroic soldiers, who have been fighting the battles of their country, and of themselves, constitute more than one-tenth of our voting population, to stand before him as petitioners for pardon and amnesty. I know his high appreciation of loyal men, of justice and right too well for this. I opposed his coming into power. I spoke and voted against him, and though I did this and in favor of another, I believe Abraham Lincoln is an honest man, and has done, and is doing, all in his power to preserve this Government and put down this infernal rebellion. [Applause.] Render unto Caesar the things that are Caesar's. I believe Mr. Lincoln is a patriot and a friend to his Government; I believe he is for free Government; and so believing, I shall stand by him. It is easy to find fault—

to complain; but the next question comes up, who would have done better than he has done? [Renewed applause.] He is the last man in the United States that would wish to circumscribe the privileges of the brave men of Tennessee in the matter of the elective franchise. Is there a Tennesseean here to-night, though he may have differed with me heretofore, who ever doubted me upon this question of free government? In an election for members of a convention or for county officers, how easy it will be for every Tennessee soldier, if he can hear who the candidates are in his district, to vote for the man of his choice wherever he may be stationed? Whether in Middle, or East, or West Tennessee, his voice can be heard and his weight goes into the ballot box in the settlement of this great question. That is the manner in which I want it settled. And when it comes to repelling and driving back the Rebel armies, then let him have on his whole armor—put on his shield and lock shield with his comrades, and never return till victory perches upon his standard. Who wants to deprive the army from Tennessee of the right to participate in the restoration of their Government? Will anybody make that allegation against me? Since this rebellion commenced, who has been hunted, persecuted, denounced, and calumniated by the Rebels? There is not one among the army of Tennesseeans but what knows that I would make any and every sacrifice by which their interest could be promoted. No, no; who ever dreamed or thought of their being deprived of participating at the ballot-box—they who have done so much for the restoration of the State?

Now upon this negro question, and I know the saying is sometimes bandied about that you are always prating and saying the negro is dead—if he is dead, why repeat it so often? Is there a man here that has observed this thing who does not know that the institution of slavery in Tennessee is dead? I have had some come to me and say, "Gov. Johnson, are you in favor of immediate emancipation?" I tell them yes. "Do you want to turn the negroes all loose upon the country? What will we do with them?" Why sir, I reply, as far as emancipation is concerned, that has already taken place. Where are your negroes? They answer, "They are running about somewhere." I ask, what do you call that? [Laughter.] They seem to be already turned loose. The institution of slavery is turned into a travelling institution, and goes just where it pleases. It is said the negroes are not qualified to be free; because they have been slaves so long they are unfitted to be freeman, and shall not be permitted to enjoy the privileges of freemen; but by way of making them competent, it is proposed to keep them in slavery nineteen or twenty years longer. In the first place it would not do to have them free, because they have been slaves, and in the next place they should be kept in slavery to qualify them for freemen. [Laughter.]

We are proceeding to put up the State government—to elect clerks, justices, trustees, legislature, Governor and other things, that constituted the State heretofore. But the institution of slavery. There it lies; will you take it back? Leave out the disturbing element I say. It is now out; and to put the State in motion, start the machinery and leave negroes out of the question. [Applause.] Then the conclusion is, that in fact negroes are emancipated in Tennessee to day, and the only remaining question for us to settle, as prudent and wise men, is in assigning the negro his new relation. Now, what will that be? There are no more negroes to-day than there were yesterday—there being no more negroes free than there were slaves. The same space will contain them in one condition as in another, and the slaveholder need not be alarmed with the fear that negroes will be increased faster than they were before. Then the negro will be thrown upon society, governed by the same laws that govern communities, and be compelled to fall back upon his own resources, as all other human beings are. The God of Nature has endowed him with faculties that enable him to enjoy the result of his own labor. Political freedom means liberty to work, and at the same time enjoy the product of one's labor, be he white or black, blue or gray, red or green, [laughter] and if he can rise by his own energies, in the name of God let him rise. In saying this, I do not argue that the negro race is equal to the Anglo-Saxon—not at all. There are degrees among white men; some are capable, others are not; some are industrious, others are not; but because we find inferiors among ourselves, shall every inferior man be assigned to slavery? If the negro is better fitted for the inferior condition of society, the laws of nature will assign him there. My own conviction is, that in less than five years after this question is settled upon the principle of hired labor, the negro's labor will be more productive than it ever was.

The argument used to be that "Cotton is King." But I think that idea is pretty well exploded. [Laughter.] For a little experience has proven that cotton is a feeble King without the protection of the United States. I used to tell them that bread and meat were King,[12] and if we look over in rebeldom now, we will find that a little bread and meat would be more acceptable than cotton. [Renewed laughter.]

I hope the negro will be transferred to Mexico, or some other country congenial to his nature, where there is not that difference in class or distinction, in reference to blood or color.[13] If in the settlement of this question the providence of God should call a number of them there, I say let them go. And about that time I would not care much to see a large portion of our gallant sons go along to Mexico, too, [Cheers,] and as they approach the city of Mexico or Jalapa, of which Louis Napoleon has taken possession, where he was going to send Prince Maximilian to govern,[14] I would like our boys to be along there inquiring into that affair, and give him to understand that while we can fight for years and head a monstrous rebellion to boot, he cannot come upon this continent to establish a government anti-republican in its character. We have not yet fulfilled our mission. We have got the negroes to dispose of. We will do that. And we have got other things to do. We should teach France and all other powers that we can crush down a gigantic rebellion at home, and that the combined armies of the world cannot subdue the United States when united. [Loud cheers.] I care not though all nations were arrayed against us in one solid phalanx. When the masses of the people of these United States stand united we can bid defiance to the combined powers of earth.

Let us go on in the performance of the great mission of restoring these States. And I fully concur in the doctrine I heard advanced here to-night, that a State cannot commit suicide—a State cannot destroy itself—a State has no right to go out of this Union, and the Federal Government has no right to put one out. None. The doctrine is as dangerous on one hand as on the other. If you accept either, your Government is destroyed and crumbles into pieces like a rope of sand, by its own weight. These States occupy a certain relation to the great whole, and the great whole to each part. The parts cannot destroy the whole, neither can the whole destroy the parts. It is undeniable: there is no way to destroy a State. We find in the Constitution that you can make States, create a Government, but there is no way to destroy it. I repudiate the doctrine *in toto*. It is contrary to the Government of our fathers—an emanation of Divinity—and we fail to discharge our duty, and commit as great a sin and error in permitting the destruction of this Government in that way, as though we had raised our sacrilegious hands to tear it down.

Though it was not my intention to speak on this occasion, in conclusion of what I have said, I am free to declare that I am for a Convention, after adopting some rule that will exclude disloyal and admit only loyal men. Under the Constitution, the people have a right to meet and appoint delegates. On the other hand, the President of the United States, through his agent, has the right by proclamation to say to the people: "On such a day elect so many delegates to take into consideration the restoration of the State." As I remarked before, sometimes we may do irregular things for the sake of returning to law and order. It might be irregular in starting, but when the Convention get together, they have the right to change, alter, or abolish, their government in their own way. I am disposed to think that the people, if they were together, would be inclined to remove the difficulties under which we labor. I am willing to trust them. I believe they are honest, and especially so in reference to governmental affairs. And even judging men by self-interest, I am willing to trust them, because it is their interest to have the best government they can get, and they will have it. I do not see why a Convention could not be trusted as well as a Legislature. Who is prepared here to-night to hesitate to admit the great principle that man is capable of governing himself? Have any of you reached that point? If you have, you had better go down and join Jeff. Davis; that is the locality for you. [Laughter.] And now I am going to tell you a truth, and you know what I say is true: If there are any here who have lived in the county of Davidson, you know many men have been afraid and alarmed even to speak upon the negro question when the large slaveholders were about.

Some of you have been deprived of your manhood so long upon this question, that when you begin to talk about it now, you look around to see if you are not overheard by some of your old masters. [Laughter.]

In 1853, when I was a candidate for Governor, it was said, "That fellow Johnson is a demagogue—an abolitionist"—because I advocated a white basis for representation—apportioning members of Congress according to the number of qualified voters, instead of embracing negroes.[15] I discussed the question alone, scarcely getting a paper to come to my support; and hundreds agreeing with me, sought me in private to give me comfort, but were afraid to strike openly. I know all about this negro question, and pardon me if I seem to be egotistical when I say that I am the only man that has dared at all times to discuss it in this State; and now some of you see what I have all along foreshadowed. I have known this question was coming, and that it was only a question of time. Standing alone, having but little means to command, and no press, but simply relying upon argument, with the great mass of the people I was sustained. Running against him who was called the "eagle orator," a lineal descendant from the forest-born Demosthenes,[16] it was expected that I would be driven from the contest; but, thank God, I have always relied upon one thing: that there was a great principle of right lying at the foundation of all things; and that truth is mighty and will prevail. Right goes forward; truth triumphs; justice is paramount; and slavery goes down. [Applause.] And now, I proclaim it, the time has come, God being my helper, I am willing to do my part, and am willing to wind up my political career in the final settlement of this question. The time has come when the tyrant's rod shall be broken, and the captive set free. [Renewed applause.] Then, now is the time to strike; and he is a coward who desires to remain inactive and will not come forward to that altar and worship. [Continued applause.] Yet while right is triumphing, they talk about compromising this question. Compromise! Compromise with what? Compromise a great principle! Will you have truth to compromise with falsehood? Will you have right to compromise with wrong? Will you have virtue compromise with vice? I say, No. In the compromise of right with wrong, right is the loser; in the compromise of virtue with vice, virtue is always violated. Deity might as well have compromised with the devil, who was the first rebel, and made war in heaven. No compromise. None. No compromise with traitors while they have arms in their hands. [Cheers.] I am no maniac or fanatic upon this question, but I feel devoted, attached and wedded to great principles. Sometimes I inquire in my own mind why this people have had no leader. Peter the Hermit led the Crusade, but was wild and visionary, yet he intended to redeem the Holy Land. The Crusaders had their leader; the Israelites had their leader; the Greeks had their leader; the Romans had their leader, and England had her leader. The Israelites had their Moses, and have this people got no Moses—no leader—or have they to rely for their deliverance upon the establishment of this great principle? The ways of Providence are incomprehensible to short-sighted, erring man. In the various periods of the world's history there have been manifestations of a power incomprehensible to us, and I believe that there is a direct and important connection between the moral and physical world, and the one is affected more or less by the other in bringing about great events. Going back to the history of the world, we find events and signs have preceded final results. This nation, many think, has been involved in a great sin. Nations as well as individuals must sooner or later be overtaken for their transgressions. Perhaps this rebellion will result in great good; the nation will become chastened and the sin removed. Who can tell? When we go back to ancient times and run over the pages of history, what do we find there? We find Pharaoh, after governing the Egyptians with an iron rod so many years, there was a rebellion there; the people were led by Moses to the shores of the Red Sea, when by the touch of his rod the waters parted and stood as a wall on either side, and Moses and his followers passed through dry-shod and reached the land of Canaan; whilst Pharaoh and his chariots and mighty hosts proceeded to follow on and were lost amid the waves, and were drowned in the sea. I do not say that this was a direct or special interposition of Providence; I will not undertake to argue that it was the result of a divine law. I refer to it as a great fact that Pharaoh and his hosts were lost in the Red Sea in pursuit of those trying to escape from bondage. If disposed, I might take you back to Babylon and there look at her people in their might, or to those mighty walls crowded with chariots. Those walls have crumbled; Babylon has gone down, and is no more. I will not say whether it was the result of a special providence, or of a general law, but I state it as a great fact. Some great wrong or some great sin had to be redressed. I might take you back to ancient Tyre, in the days of her freedom and splendor; but all her glories are no more, and her ruins are used only as a resort for straggling fishermen to dry their nets upon the rocks.[17] I might take you back to Herod, in the days of all his pomp and splendor, when, on one occasion, he appeared before the people, and they stood amazed and exclaimed, "He speaks not as a man, but as God." But he was smitten by the Almighty, and eaten by worms.[18] I will not say whether these were special interpositions of Providence or the results of a Divine law, but they are great facts. I might call attention to the journey of Saul of Tarsus to Damascus, when he was struck blind, as believed by some, on account of his persecutions of the Christians. But I will not say whether that was the result of a special interposition of Divine providence, or of a general law, but it is a great fact. I might take you to Jerusalem, and tell of the persecution by the Jews of Christ, and his crucifixion upon the cross, and now their dispersion to all parts of the globe. I will not assume that it was an interposition of Divine providence, or the result of a general law, but it is a great fact, and the Jews have been dispersed and rebuked. There are many ways in which the Almighty manifests his power. He sometimes unlocks the winds, and rends the forests, and strands whole navies upon the hidden rocks and desert shores. Sometimes He manifests His power in the forked lightning's glare, and sometimes His mutterings are heard in distant though threatening peals of thunder. Sometimes He lets the comet loose, which sweeps from one extreme of the universe to the other, shaking from its fiery tail pestilence and death. There are

> Signs sent by God to mark the will of Heaven—
> Signs which bid nations weep and be forgiven.[19]

Does not the mind irresistibly come to the conclusion that this great sin must be gotten clear of, or result in the overthrow and destruction of this nation? I say, then, remove the evil, obey the laws of Heaven, and always reach a right conclusion. As we have commenced the work of restoring the State, let us profit by past experience, and put the government in motion now upon correct and true principles. Let us go at it honestly. I know there are some that are finding fault and thinking about the places of State already. We should not be controlled by considerations of this kind. Let us forget that we have been divided into parties; let us commence the work of restoring and building the Government up, and then if we want to quarrel about local questions or questions of expediency, we will have a Government to quarrel in.

I will remark in this connection, that about the beginning of the rebellion, in conversation with Philip Clayton,[20] Howell Cobb's Assistant Secretary of the Treasury, that gentleman said, after we had argued the question pro and con: "Mr. Johnson, it is unnecessary to argue this question further; a large portion of the South is unwilling to submit to the administration of the government by a man who has come up from the ranks as Abraham Lincoln has." And let me tell you, there is a good deal of this feeling and sentiment in the hearts of the leaders of this rebellion, because Abraham Lincoln rose from the masses. Abraham Lincoln is a democrat in principle; he is for the people, and for free government, and so I am for him, [Cheers.] and will stand by him until this rebellion is put down. There are corruptions, of course, in such an immense expenditure. But what is a few millions or billions of dollars, when contrasted with the existence of this Government, and the suppression of this rebellion? What is it contrasted with the life and existence of a great nation which has not fulfilled its mission? It is easy to clamor and to find fault; but let us put the rebellion down, and then, if any body has done wrong, we will have plenty of time to punish offenders.

Gentlemen, I did not come here to speak to-night. My intention was not to participate in the meeting, but I was anxious to see some steps taken which would indicate what you intended to do. If we have correct principles, it does not need previous consultation, and the result will be the triumph of those principles. Then take this great question; it is a question of state—of the existence of free government. Take it and think about it. Turn it over in your minds. Which is the best way? What is the best mode?

How shall it be done? I stand where I have always stood, an advocate of free government. I am for the people having a fair, full, impartial trial of their capacity for self government, and I have confidence that they will triumph. And if these brave officers and gallant men, with what aid we can give them, will keep the rebel army from us, or drive them in the Gulf, (as I believe ere long they will,) before they reach the Gulf, Tennessee will "stand redeemed, regenerated and disenthralled by the genius of universal emancipation."[21] Let those of us who are for restoring the government and leaving out this element called slavery, stand together, and in language often repeated, let us give a long pull, a strong pull and a pull altogether,[22] and the union sentiment and free government will succeed. We have commenced the battle of freedom—it is freedom's battle,—and let me say it is not extended to the negro only, for this will free more white men than it will black men. I know what I say. There are men owning slaves themselves that will be emancipated by this operation. It is not my devotion to the black man alone, but a greater devotion to the white men and the amelioration of their condition. My humanity is broad enough for the white and the black man too. We have commenced the battle of freedom, and—

> Freedom's battle once begun,
> Bequeathed from bleeding sire to son,
> Though baffled oft, is ever won![23]

Make high and strong resolves; let your principles go forth to the world, and, though slave-owners and negro-drivers, though hell stand yawning before you, go forward with the banner of Freedom and Free Government; pass the fiery cross around, and Freedom will ere long triumph, and the triumph, I hope, will last for all time.

Here in Tennessee, some say, "Oh, I am afraid of the slavery question!" They are so afraid of doing wrong that they are afraid to do right. Many yet are so afraid of their former masters, they still look around to see whether Mr. Bell, Mr. Overton, or the Ewings[24] are standing about. It is time, when talking about restoring slavery, to restore manhood. They know many of them have that taken from them which constitutes a man—their manhood has been emasculated. Get your consent that you have manhood enough to stand up here and take hold of the helm of State, and convince us that you are willing to do it. Let us commence the work this night. The shackles must fall from the limbs of all. You must have laws for the punishment and protection of all. Law is what we want. There is no freedom without law. As an ancient Greek has said, "The love of law is the soul of liberty." [25] We must have law, and whether the black man is here or not, we must have government. There will be no difficulty about this question. I don't care if the negroes go to Africa or any other place more suitable to them—we can make more cotton after they are gone than has ever been made in the United States before. If you cut up these large cotton farms into small-sized farms, each man with his little family getting hold of part of it, on good land will raise his own hogs, his own sheep, beef cattle, his own grain, and a few bales of cotton, better handled, and a much better article than we have ever had heretofore.[26] With a greater number of individuals, each making a few bales, we will have more bales than ever were made before. And in addition to that, if the cotton-plant was lost, the world would not stop, for the vacuum would be filled by making a little more silk, wool, hemp and flax, and in a little while you would never know that cotton had been in the world. [Laughter.] It is all an idea, that the world can't get along without cotton. And as is suggested by my friend behind me,[27] whether we attain perfection in the raising of cotton or not, I think we ought to stimulate the cultivation of hemp, [renewed laughter,] for we ought to have more of it, and a far better material, a stronger fibre with which to make a stronger rope. For, not to be malicious or malignant, I am free to say, that many who were driven into this rebellion, I believe are repentant, but I say of the leaders, the instigators, the conscious intelligent traitors, they ought to be hung. [Cheers and applause.] Treason must be made odious, traitors must be punished and impoverished. Their social power must be destroyed, and the effects that give them power and influence must be taken away. I trust the time will come, when the Union men who have been oppressed, and the loyal heirs of those who have perished on the battle field, or starved in the mountains, will, to some extent, be remunerated out of the property of those who betrayed and tried to destroy their country. Common sense teaches that the transgressor should make restitution. What the common sense of every man suggests is but common justice.

This would not be considered a very politic electioneering speech, but I am no candidate for anything. I know some say that when traitors become numerous enough, then treason becomes respectable. I want that class hung to test their respectability. [Cheers.] Fellow-citizens, I must say in conclusion, [cries of "go on,"] that I am very much gratified to find that there has been no dissension here to-night as far as I have observed. I am proud to say that I have not seen the slightest indication of prejudice or dissension. The resolutions as adopted, as I understand them, I think will cover the whole ground, and if we carry out these resolutions[28] I think we can succeed in accomplishing the end sought for. I am also proud and gratified to see so many here participating in this meeting. Let it go to the country as an earnest of what is going to follow. Things must have a beginning, and you have put the ball in motion. I repeat, that I feel proud and more than gratified at this demonstration, and in conclusion, tender you my sincere thanks for your marked attention to this crude and desultory speech.

Pamphlet, DLC-JP5E, *Speech of Governor Andw. Johnson, on the Restoration of State Government* . . .(Nashville, [1864]); NN, *Speech of Gov. Andrew Johnson of Tenneessee* (n.p., [1864]).

1. Nashville unionists, meeting in the Hall of Representatives, had endorsed resolutions favoring the restoration of Tennessee. At this juncture the governor "was seen in an obscure corner and loudly called for"; despite his apparent unpreparedness, that worthy spoke for "some two hours" being interrupted from time to time "by loud and general applause." Nashville *Dispatch,* January 22, 1864.

2. Tennessee Constitution (1834), Art. III, sec. 14.

3. It is unclear whether Johnson refers to those chairing the meeting—Chairman Manson M. Brien and Vice Chairman Col. William C. Pickens, David W. Ballew, and Joseph Ramsey—or other speakers sharing the podium—Joseph Fowler, Col. Richard M. Edwards, and Capt. Ezra C. Hatton (of the 22nd.Mich. Inf.). Nashville *Dispatch,* January 22, 1864.

4. 1 Sam. 9:2—"from his shoulders and upward he was higher than any of the people."

5. Tennessee Constitution (1834), Art. IV, sec. 1.

6. For the text of the oath which follows, see Proclamation Ordering Elections, January 26, 1864.

7. Lincoln's Proclamation of Amnesty and Reconstruction, December 8, 1863, stipulated the following: "I, ________________, do solemnly swear, in presence of Almighty God, that I will henceforth faithfully support, protect and defend the Constitution of the United States, and the union of the States thereunder; and that I will, in like manner, abide by and faithfully support all acts of Congress passed during the existing rebellion with reference to slaves, so long and so far as not repealed, modified or held void by Congress, or by decision of the Supreme Court; and that I will, in like manner, abide by and faithfully support all proclamations of the President made during the existing rebellion having reference to slaves, so long and so far as not modified or declared void by decision of the Supreme Court. So help me God." Basler, *Works of Lincoln,* VII, 54.

8. After adoption by a majority of both houses, an amendment had to be approved by two-thirds of both houses of the next legislature and then submitted to the people for ratification. Tennessee Constitution (1834), Art. XI, sec. 3.

9. According to Mathews, *Americanisms,* I, 280, "something hidden or sinister."

10. Tennessee Constitution (1834), Art. II, sec. 31.

11. A commentary on the trustworthiness of those who presume to predict the future is found in Cicero, *De Devinatione* II, xxiv; "I wonder that a soothsayer doesn't laugh whenever he sees another soothsayer." Bergen Evans, *Dictionary of Quotations* (New York, 1968), 561.

12. See Speech at Columbus, October 4, 1861, and Speech at Nashville, May 12, 1862, *Johnson Papers,* V, 19-20, 384.

13. Johnson had first suggested this "congenial clime" solution as early as 1845. See Speech on the Admission of Texas and Other Matters, January 21, 1854, *ibid.*, I, 205.

14. Napoleon III of France had recently proclaimed Archduke Ferdinand Maximilian (1832-1867), brother of Austrian Emperor Francis Joseph, emperor of Mexico. Arriving in June, 1864, Maximilian, though supported by French armies and Mexican exiles, failed to capture popular support and, after the French withdrawal in 1866, was executed the following June. *Webster's Biographical Dictionary.*

15. As state senator, Johnson in October, 1842, had introduced his "white basis" apportionment resolution, proposing that congressional redistricting be based on the "voting population, without any regard to three fifths of negro population." Although the proposal never had a hearing in the legislature, it was an issue in the Whig arsenal during his first gubernatorial campaign. *Johnson Papers,* I, 85-86; II, 160, 163n.

16. Gustavus A. Henry, Johnson's opponent in 1853, was allegedly a descendant of Patrick Henry.

17. The fate of this prosperous Phoenician port, devastated by Alexander the Great after a seven-month siege in 332. B. C., made a lasting impression upon contemporaries and subsequent generations. Charles F. Pfeiffer, and others, eds., *Wycliffe Bible Encyclopedia* (2 vols., Chicago, 1975), II, 1753-54.

18. Acts 12:22-23.

19. A favorite Johnson couplet which continues to elude identification.

20. An incident first described in Remarks to the Third Minnesota Regiment, April 23, 1862, *Johnson Papers,* V, 327; for Clayton, see *ibid.,* 328*n.*

21. A phrase occurring in Irish orator John P. Curran's defense of his compatriot Archibald H. Rowan on trial for libel in the fight for Irish Emancipation. He who "touches

the sacred soil of Britain . . . stands redeemed, regenerated, and disenthralled by the irresistible genius of UNIVERSAL EMANCIPATION." Thomas Davis, ed., *The Speeches of John Philpot Curran* (London, 1847), 182.

22. Found originally in Frederick Marryat's *Jacob Faithful* (1834) and later used in Dickens' *David Copperfield,* this call for unity was by now an established Johnson cliché. See *Johnson Papers,* V, 386n.

23. Another of the governor's favorites, this comes from Byron, *The Giaour,* ll, 123-26. See *ibid.,* 561n.

24. For John Bell, Andrew and Edwin Ewing, and John Overton, see *ibid.,* I, 206*n,* 534*n;* II, 340*n;* V, 398*n.*

25. The source of this aphorism, highly favored by Johnson, has not been found.

26. Historians disagree regarding this point. While no one contends that the breakup of plantations would increase productivity, Ransom and Sutch insist that subdivision *per se* had no detrimental effects. Fogel and Engerman, however, marshal statistics which uphold the traditional argument that large antebellum farms were more efficient. Roger L. Ransom and Richard Sutch, *One Kind of Freedom: The Economic Consequences of Emancipation* (Cambridge, 1977), 73-77; Robert W. Fogel and Stanley L. Engerman, *Time on the Cross* (2 vols., Boston, 1974), I, 192-94, 234-37.

27. The "friend behind" could have been any one of the three speakers, Joseph Fowler, comptroller, Col. Richard M. Edwards, or Capt. Ezra C. Hatton, who preceded him.

28. Four resolutions were adopted, pledging allegiance to the Federal government, pressing for "permanent reestablishment of civil government" beginning with a constitutional convention, identifying the "unmitigated evil" slavery as the "cause of all our troubles," and urging "immediate and universal emancipation."

From James B. Bingham

Bulletin Office, Memphis,
January 22d, 1863 [1864]

Hon. Andrew Johnson, Military Governor of Tennessee:

If President Lincoln's amnesty plan is to be carried out, *how* and *when* are we to commence? We impatiently await your answer.[1]

J. B. Bingham

Memphis *Bulletin,* January 30, 1864.

1. Johnson's reply, dated January 27, reads as follows: "I have heard from Washington, and will send an answer in full in three days. Also, will send a Proclamation in regard to Reorganization." Memphis *Bulletin*, January 30, 1864.

From John A. Brown and Mortimer L. Day[1]

Jeffersonvil, Ind. January, 22'ond/63 [1864].

Hon. Gov Andrew Johnson,

Sir we the undersign desireous of going to our homes do hereby petition to you for that purpous. We have learned that some ben going home but on what terms we have not yet learned, you would oblige us very much if you would let us know upon what terms we can go hom[.] It has been four months since we came across the river. we left the Armey in August last with the exspectation of getting [to] go home,

Our homes are in west Tennessee, Madison Conty. Athogh we have no simpthy for the southern Armey, we do not wish to join the fedeal Armey, knowing that if we were everer captured, that it would go very hard with us. We do not wish to go home to remane long. We would exspect to return north again[.]

If you will give us very much.

J A Brown M. L. Day

Address M. L. Day, Jeffersonville, Ind.

ALS (Brown?), DLC-JP.

1. Probably John A. [W?] Brown (b. *c*1843) and Mortimer L. Day (1839-*fl*1900), Madison County farmers and privates, Co. B, 6th Tenn. Inf. CSA, who deserted in August. 1863. Day took the oath and was sent North; by 1880 he was a "Retired Merchant" and at the turn of the century a minister and farmer. CSR, RG109, NA; 1880 Census, Tenn., Madison, Jackson, 48; (1900), 95th Enum. Dist., 7B.

From Daniel M. Bradford

January 23, 1864, Huntsville, Ala.; ALS, DLC-JP.

Seeking an appointment to his local board of trade, "an old soldier & loyal Citizen" asks Johnson to intervene on his behalf, citing his "long & faithful services to the United States."

From Theodore Tebow

January 23, 1864, Orleans, Ind.; ALS, DLC-JP.

A unionist and former Nashville ropemaker asks compensation for losses suffered in November, 1862, "when my rope walk was toren down by Soldirs, for fire wood," thus depriving him of a livelihood and forcing him to leave Tennessee.

From Ulysses S. Grant

Chattanooga Jany 24 1864

To Gov A Johnson

Can Stokes Cavalry[1] be sent Immediately to clear out the country between Carthage & Sparta of guerillas[?][2] The work is Important & nearly all the cavalry of this department is now in distant service[.][3]

U S Grant Maj Gen

Tel, DLC-JP.

1. Col. William B. Stokes, 5th Tenn.

2. As reported to Johnson, bands of guerrillas were operating in the area, and "Several of the most prominent citisens up there Say that if you will send me or some other man . . . to breake up those large bands . . . they will all turn out soon as they can be armed and keep them out of that country." Abraham E. Garrett to Johnson, January 2, 1864, Johnson Papers, LC.

3. A week later Stokes, with about 350 men, moved toward Sparta. During February and March he reported numerous engagements with Confederate guerrilla forces under Hughs, Hamilton, Ferguson, Carter, and Bledsoe in White, Overton, Putnam, and Jackson Counties of Middle Tennessee. *Tennesseans in the Civil War*, I, 331.

To Abraham Lincoln

Nashville Tenn. Jany 24th 1864.

A. Lincoln,
Prest. U.S.

I hope that it will be Consistent with the public interest for Gen'l. Burnside to be sent back to East Tennessee.[1] He is the man[.] the people want him. he will inspire more Confidence than any other man at this time. Will be in Washington soon.

Andrew Johnson Gov.

Tel, DLC-Lincoln Papers.

1. Burnside's IX Corps was in Virginia, assigned as an independent unit supporting the Army of the Potomac.

To Nathaniel G. Taylor

Nashville Jany 24th/64

Hon N. G. Taylor
Phila. Penna.

Dear Sir. x x x I am truly gratified at the interest you are manifesting in behalf of the impoverished and suffering of East Tennessee. Whatever, by your efforts, you may succeed in doing in their behalf, has my good wishes, and you shall meet with my hearty cooperation in transporting supplies to that section. We will soon have two Rail Roads running to Stevenson,[1] and the Road from Chattanooga to Knoxville is approaching a state of completion,[2] and when these are completed I think we will have ample transportation to East Tennessee. x x x. If you conclude to send anything—in the way of supplies—to E Tennessee, and will give me due notice of it, I'll see that it reaches its destination from this point (Nashville)[3]

I am Respy Andrew Johnson[4]

Copy of extracts, MHi.

1. The Memphis & Charleston and the Nashville & Chattanooga railroads.
2. The East Tennessee and Georgia.
3. A postscript reads: "There is no difficulty in sending supplies as far as Nashville—and it will be seen from Gov. Johnson's letter that he will see that all supplies delivered at that point shall be promptly forwarded to their destination in East Tennessee[.] N G Taylor"
4. The endorsement indicates that this is an "Extract from a letter of Gov A. Johnson to Col. Taylor."

From Citizens of East Tennessee

January 25, 1864, Salisbury, N. C.; LS, DLC-JP.

Writing from the Confederate prison where conditions are "horrible almost beyond description," thirty unionists beg Johnson to "exert all your power for our release." These civilians, some imprisoned for as long as twenty months, complain that they were not exchanged the previous year and "no reasons were assigned to us for it."

From Horace Maynard

Washington Jany 25 1864

To Gov Johnson

The Oath in the proclamation may be administered by the mil Gov the Military Commander of the Dept & by all persons designated by them for that purpose[.] loyal as well as disloyal should take the oath because it does not hurt them clears all questions as to their right to vote & swells the aggregate number who take it which is an important object[.][1] this is the prests reply to your question of the fourteenth[.][2] I intend to start for Nashville in the morning[.] Will go directly through stopping a few hours in Cincinnati where a dispatch will reach me[.][3]

Horace Maynard

Tel, DLC-JP; RPB.

1. Up to this point in the original draft in Brown University Library, the handwriting is Lincoln's; the remainder is in Maynard's hand.
2. See Letter to Horace Maynard, January 14, 1864.
3. Written by the President and appended to the original is the following: "Please send the above as public business. A. Lincoln"

From L. Mino Bentley

January 26, 1864, Clarksville; ALS, DLC-JP.

Former state legislator, "A very poor Man, willing to work" but lacking "the physical strength," asks the governor's influence "to get permission to open a small trade Store & Confectionary at Columbia or Pulaski" where there are businessmen "less loyal than I am."

To James B. Bingham

State of Tennessee, Executive Department.
Nashville, Jan. 26, 1864.

To James B. Bingham, Esq., Shelby County, Tennessee:

Sir:—You are hereby authorized and empowered, to open and hold the election for county officers in the county of Shelby in pursuance of the proclamation from this department, dated January 26, 1864, and to take other steps necessary to carry out the same, and make due return thereof to the office of the Secretary of State.

I am, respectfully,
Andrew Johnson Military Gov.

Memphis *Bulletin,* March 3, 1864.

Proclamation Ordering Elections[1]

Nashville, January 26, 1864.

WHEREAS, in consequence of the disloyalty of a large majority of the persons filling the offices established by the constitution and laws of Tennessee, and of the majority of the people of the State, and as part of the legitimate fruits of secession and rebellion against the Government of the United States, the people of Tennessee have been deprived for nearly three years of all free, regular and legitimate civil government, and they are now without a Governor chosen in the ordinary way, Legislature, Representation in the Congress of the United States, and without Courts, Judges, Chancellors and the various legitimately authorized county officers.

And whereas, it is believed that a majority of the people of the State are ready and desire to return to their allegiance to the Government of the United States, and to re-organize and restore the State Government to the exercise of its rightful functions, as a State of the American Union, under the Constitution of the United States, and as an initiatory step in such re-organization and restoration, it is determined to open and hold an election on the First Saturday in March next, in the various precincts, districts, or wherever it is practicable so to do, in the respective counties of the State as prescribed by the Laws and Constitution of the State, to wit: Justices of the Peace, Sheriffs, Constables, Trustees, Circuit and County Court Clerks, Registers and Tax Collectors.

Now, therefore, in virtue of the authority vested in me, and for the purpose of bringing the State of Tennessee within the provisions of the Constitution of the United States, which guarantees to each State a Republican form of Government, I do order said elections to be holden in the various counties on the First Saturday in March next, for the officers aforesaid and none other.

But, in as much as these elections are ordered in the State of Tennessee, as a State of the Union under the Federal Constitution, it is not expected that the enemies of the United States will propose to vote, nor is it intended that they be permitted to vote, or hold office.

And in the midst of so much disloyalty and hostility as have existed among the people of this State, towards the Government of the United States, and in order to secure the votes of its friends, and exclude those of its enemies, I have deemed it proper to make known the requisite qualifications of the electors at said elections. To entitle any person to the privilege of voting, he must be a free white man; of the age of twenty-one years, being a citizen of the United States, and a citizen of the county, where he may offer his vote, six months preceding the day of election, and a competent witness in any court of justice of the State, by the laws thereof against a white man, and not having been convicted of bribery, or the offer to bribe, of larceny, or any other offence declared infamous by the laws of the State, unless he has been restored to citizenship in the mode pointed out by law. And he must take and subscribe, before the Judges of the Election, the following oath:

I solemnly swear, that I will hence forth support the Constitution of the United States and defend it against the assaults of all its enemies; that I will hereafter be, and conduct myself as a true and faithful citizen of the United States, freely and voluntarily claiming to be subject to all the duties, and obligations, and entitled to all the rights and privileges of such citizenship; that I ardently desire the suppression of the present insurrection and rebellion against the Government of the United States, the success of its armies and the defeat of all those who oppose them, and that the Constitution of the United States, and all laws and proclamations, made in pursuance thereof, may be speedily and permanently established and enforced over all the people, States and Territories thereof; and further, that I will hereafter heartily aid and assist all loyal people in the accomplishment of these results. So help me God.

And all the Judges, officers, and persons holding the election, before entering upon their respective duties, in addition to the oath now required by the Laws of the State, shall take and subscribe the same oath, and also that they will permit no one to vote who has not taken and subscribed the oath above set forth, or refuses to do so.

The Provisions of the Code, in regard to Inspectors or Judges of Election is as follows.

SEC. 841. The County Court, at the session next preceding the day of election, shall appoint three Inspectors or Judges for each voting place to superintend the election.

SEC. 842. If the County Court fail to make the appointment, or any person appointed refuse to serve, the sheriff, with the advice of three Justices of the Peace, or if none be present, three respectable Freeholders, shall, before the beginning of the election appoint said Inspectors or Judges.

SEC. 843. If the Sheriff, or other officer, whose duty it is to attend at a particular place of voting, under the foregoing provisions, fail to attend, any Justice of the Peace present, or if no Justice of the Peace be present, any three freeholders may perform the duties prescribed by the preceding section, or in case of necessity, may act as officers or inspectors.

Now, whereas, in many of the counties there are no County Courts, Sheriffs or Justices of the Peace, and in others, the persons now and heretofore filling these offices are disloyal, and therefore disqualified, in all such counties some respectable citizen of the county will be appointed to hold said elections, appoint judges, clerks and other officers, either by himself or his deputies, and administer the oath to such officers, and receive the votes and make due returns thereof to the office of Secretary of State. All other steps will be taken, looking to the election of the other officers, Federal and State, as soon as practicable.

In testimony whereof, I, ANDREW JOHNSON Military Governor of the State of Tennessee do hereunto set my hand, and cause the Great Seal of the State to be affixed at this Department on the 26th day of January, A.D, 1864.

By the Governor: Andrew Johnson
Edward H. East, Secretary of State

Nashville *Union,* January 27, 1864; DLC-JP5.

1. Responding to the crucial need for local officers, Johnson planned county elections for March 5. Apprehensive that Lincoln's proclamation and amnesty oath of December 8, enfranchising ex-Confederates who subscribed to the oath, would return local control to those who had fostered rebellion, the governor took steps to establish a more stringent test of loyalty, incorporating in this proclamation a new oath. Hall, *Military Governor,* 114-18; Maslowski, *Treason Must Be Made Odious,* 86-87; see also Letter to Horace Maynard, January 14, 1864.

Notice Concerning Pardon and Amnesty

Nashville, Tenn, Jan. 27, 1864.

A book[1] wherein to record the taking of the oath prescribed in the Proclamation of the President of the United States, of the 8th of December, 1863, by such persons in this vicinity desiring pardon and amnesty, as are entitled to take said oath, is in the custody of Edward R. Campbell, Commissioner,[2] at the Federal Court room at the Capitol in Nashville, Tennessee, who is authorized to administer said oath to such persons, and who is required to give to such persons requesting it a certificate in the following form:

"I do hereby certify that on the ______ day of ______, 186 , at ________, the oath prescribed by the President of the United States in his Proclamation of December 8, 1863, was duly taken, subscribed, and made matter of record by ________, of ________ county. The same being No. , of the book of said county."

Said certificate shall be, until some other mode of proof shall be authoritatively provided, sufficient evidence of the facts certified to entitle the rightful holder to the benefits as promised in said proclamation. Books will be opened at other points in the State, and persons authorized to administer said oath, at an early day, who will return to the office of the Secretary of State said registered oath for permanent preservation.

Andrew Johnson,
Military Governor.

Nashville *Press,* February 2, 1864; Nashville *Union,* January 29, 1864.

1. Lincoln had sent with Judge John S. Brien "a blank book and some other blanks to facilitate the taking of the oath," which the judge had delivered to the governor on the 25th, along with the President's instructions. Basler, *Works of Lincoln,* VII, 130.

2. Edward R. Campbell (*c*1843-*fl*1892), a Tennessee native, was U. S. district court clerk for more than a quarter of a century (*c*1864-*c*1892?). 1880 Census, Tenn., Davidson, 15th Dist., 17; Nashville city directories (1865-92), *passim.*

From Zwinglius C. Graves[1]

Winchester Jan. 28th 1864

A Johnson
Military Govr. of Tenn.
Dr. Sir.

I addressed you yesterday by Telegraph informing you that a Negro man by name of Marcus Combs[2] now living in Nashville came to my house yesterday accompanied by some soldiers who belong to the command of Col. Jas S Selfnage[3] of the 46 Pa. Vol. and demanded a Negro girl belonging to me, aged 13 years[.] This Negro Marcus Combs claims to be the father of the girl. This negro man Marcus formaly belong to me and the community demanded of me to sell him out of the place for theft & other mis conduct which would have put a free man into our penitentiary. Such is the character of the Negro. Now he brings a verbal order from you to the Col Selfnage commanding the Post at Dechard Depot (so the Col. informs me that the girl is to be delivered up to him) and I assure you, that I am a good loyal Citizen of Tenn, having taken the oath of allegiance at the earliest day possible for me, and received a Guarantee of Protection signed by yourself & Major Gen. Rosecrans, for all my property both real & personal[.]

Now with this statement of facts before you, I would most respectfully petition you to inform me either by mail or Telegraph immediately (for the case is very urgent) whether the Negro girl is protected by the papers I hold? Whether Col. Selfnage has a right to take the property from me without given me a voucher for the same as he is commanded to do by yourself & Gen Rosecrans in the protection papers given to me at the time I took the oath of allegiance? If you wish any further information in relation to my self and the case I present before you inquire of W. P. Marks[4] who is in a store on Union St. & he can definitely give it. I wish to be governed by the law in the matter for the sincere desire of my heart is to be a law abiding citizen.

As such I petition to you as my Gov. for instructions in the case, assuring you I shall remain what I always have been your supporter & well wisher, if you will see that justice is done in this matter.[5]

Most Respectfully your Obt. Serv.
Z. C. Graves
Pres. of Mary Sharp Coll.

ALS, DLC-JP.

1. Zwinglius C. Graves (1816-1902), Vermont-born brother of Baptist minister and editor James R. Graves, founded the Kingsville Academy in Ohio, serving as president for twelve years, before coming in 1850 to Winchester as founding president of Mary Sharp College, where he remained until 1889. 1860 Census, Tenn., Franklin, 1st Dist., 14; Thomas F. Rhoton, History of Franklin County, Tennessee (M. A. thesis, University of Tennessee, 1941), 53; Raymond A. Finney, History of Private Educational Institutions of

Franklin County, Tennessee (M. A. thesis, University of Tennessee, 1939), 28; *Goodspeed's Franklin*, 826-27.

2. He is probably the male mulatto (b. *c*1821) who had belonged to Graves on the eve of the war. 1860 Slave Schedule, Tenn., Franklin, 1st Dist., 5; see also Graves to Johnson, January 27, 1864 Johnson Papers, LC.

3. James L. Selfridge (1824-1887) was a Philadelphia clerk and businessman until moving in 1857 to Bethlehem, where he engaged in coal, iron, and real estate businesses. Commissioned colonel, 46th Pa. Inf., by Governor Curtin in September, 1861, he was promoted brigadier in 1865. After the war he served as assessor of internal revenue (1865-66) and as chief clerk in the House of Representatives (1868). Appointed health officer of Philadelphia (1882), he ran unsuccessfully for political office. Bethlehem *Daily Times,* May 21, 1887; Heitman, *Register,* I, 873.

4. Warren P. Marks (*c*1820-1877), New York-born Nashville publisher worth $38,000 on the eve of the war, was later a mathematics professor at Mary Sharp. Alderman and mayor of Edgefield (1872), he was also superintendent of schools. 1860 Census, Tenn., Davidson, Edgefield, 29; Nashville *American,* April 4, 1877; *Haddock's Directory of Nashville* (1877), 250.

5. In justifying his actions, Selfridge reported that Combs claimed the child was "born free," and further asserted that Graves "was a rebel until July 23d 63 when he took the oath— his family are now notoriously rebels[.]" Selfridge to Johnson, January 27, 1864, Johnson Papers, LC.

Authorization to Recruit

Adjutant Genl. Office
Nashville January 28th 1864

Capt. E. S. Williams[1]
71st O. V. Inft.
Captain

By virtue of the Authority in me vested by the Secretary of War I do hereby authorize you to recruit a Regiment of men to serve as Mounted Infantry in the State of Tennessee and to be mustered in the service of the United States for the term of twelve months—

The men so enlisted will rendezvous at Carthage Tenn. and such other points as may be designated from this office and will be under your Command—

Officers of the Quartermasters and Commissary Departments are requested to furnish you with the necessary Clothing, transportation and Subsistance[.]

So soon as you have enlisted the minimum number of men required for a Company they will be mustered into the United States Service and the Company officers Commissioned—

This authority to expire on the first day of May 1864—

You will make triplicate enlistment papers for all men enlisted—and enclose a monthly report to this office—and in other respects will conform Strictly to recruiting Regulations[.]

Andrew Johnson
Milt. Gov. Tennessee

LB copy, T-RG21, Adj. Gen's Papers.

1. Elihu S. Williams (1835-1903), native of New Carlyle, Ohio, studied at Antioch College and in Dayton and was admitted to the bar at Troy in 1861. He entered the service as a private (1861) and rose to captain, commanding the military post at Carthage (February, 1863). Remaining after the war, he married and served in the Tennessee house (1867-69) before returning to Troy (1875) where he practiced and was elected twice to Congress (1887-91) as a Republican. Pension file, RG15, NA; *BDAC,* 1819; McBride and Robison, *Biographical Directory,* II, 979-80.

From Cyrus A. Oakes[1]

Chicamauga Valley, Jan 30th/64
Camp of the 84th Ind Vol" Inft

Gov" Andrew Johnson

please Send me 100 copies of President Lincolns Amnesty proclamation. our Division the 1st of the 4th Corps' is now in front and I want to Supply our boys, who go on picket with the Proclamation, hoping thereby to do all the good I can. Desertions from the Enemy are frequent, 8 men belonging to one Company from Arkansas, Just passed my door. they Say our men will all take advantage of the Presidents Proclamation.

Very Respectfully Your obedient Servant
Sergt" Cyrus. A. Oakes
Company C" 84th Ind" Vol Infantry

ALS, DLC-JP.

1. Cyrus A. Oakes (1843-1918), Wayne County, Indiana, farmer, enlisted in July, 1862, as private, rising to 1st lieutenant, Co. C, 84th Ind. Inf., was wounded in May, 1864, and discharged in June. After the war, he was a journalist, residing in Chicago. Pension file, RG15, NA; CSR, RG94, NA.

From Robert Johnson[1]

Nashville Tennessee
February 1864

To, His Excellency, Andrew Johnson,
Brig. Gen'l & Military Governor,
of the State of Tennessee,
Governor,

By an order of the Secretary of War, of the United States, dated Washington, D.C. War Department, February 27th 1862, I was "authorized to raise in the State of Tennessee, one Regiment of Volunteer Infantry, to Serve for three years, or the war, of which" I was "appointed the Colonel." The Regiment to be, "Organized as prescribed and provided for, by the Act of Congress, approved July 22nd 1861, to authorize the employment of Volunteers &c."[2]

On the first day of March 1862, at Washington D. C. by Lieutenant John Elwood,[3] U. S. A. Mustering Officer; I was regularly mustered into the Service of the United States, as Colonel of the Fourth Regiment Tennessee Volunteer Infantry, U. S. A.— Said muster to date from the 28th day of February 1862. I at once proceeded to organize the Said Regiment, and had it in the field in a Short time thereafter:

On the Seventh day of August 1862 an order issued from the War Department, addressed to your Excellency, as Military Governor of the State of Tennessee, authorizing the changing of the Fourth Regiment Tennessee Volunteer Infantry, into a Regiment of Cavalry, the Same to be organized as prescribed by the Act of Congress, approved July 17th 1862, "to amend the act calling forth the militia"[.][4]

In pursuance of Said order; at Camp Dennison, Ohio, on the 6th day of December 1862, the Fourth Regiment Tennessee Volunteer Infantry, was regularly mustered out, as Infantry; and Mustered in as the First Regiment Tennessee Cavalry, by Lieutenant Robt. S. Smith,[5] U. S. A. Mustering Officer—the Said musters to date from November First 1862—and on First day of November 1862, your Excellency commissioned me as, Colonel, of the Said First Regiment Tennessee Cavalry[.][6]

By Special Field Order No 136 Extract VIII, dated Head Quarters Department of the Cumberland, Murfreesboro' Tenn—May 19th 1863,[7] I was temporarily relieved from duty with my Regiment, for the purpose of organizing, under your direction, a Brigade of Tennessee Cavalry—And as the work of organizing Tennessee Cavalry, for the present at least, is about completed,—I most respectfully tender you, for reasons, purely of a private nature, this, my resignation, as Colonel of the First Regiment Tennessee Cavalry, trusting that the Same be accepted, and forwarded to Major General George H. Thomas, Commanding the Department of the Cumberland with the recommendation, that he approve[.]

I am Governor with great respect your Ob't Serv't
Robert Johnson
Col 1st Reg't Tenn Cavalry

ALS, DLC-JP.

1. For Robert's original offer to resign, see Letter from Robert Johnson, November 17, 1863.

2. Edwin M. Stanton to Robert Johnson, February 27, 1862, Johnson Papers, LC.

3. John Elwood (d. 1862), Ohio-born Kentuckian, was appointed 2nd lieutenant, 5th U. S. Inf., in May, 1857. Detailed as mustering officer in Washington in July, 1861, he was a year later promoted to captain to serve on mustering and disbursing duty in New York City. In October, 1862, he was arrested on charges of "conspiring to defraud the government" by collecting "fraudulent claims" and "corruptly issuing money from claim agents and from his clerks to which he was not entitled." Early in December he committed suicide. ACP Branch, RG94, NA; Powell, *Army List,* 300.

4. See Edward D. Townsend to Andrew Johnson, August 7, 1862, Johnson Papers, LC.

5. Probably Robert S. Smith of Ohio, 1st Lieutenant, 2nd U. S. Cav. (1861), captain (1863), who resigned in January, 1865. Powell, *Army List,* 597.

6. Not found.

7. Special Field Orders, Dept. of the Cumberland, RG94, NA.

From Edwin H. Ewing

[Nashville, February 1, 1864]

Gov. Andrew Johnson:

Sir: I saw, a day or two since, in the newspapers a proclamation, purporting to be issued by you, as Military Governor of Tennessee, requiring a new oath to be taken as a condition precedent to voting at the March election.[1] As a citizen of Tennessee, and of the United States, I feel some interest in regard to this matter and, both for my own sake and that of the public, beg leave, with all proper respect, to ask a few questions, to which I hope a public answer will be given.

By a late proclamation of Mr Lincoln, commonly called the Amnesty Proclamation,[2] a certain oath is prescribed, to be taken by the citizens of Tennessee among others, upon the taking of which those who have been in rebellion are to be restored to all of their civil personal rights as citizens of Tennessee and of the United States. As the right of voting at elections is one of these civil personal rights, I had supposed that upon taking Mr. Lincoln's oath persons otherwise qualified under the Constitution of Tennessee, would be completely qualified, without doing anything more to exercise the privilege of voting. Then, I would ask, will it be necessary also, before a person is allowed to vote, that he should take the oath prescribed by you? If this be so, then the taking of Mr. Lincoln's oath does not restore one who has been in rebellion to all of his civil personal rights, one of which is the right of voting.

If the oath prescribed by you is necessary to be taken, I would respectfully ask upon what authority it is founded? If it is founded upon your civil authority, I should like a reference to the book and page where it is to be found. If it is founded upon your Military authority, I should like an explanation how Mr. Lincoln, who is the highest Military authority known to our laws, and from whom you derive all of your Military powers, can have given such seemingly contradictory orders?

Again: I would ask, will a person who has taken the oath of amnesty, and who is otherwise qualified as a voter under the Constitution of Tennessee, be refused his vote unless he has taken or shall take the oath required by you?

If these questions are answered satisfactorily it will be a gratification to the public; if they are not answered, it will be fair to presume that no satisfactory answer, or answer consistent with your proclamation, can be given. Your object I presume is that there should be a full and fair expression of the will of the loyal people of Tennessee at the polls. Such is my object. Mr Lincoln has said that he is *prima facie* a loyal man who shall take his oath. If Mr. Lincoln has revoked this, it is time the public should be informed of it.[3]

Yours, with respect,
Edwin H. Ewing.

Nashville *Press,* February 2, 1864.

1. See Proclamation Ordering Elections, January 26, 1864.
2. December 8, 1863.
3. The governor made no effort to reply to this "rhetorical" letter. Perhaps the defense of Johnson's oath—which occupied the first issues of the Nashville *Times and True Union* when it began publication late in February—may be regarded as a response to the *Press* and Ewing's attacks on Johnson's requirement.

From Lewis P. Firey[1]

LEGISLATURE OF MARYLAND,
Senate.
Annapolis, Feb. 1st 1864

His Excellency,
Andrew Johnson,
Governor of Tennessee, Dear Sir, Enclosed, please find a Preamble & Resolutions,[2] which I propose to cast like bread upon the waters of sectional strife, that it may be seen after many days. These Resolutions will I think, pass both Branches of the Legislature of Maryland, during the present week, & we desire to call the attention of the Border States especially, to the importance of prompt, & concerted action, in favour of *Gradual Emancipation* in *the Rebel States*, with *Compensation* to *Loyal Owners for slaves*, or other property destroyed by the armies, and also the gradual removal of the black population from the South. This strikes us, as the most, safe, & practicable way of restoring the Union, upon a firm basis, and at the same time of gradually ridding the Country of the curse, and burden, of slavery. What says Tennessee, the home of Andrew Jackson, and of Andrew Johnson! Sir, you remember meeting me, for the first time, at the President's House, two years ago, and I told you I had predicted that you would be the next President of the United States. Now sir, I have made it the rule of my life, to flatter no man knowingly, and I will not do so now; yet I will repeat what I then said, that if *you will step forth now to pacify the country, as you then did, to defend it, your election is sure*. Mark it! Then Sir take your stand—with the great men of the past, for you are one of them,—in favour of Pacification, in the way proposed by such men as Clay, Jackson, Cass, Douglass, & Dickinson, and that is by Compromise, and Conciliation. The South will gladly accept the offer And it is perfectly idle, to think of restoring the Union, & the government in any other way. It was formed in this way, preserved through every crisis in this way, & by the help of God, *it will now be saved in this way.*

I have neither time, nor inclination to argue the point. But this I will say, & I beg you to remember it, for your success for the Presidency will depend upon it. *Hostilities will cease on or before the 22nd Feb. next*, & the entire restoration of the Union will take place in the manner *proposed in these Resolutions,* on or before the 4th day of July 1864. Pardon my presumption, but ask God for guidance, and you will then think I am pretty near right, and you will help me forward in this great work. God speed you sir, & you shall have the fervent prayers, & best wishes of a, *Friend*

Lewis P Firey

Gov Andrew Johnson.

ALS, DLC-JP.

1. Lewis P. Firey (b. *c*1830), a Washington County, Maryland, unionist legislator (1861) and state senator (1862-64), had introduced compromise resolutions on February 5, 1862, urging Congress to declare an armistice and meet with Jefferson Davis to discuss restoring the Union on the basis of the Crittenden Compromise. 1860 Census, Maryland, Washington, Clearspring Dist., 96; Thomas J. C. Williams, *A History of Washington County, Maryland* (2 vols., Hagerstown, 1906), I, 305-21 *passim,* 561.

2. The resolutions, accurately summarized in the body of this letter, suffered an overwhelming defeat in the Maryland senate. Baltimore *American and Commercial Advertiser,* February, 4, 9, 10, 1864.

From John W. Gorham

February 1, 1864, Clarksville; ALS, DLC-JP.

An old friend, seeking the governor's intercession in behalf of Dr. Kindred Wilson, a former Confederate soldier who has been sent as a prisoner to Nashville, observes that "the Country is in a bad fix the People demoralized, and growing More So every day North & South, East & West White & Black Men & Women. . . . Now it Seems to me that their is a sort of go betwean-doctering that might save the Country if we had some Great Man at the head of affairs. . . . I dont know any living Man that I would prefer to yourself as a fitten Man to bring this trouble to an end, you have the confidence of the Masses of the People, and even your enemys respect and acknowlede your Talents." He concludes: "I would be glad to See you at the Head of Affares with the Constitution in your Hands Just as it is *Written*[.]"

From Daniel B. Cliffe[1] *and Others*

Franklin Tennessee Feby 2—1864

To Andrew Johnson Military Governor &c

Dear Sir

We respectfully ask you to obtain permission for Randal M. Gillespie[2] to take the oath of allegiance to the government of the United States under the amnesty proclamation of President Lincoln[.]

Mr. Gillespie is now in the Hospital at Louisville Ky in feeble health & a prisoner of war— we think his a proper case for the mercy of the government & that it can extend to him its clemency without risk— he is a poor man with a very dependent family—has a very delicate constitution & is predisposed to consumption & we think confinement in a Military Prison will cause his death— We have known Mr. Gillespie well for many years—as a peaceable-quiet-good Citizen & believe him to be truthful &

sincere in his professions— we understand & believe that he did not willingly enter the Rebel Army—but remained quietly at home until the Fall of 1862 when the retreat of the Federal Forces exposed Williamson County to the conscription & we are satisfied from our knowledge of the man & from letters from him recently—that his past experience & present convictions will make him in future a faithful & Loyal Citizen of the United States—

We address you directly because we think you know us to be true friends of the government of the United States—& that we will not knowingly or willingly do or permit anything to be done to its prejudice[.]

Very Respectfully— Dan B Cliffe
Frank Hardeman[3]
W. S. Campbell[4]

The undersigned—Father & wife of Randal M. Gillespie hereby state that we know that he entered the Rebel Army very much against his will & not until his name was entered upon the conscript Roll—& we earnestly pray that he be permitted to return home upon the within proposed terms—& we pledge ourselves that he will hereafter be entirely worthy of the confidence thus placed in him & prove in all respects a truly faithful & Loyal Citizen of the United States—

Mary R. Gillespie
George Gillespie[5]

ALS, DNA-RG249, Lets. Recd., File 140C (1864), Randall M. Gillespie.

1. Daniel B. Cliffe (1823-1913), wealthy Ohio-born doctor, as surgeon, 20th Tenn Inf., CSA, had embalmed the body of General Zollicoffer and accompanied it to Nashville. Shortly thereafter he became a unionist. Bowman, *Historic Williamson,* 106; 1860 Census, Tenn., Williamson, E. Subdiv., 8.

2. Randall M. Gillespie (*c*1829-*fl*1880), a private in Co. G, 11th Tenn. Cav., CSA, returned to his farm after the war. *Ibid.,* 117; (1880), 10th Dist., 3; *Tennesseans in the Civil War,* II, 169.

3. Franklin Hardeman (1815-1878), Williamson County native, prominent prewar Whig, and member of the Tennessee house (1847-49, 1851-53), had opposed seceession and remained a strong unionist. On the eve of the war his property, real and personal, was worth $62,000. A farmer, he was also a railroad promoter, serving as treasurer of the Tennessee and Alabama line. McBride and Robison, *Biographical Directory,* I, 329; Bowman, *Historic Williamson,* 71; 1860 Census, Tenn., Williamson, 1st Dist., 137.

4. William S. Campbell (1814-1878), native of Ireland, came to Franklin about 1839 and was cashier of the Planters' branch bank. After the war he was founding president of the National Bank of Franklin. *Ibid.*, 63; Louise G. Lynch, comp., *Bible Records of Williamson County, Tennessee* ([Franklin, Tenn.], 1970), 120.

5. Mary R. Gillespie (*c*1828-1877), Tennessee native, and George Gillespie (1787-1867), North Carolina-born Williamson County farmer with $24,500 in real and personal property. 1860 Census, Tenn., Williamson, 1st Dist., 116-17; Louise G. Lynch and Volenia W. Hays, comps., *Cemetery Records of Williamson County* (Franklin, Tenn., 1969), 67.

From John C. Gaut and David T. Patterson

Nashville Tennessee
February 4th 1864.

Gov. Andrew Johnston

Sir. We the undersigned Judges of the First & Fourth Judicial Circuits in the state of Tennessee, ask leave to State to you, that we discover upon reading the Acts of Congress of the United States; that the fifth Article of Section 5 of the Act Approved July 1862,[1] may subject our property to seizure and confiscation, because we accepted of our reelection to the office of Judges in said Judicial districts in the state of Tennessee, after the date of the pretended ordinance of Secession of the state. We were reelected & qualified before said act of Congress was aproved; and in fact we had no knowledge of the passage of the same until recently, such was the policy of the Rebel leaders, that we were not permitted to know but very litle of what was being done or had been done by the Congress of the Federal government.

Again by virtue of the Act of Congress, approved July 2nd 1862, Chap. 128, entitled an act to prescribe an oath of Office and for other purposes, we might hereafter be precluded from accepting or holding office under the United States Government. While we are not seeking office, nor expecting office under the Federal Government, we desire to have removed, if we can, every thing that may appear to place us in an unfriendly atitude to the U S. Government; not alone for our own individual benefit, but for our children. As before stated, we accepted of an reelection to said offices of Judges of the Circuit Courts, after the socalled ordinance of Secession of the state, not because, we desired to hold said offices while the authorities of the state were engaged in Rebelion; but after full consultation with the loyal Men of our respective Circuits, it was believed by many of them that the loyal citizens had been, and would be protected, to a considerable degree, by our reelections; because we had not, and would not prostitute the functions of our judicial positions, as other judges in other Circuits were doing, to cause loyal citizens to be indicted and prosecuted by the Grand Jurors for Treason to the So called Confederate States of America; because said Citizens were loyal to the Federal Government. We have tried to be loyal ourselves, and believed that it was not only the priviledge, but the duty, of all others to be loyal to the United States Government. As you are the Military Governor of our state, and as we have as yet, no representation in the Congress of the United States, we have thought it not improper to lay the foregoing statement of facts before you, and that probably, through you as the representative of the Federal Government in Tennessee, some Act of the Government might be extended to us to relieve us from the effects of said Acts of Congress above alluded to.[2] We are very respectfully

Your Obt. Servts
John C. Gaut.
David T. Patterson

ALS (Gaut), DLC-JP.

1. This section of the "Act to suppress Insurrection, to punish Treason and Rebellion, to seize and confiscate the Property of Rebels and For other Purposes," mandates that a "judge of any court," serving the Confederacy is subject to the property seizure specified in the act. *U. S. Statutes,* XII, 590.

2. Both men received presidential pardons on March 8, 1864, and in June Gaut was reappointed to the 4th circuit. Lincoln Papers, LC; Basler, *Works of Lincoln,* VII, 225; Nashville *Dispatch,* June 28, 1864.

From Robertson Topp[1]

Confidential

Memphis Feby 4th 1864.

Hon Andrew Johnson
Mily. Govr &c
D Sir

Since the commencement of hostilities between the North and South, I have been compelled, until very recently, to take up my residence in the State of Missi. that I might protect my interests in that State.

Whilst Memphis was under the control of the Confederates, my Agent and wife[2] for wild lands and town lots sold previous to the war, were compelled to take a very large amount of Confederate notes for the debts due me.

Regarding these notes as worthless if kept I employed Agents to invest it in cotton mostly in Sun Flower County Missi.

Through John C. Dyche[3] a citizen of that County I purchased 1280 bales[.] through J. H. Lawrence[4] another citizen I purchased 200 bales.

By some means or other, it has been ascertained that the cotton purchased by these agents was mine.

I have Seen a Letter addressed to a firm in this city, which leaves me no room to doubt, but that as soon as it was ascertained to belong to me, the military burned it, likewise, 205 bales of cotton raised on my own place in Bolivar County Missi[.]

In the spring of 1862 I had 359 bales burned on my place in Isaquena County Missi. In 1863, sixty seven bales in Bolivar County, all by soldiers instigated by Secessionists who were particularly hostile to me.

Very recently, a band of robbers styling themselves Soldiers, have broken open my houses, stolen my wearing apparel, money in my trunks, bed clothes, family supplies and carried off my mules—negro cloth and medicines worth over $2000.

In addition to all this these guerrilla bands have quartered on my places and are consuming my corn, hogs and cattle. The extent of the damage I have no means of knowing, as I dare not go on my own places.

Gen Grant has recently issued orders, commanding the military in their respective departments, to seize the property of secessionists and sympathizers and make good such losses.[5] My losses are so heavy, and on so large a scale as would seem to require a specific order.

I will go to Washington and try and get the Secretary of war to make a specific order, requiring General McPherson[6] to seize, on the Yazoo & tributaries, the cotton of rebels and sympathizers; sufficient, to restore to me that which has been burned—and to cover my other losses, which cannot fall short of five thousand dollars.

I will wait until I can hear from You.

If I can get Your assistance by letters to the Prest & Secretary of war, or by any suggestions you may be able to make, I shall be very greatly obliged.

Very Respectfully Robertson Topp

2161 bales cotton

N. B.

It is proper I should state, the cotton burned in Sun Flower county does not belong to me exclusively. It was purchased through me—but belongs to Capt Mitchell[7] of Illinois Mr Vance[8] of Kentucky and myself.

ALS, DLC-JP.

1. See *Johnson Papers,* II, 317*n.*

2. During the early years of the war, in an effort to protect his Mississippi property, Topp had lived in Bolivar County, returning to Memphis only when his Union sentiments imperilled his safety. The agent is unidentified, but Topp's wife, whom he married in 1837, was Elizabeth L. Vance (*c*1821-*fl*1890). Robertson Topp Papers (microfilm), Tennessee State Library and Archives; Sistler, *1850 Tenn. Census,* VI, 235; *Dow's Memphis Directory* (1890), 792; McBride and Robison, *Biographical Directory,* I, 731.

3. Probably John T. Dyche (b. *c*1814), a Georgia-born planter, who in 1850 lived in Monroe County in the eastern end of the state. By November, 1863, he was involved in cotton deals with Topp's brother-in-law. 1850 Census, Miss., Monroe, Western Dist., 146; Dyche to William Vance, November 15, 1863, General Corres., Topp Papers.

4. James H. Lawrence (*c*1834-*c*1878), native Tennessean, was a bookkeeper for a lumber yard. 1860 Census, Tenn., Shelby, Memphis, 2nd Ward, 40; Memphis city directories (1860-79), *passim.*

5. Grant's General Order No. 4, dated November 5, 1863, provided that an assessment was to be made upon secessionists of the neighborhood "for every dollar's worth of property taken from" Union citizens, "and the amount thus collected paid over to the sufferers." When the assessments could not be collected in money, "property useful to the Government may be taken at a fair valuation, and the amount paid in money by a disbursing officer of the Government." *OR,* Ser. 1, XXXI, Pt. III, 58.

6. James B. McPherson (1828-1864), Ohioan and West Point graduate (1853) who served in the corps of engineers before the war, was aide to Halleck, chief engineer for Grant, and commander of the XVII Corps at Vicksburg where he became brigadier in the regular army. Assigned the Army of the Tennessee in March, 1864, he was killed at Atlanta in July. Warner, *Generals in Blue,* 306-8.

7. Thomas D. Mitchell (*c*1823-*fl*1886), Pennsylvania-born bricklayer mustered into service as a second lieutenant in August, 1861, was promoted a year later to captain, 66th Ill. Inf., wounded at Corinth in December, 1862, and discharged at the end of his enlistment in December, 1864. After the war he was a mason, justice of the peace, notary,

and collector in Dayton, Ohio. CSR, RG94, NA; Pension file, RG15, NA; Dayton, Ohio, city directories (1865-71), *passim*.

8. William L. Vance (1815-1888) of Woodford County, Kentucky, and Memphis, was Topp's brother-in-law and a developer of South Memphis. Applying for permission to trade with the South using Confederate scrip "forced upon the union men of Kentucky, in exchange for supplies," he was refused by the President. On at least two occasions, he applied for trade permits. Lincoln to Vance, November 22, 1862, Basler, *Works of Lincoln*, V, 507; Johnson to Vance, April 24, 1865, Johnson Papers, LC; biographical data, Topp Papers; Keating, *Memphis*, I, 259.

From John W. Taylor[1]

Goshen Oldham Co Ky
Febra th 5./64

Mr: Andrew Johnston.
Dear Sir.
I take the upertunity to write you a vew lines to let you know that i am Bed fast and not able to get up and walk around in the House, but i hope that i will be able to get up again Soon. I was driven from my home last Christmas Night, and i tryed very hard to get to Nashville but it was in vain to get there as these infurnall Guerrillas was So Close after me, i had to get out of their way the best way that i Could[.] So i Came up hear into Kentuky for protection[.] The Rebles run me So fare up in to Ky that they Came within twenty Milles of Danville Ky. So you may well know that they were bound to hav me whether or not. I tore of all my Cloths by runing through the Mountians and timber, So when i got into Danville i was almost Naked. So when i got Some Cloths from a Soldier in Danville. I Came up hear with onley one Dollar, but that was not all, because i had on Soldiers Cloths that a Soldier gave me the Rebs up hear wanted To make me out a Deserter.

Mr Johnston you and my Father[2] have allways bin good frinds to gether, So i would like to hav you to Sent me Something to Show that i am a Cityzen because my Father and i hav both taken the oth that we would be loyal while Life last us, and So i Can not nor will not break that Oth let Come what will but i would like to be Safe. I am laying hear with both my feet frozen, i am not able to helep MySelf. My Doctor Bill and Board will both be very large. I will give you my Discription hight 5 feet 5 inches Eyes Blue hair Brown Age thirty year Compliction fair. Send it and you will oblige me very much[.]

Yours truly John W. Taylor

ALS, DLC-JP.

1. John W. Taylor (b. *c*1833) was a Greene County farmer. 1850 Census, Tenn., Greene, 9th Div., E. Dist., 298.

2. Jacob Taylor (b. *c*1798), Greene County blacksmith. *Ibid.*

From Martha Strang

February 6, 1864, Northwood, Ohio; ALS-DLC-JP.

Writing on behalf of her family, a teacher inquires whether there are "any openings in or around Nashville or any other suitable place where we might start a school" for "either white or black scholars or both." Is there "any confiscated rebel property" which "could be applied to this purpose for a time till a school would be self-sustaining." Her father [David Strang], a Presbyterian minister obliged to flee Blount County in 1861, has since worked for the Union cause in Ohio.

From James B. Bingham

February 7, 1864, Memphis; ALS, DLC-JP.

Editor of Memphis *Bulletin,* reporting the organization of a loyal regiment and preparations for holding state elections in March, urges Johnson and other unionists to come to "a grand mass meeting for Reorganization and Reconstruction" on February 22. "The copperheads here are awful uneasy about your oath. They shall all take it, or not vote. They may take their own course." As for Lincoln's amnesty oath, it "ought to be administered by some *true* man of our side. Appoint me and I will see that it is carried out all right."

From James F. Kirk[1]

Jessamin Co Ky Feb 7th 1864

Govner Johnson

Dear Sir I take this opportunity to in form you that from the devatating bands of the armies in East Tenn I have been Compelled to remove my family to Kentucky and had to leave evy thing I had in the world[.] this horible war has completely broke me up and under the circumstances it is imposible for me to pay you for the property I contracted for in Greenvill[.][2] therefore I wish to let you have it back with the improvements I put on it, I covered the house built a kitchen and back porch built a stone fence part of the way along the creek put a good fence round the let [left] end had new panel doors made to the front of the house and new shuters to the shop & a petition [partition] in the house all of which cost me a hundred dollars and my acount for work for your family is about sixty dollars and I am willing to give up the title bond and take back my notes[.] if you are willing to aceed to this proposition you will please write to me and I will send the title bond and the[n] you can send me my notes[.] direct your letter to Jessamin Co Kentucky Keen P.O. please write soon and oblige your un werty friend[.]

James, F. Kirk

if the proposition is acseted I will Send a reciept in full of all accounts[.]

ALS, DLC-JP.

1. For Kirk (1839-1920), a Greeneville boot and shoemaker, see *Johnson Papers*, III, 293*n*; Reynolds, *Greene County Cemeteries*, 267.

2. The original transaction, secured in a real estate bond, dated August 20, 1859, called for full payment ($500) one year later. Apparently Johnson had been "carrying him," even before the beginning of hostilities. *Johnson Papers,* III, 292-93.

From Hunter Brooke

February 8, 1864, Chattanooga; ALS, DLC-JP.

Judge advocate, Department of the Cumberland, advises that the military commission holding court in Clarksville has been dissolved. Inasmuch as "most of the business before them has been such as properly belongs to the State tribunals," Gen. George H. Thomas "hopes that you will be able to establish proper State officers there . . . fully able to dispose of all such business, and be far more acceptable to the people. All military cases can be sent to Nashville."

From Edmund R. Glenn[1]

Oak Hall Near Urbana Ohio
Febuary 8th 1864

Hon Andrew Johnston
Respected Sir

I trust you will pardon the freedom I take in thus adressing you. I want to make a few enquiries about your State and I do not know who else to enquire of, and first will Tennessee be a Free State hereafter, if so Could good improved farmes be purchased within 10 to 15 Miles of Nashville, or good farming lands near some thriving town & Good Markets, if so at about what price do you suppose they could be purchased for 1/2 cash and ballance in say 1, 2, 3, years. I mean Improved farms. I live in a Good Region of Ohio, Good farming & Stock farms and good Markets & Roads &c but it is too cold[.] we have to feed six months of the year. Our peach trees are all killed by the freeze[.] it was 20°. Below Zero for near a week.

If Good Farms Could be procured in your State on reasonable terms I think I might bring out a small Colony worth from 5 to 30 thousand Dollars each all Union Republicans.

I am a Kentuckuan by birth But always antislavery, or in other words I am an Old Abolationist of the Chase, Hale, & Gidings stripe.[2] We are all Farmers Raisers of Wheat, Corn, Barly, Horses, Mules Cattle & Hoggs &c and wish Good soil and *well watered.*

If you can spare so much time from your noble *work* in Behalf of Liberty for the *White Man* as well as for the Black, I have seen the opressions of the White Man even in Kentucky. I have plenty of relatives in the Confederate Armies, in Virginia, Carolinas, Missouri & Texas. if you are too busy or Uninformed on this subject please hand this to some one on whoom *you* and I can depend, and if Reports are Favourable I will visit your State as soon as practable.

Yours respectfully Edmund Randolph Glenn

Hon A. Johnston Gov &c

ALS, DLC-JP.

1. Edmund R. Glenn (b. *c*1805), Kentucky-born Ohio farmer, held personal property worth $25,937 and real estate valued at $15,750 on the eve of the war. 1860 Census, Ohio, Champaign, Urbana Township, 122.

2. For Salmon P. Chase, John P. Hale, and Joshua R. Giddings, see *Johnson Papers,* IV, 152*n*; I, 508*n*, 206*n*.

From George M. Stewart[1]

Near Fort Donelson
February 10th 1864

Governor Johsonn
Dear Sir
There is a gradeal of suffering of the Poor in a good many Locallities, the Nwstrn [Northwestern] R Road have foraged heavy for a Long ways on both Sides but thay havint reacht the main Corn regions that is Duck & Cumberland Rivers & those Corn rasors wont sell except at awful Pries & that in grean Backs & there is a still up running in the Neighborhood of Cumbrlin Citty about 21 miles below Clarksvill & that make a 25 or 30 Dollrs worth of whiskey out of a barrel of Corn & he has a Large amont on hand & a Lage amont in juges at Lage figurs[.] now if that Still was stopt as all the rest has bin it would give a gradeal of Corn to fead, the Poor & if it Could be it ought to have th Prce of Corn regulated & those that hav maid to Let those that dont have [and] are a seffering hav at a far Pries. There is a Plenty of men that helpt get up the rebelion & Promised men that if they would go into the servis there wives & Children should hav a plenty that is a Litting them seffer[.] in be half of those wimin & children Pleas do what you Can— I under stand that there is a nother still house abilding be Low Clarksville & hav ingaged Corn at Large figers & if there was a stop to all disstilling of grain it would help a gradeal.

I send you a Little slip from Capn Lewis[2] to Let you know that I am Loyal & I was inducted in General Rusous office on Decr 31, 63, as an imploye of the united states[.]

Yors Truly
G. M. Stewart

I Dont want my name used as to the Stillhouses[.]

ALS, DLC-JP.

1. Probably George M. Stewart (*c*1810-*fl*1870), New York native and farm laborer who had come to Tennessee by way of South Carolina and Georgia. William P. Lyon to Stewart, December 5, 1862, Johnson Papers, LC; 1860 Census, Tenn., Stewart, 10th Dist., 148; (1870), 6th Dist., 3.

2. Neither "Capn Lewis" or the "Little slip" can be found.

From James B. Bingham

Memphis, Tenn. Feb. 11, 1864

Dear Governor: You will find in the *Bulletin* of to-day a full report of our first Emancipation triumph in Memphis.[1] For some weeks past a few of the more prominent Union men of our city have been consulting upon a plan or basis for a call for a grand mass meeting of the loyal men of West Tennessee. We finally agreed upon the call upon the back of this sheet.[2] Before it was published, however, Charles Kortrecht, Pitser Miller, I. M. Hill, B. D. Nabers, and a few others, got upon another call for a meeting of the loyal citizens. They published it in the copperhead paper here,[3] circulated it in every house, and tried to get upon a strong opposition to the oath prepared by *you,* contending that as it was more stringent than that prepared by *Lincoln, you* had exceeded your authority. This was their great card. We took no direct notice of their movement, but I posted our friends, and got them to appear at their meeting in force, and instead of carrying out their plans and adopting their resolutions, we substituted resolutions endorsing your oath, Emancipation and the call already put forth by ourselves! We were overwhelmingly in the ascendant, notwithstanding our copperhead Mayor[4] was expected to muster all the city officials! It was a great triumph. It is reported that they will make another attempt, but if they do we will meet them, if possible. What adds to our triumph is this, there was not a single Federal officer in attendance. These men exercise great influence, but none of them, except Tomeny, who was tendered the appointment of Assist. Special Agent of the Treasury, but who is not permitted to enter upon the discharge of his duties, were present. The fact is, the government has sent a very poor set down here to fill civil trusts,[5] and I beg, if you have any influence at Washington, that you will use it So as to prevent the Post office here being given to any one until we can advise you who will be most acceptable to the unconditional Union men. Some of my friends have spoken of me for the post, because newspaper business here is not so profitable as it was, and because it would not necessarily interfere with conducting the Bulletin; but if I can get along without losing money, I dont want to hold office under the government. All I ask is this. We are determined that if we have any influence to command it, none but good loyal unconditional Union men shall fill offices under the government; we dont want any more corrupt scoundrels like Yeatman[6] from Cincinnati, who has done the cause all the harm it is possible for him to do it, and whose whole object appears to be to put money in his pocket.

I have now issued commissions to responsible parties to hold elections as follows: Henry county, R. H. Todd; Weakly county, O. S. Stephenson; Gibson county, Robt. E. Bogle; Dyer, Wm. Wesson; Carroll county, John

Norman; Henderson county, J. B. Davis; Madison county, Judge John Reid; Benton county, (sent a blank to John Norman, in Carroll county to fill up with the best man;) OBion county, James Caldwell; Haywood, David A. Nunn; Lauderdale county, Green W. Carson; Tipton county, Wm. A. Turnage.[7] I have thus far struck off printed sheets of the Proclamation for the election, and furnished each man with copies for each precinct. I learn from Dr. Alston[8] and W. P. Bond,[9] who are here from Haywood to-day, that the rebel Richardson[10] has advised his friends in that county *to take any oath* that the Federals may prescribe, *but to see to it and control the election at all hazards.* They therefore asked my construction of your proclamation on the point as to whether a man should be voted for who had not taken your oath. "I decided that no votes ought to be polled for any one who had not taken your oath, and who was not known to be a loyal man." Perhaps I shall publish to that effect before the election takes place.

My regiment is making progress, notwithstanding the active opposition of Hurlbut and officers under him. I have already sent to you for a copy of the order from the War Department about subsisting the men. Please send it at once. Gen. Buckland,[11] now in command, has given me quarters and subsistence for my men until I can hear from you. I have some thirty or forty men sworn in—all citizens. The first Alabama regiment, composed of Tennesseeans,[12] are to be mustered out shortly. Their time is already out, and one of a company that has already been mustered out was arrested and put in the Irving Block[13] *because he went to see about joining in service in his own State.*— Hurlbut prevented Poston, of Haywood County, from accepting a position under your authority to me.[14] I have asked our friends in Haywood to recommend to me someone who will commence operations in that quarter. I believe we shall soon get up a company, and then it will be easier to get along than now.

We shall have hard work in this end of the State, on the Emancipation Issue, as I told you. We have fixed upon the 22d instant for a mass meeting. We need all the help in the shape of speakers that we can get. Your name is a tower of Strength. We can't get along without you. You must come, and I therefore ask you to telegraph me of your acceptance of the invitation. Send dispatch to me, care of T. H. Whipple,[15] Cairo. Invite Maynard, Taylor, Brownlow, Mercer, Fowler, Netherlands,[16] in fact any man in the United States that can make a few cheering words of the right sort for us on that occasion. I am working all day and night. I write all day, and if need be talk all night. The fact is, I have a big contract on hand,[17] and if I dont keep moving, something will go wrong. I can ill spare the time I take to write so long, but I shall be more than repaid if you will be with us on the 22d, and induce any who can speak to come with you. If you can think of any one whom you would like to come with you,—any Governor from other States, write for us and get him to come along. I don't know Gov. Morton. Please send him a letter on our behalf to induce him to come. I shall send an invitation to Gov. Yates,[18] of Illinois.

Thus far the skies are bright. We have triumphed over opposition, and the cause goes onward. I have made arrangements to hold one or two public meetings every week in different sections of the city, and I think we shall give a good account of ourselves on election day. We shall have elections pretty generally throughout our section, and I expect a fair vote of those whom the rebels have not run off to Dixie.

In conclusion permit me to thank you for the happy wording of the oath. Those who can't take it are disloyal. Let them make the most of it. They wont make much "kicking against the pricks." [19]

Yours in the fellowship of a good cause,

James B Bingham

ALS, DLC-JP.

1. Although copies of the *Bulletin* for this period are unavailable, an excerpt appears in the *Missouri Democrat* (St. Louis), February 15, 1864.

2. This "call," to consider restoration of the state and immediate emancipation, bore thirty-three signatures. Johnson Papers, LC.

3. The Memphis *Argus;* no copy of this issue is extant.

4. John Park (1812-1897), Irish-born Memphis merchant with $20,000 in real and $1,000 in personal property, was mayor from 1861 through 1866, except for the year 1864, when the military set aside his election on grounds of questionable loyalty, although he had taken the oath two years earlier. Currently he was an officer in a Democratic club. 1860 Census, Tenn., Shelby, Memphis, 8th Ward, 122; Memphis *Commercial Appeal,* August 8, 1897; Hooper, Memphis, 39-53 *passim*, 83, 192.

5. Probably treasury agents David G. Barnitz and his successor Thomas Yeatman, and Reuel Hough, who, although a resident prior to the war, was appointed to the board of trade and in late 1862 named surveyor of the port of Memphis. Barnitz, chosen in July as a special agent with duty on the lower Mississippi, was replaced at Memphis in October, 1862, by Yeatman who served until his resignation in the spring of 1864. Futrell, Federal Trade, 80, 82, 99, 102, 126, 290-91.

6. Thomas H. Yeatman (1805-1878), old time Whig and Cincinnati manufacturer, currently assistant treasury agent at Memphis (1863-64) and member of the board of trade, exceeded his authority on occasion and was replaced by James Tomeny in the spring of 1864. Thereafter Yeatman became a federal purchasing agent at Vicksburg and a commission merchant, before returning to Cincinnati where he was appointed postmaster by Johnson, but the Senate failed to confirm; subsequently he served in the Ohio senate (1870-72). *Ibid.*, 117-31 *passim*, 275-77, 285, 287; M. Joblin and Co., *Cincinnati Past and Present* (Cincinnati, 1872), 93-96; Cincinnati Historical Society Name file.

7. Rufus H. Todd (1834-1894), a Henry County farmer and miller; Osker S. Stephenson (1820-*fl*1880), North Carolina-born farmer; Robert E. Bogle (b. *c*1817), a Gibson County farmer; probably William Wesson (b. *c*1808), a Virginia-born farmer; John Norman (1804-1874), farmer, sheriff (1838-44), and county judge (1856), who also served in the Tennessee house (1859-61, 1865-67) and senate (1867-69); J. B. Davis (b. *c*1810), a North Carolina-born farmer; John Read (*c*1786-1865), a Kentucky-born lawyer and judge of the 10th circuit (1836-65); James Caldwell (*c*1804-1872), Kentucky-born farmer, county magistrate, and chairman of the county court; David A. Nunn (1833-1918), a native of Haywood County and a Unionist-Republican who served in the Tennessee legislature (1866-67) and Congress (1867-69), as minister to Ecuador, Tennessee secretary of state (1881-85), and as collector of internal revenue (1897-1902); Green W. Carson (b. *c*1822), an Alabama-born Lauderdale County farmer; and William A. Turnage (b. *c*1814), a farmer who had been chairman of the Tipton County court (1850-51). 1860 Census, Tenn., Henry, 11th Dist., 178; Weakley, 4th Dist., 124; Gibson, 17th Dist., 365; Henderson, 18th Dist., 261; Madison, Jackson, 35; Obion, 3rd Dist., 168; Lauderdale, 7th Dist., 77; (1870), Dyer, 14th Dist., 21; (1880), Henry, 11th Dist., 14; Weakley, 1st Dist., 25; Lauderdale, 9th Dist., 14; WPA, Henry County, Tennessee, Tombstone Records, 34; Sistler, *1850 Tenn. Census,* VI, 250; VII, 36, 142;

McBride and Robison, *Biographical Directory,* I, 557; *Riverside Cemetery Inscriptions, Jackson,* 88; *Tenn. Official Manual* (1890), 183; *Goodspeed's Obion,* 940; *Goodspeed's Tipton,* 812; *BDAC,* 1397.

8. Auguston Alston (1825-*fl*1887), a North Carolina native, graduated from the medical university at Louisville and established a practice in Brownsville in 1849. A Whig before the war, he became a staunch Republican, moving in 1865 to Memphis where he served as clerk and master of chancery until 1871, when he returned to Haywood. *Goodspeed's Haywood,* 922.

9. William P. Bond, Brownsville laywer.

10. Col. Robert V. Richardson, 12th Tenn. Cav., CSA.

11. Ralph P. Buckland (1812-1892), Ohio lawyer, served two terms in the state senate. In January, 1862, he entered service as colonel, 72nd Ohio Vols. , fought at Shiloh, and, promoted brigadier in November, commanded the XV Corps in the Vicksburg campaign. He was in charge of the District of Memphis (1864-65), resigning to go into Congress (1865-69), and subsequently returned to his practice in Fremont, Ohio. Warner, *Generals in Blue,* 50-51.

12. Probably men of the 1st Ala. Cav., USA, at this time headquartered in Memphis; at least 150 of the 2,066 who served in this regiment were native Tennesseans. Hoole, *Alabama Tories,* 15-16, 32.

13. Consisting of three large brick warehouses, the Irving Block, used as a Confederate hospital before its conversion by Federal authorities for prison use, now housed civilians, prisoners of war, and soldiers awaiting trial. Young, *Memphis,* 128; *OR,* Ser. 2, VII, 404, 920-21.

14. Probably John L. Poston (*c*1829-*fl*1880), a Tennessee-born farmer, who seems to have been active as a recruiter and organizer of cavalry regiments. Captured at Fort Pillow, he later escaped. Following the war, he served as Haywood County court clerk. *Tennesseans in the Civil War,* I, 353-54; 1880 Census, Tenn. , Crockett, 8th Dist., 12; *Goodspeed's Haywood,* 825; *Tenn. Senate Journal,* 1866-67, App. 59; for Johnson's authority to the writer, see Letter to James B. Bingham, January 2, 1864.

15. T. Herbert Whipple was a Chicago *Tribune* reporter located in Cairo, Illinois (*c*1862-64). Whipple to Abraham Lincoln, May 24, 1864, Lincoln Papers, LC; Louis M. Starr, *Bohemian Brigade* (New York, 1954), 241.

16. Horace Maynard, Nathaniel G. Taylor, William G. Brownlow, Samuel C. Mercer, Joseph S. Fowler, John Netherland, all good Union men.

17. Possibly a reference to a pending job printing contract.

18. Oliver P. Morton of Indiana, and Richard Yates.

19. An ancient biblical and classical expression; according to *Webster's Third International,* "feel or show unusual pointless opposition to or resentment of an often necessary authority one is subject to."

From Melinda Williams[1]

Yazoo City Feb 11th 1864.

Dear Sir

The Gunboats are here for a few days, therefore, I can write freely. I detest a political woman, but, as all National troubles *seat themselves around our fire-sides,* woman clothed in modesty can speak of them.

The difficulty in this war, is we have so few men upon the tapis,[2] that understand the Southern character. Some time since I noticed in a paper, a remark of yours, given in a private conversation to a gentleman which was "Send your thrifty Yankees down to settle among us, they, will root out this rebellion"—[3]

All true union spirits agree in the wisdom of this idea, but, how is it to be carried out? How are we to get this sane population? The idea was suggested the other day by one, who would gladly use the pen of a feeble woman.— In these plantation states, (as they may be called) now out of the Union, there are many Northern claims, that have already been favorably adjudicated in the Circuit Courts; the Southern defendents having the legal privilege of an appeal to the ensuing Courts of Errors and Appeal.[4] There were no Courts held in any of these States since the spring of 1861. The higher Courts were not held according to law in the fall of 1861.—[5] Now the idea is this.

In the event of an individual failing to appear with his cause before the Courts, in proper time and order, his case would go by default. Would it not? Then why, are not States as responsible as individuals? There is a clause in the rebel confiscation acts, that secures northern creditors who were born in the South.[6] They have been waiting already three years. They are safe even from rebel vindictiveness in their debts, yet, cannot realize a dollar.—

Could Congress frame some law suitable to these facts, protecting, or giving possission of these *rich, large landed estates;* where they could be subdivided and sold to a hundred families, *your* wise idea of rooting out this rebellion could be carried out, and save millions of money and suffering to our once happy country.— The vindictiveness of these once large planters, is incredible!— In these cotton states a few rule the host. Ignorance, is the hardest thing yet to contend with.— These planters differ entirely from our simple E Tenn when left to herself. Slavery there, has been more of a patriarcal government. In the cotton States it partook of the cruelties of the task-masters of Egypt. Society is all rong here. A self made man is nothing. It is astonishing with what facility these "fire eaters" can make a virtue of necessity— "Let the negroes go" they say (when they find they are all going) "We have our Lands and we will have our independence" I have seen the Spirit of which they are made. Before the gunboats came I sat with them almost every day; sometimes half doz scouts at the time. Col White' [7] where I am, is the head quarters of rebellion. The best houses, best food, and best rooms are opened to these tattered & torn garments. My heart aches for the dignity of manhood, when I see these poor ignorant creatures (their very ignorance emboldens them) looking as Coeur de lion,[8] and truly feeling that they could live and die, in the crusade of "liberty"— So flattered are they with these attentions from Mama & daughters.— The truth is *the women keep up this war*[.][9] Tomorrow were the men willing to lay down their arms they would not *dare* come home to their wives and daughters. "We have our rich Lands they say, woman, are especially protected" &c &c &c[.] Take their Lands from them for just debts. Break up their nests and the birds will fly.— *"Verbum sat sapiente"*—[10]

With many kind wishes for your health and happiness I remain with sincere respect

Yours truly.
Melinda Williams.

ALS, DLC-JP.

1. Melinda Williams (b. *c*1822), daughter of Gen. Robert Williams of North Carolina, in 1842 married Joseph L. Williams, Knoxville congressman (1837-43). 1860 Census, District of Columbia, Washington, 2nd Ward, 99; Silas Emmett Lucas, Jr., *Marriages from Early Tennessee Newspapers, 1794-1851* (Easley, S. C., 1978), 520; for Williams, see *Johnson Papers,* III, 564*n.*

2. A misuse of "sur le Tapis," literally "on the tablecloth," or figuratively "under consideration"; she is probably thinking of men in power. *OED,* XI, 86.

3. For Johnson's invitation to "men of industry and economy to come and settle" in Tennessee, see Remarks at Nashville, October 20, 1863.

4. According to the Confederate Judiciary Act of March 16, 1861, cases formerly adjudicated in Federal circuit and district courts fell to Confederate district courts with appellate jurisdiction resting in the Confederate Supreme Court, which was never established. Unfortunately for northern creditors, after additional Confederate judiciary legislation in May, 1861, these debts "were assiduously ferreted out" and when collected went into the public treasury. However, stay laws passed in most states prohibited collection of the principal, which was deferred until war's end, so that in reality only the interest found its way into the Confederate treasury. Inasmuch as the Mississippi high tribunal was designated "Court of Errors and Appeals," Mrs. Williams may have used that term for the Confederate Supreme Court. William M. Robinson, Jr., *Justice in Grey* (Cambridge, Mass., 1941), 51, 420-36, 626; Curtis A. Amlund, *Federalism in the Southern Confederacy* (Washington, 1966), 80-84; Provisional Constitution, Art. III, secs. 1 and 2.

5. Mrs. Williams is in error in her account of the availability of southern justice during the war. Confederate district courts held terms throughout 1861, opening as early as May in Louisiana and continuing as late as December in Georgia. Moreover, state courts were also operative throughout the war in "these plantation states," and with few exceptions the the highest courts held sessions, although often irregularly and with fewer cases. Mississippi's supreme court, hearing only 19 cases during the war, nevertheless presided over 15 in the year 1861 alone. Other cases were tried in 1863 and 1864 but no terms were held in 1862 and 1865. The high courts in Alabama, Georgia, and North Carolina handled numerous cases. Henry P. Beers, *Guide to the Archives of the Government of the Confederate States of America* (Washington, 1968), 36-58 *passim;* J. G. de Roulhac Hamilton, "The State Courts and the Confederate Constitution," *Journal of Southern History,* IV (1938), 434-35; James W. Garner, *Reconstruction in Mississippi* (Baton Rouge, 1968), 40.

6. Section 6 of an act of February 15, 1862, amending the Sequestration Act, exempts those southern-born persons living in the North who have "ceased their business in the enemy's country" and been unable to remove South. *OR,* Ser. 4, I, 933-34.

7. Possibly J? J? B. White (*c*1795-*fl*1860), South Carolina-born planter, who on the eve of the war had $75,000 in real and $90,000 in personal property. 1860 Census, Miss., Yazoo, 24.

8. Apparently an oblique reference to that symbol of dedicated commitment, that inveterate crusader of medieval times, Richard the Lion-hearted of England.

9. Confederate literature is replete with examples of women's support of the war. Some, it was alleged, promised favors for enlistment, reserving "their charms 'for those who go forth to battle' while denying them to men 'who stay at home.' " In 1865 James T. Brady, New York lawyer and pundit, "warned that 'the greatest difficulty' the North would face 'in putting down the rebellion' would be the 'women of the South' who had been so intimately involved in the struggle." Mary Elizabeth Massey, *Bonnet Brigades* (New York, 1966), 25, 30, 40.

10. A word to the wise is sufficient. Hugh Percy Jones, ed., *Dictionary of Foreign Phrases and Classical Quotations* (Edinburgh, 1923), 123.

From Horace Maynard[1]

Nashville, February 13, 1864

D. Sir.

This morning the Dispatch appeared with an article upon the Oath of Allegiance,[2] which I enclose. I have heard no allusion to it & do not know how far it has been read.

Mr. Mercer hopes to start his paper next week,[3] but is not sanguine, so many & great, are the delays by the irregularity of his workmen. Has slavery anything to do in making workmen less reliable, in the slave than in the free states?

The hue & cry are still kept up pretty much as when you were here, little more so if any difference. Mr. E. H. Ewing sent in the other day to inquire if you would respond to his letter[.] The editor's reply was "no signs yet." He certainly has not been unduly flattered by the attention paid him & his officers.

I received an invitation to attend a meeting at Memphis on the 22nd inst. which I am inclined to accept—[4] Quite a delegation I understand will go to Louisville to scandalize the virtue of that conservative city.[5]

Matters move on pretty much as they did before you left.

Kind regards to Mr. William Seward, who, I presume is still with you.

I am very Truly Yours
Horace Maynard

His Excy Andrew Johnson

ALS, DLC-JP.

1. During the governor's absence in Washington, Attorney General Maynard apparently was functioning as head of state.

2. An unsigned piece of editorial correspondence in the Nashville *Dispatch* of February 13, headed "Oath of Allegiance," dealt with the necessity and sacredness of such vows. As for Johnson's oath, it contended that "No loyal citizen of the United States will hesitate to take it and to keep it according to its plain and obvious import. And he who quibbles or cavils over this oath, does not intend to keep any oath."

3. The first issue of Mercer's *Times and True Union* appeared on February 20.

4. Maynard made the trip, speaking at a Union emancipation meeting. Nashville *Union,* February 28, 1864.

5. Scheduled for February 22, "A Free Southern Convention," dubbed the "Radical Convention" by the Louisville *Journal,* called for universal uncompensated emancipation, arming the Negroes, and rescinding Lincoln's amnesty proclamation—strong meat for a city in which many prominent citizens were southern sympathizers and in which two major newspapers were by now displaying strong hues of copperheadism. Nashville *Dispatch,* January 22, 1864; Louisville *Journal,* February 25-26, 1864; Robert E. McDowell, *City of Conflict: Louisville in the Civil War, 1861-1865* (Louisville, 1962), 130, 135, 152-53, 184.

A scene on Cherry Street, *ca.*1864-65.
Courtesy Betsy Bachman Carrier.

From Robert Johnson

Nashville Tennessee
Sunday Night Feb'y 14 1864

Dear Father,

Enclosed you will please find an account of S. H. Baxter,[1] against the Government, for taking the Census in Greene County in the year 1860, which he requested me to forward to you, for Collection, Should you have time to attend to it—

Everything here about as you left them, all quite and peacable, So far as I know, but I have not been out to learn what is going on, but get the most of my information from Judge Patterson and McDannel— The "Press" comes out Semi-occasionally on you,[2] but I believe the world wags along about as usual,— The "Dispatch" has published Several excellent and well written communications in your defence—one especially, in regard to the Oath—which I enclose[.][3]

It is rumored at Knoxville, that the rebels, had taken possession of all our Books, papers &c at Greeneville— Mr Joe Allen[4] brought the information here— I hope it may prove incorrect— Mrs Fletcher got on a Boat, the Same day that you left, and I presume ere this, is with her husband—[5]

The family are in about their usual health—Stover Seems Some better the last few days—[6] Frank wrote to you to-day, and done very well—with a little pains taken with him, and practice he will learn to write an excellent hand— I think he is improving rapid— All of the Children are well, and as noisy as ever— Frank and Andrew Patterson are Sleeping in Brownings room[7]—a great thing with them— Sam is doing very well, and Seems Satisfied, but holds on to the idea that he would rather live in Greeneville than any other place that he has yet seen—[8]

I have written more than I thought I would when I commenced, and at the Same time written nothing worth reading[.]

Taking everything in Consideration, after mature reflection, I believe I will resign the 29th. inst, and try my fortune in Some of the New Territories,—perhaps it will be for the best of all, that I should do so— Next Sunday is my Birth-day, and I have, in anticipation thereof. cast away forever, my past conduct—let it be burried,—it is beyond our Control— the future alone I now deal with, and with a firm reliance on Divine aid, *I will* Succeed— Mark the prediction, and when you see me again, you will find me an altered man—*the intoxicating bowl goes to my lips no more*——

If you prefer that I should remain with you, either in my present Capacity, (have an Order to that effect) or in a private one,[9] I will do so— Otherwise I will seek my fortune in the West[.]

Your Son, Robt Johnson

ALS, DLC-JP.

1. Samuel H. Baxter (1822-1905), Greene County farmer, was 2nd lieutenant, Co. C, 4th Tenn. Inf., USA, from April to August, 1863, when he was reported missing while on recruiting service. Reappearing in Nashville about the time of Robert Johnson's letter, he was ordered to report to his regiment in Knoxville. However, in 1866 by special order he was discharged to date from September, 1863. 1860 Census, Tenn., Greene, 17th Dist., 70; (1880), 14; CSR, RG94, NA; Reynolds, *Greene County Cemeteries,* 23.

2. "For six months we have restrained an impulse," wrote the editor, "to oppose and expose the course pursued by the Military Governor." Now, dissatisfied with what it regarded as his drift to radicalism and particularly with his oath, the *Press* almost daily found fault with his administration. Asserting that Johnson came to the office, seemingly with the people's interest in mind, it charged that he was not maintaining the office in the same spirit. Nashville *Press,* February 4, 6, 8-13, 1864.

3. Quite possibly Robert sent the extended letter which had appeared over the initials J. L. (John Lellyett) three days earlier. Nashville *Disptach,* February 11, 1864.

4. For Joseph D. Allen, Greene County farmer, see *Johnson Papers,* III, 473*n.*

5. Emma H. (1843-1914), second wife of Greeneville lawyer Andrew J. Fletcher, was on her way north with two small children to join her husband in Paducah. The family ultimately refugeed in Evansville, Indiana, returning to Nashville after the war when Fletcher was appointed secretary of state for Tennessee (1865-70). Ross, *Bradley Cemetery Records,* II, 120; McBride and Robison, *Biographical Directory,* I, 251; see also *Johnson Papers,* II, 473*n;* Fletcher to Johnson, February 17, 1864, Johnson Papers, LC.

6. Johnson's son-in-law Daniel Stover, suffering from tuberculosis, had less than a year to live.

7. Frank, the family name for Andrew Johnson, Jr., the governor's youngest son, now eleven; Andrew Johnson Patterson (1857-1932), son of Martha Johnson and David T. Patterson, and Johnson's first grandchild; William Browning, private secretary and military aide.

8. For Sam, Johnson's favorite servant, see *Johnson Papers,* III, 405*n.*

9. Having been relieved of his command, Robert was now assigned as a military aide to his father.

From John L. Bridges

February 15, 1864, Camp Chase, Ohio; ALS, DLC-JP.

Arrested January 23 and held as hostage for Jesse R. Blackburn, he claims to be loyal, having twice taken the oath of allegiance and possessing a statement from seventeen Bradley countians attesting to his loyalty: "the facts are that I have only been Rebbell enough to Stay at Home." In feeble health, he asks Johnson's help in getting permission on his parole of honor "*to take the bounds of the City* of *Columbus until I can show* my *loyalty by undisputed* testemony."

From Minnissa J. George[1]

Feb 15th 1864

Gov. Johnson Sir

In the absece of civil law and legal advisers I am under the necessity of trying to get council of you. I am the widow of Jesse George (a mechanic) who lived in the fifteenth dis. of Robertson Cty in the State of Tennessee and died in 1849 leaving three small Sons and a few hundred dollars to each. The money was placed in the hands of James N. Thornhille[2] (my nephew) of Robertson County Tenn, as Guardien. My eldest Sons are of age and have received some money from their Guardien but have not made a final Settlement with him. I have had my buildings all burned by Rebel Citizens and am now without a Shelter for my head. General Payne can give you all necessary information concerning that matter. I and my children wish to move North[.] We wish to settle all our affairs here and take our little effects with us. My youngest son Thomas D George is sixteen years old.[3] He wishes to have his money drawn out of his guardien's hand and placed in myne. His elder brothers John A & James I George are willing to be my security.[4] We proposed this arrangement to the Guardien who met us the first day of this month at Springfield to make as we thought a final settlement. We met him there and were informed by the Holders of the Court Esq Hardiman and Esq Bug[5] that there could be no legal Settlement made because we had not been duly notified by a Sheriff five days before meeting[.] I asked them who our Sheriff was[.] They blushingly answered we have no Sheriff[.] I told them our civil laws were all suspended and that I could not believe there was any legality in the Court[.] I farther Said while we were all there togather we might settle our business ourselves[.] But it was not agreed to. The settlement is defered till the first monday in March. After much consultation the Court agreed that it could legally notify all parties to attend at the appointed time. The Guardien wrote his resignation and left it to be recorded and we all signed an acknowledgement that we had been duly notified by that Honorable Court to meet the first monday in March[.] I was credibly informed yesterday that the affoe said guardien intends if I become guardien for my child to compel me to take a note of over five hundred dollars on my good Brother John A Y Steuart[6] whose misfortunes render him unable to pay his debts. J N Thornhille the guardien loaned a portion of my children's money to my brother to Speculate in merchandise. He sold his goods on credit and is now a bankrupt. I am told that Thornhille says no law can compel him to give up my childs money until he is of age also that whatever situation he may have his buisness as guardien he has nothing to do but to hand it over to the next guardien[.] It is my sincere wish to have this matter legally and spedily settled. Our means are limited and expense heavy. As for my loyalty I refer you to General Payne.[7] Governor Johnson sir if you can possibly have leisure from your more important business to drop me a line informing me how I may have this matter honerably, and spedily settled that we may get us a home in time to raise us a crop You will render us a lasting Service and the God of the widow and orphan will bless you[.] If I got my childs money in my hands I want a permit from you to carry it out of this state[.] We anticipate mooving to Illinois[.] We have not positively decided in what portion to locate[.] My sons are cabinet work men. We wish to Settle Where they can carry on their trade to the best advantage. Your polittical friend

Minnissa J George

N b If your business or propriety will permit you to write to me, Please direce your letter to Mitchelville Station Sumner Cty Tennessee[.]

ALS, DLC-JP.

1. Minnissa J. George (*c*1810-*fl*1870) was a farmer who possessed $1,095 in property, moving after the war to Knox County. 1860 Census, Tenn. , Robertson, 11th Dist., 92; (1870), Knox, 9th Dist., 4.

2. James N. Thornhill (1821-*fl*1900), a miller with a combined estate of $10,000, after the war was a farmer and physician. *Ibid.* (1860), Robertson, 11th Dist., 103; (1870), 12; (1880), 18; (1900), 54th Enum. Dist. , 5A.

3. Thomas D. George (1847-*fl*1900) after the war was a cabinet builder and carpenter, living first in Knox then Hamilton County. *Ibid.* (1870), Knox, 9th Dist., 4; (1900), Hamilton, 72nd Enum. Dist., 27B.

4. John A. (*c*1840-*fl*1880) and James I. George (1842-*fl*1900) were both cabinet makers in Knox County after the war. James later moved to Roane. *Ibid.* (1860), Robertson, 11th Dist., 92; (1870), Knox, 10th Dist. , 21; (1880), 144th Enum. Dist., 12; 16th Enum. Dist., 33; (1900), Roane, 118th Enum. Dist., 13A.

5. Probably Joseph Hardaway (b. *c*1803), notary public and justice of the peace, and W. H. Bugg (b. *c*1815), a Virginia-born merchant, who was also a justice of the peace and county register (1864). Deane Porch. tr., *Robertson County, Tennessee, 1850 Census* (n.p., 1968), 123, 225; *Goodspeed's Robertson,* 837.

6. Probably John Stewart (1821-1901), a millwright with $2,500 in real estate and $3,000 in personal property on the eve of the war. 1860 Census, Tenn., Robertson, 9th Dist., 6; Durrett and Williams, *Robertson Cemetery Records,* II, 46.

7. Gen. Eleazer A. Paine.

From Melinda Williams

Confidential

Yazoo City Feb 15th 1864.

Dear Sir

Since writing to you on the 11th, while waiting for the gunboats to return, from up the river, to take my letters; I have made some discoveries of a personal nature— I transmit them to you; with a request that you will give me some counsel— Upon my arrival at this place, I was told by interested parties that my debt of $40,000 forty thousand dollars had been collected and paid into the Confederate Treasury at the beginning of the war; as a Confiscated debt: because my husband was a Federal Official—[1] This is false.— Even the rebel laws, protect me in two ways. First, I was born in the South. 2d My claim, has always stood as a Minor—As guardian & ward.

The facts are these. The debt, was placed in Lawyers hands to collect, and things went so far in the Spring of 1861, after Secession; that the Plantation with negroes, horses, mules farming utensils, were all advertised for sale; when Col White, my debtor, bought up the lawyers. I suppose thinking they would have every thing down South their *own way*.

The records are all removed, but, disinterested parties were kind enough to cut this advertisement, out of their news-paper files, for me.— What I want to counsel with you, is, can you advise me what to do in order to live through this war? My husband is virtually dead with paralysis.

Death would be a relief to him. I have two sweet little girls at the Convent in Indiana, my only son with me a boy of 15—[2] My *GOOD* husband and *these girls must* be cared for. This debt and some lands in E Tenn,[3] is now all we have to rely upon.
My purpose, is to settle myself, so soon as practicable, in Chattanooga.— In East Tenn, my husband is known, and has *many friends*. I think this will be a good point for my boy.— Are there any confiscated houses & furniture to be had in Nashville? or Memphis? All of Mr Williams rich relatives, have gone into the rebellion. Overtons, Leays &c. Mrs Lyzinka Brown, I suppose you know, has married her cousin Gen Ewell of the rebel army.[4] She is a connection of mine. In fact John Williams[5] and my husband stands *alone,* in Loyalty. I know John has his hands & heart full these times; and *would not have him know* his brothers condition.

The two Judges in the Territory sympathise with us,[6] and will cheerfully hold Mr W's Court for him; and as the public will lose nothing; I wish the matter to be kept secret until, I can know what to do; therefore; I write for your advice and aid; should there be any employment for me in Nashville.— The confusion in the country; and the dissention among friends, is why, I take this liberty. I trust you will receive it, as it was intended as a mark of esteem for your *good judgment.*

Are there any clerkships that a lady could fill? I would prefer an eligable house & furniture, could any be had. When you saw me last, I was a mere child, in experience and nerve; now, I am a woman— I trust this war will make men & woman of the Nation.— Please let me know if East Tenn is accessible.—

With Esteem Yours truly
M Williams.

NB Since writing this I hear Gen McPherson has gone into active Service—[7] Direct to The Prevost Marshal Vicksburg.

Yrs Mrs Melinda Williams
Yazoo City, Miss.—

ALS, DLC-JP.

1. Lincoln had appointed Joseph L. Williams U. S. district court judge in Dakota Territory.

2. The Williams children were: Charles (b. *c*1844), Joseph L. (b. *c*1847), Bradberry (b. *c*1849), Medora (b. *c*1850), Kate (b. *c*1856), and Melinda (b. 1860). Charles, Bradberry, and Medora were born in Tennessee, Joseph in North Carolina, and Melinda and Kate in Washington, D. C. 1860 Census, District of Columbia, Washington, 2nd Ward, 99.

3. Joseph Williams, grandson of James White, founder of Knoxville, at mid-century owned property, presumably in Knox County, valued at $200,000. He would die in December, 1865. Luttrell, *1850 Census, Knox County,* 56.

4. For John M. Lea and his brother-in-law John Overton, Jr., also a grandson of James White, see *Johnson Papers,* V, 398*n*; James Park, *The Family Record of James Park* (Knoxville, 1907), 4; for Lizinka Campbell Brown, who married Gen. Richard S. Ewell in 1863, see *Johnson Papers,* III, 372*n*.

5. For John Williams, Jr., see *ibid.,* II, 317*n*.

6. Philemon Bliss (1813-1889), Ohio-born lawyer and Republican congressman (1855-59), was chief justice of the supreme court of Dakota Territory during the war, later

associate justice of the Missouri supreme court (1868-72), and dean of law at Missouri State University (1872-89); Lorenzo P. Williston (b. c1821), New York-born Pennsylvania lawyer, had been appointed associate justice of Dakota Territory in 1861. *BDAC*, 565; *U. S. Official Register* (1863), 270; 1860 Census, Pa., Tioga, Wellsboro, 12.

7. James B. McPherson assumed command of the Army of the Tennessee in March.

From James B. Bingham

Bulletin Steam Job Printing Office,
Telegraph Building, Court Street.
Memphis, Tenn., Feb. 16th 1864.

Dear Governor: I telegraphed you yesterday to *know* certainly whether you will be with us on the 22d instant. As yet we have no answer.[1] We hope you will be with us. It would be worth many votes to us in our approaching canvass and election.

Since I last wrote, I have filled up commissions for all the Counties in the Western District, except Hardin and Decatur, which are over near the Tennessee river, and with which we have but little intercourse at present. I subjoin a full copy of all the persons to whom Commissions have been sent, as follows:[2]

Henry County—R. H. Todd; Weakly, O. S. Stephenson; Gibson, Robt. E. Bogle; Dyer, Wm. Wesson; Carroll, John Norman; Henderson, J. B. Davis; Madison, John Reid; Benton, (sent blank to Norman to be filled up for Benton;) Obion, James Caldwell; Haywood, John P. Burns; Lauderdale, Green W. Carson; Tipton, Wm. A. Turnage; Hardeman, T. J. Patrick; McNairy, John Aldridge; Fayette, George Rives. Shelby I shall attend to myself.

I fear that we shall have a thin vote in most of the Counties. All the Federal troops have moved away, and there is no protection for the people from guerrilla operations. Still we shall do our best. The rebel Richardson has instructed his friends in the upper counties to take any oath which may be necessary, but to control the elections by all means. Knowing this, we shall exclude all not known to be loyal citizens, whether they take the oath or not. At least I shall give such instructions to the judges of election in this county, as I have already done in some other counties.

My regiment is making but slow progress,[3] but it has a great deal to contend against. In the first place, I have all sorts of annoyance because you have not yet sent me a copy of the order of the Secretary of War authorizing you to call upon the nearest quartermaster or commander for subsistence, &c. A man who came to see about joining our regiment from the Alabama first—his time being out—was put in Irving prison for a day or two. Notwithstanding this opposition, however, thirty-eight others, who had never been sworn in, signified their wish to join our regiment, but we were told that we had no right to receive them! They had drawn clothes, and that was enough to keep them away from our state service![4] As soon as I can get up a company—have them armed and mounted—I intend to start them out toward Brownsville, where we can form several companies if we only had protection of armed men. In the meantime, send on the order, and then the last technicality will have been removed. Thanks to Gen. Buckland, he has given us quarters and feeds all we have been able to get as *fugitives*. So good, as far as it goes.

I am glad that you have gone to Washington to find out the probable issue of affairs. We hope to hear from you soon, and to see you in person too. We are stirring up the Smoke in this end of the State; and we are determined to bring Tennessee back as a free State or not at all!

Write soon, and oblige Yours, Truly,
J B Bingham

ALS, DLC-JP.

1. Johnson was in Washington and did not return to Tennessee until the middle of March.

2. Most of these officers have been identified in the annotation accompanying Letter from James B. Bingham, February 11, 1864. John P. Burns (b. *c*1827), had enlisted at Trenton in July, 1861, and in August was commissioned captain, Co. G, 27th Inf., CSA. By June, 1862, he was listed as a deserter from the 2nd Bde., 1st Corps, Army of Mississippi, and disappeared from the rolls. T. J. Patrick was probably Thomas G. Patrick (b. *c*1824), Tennessee-born Hardeman County farmer, possessing $7,000 real and $4,760 personal property in 1860, and formerly lieutenant, Co. E, 7th Cav., CSA. John Aldridge (*c*1823-1903), North Carolina native and McNairy County farmer, became a member of the Tennessee state senate (1865-69) and subsequently moved to Missouri. Probably George W. Reeves (b. *c*1814), North Carolina-born Somerville lawyer with property valued at $16,850; subsequently he was judge of the circuit court (1865-69). CSR (Burns), RG109, NA; 1860 Census, Tenn., Haywood, 13th Dist., 135; Hardeman, 14th Dist., 199; McNairy, 14th Dist., 490; Fayette, Somerville, 1st Dist., 5; McBride and Robison, *Biographical Directory,* II, 8-9; *Tennesseans in the Civil War,* II, 315; *Goodspeed's Fayette,* 802.

3. Bingham was raising Union guards for home militia duty.

4. If able-bodied men joined the home guard, they would be exempt from General Hurlbut's order impressing them into service to fill existing regiments. Apparently some of Bingham's recruits had earlier reported for regular service. Hooper, Memphis, 30.

From William Young[1]

[Shelbyville, *ca.*February 20, 1864]

To Governor Johnson:

Sir: In your Proclamation of the 26th of January, it is recommended, as an initiatory step in the reorganization and restoration of the State of Tennessee in the Federal Union, that an election be held for the purpose of electing civil officers; and it is desired that the friends of the Government be secured to the exclusion of its enemies. Who are to be regarded as friends, or as being true to the Union? those who voted to separate Tennessee from the Union, because they had lost their rights in the Territories, went into the rebel army, fought until they got a portion of their rights, deserted, came back and took Mr. Lincoln's Amnesty Oath and the oath you have laid down in your proclamation, and thus become loyal? That is all right as regards secessionists and enemies, but why require us Union men, who never sinned against the Government, to be classed with rebels, and take the same oath? The phraseology does not suit a Union man: "that I will *henceforth* support the Constitution, and that I will *hereafter* aid and assist all loyal persons in putting down the rebellion," implies that heretofore we have been against these things.

And there is another serious objection to being classed with them; a record is to be kept, and it will become part of the history of the country, that we assisted in breaking up this great and glorious government of ours which our fathers gave to us as an inheritance. Could you not add a codicil to your proclamation, and let Union men vote without being taunted in this manner? "Oh, yes: you have to take the same oath we do—you might as well have been secesh, for you get no credit for your Union sentiments!" We Union men of Bedford, who have stood by the government through evil as well as good report, have no objection to taking an oath that we will *continue* in the support of the State and Federal Government to the end of time as loyal men.

When the rebel army ruled over us, we were pointed out as Lincolnites, and "damned Union men;" lists were made out and furnished to forage masters, and they came and laid out six months' allowance and took the balance.

We hid our provisions, as best we could, some in garrets, some in cellars, in grave yards, and some in the tombs that stand over the honored dead, to save provision for our wives and little children to sustain life. After undergoing all this for our love and adherence to the Union cause, and then be classed as enemies. I am a friend; and, as a loyal man, would ask, with all due respect, if I am entitled to the same rights under, and the same protection of, the State and Federal Government, as I was before this rebellion. If so, I appeal to you, as Military Governor of the State, to protect my property; for, on Tuesday night, the 2d inst., some eight or ten Federal soldiers took from my lawful possession three negro women and three children, and carried them inside the lines. If they can help put down the rebellion, all right, if they are returned to me when they complete that job. If not, my rights are invaded. If I have to lose all, give me the Union, the Constitution, and the enforcement of the Laws, now and forever.

Wm. Young.

Nashville *Press,* February 20, 1864.

1. William Young (*c*1816-*fl*1870), a Tennessee native and farmer, on the eve of the war held property worth $27,000, including 22 slaves. 1860 Census, Tenn., Bedford, 3rd Dist., 47; (1870), 26; 1860 Census, Slave Schedule, Tenn., Bedford, 3rd Dist., 41.

From George D. Ramsay[1]

Ordnance Office, War Department.
Washington, Feb 23rd 1864

Genl. Andrew Johnson
Mil. Gov. of Tennessee
Nashville Tenn
Sir.

I have the honor to enclose herewith a copy of the Telegram received from the Actg. Ordn. Officer at Memphis and the reply from this Office.[2]

This Department having no authority to issue arms to the Militia of any State except upon the State quota, you are requested to inform this Office whether you are willing to receive these second class arms or such portion of them as the State may at present be entitled to, to be charged against the State quota[.]

Respectfully Your obdt Servt
Geo D Ramsay
Brig. Genl. Chf. Ordn.

LS, DLC-JP.

1. George D. Ramsay (1802-1882), Virginia-born career soldier, West Point graduate (1820), and Zachary Taylor's chief of ordnance in Mexico, had been in charge of numerous arsenals during peacetime. Still a captain at the beginning of the war and commander of the Washington arsenal, he continued there and in September, 1863, was promoted brigadier general and chief of ordnance. Retiring the following year, he later held a special assignment as inspector of arsenals. Warner, *Generals in Blue,* 388; *DAB,* XV, 340.

2. Lt. John Neily had telegraphed: "Three thousand (3000) second (2nd) class arms are asked for . . . to arm enrolled Militia . . . not mustered into the U S Service. . . . I have the arms on hand. Shall the issue be made?" To which Ramsay responded: "No arms can be issued to the militia unless the Governor of the State consents to receive such arms as part of the State quota." Neily to Ramsay, February 19; Ramsay to Neily, February 22, 1864, Johnson Papers, LC.

To James B. Bingham

Washington, Feb. 25. [1864]

To Jas. B. Bingham, Memphis:

It will be impossible for me to be with you by the 29th inst.[1] Your letter received.[2] The oath prescribed in my proclamation for elections must be observed. The President approves it as being the better mode. Will write more fully on this point soon.

Andrew Johnson,
Military Governor.

Memphis *Bulletin,* March 1, 1864.

1. Three days earlier the editor had urged the governor to come to Memphis before the election scheduled for February 29. Bingham to Johnson, February 22, 1864, Johnson Papers, LC.

2. Letter from James B. Bingham, February 16, 1864.

From Samuel C. Mercer

Nashville Tenn Feb 28/'64.

Gov. Johnson
Dear Sir,

I enclose you the leading editorial in the "Union" of this morning, and a paragraph also from our paper that you may observe the influences at work upon that paper.[1] The "Press" has been rabid in its abuse of you since you left, and the general impression among Union men seems to be that the "Union" is preparing to follow suit. Just as I Expected. The "Union" publishers are still monopolizing the patronage of the war Department and the U. S. Court, Treasury and P.O. Department. Can this not be remedied soon? The prospects of our new paper[2] are quite flattering, but the expenses are very large, and it needs liberal patronage from the Government Departments. There is a newspaper trade monopoly owned by a man named O'Neal,[3] who allows us the privelege of sending 200, or 300 copies of our paper per day to the front when I am confident we could easily sell 5000 per day if we were permitted to do so. Cannot this whole scheme be easily broken up and free trade opened? Adjutant General Thomas told me the other day that the evil should be remedied at the War Department. I earnestly hope it will be for it is an intolerable swindle at present.
The approaching county elections occasion much discussion. Intelligent staunch Unionists almost unanimously say that if your policy is to be censured at all it is that the election will be premature for the union cause. In Sumner I learn that several rebels are candidates who have never even taken the oath and the Copperheads will vote for these *en masse*[.] The "Press" advises or suggests to its friends who do *not* "ardently desire" the suppression of treason and the enforcement of the National laws, to take your oath anyhow, and then do as they please afterwards.[4] The article is an argument for perjury. I will publish it[5] and send you a copy of it, as it is a remarkable evidence of the spirit which animates the Copperheads. I earnestly hope that you may induce the President to make the amnesty Proclamation less favorable to the rebels[.] The principles of the Proclamation are correct, but it is idle to expect correct principles to be established by such traitors as we have among us.

Very respectfully, S. C. Mercer.

ALS, DLC-JP.

1. Under the head of "Colonization—Social Invasion," the *Union* editorial castigated "a rising party . . . composed of meddlesome adventurers, who have no country of their own, except Bedlam, and are forever canting about the extermination of our people, and the colonization of the country with persons like themselves. . . . They would like to do all the voting, as they now endeavor to do all the talking; for they would like to vote themselves and their tools not yet imported, into all the offices." Charging that these outsiders opposed the extension of Lincoln's amnesty "because that might break up the monopoly of loyalty" which they now enjoyed, the editor accused them of plotting "the absolute

alienation of real estate . . . so rapid that each of them could buy a farm for little more than a fair per diem to the auctioneer who sells it." To foil these invaders, "the people of Tennessee should . . . come forward *en masse,* and embrace the President's offer." Nashville *Union,* February 28, 1864.

2. With a view to promoting Johnson's vice-presidential candidacy and to support immediate emancipation, Mercer's *Daily Times and True Union* had begun publication only a week before, on February 20.

3. Not identified.

4. Claiming that the governor had no authority to prescribe an oath, the *Press* argued that, if taken, it could be regarded as "mere ceremony and sham, utterly void and of no effect"; hence, "though a man may go through the *form* of the oath, he does not *really* swear at all." Nashville *Press,* February 27, 1864.

5. See Nashville *Times and True Union,* February 29, 1864.

From Michael Burns[1]

Nashville February 29 1864

To His Excellency Andrew Johnson
Govenor of Tennessee
Govenor

I was elected President of the Chattanooga Rail Road Company at a meeting of the directors of the road on the 17th of this Month[.] I Consulted with Mr Fowler[2] in refference to the best mode of getting a Settlement with the Goverment and to get the road in the possession of the board of directors[.] he thought it most advisable to have an interview with General Grant as possibly he might be offended if the Communication was not first brought to him[.] acting on this advice Mr Fowler went with Mr Alloway[3] who is one of the Directors and myself and introduced us to the General. after Some conversation in regard to the road he told us if we would reduce what we desired to writing he would examine it and endorse his views on it and forward it to Washington to the Secretary of War[.][4] this he has done[.] I am Ignorant of the Nature of the endorsement he put on it[.] It may be unfavourable or otherwise[.] I herewith Send you a Copy of the Memorial that I left with Genl Grant which you will do me the favour of reading and if in your judgement you approve of you will place me under further obligations if you aid us in at least getting a Settlement with the Goverment and to get the Road back again in the posesion of the Company[.]

I will on the part of the Company as its President use every exertion to have the transportation of the Goverment as to men and Supplies brought over the road with more Safety and dispatch than will [be] done by partys who have No interest in the road as I intend getting the most efficient men that can be had in the Country[.]
every dollar of the earnings of the road after paying the expences of its running will applied to paying the interest on the bonds of the State[.] It is Needless to Say that all my hopes of having Justice done the Company and the State is looked for from you[.] Try and give us the Same advantages

that the Louisville & Nashville Rail Road has had and will endeavour to do our part feeling every assurance that we will give the Goverment Satisfaction in every thing we do[.]

With respt I Remain yours Obt Sev
M Burns

N B I should like to know
what Genl Grant Endorsed on My
Memorial to Mr Stanton[.]

I Still have the Same anxiety to have the N & North Western Rail Road done and to have the control of its running in the hands of the company with the Same Supervision of the Military Manager that is asked for by the Chattanooga road[.] the More I See of the way Goverment employees work the More I deem it Safe to be clear of them[.]
Trusting you may return home Soon[.]

Yours resp M Burns

ALS, DLC-JP.

1. For Burns, also president of the Nashville and Northwestern Railroad, see *Johnson Papers*, III, 376*n*.

2. Joseph S. Fowler, state comptroller.

3. Nathaniel E. Alloway (*c*1818-*fl*1891), Kentucky-born Nashville cotton dealer with $92,000 realty and $33,700 personalty, was a stockholder and director of the Nashville and Chattanooga Railroad before the war, continuing in this position until 1866. 1860 Census, Tenn., Davidson, Nashville, 5th Ward, 156; *House Report* No. 34. "Affairs of Southern Railroads," 39 Cong., 2 Sess., 304, 561; *Nashville Directory* (1891), 82.

4. Burns requested that the road be "placed in possession" of its directors, "with the Same Controul over it that the Louisville & Nashville Company are allowed to have over theirs. That is to Say the Company to run it under the orders of the Commanding General and Controul of the General Manager of the United States Military rail roads." Burns to Grant, February 22, 1864, Johnson Papers, LC.

From Thomas S. Marr[1]

Louisville Ky
[*ca.*March, 1864]

Gov. Andrew Johnson,
Sir:

Your son, Col. Robt. Johnson did me a favor of giving me a Permit in your name to ship silver and gold from Louisville to Nashville.[2] Under this Permit a sack containing about Two thousand two hundred dollars was started to me on last Saturday, which was seized by the Government Officials in this city. I would not trouble you in this matter until your return to Nashville, were it not that a copy of the Permit has been sent on to the authorities at Washington. I telegraphed you to-day of the seizure and I write you this to request you to please get an order for proceedings to be stopped until your return to Nashville.[3]

Please excuse my troubling you.

Very respectfully
Thos. S. Marr

ALS, DLC-JP.

1. For Marr (1830-1897), president of the Nashville Savings Bank, see *Johnson Papers,* IV, 90*n*.

2. While the governor was absent in Washington during the last half of December, Robert had taken it upon himself to issue this permit "By order of Andrew Johnson," although he was aware that "it is a peculiar case—let no one know any thing about it—for if you do, I will have innumerable applications—" Shipping Permit to Thomas Marr, December 20, 1863; Robert Johnson to Marr, December 20, 1863, Johnson Papers, LC.

3. Writing on March 21 to the surveyor of customs, Louisville, and on May 16 to the secretary of the treasury, the governor requested that the dollars be released and restored to Marr. Chase directed the district attorney of Kentucky to dismiss the proceedings on payment of costs and expenses. Telegram to William D. Gallagher, March 21; Johnson to Salmon P. Chase, May 16; Chase to Johnson, May 24, 1864, Johnson Papers, LC.

From Tenth Tennessee Infantry Officers[1]

Sullivan's Branch,
N. & N. W. R. R. Tenn,
March 2nd, 1864.

To his excellency, Andrew Johnson,
Military Govornor of Tennessee,
Governor;—

It is not without consideration that we take the liberty of addressing you. We are well aware, Governor, that the demands made upon your time, appertaining to the duties of the State, and the General Government, are excessive; and it is therefore with reluctance that we trouble you with this communication, and were it possible to avoid it, we certainly would not annoy you with it. But, Governor, to whom are we to look for a redress of our grievances if not to you? To be sure, we are in the Army, and there may be a military mode, but if there is, Governor, a remedy for our troubles to be found in that way, it is so tedious and uncertain, that we despair of satisfaction in seeking it by an application in that direction. You are, Governor, the political father of our State. Oour interests are allied with yours. The people, not only of Tennessee, but of the Country, look to you for Counsel. For the loyal Sentiment pervading the people to day, we believe the nation to be more indebted to you, than to any man living in this Country.

We therefore, Governor, make our petition to you as a *civilian,* and as our *political father,* for a redress of the grievances, of which we are about to complain. And knowing that you possess the remedy, and that you have never failed to show a consideration for the prayers of your people, we are persuaded that you will pay Some attention to our petition.

The thing is this;— We are officers in the regiment which has the honour to be *your* regiment, the *Governor's Guard,* and which we know prides itself on being subject, at all times, to your orders.

Nothing could give us greater pleasure than to assure your excellency, that it is our greatest wish to remain in this organization, and contribute our whole energy and influence to the harmony of the regiment. But there is a limit to human forbearance, and we, as well as the men of the Companies which we represent, are *disgusted* with the tyranny and insolence of our Major.[2] Many of our men tell us, that they are *not disposed* to reenlist as veterans, if this *pompous, insolent* and *abusive* Major is retained in the regiment.

While recently a member, and President of a Court-Martial, he insulted the whole Court, which is now in Session at this place, and of which we are members; and he was heard to Say, as he defiantly rushed from the Court-Room, that we were a *damned set of fools*[.] The members of the Court made a report of this intolerable insolence to the General Commanding the District,[3] who had an Order issued, instantly relieving him from Serving any longer as a member of the Court.

The Major is our superior officer, and we try to obey him with alacrity, in all lawful orders. But the action which we took, in relation to his being relieved from the Court Martial, we are certain, will influence him, when he gets the opportunity, to harass us more than he ever did before, if such a thing can be possible. As this might lead us to resistance, violance and disgrace, we prefer to resign, rather than incur such a risk.

If there was a certainty of our Lt Colonel[4] being always in command of the regiment, we would have nothing to complain of. But the Colonel may get sick, he may be ordered on a Court-Martial, on a Scout or on some special duty or detached service, in the event of which, the Command would necessarily dovolve on the Major. And as we have *determined* to be harassed by him *no more,* we respectfully make this application to your excellency, to remove him from the Regiment, either by causing him to resign, or giving him an office Some where else. We would assure your excellency, that we are not actuated by a Spirit of either vindictiveness or envy. We have pledged ourselves to decline any offer of a field officer's place. We are perfectly satisfied to leave the filling of such places to the pleausure of your excellency. All we ask for is, that the officers who may be placed over us, will treat us with the civility, respect and consideration which we are entitled to as volunteers in the Cause of our Country, and not treat us as a lot of vagabonds recruited in the Corrupt purlieus of vicious Cities.

As the Major has never spent a dollar or recruited a man for the regiment, he has no sympathy for the men; on the contrary, his overbearing manner, and tyranical treatment of the men, have caused many desertions; and, moreoever, we know that it is the avowed intention of whole Companies, to refuse re-enlisting as veterans, when the time comes, unless this man be removed from the regiment.

We have only to add, Governor, our profound respect for your exalted character and great public services, and to assure you of the great satisfaction which your public course affords,—

Your Obedient Servants,

Pet, DLC-JP.

1. Eight officers, captains of companies C, D, E, F, H, and I, and lieutenants in companies H and J presented this petition. This regiment was the main corps of the "Governor's Guard."

2. Louis R. Mandazy (b. *c*1830), Polish-born private in the 1st U. S. Inf. in 1852, had two five-year enlistments before joining the 10th Tenn. Inf. as 1st lieutenant, Co. K, in August, 1862, and becoming major the following February. In June, 1864, following Johnson's special order relieving him of command, he officially resigned "for the good of the service." CSR, RG94, NA; *Tenn. Adj. Gen. Report* (1866), 160.

3. Lovell H. Rousseau.

4. James W. Scully.

From J. F. Chenoweth[1]

Versailles Brown Co, Illinois
March 3d 1864

To his Excellency Gov Andrew Johnson
Nashville Tenn
Hon, Sir

I take the liberty of writing you a line, Making enquiry in regard to a Man representing himself to be Col. Hawkins[2] of a Tenn. Cav. Regt, Vols Representing himself to be Col. that was in the mountains with Parson Brownlow, & that he was wounded in the Battle of Mill Springs marched with the Gap Army to Greenupsburg Ky—& afterward participated in the Battle of Stone River, at Mill Springs was shot through both Legs, he was (if I am not mistaken) with you at Indianapolis last Spring as I Saw *him* there, & I also saw him at Springfield Ill, at the great Union Meeting on the 3d day of Aug. last, heard him Speak there, He is now in our County forming Ladies Soldier Aid Societies & raising large Amts, of Money for them, (he *not* receiving a Dollar) is doing a good work, attends to his own business, Is I Judge about 25 years of age, Dark hair, Slender & I should Judge about 5 ft 10 or 11 inches in height. Was attacked in Aug last, by a Mob at Danville this State. Represents that his Parents live near Knoxville Tenn, & that he has a Brother who is a Genl., under Butler[3] (I beleive)[.] I got the above from him in a private Conversation with him while a guest at my house, he Demeans himself as a perfect Gentleman.

Some time about the 9th of Jany last, it was published in the Knoxville Whig that a man by the name of Hutchins (Passing himself for Col Hawkins) was arrested in Louisville Ky for stealing a box of Books was imprisoned &c.[4]

The Copperhead Journals have taken it up & say this is the man[.][5] If he is not It is doing him & his cause injustice, as it has caused Some Union men to doubt him. If he is an impostor we want to know it, Will you be so kind as to let me hear from you in full. If he is the genuine Col Hawkins, your letter will do us good. If he is not he played off on yourself Gov Yates[6] & a host of others as I saw him with you.

Please Answer

Very Resply Yours J. F. Chenoweth
Post Master

ALS, DLC-JP.

1. J. F. Chenoweth (b. *c*1824), Ohio-born Illinois farmer, was postmaster (1836-66). 1860 Census, Ill., Brown, Versailles, 782; *U. S. Official Register* (1863), 353; (1865), 74*.

2. Insofar as positive identification is concerned, Colonel Hawkins, or "Huckins" or "Hutchins," remains a will-o'-the-wisp. There appears to be no information about him either before or after the war. For approximately a year after the spring of 1863, he cut a wide swath across the Copperhead country of Ohio, Indiana, and Illinois, purporting to be an East Tennessee refugee and assailing, often physically, all who in the least degree were lax in support of the war. Eliciting excitement, controversy, and even violence wherever he spoke, he was given extensive coverage by mid-western newspapers, particularly the Chicago *Times*. He would appear to have been one of those amoral soldiers of fortune who emerge in the turmoil of war with no real commitment save to their own ego-satisfaction achieved through being the focal point of mass hysteria. Chicago *Times,* May 9, June 2, August 27, 1863; Chicago *Tribune,* May 1, August 28, September 4, 1863; Louisville *Journal,* April 11, 21, 1863, January 15, 1864; Indianapolis *Journal,* March 7, 10, 1863; Knoxville *Whig,* January 9, 1864.

3 No evidence.

4. According to the *Whig* story Hawkins had been arrested and imprisoned for this offense in Kingston, Tennessee, "several years ago." Sentenced to the penitentiary, he "was afterward got off by the interference of friends who sympathized with him on the ground of his partial derangement." Knoxville *Whig,* January 9, 1864.

5. Not found.

6. Ilinois governor Richard Yates.

From Leonora Williamson[1]

Metropolitan [Washington]
March 4th '64

Gov Johnson,

Dr Sir,

I have just learned Mr Whiting[2] refuses to give up 'my papers' without an order from Sec Stanton; this astonishes me as he gives it as *his opinion* the Goverment will pay *no one* in Tennessee their losses—it matters not who they are.

When I sent my documents to the Executive Mansion, I trusted the President would see them & hoped they would not be sent to the War Department.— I had *kind* letters from Generals Sherman Hurlbut, Washbourne, Carr, Veatch & Smith[3]—also some from influential German friends— I wished his *Excellency to* see them, & know *I* had done *all I* could to vindicate the flag of my Country, & I was most unwilling to be classed among those persons who had come in & taken the Oath to save their property.

I do not consider I deserve any credit in taking care of many of the sick soldiers, it was *my duty,* & when they prefered to be at 'our house' to going to the Hospital, it was my pleasure—tho many Germans express more gratitude to me than I desire.

My case is a peculiar one, my property was within the lines, & I was assured by Gen Curtis I would be paid the same week our forces occupied Helena before my place had been foraged on much[.][4] he gave me this assurance.

My losses have been very great in destruction of buildings mills &c but my application is to be paid for the provisions the Army consumed, the mules that are in gov wagons, & the lumber that made coffins to bury the dead, & then *I have* not made out my statement, but let Officers & others connected with the Army report.

So well assured am I of the justice of the President that I am willing to abide by his decision. I expected the Emancipation Proclamation, & was very willing to abide it.

30 of the negroes which were mine once,[5] are in the Army, their wives and children *are not* & *have not* been receiving rations from the Goverment, they are living in my houses, (when they are sick taken care of at my expense), they have what crop they can make off my land. I claim nothing from them but for them to feel that I am & have been their friend. I did not buy them I inherited them— I never sold one, I hoped to provide for them as my immediate family did theirs 8 years ago—

I should be grateful to the President if he would grant me an interview[.] the boon would be granted to one who never offered up more fervent supplications to Gods throne for her children when agonizing on beds of sickness than I daily offer up that he may be the means of restoring peace to our once happy Country.

The boon I crave is that he will send to the War department & See my papers, & read them. I love my Country as much as any one—& am willing to abide his decision—

If you will go with me to see his Excellency, I will call by in a hack—at any time it will suit your convenience.[6]

With great respect
Mrs. Williamson

ALS, DLC-JP.

1. Leonora (*c*1821-*fl*1881), North Carolina native, was the wife of James M. Williamson, planter, sometime president of the Bank of West Tennessee, of the Memphis and Louisville Railroad, and of the Memphis Gas Light Company, and Shelby County clerk and master (1854-60). In 1860 their personal property was worth $260,000 and their real estate, $150,000. The property for which she sought restitution was in Phillips County, Arkansas. 1860 Census, Tenn. , Shelby, 5th Dist., 114; Memphis city directories (1855-81), *passim; Goodspeed's Shelby,* 815.

2. William Whiting (1813-1873), Harvard graduate and Boston lawyer, was solicitor of the war department (1862-65). *NCAB,* X, 147.

3. William T. Sherman, Stephen A. Hurlbut, Cadwallader C. Washburn, Eugene A. Carr, James C. Veatch, and probably Thomas Kilby Smith.

4. After his victory at Pea Ridge in March, 1862, Gen. Samuel R. Curtis threatened Little Rock in late May. Attacked by partisans and regulars under Gen. Thomas Hindman, he retreated in June to Helena, "looting as he went." The city became a Federal depot,

controlling "the trade and sentiments of a large and important scope of the country." Michael B. Dougan, *Confederate Arkansas* (University, Ala., 1976), 87-91; Ferguson, *Arkansas and the Civil War,* 176.

5. Of the sixty-six slaves owned by the Williamsons in 1860, twenty-seven males were eighteen or over and three were fourteen. 1860 Census, Slave Schedule, Ark., Phillips, St. Francis Township, 86.

6. A week later, Mrs. Williamson wrote again, asking Johnson to go with her to see the President. She ultimately won claims for damages to her Arkansas plantation in 1872 when the Southern Claims Commission, following General Sherman's corroboration of her loyalty, awarded $19,250 of the $82,185 she sought. Williamson to Johnson, March 9, 1864, Johnson Papers, LC; Klingberg, *Southern Claims Commission,* 104.

To William H. Seward

Washington City,
March 5th 1864.

Sir:

In reply to your note requesting that I should indicate suitable papers in Tennessee in which the laws of the United States should be published, I have the honor to state that it is very desirable publication of the laws should be made in the three Divisions of the State, to wit: East, Middle and West-Tennessee.

Altho parts of the same state, the geographical division as above is so distinctly marked that they are somewhat isolated from each other.

I would therefore respectfully recommend that said publication be made in Brownlow's Knoxville Whig" East Tennessee, the "Nashville Times," edited by S. C. Mercer Esq, Middle Tennessee, and the "Memphis Bulletin," edited by J. B. Bingham, West-Tennessee.

I have the honor to be Your obt. servt.
Andrew Johnson
Mil. Gov'r of Tenn

Hon W. H. Seward, Secretary of State,
Washington City.

LB copy, DNA-RG59, Corres. *re* Publishers of the Laws.

From Robert Johnson

Nashville, March 6th 1864

Dear Father,

I have nothing new to write you at this time— The election passed off very quitely yesterday— I have not heard the result, but the Unconditional Union Ticket has carried by a large majority—[1]

Secretary East has been very unwell for a few days, and I am Staying in the Office attending to the business as far as I can— he will be up, I hope, in a few days.

In December I wrote a permit for Mr Thos S. Marr[2] of this City, to Ship Some gold from Louisville to this place— he had Some two thousand Dollars Seized at Louisville the other day, and I hope you will get the Secretary of the Tresaury to have it released— The Seizure, I have no doubt was Caused by Some interested parties in Nashville, and I know that Marr intended nothing wrong, and was acting in good faith—and I ask you to have the matter set right, for Mr Marr, if you have the time to attend to the matter—

The Tennessee troops are doing very well— Col Ray has resigned and Lt Col Cook, was killed in Mississippi in the late raid—[3]

Bridges has 800 or 900 men and is filling up radidly—[4]

We are all in moderate health[.] I have had Diarrhea for the last week but am improving, and feel better than I have for a long while— my system I think is thorougly cleansed and I am a new man[.]

Frank received your letter this morning, and will write to you to-day—

Your Son
Robert Johnson

ALS, DLC-JP.

1. A total state vote is not to be found; some local reports gave no tally, only the names of those elected.

2. See Letter from Thomas S. Marr, [March, 1864], note 2.

3. Daniel M. Ray's resignation was accepted February 15; William R. Cook was wounded and captured in Mississippi on February 22. *Tenn. Adj. Gen. Report* (1866), 330; CSR (Cook), RG94, NA.

4. After a slow start—it took from October, 1863, to January to recruit Companies A and B—the regiment's growth had greatly accelerated; by March companies C through I had been mustered. George W. Bridges had recently been appointed lieutenant colonel, 10th Cav. *Tennesseans in the Civil War,* I, 344-45.

From James O. Shackelford

Clarksville March 6h 1864

Hon Andrew Johnson
Dear Sir

At our Election on yesterday we had but a small vote[.][1] 84 votes were polled here all of them native citizens Except three or four, some of our Union men shrank Back and Left me almost alone. Public Opinion is truly a Despotism, men were afraid to commit themselves, I addressed a Large meeting here on Thursdey Last in which I took the position our interest as a state demanded the Emancipation of the slaves, and Discussed the ruinous Effects of slavery, on the Country, than[k] god the time has come when it Can be Discussed. As the courts will soon be opened I suggest that all person who wish to aval themselves of the benefits of civil Law be required upon the issuing of a warrant writ or Execution to file with the Clerk or officer his oath of Allegiance to the government of the United States and in fact before the officer or Clerk shall issue the same the party suing shall take the oath of allegance Defined other wise a rebel will have all the benefits of the Law and in many instances will use it to oppress Union men[.] Our men of wealth are almost all southern sympathizers[.][2] I think An order from the Commander of the Department of this character will have a good effect. Every Excutor or Administrator who qualifies should be required to take the oath of allegiance. Men ought not to have the blessings of a government unless they are Loyal to it. Let no attorny practice in any Court without taking the oath of allegiance. It will be some-time before we can have a Legislature to regulate these matters. It will hurt no one if he wishes to sue or have an Executor from a Judgment to take the oath[.] no Loyal man will Complain, DisLoyal men will and a repetition of the oath will not hurt them, but Do them good. I hope we shall have a convention called Ere Long when the people will meet and fix the status of our state. I was gratified to see the people of the western states are Disposed to appreciate your services in the Union Cause.[3] your most bitter opponents in this section are your old Democratic friends (the Leaders)[.] with the masses you have a hold[.] I think the Skies are Brightning and Ere 12 months we shall have peace[.]

Yours Truly J O Shackelford

ALS, DLC-JP.

1. "Mockery" and "farce" are used to describe the March county elections, as Johnson's ironclad oath tended to deter moderates from participating. According to the Louisville *Journal* of March 7, as reported in the Nashville *Union* of March 10, only 87 ballots were cast in Clarksville. Maslowski, *Treason Must Be Made Odious,* 88-89; Hall, *Military Governor,* 122-23.

2. An examination of census returns and of the available clues to wartime sympathies fully supports this assertion.

3. The Indiana Republican state convention had resolved on February 23 "That the gratitude of the American people is due to Andrew Johnson of Tennessee, for his unselfish devotion to the cause of the Union . . . and that we present his name as the choice of our people for the Vice Presidency of the United States." Early in March Nebraska's territorial legislature took a similar step. Chicago *Tribune,* February 24, March 6, 1864.

From John J. Steagald[1]

Clifton March 6th 1864

Gov Andrew Johnson
Sir to you Exlency

after I left Nashville the 5 day of January last I Return to Paducah Ky and I had to ly over wating for Transpotation 4 weeks befor I could get to come up the Tennessee Rive[.] I got off at Clifton 25 day of February[.] the Gurrilais was so numers in our Country I could not gow about to Ricrut[.] I lef Lt Hardy[2] at Paducah with the under Standing that he was to gow to St Louis and Draw arms & clothing for his Men and to meet me at this place[.] the Col Hicks[3] hell his men at Paducah for Picketts untell Reasently[.] I learn he had Release them and that thy ar on their way up hear So I think If he get here now I can Soom fill up my Rigment If you will give me som five months on it[.] I would Reported soone if I had any thing to Report[.] pleas let me hear from you on this[.] write to me at Perryvill to W Stout[.][4] I am also Requsted by Henry Milum[5] the Cornor of Decatur county to say to you that he held the Election in said [county] in March 1864 with the Exception of 3 Siville Districts which he did not appoint any person to hold the Election in those Districts for the Reason he was a faird to gow thar on the account of the Gurrillas[.] they ar now cleard out of our county[.] now thy was many person that did not gow and vote at the precints on the dy of Election through fear of them[.] So thy Seams to be Som dissatisfaction of the conduction[.] on that account said Milum wants to know if he must hold the Election in those 3 districts that the Election was not held in or hold it all over the county a gain[.] we would lik your Excelency to Issue Rits of Election in Said county in order to give Satisfaction[.] if it is Rite Write to Mr Henry Milum at Perryville to the car of Mr. W Stout[.]

Your friend J J Steagald
Recruting Regmnt T. C

ALS, T-Mil. Gov's Papers, 1862-65, Corres. to A. Johnson.

1. John J. Steagald (*c*1816-*fl*1870), North Carolina native and Decatur County farmer, was commissary sergeant, 2nd Tenn. Mtd. Inf., USA, who afterward served in the Reconstruction legislature (1865-67). *Tenn. Adj. Gen. Report* (1866), 204; Sistler, *1850 Tenn. Census,* VI, 142; McBride and Robison, *Biographical Directory,* II, 861.

2. Milton Hardy (*c*1837-1864) of Carroll County enrolled in August, 1862, and mustered in November as lieutenant, Co. G, 7th Tenn. Cav., USA. Captured in December, 1862, paroled and exchanged a year later, he joined Co. G, 2nd Mtd. Inf., and was killed in action in Henry County in March, 1864. CSR, RG94, NA; *Tenn. Adj. Gen. Report* (1866), 215.

3. Stephen G. Hicks (*c*1807-1869), Georgia-born Salem, Illinois, attorney and Mexican War veteran, raised the 40th Ill. Inf. during the summer of 1861. Wounded at Shiloh the following April and discharged in October, he was reinstated the next year, serving until mustered out in July, 1865. 1860 Census, Ill., Marion, Salem, 121; Pension file, RG15, NA; CSR, RG94, NA.

4. William Stout (*c*1825-1914), Scottish-born Decatur merchant who came to Perryville in 1847, was also postmaster (1853-54, 1856, 1860). Lillye Younger, *The History of Decatur County: Past and Present* (Southaven, Miss., 1977), 188-89, 410-11.

5. Henry Milam (*c*1828-*fl*1880), North Carolina native and Decatur farmer, had also been county register. 1880 Census, Tenn., Decatur, 4th Dist. , 20; *Goodspeed's Decatur,* 816.

From Richard S. Bradford

March 7, 1864, Columbus, Ky.; ALS, DLC-JP.

Protesting that he has "never had a drop of disunion or Sessison blood in my veins," a Tennessean—"an old man Say about 50 years of age"—sentenced to hard labor by an Iowa military commission, with the only witnesses against him "4 Negro fellows," asks Johnson "to aid me before the proper authorities at Washington." This "old man" has "alage Helpless Family Wife 7 little daughters the youngest born since I have been in Prison, With one Son about 8 years old. I had a snug little Fortune about me when the War broke out on a good Farm 6 Verry Valuable Negroes, 56 Head of Hores & Mules 300 head of Hogs 100 head of Cattle was making a Stock Farm. My negroes are all gone and my Stock very nearly all gone[.] it has been taken off by both Sides in arms and by Robers and thives Since I have been Keep a way from Home[.]"

From Citizens of Shelbyville[1]

Shelbyville Ten March 8th 1864

Gov Johnson

We desire to present to you the case of J H Ivey[2] who is now a prisoner of War at Camp Chase. He was taken out in the latter part of 1862 by the conscript law and was a member of the 4 [*sic*] Confederate Commanded by Col McMurry.[3] Mr Ivey did not remain long with the armey but deserted & come home & kept out of the way of the Confederate armey until after they left Middle Tennessee, he stayed at home and was at home when some of the Federal Cavalry took him some time in August or Sept 1863[.] he had been at home quietly at work never intendig to go into the rebel armey again[.] he is at Camp Chase & was a Citizen of Franklin County Tennessee & is verey desirous to get home & will take the oath & can give a good bond[.] we state that Mr Ivey has no sympathy with the Rebellion & would make a loyal citizen if at home[.] will you please forward this petition to the war department with such recommendation as you can give[.]

Very Respectfully
John Turner[4] [and 18 others]

Pet, DNA-RG249, Lets. Recd., File 814B (1864), John H. Ivey.

1. Thomas H. Coldwell, a prominent unionist, vouched for the loyalty of the nineteen signatories. Coldwell to Johnson, March 14, 1864, Lets. Recd., RG249, NA.

2. John H. Ivey (b. *c*1833), Franklin County farmer who, according to his service record, enlisted at Ridgeville on July 24, 1861, as a private in Co. F, 4th Tenn. Inf., which subsequently became Co. C, 34th Tenn. Inf., CSA, was on "sick furlough"—presumably in consequence of a hernia—from February until September, 1862, and deserted the following July; captured by the Federals and sent to Camp Chase in August, he was transferred to Ft. Delaware in February, 1864. CSR, RG109, NA; *Tennesseans in the Civil War,* I, 246.

3. James A. McMurray (*c*1825-1863), East Tennessean in the war since August, 1861, and colonel of the 34th Inf., was mortally wounded at Chickamauga in the fall of 1863. CSR, RG109, NA.

4. John Turner (b. *c*1797) was a North Carolina-born farmer. 1860 Census, Franklin, Marble Hill, 6th Dist., 109.

From Walter Mead[1]

New York March 9th/64

To His Excelency
Govr Andrew Johnson
Dr Sir

I take the liberty of writing you for the purpose of Enquiry in relation to affairs in middle Tenn. before the Rebellion broke out I was with my son[2] Engaged in putting up works for the purpose of manufacturing salt-peter on rather a large scale[.][3] we had invested a vary considerable Capital and was progressing verry well before the Demon was fully developed after which we concluded it would be rather safer to retire[.] We are anxious to return as soon as prudence will permit that is as soon as we can do so with safety[.] our works was incomplete but when finished It will be an Enterprise of considerable magnitude and be of great importance to the surrounding Country in giving Employment to the people. May I ask you that If it should be necessary Could we Expect the protection of the authorities to such an Extent as to make us safe from raiders or others that would be Enclined to do us mischief[?] I must here state that while we was in Tenn the people of all Classes were untireing Evan profuse in acts of kindness and of Friendship, but how it may be now is what I desire to have your opinion. when our works are completed it will be at a cost of many thousands it being of Engines and Expensive steam apperatus which would be Easily damaged by an Enemy. our works are situated about twelve miles East of Sparta in White County the property known as Englands Cave. will you please state whether the Rail Road which has been talked of as a military Road from Nicholasville or Danville to Knoxville or Chattanooga will be built and if so will it run near our works.[4] I see with great pleasure that the Union ticket has been successful in all places as far as reports have been received here. my Enquirys are allready so numerous I fear I shall trespass Entirely to much upon your valuable time to give me answers.

Yours with great Esteem
Walter Mead

P. O. Box 1506

ALS, DLC-JP.

1. Walter Mead (b. *c*1801), Connecticut native and president of the Wilkesbarre Coal Company, lived at 92 E. 17th Street. 1850 Census, N. Y., New York City, 18th Ward, 186; (1860) 18th Ward, 84; New York City directories (1848-65), *passim*.

2. His namesake son, Walter (b. *c*1828), was also a coal dealer. *Ibid.*

3. Now known as Cave Hill saltpetre pits 1 and 2 at the mouth of England Cove, about a mile south of the Putnam County line, these two deep pits were mined for "nitrous earth" during the Civil War but fell into disuse, remaining virtually unexplored from 1863 until 1945. Thomas C. Barr, Jr., *Caves of Tennessee* (Nashville, 1961), 506; November 25, 1945, in "Cave Trips," notebook of Dr. Edward R. McCrady, Sewanee, Tennessee, in possession of author (1980).

4. Two railroads were projected: one from Danville to Knoxville, the other from Danville, or Nicholasville, to Tullahoma on the Nashville and Chattanooga Railroad. The latter was to pass through Sparta, and therefore would not have been far from the mine. But by June, 1864, neither route was considered militarily important, inasmuch as the Federal army held Chattanooga and could supply Knoxville from there; thus both were abandoned. Map accompanying *House Ex. Doc.* No. 1, 39 Cong., 1 Sess.; *Senate Misc. Doc.* No. 132, 38 Cong., 1 Sess., 1-2.

From Alvan C. Gillem

Nashville March 11, 1864.

Governor

I answered your inquiries by Telegraph yesterday.[1] So far as I have been able to learn the Election was a Complete success. Gen Thomas informed me that he gave all possible protection to the officers holding the elections. I have heard from Stewart, Montgomery, Dickson Hickman Maury Giles Lawrence Wayne Lincoln, Hardin & Perry, all went well[.] I speak of these Counties because they have been brought particularly to my attention. Ed Ewing & Co through their mouth peice the "Press" did everything in their power to prevent the *People* from voting.[2] So far they have failed[.]

The organization of the Tennessee Regiments now at Nashville is progressing well, but there are neither arms nor horses for them here. The Regiments taken by Gen Smith[3] to Mississippi have not returned but are expected daily. The Third and fourth are said to have distinguished themselves— I regret to say the very reverse was the case with the Second. Ray himself left the command and resigned before the battle— Lieut Col. Cook was killed & the Regiment dispersed.[4] The conduct of Major Prosser[5] is spoken of in high terms. I would recomend that he be commissioned Colonel of the Regiment. I believe he is the only officer of the Regt. who can discipline it[.] The Conduct of Lt. Col. Thornburgh[6] of the 4th is highly spoken of.

Genl Thomas has ordered the 2nd & 4th Regts to report to me upon their arrival[.] we will have 8 Tenn Cav. Regts. at this place.

Much discontent has been caused by the neglect or failure of Capt Paxton to pay bounty.[7] None of the Regiments that came from Ky have received their bounty— I enclose you a certificate showing some one in Capt Paxton's office is doing a good business. it will be observed that the men by paying two dollars each can have "their papers properly made out" & get their bounty. other certificates of the same kind can be furnished if deemed necessary[.] I merely enclose this one to show you my grounds for recomending that Capt Paxton being relieved from duty as mustering officer— I suggested Capt A. H. Plummer[8] 19th Infantry because he is here and no delay would be caused by the change, which I am satisfied Could not be for the worse.

Two of Stokes Companies were Scouting near Sparta last week, when they were attacked by Hamilton & Furgison and twenty seven of them killed— *all* six of the officers and forty men escaped[.] The disaster is charged to the ignorance & cowardice of the officers—[9] at last Stokes Regt. has been concentrated & is at Sparta. Galbraith did not go with his men. Genl. Thomas will muster him out if *you Recomend it*[.][10]

Garret[11] has 587 men at Carthage[.] Murphy[12] has between 8 & 900 at Clifton, it has been reported that Murphy is doing very good service[.] I have removed our recruiting depot from Paducah to Reynoldsburg at the request of the officers[.] two hundred and fifty men are reported at Reynoldsburg.

East has been sick for some days and I fear will not be up for a week.

The North Western Rail Road is progressing favorably from both ends.

Governor I have endeavored to carry out your views in every way— The necessities of the troops have often forced embarassing responsibilities upon me. I have done my duty to the extent of my ability.[.] I fear the Tenth Cavalry will give much trouble. Bridges is drinking to excess & old man Elliott is incompetent.[13] To get rid of Crawford[14] I have given him *ten days* leave—

If you can do So Consistently I hope you will use your influence to have me confirmed—

Hoping Governor soon to have you with us.

I am sincerely yours
Alvan C Gillem

ALS, DLC-JP.

1. The general was inaccurate; his telegram, like this letter, was dated March 11. Johnson Papers, LC.

2. Almost daily from late January until the March elections, the *Press* castigated Johnson for his efforts, according to the editor, to circumvent the use of the presidential amnesty oath for the upcoming elections. Accusing him of usurping presidential power and wanting to keep the state in the grasp of the radicals, the editor nonetheless encouraged those who had passed the amnesty test to vote or attempt to do so. Nashville *Press,* January 28-March 2, 1864, *passim*; see also Letter from Edwin H. Ewing, February 1, 1864, which the *Press* published the following day.

3. For William Sooy Smith, chief of cavalry, see *Johnson Papers,* V, 585*n.*

4. Ray resigned, but Cook was wounded, not killed.

5. William F. Prosser (1834-1911), Pennsylvania native, entered the army in November, 1861, becoming lieutenant, 15th Pa. Cav. before transferring to the 2nd Tenn. Cav. In March, 1863, he was appointed major and a year later promoted lieutenant colonel. Retiring in 1865, he settled on a farm near Nashville, served in the Tennessee house (1867-69), in Congress (1869-71), and as Nashville postmaster (1872-75). Appointed special agent of the interior department, he removed to Seattle in 1879, where he became city treasurer (1908-10). *BDAC,* 1484.

6. Jacob M. Thornburgh.

7. Joseph R. Paxton (d. 1867), a Philadelphia lawyer and captain, 15th U. S. Inf., acted for a time as mustering and disbursing officer for Tennessee troops. After the war, he returned to Philadelphia where he was employed by the Catawissa Railway. Moving to Galveston, Texas, in 1867, to engage in "mercantile pursuits," he died of yellow fever. Philadelphia *Press,* August 25, 1867; Powell, *Army List,* 522.

8. Augustus H. Plummer (*c*1832-1866), Ohio native and West Pointer (1853), served on the frontier until 1861. As captain, 19th Inf., he was captured by "Texas insurgents" in July, 1861, exchanged in August, 1862, and became an ordnance officer in the 4th Div. and XX Corps (1864-65). *West Point Register* (1970), 247; Powell, *Army List,* 533.

9. The Calfkiller River skirmish actually occurred on February 22, more than two weeks before Gillem's letter. Companies I and K of Stokes's 5th Tenn. Cav. under Capt. James T. Exum were attacked by guerrillas under Capt. J. M. Hughs and inflicted with heavy loss before 6 officers and 45 men escaped back to camp. Gillem seems to imply that cowardice was evident when *all* of the officers returned, while approximately one third of their men were killed. William B. Stokes to Capt. B. H. Polk, February 24, 1864, *OR,* Ser.

1, XXXII, Pt. I, 416; Monroe Seals, *History of White County* (n. p., 1935), 71-72; *Tenn. Adj. Gen. Report* (1866), 434, 437. For Confederate partisan leaders, Oliver P. Hamilton and Champ Ferguson, operating in White and adjacent counties, see *Johnson Papers,* V, 259*n*.

10. Lt. Col. Robert Galbraith resigned the day of Gillem's letter. Although Thomas had recommended as early as January that Stokes's regiment, because of command difficulties, be split by removing Galbraith's battalion, it was not until early April that the regiment was reorganized. It has been suggested that Stokes's influence with Johnson was the reason that reorganization was not accomplished earlier. Stokes was then assigned to command the post at Carthage and the 5th Cav. was placed under Lt. Col. William J. Clift and assigned to Gillem. *Tenn. Adj. Gen. Report* (1866), 416; *Tennesseans in the Civil War,* I, 331-32.

11. Abraham E. Garrett.

12. John Murphy (*c*1837-1871) of Iowa, on detached duty with the Governor's Guard from January to April, 1864, had enlisted in the U. S. 4th Cavalry in 1855, transferring as 1st lieutenant, 5th Tenn. Cav. in 1862 and rising to colonel two years later. After the war he returned to regular service as 2nd lieutenant, 4th Cav., resigning in 1869. CSR, RG94, NA; Powell, *Army List,* 498.

13. Lt. Col. George W. Bridges and Maj. John Elliott both had enlisted as recently as February and were destined for brief military careers, the former being discharged in December and the latter cashiered in October.

14. R. Clay Crawford, always a center of controversy, had been captain, Co. B, 1st Tenn. Lgt. Arty. until November, 1863. Although promoted to lieutenant 1st Tenn. Heavy Arty., which was not mustered in, he seems never to have served under Gillem.

From John Read

March 13, 1864, Jackson; ALS, DLC-JP.

Solicits Johnson's personal intervention in the case of Robert Hays—son of Gen. Samuel Hays, a prominent Jackson citizen—who ostensibly was serving merely as "the bearer of innocent letters . . . to Ladies beyond the line" when taken into custody by federal soldiers.

From Citizens of the Fifth Judicial Circuit

*ca.*March 15, 1864, Huntsville; Pet, T-Mil. Gov's Papers, 1862-65, Petitions.

More than one hundred citizens of the 5th judicial circuit, "desirous that *Law* may be enforced by the civil authorities," request the temporary appointment of Col. Leonidas C. Houk of the 3rd circuit to "*bring form out of chaos;* restore order to society; and vindicate the magesty of the law, thus rescuing person and property from Lawless bands and defiant desperadoes."

From Alvan C. Gillem

Nashville March 15 64.

Governor.

I have just returned from the North Western Road, it is now progressing finely[.] I passed over forty miles on the Cars—and the track laying is going on well. An Engine has gone to the other end of the Road, and there is there force enough to lay a mile daily of track. The road will all be completed except four miles from 53 to 57, by the 1st of April and will all be in running order by the 20 of April—if not sooner— I give I think the outside limit. Genls Grant & Thomas look upon it as an absolute necessity—in fact it would be impossible to subsist both Thomas & Schofields armies without the aid of this road.[1] at last the Commander of the Dept sees what you saw two years since.

I know with what avidity every detachment of recruits were Seized & put on duty when you were here[.] it has been worse Since you left. So I determined to carry the matter to Hd Qrs. and three or four days Since I went to Chattanooga to see General Thomas. The General gave orders for the 2nd, 3rd & 4th. Regiments of Cavalry to report to me & be put into a Camp of instruction and to be thoroughly Equiped & mounted[.] Those Regiments you recolect had been turned over to the U.S. he told that the Regiments organizing here should not be interfered with that they were under your orders & Commanders of Posts &C should know it. Gen: Thomas' order sending the 2nd 3rd & 4th to Nashville brings together 8 Tenn Cav. Regts at this place.—Rays, Pickens Thornburghs (Edwards), 8th Brown (Strickland) 9 Parsons 10 Bridges, 12 Spaulding & 13 Miller, about 6000 men.

Gen: Thomas of the Brigade you were authorized to raise, asked what Regiments you intended to put in it, whether Stokes was one of them, expressed, a desire to aid you in re-establishing Civil Government. his sentiments are decidedly of the *"Radical"* kind.[2] I think my time was not lost in going to Chattanooga[.] I was absent from Nashville but two days— Garret reports 650 men at Carthage—Murphy 850.

The elections went well in Obion Weakley Carroll Henderson Decatur. I think the votes will foot up at least 40,000 in the state—[3] I believe there is a decided change in public opinion in Tennessee for the better— Mr East is still sick[.]

I am Governor Yours sincerely
Alvan C. Gillem

ALS, DLC-JP.

1. The armies of the Ohio and the Cumberland, under Schofield and Thomas respectively, were wintering in East Tennessee and northern Georgia with Nashville as their major supply center. Although the L & N Railroad had been the major supply line, it was a long route, frequently crippled by raids on its many bridges and trestles; the Northwestern would be shorter and less vulnerable. Thomas had emphasized its "vital importance" in a wire to Johnson the previous fall. See Telegram from George H. Thomas, October 26, 1863; Hall, *Military Governor*, 197.

2. It may be assumed that Gillem interpreted as "radical" views supportive of greater independence for blacks. Thomas followed government policy by accepting them as contraband of war and enlisting them into service. As recently as March 6 he had written George Stearns assuring him that "in so far as it can be consistently done, any aid that may tend to promote the success of your proposed experiment in the cultivation of Tennessee lands by Freed Colored labor, will be afforded you by this Department." No doubt, Lorenzo Thomas' regulations of February 4, 1864, the employment and enlistment of freed blacks, the confiscation of plantations, if necessary, to provide employment, and the establishment of a wage scale for employed blacks would support Gillem's contention. Maslowski, *Treason Must Be Made Odious,* 114-15.

3. County returns found in the secretary of state's office are incomplete. For Henderson, Carroll, and Weakley, only the names of the officials elected are known. In Obion, 3,837 voted and in Decatur, 1,732. Tommy Adams (Tennessee State Library and Archives) to Andrew Johnson Project, January 22, 1980.

From Joseph E. Harris[1]

Law Department Yale College
New Haven Ct March 17 1864

His Excellency Andrew Johnson
Governor of the State of Tennessee Nashville
Sir—

It is gratifying to my pride to be able to inform you that nearly a year ago I was permitted to take the Oath of Allegiance to the United States, renewing in good faith all my obligations to the benificent Government under which I was born.

Ever since that period I have been here at the Law School of Yale College endeavoring to qualify myself for a profession by which I hope to get a living in my native Nashville.[2]

Every day's experience—as I become a man—convinces me the more of the utter wickedness of this most unprovoked rebellion into which as a boy I so unfortunately stumbled[3]—and I can say with truth that I most ardently desire its overthrow.

Your policy for reconstruction in Tennessee, if I understand it, is the only true policy.

I seize this opportunity to thank you for your good counsel and advice when I was a rebel prisoner at Nashville,[4] and only regret that I did not profit from it at an earlier day. I have the honor to be

Very Respectfully Your ob't serv't
Jos. E. Harris

Hon Andrew Johnson

ALS, DLC-JP.

1. For Joseph E. Harris, son of former Nashville editor and stalwart unionist J. George Harris, see *Johnson Papers,* V, 162*n*.

2. His death in London a year later precluded this hopeful future. *Ibid.*

3. After making a name for himself as an orator in "a most glowing Union Speech in the Representative Hall Feb 22, 1861, as the representative of his Society at the Nashville University," young Harris fell from Union grace and joined Rutledge's Tenn. Lgt. Arty. Bty, CSA, as a third lieutenant, only to be captured in an attack on Nashville in October, 1862. Letter from J. George Harris, February 26, 1862, *ibid.,* 162; Philadelphia *Press,* November 15, 1862.

4. Johnson's journalistic friend Benjamin C. Truman, always eager to enhance the governor's image as a sage expounder of Union principles, devoted one of his despatches to Forney's Philadelphia *Press* to reporting a "conversation" with "a Captain Harris." This "good counsel and advice" followed the well-worn path of his public addresses— reiteration of the South's unprovoked responsibility for the rebellion, the obligation of the Federal government to enforce the laws, the duplicity of the slave aristocracy in getting non-slaveholders like Harris to fight the war, and assurance of the Union's ultimate triumph. *Ibid.*

From Edward J. Read[1]

at my farm Haywood County Tennessee
19 March 1864

Honble Andrew Johnson
Military Governor of Tennessee
Nashville Tennessee
Dear Sir

Last evening I brought home from my office at Brownsville 2 of the writing Desks & a Chest containing part of my letters & papers all battered in by some of the Command of Col Hurst[.][2] you can see the prints of their guns on the folding door of my little Secretary & many of my papers are gone & feathered to the four winds of heaven[.]

Col Hurst burned 3 establishments belonging to 3 of the best Union men about Brownsville. Is that any way for him or any Federal officer to do? some of these sufferers has left since and settled in Peoria Illinois, I learned yesterday & one had before gone & opened an establishment in Memphis Tenn[.]

It appears that old Satan has been turned loose to go about and injurying the innocent[.]

Previous to the advent of Col Hurst I had shipped all of my Law Books & the most of my valuable papers to a place of safety, not knowing when one or the other of the Armies might enter and Destroy— I was always opposed to the war never was infavor of secession & never expect to be so and I have suffered more than the secessionists and it looks hard and both sides have taken from me my horses & mules &c but show the consolation of Job when his friends told him "*to curse God & die*" he told them "I Know my redeemer Liveth" and so do I—

In the summer of 1862 the Federal soldiers in passing would ride up to the field where my negroes were ploughing & try to get them to take out their mules or horses & go on with them that "*they would pay them $8 to 10$ pr month*"

My property before the war was estimated at about two hundred thousand Dollars[3] & I would willingly give it all to close the war satisfactorily now as I am young enough to make more but it appears that his majesty "*Old Satan*" is revelling in great luxury North & South & that if this war should end before he shall have been thrashed out of the people both North & South, it will soon brake out anew like an old Canser[.]

If Mr. Lincoln had had the nerve of Genl Andrew Jackson or Mr Filmore or Col James K Polk our difficulties might have been ended ere this[.]

When Genl Lew Wallace went from Corinth to Memphis in 1862, he knocked the wind out of the sails of the secessionists & made Union men out of secessionists & when the 7 Kansas Regiment went from Columbus Ky passing Jackson Tenn in 1862 robbing and hanging people they made Secessionists out of Union men[.][4]

What Caused our arms to Conquer Mexico so soon or easily in 1846, 47 & 1848? it was the mild & Gentle policy pursued by our President Col James K Polk who would not permit the Soldiers to rob pillage & plunder the Mexicans & paid for what they got[.] But Louis Napoleon landed his forces in Mexico in Novb 1860 & he suffered them to plunder & devastate the country & he is not nearer conquering them now than he was 12 mos ago Notwithstanding he has more men there than James K Polk had in 1846, 47 & 1848[.] But it appears that Mr Lincoln cannot resist the outside pressure of these heavenly sanctified preachers[5] nor Could Mr Buchanan resist the outside pressure of Floyd Toombs, Thompson & others & now where is Mr Buckanan?[6]

Had the policy of James K Polk & Genl Scott been adopted—peace now might perhaps "*have* been *restored*" & then "*those who danced could have been made to pay the Fiddler*" and I am fearful peace is far off from our once happy Country[.]

History proves that a different policy towards our enemies will produce a different & better result[.] Look at the policy of Spain towards the United Provinces in a war which lasted nearly fifty years & in which Spain lost those Provinces[.]

Look at the Policy of Charles II of England & his Parliament—he pardoned all his rebels with a few exceptions & he did not enter into this wholesale destruction & Confiscation of private property or he never could have maintained his head on the throne & those difficulties lasted 18 years before his restoration & Some of your old substantial Union friends in this part of the Country say—(I dont mean such men who are "*pig to day & pork* to-morrow".[7] Union when the Federals are about & Secessions when the Confederates are nearby such as have always been the same from the Orient to the Occident) that unless a different Policy be pursued this war will last 30 years & that there is only one way to settle it in order to have a permanent peace of which it is not my purpose now to write you[.]

My relative the Honbl John Reed of Jackson Tenn who has always been a Union man & is now in his 77 year of his age has suffered from the Federal Army more than any other man according to his property or about as much as any in that County according to his property— This is no way for officers & soldiers & a Government to treat their peaceable quiet and orderly Citizens[.]

Some times I get out of heart & think that our Dear Country is gone to old Satan or is fast on the verge & that the old maxim that "the people are incapable of self Government" has been realized[.]

I write you thus plainly because you are our Military Govenor & you were a Breckenridge Democrat and so was I and I wished to inform you how matters have been managed in portions of this Country[.]

What do you think of the English papers calling us a nation of thieves and Robbers?[8] that is tolerably tall talk[.]

Some times it does seem to me that the whole Country will get into a general row from one end to the other from the Lakes to the Gulf and from the Atlantic to the Pacific, like it was in England during her civil wars and it so much distresses me some times that it almost sickens me[.]

Several of my negroes left me in 1862 & 1863 & are in the Federal Army or waiting on the Army[.]

Please have the kindness to inform me what course should I pursue in order to get a Voucher for them[.]

If you think proper to address me, you can direct your letter thus

Yours Respectfully Edward J. Read
of Brownsville Tennessee
Care of Farmington & Howell Memphis Tennsse

To Governor Andrew Johnson
Nashville Tennessee

ALS, DLC-JP.

1. Edward J. Read (*c*1814-*fl*1880), Kentucky native, was a lawyer and farmer. 1860 Census, Tenn., Haywood, Belles Depot, 11th Dist., 128; (1880), Crockett, 5th Dist., 29.

2. For Fielding Hurst of the 6th Tenn. Cav., USA, whose command was harassing southern sympathizers in West Tennessee, see *Johnson Papers,* V, 568*n.*

3. Read either exaggerated his wealth or failed to report it accurately to the census where his worth totals $73,500 ($47,500 real, and $26,000 personal), including 3 adult male slaves and 1 female. 1860 Census, Slave Schedule, Tenn., Haywood, 88.

4. Particularly notorious for its "Negro stealing," this regiment, which had "displayed a penchant for destroying both unionist and secessionist property in Kansas . . . maintained its unenviable reputation by indiscriminate depredations on Federal and Confederate sympathizers" in West Tennessee during June, 1862. See *Johnson Papers,* V, 492n; Stephen Z. Starr, *Jennison's Jayhawkers* (Baton Rouge, 1973), 166-69.

5. An allusion to the Wesleyan doctrine of "entire sanctification" and to two Methodist bishops in particular, Matthew Simpson and Edward R. Ames, who exerted a good deal of influence on Lincoln and his cabinet, especially Stanton, from whom they secured control of the seized property of the Methodist Episcopal Church, South, including Nashville's McKendree Church. Nolan B. Harmon, ed., *The Encyclopedia of World Methodism* (2 vols., Nashville, 1974), I, 489; II, 2160; *DAB,* I, 243; XVII, 181-82.

6. Accurate as concerns Jacob Thompson and John B. Floyd, southern members of Buchanan's cabinet; inaccurate with regard to Robert Toombs, Georgia Whig. In all probability Read confused Toombs with Howell Cobb, also a Georgian, who not only was secretary of the treasury but also perhaps the President's most intimate friend. Kenneth M. Stampp, *And the War Came* (Chicago, 1950), 47-48, 53, 57; Philip S. Klein, *President James Buchanan* (University Park, Pa., 1962), 368, 371.

7. A search for the origin of this porcine figure has been unavailing.

8. It is possible that a reference to "thieves and cut-throats" in *The Times* (London) of February 15 may have been distorted in a West Tennessee paper.

From G. G. Doss[1]

Louisvill March the 20, 1864

The Governeur Johnson
at Tennessee
Dear Sir!
You moeby would not have anny Objection for to tell me of it is safed for to go to Elizabethtown Carter County East Tennessee. I would not like to fall in the Hands of Rebels—and I would Like to go to mein Farm thereself. It would be a bik favor to me if you would let me known with nacst Mail of our Armee have the Rebels driven away there; than I will come to mein loveli Home and attend to mein Farm. Sure you do not know me but you will be kind anouch to every man hoe did his duti in the Union Armee for several Months like me; and I can not find out the very Trueth about this matter without you, becaus I do not belief every report.

Yours Servent G. G. Dosse.

I find the Stamps and Umvellups for Youer Answer, Closed in here[.]

G G Dosse

ALS, DLC-JP.

1. Not identified.

From Blount County Officials

March 21, 1864, Maryville; ALS, DLC-JP.

Blount County officials—Washington L. Dearing, county clerk, Thomas Sanderson, provost marshal, and Frank M. Hood, trustee—pointing out that numerous robberies in East Tennessee endanger tax collectors on their rounds, urge a gubernatorial proclamation requiring taxpayers to pay at their respective courthouses.

To William D. Gallagher[1]

Louisville, Ky. March 21st 1864.

Dear Sir,

While at Washington City very recently, I received a telegram from Mr. Thomas S. Marr of Nashville, Tenn stating that some two thousand dollars ($2000) in gold belonging to him and shipped from this City to his Banking House at Nashville, had been seized, in transitu, by the Custom House authorities of Louisville and that the proceedings had been reported to the Treasury Department.

It appears that Mr. Marr, under a misapprehension of the Treasury Regulations governing the subject, had been granted, in my name, a permit for the shipment of the same, and seeming to act in good faith in accordance with such permit, I would therefore respectfully recommend that the said sum of money be released.

Before leaving Washington on the 16th ins't, I called at the Treasury Department, with the view of making the same statement herein made, but was officially informed that no report of the seizure of Mr. Marr's gold had been received at that Department.

I was also assured by the Ass't Secretary of the Treasury that if such Report was made, I would be advised thereof before any decision in the premise was made.[2]

Very Respectfully, Yours obt. Sert.
Andrew Johnson

W. D. Gallagher Esq.
Surveyor of Customs, Louisville, Ky.

Tel copy, DLC-JP.

1. For William D. Gallagher, customs surveyor at Louisville, see *Johnson Papers,* IV, 698*n*.

2. Two months later, Johnson, now returned to Nashville, wrote Secretary Chase reviewing the circumstances of the case and repeating his recommendation. Johnson to Chase, May 16, 1864, Johnson Papers, LC.

To Abraham Lincoln

Louisville Mch 21 1864.

His Excellency Prest. Lincoln—

The Dept of the Cumberland ought to be placed under the command of maj Genl Thomas Receiving his instructions & orders directly from Washn. I feel satisfied from what I know & hear that placing the command of the Dept under Gen. Sherman over Thomas will produce disappointment in the public mind & impair the public service[.][1] Gen Thomas has the confidence of the Army & the people & will discharge his duty as he has from the commencement of the Rebellion[.] He will in my opinion if permitted be one of the great Genls of this War if not the greatest[.] I will be in Nashville tomorrow & will dispatch you again[.]

Andrew Johnson

Tel, DLC-Lincoln Papers; DLC-JP; DNA-RG107, Tels. Recd., President, Vol. 2 (1864).

1. Sherman, whose refusal to move on East Tennessee in the fall of 1861 lived on in Tennesseans' memories, had just been appointed commander of the Division of Mississippi made up of three armies—the Ohio, the Tennessee, and the Cumberland. Meanwhile, Thomas, in charge of the latter, had earned plaudits for his conduct during several campaigns in Tennessee; as early as summer, 1862, Johnson had urged his promotion to head an East Tennessee expedition. Cleaves, *George H. Thomas,* 208; Lloyd Lewis, *Sherman: Fighting Prophet* (New York, 1932), 346; *Johnson Papers,* V, 575, 617.

From Marshall County Citizens[1]

March 24, 1864

To His Excellency Andrew Johnson
Military Governor of Tennessee
The undersigned petitioners would Represent to you that they are neighbors of James A Wilson,[2] who is now in military prison at Rock Island Illinois he having deserted the Rebel army in East Tennessee & was trying to make his way home & take the Oath of amnesty & Remain at home & was Captured & Carried to Rock Island, of which facts we are well satisfyed. we would further Represent that the said James A Wilson was forced into the Rebel army By the Confederate Cavalry about Twelve months since, against his will. He Left the Rebel army in december Last[.] Your petitioners would Represent that they are well acquainted with James A Wilson & that he is an honest upright man, & a good citizen & would If permitted to take the amnisty oath of the President of the united states & Return to his home make a good Citizen of the United States & abide by said proclamation[.] your petitioners would humbly ask your kind aid in his behalf, as his family are needing his aid at home[.]
Marshall County March 24th 1864

Pet, DNA-RG249, Lets. Recd., File 83T (1864), James A. Wilson.

1. Bearing fifty signatures, this petition had been preceded a month earlier by a similar plea with forty-three names, several of them the same. Lets. Recd., 1862-67, RG249, NA.

2. James A. Wilson (b. *c*1825), who enlisted as a private, Co. F, 17th Tenn. Inf., CSA, at Chapel Hill on February 1, 1863, was captured at Tazewell on December 15, sent to Rock Island in January, and released a year later. CSR, RG109, NA; *Tennesseans in the Civil War,* II, 438.

From William Watkins[1]

Allensville Todd Co' Kentucky
25th March 1864.

Govenor Johnson
Honored Sir

You will pardon the freedom I now take with you, I am considerably at a loss how to address you, being so little in the habit of corresponding with persons in your position. Should I, therefore, fail to comply with the usual Courtesys you will be kind enough to overlook it.
I had the pleasure of an introduction to you several years ago, but, of course, you can have no recollection of me,

I was born and raised in Logan Co Ky and has been my legacy, as was Cains, to spend a hard and laborious life, started with but little, have been tollerably successful, thoug laboring half of my life for faithless friends. One year ago last Christmas, I divided between my two Children more than

100 negroes, for whom I laboured hard, purchased the most of them. Since our unfortunate difficuties, and during the last year, many of them have been induced to run off. I understand Some are on the N Western R.R. Others are hiding about Nashville, others are in the army. The men carried of 8 or 10 small boys, too young to be of any servise to the government. I own a family of negroes whose grand mother lives in Nashville. I am told several of the boys are being harboured by her. Some of those on the road have rheumatism &c and all are anxious to come home.

I wish to inquire, if you will not assist, or permit, me to recover those harboured by the old woman and allow me to bring any others home who may wish to return?

I would like to see you in person, would like to get information on many subjects. I did hope to see civil law restored in your state, when will it be done? Would it be advisable to purchase land, with some negroes, in Montgomery Co Tennessee?

Your reply will be very kindy remembered[.]

Very respectfully your friend
W Watkins

I refer you to D. D. Holeman[2]
Address me at Allensville Ky.

ALS. DLC-JP.

1. William Watkins (b. *c*1810), a wealthy Logan County farmer, possessed $76,200 in real and $177,170 in personal property, including sixty-three slaves. 1860 Census, Ky., Logan, 2nd Dist., 91; Slave Schedule, 18-19.

2. Daniel D. Holman, a Springfield, Tennessee, tavern keeper and a lifelong Democrat.

From Horace H. Harrison

Office of Attorney of the United States
For the Middle District of Tennessee.
Nashville, Mch 28th 1864.

Gov Johnson.

I beg to State that I have carefully examined the Proclamation of His Excellency the President of the United States Explaining his proclamation of the 8 Dec 1863, and respectfully Submit the following legal construction thereof.

1st The President declares his main leading object in the proclamation of 8 Dec to be to Suppress insurrection and to restore the authority of the United States and distinctly states that the *Amnesty* therein proposed was offered with reference alone to these objects i e suppressing insurrection and restoring the authority of the national government.

2nd Persons in custody, under bonds or parole, whether as prisoners of war, or detained for offences of any kind agst the U. S. neither before or after Conviction Can take the oath in Military Naval or Civil Courts, but the offer of amnesty applies only to those who are not under Such duress.

The offer of amnesty is to those who, free from any Such duress, Shall Come forward voluntarily and take the oath with the view of restoring peace and Establishing the National authority[.]

3d Prisoners are to present their application for pardon to the Executive.

4th The oath may be taken before Any Commissioned Civil, Military or Naval officer of the U. S. in Tennessee. The Oath taken before a Justice or Notary in a State declared in insurrection would not be recognized those officers not being Commissioned officers in the Service of the U. S.

5th The remaining portion of the "Explanatory proclamation" simply directs that the record of the Oath be Sent to the State Department, registered by the Secretary & Copies or Certificates of Such record furnished.

I have the Honor to be
Very respy your obt Servt
Horace H. Harrison
U S. Dist Attorney

ALS, DLC-JP.

From Richard P. Mitchell[1]

Hd. Qrs Regimental Hospital
1st Tenn. Light Artilley Mch. 28/64

To his Excellency, Andrew Johnson
Military Governor of Tennessee

I would respectfully ask for leave of Absence for twenty[2] days to go to Blains Cross Roads, Granger Co. for the purpose of moving my family to some place where they can secure subsistence[.]

R. P. Mitchell
Major and Reg. Surgeon
1st Tenn. Light Artillery

Approved
Andrew Johnson
Mil. Gov'r.

ALS, T-Mil. Gov's Papers, 1862-65, Corres. to A. Johnson.

1. Richard P. Mitchell (1827-*fl*1890), Hawkins County native and graduate of Jefferson Medical College in Philadelphia (1854), spent one year in Gainesville, Florida, before returning to Rogersville. In the fall of 1863 he became surgeon of the 1st Tenn. Lgt. Arty. stationed at Nashville. At this time his family consisted of his wife, Mary J. Shields, the daughter of a Grainger County physician, whom he married in 1861, and an infant daughter. After the war he resumed his profession in Rogersville. *Goodspeed's East Tennessee,* 1233; Sistler, *1890 Tenn. Veterans Census,* 221; 1870 Census, Tenn., Hawkins, Rogersville, 10th Dist., 7.

2. As revealed by the endorsement and the clear evidence that this number is a correction, the original request was for thirty days.

To George D. Ramsay

Nashville Mar 29 [1864]

Brig Gen Ramsay
Chf Ord

Two thousand (2000) more Carbines are necessary for arming men now organized[.] Morrells [Merrills] Sharps or Maynards preferred[.] Horse equipments are also needed[.][1]

Andrew Johnson Mil Gov

Tel, DNA-RG107, Tels. Recd., U. S. Mil. Tel., Vol. 89 (1864).

1. This call for military supplies had remarkable success, perhaps reflecting some hard nosed interviews which the governor had during his recent Washington visit. Two days later he was assured that "Horse equipments will be sent at once—Carbines as soon as they can be procured—" and two weeks later was informed that "There have been ordered to be sent to Capt Townsend at Nashville Tenn 2000 Gallagher Carbines with accoutrements and 2000 Sabres for issue to the Tennessee troops." Moreover, the guns would "be supplied with the new soft metal cartridge which avoids the difficulty . . . in the sticking of the cartridge cases in the band after firing[.]" George D. Ramsay to Johnson, March 31, April 13, 1864, Misc. Lets. Sent, 1812-1889, Vol. 60, General Records, RG156, NA.

To James T. Shelley[1]

Nashville, March 29th 1864

Col James T. Shelley
Loudon, Tennessee,

A Soldier elected to a Civil Office is not discharged by Such election from the Service of the United States, but would be a good reason to the commander of the Department for his discharge—And no doubt would be granted—

The fact of an East Tennessean being a Soldier in the Service of the United States, would be prima-facia evidence that he was a loyal Citizen And therefore ought to vote without regard to any Oath.[2] In the present disorganized condition of the Country irregularities must be overlooked when necessary to restore law and order—

Andrew Johnson

Tel draft, DLC-JP.

1. For Shelley, colonel of the 5th Tenn. Inf., USA, see *Johnson Papers,* V, 85*n*.

2. The day before he had inquired about the status of a soldier elected to civil office and concerning the validity of a soldier's voting without taking the oath. See Shelley to Johnson, March 28, 1864, Johnson Papers, LC.

To Edwin M. Stanton

Nashville March 30 1864.

Hon E M Stanton
Sec War

Mrs Senator Foote[1] obtained a pass to go South with the understanding that she was not to return & I think that she ought to remain there at least till the Close of the rebellion[.][2] Oaths or paroles will have but little influence over her[.] Senator or Representative Foote [and] wife will do us a great deal less harm in the South than they will in Nashville[.]

Andrew Johnson Mil Gov

Tel, DNA-RG107, Tels. Recd., Sec. of War, Vol. 36 (1864).

1. Rachel D. Smiley (*c*1831-1882), widow of Nashville attorney Robert G. Smiley, in 1859 had married Henry S. Foote, formerly U. S. senator and currently Confederate congressman. Mt. Olivet Cemetery Records, II, 118; Nashville *Patriot,* June 15, 1859; Deane Porch, tr., *1850 Census of the City of Nashville* (Fort Worth, 1969), 98; for Foote, see *Johnson Papers,* III, 504*n*.

2. Two days earlier Stanton had wired: "Have you any objections to Mrs. Foote . . . being permitted to go to Nashville & remaining there on her parole[?]" Stanton to Johnson, March 28, 1864, Johnson Papers, LC.

To Abraham Lincoln

Nashville 31 Mar 1864.

His Ex. A Lincoln

Wm Bell was not arrested by my authority.[1] I presume he is a prisoner of war. I have not been able to find out much about him. There are hundreds of others, no doubt, who are more entitled to Executive Clemency than he is.—

Your late proclamation will do good;[2] I wish it had still been more stringent[.]

Andrew Johnson.
Mil Governor.

Tel, DLC-Lincoln Papers.

1. Possibly William A. Bell (b. *c*1841) of Rutherford County, a private, Co. D, 45th Tenn. Inf., CSA, who deserted at Lookout Mountain, was captured in November, 1863, and paroled from Rock Island the following October. Lincoln's wire to Johnson was prompted by Judge John Catron's intercession in behalf of William Bell's release from Rock Island, where he was held hostage, presumably on Johnson's order. CSR, RG109, NA; Lincoln to Johnson, March 29, 1864, Basler, *Works of Lincoln*, VII, 273.

2. Lincoln's order of March 26 limited his December 8, 1863, amnesty to those still "at large and free from any arrest," who came forward voluntarily to take the oath; it did not apply to those held prisoner, or under bond or parole. *Ibid.,* 269-70.

From Charles C. Alexander

April 1, 1864, Nashville; ALS, DNA-RG249, Lets. Recd., File 844B (1864), Stephen P. Doughty.

A prisoner recently released from Johnson's Island, Ohio, requests that Stephen P. Doughty of Obion County, also incarcerated there, be allowed to take the oath of allegiance and return home. Since Doughty's avowal of loyalty, other prisoners have "insulted him and treated him rudely and attempted to hang him."

From William Hoffman

April 2, 1864, Washington; LS, DLC-JP.

In response to petition, forwarded by the governor, asking for the release of David A. Rowe from Camp Chase, the commissary general of prisoners reports that "at present no prisoners of war or political prisoners are being discharged except in special cases," but assures Johnson that "the Prisoner will not be sent South for exchange against his consent."

Speech at Shelbyville

April 2, 1864, Shelbyville; Nashville *Times and True Union,* April 5, 1864.

In a three-hour harangue which received only the briefest reportage, Johnson seems to have covered the usual topics—the rise and progress of the rebellion, the culpability of its leaders, the nobility of the country's defenders, and "the glories of the future." With respect to issues currently under debate, he advocated a state convention, "opposed . . . the separation of East Tennessee," and "declared *himself* in favor of immediate emancipation, but would embrace any system of emancipation which a convention of the loyal people might deem expedient and just."

Proclamation re County Elections

State of Tennessee,
Executive Department,
Nashville, April 4, 1864.

WHEREAS, In several counties of the State, and in many districts, from various causes no election was held on the 5th of March last, for county and district officers. In all such instances where counties have failed to hold said elections, upon application to me. suitable persons will be appointed to hold the same; and in all cases where districts have failed to elect, or the officers elected to qualify, the respective county courts will order elections at such times as the same can be conveniently held. And in both cases said elections will be held in pursuance of my proclamation of the 28[26]th of January, 1864. In all cases, where questions arise as to the capacity of the party elected to hold, either from any of the disqualifications mentioned by law, or of failure to comply with said proclamation in the election, or by reason of said person's known and continued disloyalty to the Government of the United States, the questions are referred to the county courts of the county, who will hear and determine the same, and shall enter the same, if the person is found to be disqualified, upon the records of the courts, and striking such name from the commission, if he be elected to an office requiring a commission by law.

In testimony whereof I have hereunto subscribed my name, and caused the Great Seal of the State to be affixed, at the Department at Nashville, this the 5th day of April, 1864.

Andrew Johnson.

By the Governor:
Edward H. East,
Secretary of State

Memphis *Bulletin,* April 13, 1864.

To Abraham Lincoln

Nashville, April 5th 1864

His Excellency Abraham Lincoln.
Washington City,
Mr President,

Enclosed you will please find charge of the Criminal Judge to the Grand Jury of this County[.][1]

The meeting at Shelbyville on the 2nd April, went off well.[2] Indications on the part of the people were much better than I anticipated in regard to the emancipation of Slavery— As Soon as practicable there must be a Convention, which I believe will Settle the Slavery question definitely and finely— I hope that Congress will soon propose an Amendment to the Constitution of the United States, to the different states upon this subject— the Sooner it is done, the better— Our Marshall will make Some arrests this week for treason—[3] If we have one or two Convictions in this state, it will exert a powerful influence upon rebels and hasten restoration more than anything which can be done—

With great respect
Andrew Johnson Mil Gov

LS, DLC-Lincoln Papers.

1. Opening court the day before, Judge Manson M. Brien had charged the jury to disregard all Confederate laws. After remarks on "Homicide . . . and other heinous offences," he spoke briefly about larceny and receiving stolen goods, and then proceeded to lay down a stern, intractable line on treason, defining it according to the state code and warning that taking the President's amnesty oath "does not excuse or pardon a person who has committed treason against the State of Tennessee." Offering a ringing defense of Johnson's much-criticized supplementary oath required for voting in the recent elections, he endorsed the right of soldiers and others recently come to the state to vote, if they could and would take the requisite oaths. All who had violated their oaths, whether Lincoln's amnesty or Johnson's supplementary, "you will indict for perjury." Nashville *Dispatch,* April 5, 1864.

2. Some 2,500 people attended, with Edmund Cooper, presiding. In addition to speeches by General Rousseau, Col. Lewis Tillman, and others, the governor spoke for three hours on slavery and reorganization. Advocating an immediate constitutional amendment to abolish slavery, he opined that free Negroes worked better than slaves, and that "Negroes could only be valuable to the community, now, as free men." He had emancipated his own, was now paying them wages, and "never before were they so valuable to him; and they never were so contented to remain in his service." Nashville *Union,* April 5, 1864. No extended report of this speech has been found.

3. There were numerous trials for treason reported in the Nashville press during April and May, principally in Connelly Trigg's U. S. District Court, but most of those indicted had been under arrest for a year or more. Perhaps Johnson's use of "arrest" is a euphemism for the commencement of formal proceedings. Most cases were dropped, however, because those charged had subscribed to the amnesty oath. For Edwin R. Glascock (*c*1816-1891), U. S. marshal (1863-67), see *Johnson Papers,* IV, 337*n;* Nashville *American,* February 13, 1891; *U. S. Official Register* (1863-67), *passim.*

To Abraham Lincoln

Nashville Apl. 5 1864

His Excellency Abraham Lincoln
Prest

The papers state that Genl Buell is to be sent to Knoxville to take Command[.] I trust in god that Gen Buell will not be sent to Tennessee.[1] We have been cursed with him here once and do not desire its repetition[.] We had a fine meeting at Shelbyville. Went off well[.] General Rosseau made a fine speech taking high ground on the negro question which will I think do great good in Kentucky and Tennessee[.][2] If Genl Rosseau had leave of absence for a short time which would Enable him to visit Kentucky and make some speeches in that state such as he made at Shelbyville it would do much good in putting down Copperheads and traitors. If this suggestion was made to Genl Thomas I have no doubt he would grant him leave of absence for the present[.] His services would be invaluable in Kentucky[.][3]

Andrew Johnson

Tel, NHi-Andrew Johnson Papers.

1. On April 2, a despatch from its special correspondent at Chattanooga appeared in the Louisville *Journal* to the effect that "Gen. Buell is to take command of the Department of the Ohio, headquarters for the present at Knoxville." A conflict of personalities and functions, together with Buell's lack of aggressiveness, particularly as concerned the early redemption of East Tennessee, had made that general anathema to the governor. Never again assigned a field command, Buell was about to be mustered out of volunteer service in May, resigning his regular commission in June. See Letter to Abraham Lincoln, September 1, 1862; Warner, *Generals in Blue,* 52.

2. Rousseau came out strongly for the abolition of slavery and the use of Negro troops. As a southern man he had many prejudices; but "I thank God that I love my country better than slavery, and my prejudices." Predicting that the institution would perish with the end of the war, he counseled slaveholders to enlist their Negroes and collect the three hundred dollars' bounty. Admitting his distaste for black troops, "he had always believed that a nigger with a musket on his shoulder fighting for the government, was far better than a rebel fighting against it." Rousseau assured his listeners that he was willing to sacrifice everything in crushing the rebellion, that "love of, and devotion to, his country was his guiding star," and that although "to be assigned to the command of negro troops would be

most repugnant indeed," yet he would do so "if the safety of his country demand it." Nashville *Times and True Union,* April 5, 1864.

3. On April 5, Lincoln endorsed Johnson's communication: "I leave to the Sec. of War whether this shall be brought to the notice of Gen. Grant." Basler, *Works of Lincoln,* VII, 287.

From Charles A. Dana

April 6, 1864, Washington; LB copy, DNA-RG107, Mil. B: Copies Lets. Sent, Vol. 55A (1864).

Asserting that "it is found to be inconsistent with the exigencies of pending military operations to comply with your request," the assistant secretary of war refuses to authorize the purchase of "5,000 horses to mount cavalry enlisted by" Johnson.

From Mary B. Howard[1]

Lebanon April 6th 1864

Govenor Johnson:

You may be apprized of the fact, that my Husband is buried in Greeneville—[2] It is my desire as soon as possible, to have his remains brought to Lebanon, that he may rest by the side of our children. I see from the Nashville papers, that Genl Longstreet has retired from Greeneville, and that his headquarters are now at Watauga.[3] If this is true, is not the communication from Nashville to Greeneville unbroken, and will not the cars run all the way, so soon as the damage done the railroad is repaired? I write to you to ascertain the truth of the dispatch. I feel that you will cheerfully give me any information in your power, or any assistance which I may call for at your hands— If it is practicable for me to start to Greenville, can I get a pass through the lines, and will *transportation returning* be granted me? If the way is open, it is my intention to go immediately, and if any obstacles are thrown around me, will you aid me in removing them? Is there any gentleman now in Nashville from Greeneville who will return soon? If you advise me, that it is practicable to undertake it, I will be obliged to you if you meet with any company suitable for me, that you will advise me of it immediately. I have understood, that there are a good many East Tenneseans in Nashville—and you will most likely know their movements— I have written to Gen Milligan—

Hoping to hear from you very soon,

I am Respectfully
Mary B. Howard

ALS, DLC-JP.

1. Mary Ann Burford Howard (1838-1916), daughter of former state senator David Burford of Smith County, was the widow of Confederate Col. John K. Howard. Nashville *Banner,* November 13, 1916; Acklen, *Tenn. Records,* I, 288.

2. John K. Howard, Sam Milligan's brother-in-law, who died in Richmond in July, 1862. Temporarily interred in Greeneville, his body ultimately was returned to Lebanon.

3. In order to shorten his lines, Longstreet began withdrawing from Greeneville in late March; by the thirty-first he was reported at Watauga but had established his headquarters at Bristol. Nashville *Union,* April 1, 1864; *OR,* Ser. 1, XXXII, Pt. III, 720.

From William P. Lyon[1]

Head Quarters 13th Wis. Vet. Vol. Inftry,
Edgefield, Tenn. April 6th 1864.

Hon. Andrew Johnson
Mil. Gov. of Tennessee:

I have the honor to state that there are a number of refugee families residing in this village—nearly all of whom are in very destitute circumstances—who are threatened by persons claiming to own the premises occupied by them—(or to be the agents of such claimants)—with forcible ejection from their homes. In many cases this would be a great calamity to these people, as it is quite impossible for them to procure other houses. An increased demand for residences and the consequent advance of rents, are the causes of this onslaught upon these poor people.

I made enquiries at the different military Head Quarters in town yesterday & was informed that you had jurisdiction in these matters. I called at your office, but did not see you. I, however, had a conversation with Col. Johnson on the subject, and requested him to say to you that I would gladly execute your orders for the protection of these families, for I beg to assure you that they need protection and the Government owes it to them for their unswerving loyalty.

I shall not allow any of them to be ejected—except by civil process—without your orders or other competent military authority; and I will cheerfully investigate and report upon any of these cases which you may think proper to refer to me.

I am, Governor, Very Respctfly,
Your Obdt. Sert. Wm. P. Lyon
Col. Comdg. Regt.

You will please excuse me for addressing you direct, as I have not the name of your Adjt. Gen.

W. P. L.

In connection with the enclosed general statement, I wish to call your attention to two particular cases.

A house formerly used as a Hospital by our troops is occupied by two families.[2] They found the building empty & moved in it. One of these families named Jenkins is unable to go by reason of the serious illness of one of its members. Jenkins is an Employee of the Govt.[3] The other is a family from Jasper, Tenn. The mother recently died. The step-father named Beck, said to be a drunken, worthless vagabond, has abandoned them entirely. There remains an old grandmother who is bed-ridden—a young woman, Miss Tipton, & two young children, all dependant upon Miss. T.

for support. She is a person of more than ordinary intelligence, and is making earnest exertions to support the family thus left upon her hands.

Both these families have been notified that unless they get out of the house immediately they will be put into the street. This comes from some person in town who says he owns the premises.

I respectfully request you to make an order that these families be allowed to remain where they are until further orders.

There is no injustice in this. The relation of landlord & tenant does not exist between the parties. They (the occupants,) have not admitted the title of the claimant—and the civil courts are open to him—if he is really entitled to possession.

Wm. P. Lyon Col &c.

ALS, DLC-JP.

1. William P. Lyon (1822-1913), New York native, moved to Wisconsin, taught school, passed the bar in 1846, and served in the legislature (1859-60). Enlisting as captain in the 8th Wis., he transferred to the 13th as colonel. Subsequently he was judge of the 1st circuit court (1865-71) and of the state supreme court (1871-94), the last two years as chief justice. *NCAB,* XIII, 98.

2. None of these squatters can be identified with any degree of certainty.

3. Possibly William Jenkins, an assessor. *Singleton's Nashville Business Directory* (1865), 254.

To William G. Brownlow

Nashville, April 6th 1864

Rev W. G. Brownlow
Knoxville, Tennessee,

Upon what day does the Knoxville-Greeneville Convention assemble.[1]

The meeting at Shelbyville went off well— Indications on the part of the people, were decided for a Convention and emancipation. They are for Settling the Slavery question now, and Settling it finely— Can I do any good by being at your Convention[?]

Andrew Johnson Mil Gov

Tel draft, DLC-JP.

1. Brownlow answered immediately that the "Convention meets Tuesday next 12th." Actually a reconvening of the 1861 Knoxville Union Convention, the meeting ended *sine die* in rancor without adopting any of the resolutions offered. Brownlow to Johnson, April 6, 1864, Johnson Papers, LC; Temple, *Notable Men,* 407.

To James R. Hood

Nashville, April 6th 1864

James R. Hood Esqr
Chattanooga, Tennessee,

I am Satisfied that it is best to have a convention—[1] The Convention can do all that a Legislature can, and more too, if necessary and fix the proper time for the meeting of the Legislature— Now is the time to Settle the Slavery question, and a convention will have the power to do so. Convention and immediate emancipation is the true position to occupy—[2] At what time would be best for the convention to meet[?][3]

Andrew Johnson Mil Gov—

Tel draft, DLC-JP.

1. Johnson was responding to the telegraphed query: "Would it not be wise to call a Convention of the people and have it published before the 12th[?] rely on the Cooperation of our people[.]" Hood to Johnson, April 6, 1863 [1864], Johnson Papers, LC.

2. Seeking party unity on the question of immediate emancipation, the governor is attempting to sway Hood on an issue about which the editor apparently was undecided. New York *Times,* February 22, 1864.

3. Hood replied the same day: "A two months canvass ought to be sufficient[.] Immediate Emancipation & repudiation of all harris appropriations should be incorporated in Constitutional Amendments[.] East Tenn can be carried for these with tremendous Majorities[.] if you issue a proclamation telegraph it verbatim[.] A Legislature would breed interminable feuds[.] it is important to forestall indescreet men at Knoxville on the 12th[.]" Hood to Johnson, April 6, 1864, Johnson Papers, LC.

To Edwin M. Stanton

Nashville, April 6, 1864.

Hon. E. M. Stanton, Secretary of War:

I do hope that General Buell will not be sent to Tennessee; anybody before him. He is not the man to send into Kentucky or Tennessee at this time. His influence will be with George D. Prentice[1] and that class of men.[2]

Andrew Johnson,
Military Governor.

OR, Ser. 1, XXXII, 278.

1. The Louisville *Journal,* edited by George D. Prentice, supported Lincoln until cooled by the Emancipation Proclamation; later it endorsed McClellan's candidacy. For Prentice, see *Johnson Papers,* IV, 547*n*.

2. By return telegraph, Stanton assured the governor that there was "no design to put General Buel again in command in Tennessee." Sec. of War, Tels. Sent, Vol. 23 (1864), RG107, NA.

To William P. Mellen

Nashville Apl. 7, 1864

W. P. Mellin
Spec'l Sup. Ag't. Treasy Dept.
[Cincinnati, Ohio]

Mrs James K. Polk gives many reasons why the sale of Mr J. W. Childrers and Mr Avants personal property[1] should not take place on tuesday next[.] she desires a postponement of the sale until she can confer with you or the Sec'y of the Treas'y. I hope her request will be granted. will you dispatch to me the result.[2]

Andrew Johnson Mil Gov.

Tel, DNA-RG366, Records of the General Agent, Tels. Recd., 1863-66; DLC-JP.

1. If the personal property involved were slaves, in 1860 Childress owned 45 and Avent, 23; however it was more likely to have been household goods. 1860 Census, Slave Schedule, Tenn., Rutherford, Fose Camp, 32; *Goodspeed's Rutherford*, 1022; for John W. Childress and his son-in-law James M. Avent, see *Johnson Papers*, III, 393*n*; IV, 694*n*.

2. The former first lady had her way! Barnitz to Johnson, April 7, [1864], Lets. Sent by Special Agent William P. Mellen, Vol. 41, RG366, NA.

To William T. Sherman

Nashville, April 8th 1864

Major Gen'l W. T. Sherman
Comdg Mil Div of the Miss
Nashville, Tenn,
General,

I have been informed that Mrs Dr Waters,[1] who left this City, at the time of its evacuation by the rebel Forces, and who has been closely allied, ever Since, with Gov Isham G. Harris, formerly of this State, has returned to this place—

I consider her presence here inimical to the Federal cause, and that she ought to be removed beyond our lines, or at least, north of the Ohio River, there to remain until permitted by the proper authorities to return[.][2]

I Am Gen'l very respectfully Your Obt Sert
Andrew Johnson, Mil Gov

L, DLC-JP.

1. Anna M. Rawlings (1826-1910) in 1846 married Maryland-born Dr. John Waters, brother-in-law of Felix Robertson. Their property, real and personal, in 1860 was worth $350,000. After Waters' death in 1867, she married Col. Beverly Williams, a Union officer, and moved to Little Rock. Acklen, *Tenn. Records*, I, 51; 1860 Census, Tenn., Davidson, Nashville, 3rd Ward, 93; WPA, Davidson County Marriage Books 2-3 (1838-1849), 81; Thomas, *Old Days in Nashville*, 49.

2. On April 9 Sherman endorsed this letter: "Genl. & Gov. Johnson will select for her an escort, one officer of Tennessee. Let her have time to lay in a little money, and then convey her to Canada. Quartermaster Dept. will furnish transportation."

To Unknown

Nashville, April 8th, 1864.

My attention having been directed to a communication from Hon James A. Hamilton addressed to Maj W. B. Lewis[1] upon the subject of proposed Congressional legislation with the view of the adoption of an Amendment to the Constitution forbidding the existence of slavery in the States and Territories &c, and also making enquiries as to the time of election of Members of Congress from this State, I have to state that I most fully concur in the views of Mr. Hamilton as expressed in said letter, and regard it as highly important that the Joint Resolution now pending should receive the sanction of Congress—the sooner the better.

In regard to the action that may be had in this State, I can only say that every effort will be made to secure its representation in the proposed measure.

Andrew Johnson Mil. Gov'r.

Copy, T-MsD, AJ Corres., 1865-75.

1. James A. Hamilton (1788-1878) was the third son of Alexander Hamilton. A New York lawyer and Jacksonian Democrat, he was an influential politician through the Van Buren period; in 1840 he became a Whig and during the war, as a Republican urged emancipation as a military measure. William B. Lewis (1784-1866), a Virginian who moved to Nashville about 1809, was a member of Jackson's "Kitchen Cabinet," having been his quartermaster in the War of 1812. Serving as 2nd auditor of the treasury until 1845, he returned to Nashville to live out his life quietly. The letter has not been found. *DAB*, VIII, 188-89; XI, 226.

From David C. Beaty[1]

Fentress County, April 10th, 1864.

Gov. Johnson—

Sir; Necessity forces me to address you this note. The time has come when I must make some exertions to save my men & the citizins of this section who have ever been my friends[.] I have waded through difficulties that but few would have endured. I have held this county with a small band, without the aid of state or government. My duty demanded all this of me, & now my duty demands more. I must have some assistance from some source, & knowing as I do that you are the head of state, I ask you to do something for me. This county, as you are awear, has been hemed in without any outlet to supply herself with the necessaries of life, until the citizens as well as my men are almost without provisions. The citizens have done all they can do—they have fed us—befriended us in the hour of danger, & now I think it is my turn to do all I can for them. We need something here that will answer insted-of or for *bread*; & the fact is we must have it, or starvation will appear among us soon—families are to day suffering for the want of bread, & this section of country unable to farnish enough of that. Our stock is gon, or unable to do service—& we have no where to go to obtain any thing though they were competent. Therefore our only means of releaf is in apply to you, & be assured that we have great confidence. My plan to furnish this country is to get you to send something up the river to the nearest point, Mill Springs I suppose—corn, flour, *crackers*, or anything that will sustain life. To prevent women, & children from starving something of this character must be brought into the country.— I will make the best distribution of them possible.

One other thing I desire to mention, I have written to Horace Maynard, asking for pay. He offers to do all he can in that way. We have never drawn any, & now we need it. Can you do anything for us. I think I am enti[t]led to pay or I would not ask it,—& if you do not of cours you will not attempt to get it or put me in any way so that I can draw it. Write to me, & let me know whether you can do any thing for me or not.

Capt. David Beity.

ALS, DLC-JP.

1. David Crockett ("Tinker Dave") Beaty (1823-1883), a Fentress County native, early in 1862 formed a partisan company known as Dave Beaty's Independent Scouts, USA, which operated against Confederates in Overton and Fentress counties. Never receiving pay from the government, this band fluctuated between five and sixty. Beaty was a prominent Conservative Republican in Fentress County during Reconstruction. Robert and Mary Aldridge, *History of Overton County, Tennessee, 1776-1976* (Livingston, Tenn., 1976), 61; *Tennesseans in the Civil War*, I, 413; Daniel, Special Warfare in Mid. Tenn., 146-47; Nashville *Republican Banner*, January 8, 1869.

From James P. Thompson[1]

McMinnville April 10/64

His Excellency Andrew Johnson

Sir, The Board of Claims now in Session have disposed of Some 25. or 30 Claims; The inquiry is frequently made by my clients, when will these accounts be paid? has any appropriation been made by Congress to meet these demands? They further inquire if any Scrip or Voucher will be issued?[2]

It is obvious why the above Interrogatories are made. The class of claims the Court is daily passing are for Qr Masters and Commissary Supplies, which includes Horses, Beef cattle, Sheep, Pork, Irish Potatoes and Forrage, Corn, wheat, Rye, oats Hay and Fodder. Such are the articles necessarily used by the army and for which our people are presenting their claims. 1st Qr Master Supplies; 2nd Commissary Supplies, leaving all other damages done to private property yet to be considered.

The waste and distruction of property of the discription above refered to, you cannot have an adequate Idea unless you would or Could Visite the Sufferers in this wretched war. The country around us, Say all the adjoining counties are coming in filing claims for, Horses, corn & forage, with the hope that the Government would relieve them to the extent of what may be allowed them, even then in many cases, it will not be compensation for all the citizens have lost, for this reason, many articles are not Subject to be accounted for as necessary Supplies for an army, but such losses is incident to the occupation of a country in all wars[.]

If you have the information desired by my clients will you advise me of the fact by the earlies opportunity?

Should there be no fund dedicated by law, to discharge these claims, can you induce the government to issue Certificate or Scrip, that can be made available to the claimants, in these cases and Stead of money? The great majority of these claimants have been reduced to want, they have neither, corn, forage nor horses to make a crop this year[.] Such destitution I never expected to See in Tenn, all the Horses and Valuable mules have been, taken by the armies that have alternately occupied this place, in process of depletion that has been going on now nearly 3 years, until this country & Surrounding counties are completely exhausted.

Col. Gilbert commandant of this Post,[3] is President of the Board and is discharging his duties, promptly and intelligently and Satisfactorily, I hope to the Government & Citizens. He is acceptable to our people & quite energetic and with all popular. I think he ought to be retained here as his administration has resulted So far, in restoring Security and tranquility to this Section of the country[.]

Respy yr obt svt
J. P. Thompson

ALS, DLC-JP.

1. James P. Thompson (1793-1886), Virginia-born McMinnville lawyer and veteran of the War of 1812, served in the Reconstruction legislature (1866-67). Robison and McBride, *Biographical Directory,* II, 899-900.

2. The quartermaster and commissary departments rarely issued any form of compensation for these claims during the war; on July 4, 1864, Congress prohibited them from processing any claims from states in rebellion. Klingberg, *Southern Claims Commission,* 23-24.

3. Henry C. Gilbert.

From Alexander E. Wagstaff[1]

Head Quarters 103d Reg't Ills. Infty Vols
Scottsboro, Ala., April 11th 1864

To His Excellency Andrew Johnson
Governor of Tenn.,

Sir—I have been requested by the Division and Brigade Post Masters of the 4th Div. 15th Army Corps, and by officers, to state to you, that for some time past the mails have been forwarded from the Nashville P. O. in such a loose and careless condition that many soldiers will never be able to receive the letters intended for them by their friends at home. In this regiment, the Postmaster has received almost as much mail, at times, belonging to other and distant regiments as for our own, and often the letters intended for persons in this regiment and Division have been sent to Chattanooga, Athens, Cleveland and other points, finding their proper places, perhaps after weeks, and often a longer time. Would you, sir, be so kind as to use your influence with the authorities to have this evil eradicated? I know of no one else who might be successful, and as the matter must rest at the Nashville, office, it can be seen to. By so doing, sir you will confer a lasting favor, and you will have the thanks of many a good soldier, as well as those of mine.[2]

I have the honor, sir, to be
Very respectfully Your obd't Serv't
A. E. Wagstaff
Adj't 103d Regt Ills. Infty Vols.

ALS, DLC-JP.

1. Alexander E. Wagstaff (b. *c*1833), 1st lieutenant and adjutant, 103rd Ill., was an Ohio-born editor living in Canton, Illinois, when he enrolled in the service in 1863. In June of the following year, he was "dishonorably discharged" for "cowardly and disgraceful conduct" at Resaca and Dallas, Georgia. CSR, RG94, NA.

2. Nashville postmaster, A. V. S. Lindsley, to whom Johnson forwarded the complaint, replied that the mail left the central post office "properly put up & in good order" and that, inasmuch as the military authorities take "charge of the mails" at the post office doors, any complaint should be addressed to Wagstaff's superiors. Lindsley to Johnson, April 15, 1864, Johnson Papers, LC.

To Abraham Lincoln

Loudon Tenn Apl 11 1864.

His Excellency A Lincoln.

I am by accident detained here on my way to Knoxville to attend the Convention to assemble there tomorrow[.][1] Things do not look as I would like to find them[.]

I learn that Gen Granger[2] has been relieved from his command.[3] I regret this for I find that he has the confidence of the people his officers & men, that he has given entire satisfaction & am satisfied he should be retained here in his present command[.] East Tenn should without delay be placed in the Dept. of the Cumberland.[4]

Genl Granger is on the eve of leaving & I hope he will be at once retained in his former position.

Andw Johnson

Tel, DLC-Lincoln Papers; DNA-RG107, Tels. Recd., President, Vol. 2 (1864).

1. A reconvening of the Greeneville-Knoxville Union meetings of 1861 was held in Knoxville on Tuesday, April 12. Nashville *Dispatch*, April 13, 1864.

2. Gordon Granger (1822-1876), West Point graduate (1845) and Mexican War veteran, had risen to major general by September, 1862. Playing a prominent part in the relief of Rosecrans at Chickamauga, he commanded a corps at Chattanooga and thereafter a corps or division in operations in East Tennessee and at Mobile, Alabama. After the war he commanded the districts of Memphis (1867-69) and New Mexico (1871-76). Warner, *Generals in Blue*, 181.

3. Granger, himself, from his headquarters in Loudon on April 10, had issued an order to his IV Corps indicating that he had been relieved; Maj. Gen. O. O. Howard assumed command. Nashville *Union*, April 17, 1864.

4. The change was not made until January 17, 1865. Dyer, *Compendium*, 254.

Speech at Athens: Two Versions[1]

April 11, 1864

I.

(Chattanooga *Gazette*)

Gov. Johnson addressed a large number of citizens at this place to-day. He declared that he thought the negro had worked the rich land of Tennessee long enough and that the white men should now have a chance. He said this question of slavery had always been a source of trouble, and that it had hindered the developement of the boundless resources of Tennessee, that it was now to be settled and settled forever, that the time was when they would not allow a man to speak his mind on this subject, "out" he meant to talk now. The only question was, what should be done with the negro; somebody says, "oh dear, you ain't going to turn them loose are you?" Are they not loose now and will there be any more of them when they are legally loose than there are now? The day of peace and quietness and of all of God's blessing were at hand if the people were but true to themselves and to the Government. The devastating blasts of war would sweep through these valleys no more.

II.

(Louisville *Journal*)

Not being prepared to transcribe the Governor's few well-timed remarks to the citizens (?) of Athens, I could give no more graphic account of what I did hear than a few words from the radical dictionary:

"Gentlemen, slavery is dead! dead!! dead!!!" "You know it as well as I do." "I am on my way to Knoxville to assist East Tennessee in ridding herself of the accursed institution which has caused you to leave your peaceful homes to fight this slavery aristocracy." "I own slaves which were bought by their own toil and labor on Tennessee soil." "The time will come, dear friends, when slaves shall not till the soil of Tennessee, *unless they can come forward and compete with the labor of white men*. If they cannot, they will have to stand back; yes, sirs, stand back."

"We of East Tennessee intend to make a new State out of her, although we have been disturbed in the undertaking more than once—yes, twice." [2]

Between the whistling and hissing of three over-charged engines, your special catches no other sound or words than "nigger, free labor, equality—dead, irrevocably dead," &c.

Nashville *Times and True Union*, April 15, 1864, and Louisville *Journal*, April 22, 1864.

1. When his train stopped briefly in Athens en route to the Knoxville Union Convention, the governor spoke to an assemblage variously described by a friendly observer as "a large number of citizens," and by a less sympathetic and somewhat facetious reporter as "a small crowd of convalescent soldiers and a few butternut teamsters who had been called together more through his voice stentorian than musical." These accounts, though not verbatim, convey the atmosphere of such a "whistle stop" harangue, and in their sharp difference in tone illustrate the ways in which the personality of the reporter, perhaps compounded by his political bias, can affect the record left to posterity.

2. The *Journal* reporter was not only unfriendly; he was inaccurate. Far from seeking "to make a new State out of her," Johnson was on his way to forestall such a move at the impending convention.

Speech at Knoxville[1]

1864, April 12

The time has arrived when treason must be made odious, when traitors must be punished—impoverished; their property taken from them, whether it be their horses, their lands, or their negroes, and given to the innocent, the honest, the loyal, upon whom the calamities of this unprovoked and wicked rebellion have fallen with such crushing weight. It is easy to stand here and declaim, but I am not declaiming. It is easy to utter mere bombast, but I am not uttering bombast. You know me. You know something of what I have done for you—for Tennessee—for East Tennessee. But I will not speak of that. If I have made sacrifices, if I have endured sufferings, if I have undergone hardships, so let it be. God grant that I may have helped you, and that I may help you again. But you must help yourselves. You must join hands with me and with one another, and swear to do what I have already told you must be done—to make treason odious, [this he said with tremendous emphasis,] and to make traitors suffer, as you have suffered, as your wives and children have suffered, as your country has suffered.

What has brought this war upon us? Let me answer in one word, let me speak it so loud that the deafest man in all this multitude can hear me—Slavery! [Hundreds of voices: "That's so, that's a God's truth."] Men talk about the Constitution and State rights. They sneer at the Emancipation Proclamation, and call it a tyrannical assumption of authority, a despotic usurpation of power. Listen to what I now say: all such talk is the language of treason. But I am not here to discuss the constitutionality of slavery, or the unconstitutionality of the President's Proclamation of Freedom. I am here to present facts; to address your intellects; to appeal to your common sense. Here is one fact to which I want you to attend: Why is the soil of your beloved Tennessee—a soil as rich as any in the world—so far behind the States of the North in its productiveness? Why have you but few such farms, but few such granaries, as they have all over Indiana and Ohio and Pennsylvania?[2] Here is the explanation, and let me speak it so loud that the deafest man in all this multitude can hear me— Slavery! Thank God, the people are beginning to see that slave labor has impoverished the soil of Tennessee about long enough. [Cries of "Good, good—that's so."]

Men sneer at the doctrine of emancipation. Let them sneer; but this I tell you—mark me—it is the *white* man that we propose to emancipate; it is the *white* man that is even now being emancipated; and may Heaven hasten the work of emancipation, and carry it on until all are free. [Loud and prolonged applause.]

Thank God that I can say these things to-day in Knoxville! that I can say them and be applauded! Thank God for free speech and a free press, and the prospect of a free country! May He who is our Maker, and who will be our Judge, break every yoke, loose every shackle, open every prison door and let every bondman, white and black, go free! [Loud applause.]

Sometimes the clouds appear dark and lowering—sometimes I confess to a feeling of gloom; but when I remember that there is a God, I am encouraged.[3] Though not religious as I ought to be, I sometimes walk by faith, and I have found it a convenient way of walking when it is too dark to see. And on the whole, though our suffering has been great, our blessedness will be all the greater when the day of our triumph shall come!

My countrymen! my heart yearns toward you; I love you; I am one of you. I have climbed yonder mountains that you have climbed—yonder mountains, rock-ribbed and glowing in the sunshine—in whose gorges, in whose caverns, your sons, hunted like wild beasts, have fallen to rise no more. I do not speak of these things to draw your tears. It is not a time for tears, but for blows. I speak of them that I may fire your hearts with holy indignation, and nerve your arms for unconquerable fight. And I speak of them because the mountains seem to talk to me. My home is among the mountains, and though it is not far away, yet I cannot go to it. It is the place where I met her, and loved her, and married her who is the mother of my children. Do I not love the mountains, then? And if liberty is to expire, if freedom is to be destroyed, if my country, in all its length and breadth, is to tremble beneath the oppressor's tread, let the flag, the dear old flag, the last flag, be planted on yon rocky hights; and upon it let there be this inscription: "Here is the end of all that is dear to the heart and sacred to the memory of man."

But I must not go on in this strain. Why is it that there is so much that is mournful in the contemplation of this broad, beautiful country? Who are the men that are to be held responsible for the terrible war whose ravages we see to-day wherever we cast our eyes? Jefferson Davis, Robert Toombs, Yancey, Stevens—but I will not continue the hated list. You know them. You have felt them. And for what cause have they made us to suffer thus? I have told you again and again. Shall I repeat it? Well, it is slavery! What right have I, what right have you, to hold a fellow-man in bondage, except for crime. What right have you to use his labor without compensation? to separate him from his wife and children, and sell him or them like dumb brutes? And yet because the whole nation would not recognize this right, and bow to those who claimed it, we have war, we have wasted fields, desolated homes, broken hearts. There are those here who will sneer at me as I talk thus—who will button their mouths and think—not daring to say it—"damned Abolition Yankee, he wants office." I spurn all such from me as I would a filthy dog; I trample them under my feet as I would a venomous reptile.[4]

Cincinnati *Gazette*, April 19, 1864; Milwaukee *Sentinel*, June 16, 1864.

1. Claiming that they were merely reconvening the Greeneville-Knoxville Union conventions of May and June, 1861, East Tennessee extremists, hoping to divorce the region from the state, even as Virginia had recently been dissevered, organized a mass meeting, using as the occasion the third anniversary of the destruction by Texas Rangers of a liberty pole and American flag. The ceremonies associated with erecting another pole and the same flag on the exact spot of the desecration included music by the 6th Tenn. Inf. band and short speeches by William B. Carter, John P. Holtsinger, and Oliver P. Temple. Johnson followed with the main oration of the day; "the citizens concurred most enthusiastically" with his comments on slavery. What follows "is not more than a fourth part of Governor Johnson's eloquent and deeply affecting speech," according to the *Gazette* reporter.

"After he left the stand, he told me that in the former part of his speech which I had not heard—he made a bare allusion to the subject of making a new State out of East Tennessee; that the time had not come for decided action on a question so vital; but that other questions, involving present interests, and demanding immediate action on our part were upon us; that we are called upon to meet them face to face, and must meet them, and in meeting them quit ourselves like men, like Christians, and like patriots." Paul E. Rieger, ed., *Through One Man's Eyes: The Civil War Experiences of a Belmont County Volunteer* (Mt. Vernon, Ohio, 1974), 92-93; Knoxville *Whig and Rebel Ventilator*, April 16, 1864; Cincinnati *Gazette*, April 19, 1864.

2. With his Speech on Restoration of State Government, January 21, 1864, Johnson began to blame the failings of the southern economy on slavery, a point of view he had not earlier expressed.

3. A striking invocation of the divine from a man whose speeches were, except for his notorious "Jacob's Ladder" harangue, decidedly secular in tone.

4. Phraseology strikingly reminiscent of Johnson's attacks upon the Know-Nothings during the gubernatorial canvas of 1855.

Speech at Knoxville[1]

April 16, 1864

Fellow Citizens: I appear before you to-day under very different circumstances from those which surrounded me here three years ago. The Rebellion was then just inaugurated. I see before me many with whom I then differed in opinion, and there are some who then stood by me who are now on the other side. We were then united in endeavoring to convince the public mind of the evils of this Rebellion. He would ask a question. What condition are we involved in, and what brought it about? We were involved in a Rebellion. Our fathers who formed the Constitution foresaw that rebellion and insurrection were liable to occur, and provided against them, as well as for the punishment of treason. So we see a Rebellion, in the wise forecast of the fathers of the Republic, was expected. It has come, but the Government has the power to put it down. He would vindicate the North against the charge of wishing to interfere with us; but there was a constitutional right to interfere, and there was, beside the right, a high constitutional obligation to do so. We hear complaints about the invading army. No one had a right to complain. They had come in compliance with our request, to unfurl here in Tennessee the good old flag which our fathers fought under. I tender them my sincere thanks for what they have done. I was going to say that as soon as the Government of the United States had fully performed its high constitutional obligation in expelling the Rebels from Tennessee, we commence the Government of the State. The result of the Rebellion was the suspension of all civil authority. We have no Legislature; the Governor has run away, fled to find protection among another people beyond the borders of the State, carrying off with him \$3,000,000, the sacred fund for the common schools,[2] and the State is prostrate. Another obligation imposed by the great charter of our liberties is the obligation to guarantee to every State a republican form of Government. One of the fundamental principles lying at the base of this great political structure is, according to the fourth article of the Constitution, "the United States SHALL guarantee to every State a republican form of Government, and shall repel invasion," and the Chief Magistrate takes an oath to support the Constitution of the United States, and to see that the laws are faithfully executed. Our republican form of Government has given way, and we are now engaged in the great work of restoring the authority of the law and Constitution over the whole people. It is the duty of the Chief Executive to inaugurate those measures which shall guarantee a republican form of government. If the Rebellion, in its wicked and headlong course, wipes out Slavery, it is not the duty of the Government to bring it back. It is one of the works of the Rebellion, done by its own friends. If the President finds it necessary in the discharge of his duty to supply a government for a State, where the Government has been overthrown, he must guarantee one to them that is republican in form—and no other. Suppose one of these States should set up a monarchy, and set up a prince here and a duke there to rule over the people. Would there be any doubt as to the duty of the President in such a case, and wouldn't he be derelict not to interfere and change that Government? Now I reckon we can have a republican form of government without Slavery, as well as we can with it, and a great deal better. The first article of the Bill of Rights declares that all power is inherent in the people. And among the rights is that to alter and amend their Constitution in any manner they shall think proper, whenever in their judgment it may be deemed proper. With this right is the correlative one to elect such men as they may choose to do their work, and restore a Government which has been taken away. Somebody must move, must start it, and the people were the proper power to begin. Some say you have no right to call a Convention, but you can call the Legislature together. I would like to know where you get it? You can eject a Governor—he ran away and carried off the public archives [laughter]—but you have no right to go to the source of all power, the people themselves! It is a duty we owe to the State to dissipate this shallow delusion. Let us try to get at the animus of these men. I think I understand them. By the Constitution of the State of Tennessee, the Legislature cannot emancipate without the consent of the owners.[3] Now the people have the power to call a Convention, and they have the power to convene either. A Convention is clothed with sovereign power. It can do all that a legislature can do. It can do more. Why? The Legislature as soon as it convenes commences pleading the Constitution. They cannot emancipate Slaves without the consent of their owners. A secret power is at work. Don't you see? They say, let us have the Legislature called together and not the Convention, for then we shall have the power to hold on to Slavery for six years longer, and we can keep this question alive in the State, and thus be ready to throw Tennessee into the hands of the South, in any plan of adjustment that may arise. This thing called Slavery is lying dead; we can't hold on to it any longer. Then why not determine the question at once. Now is the time to exercise this power.

He believed that if the State had moved rightly in this matter they might have got something out of the Federal Government for their slaves; but he was free to say, and he would not conceal anything from the meeting—the time had now gone by for getting much for the negroes. To state what he really felt, he was not so much in favor of paying for them himself as formerly.[4] They were free already. Then call the Convention and recognize the fact as it exists. You haven't to abolish Slavery; it is already effectually done, and it only remains for you to legalize freedom. Who is going to hurt you? Who is afraid to trust you with this power? Hence there is nothing to do, after legalizing the question, but to pass laws for the equitable government of all. All men by nature are lazy; I know I am myself [laughter]; but by habit we become industrious and economical. You say the negro won't work if the stimulus of the lash and of force is removed. How do you know that? Have you tried the stimulus of wages and of kind treatment? I had some slaves myself; one of them is here now. They followed me to Nashville, and came to see me. I said to them, go to the Quartermasters, the Commissaries, to the citizens, and find out the best wages you can obtain for work, and then come back to me and I will pay you more than you can get any where else. The consequence is, I have the most obedient, attentive, and kind lot of servants of any man in the State. Then when all else fails, haven't you vagrant laws. Can't you bind out the improvident and lazy to serve, to learn trades, &c. He had been a witness himself in the case of a boy who was bound out to a master, who was held by the indenture to teach the boy to read, write, and cipher as far as the single rule of three.[5] And the master quarreled with the lad about fulfilling his part of the contract on the schooling question. The Governor was referring to his own case. The labor question was easily settled. The emancipated or the free black man must bestir himself. Freedom did not mean the liberty to lay off and do nothing while you feed on milk and honey. Freedom meant the liberty to work and to enjoy the product of your own labor: that is nature's—it is God's decree for all—white and black alike; and I will say to the black man, for I see many of them before me, that you must be a little more industrious and a little more economical if you expect to hold your way alongside of the free white laborer. The time was when we could not speak to the black man, but thank God the time has come when speech is free, and the Press is free also. [A voice from the reporter's stand—Amen!] The slaveholders of East[6] Tennessee have controlled the Government on this as upon all other subjects connected with the negro. But in violating the great fundamental axiom that all the institutions of the Government should be controlled by the Government, and attempting to make Slavery control the Government, they have brought out the Rebellion, and destroyed their darling institution with an everlasting overthrow. The first gun fired upon Fort Sumter emancipated the last slave in this country. [Laughter and applause.] I tell you, my countrymen, this institution will be removed from among us, and the collaterals will all conform, just as the sparks fly upward, or as water runs down hill. Are you willing to trust yourselves? Are you not fit to decide this question? The Rebels wanted a Convention to carry the State out of the Union. We want one to restore the Government and build it up. [Applause.] Elect your Members of Congress. "But," the objector says, "Mr. Lincoln will not let us in." The two branches of Congress each passes upon the qualifications of its own Members. Call this Convention, and wipe out one little article from her Constitution, and the State stands redeemed, regenerated, disenthralled. The Government of the State must ultimately fall under the control of the loyal citizens. If there are five thousand, or only one thousand loyal men in Tennessee, the Government must pass into their hands.[7] The moment a citizen of Tennessee joined the Rebellion, that moment he ceased to be a loyal citizen of the United States Government, and thereby lost all claim to participate in the Government, and forfeited all its protection. Hence if there are only five hundred good and loyal men, when the time comes to set up civil rule, the Government will pass into their hands, and the United States Government will stand by them. He never intended to lie down and sleep beneath the flag of treason. The question then arises as to the right of a traitor to vote at all. When the foreigner comes forward to vote, we say to him stand back for five years. Which, he would ask, is best qualified to vote, the foreigner seeking an asylum here from the tyranny of the Old World, with all his hopes and aspirations, for the future, for himself and his children, centered in the maintenance of this great republican form of government, or the renegade and traitor who has turned his back upon free institutions, and whose hands are crimsoned with the blood of loyal men? They have come back, and they will continue to come, and they will make a code intended to perpetuate Slavery as a politician's capital in which to speculate. He had heard of some of these men, with the oath of amnesty still fresh upon the their lips, and before the ink with which they had signed their names was dry upon the paper, turn round and impudently interrogate loyal men and officers as to their authority for doing this or that (the speaker particularly mentioned Ed. H. Ewing, a wealthy and influential Rebel). Here were these men, tried, condemned, and the order for their execution had gone forth. They stood upon the scaffold, with the rope adjusted about their treasonable necks and the cap drawn down over their heads, awaiting the hangman's ax to sever the rope and launch them into eternity. At this critical moment a person is seen rushing through the crowd of spectators with outstretched hand, in which he holds a paper. He commands the execution to be stayed. He holds in his hands the Amnesty Oath of the President of the United States. The culprit takes the oath, the cap is withdrawn from over his face, the rope taken from his neck, and the criminal turns round, kicks the Sheriff out of the way, and impudently asks, "I want to know, Sir, by what authority you have me here?" Such is the effrontery, the insolence of traitors. They do not scruple to say, "I took the oath to save my little property." Gov. Johnson here referred to the oath he had prescribed as a qualification for voters at the late election, which he commented upon at some length, showing how it affected the disloyal. It required them to swear that they earnestly desired the suppression of the Rebellion, the defeat of the Rebel arms, and the success of the Union forces, and pledged them to do all in their power to accomplish this result. This, as soon as it was published, created a great fluttering in the Secession camp. They said, "Oh, he requires more of us that [*sic*] Mr. Lincoln does." But he never found a good, loyal man, who objected to taking this oath. He thought it likely even some disloyal persons took it. If there was a better test than that he was in favor of it. He thought that traitors and Rebels should be put upon probation, and let their conduct decide what constitutional test they shall be required to subscribe to before again being admitted to full political fellowship. But all these things would follow in their natural order. Let us do one thing at once—put the State upon its legs. There were complaints of outrages; of corn taken without vouchers, and Mr. Lincoln was responsible. Mr. Johnson proceeded to vindicate the President and the Government against these silly charges, and to put the responsibility where it belonged—upon the incompetent and dishonest officers; the rest was but the natural results of all war, and the presence of armies in a country, and, to a great extent, was an unavoidable incident of the war. They, and they only, were to blame who had begun the war and brought these armies into Tennessee. He had seen the President and the officers of his Cabinet almost in tears over these outrages. We should not be soured by these things, but organize the State Government. The issue is the life of the Government itself. Let us take the sick man out of bed (we know who put him there), and get the patient well. The Governor next referred to the Bill of Rights of the State of Tennessee, which gives *to the people* the power to alter or amend their form of government—always observing that it must be republican in form. He spoke of the great sympathy attempted to be expressed for Rebels, and the proposed invitation for them to return. He was in favor of their return, but he wanted to see the proper evidence of their repentance and reformation. Let these, then, come in here *ad libitum*,[8] and how long would it be before they would run loyal men away from the polls by the use of bowie knife and pistol—playing their old game of bullying all who were opposed to them. What do you think of the fitness of that man to come up to the polls and vote with you, loyal citizens of Tennessee, who publicly offered $50 a piece for the best bloodhounds,[9] to hunt the Union men in the mountains and caves of the earth, fleeing from the infernal conscription? He referred to the enlistment of blacks in the army, and showed that it was no new thing, but had been practiced in every war from the Revolutionary War down. He demonstrated that the Rebels began the employment of negroes, the Cherokee Indians, &c.[10] He warned these leading Rebels, who had perpetrated these acts of outrage and murder upon Union men in Tennessee, that they could not stay, return, or live here, and he advised all men of this class that the time was come for them to take up their beds and walk. He referred to the bridge-burning business, the sacrifice of innocent lives, and the sufferings of their widows and orphans, and strongly hinted that the man[11] who received the Government money to accomplish the work, and by whose agency they suffered, while the principal fled for safety to Kentucky, ought to commisserate the condition of the helpless widows and orphans now suffering from want. The blood of these men, like that of Abel, cried aloud from the ground against the author of their death, and for succor to their wives and little ones. He read the order of Judah P. Benjamin, the Rebel Secretary of State, directing their execution, with directions that their bodies be left hanging near the burned bridges.[12] He ventilated the conduct of this doubly-dyed traitor as a Member of Congress, on the Crittenden and other propositions of Compromise, and showed him up to the detestation of every honorable-minded man. He declared in favor of immediately legalizing the freedom of the slaves in Tennessee; and when that measure was completed, he was in favor of compensating loyal men, but not one cent would he pay to Rebels. [Laughter and applause.]

New York *Tribune*, April 30, 1864.

1. Between these two Knoxville speeches, the reconvened Knoxville Convention, which Conservatives attended in force, badly embarrassed Johnson by refusing to endorse his efforts to restore civil government in Tennessee. In an attempt to save face, supporters called a mass meeting to consider resolutions—written by Johnson, according to Oliver P. Temple—which endorsed his program. Brownlow, Temple, and John Caldwell preceded the governor on the speaker's stand; John P. Holtsinger followed him. A "long and unanimous 'yea' from the assembled multitude" passed the resolutions. Cimprich, Slavery Amidst Civil War, 240; New York *Tribune*, April 30, 1864.

2. Upon Nashville's fall to Federal troops in late February, 1862, Harris fled to Memphis, taking the public archives and the assets of the Bank of Tennessee, last reported as over three and one-half million dollars. Included was the common school fund, "sacred" because it was ordained by the Constitution of 1834 as a perpetual fund, never otherwise appropriated, the interest to be distributed for school purposes. When Memphis was invested, the governor, along with other state officials still guarding the public archives and treasury, became a refugee, encamping with the Army of Tennessee beyond state borders. Cave Johnson to the Legislature, October 8, 1859, *Tenn. Senate Journal*, 1859-60, App. 76; William G. Brownlow to the Legislature, October 3, 1865, *ibid.*, 1865-66, pp. 17-18; Tenn. Constitution of 1834, Art. XI, sec. 10.

3. In section 21 of Tennessee's Declaration of Rights (1834 Constitution, Article I) is the guarantee that "no man's . . . property [shall be] taken or applied to public use, without the consent of his representatives, or without just compensation being made therefor."

4. The Johnson papers afford no evidence that he had ever supported compensated emancipation.

5. A "method of finding a fourth number from three given numbers, of which the first is in the same proportion to the second as the third is to the unknown fourth." *OED*, VIII, 882.

6. This cannot have been but a slip of the reporter's pen; surely the speaker must have been indicting the slavocracy of Middle or West Tennessee.

7. It might be noted that although the "reconvened convention" had displayed some interest in divorcing East Tennessee from the remainder of the state, Johnson would have no part of such maneuverings. It is perhaps symbolic that his April 12 speech was delivered outside the courthouse where the assemblage was convened. This current speech, also before a mass meeting, makes clear the considerations underlying his stance; the governor intended that the loyal men of East Tennessee should not only remain as part of the state but, even more to the point, should take control of a restored Tennessee and guide it in the dual paths of virtue and vengeance.

8. That is, at will.

9. Johnson is suggesting the possibility that men like William H. Harris and Frank N. McNairy, whom he considered partisan rangers or guerrillas, being pardoned, might eventually vote alongside good unionists. Back in December, 1861, Harris and McNairy had advertised that they would pay for bloodhounds to hunt down "the infernal cowardly Lincoln bushwhackers." See *Johnson Papers*, V, 404*n*.

10. Early in the war Negroes, while not armed and usually assigned to labor battalions or as servants, cooks and teamsters, were seen in Confederate forces. In January, 1864, Gen. Pat Cleburne had presented a petition among brother officers for using Negro soldiers. Although Jeff Davis squelched the proposal, rumors of such use circulated. These reports became arguments for the North to raise black units. Regiments of western Indians—Cherokee, Chickasaw, Choctaw, Creek, and Seminole—had been engaged in Arkansas, most notably at Pea Ridge. In East Tennessee Indian companies in Col. William H. Thomas' 69th N. C. (Thomas' Legion) were used for guard duty and participated in several skirmishes during the winter of 1863-64. Cornish, *The Sable Arm*, 16-17; Frank E. Vandiver, *Their Tattered Flags* (New York, 1970), 260-63; John R. Finger, "The North Carolina Cherokees, 1838-1866," *Journal of Cherokee Studies,* V (1980), 23.

11. For the Reverend William B. Carter and the bridge-burning, see *Johnson Papers*, IV, 670*n*; V, 42n, 75n.

12. For this order, see Benjamin to Col. William B. Wood, November 25, 1861, *OR*, Ser. 1, VII, 701.

From Polk County Citizens[1]

[*ca.*April 20?], 1864

To Gen. Andrew Johnson Military Governor of Tennessee.

Dr Sir. We the undersigned citizens and loyal men of Polk county Tennessee make this appeal to you in behalf Major H. Hancock[2] a citizen of said county of Polk; who was arrested by the Federal authorities in said county about the first of December 1863. Said M. H. Hancock is now reported to be held by the Federal government a prisoner at Rock Island. He was a Rebel and was a capt in the Rebel Army for about ten months. Shortly after the battle at Corninth, his health having failed, and upon the reorganization of the Rebel army he got out of the Rebel service and arrived home in May 1862. He remained at home with his family from that time forward until the time of his arrest as before stated. When the Rebel conscript law was inforced in said county of Polk the said Hancock accepted of the position of Enrolling officer to keep out of the army himself. He has always maintained the reputation of an upright, honest and honorable man. He has been the high Sheriff of said county of Polk before the Rebelion. He has a wife and seven children. There never was any charges against him, except that he took sides with the Rebelion and raised a company and served in the army for ten months and afterwards served as enrolling officer. But at no time did he ever arrest any union men or force them into the Rebel army, but after his return from the Rebel army he lived with his union neighbors on terms of friendship, and when the federal forces came to our county he did not flee at their approach but staid at home and announced publically that he would stay at home and submit to the laws. We are informed that after his arrest he desired to take the oath alligeance to the Federal Government and afterwards the Oath of Amnesty under the Presidents Proclamation, but it was denied him and he was sent from Tennessee North and as we are advised to Rock Island. If it is desired Mr. Hancock will give any bond that the Government may require in addition to the Oath. We believe he is an honorable man and would live up to his oath. Thousands of Rebel citizens of Tennessee & nearly all of that class of said county of Polk have been permitted to take the Oath of Amnesty and are living at home with their families, and we respectfully ask that the said Hancock be permitted to take the Oath and return to his family as many thousands of others have done and are doing, but if in addition a bond is required the citizens of Polk will be his surety on such bond. We respectfully ask of you Gen. Johnson to attend to this matter in behalf of the said Hancock & his family. We are advised that the application can alone be made through you.[3]

We are your obt. servts.

Pet, DNA-RG249, Lets. Recd., File 660M(1864), M. H. Hancock.

1. Signatories were James Parks, James Gamble, Charles M. McClary, William M. Biggs, Robert N. Fleming, and George M. Coleman.

2. Major H. Hancock (1827-*fl*1900), Polk County sheriff (1854-62, 1870-74), enlisted at Knoxville in July, 1861, as captain, Co. B, 29th Tenn. Inf., CSA, and resigned at the regiment's reorganization in May, 1862. During the fall, to avoid conscription he served as an enrolling officer, and, according to some Polk countians "was exceedingly mild towards the Union citizens" prior to his arrest and incarceration. CSR, RG109, NA; *Goodspeed's East Tennessee*, 806; Jacob McClary, et al. to E. M. Stanton, June 6, 1864, Lets. Recd., RG249, NA; 1900 Census, Tenn. , Polk, 124th Enum. Dist., 12A.

3. In an endorsement of April 25 the governor responded, restating, in his own hand, the gist of the petition; a month later he "recommended for the most favorable action" a similar appeal by Jacob L. McClary et al to Secretary Stanton, dated June 6.

From James B. Bingham

Memphis, April 23, 1864.

Dear Johnson: I have been very ill since the 3d of March. By the assistance of an amanuensis I have sent you several letters, but thus far, notwithstanding your promise to write me fully from Washington, I have not received a word, either in reply to letters or dispatches.

If you noticed my controversy with the leader of the half-reclaimed Secessionists[1] you have seen that I construed my commission to empower me to act as a special election agent and not as a Sheriff, and consequently that certificates of election or Commissions as officers must emanate from Nashville. Our men have been anxiously awaiting the arrival of such commissions, in order to enter upon the discharge of their duties; but thus far none have come, and nothing has been done. I understand that Harrison has written here that it is doubtful whether the commissions will be sent or a new election ordered.[2] I am opposed to any more elections, State or Municipal, until we have one for the election of members of a State Convention, and I am in favor of putting that off for several months—at least until we can get some Federal Commanders here who will not show rebels more favors than they do Unconditional Union men. I am particular in desiring that you will appoint municipal officers for us in June, and not permit another farce of an election. With a very few exceptions, the men now in possession of our municipal government are unprincipled, disloyal and even dishonest. They were elected by fraud, and have used their power to put money in their pockets and secure a re-election. They control the entire Irish element, and are now busy preparing the ropes for another lease of life. Out of about 6000 voters in our lines in March, there was only about 1200 votes polled.[3] Although the pretext was that your oath was a hard one, the real difficulty was, with a large portion, hatred of the Union. If you permit another farce of a municipal election, *before the election for* members to a State Convention, the effect will be all injurious to *our* Side, because in the small vote usual in a municipal election, they will probably be able to triumph, which will give them strength in the State elections to follow. By appointing our officers, we break up the foul combination, put better men in their places, and have all the advantage for our own side. I trust you will think of this matter seriously, and let me know how far you are willing to accede to our wishes in this matter.

I understand that some of our copperheads have got up a recommendation of Mr. Nooe for Judge of our Common Law and Chancery Court.[4] Nooe was a Union man, of the half-and-half order, until Dr Fowlkes,[5] Sam Walker and a few others got disgusted with Lincoln's proclamation, and since then he has been just as I would have him. In a conversation with him about your willingness to appoint a Judge for us, about 12 months ago, he expressed himself clearly that you had no such power, and that no man was fit to fill the position who conceded that *you* had any such power. It seems now that a change has come over the spirit of their dreams.[6] *Now* they appreciate the advantage of having a Judge who will register their wishes, and save their property for them and hence their activity. As I have already told you I will never recommend an unworthy man for that position, but I believe we have a man in view for Judge that will fill the bill. He is a lawyer from Ohio, has been in the Army, is intelligent, and says he is for *your* policy. If I find out that he is all right, in every particular, I will recommend him; if not, not, and I have so told him. His name is Irving Halsey.[7] Please make no appointment until you hear definitely from us.

Hurlbut—thank the Lord,—has left Memphis, and I hope never to return again. He was permitted to remain too long for our good. Old Buckland was a great improvement on Veatch,[8] but he lacks energy, positiveness and force. There will be some help for us when our Commanders co-operate actively with us, and not against us.

Hurlbut has done his best against my regiment, in an indirect way, but still it prospers. I have some eighty men out in corps drilling, and only need the mustering-in of Some officer to receipt for clothing, &c. If you have not already done so, please send a Commission for John Snyder as first Lieutenant Company F Union Guards.[9]

But I have exhausted my strength and must close. You must fulfil your promise and write to me fully.

Your friend James B Bingham

ALS, DLC-JP.

1. Charles Kortrecht, a Memphis attorney, had challenged the election results, particularly at Germantown, and in response the provost marshal had taken testimony on alleged voting fraud. Especially concerned over the posts of clerk of common law and criminal court, Kortrecht objected that Bingham should not have reported election returns until after the investigation; the editor argued that higher authorities should handle the matter, promising to send Kortrecht's letter to the secretary of state. Memphis *Bulletin*, March 13, 16, 19, 1864; Hooper, Memphis, 77.

2. Probably Horace H. Harrison; the letter has not been found.

3. Bingham's figures are distorted—not only "6000 voters in our lines," but also the "1200 votes polled." Probably the first figure included a sizeable number of transients and the second understated the total ballots, ranging from 1,407 for circuit court clerk to 1,528 for sheriff, as reported in his own paper. Before the March election, Bingham and the "unconditional Union" men tried to win the labor vote, mainly German and Irish, by charging that the opposition, basically slaveowners, had "used" them to fight a war for slavery and planned to "use" them to reconstruct a pro-slavery state. Memphis *Bulletin*, March 9, 1864; Hooper, Memphis, 76, 77.

4. John A. Nooe (1812-1865), a Virginia native who entered the legal profession in Alabama, served as a Democrat in the legislature (1835) and in several local offices before moving to Memphis in 1855. Thomas M. Owen, *History and Dictionary of Alabama Biography* (4 vols., Chicago, 1921), IV, 1284.

5. For Jeptha Fowlkes, see *Johnson Papers*, III, 602*n*.

6. Byron's "The Dream," st. 5.

7. Despite the fact that Irving Halsey (*c*1837-*fl*1878), a lawyer and captain 5th Ohio Cav., had as recently as March 24 been dishonorably dismissed the service for disobedience of orders, disrespect to his commander, and conduct unbecoming an officer, he had the temerity to seek a judgeship. Remaining in Memphis after the war, he formed a law partnership with T. B. Edington and eventually became judge of the Shelby 2nd circuit court (1870-78). CSR, RG94, NA; *Official Army Register: Volunteers*, V, 10; Memphis city directories (1866-73), *passim*; *Tenn. Official Manual* (1890), 184.

8. Ralph P. Buckland had replaced James C. Veatch as commander of the District of Memphis the preceding January.

9. Possibly John Snyder (b. *c*1828), Shelby countian living with his parents in 1850. Sistler, *1850 Tenn. Census*, VI, 119.

From Franklin County Citizens[1]

State of Tennessee
Franklin County, April 23, 1864

To Brig. Genl. Andrew Johnson—
Military Governor of the State of Tennessee—
General:—

The undersigned, citizens of the county of Franklin, and state of Tennessee, have the honor to address you on behalf of John B. Prince and John M. Kelly,[2] formerly of this county, but now held as prisoners at Fort Delaware, in the state of Delaware, and respectfully ask your attention to the following statement of facts.

The said John B. Prince and John M. Kelly were both formerly connected with the so-called Confederate army, but at the time they were made prisoners they had left said army with the intention of never again participating in the military service of the rebellion. John B. Prince deserted said service at the time of Bragg's retreat, in July, 1863. John M. Kelley, served about one year in the rebel army, and was discharged from said service about the first of April, 1863, upon application of his mother in consequence of being under age.

Both said Prince and said Kelly remained at their homes, engaged in peaceful pursuits from the time of leaving the rebel service until the arrival of the federal forces south of Cumberland Tunnel, in the summer of 1863. They then reported themselves to the commander of said forces, for the purpose of taking the oath of allegiance to the Government of the United States, and availing themselves of the privileges guaranteed to rebel deserters by Maj General Rosecranz, in General Orders[.] For that purpose they crossed the mountain with the federal forces, to Cowan, Tenn, but were never allowed to return, nor has any information been received by their families or friends of the nature of the charges under which they were held as prisoners.

Your memorialists would further represent that the said Prince and the said Kelly do not wish to be treated as prisoners of war, but are anxious to take an oath of allegiance to the Government of the United States or give any other surety which may be required for their good behavior as peaceful citizens.

Your memorialists, therefore, humbly pray, that if within the province of your authority as Military Governor of this State, you would take the necessary steps to secure the release of said prisoners, and their return to their homes and families.

And for this, your memorialists, as in duty bound, will ever pray,[3]

Mem, DNA-RG249, Lets. Recd., File 472C(1864), John B. Prince and John M. Kelly.

1. The name of Meredith Catchings (*c*1815-*fl*1866), long-time Franklin County justice of the peace (*c*1838-66), headed the twenty-six signatories. Billie and Hall Burks, trs., *Marriage Records of Franklin County, Tennessee, 1838-1875* (Sewanee, 1979), *passim.*

2. Prince (*c*1834-*fl*1900) and Kelly (1846-*fl*1887), both farmers, had enlisted at Tullahoma, February 28, 1863, as privates in Co. I, 17th Tenn. Inf., CSA. They came from neighboring farms and would appear to have been uncle and nephew, though only twelve years apart. According to his service record, Prince was captured at Cowan July 13, 1863, and remained a prisoner until May, 1865, when he was released after taking the oath of allegiance. Kelly's record is less complete, indicating only that he was sent to a hospital, May 1, 1863, and subsequently was a prisoner of war. CSR, RG109, NA; 1900 Census, Tenn., Franklin, 30th Enum. Dist., 4B; Carpenter, *1850 Census, Franklin*, 112; *Goodspeed's Franklin*, 830.

3. On May 17 Johnson forwarded this petition to commissary general of prisoners, William Hoffman, who, in reply, indicated that the two would not be released "at present." Hoffman to M. Catching, May 25, 1864, File 472C(1864), Lets. Recd., RG249, NA.

From James H. Kile[1]

Fort Johnson Nashville Tenn,
Apl. 23d, 1864

Andrew Johnston
Honored Sir,

Necessity compells me to make a few statements of facts and to request your interference in behalf of my family—

I am a citizen of Bradley Co. Tenn, and have been in the United states service for more than two years.—

some time in last February my family was compelled to leave home for want of subsistence. I met them at this place Feb. 18th, and have been trying from that time to this to rent a house or room for them to live in but have, as yet, failed to get one—

I find that nearly all of the confiscated, as well as individual houses are occupied by contraband negroes, poor white soldiers families are left out of doors, more than once have I tried to rent vacant houses only to receive the assurance from some rebel citizen that they were rented to negroes,[2] this being the case I would most respectfully ask that you grant my family a pass to Charleston Tenn and the privilege of transporting provisions over the Rail Road to them— my family consists of, my wife and four children, my wifes sister and five children, and my sister (twelve in all)[.] if you will aid me in procuring a house, or pass them back home I will ever hold you in most greatful remembrance[.][3]

Most Respectfully Sir Your Obdt Servt
James H. Kile
1st Sergt Battery "D" 1st Tenn Arty

ALS, DLC-JP.

1. James H. Kile (b. *c*1831), enlisting as a private at Sale Creek (Hamilton County) in November, 1861, served in the 1st Tenn. Lgt. Arty., rising to second lieutenant in September, 1864. During May and June of this year he would be on recruiting service. CSR, RG94, NA.

2. Nashville's conversion into a major Federal military base brought a critical housing shortage. Many black and white refugees secured remunerative employment there; it is not clear which group, if either, had the greater success in securing the limited housing available. Cimprich, Slavery Amidst Civil War, 114, 131.

3. An endorsement by the battery's commanding officer, Lt. Victory R. Williams, attests to the accuracy of Kile's statement and that "his family is large and in destitute circumstances."

From Alfred Bearden[1]

Fayetteville Tenn Aprile 27, 1864

Gov Andrew Johnson
Nashville Tenn
Dear Sir

John. S. Downing[2] Private Capt Williams[3] Company, 45 Regment Tenn. Infantry, was Conscripted in Williamson Cty Tenn, and taken off on the 11th of May 1863, and captured by the U. S. Forces near Wincester Tenn about the 21st June /63. Said Downing is at this time a Prisoner at Camp Chase Ohio and is verry anxious, to take the Oath and return Home; His Father[4] is some Eighty years of age, is and has been, all the time Loyal, so has his sons. Gov, anything that you may feel willing to do to aid in restoring this favorite son, to a worthy old Father will be duly apreciated, and gratefully remembered, by Your Friend[5]

Alfred Bearden

P S. Enclosed, see his last letter to his Father[.][6]

ALS, DNA-RG249, Lets. Recd., File 489J(1864), John S. Downing.

1. Alfred Bearden (*c*1811-*fl*1880), South Carolina native, was a Lincoln County gunsmith. Deane Porch, tr., *1850 Census, Lincoln County, Tennessee* (Nashville, 1970), 7-8; 1880 Census, Tenn., Lincoln, 129th Enum. Dist., 22.

2. John S. Downing (b. *c*1834), enlisting in January, 1862, as a private, Co. A, 45th Tenn. Inf., CSA, was "Sick at home," September and October, 1862, and from late December, 1863, to early January, 1864, and absent without leave until March when he was listed as "Deserted." However the records are contradictory, inasmuch as he also appears on the roll as "Captured on the retreat" from Middle Tennessee in July, 1863. Bearden and Downing apparently were related, although the precise kinship is unclear. CSR, RG109, NA; 1850 Census, Tenn., Williamson, 24th Dist., 433.

3. The captain of Co. A, made up of men from Williamson County, after the reorganization in 1862, was S. B. Wilson. *Tennesseans in the Civil War*, I, 273.

4. Willam H. Downing (b. *c*1785) was a well-to-do ($20,385 in 1860), North Carolina-born, Williamson County farmer. 1850 Census, Tenn., Williamson, 24th Dist., 433; (1860), E. Subdiv., Eaglesville, 123.

5. A later petition secured Downing's release on November 28, after Johnson had endorsed it: "I am thoroughly satisfied that this case should go outside the ordinary course and that the party should be promptly released. He is undoubtedly and has always been a Union man." Petition of Presly Jones et al, July 11, 1864, Lets. Recd., File 489J(1864), RG249, NA.

6. John S. Downing to W. H. Downing, March 14, 1864, *ibid.*

From Fielding Hurst

Headquarters 6th Tenn Cavalry
Memphis Tenn April 29th 1864

Govenor Andrew Johnson
Dear Sir.

I take pleasure in thus introducing to you Major Robert M Thompson of my Regiment, who is ordered to report to you on Business Connected with the recruiting Service.[1]

Major Thompson will give you in detail the deplorable State of affairs which now, exist in West Tenn, but I cannot help giving you a few facts[.]

Forrest is now, and has been for forty days in the Counties between the Missippi and Tennessee Rivers, Carrying devastation and destruction as he goes.[2]

West Tennessee has furnished a number of men for the United States Service, who entered the Service for the purpose of defending their homes from the invasions of the enemy, and yet these men are Compelled to Stay here, and at other points remote from their homes, while the Rebels are allowed to float at large, Sacking, burning, and plundering, their familes of all they have to Subsist upon.

This State of affairs has existed to a more or less degree, ever Since the war began, and yet the Military Authorities do nothing to alleviate their Suferings but on the contrary, frequently taunt us with being "Conquered Rebels" and *insinuate* that they had just as leive have us on the other Side as not.[3]

This does not at all Suit me. I don't like to be compelled to keep my Regiment, where a Rebel has more influence over the authorities than a loyal man, neither do I like the idea of guarding Rebel Property, whilst the owners of Said Property are living luxuriently under the protection of *my* Government, and at the Same time plotting treason against that Government, neither do I like to be under the *immediate* Command of men, who have "Cotton on the brain" to Such an extent as to Cause them to neglect their duty to the Government.[4]

Now, what I desire is, to be Stationed at Some point on the Tennessee River, above Fort Henry, where I can be of Some Service to the familes of the men in my Regiment. I know I cannot go there now, but I do not think the time is far distant when I can, and I therefore *earnestly* request you, to use your influence to that effect and if *possible* have us ordered there.

I have nearly a full Regiment yet Numbering (969) Nine Hundred and Sixty Nine enlisted Men. I had on the 1" March (1026) one thousand and twenty Six. we have been in Several engagements, in one of which the loss was forty, and three officers.[5]

For further information I refer you to Major Thompson, who can give you a correct history of the Suferings of the Union families in West Tenn[.]

I have the honor to be
Very Respectfully Your Obt Servant,
Fielding Hurst
Col 6th Ten Cavalry

ALS, T-Mil. Gov's. Papers, 1862-65, Corres. to A. Johnson.

1. Robert M. Thompson (1830-1903), a North Carolina-born McNairy County clergyman and merchant, who enrolled in August, 1862, as a lieutenant and rose to major in July of the next year, was from January to June, 1864, on detached service for recruiting; he resigned in December. After the war he served as county court clerk (1866-70) and was a lawyer, practicing in Tennessee and various eastern cities. CSR, RG94, NA; 1860 Census, Tenn., McNairy, 2nd Dist., 55; Marcus J. Wright, *Reminiscences of . . . McNairy County* (Washington, 1882), 13; Pension file, RG15, NA.

2. On March 16 Forrest began a month-long expedition into West Tennessee and Kentucky, during which he captured Union City, attacked Paducah, skirmished near Columbus, Kentucky, Bolivar and Raleigh, Tennessee, captured Fort Pillow, and ended the campaign with a skirmish at Paducah, April 14. Hurst had been ordered "to hang upon and harass the enemy, with a view of impeding his movements as much as possible," and, while evading "a general engagement . . . cut off and capture his foraging parties, stragglers, &c." Long, *Civil War Almanac*, 475-85 *passim*; Benjamin H. Grierson to Hurst, March 24, 1864, *OR*, Ser. 1, XXXII, Pt. III, 145.

3. Inasmuch as West Tennessee had been so preponderantly Confederate, it would appear that the Federal military authorities were skeptical that there could be any bona fide unionists and hence were the more suspicious of those who claimed to be. Hooper, Memphis, *passim*.

4. Both treasury agents and military officers were involved in illicit cotton trading; prices spiraling to a high of over $1.00 per pound by the end of June, 1864, brought a suspension of the trade in mid-summer. *Ibid.*, 98; Futrell, Federal Trade, 289.

5. According to Confederate sources, Hurst, in an encounter with Col. J. J. Neely near Bolivar, lost sixty-five men killed or captured, including three captains, and his entire wagon train. Forrest to L. P. Polk, April 2, 1864, *OR*, Ser. 1, XXXII, Pt. III, 733.

From Daniel E. Sickles[1]

[Nashville], Sunday Ev'g [May 1864][2]

My dear Governor,

Can you go to the Hermitage to-morrow morning? Gen. Smith[3] will furnish an escort and Carriage and start at any hour Convenient to yourself— he suggests an early hour—say eight o'clock—but name your own hour and if Tuesday will suit you better it is the same for me— the Carriage will Call for you at the time you name.[4]

TrulYrs D Sickles
Maj Genl

Gov. Johnson &c &c &c

ALS, DLC-JP.

1. Daniel E. Sickles (1825-1914), New York congressman (1857-61) and major general in the Army of the Potomac, served with the III Corps at Sharpsburg and Fredericksburg and commanded the Corps at Chancellorsville and Gettysburg, losing his leg in the latter battle. His field service ended, he was dispatched on a southern tour by Lincoln in the spring of 1864 and subsequently on a diplomatic mission to Colombia. Military governor of South Carolina (1866-67) and minister to Spain (1869-74), he returned to Congress for one term in 1893. Warner, *Generals in Blue*, 446-47; see also, W. A. Swanberg, *Sickles the Incredible* (New York, 1956).

2. Sickles departed Washington in April with the object of ascertaining the progress of reconstruction in Union-held cities in Tennessee, Louisiana, and South Carolina, the condition of blacks, and the effect of the Amnesty Proclamation upon the South, particularly the southern army. This letter could have been written in April, but hardly later than the early days of May, inasmuch as he left Nashville for Memphis on May 18 and for about ten days preceding had been with Sherman's army as it moved south from Chattanooga until it attacked Johnston at Resaca on May 15. Sickles to Lincoln, May 16, 1864, Lincoln Papers, LC; Long, *Civil War Almanac*, 492; Swanberg, *Sickles*, 260-62.

3. Probably William Sooy Smith.

4. Subsequently it was speculated that Lincoln had sent Sickles to "explore" Johnson's suitability for vice president, a purpose which Sickles himself denied. Interviewed in 1891, the general declared that his mission was confidential, but not related to the Tennessean's nomination; rather, Sickles was to investigate the accuracy of reports about the harshness of Johnson's administration, and, if they were true, whether it could be "modified to come more nearly to Mr. Lincoln's ideas." New York *Times*, July 10, 1891.

From Montgomery Blair[1]

[Washington], May 4, 1864

Dear Govr.

I submit this letter[2] to you to enable you to decide what course I shall[3] take in the matter[.]

If you for any reason do not wish to appt Mr. G[4] at this time but would recommend him hereafter—I will not give him the appt due to him— He is a valuable officer & has the recommendations of evy one almost for the P o at Memphis but you will see by this letter that I look to you alone because I mean to sustain you—

I dont want you to take Mr Gist unless you are satisfied he will best serve you in the office— He is to all eyes the best officer in our service—

yrs trly M Blair

My 4, 64

ALS, DLC-JP.

1. For Postmaster General Blair, see *Johnson Papers*, V, 222*n*.

2. Writing Blair the previous day, Robert C. Gist had indicated that he would like the postmaster appointment in Memphis and that he knew the post depended upon Johnson's approval. As one of the governor's "most ardent admirers," Gist had "never disguised my sentiments, & . . . acted uniformly with the Johnson Emancipation party." Johnson Papers, LC.

3. "You will" has been crossed out.

4. Robert C. Gist (*c*1824-1878), native Kentuckian, was a special post office agent at Memphis (1863-64) before his appointment as postmaster (1864-*c*69). Remaining in the city, he became an insurance agent and cotton solicitor, perishing in the great yellow fever epidemic. 1870 Census, Tenn., Shelby, Memphis, 2nd Ward, 62; *U. S. Official Register* (1863), 630; (1865), *347; (1867), 657; Memphis city directories (1867-78), *passim*; Memphis *Appeal*, September 11, 1878.

From Henry Marsh

May 4, 1864, Warrington, Ind.; ALS, DLC-JP.

Washington County refugee who wants to return to rescue his family, asks about the possibility of travel by public conveyance to Knoxville via Nashville and what chance he might have to get his family out of East Tennessee.

From Joseph P. Wilson

May 4, 1864, St. Cloud, Minn.; ALS, DLC-JP.

Old settler, familiar with public lands in Upper Mississippi Valley, offers services (at rate of "5 per ct upon a valuation of $1. per acre or $8. for each 1/4 sec of 160 acres—or 1/20 of the land located") to select the 125,000 acres due Tennessee under the Morrill Act of July, 1862; "can select the lands by careful examination of each particular tract and furnish Plats of the surveys . . . together with a description of each tract[.]"

From William G. Brownlow

Knoxville, May 5th, 1864.

Gov. Johnson:

I wish you to *read* and *consider* well the enclosed letter.[1] Rev. Mr. Bayless, is the chaplain of a Kentucky Regiment, and is the right sort of man, in all respects. He has settled in East Tennessee, permanently, and will be a Bradly County man.[2] His son is all, and even more than he represents him to be. If you can find a place for him, he will honor it, and himself.

Things are working well in regard to the political question— the people will sustain us at the ballot-box,[3] against those copperhead leaders, and they feel and know it.

Thousands are coming in from the upper counties, destitute, and fleeing because our forces fell back. We are sheltering and feeding as well as we can. The great point we have now to guard against is the driving of our *Union voters* out of the Country. Thousands are going, to Indiana & Illinois, and will never get back. The rebels want them gone, so they may be able to vote us down.

We are all looking with interest to the results at Dalton.[4]

I am, &c, W. G. Brownlow

ALS, DLC-JP.

1. Not found.

2. Capt. John S. Bayless (*c*1811-1865), chaplain, 16th Ky. Inf., apparently did not settle in Bradley; reenlisting in January, he died at Kinston, North Carolina, April 4, 1865. His son has not been found. CSR, RG94, NA.

3. The balloting in question does not seem to be national, but rather the election intended to restore the state government. Far from being imminent, as Brownlow implies, this event would not take place until the following March 4, the day Johnson was sworn in as vice president.

4. Gen. Joseph E. Johnston was entrenched at Dalton as Sherman began his Atlanta campaign in early May. Unable to pierce the Confederate defenses head on, Sherman launched a flanking movement, thereby forcing the enemy to evacuate their position on May 12 and turn to meet at Resaca the threat to their rear. Long, *Civil War Almanac*, 495, 497, 500.

From James F. Rusling

May 6, 1864, Nashville; ALS, DLC-JP.

Captain and assistant quartermaster of the "Senior and Supervising Quartermaster's Office," Department of the Cumberland, suggests reorganizing the state's military department by appointing a quartermaster general in addition to the adjutant general, inasmuch as "the Public Business has so largely increased, that a subdivision of the duties and a separation of the two Departments has become a matter of necessity." Such officer could be detailed by the President from the army with rank and pay of lieutenant colonel or appointed by Johnson from Tennessee troops with rank of colonel. Offers himself as a candidate.

From James Hilderbrand[1]

Jeffersonville, Clark County, Indiana.
May 7, 1864.

To His Excellency Andrew Johnson
Governor of Tennessee.

It is under a severe penalty, and perplexing Circumstances, that I appeal to you, and respectfully pray you to release me from my oath, to remain North of the Ohio River under the penalty of death. What have I done to merit this severe punishment, or what charges are there prefered against me, that I should have the severe sentence of death carried out as my punishment, should I cross the Ohio River to go South. Of the reasons—and the charges that should put me under such severe restrictions I have never been informed. They charge or charges must be filed in your department, and please inform me what they are. I shall be much obliged to you[.]

I was born and raised in Tennessee. My former home was in Bradley County, near Cleveland. My Mother is still there, I have two Brothers in the Federal Army, 10th Tenn Cavalry, Col Bridges, so I was informed.[2]

Of one thing I am certain, my conscience are clear of Ever Casting my vote for the Ordinance of the secession of Tennesse from the Federal Union or to give any aid or countenance to it, or to ever vote for any man that favored the Secession, or the Rebellion, in any shape or form[.] I with other Union men were, persecuted, and driven from home[.] We had to keep concealed in the mountains, caves, and woods, Suffer hunger, thirst and cold, and hunted like wild beasts, and for what, because we are conscionciously opposed [to] the disruption of the Union, and with your Excellency and Mr Brownlow would not succomb to their demands. I was hunted down, and taken by a detachment of Rebol Cavalry about the Middle of March 1863—(the first time I was ever taken and in the Rebel Army) I was tied, and handcuffed and in irons carried to Port Hudson on the Missi' River[.] I was kept in that position about one month, up to the first week in May— I was then put into the first Tennessee Battallion, and we were marched to Jackson, Missi'[.] there we made a halt, but soon were ordered to a march Eastward, and the first night after we left Jackson I deserted them, with a determination to sooner face death than to fight for their Cause, I left knowing if I was captured it would be death[.] I travelled and kept my self concealed, passing near Rebel Squads at night, Barefooted, with Scarcely clothing to keep me covered. I made my way to Cowan Station,[3] and delivered myself up to the U. S Military authorities. I was there requested to take an Oath *"Prisoners Parole"* of which I enclose you a Copy[.] From Cowan Tenn I was sent to Louisville and there requested to take an Oath, to cross the Ohio River and not return without a written permission from you or Genl Rosecrans—unter the penalty of Death. Sir, I have made a fair, a candid & true Statement, of my Case[.] If I had an opportunity, I could prove to your Satisfaction my former Union Sentiments. I refer you to the following Gentlemen who now are freemen again old Citizens of Bradly County Tennessee, A. J. Hicks—was (in the Federal Army), John Blackburn Esq. formerly, a Justice of the Peace, Uriah Hunt, Gabrael D Ford,[4] & others who were acquainted with me. Other deserters from Tennessee in the Rebel army have Came across the Ohio River by the hundreds. those too who volunteered in the Rebel Army—they have had permission to go home, and I appeal to your Excellency what have I done that I must, remain here. I respectfully pray you to release me to let me return home to my aged mother, and take care of her. I have no apologies to make for being in the Rebel service. I cannot change my sentiments[.] I voted and done all I could against the secession of Tennessee, to uphold the Union of the States[.] I never fired a musket against my will and for the disruption of the Union. The Short time I was with them I was taken by force kept by force and I had to desert them by force. I leave the subject with you. I again ask what have I done. You have it in your power to release me and as an East Tennesseean I pray you most respectfully to grant me this request[.]

Enclosed I send you 3 Po Stamps[.] please answer as soon as convenient[.]

Respectfully yours—
James Hilderbrand

P. S. On the back of my first obligation I took at Cowan, there is an endorsement, "dont want to be Exchanged"[.] I cannot see why that endorsement was written. It never was Customary I believe to Exchange deserters from one hostile Government to another.

This is the first effort I have made to be released from [m]y parole to remain North during the war.[5]

J. H.

ALS, DLC-JP.

1. If we are to believe him, James Hilderbrand (*c*1832-*fl*1870), a Bradley County farmer, was apparently conscripted into the 1st (Colm's) Tenn. Inf., CSA, which from early May to July, 1863, served in and out of Jackson, Mississippi. 1860 Census, Tenn., Bradley, 3rd Dist., 245; (1870), 5th Dist., 10; *Tennesseans in the Civil War,* I, 164-65.

2. Nisa Hilderbrand (*c*1805-*fl*1870), lived with her son James; the brothers were John (1841-1916), a private, Co. D, 10th (Bridges) Tenn. Cav., USA, who lived in Cleveland after the war, and William A. (b. *c*1839), a private in the same company. Enrolled at Calhoun in January, 1864, both were mustered out at Nashville in August, 1865. 1860 Census, Tenn., Bradley, 3rd Dist., 245; (1870), 4th Dist., Cleveland, 10; Sistler, *1890 Tenn. Veterans Census,* 146; Ross, *Bradley Cemetery Records,* II, 154; *Tenn. Adj. Gen. Report* (1866), 560; CSR, RG94, NA.

3. A station in Franklin County on the Nashville and Chattanooga Railroad.

4. Andrew Jackson Hicks (*c*1826-*fl*1890), Bradley County farmer and Hilderbrand's neighbor, who after the war moved to Rhea County, enlisted in March, 1862, as a private, Co. F, 1st Tenn. Cav., USA, serving until March, 1865; John Blackburn (1813-1880) was a North Carolina-born farmer and schoolteacher, who also served as county surveyor

for twenty-six years; Uriah Hunt (b. *c*1815), also a farmer; and Gabriel W. Ford (1817-1880), a physician. CSR (Hicks), RG94, NA; 1860 Census, Tenn., Bradley, 3rd Dist., 243, 245; 5th Dist., 72, 77; Ross, *Bradley Cemetery Records,* I, 353; II, 121; Sistler, *1890 Tenn. Veterans Census,* 145; Cleveland *Banner,* June 18, December 17, 1880.

5. An extended endorsement "By Command of Maj. Genl. Thomas" observes: "it appears that at the time he took the oath he was considered a Prisoner of War and by accepting the same acknowledged himself to be," concluding that "he must still be considered as such and will be required to observe the oaths he has taken until regularly Exchanged or properly released under existing Orders of the War Department—"

From William G. Bewley[1]

Federal Prison
Knoxville Tenn May 8/64

Govorner Andrew Johnson
Military Govorner of Tenn
Govorner;

I am under arrest in this place for shooting a reble in self defence.

In 1862 I made up a Company of 125 men, and started to Kentuckey to join Robert Johnson's Regt, by [but?] the man with whom I had the diffaculty, and his Sons they caused my arrest, by giving information to the rebles.[2] I was captured and brought to this place and confined in Prison by the rebles, and from this place I was sent to Madison G.a. I was released from their by taking the oath of allegence to Confederate Government, and went home. I then went to work and recruited an other Company and was followed by this mans Sons but Sucseed in making my way to Kentuckey although several of my men were killed by those same men.

At the time Thomas A. R. Nelson and yourself was canvesing this Section of the Country for the Federal Government, two of this mans Sons pushed an Umberlla through the window of the Car in which you rode and Spit at you through the hole at Russellville and proposed thre times thre groans for you. I was an eye witness to this as well as meny other of my acquaintences.

Those boys of whom I speak are Sons to Hugh Kane a rank Seecessionist, and a man who has done evry thing in his power to render assistence to the caus of the Confedracy.

In the first place they were to cowardly to enter the Army themselfs, and consequently hired Substituters. They afterward acted as agents for the Confederate government, and one of those Genteel-men after serching 3 days for a Union Soldier, and did not Sucseede in finding him took his wife out and raveshed her, and then made his brags that he would have a good time whil the "Union Soldiers" was gone. He said he would Stand him-self in the Country for their (the Union mens) wives. They also took the grain out of their Store House, and rendered it a place of confinement for the men they had conscripted for the Confederate Army.

Now General; I humbly ask if this is the way to use a man who has Sacrafised a home, and his evrthing to be used. Take it to be your own

Case. You know what the rebles of East Tenn are, and, what the Union men had to suffer from their hands. I have worked for, and done all in my powr for the Federal Government, and now those reble scoundrels laugh, and grin at me, for to think their influence got me into this[.]

Please look into and investegate my case as soon as convenient, and caus me to be released from Prison. I have bin in the Federal Army fourteen months and will refer you to Colonel Crawford[3] fro my abilaties as a Soldier and my good conduct as an Officer[.]

I am Governer with Respect your humble Servent
W. G. Bewley
Lieutenant Comp "B." 1st Tenn Arty.

Gov. Johnson
Military Governer of Tennessee
Nashville, Tenn

ALS, DLC-JP.

1. William G. Bewley (b. *c*1836), previously a farrier and enlisted man, and since early April first lieutenant, Co. B, 1st Tenn. Arty., USA, was arrested for killing Hugh Cain "on or about the 27th day of April" in Russellville, Jefferson County. Acquitted in September, he resigned the following March; his service record carries the notation "Incompetency." CSR, RG94, NA.

2. Bewley's nemesis was Hugh Cain, Jr. (1801-1864), a prominent Hawkins (now Hamblen) County farmer who had sired at least five sons, two of whom lived with their father on the eve of the war. It was undoubtedly the older three—James L., Samuel (b. *c*1836), and William Crockett (1838-1865)—Jefferson County merchants who made life miserable for Bewley. Sistler, *1850 Tenn. Census,* I, 269; 1860 Census, Tenn., Hawkins, 13th Dist., 140; WPA, Hamblen County Tombstone Records, Russellville Cemetery, 188.

3. R. Clay Crawford, lieutenant colonel, 1st Tenn. Lgt. Arty. Btn.

From James L. Cain[1]

Knoxville Tenn. 8th May 1864.

Hon. Andrew Johnson,
Military Governor of Tennessee,
Sir.

I understand that a letter has been addressed to you by W. G. Bewley Lieutenant Company B 1st Tenn. Artillery, who is under military arrest in this place, for the murder of my father, Hugh Cain, requesting you to order or obtain his release.

Strong representations are said to have been made in the letter as to the disloyalty of my father and one of my brothers.[2] It is true that one of my brothers was disloyal, but my father was always a Union man and had a conversation with you, as I hear, when you were last in Knoxville.

Bewley has been at enmity with my father, since last October, because he alleged that my father had sent soldiers to forage on his mothers place.[3] Father alleged that she had sent the soldiers on him and that he merely sent them back.

Bewley, as I can prove, made repeated threats against my father, and, while he was sitting quietly at the Depot in Russellville on the 27th April last, came up and after a few words, struck him with a large stick, and, as father pushed him back, he attempted to draw his pistol and threatened to kill a bystander who attempted to prevent his using it. Father, when he saw the pistol, retreated some twenty yards and crawled under the depot, through a small hole on the upper side. Bewley fired at him as he went under, but missing his aim, went round to the end of the depot, took deliberate aim at him and shot him when all resistance had ceased.[4]

I can prove the substantial correctness of the above statement by respectable witnesses and am advised that the case is clearly murder at the common law, and murder in the first degree by the statute law of Tenne.

Having thus shown that the case is not one for executive interference or clemency, I have to ask, respectfully, that you forward to me or to Brig. Gen. S. P. Carter, a copy of the appointment or commission of Bewley as Lieut. as I am told this will be necessary on his trial before a Court Martial or Military Commission.[5]

Very respectfully, Your Obt. Serv't,
J L. Cain

ALS, DLC-JP.

1. James L. Cain (1833-*fl*1887) had within the year moved from Jefferson County, where he and his brothers had been merchants, to Greene where he became "one of the largest and most prominent farmers in the Fourth Civil District." In 1878 and 1885 he opened "merchandizing" establishments in Riverton, Mississippi, and Pine Bluff, Arkansas, although he continued to be a Greene County resident. *Goodspeed's East Tennessee,* 1242-43.

2. Although the "disloyal" brother has not been positively identified, it may have been Samuel; an S. R. Cain served as a private in Co. B, 12th Tenn. Cav. Btn, CSA, recruited in upper East Tennessee. *Tennesseans in the Civil War,* I, 33; II, 72.

3. Bewley's mother Mahaly (b. *c*1805), a Virginia native and Cain's neighbor, had been raising a family alone since 1850. Byron Sistler, tr., *1830 Census, East Tennessee* (Evanston, Ill., 1971), Hawkins, 19; Sistler, *1850 Tenn. Census,* I, 125.

4. Allegedly, Bewley went to the railroad depot, where he "did . . . unlawfully and maliciously shoot and kill one *Hugh Cain*" with "a revolving pistol." The general court, though finding him guilty of the act, acquitted him of murder. This verdict was overturned in September at the Knoxville 4th Division Headquarters on the ground "that the evidence shows that it was not an act of self defense, and does not justify an honorable acquittal." Nonetheless, Bewley was released to return to his regiment. General Orders No. 21, September 21, 1864, CSR, RG94, NA.

5. An endorsement by prominent Hawkins County unionists John Netherland, Absalom A. Kyle, and William C. Kyle, attests to Cain's "good character" and truthfulness. They observe "that the whole Community at Russellville was shocked at the deliberate murder of a Citizen who was well known as peaceful in his habits and deportment, and who was regarded as a worthy man by all who knew him."

To James B. Bingham

State of Tennessee,
Executive Department,
Nashville, May 10, 1864.

James B. Bingham, Memphis—
Dear Sir:

I have caused all the papers enclosed by you,[1] to be examined in reference to the election of County and District officers holden in Shelby County, on the 5th day of March, 1864, as also the papers relating to the same matter, forwarded to me, by the contestants, and have concluded to hold the election void, so far as relates to the following offices, to-wit: Sheriff, Clerk of County Court, Register, County Trustee, and Clerk of Common Law and Criminal Court. I see no reason, from any of the papers or otherwise why the other officers elected should not go on. In pursuance of this conclusion, I herewith enclose to you a blank commission authorizing you, or such other person as is suitable and proper to hold the same, such other person to be selected by yourself, and the friends of the Government resident in Shelby county, and make publication of the same.

I am, respectfully,
Andrew Johnson,
Military Governor.

Nashville *Times and True Union,* June 3, 1864.

1. Some time between March 8 and 13, Bingham had sent Johnson the official election returns for Shelby County; these records are now in the office of the secretary of state. Memphis *Bulletin,* March 9, 16, 1864.

To Joseph D. Webster[1]

Nashville, May 11th 1864.

Brig. Gen'l Webster,
Chief of Staff &c Nashville, Tenn.
General:

I am advised that it is contemplated by the Military authorities to take possession of the West-Wing of the Penitentiary (for military purposes) in addition to the portion now so used by them.[2]

I have to state in regard thereto that there are now, as I understand, upwards of one hundred and sixty prisoners convicted of crimes in the U. S. Courts, before Military Commissions &c. The capacity of the West-Wing (that proposed to be taken) is one hundred and twenty cells, and I would respectfully recommend that a number equal thereto be transferred to that Wing to be controlled by the same authority as that exercised over the other prisoners confined in that portion of the building.

I respectfully suggest that as the better course, and that you will thereby secure the additional room you now require, at the same time promoting the public interests in the proper confinement of convicts.[3]

Very Resp'y Your Obt. Sevt.
Andrew Johnson Mil. Gov'r.

Copy, DLC-JP.

1. Joseph D. Webster (1811-1876), New Hampshire native and Dartmouth graduate (1832), was commissioned in the army's topographical engineers (1838). Returning to civilian life after the Mexican War, he settled in Chicago in 1854. Having reenlisted in 1861, he became Grant's chief of staff early in the following year, was promoted brigadier in the fall, and during the Vicksburg campaign was in charge of all the railroads supplying Grant's army. Subsequently chief of staff to Sherman and Thomas, he retired to Chicago where he was city assessor (1869-72) until appointed collector of internal revenue. Warner, *Generals in Blue,* 546.

2. In July, 1863, Johnson had granted permission for army use of the penitentiary for military prisoners to be transferred from the city jail. James A. Garfield to Gordon Granger, July 27, 1863, Vol. 6, Lets. Sent, RG393, NA.

3. Apparently the transfer was made; in December, both east and west wings "together with portions of the middle building" were being used by the military; as a result, many civilian "convicts were compelled to sleep two in a cell, upon the stone slab floors." *Tenn. House Journal,* 1865-66, App. 100.

From Nelson D. Oviatt[1]

Nashville Tenn May 14th/64

His Excellency Andrew Johnson
Milr Gov of Tenn
Dr Sir

I have been waiting for several days now in hopes to be able to get to your Office & have been in hopes to again resume labors for you, but although my health has improved 'till I feel quite well I am still weak & my disease seems to have settled in my left hip rendering it impossible for me to walk to any Extent & the present prospect is that it will be some days yet before I will be able to walk enough to resume business.— This being the case & having heard that you was making Enquiries about an Express Box that has been recd since I was taken sick & also about the horse I thought I had better write you a few lines & Explain how those things were.

About the time I was taken Sick I sent to Ohio to my Brother[2] to send me some Garden Seeds, that I could not get here, as I had a friend coming who I expected would bring them, for him, but he failed to get them brought in that way, & the first I knew I Recd a Letter that he had sent them by Express & directed them to me in your care. The Box arrived & the Seeds were all Sown whilst I was Sick & I never Saw Either, Box nor contents, but if you wish I will get the Box (if not destroyed) that you may see the Size &c—& a list of the contents for I do not remember now what I ordered & consequently cannot tell what was in it. This is all that I have recd by Express or otherways directed to your care Except the two Boxes for the refugees sometime since.—

About the horse I have always assumed the Control of him, of course since you put him into my care, though I don't think I had been on him more than twice in Six weeks myself when I was taken Sick. Still he was a great help in conducting my business, & he was & has been all the time well taken care of & kept in readiness for the use of such persons, as were conducting public business under you, never using him myself nor having him used for any private purpose when he was wanted for public use.—

Since I have been sick he has been used by Mr Davis Mr Gaut & Mr Hall[3] Entirely, by Mr Hall whilst acting as Agent for the "East Tenn Relief Association"[.]

In this I supposed I was fulfilling you wishes, (Keeping a Boy at my own Expense to take care of him all the time) but if not please notify me, or if you wish to make any other disposition of the horse.—

You will of course know whether I am likely to need him any more or not, though I am in hopes you will give me employment & that I may resume work again soon.—

I have to add that I am now a Married Man again[4] & that I reside on Spruce Street 3d door South of Cedar. (*Ea Side Spruce*)

Hoping these Explanations will prove Satisfactory to you I remain

as Ever Your humble Servt
N. D. Oviatt

ALS, DLC-JP.

1. Nelson D. Oviatt (*c*1831-*fl*1882), Connecticut-born resident of Cleveland, Ohio, during the mid-fifties, appears in Nashville in the summer of 1863 working with refugees—finding temporary housing, obtaining rations, clothes, and blankets from the military, and arranging travel north for them to seek employment. Begun "as an act of humanity . . . his unselfish labors attracted the notice of Gov. Johnson, who urged him to devote his whole time to it in an official capacity." From September to April, 1864, "in the quality of an agent for the destitute," he assisted some ten thousand persons. Settling in Humphreys County as a farmer after the war, he subsequently returned to Cleveland where he was proprietor of the Pearl Street House in the 1880's. 1860 Census, Ohio, Summit, Copley Township, 86; (1870), Tenn., Humphreys, Waverly, 19; Cleveland city directories (1856-82), *passim;* Nashville *Dispatch,* December 30, 1864.

2. Not identified.

3. Davis and Hall are unidentified. John M. Gaut was a charter member of the Nashville Refugee Aid Society. Nashville *Times and True Union,* June 30, 1864.

4. During the preceding week a marriage license had been issued to Oviatt and a Margaret Howard. *Ibid.,* May 9, 1864.

To Manson M. Brien

Nashville, Tenn., May 15th 1864.

Judge:

We have information, deemed sufficiently reliable to warrant some notice, to the effect that at the election lately held in this State, there were voted for and elected, in some one of the Civil Districts of Wilson County, a certain free man of color as magistrate, and a certain man of color, held as a slave, as Constable.[1]

I have to request that you will enquire into the facts connected therewith, as far as it may be in your power so to do, secure, if possible, the Poll Books, and cause to be arrested all the parties in any manner connected with this expression of contempt for the Government and its efforts to restore civil law in Tennessee, and have said parties sent under guard to this City for such disposition as may be hereafter determined upon.[2]

I will add that it may be deemed proper to take immediate steps to gratify the people of that District in which said proceeding is alleged to have taken place, now that they have so clearly indicated their views and wishes.

Very Truly Yours etc
Andrew Johnson Mil. Gov'r.

Hon M. M. Brien
Judge of Criminal Court etc.

L, Jack Reynolds, Smyrna, Georgia [1972].

1. Records in the secretary of state's office show that four magistrates were elected in Wilson County: Marcus D. Allen, Ezekiel Holloway, Edward Patton, and Zadock McMillan; all, according to the censuses of 1850, 1860, and 1870, were white. There is no extant report of the election of a constable. Tommy Adams (Tennessee State Library and Archives) to Andrew Johnson Project, January 22, 1980.

2. Absence of any current or subsequent comment on this alleged abnormal situation suggests that the "information" was without foundation.

From Alvin Hawkins

Green Castle Ind May 17th 1864

Hon A. Johnson
Dear Sir—

I have just learned that while Forrest's forces were in West Ten, they arrested and Carried off, B. F. Harrison, Lewis A Williams, A. D. Bennett, and Jno. B Britt,—[1] Harrison has for many years been Clerk of the Circuit Court, & was Re-elected in March last—[2] Williams, was for Several years the Tax Collector and has or had one son in the Union Army 7th Te. Cavalry—[3] Britt, has or had Several Sons in the same Regt. and is about—60 years of age—[4] They are all good Citizens and have all the time been influential Union Men—Resideing in Carroll Co, Ten.

In their behalf and in behalf of the Union Men still there—I appeal to you[.] Let prominent secessionists of that County be imprisoned or banished south of the Union lines untill these Union Men are Released— by this mean we may not obtain "indemnity for the past" but we may have "Security for the future."[5] I would Suggest that at this time a Single Company of Cavalry, Can be put across the Te. River at Johnsonville proceed to Carroll & Huntington make the necessary arrests and Return in 48 hours—without danger.

I may be mistaken but it occurs to me that unless a *Rigid System of Retaliation be adopted and enforced;* it is idle to talk of protecting or encourageing Union Men in Tennessee— All other means have failed— Hopeing that you are so situated that you can accomplish the end suggested, I am

Respectfully yours
Alvin Hawkins

ALS, DLC-JP.

1. Benjamin F. Harrison (*c*1824-*fl*1880), Carroll County register (1852-56), circuit court clerk (1856-70), and "hotel keeper"; Lewis A. Williams (*c*1818-*fl*1880), North Carolina-born Carroll County farmer; A. D. Bennett (*c*1820-*fl*1900), Huntingdon merchant; and John B. Britt (*c*1806-1864), North Carolina native and substantial farmer. 1860 Census, Tenn. , Carroll, 11th Dist., 207, 202, 208, 191; (1880), 16th Enum. Dist., 9, 35; (1900), 138th Enum. Dist., 18A; *Goodspeed's Carroll,* 802; WPA, Carroll County Wills, Book A, 1822-64, p. 202.

2. See Proclamation Ordering Elections, January 26, 1864.

3. John F. Williams (*c*1845-*fl*1900), enlisting in September, 1862, was captured four months later, paroled the following September, and re-enlisted in January, 1865. After the war he became a physician. CSR, RG94, NA; *Tenn. Adj. Gen. Report* (1866), 484; 1900 Census, Tenn., Carroll, 133rd Enum. Dist., 10A.

4. Of Britt's three sons of military age—23, 22, and 17 in 1860—only the youngest Dempsey (b. *c*1843), a private, Co. F, 7th Cav., has a service record. CSR, RG94, NA; *Tennesseans in the Civil War,* II, 476.

5. An allusion to an 1801 letter from Charles James Fox to Thomas Maitland, commenting that "Indemnity for the past and security for the future" might be found in the terms of the pending Treaty of Amiens with France. John Russell, ed., *Memorials and Correspondence of Charles James Fox* (4 vols., New York, 1970 [London, 1853-57]), III, 345.

To Abraham Lincoln[1]

Nashville, Tenn., May 17th 1864.

His Excellency Abraham Lincoln,
Washington City.

I am thoroughly satisfied that the Amnesty will be seriously detrimental in reorganizing the state government, and that Tennessee should be made an exception. We have gained all the benefit so far as the Army is concerned that can result from it. Let all the pardons granted to Tennesseans be upon the application of those desiring[2] it directly to the President.[3] The influence will be better and they will feel a much greater obligation to the Government. As it now operates its main tendency is to keep alive the rebel spirit in fact reconciling none. This is the opinion of every real union man here.[4]

Andrew Johnson Mil. Govr.

Tel copy, DLC-JP; DLC-Lincoln Papers; DNA-RG107, Tels. Recd., President, Vol. 2 (1864).

1. Because the recipient's several copies of this wire contain multiple errors committed by the telegrapher, the text printed, contrary to our usual practice, is that of the sender's copy.

2. One wonders what the President's reaction may have been when he read in his garbled copy "deserving" in place of "desiring."

3. Under Lincoln's amnesty oath, which could be "taken and subscribed before any commissioned officer, civil, military or naval, in the service of the United States," rebels might gain full political rights—a policy supported by the more conservative unionists but

Andrew Johnson.
"Likeness from a recent Photograph from life."
Painted by Alonzo Chappel; published by Johnson, Fry Co. in volume II, Evert A. Duyckinck, *National Portrait Gallery of Eminent Americans* (New York, 1862-[64]).

denounced by radicals as "a cheap way for treason to avoid punishment." The President had, however, agreed that Johnson's stiffer oath should be required for county elections. Maslowski, *Treason Must Be Made Odious,* 86-88; Basler, *Works of Lincoln,* VII, 270.

4. Lincoln responded two days later: "Will write you on the subject within a day or two." No subsequent letter has been found. *Ibid.,* 351.

Speech at Johnsonville[1]

May 19, 1864

Governor Johnson, after acknowledging the compliment of the toast, said that this day gave Nashville and Middle Tennessee direct communication with the glorious northwest and if the people were wise they would cultivate the connection. We had come down to the waters of the Tennessee and taken possession, not as olden conquerors used to do, in the name of some monarch, but in the name of Freedom and of the United States. To-day we had a direct communication with the great northwest, God bless her! instead of making a circuitous route through conservative Kentucky.[2] There was more loyalty to-day in Tennessee than there was in Kentucky. We have had slaves and bondmen among us, to-day the great idea of freedom is abroad, and this struggle which agitates the land is a contest of merit, of human right, and freedom. Let the people see facts as they are and no longer delude themselves with old prejudices. Let the blacks understand that they must assume responsibilities, and take that position which their merits or demerits may assign them. In the words of Mr. Lincoln: "Let all have a fair start, and an equal share in the race of life."[3]

Go the the ballot-box and put down this infernal and damnable system of slavery, and restore your State. The slaves are free to-day. As soon as you can acknowledge the legality of emancipation. Unless you people show a desire to put down these guerrillas and restore the law no Generals can save you from ruin. Do your part and the soldiers will protect and sustain you. I have been denounced as a despot and an enemy of the people by a little newspaper,[4] which is always railing at Andy Johnson. Thank God I can live all traitors down. They know their accusations are false and absurd. I have sought to deliver and redeem my State, where I grew up[5] and where my children live. If I had been the lover of power which my enemies say I am, I had offers of place and power, far higher far less harrassing, and far more profitable than the office of Military Governor.[6] I have sought faithfully to serve and save my State. You may discard me; I care not. You may trample me under foot; I care not: for the proud satisfaction of having stood up for free government against an iniquitous and atrocious rebellion is stronger than all that.

Nashville *Times and True Union,* May 21, 1864.

1. To celebrate the Nashville and Northwestern Railroad's completion to the Tennessee River, Johnson and other dignitaries, traveling by special excursion train, arrived at Johnsonville. Following a reception at the depot in which Nashville mayor John Smith led a toast to "Andrew Johnson—amid storm and tempest, treason and rebellion, he remained

faithful and true to the Union and Constitution," the governor addressed the assemblage. Nashville *Times and True Union,* May 21, 1864.

2. An allusion to the Louisville and Nashville Railroad, the main supply line.

3. A sentiment found in an early Lincoln message to Congress in 1861 and in other speeches that same year, notably at Philadelphia in February. Basler, *Works of Lincoln,* IV, 240, 438.

4. The Nashville *Daily Press,* organ of the conservative unionists, whose editors had particularly attacked Johnson's iron-clad oath.

5. Here the reporter would appear to have misquoted; Johnson was a young man when he located in Tennessee.

6. Although "had" seems to imply a condition prior to acceptance of the governorship, he may have been thinking of his prospects for the vice presidency.

Memorial of Augustus R. Brown[1]

[Nashville], May 24, 1864

To his Excellency Andrew Johnson
Governor of the State of Tennessee

Your Memorialist Augustus R. Brown of Nashville respectfully represents to your Excellency, that on last Saturday evening he was waited upon by an Officer from the department of Col Horner[2] Provost Marshall of this Post, bearing a paper charging your Memorialist with disloyalty and assessing him *by your order* in the Sum of Five Hundred Dollars ($500), and requesting the Same to be paid promptly.

Knowing your Excellency's character for Justice your Memorialist beleives that this order based upon *ex parte* evidence, with no opportunity being allowed him of explanation or justification, was predicated upon an exaggerated Statement Such as were utterly unwarrented by the facts.[3]

Your Memorialist begs leave to submit the following Statement of the occurrence on account of which or rather as he beleives upon an exaggerated Statement thereof, he is mulcted in what is to him an enormous fine.

On Saturday last Mr Dillon Collector of the Customs of this Post, called into the Store of Driver & Brown[4] (of which firm your memorialist is Junior Partner,) and in a peremptory and blunt manner demanded One hundred Dollars for the refugees funds. The members of Said firm are young men of limited means who purchased on credit the Stock of the old firm of James Erwin & Son,[5] and have by close attention to their business, been Striving to meet their obligations and to make a Start in the world—like all other Merchants they are called upon almost daily for aid and assistance for every Species of charity, and have in no instance ever refused to give whatever amount they thought their means would justify[.] Acting upon this principle Your Memorialist on the advice of his Partner (Mr Driver) gave Mr Dillon Five Dollars which they then beleived and now aver was a liberal gift on their part considering their circumstancs & indebtedness &,

Mr Dillon was not Satisfied but demanded a further Sum of ten dollars. Irritated by the demand and Still more by the manner of Mr Dillon making the demand,

Your Memorialist who admits being of quick temper replied with Some heat "Dam the refugees let them go to work like I have to do," or words to that effect as near as he can remember. Your Memorialist urges that his expression was not the result of any premeditation or any intented insult towards a class of people many of whom are doubtless worthy and derserving persons driven from their homes by the unfortunate State of affairs now extending throughout the State, but the result mearly of a momentary indignation that a person already holding in his hand a gift of money which the giver thought adequate, Should demand more and demand it in So rude a manner.

Your Memorialist avers that the above Statement embraces every charge to its full extent that can be made against him. as to my general charge of disloyalty, it is unnecessary to make any Statement, except So far as to Say that although your Memorialist is not nor has ever been guilty of active or constructive treason, nevertheless as a citizen of Tennessee he has thought it his duty to take the oathes required as proofs of loyalty, and that he has conformed himself to all the laws orders and regulations as becomes a loyal citizen.

Your Memorialist holds himself ready to qualify to the entire truth of the above Statement, and lays it before your Excelency with a firm beleif that upon a further investigation into the merits of the case, you will direct the order to be withdrawn and the fine to be remitted[.]

With respect Your Excellencys Obt Servant
A. R. Brown

Nashville May 24th/64

Mem, DLC-JP.

1. Augustus R. Brown (*c*1840-*fl*1881), native Tennessean engaged in the hardware and cutlery business at "32 ws Public Square," was later in business with S. N. Macy and/or E. R. Driver, at least until 1881. He seems to have boarded most of the time at the Commercial Hotel until 1870—and at the Maxwell House thereafter. Nashville city directories (1865-81), *passim*; Henry McRaven, *Nashville: "Athens of the South"* (Chapel Hill, 1949), 107; 1870 Census, Tenn., Davidson, Nashville, 3rd Ward, 5.

2. John W. Horner (b. *c*1836), New York native, Detroit schoolteacher, and a three-months' volunteer in 1861, reenlisted in July, 1862, as captain, 18th Mich. Inf., becoming lieutenant colonel in February, 1864. During the first six months of that year, his regiment was stationed in Nashville. 1860 Census, Mich., Lenawee, Adrian, 2nd Ward, 159-60; Robertson, *Michigan in the War,* 386, 852.

3. According to Joseph R. Dillin, a former salesman for Fall and Cunningham, hardware merchants, and since April, 1863, a treasury agent, now collecting for the Nashville Refugee Aid Society, his efforts were well rewarded, except for Brown's announcement that "He would not give them one cent to save their lives. He wished they were all in *Hell.*" Dillin urged that "we use every effort to have the Authorities Assess Mr Brown five hundred dollars." This letter, together with the relief committee's (David T. Patterson, Joseph S. Fowler, Alvan C. Gillem, and John M. Gaut) assertion that Brown's "humanity can only be reached through his pocket," elicted Johnson's order that Horner collect "the sum of Five Hundred Dollars" for the Relief Association. "Such language as that attributed . . . to Brown," wrote Johnson, "could only proceed from an ardent sympathizer with the cause of the Rebellion." He is "undoubtedly of that class, who have brought about the necessity of establishing . . . 'Union Relief Associations' for the benefit of the destitute Union families," and "should be compelled to contribute towards the alleviation, in some manner, of the suffering he has aided in imposing on them." Endorsements on Dillin to Gaut, May 17, 1864, Johnson Papers, LC.

4. In addition to his hardware business Eban R. Driver (1836-1882), Massachusetts native and son of William Driver, sometime Nashville alderman, was also the first president of the Edgefield and Nashville Manufacturing Company (1874). He had been arrested the previous summer and temporarily sent North. Acklen, *Tenn. Records,* I, 22; Clayton, *Davidson,* 223; 1860 Census, Tenn. , Davidson, Nashville, 1st Ward, 16; Porch, *1850 Census, Davidson,* 359; Richmond *Dispatch,* June 26, 1863.

5. James Erwin (*c*1797-1870), was a wealthy Irish-born hardware merchant ($260,500 in real, $82,000 personal property in 1860); son James (*c*1833-1862) had clerked for the store and possessed personal property worth $27,000. 1860 Census, Tenn., Davidson, Nashville, 2nd Ward, 58; Nashville city directories (1855-61), *passim*; *Nashville City Cemetery Index,* 25; Acklen, *Tenn. Records,* I, 93.

From William G. Brien[1]

Nashville May 25th 1864

Gov Andrew Johnson
Dear Sir;

Please allow me to state the facts in the case of Mrs Brown[2] ap[pelant] vs Lallaland,[3] which was tried before G M Southgate[4] and two other Justices on the 23rd inst.

Upon the trial we though defending were required to assume the burthen of proof and when we had established our contract by the brother and agent of Miss Ida Bunch[5] the plaintiff herself was offered as a witness[.] Thereupon I objected to her competency and seeing that the Court were determined to accept her, notwithstanding the proof shewed that the rents belonged to her, I informed the Court that if She were permitted to testify I would withdraw all defence, let them render a judgement and appeal. All of which was done. I am farther informed by Mrs Lallaland that when the rent was raised she and her husband wanted to vacate the property because they could get another house for less. Miss Bunch's Agent would not allow it and now that there is no vacant house to be found they want to turn them out to rent the property at the same rate to some one else, and will not accept rent from Mr Lallaland.

Mr and Mrs Lallaland say farther that they have taken good care of the property and promptly paid the rents as their receipts will show. Govenor I therefore in behalf of the laws of the land as well as the merits which these facts disclose earnestly entreat that you will [allow] the law to take its course and justice to be administered between the parties.[6] I am with very high regard

Your friend W G Brien

ALS, DLC-JP.

1. William G. Brien (1831-*fl*1913), son of Judge John S. Brien and a graduate of Nashville Medical College, was a lawyer who subsequently served as judge in both criminal and circuit courts and as professor of medical jurisprudence at the Medical College. Nashville city directories (1868-1915), *passim; Who's Who in Tennessee* (Memphis, 1911), 405; Clayton, *Davidson County,* 294.

2. Perhaps Mrs. Lizinka Campbell Brown, who the preceding May had married her cousin, Confederate General Richard Ewell.

3. For French-born Eugene Lallemand, see *Johnson Papers,* V, 563*n;* his wife Matilda was a native of Virginia. 1880 Census, Tenn., Davidson, 21st Dist., 2.

4. George M. Southgate (b. c1801), Virginia-born, was a Davidson County justice of the peace. *Ibid.* (1860), Nashville, 2nd Ward, 56.

5. Neither has been identified.

6. Evidently convinced by Brien's argument, the governor ordered Southgate to "allow the appeal of Defendant [Lallemand] be taken" and to postpone "execution of judgment & verdict . . . until otherwise advised by this office." [Johnson] to Southgate, May 25, 1864, Johnson Papers, LC.

From Gordon Granger

New York City May 26th. 1864.

My Dear Governor.

I regretted being compelled to leave Nashville before your return from East Tenn. After Seeing Sherman I was able to form Some idea as to the reasons of my removal from the 4th Corps & from the Dept. of the Cumberland—[1] It would appear from the best information I could get that it was personal vindictiveness on the part of Grant & that Sherman wanted me out of the way as being a *rising* & dangerous man who might Some day overthrow & Supercede him. The reasons trumped up for my decapitation are ficticious & false from beginning to End.[2] It is now nearly two months Since they Sent me into Exile. Not a word nor intimation have I recd from the War Dept. as to what disposition is intended to be made of me— Well may I exclaim "Save me from my friends"—[3] You have Seen Something of my Energy, fighting & labor to Support the administration & kill this damnable rebellion. Thousands in Tennessee & Ky will bear witness to my zeal & Earnestness in our righteous Cause. Few Generals have Struck Such heavy blows upon Every battle field & Slaughtered the rebels as I have done or have led their troops with more judgement & efficiency— (*pardon my Egotism*) While I have been a terror to the Sneaking rebels who hide behind their oaths Stay at home to give information & act Spy & guerrilla, I can but regard my downfall as certain & complete & that Grant Sherman & their unscrupulous Sattelites have deliberately planned my destruction Simply from Envy & to get rid of one whom [they] regarded as a dangerous rival.

The present moment is So pregnant with important Events that it will be impossible for me to do any thing to recover lost ground for Some time to come— If I am Saved from ignominy & injustice & permitted to exert my Energies for the good of our Country, it can only be accomplished by my friends. Since our acquaintance you have proven yourself my friend & have already laid my Case before the president. Whether he has taken any notice of your request I know not.— As the Convention meets in June at Baltimore I have thought it more than probable that you would come East.[4] If you Should come I believe we could get a hearing at the War Dept & that I could be restored to my proper place & command[.] my ambition is to Serve in Tenn or against the rebels on its borders— A Resolution has passed the House to drop all unemployed Generals on the 1st of July next[5]

& if it passes the Senate my Military Carreer will terminate on that date. Ah what gratitude for 20 years (the prime of my life) of incessant labor Exposure of life in many battles of health, Everything in fact that is dear to the Soldiers. Yes what a return for Saving the Army at Chicamauga & again Covering it with glory & winning the day at Mission Ridge—[6] In God's name what incentive have I to be an American citizen, to hazzard my life, my honor, Every thing in the Sacred cause of my Country? humiliation & dishonor!!! Gov I wish you would come on if possible, if not please write in my behalf if you think it best to do So.[7] If you come telegraph me to *N. Y. Hotel.*

please accept my best wishes for yourself & the Early regeneration of your beloved State[.]

Sincerely Yr friend
G. Granger

His Excy Gov Johnson.

ALS, DLC-JP.

1. In late March, Sherman, stopping at Loudon where Granger was headquartered, found him "full of complaints at the treatment of his corps" and ready to take a leave of absence; whereupon Sherman relieved him, transferring Gen. Oliver O. Howard to command. William T. Sherman, *Memoirs* (2 vols., New York, 1875), I, 396; II, 8.

2. Having lost favor with Grant over his apparent "lack of energy and capacity" in December when ordered to reinforce Burnside at Knoxville, Granger's "language and manner" on that occasion had created "a bad impression" on Sherman who wrote: "it was one of the causes which led me to relieve him as a corps commander." *Ibid.,* I, 396; Jesse Burt, "East Tennessee, Lincoln, and Sherman, Part II," ETHS *Publications,* No. 35 (1963), 65; Glenn Tucker, *Chickamauga* (Indianapolis, 1961), 106, 341.

3. A saying, generally attributed to Marshal Villars upon taking his leave of Louis XIV, although also expressed by Voltaire as "May God defend me from my friends; I can defend myself from my enemies." Burton E. Stevenson, *Home Book of Quotations* (New York, 1964), 734.

4. Johnson did not attend the nominating convention.

5. Joint Resolution No. 49 passed the House on May 11; the next day it was referred to the Senate military affairs committee, where it apparently died. Granger remained in service, seeing action at Mobile and later commanding the Districts of Memphis (1867-69) and New Mexico (1871-76). *Cong. Globe,* 38 Cong., 1 Sess., 2238, 2239; Warner, *Generals in Blue,* 181.

6. During the battle of Chickamauga, Granger, without awaiting orders, had marched to Thomas' relief in an engagement which averted disaster for Rosecrans' army. Charles A. Dana wrote from Chattanooga that the general, "his hat torn by bullets, raged like a lion wherever combat was hottest with the electrical courage of a Ney." In November, his two divisions, serving under Thomas, stormed the rifle pits at the foot of Missionary Ridge and participated in the general assault which followed. *Ibid.*; Dana to Stanton, September 21, 1868, *OR,* Ser. 1, XXX, Pt. I, 195; Thomas' official report of December 1, 1863, *OR,* Ser. 1, XXXI, Pt. II, 94-96; Powell, *Army List,* 337.

7. In response to Granger's request, the governor, who had earlier protested his removal, sent a strongly favorable letter to Lincoln. "At the time he was removed from his command I looked upon it as a public loss. . . . I regard him as bold, energetic & efficient— I sincerely hope that the services of such a man will not be dispensed with for the want of a command." Telegram to Abraham Lincoln, April 11, 1864; Johnson to Lincoln, June 30, 1864, Lincoln Papers, LC.

From John Netherland

Knoxville 26th May 1864

Govr Johnson,
Dear Sir

The forces of the Goverment, as you know, have for sometime, been withdrawn from the upper part of Eastern Tennessee.[1] We now, have no troops above Strawberry Plains, leaving all the country from that point to Bristol in the hands of about *Two Hundred and fifty Rebels,* who are ravaging the country at pleasure, committing daily robberies, and occasional murders. I learn to day, that they are pasturing our wheat fields. This is to be the ruin of the people, as our people in a great measure, depend on their harvest for the means of living—

I mention these things to you, as I trust you will do something to releive our part of the country. There are two squads of Rebels, who stay about Greeneville, and Rogersville. They do not exceed 150. men.[2]

If you will have one *good* Regiment of East Tennesseans, sent to the upper country, you will releive us, and get the lasting gratitude of the people of that section. Unless *you* do something I feel that there is no hope, and therefore, in the name of your old neighbors, and in my own, I earnestly call on you, for *prompt* action. We want *our own men,* who know the *roads* & the *fords,* & who feel an interest in the country and it's inhabitants.

Please answer

Truly Yr Friend
J Netherland

ALS, T-Mil. Gov'r Papers, 1862-65, Corres. to A. Johnson.

1. Although writing from Knoxville, Netherland was a resident of Hawkins County.
2. Following the siege at Knoxville, Longstreet had retired to Virginia in April. By mid-month there were only scattered Confederate forces, at Kingsport, Zollicoffer (now Bluff City), Carter's Depot, and Blountville; there were also partisan rangers under John T. Reynolds. *OR,* Ser. 1, XXXII, Pt. III, 344.

From "Mercy"[1]

Private Nashville May 28th 1864

Govr. Andrew Johnson
Governor.

On Saturday last I wrote you a hurried letter in behalf of the Son of my old friend Dr. John S Young who is confined in the Penitentiary on a charge of Murder Robbery etc—awaiting promalgation of sentence[.][2] Since then I have seen an old School teacher of Young & a Mrs Richardson daughter of the late Mr Bosworth who owned an factory in South Nashville.[3]

Mrs Richardson says Young was amiable well disposed boy and she cannot believe he is guilty of the charges preferred against him. Many others corroborate this opinion. I am not acquainted with the youth, but 'tis enough for me to know that he is the son of my old friend Dr Jno S. Young, a noble—honest, warmhearted man, and for the sake of Dr Young and his kindness to me, I would be unfaithful to the memory of an old friend, did I not use my influence in behalf of his unfortunate son. I have no doubt Governor some man or *woman* have endeavoured to prejudice you against Young[.] But I *know* you have a sympathetic heart, and that you do *feel* for the unfortunate—victims of this cruel war. Why Sir thousands and thousands of men and women have lost their Senses—and can it be expected that people will act as in peaceful happy times. War is an *emanation* from the *Devil* and can *never* be *Christianized,* and it seems it cannot even be *civilized.* But in the great land of the Hereafter, when every man must stand in naked ugliness before the throne of the *"Great I Am"* How pleasant will that man feel Should an Angel in Heaven once a poor care worn widow on Earth, accost him thus, You once saved my unfortunate boy from an ignominious death.— God bless you Governor Johnson for that noble act. Methinks I can hear that mother *pray* the Father of all good.— Oh! Father for the *good* this man did unto my boy, blot out I *implore thee* many of his sins from thy Book of Remembrance[.] Is this a fancy sketch. By no means. Use your influence, save poor Young and his Mother, and good Angels will beseige the throne of Grace in your behalf[.] "Religion pure and undefiled is to visit the widow and fatherless in their affliction" etc[.][4] If you cannot visit his widowed mother[5] You can cause joy and not grief to visit her widowed heart!! *Be good* and *do good* and *then you will* be happy— It was a principle with the great and good Wesley to do everything as if in the immediate presence of God, believing that a man would at the final judgment be answerable to God for every act *done on Earth.* And in view of my responsibility to God—and being a professed follower of his son Christ Jesus, I tell you today while I recognize—in you a man of *great* intellect, personal courage, and Iron will, I find alas! you want the *crowning virtue* of *Christianity*— The Grace of God alone can change our hearts and make us love our enemies— Enemies aid I say— Can it be possible that Gov Johnson can regard the son of his old friend John S Young—(a mere thoughtless boy) as his enemy. It cannot be that a man of Gov Johnsons intelligence can *regard* the son of his old friend as his enemy rebel though he be. Well if you are a friend and not an enemy—you can exert an influence with the President or Jdg Advocate Holt[6] that will save Young—and wherever you use your influence you *know full well* it *is not in vain.* Again whenever a man or woman endeavors to *influence* or prejudice you against another, Ask the question to *yourself?* what motive influences them? A *good man* or *woman* will always seek to do *good* for the *unfortunate* and not *add* to *their miseries.* Before a man or woman attempts to injure another he or she should ponder well the following verse in Pope's universal prayer.

Teach me to *feel another's wo.*
To hide the *fault I see,*
That *mercy I to others show,*
That *mercy show TO ME*.[7]

A few years ago a majority of the Tennessee rebels were like the father of poor Young the fast friends of Gov. Andrew Johnson. While most of those who now surround Gov. Johnson, he denounced as God forsaken Know Nothings who could not look an honest man in the face.[8] Well if they would persecute the Catholics, then may they not to day persecute the rebels more than justice mercy or Christianity will sanction. Be assured that the religious test in Know Nothingism was a plant of New England, growth[.] No Sir I am opposed to all persecution Religious or political— For Republican government is founded in the *virtue, intelligence, affection* and *confidence* of the *people*— And Remember *this war will not last* always. (*At least I hope not*—) for what is War *but madness ruin, death, desolation—and every thing that is deplorable*—

During the progress of this cruel war many persons have used all their influence to persecute rebels, to prove by their feats how intensely *loyal they were,* while *many* of this *class* were loud mouthed rebels, before the fall of Fort Donelson. A truly *Loyal Man* or woman, loves law & order and reverences the Constitution, and hates tyranny cruelty and oppression. The *healing-balsam* is oftener *successful* than the *Surgeons knife. Kindness* and not *cruelty,* will convince *mans intellect* and *win* his *heart, while* the contrary tramples Republican liberty in the dust. Oh! for the spirit of A, Clay or Webster in this hour of *desolation death* & *ruin*[.] To learn political wisdom and to be imbued with a lofty unselfish patriotism a man should read—and reread Washingtons Farewell Address until he can feel his universal love of country, as [illegible] of *party spirit.* Had your proclamation of March '61[9]—been adhered to a different state of things would greet our eyes today— "*Physician heal thy self*—"[10] Governor Johnson, you cannot forget the fact, or do away with the obligations you owe the Tennessee Democracy— And may God in Mercy cause you to retrace your errors and lead you in right paths, and help save the people of Tennessee from endless ruin is the prayer of "*Mercy*"

"Blessed are the *Peace makers*"[11]

ALS, DLC-JP.

1. "Mercy" may possibly be the person who wrote November 17, 1862, as "A Peace Democrat."

2. John S. Young (1840-1899), a private in Co. H, 11th Tenn. Cav. (originally a partisan ranger unit) and son of the Nashville physician and former Tennessee secretary of state, was sentenced by a military commission to be hanged for murder, robbery, conspiracy, and violation of the laws of war. Denominating him a "citizen," Johnson wrote the President that "the proof does not show that he was personally involved but with a gang a portion of whom committed it." The governor recommended life imprisonment, asserting that Young "was influenced to enter the rebel army" and, confusing John with an older brother Walter listed in the 1860 census as "helpless," added "he is not more than one or two degrees removed from idiocy." His sentence suspended, John was shipped with other prisoners to Point Lookout in February, 1865, to await special exchange. A graduate of

Cumberland University (1859), he attended Union Theological Seminary in Richmond (1865-68), was licensed, and served numerous Tennessee pastorates until his death. Young to Johnson, June 2, August 15, October 22; Johnson to Lincoln, August 17, 1864, Johnson Papers, LC; Basler, *Works of Lincoln,* VII, 502-3; E. C. Scott, *Ministerial Directory of the Presbyterian Church, U. S., 1861-1941* (Austin, 1942), 84; for father, John S. Young, see *Johnson Papers,* I, 27*n*.

3. William Bosworth (*c*1785-1858), Kentucky-born ropemaker and early settler in Nashville, had a hemp factory on Water Street. The daughter in question has not been identified. Porch, *1850 Census, Davidson,* 132; *Nashville City Cemetery Index,* 8; Edythe R. Whitley, *Tennessee Genealogical Records: Davidson County* (n. p., 1965), 25.

4. James 1:27.

5. Jane Colville Young (b. *c*1810), of McMinnville. Acklen, *Tenn. Records,* I, 423; Porch, *1850 Census, Davidson,* 36.

6. For Joseph Holt, see *Johnson Papers,* III, 430*n*.

7. Alexander Pope, *The Universal Prayer,* st. 10.

8. The governor's wartime allies—Brownlow, Temple, Nelson, Etheridge, Campbell, and other former Whigs and Know Nothings—had been his bitterest political foes.

9. See Appeal to the People of Tennessee, March 18, 1862, *Johnson Papers,* V, 211, in which Johnson offered "the erring and misguided" a welcome back on lenient terms.

10. Luke 4:23.

11. Matt. 5:9.

To Lovell H. Rousseau

Nashville, Tenn., May 28th 1864.

Maj. Gen'l L. H. Rousseau
Comd'g &c Nashville, Tenn.

General! I have the honor to enclose herewith, for your information, Official copies of War Dep't orders dated respectively March 28th & April 22nd 1863,[1] the last of which detaches the 1st Mid: Tenn Inf'y (now 10th Tenn Inf'y) from general service and places it under my command, while the former authorizes the organization of one Brigade for the purpose of a Governors Guard. It was thought that such an organization, under State control as it were, might be exceedingly useful in sustaining and strengthening, more directly, the Civil Authorities, at the same time rendering such military service here and in this section as might be required of them under proper authority. The 1st Mid Tenn Inf'y formed a part of such organization and it was expected that the contemplated force would be promptly raised. In view of the orders of the War Department, so fully explaining the object of this command and further the positive order that such force should be under my exclusive control, I would respectfully suggest that there should be no interference with said organization for the purpose of withdrawing any part thereof for other service than that contemplated in said orders, unless it be done in the manner therein indicated.[2]

Very Resp'y Your obt. Sevt
Andrew Johnson Mil Gov'r.

Copy, DLC-JP.

1. On June 6, Gen. George H. Thomas directed that the 10th Tenn. Inf. be detached from the Army of the Cumberland and transferred to Johnson as a governor's guard. William D. Whipple (for Thomas), Special Field Orders No. 154, June 6, 1864, Tels.,

Dept. of the Cumberland, RG393, NA; see Authorization to Raise Troops, March 28, 1863.

2. This admonition reflects the difficulties which attended the overlapping relationship between the military and civil administrations. Ever since his appointment, Johnson had been trying to implement the authority given him for raising a body of troops under his personal control; now, his efforts realized, he was exceedingly proprietary about this Governor's Guard—unquestionably an instrument of power and, in one sense, a "state army."

From Horace Maynard

Knoxville, May 30. 1864.

Dr. Sir,

From this point eastward the people are annoyed by occasional small parties of guerillas—some marauding parties, contemptible as a military force, but capable of doing much mischief. The people would unite, I am assured in suitable organizations for the local defense if they could be assured of not being called away out of the country for the general purposes of the war. This they do not wish to do, as the labor is already largely withdrawn into the army & to take away any considerable numbers in addition would leave few but women, children & old men.

I have been requested to inquire of you whether you could not call out a militia force, equal to some two or three regiments for a limited time to defend against predatory bands, raids & the like. They might also be employed in prrison & guard duty, releasing for active service, quite a number of old troops now scattered at different points.

The court has been in session two weeks. Much business is likely to be done. A grand jury of twenty three is in session, composed of solid & substantial citizens from different parts of East Tennesseе. The sitting will be prolonged two weeks more, I suppose.

I am very Respectfully Your Obt. Servt.
Horace Maynard

His Excy. Andrew Johnson
Gov. Tenn &c—&c.

ALS, DLC-JP.

From Thomas Chadwell[1]

[Nashville, June, 1864]

Hon Andrew Johnson
Dear Sir

On or about 10th day of March 1864, one of my Tenants left a house of myne in lower edgefield & before my agent could lock the doors & get the Keys a man by the Name of Roney[2] moved in & took possession of my house, Made threats, that he intended to live there, & defied me or any one else, to get him out. he has been there, since that time over 3 months, paid no rent & says, so I am informed, he intends to pay no rent, & that you said he could stay as long as he wanted to. I think I have been very liberal to him made a proposition to his Wife to give her rents to the time provided they would give me the house. No answer recd to the proposition. I have agreed to let a poor family, have the house who has no home, & they are waiting to hear whether they Can get the house within a reasonable time. Please let me know, whether atall I can get the house & about what time.

Thos. Chadwell

ALS, DLC-JP.

1. Thomas Chadwell (*c*1822-*fl*1879), a Davidson County farmer before the war, became a Nashville lawyer and a wealthy real estate agent, possessing $160, 000 in 1870. Porch, *1850 Census, Davidson,* 163; 1870 Census, Tenn., Davidson, 18th Dist., 11; Nashville city directories (1867-79), *passim.*

2. Probably John Roney (*c*1840-*fl*1881), Nashville shoemaker, and his wife, Bridget, both Irish-born. On June 6, General Rousseau ordered the Roneys to vacate within five days or report upon whose authority they occupied the premises; the following day Johnson wrote the general that Roney "holds possession of it at my instance. His family is now sick, and the Civil Authority affords ample redress in all such Cases." 1870 Census, Tenn., Davidson, Nashville, 5th Ward, 22; Nashville city directories (1867-81), *passim;* T. O. Bigney to John Roney, June 6; Johnson to Rousseau, June 7, 1864, Lets. Recd., Dept. of the Tenn. (Mid. Tenn.), RG393. NA.

From Mary E. Clements[1]

Assistant Quartermaster's Office,
Forage Department.
Nashville, Tenn., [June?], 1864.

Gov Johnson

I am here with my family which is my 5 little boys 2 Servants and myself[.] I do pray you to try and get me a House or some rooms[.] I am not hard to pleas at this time[.] I have bin in Secret Service for Gen Sherman[2] for some time and had an order from the Gen to Gen Webster[3] for a House[.] I want to get my family Setled and I am ready for work again[.] do let me know if you can do any thing for me[.]

I am very respectfuly Mrs M E Clements

ALS, DLC-JP.

1. Mary E. Clements (b. *c*1833), a dressmaker, was by 1865 living at 120 S. Summer Street. 1870 Census, Tenn., Davidson, 5th Ward, 40; *Singleton's Nashville Business Directory* (1865), 167.

2. William T. Sherman.

3. Joseph D. Webster.

From Thomas B. Sevier

June 1, 1864, Tullahoma; ALS, DLC-JP.

A Tennessean, unhappy in 2nd Ky. Bty.—considered "by outsiders the Rebel Battery," composed of "bitter Pro-Slavery men"—and eager for action, wants appointment in a regiment under Meade or Sherman.

From Montgomery McTeer[1]

Knoxville Ten June 2nd 1864

Governor Johnson

I write you this hasty line merely to say to you that I am the Attorney for something over One hundred and fifty Citizens of Blount County, from whom their forage and provisions have been taken for the use of the United States Army—many of them being strongly represented in the U. S. Army by husbands, sons or brothers and whose families are now in want of the Common necessaries of life. Many of their claims are audited and recorded by the Commission at Knoxville but the Government has not authorized their payment and they have no means to purchase if it was in this country and so far the "Relief" furnished from the north is of no moment to them.[2]

For them and in their behalf I would request you to use your influence with the Government for an early liquidation of their claims, and I would ask of you the favor to procure and forward me a permit from the proper authority, authorizing me to go to Nashville, purchase & ship on the M. N. R. R.[3] a limited supply of provisions for them—specially.

Yesterday I handed in to the office of Dr Brownlow the proceedings of a public meeting in Blount of Unconditional Union men but too late for publication this week.[4] It should have appeared sooner but I have been too unwell to prepare it. For the same reason I have not furnished you a Manuscript Copy as requested. I do not belive there are twenty-five male slave devotees left in Blount. The question now is how is the right way to get clear of it.

Respectfully Montgomery McTeer
at Maryville

The resolutions as passed in Blount Endorses President Lincoln & his war policy and pledges support to his election should he be the nominee of the Baltimore Convention—Favors the Call of a State Convention for the revision of the State Constitution and a Constitutional prohibition of Slavery and an Unconditional Union of these States—

Very Respectfully M. McTeer
Cir. Court Clk Elect Blount Co

His Excellency A Johnson
Nashville Ten

ALS, DLC-JP.

1. Montgomery McTeer (1811-1876), a Blount County millwright, published a bi-monthly, *The American Journal of Productive Industry,* and served as circuit court clerk (1864-68). 1850 Census, Tenn., Blount, 1st Dist., 1; Worth S. Ray, *Tennessee Cousins* (Austin, 1950), 328; *Goodspeed's East Tennessee,* 830, 833.

2. Funded by northerners, mainly from Boston and New England, after ardent appeals from former Tennessee congressman N. G. Taylor, the East Tennessee Relief Association was organized as the result of Longstreet's presence in that area, the brunt of which fell heavily on the unionists who had been obliged to flee their homes, seeking safety in

Knoxville during Burnside's occupation in the winter of 1863-64. Temple, *East Tennessee,* 514-15.

3. Evidently McTeer was confused; the only existing rail link between the capital and Knoxville was provided by the Nashville and Chattanooga connecting with the East Tennessee and Georgia.

4. The writer was secretary of this gathering held in Maryville on May 14. Knoxville *Whig and Rebel Ventilator,* June 11, 1864.

From Eli Thayer[1]

New York City No 1 Park Place
6th June 1864

Dear Sir

Ever since the beginning of this rebellion I have been urging upon the administration the necessity of confiscating the lands of rebels & of dividing them among loyal men—

We should open the doors to the whole civilised world & invite all to come in & occupy.

The region of country now in rebellion is one hundred times as large as Mass & could well support fifty millions of people.

We should have begun somewhere & occupied as fast as the army advanced. In this way we should have had a base line of productive industry always keeping pace with the military & whatever we gained by arms would have been held by free labor— For example: If we had put a line of forts from the Suwanee to the St Mary's rivers in Fla about 30 miles & held them by a part of our troops we could in a short time have filled the peninsula with assured laborers. These forts could then have been placed 50 or 100 miles further northern & the territory south of the new line filled in the same way. By this method we should have no need of going over the country a second time & when the war was ended there would be no need of a standing army. But the President has persistently opposed this confiscation of the property of rebels & has adhered to the plantation system.[2] By this foolish & ruinous policy he has cost the country a million of men many millions of dollars. The war could have been ended & democratic institutions established through all the rebel States eighteen months ago had it not been for his timid & stupid policy.

Now if you were candidate for President I would vote & work for you with all my heart as I told you two years ago in Washington I hoped you would be. But to be Vice President is to be a cypher as we all know[3] & I am sorry to see you lose the power for good you now have by being the shadow of a man who opposes your views at every point.[4]

I wish however you would give us a practical illustration of your principles as you *now* have a chance of doing, by the state action of Tenn. If treason exists anywhere it [is] as much against the individual States as against the U.S. & may be punished by *each state. Your own state can properly confiscate the lands* of *your own rebels.*

As Gov. Wise said about John Brown "The state has the first right to a traitor & after we are done with him the U. S. may have him" [5] Here then is a chance for you to begin to apply the only remedy there is for this rebellion & I hope you will see fit to do it *now*[.]

Very truly yours
Eli Thayer

Hon Andrew Johnson Gov Tenn

ALS, DLC-JP.

1. Eli Thayer (1819-1899), abolitionist and one of the founders of the New England Emigrant Aid Company, had served as a Republican congressman (1857-61). During the preceding session (1863), he had urged that rebel lands be confiscated and given as 160-acre homesteads "to each private in the naval service, and to each man in the rank and file of the union army, and of the rebel army, who will take the prescribed oath of allegiance." Any land remaining should be open for settlement under the Homestead Law. *DAB,* XVIII, 403; undated, printed petition attached to Letter from Eli Thayer, June 7, 1864.

2. Lincoln's opposition to the Confiscation Act was well known. Not until Congress, by a hastily added "explanatory resolution," had corrected what he regarded as a major flaw—extending the forfeiture beyond the lifetime of the alleged criminal—did he sign the bill in July, 1862, and even then attached the message he had planned as a veto. James G. Randall, *Lincoln the President* (4 vols., New York, 1945), II, 226-29; III, 120.

3. This observation accurately reflects not only contemporary assessment but also the actual state of the office at that time. Irving G. Williams, *The Rise of the Vice Presidency* (Washington, 1956), 1.

4. Thayer and his fellow extremists saw Johnson's "radicalism" as more deep seated than the anger and political expediency which had prompted his recent public statements. From such misreading would arise dire consequences for the nation during the ensuing four years. In reality, except for differences about the terms of restoring citizenship, the views of the President and the governor were remarkably similar.

5. At the time of Brown's capture in 1859, Henry A. Wise was quoted as having "no objection to the general government proceeding against the prisoners—that is, what will be left of them by the time the Virginia authorities have done with them." New York *Herald,* October 20, 23, 1859.

From Eli Thayer

New York 1 Park Place
7th June 1864

Dear Sir

Since writing you yesterday I have met D. Dudley Field Esq.[1] one of the leading lawyers of this city to whom I explained my position in relation to the power of a state to confiscate the property of traitors & also my position that treason against the United States was also treason against the individual states[.]

Mr. F. says both positions are correct. If this be so, you have it in your power to illustrate in Tenn. how the rebellion can be ended & the Southern States regenerated. Should you at once begin this Confiscation on State authority you would secure an immense immigration from the North & from Europe.

If we are still to retain the plantation system there is no hope for the masses of the Southern people[.] Slavery though nominally abolished will virtually exist & in its worst form. The negro will suffer all the evils of servitude & enjoy no protection of ownership. It will come in competition with the whites & probably in collision as well. To strike at the root of the rebellion you must strike at the landed power of the rebels for it was by that power that they made the rebellion. Give the rank & file of the rebel army farms if they will take the oath of allegiance[.]

It is not enough to offer them starvation as Lincoln does in his miserable amnesty proclamation. They went into the rebel service to escape that & it is folly to expect they will come out to secure it.

I hope most earnestly that you will set the right example in your own state & thus solve the entire problem at once. I know that your heart & mind are right & would impel you [to] act in this direction[.]

Very truly yours
E. Thayer

Hon Andrew Johnson Tenn.

ALS, DLC-JP.

1. David Dudley Field (1805-1894), Connecticut-born New York attorney and chairman of the state's delegation to the Washington Peace Conference (1861), was a leader in law reform, writing a number of treatises on political, civil, and criminal procedures. Quitting the Republican fold after Lincoln's death, he was elected to Congress as a Democrat to fill a vacancy from January-March, 1877, returning afterwards to his practice. *DAB*, VI, 360; *BDAC*, 885.

A Nashville Housing Problem[1]

June 8-9, 1864.

I

Nashville, Tenn., June 8th 1864.

The parties purposing to take the property now in possession of the bearers hereof will please furnish this office with information as to the authority under which it is required.

Andrew Johnson Mil Gov'r

II

Post Qr. Mr's Office
Nashville Tenn
June 9th 1864

Respectfully returned to Gov Johnson. This Building for more than a year has been used as Hospital #11.[2] At one time Surg Chambers[3] in charge thought it could be permanently released and reported it vacated— In a few days after he applied for the use of it, as his patients had largely increased,[4] it was therefore reassigned to him by an Order from this Office—

Very Respectly Jno F Isom[5]
Capt. a. a. Q. M. Post

III

Executive Office
Nashville, Tenn. June 9th 1864.

Respectfully referred to Brig. Gen'l Miller,[6] Comdt of the Post.

I am reliably advised that this house is now in the occupancy of eleven families of U. S. Soldiers, and that they are to be dispossessed for the benefit of a *class of women of more than doubtful character*.

I hope that Gen'l Miller will investigate the matter, and act in the premises as his good judgment may dictate.

Andrew Johnson Mil. Gov.

IV

Post Hd. Qs Nashville
June 9, 1864

Respectfully returned to Gov. Johnson. Attention is called to the endorsement of Surgeon Chambers who it seems upon investigation had some time ago prepared the house in question for Hospital purposes and a portion of the building for some people who had been dispossessed by the Military in order to obtain their houses for Military purposes. The people now claiming to hold the house as soldiers families it seems took possession of the house without authority, & have been in possession for some time. Chambers now requires half or more of the house for hospital and the ballance for the people dispossessed by Military authority as stated. The Hospitals in charge of Surgeons Chambers are authorized by Department Orders the same as other hospitals notwithstanding the inmates are of disreputable character, and this building it seems is necessary for his purposes. The soldiers families would not probably desire a joint occupancy with this class of hospital patients and if a part of the house is taken for a hospital according to original orders & design it would in my judgment be better for families of the soldiers to have other quarters. I am ready to assist them in any way I can. Chambers proposes to give some of the people other places[.]

Jno. F Miller Brig Genl.

Memo and endorsements, DLC-JP.

1. Although much about the following items, including the identity of "the bearers" and the ultimate outcome, remains obscure, they provide an example of a wartime human problem which embroiled the "civilian" governor with the regular military authorities.

2. The Pest House on University Pike was the structure in question. Nashville *Union*, March 7, July 23, 1863; Nashville *Times and True Union*, July 1, 1864.

3. William M. Chambers (*c*1814-1892), native Kentuckian living in Charleston, Illinois, was a surgeon of volunteers (1861-65) who returned to his practice following the war. 1860 Census, Ill., Coles, Charleston Twp., 189; Heitman, *Register*, I, 294; File C-309-C.B. (1865), ACP Branch, RG94, NA.

4. During the summer of 1863, in the face of a growing incidence of venereal disease, the military authorities set up a system of licensed prostitution, requiring weekly examinations; those who were healthy received a certificate of soundness; "those in the slightest degree diseased" were ordered into a hospital for treatment. Chambers, in charge of Hospital No. 15, converted in February, 1864, into a venereal disease facility, reported on

June 30, that 994 cases had been admitted. Such were the patients who "had largely increased" and for whom Chambers was being "furnished with rooms &c by the Quartermaster." *Ibid.;* U. S. Surgeon General's Office, *The Medical and Surgical History of the War of the Rebellion,* Part 3, Vol. I, Charles Smart, ed. (Washington, 1888), 893-94.

5. John F. Isom (b. *c*1836), a lieutenant and captain, 25th Ill. Inf. (1861-64), was at this time acting assistant quartermaster. Early the next year he formed a partnership in the city to adjust and collect war claims against the Federal government. CSR, RG94, NA; Nashville *Union,* January 4, 1865.

6. For Miller, see *Johnson Papers,* V, 557*n*.

From Enoch T. Carson

Cincinnati Ohio June 9th 1864.

Dear Governor,

Allow me to congratulate you and to express to you my great satisfaction and joy at your nomination for Vice-President of the U. S. this nomination gives me the greatest satisfaction, My motto has been Johnston and Brownlow of Tennessee[.] they have done more by their own example and personal influence for the cause of the Union, than any dozen other civilians in the U. S. You have both been much traduced by the Butternuts in the North,[1] and I am sorry to say by the Union men too because they did not know you as I did. thank God you are now in a fair way to receive a proper acknowledgement from the Loyal people of the U. S. of their appreciation of your sacrifices, and services. God bless "old Brownlow for his speech at Baltimore,[2] he did it, and he has only added another "notch" higher in my estimation of him[.]

The only fault I have to find with the nominations is that they were not *reversed* and you on the head of the ticket. what we want in the next administration is the real old jackson democracy, which I fear but few, if any old line Whigs have.[3] I feel that I have the right to say so—as I was an "old line Whig"[.]

A word about business, you have my Certificate of Deposit for Temporary Loan to the U. S. at 5 pr cent interest. I was authorised *yesterday* to raise the rate to 6 per cent—[4] If you will Send your present certificate endorsing upon the back of it "*pay E. T. Carson, Depository for conversion in 6 per cent certificate*" I will take that one up send you a new one for same amount bearing *6 per cent interest.* together with the accummulated interest of 5 per cent to date of new certificate.[5]

Hoping that you are and yours are well, and that you will be in good condition for the campaign I am very Truly Yours

E. T. Carson.

ALS. DLC-JP.

1. Originally applied to Confederates, the term had become a synonym for northern "copperheads." Mathews, *Americanisms,* 232.

2. Parson Brownlow had attended the National Union Convention and, though ill and unable to make a lengthy speech, pleaded for the seating of Tennessee's delegates, then an issue because of the state's Confederate status. As a result, the delegates were accredited and seated. Coulter, *William G. Brownlow,* 259.

3. The writer does not elaborate on the particular aspects of Jacksonian ideology which Lincoln, "an old line Whig," lacks.
4. Carson may have been notified by the treasury department in anticipation of passage of the Legal Tender Act of June 30, 1864, which granted discretionary power to the secretary of the treasury to raise to 6%, or lower, interest rates on temporary loans. *U. S. Statutes,* XIII, 219.
5. A notation on the letter indicates that W. A. Browning on June 28 sent Carson—"endorsed as directed within"—two certificates, one for $2,500 and the other for $1,400.

From Robert Lowry

June 9, 1864, Boston, Mass.; ALS, DLC-JP.

Former Nashville woodturner, temporarily employed in Boston, reports that "three rouseing cheers in honour of Abe Lincoln and Andy Johnston" were given at the Chickering Piano Forte Factory when the nominations were known.

From Blackston McDannel

Knoxville Ten June 9, 1864

Gov. A. Johnson
Nashville Ten

I am somewhat interested in the request of Capt. Anderson W. Walker[1] of our County (Greene) which you will find herewith enclosed, and only intended for me. Walker requested me to write you concerning his Commission as Captain of Co. S [F]. 8th. Tennessee Infantry. I asked him to make a statement of his case, and he handed me the paper in pencil. You will see what he wants. If you can possibly grant his request, I hope you will do so at once, as I think he richly deserves the Commission. I know a good deal about Walker's movements since this war began. The Rebs had him *under* at the commencement of our troubles, but it was only the smothering of a Volcano. He was a prisoner, and was deeply implicated with Dave Fry as a Bridge burner and as an active participator of the fight at Cedar Creek,[2] but he and his friends managed to effect his release, and as soon as he could show his hand he did so fearlessly and risked his all.

He has been engaged principally in the Scouting and Spy service, acting as guide to various parties, and is now in that kind of service. His last service was as a guide to a detachment under Col. Foote, in the late expedition to Greenville, which resulted in the route of the rebel John Arnolds Company of thieves of 60 men. 20 odd were killed 27 prisoners, the balance scared to death.[3]

Arnolds Co. was encamed at Greenville in the Williams Grove, but at the time of the surprise, were Scattered in town and at old Phenis Jones' farm grazing their stolen horses on John & Alek Jones' meadow.[4] It was a running fight for 10 miles southward. Arnold escaped, but in a few days afterward that great Scoundrel and notorious villian Col. Sam. Davis was killed at Mat. Rose' house by some of our boys, called Bushwhackers. Sam was buried at Mount Bethel.[5] There is no mistake in this. Do all you can for Walker. I am satisfied he deserves the Commission.

He came up here to get some few recruits to fill out his company, and while here was detailed to guide in the Scouting service, as he informs me.

There is some talk here that you have promised to Send us, at least one reg't for our relief in the upper counties of E. Ten. For God's sake send them, and that quickly. The presence of one reg't in upper E. Ten. will enable the people to go home and save their harvest, meadows &c.

From Strawberry plains to the Virginia line, every thing is fearfully uncertain, and subject to marauding parties of Rebs. In fact they have been pillaging, and taking prisoners all over the country. I wish you would let me know, whether or not, you can send us a reg't.

Yours truly B. McDannel

Say to Glascock[6] that we have recvd. the Books & Stationery. But that the Court Seal has not yet come to hand.

Hope he will send it immediately, if not already sent.

B. McD.

ALS, DLC-JP.

1. Anderson W. Walker (1813-1883), Greene County farmer, three times sheriff (1866-74), clerk and master of chancery court (1876-80), had, according to his representation to McDannel, spent much time and effort in recruiting, scouting, and guiding for the Union forces. There is no record that he received the captain's commission he sought. 1860 Census, Tenn., Greene, Caney Branch, 3rd Dist., 70; Walker to McDannel, [June 9, 1864], Johnson Papers, LC; Reynolds, *Greene County Cemeteries,* 281; *Goodspeed's East Tennessee,* 890.

2. During the fall of 1861, East Tennessee unionists under Colonel David Fry harassed the Confederate authorities, precipitating in September an incident near Cedar Creek in Greene County, in which a Confederate soldier was shot and killed, and in November burning the bridge over Lick Creek, some fifteen miles west of Greeneville. Temple, *East Tennessee,* 384; Knoxville *Whig,* September 14, 1861; Atlanta *Southern Confederacy,* September 17, 1861.

3. Thaddeus Foote (*c*1821-1903), Massachusetts-born Michigan lawyer, was colonel, 10th Mich. Cav. until discharged in July on a physical disability, having accidentally shot himself in the foot while returning to camp on May 31 after the Greeneville raid which started out as a reconnaissance from Strawberry Plains. On May 30 with 160 men, Foote surprised John Q. Arnold's partisan rangers and, depending on the source, killed either 22 or 24, captured 26, and wounded 10 or 14. 1880 Census, Mich., Kent, Grand Rapids, 2; Robertson, *Michigan in the War,* 718; Pension file, RG15, NA; for Arnold, see *Johnson Papers,* IV. 190*n*; V, 531*n*.

4. For Johnson's old antagonist, Alexander Williams, whose home and "grove" were between Main and Irish streets, see *ibid.,* I, 14*n*. Although Phineas Jones (b. *c*1788) was dead by 1860, his widow Sarah and sons John (*c*1803-*fl*1870) and Alex (b. *c*1808), lived on adjacent farms. Sistler, *1850 Tenn. Census,* IV, 3; 1860 Census, Tenn., Greene, 10th Dist., 100; (1870), 65.

5. Samuel W. Davis, who lived near the Williamses in Greeneville and was a Confederate sympathizer, in trying to escape to North Carolina was overtaken and killed. Mat Rose would appear to have been Henry M. (b. *c*1824), a millwright. Mt. Bethel Presbyterian Church Cemetery is now known as Old Greeneville Cemetery. For Davis, see *Johnson Papers,* V, 531*n;* Carl N. Hayes, Neighbor Against Neighbor, Brother Against Brother (typescript, University of Tennessee Library), 11; 1860 Census, Tenn., Greene, 3rd Dist., 42; Acklen, *Tenn. Records,* I, 132.

6. Edwin R. Glascock.

From National Union Convention Committee[1]

Baltimore Md. June 9, 1864.

Hon Andrew Johnson
Dear Sir.

The undersigned have great pleasure in performing the duty assigned to them of informing you of your unanimous nomination for the office of Vice President of the United States, by the National Union Convention, which closed its sittings in this City, yesterday—

We enclose also, a copy of the resolutions or platform of principles unanimously adopted by the Convention to which your attention is respectfully invited, and, which, we trust, will have your approval.

The Committee need hardly add the assurance of their hearty Concurrence in the action of the Convention in selecting you as the Candidate of the great majority of the loyal people of the Country for the Vice presidency of the United States, nor of their conviction, that in so nominating you, the Convention but faithfully interpreted the wishes of their patriotic Constituents.

Earnestly requesting your acceptance of the position to which you have been assigned, and congratulating you upon the encouraging prospects for the speedy suppression of the rebellion, and the extinguishment of its cause, we have the honor of subscribing ourselves,

Your Obt Servts.
W Dennison, of Ohio, Chmn[2]

ALS (Dennison), DLC-JP.

1. A committee, consisting of one person from each state, was selected on June 8 to inform the candidates of their nomination. Johnson did not receive this formal notification until June 25 and did not respond until July 2. Washington *Evening Star,* June 9, 1864; Nashville *Times and True Union,* July 20, 1864.

2. Besides Chairman Dennison, there are thirty other signatories. For William Dennison, see *Johnson Papers,* IV, 584*n*.

From George L. Stearns

Boston June 9th 1864.

Dear Sir

If any thing can reconcile me to the renomination of Abraham Lincoln, it is the association of your name on the same ticket. Indeed I should have been much better pleased if your name had been placed by the Convention before our people, for the Presidency.

Your broad and sound views of public affairs, deeply impressed me in our early interviews, and subsequent intercourse confirmed the impression.

At present there appears to be no opposition that will be likly to defeat your election, and I trust you will, when in power be able to carry out those plans for the regeneration of the south so freely canvassed by us in Nashville,[1] in which you may safely count on the cooperation of myself and those working with me[.]

Truly Your friend
George L. Stearns

H. E. Andrew Johnson
Military Gov. of Tennessee
Nashville Tenn.

ALS, DLC-JP.

1. Following Johnson's accession to the presidency, the commissioner of colored troops wrote reminding him of their "conversations . . . on the policy to be pursued towards the Rebel States." In that letter, Stearns expostulated on a subject near and dear to the Tennessean—the war between capital and labor and the need to put down the one and advance the other. But this 1865 letter does not necessarily reveal their attitudes in 1863. Stearns to Johnson, May 17, 1865, Johnson Papers, LC.

To Joseph D. Webster

State of Tennessee, Executive Department,
Nashville, Tenn., June 9th 1864.

Brig. Gen'l J. D. Webster,
Cheif of Staff &c
General:

Col Donaldson[1] has sent me a copy of a letter, addressed to him by Mr. A. Anderson, Gen'l. Sup't. U. S. Mil't R. Rd's,[2] of which I enclose a copy, informing him that you had instructed him (Mr. Anderson) to use the Nashville & North Western R.R. as a Military Road, although not formally transferred by me.[3]

It is my desire that the Road should be made available for any and every purpose by the Government, and I so made known my wishes in the matter to Col Donaldson, as the Senior and Supervising Quartermaster of this Military Department, before the receipt of Mr. Anderson's letter; but I would respectfully state that the Road is not yet completed, so as to be transferred to the General Manager of U. S. Military Railroads, and therefore, being still under my control, should not be removed therefrom, until completed under my orders and in accordance therewith.

Of course the Road can be used to its full capacity for all Army purposes, but till it is completed, and turned over by me to the War Department, I shall expect to retain control, so far as it may be deemed necessary in accordance with my instructions from the Secretary of War both verbal and written.

I am, General, Very Respectfully
Your Obt. Sert. Andrew Johnson
Mil: Gov'r &c

Copy, DLC-JP.

1. James L. Donaldson, chief quartermaster, Department of the Cumberland.

2. Adna Anderson (1827-1889), a civil engineer who worked for a number of railroads, including the Tennessee and Alabama and the Edgefield and Kentucky, was chief of construction corps for the Army of the Potomac and subsequently chief engineer of military railroads in Virginia. At this time he was responsible for the Division of the Mississippi; before the end of the year he would become chief superintendent and engineer of all military railroads (1864-66). After the war, he continued his career in railway construction. *NCAB,* XXXIII, 47-48.

3. Anderson to Donaldson, June 7, 1864, Johnson Papers, LC.

Speech on Vice-Presidential Nomination[1]

June 9, 1864

After thanking the assembly for the compliment they had bestowed upon him, and a few other preliminary remarks, Governor Johnson proceeded to say, that we are engaged in a great struggle for free government in the proper acceptation of the term. So far as the head of the ticket is concerned the Baltimore Convention has said, not only to the United States, but to all the nations of the earth, that we are determined to maintain and carry out the principles of free government. [Applause.] That Convention announced and confirmed a principle not to be disregarded. It was that the right of secession, and the power of a State to place itself out of the Union are not recognized. The Convention had declared this principle by its action. Tennessee had been in rebellion against the Government, and waged a treasonable war against its authority just as other Southern States had done. She seceded just as much as other States had, and left the Union as far as she has the power to do so. Nevertheless, the National Convention[2] had declared that a State cannot put itself from under the national authority. It said by its first nomination, that the present President, take him altogether, was the man to steer the Ship of State for the next four years. [Loud applause.] Next it said—if I may be permitted to speak of myself, not in the way of vanity, but to illustrate a principle—"We will go into one of the rebellious States and choose a candidate for the Vice Presidency." Thus the Union party declared its belief that the rebellious States are still in the Union, and that their loyal citizens are still citizens of the United States.[3] And now there is but one great work for us to do, that is to put down the rebellion. Our duty is to sustain the Government and help it with all our might to crush out a rebellion which is in violation of all that is right and sacred.

Governor Johnson said he had no impassioned appeal to make to the people in his own behalf. He had not sought the position assigned him by the National Convention.[4] Not a man in all the land can truthfully say that I have asked him to use his influence in my behalf in that body, for the position allotted me, or for any other. On the contrary I have avoided the candidacy. But while I have not sought it, still being conferred upon me unsought, I appreciate it the more highly. Being conferred on me without solicitation, I shall not decline it. [Applause.] Come weal or woe, success or defeat, sink or swim, survive or perish, I accept the nomination, on principle, be the consequences what they may. I will do what I believe to be my duty. I know there are those here who profess to feel a contempt for me, and I, on the other hand, feel my superiority to them. I have always understood that there is a sort of exclusive aristocracy about Nashville, which affects to contemn all who are not within its little circle.[5] Let them enjoy their opinions. I have heard it said that

> Worth makes the man, and want of it the fellow.[6]

This aristocracy has been the bane of the slave States, nor has the North been wholly free from its curse. It is a class which I have always forced to respect me, for I have ever set it at defiance. The respect of the honest, intelligent and industrious class I have endeavored to win by my conduct as a man. One of the chief elements of this rebellion is the opposition of the slave aristocracy to being ruled by men who have risen from the ranks of the people. This aristocracy hated Mr. Lincoln because he was of humble origin, a rail-splitter in early life. One of them, the private Secretary of Howell Cobb, said to me one day, after a long conversation, "We people of the South will not submit to be governed by a man who has come up from the ranks of the common people, as Abe Lincoln has." [7] He uttered the essential feeling and spirit of the Southern rebellion. Now it has just occurred to me, if this aristocracy is so violently opposed to being governed by Mr. Lincoln, what in the name of conscience will it do with Lincoln and Johnson.[8] (Great laughter.) I reject with scorn this whole idea of an arrogant aristocracy. I believe that man is capable of self-government, irrespective of his outward circumstances, and whether he be a laborer, a shoemaker, a tailor or a grocer. The question is whether man is capable of self-government. I hold with Jefferson that Government was made for the convenience of man, and not man for the Government.[9] That laws and constitutions were designed as mere instruments to promote his welfare. And hence from this principle, I conclude that governments can and ought to be changed and amended to conform to the wants, to the requirements, and progress of the people, and the enlightened spirit of the age. [Loud applause.] Now if any of you secessionists have lost faith in man's capability of self-government, and feel unfit for the exercise of this great right, go straight to rebeldom; take Jeff. Davis, Beauregard and Bragg for your masters, and put their collars on your necks.

And here let me say, that now is the time to recur to these fundamental principles, while the land is rent with anarchy, and upheaves with the throes of a mighty revolution. While society is in this disordered state, and we are seeking security, let us fix the foundations of the government on principles of eternal justice which will endure for all time. There is an element in our midst who are for perpetuating the institution of slavery. Let me say to you, Tennesseans and men from the Northern States, that slavery is dead. It was not murdered by me. I told you long ago what the result would be if you endeavored to go out of the Union to save slavery,[10] and that the result would be bloodshed, rapine, devastated fields, plundered villages, and cities; and therefore I urged you to remain in the Union. In trying to save slavery you killed it, and lost your own freedom. Your slavery is dead, but I did not murder it. As Macbeth said to Banquo's bloody ghost:

> Never shake thy gory locks at me.
> Thou canst not say I did it.[11]

Slavery is dead, and you must pardon me if I do not mourn over its dead body; you can bury it out of sight. In restoring the State leave out that disturbing and dangerous element, and use only those parts of the machinery which will move in harmony.[12]

Now in regard to emancipation, I want to say to the blacks that liberty means liberty to work and enjoy the fruits of your labor. Idleness is not freedom.[13] I desire that all men shall have a fair start and an equal chance in the race of life, and let him succeed who has the most merit. This I think is a principle of heaven. I am for emancipation for two reasons; first, because it is right in itself, and second, because in the emancipation of the slaves, we break down an odious and dangerous aristocracy. I think that we are freeing more whites than blacks in Tennessee. I want to see slavery broke up, and when its barriers are thrown down, I want to see industrious, thrifty immigrants, pouring in from all parts of the country. Come on! We need your labor, your skill, your capital. We want your enterprise and invention, so that hereafter Tennessee may rank with New England in the arts and mechanics, and that when we visit the Patent office at Washington, where the ingenious mechanics of the free States have placed their models, we need not blush that Tennessee can show nothing but a mouse-trap or something of about as much importance.[14] Come on! We greet you with a hearty welcome to the soil of Tennessee. Here is soil the most fertile in every agricultural product; a delightful and healthy climate, forests, water-power, and mines of inexhaustible richness; come and help us redeem Tennessee, and make her a powerful and flourishing State.[15]

But in calling a convention to restore the State, who shall restore, and re-establish it? Shall the man who gave his influence and his means to destroy the government? Is he to participate in the great work of re-organization? Shall he who brought this misery upon the State be permitted to control its destinies? If this be so, then all this precious blood of our brave soldiers and officers so freely poured out, will have been wantonly spilled. All the glorious victories won by our noble armies will go for nought, and all the battle-fields which have been sown with dead heroes during this rebellion will have been made memorable in vain. Why all this carnage and devastation? It was that treason might be put down and traitors punished. Therefore I say that traitors should take a back seat in the work of restoration. If there be but five thousand men in Tennessee, loyal to the constitution, loyal to freedom, loyal to justice, these true and faithful men should control the work of reorganization and reformation absolutely.[16] (Loud and prolonged applause.) I say that the traitor, has ceased to be a citizen, and in joining the rebellion, has become a public enemy. He forfeited his right to vote with loyal men when he renounced his citizenship, and sought to destroy our Government. We say to the most honest, and industrious foreigner who comes from England, or Germany, to dwell among us, and to add to the wealth of the country, "Before you can be a citizen you must stay here for five years."

If we are so cautious about foreigners who voluntarily renounce their homes to live with us, what should we say to the traitor, who although born and reared among us has raised a paricidal hand against the Government which always protected him?[17] My judgment is that he should be subjected to a severe ordeal before he is restored to citizenship. A fellow who takes the oath merely to save his property, and denies the validity of the oath is a perjured man and not to be trusted. Before these repenting rebels can be trusted let them bring forth the fruits of repentance. He who helped to make all these widows and orphans, who drape the streets of Nashville in mourning should suffer for his great crime. The work is in our own hands. We can destroy this rebellion. With Grant thundering on the Potomac, before Richmond, and Sherman and Thomas on their march towards Atlanta, the day will ere long be ours.[18] Will any madly persist in rebellion? Suppose that an equal number be slain in every battle, it is plain that the result must be the utter extermination of the rebels. Ah, these rebel leaders have a strong personal reason for holding out, to save their necks from the halter. And these leaders must feel the power of the Government. Treason must be made odious, and traitors must be punished and impoverished. Their great plantations must be seized and divided into small farms, and sold to honest, industrious men.[19] The day for protecting the lands and negroes of these authors of rebellion is past. It is high time it was. I have been most deeply pained at some things which have come under my observation. We get men in command, who, under the influence of flattery, fawning and caressing, grant protection to the rich traitor, while the poor Union man stands out in the cold, often unable to get a receipt or a voucher for his losses.[20] [Cries of "That's so!" from all parts of the crowd]. The traitor can get lucrative contracts, while the loyal man is pushed aside, unable to obtain a recognition of his just claims. I am telling the truth. I care nothing for stripes and shoulder-straps. I want them all to hear what I say. I have been on a gridiron[21] for two years at the sight of these abuses. I blame not the government for these wrongs which are the work of weak or faithless subordinates. Wrongs will be committed under every form of government and every administration. For myself I mean to stand by the government till the flag or the Union shall wave over every city, town, hill-top, and cross-roads, in its full power and majesty. The nations of

Europe are anxious for our overthrow. France takes advantage of our internal difficulties and sends Maximilian off to Mexico to set up a monarchy on our borders. The day of reckoning is approaching. The time is not far distant when the rebellion will be put down, and then we will attend to this Mexican affair and say to Louis Napoleon, "You can set up no monarchy on this continent." [Great applause.] An expedition into Mexico would be a sort of recreation to the brave soldiers who are now fighting the battles of the Union, and the French concern would quickly be wiped out.[22] Let us be united. I know that there are but two parties now, one for the country, and the other against it, and I am for my country.

I am a democrat in the strict meaning of the term. I am for this government because it is democratic—a government of the people. I am for putting down this rebellion, because it is war against democracy. He who stands off stirring up discontent in this State and higgling about negroes, is practically in the rebel camp and encourages treason. He who in Indiana or Ohio, makes war upon the Government out of regard for slavery is just as bad. The salvation of the country is now the only business which concerns the patriot.

In conclusion, let us give our thanks, not formal but heartfelt thanks, to those gallant officers and soldiers, who have come to our rescue, and delivered us from the rebellion. And though money be expended, though life be lost, though farms and cities be desolated, let the war for the Union go on, and the Stars and Stripes be bathed, if need be, in a nation's blood, till law be restored and freedom firmly established.[23]

Nashville *Times and True Union,* June 11, 1864; Milwaukee *Sentinel,* June 18, 1864.

1. Troops at Fort Negley celebrated the news of Johnson's nomination with thirty-four-gun salutes at both noon and sunset. That evening an impromptu committee decorated the St. Cloud Hotel with American flags, illuminated it "in good style," and invited Johnson to speak. As the band of the 18th Michigan Infantry played, a crowd of around two thousand—mostly northerners, according to the hostile Nashville *Press,* mostly Tennesseans, according to the friendly Chicago *Tribune*—gathered for the event. The ensuing version, according to the Cincinnati *Gazette* of June 14, represents "a full report, corrected by the Governor." New York *Times,* June 20, 1864; Nashville *Press,* June 10, 29, 1864; Chicago *Tribune,* June 15, 1864; Nashville *Times and True Union,* June 10, 1864.

2. The Union party convention which met at Baltimore on June 7 and 8. Long, *Civil War Almanac,* 516-18.

3. Johnson's interpretation of the inference to be drawn from his nomination was not universally held. Thaddeus Stevens had questioned the legitimacy of a candidate from a "damned rebel province"; James B. Bingham later informed the governor that the convention did not intend his selection to be a recognition that Tennessee was in the Union. Yet, as several politicians realized, the action could be viewed as setting just such a precedent. Herman Belz, *Reconstructing the Union: Theory and Policy during the Civil War* (Ithaca, 1969), 214-15; Letter from James B. Bingham, June 26, 1864.

4. Benjamin C. Truman subsequently claimed that the governor had asked several friends to mobilize support for his nomination; no evidence of this has been found, yet others did campaign in his behalf, and he must have at least known of their efforts. A. K. McClure, *Abraham Lincoln and Men of War Times* (Philadelphia, 1892), 443-44; Benjamin C. Truman, "Anecdotes of Andrew Johnson," *Century,* LXXXV (1913), 437; *Frank Leslie's Illustrated Newspaper,* April 9, 1864.

5. See *Johnson Papers,* V, xxxiii.

6. Alexander Pope, *Essay on Man,* Epistle IV, l. 203.

7. Philip Clayton. See Speech on Restoration of Government, January 21, 1864, note 21.

8. The Nashville *Press* of June 10, 1864, reported this observation as: "when A. Lincoln was nominated, some folks didn't like it because he, Lincoln, was one of the people. To all such, he would say, what the devil would they do when there was a ticket with *two* on it that came from the people."

9. Jefferson developed this principle best in the second paragraph of the Declaration of Independence. Johnson's earlier speeches had discussed this point in words similar to those used here. *Johnson Papers,* II, 355.

10. More than three years earlier, in his senatorial Speech on the Seceding States, February 5-6, 1861, he had declared: "I believe the dissolution of this Union will be the commencement of the overthrow and destruction of the institution of slavery." *Ibid.,* IV, 237.

11. Shakespeare, *Macbeth,* Act III, sc. 2.

12. According to one report, the governor addressed this topic "with much vehemence of manner, and in a tone of voice and with a peculiar gesture with his right forefinger, which serves to, as it were, italicise his words and to attract the attention of his audience." *Universal Suffrage and Complete Equality in Citizenship . . . in Discourses by Henry Ward Beecher, Andrew Johnson, and Wendell Phillips* (Boston, 1865), 13.

13. In testimony before the American Freedmen's Inquiry Commission on November 23, 1863, Johnson had said "The idea of freedom is not to do nothing; you must go to work."

14. While Tennessee had 3.5% of the nation's population in 1860, its citizens received only .9% of the patents granted that year. Although one of the patents issued was for a mousetrap, Johnson greatly underestimated the creativity of the state's inventors whose innovations covered a wide range of agricultural and industrial machinery. *Senate Ex. Doc.,* No. 7, 36 Cong., 2 Sess., *passim;* Joseph C. G. Kennedy, comp., *Population of the United States in 1860 . . . The Eighth Census* (Washington, 1864), 465, 597.

15. As the Nashville *Press* pointed out, Johnson's conversion to emancipation had led him to reverse his prewar contention that slave labor sustained high wages and economic opportunity for whites while its absence reduced workers to a subsistence level. His new position also anticipated the Brownlow administration's decision two years later to establish a state bureau of immigration. Nashville *Press,* June 30, 1864; *Johnson Papers,* II, 354-55; Coulter, *William G. Brownlow,* 288.

16. This is the first hint in Johnson's wartime speeches that, contrary to the vision which he frequently conjured up for northern politicians, the majority of Tennesseans might not be unionist.

17. The idea of equating rebels with immigrants, which may have been original with Johnson, clearly differed from the thinking behind the Wade-Davis bill then under consideration by Congress. The latter would have prevented only the higher Confederate officials from voting after the reestablishment of state governments but would have made their disfranchisement permanent. *Cong. Globe,* 38 Cong., 1 Sess., 3348.

18. Grant's army, having just fought the battle of Cold Harbor, was actually much closer to the James River than the Potomac; Sherman had reached the mountains northwest of Marietta, Georgia. Long, *Civil War Almanac,* 514-18.

19. Johnson had advocated confiscation for some time; however, only in 1864 did he publicly couple it with land reform. *Johnson Papers,* V, 538; Speech on Restoration of State Government, January 21, 1864.

20. Numerous complaints in Johnson's correspondence undoubtedly affected this view. For two recent examples, see Letters from Robertson Topp, February 4, and Edward J. Read, March 19, 1864.

21. "An iron grating formerly used for torture by fire."

22. For his earlier expression of this solution to the Mexican crisis, see Speech on Restoration of State Government, January 21, 1864.

23. Although a hostile newspaper described the crowd reaction as "not very terrific," journals friendly to the governor reported that the listeners responded enthusiastically. Nashville *Press,* June 10, 1864; Nashville *Times and True Union,* June 11, 1864; Chicago *Tribune,* June 15, 1864; New York *Times,* June 20, 1864.

From P. H. and William Adams[1]

[Danielsville], June the 10the/ 64

Gov Andrew Johnson Sir pleas allow me to Say to you that I have Bought timber on Land lying in Dickson County Tenn from the true Agent of the Esstate of James L. Bell[2] on the South Side of the N. & N. W. R. R. on. Sec 46 and at preasant Aman named F. B. Andres,[3] is choping the Timber By forse[.] he Says he is going to take the timber By gitting orders from you[.] he has A. goverment contract fer to deliver So much wood on the Roade any Wher on the line to "Sec" 57, and is giting $3 per cord and all So transportation over the Road for him Self his men and his Rations free of charge[.] we cut fifteen hundred cords for which we had to Sell jest as we could as we cood not get a contract from the goverment[.] we only got $2 per cord fer ours[.] we will chop the timber fer less money the [than] he will and I wish you ef you please to Stop him from choping our timber ef you please and oblige yours[.][4]

P. H. & W Adams

ALS, DLC-JP.

1. P. H. Adams (b. *c*1842) and his younger brother William (1844-*fl*1900), Tennessee-born farmers, were sons of Nelson Adams. 1860 Census, Tenn., Dickson, Danielsville, 33; (1900), 12th Enum. Dist., 8B.

2. James L. Bell (*c*1795-*c*1860), nephew and an heir of Montgomery Bell, was a Maryland-born "Agent Iron Works." *Ibid.* (1850), Davidson, 655; Robert E. Dalton, "Montgomery Bell and the Narrows of Harpeth," *Tenn. Hist. Quar.*, XXXV (1976), 26; WPA, Cheatham County, Tennessee, County Court Minutes, 1856-1860, p. 284.

3. Possibly B. Anders (b. *c*1841), a farmhand. 1860 Census, Tenn., Dickson, Danielsville, 172.

4. Johnson forwarded this letter to Capt. F. H. Rugar, assistant quartermaster, Nashville and Northwestern Railroad, who replied that he knew "nothing of the facts of this case" and could say only "that Mr. Andres has a contract for wood" along that railroad. Rugar's endorsement, June 14.

From Charles A. Fuller

June 10, 1864, Nashville; Copy, DNA-RG366, Lets. Sent (Press Copies) by Special Agent William P. Mellen (January 10-May 28, 1864).

Assistant special agent, answering inquiry concerning "probable time of the establishment of trade at the Western terminus of the Nashville & N. W. Railroad—Johnsonville," indicates that, pending an inspection tour, he will soon "recommend the opening of trade at Johnsonville, and perhaps at one or two other points."

From John M. Hale

June 10, 1864, Reading, Pa.; ALS, DLC-JP.

Former assistant quartermaster, earlier stationed in Nashville, congratulates the governor, assuring him that "no nomination not even that of Mr. Lincoln could have been more acceptable to the people of Pennsylvania," all of whom "feel it is but a just tribuit to your eminent services in the cause of the Union . . . and that it is but a stepping stone to the only other position that could add luster to your name."

From S. Newton Pettis[1]

ASTOR HOUSE

New-York, June 10 1864

Dear Sir

I came here yesterday from Washington in company with Genl. Carey of Cincinnatti[2] for the purpose of addressing a Union Ratification meeting at Brooklyn last night—[3] We did so—I thought it too soon to attempt to ratify, but am satisfied of my error— The people are in advance of the politicians— The meeting was more than *enthusiastic*, it was *tumultuous* from the beginning to its close— It was kept up until a late hour— I return to Washington to day to complete my business before returning home to Penna.

I shall urge our friends at Washington to lose no time in a vigorous opening of the campaign, believing as I do that if we act with promptness and energy we can well nigh win the battle before the assembling of the Democratic Convention at Chicago— I enclose you a slip of the Tribune this morning—[4]

I was with the President ten minutes after receiving the intelligence of your nomination— I need not tell you of the satisfaction felt and *expressed* by him at the result! you know full well what his feeling would be and more— Genl Careys tribute to you last evening was both touching and eloquent—[5]

I feared the defeat of Mr Dickinson[6] at Baltimore might produce a bitter heart burning here in New York, but our friends say not, that Judge Daily, Tremain, Brady and Meagher[7] are satisfied as well with your War Democracy, as though you lived in the Empire State, while outsiders are better pleased with your present locality in view of your political record & your sympathies and labors in the cause in which all lovers of country are engaged— I suppose you remember me— If you receive this, & acknowledge its receipt please do so at Meadville Pa.

I have the Honor to be as ever

Yours Faithfully
S. Newton Pettis

Hon Andrew Johnson
Nashville Tenn—

ALS, DLC-JP.

1. Solomon Newton Pettis (1827-1900), Ohio native and Meadville, Pennsylvania, lawyer, had been associate justice of Colorado Territory (1861-62) and one of Lincoln's strongest supporters at both nominating conventions. Allegedly, during an interview with the President on the morning of the Baltimore convention, Pettis asked whom he wanted on the ticket; Lincoln "leaned forward and in a low but distinct tone of voice said, 'Governor Johnson of Tennessee.' " Subsequently Pettis filled a congressional vacancy

(December, 1868-March 3, 1869) and served as minister to Bolivia (1878-79). *BDAC*, 1450; McClure, *Lincoln and Men of War Times*, 439.

2. Samuel F. Cary (1814-1900), Ohio lawyer and delegate to Baltimore, had been paymaster general of Ohio troops during the Mexican War and as assistant provost marshal had helped raise recruits at Cincinnati in 1862. Elected to Congress in 1867, he was the only Republican who voted against Johnson's impeachment. In 1876 he was the Greenback vice presidential candidate. Greve, *History of Cincinnati,* II, 529.

3. Both Pettis and Cary spoke before the "large and enthusiastic gathering" at the Central Union Club. New York *Tribune*, June 10, 1864.

4. Probably the column on the "Union Ratification Meeting." *Ibid.*

5. Cary's remarks were made during his seconding of the resolutions. *Ibid.*

6. For Daniel S. Dickinson, a vice-presidential candidate, see *Johnson Papers*, III, 461*n*.

7. Charles P. Daly, Lyman Tremain, James T. Brady, and Thomas F. Meagher. Daly (1816-1899), New York City native, state assemblyman (1843) and judge of the city's court of common pleas (1844-85), was a War Democrat who enthusiastically supported the Lincoln administration. Tremain (1819-1878), New York lawyer and former Democrat, was a state legislator (1866-68) and congressman (1873-75), before returning to his practice in Albany. James T. Brady (1815-1869) was a prominent New York City lawyer. Meagher (1823-1867), Irish-born patriot whose death sentence had been commuted to exile in Tasmania, escaped to the United States in 1852. Studying law and becoming a leader among New York City Hibernians, he organized and commanded the Irish Brigade, resigning after the Battle of Chancellorsville. Reappointed as a brigadier in 1864, he served with Sherman; after the war Meagher occupied temporary government posts until 1867 when he drowned near Fort Benton. *DAB*, V, 41; II, 583-84; XII, 481; *BDAC*, 1727; New York *Times*, December 1, 1878; Warner, *Generals in Blue*, 317-18.

From Nathaniel P. Sawyer

June 10, 1864, Pittsburgh, Pa.; ALS, DLC-JP.

Congratulates Johnson on his nomination: "Oh how I wish it had been for the Presidency then the Union Party would not have been divided[.] Fremont would have Supported you and we could have taken you to the White House without any trouble. I am sorry very sorry that you have not been associated with a better man than Lincoln."

From George B. Lincoln[1]

Post-Office, Brooklyn, Kings Co., N. Y.,
June 11th 1864

My dear Sir

I congratulate you upon the deserved compliment paid you by the great convention which met in Baltimore last week.

In a conversation with President Lincoln the evening after the Convention made their nominations, I stated to him that I intended to write you at my earliest convenience, and I stated to him what the purport of my letter would be. I was rejoiced to hear him speak, as he did, of the perfect accord of feeling and sympathy upon public questions between yourself and himself and his satisfaction at your nomination.

I was not a member of the convention and regret that any one holding office should have consented to act as a Delagate there—but I was present while the preliminary work of the convention was going on.

In canvassing for the candidate for the Vice Presidency—your name was from the first most favourably considered—and but one objection—so far as I heard was made. That was the fear expressed by those representing strong Anti slavery districts that their constituents would fear that what had been known as "*Border State influence*!" would thereby prevail in case this ticket should be elected. To such as I met, I endeavoured to convince them—as I thought I was right in doing—judging by what I had seen of your writings & from the general tenor of a conversation between yourself & *Senator King*[2] of our State myself being present at the Presidents House some time since, that they would have no occasion to regret favouring your nomination on that account—believing as I did that your conviction now was, that not only the Rebellion must be put down—but that it must not be allowed to break out again from the same *cause*.

In view of this feeling manifested there and presuming it to exist to greater or less extent over the north—I write this as a word of encouragement for you in your letter of acceptance (trusting that you will not decline the nomination) to express as clearly and as firmly as your *judgement* and your *conscience* will allow your *anti slavey policy*[.]

I deem your letter of more importance that Mr. Lincolns—just at this time—and believe that the *Fremont Gun*—will be effetually *spiked* thereby.

This Fremont movement is a weak concern—but just about as strong as the *Birney* movement which defeated *Henry Clay* in 1844.[3]

The Loyal people of my section are ready for the campaign—and were the first (that I have noticed) to ratify the doings at Batimore.

Trusting that ere long the *army* of soldiers will overthrow their fierce adversery—and conquer a Peace—and that the *army* of Citizens may elect the ticket nominated at Baltimore

I remain Dear Sir with great Respect
Your obt Servt. Geo. B. Lincoln

ALS, DLC-JP.

1. George B. Lincoln (*c*1817-*fl*1869), Massachusetts native and salesman with $1,200 real and $1,700 personal property on the eve of the war, was Brooklyn postmaster (*c*1862-66) before being associated with the New York *Tribune*. 1860 Census, N. Y., Kings, Brooklyn, 1st Ward, 46; Brooklyn city directories (1860-69), *passim*.

2. For Preston King, senator from 1857 to 1863, see *Johnson Papers*, I, 461*n*.

3. James G. Birney (1792-1857), Kentucky-born lawyer and longtime abolitionist, was the Liberty party presidential candidate in 1840 and 1844, receiving 62,300 popular but no electoral votes in the latter canvass; it has been argued that Clay's equivocal position on the annexation of Texas cost him the support of many Liberty men in New York, and thereby the election. *DAB*, II, 291-94.

From William H. Robinson[1]

Nashville Tenn June 11th 64

Andrew Johnson
Mil Governor.

I would respectfully represent that I am a loyal Citzin of Wilson County.

That on the 9th Inst, Capt Wyatt[2] of the 13th Tenn Cavalry, in command of about thirty soldiers, and while I was absent, visited my house, entered it with pistols drawn, and in a state of intoxicatin, himself and men, Cursed my wife—entered my drawers, destroyed papers, took thirteen hundred and fifty dollars in different kinds of money, drank whiskey, and played at cards, laid and rolled on my beds with their boots on—also took one shot gun, one saddle, one horse, and one pr of silver specticacles & one watch seal, and after staying in this manner some three hours, left word with my wife that if I did not report at Gallatin to day they would again visit my house and hang me to the first lim.

Respectfully Yr obt Svt
William H. Robinson

ALS, T-Mil. Gov's Papers, 1862-65, Corres. to A. Johnson.

1. William H. Robinson (*c*1835-*fl*1870) was a Tennessee-born farmer with $4,050 in real and $7,865 personal property on the eve of the war. He and his wife Elizabeth (b. *c*1837) had three young children. 1860 Census, Tenn., Wilson, 25th Dist., 218; (1870), 6.

2. James B. Wyatt (*c*1838-1864), enlisting at Taylorsville in August, 1861, as a private, Co. F, 4th Tenn. Inf., was captured and paroled near McMinnville in October, 1863, and transferred to Co. M, 13th Tenn. Cav. as captain. In December, 1864, he was killed near Abingdon, Virginia, his birthplace, by irate citizens who claimed he set fire to some buildings in town. CSR, RG94, NA; Scott and angel, *13th Tenn. Cav.,* 222.

From John H. Wilson

June 11, 1864, Fort Snelling, Minn.; ALS, DLC-JP.

Private, Co. G, 1st Conn. Cav., was arrested in 1861 by the rebels "on account of my known Union sympathies and thrown into jail" for five months. Still "refusing to swear allegiance to Jeff. Davis," he "was forced into the ranks of the rebel army" for eighteen months until he deserted and enlisted in the Union army where he has been some ten months. Noting that his wife died soon after his capture, he has the "greatest anxiety" for his two children and "hopes that if you have communication with your own family you could perhaps send word to my children who I think are at Preacher Sam. Gaines four miles from Kingsport."

From Johann P. M. Epping

June 12, 1864, Washington; ALS, DLC-JP.

An antislavery German-American, doubting that "Without your name and your great popularity . . . Mr. Lincoln's Ticket could have secured the majority of the people," opines that the conservative vote is now safe. "Sorry to see the majority of the people of the western portion of your state so reluctant to give up their so long cherished but pernicious slavery system"; suggests that he join the nominee "and stump the state" to persuade them to accept a reorganization scheme based on the ideas propounded in attached essay entitled "The Freedman's Future."

From Loyal Citizens of Upper East Tennessee[1]

Knoxville Tenn June 12th 1864

Gov. A. Johnson
Nashville Tenn

Dear Sir:—We a portion of the loyal Citizens of Upper East Tennessee, who have heretofore been your personal and political friends, and who have known you from your first advent into political life, and supported you through all of the hard struggles you have had, to the present time, and now when the time of all other times has arrived—when the Sons, Fathers & Brothers of all those who in times passed, have done all they could to elevate you to what you now are,— What should those same friends expect of you when all that is near and dear to them are suffering from oppression? And not a single instance is noted in which you have ever made an effort to releave us, When we know full well that you have had, and now possess an influence that if exerted at all on your part, would have *long since* been to our advantage.

But instead of this how are the men and regiments that was raised for the express purpose to protect the upper Counties of East Tennessee been treated. Where are they now? They are guarding the rebels property of Middle Tennessee.[2] While their families are now exposed to the Rebels, and suffering from their tyranical rule—being robed & murdered daily by them. When a few regiments that you could easily spare would most certainly give the releaf they so much desire.

And now Governor as you have been nominated for the Vice Presidency with Mr. Lincoln for whom all in our State would proberbly vote with pleasure. We therefore take the liberty to inform you that unless you do send us aid and assistance and that soon, *Your* name will be stricten from thousands of tickets in this end of the State.[3] We will also furnish a Copy of this letter to the Chicago Times for publication.[4] For as we said before, we cannot see what *you* have done for our once happy Country. If this be fully shown which it can be, you must only blame yourself for the Mortification that you will experience from it,

Many Many Very Many
Voters of Upper East Tenn.

L, DLC-JP.

1. In effect, this is an anonymous letter, which, purporting to speak for many, may very well have emanated from only one.

2. This statement has some validity, in that several regiments consisting mainly of East Tennesseans, or which had been raised for an East Tennessee expedition, were on duty in the mid-state area. However, their assignments there were to guard Sherman's supply

lines, mainly the Nashville and Chattanooga Railroad. The 10th Cav. and the 4th Inf. had been assigned to East Tennessee until January and April, when they were transferred to Nashville. Four other infantry regiments had been in East Tennessee until April when they were moved south for the Atlanta campaign. Only the 11th Cav., on guard duty at Cumberland Gap, and the 2nd Inf., stationed at Knoxville and Loudon, were still in the area. Dyer, *Compendium*, 1637-45 *passim; Tennesseans in the Civil War*, I, 317-96 *passim*.

3. Johnson's name, of course, was not stricken; the Lincoln-Johnson ticket carried the region, very few votes being cast for McClellan.

4. This sentence is apparently to be read as a threat which was not carried out; a search of that paper from this date to the end of August has failed to produce a copy of this or any comparable letter.

From Absalom A. Kyle

Knoxville Ten 13th June 1864.

Gov. A. Johnson,
Dr Sir,

At the request of very many of our up Countrymen I write to ask you to send us one Regt. of East Ten: troops.

We understand that you control 2 or 3 Brigades in & around Nashville, hence this request.

The Country from Strawberry Plains to Bristol, is given over to the Rebels, & they control it with a small scouting force of 50. to 100— Our Union Citizens who remain at home, many of them are not only robed; but Shot down on their own door-cills in the presence of their families—[1] The Country is being desolated & depoulated & not one fourth of a crop being raised for the next year—

Our harvest will be on hand in 15 or 20 days, and unless the up Country is protected, we cant possibly save our harvest, which upon average is not more than half a crop—

One Regt, at Bulls Gap of 6 or 800. E. Ten: troops Can be fed there by the R.R. & Can scout & protect the whole of Upper E. Ten to Bristol— I entreat you, to at once attend to this request if it be in your power to do so— These people in a great measure, look to you for releif & will be greatly disappointed, if they fail to get it—

I am pleased with the Presidential Ticket, (and without intending to flatter) would have been better pleased with you at the head of the ticket— Please let me hear from you on recpt of this— Say what you can do for us—

How long, before we will have a chance at reorganization? Let it come as soon as possible, but, not however 'till the country is cleared of Rebels above this[.]

Very truly Yr freind,
A. A. Kyle

ALS, DLC-JP.

1. Although atrocity stories were rife in Brownlow's *Whig* during the preceding months, none report victims' being "Shot down on their own door-cills in the presence of their families—"

From Andrew J. Marshall[1]

Jefferson ville Indiana
June 13 1864

onerable Govenor Andrew Johnson I take this oppertunity to inform you that theare is a goodley nomber of your States men and frends and nabors at this hospittle and how they are treated heare[.][2] The wards are kept nice and Clean but when we gow to the dining Room theare we hav all Reasons to Complan[.] they diets that we hav to eat would mak a well man Sick in plase of making him well— theare is plenty of Sanatary provision sent in heare but it is all Consumed by the Cooks and waters and useles woman on Side tables[.] weakley men never will Recrut up[.] heared Speech by tennisseeians[.] they diet and water does not a Gree with us heare[.] I live in two miles of old Greenville tenn wheare the water and are is pure[.] we Call uppon you as a frend and as a man posest of a kind feeling for youre States man who Sacrefised thear lives there famleys and there property for there Country as did you to Call us back to our own State[.] the govenors of those States hav ageants hear transfuring the men to there own States wheare they will be better taking Care of than they are hare at this pore hows[.] we duo think you Should Send a man from our state to Get us back to our own State[.] if we ware able to duo duty, we would much Reather bee with our Ridgment[.] we Could fare much better[.] we duo not know whether we evry will bee able to duo duty aney moore ore not but heare is long to live and well to duo and dam the Rebble that hurts mee or you[.] So nothing more at presant but I Still Remane

your frend Andrew J. Marshall
June 13 the 1864

ALS, T-Mil. Gov's Papers, 1862-65, Corres. to A. Johnson.

1. Andrew J. Marshall (1823-1884), Tennessee-born Greene County farmer, enlisted in July, 1863, as sergeant, Co. E, 8th Tenn. Cav., USA. "Sick in Hospl Mar 21/64," according to his service record, and with "chronic rheumatism" at Jeffersonville, Indiana, he was transferred to a Knoxville hospital in July, and mustered out in September, 1865. CSR, RG94, NA; Reynolds, *Greene County Cemeteries*, 205; 1860 Census, Tenn., Greene, 24th Dist., Greeneville, 105.

2. Jefferson Hospital was built for army medical use during the fall of 1863 on the north bank of the Ohio River at Jeffersonville. U. S. Surgeon General, *Medical History of the Rebellion*, Pt. 3, I, 932.

From William T. Sherman

Hdqrs. Military Division of the Mississippi,
In the Field, Big Shanty,
June 13, 1864.

Governor Andrew Johnson,
Nashville:

My congratulations on your nomination.

I think it will simplify matters and insure the responsibility of agents, if you will turn over the management of the Northwestern road to Mr. Anderson,[1] and the guarding and protecting it to General Rousseau. I am informed the road is now done, and it will soon be needed to the full extent of its capacity. I have no doubt the enemy contemplated that Forrest should enter Tennessee about Florence, at the same time that Morgan slipped into Kentucky.[2] It would be well for Gillem to be on the *qui vive* about Lamb's Ferry;[3] but I think the late rains have rendered the passage of the Tennessee difficult, and Forrest is occupied elsewhere.

W. T. Sherman,
Major-General.

OR, Ser. 1, XXXVIII, Pt. IV, 466.

1. Adna Anderson.

2. Morgan entered Kentucky from Pound Gap, Virginia, on June 2. Confederate strategy called for Forrest to move north from Alabama into Middle Tennessee where he could threaten Sherman's supply line, or join or relieve Johnston. Howard Swiggett, *The Rebel Raider* (Indianapolis, 1934), 225-26; *OR*, Ser. 1, XXXVIII, Pt. IV, 462; Henry, *Forrest*, 280-81.

3. Located near Rogersville, Alabama. Sherman knew Forrest was "occupied elsewhere" because a Federal expedition sent out from Memphis on June 1 was designed to divert him from either reinforcing Johnston in north Georgia or attacking the Middle Tennessee railroads. *Ibid.*; Sherman to William Sooy Smith, June 12, 1864, *OR*, Ser. 1, XXXVIII, Pt. IV, 462.

From Charles Watson

June 13, 1864, "Section 55 N & N. W. R. Rd."; ALS, DLC-JP.

Having learned that Johnson wishes to "secure the services of some one having some knowledge of military affairs and scouting service" for secret service duty in Davidson and "two counties on other side of the Cumberland river," a deserter from the rebel army, who has been in the employ of the federal army since the preceding October, applies for the position, enclosing a recommendation from Maj. Amasa J. Finch, 12th U. S. Cld. Troops.

From Daniel Mace[1]

La. Fayette, Ind.
June 14, 1864

My dear Sir,

I Send you Slip from the Baltimore American giving an account of your nomination for the Vice Presidency, which you have no doubt Seen ere this. I was prompted to take the course I did in your case[2] by a full approval of your course before and after the rebellion. You were one of my first acquaintances when I went to Congress, and I found in you a true friend to the poor man, a warm decided friend of the bill, giving homesteads to actual Settlers, when at the Same time, in this measure you were opposed by Jeff Davis & Co, and every trater at heart in or out of Congress. These traitorous rascals under the name of democracy had no regard whatever for the interests of the great labouring masses of the Country,

Enough of this[.] you are nominated and will be elected, and nothing preventing I will See you inagurated[.] Maynard acted nobly in your behalf.[3] God bless you.

Your friend Danl Mace.

Gov. Johnson

ALS, DLC-JP.

1. Daniel Mace (1811-1867), Ohio-born Hoosier lawyer, had served in Congress as a Democrat (1851-55) and a Republican (1855-57). Soon after Johnson became President, Mace solicited a southern judgeship or diplomatic post—not "as one begging appointment . . . but as a personal and political friend who is willing to accept an appointment, if in your judgment it is proper to confer it." In 1866 he was rewarded with the postmastership at Lafayette. *BDAC*, 1248; Mace to Johnson, June 16, 1865, Lets. Recd., President, RG60, NA.

2. It was Mace who, on behalf of the Indiana delegation, presented Johnson's name to the convention. Washington *Morning Chronicle*, June 9, 1864.

3. Horace Maynard seconded Johnson's nomination with a rousing peroration described by Hannibal Hamlin's grandson as "a political classic." Praising the governor as a patriot who "stood in the furnace of treason," the congressman provoked "wild and patriotic applause" and a spontaneous demonstration. Burton C. Cook, chairman of the Illinois delegation, credited the Tennessean with swaying the convention. "It was that speech by Maynard that defeated Hamlin," Cook recalled. "He spoke in the most passionate way of the great sufferings that had been endured by Union men living in the South," producing "a stampede from our ranks by the Hamlin men." With Illinois Republicans expressing support for Johnson, other delegates followed suit, presuming that the action had the president's blessings. Charles E. Hamlin, *The Life and Times of Hannibal Hamlin* (Cambridge, Mass., 1899), 476; New York *Tribune*, July 10, 1891; Hardison, In the Toils of War, 336-38.

From William P. Jones

Tennessee Hospital for the Insane
June 15 1864

Gov Johnson

Mr Garrett[1] will today appear before the Secretary of State, & testify as to damages perpetrated upon this place by the US Soldiery. Other witnesses will be present as required.[2]

I have no question where the damages shall be thus fairly & impartially assessed; with *yr recommendation* they will be paid.

Perhaps the Government ought to know, that but for yr presence in this State, and assuming the responsibility of supporting *this Charity*, the burden of sustaining it, would long since have devolved upon the Military Authorities[.][3]

You, probably, are familiar with the fact, that an Asylum for the Insane, in Virginia—one full of the frinds of Traitors—has now for more than two years, been wholly supported, at the expense of the General Government.[4]

Having done so much for Va, will they refuse to pay for damages upon this place? I think not[.][5]

Yrs truly W P Jones

ALS, DLC-JP.

1. Andrew D. Garrett (*c*1817-*fl*1870), Tennessee-born clerk of the hospital, was by 1870 its supervisor. 1860 Census, Tenn., Davidson, 5th Dist., 76; (1870), 32.

2. Jones, reporting to the legislature in 1865, wrote that, shortly after his appointment in 1862, two Federal divisions encamped upon the grounds and "within a few days burnt our supply of wood and about five miles of excellent, cedar fence." *Tenn. House Journal*, 1865, App. 95, 106.

3. As military governor Johnson assumed control of the asylum, spending a significant portion of his allocated funds to maintain the institution. *Tenn. Senate Journal*, 1865, App. 11-14.

4. Although Gen. George B. McClellan had taken over the Virginia Lunatic Asylum in 1862, it did not become an official Federal institution until March, 1864, when it became an army hospital. Henry W. Flournoy, ed., *Calendar of Virginia State Papers* (11 vols., Richmond, 1875-93), XI, 228-33.

5. The available evidence suggests that Jones was mistaken in his confidence. There was neither direct assistance from the Federal military authorities during the war nor yet later reimbursement for losses. An account, "never collected," totalling $4,130.00 "For the destruction of . . . property . . . during the months of November and December, 1862," was included in the Superintendent's Report to the Trustees of the Tennessee Hospital for the Insane several years after the close of the war. *Tenn. House Journal*, 1867-68, App. 159.

From William Driver

Nashville June 16/64

To His Excellency
Hon. Andrew Johnson Mil. Gov. &c
Nashville Tenn.
Dear Sir

having recently visited the Building formerly owned by V. K. Stevenson[1] on Church Street opposite the St. Cloud Hotel, I find it occupied by Negro families who are paying rent to a B. F. Skinner,[2] who has been a Ward Master in Hospital No. 4 as follows

for	1	Room	pr	Month		$14 00
″	1	School Room	″	″		15 00
″	1	Room	″	″		7 00
″	1	″	″	″		6.00
″	10	Rooms	″	″	Each $10.00	100.00
″	1	Room	″	″		15 00
″	1	″	″	″		12.00
						$169 00[3]

Making an aggregate of ($169 00) One Hundred and Sixty Nine Dollars pr. Month which is passing into the hands of said (Skinner) from these Occupants, receipts for part of the Same Signed by him I have seen and have some of them Now in My possession[.]

deeming it my duty to state these facts and Call your attention to the Matter immediately, that a prompt investigation of this Man s case May be had, and by what right he is collecting rents on this property, when if Rents are collected the Government Should be the recipient[.]

Very Respectfully Your obt Servt.
William Driver

ALS, DLC-JP.

1. For Vernon K. Stevenson, former president of the Nashville and Chattanooga Railroad, see *Johnson Papers*, II, 251*n*.

2. B. F. Skinner was listed as a grocer in *Singleton's Nashville Business Directory* (1865), 235.

3. Five days later, in the Nashville *Times and True Union*, Driver presented his complaint with somewhat greater elaboration of this "federal" housing.

> That ruin has been renting, and now rents as follows: One room $14; two rooms, $15 each, $30; one eight feet square, without light, $7; another of the same kind, $6; eight rooms, at $10 each, $80; one at $12, and two in the stable at $10 each, with a chamber over the same at $10, amounts to $179 per month for a roofless ruin, owned by a rebel. The rentees are contrabands. I saw as many as one hundred of these in and about the place yesterday—a school being kept in one room. These creatures, sick, worn and weary looking, are passing away; no roof over their heads but the wild elements, when it storms; no friend but God. What a price they are paying for what God made their birthright —LIBERTY.

From William G. Brownlow[1]

Philadelphia, June 17, 1864.

Gov. Johnson: I am detained looking after a new Press, which I propose to ship to Louisville, and when there, I have *Secty Stanton's* special permit to ship upon the Louisville and Chattanooga Railroads. I shall go to New York and get a Press of Hoe.[2] I think I am doing quite as much good here, as if I were at home.

No ticket that can be formed at Chicago or elsewhere, can defeat our Baltimore ticket.

The Chicago Convention, it is believed, will nominate Vallindigham.[3]

Lincoln is here, Everett is here, and thousands in attendance at the great Sanitary Fair. Thus far the receipts have been $700,000, with ten days more to run, at an average of $50,000 per day![4]

I wrote out a long dispatch to you at Baltimore, but the rascally operator refused to send it *without pay in advance*, and charged three prices, and I declined. He was evidently Secesh, for he turned up his nose at the names of youself and me. I knew, however, that our delegates could tell you particulars.

One word in conclusion. We must make extra efforts to carry Tennessee. The Copperheads of our State will be represented at Chicago.[5] If they are not, they will do all they can against us. We ought to have a state Convention, to form an Electoral Ticket. Perhaps the *Constitutional State Convention* should assemble first[.]

I expect to reach Nashville in ten days, and then we will confer more fully.

I am, &C, &C,
W. G. Brownlow

ALS, DLC-JP.

1. Brownlow used the stationery of Philadelphia publisher George W. Childs on which was depicted a sword crossed by a feather and a quill, with the inscription: "The Pen is Mightier than the Sword."

2. This rotary press, invented by Richard M. Hoe and sold by his company, revolutionized the newspaper printing industry after its installation at the Philadelphia *Ledger* in 1847. *DAB*, IX, 104.

3. The national convention of the Conservative Unionists chose McClellan, not Vallandigham, as its candidate. For Clement L. Vallandigham, former Ohio senator and leader of the Copperheads, or Peace party, mainly Democrats who refused to support McClellan, see *Johnson Papers*, IV, 284*n*.

4. "The Great Central Fair for the United States Sanitary Commission" had opened June 7 and would close June 28. With a total attendance of 442,658, the daily average being about 29,510 persons, cash receipts at the end of the three weeks amounted to $597,931.26, which grew to $624,508.77 at the final report on July 5. Lincoln and New England orator Edward Everett had spoken the previous day. Philadelphia *Evening Bulletin*, June 8, 27, 28, July 5, 1864; Philadelphia *Press*, June 17, 1864; Earl S. Miers, ed., *Lincoln Day by Day* (3 vols., Washington, 1960), III, 265; Winnifred K. Mackay, "Philadelphia During the Civil War," *Pennsylvania Magazine of History and Biography*, LXX (1946), 28-30; for Everett, see *Johnson Papers*, IV, 479*n*.

5. William B. Campbell, who led the Tennessee delegation, was considered as a candidate for vice president, but withdrew his name before nominations began. Other prominent Tennesseans were John S. Brien, Jordan Stokes, Balie Peyton, and William Lellyett. Nashville *Times and True Union*, September 1, 1864; Chicago *Tribune*, August 31, 1864.

From William M. Thayer

June 17, 1864, Franklin, Mass.; ALS, DLC-JP.

Author of a number of books on the early life of famous Americans desires to do one on Johnson, "which will close with a recital of your achievements in later life, showing that 'the boy is father to the man,' this being the point of this class of books of mine." Considers it is appropriate, inasmuch as he has written one on Lincoln, and "we expect to instal you with him at Washington." Wants to interview the governor and "a few of your early associates now living, provided they are loyal so as to be reached."

From James B. Wyatt

Head Qrs 13th Regt. Tenn Cav.
Near Gallatin Tenn. June 17th 1864.

To His Excellency Gov. Johnson.
Sir:

Having learned that there is an order from Your Excellency for my arrest upon the charges of having visited the house of one Mr Robison[1] in his absence with a Party of drunken soldiers from the 13th Tenn Cav.—entering his house drunk—wallowing on his bed with muddy boots and vomiting on his bed stealing three (3) horses from him and one saddle one pr scissors one shot-Gun and ($1300.) thirteen hundred dollars in different kinds of money, I deem it my duty to make a statement of the facts in the case with the testimony of Henry M Walker 1st Lieut Co. "K" 13th Tenn cav. and Sergeant A. G. Parks of Company of "I" [2] who were present during the whole of my stay with Mr Robison.

I was ordered by Lieut Col Ingerton[3] of the 13th Tenn cavalry to take charge of a Detachment of men provided with 3 days rations and proceed in a direction South of the Cumberland River for the porpose of "impressing horses to mount the 13th Regt Tenn cavalry." accordingly on the night of the 4th of June I left camp pursuant to order, I was ordered also to disperse "gangs of guerrila's reported to be very troublesome to the Citizens of Wilson Co." my order stated also that I was not limited to 3 days time though I was only ordered to provide the party with 3 days rations. On the 8th day of June I arrived at the house of Robison in Wilson Co. Tenn. having traced 2 stolen mules into that neighborhood and found them turned loose in the road. I was there creditably informed by Sanford Casteman[4] that the above named Robison had been harboring guerrillas'—that he would pilot me to the house and if I would surround the house instantly I would probably catch some of them there, according to

Mr Castleman's directions I surrounded the house but found no guerrillas there. I found a horse there suitable for the cavaly service which Mrs Robison could give no account of stating that she did not know how he came there. I took this horse for the use of the 13th Tenn Cavalry and reported him to the Command where he may be found at any time. I took a Rebel Officer saddle which I told Mrs Robison I would return the next morning, on my return to Camp I came back to Robison's the next morning finding neither Mr. nor Mrs Robison at Home[.] in the mean time I learned that the horse was a strange horse in the neighborhood[.] taking this fact in connection with the finding of the rebel saddle I regarded it very suspicious and my suspicions were confirmed by his general character in the neighborhood, I concluded I would bring the saddle to Camp. This horse and saddle were the only things taken from Mr. Robison to my knowledge. There was no man in my Command under the influence of intoxicating liquor. I called upon Mrs Robison for dinner the first day I was there[.] she refused to get us dinner remarking that if we were Bushwhackers she would feed us but as we were Yankee soldiers she would not or language to that effect, I then told her that we would have to have dinner and if she would not get it some of the soldiers could. She baked some corn bread and fried some meat but would not furnish any plates or chairs for us.

I certify that the above are facts which I can substantiate by a nuber of men who were with me and who are known to this Command as men of veracity.[5]

I am Gov. With much Respect
Your Obt. Svt. James B Wyatt.
Capt. 13th Tenn. cav Comd'g Co "M."

ALS, T-Mil. Gov's Papers, 1862-65, Corres. to A. Johnson.

1. See Letter from William H. Robinson, June 11, 1864.

2. Henry M. Walker (1833-*fl*1900), Tennessee-born Washington County farmer who enrolled at Crab Orchard, Kentucky, in October, 1863, was commissioned by Governor Johnson 1st lieutenant, Co. K, 13th Tenn. Cav., USA. Alfred G. Parks (*c*1822-1865), enlisting as a private, Co. I, 13th Tenn. Cav. in Washington County in September, 1863, was wounded in November, 1864, and died several months later. CSR, RG94, NA; 1900 Census, Tenn., Washington, 155th Enum. Dist., 11A.

3. William H. Ingerton (d. 1864), career soldier and lieutenant, 4th U.S. Cav., was promoted to lieutenant colonel, 13th Tenn. Cav., in May, 1864, dying from a pistol wound in December. CSR, RG94, NA.

4. Probably Sandifer Castleman (*c*1824-*fl*1880), a Tennessee-born farmer living with his parents at the outbreak of the war. 1850 Census, Tenn., Davidson, 4th Dist., 404; (1860), 16th Dist., 46; (1880), Wilson, 267th Enum. Dist., 11.

5. Appended is a certification by Walker and Parks.

From Francis C. Messinger

June 19, 1864, Oshkosh, Wis.; ALS, DLC-JP.

Massachusetts-born printer, commenting on Johnson's recent Nashville speech, declares that the "Government should *act* upon the principles you . . . enunciated," especially "the doctrine that none but the truly loyal and faithful Union men" should be allowed "any control or voice" in the reorganization of Tennessee. Welcoming back "those persistent rebels who only pretend to repent" is "abhorrent to every principle of right and justice"; it "would serve as a precedent" that rebellion "is no crime worthy of punishment." Feels "some apprehension as to the course likely to be pursued at Washington" in bringing the rebellion to a close. Has concluded that Seward "does not think it expedient to *punish,* but rather to forgive, the sin of rebellion," and fears "that the heart of the President, if not his judgment, will lead him to be lenient where justice alone should rule." Prays that "your timely and strong support of what I believe to be right may have its influence with him." Messinger would move to Tennessee "had I the *capital,*" but "there will be found enough without me."

From Campbell C. Reed

June 19, 1864, Clinton; ALS, DLC-JP.

Recently elected Scott County court clerk, a private in Co. G, 2nd Tenn. Inf., wants separation from service to attend to his office, having been notified that the "court were dissatisfyed" with his absence and "Talk of Electing an other clerk at the next Term of the court."

To John G. Parkhurst[1]

Nashville, Tenn., June 19. 1864.

Col. Parkhurst
Col. Pro. Mar: Genl. Dept. Cumb.
Big Shanty, Ga.

I have just received a copy of your to Capt. Goodwin in regard to the State Prison.[2]

There are a large number of convicts in the Prison sentenced by State Authority for a term of years, who will be practicably released and turned loose upon the country if this order is executed. One Division of the building is now occupied by the military authorities[.] The West Wing of the building refered to in your order contains one hundred & twenty cells. The proposition was made through Genl. Webster to receive prisoners convicted by military authorities to the utmost capacity of the West Wing.

There were one hundred and seventy military convicts confined at the time, whon we proposed to receive or so many of them, as could be accommodated in the West Wing.

I feel assured that Genl. Thomas does not understand the true condition of the state Convicts, and hope all proceedings will be suspended until he can be confered with on the subject[.] There are circumstances connected with this effort to take exclusive control of the State Prison which should be understood & considered.

Has Gen Thomas or yourself received my communication on this subject to Gen Webster?[3]

If so I respectfully call your attention to it,—if not received it will be forwarded immediately with other information upon the subject.

A number of convicts have already been recieved, and are now confined, who were sentenced by Military Commissions & courts. Gen Thomas & Col Parkhurst may [be] fully assured that every effort will be made to promote the public interest & secure the success of our army.

Andrew Johnson Mil Gov

Tel draft, DLC-JP.

1. For Parkhurst, provost marshal at Nashville, see *Johnson Papers,* V., 377*n*.

2. On June 13 Parkhurst authorized Goodwin to take possession of the "West" and "new wing" of the penitentiary, returning the balance of the prison to the state for civil use. Five days later Goodwin forwarded this communication to Johnson. Goodwin to Parkhurst, May 7; Parkhurst endorsement, June 13; Goodwin's and Webster's endorsements, both June 18, 1864, Johnson Papers, LC.

3. See Letter to Joseph D. Webster, May 11, 1864.

From John C. Gaut[1]

Cleveland Tennessee
June 21st 1864

Gov. Andrew Johnson
Nashville Tennessee

Dr Sir. When I last saw you I promised to write you on my arrival home. I have not done so, until now, because, it was my misfortune, soon after I got home to take sick & I am now just getting so that I can walk about. I do not believe that I have any thing to write you of any interest. We can have but little news from the front. We have no mails, nor Post Office, except a military mail, and that, now rarely brings any thing for citizens. We believe, and so I suggest to you, that as a Presidential canvass is about commencing, that it is not only just to the loyal Union men, but that it will be of advantage to the Government & to the *Nominees* of the Baltimore Convention, to have our mails & Post-officices established; and also the restrictions upon trade so removed as to let in some goods for the benefit of loyal citizens as soon as we can have protection. I assure you, unless I am greatly mistaken, that the Ticket nominated at Baltimore will receive a very large majority in E. Tennessee in November next. I may say almost the unanimous vote of the Union element. And the Union Men desire to see the Ticket elected and will work for it. I think many of the Rebels will vote the Ticket through fear, if the Union element is protected. Some Rebels or who have been Rebels may vote for the ticket because they are subjugated, and believe they have done wrong.

But now at this time the whole Union element in E. Tennessee suffer from fear and alarm by day and night. The Federal soldiers have all been sent to the front, and left us without protection. The Rebel Cavalry have been pitching in to Bradley & Polk ever since last Thursday. Since I came home we have only had a part of an Artillery regiment at this place, Col. Gibson commanding,[2] and they had not a single piece of Artillery. The only thing which saved them from capture & our town from ruin last Friday was the accidental & fortunate arrival of two Cavalry regiments who had been ordered to this place for organization to go to the front. They had been scattered about in E. Tennessee, garrisoning various points and were ordered to rendivous at this place, preparatory to go to the front. Some arrived on Thursday evening, and the balance on Friday morning, and at one oclock on Friday Four Hundred of Wheelers rebel Cavalry[3] approached in less than four miles of the town with 3 pieces of Artillery, intending to capture the garrison & destroy the Town & Rail Road but learnt before they got to Town of the arrival of said Union Cavalry and be at a retreat back to the Georgia line. They are rebel troops from Texas a part of Wheelers command, commanded by a rebel Col. Christie[4] with some of our rebel Tennesseans with them as guides &c. That Rebel command was yesterday & last night encamped at Westfields old stand[5] in Murray County, Georgia. The Federal Cavalry here have orders to go to the front and will leave this evening, which will leve us without any protection, except the small garrison above described, and not a federal soldier this side of Knoxville, except a garrison at Loudon. If you could spare a Regiment of E. Tennessee Cavalry they could help defend this place and extend protection to Bradley & Polk. If Col Thornburg and the 4th E. Tennessee Cavalry[6] were here I think we could get along. Many of our Union men try to work in day time & lie in the woods at night. Now and then one is killed or captured. We do not understand how it is, that the Rebels can spare their Caverly to send around in the rear to kill, capture & burn and that Gen. Sherman cannot send a force to attend to them.

Our people have been exceedingly anxious to see the circuit & chancery courts established and the laws executed upon the thieves, robers & murderers. The military do not reach them well, and it is probable that the convention to meet at Chattanooga tomorrow[7] may make some request on that subject. But I say to you that it is impossible for courts to be held in our present condition and it would be rashness and folly to attempt it. You must have things better settled and have protection before courts can be held and thus I wish to see the laws fully & faithfully executed against all violations of law. We will then need an able and vigorous Attorney General as well a good lawyer for a court. The stealing, robing and murder cases throughout the rebelion will come up for trial.

When I mentioned the 4th E. Tennessee Cavaly I only did so because so many of them are from this locality. We have no preference and would be rejoiced to see any Cavaly force sent here, and particularly Tennesseeans. If there is any thing which I can do or have done, you can command me. I am for the Batimore ticket first last and all the time and hope and trust in the Providences of God that it will be elected by milions of majority and believe it will be. And you need have no uneasiness about E. Tennessee. It is true they are unprotected, but give them protection, mails and Post offices and the majority that they will give in November next will test their loyalty to the Goverment of their fathers. Excuse these scraps of paper as I have not the time, nor am I yet able to get about to buy some paper.

Very respectfully
John C. Gaut

ALS, DLC-JP.

1. Gaut was currently in process of being re-commissioned by Johnson as circuit court judge.

2. Horatio G. Gibson (1827-1924), Maryland-born West Point graduate (1847), became an artillery captain in 1861 and colonel, 2nd Ohio Heavy Arty., in 1863. Mustered out of volunteer service at war's end, he rose to a permanent rank of colonel in 1883 and retired eight years later. Heitman, *Register,* I, 453; Washington *Post,* April 18, 1924.

3. As Gen. Joseph E. Johnston retired southward along the Western & Atlantic Railroad toward Atlanta before Sherman's advance, Wheeler's cavalry covered the Confederate movement and occasionally attacked Sherman's rear, menacing his supply lines along the railroads. Although the major portion of Wheeler's command between May 27 and June 18 was dismounted behind breastworks protecting Johnston's withdrawal, the troops in question may have been a raiding party approaching Cleveland, which is on a line direct north from Dalton. W. C. Dodson, ed., *Campaigns of Wheeler and His Cavalry* (Atlanta, 1899), 185-92; John P. Dyer, *"Fightin' Joe" Wheeler* (Baton Rouge, 1941), 167-75; Gilbert E. Govan and James W. Livingood, *A Different Valor: The Story of General Joseph E. Johnston, C. S. A.* (Indianapolis, 1956), 278-88.

4. Samuel P. ("Pat") Christian (b. *c*1834), a Virginia-born steamboat pilot, was major of the 8th Tex. Cav., CSA. 1860 Census, Tex., Harris, Houston, 2nd Ward, 106; *OR,* Ser. 1, XXXVIII, Pt. III, 650.

5. Probably the farm of David Westfield (b. *c*1786), a South Carolina native, located near Hossler's Mills, Georgia, along the road between Dalton and Cleveland, Tennessee. 1860 Census, Ga., Murray, Hossler's Mills, 1013 Dist. G.M., 96.

6. On June 26 Jacob M. Thornburg was ordered to move to Decatur, Alabama. Eckel, *Fourth Tenn. Cav.,* 49.

7. Delegates from the 4th judicial circuit, 2nd chancery division, and old 3rd congressional district met on June 22. Among the resolutions were a call for the unconditional abolition of slavery; an endorsement of the Lincoln-Johnson ticket; a request that the military governor, when the time is right, "take such steps as may be necessary to reorganize the State of Tennessee upon a basis which will insure permanent State and national tranquillity"; a recommendation of D. C. Trewhitt for chancellor and Gaut for circuit court judge; the assertion that "no citizen of Tennessee has forfeited any right he had as a National citizen, who has all the time adhered to the Federal Government"; and an affirmation that Tennessee unionists are "constitutionally and justly entitled to representation in the Federal Government, and a voice in the election." Chattanooga *Gazette,* June 23, 1864.

From John L. Plemons[1]

Jeffersonville, Indiana, June 21st, 1864.

His Excellency, Andrew Johnson,
Governor of Tennessee,

Sir. I a Citizen of Tennessee, having been forced into the Rebel Army—and makeing my escape, takeing refuge in the Federal army, and being sent across or North of the Ohio River under oath not to return during the War.

I am unable to work, or do any labor of any kind to support myself, being in a strange place, and having no refuge. What shall, or can I do in my present condition. Beleiving that if I can establish my loyalty, If I can induce any one to make the necessary enquiry—I would be liberated and allowed to return home. I therefore appeal to you, having no one else to make any investigation of my loyalty, or any one that has the facilities that you have—to ascertain the facts, that you enquire into my Case— If you find my statements correct, O, will you please to reccommend me favourable to the powers that be to release me to return to my home in Linchburg, Lincoln County Tennessee. My Mother resides at Elegay, Gilmore County Georgia[.][2] When the War broke out, and the Rebels in Tennessee, required all able bodied men in Lincoln Co to volunteer, I left and went to my mother in Georgia. I was there, for some time, a Press gang came around, and conscripted me— I was examined, and pronounced unfit for duty, but was taken to Richmond, and put into the Quartermaster's department. I done all I could—my disease being effects of Gravel. I could not do much. I remained at Richmond til May 4th 1864. I made my escape, and by a furlough—I received from a friend I made my way to Georgia, and to Cleveland, Tennessee, I delivered myself up to the U. S. Authorities. I was taken to Chattanooga, & to Nashville, & to Louisville Ky—where I was released, on takeing an oath to go immediately North of the Ohio River, and not return during the War, My Oath is dated at Louisville June 13th 1864, Signed by C B Pratt, Capt. 25 Mich Vols[3]— and approved by order of Brigadier General Burbridge, Stephen E. Jones, A.D.C P.M.G. Dist of Kentucky.[4] As for the support to the Rebellion I never give any—excepting by force. I did not dare go to the Election at Linchburg, to cast my vote against Secession as I would have done—had no threats been made to kill every man that voted against the ordinance. I was "Spotted" and had to leave. I have still a house and lot in Linchburg Tenn. also a Shoemaker Shop—if not distroyed, and still hold that as my place of Residence[.] While I was in Georgia, I also had some property there[.] The Rebels took every thing I had also served my mother the same way— we have with other Union men suffered their persecutions severely— I will refer you to John Gibson, Adolphus Jones, William Meace, Coke Ellington Esq, L M. Greer, & other citizens of Elligay Gilmore County Georgia[.][5] These Gentlemen are all prominent Union men. I will let them speak as to my Character, & my losses in Georgia[.]

I also refer you to T. P. Green, Jefferson M. Stone William Hague Sr. William Hague Jr. & other Union men at Linchburg—Lincoln Co. Tennessee as to my Character, & Union Sentiments.[6] Your Excellency may be personally acquainted with some of the above named Gentlemen. I do not wish to return to Georgia, but wish to return to Linchburg Tenn. I may there do something to maintain myself— I cannot labor[.] I have no money to support myself— I am in a strange place where Refugees—from oppression and persecution in the South are sent here, and here are viewed with suspicion. If a man has his health he can get along—but what shall I do— If I am released from my parole I will go to Nashville and let any physician examine me, or will send you a certificate from here if you wish. I am a native of Tennessee, and in my present Situation I pray you, to Examine my Case— I appeal to you as Governor of my native State, to sift my character thoroughly[.] If you find that I am intitled to your consideration will you use your influence to have me released— I ask a fair, and open investigation. If I could work at my trade or do any other work to maintain myself I would not ask these favors at your hands at present. My Oath or Parole is dated at Louisville Ky June 13th 1864, and Commences— I John L. Plemons of the County of Gilmore, State of Georgia, do Solemnly Swear &c &—

I leave the subject with you— will you please Grant my request. Enclosed find 3 P. O Stamps to prepay postage if necessary— please answer soon.

Respectfully yours
John L. Plemons

ALS, DLC-JP.

1. John L. Plemons (*c*1836-*fl*1870), born in North Carolina and reared in Georgia, operated a grocery in Shelbyville after the war. 1850 Census, Ga., Gilmer, 33rd Subdiv., 836; (1870), Tenn., Bedford, Shelbyville, 6th Ward, 1.

2. Sarah M. Plemons (b. *c*1806), native of North Carolina, was a widow with eight children. *Ibid.* (1850), Ga., Gilmer, 33rd Subdiv., 836.

3. Charles B. Pratt (1829-1890), New York-born shoe dealer of Marshall, Michigan, was mustered in September, 1862, and detailed to recruiting service until sent on detached duty to Louisville, April, 1863. He was in command of the military prison at Louisville from September, 1864, until mustered out in August, 1865. 1860 Census, Mich., Calhoun, Marshall, 1st Ward, 12; CSR, RG94, NA; Pension file, RG15, NA.

4. Stephen G. Burbridge (1831-1894), Kentucky lawyer, became brigadier in June, 1862, fought at Shiloh and Vicksburg, and early in 1864 succeeded Jeremiah Boyle as commander of the District of Kentucky. He was extremely unpopular with the local citizenry and civil authorities for arresting those suspected of opposing Lincoln's reelection, regulating prices "to force farmers to sell to the Federal government at figures below the Cincinnati market," and initiating "a system of reprisals against civilians to suppress guerrilla depredations." Relieved of his post in January, 1865, he resigned the service in December. After the war he was socially ostracized and financially ruined. Warner, *Generals in Blue,* 54.

5. John Gibson (b. *c*1800), North Carolina native and farmer; Adolphus Jones (b. *c*1817), North Carolina-born farmer; William Meace (b. c1812), Tennessee native and farmer; Coke Ellington (1812-1895), native Georgian, served as a Whig in the state senate (1838) and was an active unionist, joining the Republican party after 1860. A wartime refugee, he returned home to serve in the constitutional convention of 1865 and was elected to the legislature (1865-66). Levi M. Greer (*c*1830-1896), South Carolina-born merchant, was clerk of the inferior court (1864-66) and sometime postmaster. 1860 Census, Ga., Gilmer, 33rd Subdiv., 76, 78, 13, 5; George G. Ward, *The Annals of Upper Georgia, Centered in Gilmer County* (Carrollton, Ga., 1965), 228-29, 245, 596-99.

6. Townsend P. Green (b. *c*1813), Virginia-born farmer and tanner with $7,000 real and $24,000 personal property; Jefferson M. Stone (1823-*fl*1900), a tanner; William L. Hague (1804-1871), North Carolina-born millwright-farmer; and possibly William F. Hague (b. 1834), his nephew. Deane Porch, *Lincoln County, Tennessee, 1850 Census* (Nashville, 1970), 85, 187; 1860 Census, Tenn., Lincoln, 1st Dist., 8; 2nd Dist., 91; 4th Dist., 118; (1900), 59th Enum. Dist., 1B; Mabel A. Tucker and Jane W. Waller, *Lincoln County, Tennessee, Bible Records* (3 vols., Batavia, Ill., 1971-72), III, 3; "First Presbyterian Church of Fayetteville: Baptisms," *Lincoln Co. Tennessee Pioneers,* Vol. I, No. 5 (1971), 80.

From George W. Pohlman[1]

Cincinnati June 21st 64.

Gov A Johnson
Nashville Tenn

Your Exellency will excuse me for addressing myself [to] you.

I have furnished & clothed a great many Tennessee Officers when they were organized into Regiments & have trusted them on their honor as officers to pay when they drew their pay and the greater part have paid like honorable men but a great many have refused their bills altho they have been paid regularly[.]

The object of this is to ascertain if, there is remedy for me through you or the Adjt General of the State to get these Officers to pay me[.]

I have furnished the 1st 2d 8th 12th Tenn Cavalry and 1st Tenn Artillery and was induced to trust all these men throug Mr Brownlow & his sons who assured me that they were all honorable men but poor & destitute & that if I trusted them with theire Equipment that they no doubt would pay.

If you can possibly advise me in this affair I should esteem it a great favor[.]

very respectfully
Geo.W Pohlman

ALS, DLC-JP.

1. George W. Pohlman (*fl*1872) operated a Cincinnati military trimmings store prior to and during the war, later becoming associated with an insurance company. Cincinnati city directories (1858-72), *passim*.

From John Netherland

Knoxville 22nd June 1864—

Gov Johnson—
Dr Sir

I sent a telegram, some days since, to you or my friend Judge Patterson,[1] asking information, what steps were necessary for a loyal man, to take to get some cotton out [of] our lines in Georgia. I received no answer. I now write you again, and send it by John Crawford, giving you a list of the cotton,[2] and the owners, which I endorse to you, as it was made out by one of the Firm, Mr John F McEwen.

The cotton belongs to J C. Gillespie & Co—of Roane County Tennessee. The firm is composed of J. C. Gillespie, John F McEwen & John Strong.[3] They are all loyal men, and of the kind to be relied on—

If you can give Col. Crawford any assistance in getting this cotton out you will confer a benefit to worthy loyal citizens, and will confer a personal favor on me.

I would have come out to see you, but it is out of my power at present. There are many things about which I should like to see you, and much of our conversation would turn on men & things, in this end of the state. Let me say to you, that things here, need more attention, than they are receiving— A small amount of work done *now,* will save a *vast amount hereafter*—

You will find me at all times in the coming contest where I told you I would be, when we were last together—

I should be glad to hear from you— you can make your communications as private as you choose, and they will be so used and regarded—

My respects to the Judge & your families[.]

Truly Your Friend
J. Netherland

ALS, DLC-JP.

1. The telegram directed to Johnson and his son-in-law, David Patterson, is not extant.

2. Neither the man nor the list has been found.

3. John C. Gillespie (*c*1815-1873) was a Kingston merchant in business with his brother-in-law John F. McEwen (b. *c*1840). Following the war he moved to Chattanooga where he was a miller. McEwen remained in Kingston as a dry goods merchant. Strong has not been identified. Sistler, *1850 Tenn. Census,* III, 17; 1870 Census, Tenn., Roane, Kingston, 3; Hamilton, Chattanooga, 1st Ward, 17; T. J. Campbell, *Records of Rhea* (Dayton, Tenn., 1940), 132.

From Elbert A. James[1]

Chattanooga Tenn June 23d 1864

His Excellency Andrew Johnson
Mil. Gov. of Tenn
Governor—

I herewith send you a copy of the proceedings of the Convention held at this place yesterday as per instructions[.][2]

Col D. C. Trewhitt[3] drew up the resolutions for both committees though chairman of one only[.]

The Convention was a decided success; as it was composed of a greater num[ber] of *citizens, actual residents,* of this Congressional District than have assembled at any place within the same for years.

The persons recommended for the different offices are the unanimous choice of the convention[.][4]

Hoping that these proceedings may meet your approval and that the persons recommended may be commissioned as early as is thought practicable I reman vry respectfully

Your Obt Servt E. A. James

ALS, DLC-JP.

1. Elbert A. James (1841-1885), Tennessee native and co-editor of the Chattanooga *Gazette,* was postmaster (1865-69), state representative (1869-71) and senator (1873-75), and Democratic presidential elector (1868,1876), as well as farmer, ironmonger, superintendent of the Chattanooga Gas Light Company, and a participant in river improvement conventions (1868-74). McBride and Robison, *Biographical Directory,* II, 455-56.

2. See Letter from John C. Gaut, June 21, 1864, note 7.
3. Daniel C. Trewhitt was chairman of the committee on resolutions.
4. Trewhitt was recommended for chancellor, John C. Gaut for circuit court judge, and A. A. Hyde for attorney general. *Ibid.*

From Andrew J. Pemberton and Others[1]

Nashville, June 23rd, '64.

Gov. Andrew Johnson,
Dear Sir:

We, the undersigned, would very respectfully call your attention to the following statement and earnestly ask of you your good offices in behalf of those for whom this petition is written. Joseph Berryman, H. T. Berryman, T. Berryman[2] are now confined as Prisoners of War at Rock Island, Bar. 57. They are citizens of Humphrey County, Tenn. About the 10th of Feb. 1863 they were conscripted by Forrest wholly against their will. About the 1st of June following—the first chance that had presented itself—they deserted the Confederate Service and returned to their homes where they remained until Christmas last, quietly engaged in their civil pursuits. At that time, they of their own free act, delivered themselves up to Major Price,[3] then commanding at Station Forty Nine on the N. W. R. R. with the request that they should be allowed to take the oath of amnisty or any oath or bond that might be required in order for them to resume their occupations as citizens, from which they had been forcably withdrawn. They were not permitted to do this but were sent immediately North for exchange. They now and have at all times refused to be exchanged—only desiring to take the oath of allegiance and return to their homes.

They have recently addressed one of us a letter earnestly asking that a petition be drawn up to you with the hope that, when you know the circumstances under which they became Prisoners of War, you will exercise that kind influence, which has alleviated the sufferings of so many other unfortunate men, in procuring their release. They are and have always been true, unflinching Union men and two of them voted *against* Separation and Representation on the 8th June 1861. The other was not old enough or he would have voted the same ticket. The letter they have written in this matter is herewith enclosed[4] that you may be convinced of their earnest desire to be released from Prison and restored to the rights of citizens under a government against which they were *forcably* enlisted.

Entreating, Gov. Johnson, that this petition will obtain your welknown kind consideration, we remain[5]

Very Respectfully
Your obedient Servants,

Mem, DNA-RG249, Lets. Recd., File 409P (1864), Joseph, H.T., and T. Berryman.

1. Andrew J. Pemberton (1836-1915), who had enrolled as a private, Co. F, 10th Tenn. Cav., CSA, in January, 1863, was listed as a deserter in June. Gladys P. Anderson and Jill K. Garrett, comps., *Humphreys County, Tennessee, Cemetery Inscriptions* (2 Pts., Columbia, Tenn., 1966-69), II, 74; CSR, RG109, NA.

2. Joseph (b. *c*1837) and his father Taliaferro Berryman (b. *c*1810), a farmer with $1,000 real and $632 personal property, enlisted as privates in Morton's Lgt. Arty., CSA, early in 1863, deserted in June, were captured December 18, and sent to Rock Island in January, 1864. In October Joseph enlisted in the U. S. Army for frontier service, while Taliaferro, taking the oath of allegiance, offered to serve on the frontier but was rejected by the mustering officer. Henry Thomas Berryman (b. *c*1840), another son, is the Thomas Berryman, found in Co. C, 24th Btn., Tenn. Sharpshooters, CSA, who apparently deserted to join Morton's Arty. CSR, RG109, NA; 1860 Census, Tenn., Humphreys, Waverly P.O., 10th Dist., 99.

3. Avalo J. Price (b. *c*1843) of the 8th Iowa Cav. CSR, RG94, NA.

4. Taliaferro, Joseph, and H. T. Berryman to Andrew J. Pemberton, June 5, 1864, File 409P (1864), Lets. Recd., RG249, NA.

5. In addition to Pemberton the memorialists were G. W. Johnston, W. O. Garden [?], Jos. M. Mitcham, S. L. Graham. W. H. Wilkinson endorsed the statement. Subsequently, William Hoffman, commissary general of prisoners, declined to release the Berrymans. Hoffman to Pemberton, July 14, 1864, *ibid.*

From William A. Sorrells[1]

Jasper, Tennessee, June 23rd, 1864.

To His Excellency, Andrew Johnson,
Military Governor, Nashville, Tenn.

I am fully convinced that there is a deep laid Conspiracy on hand in this county to draw from the United States Treasury a large amount of money—how large I am unable to say—wrongfully, as I think. In December last, if I remember well, there was a Board of claims established here to assess the damages done to the citizens by the Federal troops since the commencement of the rebellion. The Board was composed of five members, three Military, and two citizens, Brig' Gen Steedman, Chairman.[2] The Board was imposed upon by enemies of the Government, as can be proved, if necessary; but the Board, or most of it were innocent. I understand an Agent is now gone to Washington City to urge the payment of these claims as early as possible. I know that there were Conspiracy, fraud and perjury on the part of some of the claimants, but not all; and my opinion is that fifty thousand dollars or more in consequence was allowed by the Board, than would have been allowed, if truth alone had been introduced. Since the Army of the Cumberland drove Bragg from this Country, and took possession of it,[3] many of the enemies of the Union came forward and took the oath of allegiance, but if there is one in the County in reality converted to the Union Cause, in all candor, truth and Sincerity, I know not who it is: and I have been here nearly all the time for forty years. If rebels are suffered for nearly three years to do all they can to break down the Government, and then when they are conquered, come forward and take a hypocritical oath to save property, an awful doom awaits the loyal portion of the American people. It seems to me that the loyal only should be paid for damages; but if it is the policy of the Government at Washington to place all, loyal and disloyal alike, upon an equality in deriving benifits from it, then I can see no good that can result from the loss of so much blood and treasure, already shed and spent. I know it will be hard for the truly loyal and needy to be out of the use of their just claims the length of time it would require to reinvestigate all the claims considered by the Board; but some special relief might be afforded to them.

No truly loyal man who is able to live without immediate aid from some quarter, will murmur at the postponement of the payment of his just claim against the Government, when the postponement of the collection will prove a saving to the Government of so large a sum. If this system of wrong upon the Government shall be successfully carried out in all other sections of the country, in the manner it is sought to be carried out here, what will become of us? As one who has ever been loyal to the Union, I have thought it my duty to say thus much to you now, as a faithful sentinel on the watch tower. If, however, the rebels are to be dealt with by the Government in the same manner that we are to be dealt with, I shall not deem it necessary to say more on the subject; but whatever may be done in the matter, I would be pleased to hear from you on the subject, and as early as your convenience will permit.

And as there is but little or no regularity in the post office at Shellmound, on the Nashville and Chattanooga Rail Road, which is the nearest post office to me, it is deemed best to address me at Bridgeport, Alabama, where this letter is written[.]

Very Respectfully, Wm. A. Sorrells.

ALS, DLC-JP.

1. William A. Sorrells (*c*1813-*fl*1870) was a North Carolina-born lawyer. 1870 Census, Tenn., Marion, 7th Dist., 30.

2. Others on the board were: from the military, Col. P. Sidney Post, Lt. Col. J. P. Kerr, Capt. Seth B. Moe, and civilians William Pryor and A. Kelly, both of Marion County. The board sat from December 12, 1863, until February 11, 1864. Draft inventory Records of the Steedman Board of Claims, 3rd Auditor, RG217, NA. For James B. Steedman, see *Johnson Papers,* V, 631*n*.

3. Bragg withdrew from Marion County in late August and early September, 1863, in the face of Rosecrans' advance. Long, *Civil War Almanac,* 397, 398, 404.

From Thomas H. Coldwell

Shelbyville Ten June 24th 1864

Gov Andrew Johnson
Sir

David M Burks[1] a citizen of Coffee County Ten was arrested on the 12th day of November 1862 as a conscript and placed as a private in the 44th Ten (Reb) Reg[.] after he was conscripted they gave him permission to go home for a few days[.] when he go home he hid himself & kept himself concealed until the 14th day of June 1863 when he was again caught by the conscript cavalry and was kept under arrest until they Rebal armey left Tullahoma[.] On the 8th day of December 1863 he again deserted and came to the Federal lines & was sent to Rock Island as a prisoner of war[.]

Mr Burks deserted in good faith & under order *No 10* of *Lt Gen Grant*[2] he & his friends claim his *discharge*[.] he is & has always been willing to take the amnesty oath[.]

We state that Mr Burks was conscripted & forced into the rebel army against his wishes & forced to fight against his principles for he is & has been for the Government of the United States and will if permitted to return make a true and loyal citizen[.]

Very Respectfully [no signature]

Shelbyville Ten June 27th 1864

Gov Johnson

From my knowledge of Mr Burks I am satisfied that he had been a union man and is yet & that he did all he could to keep out of the armey and by the most perfect accident he was caught in June 1863 after he had deserted the first time & there is as little doubt about his deserting in December 1863[.]

Respectfully Thos H Coldwell

ALS, DNA-RG249, Lets. Recd., File 631C (1864), David M. Burk [*sic*].

1. David M. Burks (1834-*fl*1900), a farmer who was enrolled in June, 1863, deserted in December, was captured by Federal authorities and sent to Rock Island where he remained until released in May, 1865. 1860 Census, Tenn., Coffee, 4th Dist., 156; (1900), 33rd Enum. Dist., 3A; CSR, RG109, NA.

2. The order of December 12, 1863, specified that "deserters from the enemy, coming within our lines," would be protected and permitted to go home upon satisfying field commanders of their sincerity and upon taking the oath. Letter Book, Vol. 14, Series V, Grant Papers, LC.

From Thomas H. Coldwell

Shelbyville Tenn June 25th 1864

Gov Andrew Johnson

I write to you this morning to ask some information & to obtain some action on your part if you are authorised to act in the premises. There is now in and around this place, a Number of Negroes that have left their former masters, many of whom are without work, and the services of all are required, in the growing crops & the harvest that is now matured—

The trouble is that there is no one here authorised to act in such cases, and persons fear to hire the Negroes as many of them belong to persons in this vicinity & trouble might grow out of it, under existing laws. It would be better for the Community for the Negroes to have work for then they can get provisions honestly & if they cannot git work they must eat & will eat.

There is a gentlem[an] here by the name of (Horner A F)[1] who rented of Gen Cannons Exr[2] a farm which he has planted in cotton about 125 acres and he has done all he could to avoid difficulties about Negroes, & he finds it very difficult to procure hands by this course. If there was any one here from whom he could hire Negroes he would pay them from 20 to 26 dollars per month and others here who have medows & harvest fields want hands badly & the same difficulty arises with them[.]

If you have the authority if you will appoint some one here to take charge of the contrabands and hire them out, or if you will authorise A F Horner to hire the hands he wants I will pledge my word for it, that he will not interfear with any negro that is at home, nor will he try to get one to quit his home as there is plenty here that have been here for 5 to 10 months to do all the work he & others want. I know him well, he is for the present living at my house & will not do any thing that is not strictly honest[.] he is from Ohio and an acquaintance of my wife & has been here for about 12 months & intends to make this his home & is one of the most active energetic & business men of my acquaintance, & I feel a strong desire to keep such men with us[.]

You will please examine the orders & grant the request if you have the power[.]

Very Respectfully Thos. H. Coldwell

ALS, DLC-JP.

1. Probably Abram F. Horner (b. *c*1828), a Pennsylvania-born cooper living in Steubenville on the eve of the war. 1860 Census, Ohio, Jefferson, Steubenville, 207.

2. Robert Cannon (*c*1790-1863), brother of Newton Cannon, onetime governor of Tennessee, and a North Carolina native who came to Bedford County about 1810, had been a major general in the militia and a state representative (1833-35). McBride and Robison, *Biographical Directory,* I, 121.

From John F. Miller

June 25, 1864, Nashville; LS, DLC-JP.

President of military commission which found Robertson countian Robert Gossett "guilty of murder and of being a guerrilla" and sentenced him to death, urges that Johnson deny appeal of prisoner's father for a pardon: he "deserves to die for his crimes."

From James B. Bingham

Cincinnati, June 26, 1864.

Hon. Andrew Johnson—

Dear Governor— After an absence of over two months, I have reached this place enroute for home. My health is much better and I hope to labor with some efficiency in the present canvass. Though I was not the first to congratulate you on your nomination, I labored all I could to bring it about,[1] and mean to labor efficiently to make it a triumph. I was in Washington last Wednesday, and I was sorry to learn from some of our friends that they did not feel certain of triumph. One of them—Judge Kellogg of Michigan[2]—asked me to write to you asking you to take the stump and make speeches in all the North in behalf of the cause. He says you can do more good in that way than any man in the nation. He thinks we should omit nothing that will make success certain. He begged me to urge you to take this course at once, even if it was necessary for you to resign your present position.

I asked his opinion about the propriety of forming an Electoral ticket in our state. He said we ought not to do it—that Lincoln and Johnson would be elected without tickets in the Seceded States or not at all—that that was the determination in Congress &c. I know it is not the intention of Congress to admit the Arkansas delegation.[3] They wont let any body from the Southern States vote for President this time. Still if you think it best for us to form a ticket, we can hold a convention next month or thereafter and get up one— I only wanted to let you know what our friends in Congress think about it. Before I went to Washington Brownlow and myself had agreed to have a convention to get up a ticket, but if it is likely to embarrass our friends, or prove a bad example, why I am willing to let it drop, and I shall do it any way till I hear from you.

I see you have fallen into error in your Nashville speech. It was your known patriotism and fidelity, in the darkest hour of the country's history, and your unswerving support of the government since the inauguration of the war, and not any recognition of the Southern States as in the Union, which placed you on the ticket.[4] This I know from personal observation and from the declaration of those who voted for you in Convention. You were bitterly opposed by Cameron and the Pennsylvania delegation with but few exceptions, and they afterwards came in only from necessity.[5]

Great fears are entertained that Grant's movements may place him in the field, or that a Union of the democractic elements with Fremont and the radicals may make a disastrous change in the present programme.[6] It is rumored around Washington that Thad. Stevens[7] is not very warm for the ticket—in fact that he, Winter Davis, Blow, and others, rather desire its defeat.[8]

The Blairs are awful unpopular among the Congressmen. It is believed that Lincoln will be compelled to throw Montgomery out of the Cabinet.[9] I know, from his own confession, that Blair is no friend of yours, and not only did not use his influence for you, but expressed his opinion that Hamlin would be renominated.[10] It made the deeper impression on my mind at the time because I had reason, from what you had said to me, to believe that you thought him a friend of yours. I think it very likely that Blair is the friend of no one unless it will promote the interest of the Blair family.

The government needs money, and Chase is in a bad fix. His Schemes of late have not worked well.[11] Thad. Stevens very imprudently admitted the possibility of the repudiation of the public debt in a debate last Thursday[12] and I fear the worst possible results therefrom. Pomeroy, from Seward's district also intimated the same thing.[13] The truth is, there is a general want of harmony between the President, Cabinet and Congress. Hence the necessity of your making a tour to put things to right.

I see that Washburn has intimated that there shall be no disloyal municipal government at Memphis.[14] If the people cant elect better men, he will appoint them. This is what I wanted you to do six months ago.

Write soon and oblige
Yours, truly, J B. Bingham.

P.S. I leave for Memphis Tuesday[.]

ALS, DLC-JP.

1. Bingham, who went east in June "in quest of lost health," attended the Baltimore Convention only as a spectator, but perhaps busied himself "pulling the wires" behind the scenes. Memphis *Bulletin,* June 29, 1864.

2. Massachusetts-born Francis W. Kellogg (1810-1879), arriving in Michigan in 1855, engaged in the lumbering business and served as a Republican in the legislature (1857-58) and in Congress (1859-65). During the war he organized several regiments and was colonel of the 3rd Mich. Johnson appointed him collector of internal revenue at Mobile (1866-68), where he served until elected to Congress from Alabama (1868-69). *BDAC,* 1150.

3. Qualifying under Lincoln's "ten percent plan," Arkansas throughout 1864 attempted to regain admission to the Union—by sending representatives and later senators-elect, none of whom were seated, and by having Kansas Senator Lane introduce on June 10 a direct resolution for recognition. Referred to the judiciary commitee, it was reported adversely June 25, and defeated four days later by the full Senate. The opposition was led by radical senators, who, like some Democrats, questioned Lincoln's motives in restoring Arkansas, Tennessee, Louisiana, and Florida during a presidential election year. Ferguson, *Arkansas and the Civil War,* 272-75.

4. Johnson, in accepting the nomination, was quoted as saying that "the Union party declared its belief that the rebellious States are still in the Union, and that their loyal citizens are still citizens of the United States." See Speech on Vice-Presidential Nomination, June 9, 1864.

5. In the Pennsylvania caucus poll, Johnson had been third. It was decided that Cameron, as chairman, would present Hamlin's name for renomination and cast a "solid complimentary vote" for him but switch to Johnson before the votes were tallied. Lincoln had asked Cameron—who had secretly "coveted" the post and was disappointed when no support materialized—to serve as "liaison to contact his choice for Vice-President." Erwin S. Bradley, *Simon Cameron: Secretary of War* (Philadelphia, 1966), 236-44.

6. Radical dissidents, unhappy with the administration's emancipation policies, had met in Cleveland on May 31, to organize a new party with the suggested name "Radical Democracy." The two factions, a majority favoring John C. Frémont and a minority, mainly from the east, supporting Grant, joined to adopt a platform which advocated a constitutional amendment prohibiting slavery, a one-term presidency, and a reconstruction dictated by Congress, and nominated Frémont and John Cochrane. Within a few days a convention of New York War Democrats named Grant, and just prior to the Baltimore convention, a New York City mass meeting applauded the general as a possible candidate. Ruhl J. Bartlett, *John C. Frémont and the Republican Party* (Columbus, Ohio. 1930), 103; Carl Sandburg, *Abraham Lincoln: The War Years* (4 vols., New York, 1939), III, 71-76.

7. Thaddeus Stevens (1792-1868), Vermont-born Pennsylvania lawyer, served as a state representative (1833-41) and as a Whig and Republican Congressman (1848-53, 1858-68). Long identified with the Free-Soilers and abolitionists, he opposed any concessions to the South and helped organize the Republican party in 1856. Although differing with Lincoln on a number of issues, he was especially critical of the administration on the matter of reconstruction. Subsequently in the forefront of opposition to Johnson's reconstruction policies, he was a member of the committee which drafted the impeachment resolutions and one of the managers for the Senate trial. Ralph Korngold, *Thaddeus Stevens* (New York, 1942), 226-28; Richard N. Current, *Old Thad Stevens* (Madison, Wis., 1942), 197; *DAB,* XVII, 620-25.

8. Henry Winter Davis (1817-1865), a Baltimore lawyer, served in Congress as a member of the American party (1855-61) and of the Union party (1863-65). Henry T. Blow (1817-1875), Virginia native and Missouri Republican congressman (1863-67),

had moved to St. Louis in 1830, engaged in business, was a state senator (1854-58) and minister to Venezuela (1861-62) and later to Brazil (1869-71). Stevens, who had told Lincoln that the Tennessean was a "rank demagogue" and a "damned scoundrel," voted for him only at the direction of his state caucus. *DAB,* V, 119-21; II, 391-92; Current, *Thad Stevens,* 200.

9. The Blair family—old Frank, young Frank, and Montgomery—who had influence and patronage in both Missouri and Maryland, were anathema to Davis, a protégé of Stevens, and Blow. All the Blairs favored a mild reconstruction: Congressman Francis, Jr., had attacked Chase, the Radicals, and their policies in the House in April, 1863, and Montgomery, advocating compensated emancipation and colonization, had opposed Lincoln's proclamation. With such moderates as Attorney General Edward Bates and Navy Secretary Gideon Welles, he was considered to have too strong an influence with the President. Frémont's withdrawal from the race was predicated upon Lincoln's dismissal of Montgomery as postmaster general. When the latter resigned on September 23, Frémont dropped his candidacy. William F, Zornow, *Lincoln & the Party Divided* (Norman, Okla., 1954), 145-46; T. Harry Williams, *Lincoln and the Radicals* (Madison, Wis., 1941), 354-55; Hans L. Trefousse, *The Radical Republicans* (Baton Rouge, 1968), 291-92.

10. Although Montgomery personally favored Johnson, he joined with Seward, Welles, and Bates in supporting Hamlin's renomination. William E. Smith, *The Francis Preston Blair Family in Politics* (2 vols., New York, 1933), II, 268.

11. Largely at Chase's insistence, Congress had passed a new loan bill in March, 1864, for a $200 million bond issue, redeemable in ten to forty years, popularly referred to as the ten-forty loan, at six percent interest. Given wide latitude in administering the act, the secretary had lowered the interest rate to five percent; as a result the bonds were not selling well by June, and the treasury had to fall back upon short-term six percent loans, which had greater appeal to investors. Moreover, the Gold Bill, which he had sponsored to reduce speculation in gold, was damaging to the economy, so much so that Congress rescinded it on July 2, four days after Chase's resignation. D. Rich Dewey, *The Financial History of the United States* (New York, 1928), 295, 313-15; David Donald, ed., *Inside Lincoln's Cabinet: The Civil War Diaries of Salmon P. Chase* (New York, 1954), 212.

12. During the House discussion of a loan bill on June 23, Stevens, as chairman of the ways and means committee, spoke against continuing debt payment in gold when it was no longer the circulating currency. This insistence on gold payments, he declared, was the cause of speculation in the precious metal, forcing the price up. While "I abhor repudiation . . . I see it staring us in the face, at no great distance in the future, just as plainly as if I saw it here to-day, if this policy be continued any longer." *Cong. Globe,* 38 Cong., 1 Sess., 3213.

13. Theodore M. Pomeroy (1824-1905), Auburn, New York, lawyer who had studied with Seward, served as congressman (1861-69), mayor of Auburn (1875-76), and state senator (1878-79). In the House debate on the loan bill, Pomeroy expressed the fear that if the gold standard were weakened, the country would be heading toward repudiation. *BDAC,* 1469; *Cong. Globe,* 38 Cong., 1 Sess., 3210.

14. Cadwallader C. Washburn (1818-1882), Maine native, moved successively to Iowa, Illinois, and finally to Mineral Point, Wisconsin, where he practiced law and became wealthy through banking, lumbering, and land speculation. A Republican congressman (1855-61, 1867-71) and delegate to the Washington Peace Conference (1861), he joined the Wisconsin Volunteer Cavalry in 1862, rising to major general in November of that year. After the war he returned to his business interests and served one term as governor (1872-74). As commander of the Department of West Tennessee with headquarters in Memphis (1864-65), he publicly warned Mayor John Park that if the latter were reelcted, he would suspend the government and appoint municipal officers; when Park was reelected by a plurality, the general kept his word. *BDAC,* 1779; Warner, *Generals in Blue,* 542-43; Boatner, *Civil War Dictionary,* 892; Memphis *Bulletin,* June 19, 1864.

From David F. Harrison

June 27, 1864, Loudon; ALS, DLC-JP.

Complaining that many Nashville postal workers are "Copperheads or anti War Rebels," asks, "is it good policy to feed and foster an Adder to sting you[?] *I think not*[.]" Observes that Michael L. Patterson, in command at Loudon, "pleases the Loyal people but the Rebels hate him awfully which you know is a good sign[.]" Proposes in view of the small garrison to organize a military company "to be called into service in case of an attack on this place[.]"

From Jacob G. Hornberger

June 27, 1864, Clarksville; ALS, DLC-JP.

A longtime Johnson supporter asks that Judge Herbert S. Kimble, "ready and willing to open our County Court," be allowed to do so upon taking the oath to support the Constitution without "other & additional oaths"; for "a little civil law in this portion of the state" is needed, especially in probate cases, inasmuch as "widows who wish to dissent from the wills of their husbands" must do so within twelve months.

From Samuel E. Hare

June 28, 1864, Nashville; ALS, DNA-RG249, Lets. Recd., File 546H(1864).

Asks help in procuring the release from Fort Delaware of his son, Henry, "Seduced into the Rebellion in 1861 . . . before he was 18 years of age." Eager now to take the oath of allegiance and amnesty, "He was young thoughtless indiscreet, and was influenced by bad designing men, much older than he . . . . The bitter lessons he has learned since his imprisonment will . . . make a new man of him, and teach him, in the future, to reverence a government he once So Cruelly wronged."

From William Oland Bourne[1]

New York, June 29, 1864.

Honored and Dear Sir,

Several Months since I wrote you[2] informing you of your nomination as an Honorary Member of the Workingmen's Association of this city, and enclosing at several times copies of the Constitution and By Laws, and also copies of the "True Platform"[3]—containing our publications, Addresses, and Correspondence from many of the leading men of the Country.

I have taken it for granted that the pressure of public business has Compelled you to delay writing from time to time, but as the time for earnest action has come, I am induced to write you again to remind you of the circumstance.

Our Association is organised to promote the principles of loyalty and union among the Workingmen of the whole Country, North and South, and to appeal to them to sustain our institutions of popular freedom. Politically, our key note is the same as you advanced in your recent speech, where you said the War on the part of the Southern leaders, is a "*War against democracy*."[4] The enclosed resolutions will define our ground.[5] We wish to Carry these principles before the Workingmen of the Country, in order to support the Union cause.

It appears to me that you can render good service to the cause by writing a Letter accepting the membership, and in it make a statement of the whole question as it affects the interests of working men throught [*sic*] the Union. Such a letter coming from you to the workingmen thr[ou]gh our Association and our publications, would do us an honor we covet, and also be of great service to the Cause.[6]

Should you be willing to honor us, allow me to beg of you a reply at the earliest day possible.

I have the honor to be Your Obt Servant
Wm Oland Bourne,
Cor Secretary 13 Vandam St.

His Excellency Andrew Johnson,
Governor &c.

ALS, DLC-JP.

1. William Oland Bourne (1819-1901), Pennsylvania native, moved to New York with his family in 1829. Apprenticed to a publisher, he became editor of the Lowville (N.Y.) *Journal* and ultimately of *The Iron Platform,* a workingmen's publication, published in New York City (1856-64). During the war he established the Soldier's Friend to aid disabled veterans and sponsored prizes for amputees who learned to write after losing a hand. Author, poet, reformer, and patriot, he published patriotic verse and numerous books, donated his services to libraries and schools, and spent nearly every Sunday visiting the sick and prisoners in city institutions. New York *Times,* June 7, 1901; see also *Johnson Papers,* IV, 585-86.

2. See New York City Workingmen's Association to Johnson, December 24, 1863, Johnson Papers, LC.

3. Although the constitution, the by-laws, and a printed letter from the president appealing for funds are to be found in the Johnson Papers, issues of *The Iron Platform* are missing. For this newspaper, see *Johnson Papers,* IV, 586n.

4. "I am for putting down this rebellion, because it is war against Democracy." Speech on Vice-Presidential Nomination, June 9, 1864.

5. Not found.

6. There is no evidence that Johnson replied.

Appendix

Andrew Johnson: Military Governor

by

John A. Martin

A Friendly Contemporary Assessment[1]

The Northern public have but a very faint idea of the character and services of Governor Andrew Johnson, Vice-President elect, notwithstanding the unanimity with which they hailed his nomination and gave him their suffrage. They know how, starting in life a poor, friendless, uneducated boy, he forced his way to distinction and greatness by an industry as herculean as it was rare, a power of will that nothing could dishearten, and a genius that made itself acknowledged and felt among the greatest minds of a State celebrated for its Jacksons, and Polks, and Grundys, and Bells. They know, also, with what earnest bravery and unswerving determination he has opposed the rebellion from its very inception, and how his influence made the mountain homes of East Tennessee ring with the songs of Union, and her sons suffer and die for its cause. But they have not seen nor do they know of or appreciate the daily evidence of his thorough devotion to the Union, his patient, earnest work for it, and his innate and never changing faith in the principles of true Democracy.

It was our lot to be thrown into intimate connection with him during the winter of '62 and '63, when for six months we acted as Provost Marshal of the city of Nashville. Our office adjoined his, in the State Capitol, and hardly a day past that we did not see and consult with him, and witness his wearing labors and harrassing tasks. The city was at that time crowded with Union refugees, and filled to overflowing with poor, friendless slaves who had escaped from bondage, and came thronging to our lines, expecting the beneficent protection of the Government, when as yet no provisions had been made for either their employment or their maintenance. The negroes were ignorant and unlettered; only one idea had crudely taken possession of their brains, and they clung to it with a tenacious reliance that no ill-treatment or disappointment could destroy or obliterate—that was a childlike faith and confidence that the Government of the United States and its army was friendly to them, and the rebel Confederacy their natural oppressor and enemy. They had heard our enemies and theirs talk of the Yankees establishing "negro equality and Freedom," and their idea of Freedom was generally the crude expectation of perfect immunity from labor and bountiful provision for sustenance, comfort and ease.

As the civo-military representative of the Government, they looked up to Gov. Johnson as children regard a father, and depended on his fostering protection as implicitly as they had before looked to their masters for food, clothing and shelter. Our soldiers sent them to him because they did not know to whom else to direct them to; civilians sent them to escape their importunities and avoid their petitions for advice and aid; and so they flocked to his office by scores.

His patience never wearied in listening to their simple stories; his kindness never tired in giving them aid or advice; he explained to them, with cheerful and encouraging words, and in a plain and simple manner, so that their poor understandings could comprehend his ideas, the new relation they occupied, their rights, their duties, their wants; that although the[y] were Free, Freedom did not mean idleness and vagabondage; that the Government would help them, but it could not support them in ease and worthless[nes]s; they must work, as before, but their earnings would be their own, for themselves and their families; that they should learn to depend on themselves, learn to read and write; be honest, sober, and industrious, and they would make themselves useful and respectable members of community. He got them work in the Quartermaster's and Commissary Departments, Hospitals, and business houses; he directed them where they could find employment; if there were houses of Secessionists empty, or with room to spare, he gave them shelter for their families; if they were defrauded, he listened with calm and attentive patience to their stories, sifting with quick intuition and ready clearness, the grain from the chaff of their verbose complaints, and righted their wrongs; he organized a working committee to furnish them with provisions until they could supply themselves by their own exertions; he sent them North to better homes and care, whenever opportunity offered.

Thousands of times we have seen him surrounded by a crowd of these poor, ignorant, helpless people—his earnest, manly, intelligent, and usually stern face lightened and softened with divine pity for their woes and sufferings; his clear, brilliant eye occasionally flashing his hearty indignation at some story of deeds meaner and more ignoble than common; and his kindly voice giving counsel and instruction with a touching cheerfulness that came from a heart in the right place; as courteous as though he were talking to the greatest potentate in the world, and as patient, untiring, parential, and kind as though it was the business of his life to listen and to advise—and we thought, here is a man who wears God's patent of nobility stamped upon his brow; one who was born to rule, and govern, and command, but standing in his pride of place is yet the truest representative of real and pure democracy in all the world.

The refugees were hardly less troublesome than the blacks, and they were almost as helpless. He cared for them; he listened to their stories of the wrong and outrage which had forced them to leave their home, while his eyes blazed with the fury of an honest man's just indignation against the villainy; he helped them on their way to a better and safer home; he provided for their temporary wants by procuring work or provisions for their support; he gave them shelter in the houses of the friends of those who had driven them from their own.

And all this was outside of the greater duties and daily cares of his important and responsible position as Military Governor. He had Regiments to organize and equip; Courts of Justice which had been destroyed by the Rebellion, to re-institute and place in their proper functions; laws to establish, regulate and enforce; a people, sadly strayed from the principles which Jackson taught, to bring back to reason and fidelity to country; and a great State, wild with frenzy of secession, to restore to its old place among the Stars. He worked for the accomplishment of all these objects with an industry and energy that never grew weary or asked repose, and an intelligence and capacity that was as wonderful in its patience as it was comprehensive in its ability. He gave to their execution all his courage, all his might and all his heart.

Our Military Commanders often clogged his way with obstacles, or made his duty the harder by failing to give him the assistance they should have conferred, to further his plans and purposes. He protested against this with just earnestness, but rarely with complaining bitterness, and their actions could never disturb the stately courtesy of his bearing or change the intention of his work and aim. He labored on, sincere in his actions, to bring back his State to the Union, and save his fellow-citizens, even to the humblest and most helpless, from want, and suffering, and outrage.

Few, perhaps none, in this country, have made so many sacrifices or labored with as ardent zeal for the people as the Nation as Andrew Johnson, and few have ever reached his height of pure and practical Democracs. His modest and unostentatious labors have been rarely understood or appreciated as they deserve, and if, by bringing them to the notice of the public we can make them valued, we shall have done only an act of simple justice to one who, of all the elements that adorn and beautify his character, is a PATRIOT, A STATESMAN, AND A MAN.

Nashville *Times and True Union,* January 7, 1865.

1. This laudatory, effusive, even sentimental, account of Governor Johnson's relations with the floundering blacks and whites whose lives had been irreparably disrupted by war was written by a young antislavery newspaperman who, two years earlier, at the tender age of twenty-three, had been in the midst of the incivilities of a truly civil war. Clearly, the older man, now ascending to the second highest place in the land, had awed and impressed Martin, politically influential colonel of the 8th Kans. Vol. Inf., who in the fall of 1861 had left the editorial desk of his *Freedom's Champion* (Atchison) for the camps of war. Now, in the last days of 1864, recently mustered out and resuming pursuit of both his journalistic career and his political ambitions, he wrote to pay tribute to his former associate; to say that he was exploiting a rising star would perhaps do him an injustice. For Martin, see Letter from Edward H. East, May 13, 1863, note 3.

Index

Primary identification of a person is indicated by an italic *n* following the page reference. Identifications found in earlier volumes are shown by a parenthesized Roman numeral and page number immediately after the name. Abbreviations beyond those found in Editorial Method are VP (Vice President), Co. (County), and illus. (illustration).

The Papers of Andrew Johnson

Monticello, the type chosen for this series, is a Linotype design based on the first successful American face, which was cut by Archibald Binney at Philadelphia in 1796. The clean legibility of Monticello, especially in the smaller sizes, suits it admirably for a series in which documentation is extensive.

Volume 6 of *The Papers of Andrew Johnson* was composed on a Merganthaler Linotron 202, utilizing computerized photocomposition, and printed offset by McNaughton & Gunn of Ann Arbor, Michigan, and bound by John H. Dekker & Sons of Grand Rapids, Michigan. The text paper is Olde Style Wove, which adheres to the specifications of the National Historical Publications and Records Commission, and was manufactured by the S. D. Warren Company, Boston, Massachusetts. The Holliston Mills, Inc., Hyannis, Massachusetts, manufactured the binding cloth. The book was designed by Hugh Bailey and Helen Orton.

THE UNIVERSITY OF TENNESSEE PRESS